Alexander

Christmas 2013

from

Granny and Grandpa

ORIEL COLLEGE

John Eveleigh (1748–1814), fellow 1770, provost 1781–1814
Oriel College

ORIEL COLLEGE
A HISTORY

Edited by
JEREMY CATTO

OXFORD
UNIVERSITY PRESS

OXFORD
UNIVERSITY PRESS

Great Clarendon Street, Oxford, OX2 6DP,
United Kingdom

Oxford University Press is a department of the University of Oxford.
It furthers the University's objective of excellence in research, scholarship,
and education by publishing worldwide. Oxford is a registered trade mark of
Oxford University Press in the UK and in certain other countries

© Oriel College, Oxford 2013

The moral rights of the authors have been asserted

First Edition published in 2013

Impression: 1

All rights reserved. No part of this publication may be reproduced, stored in
a retrieval system, or transmitted, in any form or by any means, without the
prior permission in writing of Oxford University Press, or as expressly permitted
by law, by licence or under terms agreed with the appropriate reprographics
rights organization. Enquiries concerning reproduction outside the scope of the
above should be sent to the Rights Department, Oxford University Press, at the
address above

You must not circulate this work in any other form
and you must impose this same condition on any acquirer

Published in the United States of America by Oxford University Press
198 Madison Avenue, New York, NY 10016, United States of America

British Library Cataloguing in Publication Data

Data available

ISBN 978–0–19–959572–3

Printed in Great Britain by
CPI Group (UK) Ltd, Croydon, CR0 4YY

Links to third party websites are provided by Oxford in good faith and
for information only. Oxford disclaims any responsibility for the materials
contained in any third party website referenced in this work.

Preface

Writing a history of an institution which is almost 700 years old is a daunting prospect. This is not only because there is, inevitably, a lot to say. The sources which survive are likely to be both patchy and partial; and to retrieve a real sense of what it was like to be part of the institution through the varying phases of its existence is likely to be very difficult. Moreover, such a task also raises particular questions—tantalizing but compelling questions for both the historian and the general reader—which may well prove impossible to answer. Is there any discernible or important continuity over seven centuries, in purpose, in operation, in achievement? How has the 'same' institution managed to sustain itself through the utterly different worlds of medieval times, the Renaissance, Civil War, industrial revolution, and a globalized twentieth century? Does it affect its current aspirations, or how well it achieves them, that it *has* a 700-year history? Perhaps most tantalizing, would Adam de Brome, if he were to reappear from his resting place in St Mary's, recognize *anything* at all of the college which he founded in 1326?

Another daunting aspect is that, while all institutions exist in, and relate to, their external environment, this is a particular problem in the case of an Oxford college. It is quite difficult to describe even the current nature of the relationship between the colleges and the university, much of which operates rather informally; and to unravel this for past centuries is harder still. In addition, being an educational institution, the college's history is as much about who or what manner of person it produced—and what they then did in the light of their time here—as it is about the activities of the college itself.

Added to which is the problem of perspective. Most if not all historians no doubt seek as part of their profession to understand the object of their study in terms of the ideas, norms, and perceptions of the times they study; and strive to be relatively unfettered by contemporary views, conditioned as they are to some extent by today's world. But where they are faced with the same institution, arguably at least pursuing a rather similar objective today as in previous times, the need to leap back rather than look back becomes ever more necessary.

So, the project is a difficult task, raising difficult questions but, by very much the same token, a fascinating task as well. Fortunately, there are enough records, and the editor of this volume has brought together the necessary historical expertise, to allow a new look—the first for over 100 years—at why and how Oriel evolved the way it did; how both external forces and numerous individuals shaped it over the centuries; what role it played and what impact it made; and, in these ways, provide a scholarly framework for thinking about those tantalizing questions.

Another issue that faces all such projects is whether to pursue a chronological approach or a thematic one. Both have evident advantages and disadvantages. The solution adopted by the editor for Oriel's History, which I believe has worked well, is to pursue a chronological approach for much of the life of the college; but with a number of thematic chapters appearing later on, the latter providing the opportunity for various authors to explore particular aspects of Oriel in more recent times, while not disrupting the chronological flow provided by other authors.

Getting together and coordinating the work of thirteen authors in twenty-three chapters is, of course, a very major undertaking; and this project would not have taken flight without the work and support of a number of key people. These include both Dr Lee Seng Tee and Sir Ewen Fergusson (1951) who provided financial support, respectively for the lecture series that underpinned the preparation of the volume and work on the book itself. Sir Ewen also chaired a small committee to oversee the work; Professor Robert Fox (1958) in addition to being a contributor also sat on the steering committee; and essential to the whole enterprise, Dr Jeremy Catto, Emeritus Fellow, contributor to the volume, and its editor. I know from undertaking a similar exercise some years ago how totally draining the role of editor can be—far more so than producing one's own work—and the college is very indebted to Dr Catto for undertaking this project.

Sir Derek Morris

Contents

List of Plates	x
List of Illustrations	xi
List of Maps	xv
List of Plans	xvi
Acknowledgements	xvii
Abbreviations	xix

Introduction *Jeremy Catto*	1
1. The Foundation *Jeremy Catto*	12
2. Patrons and Pastors, 1385–1479 *Jeremy Catto*	35
3. Oriel in Renaissance Oxford, 1479–1574 *Jeremy Catto*	60
4. Expansion and Retrenchment, 1574–1660 *Kenneth Fincham*	94
5. A Protestant College, 1574–1660 *Kenneth Fincham*	135
6. Politics and Interest, 1660–1781 *Paul Seaward*	160
7. An Anglican Foundation *Paul Seaward*	193
8. A Society of Gentlemen *Paul Seaward*	219
9. Eveleigh and Copleston: The Pre-Eminence of Oriel *Ernest Nicholson*	247
10. Oriel and Religion, 1800–1833 *Peter Nockles*	291
11. A House Divided: Oriel in the Era of the Oxford Movement, 1833–1860 *Peter Nockles*	328

12.	Oriel to Oliver Twist: Noetics and Tractarians at Large *Simon Skinner*	371
13.	Hawkins, Monro, and University Reform *Ernest Nicholson*	408
14.	Oriel and the Wider World *Alexander Morrison*	444
15.	The Estates of Oriel, 1324–1920 †*Ralph Evans and J. P. D. Dunbabin*	476
16.	Property and Investments, 1920–1990 *Wilf Stephenson*	526
17.	The Buildings of Oriel *Matthew Bool*	549
18.	Oriel and Sport *Clive Cheesman*	597
19.	Science at Oriel *Robert Fox*	645
20.	Government, Oxford, and Oriel, 1914–1990 *John Stevenson*	678
21.	The College Community, 1905–1950 *John Stevenson*	707
22.	The College Community, 1950–1990 *John Stevenson*	749
23.	Epilogue: Oriel 1990–2013 *Jeremy Catto*	785
	Appendix: College Officers	793
	(a) Provosts	793
	(b) Vice-Provosts	794
	(c) Deans	795
	(d) Treasurers	803
	Index	815

Very sadly Ralph Evans died on 3 September 2011. He is greatly missed by his fellow contributors and editor. His draft chapter has been generously completed by John Dunbabin.

List of Plates

Frontispiece John Eveleigh
1. Edward Copleston
2. Richard Whately
3. Thomas Arnold
4. Edward Hawkins
5. Matthew Arnold
6. David Binning Monro
7. Cecil John Rhodes
8. Charles Lancelot Shadwell
9. James Bryce
10. Lancelot Ridley Phelps
11. The Dean Estate Map (detail)
12. Sir David Ross

List of Illustrations

1.1	The foundation charter of Edward II, 21 January 1326	19
1.2	The college seal	20
1.3	Adam de Brome petitions for the college	20
1.4	Brome's dossier on the foundation: note on Hugh Despenser	22
2.1	Archbishop Arundel inquires into the fellows' conduct, 1411	36
2.2	The earliest treasurers' account, 1409–10	38
2.3	The Founder's Cup	59
3.1	John Bereblock's view of Oriel, 1566	68
3.2	Thomas More	70
3.3	The Coconut Cup	79
3.4	George Dudley seeks a place, 1536	81
3.5	William Allen	88
3.6	Sir Walter Raleigh	92
4.1	Anthony Blencowe	95
4.2	Sir Henry Unton	96
4.3	Sir Matthew Lister	104
4.4	Robert Pierrepont, earl of Kingston	112
4.5	John Rouse	114
4.6	William Lewis	116
4.7	John Tolson	119
5.1	Sir Robert Harley	142
5.2	William Prynne	150
6.1	Robert Say	165
6.2	Charles Somerset, duke of Beaufort	189
7.1	John Robinson, bishop of London	215
7.2	Joseph Butler, bishop of Durham	217
7.3	Gilbert White	218
8.1	The benefactors' book	225
8.2	Joseph Warton	244
9.1	Richard Mant	268

9.2	Baden Powell	282
9.3	Richard Temple, duke of Buckingham	285
9.4	Sir George Grey	286
9.5	Charles Wood, viscount Halifax	287
9.6	James Harris, earl of Malmesbury	289
9.7	William Palmer, the college butler	290
10.1	John Keble	311
10.2	James Endell Tyler	318
10.3	Joseph Blanco White	321
10.4	Richard Jelf	323
10.5	Edward Bouverie Pusey	326
10.6	The Oriel Teapot, emblem of Noetic temperance	327
11.1	John Henry Newman	329
11.2	Newman at St Mary's	330
11.3	Hurrell Froude, Thomas Mozley, and Newman in the common room	332
11.4	Renn Dickson Hampden	334
11.5	Charles Marriott	345
11.6	Frederic Rogers, Lord Blachford	348
11.7	Richard William Church	349
11.8	James Anthony Froude	361
11.9	James Fraser	363
11.10	Charles Neate	365
11.11	The Oriel Auto da Fé	366
11.12	'Ye Provost and his Satellites', c.1849	367
12.1	Nassau Senior	374
12.2	Thomas Mozley	393
13.1	George Anthony Denison	413
13.2	John William Burgon	425
13.3	Arthur Hugh Clough	425
13.4	Edward King	425
13.5	Samuel Wilberforce	425
13.6	Harry Vane, duke of Cleveland	436
13.7	John Spencer-Churchill, duke of Marlborough	436

LIST OF ILLUSTRATIONS

13.8	Gathorne Gathorne-Hardy, earl of Cranbrook	436
13.9	George Goschen	436
14.1	Orielenses dine in Khartoum, 1936	470
14.2	The Oriel bishops, 1930	473
15.1	The Treasurers' Pistol	486
17.1	Agas's map of Oxford, 1578 (detail)	555
17.2	The first quadrangle, south and west sides	556
17.3	The first quadrangle, north and east sides	557
17.4	Loggan's engraving of Oriel, 1675	560
17.5	Loggan's engraving of St Mary Hall, 1675	560
17.6	The Robinson Building	562
17.7	The Carter Building and its extension	563
17.8	The Leigh Library	565
17.9	The garden quadrangle: the proposed 'infill'	567
17.10	Daniel Robertson's improvements to St Mary Hall, 1826	571
17.11	A projected provost's lodging, 1874	583
17.12	Tackley's Inn restored: the east front	589
17.13	The entrance to the Harris Building, 1993	593
17.14	The James Mellon Building	595
17.15	The Provost's Mouse	596
18.1	The Oriel eight, *c.*1860	604
18.2	Thomas Hughes	605
18.3	Francis Henry Hall	606
18.4	College sports day, 1903	611
18.5	The bump supper, March 1908	612
18.6	P. F. Warner, 1905	618
18.7	The Minnows Cricket Club, 1907	619
18.8	The college barge with swimmers, 1908	623
18.9	Head of the River, 1933	628
18.10	Oriel four at Henley, early 1930s	629
18.11	Soccer cuppers, 1908	636
18.12	Coxless four, 1937	637
18.13	Coxless four, 1949	638
18.14	Head of the River, 1976	639

19.1	The Oriel Astrolabe	646
19.2	Richard Dyer's Cabinet of Specimens	651
19.3	Francis Harrison	664
19.4	Dalziel Llewellyn Hammick	667
19.5	Kenneth James Franklin	668
21.1	The Rhodes Building opening ceremony, 1911	708
21.2	First World War: Roll of Service	723
21.3	Sir Henry Tizard	726
21.4	The second eight, 1926, with A. J. P. Taylor	732
21.5	J. W. C. Wand as archbishop of Brisbane	735
21.6	The college servants, 1939	740
21.7	The fellows, 1941	741
21.8	Sir George Clark	747
21.9	The library fire: the aftermath	747
22.1	W. A. Pantin in his rooms, 1966	757
22.2	Kenneth Turpin	758
22.3	Lord Swann	759
22.4	Sir Zelman Cowen	760
22.5	The dons' eight, 1975	772
22.6	The Regius Professors of Modern History, 1998	776
22.7	The fellows, October 1991	782
22.8	Oriel women with Bill Parry, 1995	783

List of Maps

1. College properties in England — 499
2. Oriel estates in the Oxford region — 500
3. Wadley and Littleworth — 501
4. Dean and Chalford — 502
5. Shenington — 503
6. Swainswick — 504

List of Plans

1.	The college site	573
2.	The college garden *c.* 1730	574
3.	Williams's plan of Oriel, 1733	575
4.	Williams's plan of St Mary Hall, 1733	576
5.	The principal's lodgings, St Mary Hall, 1733	576
6.	The proposed rebuilding of St Mary Hall, 1746	577
7.	Oriel in 1814	578
8.	Plan for the Rhodes Building	579
9.	Waterhouse's first plan for an Oriel Square building, 1876	579
10.	Plan and elevation of Tackley's Inn	580

Acknowledgements

The editor and contributors owe a great debt to those who have facilitated this book. First of all, to Sir Ewen Fergusson, without whose generous support the project would not have been possible, and whose constant encouragement on the steering committee has kept us in good heart and on the right path. To Professor Ernest Nicholson, whose idea the history originally was when he was provost, we owe the concept and the plan which we have adopted. The other members of the committee, Sir Derek Morris and Professor Robert Fox, have been supportive throughout, and their suggestions have done much to improve the shape of the volume. All contributors owe a very great debt to the exemplary efforts of the Librarian of Oriel, Marjory Szurko, and the Archivist, Robert Petre, who have both gone to great lengths to produce promptly for us the material held within the college on which we have principally worked. Robin Darwall-Smith, the Archivist of University and Magdalen Colleges, has put his considerable experience of writing college histories at our disposal, and has made valuable suggestions for improvement to several chapters. Julian Munby's deep knowledge of the buildings has kept us from several errors, and the expertise of two former bursars of Oriel, Brigadier Hugh Browne and Brigadier Mike Stephens, on the rebuilding of the Island Site has enabled us to understand that complex operation. Other archivists, especially Simon Bailey, the University Archivist and his staff, Judith Curthoys, the Archivist of Christ Church, and the staff of the Lincolnshire Archives Office and the Oxford County Record Office, have facilitated many enquiries, as have the always helpful staff of the Bodleian Library. Keiko Ikeuchi at the Museum of the History of Science in Oxford has kindly provided illustrations of items in the collection. Individual contributors have also benefited from the kind help of John Albert, Nigel Aston, Robert Beddard, Glenn Black, Casey Charlesworth, Pietro Corsi, Richard Cross, Mark Curthoys, Brian Escott-Cox, John Foot, Andrew Foster, Lawrence Goldman, S. J. D. Green, Jasper Griffin, Robin Harland, Andrew Hegarty, Gerard Kilroy, Simon King, Peter Lake, Paul Langford, Philippe Lefebvre, David Maskell, James Methven, Leslie Mitchell, Geoffrey Neate, Kenneth Parker, Bill Parry, James Pereiro, Mary Porter, Daniel Robinson, Michael Sheen, Johanna Stephenson, Nicholas Tyacke, Eric Vallis, Graham Vincent-Smith, Tony Ward, Rebecca Warren, Thomas Welsford, John Whitehead, Mark Whittow, and David Wigg-Wolf. Sarah Holmes has expertly guided the volume through the press, and we are grateful too to Jonathan Bargus for his sure hand in organizing the illustrations, and to Jackie Pritchard and Carol Carnegie for their prompt and effective copy-editing and production of the volume.

We thank the Trustees of the Imperial War Museum for permission to quote from the papers of Sir Henry Tizard, and for permission to reproduce portraits and images, we are grateful to the National Archives for 1.3, The Curators of the Bodleian Library for 3.1 and 17.1, the Trustees of the National Portrait Gallery for 9.3, 9.5, 10.3. 12.1, 13.1, 13.6, 13.7, 13.8, 13.9, and 18.6, the Warden and Fellows of Keble College for 10.5, Dr Douglas Hamilton for 17.2, 17.3, 17.6, and 17.13, the President and Fellows of Magdalen College for 18.1 and 21.3, the Trustees of the Oxford Museum of the History of Science for 19.1 and 19.2, and last but not least, the Provost and Fellows of Oriel for all remaining images, as well as for innumerable other benefits.

Abbreviations

BRUO	A. B. Emden, *Biographical Register of the University of Oxford to A.D. 1500*, 3 vols. (Oxford, 1957–9)
BRUO 1501–40	A. B. Emden, *Biographical Register of the University of Oxford A.D. 1501 to 1540* (Oxford, 1974)
Cat. Mun.	C. L. Shadwell, *Catalogue of the Muniments of Oriel College*, 8 fascicules (Oxford, 1893–1905)
CCEd	Clergy of the Church of England 1540–1835, Database
CCR	Calendar of Close Rolls
COS	Charity Organization Society
CPR	Calendar of Patent Rolls
CSPD	Calendar of State Papers Domestic
DR	*The Dean's Register of Oriel*, ed. G. C. Richards and H. E. Salter (Oxford, OHS 1926)
EETS	Early English Text Society
EHR	*English Historical Review*
Hearne, *Collections*	Thomas Hearne, *Remarks and Collections of Thomas Hearne*, ed. C. E. Doble, D. W. Rannie, and H. E. Salter, 11 vols. (Oxford, OHS 1885–1911)
HMC	Historical Manuscripts Commission
HMSO	Her Majesty's Stationery Office
HUO	History of the University of Oxford, i: *The Early Oxford Schools*, ed. J. I. Catto (Oxford, 1984); ii: *Late Mediaeval Oxford*, ed. J. I. Catto and Ralph Evans (Oxford, 1992); iii: *The Collegiate University*, ed. J. K. McConica (Oxford, 1984); iv: *Seventeenth Century Oxford*, ed. Nicholas Tyacke (Oxford, 1997); v: *Eighteenth Century Oxford*, ed. L. S. Sutherland and L. G. Mitchell (Oxford, 1984); vi: *Nineteenth Century Oxford, part I*, ed. M. G. Brock and M. G. Curthoys (Oxford, 1997); vii: *Nineteenth Century Oxford, part II*, ed. M. G. Brock and M. C. Curthoys (Oxford, 2000); viii: *Twentieth Century Oxford*, ed. B. H. Harrison (Oxford, 1994)
ICS	Indian Civil Service
LAO	Lincolnshire Archives Office

ABBREVIATIONS

LDN	*Letters and Diaries of John Henry Newman*, ed. C. S. Dessain, I. T. Ker, T. Gornell, G. Tracey, and F. J. McGrath, 32 vols. (London, 1961–2008)
Letters and Papers, Henry VIII	[Public Record Office] *Letters and Papers Foreign and Domestic of the Reign of Henry VIII*, 23 vols. in 35 (London, 1862–1932)
OC	Order of Carmel (Carmelites)
OCA	Oriel College Archives
OCL	Oriel College Library
OCR	*Oriel College Records*, ed. C. L. Shadwell and H. E. Salter (Oxford, OHS 1926)
ODNB	*Oxford Dictionary of National Biography*, ed. H. C. G. Matthew, B. H. Harrison, and L. Goldman, 60 vols. (Oxford, 2004)
OFM	Order of Friars Minor (Franciscans)
OHS	Oxford Historical Society
OR	*Oriel [College] Record*
OSA	Order of (canons of) St Augustine
OUA	Oxford University Archives
OUBC	Oxford University Boat Club
Parl. Deb.	*Parliamentary Debates*, 199 vols. (London, 1892–1908)
PP	*Parliamentary Papers*
Provosts and Fellows	G. C. Richards and C. L. Shadwell, *The Provosts and Fellows of Oriel College, Oxford* (Oxford, 1922)
Rannie, *Oriel*	D. W. Rannie, *Oriel College* (London, 1900)
Registrum Orielense	C. L. Shadwell, *Registrum Orielense*, 2 vols. (Oxford, 1893–1902)
SA	*Statuta Antiqua Universitatis Oxoniensis*, ed. Strickland Gibson (Oxford, 1931)
SPS	Sudan Political Service
TNA PRO	National Archives, Public Record Office
VCH	*Victoria History of the Counties of England*
Wood, *Athenae Oxonienses*	Anthony Wood, *Athenae Oxonienses*, ed. P. Bliss, 4 vols. (London, 1813–20)
Wood, *Life and Times*	*The Life and Times of Anthony Wood*, ed. A. Clark, 5 vols. (Oxford, OHS, 1891–1900)

Introduction

Jeremy Catto

Oriel was the fifth college to be founded in Oxford, in 1326, and was always thereafter a comparatively small body, which has only come into national prominence for two or three generations in the early nineteenth century. The contributors to this book not only explore that brilliant episode but the society in which it incubated and which continued after it had ceased. They have seen the history of the college as the development of the body of Orielenses as a whole: that is, not just their usually brief years at Oxford, but their origins, careers, and destinies, which in some phases of college history were intertwined through networks of enduring friendship and patronage. Whether they shared a distinctive body of ideas in any period is more dubious, but the interests and opinions which some of them had in common, if they can be detected, are an integral part of the story. In the following chapters the fortunes of the Oriel community, originally a body of fellows but later a society of undergraduates as well, is therefore the subject of attention as well as the institutional history of the college. Oriel's history is not, of course, a virgin field. In these introductory remarks its historiography, almost all of it from the pens of Orielenses, will be briefly surveyed, with the materials from which college history can be reconstructed. Any enduring features which seem to distinguish the college from its sister communities are noted with appropriate caution.

A measure of caution is necessary, because tracing a distinctive character through the history of institutions such as Oxford and Cambridge colleges is not on the face of it an exercise likely to bear fruit. Successive social pressures, and the attraction of passing ideas, will inevitably have distorted the intentions of its original members, however strongly they were framed in custom and statute, and altered the terms of association. Residential societies within larger bodies, they have been especially subject to the constant refreshment of their members, the fellows largely from other colleges in the university and the undergraduates from every part of the realm or beyond it, even if a regional bias has sometimes prevailed. They have been torn between the competing demands of intellectual enquiry, religious mission, and service to the state, and in times of stress have generally taken refuge in their statutes and received customs, at Oxford for instance in the face of parliamentary commissioners after the Civil War. A few have invented college traditions with the appearance of immemorial antiquity, as the fellows of University College did in the 1380s by appropriating King Alfred as their founder—a myth which survived its demolition in the 1720s at least as far as the Millenary Dinner of 1871.[1] But most Oxford colleges, including Oriel, had no founding myth. They had a collective memory of the original founder and of subsequent benefactors, ritually expressed in college prayers and ceremonies. There is early evidence of Oriel's corporate memory: in 1397 one of the fellows, almost certainly Thomas Leintwardine, compiled a register of the Oriel muniments with a record of the corresponding obligations the college had incurred, and a calendar in which the date of their annual celebration could be entered. Within two generations of the foundation in 1326, therefore, the commemoration of benefactors had begun, and as new entries in the calendar indicate, the fellows acknowledged further benefactors with annual prayers and masses. Their Protestant successors, though they changed the form of commemoration, remembered their benefactors and added new names to a weekly prayer, still recited at college evensong, of which the earliest extant form is in the register of muniments in a sixteenth-century hand.[2] Meanwhile a bare list of the first fifteen provosts was recorded in the college precedents book, later the Dean's Register, in John Hals's brief provostship (1447–9), which was periodically added to, with occasional comments, when new provosts were elected; a custom still observed in the twentieth century.[3]

In this unpretentious form the outlines of Oriel's history were preserved for future generations, without attracting more than passing attention from the Oxford antiquaries of the seventeenth and eighteenth centuries. Though Anthony Wood included the foundation and some of the notables of Oriel in his compilations on the university, he did not it seems examine the college archives. The Oxford librarians Thomas James and Gerard Langbaine made lists of the college manuscripts, but made no further foray into Oriel's past. The college had no antiquary of its own among the fellowship: the only fellow to give any attention to the college records was James Davenant, fellow from 1662 to 1717, who according to Thomas Hearne 'made an Abstract of all the Writings in the College Treasury and digested them in order', perhaps in

---

[1] Robin Darwall-Smith, *A History of University College, Oxford* (Oxford, 2008), 38–9, 256–7, 390.
[2] British Library Lansdowne MS 386, fo. 53ʳ.
[3] G. C. Richards and H. E. Salter (eds.), *The Dean's Register of Oriel, 1446–1661* (OHS, Oxford, 1926), 345–7.

1671–2 or 1683–4 when he was senior treasurer.⁴ His abstract does not seem to survive. It may have been useful in the 1720s, when the statutes of Edward II and Bishop Burghersh's revision were consulted in the lawsuit over the visitorship; in consequence of the case, the ancient register of muniments and calendar were called into the Court of Common Pleas and never recovered. In the 1740s another fellow made an attempt to trace the succession of the fellows since 1661, making a chart at the back of the Dean's Register; it was carried on periodically into the nineteenth century. The writing of the original hand seems to be that of Edward Bentham, the energetic tutor and writer on logic and divinity, who was a fellow from 1730 to 1755 and several times dean between 1737 and 1749. His motive was probably more antiquarian than practical, as he seems in addition to have annotated the list of St Antony's and Dudley exhibitioners—undergraduates supported by fifteenth- and sixteenth-century benefactors—in the Dean's Register in an attempt to establish their order of succession, an exercise with no practical application in his time. Ninety years later, the foundation charter and statutes were appealed by John Henry Newman as justification for his vision of a Christian fellowship 'pursuing', in Tom Mozley's words, 'their own studies and exchanging daily assistance in brotherly love and confidence'.⁵ His idealized evocation of fourteenth-century Oriel may have inspired his friends in their battle with Provost Hawkins over the office of tutor; it was never likely in the very different conditions of nineteenth-century Oxford to be the basis of a practical programme.

The Tractarian appeal to the founder's intentions did not stimulate research into the working of the medieval college. The statutes themselves were jealously kept confidential, in accord with general Oxford practice, and were only published in a pirate edition by the parliamentary commissioners, from copies in the public domain, in 1853.⁶ It was left to a later fellow out of sympathy with the Oxford Movement to sort out the college records and put together the first coherent account of its history. Charles Lancelot Shadwell (1840–1919) came from a distinguished legal family; his grandfather had been the last vice-chancellor of England. Coming up to Christ Church from Westminster in 1859, he read classics and then the new school of law and history, and was elected to an Oriel fellowship in 1864, lecturing both in history and in law. He occupied one or both of the treasurerships for most of the years 1866–87. From his undergraduate days he had been a member of the literary essay club Old Mortality and one of Walter Pater's circle of aesthetes; Pater described his translation of Dante's *Purgatorio* as 'full of the patience of

---

⁴ Hearne, *Collections*, viii. 166.
⁵ Thomas Mozley, *Reminiscences Chiefly of Oriel College and the Oxford Movement*, 2 vols. (London, 1882), i. 141–2.
⁶ *Statutes of the Colleges of Oxford*, 3 vols. (Oxford, 1853).

genius', and had been inspired by his personality to write *Diaphaneité*, whose hero was 'the ethical equivalent of light...the regenerative principle, the creative spark'.[7] Shadwell, whose private fortune effectively made him an independent scholar, eventually exchanged his official fellowship for an honorary equivalent and finally, in 1905, was elected provost. In the treasurer's office he was able to devote his energies to the records in his care. He rearranged, rehoused, and renumbered them, and transcribed the early treasurers' accounts; he systematically if incompletely calendared the deeds relating to college properties, in a privately printed edition, and produced an annotated private edition of the calendar of 1397 from its alienated exemplar in the British Museum. The collotype facsimile which he had made of the calendar and register of muniments was bound and labelled *in usum decani*, to remind that officer of ancient college customs. He collected but did not publish material on the provosts and fellows, but did publish in two volumes a register of the junior members of the college up to 1900, with a few biographical notes, compiled from university and college records, and accompanied with essays on the various classes of college membership.[8] His researches were summarized in the essay on Oriel which he contributed to Andrew Clark's volume on Oxford colleges: a study based directly on college records, which however (unlike the other essays in the volume), stopped short of the nineteenth century, with only a veiled and non-committal reference to Newman.[9] Shadwell's Oriel was a traditional body guided by past custom; it was not to be, as was Newman's in 1830, a romantic reconstruction of the founder's intent in the light of modern controversies. Nevertheless, the dramatic circumstances of the Tractarian controversies themselves imprinted in the fellowship, by Shadwell's time, a sense of the historic significance of the college's recent past. At attempt was made to collect relevant manuscript and pamphlet material, stimulated perhaps by the collections deposited in the library after Provost Hawkins's death in 1882. The 'Orielensia' collection, placed in the Cedar Room on the western end of the senior library gallery and assigned its own callmark, seems to have been formed at that time, though whether Shadwell had any part in it is quite uncertain; the logician John Cook Wilson was then librarian and may have assembled it himself.

All subsequent historical work on Oriel, including the present volume, is dependent on the labours of Shadwell. They provided the underpinnings of David Watson Rannie's volume on Oriel in the college history series published by F. E. Robinson and Co. in 1900, the first and until now the only

---

[7] ODNB s.n.; Gerald C. Monsman, 'Old Mortality at Oxford', *Studies in Philology*, 67 (1970), 359–89, cf. 386; *Provosts and Fellows*, 183.

[8] C. L. Shadwell, *Catalogue of the Oriel College Muniments 10 parts* (Oxford, 1893–1905); *Oriel College Calendar, 1397* (Oxford, 1899); *Registrum Orielense*, 2 vols. (London, 1893–1902). His transcriptions of the treasurers' accounts are in Oriel College archives.

[9] Andrew Clark, *The Colleges of Oxford* (London, 1891), 87–123.

full-length history of the college.¹⁰ Rannie (1857–1923) was a graduate of Edinburgh University who had come to Oriel in 1888 as a mature student, to read modern history; he achieved numerous academic successes, including the Stanhope and the Chancellor's English Essay Prizes and a first class in modern history in 1892. Though he had been called to the Bar in 1888, he had devoted himself to literature and history, publishing outlines on the English constitution and the history of Scotland, and works on Wordsworth, 'avowedly desultory', and Shakespeare; he edited two volumes of Hearne's collections for the Oxford Historical Society. Once at Oxford he 'gave himself to the studies of the place with the earnestness of a mature mind', in the words of F. C. Montague's obituary. He lived in Oxford for some years after graduation, and served as a lecturer at Exeter College.¹¹ His history of the college was supported by Provost Monro, by the dean, F. H. Hall, and the librarian, F. C. Montague, who afforded him access to materials; but his overwhelming debt to Shadwell is fully acknowledged. It is clear on even a rapid perusal of Rannie's history that he worked through not only Shadwell's notes and transcriptions but the unpublished Dean's Register; his account of the first five centuries of Oriel filled out Shadwell's sketch and added material on some notable members of the college, but did not depart far from his mentor's interpretation. Once he reached the nineteenth century, however, he walked on territory not charted by Shadwell; and here he showed a fine judgement, confidently negotiating the crevasses opened up by acrimony not yet quite extinguished. He could rely on substantial materials, including Provost Hawkins's private communications with the Oriel tutors, shown him by Monro, on the 'Orielensia' collection, and on a mass of memoirs and published correspondence. The Tractarians were amply remembered in Thomas Mozley's *Reminiscences*, the memoirs of Mark Pattison, Newman's correspondence edited by Anne Mozley, and the scattered memories of Dean Church in his occasional publications. Rannie, writing a decade before William Tuckwell's *Pre-Tractarian Oxford* was published, reached behind them to reconstruct the college brought to distinction by Provosts Eveleigh and Copleston and by the rationalizing Noetic circle. He made use both of William Copleston's memoir of his uncle and Archbishop Whately's edition of Copleston's *Remains*, together with the recollections of John Keble; he was aware of the precocious statistical work of Henry Beeke on the income tax, and sensitive to the satirical potential of Noetic earnestness symbolized by the Oriel common room teapot. Rannie was no less well balanced about the Tractarians and their critics; his account of the relations of Hawkins with

---

[10] D. W. Rannie, *Oriel College* (London, 1900).
[11] On Rannie see *Registrum Orielense*, ii. 660; F. C. Montague in OR (December 1923), 175–7. Though stated in the Register as from Edinburgh University, he is not recorded in the *Alphabetical List of Graduates of the University of Edinburgh 1859–1888* (Edinburgh, 1890).

Newman and the other tutors in 1830, using the confidential material in Monro's custody and Copleston's advice to his successor, is eminently judicious. His sympathies were clearly with Hawkins, to whose daughter he dedicated the book; but he respected Newman and Hurrell Froude, and included sympathetic sketches of Charles Marriott and Charles Page Eden. His broad sympathies and irenic tone amply justified the provost's confidence in him, and allowed his book to establish a conciliatory interpretation of the recent past which must have suited the college authorities in the difficult situation of 1900. Shadwell for all his learning could not have achieved it. The college was fortunate to find in Rannie, an unusual alumnus, such an intelligent and eloquent spokesman.

It was left to Shadwell's younger colleague, the Hellenist George Chatterton Richards, to bring his unpublished work into print. A former proctor and active member of the fellowship, Richards had his own antiquarian interests and had compiled material on the provosts and fellows before Shadwell's notes on the subject became available to him. He published their combined work in 1922, completing the prosopography of the college which Shadwell had initiated in *Registrum Orielense*, and incorporating a number of learned appendices; they included a partly speculative table of the order of succession of the fellows, an exercise clearly inspired by Edward Bentham's researches, but attempted on a grand scale by no previous Oxford antiquary.[12] His *Provosts and Fellows* set a new standard in Oxford biographical registers, prefiguring on a small scale the monumental register of medieval Oxford alumni undertaken by A. B. Emden a few years later. The forthcoming sixth centenary of Oriel, due in 1926, elicited two further publications. The first volume of the so-called Dean's Register, in fact the college register, was prepared by Richards with the help of H. E. Salter of Magdalen, the indefatigable leading light of the Oxford Historical Society; it was an invaluable record of college business from 1504 to 1661. Richards, preparing to leave for a chair at Durham, had no part in the second publication, an edition of medieval college records prepared by Salter on the basis of Shadwell's organization and catalogue of the muniments; Salter, in deference to his predecessor, included Shadwell's name on the title page, but the work was effectively his own. Though it covered only the Oxford deeds of the college, it made possible the systematic study of medieval Oriel, and included a critical edition of the foundation statutes.[13] It was the last work published in Shadwell's wake.

The treasurer's office with its custody of the records continued after 1926 to be the centre of investigation of Oriel's history. C. S. Emden was treasurer

---

[12] *Provosts and Fellows*.
[13] G. C. Richards and H. E. Salter (eds.), *The Dean's Register of Oriel, 1446–1661* (OHS, Oxford, 1926); C. L. Shadwell and H. E. Salter (eds.), *Oriel College Records* (OHS, Oxford, 1926).

from 1928 to 1946; a graduate in jurisprudence and an authority on the British constitution, he developed an interest in aspects of college history especially in the eighteenth century. Individual Orielenses, however, were the subjects of his researches; only a few documents in the archives engaged his attention, such as the common room account book from 1744 to 1900; his debt to Shadwell was confined to the names in the register. His work was organized in a number of short papers, which were published in a collected edition in 1948.[14] In accord with the spirit of the times, he concentrated on family and friendship networks: Sir Walter Raleigh and his friends, Virginians at Oriel, the Oriel friends of Dr Johnson, loyal Oriel families. Relying largely on materials outside the college, including numerous family papers, he restored a considerable body of distinguished alumni to college attention, among them Sir Robert Harley (1579–1656), Lord Chief Justice Holt (1642–1710), William Cadogan the physician and pioneer paediatrician (1711–97), and Joseph Warton the literary scholar (1722–1800). The ever popular Gilbert White of Selborne (1720–93), to whom he devoted three studies, was later the subject of a longer work.[15] Though his tone is that of a dilettante, and his references are not very explicit, these papers are models of scholarship. He may well have been the moving force behind the remarkably large collection of portraits and drawings of Orielenses which hang in the small common room.

A number of other scholars made use of the reorganized archives to investigate aspects of Oriel's past, often publishing the results in the *Oriel Record*: among them were F. J. Varley, who used the treasurers' accounts to elucidate the history of the buildings, and G. N. Clark, the tutor in modern history. The largest contribution was made by W. A. Pantin, one of Clark's successors as a tutor, who was a pioneer of the study of vernacular architecture and had an unrivalled knowledge of the surviving remains of medieval buildings in Oxford. Among them Tackley's Inn in the High Street was an ancient property of the college with thirteenth-century features; Kylyngworth's in Oriel Street, a college property since 1367, had been rebuilt about 1600. Pantin brought documentary sources and the material remains together in studies in the *Oriel Record* and elsewhere.[16] In 1954 he wrote a brief account of college history, with a survey of the development of the buildings, for the Victoria County History: it was an effective updating of Shadwell's account in 1891, especially as to the material structure of the college.[17] The

---

[14] C. S. Emden, *Oriel Papers* (Oxford, 1948).
[15] Emden, *Gilbert White in his Village* (London, 1963).
[16] W. A. Pantin, 'Tackley's Inn', OR (1941), 139–55; 'Kylyngworth's', OR (January 1944), 246–53; 'The Halls and Schools of Medieval Oxford', in R. W. Southern et al. (eds.), *Oxford Studies Presented to Daniel Callus* (Oxford, OHS, 1964), 31–100, which in addition considered the halls incorporated in the St Mary quadrangle.
[17] Pantin, 'Oriel College', VCH *Oxfordshire*, iii. 119–31.

basis of all these studies was the accumulated muniments and other records of the college, now stored in the basement of the Rhodes Building in ever increasing disorder as recent office papers were progressively added to the stock. Eventually in 1993–6, through the generous support of the Sunley Foundation, a new archive room was constructed above the library stack, and the muniments were reorganized to modern standards by the strenuous efforts of two successive archivists, Elizabeth Boardman and Robert Petre. Their work is the foundation on which the present volume stands.

The reorganization of the archive has made access to the materials used by Shadwell and his successors easier, but has not brought to light any substantial additions to what was known in 1890. The largest corpus, naturally, is the muniment proper, the deeds on which the college's title to its property rests. Some, though not all, of the early deeds were calendared by Shadwell, and the deeds to Oxford properties were printed by Salter; the remainder, and especially the archive of the college manor of Wadley, have much to reveal about both the circumstances of the original benefactions and the subsequent administration of college property. Estate documents and maps throw further light on the agricultural properties after 1700. Of more general significance are the annual treasurers' accounts, which survive for 1410–15, 1450–1526, and (as the 'Style') from 1582 onwards, from which evidence of the college's social life, its building, and its external relations can be derived. After 1643 the buttery books have information on individual members' expenses in college. In the Dean's Register a few documents of 1446–50, preserved as models for correspondence, precede the record of college decisions which begins in 1504; the first volume to 1661, which has been printed, contains matters of substance, as do parts of its unpublished successors though their character becomes increasingly formal. Occasional records of special circumstances, such as the inquiry into the conduct of the fellows in 1411, surviving correspondence of the sixteenth century, and the benefactors' book in the seventeenth and eighteenth centuries, add further details. Provost Carter's memorandum book, with drafts of letters of the second and third decades of the eighteenth century, throws light on the turbulent internal affairs of early Georgian Oriel, on which from another viewpoint the notes and collections of the antiquary Thomas Hearne are equally eloquent. From the beginning of the nineteenth century notes and documents of successive provosts survive, and from the 1860s their notes of college meetings, sometimes with voting records, are extant. From this time the archive contains records of college clubs and societies, including sporting clubs, as well as governing body and committee minutes and the college accounts.

A large body of material has been collected in addition in the college library. The earliest collection of about a hundred manuscripts, catalogued possibly in 1349, was evidently divided into a reference and a lending library;

but none of them appears to be among the current Oriel manuscripts.[18] Seven among the present holdings, including two given before 1349, provide evidence of the fellows' studies in the fourteenth century; thirty more were given or bought during the fifteenth century, while an equal number of uncertain origin very probably include some acquired before 1500. In addition there are thirteen manuscripts from the medieval collection now in other libraries. The intellectual life of the fellows and their work of instruction can partly be followed in these texts with the fellows' occasional annotations. Those of the sojourner Dr Thomas Gascoigne, who lived in Oriel from about 1430 to 1458, are particularly eloquent, though most of the hundred manuscripts known to carry his notes are in other collections. From about 1540 the college set about expanding its exiguous and serendipitous collection of printed books, to which the legacies of Thomas Cogan, John Jackman, and Anthony Blencowe contributed further. The library was probably situated on the eastern range of the front quadrangle until the rebuilding of the 1630s, when it was on the northern side. Surviving callmarks seem to refer to the library in its latter position. It continued to increase in the eighteenth century, especially with acquisitions in the fields of theology and church history, until with Lord Leigh's bequest of a more elegant and up-to-date collection the present senior library was constructed to house them. All these books have a potential bearing on the studies and intellectual life of the fellows, though without annotations, which are not common, it is difficult to pin it down. The library expanded considerably during the nineteenth century, and about 1900, building on the 'Orielensia' collections, a deliberate effort was made to accumulate private correspondence relating to the Noetics and the Oxford Movement, of which the core was the correspondence of Provost Hawkins. This collection has proved to be the most extensive primary source for both Noetics and Tractarians, matched only by the published memoirs and papers of the protagonists. It is supplemented for the early twentieth century by the prolific correspondence of Provost Phelps with members of the college, many of whom were in government service in distant parts of the empire, and most of whom of the appropriate age fought in the First World War. The present authors are greatly indebted to Marjory Szurko, the Librarian, for her expert organization of these materials and readiness to produce them in response to the contributors' constant demands.

Other sources of college history are more adventitious. University records, especially those of the vice-chancellor's court, include a number of Oriel wills

---

[18] The catalogue is dated to 1375 by Shadwell, 'The Catalogue of the Library of Oriel College in the 14th Century', in C. R. L. Fletcher (ed.), *Collectanea*, i (OHS, 1885), 57–70, but assigned to 1349 by W. J. Courtenay, 'The Fourteenth-Century Booklist of the Oriel College Library', *Viator*, 19 (1988), 283–90.

and an occasional lawsuit. The occasional admonitions and directions of the Visitor are found, up to 1727, among the records of the diocese of Lincoln. The public records contain, on this as on any other English institution, significant information in unpredictable places; and the private papers of members of the college are of course to be found in a great variety of archives and libraries. Doubtless some of them have yet to be identified; but a great number have been pressed into service in the present volume, as will be seen.

The most prominent distinctive feature which historians of the college noticed was the relative freedom of the fellows under the statutes to elect colleagues from any part of the realm. The early colleges, whether by statute or custom, favoured their founders' kin or students from particular dioceses, or from places where they had property, in elections to fellowships; New College was bound to elect scholars of Winchester College, and Balliol, in the statutes of 1507, to give preference to its own junior members. Oriel was an exception: Adam de Brome had no kin, and made no provision for regional privilege; an early bias to the north Midlands did not last, and the internal dissensions of the fellows between 1385 and 1426 may well have been due to the uneasy cohabitation of northerners and southerners under the same roof. This was explicitly confirmed in 1426, under a new statute which laid down that no more than two fellows from the same 'town, city, county or diocese' should be in post together. Restrictions were however placed upon the Frank fellowships, endowed in 1441 with preference to candidates from four southwestern counties, and on two further fellowships for which scholars of the dioceses of Worcester and Lincoln were favoured. Renewed dissensions over regional bias broke out in the early sixteenth century. But the clear preponderance of the western and south-western counties in fellowship elections was gradually diminished during the late seventeenth and eighteenth centuries, and in 1674 new injunctions of the Visitor laid down procedures for the election of fellows, which included a wide quorum of electors, and provision for disputations and a written examination.

These new arrangements should on the face of it have allowed intellectual merit among a broad body of potential candidates to prevail in fellowship elections. But did it? Nearly 60 per cent of fellows between the Restoration and the election of Provost Eveleigh had matriculated elsewhere. It is less clear that they were preferred on merit: some who despaired of election in their own colleges were advised to apply to Oriel, but the grounds on which they failed to find favour in their original societies but were more fortunate in Oriel are not obvious. Learning certainly counted for something to Provost Carter in the 1720s; affection to the Hanoverian government perhaps for more. It is telling that few fellows elected between 1660 and 1770 made much of a mark beyond the college walls; John Robinson, Richard Dyer, and Gilbert White were notable, though perhaps accidental exceptions. In Provost Clark's time criteria were perhaps changing, with the election of John

Eveleigh (1770), Henry Beeke (1775), and Daniel Veysie (1776). The fellows were free to choose without restriction to their own matriculated members or (with a few exceptions) to candidates from designated regions, but Rannie was surely right to remark that 'what directly led to the pre-eminence of Oriel in the first thirty years of the nineteenth century... was the use it made of this exceptional freedom'.[19] Only in 1795, with the election of Edward Copleston to a restricted fellowship on grounds of merit, is there incontrovertible evidence of a new spirit in the college. The statutes might make the improvement of the fellowship possible; but only the spirit of the age made it necessary.

One distinctive feature may, tentatively, be observed. Among the ranks of solid citizens and grave senators of the college, a tendency to resist fashionable ideas is sporadically evident, notably in Reginald Pecock's idiosyncratic theology, Edward Powell's rejection of the Henrician Church, Sir Walter Raleigh's scepticism, William Prynne's defiance of Archbishop Laud, and the Tractarian campaign against progressive liberalism. Newman escaped formal censure, but his opponent Renn Dickson Hampden, like Pecock and even the saintly bishop Edward King in 1887, faced the indignities of ecclesiastical tribunals, while Prynne suffered more materially, and Powell and Raleigh capitally, for their willingness to stand out in unsympathetic company. While this trait should not be exaggerated—most of them had fierce opponents within the college—equally it should not be ignored. Subversives and troublemakers, with whom a more recent member of the college, A. J. P. Taylor, gladly identified, were a necessary product of the intellectual independence which every generation of Orielenses nurtured.

Some of the chapters presented here are chronological in scope; others focus on topics such as the college's buildings, its estates, and the sporting activities of its members which are better treated separately. The contributors have sought to present a portrait of this community, or more accurately a succession of college communities, in the widest sense of the term, that is of its members in any capacity, their background and subsequent lives. In some periods Orielenses have constituted a network of patronage, or a body offering mutual advantage, though only to a limited extent. At other times they have made a forum for intense ethical and religious debate, in which the only constants have been profound differences of principle, maintained with passion. A placid stream has alternated with an angry torrent. If we have succeeded in conveying something of these changing faces of the college community, we will have achieved our modest objective; but our success will be judged by the readers of the following chapters. The inevitable omissions and inaccuracies are of course the responsibility of the editor.

[19] Rannie, *Oriel College*, 163.

I

The Foundation

Jeremy Catto

In 1326, when we have the first evidence of a community of scholars at St Mary's, later to be the college commonly known as Oriel, the University of Oxford was entering its era of maturity as a primary European centre of thought. For the first time, a critical mass of trained thinkers was in formation, whose distinctive logical, philosophical, and theological ideas were now received and absorbed beyond English shores and notably in the older and more prestigious schools of Paris.[1] In the previous generation its most brilliant philosopher, the Franciscan Duns Scotus, had been the first Oxonian substantially to influence European thought. By 1326 Oxford was the centre of a prolific variety of intellectual developments: the recast terminist logic of another Oxonian, the Franciscan William of Ockham; the new mathematical physics of the 'Oxford Calculators' who attempted a mathematical description of physical changes of all kinds; and the exploration by theologians of the limits of human knowledge of God and of God's omnipotence. In the course of these debates an immense body of literature was produced, for the most part formally organized questions within commentaries on the works of Aristotle or the *Sentences* of Peter Lombard, with a few tracts on special topics. The majority of this work is still confined to manuscripts or at best early printed texts, but some of the material which has been read by modern thinkers is surprisingly relevant to current debates on analytical philosophy and even psychology. Its writers cannot really be classified, contrary to what used to be assumed, into particular philosophical schools, Scotist, Thomist, or nominalist; they had independent minds and disputed with one another on particular issues. No master however prestigious could escape the critical appraisal of his colleagues, usually expressed with professional courtesy, though profound and strongly felt disagreements lay beneath the surface.

---

[1] On what follows see above all William J. Courtenay, *Schools and Scholars in Fourteenth-Century England* (Princeton, 1987).

Some debates were the business of the arts faculty, where questions of logic and natural philosophy were the central topics. They formed a continuum with the issues discussed in the faculty of theology, where somewhat older masters, having completed their study of arts, disputed the deepest philosophical and theological questions. Very few of the masters can have been over 40 and almost all, at this time, looked forward to a career beyond the schools.

Masters and students, then, were a community in which each age cohort helped to instruct their juniors. They lived in distinct smaller communities, some bound by a common religious rule, like the large houses of the four orders of friars or the smaller colleges of monks, others joined together in one of the hundred or so 'academic halls', a lodging house governed by a master or 'principal' who might also provide informal instruction. From the 1260s a new form of community, colleges for scholars outside the religious orders who had with some exceptions attained a first degree, was coming into existence. Endowed by external patrons, with funds to support a limited number of fellows who could enjoy the advantages long possessed by the friars, these new associations would slowly come to encapsulate the way of life of the university. But in 1326 only four had established themselves: Balliol, for masters of arts from a northern background; University College, a smaller community with a similar bias; Exeter, founded for scholars from the south-west; and Merton, much larger and richer than the others, and with a less developed regional bias, which catered for all faculties. The motives of their mainly ecclesiastical founders varied, but they attest the growing prestige of a university education, which could fit its beneficiaries to give intelligent service to potentates and dignitaries in numerous ways. Participation in the intellectual awakening of Oxford in the years around 1326 was probably not what the founders of colleges expected of their members, since the friars were, at that time, the main protagonists in the great debates. Nevertheless, and particularly as the work of the arts faculty in which friars were not represented grew in maturity and originality, the colleges and especially Merton took an increasing part in it. The English governing cadre was not slow to notice and to appreciate the new intellectual confidence of Oxford scholars. That a clerk of the king's chancery, an institution at the heart of government, should seek to support them with a college of his own was therefore in accord with the spirit of the times.

The first indication that a community of scholars of the University of Oxford was actually residing in part of the premises of the modern college of Oriel is to be found in the statutes issued by Edward II at Norwich on 21 January 1326. Envisaging a future removal to more convenient quarters, the charter refers to an earlier assignment of the *mansum rectorie* of St Mary's Church for the scholars' residence, implying that they were now ensconced in the rector's house.² This earliest code of statutes was for the most part a somewhat simplified version of the Merton statutes of August 1274; the points of difference from its model reveal, perhaps, the actual characteristics of the new community.³ The number of scholars, or fellows, was still flexible: a potential future increase in the number of beneficiaries in step with a growing income was in the mind of the statutes' framer, and arrangements for a dean, sub-deans, and supervisors for young scholars seem appropriate for a larger body than the ten fellows who constituted the college before 1441. It is unlikely, however, that resources were available to sustain as many as ten in January 1326. The statutes were more specific than Merton's on the scholars' studies: though they could be admitted if they were bachelors of arts, they were expected to proceed, once they were masters, to study in the higher faculty of theology, or as a variant in the faculties of civil and canon law.⁴ Above all the statutes, like the foundation charter issued on the same day, underlined the role of the central figure, Adam de Brome 'whom we have preferred to the place of provost of the same, and whom we desire to choose the scholars of the college'.⁵ In every charter, set of statutes and transaction associated with the establishment of the college, Adam appears as the prime mover, his name alone cited in all of them. His intentions, and his success in implementing them, must be the focus of any enquiry into the circumstances in which this body of scholars came together and perpetuated itself.

The founder, for such he clearly was in reality under the formal and prestigious umbrella of a royal charter, was on the face of it an unlikely benefactor of Oxford. Adam de Brome was an experienced clerk of chancery who had achieved some measure of success: he had served in the multiple roles expected of kings' clerks at the beginning of the fourteenth century, as an army procurer in the wars of Edward I, as an auditor and collector of taxes, and a justice in inquisitions and commissions of oyer and terminer.⁶ Earlier founders of colleges had been grander: bishops like Walter de Merton and Walter de Stapeldon, the founder of Exeter College, or nobility such as John de Balliol earl of Galloway and Dervorguilla his wife. Moreover, the donors of Oxford loan-chests had all been, until Brome's generation, royalty, earls, and bishops. Adam was therefore a founder of a new kind, exemplified in the two contemporary donors of loan-chests, the judges Henry Guildford and Gilbert de Rothbury, and in the king's clerk Robert de Eglesfield, the

---

² OCR 12–13.
³ *Statutes of the Colleges of Oxford* (Oxford, 1853), i, Oriel, 6–16; cf. the Merton statutes, *Statutes of the Colleges of Oxford*, i, Merton, 23–37.
⁴ OCR 6.
⁵ OCR 6.
⁶ CPR 1292–1301, 344–5, 585; CPR 1301–7, 309; CPR 1307–13, 327; Cal. Inq. Misc. 1307–47, 72, no. 293; CPR 1317–21, 98.

founder of Queen's College in 1341.⁷ There is no certain indication of the origins of Adam de Brome. Among many suggestions, the most plausible is that of Sir Maurice Powicke, who was inclined to think him a member of a fairly humble family from Brome in Suffolk, close to Eye, which was the centre of an honour in the possession of Edmund earl of Cornwall, cousin of Edward I, until his death in 1300. In Edmund's inquisition *post mortem* Adam was stated to hold a moiety of a knight's fee worth 13*s*. 4*d*. a year.⁸ His entry into the king's service might well have been effected by a patron such as Earl Edmund. He must have been born before 1270, as his first mention in the records of government seems to have been entered in June 1292, an acknowledgement of a debt of 26*s*. 8*d*. to Adam by Gilbert de Sancta Fide, enrolled in the Close Rolls.⁹ The record of a private transaction in so solemn a manner is the first of many relating to Adam's affairs, and indicates with high probability that he was already a clerk in the chancery. Thereafter he was mentioned fairly frequently, at first (1297–1301) in the role of procuring supplies in southern England and in Ireland for Edward I's armies in Scotland.¹⁰ The unpopular role of tax-collector regularly fell to him: he was auditor of the clerical tenth in 1305, assessor of tallage in 1312, and collector of the sixth in 1323.¹¹ The law played a large part in his career, with experience as an attorney and later, in 1315, as a commissioner of oyer and terminer and justice of the Staple, and as chancellor of Durham *sede vacante* in 1311 and 1316–17.¹² His services were important enough after 1315 to allow him regular letters of protection as a king's clerk from legal proceedings against him, and until at least 1329 he was deemed to be constantly in the chancery on the king's business.¹³ By 1323 he was present at the council meeting held at Thorpe, by which time he must have had more or less close access to the king.¹⁴ By the 1320s, an era of active and in many contemporary eyes oppressive government, he must have had distinct personal authority and concomitant opportunities for patronage. The records of chancery provide evidence that Adam was also involved throughout his career, like other clerks, in private transactions of a more or less lucrative character. He was able to act as attorney in the Westminster courts for numerous individuals including the prior of Hertford, Oliver d'Eyncourt, and John Lutterell,

---

[7] On the judges see J. Sainty, *The Judges of England, 1272–1990* (London, Selden Society supplementary series 10, 1993), 60, 61. On Eglesfield see ODNB s.n.
[8] CCR 1296–1302, 436. See F. M. Powicke, 'More Notes on Adam de Brome', *Oriel Record* (June 1941), 135–9.
[9] CCR 1288–96, 267.
[10] CPR 1292–1301, 242, 344–5, 488, 585.
[11] CPR 1301–7, 309; CPR 1307–13, 521; CPR 1321–4, 324.
[12] CPR 1313–17, 423.
[13] CPR 1313–17, 347; CPR 1324–7, 62; CPR 1327–30, 454.
[14] List of persons present at the meeting, printed from TNA PRO C.49/45/13 by J. C. Davies, *The Baronial Opposition to Edward II* (Cambridge, 1918), 584.

sometime chancellor of Oxford. The series of appointments to this role recorded in chancery begins in 1299 and extends to 1325.[15] More difficult to interpret are the recognizances of debt, usually in favour of Brome, which are recorded from 1292. They seem to be contracted with other chancery clerks like Robert de Bardelby and Henry de Clif, but sometimes with other parties, and to involve sums ranging from £1 10s. to £54 13s. What lies behind them can only be guessed, but they do indicate an additional business of some kind, in which Adam is likely to have made a profit.[16] In one transaction of 1302 in which he was the debtor he funded his debt on lands in Yorkshire, otherwise unmentioned: they had been acquired perhaps when Edward I's government had been set up at York, and may explain why he sought an endowment for his college in the Yorkshire church of Aberford.[17] He received in addition benefices appropriate to a clerk of chancery after his ordination in 1301: Wyck Rissington in Gloucestershire in 1301, the mastership of Dunwich Hospital (1306–12), Bridford in Devon (1311–12), St Creed, Cornwall (1314), the prebend of Bathwick, Somerset (1314–20), Handsworth, Yorkshire (1314–16 or later), the archdeaconry of Stow (1320), St Mary's, Oxford (1320–6), and a moiety of Eckington, Derbyshire, in 1328.[18] This is probably not a complete record, but it shows the level of remuneration, substantial but not excessive, which Adam's services were thought to merit.

It is not clear at what point Adam de Brome became interested in Oxford and its university. No evidence remains of any connection between the chancery clerk and the schools until 16 June 1320, when he was presented to the living of St Mary's. Even after that date, and until his death in 1332, his work as a justice of the Staple and on various commissions must have kept him in London or on the road: his presence is recorded on a number of formal occasions in the chancery, where, according to his letters of protection, he was constantly in attendance. The rector of St Mary's had, however, a substantial rectory across the High Street, and references to his activities in Oxford through the 1320s may indicate that he spent some time there. It is probably coincidental that one of his tasks was the inspection of weirs in Oxfordshire, Berkshire, and Buckinghamshire (1 December 1320); it was more indicative, perhaps, of periods of residence that another was to enquire into lands in Oxfordshire in the king's hand (30 December 1322).[19] By 1323 he was hearing the plaints of the abbot of Rewley, and in 1325 he was entrusted with part of the municipal seal for the recognizance of debts, and commissioned to enquire into the state of the town walls.[20] The rector's standing at Westminster

---

[15] CPR 1307–13, 112; CPR 1324–7, 106; CPR 1292–1301, 455.
[16] See for example CCR 1288–96, 267; CCR 1313–18, 81; CCR 1318–23, 354; CCR 1330–3, 178.
[17] CCR 1296–1302, 578.
[18] BRUO i. 274–5, s.n.
[19] CPR 1317–21, 547; CCR 1318–23, 620.
[20] CPR 1321–4, 258, 308, 311; CPR 1324–7, 223.

enabled him to do service for the university. His position may have persuaded Thomas Cobham, bishop of Worcester, to promise funds to build a new congregation house and university library in the churchyard, a project which Adam undertook and which was partly achieved by the bishop's death in 1327.[21] Besides representing the former chancellor Lutterell during his absence, he may have protected the chancellor from prosecution for failures in his responsibility (together with the mayor) for the assize of bread and ale, as is implied in a letter to John de Everdon, baron of the exchequer.[22] A powerful and well-disposed royal judge installed at St Mary's must have been a valuable asset from the university's point of view.

These activities offer no direct clue to his motive in turning his rectory into a college, and himself into its provost with duties of residence, while continuing (unwillingly perhaps) to perform the arduous round of the king's service. No other founder or benefactor had so involved himself in the ordinary business of the university, though none of course had been rector of a town church and thus already, if only nominally, under the jurisdiction of the chancellor of the university. Perhaps the most plausible context of his foundation is to be found not immediately in Oxford but in the chancery. From at least 1325 he associated senior clerks of chancery with his property transactions on behalf of the college: he took seisin of the church of Aberford together with William de Herleston, and the deed which admitted James of Spain, the king's cousin and sometime chamberlain of the exchequer, to the fraternity of the college was witnessed by Herleston, Mr Henry de Clif, and two other chancery clerks. Robert de Bardelby, another clerk, though not associated with Brome in assembling property, was remembered as a benefactor, with his obit observed.[23] All three were among the most senior clerks of chancery, who acted as keepers of the great seal on several occasions in the reign of Edward II.[24] Clif seems to have been a university master, probably of Oxford. Further, two of Adam's proxies in deeds from 1327 onwards, Richard Overton and Alan de Horncastle, may well have come from the same circle. Overton was certainly a king's clerk in 1340 and seems to have been a clerk in a more junior position at an earlier date; if so, he took leave to study at Oxford about 1335 and is likely to have been a fellow or sojourner at Oriel during his residence. Horncastle is less clearly connected with the others, but he must have been a practising canon lawyer, as he represented the bishop of Llandaff at the Roman curia in 1326.[25] Finally, the role of James of Spain, an

---

[21] OCR 24–7. [22] TNA PRO SC 1 (Ancient Correspondence) 35/148.
[23] OCR 120–1, 24.
[24] T. F. Tout, *Chapters in the Administrative History of Medieval England*, 6 vols. (Manchester, 1920–33), vi. 7–11.
[25] BRUO i. 438–9, s.n. Cliffe; BRUO ii. 1412, s.n. Overton and ii. 965, s.n. Horncastle. Overton's chancery duties in 1327 are proved by his writing the college's licence in mortmain (14 March), OCR 18.

older and grander figure than any of the others, whose Oxford career went back to the 1270s, and who must as a cousin of Edward II have had an entrée into the king's presence unavailable to any other clerk, is unclear. His legacy of the house of La Oriole to Brome's college in 1328 may have been anticipated in the statutes of 21 January 1326, in the provision for the site of the college to be moved to other premises in the parish of St Mary; if so, he must have encouraged the project.[26] In any case, from one perspective the new foundation could be seen as the work of a body of senior chancery clerks. In the chancery, as in other organs of the king's government, the value of university training was coming to be appreciated, as much among those who had not experienced it as among graduates themselves: the judicial founders of university loan-chests, as well as royal servants such as John Hotham, bishop of Ely, who had been intimately associated with the origin of the King's Hall at Cambridge, exemplify the desire to encourage it. Their sentiment is neatly encapsulated in the words of Edward II's foundation charter of January 1326, words penned in all probability by Adam of Brome: 'the profuse fruit which the university of Oxford.... has up to now conferred on us and on our kingdom in counsel and in the conduct of business...'[27]

Adam's original idea, in April 1324, was to establish a community of scholars under the control of the rector of St Mary's. His licence from the king, dated 20 April, allowed him to accumulate property, notwithstanding the Statute of Mortmain, to the annual value of £30.00, enough for about five scholars.[28] In the same year he acquired two properties for them. One was a house or garden in the northern suburb, now on the north side of Broad Street where the gate of Trinity stands, named Perilous Hall. It was intended only to be let for rent; it probably brought in very little, and in the earliest rental of 1363 it is omitted.[29] More substantial was his purchase, in September 1324, of Tackley's Inn, a hall 'inhabited after the manner of scholars', with a row of shops in front, which had been built as recently as 1291–1300. The shops will have brought in more rent, but the hall range behind, albeit consisting only of a hall and two large solars, was intended, according to his deed of 6 December, to accommodate his scholars.[30] They were to be under the guidance of John de Laghton, the 'rector'. We know nothing further of Laghton, save that he had the reservation of a benefice in 1331 and died while still a fellow by May 1332.[31] He was not termed a master

---

[26] BRUO iii. 1736–8, s.n. Spain; OCR 12–13.   [27] OCR 3.

[28] At the rate of 12*d*. per week per scholar established in 1326, and allowing for half the income to be spent directly on their maintenance.

[29] OCR 274, 383.

[30] 106 High Street; OCR 2. On Tackley's Inn see W. A. Pantin, 'The Halls and Schools of Mediaeval Oxford', in *Oxford Studies Presented to Daniel Callus* (OHS, Oxford, 1965), 38–41.

[31] BRUO ii. 1064, s.n. Laghtone, corrected by L. T. Nau, 'A Note Regarding Four Early Fellows of Oriel College, Oxford', *Mediaeval Studies*, 37 (1975), 543–5.

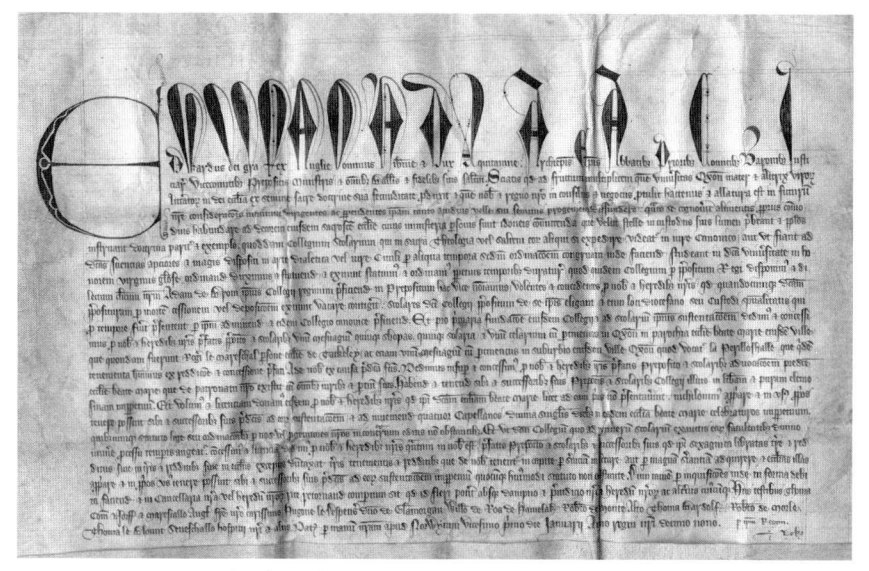

ILLUSTRATION 1.1 The foundation charter of Edward II, 21 January 1326, *OCA*

in 1324, so may simply have been the most senior of the scholars. No others are known by name, though it is a reasonable guess that Ralph de Kevelyngworth, ordained to the title of a fellow in March 1326, William de Kirkham, granted reservation of benefice in 1331 and dead while still in fellowship by 1332, William de Leverton, fellow in 1332 and the second provost, and John de Aston, another fellow in 1332, were among the original scholars.[32] In any case, they seem to have also been accommodated in the rectory of St Mary's, later St Mary Hall, by 1326, as the foundation deed and statutes of 21 January indirectly imply.[33] We know nothing further of this embryonic community.

Adam however continued to be active on behalf of his college. On 18 May 1325 he acquired the advowson of the church of Aberford in Yorkshire, together with William de Herleston; it was later, in 1332, appropriated to Oriel.[34] It must have been about the same time that Adam conceived the more ambitious idea of persuading Edward II to refound the college in his own name, with the rectorship of St Mary's appropriated to it and with himself as the provost. There was nothing out of the ordinary in the appropriation of churches to Oxford colleges: the several precedents of which

---

[32] BRUO ii. 1044 (Kevelyngworth), 1056 (Kirkham), 1138 (Leverton), i. 66–7 (Aston); see Nau, 'A Note', 544–5.
[33] OCR 4, 9.   [34] *Cat. Mun.* vi, nos. 5–8, 17.

20   THE FOUNDATION

ILLUSTRATION 1.2 The college seal, probably made in 1326, *OCA*

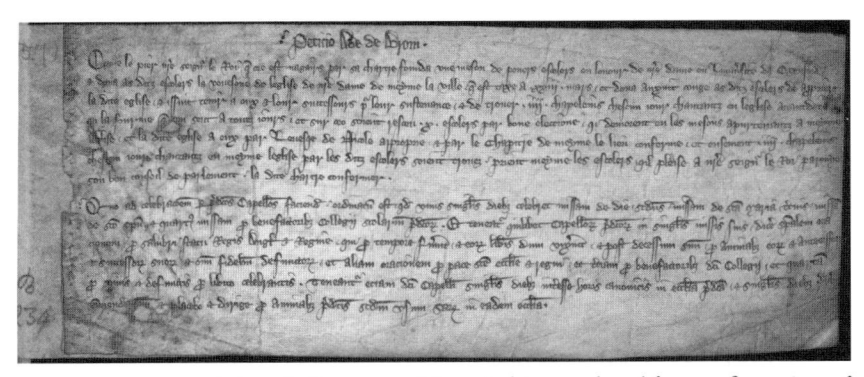

ILLUSTRATION 1.3 Adam de Brome petitions in his own hand for confirmation of his charter, 1326

National Archives

Merton's appropriation of Ponteland, Northumberland, was perhaps the first, and the latest, in 1314, was that of Gwinear in Cornwall to Exeter College. But it was the first appropriation of an Oxford church, and among Oxford churches St Mary's was the most intimately associated with the university. It was the place of debates in congregation and the venue of numerous academic acts. But there is nothing to indicate opposition on the part of the university. The chancellors of the 1320s were primarily men of business who are likely to have shared the values and perspectives of Adam and his chancery colleagues: Henry de Gower (chancellor 1322–5) was a future bishop of St David's, William de Alberwyk (1325–7) would later be a king's clerk himself, Thomas Hotham (1327–8) had earlier been in royal service, and Ralph of Shrewsbury (1328–9) would be bishop of Bath and Wells and would leave a book to Oriel.[35] Until the conflict over Cobham's books came to a head in 1338 there is no sign that the interests of college and university would clash on the common ground of St Mary's. Adam's change of plan did however put his foundation more prominently into the political arena. In the last months of 1325, when he must have been carrying the project towards completion through a royal charter and set of statutes, opposition to Edward II's rule was beginning to focus on the group of exiles round Queen Isabella; but the primacy of the Despensers at the king's court was still undimmed. There was a price to pay for the favour, the beneficiary of which was the king's intimate, Hugh Despenser the younger. The evidence that the issuing of the charter and statutes was not entirely a harmonious proceeding comes partly from the text of the statutes, and partly from a quire among the college muniments which, like two other similar records, appears to have been drawn up by Adam de Brome in his own hand as a note of his property transactions on behalf of the college. The statutes, which must have been drawn up by Adam himself on the basis of the Merton statutes, make provision that the college chaplain should say prayers daily, not only for the king's soul, those of his children, and of the kings of England succeeding him, but for that of 'our cousin and liege Hugh Despenser the younger, the souls of his parents and his friends...at the Corpus Christi altar in the church of [St Mary]'.[36] The statutes and royal charter were issued on 21 January 1326, the charter being witnessed by Despenser among others. Little more than a week later, on 2 February, according to a deed recorded in the parchment quire, Adam acknowledged in final concord at the king's court at Westminster that Hugh Despenser was the rightful owner of the advowson of the church of Aberford, his recently acquired property, relinquished in return for a brown sparrowhawk (*spervarius sorus*). The indignation which Adam felt at being obliged to conclude this humiliating exchange can be inferred

[35] BRUO i. 18; ii. 797, 970; iii. 1698–9.   [36] OCR 13.

from the note which he appended: 'Afterwards the said Hugh became an enemy of and rebel against king Edward son of king Edward son of king Henry, in the twentieth year of his reign [8 July 1326–20 January 1327], and as a result all his lands and tenements, including the advowson of this church, came by forfeiture into the hands of the king; and the following is [Edward III's] charter for the provost and scholars of St Mary's of Oxford.'[37] But in February 1326 his foundation was much diminished by the loss of Aberford: only Perilous Hall and Tackley's Inn could bring in some rent. Some meagre compensation was made on 5 March when Edward II granted the wardenship of St Bartholomew's Hospital (Bartlemas) on the road to Cowley.[38] Not until the acquisition of the advowson of Coleby, the regrant of Aberford, and the gift outright of Bartlemas in 1327 and 1328 could it have seemed secure.

Distaste for the obligation to pray for the Despensers may explain Adam de Brome's rapid supersession of the January statutes. He must have sought, almost immediately after the transaction of 2 February, the approval of

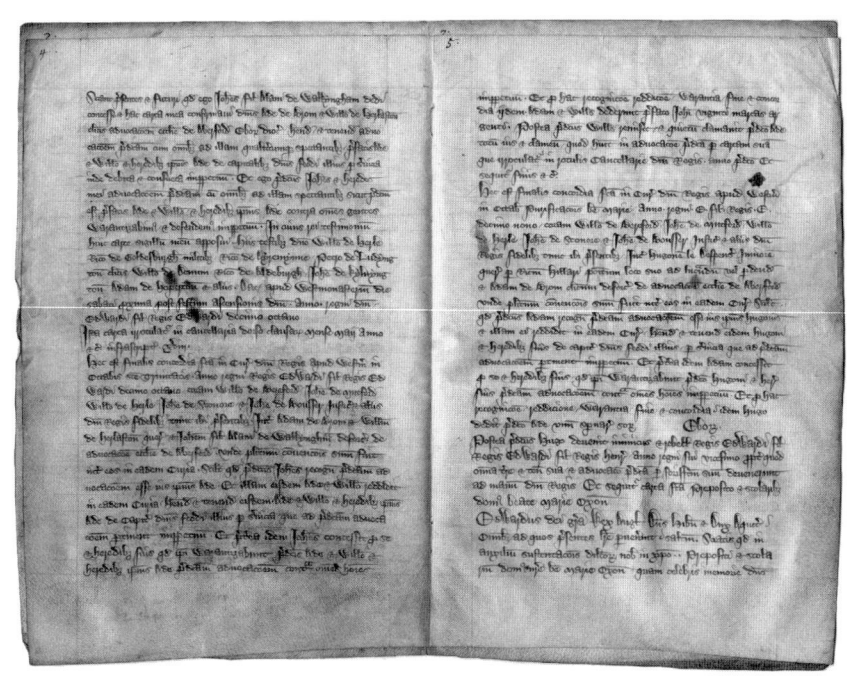

ILLUSTRATION 1.4 Adam de Brome's autograph account of the loss and recovery of Aberford, c.1327, *OCA*

[37] OCA DL14/Z.10, *Processus de Aberford*, 5.   [38] OCR 291–2.

the bishop of Lincoln for the new college, which was forthcoming on 13 March.[39] No hint of anything but praise for Edward II's munificence, described in the context of a long royal tradition of religious foundations and couched in the terms used in the king's foundation charter, can be found in the document. Bishop Henry Burghersh as diocesan of Oxford merely claimed the right of approbation of the charter, and that of confirmation of election where heads of religious foundations were chosen by common vote of the scholars. A few weeks later (19 May) he formally admitted the provost at Stowe Park, Adam presumably being present on that occasion. The college copy of this ratification, which Adam must have brought back with him, was given a title in what appears to be the hand of the Aberford parchment quire, which may well be that of Brome, *Ratificacio et approbacio prepositi et colegii per Episcopum Lincolniensem Diocesanum.* It is also endorsed, in the text hand (with three cancelled phrases and corrections), *dominus Robertus Borwas miles et Matild' eius uxor, magister Rob' Borwas, dominus Stephanus Borwas ac alii liberi.*[40] Four days later these words were inserted in slightly different terms into a revised set of statutes, as Burghersh's parents and siblings for whom the scholars are enjoined to pray, substituting for prayers for the Despenser family as directed in the January version of the statutes.[41] The new document was issued on the college's authority and sealed with the college's seal. This appears to be the evidence leading up to the making of the revised college statutes. What are we to make of it? In the traditional version, best expressed by W. A. Pantin in the Victoria County History, the alteration is explained in terms of national history: 'political events made it necessary to find a new patron for the college in Henry Burghersh, Bishop of Lincoln, in whose diocese Oxford lay...' This will not quite do, since the statutes were issued in May, before Queen Isabella's return and the violent events which led up to Edward II's deposition had destroyed his authority, events which initially had Burghersh himself running for cover.[42] He was in no position to protect an Oxford college, and there was no reason why it should need protection. There was no question of displacing the king; Burghersh's approbation of 13 March had expressly recognized the royal foundation. The revised statutes differed from the original only in two respects. They are more specific in detail, for instance in specifying the number of scholars permitted to read canon or civil law. Such changes were the adjustments natural to a functioning community. Secondly, reference is made to the powers of the bishop of Lincoln, powers of confirming the election of the provost and interpreting the statutes; there is provision for prayers for

---

[39] OCR 14–17. [40] OCA PRO 1 A/2/2; OCR 17 and note 2.
[41] OCR 18 and *Statutes of the Colleges of Oxford*, i, Oriel, 6–13, cf. 12.
[42] W. A. Pantin, 'Oriel College', VCH *Oxfordshire*, iii (London, 1954), 119; Oxford DNB s.n. Henry Burghersh.

Burghersh's relatives and for future bishops of Lincoln, and a declaration that no statutes shall be made in derogation of the bishop's rights and privileges. These changes may be seen as responses to the episcopal assertion of powers in the approbation of 13 March. It is clear that the revised statutes were made by the college, not the bishop. The Oriel text of the ratification of 19 May is written in what is probably an Oriel hand, though not Brome's evidently; and we may reasonably speculate that one of the fellows accompanying Brome took a copy of the original and added a note on the dorse, specifying (with some trial and error) which of Burghersh's relatives were to be named and in what form, at the dictation of a member of the bishop's household. This note was then faithfully reproduced in the revised statutes. In this way, the royal foundation was fully recognized, but the offensive injunction to pray for the Despenser family was removed. In later years, the bishop's ordinary authority was deemed to make him the Visitor, an office which had not emerged in Oxford in 1326; and the King's Bench judgement of 1727, which purported to restore the royal visitorship and the original statutes (though not, evidently, prayers for the Despensers), was equally anachronistic. In May 1326, Brome was merely careful to pay court to both the civil and the ecclesiastical power.

The appropriation of St Mary's to the new college proceeded through its various stages during the summer of 1326. At some point Brome seems to have solicited a letter to Burghersh from Thomas Cobham, the bishop of Worcester and benefactor of the new congregation house and library. Cobham reminded his colleague of their common friendship and patronage of learning, referring to his impending gift of books.[43] Whether his letter had any effect or not, the formalities were completed by 9 August: the Lincoln chapter's concurrence, Adam's resignation of the rectory (both on 4 August), and the induction of Brome into his provostship and the college into the rectory on 9 August, with the prior of St Frideswide's representing the bishop.[44] A few weeks later Queen Isabella landed in Suffolk and threw all political calculations into doubt. Henry Burghersh, who had only precariously regained favour with Edward II in 1324 (having been the protégé of his rebel uncle Lord Badlesmere, executed in 1322), hedged his bets initially and retreated to his fortified manor house at Banbury, but joined the queen in

---

[43] *The Register of Thomas de Cobham, Bishop of Worcester, 1317–27*, ed. E. H. Pearce (Worcester Historical Society, Worcester, 1930), 201. It is not clear why the editor thought this letter should be dated to 1325, when the royal foundation (referred to here) and the appropriation occurred in 1326. The letter is not dated, but is inscribed in a group of undated letters among 1326 entries in chronological order between an entry dated 6 May and a citation to appear on 13 July. It is followed by a note apparently from Cobham's registrar to Brome, apologizing for not sending the draft for Brome to check. This implies that Brome had asked Cobham to write the letter.

[44] OCR 85–8.

November. He was rewarded with a place in the council of the new king Edward III, and in March 1327 with the office of treasurer. Adam de Brome cannot have had any hesitation in adhering to the new regime, given his treatment at the hands of Hugh Despenser and the support given him by Burghersh. He energetically set about rebuilding the material basis of his college, beginning with the new king's immediate confirmation of the charter (but not the statutes) of 21 January 1326, with Burghersh among the witnesses (20 February 1327) and licence in mortmain to acquire new property (14 March).[45] He sought to replace the advowson of Aberford with that of Coleby in Lincolnshire (15 August) and shortly afterwards regained Aberford itself by royal grant (9 October); on 24 February 1328 he had another royal grant of St Bartholomew's Hospital on the road to Cowley, of which he already had the wardenship. He acquired Baner Hall in Broad Street with Richard Overton on 6 June 1329, and Moyses Hall, also with Overton, on 11 June 1330.[46] All these properties produced rent for the college, perhaps about £7 together in the 1348 and 1363 returns.[47] A more momentous acquisition had been effected shortly after the regrant of Aberford. This was the reversion of the royal grace and favour house at the southern end of the block of property on which the rectory of St Mary's stood, known as Seneschal Hall or, more recently, as La Oriole. This very large square house, which was approximately of the same dimensions as the present front quadrangle of Oriel, had been built in the twelfth century. Its 'chambers and outbuildings, kitchen gardens and pleasure gardens' were a spacious contrast to the crowded rectory of St Mary's and Tackley's Inn.[48] It was probably, after Oxford Castle, the largest single residence in the city. Accordingly, it had usually been the perquisite of persons of national or at least regional importance: it had passed from Sawy son of Langrif, otherwise unknown, to Richard of St Germans the sheriff of Berkshire (1176–86), whose position as seneschal or steward of Bernard of St Valery gave the house its earlier name. In the 1190s it had belonged to Hubert Walter, the justiciar and archbishop of Canterbury, and in 1241 to Andrew Blund, the nephew of Henry of London, late archbishop of Dublin. How its transfer between these various owners was effected is unknown in the absence of deeds; when deeds begin, in 1246–7, they show it successively occupied by Mr John de Offinton, his heir Robert de Offinton, Adam Feteplace, and eventually, before 1272, by Bogo de Clare, dean of Stafford. He gave or sold it to the queen, Eleanor of Castile, who granted it for life, about 1280, to her nephew and servant James of Spain, natural son of King Alfonso X of Castile. James may have lived there during his Oxford studies, but let it at least for one period, in 1306, as an academic hall: Dr Walter Stapeldon made an agreement there, 'in his hall at La Oriole'

---

[45] OCR 17–18.   [46] OCR 290–1, 277, 261.   [47] OCR 381–3.
[48] The description is in a deed of about 1280, OCR 117–18.

on 22 April 1306.[49] It is unlikely that James of Spain, who must have been nearly 70 in 1327, resided personally at La Oriole: the deed by which he acknowledged his new landlord was sealed at his London residence in Newgate (28 September 1328). His benevolence to the college was clearly shown on 16 May 1329 when he delivered seisin, or actual possession of the property, to the provost and fellows, receiving in return, together with his deceased aunt, its prayers and the fraternity of the college.[50] Adam de Brome must have moved his college there during the long vacation following, and its continuous residence there, whence it derived its traditional name, may be counted from the academic year 1329–30.

Edward III's confirmation of the new statutes on 18 March 1330 marked the end of the Crown's series of benefactions to Adam's foundation. The bishop of Lincoln concluded his own gifts with an increase in the stipend of the vicar of St Mary's from £5 4s. to ten marks (£6 13s. 4d.) on 17 October 1331.[51] Thereafter the college was to stand on its own with only an occasional helping hand from the king or the diocesan bishop. This did not preclude favours for individual fellows. In the summer of 1331 a list of twenty Oxford masters was submitted to the Roman curia at the king's request, of whom four were fellows (or, less likely, sojourners) of Oriel, and seven Mertonians; these requests were granted on 26 September. The four Oriel beneficiaries were John de Laghton, Brome's deputy in 1324, William de Kirkham, John Ingolmeles, and Richard Kilvington. On 19 May 1332 the Crown requested a variation, substituting John Aston for Laghton who had died, and on 28 May a second variation was sought, with William de Leverton in place of the deceased Kirkham. Copies of the grants of reservation of September 1331 were forwarded to Ralph of Shrewsbury, former Oxford chancellor and now bishop of Bath and Wells, the bishop of Ardfert, and the Keeper of the Privy Seal, Richard de Bury.[52] The bishop of Bath and Wells, a future benefactor of Oriel, and Richard de Bury, a future employer of Kilvington, must be presumed to be the promoters behind this royal request.[53] We thus know the names of six fellows in 1331–2, a viable community.[54] It was not yet large

---

[49] Exeter, Dean and Chapter Archives 2916; see A. G. Little and R. C. Easterling, *The Franciscans and Dominicans of Exeter* (Exeter, 1927), 76–8.

[50] OCR 120–1. On the previous history of the property see OCR 114–20. The fraternity of the college, like honorary fellowships subsequently, will have made its beneficiaries, in modern parlance, members of the community. Its conferment on Queen Eleanor of Castile (died 28 November 1290) made Oriel the first Oxford college to admit a woman.

[51] OCR 19, 88–90.

[52] *Cal. Papal Letters* ii. 363–5 and 361, and for the variations, Nau, 'A Note', 544–5, where a reference to the four Oriel scholars or fellows favoured in 1331 must indicate Kilvington and Ingolmeles as the two others.

[53] The bishop of Ardfert, presumably Edward of Carmarthen OP who had just been promoted to the see, may have been their agent at the Roman curia. Nothing further is known about him.

[54] Mr Ralph de Kevelyngworth had also been named in 1326 (BRUO ii. 1044).

enough for college disputations to be held as laid down in the 1326 statutes, though the new statutes of 8 December 1329 made arrangements for them 'when there will be (*dum fuerint*)' enough scholars or fellows preparing for the MA and B.Th. degrees; but the new statutes looked ahead to the election of the next provost, specified further fees for various offices, and laid down procedures for settling internal disputes.[55] When the founder died, apparently on 16 June 1332, he could have taken satisfaction in a small but comfortably housed and very well-favoured college, with good prospects for survival and for further endowment. He left Moyses Hall and Baner Hall to trustees, Richard Overton and Alan de Horncastle, to be handed over to the college at a later date.[56] More significantly for the future, alone among Oxford college founders, he left no founder's kin or local connection to bind his colleagues. His impression on his community was still decisive. We have no way to assess Adam de Brome's character beyond the bare record of his activities, with one surviving letter. They indicate a tough, energetic, perhaps understated but certainly determined and resourceful individual, thoroughly at home in the chancery and the royal service which must have been his effective family, whose regard for the benefits of education he must have shared. His foundation could easily have failed. If it did not, the outcome was due to the energy and perspicacity of the founder, and to the unifying effect he evidently had on the fellows who survived him.

William de Leverton, who incepted as doctor of medicine in 1334, was elected to succeed Brome. He remained in post until his death on 21 November 1348. Leverton had been a fellow and master of arts of Balliol in 1321 who joined Oriel presumably to pursue his higher degree; he seems to have originated in the Newark area, taking his name probably from North or South Leverton and receiving a benefice at the local priory of Southwell.[57] He was one of a group of fellows from eastern Nottinghamshire who were perhaps recruited by John de Laghton, and who included Richard Kilvington and probably John Aston; they would shortly be joined by Nicholas Misterton and William Hawkesworth.[58] This connection gave a local flavour to the fellowship which Brome had failed to establish in the interest of his Suffolk compatriots; if the north Midlands bias did not last beyond the

---

[55] *Statutes of the Colleges of Oxford*, i, Oriel 13–16.
[56] See the extract from his will, Oxfordshire Record Office DC2/C2/A3/2, Liber Albus Civitatis Oxoniensis fo. 12ᵛ; summarized in H. E. Salter (ed.), *Liber albus civitatis Oxoniensis* (Oxford, 1909), 13. Overton would continue to serve the college as a trustee until 1345.
[57] BRUO ii. 1138.
[58] BRUO ii. 1084 (Laghton), ii. 1050–1 (Kilvington); i. 66–7 (Aston); ii. 1286 (Misterton); ii. 890 (Hawkesworth). Laghton was from York diocese (which included Nottinghamshire) but his family origin was perhaps at Laughton in Lincolnshire, close to Newark; Kilvington, from the same diocese, shared the name of a village a little south of Newark and had the reservation of a benefice in the gift of the local priory of Thurgarton; Aston became vicar of Sutton-on-Trent; Misterton and Hawkesworth are villages in the same district.

mid-century, it was probably maintained in Leverton's time. In Richard Kilvington, however, it gained for the college one of the most original of a brilliant generation of philosophers and logicians, who would also enter the king's service and the ecclesiastical hierarchy, at the end remembering Oriel with a bequest. Kilvington's patron, Richard de Bury, was probably the most influential of Edward III's ministers in the early 1330s. He must have known Brome and shared the chancery's appreciation of graduates in its ranks, as the mass promotion of Oxford masters in September 1331 attests. His circle included the great names of Oxford philosophy and theology, including Richard Fitzralph, Thomas Bradwardine, Robert Holcot OP, and Thomas Buckingham.[59] Towards the end of the 1330s many of them, including Kilvington, would enter the king's service; but for the time being Bury was content to leave them in the Oxford schools where they disputed the current issues of grace, free will, and divine omnipotence. Among several Mertonians, Kilvington was the only fellow of Oriel, so far as we know, to participate in these debates and to be cited by other disputants; his writings must represent such college disputations as there were in that earliest generation. Only the first, his *Sophismata* or collection of logical puzzles, has been printed: it is likely to have been based on lectures of c.1326–9 when he was probably but not certainly a fellow.[60] He lectured on Aristotle's *De generatione et corruptione*, *Physics*, and *Ethics*, all texts used in the arts faculty, and on Peter Lombard's *Sentences*, the primary set text for theology, the last probably in 1333–4.[61] All these works give the impression of a philosopher interested above all in the application of an almost mathematical logic to the material world and to the changes observable in matter, and in his *Sentences* commentary to theological ideas like the measurement of charity, asking questions such as 'whether the habit of charity, through which God is above all to be loved, is increased through meritorious acts'.[62] On one topic, infinity, he had argued against the position of Richard Fitzralph. An independent spirit is in evidence throughout his surviving works; they are characterized by an unusually firm and clear exposition of his own view, almost in defiance of the judicious conventions of scholastic disputation. In his commentary on the *Ethics*, for example, discussing whether every virtuous man takes delight in his own (virtuous) works, he asserted, 'and I prove that he does not; since delight is a virtuous operation intrinsic to itself, it would then follow that the virtuous man would delight in his own

---

[59] See Oxford DNB s.n. Bury.
[60] Ed. N. Kretzmann and B. Kretzmann, *Ricardi de Kilvington Sophismata* (Oxford, 1990), and see their *The Sophismata of Richard Kilvington* (Cambridge, 1990). The editors implausibly date the work to 1324–6, but it is more likely that it reflects his lectures as a master of arts.
[61] On the date see W. J. Courtenay, *Adam Wodeham: An Introduction to his Life and Writings* (Leiden, 1978), 88–9.
[62] Kilvington, *Super sententias*, Bruges, Stadsbibliotheek MS 503, fo. 89va.

delectation, and by the same logic would delight in the delectation of his delectation, and so on ad infinitum'.⁶³ Was his confident and argumentative spirit the quality that persuaded Bury to attach him to an embassy in 1339? Kilvington was evidently successful in this broader sphere. His future career took him through Bury's and the public service to be dean of St Paul's in 1354, from which eminence he actively promoted and supported Richard Fitzralph's controversial campaign against the friars from 1356 to 1360. At his death in 1362 he left a bequest of books to his old college.

Kilvington was the only fellow of this early group of north Midland scholars to distinguish himself intellectually and politically. Provost Leverton continued to augment the college property in a modest way. His most notable success, and his one distinct setback, however, concerned its academic resources. The success was the series of gifts of over fifty books made to the library. But books were also the crux of Oriel's long-running dispute with the university, occasioned by Bishop Cobham's scheme, in which Adam de Brome was an important instrument, for a university library at St Mary's which would house his own collection. That scheme had foundered at Cobham's death in 1327 with insufficient funds even for his funeral. His executors had made the best of a bad job by selling the books to Brome for his new college for fifty pounds, and they had duly been placed in Oriel. This had caused resentment in the university, and in 1338 or so Mr John Reynham, one of the proctors and a fellow of Merton, went to Oriel with a great crowd of scholars and seized the books. The college, unable to prevent them, had responded by denying the university the use of the room above the new congregation house originally intended for the common library: William of Daventry, then the bursar (or *proctor redituum*) and later provost, took advantage of the strong door and the locks fitted by Brome, and filled the room with the college's timber store. This seems to have prevented the use of the books for a generation: they remained packed in two chests, presumably in the congregation house below, unavailable either to the scholars of Oriel or to the masters of the university. Eventually, about 1367, the chancellor cited the college before his court, allegedly denying the masters time to respond, found in the university's favour, and with the regents in arts had the door knocked down and the locks removed. Congregation ordained that the books should be chained there, some of them being sold and replaced with more useful texts. The college complained to the bishop of Lincoln and to Edward III, which drew an injunction from the Crown to permit no injury to his college.⁶⁴ This may have been enough to

---

⁶³ Kilvington, *Super Ethica*, Bruges, Stadsbibliotheek MS 503, fo. 56ᵛᵇ.
⁶⁴ The memorandum drawn up, presumably for the king and bishop, by Provost Daventry on this occasion provides most of the information on this dispute; see OCR 24–7. For the appeal to the bishop of Lincoln see OCR 27–8 and for the royal injunction OCR 28–9. The university statute on the library is in *Statuta antiqua Universitatis Oxoniensis*, ed. Strickland Gibson

inhibit the university's plans: the library was not opened until Archbishop Arundel, an Oriel man himself, bought off the college's claims for fifty marks (19 April 1410).[65] The dispute, which showed neither side much to advantage, did not prevent the fellows of Oriel from taking a full part in university affairs, providing proctors in 1355, 1361, and 1382. Nor did it inhibit the development of their own library. Brome's concern with building up a college library is evident in his acquisition of Cobham's books. In the following years numerous benefactors seem to have given at least fifty-three books which appear in the catalogue now dated with some probability to Ascension Day (21 May) 1349.[66] Some of those who can be identified were either associates of Brome in Oxford or the king's service, or colleagues of Bishop Burghersh at Lincoln; among the latter, perhaps, was John Cobbledik who left twenty-nine books of philosophy and theology at his death about 1337. The full list of ninety-nine volumes seems at first sight rather old-fashioned; one side of the vellum strip on which it was inscribed lists sixty-seven of them according to the different faculties or subjects, grammar, logic, astronomy, civil and canon law, theology; they include the set texts and standard authorities. They reflect nothing of the contemporary debates on free will and other topics in which Kilvington had participated. However the last 32 books were listed separately on the back without distinction; they include a number of books of disputed questions without attribution, of theology, logic, and natural philosophy, and on Aristotle's *Metaphysics*. They sound suspiciously like the characteristic notebooks of the 1330s in which the explosive new ideas of the hour were formulated, ideas which resulted from the application of the new logic and mathematical physics to large questions of metaphysics and theology. It may be speculated that this final third of the list comprises the books circulating among the fellows, according to the system of periodic borrowing already familiar in Merton, while the first two-thirds represents the reference collection, available as the master's texts when lecturing in the schools but not to be taken away to their private studies.[67]

The catalogue of 1349, therefore, is not a complete guide to the intellectual life of the college, and the fellows' own books must have further tipped the balance from ancient to modern learning. The following generation saw new developments in logic and new theological controversy in Oxford, reflected in Oriel by the work of John Huntman and perhaps by the stirs and conflicts in its fellowship. Further bequests to the library in the 1360s included books of Richard Kilvington himself, a bequest large enough to be noted specifically

---

(Oxford, 1931), 165–6, with some account of the affair from its own point of view. See the summary of M. B. Parkes, 'The Provision of Books', HUO ii. 470–1.

[65] CPR 1408–13, 190–1.
[66] See W. J. Courtenay, 'The Fourteenth-Century Booklist of the Oriel College Library', *Viator*, 19 (1988), 283–90.
[67] On book circulation in colleges see Parkes, 'The Provision of Books', HUO ii. 456–8.

with those of the founder and of Cobbledik in the 1390s inventory of the college's property.⁶⁸ But three alone survive, and it cannot be coincidence that they are all voluminous guides to canon law and moral theology, the reference books of an active dean of St Paul's. If the books of his dynamic Oxford years came to Oriel, they have now disappeared. All three, now MSS 27, 68, and 72, must have sat in the reference collection, consulted perhaps like indexes but not annotated. The spidery and characterful scholar's hand which seems to occur in the margins of all three also signs every leaf of one of them *magister Ricardus de Kylvington*, and is presumably his own. One manuscript, MS 25, at least, however, supplies evidence of their engagement, perhaps with instruction in mind, with Aristotelian ideas. It is one of Cobbledik's books, listed as such in the catalogue and with his note of ownership on a flyleaf, a simple text of Aristotle's *Ethics*, *Metaphysics*, and *Rhetoric* in a large early fourteenth-century script, with ample margins to invite commentary. This was supplied on a large scale with a profusion of notes, filling the margin and glossing every point sometimes more than once; notes by several successive hands datable to the later fourteenth and early fifteenth century, when the manuscript was in the college library, and which therefore must be Oriel hands. At least five separate writers contributed their notes, each of them having something to say on virtually every page of the *Ethics* and *Metaphysics*, though they have little on the *Rhetoric*. The manuscript was evidently being used as a text for regular lectures on the *Ethics* and *Metaphysics*, either formally in the university schools or for private exposition in the college. Aristotle's *Ethics* became a set text sometime before 1390 and the *Metaphysics* shortly afterwards, but they had long been popular texts for lectures. Notes in the flyleaves and other blank spaces show that the manuscript was borrowed by Walter Wandesford, who was a fellow about 1360; his may be one of the annotating hands. Other notes seem to be draft questions for disputation on the basis of the text, with lists of names attached presumably of bachelors and scholars assigned to take part in them.⁶⁹ One annotator is John Felkirk, fellow and master of arts in the 1390s. In these notes we can observe more or less directly a process not clearly visible elsewhere: the teaching activity of two or three generations of Oriel fellows on two of the more difficult texts of Aristotle, possibly in the university's lecture halls but more likely, in view of the draft list of questions, in college. But the presumably undergraduate hearers of the lectures and participants in disputations must have been members of halls in which fellows offered instruction. From 1436, when the Register of Congregation begins to record the names of principals of halls, it is possible to detect the dependent halls of numerous colleges, and it is

⁶⁸ OCR 490.   ⁶⁹ Oriel MS 25, fo. 225ʳ.

reasonable to suppose that these traditional relationships were not new.⁷⁰ In Oriel's case St Mary Hall, on the site of the rectory of the church, Martin Hall, on the site of the present chapel, and perhaps Bedel Hall (now the southern range of the third quad) were the halls most closely connected with the college, in one or more of which Walter Wandesford and John Felkirk may have expounded Aristotle's *Ethics* and *Metaphysics*.

MS Oriel 25, together with the evidence of the texts in the 1349 catalogue which circulated among the fellows, strongly indicates that even if they were themselves studying in a higher faculty, instructing undergraduates or bachelors in the faculty of arts formed an important part of their activity. The contribution to logic made by John Huntman, who was a fellow between 1373 and 1387 and is probably to be identified with the author known in surviving texts as Johannes Venator, confirms the predominant place of the study of arts in Oriel: like Kilvington, he participated in the lively debates on points of propositional logic which were maintained by numerous Oxford masters, including Richard Feribrigge, Henry Hopton, and John Wyclif.⁷¹ His contribution to the question of what is signified by a proposition such as 'God exists' or 'Socrates runs', discussed by most contemporary logicians, was that while it signified exactly what it predicated, i.e. God, or the running Socrates, the converse was not the case. He was therefore an independent thinker, but in a well-established Oxford tradition; there is no indication in the 1370s, any more than in Kilvington's generation in the 1330s, that Oriel had a continuous intellectual character of its own, as might be predicated of Merton or Queen's during the fourteenth century. Like Kilvington but on a less exalted level, Huntman went on to serve bishops of Lincoln and Durham until his death, perhaps in 1427. But his intellectual legacy, like that of other logicians of his generation, seems to have been most appreciated in Italy. Kilvington and Huntman apart, the intellectual activity of the Oriel fellows in these first generations was expended, on the evidence of the book catalogue and teaching manuals such as Oriel MS 25, on the daily grind of teaching in the arts and perhaps theology faculties. They were still in Provost Leverton's time a cohesive community, whose core, his Nottinghamshire compatriots among the fellows, was still intact. The recruitment of William Hawkesworth in 1341 as a fellow and as provost (after a period as fellow of the new Queen's College) on Leverton's death on 21 November 1348 reinforced the group, if only briefly. Hawkesworth's election was legally flawed, apparently by the absence of a number of fellows, and was technically quashed by the bishop of Lincoln, who

---

⁷⁰ See Jeremy Catto, 'The Triumph of the Hall in Fifteenth-Century Oxford', in Ralph Evans (ed.), *Lordship and Learning: Studies in Memory of Trevor Aston* (Woodbridge, 2004), 209–23.

⁷¹ On Huntman see Emden, BRUO ii. 987–8, and E. J. Ashworth and P. V. Spade, 'Logic in Late Medieval Oxford', HUO ii. 35–64, esp. 58–9. Parts of his *Logica* have been translated by M. M. Adams in Paul of Venice, *Logica magna*, part ii, fascicule 6 (Oxford, 1978), 237–51. His copy of the Franciscan finding list, the *Tabula septem custodiarum*, is Oxford, Magdalen College MS lat. 78.

then reappointed him.⁷² But he was also a prominent northern master, who had been chancellor's commissary only a few months before, and whose controversial election as chancellor of the university shortly afterwards resulted in a notorious disturbance in the chancel of St Mary's on 20 March 1349. His rival, Dr John Wylyot of Merton, with a crowd of supporters, interrupted the exequies of a university benefactor, 'obstructed the priest, Master John de Lollington, from celebrating mass, making a great noise and tumult, attempted to eject Master William Hawkesworth, who claimed to be chancellor, from his place in the choir, and otherwise obstructed and perturbed the priest, the chancellor and proctors and the regent masters in arts'.⁷³ Whether or not the riot was the cause of Hawkesworth's death on 8 April is not recorded on his memorial brass in St Mary's nor elsewhere; but as the royal order to Wylyot to keep the peace mentions deaths and injuries incurred during the fracas, it is not unlikely.⁷⁴ Wylyot thereafter was chancellor unopposed, which might imply that Hawkesworth's election was not considered fully legal. In any case, the election as provost of Oriel of William Daventry, who had been active in the affair of Cobham's books, seems to mark a break with the Nottinghamshire connection in the college, for which there is no later evidence. Daventry's fellows were recruited from any part of England on principles now irrecoverable, though there may have been a bias towards northern masters.⁷⁵ In his time and that of his successor, John Colyngtre, elected in 1373, they seem to have cohered well, though internal tensions, inevitable perhaps without the mutual trust of close compatriots, would be evident in the next generation. Daventry had shown his determination to defend college interests as early as 1337, when he was *procurator reddituum*, and again in 1367, over the affair of Cobham's books. His sense of college tradition was evident in his foundation of a chantry in memory of Adam de Brome and his chancery colleague Robert de Bardelby in 1362, and he both expanded the college's endowment of Oxford properties, acquiring most of the houses and plots between La Oriole and St Mary Hall between 1357 and 1362, and built its first chapel.⁷⁶ Perhaps most significantly for the future, he brought in, presumably as sojourners rather than fellows, two young men of

---

⁷² 20 December 1348. See LAO, Reg. Gynwell fo. 245ᵛ. Gynwell's direction on the conduct of elections on 28 April 1349 (OCR 64–6) refers to elections without notice to absent fellows.

⁷³ OCR 19–22.

⁷⁴ The brass is recorded in T. G. Jackson, *St Mary the Virgin, Oxford* (Oxford, 1897), 191–2. See CCR (1349–54), 74 (2 April 1349).

⁷⁵ For the eight years in which the names of proctors are known between 1355 and 1368, all the northern or junior proctors (that is, from north of the Nene) were fellows of Oriel and all the southern or senior proctors were Mertonians. See A. B. Emden, 'Northerners and Southerners in the Organization of the University to 1509', in R. W. Southern et al. (eds.), *Oxford Studies Presented to Daniel Callus* (OHS, Oxford, 1964), 1–30.

⁷⁶ OCR 23–4, 29–30. His acquisitions on the college site can be followed in OCR 121–46. For his will, see OCR 30–1. A rental for 1363–4 (OCR 382–4) shows the college receiving a modest rent from some forty-eight Oxford properties.

prominent social position. The first, Philip de Beauchamp, a godson of Queen Philippa, was resident about 1357, when he witnessed a deed. He was already a canon of Exeter and had he survived would probably have been made a bishop, but he died in 1371.[77] Thomas Fitzalan better known as Thomas Arundel, younger son of Richard, the 3rd Fitzalan earl of Arundel, was resident in 1373 when he witnessed Daventry's will. Though he was never more academically than a bachelor of arts, his later literary interests and learning impressed his contemporaries, including the Florentine humanist Coluccio Salutati. He was promoted to the see of Ely in August 1373 and as archbishop of Canterbury would be a benefactor of the college, redeeming the seizure of Cobham's books and contributing to the college chapel, as well as a firm judge, in 1411, of the fellows' unruly conduct.[78] The presence of these potential future patrons in college was an early indication of the need and desire for external protectors which would be a feature of both colleges and the university in the following centuries.

John Colyngtre, apparently from Collingtree in Northamptonshire, was elected provost in 1373 by ten fellows, the full complement which custom, though not the statutes, determined. It would be nearly the last undisputed election for some time. Virtually nothing is known of this provost, who seems to have slightly expanded Oriel's Oxford properties before his death in 1385.[79] His tenure was effectively a continuation of his predecessor's domestic regime, and it serves to conclude the era of the college's foundation. The sixty years or so since Adam of Brome's initiative of 1324 had firmly established the new community in Oxford. It was unique in the university in its founder's lack of kindred: his official family, the clerks of chancery, was to some extent the substitute, bringing the infant college into unusually close relationship with the king's government: as a result, the college's leading intellectual light in these early years, Richard Kilvington, was also highly successful in the service of the Crown. With the passing of the first generation, the circumstances which had bound the first fellows together no longer applied. The support of the king and the bishop of Lincoln were now at best sporadic; the chancery connection ceased to be close, and the bond of a common Nottinghamshire origin which linked several early fellows had been dissolved. William Daventry's college was a body of young masters recruited without the dead weight of regional interest: if this may have made them rather more inclined to internecine quarrels, as would appear in the following years, it would be, in the long term, a source of resilience and strength.

---

[77] BRUO i. 136–7.
[78] BRUO i. 51–3. On Arundel see Margaret Aston, *Thomas Arundel* (Oxford, 1967). On his intellectual interests see Catto, 'Shaping the Mixed Life: Thomas Arundel's Reformation', in Linda Clark, Maureen Jurkowski, and Colin Richmond (eds.), *Image, Text and Church: Essays for Margaret Aston* (Toronto, 2009), 94–108, cf. 99–100.
[79] BRUO i. 471. For property transactions under his provostship see OCR 136, 155–6, 218–20.

2

Patrons and Pastors, 1385–1479

Jeremy Catto

The period of rather more than ninety years from the death of Provost Colyngtre to that of Provost Hawkins was a period of transformation for the University of Oxford. At its beginning the bitter dissensions over the evangelical reforms of John Wyclif, which had been championed in Oxford if not universally popular there, were embroiling the masters in national controversy and subjecting the Oxford schools to unwelcome ecclesiastical discipline. In contrast, by the beginning of the final quarter of the fifteenth century the university was a more or less harmonious part of a clerical establishment, its leading masters, learned and civilized on the whole, filling, with their counterparts from Cambridge, the episcopal bench and the prebendal stalls of the English cathedrals. Older and graver than their fourteenth-century predecessors, they were dignitaries such as Dr Thomas Chaundler, chancellor of Wells (1452–67) and late warden of New College (1454–75), who had served long years as chancellor of the university and had instilled into generations of students high standards of pastoral care and a modicum of humanist Latinity. His Wykehamist pupils would lead the renaissance of humanist learning in England which would culminate with John Colet and Thomas More; they would also form a clerical connection dominant in the early Tudor state, and first in the queue for its rewards. Oxford and Cambridge colleges would all to some degree conform to this pattern, dependent on successful alumni for their enrichment and the preferment of their fellowship; if they no longer harboured the pioneering young logicians who were in evidence so late as 1410, their quadrangles were filled with much better-read masters, capable of a superior Latin style and sometimes sporting a little Greek learning, as well as a more balanced understanding of the fathers of the Church. The quadrangles themselves had acquired their familiar foursquare look, if not, except at New College, on the scale of the following century, and the colleges (again, apart from New College and Magdalen), though legally composed only of the graduate fellows on the foundation, had already in practice incorporated numerous academic halls, in which the fellows instructed undergraduates. They thus transformed themselves into large pedagogic institutions which observed the principles of humanist education. In this distinctly national and almost Anglican clerical world, the sodality of European universities which had been led by Paris had somewhat faded from view, though even in the 1470s an Oxford scholar could edit at Padua the *editio princeps* of Duns Scotus, one of the brightest stars in the international scholastic firmament. The Italian travels and

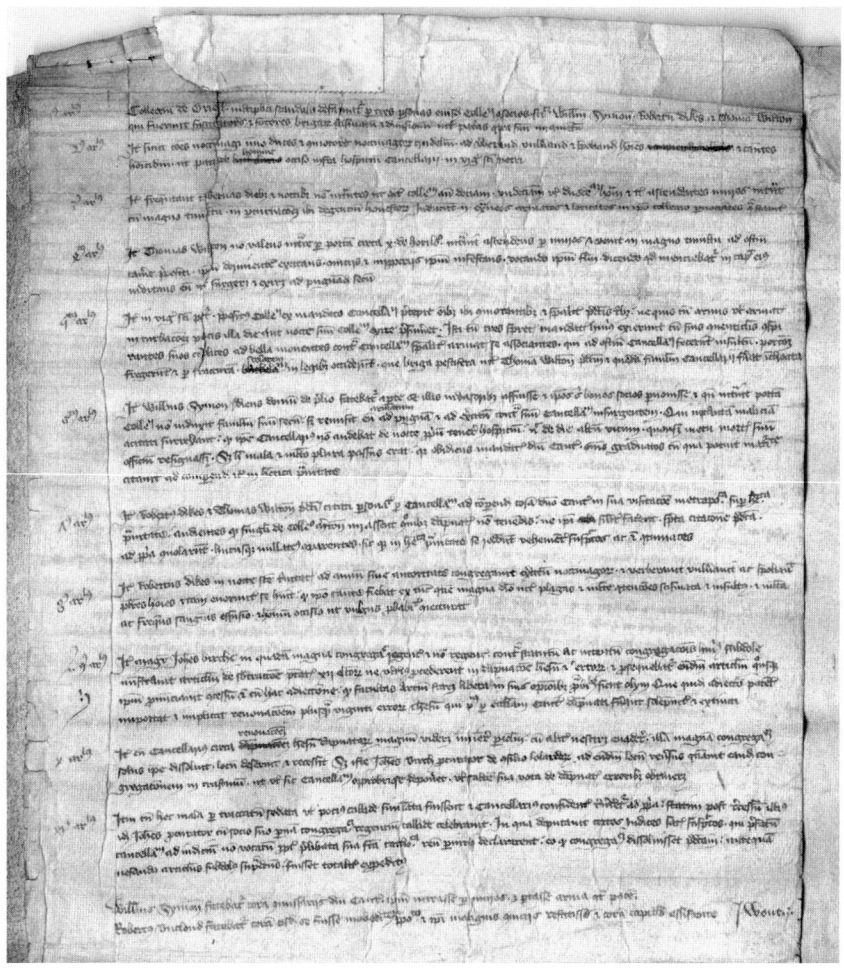

ILLUSTRATION 2.1 Archbishop Arundel inquires into the conduct of the fellows of Oriel, 1411, *OCA*

correspondence of Oxford humanist scholars would however help to bring into existence an alternative fellowship of European intellectuals. In all of these developments, from the Oxford logicians to the English humanists, a now enlarged Oriel would play its part.

It was a part which, to all appearance, was overshadowed by internal dissensions and repeated interventions of the Visitor. The disputed election to the provostship of 1385 was followed in the next forty years by six others, only two of which failed to end in lawsuits. In addition, in 1411 the riotous conduct of several fellows, compounded by their prominent part in the university's resistance to ecclesiastical visitation, brought down an archiepiscopal inquiry and a charge that the college was causing a public scandal. These events should not be seen entirely in the lurid light in which they appear in the documentary record. They were obscurely related to university disputes, and one of the characteristics of this period is the prominent part played by provosts and fellows of Oriel in university affairs, as chancellor or as one (or occasionally both) of the proctors. Moreover the fellows, whatever their internal disputes, were developing a wider community in which they instructed the undergraduate scholars of St Mary Hall, Martin Hall, Bedel Hall, and sometimes others; some of this activity can be traced in the books they seem to have used for instruction, a few of which still survive. More than one had a reputation among the Oxford logicians whose originality was still recognized in the early years of the fifteenth century. By the 1430s some of them were making their mark in the service of government. Three successive provosts became bishops, while another sojourner (or rent-paying resident) who was very much part of the community, Dr Thomas Gascoigne, was several times chancellor of the university. This political connection brought wealth and influence to Oriel, though its distinctly Lancastrian bias for a time limited the advantage it conferred. By 1479 a larger fellowship, a thriving body of undergraduates in the college's dependent halls, and a richer endowment would open the prospect of a vigorous part for Oriel in Renaissance Oxford.

It is possible, through the survival of treasurers' accounts for 1409–15, together with the charges and witnesses' statements included in the record of Archbishop Arundel's inquisition in 1411 and the account of the expulsion of two fellows in 1426, to form some idea of the way of life of the fellows in the early fifteenth century.[1] They lived in the premises given by James of Spain in 1329, and had adapted the properties later collected to the north—now the second quadrangle—as their garden. They had probably rebuilt already much of the original house of La Oriole: about 1373, at the expense of

---

[1] The first of the treasurers' books to survive, covering the years 1409–15, is OCA TF A1/1; for the inquisition of 1411, *Snappe's Formulary*, ed. H. E. Salter (OHS, Oxford 1924), 194–215; for the expulsion of 1426, OCR 47–58.

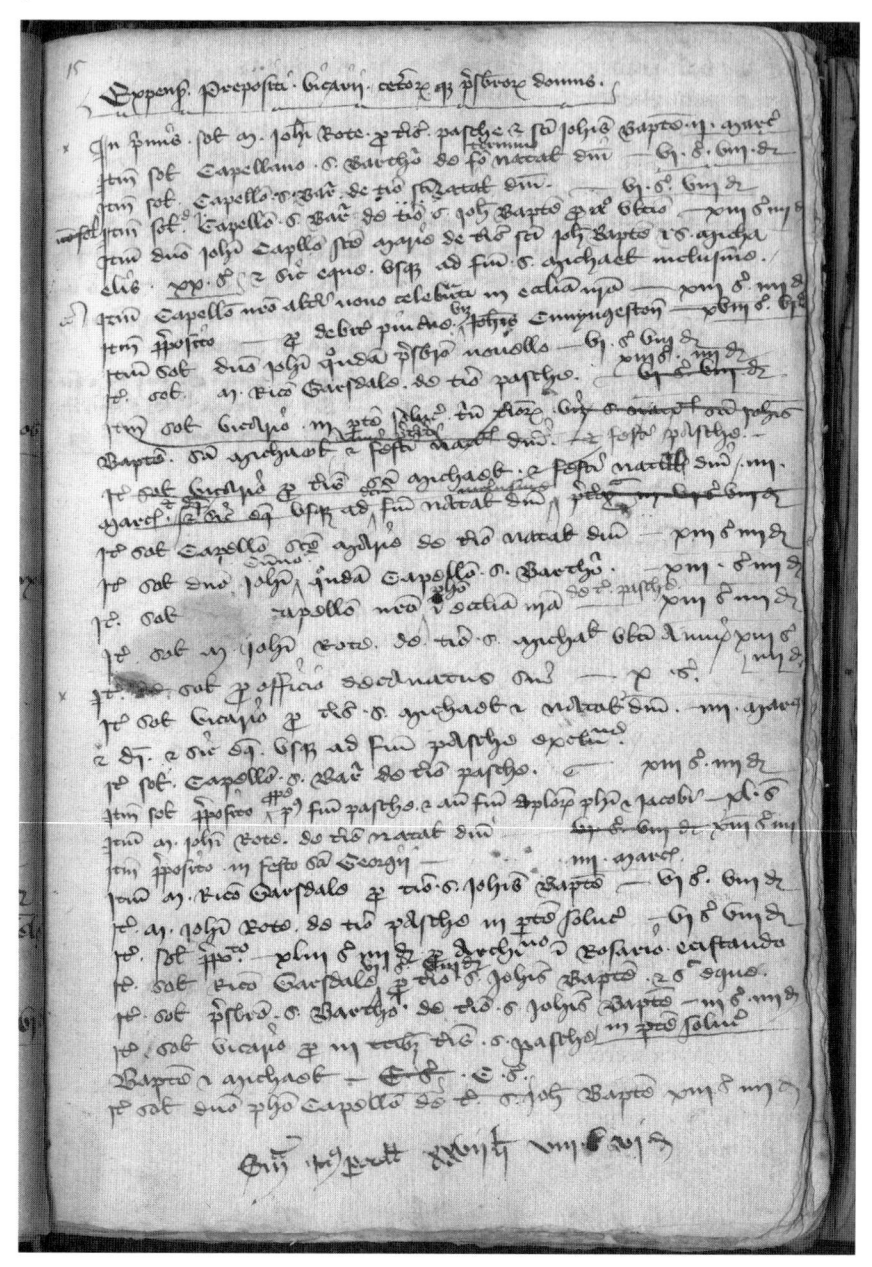

ILLUSTRATION 2.2 The earliest treasurers' accounts, 1409–10, *OCA*

Thomas Arundel, the young bishop of Ely, and his father, they had put up a chapel in the north range. John Bereblock's drawing of 1566 shows what was left of the fifteenth-century quadrangle, modified by the extensive rebuilding of 1534–5. By then Arundel's chapel had been superseded by a new building in the south or Merton Street range, identifiable in Bereblock's drawing by crosses on its roof; it was consecrated, and presumably completed, in 1437. The original hall seems to have been next to the chapel, at the western end of the south range; it was replaced, before 1449, with a new hall on an upper level along the western end of the north range. Bereblock shows four large windows of sixteenth-century design on the upper level of the east range; they were perhaps the windows of the library which was refurbished about 1449. The other windows, including the chapel's, have rounded tops and were presumably made in the fifteenth century or earlier. The main gate, built in 1409–10, appears toward the south of the west range.[2] The whole quadrangle has a foreshortened look, too narrow on the east and west, which may simply represent Bereblock's imperfect perspective, if the quadrangle of 1566 was of the same dimensions as the present front quadrangle.[3] The gradual acquisition of tenements to the north had virtually joined the college site to that of St Mary Hall by 1400. The only gap was Bedel Hall, which the college occupied and used as a dependent academic hall before its acquisition in 1455. These properties, developed as a garden, like many formerly inhabited sites of central Oxford after the Black Death, were probably where the vines pruned in 1413–14 were situated, and the apple trees whose surplus produce was often sold.[4]

Contiguity must have drawn together the college proper and its group of halls, all of which adjoined either the college or its garden. The process by which colleges rented groups of such halls, independently of ownership of their sites, was well advanced by the time of the first comprehensive evidence of it in the caution list (the annual list of pledges given by prospective principals to the chancellor) of 1436; by 1446 the college could appeal to its patron Bishop Carpenter for help in rebuilding St Mary Hall; and the principals of Bedel Hall and Martin Hall, a small property on the site of the present chapel, were consistently fellows of Oriel. Both Bedel Hall and St Mary Hall were listed in 1444 as halls of artists, and therefore housed undergraduates, instructed by fellows of the college and perhaps by the chaplains, who tended to be bachelors of arts if the lists of them mentioned

---

[2] Treasurers' accounts 1409–15, OCA TF A1/1, 77; OCR 61. For the chapel of c.1373 see OCR 29–30; its site in the north range is ascertained by a reference in 1397 to the next property on the north as *adjacens capelle* (OCR 491). See Chapter 17 for further references.

[3] Bereblock's drawing is reproduced from Oxford, Bodleian Library MS Bodley 13, fo. 6^v, in HUO ii. lxviii.

[4] Treasurers' accounts 1409–15, OCA TF A1/1, 164, 40.

in the treasurers' accounts of 1409–15 are representative.[5] The text of Aristotle's *Ethics*, *Metaphysics*, and *Rhetoric*, now Oriel MS 25, which was described in the last chapter, throws light on the process of instruction in the fifteenth-century halls. Its profusion of notes, which gloss almost every point of the first two texts, include contributions in early fifteenth-century hands, which, as the manuscript appears to have remained in Oriel throughout, must be those of fellows engaged in expounding it. The only fellow after 1385 named in the marginal notes is John Felkirk, who was in residence in 1394 and by 1410 was vicar of Aberford. There is also a note in a hand of about 1400 which appears to refer to arrangements for disputations, naming two or three bachelors (*domini*), evidently as participants. It may refer to formal university exercises, but it is perhaps more likely, in the light of this text's use by fellows over several generations, that the informal exercises in one of Oriel's dependent halls are intended.[6] It throws light on what was clearly the main business of the fellows, the instruction of undergraduates in arts, which was undertaken by young masters or bachelors among the fellowship studying, if the statutes were being observed, for a higher theological degree.

We can know very little of the life of the halls from surviving sources.[7] What the treasurers' accounts and the inquisition of 1411 do throw light on is the internal life of the fellows within the college walls. The accounts show weekly commons for up to eleven fellows in 1409–10, and as many as thirteen on 24 February 1415; the number may be inflated by including both probationary fellows and masters going out of fellowship. Bishop Repingdon's confirmation of Thomas Leintwardine's election in 1417 records nine fellows voting (with one presumably ex-fellow, John Rote, present at the election), which with the unsuccessful candidate Richard Garsdale makes ten. In 1424 nine fellows voted for or against a tenth, Nicholas Herry.[8] Ten, therefore, the statutory number, seems to have been the norm. Besides the fellows, a number of persons rented rooms within the college, and played a part in the community, as Philip Beauchamp and Thomas Arundel had a generation before. There were three or four chaplains, as the statutes provided, usually bachelors of arts; besides their ecclesiastical duties, perhaps they helped to instruct undergraduates in the dependent halls. The vicar of St Mary's, up to about 1405 a former fellow but from then to 1432 Dr John Plummer, the first

---

[5] On the informal rise of the undergraduate college see Jeremy Catto, 'The Triumph of the Hall in Fifteenth-Century Oxford', in Ralph Evans (ed.), *Lordship and Learning: Studies in Memory of Trevor Aston* (Woodbridge, 2004), 209–23.

[6] BRUO ii. 674; *Provosts and Fellows*, 18. Oriel MS 25, fo. 225^r.

[7] What can be known about the buildings of academic halls is collected in W. A. Pantin, 'The Halls and Schools of Medieval Oxford', in R. W. Southern (introd.), *Oxford Studies Presented to Daniel Callus* (OHS 1964), 31–100, see 41–6.

[8] OCA TF A1/1, 9, 201; LAO Reg. Repingdon fo. 415^v; OCR 37.

of a series of non-Oriel vicars, had a room in college for which a new lock and key were provided in 1413–14.⁹ More weighty, at times, in college affairs were the rent-paying sojourners. In 1409–10 rooms were rented to Thomas Leintwardine, formerly a fellow and trustee for various properties, who would be elected provost in 1417; to Richard Snetisham, another former fellow, a contributor to the new stalls in St Mary's, a benefactor of the library, and a theologian who had compiled an abbreviation of the *Sentences* commentary of Robert Cowton OFM and who died studying at Paris in 1416; to Roger Radcliffe, a master on leave of absence from his cure who died in 1413; to William Scrope, a young master of the noble Yorkshire family of Scrope, who would die in 1463; and to one Colne, perhaps an undergraduate scholar, who is not otherwise known. Apart from Scrope and Radcliffe they were still paying rent in 1412–13; Radcliffe had moved to a house in the parish. William Penbegyll, a notable logician, joined them in the same year. Closely associated with Snetisham and Penbegyll, but not mentioned as a tenant, was Ralph, son of John Lord Lovel, another benefactor of the college at his death in 1413; perhaps he lived in one of the halls.¹⁰ Clearly they were members of the community; some, as former fellows and future benefactors, felt affection for or at least obligation to it; others were perhaps only tenants. As Dr Thomas Gascoigne, a major benefactor and probably the longest resident in college from about 1428 to 1458, fell into this category, it cannot be ignored in any account of college affairs. A community of perhaps thirteen or fourteen masters, therefore, made up the active part of the college at any one time up to the augmentation of the fellowship in 1441.

The age of the masters varied: in 1411 Provost John Possell is described as about 60; Thomas Leintwardine must have been about 45; John Martill, a fellow, was a little over 30; Henry Kayll, another fellow, was 21 or more.¹¹ This goes some way to explain the riotous behaviour attributed to some fellows in 1411; Thomas Wilton, William Symond, and Robert Dykes, allegedly the chief perpetrators of the troubles, were probably in their twenties, Robert Buckland and Thomas Hardy perhaps even younger. The first three were accused, and the witnesses confirmed it, of bringing the college into disrepute as common *noctivagi*, leaders of nocturnal riots and frequenters of taverns who came back to college after midnight and climbed in with much noise and tumult, offering violence to the provost. Conduct of this kind was not confined to the troubled years of 1410–11; in 1426 Thomas Bedmystre was expelled from the college as a companion of *noctivagi* who brought them riotously into college, causing the scholars to fear for their

---

⁹ OCA TF A1/1, 164.
¹⁰ OCA TF A1/1, 8, 126, 158; on Lovel see BRUO ii. 1166.
¹¹ Inquisition, *Snappe's Formulary*, 207, 212, 214; see also 195. Leintwardine was first a fellow about 1386, see BRUO ii. 1131–2.

lives and property. He had been known to cause disturbance at common table, pulling off the table-cloth and the vessels upon it, seizing those placed in front of the dean, and driving the fellows from the table.[12] Another fellow, Robert Morton, was accused of having, on Wednesday 28 June 1424, brought some bachelors of arts into college by force, bringing them to dine at the common table, and prevented the fellows from the enjoyment of their dinner.[13] These charges, both in 1411 and in 1426, may not reveal the whole truth. Further accusations in 1411 were directed at other fellows: Mr John Birch, a proctor at the time, was charged with resisting Archbishop Arundel's proceedings against Oxford Lollards, and causing congregation to dismiss the chancellor in his absence in an irregular session. He and William Symond had refused to renounce Boniface IX's bull of exemption for the university as directed by the archbishop and agreed by the college. Further, they had resisted the archbishop's entry into St Mary's to conduct his visitation. They had been supported by the provost's deputy the dean, John Rote, who had been a fellow since 1394; he had been roused to fury by the visitation, and had been heard to say of Arundel, 'May the devil take him and break his neck'.[14] He was charged with being the *radix malorum omnium* and their silent abetter. The masters and scholars of the whole university, therefore, were divided by bitter controversy at this time; over Arundel's campaign against Lollard masters, and more traditionally by a new outbreak of violence between northern and southern scholars in 1410. Wilton, Symond, and Dykes were all northerners who incited violence against their southern colleagues; even worse, they had encouraged the Irish scholars, by custom included in the southern nation, to join with them.[15] In 1424 Morton and Bedmystre had been opponents of Herry's election as provost; further, Morton had been proctor in 1420–1 and Bedmystre from 1424 to 1426, in his second year together with another Oriel fellow, Thomas Greenley.[16] They were notable members of the university and had been involved in a recent college lawsuit; the violence with which they were charged may have been taken out of context in the heat of the battle. Perhaps most of the younger fellows were chargeable with similar offences against the peace of the college; the evidence of judicial proceedings can distort the context, even if, as seems likely on the evidence, Wilton and his colleagues were guilty more or less as charged. The strife and division among the fellows which the 1411 inquisition seems to imply may be further modified by the evidence of the account book for 1409–15, which, admittedly, is equally indirect and uncertain. The treasurers for this period were John Rote the dean, and Richard Garsdale, another northerner who would be a

---

[12] OCR 51–4.   [13] OCR 55–6.
[14] Inquisition, *Snappe's Formulary*, 198–201.   [15] Inquisition, *Snappe's Formulary*, 206.
[16] OCR 37; A. B. Emden, 'Northerners and Southerners in the Organization of the University to 1509', in Southern (introd.), *Oxford Studies*, 1–30, see 23.

PATRONS AND PASTORS 43

candidate for the provostship in 1417. In the same year as the alleged disturbances both the accused and the witnesses against them were contributing to the cost of the new stalls in St Mary's: William Corfe (former fellow and future provost), Thomas Leintwardine, Richard Snetisham, 13s. 4d.; William Symond, John Martill, 3s. 4d.; Thomas Wilton, Henry Kayll, Robert Buckland, 20d.[17] John Rote and John Birch, whatever they may have said about Archbishop Arundel in 1411, had only a year before helped to expedite his settlement of the old dispute between Oriel and the university over Cobham's books, which entailed a payment by Arundel to the college of £100, about two-thirds of the college's annual income; they had appeared *in curia* in London, presumably Arundel's own court, to represent Oriel's interests, and their expenses were noted in the accounts. In 1411, while trying to prevent Arundel's entry into St Mary's to conduct his visitation, they (or perhaps other fellows) were entertaining him to spiced wine.[18] The fellows simultaneously cooperated and disagreed, sometimes violently—a situation which would be common enough in Oxford in later periods.

The accounts reveal a few other details of life in Oriel about 1410. John Kent was perhaps the manciple, though he is nowhere so named. There was a butler, a cook, and a subcook; laundresses and barbers were employed (the barbers had to maintain the tonsure which even clerks in minor orders, a category including undergraduates in academic halls, were required to sport). The constant payments to tilers and carpenters indicate the endless round of repairs to the premises. In 1413–14 they were mending the paving stones of the quadrangle; the next year new tables were needed for the hall.[19] Some kind of examination was held in 1412–13, perhaps for probationary fellows on confirmation; an external examiner, Thomas Ward of Canterbury Hall, was engaged, to whom 3s. 4d. was paid, which implies substantial work.[20] There were various guests, including the town bailiffs, Arundel's commissioners Richard Courtenay and Roger Coryngham (in 1410–11, perhaps when they were conducting the 1411 inquisition), various canon lawyers. In 1414 the college conducted and paid the expenses of the exequies of Provost Possell, for which his old persecutor Thomas Wilton had to provide some ready cash.

Nevertheless the dissensions of the forty years or so between the election of Provost Middelton in 1385 and that of Provost Carpenter in 1427 require some explanation. They did not happen (so far as extant sources reveal) in other colleges; and they were the subject of comment to outsiders, both in the inquisition of 1411 and in the statute made by Archbishop Chichele's commissioners in 1426. To the later observer their obvious manifestation was the series of lawsuits which followed the elections of Middelton, Possell,

[17] OCA TF A1/1, 52.
[18] OCA TF A1/1, 23, 52.
[19] OCA TF A1/1, 164, 204.
[20] OCA TF A1/1, 152.

Rote, Leintwardine, and Herry. The election of John Middelton in 1385 was contested by another fellow, Thomas Kyrton, whose claims were initially upheld by the Visitor; but on appeal Middelton was confirmed by the archbishop of Canterbury. These proceedings were not concluded until February 1387. In 1394, the election of John Maldon was not challenged, but in 1402, that of John Possell was unsuccessfully contested by another fellow, Thomas Leintwardine, on behalf of his opponent John Paxton, before the Visitor and then the archbishop of Canterbury. In 1414 the election of John Rote was challenged by his colleague John Martill, who alleged he had not been summoned to the election meeting; Rote's election though confirmed by the Visitor was annulled by Archbishop Chichele, and William Corfe was elected. In 1417 Thomas Leintwardine's election was contested by Richard Garsdale, who secured confirmation by the Visitor, but was eventually settled in his favour. Henry Kayll's election in 1421 was unopposed, but on his death in 1422 there was an interregnum of two years. In 1424 the election of Nicholas Herry was contested, but confirmed first by the archbishop's commissioners during the vacancy of the see of Lincoln, and then on appeal by the archbishop himself.[21]

If these disputes were the outward signs of a long-term factional division among the fellows, it is now impossible to reconstruct. There may have been a rivalry of northern and southern masters in a college not clearly aligned with either nation: John Middelton, elected provost in 1385, was probably a northerner, his rival Thomas Kyrton was probably not. But in 1402 neither John Possell nor his opponent John Paxton seem to have been northerners; nor were Provost William Corfe and his unsuccessful colleague John Rote, in 1414. In 1417 we have a list of the voters on either side; Thomas Leintwardine and all his supporters were from the southern nation, his rival Richard Garsdale and most but not all of his partisans were northern. The latter group seem to be those accused of making trouble in 1411, with Robert Morton, who was deprived for similar reasons in 1426.[22] A similar alignment occurred at the next election but one in 1424, when Provost Herry was supported by southerners whereas the veteran northern master, Thomas Wilton, favoured his unnamed opponent.[23] No doubt this regional distinction, if it existed at all, applied only in broad outline. But the commissioners of 1426 did not seem to regard the tumultuous election of successive provosts as the heart of the problem, and made no modification to the election statute of 1349,

---

[21] On Middelton's election see OCR 32–3; Maldon's, OCR 34–5; Possell's, BRUO ii. 1440 and Lambeth Palace, Reg. Arundel fo. 107^v; Rote's, LAO Reg. Repingdon fo. 400^v and *The Register of Henry Chichele, Archbishop of Canterbury*, ed. E. F. Jacob, 4 vols. (Canterbury and York Society, Oxford, 1938–47), iv. 113–14; Leintwardine's, LAO, Reg. Repingdon fo. 415^v; the votes of fellows, Trinity College, Cambridge MS O.10.21, fos. i–ii; Kayll's, LAO, Reg. Fleming fo. 137^v; Herry's, OCR 37–47.
[22] OCR 47–58.   [23] OCR 37.

although they claimed to have examined the root causes of disturbances in the college. They focused instead on elections to fellowships, on which no specific evidence has survived. They decreed that no such elections should be made without the provost's express consent, and, significantly, they further laid down that no two fellows who originated in the same town, city, county, or diocese should hold office at the same time. It seems clear, therefore, that the regional heterogeneity characteristic of the college, whatever its advantages in opening the fellowship to merit, had the drawback that the fellows, having little mutual trust, could easily descend into faction. In the frequent absences of the provost and many fellows—Provost Corfe seems to have been away at the Council of Constance for virtually the whole of his tenure—it is all too likely that a rump of fellows elected friends and associates, without the full consent of their colleagues. The commissioners, assuming that any provost would not be in residence for much of the time, emphasized the authority of the dean, who, if he also were to be absent, should have as his deputy a senior fellow appointed by his colleagues. The fellows, then, would always be subject to clear authority.[24]

It is less clear that the fellows were divided, as has sometimes been asserted, by the conflict between the protagonists of John Wyclif and their orthodox opponents. It is true that the two proctors in 1382–3, when the Wycliffite masters were condemned by Archbishop Courtenay, Walter Dash and John Huntman, both fellows of Oriel, were reprimanded for their partisanship with the radical party.[25] Their stance would not have distinguished them at this stage from the majority of masters of arts, who were jealous of the university's privileges and regarded the friars, whom the Wycliffites Nicholas Hereford and Philip Repingdon OSA had denounced, as the principal threat to Oxford's independence. A quondam fellow, John Aswardby the vicar of St Mary's, renewed the onslaught on the friars in a sermon, which brought down on him accusations of sympathy with Wyclif but no ecclesiastical condemnation.[26] In 1411 another Oriel proctor, John Birch, defied Archbishop Arundel's visitation of the university and demanded that masters in the arts faculty be free to defend probable opinions as in the past, while his colleagues Robert Dykes and Thomas Wilton refused to take the oath not to maintain condemned Wycliffite propositions.[27] None

---

[24] OCR 37–47. The stipulation that only one fellow from each county, etc., should be in fellowship at the same time was modified to two fellows in 1441; *Statutes of the Colleges of Oxford*, i, Oriel, 22.

[25] W. W. Shirley (ed.), *Fasciculi Zizaniorum*, Rolls Series (London, 1858), 304–5. John Huntman, a notable logician, shared some of Wyclif's opinions on logic.

[26] The sermon was preached some time between 1384 and 1395. It does not survive but was answered by Richard Maidstone OC; see his *Determinatio*, ed. V. Edden, *Carmelus*, 34 (1987), 120–34.

[27] Inquisition of 1411, *Snappe's Formulary*, 198.

of these protests took their perpetrators out of the mainstream of university opinion, in contrast to the committed Wycliffite stance of Peter Payne, the principal of St Edmund Hall, or of the group of fellows of Merton headed by William James. It is more likely that the active part taken by fellows of Oriel in university affairs brought them to the forefront of conflict in a difficult period in Oxford's relations with the Crown and with church authorities.

Several fellows of this generation were prominent in the development of Oxford logic, one of the main preoccupations of the faculty of arts.[28] John Huntman, whose *Logica* had been a notable text of the previous generation, cannot have been their direct master; he had been chancellor of Lincoln since 1390. Richard Garsdale, a fellow since perhaps 1404, John Martill, fellow from 1409 or earlier, and the sojourner William Penbegyll contributed to the growing collection of brief tracts known collectively as the *logica oxoniensis*, though it is difficult to identify individual writings. We know that Martill together with another logician, William Milverley, provided a solution alternative to that of Robert Alington for a problem in a collection of *insolubilia*; their answer survives in a manuscript in Rome.[29] Richard Garsdale is also associated with them as a logician.[30] His brief commentary on the *termini naturales* is his only surviving attributable text, though a list of titles of historical works and one theological tract or sermon, *De dilatatione fidei*, is preserved by bibliographers.[31] William Penbegyll, who had been a fellow of Exeter, had perhaps written his tracts on universals before his stay in Oriel, but he was generally associated with the other Oxford logicians of the age.[32] Besides their identifiable tracts, they are likely to have contributed to the collection of logic teaching aids put together about 1410, the *logica oxoniensis*.[33] The teaching and honing of Oxford logic, the most distinctive contribution of the university to European philosophy at this time, must be seen as a cooperative activity always in the background of the stirs and quarrels of Oxford in the wake of John Wyclif. If the fellows of Oriel were prominent in controversy it was, ultimately, the consequence of their active involvement in the faculty of arts.

---

[28] On logic see E. J. Ashworth and P. V. Spade, 'Logic in Late Medieval Oxford', HUO ii. 35–64.

[29] It is attributed to them in the logic notebook of a monk of Worcester Cathedral Priory, Worcester Cathedral MS F.118, fos. 150ʳ–151ᵛ; The text, unascribed but identifiable by its incipit, is in Rome, Biblioteca Angelica MS 1017, fos. 14ʳ–19ᵛ. See Ashworth and Spade, 'Logic in Oxford', 61–2. William Milverley had no known connection with Oriel; he rented a school from Exeter College in 1400; see BRUO ii. 1284, 1333 (s.n. Mylverley).

[30] Worcester Cathedral MS F.118, fo. 115ᵛ.

[31] His extant work (ascribed to John Garisdale) is in Oxford New College MS 289, fo. 38; for the others see John Bale, *Index Britanniae scriptorum*, ed. Mary Bateson and introd. Caroline Brett and James Carley (Woodbridge, 1990), 347.

[32] His *Universalia* is edited by A. Conti, *Medioevo*, 8 (1982), 178–203.

[33] See L. M. de Rijk, '*Logica oxoniensis*: An Attempt to Reconstruct a Fifteenth-Century Oxford Manual of Logic', *Medioevo*, 3 (1977), 121–64.

Thomas Leintwardine, a fellow until 1401, a sojourner thereafter, and briefly provost (1417–21), was exceptional in the Oriel community as a theologian and notable preacher, whose lost commentary on the epistles of St Paul was admired and copied by Abbot Wheathamstead of St Albans. Elected in 1386 or earlier, he seems to have been active in college affairs in the 1390s as a trustee of property, and he was evidently the compiler of the register of its muniments in 1397, together with a calendar in which its obligations to benefactors are recorded. The unusually acute sense of the community which the compilation implies must have made him a force for stability in the troubled college of his time, as his evidence to the inquisition of 1411 seems to confirm. But we know nothing of his theological work.[34] His younger colleague Henry Kayll seems to have made a study of solid geometry, on the evidence of his annotations in a college manuscript. Kayll had been about 21 when he was called to give evidence in the inquisition of 1411; in 1421 he was elected provost, but died within the year.[35] At some intervening date he borrowed and annotated the college copy of Euclid's *Geometry* and other mathematical texts, to which he seems to have contributed headings and a table of contents, as well as marginal notes signed *quod Kayll*. The notes are designed to help future readers of a difficult text who might be instructing students in the arts faculty; he did not disguise his own struggle to understand it, commenting on a passage of Theodosius of Tripoli on spheres, 'as I, Kayll, have understood it with great labour'.[36] His interest was perhaps not that of a pure mathematician, but of an astronomer trying to apply the rules of solid geometry to the heavenly spheres, as is indicated in another note on Theodosius' useful theorems on spheres: 'if you understand this clearly, it can be used to explain how the days grow longer when the sun is in Aries... because Aries ascends more in an oblique circle than an oblique straight line in respect to Taurus, and vice versa.'[37] This is confirmed by another book which Kayll owned and left to Oriel, his copy of the *Summa judicialis* of John Ashenden, a fourteenth-century book of prognostications of dubious intellectual merit which may well be written in Kayll's hand. If his laborious study of ancient mathematical texts looks forward to the science of a later century, his astrology was distinctly traditional.[38]

At the same time as Henry Kayll was reading the geometers, the college was slowly becoming more involved in larger public issues. The rise to prominence of Thomas Arundel, once a young resident and later an affectionate patron, must have opened career opportunities. Provost Middelton

---

[34] On Leintwardine see BRUO ii. 1131–2. His compilation of the register of muniments is argued by C. L. Shadwell in his edition of *The Calendar of Oriel College, Oxford* (n.p., 1899), 15.
[35] BRUO ii. 1027–8 (s.n. Kayle).
[36] Oxford, Bodleian Library MS Auct. F.5.28, fo. 48r.
[37] MS Auct. F.5.28, fo. 47r.   [38] Oriel MS 23.

(1385–94) was also a canon of Hereford, where he was buried, but of his activities at Oriel we know only of his part in various property transactions on its behalf.[39] Provost John Maldon (1394–1402) was a bachelor of medicine who left his medical books to the college, but is chiefly distinguished for the cartulary of deeds and the calendar drawn up for him, probably by Thomas Leintwardine, in 1397.[40] His successor John Possell (1402–14) was able to secure Arundel's good offices in the final settlement of the issue of Cobham's books, but had to endure the indignity of his inquisition into the fellows' conduct. William Corfe (provost 1415–17), perhaps through his Wykehamist brother John, was favoured by Archbishop Chichele enough to represent him at the Council of Constance; he was therefore absent for almost the whole of his tenure, dying at the Council.[41] The final defeat of the long-serving John Rote in this disputed election, and his departure from the college (with a large claim for debts allegedly owed him by the college), perhaps marks the tipping of the balance away from the exuberance of the struggle for university privileges, towards the more stable, safer college of Carpenter and Gascoigne.[42] Corfe's successors Thomas Leintwardine (1417–21), Henry Kayll (1421–22), and Nicholas Herry or Henry (1424–27) continued the turn to stability, not without opposition.[43] But with the election of John Carpenter in 1427 a new era began.

John Carpenter had been a fellow since 1417 at latest. Reginald Pecock, who would be his friend on the episcopal bench until the latter's condemnation for heresy in 1457, was his ally in 1417 and 1424 in support of Provosts Leintwardine and Herry; Pecock resigned about 1425 and made his career largely in London; his advancement and that of Carpenter were closely related, both in London networks and in the service of the Lancastrian court. They and their colleagues and successors, Richard Praty, Thomas Graunt, Walter Lyhert, John Hals, and Henry Sampson, would pursue careers in royal service, for which they were well rewarded, but as part of a recognizable Oriel connection, in which the college would be the beneficiary of their success. Five of them would be bishops. In retrospect—it is unlikely that the process was perceptible at the time—this would prove to be the agent of a great change in the fortunes of Oriel. A better-endowed college, its fellows, and, increasingly, the scholars educated under its aegis in its dependent halls would participate in the burgeoning business of the English state and Church more actively than they had done since the time of Richard Kilvington. In the exigent service of the Lancastrian kings, John Carpenter

---

[39] BRUO ii. 1276.
[40] BRUO ii. 1208. The cartulary is now London, British Library MS Lansdowne 386.
[41] On Possell see BRUO iii. 1505; on Corfe, BRUO i. 487; for his funeral oration see Andreas von Regensburg, *Sämtliche Werke*, ed. G. Leidinger (Munich, 1903), 253–4.
[42] For Rote's claims see OCR 36–7.   [43] BRUO ii. 1131–2; 1027–8; 910 s.n. Henry.

and his colleagues had to have something to offer. None of them were canon or civil lawyers: New College, and All Souls after 1438, would provide an ample supply of legal expertise to government. Nor were they logicians like Garsdale and Martill, for whom career openings were meagre. They were theologians, not of the speculative kind like Kilvington and Wyclif, but masters of the art of *doctrina*, the art of propagating an established body of orthodox religious teaching firmly based on biblical and patristic scholarship. It is unfortunate that none of them, except the rather eccentric Dr Pecock and the perhaps equally singular Dr Thomas Gascoigne, have left any writings. Some, probably all of them, had extensive libraries and, to judge from the homiletic materials among their books, habitually preached.[44] Fifteenth-century governments, always anxious about the temper of their subjects, welcomed learned and orthodox preachers, and the Oriel connection may well have originated, in the late 1420s, from its comparative wealth in pastoral theologians.

Dr John Carpenter left nothing directly, whether as provost or bishop of Worcester, by which his intellectual interests can be judged. He was, however, a notable founder of public libraries at Worcester and Bristol, on the model of his relative and namesake John Carpenter, the common clerk of the City of London who established the Guildhall Library; the London milieu in which Provost Carpenter moved was inventive in promoting the circulation of books.[45] It was not surprising that he should advance the careers of two contrasting scholars among the book-collecting theologians just mentioned, neither of whom can have been easy to help. One was his early colleague Reginald Pecock, whose connections with the powerful London mercers' guild and later with the royal household whose leading figure was William de la Pole, earl of Suffolk, must have owed something to Carpenter.[46] His promotion as a bishop, first of St Asaph and later of Chichester, was, according to his critic Gascoigne, due to Suffolk and Lyhert. Pecock's later trial, condemnation, and imprisonment for heresy has obscured the fact that the original purpose of his writings was an exercise in *doctrina*, the defence of

---

[44] Dr Walter Lyhert (fellow 1425–35, provost 1435–46, bishop of Norwich 1446–72) had a copy of Philip Repingdon's *Sermones dominicales* (BRUO ii. 1187–8); Dr Thomas Graunt (fellow 1424–35, precentor of St Paul's, 1454–74) owned numerous biblical commentaries and a copy of Roger of Waltham's *Compendium morale*, which he indexed (BRUO ii. 802–3); Thomas Wyche, B.Th. (fellow 1435–61), had an extensive collection of biblical and apologetic materials (BRUO iii. 2102).

[45] On Carpenter's library initiatives see James Willoughby, 'Common Libraries in Fifteenth-Century England: An Episcopal Initiative', in Vincent Gillespie and Kantik Ghosh (ed.), *After Arundel: Religious Writing in Fifteenth-Century England* (Turnhout, 2012), 209–22.

[46] On Pecock see Wendy Scase, *Reginald Pecock* (English Writers of the Late Middle Ages, Aldershot, 1996). See also Jeremy Catto, 'The King's Government and the Fall of Pecock, 1457–58', in Rowena E. Archer and Simon Walker (eds.), *Rulers and Ruled in Late Medieval England: Essays Presented to Gerald Harriss* (London, 1995), 201–22.

the faith by argument and authority, against London critics whom he termed Lollards. But whereas most contemporary apologists were preachers, Pecock thought personal contact and the circulation of books in English was more effective in the defence of orthodoxy, and was prepared to say so in public. Worse, his books contained eccentricities such as a new scheme of virtues and vices and the opinion that the article on Christ's descent into Hell in the Apostles' Creed was an interpolation. From about 1447 he was, albeit a bishop, a subject of grave suspicion and in 1457–8 he was condemned to deprivation and imprisonment. His tragic end was the result of a highly individual parabola. He began however as a straightforward apologist for orthodoxy, and this probably reflects the common standpoint of his Oriel colleagues.

Several of Pecock's more original notions were scholarly adjustments to the body of Christian tradition, like his doubts about the authenticity of the Donation of Constantine, the legal foundation of the papacy's temporal power.[47] Research into the history of the Church and the writings of the fathers was central to the work of his Oriel successor and sharp critic, Dr Thomas Gascoigne, whom Carpenter must originally have promoted. Though Gascoigne, who was born about 1403 and lived in Oriel from about 1428, was a sojourner, being ineligible for a fellowship on account of his independent means, he was a valued member of the community, a benefactor of the library whose benevolence was recognized by the college in 1449 with the concession of free occupation of the 'first-floor room next to the Hall, where he has lived for many years'.[48] His circulated works amounted only to a life of St Jerome and a tract on indulgences, but his wide reading of the fathers and early medieval authors was recorded in notebooks, one of which survives, and transcribed into a vast dictionary of preaching topoi, his *Liber de veritatibus*, together with topical comments which bear witness to his many prejudices.[49] Though no sermon of Gascoigne's is extant, he shared to the full his contemporaries' enthusiasm for evangelical preaching, and preached often, only regretting that he had not preached 'as often as, or as well as, or where he ought to have preached'.[50]

---

[47] Pecock, *The Repressor of overmuch Blaming of the Clergy*, ed. C. Babington, 2 vols. (Rolls Series, London, 1860).

[48] DR 369–70; the room is perhaps represented on Bereblock's drawing by the window or windows next the hall, north of the main gate (see Ill. 3.1, p. 6).

[49] Gascoigne, *Tractatus de indulgenciis*, British Library Royal MS 8.G.vi, fos. 189^r–191^r; *Vita Jeronimi*, Oxford, Magdalen College MS lat. 93, fos. 199^r–202^v and 192^{r-v}. His surviving notebook is Oxford, Bodleian Library MS Lat.Theol. e.33; his *Liber de veritatibus* is Oxford, Lincoln College MSS lat. 117 and 118, extracts ed. J. E. T. Rogers, *Loci e libro veritatum* (Oxford, 1881). See W. A. Pronger, 'Thomas Gascoigne', EHR 53 (1938), 606–26 and 54 (1939), 20–37, and R. M. Ball, *Thomas Gascoigne: Libraries and Scholarship*, Cambridge Bibliographical Society Monograph 14 (Cambridge, 2006).

[50] *Liber de veritatibus*, Lincoln Coll. lat. MS 118 p. 397, *Loci*, ed. Rogers, 179.

The essence of his sermons was the exposition of Scripture, the starting point of which was the scholarship of his model and mentor, St Jerome. The deposit of authentic Christian teaching needed to be uncovered by historical scholarship especially of the early Church, and the task of the theologian was to sift Christian authors, who needed to be sought out in the whole range of libraries within his reach. Gascoigne was the precursor of scholars such as Erasmus, Archbishop Ussher, and the editors of ancient texts in seventeenth- and eighteenth-century Oxford; though he was not an editor himself, his search through some thirty libraries (and one bookshop) in Oxford and elsewhere uncovered the materials for later editorial work.[51] His hand can be seen in annotations in at least a hundred manuscripts; the notes are often the basis of entries in his *Liber de veritatibus*.[52] He collected (and gave away) a large personal library in addition. His interests and wide reading seem to have been characteristic of the Oriel fellows of his time, such as Dr Thomas Graunt and Dr Thomas Wyche, some of whose theological books are recorded; it marks a break from the logic and metaphysics of the previous generation. The rapid expansion of the Oriel library (to whose refurbishment he contributed) through his and his colleagues' donations aptly marks the change of direction in the intellectual interests of the age.

Gascoigne was far more than a college character; he was several times chancellor of the university, or chancellor's commissary, between 1434 and 1453; Henry VI once asked him why he was not a bishop, the true answer to which was his disdain for the ecclesiastical preferments which were enjoyed by all the provosts and several fellows of his time. His criticism of absentee placemen must have included both John Carpenter and Walter Lyhert; in addition, the latter's part in the promotion of Pecock to the see of Chichester was singled out for critical comment.[53] Gascoigne's financial independence permitted him this luxury; for graduate careerists on the make, however, the influence at the Lancastrian court forged by Carpenter and honed by Lyhert was a priceless advantage, without which Pecock, John Hals, and perhaps Richard Praty would not have reached the episcopal bench, nor Thomas Graunt been installed as canon of St Paul's. The origin of the connection must have been the near relation of Provost Carpenter to his namesake the common clerk of the city of London, who was inevitably close to the council of Henry VI's minority. Through the common clerk's influence, it is probable, the provost was made king's clerk and chaplain in the 9-year-old king's household, which involved his accompanying Henry VI, in 1430, to Paris to be crowned, and permitted him to be present at the trial of Joan of Arc at

---

[51] Listed by Ball, *Thomas Gascoigne*, 103–46.

[52] 99 manuscripts listed by Ball, *Thomas Gascoigne*, 147–55, to which can be added Bern, Stadtbibliothek MS 69, an Oriel manuscript.

[53] Gascoigne, *Liber de veritatibus*, Lincoln College MS lat.117, 401; *Loci*, 40.

Rouen the following year.⁵⁴ Further favour was shown him by his presentation to the mastership of St Antony's Hospital in London in 1433, and by 1435 his court duties were onerous enough for him to resign the office of provost. The college was not forgotten: his new eminence, culminating in his elevation to the see of Worcester in 1443, enabled him to confer on it a series of benefactions and a notable legacy. More immediately, it led to preferment for a series of Oriel colleagues: for Richard Praty, dean of the Chapel Royal in 1432, the see of Chichester in 1438; and for Pecock, already ensconced in London as master of Whittington College, the see of St Asaph in 1444. Two fellows were promoted to the king's foundation of Eton, the object of Henry VI's closest affection: John Mawnsell was made a fellow in 1447, and his Oriel colleague Richard Hopton was appointed headmaster in the same year.⁵⁵ Carpenter's colleague and friend Walter Lyhert was elected to succeed him without dissent on 1 June 1435; Lyhert, a Cornishman who had been fellow of Exeter, but had migrated to Oriel in 1425, would himself be master of St Antony's Hospital in 1444, in succession to Carpenter, and bishop of Norwich in 1446, and was the fourth Oriel fellow to be promoted to the episcopal bench in a single decade.⁵⁶ Like the others he was an active supporter of the unpopular minister William de la Pole earl and then duke of Suffolk, and later of Queen Margaret; like his patron Bishop Carpenter, he would lose his influence with the change of dynasty in 1461. But in the mid-century the Oriel connection would be well established in the royal household and in the patronage of the Crown.

If numerous fellows benefited from Provost Carpenter's fortune, the college was enriched and expanded. By the will of John Frank, the Master of the Rolls, who died in 1438, Oriel was left £1,000 for the reversion of the manor of Wadley in Berkshire, the profits of which were to support four new fellows; they were to be chosen if possible from the south-western counties of Devon, Dorset, Somerset, and Wiltshire. Frank appears to have had no direct connection with Oriel; but he was an important official and judge; he must have been well known at court and in the City of London; it is likely that Carpenter as Oriel's most prominent patron in the royal household had elicited the legacy.⁵⁷ After his elevation to Worcester Carpenter was more directly a benefactor. In 1446 the college appealed to him directly for help in the rebuilding of St Mary Hall, the western range of which had become ruinous. He responded magnificently, not only having the range rebuilt, but

---

⁵⁴ BRUO i. 361.   ⁵⁵ BRUO ii. 1246, 960–1.

⁵⁶ For Lyhert see BRUO ii. 1187–8; his confirmation as provost, listing the fellows voting in order of seniority, is in LAO, Reg.Gray fo. 64ʳ⁻ᵛ. Like Carpenter he seems to have founded a public library at Norwich, on which see Willoughby, 'Common Libraries', 218–20.

⁵⁷ *Statutes of the Colleges of Oxford*, i, Oriel, 23–4, college ordinance of 13 May 1441. On Frank see BRUO ii. 721, and John Sainty, *The Judges of England* (Selden Society, London, 1993), 147. The deeds for the acquisition of Wadley are in OCA DLL 2.

acquiring Bedel Hall, which the college had long used but which belonged to the university, in addition, thus creating a continuous block of college land from La Oriole to the High Street.[58] A communicating door between Bedel Hall and Oriel, ordered to be blocked up in 1545, gave internal access.[59] By another series of transactions, which seem to go back to 1442 at latest, he gave the college lands in Essex, which were transferred to St Antony's Hospital for the provision of nine scholars who were to live in Bedel Hall; Oriel, the master of St Antony's, and the dean and chapter of Carpenter's rebuilt college of Westbury on Trim were to have the right of presentation.[60] Finally, in his will of 1476 he left the manor of Dean and Chalford to Oriel, for the maintenance of two fellows from Worcester diocese, the first to be one of the original fellows, and the second to be additional. The college was to observe his obit on the feast of the Eleven Thousand Virgins (21 October), with prayers in memory of himself, Bishop Lyhert, and Henry Sampson, his executor—three provosts who had presided over a spectacular rise in the college's fortunes.[61]

Provost Lyhert resigned his office on 28 February 1446, two days after receiving the temporalities of Norwich, writing from an upper room at St Antony's Hospital where he was perhaps already a habitual resident. Following his predecessor's evident practice, he had been largely an absentee, as the college's ordinance of 1441 implies; his successors too would be largely non-resident for at least sixty years.[62] The college had evidently been prepared for the vacancy for some time, as the dean had already written to the bishop of Lincoln on 25 January to ask for a dispensation to elect a quondam fellow, John Hals, in spite of his not having completed his probationary year (1427–8). Hals's connection with the college was therefore minimal; he was a chaplain to Queen Margaret and close to the court, and would be, two years later, Lyhert's archdeacon of Norwich. His election was presumably due to

---

[58] DR 366; OCR 137–9 for the acquisition of Bedel Hall (1452–5); Pantin, 'Halls and Schools', 41–6.
[59] *Statutes of the College of Oxford*, i, Oriel, 39; Pantin, 'Halls and Schools', 46.
[60] OCA DR 5 (912–28); *Cat. Mun.* viii. 27–32. The first mention of the scholars is on 14 November 1451 (OCA DR 5 (925)). For the operation of the scholarships see *Dean's Register of Oriel*, 10, 93; *Cat. Mun.* viii. 32 no. 129 (30 September 1504).
[61] *Statutes of the Colleges of Oxford*, i, Oriel, 25–6, ordinance of the college, 31 January 1483. This plan must have been formed at least as early as 1471, when a body of feoffees on behalf of Oriel, headed by Carpenter, acquired by purchase the reversion of Thomas Wilcottes's rents and services in the manor of Over Chalford annexed to Dean: *Statutes of the Colleges of Oxford*, i, Oriel, 31–4.
[62] *Statutes of the Colleges of Oxford*, i, Oriel, 22. Lyhert remained a friend to the college, and was ready with a loan when the college needed to raise money to expedite Edward IV's confirmation of its statutes. He also established exhibitions for poor scholars at Oxford and Cambridge, the first of whom at Oxford was Walter, the son of his former neighbour John Paston I; cf. his will, TNA PRO Prerogative Court of Canterbury wills, 7 Wattys.

the patronage of his predecessor.[63] He was probably an absentee and possibly a reluctant provost in the first place; after three years he resigned. Ten years later he would be bishop of Coventry and Lichfield, in which office he would survive until 1490, always at heart a loyal Lancastrian who served briefly as Keeper of the Privy Seal in Henry VI's readeption of 1470–1. Hals however was a benefactor, acquiring in 1478 the manor of Littleworth, which abutted Wadley in Berkshire.[64] He was succeeded by Henry Sampson, a more involved fellow who had been principal of St Mary Hall and therefore an active participant in the college's pedagogic activities. He seems to have been close to Bishop Carpenter, who promoted him to most of his benefices and for whom he would act as executor.[65] Sampson was an active provost; when the series of treasurers' accounts resumes in 1450, he can be traced on college business, in London during sessions of parliament and frequently at various of the Oriel manors. He must have been central to the negotiations which resulted in the acquisition of Bedel Hall and the endowment there of the St Antony's exhibitioners, as well as to Carpenter's final benefaction. He also had to deal with the loss of favour at court which followed Edward IV's accession in 1461, when the manor of Wadley was taken back into the king's hand; Oriel, like New College, the other Oxford institution favoured by the Lancastrian court, had to make a loan, in its case of 100 marks, which the college raised by further loans from Sampson himself, Thomas Wyche, and Bishop Lyhert.[66] In later years he seems to have spent longer at his rectory of Tredington, where after his retirement from the provostship in 1476 he spent the last six years of his life.

Sampson may have been a learned preacher; his books of biblical exegesis and his copy of Eusebius's *Historia ecclesiastica* were bequeathed to the college.[67] Certainly he was one of an active group of fellows whose service can be traced in the accounts, but whose intellectual interests were largely theological and pastoral. They were active, too, in acquiring theological works for the library, including in 1454, remarkably, three works of Wyclif openly avowed in the treasurers' accounts.[68] Among these masters Thomas Wyche (fellow c.1435–61), Roger Stevenes (fellow c.1445–84), Henry Popy (fellow c.1451–64), and Robert Grafton (fellow 1456–67) stand out; in Sampson's later years, Robert Sheffield (fellow 1461–c.1476), Edmund Alyard (fellow 1463–1501), and John Taylor (fellow 1467–79, provost 1479–92) seem to have been prominent, filling in turn the offices of collector of

---

[63] DR 348–64, a very full collection of documents on this election preserved, evidently, as a precedent for future dispensations. On Hals see BRUO ii. 856–7, s.n. Halse.
[64] OCA DLL 3 (828).
[65] BRUO iii. 1635–6.
[66] Treasurers' accounts 1450–82, OCA TF A1/2, 144, 154 (18 June to 30 July 1461).
[67] Oriel College MSS 1 (Eusebius); 13 (Aquinas, *Catenae super Lucam et Johannem*); 51 (Hugh of St Cher, *Postilla super Johannem et Psalmos*).
[68] OCA TF A1/2, 10, 23, 38, 50.

rents, chaplain, treasurer, dean, and principal of St Mary Hall and other dependent halls. Their undoubted record of service in pursuit of the college's business, which the accounts reveal, must be modified by the evidence of their books, many of which survive in the college library and elsewhere. These books were largely theological; there is little evidence of active interest in logic or natural science, though works of Avicenna and Averroes were bought for the library in 1450.[69] Instruction of undergraduates in the arts and natural philosophy continued, however, in the halls; perhaps they had their own libraries, or the college library was already well supplied. Wyche's books are perhaps representative. He had borrowed from the library at least one work of traditional theology, the *Quodlibeta* of Henry of Ghent which Gascoigne had given; either he or another borrower of the fifteenth century annotated it in a few places, on the way of life of prelates and mendicants.[70] He owned another copy of Henry of Ghent, some of Nicholas of Lyre's commentaries on Scripture, a book of scriptural concordances, some fourteenth-century inquisitors' tracts against heresy, an *Opus juridicale*, and the letters of Peter of Blois; many of his books were purchased from the bookseller and stationer John More. The first was perhaps a text for his theology degree; the rest were equipment for the life of a preacher and churchman.[71] Stevenes had two theological textbooks, the *Sentences* commentaries of François de Meyronnes and of Scotus.[72] Robert Grafton, perhaps under the influence of Gascoigne, had copies of Robert Grossesteste's *Dicta*, *De lingua*, and *De oculo* and works of Bede and Gregory, all of them of interest to a pastoral theologian.[73] Robert Sheffield had some works of Bernard of Clairvaux.[74] John Taylor, the future provost, left to Oriel his texts of the early Christian poet Prudentius, together with the *Summa theologica* of Praepositinus and Aquinas's commentary on the *Physics*, to Merton his patristic books and Josephus, and to the warden of Merton, Dr Fitzjames, his copy of the works of St Ambrose: his distinct interest in the early Church perhaps signifies a shift of attention to topics which would be studied more closely in the following century.[75] If the fellows did not leave writings of

---

[69] OCA TF A1/2, 50. This volume is possibly the collection of medical texts now Oriel College MS 61.

[70] Oriel College MS 31; for the annotations see fo. 188ra, and for the borrowing note fo. 319^r.

[71] The books are now Oxford, Lincoln College MS lat. 109, Trinity College Cambridge MS B.4.22, London, British Library MS Add. 4356, Oxford Magdalen College MSS lat. 4 and 134, and Bodleian Library MS Laud misc. 6 respectively. He also owned the theological tracts now Magdalen MS lat 16. See M. B. Parkes, 'The Provision of Books', HUO ii. 409–83, cf. 412, 419, 422.

[72] Oriel College MS 37; London, British Library MS Sloane 3884, fo. 70 (one leaf only).

[73] Oriel College MSS 20 and 41.

[74] Antwerp, Plantin-Moretus Library MS 107.

[75] Oriel College MSS 3, 24, 48; Oxford, Merton College MSS 2, 316 (his Isidore does not survive); Bodleian Library MS Bodley 700.

their own, they certainly read widely and probably applied what they read in sermons.

Two sources throw light on the pedagogic activities of the fellows in the middle and later fifteenth century. One is the series of letters about the residence of Walter Paston in Oxford from about 1473 to 1479, which includes a letter from Edmund Alyard to Walter's mother Margaret. Walter was the youngest son of the late John Paston I, the Norfolk lawyer whose property transactions had brought his family, through many troubles, to the front rank of gentry families of the county; he was destined for a career in canon law, which he was to study after reaching the standing of bachelor of arts. He seems to have been the beneficiary of an exhibition founded by the bishop of Norwich, apparently Walter Lyhert who had died in 1472, the patronage of which was in the hands of his executors. He completed his course in arts, but died in the long vacation before he was able to embark on canon law.[76] Alyard wrote to Margaret Paston on 4 March 1479: '... as for your son Walter, his labour and learning has been and is in the Faculty of Arts, and is well sped therein, and may be bachelor at such time as shall like you, and then to go to law. I can think it to his preferring, but it is not good he know it on-to the time he shall change. And as I conceive there shall none have that exhibition to the Faculty of Law. Therefore move ye the executors that at such time as he shall leave it ye may put another in his place such as shall like you to prefer...' He suggested that Walter should take his degree at midsummer, go home for the long vacation, and return to study law at Michaelmas, a plan frustrated by his pupil's death.[77] Walter was clearly a privileged undergraduate, and Alyard must have had college interests in mind in maintaining the exhibition; but the trouble taken by a senior fellow on behalf of a single individual is in accordance with the contemporary ideal of tutorial care, as expressed rhetorically by his contemporary Dr Thomas Chaundler, late warden of New College and sometime chancellor.[78]

The other item of evidence is a small quire of theological notes, found 'in the back of a study', apparently in the wainscoting, in the 1870s at St Mary

---

[76] See *Paston Letters and Papers of the Fifteenth Century*, ed. Norman Davis, 3 vols. (Oxford, 1971–6 and EETS, London, 2006), i. 644–8 and ii. 366–7. That Walter resided in Oriel or one of its halls is clear not only from his pupillage with Alyard, but from his payments to John Skelton in his will (i. 647). Skelton appears as a former college butler in the treasurers' accounts, OCA TF A1/2, 520, before December 1478, when his account was settled; he had been underbutler in 1473–4 (OCA TF A1/2, 414). The description of Skelton as *principali* in his will is therefore probably a mistake for *pincerne*. Paston did not, on the evidence of the treasurers' accounts, rent a room in college; he may have resided in St Mary Hall, or shared his master's room, in accord with contemporary practice.

[77] *Paston Letters*, ii. 366–7 (spelling modernized).

[78] Thomas Chaundler, *Collocutiones*, Oxford New College MS 288, fos. 5^r–31^r. See Catto, 'Triumph of the Hall', 221.

Hall.⁷⁹ This has recently been dated to 1440–60 on palaeographical grounds; it consists of ten leaves apparently of fragments of lectures on Aristotle's *Ethics*, *De sensu et sensato*, and *De anima*. Inserted among them, in the same hand, is a single bifolium of passages from a tract of the late fourteenth-century anti-Lollard polemicist John Deverose, *De advocacione imaginum et de peregrinacione*, and perhaps from another work of the same author.⁸⁰ Lectures on these texts of Aristotle were commonly given in fifteenth-century Oxford by bachelors of arts; they might be given in halls, and if they were, were recognized by the university as of the same standing as lectures in the schools.⁸¹ These notes, therefore, appear to be those of a bachelor assisting in the instruction given to undergraduates in St Mary Hall, who may or may not have been a fellow of Oriel; but he will have been part of the team, which included Henry Sampson, Richard Wiltshire, Clement Smith, Henry Popy, and Thomas Parys in the mid-century, that maintained the teaching of undergraduates in St Mary Hall and its newly incorporated annexe of Bedel Hall. At least three of them, Provost Sampson himself, Popy, and Paris, had theological books, mainly of a pastoral nature, and it is therefore not surprising to find the unknown bachelor reading a tract in defence of the cult of images, still a sensitive subject in the wake of Lollard objections. Beside this more private interest, he lectured on such topics as the *summum bonum* and the nature of felicity, the qualities of colour, and the powers of the soul. It is evident that the distinguished tradition of Aristotelian study, active since the early thirteenth century, continued in fifteenth-century Oxford, and in the purview of Oriel, as the living principle of advanced education.

By the 1470s Henry Sampson may have ceased to live primarily in the provost's quarters: he was probably resident for most of the year at his residence of Tredington in Gloucestershire. In September or October 1476, after the recent death of his patron Bishop Carpenter on 15 July and perhaps as a consequence, he retired from his college office to live there permanently.⁸² The college had elected a successor by 6 November, though the provost-elect seems to have hesitated to agree: he did not accept the office until shortly before 17 July 1477.⁸³ It was perhaps not surprising that Thomas Hawkins, who had been a fellow in 1451–3 (and probably longer) and was now comfortably precentor of Salisbury, should have been reluctant,

---

⁷⁹ Oriel College MS 88.
⁸⁰ Oriel College MS 88, fos. 1ʳ–6ᵛ and 9ʳ–12ᵛ (lectures on Aristotle); 7ʳ–8ᵛ (Deverose etc.). Fos. 7ʳ⁻ᵛ correspond to the text of Deverose, *De advocacione*, in Oxford, Worcester College MS 233, fo. 143ʳᵇ⁻ᵛᵇ. For the date, see the notes of Dr Malcolm Parkes bound with the manuscript.
⁸¹ See J. A. Fletcher, 'Developments in the Faculty of Arts', in HUO ii. 337–8.
⁸² Before 30 October, when his expenses (presumably for removal of his effects) were paid; OCA TF A1/2, 485.
⁸³ OCA TF A1/2, 486. The 1349 statute on election of the provost was confirmed by Thomas Rotherham, bishop of Lincoln, on 17 October; see OCR 64–6.

given his current circumstances; but his patrons were Carpenter, who had conferred on him his first preferment in 1454 and the archdeaconry of Worcester in 1467, and John Hals the bishop of Lichfield, whose first archdeacon of Stafford he had been (1459), and he perhaps saw it as his duty. He does not seem to have resided or to have taken the provost's stipend. However he was the last provost to have been a beneficiary of the powerful network of influence woven by John Carpenter and further developed by Walter Lyhert and John Hals, and he played some part in the final benefaction it conferred on the college. In 1478 Bishop Hals acquired for Oriel the estate of Littleworth, near Faringdon and adjacent to its Wadley property, conferring it on trustees who included, besides himself, his three successors Henry Sampson, Thomas Hawkins, and John Taylor, the dean and after 1479 the provost. Taylor and presumably Sampson and Hawkins travelled to Staffordshire to be present for the deed of feoffment on 1 September.[84] But within a few months the provost was dead; his exequies were performed in college on or before 2 March 1479, and a fortnight later the first consignment of his bequest of books was received at Oriel.[85]

In retrospect, the death of Hawkins was the end of an era in Oriel. The previous century had marked the ascent of the college from being a distinct, lively, but not very influential society in Oxford to become the core of a powerful Lancastrian connection. Its accommodation of the future Archbishop Arundel in the early 1370s had perhaps pointed the way; certainly, Arundel's patronage would prove a critical benefit in the uncertainty of Oxford's painful divestment of its Wycliffism. In the event, as Oxford came to be an important node of the proto-Anglican church establishment of Henry V and his successors, Oriel under the guidance especially of its great provost and patron John Carpenter played a willing and highly profitable part in the Lancastrian system. When the house of Lancaster foundered, in the course of 1461, the college and its patrons were placed in danger; but since Edward IV needed the support of the Lancastrian bishops, the price to be paid for the college's rehabilitation turned out to be moderate and its prosperity actually increased at the hands of its old patrons. These years were not only, however, a time of merely material success. A college whose fellows had been deeply involved in Oxford's governance during the phase of its Wycliffite sympathies also harboured, in the same generation, some distinguished logicians. In the following generation it accommodated, consistently if probably not without tensions, Dr Thomas Gascoigne, the most distinguished English patristic scholar of the century, whose book-hunting and

---

[84] OCA, LL 2 A bis 1. Taylor's expenses for the journey (14s. 10d.) were paid on 2 October (OCA TF A1/2, 504). The college had livery of the estate on 10 February 1483; see OCA, LL 2 A bis 6. On Hawkins see BRUO ii. 891–2.

[85] Treasurers' accounts 1482–1513, OCA TF A1/3, 510, 521, 524.

ILLUSTRATION 2.3 The so-called Founder's Cup, made in Paris *c*.1350 and bought in 1493
Oriel College

collecting almost certainly influenced the fellows of the mid-century and beyond, as well as enriching the library. It had also housed his particular bugbear, the older and more controversial Dr Reginald Pecock, an eccentric but distinctly original scholar who was the victim of his own outspokenness. Throughout the period the fellows had continued to instruct undergraduates in logic and philosophy in its dependent halls, which gradually evolved into the large community of St Mary Hall; their own studies were, for the most part, in the theology faculty as they had always been. The fellows who became bishops, Richard Praty, John Carpenter, Reginald Pecock, Walter Lyhert, and John Hals, seem mostly, so far as the evidence goes, to have put their theological training to use as active pastoral prelates. During the century after 1385 Oriel had established itself, in common with other colleges, as an integral element in Oxford's pervasive influence on a national Church and an intelligently ordered government. Together with the other parts of the system, it would face a painful challenge in the succeeding era.

3

Oriel in Renaissance Oxford, 1479–1574

Jeremy Catto

Amid the profound cultural changes of the Renaissance, European universities, and especially perhaps Oxford, appeared to cling to the models of learning of the past. The requirements of the Oxford curriculum in the arts, theology, and law faculties were much the same as they had been in 1400; the works of Aristotle continued to be the backbone of the study of arts, as the traditional lectures on the *Sentences* of Peter Lombard and on the Bible dominated the teaching of theology. No radical statutory changes were enacted in any faculty before 1549, with the exception of the abolition, on royal authority, of the study of canon law in the 1530s. Even the statutes of 1549 and the *nova statuta* of 1565 were conservative in comparison with enactments at Cambridge and at foreign universities. The registers of congregation show no sign of innovation in the university's ancient system of teaching, beyond relaxing to a limited extent, as had been the practice for over a century, the requirements of the statutes in individual cases.[1] The Dean's Register at Oriel, which was kept almost continuously from 1505, records the college's similar academic requirements laid on fellows proceeding to the degree of master of arts.

Beneath the carapace of university custom, however, the Oxford masters like their counterparts elsewhere were adjusting to the changing values of society. The most immediate novelty was the new emphasis on the education of youth, which in the fifteenth century had already borne fruit in a wealth of endowed schools, Winchester, Eton, Wells Cathedral School, Magdalen College School, and many others where a more elegant Latinity and more acceptably courtly manners were imposed on an increasing number of

---

[1] On graces in the early sixteenth century see W. T. Mitchell (ed.), *Register of Congregations, 1505–1517*, 2 vols. (Oxford, OHS 1998), i. 18–40.

children. Oxford colleges and academic halls received and nurtured many of their alumni, taking pride in imparting to them a more all-encompassing education than the limited training of the traditional faculties had allowed; the prevailing values of late fifteenth-century New College were articulated in the *Collocutiones* of its warden, Dr Thomas Chaundler, with emphasis on individual pastoral care and a Ciceronian sense of public responsibility. A more robust version of Chaundler's approach was taken in the *Statuta aularia*, a code drawn up about 1490 for undergraduates in academic halls and applicable therefore to the vast majority of scholars.[2] About 1500, therefore, university education was no longer predicated on the ideal, however unattainable for most scholars, of the fullness of learning represented by the doctor of theology, laws, or medicine. Bypassing the professionalism of the schools, many undergraduate scholars might seek a more general and humane education in which residence at Oxford was only part of a *cursus* which might also include a season at the Inns of Court—the path followed by the young Thomas More—or a period of study of Greek or humane letters in Italy, such as William Grocyn of Magdalen would enjoy. These broader accomplishments and the manners which were acquired alongside them offered increasing opportunities for advancement in the court and metropolitan world of sixteenth-century England. A related new feature of Oxford education was the growing interest in classical and patristic literature which scholars evinced at every level and in every faculty. There was a ready market for printed texts, including the newly edited works of Plato and in due course for scholarly editions of the Polyglot New Testament and Augustine, which were extensively used by theologians lecturing in the schools. Humane letters were cultivated by numerous leading scholars such as Thomas Linacre and John Colet, and were intrinsic to the education laid down at the new foundation of Magdalen, where the humanist Cornelio Vitelli seems to have taught in the 1490s; humanist ideals would explicitly inspire Richard Fox's new foundation of Corpus Christi College in 1517.

In Oriel, as in other colleges, the formal records give little indication of these profound changes, but casual references to the learning of the fellows and the evidence of their books make clear that new concepts of education and literary scholarship were powerfully present there as elsewhere. The body of fellows, supplemented by a few sojourners and a small number of undergraduates within the walls, was still in 1479 of no distinct geographical origin, though a bias to the west country and the south-west, brought about by the Frank and Carpenter fellowships, would be evident in later decades. The new provost, Dr John Taylor, conformed to the pattern: his origin was in

---

[2] Chaundler's *Collucutiones* are in Oxford, New College MS 288, pp. 1–55; the *Statuta aularia* are printed in *Statuta antiqua Universitatis Oxoniensis*, ed. Strickland Gibson (Oxford, 1931), 574–600.

Carpenter's diocese of Worcester, and since his election in 1467 had filled most college offices, including that of dean during the non-resident provostship of Thomas Hawkins.³ Taylor was a theologian who played an active part in university affairs; his copy of Aquinas on the *Physics* and other texts used in the arts faculty (Oriel MS 48) was perhaps acquired when he was lecturing in arts, but most of his books, left to Oriel and Merton, were patristic texts including an ancient copy of the *Carmina* of Prudentius (Oriel MS 3), in accord with current taste. In 1483 he debated theological questions with William Grocyn before Richard III, whose almoner he became. Taylor probably shared Grocyn's interests and rhetorical skills, and though his visit to Rome in 1492, shortly before his death, is likely to have been for business reasons (his expenses do not seem, however, to have been paid by the college), he must, like Grocyn, have been affected by contact with a Renaissance court. He died on 23 December, and was succeeded, on 5 February 1493, by his former colleague Thomas Cornysh, who had been a fellow from about 1475 to 1484 and was now *episcopus Tinensis in partibus infidelium* and suffragan bishop of Wells.⁴ It was a curious choice insofar as Cornysh was a busy diocesan official, fully involved in the affairs of Wells, who must have continued to spend most of his time there; the fellows probably sought a man of wider influence in the Church. As it turned out the new provost spent at least part of most years at Oriel, as is shown by his personal appearance at Wadley almost every year to hold the college's court.⁵ He was probably the instigator of the new college register, to be kept by the dean, which was instituted in 1504. The only book of his to have survived is a collection of excerpts from Augustine in defence of Christian philosophy, which had probably been compiled in the thirteenth century: he shared his predecessor's reading of the fathers, but perhaps only as a preaching aid.⁶

If the fellows hoped to find in Provost Cornysh a new episcopal patron after the death of John Hals in 1490, they were disappointed. The final benefaction of the Lancastrian network set up by John Carpenter had been the transfer of Littleworth, Bishop Hals's gift, into college hands in 1483. It is noticeable that the cathedral canonries and other plums available to at least some Oriel fellows in the mid-century were not granted to their successors who bore the burden of college business in its final decades: Thomas Wormeswell, treasurer, chaplain, and dean in the 1480s, was vicar of Littleham in Devon; William Wright, who laboured in Oriel's interest at the 1484

---

³ For his career see BRUO iii. 1850–1.
⁴ See BRUO i. 491–2. The bishopric intended by the adjectival form *Tinensis* is not identifiable, and seems to be a fiction of the Roman curia; it is not Tenos in the Aegean, which was under Christian rule and had its own line of bishops.
⁵ See treasurers' accounts, OCA TF A1/3, 250 (1493–4); 270 (1494–5); 291 (1495–6); 328 (1497–8); 393 (1500–1); 441 (1502–3); 463 (1503–4); 487 (1504–5).
⁶ London, Lincoln's Inn Hale MS 75 (70).

parliament, became rector of Fornham, Suffolk; Roger Sutton, treasurer and principal of St Mary Hall, was made a fellow of Eton, as was Richard Martyn, treasurer and chaplain.[7] The only exception was Dr Edmund Wilsford, collector of rents, treasurer, chaplain, and dean on occasions from 1484 to 1498, who was probably the first Lady Margaret lecturer in theology (1497–1500); he was made canon of Lichfield in 1500, but evidently on the strength of his position as a leading Oxford theologian.[8] Wilsford would become the most forceful of the provosts of this period.

If powerful competition from the nexus of patronage of newer and richer colleges such as Magdalen had dimmed the prospects of Oriel fellows, however, the resources of previous benefactors allowed the college to prosper. In 1493 the fellows marked their new-found well-being by acquiring a handsome silver-gilt cup, later known inaccurately as the Founder's Cup.[9] A few years later they felt sufficiently in funds to acquire a new manor.[10] The cost of the manor of Shenington (Gloucestershire, now Oxfordshire) was covered by the generous gift of £300 donated in 1504 by William Smyth, bishop of Lincoln, and from Shenington's revenues the college established a new fellowship for scholars from the diocese of Lincoln, as well as increasing the allowances of the provost and fellows.[11] He seems to have had no previous link with Oriel, earlier than his *ex officio* position as Visitor; he had probably studied at Brasenose Hall, which he endowed and incorporated as a college in 1509.[12] It is not very surprising in the circumstances that at the next fellowship election, on 27 April 1506, one of the successful candidates should be Matthew Smyth BA, nephew of the bishop, albeit from the diocese of Lichfield from where there was already a fellow.[13] Smyth remained a fellow until the end of Trinity Term 1510 (despite being collated to a canonry at Lincoln in 1509); in August 1510 he became principal of Brasenose Hall and the first head of Bishop Smyth's newly endowed Brasenose College, dying in office as late as 1548.[14] The first Smyth fellow was elected on 8 November 1508, a protégé of the bishop from the humanist foundation of Banbury School: this

---

[7] BRUO iii. 2088 (Wormeswell), iii. 2094–5 (Wright), iii. 1894 (Sutton), ii. 1237 (Martyn).

[8] BRUO iii. 2115–16.

[9] Treasurers' accounts, OCA TF A1/3, 248. See E. Alfred Jones, *Catalogue of the Plate of Oriel College, Oxford* (Oxford, 1944), 1. See Ill. 2.3, p. 59.

[10] For the acquisition of Shenington see OCA DLR/860, the grant of a moiety of Shenington by Sir Reginald Bray to Thomas Cornysh, 10 November 1502.

[11] The college thanked the bishop on 20 March 1504 and again in November (OCA DR 13, 7), and made a new statute on allowances on 23 October, confirmed by Smyth on 20 November (OCA DR 5–6; *Statutes of the College of Oxford*, i, Oriel, 26–8). The money only reached the college accounts in the financial year 1505–6 (treasurers' accounts, OCA TF A1/3, 521). The fellowship statute was made on 5 May 1507 and confirmed by the bishop on 7 May (*Statutes of the Colleges of Oxford*, i, Oriel, 26–8).

[12] BRUO iii. 1721–2; J. Mordaunt Crook, *Brasenose: The Biography of an Oxford College* (Oxford, 2008), 11–12.

[13] DR 10. [14] BRUO 1501–40, 523–4; Mordaunt Crook, *Brasenose*, 10, 19.

was Roger Edgeworth, who would become a distinguished preacher and theologian. As he too was from the diocese of Lichfield, the limiting statute had to be waived 'with the unanimous assent of the fellows and the consent of the bishop'.[15] As was often the case, an election which owed so much to a patron's influence gave the college a scholar of distinction.

This fortunate benefaction can hardly have come about without the full support of Provost Cornysh. But the first college row of which we know since 1424 arose shortly afterwards, and led directly to his resignation in acrimonious circumstances. This is because its various stages are recorded in the new college register, which was to be kept by the dean or his assignee according to a decision of 23 October 1504.[16] The Dean's Register, as it came to be known, was kept as a continuation of a book of precedents begun in 1446 and sporadically added to thereafter, even after 1504. In the early years documents were inserted both after the precedents and at the back of the volume.[17] But the entries can hardly be understood from the printed edition: they are in numerous hands some of which can be identified, including that of Cornysh, who inserted doubtless tendentious accounts of his side of the affair in his own hand. Other entries are in the hand probably of his deputy and opponent, John Goodrich, who was dean from 1505 to 1507. The issue was once again, as in the previous century, the competing passions of local loyalties, which the 1426 statutes had been designed to resolve. But it was exacerbated by the personality of the dean. Goodrich's first record, of 18 February 1506, was hardly that of a man used to writing emollient college minutes: *orta est... contentio*, 'a dispute arose' on the terms of the lease of the college manor of Dean. Who argued what is unknown to us; the argument was settled amicably at the college meeting of 27 April.[18] But the framing of the minute is a pointer to the character of a dean who relished an argument.[19]

At the same April meeting, three new fellows were elected for a probationary year. One was Matthew Smyth, already bachelor of arts; the others, Thomas Stock of Hereford diocese and John Parker of Dorset and Salisbury diocese, had not yet graduated. Their regional origins were important because of the college statute, confirmed in 1441, that there should be no more than two fellows from any one county or diocese.[20] The provost's clear duty, as Cornysh recognized, was to uphold the statute. He was confronted by the powerful determination of Goodrich to elect a protégé from his own home county of Gloucestershire: for it emerged during the summer that Stock was

---

[15] DR 17; see BRUO 1501–40, 184–5. He was originally from Denbigh.
[16] *Statutes of the College of Oxford*, i, Oriel, 28.
[17] The first volume of the Dean's Register is OCA Gov 4 A1.
[18] DR 9.
[19] On his angry refusal of a conciliatory gesture in the chancellor's court see *Chancellor's Register 1498–1506*, ed. W. T. Mitchell (OHS, Oxford, 1980), 130, 263–4.
[20] *Statutes of the Colleges of Oxford*, i, Oriel, 22.

actually a Gloucestershire man, a county which had already supplied two fellows, Goodrich himself and Robert Doll. Accordingly, shortly before the beginning of Michaelmas Term (10 October) the provost, supported by a majority of five fellows (Edward Trowbridge, Thomas Richards, William Broke, John Lewis, and Doll), declared his and Parker's election to be contrary to the statutes, against the opposition of Goodrich and three other fellows (John Baker, Thomas Heritage, and Henry Myn).[21] But on the first day of term, presumably in the provost's absence and against the will of the majority, Goodrich and his associates admitted them to fellowship. The dean omitted to record these proceedings in the register; instead, he inserted two entries of a subsequent meeting, in December. In the first, he recounted, not without a note of mockery, *quedam pia contentio*, 'a respectful dispute' over whether the provost could exercise a casting vote in the election of John Lewis and Robert Doll to permanent fellowships, a question which was resolved, according to Goodrich, against the provost. Goodrich, of course, had an interest in removing Doll, the second Gloucestershire fellow, with whom he was clearly not on good terms, since that would remove the objection to Stock. The second entry reverts directly to the question of Stock, who is admitted to be not from Hereford but from Worcester diocese (no mention is made of Gloucestershire, which was part of that see). It was agreed that at the time of Stock's election there was an existing fellow, Thomas Jokys, from that diocese, but as he had now died, the provost and fellows allowed Stock to complete his year of probation, after which the facts would be re-examined. This rather dissembling minute seems to mark at least a partial victory for Goodrich and his party at the December meeting; Stock, and presumably Parker, remained a fellow. But he had lost the battle to remove Doll and Lewis, who were elected to full fellowships. At that point the provost seems to have regained the register from the dean's hands, as he then inserted his own memorandum of the omitted October meeting.[22] But his inevitable absences seem to have prevented him from carrying his point.

Nothing further is recorded until 12 July 1507, when we have another minute in Goodrich's hand. In the interval he must have presided over the college, and seems to have appealed to the Visitor to reopen the question of Doll's and Lewis's election; the bishop mandated them not to appear at college meetings until he or his chancellor appeared in person to adjudicate the case. Then at a college meeting on 12 July, in the provost's absence, Doll (who was said to have taken advice) appeared in spite of the Visitor's

---

[21] DR 12, from the memorandum inserted later in Cornysh's hand. The case of Parker is not mentioned, but if as is likely he is the Parker elected to All Souls in 1509, he was from Exeter diocese (the origin of at least one existing fellow, John Bowerman) and had deceived the college on this point. For Parker see BRUO 1500–40, 432.

[22] DR 12.

prohibition, and was challenged by the dean; he declined to leave, and seems to have been allowed to remain.[23] If the provost was unable to have Stock removed, the dean was equally powerless to expel Doll. Meanwhile the provost returned in time for another college meeting, on 9 August, to receive the accounts for the previous year. This time the provost (who wrote the minute of the proceedings) and his party were present, but the dean and his supporters Henry Myn and Thomas Heritage arrived late. In the meantime the provost and his supporters took the opportunity to remove Goodrich from the office of dean, electing Edward Trowbridge, a firm partisan of Cornysh, in his place. Goodrich and his supporters, including John Baker who had been present throughout, withdrew, went to the chapel and made a new election; the other party pronounced them to be *periuros et inobedientes*, in breach of the statutes.[24] The schism in the deanship seems to have lasted all summer. Finally, on 14 October, according again to the provost's account, he required Goodrich to hand over the statute book and insignia of his office; but the erstwhile dean declined to do so unless his acts as dean, 'whether just or unjust', were ratified, a condition rejected by the provost. The next day at a college meeting the provost and his party (including Doll and Lewis) annulled the election of Stock and Parker, his four opponents declining to appear; they were declared to be contumacious and the whole affair was to be reported to the Visitor.[25]

In the provost's account this looks like a clear victory for himself and his supporters. But in reality he seems to have been unable to enforce their decisions, perhaps because his other responsibilities prevented him from being present continuously. A few days later, he sent a message through his supporter William Broke, resigning his office. Edward Trowbridge, the new dean, lost no time in holding an election at which Dr Edmund Wilsford was summoned back to be provost.[26] Trowbridge was no more successful than Cornysh had been at enforcing the decision to expel Stock and Parker: at a college meeting on 2 November they were again directed to leave, but refused. Stock, if not Parker, kept his place, and was eventually dean himself.[27] Doll and Lewis kept their fellowships too, and Trowbridge on the same day made them keepers of the library. Provost Cornysh retired to Wells, where he died in 1513. He probably did not forgive the fellows for the circumstances of his resignation; unusually, he did not mention the college in his will, though he left a legacy to one fellow, William Canynges.[28]

---

[23] DR 13–14.   [24] DR 6–7.   [25] DR 14–15.
[26] DR 15–16. On Wilsford, elected on 30 October, see BRUO iii. 2115–16, s.n. Wyllesford. It was evidently a contentious election: Trowbridge was enjoined to keep the peace with other fellows in the chancellor's court next day (OUA, Chancellor's register F reversed, fo. 30ᵛ).
[27] DR 16. On Stock see BRUO 1500–40, 542, s.n. Stoke.
[28] *Somerset Medieval Wills*, series ii, 1501–30, ed. F. W. Weaver (Somerset Record Society, London, 1903), 167–70.

The episode has been recounted in detail for the vivid glimpse of life in Oriel that it affords. Goodrich's determination to promote another Gloucestershire man revived the quarrels which had been endemic before Carpenter had suppressed them, nearly a century earlier. His persistence succeeded: admission, however irregular, entrenched Stock's position and both the provost and a majority of fellows were powerless to remove him. Doll too was impossible to dislodge. The bishop of Lincoln as Visitor, though appealed to, seems not to have acted in either case. A provost who must have been attending to other duties in Wells much of the time was not in a strong position, but with the agreement of the majority he did his best to uphold the statutes' prohibition on regional bias, a principle unique to Oriel among Oxford colleges, but one which must have come under pressure from the provisions of the Frank and Carpenter benefactions. His successor, with fewer external duties and probably more continuous residence, would be able to enforce the statutes more firmly and to restore the prerogatives of his office.

With the institution of the Dean's Register, the preoccupation of the fellows with their own number and with the distribution of offices comes into sharp focus. It may, however, distort the reality of their constant involvement in teaching and the work of the university. The fellows were at the centre of an educational enterprise which included, certainly, the progress of their younger members through the faculty of arts, but which also involved, through the academic halls which the fellows ran and especially St Mary Hall, the teaching of undergraduates. Only occasional evidence of this work survives. Throughout the controversy over fellowships Goodrich's opponent Edward Trowbridge was principal of St Lawrence Hall in Ship Street (1505–7) and later of Beam Hall in Merton Street (1508–11), while his supporter Thomas Heritage was principal of St Mary Hall by agreement with the college from 1504 to 1514.[29] St Mary Hall was now incorporated with Bedel Hall to make one of the larger halls of sixteenth-century Oxford: it had inherited from Bedel Hall the obligation to house the St Antony's exhibitioners in its better chambers, as the college reaffirmed in September 1504.[30] When Richard Dudley funded the Dudley exhibitioners they too would be put up in St Mary Hall.[31] It is reasonably clear that the hall was regarded by the fellows as Oriel's undergraduate wing. But there is also evidence that a small number of scholars resided in Oriel too. The case of Walter Paston, Edmund Alyard's scholar in the 1470s and apparently a batteler, paying for his commons, was mentioned in the last chapter. William Canynges was probably another: ten shillings were paid for his keep in 1503–4.[32]

---

[29] DR 8–9; BRUO ii. 917.
[30] OCA DR 5 (928); *Cat. Mun.* viii, no 129, 30 September 1504.   [31] DR 75–6.
[32] Treasurers' accounts, OCA TF A1/3, 460. On battelers at a later date see *Registrum Orielense*, i. vi–ix. Shadwell's distinctions, *commensales* and *communarii*, are anachronistic as specific categories for this period.

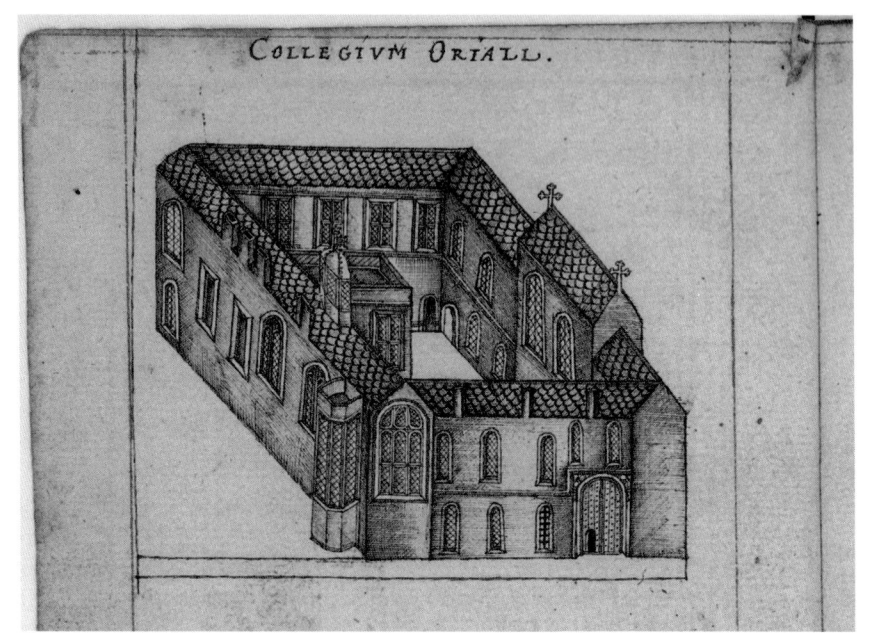

ILLUSTRATION 3.1 John Bereblock's view of Oriel, 1566
Bodleian Library MS Bodley 13, fo.6v

If he was a member of the well-known Bristol family he was probably a protégé, as he was certainly a legatee, of Provost Cornysh; he was elected a fellow in 1509.[33] In 1516–17 a poor scholar, Roper, was paid for working in the garden, and six others for cutting wood. About this time the college's other academic hall, Martin Hall on the site of the present chapel and kitchen, was rebuilt, largely for sojourners' use, but in 1523–4 it also accommodated the sons of Thomas Unton the lessee of Wadley. According to the antiquary Miles Windsor, his father Anthony, the son of Andrew Lord Windsor, was a batteler at Oriel, apparently about this time.[34] Two well-placed scholars, William and Richard Scudamore, sons of John Scudamore, gentleman-usher of the King's Chamber, were in residence sometime in the 1530s; William wrote to his father by the hand of his unnamed master, whom he warmly recommended: 'we fynd hym good';

---

[33] BRUO 1500–40, 99; *Provosts and Fellows*, 49.
[34] For the Untons, see treasurers' accounts, OCA TF A1/4, 545–6, 576, 578, 710. Presumably the sons were Alexander and Thomas; see J. G. Nichols (ed.), *The Unton Inventories* (Berkshire Ashmolean Society, London, 1841), xxv–xxviii. Miles Windsor describes his father as *huius olim commercii*, presumably a resident paying battels, in an inscription in *The Workes of Sir Thomas More* (London, 1557), presenting the volume to the college as it had once belonged to the elder Windsor; see the *Workes*, OCL V.f.3, title page.

and took the opportunity to request a doublet to wear on feast days.[35] In 1537, according to evidence given in proceedings for treason in the aftermath of the Pilgrimage of Grace, an unnamed schoolmaster of Knutsford had a son, Philip, at Oriel, to whom he sent a possibly subversive letter.[36] These were exceptional cases who were probably in the care of individual fellows; but by 1568 Oriel was reported to have thirty-one students and four *famuli*, while St Mary Hall had seventy-five students and three *famuli*.[37]

This distribution is confirmed by the evidence of the Cardinal Morton scholars at Oxford. John Morton, cardinal archbishop of Canterbury, in his will of 1500 had left funds to continue his practice of providing exhibitions for undergraduate and graduate scholars at Oxford; the funds were to be administered by the warden of Canterbury College, while the exhibitioners would be housed in one of the colleges or halls of the university. Records survive for the years 1501–8.[38] They show provision at St Mary Hall for Edward Bowden, first scholar and after 1505 a bachelor of arts, Thomas Burton, and John Glower; Bowden is described in 1505 as *collegiatus*, perhaps implying that he and not the others resided there.[39] Other beneficiaries resided in Oriel: three were fellows, Richard Vaughan, John Dalby, and William Broke; a fourth, Robert Hopton, *in regali collegio moranti* in 1508, later became fellow of All Souls.[40] So at least one scholar was residing in 1508. They were probably exceptional until the second half of the century; St Mary Hall even then seems generally to have presented more scholars for matriculation than Oriel did.[41] We know of one further Morton scholar, this time promoted during the cardinal's lifetime, who probably resided at St Mary Hall in conformity with the scheme put into practice after 1501. This was Thomas More, who was at Oxford in the years 1490–2, and according to the statement of Miles Windsor, a scholar in the hall. Windsor probably relied on his father's information, which must have been garnered at St Mary Hall in the 1520s, only a generation after More's residence in Oxford. This was in contradiction to the assertion in Cresacre More's *Life of Sir*

---

[35] TNA PRO C.115/100, letter of William Scudamore 'wryten at Oxford yn Oryall Colege', 21 January, year unnamed. This is probably William Scudamore of Holme Lacy who died in 1560.

[36] *Letters and Papers, Henry VIII*, xii part i, no. 389, 10 February 1537.

[37] In October 1506 'thirteen fellows and five of the scholars' were present at the annual exequies of Bishop Carpenter (OCA TF A1/3, 460); this sounds like a regular contingent, but must actually refer to the St Antony exhibitioners housed in St Mary Hall, who were expected to attend this ceremony. The figures for 1568 are given in *Epitome chronographica collegiorum Oxoniensium*, Washington, DC, Folger Library MS V.a.176, fos. 173–4.

[38] W. A. Pantin (ed.), *Canterbury College, Oxford* (OHS, Oxford, 1941–85), iii. 227–43.

[39] BRUO 1501–40, 62–3, 88, perhaps 234 s.n. Glover.

[40] BRUO iii. 1942–3 (Vaughan); i. 533 (Dalby); i. 273 (Broke). BRUO 1501–40, 298–9 (Hopton).

[41] A. Clark (ed.), *Register of the University of Oxford* (Oxford, OHS 1884–9), ii. 10–46 (matriculation lists 1565–83).

ILLUSTRATION 3.2 Thomas More, former scholar of St Mary Hall
Oriel College

Thomas More, published in 1627, that he was at Canterbury College, but Windsor's information is earlier and the error easy to understand as the warden of Canterbury College administered the scheme.[42] More showed no later favour to Oriel, though some affection for at least one of its fellows: but then his opinion of the Oxford schools was never very high.

So the fellowship still constituted the overwhelming majority of the college community in the first half of the sixteenth century. We have lists of them in 1510, signing their acknowledgement of the bishop of Lincoln's visitation, in 1516 at James More's election, in 1520 at Bishop Atwater's visitation, in 1530 at the election of Thomas Ware, in 1534 taking the oath of supremacy and at the visitation of 1539.[43] The bias towards the west and south-west is visible throughout; it was the inevitable result of the Frank fellowships and that of Carpenter, but was increased by the predilection of fellows such as Goodrich, and by further elections of Welsh fellows such as the recalcitrant Lewis,

---

[42] Anthony Wood, *Athenae Oxonienses*, i. 79–80; Cresacre More, *Life of Sir Thomas More, Knight, Lord High Chancellor* (London, 1726), 9.

[43] DR 381–2 (1510), OCR 70–1 (1516), A. Hamilton Thompson (ed.), *Visitations of the Diocese of Lincoln*, 3 vols. (Lincoln Record Society, Lincoln, 1940–7), iii. 72–4 (1520), DR 80 (1530), DR 382–3 (1534), DR 111 (1539).

William Griffith of Bangor, and Roger Edgeworth, the bishop's protégé, from Denbigh. They were afforced by the presence of distinguished sojourners, some of whom like Fulk Salisbury, the future dean of St Asaph, took a room for a year only; others like James Bennett stayed for a decade (1491–1502), or Dr John Roper the divinity lecturer, vicar of St Mary's and influential churchman for a shorter period (1507–12). Both Bennett and Roper established a friendly relationship with their hosts.[44] Most of them were former fellows, with whose success the college hoped to be associated: Richard Dudley, the cousin of Henry VII's minister Edmund Dudley, had been a fellow from 1497 to 1506 and returned as a sojourner in 1511–12; he would be an important future benefactor. He would that year find Dr Edward Powell for company: Powell, a fellow from about 1494 to 1501, had evidently studied in Paris (*c*. 1501–3) and then become a canon of Lincoln; he would long be favoured by Wolsey and Henry VIII for his polemic against Luther. He would be entertained by the college at regular intervals.[45] Rowland Phillips, fellow from 1491 to 1506, was assigned a room after his resignation; a future chaplain to the king and occasional preacher before him, he would be briefly warden of Merton (1521–4).[46] And in the 1520s Roger Edgeworth would compose some of his great body of sermons in Oriel.[47]

The election of Provost Wilsford was something of a turning point. Wilsford was a great university figure, who had been the first Lady Margaret lecturer in divinity; though none of his books survive, his scholarship is likely to have resembled that of John Colet, who lectured on the Epistles of Paul in Oxford about 1500. He was ready to enforce higher intellectual standards in a college too plainly devoted, in the wake of its old Lancastrian connection, to worldly advancement. But first he had to re-establish the provost's authority, which had been flouted by Dean Goodrich's party. That it was not easy is made clear by the meticulous care with which, in his own hand, he recorded his proceedings against the unsatisfactory John Lewis in the college register. It was probably on account of Lewis's conduct that in October 1508 the college revoked the terms it had exacted for his inception in arts, and left the provost to draw up more severe conditions at his discretion. Lewis's boisterous demeanour and defiance of college

---

[44] BRUO iii. 1631, i. 165–6, iii. 1590. Sojourners were referred to in the treasurers' accounts and the Dean's Register sometimes as *commensales*, sometimes as *communarii*; the distinction is not obvious in this period and always referred to masters of arts. For its later use see *Registrum Orielense*, ed. Shadwell, i. ix–xii.

[45] BRUO i. 598–9, iii. 1510–11; treasurers' accounts, OCA TF A1/3, 677. For his entertainment see OCA TF A1/3, 758 (1513–14), OCA TF A1/4, 556 (1517–18), 747 (1525–6). He seems to have had the old congregation house in St Mary's re-roofed at his own expense in 1507 (OUA Chancellor's register F reversed, fo. 18^r).

[46] BRUO iii. 1477–8.

[47] *Sermons very Fruitfull, Godly and Learned by Roger Edgeworth*, ed. Janet Wilson (Woodbridge, 1993), 20.

discipline led to a second warning in August 1509 and a final admonition in February 1510, after which a formal inquiry was held in April, specifying his offences and ending in his expulsion, on a majority vote. This time there was no question of defiance, though he appealed to the chancellor's court. He disappeared from the record in 1513.[48] Most of Goodrich's party—Goodrich himself, Baker, and Henry Myn—had resigned on collation to benefices by 1509. Thomas Heritage was expelled in 1513 for an unspecified offence, perhaps unpaid debts; he would later be surveyor of the king's works and would advise the college, in 1535, on the rebuilding of the hall.[49] It was probably at Wilsford's instigation that a statement of the college's 'laudable customs', including presence at college disputations, was inserted on the first page of the college register.[50]

Having asserted his authority, Wilsford initiated the practice of imposing college conditions for young fellows who were bachelors to incept as masters of arts. They were enjoined to observe the formal obligations imposed, though often moderated by graces, by university statute; but they were also obliged to conduct disputations 'here in college' on the evenings when they were customarily held.[51] The conditions laid down tended to be elaborated in time: the five fellows permitted to incept in December 1511 were each assigned to lecture on either a work of Aristotle or the commentaries of John Canonicus. Though the text is not explicit, the provost seems here to be laying down an educational programme for undergraduate scholars, presumably at St Mary Hall, not just for the bachelors themselves, since otherwise there would be no point in differentiating the books to be studied and expounded. The conditions of inception could be relaxed both by the college and by the university congregation, but the requirement to hold disputations in college for the instruction of scholars was maintained.[52] College licences to incept in arts continued to be granted, though eventually only as a matter of form, into the seventeenth century; the lectures and other academic exercises were sometimes to be held in Martin Hall, another indication of their intended college audience.[53] They certainly drove the bachelor fellows

---

[48] DR 18–25; BRUO 1501–40, s.n. Lewys, 355; OUA, Chancellor's register F reversed, fo. 150ʳ. Lewis was at this time a scholar of civil and canon law, which may explain if not excuse his reluctance to perform the duties of a regent master of arts: see *Register of Congregations, 1505–17*, ii. 33, 46, 48.

[49] DR 33, 34–5; H. M. Colvin, *History of the King's Works*, 6 vols. (London, 1963–82), iii. 15; BRUO ii. 917.

[50] DR 343–4. The custom prohibiting familiarity between bachelors and masters was cited against Lewis (DR 23).

[51] DR 18 (conditions for Robert Doll and John Lewis), 25–6 (for Thomas Stock, including the words quoted), 28–30 (for William Griffith, Thomas Ware, John Stephens, John Morris, and Roger Edgeworth).

[52] DR 30–1, terms of relaxation for Ware and Stephens. Ware and Griffith had already been excused the remainder of their university regency (*Register of Congregations*, ii. 194).

[53] In 1539 for instance: DR 111.

into the library: William Griffith's name is found, with the date 1510, in a text of Antonius Andreas on the *Metaphysics*, the book assigned to him in the following year.⁵⁴

The library at this time seems to have been situated on the present site of the hall. Keepers of the books were regularly elected, though the election of John Lewis in 1507 was not likely to have contributed to their safekeeping. We know too that there was a system of periodic, probably annual, 'election' of books, through which fellows could borrow texts, which probably went back to the foundation and was certainly in operation in 1349.⁵⁵ Griffith had presumably borrowed the two manuscripts in which his name is found. As his choice indicates, the backbone of the library was still its manuscript collection, which if it still retained the ninety-nine books held in 1349 and the forty-four known to have been given between then and 1510, together doubtless with others unrecorded and subsequently removed from the library, must have been a respectable collection slightly over half the size of Merton's, the richest in the university among secular colleges. Though there had been some purchases in the mid-fifteenth century, books no longer appeared in the accounts from about 1460 to the end of the extant series in 1526, and its further growth was due to gifts alone. As to printed books, there is no reliable information. At present the college possesses slightly more than 140 books printed before 1540, but there is no indication that any of them were acquired by then: where there is a note of gift, legacy, or acquisition, it indicates that the volume in question came into college possession after 1540. The great majority, however, carry no information on the date at which they came into the library. A few, such as the copy of Scotus on the *Sentences* (Paris, 1513), which has early sixteenth-century annotations, or the Revelations of St Brigit (Nuremberg, 1521) are unlikely, though not impossible acquisitions after the religious reforms of the 1530s. It is probable that Oriel, like other Oxford colleges, did not generally purchase printed books before the 1540s.⁵⁶ On 3 August 1544 it was determined to sell college silver to the value of thirty pounds in order to buy books of theology and other subjects; by then it may well have been obvious that the collection was not keeping up with the mass of learned works currently available. The shortfall was largely made up by donations from fellows of the late sixteenth century, notably Richard Pigot, John Jackman, and Anthony Blencowe.⁵⁷

---

⁵⁴ Oriel College MS 26, fos. iv recto, 174ᵛ. His name and that of Thomas Ware are found as well in Oriel College MS 33, fo. 191ᵛ, a text of numerous commentaries on Aristotle.

⁵⁵ See Chapter 1, and cf. Oriel MS 67, fo. 185ᵛ, *Liber de Oriell de eleccione Magistri J. Bedmester*.

⁵⁶ See N. R. Ker, *Oxford College Libraries before 1556* (Oxford, 1956), and 'The Provision of Books', in HUO iii. 441–519.

⁵⁷ DR 124. For later gifts see *Provosts and Fellows*, 70, 71, 73.

If the fellows, or at least the younger fellows, were occupied throughout this period in their own and their scholars' progress through the faculty of arts, the statutory duty of the senior members of the fellowship was to study in one of the higher faculties. In this respect there was a real break with the relaxed habits of the late fifteenth century, when the fellowship was almost entirely a body of masters teaching in the faculty of arts, though several fellows had theological books. Between Provost Sampson, who was a scholar of theology in 1457, and Wilsford, whose doctorate in theology dated from 1497, only John Taylor had persisted in that faculty, incepting as doctor in 1479, the same year that he was elected provost. The change came about in the 1490s, probably under Wilsford's influence as the only bachelor of theology in the college; several younger fellows, Rowland Phillips, James More, and Edward Powell, followed his lead, and in the next decade Richard Dudley, John Baker, and John Goodrich would do likewise. As provost Wilsford seems to have encouraged another generation to incept in theology, including Thomas Ware, Roger Edgeworth, and William Canynges; Walter Mey was a bachelor of theology. The practice was maintained under his successors into the 1550s. Though it is likely that all these theologians were primarily biblical and patristic scholars in the manner of Colet, and in accordance with the humanist scholarship enjoined on his theology lecturer at Corpus Christi College by Bishop Richard Fox in 1517, most of them have left no writings. The works of only two, Edward Powell and Roger Edgeworth, throw some light on the Wilsford school, if school it was. Though Powell may have studied in Paris about 1502, he was formed by the traditions of Oxford theology; a successful church career and his favour with Cardinal Wolsey encouraged the fellows of Oriel to allow him a college room and entertain him on occasion. His *Propugnaculum* against Luther, printed in 1523, is a polemic founded on the Bible and the fathers and written in humanist Latin. This did not inhibit Powell from criticizing Erasmus: 'Here Luther erasmizes, and indeed Erasmus lutherizes...both are to be blamed, Luther for writing blasphemously, Erasmus for cravenly keeping silent.'[58] The work received the university's commendation and the approval of Wolsey. His younger colleague Edgeworth, who resigned his fellowship in 1519, was equally favoured with a room in Martin Hall from 1524 to 1530, where he seems to have composed his first set of sermons. Another followed in the late 1530s when he was a canon of Wells, and both were printed in Mary's reign. In the second set Edgeworth endeavoured within the constriction of official doctrine to put the orthodox case against radical preachers in the diocese such as Hugh Latimer; the first is less polemical. Edgeworth, like Colet, avoided the speculative theology of the past and concentrated on the

---

[58] Edward Powell, *Propugnaculum summi sacerdotii evangelici* (London, 1523), fo. 119^r.

critical and historical explication of the biblical text; he used Erasmus's scholarly edition of the New Testament and his annotations on the text, and relied on his own extensive knowledge of the Latin fathers.[59] Between them Powell's work against Luther and Edgeworth's sermons allow us to see the nature of the theology which they learnt under Wilsford's guidance: scholarly, and open to new work on texts, but content to define and explain orthodox teaching, and distinctly resistant to the controversial theology coming from Germany.[60]

The legal faculties were barely represented in Oriel in these years. John Bowerman, a fellow since 1503, was admitted as bachelor of civil law in 1507, but died the same year.[61] His contemporary John Lewis was a scholar of both laws, but as we have seen was expelled in 1510. Two contemporary fellows, Thomas Freeman elected in 1510 and William Rose in 1512, after becoming masters of arts in 1516 desired to study medicine. There seems to have been some resistance to this: the Visitor was asked to adjudicate in 1520, and reserved judgement. Freeman in any case resigned in 1522, married, and was granted the reversion of Littlemore farm, which enabled him to reside and become doctor of medicine (1528). His distinguished medical career culminated in his presidency of the College of Physicians in 1545–6.[62] William Rose had already become bachelor of medicine in 1518, but about 1522 left Oxford for Venice where he was one of the four English scholars who helped to complete the Aldine edition of the Greek text of Galen. Like at least one other member of the team, Thomas Lupset, he must have become an intimate of Sir Thomas More as well as a Greek scholar; More published his pamphlet against Luther under Rose's name, and perhaps inspired the affectionate description of his friend as 'a mad companion that then wandred in Italie, and for the manner of his behaviour he was well knowne of most men'.[63] His early death in Rome about 1525 cut off a career which would perhaps have been as notable for literature as for medicine.

As Rose's associations suggest, there was probably a greater informal interest in humane letters in Oriel than college records imply. Dr Goodrich, the controversial dean of the first decade of the century, had in later life at least a local reputation as an arbiter of literary elegance. After leaving Oxford he had become penancer in Worcester diocese and a well-known local figure;

---

[59] Edgeworth, *Sermons very fruitfull* (1st edn. London, 1557); ed. Wilson, introduction, 37–59.
[60] On Oxford theology in the sixteenth century see S. L. Greenslade, 'The Faculty of Theology', in HUO iii. 295–334.
[61] BRUO i. 235.
[62] *Visitations of the Diocese of Lincoln*, iii. 73; BRUO 1501–40, 217.
[63] BRUO 1501–40, 492; *The Complete Works of St Thomas More, Responsio ad Lutherum*, ed. J. M. Headley, 2 vols. (New Haven, 1969), i. 1, ii. 800–1; *The Life of Syr Thomas More &c* by Ro: Ba:, ed. E. U. Hitchcock (London, EETS, 1950), 64.

in 1530 he was the recipient of an elaborate letter from Robert Joseph, the humanist monk of Evesham, who politely implied that Goodrich was a past master in the epistolary art, and asked for his learned guidance on the seven names of demons. In his native Gloucestershire at least, Goodrich was a member of a circle of university-trained humanist correspondents.[64] Both Rose and William Griffith, whom we last saw reading Aristotle commentaries in the library, were the recipients of elegant *epigrammata* from John Constable, the poet of Beam Hall in Merton Street and another likely disciple of Sir Thomas More. Griffith, who had died in 1512, was memorialized as a philosopher who knew the secrets of nature, and an astronomer familiar with the motions of celestial beings. Similar praise was bestowed on Rose, with the additional laurel of medical erudition, and the less respectful information that he was soaked in liquor as well as learning.[65] Rose was the first fellow of Oriel known to have learnt Greek. A further hint appears from the injunctions of the Visitor, the stern upholder of solid learning Bishop John Longland, in 1531: 'We enjoin each and every bachelor to put aside modern literature, the study of Latin and works of poetry, to concentrate on the writings and language of ancient doctors, which they can employ more usefully in their ordinary disputations.'[66] Perhaps the Visitor had in mind the Dudley exhibitioner Thomas Roberts, elected fellow in 1531, who was later the recipient of an *epigramma* from his contemporary John Parkhurst of Merton.[67] In any case a lively cult of stylish poetry seems to have flourished, beneath the purview of more formal college documents.

Edmund Wilsford died on 3 October 1516, and the college, with Thomas Stock the dean presiding, elected another theologian, Dr James More, eleven days later.[68] More seems to have continued the policy of his predecessor and maintained the college as a place of traditional learning; his provostship was a period of comparative calm after Wilsford's strenuous tightening of college discipline. It is perhaps an appropriate point from which to survey college life in the early sixteenth century, as far as the meagre records permit. Oriel was still, as it had always been, a society of comparatively young men, between 20 and 35, leavened by a few sojourners or *commensales* of an older generation, and of course by a provost normally senior to the fellows. Since the benefactions of the previous century they had lived in greater comfort: the allowances for common table and the provost's stipend were

---

[64] *The Letter Book of Robert Joseph*, ed. Hugh Aveling and W. A. Pantin (OHS, Oxford, 1967), xxiv, 39–40, 276.
[65] John Constable, *Epigrammata* (London, 1520), sig. d.ii verso, d.iii recto.
[66] *Statutes of the Colleges of Oxford*, i, Oriel, 37.
[67] BRUO 1501–40, 486–7 (Roberts), 433–4 (Parkhurst). See John Parkhurst, *Ludicra siue Epigrammata* (London, 1573), 161.
[68] The formal report of the election to the Visitor, dated 23 October, is in OCR 69–72.

increased out of the revenues of Shenington in 1504.⁶⁹ The treasurers' accounts show constant repairs and improvements throughout the period, with the rebuilding of Martin Hall for the accommodation of sojourners and for college disputations in 1517–18; after 1535 a new hall in a more elaborate style was constructed, as Bereblock's drawing of 1566 portrays it.⁷⁰ On the other hand there seem to have been more visitations of the plague in Oxford in the early sixteenth century: they are mentioned in the register in 1513, 1518, and 1522, and there were several other epidemics. Arrangements were made for the fellows to retreat to the manor of Dean, or to Bartlemas, when the plague struck, though several elected to remain in college.⁷¹ Meanwhile the rhythm of college life continued in its long-established way: morning mass, at which the bachelors were required to attend as the 'laudable customs' firmly state, study or disputations, dinner at 11.00 a.m., supper at 5.00 p.m. or so, study in the library (enjoined on bachelors 'especially at night').⁷² Dr Cogan remembered the fare about 1560: 'they had commonly at dinner, boyled Beefe with pottage, bread and beere and no more', and at supper 'pottage, brothes and such like', which he regarded as healthy; he did not recommend study at night, however.⁷³ The college observed its own special commemorations, written in the calendar in 1397 and constantly added to: on 2 January the mass and dirge for Bishop William Smyth, its benefactor, who died in 1514; on 22 January a mass and distribution of bread in memory of Joanna Ludwell and William Rauton who had given two shops in 1394; the great feast of Candlemas on 2 February; the mass for Robert Karver, fellow, who had died about 1505, on 25 March; the placebo and dirge for Adam de Brome on 16 June, for Edward II on 21 September, for Richard Dudley, after his death in 1536, on 18 October and on 21 October jointly for the great fifteenth-century provosts, John Carpenter, Walter Lyhert, and Henry Sampson 'to which some scholars at Bedel Hall should come'—doubtless the St Antony exhibitioners; on 21 November the obit of Provost William de Leverton, and on 29 November that of Bishop Burghersh the first Visitor; and on 21 December the obit of Richard Martin, formerly fellow, who had died in 1503.⁷⁴ In addition the bachelors and masters should accompany the provost to attend church or to hear sermons 'for the honour of the college'.⁷⁵ Besides their spiritual obligations there were annual college offices to fill: the keepers of the library, the collector of rents, the chaplain, the two treasurers, the dean; and the college assigned two senior fellows, or more usually the provost himself with a fellow, to hold court at Dean or

---

[69] DR 5–6. [70] Treasurers' accounts, OCA TF A1/4, 576; DR 99, 102.
[71] DR 32, 44, 57. See J. K. McConica, 'The Collegiate Society', in HUO iii. 648–50.
[72] DR 343.
[73] Thomas Cogan, *The Haven of Health* (London, 1589), 185, 190, 16.
[74] C. L. Shadwell (ed.), *The Calendar of Oriel College, Oxford, 1397* (Oxford, 1897).
[75] DR 343.

Wadley. Frequently there was business in London: the provost often attended during sessions of parliament, on occasion taking the charters with him, as Provost Taylor did on 16 February 1484.[76] In 1522 Walter Mey the dean and Richard Crispin attended Cardinal Wolsey 'bending the knee in the royal palace', to obtain a favourable verdict in their dispute with the city of Oxford over Bartlemas. Dean Mey appended a note in the register: 'if this matter comes into dispute in future, beware of the Exchequer court: I think we would have nothing of the fee farm left if we were to continue our suit there.'[77] On one occasion in 1509 two fellows had to accompany a colleague who had gone out of his mind to Bedlam; this was Robert Norreys, fellow since 1493, who had had to be put under restraint before his removal.[78] There were rules about dress: bachelors were not to wear shoes without buckles, and secular head-covering (*pilio siue caleptra*) only on journeys; and all fellows of course must wear their gowns to university acts.[79] In April 1513, Dean Broke presided over a college meeting at which the fellows debated the colour of the college livery for the coming year, 'all the fellows agreeing on the colour called light tawny'.[80] In the relaxed period before Wilsford's reforms, it must have been easy for the fellows to fill their days with college trivia to the neglect of higher studies. Conversely, the provost's insistence on academic values may have accounted for the unusually high rate of turnover in fellowships between 1508 and 1513.

In a college largely composed of men in their twenties it hardly needs pointing out that boisterous behaviour and disrespect of seniors was the usual theme of warnings to junior fellows.[81] Bishop Atwater's visitation of 1520 detected the masters falling away from their duty of conducting college disputations in arts, and some of them were criticized for prolonged absences; one, Thomas Slade, was asked either to reside or resign; he chose the latter. Thomas Stock, a more senior fellow, had delayed his resignation until he was sure that another Gloucestershire man, John Throckmorton, would be elected to take his place. This curious echo of the stirs of 1507 shows the strength of regional connections, or at least Gloucestershire connections, in college affairs. Walter Mey had been found to make astrological predictions, a practice which he compounded in the following year by physical violence against a colleague; these misdemeanours did not prevent his becoming dean in 1523. The fellows in general did not come to college meetings or hear the statutes read.[82] Bishop Longland in 1531 blamed the provost (probably More, who had resigned the previous November, not his successor) for prolonged non-residence, and the dean, Richard Lorgan, for

---

[76] Treasurers' accounts, OCA TF A1/3, 25. [77] DR 60.
[78] OCR 68; treasurers' accounts, OCA TF A1/3, 605, 606. See DR 4 and n. 1.
[79] DR 343–4. [80] DR 32. [81] DR 22–3 (Lewis), 124 (Edmund Crispin).
[82] *Visitations of the Diocese of Lincoln*, ii. 72–4; for Mey's assault, DR 52.

ILLUSTRATION 3.3 The Coconut Cup, bequeathed by Richard Dudley, 1536
Oriel College

slackness in enforcing the statutes and customs and especially attendance at college disputations. Further, the treasurers had been found at fault in not putting the monies they received into the college chest, and in failing to draw up the accounts properly.[83] In 1538 one of the treasurers, William Pye, was found to have retained college monies in breach of the Visitor's injunction, and was declared to owe over £40 as a result. Though judged worthy of expulsion, he was not deprived, but allowed to repay in instalments, and shortly afterwards was elected dean.[84] Visitations of course highlighted defects out of context, but it is difficult not to conclude that college solidarity, by 1540, was covering up abuses that Provost Wilsford would not have tolerated.

Dr More may have been absent at his Monmouthshire parish in longer stretches than the Visitor could approve, but extant treasurers' accounts show him invariably present to receive the accounts in August, and for his

---

[83] *Statutes of the Colleges of Oxford*, i, Oriel, 35–7. There are no extant accounts between 1526 and 1585.
[84] DR 108, 113, 119.

first two years copying them in his own hand.⁸⁵ He was in any case served by a group of senior fellows, theologians in the tradition of Wilsford like himself, including William Canynges (fellow 1509–21), Thomas Ware (fellow 1507–26, and sojourner thereafter), Richard Crispin (fellow 1513–27), and Richard Lorgan (fellow from 1519 to his death in 1536, and principal of St Mary Hall 1521–30).⁸⁶ The great success of More's provostship was the benefaction of Richard Dudley, who had been a fellow from 1495 to 1506, and who was now precentor of Salisbury. The college had wisely kept in touch with Dudley even after the disgrace and execution in 1510 of his cousin Edmund, Henry VII's minister, renting him a room in 1511–12.⁸⁷ About 1521 Dudley reciprocated, offering to endow three new fellowships; the college, fearing the expense if they were not sufficiently endowed, sent More, Crispin, and later William Upton and Robert Charde to Salisbury to work out the terms, and it was not until April 1529 that it was settled that there should be two Dudley fellows and six exhibitioners who, like the St Antony exhibitioners, would live in St Mary Hall.⁸⁸ The college's preference for exhibitioners is a sign of the increasing emphasis placed on undergraduate education. The expense was carried by Dudley's acquisition for Oriel of the manor of Swainswick outside Bath.⁸⁹ Oriel's claim was not secured without litigation, but the fellows and exhibitioners were appointed from 1529.⁹⁰ The benefaction completed the series of endowments by well-connected former provosts and fellows (and one episcopal Visitor) which had begun with John Carpenter nearly a century before.

The most active of More's colleagues in college business was Thomas Ware, who had been dean three times (1517–19, 1521–2, and 1524–5), and who even after resigning his fellowship in 1526 was granted a room in Martin Hall and a garden. When More resigned on the ground of old age and ill health in 1530, he was a natural successor both as a college man, a former proctor and a theologian of some reputation. In 1529 his colleagues showed their regard by allowing him to nominate one of the Dudley exhibitioners, and a year later they elected him provost.⁹¹ Ware was the right man for unexpectedly turbulent times. He was able to plan and carry out the rebuilding of the hall, which

---

⁸⁵ Treasurers' accounts, OCA TF A1/4, 527–620 (1516–18) are fair copies in the provost's hand.

⁸⁶ BRUO 1501–40, 99 s.n. Cannynges, 606, 155–6 s.n. Cryspyn, 362.

⁸⁷ Treasurers' accounts, OCA TF A1/3, 577.

⁸⁸ DR 62–3, 67–8, 73–4, 75–6.

⁸⁹ The first step in Dudley's plan, the acquisition of Swainswick, was completed on 4 February 1521 (OCA DR4/1040).

⁹⁰ Richard Dudley died in 1536, leaving in addition 'a nutte with a cover', presumably the coconut cup, to Oriel, as his brother George wrote to Provost Ware, with a request that his nephew 'may be one of the scholers of that same fundacion when any rome is voyde' (OCA DLR 1/1160, 26 June 1536). The Dudley family of Yanwith won the right to nominate two Dudley exhibitioners in 1544 (OCA DR 4/1039).

⁹¹ DR 77, 79–82.

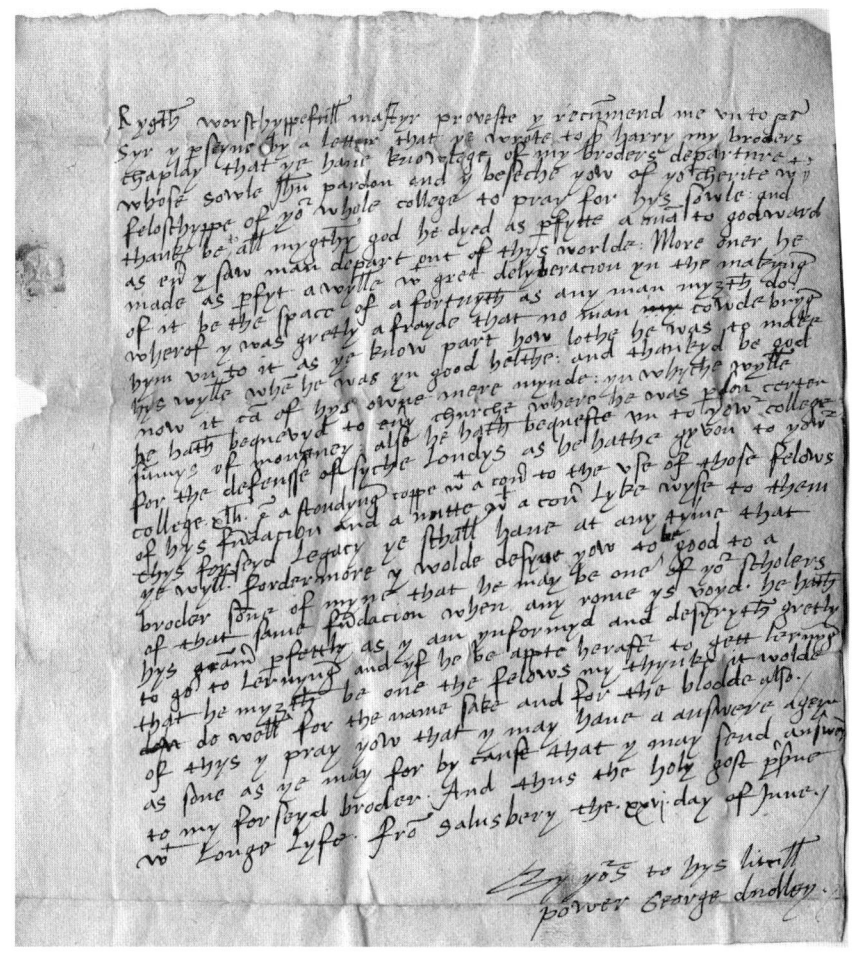

ILLUSTRATION 3.4 George Dudley requests a place for his nephew, 1536, OCA

must have been the most visible achievement in his provostship.[92] But public affairs intruded into college life in his term of office more insistently than he can have wished. Like the other heads of Oxford houses and especially theologians, he was shortly afterwards exposed to the urgent need of Henry VIII for theological support for his divorce; he was listed, oddly among 'such persons as be well learned and not residing in the University of Oxford', as one who might be consulted, in the company of his Oriel predecessors

[92] DR 86, 99, 102.

Dr Powell and Mr Goodrich, his colleague Dr Crispin, and in Oxford his junior, Mr Lorgan.[93] What answer he gave is not recorded. Three years later he had to receive Dr Richard Cox, Archbishop Cranmer's chancellor and Visitor, for the purpose of securing the subscription of each fellow to the king's declaration 'concernyng the bishop of Rome hys autoryte within thys reallme'. On 27 July 1534, assembled in the chapel, he and the fellows subscribed the king's articles, apparently without exception.[94] What they really thought is not, of course, recorded. Nearly all the Oriel theologians of the Wilsford school conformed without being known to have objected: Dr Rowland Phillips the vicar of Croydon, John Goodrich BD at Bristol, Dr Roger Edgeworth at Wells, Dr Richard Dudley and William Canynges BD at Salisbury, Dr Richard Crispin in Devon, and within Oriel, besides Ware, his close associates Richard Lorgan BD, John Ryxman BD (dean 1531–5), and Mr Alexander Ryshton (dean 1535–6, died 1537). Several of them, however, showed Catholic sympathies: Rowland Phillips, reputed to be 'of the popish sort', was imprisoned for much of the 1530s, though he claimed to have tried to bring the Carthusians round to the king's obedience.[95] Richard Crispin preached a sermon in Edward VI's reign in favour of Catholic practices, and died in the Tower as a consequence.[96] Roger Edgeworth was a notable opponent of the Protestant preacher Hugh Latimer at Wells, and showed his true colours in Mary's reign.[97] So did John Ryxman, who was chaplain in 1557 to the Catholic bishop Turberville of Exeter, and the former treasurer William Pye, who was appointed in 1554 to dispute with Cranmer and Latimer.[98] Two former fellows went further. George Croft, who had been a fellow (1514–19), junior proctor (1520–1), but not apparently a theologian, had preached before Henry VIII as late as Lent 1531 and had conformed in 1534, but four years later, in the course of proceedings against the Pole family, was detected in private disapproval of the royal supremacy, tried, and executed.[99] Dr Edward Powell, the veteran polemicist, was even more obdurate, refusing the oath in 1534; he was imprisoned in harsh conditions in Dorchester Gaol and in the Tower, and eventually hanged at Smithfield in 1540.[100] It is likely that the opinion of these theologians was reasonably representative of the views of the fellows in the 1530s, and it explains the attitude of William Allen in the next generation. Only two of them seem to have inclined to the

---

[93] *Letters and Papers, Henry VIII*, v, p. 6, no. 6 (1531).   [94] DR 382–4.
[95] BRUO iii. 1477–8; ODNB s.n.   [96] BRUO 1501–40, 156.
[97] *Sermons very fruitfull*, ed. Wilson, introduction 13–36.
[98] BRUO 1501–40, 499, 468–9. Ryxman was principal of St Mary Hall in 1534 when Thomas Goldwell was studying theology there; Goldwell, a firm Catholic, left for Louvain in 1536, became an associate of Reginald Pole, was briefly bishop of St Asaph (1556–9), and died in Rome in 1585 as a priest of the Theatine Order (BRUO 1501–40, 239–40; ODNB s.n.).
[99] BRUO 1500–40, 150; ODNB s.n. Crofts.
[100] BRUO iii. 1510–11; ODNB s.n. He was beatified in 1886.

reformed point of view, but in 1534 they were the seniors. One was Thomas Ware himself: according to the former sojourner Dr Henry Morgan (as reported by Bernard Gilpin the Protestant pastor), the provost, 'a man most famous for life and learning, had affirmed unto him that the principall sacrifice of the Church of God was the sacrifice of thanksgiving. This was his answere when I demanded of him what could be said for the sacrifice of the Masse.'[101] This careful statement certainly sounds more Protestant than otherwise. The other was Richard Lorgan, who was recommended to Thomas Cromwell by Dr Thomas Knolles, president of Magdalen, as suitable to be reader in divinity, being of good qualities and one who had always used himself discreetly in all the king's causes.[102] Doubtless the overriding consideration for most of them, whatever their sympathies, was to survive.

In 1538, when Provost Ware resigned, the fellows made the surprising choice of an older master: Henry Myn, who was not a theologian, and who had long before been a partisan of John Goodrich in the quarrels of 1507. He had ceased to be a fellow in 1509, though in 1523, as the executor of Robert Karver, he had urged the college to separate the day of his obit from that of Richard Martyn.[103] It is not even clear that he resided very often in the two years of his provostship; the business was mostly conducted by John Griffith, the dean.[104] The election of another theologian, William Haynes BD, on 18 October 1540 marked the return to normality: Haynes had been a fellow from 1524 to 1534 and had then been a fellow of Eton and prebendary of Chichester; his appointment as a royal chaplain in 1539 implies a degree of favour at court, which may explain his election. He combined his provostship with a canonry at Osney (1542–5), where the new see of Oxford was briefly established, and may have resided in Christ Church thereafter, where he died on 8 July 1550.[105] His first concern was probably the defence of Richard Dudley's bequest, which had been disputed by his nephew and namesake Richard Dudley of Yanwith; in July 1541 as a matter of 'urgent necessity' William Pye was transferred from his Dudley fellowship to one on the old foundation, and the other Dudley fellow, Morgan Phillips, was lined up for the next vacant fellowship. The reason, as the Dean's Register explains in an entry in January 1542, was that Dudley's legacy had been entirely expended on litigation rather than the amortization of Swainswick; it was essential that the college's resources were not used to maintain the Dudley fellowships.[106]

---

[101] G. Carleton, *Life of Bernard Gilpin* (London, 1628), 115–16, quoting an original letter in his possession.
[102] *Letters and Papers, Henry VIII*, ix (1535), 384, no. 1120.
[103] DR 109, 59. BRUO ii. 1334–5, s.n. Mynne.
[104] He presided over college meetings on 8 March, 31 October, and 3–4 November 1539, and probably died in college on 13 October 1540, since he was buried in St Mary's: DR 110, 113–14.
[105] BRUO 1501–40, 277–8.
[106] DR 116–17.

The dispute was not settled until 1 February 1544, when it was agreed that Oriel would have peaceful enjoyment of Swainswick and in return that the younger Dudley and his heirs 'for the good and entiere zele love and favor that he beareth to lernyng and study and specially of divinitie which the studentes and fellowes of the said Oreall Colledge chiefly do professe', should have the nomination of two of the six Dudley exhibitions.[107] The concession would itself soon benefit the college: in 1560 he used his nomination to promote his son and a *cognatus* to exhibitions; the latter was the great future provost Anthony Blencowe.[108]

The arrangement underlines the fellows' engagement with the education of undergraduates. The Dean's Register had for some time noted the election or nomination of St Antony's and Dudley exhibitioners; they were sometimes referred to as *scholastici*.[109] In December 1545 Bishop Longland addressed his injunctions to the provost, dean, fellows, and *scholastici*; the principal of St Mary Hall must be suitable for and diligent in their education and must provide lectors of sufficient learning to conduct their lectures and disputations. The door between the hall and the college must be blocked up to prevent too easy social access.[110] The *scholastici* were distinct from the exhibitioners; John Herniman, a Dudley exhibitioner in 1551, was elected a scholar in 1554, to be educated at college expense until he became a bachelor of arts and eligible for a probationary fellowship, on condition that he swore not to remove to any other society in the meantime.[111] For a brief period, from about 1549 to the mid-1560s, the college seems to have abandoned its traditional custom of electing fellows from the pool of talent available generally in Oxford in favour of the practice common in many colleges, of promoting its own *scholastici*. It did not last: the election of Richard Barret from Brasenose in 1565 marked a return to the old practice.[112]

Longland was equally concerned with the fellows' own studies. He was determined to enforce their commitment to study theology, and to hold them to the philosophical exercises and disputations of the arts faculty until they were qualified to read the subject. This had been college policy, in accordance with the statutes, pursued consistently since at least the time of Provost Wilsford, but not for the first time it was in conflict with the desire of a number of fellows to study medicine. The Visitor was constrained to

---

[107] OCA DR 4/1039, Indenture of agreement to convey, on conditions, the manor of Swainswick to Oriel.
[108] DR 145; *Registrum Orielense*, 28.
[109] OCA GOV 4A1, 554–96 (1540–1604); not in the printed edition, but listed by Shadwell, *Registrum Orielense*, where Dudley exhibitioners are noted, i. 17. An entry for 1548 not quite accurately calls Dudley exhibitioners *scholastici*.
[110] *Statutes of the Colleges of Oxford*, i, Oriel, 38–40.
[111] *Registrum Orielense*, i. 22.
[112] *Registrum Orielense*, i, v–vi; *Provosts and Fellows*, 65–74.

recognize the legitimacy of this ambition, and strove to reconcile it with the promotion of theology in the hard case of Edmund Crispin. Presumably a relative of Dr Richard Crispin, he had been elected with Morgan Phillips in 1538, and as both of them had been negligent in their studies they were only confirmed in 1539 on condition that they lectured on Aristotle's *De caelo*. He was admonished again in 1542 for not taking part in disputations, and two years later for disobedience and indiscipline. He had had permission to study abroad in 1542, but had evidently not taken it up. His recalcitrance was in part due to his studying medicine, in which he qualified as a bachelor in 1543. The bishop allowed him to be dispensed from philosophical exercises while he pursued his medical course, but sought to bring him back afterwards to theology, and enjoined him meanwhile to say his offices in St Mary's and to refrain from blasphemies.[113] In fact Crispin resigned his fellowship a few weeks after Longland's injunctions were issued, being already university lecturer in medicine; he became doctor of medicine in 1548, married, and was dead by 1550. His misdemeanours were not entirely the result of his medical preoccupations, but may have been provoked by his frustration in the face of pressure to study theology. A joshing note in a college text of Aquinas's *Physics* commentary, datable to June 1545, pokes fun at him: 'Nota quod crispyn was at morow masse on seynt petroc...nota quod crispyn comyth unto the lybrarye when he he may dreede his quisquis...nota quod crispyn doth oft tymes play the knav yn the lybrary...rara avis in ambobus locis.'[114]

Crispin was an exception: the great majority of the fellows in the provostships of Haynes and his successor read theology, though few took a degree in it. All of them whose views can be deduced leant to the Catholic tendency all but universal in Oxford; Morgan Phillips, who had been Crispin's fellow probationer, was one who qualified as bachelor of theology, and was put up to dispute with Peter Martyr, the Protestant controversialist, in the schools in 1549.[115] As principal of St Mary Hall (1547–50) he had the future recusant William Allen as his scholar; Allen was elected fellow in 1550, and in due course was principal of St Mary Hall himself (1556–60). Phillips must have been closely associated with Mr John Smyth, who acted as dean from 1545 to 1549, as Provost Haynes retired to his canonry at Christ Church sometime after 1547; in the provost's last illness, and perhaps in the temporary absence of the dean, William Collinge, he signed himself in the register as the provost's vice-gerent *dum egrotus erat*.[116] In his role as principal, and

---

[113] *Statutes of the Colleges of Oxford*, i, Oriel, 38–9; DR 113, 120, 121, 123; BRUO 1501–40, 155.
[114] Oriel College MS 48, fo. ii recto. The note can be dated to 1545, after the admission of William Norfolk, mentioned here too, and before Crispin's resignation; St Petroc's day is 4 June.
[115] Jennifer Loach, 'Reformation Controversies', in HUO iii. 370.
[116] On Phillips see ODNB and BRUO 1501–40, 448; see his acts in DR 129–30.

together with Smyth, he must have received the Edwardian commissioners in 1548, but if they ordered any changes in the college's affairs no record has survived. But on the morning of 17 June 1550, when the provost resigned, he lost no time in proceeding to an election. The fellows were summoned for two o'clock, and after the resignation was read to them they proceeded to elect John Smyth, who went to seek the bishop of Lincoln's confirmation as Visitor the next day. Their haste was deliberate: the Edwardian government under Protector Somerset had already leant on Haynes to elect John Edwardes a fellow, and as soon as they heard of the vacancy had commanded the election of Dr Gilbert Turner, a Cambridge botanist and strong Protestant. On 9 July Dean Collinge was instructed to ride to the Privy Council to explain that the provostship had already been filled.[117]

John Smyth was first and foremost a domestic provost. He had been a fellow since 1529, and had been present at the election of his three predecessors; brief notes on them in the list of provosts, including the compliment to Haynes as *vir ad clementiam natus*, are probably in his hand.[118] He was a bachelor of theology and had been senior proctor (1546–7). Having no preferment, beyond the rectory of East Ilsley which he held in 1550, he seems to have resided in college for twenty years.[119] He must have kept his head down for the remaining years of Edward VI's reign, as his close association with Morgan Phillips allows little doubt of his religious sympathies, but the accession of Queen Mary opened numerous opportunities for him, above all the post of Lady Margaret Praelector of Divinity once held by Edmund Wilsford and Richard Lorgan. He was preferred to a canonry at Westminster and made treasurer of Chichester, perhaps through the influence of William Pye, who held office in both chapters. Though his Catholic leanings ensured that he was deprived of all these positions on the accession of Elizabeth, he must have been discreet enough to keep his office of provost, when at least eleven of his fellow heads resigned or were ejected.[120] He must therefore have outwardly conformed. Within the college, though the sources and notably entries in the register are sparse, he seems to have made no innovations, beyond perhaps the new custom of electing fellows from the existing body of scholars, a practice which began when he was dean and ceased with his provostship. The core of the fellowship, Morgan Phillips, William Norfolk, William Wood, and probably William Allen, followed his lead and read theology; they were successively principals of St Mary Hall and therefore responsible for college undergraduate teaching. Outside this group,

---

[117] DR 128–31. [118] OCA GOV 4A1, 5.
[119] *Provosts and Fellows*, 59–60; Emden, BRUO 1501–40, 522–3.
[120] Penry Williams, 'State, Church and University, 1558–1603', in HUO iii. 397–440, cf. 406. William Allen claimed fifteen heads in Oxford and Cambridge had been removed: *A true, sincere and modest Defence of English Catholiques* (Rouen, 1584), 46.

however, fewer fellows seem to have studied theology after graduating in arts: John Edwardes and Thomas Griffith read medicine, and John Belley civil law, while Richard Sewall went off with leave of absence to teach in a school in Nottinghamshire, and did not return. His failure to resign in due form followed a pattern set by his seniors, five of whose fellowships lapsed on 20 December 1554, including that of Morgan Phillips himself. The preferments open to conservative churchmen in Mary's reign must have exacerbated the problem of absentee fellows, but their failure to observe the 'statutes and laudable customs of the college' is surprising.[121] On the other hand, the internal affairs of the college were vigorously tended; Henry Mitchell and William Allen (1553), John Hemming, Peter White, and Robert Hughes (1555), and John Herniman and John Belley (1559) were granted leave to incept as master of arts on the strict condition of participating in the college disputations in arts which were an essential part of undergraduate education.[122] Plate was to be sold to purchase lands, fines for leases were not to benefit absentees from the sealing ceremony, and annual inventories of furniture were to be drawn up both in college and in St Mary Hall.[123]

Without extant treasurers' accounts of this period, we cannot know whether former fellows such as Roger Edgeworth or John Ryxman, now active in the Marian Church, returned to college and exercised the same influence as Edward Powell and Richard Dudley had in the previous generation. William Pye, who was appointed to dispute with Cranmer and Latimer in 1554, must have stayed in Oxford for a time and probably in Oriel. Not surprisingly, the biblical and patristic theology found in Edgeworth's newly printed sermons underpinned the later polemic of the one figure among the fellowship in the 1550s to have left theological writings, William Allen. As a student of Morgan Phillips and then a fellow of Oriel, he must have laid the foundations of the wide reading in the fathers and in biblical scholarship which is evident in his later writings as a Catholic apologist at Douai and Rheims. There is nothing, however, to distinguish his theological training in Oriel from the general character of the subject in mid-sixteenth-century Oxford. Allen seems to have written nothing which casts light on his early years; in his one indirect reference to the last years of Edward VI, he castigated the treason of 'duke Dudley (a hateful name to England since Henry the seventhes tyme)'; he must have forgotten the positive connotations of the name of Dudley in Oriel.[124] After 1559, he was only one of the hundred or so fellows of Oxford colleges to leave the university for reasons of religion. He was, however, one of the most creative, and his enterprise in founding the English college at Douai was shared with his former master Morgan Phillips. Deprived of his precentorship of St David's, Phillips went to Louvain, visited

[121] DR 138–9, 141, 142.
[123] DR 135, 138, 139–40, 142–3.
[122] DR 137–8, 140, 144–5.
[124] Allen, *A modest Defence*, 56.

ILLUSTRATION 3.5 William Allen, fellow 1550–65, cardinal 1587, died 1594
Oriel College

Rome with Allen, and from 1568 to his death in 1570 lectured at Douai. The active centre of recusant resistance to the Elizabethan settlement was therefore an offshoot of Marian Oriel, with the further recruitment, after 1576, of another fellow, Richard Barret, who eventually succeeded Allen as the president.[125] Besides Phillips, Allen, and Barret, two other fellows, John Hemming and John Herniman, seem to have lost their fellowships as absent recusants; William Holte followed them in 1574, and a St Antony exhibitioner of 1564, John Lane, became a Jesuit about the same time. An Irish fellow, Peter White, dean of Waterford, was deprived in 1570 and kept a Catholic school thereafter. Finally Francis Webber, who was briefly dean in 1565, was expelled from his fellowship that year for refusal to take the oath of supremacy.[126]

---

[125] James McConica, 'The Catholic Experience in Tudor Oxford', in Thomas M. McCoog (ed.), *The Reckoned Expense: Edmund Campion and the Early English Jesuits* (2nd edn., Rome, 2007), 43–73. On Barret see also *The Letters of William Allen and Richard Barret*, ed. P. Renold (Catholic Record Society, London, 1967).

[126] *Provosts and Fellows*, 67, 68, 75; *Registrum Orielense*, i. 33.

The Oriel theologians who followed Edmund Wilsford had proved, not surprisingly, to be overwhelmingly Catholic in sympathy, though some were prepared to conform to the Henrician and Elizabethan Church. If their final generation was most fruitful abroad, promoting the recusant cause, in Oriel they were succeeded by fellows who, if they stayed in Oxford for any length of time, either remained teaching in the arts faculty or studied medicine or civil law. The last fellow in this era to read theology was John Hurlock (*scholasticus* 1560 and fellow 1561–70), who, significantly, was principal of St Mary Hall (1565–70).[127] His contemporaries were content to remain masters of arts until they were appointed to a country living or some other employment. Another group read medicine, among them John Jackman (fellow 1562–84, dean 1575–9 and 1581–2, bachelor of medicine 1584), who after vacating his fellowship married, practised medicine in Oxford, and left numerous books to the library.[128] His colleague Thomas Cogan, the author of the *Haven of Health*, was elected in 1563 and resigned in 1575, after becoming high master of Manchester Grammar School.[129] A further contingent were almost the first Oriel fellows to read civil law, notably John Belley, elected probably in 1555 and provost 1566–74, who having qualified as bachelor of civil law in 1564, gave up the provostship to practise as a master in chancery and chancellor of the diocese of Lincoln (1574–1608).[130] He was followed by Anthony Blencowe (fellow 1563–74, dean 1571–2, provost 1574–1618), bachelor of civil law 1586, Thomas Philipson (fellow 1563–79, dean 1573–5, and principal of St Mary Hall 1578–87), who was licensed to study civil and canon law in 1570, and Robert Garvey of Kilkenny diocese (fellow 1563–1580), who was bachelor of civil law in 1575.[131] In default of a school of Anglican theology in Oriel after Smyth's provostship, the core of the fellowship concentrated on less controversial subjects.

On the resignation of John Smyth on 2 March 1565, the dean, Francis Webber, and the fellows moved as quickly as their predecessors in 1550, but in a surprising direction. On 3 March they applied to the bishop of Lincoln for a dispensation from the statutes to elect a person from outside the fellowship, which being granted they proceeded to elect the 29-year-old Roger Marbeck, canon of Christ Church and public orator. This can only have been designed to draw a line under the conservative regime of his predecessor, now clearly out of favour with government; Marbeck, who perhaps had the backing of Sir William Cecil, the queen's secretary of state, was a high flyer in Oxford with a great reputation for rhetoric. He was no

---

[127] *Provosts and Fellows*, 70.   [128] *Provosts and Fellows*, 71.
[129] *Provosts and Fellows*, 71; ODNB s.n. It is not certain that Royal College of Physicians MS 201, a medical notebook, is in his hand, but it contains notes of Cogan's formal medical disputation with John Jackman (fellow 1562–84), which may be either a college or a university exercise, and must date before 1574 when Cogan departed for Manchester.
[130] *Provosts and Fellows*, 68–9.   [131] *Provosts and Fellows*, 71–2.

theologian and had not taken major orders; his ecclesiastical preferments were sinecures. But he was keen to reduce Oriel to obedience to the state religion. He proceeded to fill up the places of Allen and Herniman, who had long gone, and of a more recent absentee fellow, Richard Muckleston, and on 18 December, after failing to persuade Dean Webber to take the oath of supremacy, he had his deputy expelled from the fellowship. On the one substantial matter of policy in his provostship, he may not have been the prime mover. Shortly before Webber's expulsion, on 31 October while the office of principal of St Mary Hall was vacant, the vice-chancellor had exercised the university's dormant power of appointment in favour of the senior graduate of that society, Nicholas Sheffield. Sheffield, a Dudley exhibitioner, may not even have been in Oxford as he had been deemed to have left Oxford and given up his studies the previous May. The college's reaction was sharp. On 9 November, in the absence of the provost, Webber led the fellows in resolving, in accordance with college custom 'as the common opinion of the lawyers confirms', not to admit any principal not a fellow unless by their consent. They claimed that their colleague Alexander Brechin was about to be duly nominated and elected by the scholars of the hall. The college must have appealed to Congregation, as on 13 November the vice-chancellor appointed a panel to hear the case; and on 19 November, Brechin having presumably withdrawn and another fellow, John Hurlock, been nominated, the college further affirmed their rights by assigning funds for the repair of the hall. Nothing further is heard of the appeal, the vice-chancellor doubtless being now satisfied on the proper governance of St Mary Hall. The episode in retrospect was the first indication of the university's tendency to treat the hall as an independent society and not as Oriel's undergraduate wing, which would ultimately prevail.[132]

On the queen's first visit to Oxford, early in 1566, Marbeck made an elegant Latin speech which found favour with her: an important consideration for him, in pursuit of which he was even prepared to reverse the lease of the manor of Dean to his relative Edward Marbeck in favour of the earl of Leicester's nominee Ralph Sheldon. However, at some point that summer he seems to have married Anne Williams, the daughter of an Oxford alderman and a Catholic, and in consequence he resigned all his preferments, including on 24 June the office of provost. His renunciation does not seem to have implied the loss of royal favour, as he welcomed the queen on her second visit, on 31 August, with another speech, but it altered the scope of his career. He turned to medicine, an interest of more than one of his former Oriel colleagues, and eventually became the queen's doctor and a pillar of the

---

[132] See *Registrum Orielense*, i. 29 (departure of Sheffield); OUA NEP Reg. Kk 9 (1564–82) fos. 14^v, 15^r (nomination of Sheffield and appeal proceedings); DR 154–5 (Oriel's response and repairs to the Hall).

Royal College of Physicians. His brief but decisive rule in Oriel marked the end of its government by theologians.[133]

The new regime must have represented the settled will of the fellowship and not just the reforming spirit of Marbeck, since the day after he resigned they chose not to have a theologian but (reverting to their ancient practice of a domestic election) the civil lawyer John Belley, who had been active in university business. He had been a fellow from about 1555 to about 1563. The only theologian in fellowship at the time was a younger man, John Hurlock, the principal of St Mary Hall, who became dean in September 1566. He may have harboured a certain sympathy for colleagues expelled for their religious sympathies, since his was probably the hand which added a gloss in the register to Marbeck's entry on Webber, that he was 'judged unworthy of fellowship' with the words *sed utrum Marbekke non potiori sententia*, 'rather, perhaps, the judgement of Marbeck'. The words were however later scratched out.[134] Belley, like Marbeck, showed signs of assuming the later grandeur and influence of the office, securing additional commons for himself and the farm of Swainswick for his brother George. His rule was otherwise uneventful, and unlike his predecessors he seems to have made no entries personally in the register, the business being undertaken by his deans, Hurlock, Richard Pigot, Thomas Cogan, John Jackman, Anthony Blencowe, and Thomas Philipson. In 1574 he was granted a final privilege, the right of next presentation to the college living at Aberford, and shortly afterwards resigned. As chancellor of the diocese of Lincoln, he indulged his antiquarian interest in church inscriptions by adding his name to at least five in churches in Cambridgeshire, Hertfordshire, and Bedfordshire.[135] The day after his resignation the fellows elected the late dean, Anthony Blencowe, inaugurating a provostship which would last forty-four years.[136]

In 1570 Belley had appointed Richard Pigot to succeed Hurlock as principal of St Mary Hall. He was the first principal not to be a theologian; he seems only to have been a master of arts until in 1595, long after his principalship, he was admitted to study civil law. His students, some of whom formed a distinct social circle, were the first we can trace who pursued secular careers and achieved notable success. He was the tutor of Sir Henry Unton, as his funeral verses on Unton's death in 1596 explicitly state, and it is likely that Unton's two brothers, Francis and Edward, and his friends Charles Champernowne and Walter Raleigh, all of whom appear in the list of Oriel students in residence in 1572, were Pigot's charges too. Both Henry

---

[133] On Marbeck see ODNB s.n., and DR 151–8.   [134] DR 155.
[135] L. W. G[rensted], 'A Provost's Signature', OR (January 1940), 58–9.
[136] On Belley see *Provosts and Fellows*, 68–9; DR 158–66. His right of presentation to Aberford was exercised in favour of William Bucketrowte, an Oxford scholar but apparently not an Oriel man; see CCEd database, s.n. Bucketrowte.

ILLUSTRATION 3.6 Sir Walter Raleigh (1554–1618), scholar at Oriel c.1572–4
Oriel College

and Edward Unton had distinguished though short military careers, and Henry in addition was the queen's ambassador in Paris. Raleigh was associated with Edward Unton in two expeditions, and the families later intermarried. Champernowne was Raleigh's cousin, and an officer in his ship in the 'voyage of discovery' of 1578. In addition, Raleigh's connection with Thomas Harriot, the future mathematician who was at St Mary Hall in the later 1570s, may have originated through Pigot. They were the first fruits of Oriel's change of direction from a body predominantly composed of theologians to a more variegated fellowship, whose primary business was the humane education of students destined for secular careers.[137]

The ninety-five years from the election of John Taylor to that of Anthony Blencowe were years of consolidation and quiet achievement. The prosperity bestowed by the fifteenth-century court bishops had been augmented; the standard of living of the fellows was somewhat better, and the hall had been

---

[137] For Pigot's verses see *Funebria nobilissimi ac praestantissimi equitis, domini Henrici Unton* (Oxford, 1596), unpaginated. On the circle of Raleigh at Oriel, C. S. Emden, *Oriel Papers* (Oxford, 1948), 9–21. For the scholars in residence in 1572 see *Registrum Orielense*, i. 40–4.

rebuilt. It had been possible to fund three more fellows and six more exhibitioners. Oriel's share of the benefactions to Oxford colleges was comparatively smaller than had been the case in the mid-fifteenth century, as Magdalen, Corpus Christi, and Christ Church had successively attracted rich endowment, but it had been effective. A large proportion of the fellows who had enjoyed these benefits had applied themselves to the study of theology, under the influence of Edmund Wilsford as fellow and provost, and those who had not had been constrained to teach arts to the scholars of St Mary Hall. The learning of the Oriel theologians, as revealed in the polemic of Edward Powell and the sermons of Roger Edgeworth, was substantial; it was indebted to the scholarship of Erasmus and its language betrayed an education in humane letters. Fellows like William Rose and Thomas Roberts were recipients of elegant Latin epigrams, and Rose certainly had some Greek. But the most pervasive change of these years was the gradual integration of an undergraduate body into the college. Undergraduate scholars had been accommodated in St Mary Hall since the foundation, and the fellows of Oriel had always instructed them in arts, a practice which survived beyond 1574. A few, however, had lived within the college since the 1470s, when Walter Paston was Edmund Alyard's scholar, at least. This was a privilege allowed to the scions of persons whom the provost and fellows wished to please: Walter Paston on account of Bishop Lyhert, William Canynges probably as a member of a powerful Bristol clan, the Unton boys as sons of the college's lessee at Wadley, which incidentally proved to be the beginning of a great Elizabethan connection.[138] With the number of undergraduates growing, both in college and in St Mary Hall (which though independent was ruled by current or quondam fellows up to the Restoration), and underlying the religious changes of the second half of the period, more varied and more secular occupations were opened both to fellows and scholars. An Anglican Oriel would play an active part in a renewed university and a more variegated national life.

---

[138] On this see Emden, *Oriel Papers*, 1–8.

4
Expansion and Retrenchment, 1574–1660[1]

Kenneth Fincham

In the second half of the sixteenth century, Oxford and Cambridge, like their counterparts abroad, faced a series of novel challenges and pressures—social, intellectual, religious, and political. The increasing expectation that young men receive a university education led to a steady rise in demand for places, and the transformation of colleges from graduate bodies into a mixed economy of fellows and undergraduates, which offered a broad education to prepare students for public life in government and the law, as much as in the Church. To cope with this influx, new colleges were established, such as Jesus and Wadham in Oxford, and Emmanuel and Sidney Sussex in Cambridge, and older colleges built additional ranges and sometimes new quadrangles. Teaching changed, too, to incorporate humanist ideas within the traditional curriculum and to disseminate new Protestant doctrines. For following the Elizabethan settlement of religion in 1559, both universities were expected to be citadels of Protestantism, and agents of conformity among their burgeoning population, but in truth they also became arenas for debate and division about the character of the new religion. These theological disagreements played their part in producing the political meltdown of the 1640s, as Oxford became Charles I's headquarters in the first Civil War, and the university found itself on the front line, ravaged by plague and plummeting student numbers and estate rentals. On the defeat of the royalists, the victorious Parliament took control the university and from 1648 attempted to purge it of those who did not share its political and religious convictions.

---

[1] I am most grateful to the editor, as well as to Andrew Foster, Andrew Hegarty, Peter Lake, Nicholas Tyacke, and Rebecca Warren, for comments on a draft of these two chapters, and for the invaluable assistance of Simon Bailey, Alice Millea, and Anna Petra in the University Archives.

ILLUSTRATION 4.1 Anthony Blencowe (c.1544–1618), fellow 1563, provost 1574–1618
Oriel College

The next two chapters follow the fortunes of Oriel, a college of middling size and modest means, during these years of change and upheaval. While Oriel's history, in its broad outline, mirrors that of other colleges in this period, it also contains distinct characteristics of its own, subtle differences in the timing and nature of its response to external pressures, and occasionally its own independent initiatives, most conspicuously the rebuilding of the entire college between 1613 and 1642. Religious changes in this period will be considered in the next chapter; here we explore the college's growth in numbers and ambition up to the Civil War, and the ways in which it weathered the troubles of the 1640s and 1650s.

The sources for this study are rather diverse. The college records are not rich for this period, beyond the official or Dean's Register, the treasurers' or Style accounts, and the benefaction register. These are supplemented by the university archives, principally probate and disciplinary records of the chancellor's court, and private, scattered sources such as letters and notebooks of Orielenses as well as their occasional forays into print. The writings of Anthony Wood, the seventeenth-century Oxford antiquary, have been

ILLUSTRATION 4.2 Sir Henry Unton (c.1557–96), scholar of Oriel c.1570–3
Oriel College

indispensable, with their pleasurable mix of fact, gossip, insight, and prejudice.[2] Among modern scholarship, pride of place must go the relevant volumes of *The History of the University of Oxford* (1986, 1997) and the recent college histories following in their wake, which have made Oriel's place in Oxford, and the distinctiveness of its experience, much more intelligible.[3]

Of all the changes which Oriel experienced in the ninety years after 1570, none was more momentous than its development from a predominantly graduate society of provost and fellows into a fully-fledged undergraduate college with the fellowship providing lectures and tutorials. This was a

---

[2] Principally A. Wood, *Athenae Oxonienses* and *Fasti Oxonienses*, ed. P. Bliss, 2 vols. (Oxford, 1815–20).

[3] HUO iii; HUO iv; J. Jones, *Balliol College: A History* (2nd edn., Oxford, 2005); R. Darwall-Smith, *A History of University College Oxford* (Oxford, 2008); L. W. B. Brockliss (ed.), *Magdalen College Oxford: A History* (Oxford, 2008); J. Mordaunt Crook, *Brasenose: The Biography of an Oxford College* (Oxford, 2008). See also A. Hegarty, *A Biographical Register of St John's College, Oxford 1555–1660* (OHS ns xliii, Oxford, 2011).

gradual process, signalled by the brief experiment of electing scholars to the foundation in 1549–64, and the presence in college, by 1552, of ten undergraduates. It was given further impetus with the university's requirement in 1565 that all matriculating students had to be attached to a college or hall. Nevertheless, the decisive period came in the 1570s and 1580s. A census of 1572 shows that the college contained, aside from its senior members, nineteen others—including Henry Unton and Walter Raleigh—who seem to have been, for the most part, undergraduates. From the 1580s, we possess university matriculation registers and college admission figures, and though the totals for the two sets of records differ, they indicate that significant numbers of students were now entering Oriel. Matriculands certainly fluctuated in number: twenty undergraduates matriculated from the college in 1581, four in 1582, fifteen more in 1583, and then a mere three in 1584. Nevertheless, for the whole period 1585 to 1600, there were 200 matriculations from Oriel, an average of twelve a year. The actual figure of new students was higher than 200, since some chose not to matriculate and others joined as graduates. So over the same fifteen years, the college admitted 261 men, an average of 18 p.a.[4]

Robert Pierrepont, future earl of Kingston, was the first undergraduate *commensalis* or fellow commoner at Oriel, in 1596, and he enjoyed privileges of dress and of dining with the fellows at the cost of higher fees.[5] Others of the same rank among Pierrepont's contemporaries were Robert Harley (admitted in 1597) of Herefordshire, afterwards a knight and member of parliament, and Richard (1602) and Thomas Cave (1608), sons of Sir Thomas Cave of Stanford, Northamptonshire. Richard took his BA in 1605 but died the following year in Padua, while Thomas was knighted in 1616 and created a baronet in 1641. These gentlemen commoners were often generous contributors to the rebuilding fund in the later 1630s.[6]

Commensales were the top of three ranks of undergraduate. Beneath them were the most numerous group of commoners, who paid lower fees and were entitled to take their 'commons' or food in hall, and below them were servitors or 'battelers', as they were interchangeably known in Oriel, from poorer backgrounds, who earned their keep. Some worked as servants to

---

[4] C. W. Boase (ed.), *Register of the University of Oxford*, i, 1449–63; 1505–71 (OHS, 1885), xxiii; A. Clark (ed.), *Register of the University of Oxford*, ii (1571–1622), part ii (OHS, 1887), 39–40; HUO iii. 49–50, 62; *Registrum Orielense*, i. 38, 41–4, 51–97; OCA TF 1 A1/5, fos. 16ʳ–90ᵛ; C. S. Emden, *Oriel Papers* (Oxford, 1948), 11–13. A survey of 1568 states that Oriel then had 31 *studentes*, the smallest number of any college: Washington, DC, Folger Shakespeare Library MS V.a.176, fo. 173; I owe this reference to Gerard Kilroy.

[5] For the contemporary nomenclature of fellow commoner, see DR 334; J. Day, *Day's Festivals* (Oxford, 1615), ¶ sig. 2ʳ.

[6] DR 284; OCA BT 1 A/1, p. 7; *Registrum Orielense*, i. 83–4, 86, 102, 123.

individual fellows, sometimes sleeping in truckle-beds in their rooms; Barton Daniell, a fellow who died in 1620, left his best apparel to 'his owne poor scholler or boy'. Anthony Tye, fellow 1571–84, bequeathed to Oriel a lease of land in Devon in 1584 which would provide 16*d*. per week to two servitors, while John Jackman, fellow 1561–84, in his will of 1600 left property in Oxford to support a poor scholar as college porter. Other servitors earned money as bible clerks or received one of the twelve St Antony and Dudley exhibitions.[7] Through such devices, those with limited means could receive a university education and sometimes achieve academic advancement beyond this. Four future fellows were bible clerks and Dudley exhibitioners as undergraduates at Oriel. One of them was Thomas Sheppard, who held a St Antony exhibition, worth 8*d*. a week, served as bible clerk in 1633–8, took his BA in 1636, and was elected in 1638 to the fellowship. He was a theologian, eventually acquiring a BD, and remained on the fellowship until 1661.[8]

The social composition of undergraduates at Oriel broadly matched those of the wider university in the early seventeenth century. The largest contingent (40 per cent) was of plebeian origin, followed by 26 per cent from the gentry, 21 per cent from the armigerous gentry, knights and peerage, and 13 per cent from the clergy. Of 164 students entering Oriel in the 1630s, 85 (52 per cent) were commoners, 52 (32 per cent) were servitors, and 27 (16 per cent) were *commensales*. In short, the more socially exclusive Oriel was a product of the later seventeenth century.[9] Sons of clergy were of course a new feature in the English social landscape, since it was only from 1549, as part of the Edwardian Reformation, that ministers were permitted to marry. The first clerical offspring to join the college was William Cooke, son of a Northamptonshire minister, in 1586 at the tender age of 11. Most matriculands were older, usually in their mid-teens. Cooke's later career is unknown, but it is from this period we begin to see many sons following their father into the clerical profession, and occasionally also inheriting their benefices. Thus Samuel and Richard Sankey, sons of a Shropshire minister, matriculated together on 20 October 1598, one aged 17 and the other 16. Each, after taking his BA at Oriel in 1602 and MA at St Edmund Hall in 1605, was ordained by the bishop of

---

[7] VCH *Oxfordshire*, iii (1954), 123; P. Agius, 'Late Sixteenth- and Seventeenth-Century Furniture in Oxford', *Furniture History*, 7 (1971), 80; OUA Hyp/B/24, fo. 6, B/34, fos. 97–8; *Provosts and Fellows*, 71, 75. Tye's will was not settled until 1626: see *Provosts and Fellows*, 76, 78; OCA DLR 8, no. 6.

[8] OCA BT 1 II/2/3; *Provosts and Fellows*, 104. The other three were Robert Forward, John Taylor, and Richard Owen, *Provosts and Fellows*, 93, 94, 98.

[9] HUO iv. 55, 63; *Registrum Orielense*, i. 95–296.

Oxford, Samuel becoming a clergyman in Hampshire, while Richard succeeded his father Peter as incumbent of Wem.[10]

From where were these undergraduates drawn? A study of their geographical origins in the period c.1570 to 1660 shows that while they came from all parts of England and Wales, just over half (51 per cent) came from Devon, Dorset, Somerset, and Gloucestershire, from Wales and its marcher counties, and from Cumberland. This pattern reflected long-standing regional associations with the west and north via the Frank and Carpenter fellowships and Dudley benefactions. The connections with Wales are less straightforward. Welsh undergraduates were a rarity until the late 1580s, when they began entering the college in some number, with forty-eight being admitted in the 1590s, including a bumper crop of twenty in 1599.[11] This influx must be connected with the presence of two long-serving Welshmen on the fellowship, David Griffith (1584–1604) from mid-Wales and Cadwallader Owen (1584–1602) from north Wales. Both were later beneficed ministers in the principality, and presumably continued to recruit their fellow countrymen; indeed, Cadwallader Owen's son Richard entered the college in 1622 and in turn became a fellow.[12] When William Lewis from north Wales was elected provost in 1618, it was, according to the antiquary Anthony Wood, writing years after the event, thanks to a faction of Welshmen on the fellowship; inaccurate, as we shall see, but interesting for that link of Welshmen and Oriel.[13]

No sources directly address undergraduate recruitment in this period, but we can deduce a good deal from family and personal connections about why some students were sent to the college. At least seven members of the Blencowe clan were enrolled at Oriel under Provost Blencowe, including his nephew John Tolson, a future provost, while the numerous Sheldons in college in the 1580s was a result of Ralph Sheldon of Beoley, Worcestershire, being a college tenant and friend to Blencowe.[14] So too with the fellowship: John Day was elected fellow in 1588, and his brother Lionel was admitted BA at Oriel in 1591. Thomas Prynne, college tenant at Swainswick near Bath, sent his two sons William and Thomas to Oriel, in 1616–17, who were followed by their nephew Arthur Kemys twenty years later.[15] Several generations of the same family could attend the college: Edward Kynaston was a

---

[10] *Registrum Orielense*, i. 62, 90; CCEd, 'Samuel Sanky' (Clergy ID 15237) and 'Richard Sanky' (29325).

[11] *Registrum Orielense*, i. 92–5.

[12] *Provosts and Fellows*, 81–2, 98; CCEd, 'David Griffith' (Clergy ID 135589) and 'Cadwallader Owen' (73149).

[13] Wood, *Fasti Oxonienses*, i. col. 437.

[14] DR 156.

[15] Thomas Prynne was tenant from 1616–17 until his death in 1619–20, when first his widow Mary (until 1622–3), and then his son William (1631–2 to 1637–8) took over the lease. Charles I confiscated it from Prynne in 1637–8 after his prosecution in Star Chamber. OCA TF 1 A1/5, fos. 198r–321r; K. Sharpe, *The Personal Rule of Charles I* (New Haven, 1992), 763.

commensalis at Oriel in the 1580s, and was followed by his son Francis (1601), his grandson Edward (1631), and his great-grandson Francis (1655).

The influx of undergraduates created new challenges—financial, disciplinary, and educational—which the college had to address. A sweeping series of regulations were adopted between 1585 and 1594. Only the provost or his immediate deputies were entitled to admit commoners into the college; each fellow could only have one batteler to serve them at any one time; battels were to be paid punctually by fellows, on behalf of their pupils, and those that failed to do so were to be 'put off the commons' or banned from receiving their daily allowance of food and drink. Oriel was among the first of Oxford colleges to require 'caution money', or a down payment, to be made by fellows for their pupils. Fellows were charged with seeing that their pupils took holy communion regularly, and instructed to be more severe in checking unruly conduct, especially in suppressing running about and yelling in college, with the sensible qualification 'as far as may be possible' ('*quoad fieri posset*').[16] Teaching too was expanded, with a college catechist appointed in 1585 and a logic lecturer in 1591.[17]

The actual practice of undergraduate teaching, however, is poorly documented. We can glean something from the presentments made to the vice-chancellor at periodic visitations of St Mary Hall, Oriel's younger academic sibling, and governed by a succession of current or former fellows of Oriel. In 1613, under Ralph Braddyll (principal 1591–1632), it was reported that there were weekly 'logicke lectures, disputations for scholars and bachelars, themes and corrections', sometimes declamations, but 'noe other exercise of lerninge publique'. This was reformed under Braddyll's successor John Saunders (principal 1632–44 and then provost of Oriel 1644–53). Disputations were now kept 'constantly twise every day by the commoners, except Thursdayes and Satterdayes in the afternoon, and lecuters [*sic*] in the Hall twice every week' and well as two declamations every week in term. The declamation was an academic exercise introduced in the mid-sixteenth century to teach both undergraduates and BAs to speak eloquently in Latin. It may well be that a similar diet of disputations and lectures were observed in Oriel, although the adoption of declaiming in 1586–7 as a requirement for BAs there was effectively blocked by the bachelors themselves.[18] Lectures and disputations were accompanied by personal tuition from some of the fellows, but the record is silent on their form and frequency.

---

[16] DR 182, 186–7, 205–6; see DR 214; HUO iv. 75–6; C. Hopkins, *Trinity: 450 Years of a College Community* (Oxford, 2005), 65. Lists of caution money survive from 1618: OCA TF 1 A1/5, fos. 278ᵛ–81, TF 1 B1/1.

[17] DR 182, 201.

[18] OUA NEP/supra/45, fos. 87ʳ, 143ʳ; HUO iii. 193–4; DR 187–91. See Archbishop Laud's remark in 1639 that Braddyll had 'lived well, but in too free a fashion': William Laud, *Works*, ed. W. Scott and J. Bliss, 7 vols. (Oxford, 1847–60), v. 247.

Book ownership is one way into the intellectual outlook of the fellowship. We possess the inventory of books for Thomas Powell, MA and fellow 1565 until his death in 1575, and university praelector in natural philosophy. Powell's small collection of forty-two books was rather conventional, containing volumes on natural science, history, law, and theology, including Cicero's *De officiis*, Aristotle's *Physics*, and Justinian's *Institutiones*. His teaching was likely to have run along traditional tracks.[19] We move into a rather different mental world with the library of Powell's contemporary Anthony Tye, fellow 1571–84. His inventory of 140 books reveals the imprint of the new humanist learning. There are numerous books by Greek authors, often in the original tongue, on literature (Homer, Aeschylus, and Sophocles), rhetoric (Demosthenes), and theology (Eusebius, Justin Martyr), biblical works in Hebrew, modern works on Aristotle's *Physics* (Ammonius and Francisco de Toledo), and strong holdings in astronomy, astrology, and medicine, including two treatises on urine. This impressive range could not be anticipated from the formal academic record of Tye proceeding MA in 1573 and taking up civil law in 1581.[20] Unfortunately, we know nothing of Tye's activities as a college tutor or lecturer.

Another humanist was John Day, elected to the fellowship in 1588, four years after Tye's death, and his lectures and notebooks do provide some insight into teaching at Oriel. As a newly elected fellow, Day was required by the provost and fellows to lecture on Aristotle's *Physics*, and, as the text was prescribed for the arts degrees of BA and MA, he probably attracted a mixed audience of undergraduates and bachelors. He also devised over a hundred propositions from other Aristotelian works, *De anima*, *Metaphysica*, *De meteoris*, and above all the *Ethics*, which may have formed the basis of college disputations. As a disciple of John Case of St John's and John Rainolds of Corpus, Day offered a humanist interpretation of Aristotle. His lectures drew on medieval scholastic authorities such as Aquinas and a range of modern commentators from across Europe, including three Jesuits—Cardinal Francisco de Toledo, Benito Pereira, and Pedro de Fonseca—whose scholarship Day particularly admired. The academic republic of letters could thus transcend narrow confessional divisions. In one proposition he devised—'is monarchy the best form of government?'—Day cited Jean Bodin's recent work *The Six Books of the Commonwealth* (1576), which addressed the problem of government from the experience of the French wars of religion, a citation which typifies Day's engagement with Aristotle's

---

[19] *Provosts and Fellows*, 73; Clark (ed.), *Register of the University of Oxford*, ii (1571–1622), part i, 99; R. J. Fehrenbach and E. S. Leedham-Green (eds.), *Private Libraries in Renaissance England*, iv (Binghamton, NY, 1995), 205–11.
[20] *Provosts and Fellows*, 75–6; Fehrenbach and Leedham-Green (eds.), *Private Libraries*, vi (Tempe, Ariz., 2004), 47–64.

thought in a thoroughly contemporary context.²¹ Years later, in 1612, Day became college catechist, and subsequently published his lectures for the benefit of future generations of students who had missed hearing them.

Relatively little survives of the academic work of undergraduates. John Gray, elected to a Dudley exhibition in 1574, died probably of the plague in 1577 and left behind him a fairly typical library for a student in the arts faculty, consisting of forty books, mostly in Latin, on rhetoric, logic, ethics, and theology, including Aristotle's *Organon*, Cicero's *De officiis*, Aesop's *Fabulae*, the English Bible, and an unspecified work by the Lutheran Philip Melanchthon.²² Sixty years on, a notebook of 1633 belonging to 'G.S.', probably Griffith Smith, of 'Coll: Oriel' underlines the wide general reading that undergraduates undertook. Much of the volume is concerned with law and history, with numerous quotations in English, Latin, and occasionally Greek from the Scriptures, Herodotus, Plutarch, and particularly from *The History of the World* (1614, and later editions) by a fellow Orielensis, Sir Walter Raleigh. Smith also cites theologians such as Gregory Nazianzen, philosophers such as Aquinas and Pico della Mirandola, and the essayist Michel de Montaigne. Amidst all this are shorter notes, such as '3 thinges requisite to a long life' (health, air, and diet), the three ways the devil works, four sorts of witches, '4 propertyes of a good law', and the five prerogatives belonging to an absolute monarch.²³

Personal financial accounts throw a rather different light on undergraduate life, beyond the tutorial and lecture hall. The earliest for Oriel dates from the 1650s, but one set survives for William Freke, sixth son of a Dorset gentleman and an undergraduate at St Mary Hall in 1619–22, from the age of 14 to 17. Much of his expenditure was on clothes, such as a hat band and hat brush, laced ruffs and cuffs, waistcoat, a scabbard for his sword, green stockings, spurs, and no fewer than twenty-two pairs of boots and shoes in three years. There is a quarterly payment of £1 to 'my Tutor Paule', a fee to be admitted to Mr Saunders's fencing school, and charges for lessons on the viol and strings. Conspicuously few books were purchased. Freke did buy several on geography, including George Abbot's popular *A Briefe Description of the Whole World* and Robert Johnson on the new plantation in Virginia, as well as Francis Bacon's *Essays* and an expensive volume on hawking and hunting.²⁴ Martin Sandford was another gentleman's son, admitted as a gentleman

---

²¹ Oxford, Bodleian Library MS Rawlinson D 274, fos. 1ʳ–127ʳ (*De auscultacione physicae Aristotelis*) and fos. 217ʳ–59ʳ (*Obiectiones et solutiones Aristotelicae*), the latter of a slightly later date; J. McConica, 'Humanism and Aristotle in Tudor Oxford', EHR 94 (1979), 291–317; C. B. Schmitt, *John Case and Aristotelianism in Renaissance England* (Kingston, Ont., 1983), 56–7.

²² *Registrum Orielense*, i. 45; Fehrenbach and Leedham-Green (eds.), *Private Libraries*, v (Tempe, Ariz., 1998), 94–7.

²³ Northamptonshire RO, Fitzwilliam (Milton), Misc. Vol. 302.

²⁴ H. V. F. Somerset, 'An Account Book of an Oxford Undergraduate in the Years 1619–1622', *Oxoniensia*, 22 (1957), 85–92.

commoner in 1654. He was initially given an allowance of £60 per year, which proved to be insufficient so it was raised in 1655 to £80. There were payments for his accommodation, to a servitor, barber, laundress, and bedmaker, for music lessons, clothes, 'combes and powder', and also books, all approved and signed off by his tutor, Arthur Acland (fellow 1640–59).[25]

Oriel was unusual among Oxford colleges for having only a handful of its fellowships tied to particular counties or dioceses, and without a body of scholars on the foundation to apply for vacancies. As a result, fourteen out of the eighteen fellowships were open to candidates from the wider university and, in theory at least, were more competitive than most. The process of electing fellows is poorly documented, though ties of kinship, friendship, and patronage, mostly invisible to us, must account for the selection of some outsiders to the fellowship. Kinship was certainly evident in 1590 when Richard Butler, a St Antony exhibitioner, was recommended by Provost Blencowe on the grounds of his affinity to the college benefactor Dr Dudley and was duly elected, but this was the only time in the period that such preference was exercised. Very occasionally, objections break through the silence of the record. In 1610 an outsider, Giles Widdowes, was presented for election by the Visitor, William Barlow bishop of Lincoln, who overruled opposition from the fellowship, and Widdowes was admitted. The Dean's Register provides no details as to why Widdowes's candidature was opposed. In time, Widdowes would become a controversial Laudian and be involved in a public spat with William Prynne, Orielensis and puritan pamphleteer.[26] From the 1580s, with a growing number of resident undergraduates, the college began to recruit fellows from within its walls. A small majority of fellows (51 per cent) elected between 1588 and 1648 had some prior connection with the college, and for the period 1620 to 1648 the figure rises to 63 per cent. Among them were two future provosts, John Tolson and John Saunders, the eminent physician Sir Matthew Lister, and the future bishop Humphrey Lloyd; equally, from elsewhere in Oxford came two other future provosts, William Lewis and Robert Say, John Rouse, Bodley's second librarian, John Day, a distinguished theologian and preacher, and Richard Quiney, a grandson of Shakespeare, who was elected fellow in October 1638 and died the following January. The success of internal candidates for the fellowship in the years 1588–1648 was to drop in the century after 1660, when only 41 per cent of fellows had links to the college before their election.[27]

There was a distinct shift in the intellectual interests of the fellowship in Provost Blencowe's lengthy tenure (1574–1618). In the 1570s, the majority of fellows specialized in civil law or medicine, or else remained masters of arts,

---

[25] Somerset Heritage Centre, DD/SF 6/1/2-4. His father was Francis Sandford, admitted to Oriel in 1602–3 as a commoner (*Registrum Orielense*, i. 103, 276).
[26] DR 199, 229–31.
[27] *Provosts and Fellows*, 104; Hegarty, *St John's*, 401–2.

ILLUSTRATION 4.3 Sir Matthew Lister (1571–1656), physician, fellow 1592–1605 Oriel College, from a line engraving by Paul van Somer, 1646

and there were notably few theologians as the college adjusted, slower than many others, to the new religion. Blencowe himself was a civil lawyer, who took his DCL in 1586 and from c.1593 to his death in 1618 was chancellor of Oxford diocese, appointing as his surrogates in the church courts a number of civilians who were current or former fellows, including George Dale DCL (fellow 1578–88), Ralph Braddyll (fellow 1584–91), Abel Gower (fellow 1585–1616), and William Wilmott (fellow 1585–1610).[28] There was a small

---

[28] *Provosts and Fellows*, 72–3, 78, 82–3; Oxfordshire RO, Oxford diocesan papers MS d 4, fos. 2^r, 91^r, 101^r; c 264, fos. 4^v–5^r, 6^v–7^r. From 1615 Gower also served as commissary of the peculiar jurisdiction of Thame (OUA Hyp/A/31, fo. 45^r).

number studying medicine, among them John Jackman (fellow 1562–84), who took his BM in 1584, and Henry Ashworth (fellow 1574–85), who received his BM in 1585. Both resigned to practise medicine in the city of Oxford, Jackman dying in 1600, Ashworth in 1633. Ashworth lived in Catte Street, with Provost Blencowe among his patients, and was elevated to an MD in 1605 on being chosen to participate in the faculty's academic exercises performed at James I's visit to Oxford. Ashworth evidently took on pupils, among them William Denton of Magdalen, who became a royal physician in the 1630s. He also supported in print the attack by Dr John Cotta, a physician in Northampton, on clergy who practised medicine. Cotta's particular target was the *'aurum potabile'* or life elixir peddled by a local minister, John Markes, and Ashworth testified that in his recent illness he had taken the potion, to no benefit, and went on to denounce priest physicians as dispensing dubious remedies while neglecting their ministerial function. They should heed the words of St Paul

> who counselleth them to attend their reading, to attend their flocke, to attend their office and function, rather than to watch at the furnace as laborants, or to keepe a shop of medicines as apothecaries, or to practise phisicke as intruders... or to give doubtfull answers as wizards, or to erect false figures as impostors; or to professe soothsaying as magitians, or to pervert sicke men from religion as dissemblers...

Thomas Wyatt, a former fellow, recorded a nice anecdote about Ashworth, calling on his deathbed in 1633 for a bible and saying *'haec est vera medicina'*. In his will, Ashworth bequeathed £5 to Provost Tolson for a silver cup and £3 for 'a common dinner or supper' for the fellowship.[29] Another physician on the fellowship was John Saunders (1602–17), a BM in 1611 and DM in 1628, and much later still, provost. The most prominent was Matthew Lister, fellow 1592–1605, who moved to London to become physician to the Crown and to courtiers, and was knighted by Charles I in 1636. The importance of the discipline to Oriel was recognized in 1612, when one of the three fellowships reserved for civil law was transferred to medicine, an act of real commitment at a time when the faculty was still numerically small and politically uninfluential.[30] Similarly, in the 1570s and 1580s, Blencowe's key lieutenants were not theologians but John Jackman, who studied medicine,

---

[29] *Provosts and Fellows*, 71, 76–7; TNA PROB/11/131, fo. 150ᵛ, 11/164 fo. 407ʳ; ODNB s.n. William Denton; HUO iv. 506; J. Nichols, *The Progresses, Processions and Magnificent Festivities of King James the First*, 4 vols. (London, 1828), i. 534 n. 7; I. Cotta, *Cotta contra Antonium* (Oxford, 1625), 60, 64–8, 95–6; D. Harley, 'James Hart of Northampton and the Calvinist Critique of Priest-Physicians: An Unpublished Polemic of the Early 1620s', *Medical History*, 42 (1998), 362–86; J. H. Raach, 'Five Early Seventeenth Century English Country Physicians', *Journal of the History of Medicine and Allied Sciences*, 20 (1965), 215–17; Oxford, Bodleian Library, MS Top. Oxon c 378, p. 522.

[30] *Provosts and Fellows*, 85, 88–9; ODNB s.n. Matthew Lister; Hegarty, *St John's*, 348–9; OCA GOV 3 A14c; HUO iv. 506, 514.

and Richard Pigot, fellow for fifty-two years (1561–1613), who belatedly took up civil law. Pigot remained influential until his death, and after 1585 was joined by two other future civilians, Abel Gower and William Wilmott.

By the 1590s the balance had begun to shift, as theologians gained ground in the fellowship. The decision to revive disputations in theology in 1593 was one sign of changing times. Increasing numbers of fellows took degrees in theology, with no less than five past and present fellows—Day, Tolson, Fawconer, Wyatt, and Lloyd—graduating BD in 1611–13. In 1611 the Visitor, Bishop Barlow of Lincoln, reviewed the rules for those studying for higher degrees in theology. Theologians should take holy orders within six years of receiving their MA, and within nine years proceed to BD. Disputations lasting two hours were to be held in chapel three times each Michaelmas Term, and twice in other terms. The question under debate should be posted in the chapel and hall four days before the disputation, at which one respondent should face two opponents, with the dean, were he a theologian, or else the senior in theology, as moderator.[31] Theologians also played increasingly important roles in college. The first was Richard Wharton, who held a number of college offices from the 1580s to his resignation in 1608; from 1600 he was joined by two theologians, John Tolson, Blencowe's nephew and successor-but-one, and John Day. The latter, for example, served as dean (1601, 1611, and 1616), senior treasurer (1593, 1601, 1604, and 1609), and catechist (1612–20).

Day was also one of a number of fellows who was granted leave of absence to study abroad, one indication of intellectual vitality among the fellowship. Day went to France in 1605–8, probably to the Protestant seminary at Saumur, and references to his travels occur in his published sermons in the 1610s.[32] Matthew Lister was given permission to study at Padua, renowned for its teaching of medicine, and proceeded DM from Basel about 1603. John Rouse, fellow 1601–52, spent 1611–16 abroad visiting Heidelberg and its famous library, obtaining an extension from the Privy Council in June 1614 for up to two more years overseas for his 'experience in the languadges'.[33] Such travel was not always for academic reasons: two fellows, William Clavell and Ralph Braddyll, were permitted to spend two years in the service of Sir Henry Unton, an Orielensis, on his appointment as resident ambassador at the court of Henry IV of France in 1591. Braddyll returned to academic life, as principal of St Mary Hall (1591–1632); Clavell's vision was

---

[31] DR 204; *Provosts and Fellows*, 84–8; OCA GOV 2 D2. These regulations may have been influenced by university statutes of 1564–5 and 1583. See S. Gibson, *Statuta antiqua Universitatis Oxoniensis* (Oxford, 1931), 383, 427–9.

[32] DR 221; J. Day, *Davids Desire to go to Church* (Oxford, 1612), 48; J. Day, *Day's Festivals* (Oxford, 1615), 309, note a.

[33] DR 213, 217, 236; OCA TF 1 A1/5, fos. 90ᵛ, 159ᵛ, 166ʳ, 173ʳ, 180ᵛ, 187ʳ; *Acts of the Privy Council 1613–1614*, 475. A fourth traveller was Abel Gower, permitted to study abroad in 1598–9 with a stipend of £6 13s. 4d.: DR 211–12; OCA TF 1 A1/5, fos. 86ᵛ, 90ᵛ.

broader. He had been elected fellow in 1583, given two years leave in 1587, and enrolled in the Middle Temple. He resigned his fellowship in 1598, was knighted for his services in the Irish war which ended in 1603, and later, as we shall see, became a rather unsuccessful entrepreneur.[34]

From the last years of the sixteenth century, colleges in both universities began to expand their libraries, soliciting donations, cataloguing their holdings, and improving the library furniture.[35] This process began at Oriel just after 1600, and the immediate impetus may have been the gifts, in 1595, and then in 1600, of books on medicine and botany from two former fellows, first from Thomas Cogan and then a much more substantial benefaction of thirty-eight volumes from John Jackman. Yet it was precisely at this time that Provost Blencowe was an active member of the university committee supporting the foundation of the Bodleian Library, and later as chancellor of Oxford diocese would solicit money from local clergy for the building of the schools quadrangle, so the example of Bodley may have prompted Blencowe to develop the college's own collection and encourage a culture of donations.[36] Individual items begin to appear in the treasurers' accounts: in 1601–2 a gift of a book by Tertullian from Nicholas Bond, president of Magdalen, and a bequest by former Provost Smyth (1550–65) of works by Plato and St Basil; then in 1607–8 John Lewis, yeoman of Iffley and an admirer of Cadwallader Owen (fellow 1584–1602), left 20 marks (£13 6s. 8d.) to buy 'the kings great bibles', probably the *Biblia Regia* or Antwerp polygot bible, published in eight volumes in 1568–73. These were to be chained in the college library, 'as a testimonie of my love to that house, and zeale that I beare to learninge'.[37] Unlike some colleges, Oriel did not rely exclusively on donations, and from 1608 purchased new books using the 50s. paid by incoming fellows, which often went to strengthening the holdings in theology.[38] Fellows also gave individual items, and were guided by gaps in the current collection. John Day presented a commentary on Cicero's *Orations* in two volumes in 1605, and his own *Day's Descant on Davids Psalms* in 1620, while in 1615 Richard Cluett donated *The Vision of Pierce Plowman*.[39] Further books came from fellows at their resignation, and from valuable

---

[34] DR 200; *Provosts and Fellows*, 81–2; J. Hutchins, *The History and Antiquities of the County of Dorset*, 4 vols. (London, 1973), i. 567.
[35] K. Jensen, 'Universities and Colleges', in E. Leedham-Smith and T. Webber (eds.), *The Cambridge History of Libraries in Britain and Ireland*, i (Cambridge, 2006), 345–62; HUO iv. 672–3, 678; J. F. Fuggles, 'A History of the Library of S. John's College Oxford from the Foundation of the College to 1660' (Oxford B. Litt. thesis, 1975), 57–100.
[36] DR 208; OCA BT 1 A/1, pp. 14, 17; OUA NEP/supra/register M, fo. 32^r; HUO iv. 139.
[37] OCA TF 1 AI/5, fos. 104^r, 133^r, 137^r; TNA PROB/11/100, fo. 183^v.
[38] Darwall-Smith, *University College*, 143. Fuggles notes that St John's steered donors towards presenting certain books, to avoid duplication, and this may have happened elsewhere; 'Library of S. John's', 64.
[39] OCA BT 1 A/1, pp. 18–23; OCL shelfmarks X d 20–1, 3 Wd 17.

legacies from former fellows such as fourteen books from Richard Wharton in 1610, twenty-eight from Richard Pigot in 1613, and sixty-six volumes, mostly on civil law, from Provost Blencowe himself in 1618.[40] Folio books were chained throughout this period, and from c.1600 the college accounts show increased expenditure for binding, clasps, chains, loops, and iron bars, but also, from 1608, for shelving. The college followed the example of Merton and Duke Humphrey's Library, and began to remove books from chests and place them, spine inwards, in 'presses' or bookcases. In 1630 William Combe, fellow 1624–30, left up to £100 for 'the making upp of new desks in the library' which may have been placed beneath or between these bookshelves.[41] The earliest surviving catalogue of the library dates from 1625, and by this time donations of books had become an established part of college life, and were memorialized in the benefactors' book started in about 1636. It was not until 1655, however, long after some other colleges, that a librarian was appointed.[42]

What can we learn of the character of Provost Blencowe, who presided over the dramatic changes from 1574 to 1618? Blencowe had joined the college in 1560 as a Dudley exhibitioner, took his BA in 1563 and his MA in 1566, became a fellow in 1563, served as senior proctor to the university in 1571–2, and was elected provost in 1574. He studied civil law, receiving his BCL and DCL in 1586, and was respondent in law at royal visits in 1592 and 1605. However, he was never a major figure within the university, only ever serving as deputy to the vice-chancellor and discharging unglamorous administrative roles such as university auditor.[43] Something of Blencowe's personality emerges from *Iter boreale*, a Latin poem of 600 hexameters composed by his friend Richard Eedes, future dean of Worcester, which recorded the occasion in the summer of 1582 when the two accompanied Tobias Matthew, dean of Christ Church and future archbishop of York, on his journey north as Matthew took up his new position as dean of Durham Cathedral. Eedes's tone is light and at times satirical, and Blencowe is dubbed as a crafty and duplicitous companion—'no man more deceitful', full of 'empty promises and lying talk'. This is banter, of course, but it suggests that Blencowe may have been a smooth operator, and a man able to get his own way, all at the price, here at least, of a little teasing. Blencowe also knew how to combine work and pleasure. The party stayed with Oriel tenants going north and then on the way home, and at one of these Eedes enjoyed the beauty of the tenants' daughters ('thanks be to dominus Anthony, to whom

---

[40] OCA BT 1 A/1, pp. 13–15, 18.
[41] OCA TF 1 A1/5, fos. 100^r, 104^v, 120^r, 137^r, 152^r, 159^v, 166^r, 174^v 180^r, 194^r, 215^v, 268^v, and *passim*; TNA PROB/11/157, fo. 204^v; VCH *Oxfordshire*, iii. 124. In the event, only £28 of Combe's legacy was spent on desks (OCA BT 1 A/1, p. 2).
[42] DR 285, 334; OCL shelfmark D. C. V. 22; OCA BT 1 A/1; HUO iv. 678.
[43] A. Clark (ed.), *Register of the University of Oxford*, ii (1571–1622), part i, 230, 232, 246–7; Nichols, *Progresses*, i. 535; OUA Hyp/A/21, fos. 212^v, 213^r; WP/β/21/4, pp. 101–2, 122.

our gratitude is expressed with a wide grin'); at another, they planned to spend one day hawking for partridge, and another coursing rabbits. Blencowe evidently had a gift for close and often enduring friendships: not just with Eedes and Matthew but others, as we shall see, such as the Sheldons of Beoley, Worcestershire, and with Thomas Allen of Gloucester Hall.[44]

From the 1590s, unusually but not uniquely for a head of house, Blencowe carved out a profitable legal practice in diocesan administration, as chancellor of the dioceses of Oxford (c.1593–1618) and Chichester (1590–1607).[45] Blencowe left the running of Chichester to his deputies, although his brother George resided there and looked after his interests. At Oxford, however, he was a tireless administrator, ruling the diocese during the long vacancy between bishops in 1592–1604 and directly answerable to Archbishop Whitgift of Canterbury. When a new bishop, John Bridges, was finally appointed in 1604, Blencowe had to move fast to have his patent renewed. As it turned out, Bridges and Blencowe worked together well, and in his will Blencowe left the bishop a ring of angel gold displaying a death head as a remembrance, as well as another to the diocesan registrar Thomas Flaxney, whose son had been an Oriel undergraduate in 1607–11. Throughout his time as chancellor of Oxford, Blencowe regularly presided in the consistory court, held in All Saints on the High Street, even on the day before his death on 25 January 1618, and also transacted diocesan business from his lodgings in Oriel.[46]

Blencowe seems to have brought the same energy, sharp legal mind, and administrative acumen to bear on his rule as provost. At his death in 1618, he was eulogized by the dean, William Lewis, as a most benevolent head ('*caput charissimum*') who ruled fruitfully and judiciously. On occasion he had to stamp his authority on the fellowship, in 1591 overturning the decision of the dean to oust a fellow for accepting a benefice incompatible with his fellowship, since the decision was reached in his absence; on other occasions handling accusations and counter-accusations between fellows, in one case involving charges of theft and adultery, and in 1588 admonishing Simon Lee, acquitted of committing 'grave crimes', to avoid any scandal in the future. It

---

[44] D. F. Sutton, *Oxford Poetry by Richard Eedes and George Peele* (London, 1995), 33, 59, 87, 91–3.

[45] Other examples, all from Cambridge, are Barnaby Gooch (Magdalene), Clement Corbett, and Thomas Eden (Masters of Trinity Hall) who at the same time were diocesan chancellors.

[46] B. P. Levack, *The Civil Lawyers in England 1603–1641* (Oxford, 1973), 212; CCEd, 'Anthony Blencowe' (Clergy ID 55594); CSPD (1603–10), 59; A. Thrush and J. P. Ferris (eds.), *The House of Commons 1604–1629*, 6 vols. (Cambridge, 2010), iii. 239–40; TNA PROB/11/131, fos. 150^v–1^r; Hegarty, *St John's*, 274–5; *Registrum Orielense*, i. 120; Oxfordshire RO, Oxford diocesan papers MS d 4, fo. 54^r, d 5–6, 9, 10, fo. 188^r, c 264, fos. 2^v–4^r, 23^r, 27^v–8^r, 56^v, c 265, fo. 10^v. Blencowe died on 25 January not 15 January 1618 as stated in the Dean's Register and, following it, by Shadwell: see J. Day, *Day's Descant on Davids Psalms* (Oxford, 1620), 72; Oxfordshire RO Oxford diocesan papers MS d 10, fo. 188^r; OCA GOV 4 A1, 298; *Provosts and Fellows*, 73.

may have been Blencowe who in 1610 brought to the attention of the Visitor, Bishop Barlow of Lincoln, the case against William Whetcombe in the chancellor's court. Whetcombe, a senior fellow, was accused of frequenting the company of Katherine Badcocke, a married woman and described as a 'notoriouse strumpet' who 'gloried in her leawdnes'. After summoning him to a hearing, Barlow had Whetcombe removed from the fellowship.[47]

The college accounts indicate Blencowe's personal involvement in college business outside Oxford, including visits to London and Winchester to obtain letters patent for the refoundation of the college in 1603 and its confirmation by parliamentary statute in 1606. Advancing age did not diminish his drive. In 1614–16 Blencowe tried to extract more money from the dean and chapter of Windsor for the St Antony exhibitioners, on the grounds that his predecessors had negligently allowed the annual payment to diminish from 25 marks (£16 10s.) to £10 8s. p.a.; the case went to arbitration and the college's case was rejected. A single entry in 1617–18 is very telling: it is a payment of 25s. to Blencowe, aged about 74 and in the last year of his life, for the cost of journeying to London on college matters.[48] His high standing at least amongst some in college is evident from the will of William Stockdell, manciple of Oriel, in 1591. Stockdell appointed Anthony Morebreade, a fellow of Magdalen, as his executor, and 'my welbeloved Mr Anthonye Blincow' as his overseer, 'in whome above all creatures I do repose my chiefest and moste speciall trust to have this my last will performed in all points according to my true meanynge', and instructed that, contrary to usual practice, the executor be directed by the overseer.[49]

Blencowe was evidently an active and conscientious provost. But was he primarily responsible for the two most important developments in his time as provost—the re-foundation in 1603–6 and the commitment to rebuilding from 1606? Both occurred very late in his forty years as provost. The college was slower than many others to receive confirmation of its possessions and status, while on Blencowe's watch the fabric was allowed to deteriorate, in parts to the point of ruin ('*in ruinam vergentis*'). It seems likely, therefore, that the drive for these changes came from a new generation of fellows, in particular Gower, Wilmott, and Tolson. Nevertheless, even if he was not the initiator, Blencowe became an enthusiastic supporter of both projects and furthered them in significant ways.

The re-foundation of 1603–6 is a major event in the history of Oriel. In the later sixteenth century many colleges followed the example of both

---

[47] DR 189–90, 195–6, 230–1; OUA Hyp/B/4, fos. 145^v–6^v, Hyp/A/30, 10, CC Papers 1610 p/10. For Whetcome's chequered career as a young fellow, see DR 188–9, 196.
[48] OCA TF 1 A1/5, fos. 12^v, 26^v, 108^r, 109^v, 113^r, 115^v, 124^r, 153^r, 186^v, 208^r; OCA BT 1 II/2/1, pp. 3–5, 7, 10.
[49] OUA Hyp/B/33, fo. 89.

universities, which had been incorporated by parliamentary statute in 1571, and obtained letters patent from the Crown and sometimes a statute confirming their corporate status and lands.[50] The case of Oriel presents a highly distinctive variant in this process. Why the college waited so long for letters patent is unclear, but it appears that by 1603 they could delay no longer. Preaching before James I in 1612, William Westerman, an Orielensis, recalled 'the new life, which Oriall Colledge, when shee was almost at the last gaspe, and on the hazard, receaved by the royall charter and confirmation', which mixed flattery to the king with an uncomfortable truth: that the multiplicity of names used by the college over the last century or so had called into question its possessions and manors and left it potentially vulnerable to legal challenge. The twenty-nine different titles by which Oriel was variously known were recited in the letters patent obtained from the new king on 18 June 1603. The shortest was '*collegium Oriell in Oxonia*', while the longest betrays the confusion which had arisen:

Prepositi Collegii Oxon vocat le Oriell et eiusdem Collegi Scholaroium alias dict Prepositi et Scholarium Colleg in Oxonia vocati Le Oriell alias dict Prepositi et Scholarium domus sive Collegii de Oriell in Oxonia alias dict Prepositi et Scholarium Societatis Collegii Regis vocati Le Oriell in Oxonia dict Collegii Regis Oxon vocatt Oriell Prepositi et eiusdem Collegium Scholarum.

In place of these, James I determined that the college be incorporated as the 'Provost and Schollers of the House of the Blessed Mary the Virgin in Oxford commonlie called Oriell Colledge of the foundation of Edward the Second of famous memory', which henceforth might safely and quietly enjoy possession of all its manors, lands, and tenements. Given that it was intended to nail any doubts about the legality of Oriel as a corporation, it comes as something of a surprise to find that the letters patent carry the great seal of Elizabeth I. Evidently the king's new seal had not yet been cast.[51]

Emboldened with this legal title, the college immediately decided to unpick the lease of Wadley and Wickensham manors in Berkshire, its most valuable possession. These manors were worth an estimated £500–600 p.a., but by a disastrous grant in 1538 of three leases totalling 208 years they yielded a paltry annual rent of £58, which would eventually rise to £60. The college decided to challenge the validity of the second lease, which was to

---

[50] Such as University College (1573), Balliol (1588), and Corpus (1606); see HUO iii. 402; Darwall-Smith, *University College*, 111; Jones, *Balliol College*, 80–1; Corpus Christi College Oxford Archives A/50/3.

[51] W. Westerman, *Iacobs Well: or, a Sermon preached before the Kings most excellent Maiestie at St Albans, in his Summer Progresse 1612* (London, 1613), 66; OCA GOV 1 B6–7. James I's great seal was not ready until 19 July; see 'The Journal of Sir Roger Wilbraham', ed. H. Spencer Scott, *Camden Miscellany x* (Camden Society 3rd series, iv, 1902), 61. The new title took time to be adopted: in 1611, the Visitor referred to '*domus Beatae Mariae sive Collegii Regalis vocat Oriel*'; OCA GOV 2 D2.

ILLUSTRATION 4.4 Robert Pierrepont (1584–1643), 1st earl of Kingston, *commensalis* 1596–9
Oriel College

begin in 1616. The current lessee was Valentine Knightley, recently knighted by James I, who responded by procuring a letter from the king, dated 19 October 1603. James rebuked the provost and fellows 'for that our meaning was not in the newe graunting of your foundation to preiudice your tenants estate', and demanded that they find ways to confirm the leases. An ally for the college in this dispute was Henry Howard earl of Northampton, an intimate counsellor of the king, who was presented with a gift of gloves in 1604–5 in gratitude for his assistance with college business at court. The matter was settled by a private act of parliament of 1606, guided through the House of Commons by a committee which included Blencowe's brother George, MP for Chichester. Provost Blencowe and Abel Gower were also at Westminster for most of the parliamentary session, lobbying on behalf of the college. The act gave statutory ratification to the letters patent of 1603, but also declared the leases of 1538 as 'ajudged good, sufficient and effectual in law'. However, the college had not been cowed by the royal letter, and agreed with Knightley that in return for an undertaking that there would be no fines imposed when the second lease replaced the first, the annual rent would immediately rise to £100. The first payment appears in the college accounts in 1606–7 and represented both a victory for Oriel and a tribute to Blencowe's stewardship. The entire rental income of the college in 1602–3 had been £250, so an extra £42 p.a. was a valuable increase. The letters patent and the private act also gave the college the legal security to pursue suits against, say, the dean and chapter of Windsor in 1614–16, which Blencowe stated could not have been contemplated before the re-foundation.[52]

It is no coincidence that plans to rebuild the college followed hard on the heels of the re-foundation. With their corporate status and lands assured, the college could address the dilapidated condition of the fabric and the pressing need to maximize space. Accommodating a sizeable number of undergraduates from the 1570s within the medieval quadrangle cannot have been easy. Just how large was the college community at the start of the seventeenth century? There is no regular listing of resident members in college in this period, and the extant series of buttery books, unreliable as they sometimes may be, only begin in 1643. Two surveys in the long vacations of 1611 and 1612, when not all were likely to be in Oxford, stated that the entire society of Oriel numbered sixty-four and then seventy-nine, but we get a very different total using the detailed list of college members 'who took or were to take' the Oath of Allegiance in July 1610. It contains the names of about 130 resident members, 100 of whom are recorded as taking the oath. A later census of 1634 supports this larger total by putting Oriel at 106 members. If precision is not possible, it is clear that space was at a premium.[53]

The first evidence of planning for the rebuilding occurs in December 1606, when the college agreed to sell timber to the value of £100 and put the money towards a construction fund. In 1613–14 a new provost's lodging was erected in the south-west corner of the garden, perhaps because Blencowe's existing accommodation in the main quadrangle had become dilapidated, but more likely as a first step in a bigger scheme, to create a separate lodging and free up space in the projected new quadrangle.[54] A year later, in 1614–15, £11 4*s*. 8*d*. was spent on quarrying and transporting stone for the planned rebuilding of the west or front range of the college ('*ad futuram aedificationem occidentalis partis*'). Blencowe died in January 1618, but his will, written over four years earlier in September 1613, spells out the envisaged programme. He left the bulk of his estate, totalling £1,300, to the college, and 'my desire is

---

[52] OCA GOV 1 B7; DLL 2; TF 1 A1/5, fos. 106^{r-v}, 120^r, 124^r, 127^r; BT 1 II/2/4; CSPD (1603–10), 44; *Commons' Journals*, i. 283. The earl of Salisbury may have also been an ally, for in October 1606 the college complied with his request to grant the valuable lease of Coleby to his nominee, John Dackam (DR 223). I owe this reference to the kindness of John Dunbabin.

[53] DR 224; OCA TF 1 E1/1; Oxford, Bodleian Library Twyne MS 21, 513–14; OUA, SP/E/6/1, fo. 5^r,/ 9–10; John Scot, *The Foundation of the Universitie of Oxford with a Catalogue of the Principall Founders and Speciall Benefactours of all the Colledges, and totall number of Students, Magistrats and Officers therein being, anno 1634* (Cambridge, 1634). The protestation returns of February 1642, with 75 names for Oriel, may be incomplete. C. S. A. Dobson, 'Oxfordshire Protestation Returns', *Oxfordshire Record Society*, 36 (1955), 114.

[54] F. J. Varley, 'The Provost's Lodgings at Oriel College', OR (April 1946), 15–18; OCA TF 1 A1/5, fos. 179^v, 181^{r-v}.

ILLUSTRATION 4.5 John Rouse (1574–1652), Bodley's Librarian, fellow 1601–52
Oriel College

that it may be bestowed towardes the new buildinge of some part of those ruinous buildinges of the sayd colledge, which have most neede to bee reedified, which I take to be, the weste side'.⁵⁵ Blencowe's wishes were observed by his two successors, Provost Lewis and his nephew and executor, Provost Tolson. In 1620–3 first the west and then the south ranges were rebuilt, with Provost Lewis laying the foundation stone.⁵⁶ As money ran short, at the suggestion of Bacon, Lewis penned some persuasive appeals for donations to all eminent Orielenses. Or so his contemporary, Bishop Robert

---

⁵⁵ OCA TF 1 A1/5, fo. 187ᵛ; TNA PROB/11/131, fo. 151ʳ.
⁵⁶ DR 248–9, 255; TNA PROB/11/325, fo. 310ᵛ. Lewis's will of 1667 reads: 'I had the honor to be Fellowe and Provoste and to lay the first stone of their new Colledge whereof I caused the modell to be by [a] shilfull [*sic*] surveyor exactly drawne.' Was this a drawing (or model) of the entire projected quadrangle?

Skinner, stated in a letter in 1665.[57] We should note that no such letters have survived and the donations for the fabric fund recorded in the benefactors' book relate to the late 1630s rather than the early 1620s. Given that Lewis had written such letters in 1612–15 on behalf of the university as it raised money for the new schools quadrangle of the Bodleian, it is likely that Skinner was confusing Lewis's earlier fund-raising with the letters written by Provost Tolson for the second phase of the rebuilding programme in 1636–42.[58] As for Blencowe, verses were composed after his death comparing him to Adam de Brome, both of them provosts, munificent patrons, and builders: 'One House holds both, both Builders are, and both she holds together.'[59]

Blencowe's death in January 1618 led to a disputed election. The winner was not one of the senior fellows but William Lewis, who had been elected a fellow in 1609 aged only 17. Now aged 26, Lewis had just been appointed dean and therefore was responsible for overseeing the election of a new provost. Elections of heads of house were usually conducted in a few days, to avoid outside interference, but in this case nearly a month elapsed before votes were cast, since Lewis was intent on winning the ballot. His opponent was John Day BD, aged 53 and fellow since 1588, with limited connections outside Oxford, although he looked to George Abbot, archbishop of Canterbury, for support.[60] In contrast, Lewis was domestic chaplain to Francis Bacon, who had just been appointed Lord Chancellor and was at the height of his power. Bacon evidently used his influence with the chancellor of the university, William Herbert earl of Pembroke, and the Visitor, George Montaigne bishop of Lincoln, on Lewis's behalf, and faced down the opposition of Archbishop Abbot and John King bishop of London, both former heads of Oxford colleges. When King protested at Lewis's relative youth, Bacon could reply sententiously that 'he respected not minoritie of years where there was majoritie of parts'; for, at the age of 26, Lewis was significantly younger than almost all his fellow heads at Oxford had been at the time of their election, the closest being Richard Kilby, elected rector of Lincoln in 1590 aged 29. By 14 February 1618, a week before the election, London gossips had learned that Lewis had secured the promise of votes and would be the new provost. On 21 February, he was duly elected by five votes to three, with nine of the fellows including John Day absent, perhaps a mark of dissent. A month later, at Lewis's installation, four of the eight fellows

---

[57] A. Wood, *The History and Antiquities of the Colleges and Halls in the University of Oxford*, ed. J. Gutch (Oxford, 1786), 327 n. 65.
[58] Oxford, Bodleian Library Add. MS C 206, fo. 56^r, and see also fos. 24^r, 63^r, 120^r; DR 284–5; Rannie, *Oriel College*, 97, also attributes Tolson's letters to Lewis.
[59] Day, *Day's Descant*, 72.
[60] In 1620 Day dedicated *Day's Descant* to Abbot and wrote of his obligations to the archbishop (sig. ¶3i^{r-v}). Day's presentation copy to Abbot is in Lambeth Palace Library, 1620.12.

present—Tolson, Rouse, Taylor, and Forward—walked out in protest. The split in the fellowship was not generational, for while Tolson and Rouse were senior fellows, Taylor and Forward were Lewis's contemporaries. On the other hand, the five fellows who seem to have supported Lewis had all been appointed since 1610 and none of them, *pace* Anthony Wood, was Welsh. With the division in the fellowship over Lewis's election, appeals were made to the Visitor, chancellor, and archbishop, and it was only settled by direct intervention from Lord Chancellor Bacon. Citing the original statutes of the college of 21 January 1326, which in fact had been superseded by the Lincoln statutes of 23 May 1326, Bacon claimed the right as Lord Chancellor to settle the disputed election, and 'upon due consideration' of the merits of the candidates and other circumstances, judged in favour of Lewis and confirmed his appointment.[61] Not merely was Bacon here exceeding his jurisdiction but he was also the known backer of one of the parties; in an age of bitterly fought elections over headships, this case is still remarkable for Bacon's effrontery and legal chicanery.

ILLUSTRATION 4.6 William Lewis (1592–1667), fellow 1609, provost 1618–21

Oriel College

---

[61] DR 241–6; N. E. McClure (ed.), *Letters of John Chamberlain*, 2 vols. (Philadelphia, 1939), ii. 139–40; Wood, *Fasti Oxonienses*, ii col. 437; *Reports of Divers Special Cases, adjudged in the Courts of King's Bench, Common Pleas, and Exchequer...Collected by Sir Thomas Raymond* (London, 1803), 31.

William Lewis's brief tenure as provost (1618–21) was punctuated with lawsuits. Having imposed an oath on college servants 'to deal truly in their severall places', Lewis then sacked William Walter, one of the college cooks, as being 'unfitte and unsufficient'. Walter appealed to the university chancellor and to the Visitor, although without success, and then sued his successor Thomas Hayles through the vice-chancellor's court, where five fellows were summoned as witnesses. The sentence went against Walter, who had to pay costs.[62] A more significant dispute involved the Company of Ironmongers. One of their number, William Chapman, had left money in 1580 to support two poor scholars at Oriel in the study of divinity. In Blencowe's time, the college and company appears to have worked together fairly harmoniously in selecting candidates as Chapman scholars. In 1618, however, the college's candidate, Joshua Eliot, was rejected by the company on the grounds that he could maintain himself without the scholarship, and they conferred it instead on another fellow, Hugh Yale. Led by Provost Lewis, the college accused the company of corruptly backing Yale, and maintained that Yale was ineligible since he was studying philosophy for his MA and not theology. Nor, they alleged, was the company capable of making academic judgements on the suitability of candidates. The company in turn claimed that 'lately' the scholarship had been awarded by seniority rather than by need, and accused Lewis of attempting to dictate the choice of candidates. The case went to Chancery and in November 1620 was resolved by Lewis's patron, the Lord Chancellor. This time, Bacon exercised some impartiality. The college was given absolute right to elect the scholars, since the company 'cannot soe well iudge and discerne of the merit and inclination of the scholler', but he upheld the choice of Yale on the grounds that an exhibitioner might study a variety of disciplines for a time before settling on divinity. Bacon also backed the Ironmongers' demand that the exhibition should be awarded to those in poverty.[63]

The link with Bacon shaped much of Lewis's brief provostship. In 1619 Michael Wigmore, a former fellow of Oriel in search of a patron, was invited to preach before Bacon at his residence in York House, London. Bacon also wrote on behalf of Charles Child, an Orielensis, for a vacant fellowship at All Souls. Both no doubt occurred at Lewis's instigation.[64] Just as Bacon was decisive in Lewis's appointment, so he may have been in Lewis's abrupt departure. After just three years in office, on 30 April 1621 Provost Lewis acquired a licence from the Privy Council to travel abroad for three years. He resigned on 29 June 1621 and headed for Paris. The reasons for his

---

[62] OUA Hyp/B/5, fos. 33ᵛ–5ᵛ, 38ᵛ, 48ᵛ–9ʳ; CC Papers 1620/47 1–12.
[63] HUO iv. 79; OCA BT 1 I/1, I/6, I/3/1–8.
[64] M. Wigmore, *The Holie Citie* (London, 1619); All Souls College Archives, Anstis MS 5, fo. 8.

resignation were a matter of speculation then and remain so now. In the spring of 1621 his patron Bacon had been impeached by parliament, found guilty of corruption, and in June dismissed from office. As Bacon awaited his sentence, Lewis wrote a lengthy poem defending his patron, more striking for its loyalty than for its literary merits:

> O that I could but give his worth a name
> That if not you, your sonnes might blush for shame!
> Who in Arithmatick hath greatest skill
> His good partes cannot number, yet his ill
> Cannot be calld a number since; tis knowne
> He had but few that could be calld his owne...[65]

Perhaps Lewis felt uncomfortably exposed to enemies with the fall of his patron and effectively fled abroad. The London newsletter writer John Chamberlain reported alternative reasons for his resignation: 'some say for debt, some for a fowler fault, and that he was *Domini similis*', 'similar to his Master', Bacon, who was rumoured to be homosexual. In 1619 a preacher at Paul's Cross, the most celebrated pulpit in the land, had even alluded 'somewhat scandalously' to Bacon 'and his catamites as he called them'. William Prynne was an undergraduate at Oriel in Provost Lewis's time, and years later, in the course of attacking Archbishop Laud, a later patron of Lewis, could state bluntly that the provost had 'fled hence for sodomy'.[66] Such accusations were not unknown in Oxford of the 1620s, and were one of the charges laid against President Anyan at neighbouring Corpus Christi in the parliament of 1624. There may also be a less colourful explanation. Lewis spent some of his time as provost in London, attending on Bacon, and may have acquired a taste for high politics outside academic life. Certainly by the mid-1620s he undertook diplomatic business for George Villiers duke of Buckingham, and in 1627 was commended by Charles I for his work in 'some affairs of weight' in 'foreign parts'.[67] What is clear is that Lewis and the fellowship parted on good terms, notwithstanding his contested election in 1618 and his sudden resignation. The college granted him his full annual stipend, chantry income, and even fodder for his horses despite his resignation three months before the end of the financial year. In return, Lewis was a generous benefactor to Oriel, giving thirteen volumes of commentaries by Alfonso Tostado, bishop of Avila, £100 in the late 1630s to the fabric fund, and on his death in 1667 wrote in his will in the warmest terms about the

---

[65] See 'Early Stuart Libels' at http://parl.oclc.org.emls/texts/libels/; T. Lockwood, 'Poetry, Patronage and Cultural Agency: The Career of William Lewis', in H. Adlington, T. Lockwood, and G. Wright (eds.), *Chaplains in Early Modern England* (Manchester, 2013), 103–22.

[66] McClure, *Letters of Chamberlain*, ii. 243, 385; W. Prynne, *Canterburies Doome* (London, 1644), 356 and 'The Table' [index], sig. C2v. See also Wood, *Fasti Oxonienses*, i. col. 437.

[67] ODNB s.n. Thomas Anyan; DR 248; Wood, *Fasti Oxonienses*, i. cols. 436–7.

college and left a silver chalice for the chapel and more books for the library, including Brian Walton's Polygot Bible in six volumes.⁶⁸

This time the fellowship avoided a divisive election, and by unanimous consent it elected John Tolson, Blencowe's devoted nephew, to succeed Provost Lewis. John Day may have put himself forward again, but attracted no votes. Day retained his fellowship but 'not without some discontent for the loss of the said provostship', and retired to a Suffolk living until his death in 1628. He did remember the college, however, in his will.⁶⁹ Like Day and Lewis, Tolson was a theologian, who proceeded BD in 1611 and DD in 1622. The new provost was also an experienced hand at college business, having served as dean (1606, 1612), junior and senior treasurer (1599, 1603, 1610, 1614), and catechist (1620), as well as junior proctor of the university (1607). Tolson was also a beneficed minister, holding livings at Hampton Poyle near

ILLUSTRATION 4.7 John Tolson (1576–1644), fellow 1596, provost 1621–44

Oriel College

---

⁶⁸ OCA TF 1 A1/5, fos. 225ʳ, 226ᵛ, BT 1 A/1, pp. 3, 18; TNA PROB/11/325, fo. 310ᵛ.
⁶⁹ Wood, *Athenae Oxonienses*, ii. col. 412. Day left the college Erasmus's annotations on the New Testament, 'for asmuch as that booke is not amongst his workes in that Colledg library', and also commentaries on Juvenal and Persius. TNA PROB/11/325, fo. 208ᵛ.

Oxford and Marston Sicca in Gloucestershire, both on the presentation of old friends of his uncle, Provost Blencowe.[70] Tolson evidently owed a great deal to Blencowe, and was duly respectful of his uncle's memory and legacy. Soon after taking office, he had Blencowe's portrait repaired and protected with curtains; in his study he had a cabinet, frame, and other furniture bequeathed by Blencowe; and in his will, proved in 1644, he asked to be buried in the chancel of St Mary the Virgin 'neere to the corps of Dr Blencow my praedecessor and my reverend uncle deceased'.[71] But Tolson was his own man, an energetic administrator and disciplinarian, and in his time, intellectual life in the college continued to develop. A public lectureship in Greek was established in 1624, nearly a century after similar appointments at the bigger colleges in the university; more promptly, Oriel was one of several colleges to give financial support in 1627–9 for the public lectures on Arabic at Exeter given by Matthias Pasor, who had fled from war-torn Heidelberg and settled briefly in Oxford. From about 1628, the £5 charged to each fellow commoner on admission was earmarked for books for the library, which helped to swell the collection.[72]

There is no doubt, however, that Provost Tolson's greatest achievement was to complete the rebuilding of the college. To do so required energy, dexterity, and perseverance. As incoming provost, Tolson oversaw the completion of the south range in 1622–3, which was financed by the sale of timber and college plate, and the remainder of Blencowe's legacy of £1,300. A gap of thirteen years ensued before the second phase of reconstruction began. In October 1636, a series of resolutions were adopted in order to proceed with the building of the north and east ranges. Money was to be raised through a fine of £700 for a new lease of college land at Littleworth, Berkshire; admission fees from fellow commoners were to be diverted into the fabric fund; Tolson himself promised £500 or (if necessary) £600; and most significantly of all, former fellows and fellow commoners were to be asked for donations. The resolution recalled that a similar appeal had been made to former fellows in the 1530s for the rebuilding of the hall; in widening the field, Tolson was using the same fund-raising device which had been used successfully for the building of the schools quadrangle of the Bodleian and at Jesus College. Adopting another idea of Bodley's, the college opened a benefactors' book, to record the gifts of all donors, including the provost and fellows.[73]

Several of these appeals from Tolson survive in gentry archives. Writing in October 1637 to Sir Robert Harley (*commensalis*, 1597), Tolson recalled 'the

---

[70] Sir Michael Dormer and Edward Sheldon. For his clerical career, see CCEd, 'John Tolson' (Clergy ID 15685).

[71] OCA TF 1 A1/5, fo. 231ʳ, AH 3 A6/1.

[72] HUO iii. 21–2, 27, 36, 59–60, 342, HUO iv. 479–80; DR 257; OCA TF 1 A1/5, fos. 262ʳ, 268ʳ, 275ʳ, BT 1 A/1, pp. 101–11.

[73] DR 255, 284–5, 287–9; HUO iv. 138, 139–42.

mutuall respect and familiaritie between us' when Harley had been at Oriel as 'a pupill of the famous Mr Owen' (Cadwallader Owen, fellow 1584–1602), and now, 'by his sonne' (Richard Owen, currently a fellow), 'his living image, I have taken the oportunitie to renew' the connection. He went on:

> We have adventured upon a great worke, no lesse then the fabricke of a new a[nd] well composed building out of the ruines of an old castle of ragges. A taske so heavie that without farther supporte we cannot so soone finish as sinke under it.

The appeal to help with rebuilding 'your decayed mother' elicited £20 from Harley. A similar letter to Bishop Bridgeman of Chester, father of George, a commoner of 1632, produced another £10. That to Sir Thomas Cave of Stanford Hall, Northamptonshire, *commensalis* in 1608, reminded him of his generosity in giving a gilt goblet to the college, and asked for money since 'our walls are tottering'. In response, Cave also sent £20.[74] Although no building accounts have survived, the benefaction book allows us to assess the scope of this fund-raising campaign. The net was cast wider than anticipated in the college resolution of October 1636, to include former fellows and ex-commoners as well as a broader circle of friends of the college. The provost and fellowship led the way, with a contribution of £50 each, totalling £950, to which Tolson added £1,150. Sixteen ex-fellows contributed £315, twenty-eight former fellow commoners and commoners another £468, while twenty-nine tenants and associates raised £179, a total figure of £3,062 of which Provost Tolson contributed no less than a third.[75]

As expenditure rose, additional sources of revenue had to be found. In 1637 all college tenants were requested to loan the equivalent of a year's rent and, if they refused, then timber on their land was to be felled; and in 1639–41, in order to pay for the new chapel, the final stage of the reconstruction project, the college agreed to sell its presentations to three livings, and dispose of some of its plate.[76] As a result of these expedients, the rebuilding proceeded quite rapidly. Gerard Langbaine of Queen's noted in September 1639 that the college was now much enlarged, 'with a fair stately new building now almost finished, at the charge, or at the solicitation, of Dr Tolson, the provost', while a fellow of Brasenose commended it as 'a most brave quadrangle'.[77] The chapel was consecrated in the summer of 1642 by Bishop Prideaux of Worcester, the vice-chancellor and a contemporary of Tolson, who preached the sermon. At the same time, the college Visitor authorized a

---

[74] BL Add. MS 70,002, fo. 168^r; see also fos. 184^r, 188^r, 219^r; OCA BT 1 A/1, 7, 10; Staffordshire RO, Weston Park MSS, D1287/18/2 (P399/164); HMC, 10th Report, Appendix VI, Abergavenny MSS, 134.
[75] OCA BT 1 A/1, 1–11, 113–16.
[76] DR 286–7, 293–5, 296.
[77] HMC, 12th Report, Appendix VII, Le Fleming, 17; Brasenose College Archives, Legh Papers, no. 52.

change in the college statutes so that members of Oriel were now required to attend daily service in their own chapel, newly erected, rather than at St Mary the Virgin church. We know nothing about its furnishings, but given the puritan backlash taking place against Laudian ceremonialism at precisely this time, just before the Civil War, the chapel is unlikely to have had a railed altar.[78]

The rebuilding of Oriel was one reason, among several, for the loosening of ties between the college and St Mary Hall in this period. It is true that from the 1570s to the 1650s the principal of St Mary Hall was usually a current fellow of Oriel who either retained his fellowship (as in the case of Richard Pigot, 1570–8, and Nicholas Brookes, 1644–56) or resigned it on or after taking office (Thomas Philipson, 1578–87, George Dale, 1587–91, and Ralph Braddyll 1591–1632).[79] The exception was John Saunders, who resigned his fellowship in 1617, was chosen as principal of St Mary Hall in 1632, and moved from there back to Oriel in 1644 on his election as provost. In 1656 this sequence was broken, with the appointment by the chancellor, Oliver Cromwell, of Thomas Cole, a Christ Church man, who was replaced at the Restoration in 1660 by Martin Llewellin, another outsider.[80] Traditionally, St Mary Hall had housed undergraduates taught by the fellows of Oriel, in particular the six Dudley and six St Antony exhibitioners. Both groups of exhibitioners took an oath of obedience to the provost and dean of Oriel as well as the principal of St Mary Hall, but from 1592 onwards the principal was omitted from the oath, which suggests that the exhibitioners were now housed elsewhere. In fact, some remained for a time at St Mary Hall, although space became increasingly tight, as the number of its own undergraduates rose. A list of 1610 records a community of forty-four—Principal Braddyll, five MAs, four BAs, and thirty-four students.[81] As Provost Blencowe explained in 1610, several of the Dudley exhibitioners, as poor scholars, found it difficult to maintain themselves there, and 'because the sayd hall hath bene for this manie years paste verie well furnished and stor[e]d of scollers and students (thanks be to God)', they were permitted to reside in Oriel or in other colleges, provided they were ready to settle in St Mary Hall if rooms became available. In fact Dudley exhibitions were often conferred on students who had already matriculated from Queen's, since the college, like the benefaction, had close ties to

---

[78] Wood, *Colleges and Halls*, 135; OCA TF 1 A1/5, fo. 341^r, GOV 2 D3; HUO iv. 689–90.

[79] When Principal Braddyll was absent from Oxford in 1594–5, his deputy was Richard Wharton, fellow of Oriel: OUA Hyp/A/23, fos 145^r, 250^r. From the 1570s, principals of halls were usually chosen by the chancellor, though there is no extant evidence for appointments at St Mary Hall until 1656. HUO iii. 429 n. 3; Laud, *Works*, v. 35.

[80] R. A. Beddard, 'A Projected Cromwellian Foundation at Oxford and the "True Reformed Protestant" Interest, c. 1657–8', *History of Universities*, 15 (1997–9), 156, 158–9, 172–3, 177–8.

[81] OCA GOV 4 A1, p. 589; OUA SP/E/6/1, fo. 11^r. Another list of 1613 listed 41 members (NEP/supra 45, fo. 89^r).

the north-west, so these exhibitioners may have continued to reside there. The problem of lodging at St Mary Hall was finally resolved by the rebuilding of 1620–3. The annual payment of 10s. 6d. to the principal to house six Dudley exhibitioners ceased in 1625–6 as evidently accommodation was now provided in Oriel.[82]

The most radical proposal for St Mary Hall proved to be abortive. In 1657–8 a group of Cromwellian administrators, led by Bulstrode Whitelocke, proposed to transform St Mary Hall into a new college, dedicated not to teaching but to the research and publication of 'a generall synopsis of the true reformed Protestant, Christian religion professed in this commonwealth'. This would be a defence of the religious changes in England of the 1640s and 1650s as well as a fillip to promote Protestant solidarity across Europe. The idea never got beyond the drafting stage, and was probably shelved on Cromwell's death in 1658, so that St Mary remained a hall until its absorption by Oriel in 1902.[83]

The provost and fellows of Oriel rarely filled the senior academic or administrative positions within the university. Orielenses who had been undergraduates certainly made their mark, but often their links to Oriel were slender. Thus John Rainolds (d. 1607), who occupied a special lectureship in controversial theology supported by Sir Francis Walsingham and Robert Devereux earl of Essex before becoming president of Corpus Christi, had entered Oriel aged only 8 as a St Antony exhibitioner in 1557, then left Oxford to return to Merton and then Corpus.[84] The record is much less impressive for the provost and fellows. Oriel, of course, supplied a number of university proctors, including Blencowe in 1571–2 and Tolson in 1607.[85] Tolson was the only provost of Oriel to serve as vice-chancellor in this period, nominated by the chancellor, Philip Herbert earl of Pembroke, for the first year of the Civil War, 1642–3. However, from Blencowe onwards, successive provosts were drawn into the regular meetings of the heads of houses at which, under the direction of the vice-chancellor, university business was increasingly conducted, and in the 1630s was formally constituted as the Hebdomadal Board. Its activities, however, remain shadowy.[86]

---

[82] OCA DLR 8 no. 6, TF A1/5, fos. 8ʳ, 255ʳ, 261ᵛ. Blencowe himself as a Dudley exhibitioner had been permitted to spend two years at Queen's. For the link, see *Registrum Orielense*, i. 28–9, 103, 113, 115, 121, and *passim*.

[83] Beddard, 'Projected Cromwellian Foundation', 155–91; for Whitelocke, see Hegarty, *St John's*, 480–1.

[84] *Registrum Orielense*, i. 25; ODNB s.n. John Rainolds.

[85] Oriel supplied proctors on nine occasions between 1571 and 1660; see Wood, *Fasti Oxonienses*, i, cols. 187, 195, 239, 272, 320, 422, 496; ii, col. 90. Those serving before 1629 were elected by the university, and thereafter a proctorial cycle amongst the colleges regularized such appointments. See Laud, *Works*, iii. 209.

[86] HUO iii. 401–3; HUO iv. 202; see Gibson, *Statuta antiqua*, 520.

Two fellows of Oriel certainly carved out a name for themselves within the university. One was John Day, vicar of St Mary the Virgin in the years 1608–22 and celebrated as 'the most frequent and noted preacher in the university'. His writings are considered in the following chapter.[87] The other was John Rouse, who served as Bodley's second librarian from 1620 to his death in 1652. Rouse was responsible for producing the *Appendix* to the Bodleian's Catalogue in 1635, listing 3,000 new volumes acquired since 1620. Rouse himself broadened the collection, acquiring literary works such as Shakespeare's *Venus and Adonis* and *The Rape of Lucrece* as well as the political works of his friend John Milton, on the freedom of the press and in favour of divorce. Unsurprisingly, Milton's verdict on Rouse was 'a most learned and good judge of books'. It is well known that Rouse politely declined Charles I's request in 1645 to borrow a book from the Bodleian and thereby break its statutes; it is more often forgotten that he was forced to comply with a similar demand for six books from the parliamentary visitors in 1648. Rouse faced the awkward challenge of protecting the interests of the library through successive regime change—royalist Oxford in 1642–6 followed by the rule of parliament and after 1649 the English Republic—which he managed with no lasting damage to the Bodleian's wealth, collections, or fabric.[88] At his request, Rouse was buried in the new college chapel, and in his will he left twenty books to Oriel library and £20 to the Bodleian.[89]

By the mid-seventeenth century, the college had been educating two generations of undergraduates, the majority of whom pursued careers beyond Oxford and academic life. Some went into the professions, as lawyers, clergy, and physicians. Orielenses from wealthy backgrounds often spent a year or two in Oxford, and left without taking a degree, and enrolled in one of London's Inns of Court, colloquially known as the country's 'third university', where they could enjoy metropolitan life and acquire a working knowledge of common law which they would need as future landowners and magistrates. Thus Richard Best, son and heir of John Best of Allington Castle, Kent, was admitted a commoner at Oriel in 1614–15, aged 17, and two years later entered the Middle Temple. Many undertook public office, such as Robert Pierrepont (entered 1596), who, after a spell at Gray's Inn, became a justice of the peace, subsidy commissioner, and high sheriff in Nottinghamshire. Pierrepont was elected to parliament in 1601, aged only 17, through the influence of his relative Gilbert Talbot earl of Shrewsbury, and eventually bought his way into the aristocracy in 1627–8, as Viscount Newark and then

---

[87] Wood, *Athenae Oxonienses*, ii col. 412.
[88] W. D. Macray, *Annals of the Bodleian Library Oxford* (Oxford, 1984), 56–105; E. Craster, 'John Rous, Bodley's Librarian 1620–52', *Bodleian Library Quarterly*, 5 (1955), 130–46; ODNB s.n. John Rouse. Francis Yonge, MA of Oriel, served as the library's janitor (c.1644–7) and then as sub-librarian.
[89] TNA PROB/11/221, fo. 326ᵛ; Wood, *Colleges and Halls*, 135.

earl of Kingston, and thereafter took a less active part in local politics.⁹⁰ Others built a career in the law. William Prynne (1616), the anti-Laudian writer whose footnotes were so copious that he received the nickname 'Marginal Prynne', was a Bencher at Lincoln's Inn, where he resided from the 1620s to his death in 1669, and was buried in the chapel there. Others found posts in the Westminster courts or in the localities: Henry Barker (1641) studied at the Middle Temple and became a Clerk of the Crown in Chancery, while Edmund Petty (1636), a supporter of the English Revolution, became Recorder of Chipping Wycombe in the 1650s, a Buckinghamshire JP and MP in the Convention Parliament of 1660.⁹¹ Oriel's tradition in studying civil law produced a small number of prominent civilians, principally Charles Tooker (fellow 1618–24), who became official to the archdeacon of Berkshire in the 1630s, and Giles Sweit (BA 1605, MA 1611), who combined an academic with a legal career, so that by 1661 he was dean of the Arches, the principal ecclesiastical lawyer in the province of Canterbury, as well as Regius Professor of Civil Law.⁹² Medicine, another string to Oriel's bow, produced among its former fellows provincial practitioners—Thomas Cogan (fellow 1563–75) in Manchester, John Jackman (fellow 1562–84), and Henry Ashworth (fellow 1574–85) in Oxford—as well as those who worked in London. Both Matthew Lister (fellow 1592–1605) and Maurice Williams (fellow 1621–31) became physicians to Charles I and were knighted. At the Privy Council's request in 1631, Lister helped propose a scheme to combat plague by establishing an Office of Health which would supervise the building of hospitals in London and recruit a corps of specialist physicians, an ambitious plan which was shelved when the plague receded. For much of the 1630s, on Archbishop Laud's recommendation, Williams attended the Lord Deputy, Thomas Wentworth, in Dublin.⁹³

Many Orielenses entered the Protestant ministry, at a time when the clerical profession was increasingly a graduate occupation. Typical amongst them was Bartholomew Parsons, who proceeded BA at Oriel in 1600 and MA in 1603, and then took orders while reading to be BD. He became a pluralist in Wiltshire, enjoyed cordial relations with the local gentry, and published a number of sermons. These included a conventional defence of

⁹⁰ *Registrum Orielense*, i. 83–4; ODNB s.n. Robert Pierrepont.
⁹¹ *Registrum Orielense*, i. 224, 244; B. D. Henning (ed.), *The History of Parliament: The House of Commons 1660–1690*, 3 vols. (London, 1983), iii. 232.
⁹² Others were George Dale, fellow 1578–88, and Pauncefoot Wall, fellow 1626–35, who became a registrar in the peculiar courts in Hereford diocese: see CSPD (1636–7), 297. Dale, Tooker, and Sweit were admitted to Doctors' Commons: G. D. Squibb, *Doctors' Commons: A History of the College of Advocates and Doctors of Law* (Oxford, 1977), 165, 173, 175. For Sweit see also HUO iv. 691–2; Hegarty, *St John's*, 447.
⁹³ ODNB s.n. Matthew Lister; H. Trevor-Roper, *Europe's Physician: The Various Life of Sir Theodore de Mayerne* (London, 2006), 8, 171, 307–11; *Provosts and Fellows*, 85, 96; Hegarty, *St John's*, 348–9; Laud, *Works*, vii. 56.

non-resistance to anointed princes, against the views of Cardinal Bellarmine; a staunch defence of the clergy's right to tithes; and public praise for Sir William Doddington, a Hampshire gentleman, for restoring impropriated revenue to the Church.[94] Clergy often supplemented their income with school teaching, but only a minority had formal positions, such as John Barclay (1599), who in 1606 took a Denbighshire living and the post of headmaster of Oswestry School. Others taught while still studying at Oriel, such as William Wilson (1609), who was dispensed from attending lectures for his baccalaureate in January 1613 since he was teaching boys in the country.[95] Samuel Yerworth (1610) was an accomplished Hebraist, who may have remained in Oxford after graduation to teach in a private capacity. In 1618 Yerworth was ordained, served for many years in the ministry in the West Country, taught for a while in Bristol, and in 1650 published a short Hebrew grammar, *Introductio ad linguam Ebraeam brevissima*. In it, he promised a 'full and compleat grammar' were it to be well received. Whatever its reception, Yerworth published nothing more.[96]

Having benefited from a broad humanist education, and in some cases with the leisure which accompanied inherited wealth, it is unsurprising that some Orielenses became writers and poets. A good example is Robert Vaughan (1610–11), a Welsh gentleman, JP for Merioneth and a noted antiquary in Welsh history. Hannibal Baskerville (1623), on the other hand, has been labelled an 'antiquarian dilettante' who wrote little of real substance. Ferriman Rutter (1618) was a cleric and minor poet, who contributed to a collection of verses published in 1636 celebrating Robert Dover's 'Olimpick Games', which were held on the hill above Chipping Camden in the Cotswolds each year from 1612 to 1644. Rutter lavished praise on Dover, though he candidly confessed he had never attended the games![97]

The most distinguished of the literary Orielenses were two contemporaries, Francis Kynaston (1601) and Richard Brathwaite (1604). Kynaston was the eldest son of Sir Edward Kynaston (1583) of Oteley, Shropshire, and attended Lincoln's Inn and Cambridge after leaving Oxford. Elected to parliament in 1621, he joined the household of the new king, Charles I, as an esquire of the body, in 1625. In the 1630s he published three works of translation, including Chaucer's *Troilus and Criseyde* in Latin verse, with the intention that a foreign

---

[94] ODNB s.n. Bartholomew Parsons; CCEd, 'Bartholomew Parsons' (Clergy ID 73290); B. Parsons, *The Historie of Tithes* (Oxford, 1637), sig. A2ᵛ. See Chapter 5 for an analysis of Orielenses in the ministry.

[95] *Registrum Orielense*, i. 93, 125; see also DR 188.

[96] HUO iv. 460–1; Wood, *Athenae Oxonienses*, iii. cols. 276–7; CCEd, 'Samuel Yerworth' (Clergy ID 51833).

[97] ODNB s.n. Hannibal Baskerville; Wood, *Athenae Oxonienses*, iii. cols. 728–9; C. Whitfield (ed.), *Robert Dover and the Cotswold Games* (London, 1962), 95, 175–7; CCEd, 'Ferriman Rutter' (Clergy ID 81431).

audience would come to appreciate Chaucer, and to give the poem a linguistic stability which changes in the English language could not guarantee. Part of it was dedicated to John Rouse, his tutor at Oriel. In 1635 Kynaston founded the *Musaeum Minervae*, an academy of learning, with a £100 gift from Charles I, a licence under the great seal, and a grant of arms. His aim was to match continental academies and provide a finishing school for the upper classes, teaching them 'the sciences of navigation, riding, fortification, architecture, painting' and other 'most usefull accomplishments', including music and modern languages. Kynaston appointed himself the first regent, to oversee the teaching of heraldry, common law, antiquities, and husbandry; other subjects were to be supervised by six professors and their assistants. The academy did not survive Kynaston's death in 1642.[98]

Richard Brathwaite lived not in London but in Kendal in Westmorland, and was JP and deputy lieutenant as well as a prolific poet and writer; he moved easily between different genres, including elegies, conduct literature, history, and dramatic dialogue. One of his most popular works was *Barnabas itinerarium, or Barnabee's Journal* (1638), a satirical account in Latin and English of four journeys between Kendal and London. In the first part, Barnabee visits Banbury, infamous for its puritans and their strict observation of the Sabbath:

> To Banbery came I, O prophane one!
> There I saw a Puritane-one,
> Hanging of his Cat on Monday,
> For killing of a Mouse on Sonday.

A constant refrain is the charms and temptations of drink. In the third part he reaches Richmond in Yorkshire:

> Thence to Richmond, heavy sentence!
> There were none of my acquaintance,
> All my nobles cumrads gone were,
> Of them all I found not one there,
> But lest care should make me sicker,
> I did bury care in liquor.

Brathwaite also engaged with contemporary politics, producing in 1641 *Mercurius Britanicus*, a drama in pamphlet-form, which immediately ran through five editions. In it he roundly condemned the judges who had backed the king in the Ship Money trial of John Hampden in 1637–8, while vindicating the minority amongst them who had supported Hampden,

---

[98] *Registrum Orielense*, i. 55, 99; ODNB s.n. Francis Kynaston; *Amorum Troili et Creseidae: Libri duo priores Anglo-Latini* (Oxford, 1635), sig. P^r–P2^r and *passim*; *The Constitutions of the Musaeum Minervae* (London, 1636), sig. ¶2i^v and *passim*; Wood, *Athenae Oxonienses*, iii. cols. 38–9 TNA SO 3/11 (June 1636, May 1637).

including his own godfather Sir Richard Hutton. But Brathwaite positioned himself among those who welcomed justice and measured reform rather than wholesale reformation, and had some sharp digs at religious sectaries and puritan plans to remodel the entire Church. This perspective makes him very likely to have been a royalist in the Civil Wars which soon followed. Brathwaite lived until 1673, and his satires and poems continued to appear well into the 1660s.[99]

Few Orielenses in this period made their fortune in commerce and trade. The clear exception is Henry Box (1600), who began as an apprentice in the Grocers' Company in London in 1604 and by 1640 was elected its master. Box became a highly successful druggist, importing goods from Amsterdam and elsewhere which, as he explained in 1651, 'are here much wanting both in the use of phisick and surgery'. In 1641 he presented communion vessels to the newly built chapel of Oriel, and in 1660–3 with his wife Mary founded a free grammar school at Witney. Its governors were drawn from the Grocers' Company and its Visitors were four senior fellows of Oriel. It is still with us, now a large comprehensive, and renamed the Henry Box School.[100] Much less successful was Sir William Clavell, a fellow (1583–98), and later 'a great but unfortunate projector'. At Kimmeridge bay, on the Dorset coast, Clavell used oil shale for boiling salt, producing alum, fixing cloth-dyes, and finally for the production of glass. He ran foul of Sir Robert Mansell, who held the monopoly in glass manufacture, and was imprisoned twice in the 1620s, while his coal-fired glass-furnace, one of the first of its kind, was deliberately destroyed. Clavell lost £20,000 in such ventures, according to a later estimate.[101]

At the very moment when the rebuilding programme was finally completed, with the consecration of the college chapel in June 1642, the country was moving rapidly towards civil war. Oxford became the royalist headquarters in 1642–6, so that the period of sustained growth for Oriel since the 1570s came to an abrupt halt, and was followed by financial hardship, falling enrolment, and all the privations of war. The defeat of Charles I led to the parliamentary visitation of the university and external interference in the running of the college. Throughout the 1640s and 1650s Oriel remained a bastion of royalism, but with a strong streak of pragmatism, so outward conformity enlivened with the occasional gesture of muted defiance allowed

---

[99] ODNB s.n. Richard Brathwaite; Wood, *Athenae Oxonienses*, iii. cols. 986–92; Corymboeus, *Barnabae Itinerarium, or Barnabees Iournall* (London, 1638), sig. B4^r, V4^r; *Mercurius Britanius, or the English Intelligencer* (London, 1641); M. Butler, 'A Case Study in Caroline Political Theatre: Brathwaite's "Mercurius Britannicus"', *Historical Journal*, 27 (1984), 947–53.

[100] ODNB s.n. Box later gave a copy of Walton's Polygot Bible to the library: OCA, BT 1 A/1, p. 11. For his gift of a chalice and patens, see E. A. Jones, *Catalogue of the Plate of Oriel College Oxford* (Oxford, 1944), 3 and plate 3.

[101] *Provosts and Fellows*, 81; J. Hutchins, *The History and Antiquities of the County of Dorset*, 4 vols. (London, 1870–4), i. 556, 567–7, 570; D. Crossley, 'Sir William Clavell's Glasshouse at Kimmeridge, Dorset: The Excavations of 1980–81', *Archaeological Journal*, 144 (1987), 340–82.

the college, by the mid-1650s, to have recovered its numbers, revenue, and self-governance.

Provost Tolson's royalism was never in doubt. In February 1642, when parliament imposed the Protestation oath on the university, which was intended to unearth Catholics, Tolson and six other heads subscribed with a rider stressing their loyalty to the Crown. In the summer of 1642 the university lent Charles I over £14,000, to help finance the raising of an army, and £766 of this was provided by Tolson. He was acting vice-chancellor in the autumn of 1642, and served as vice-chancellor from February to November 1643, taking a major role in the transformation of Oxford from a university into a garrison town.[102]

Oriel itself housed about thirty-five royalists in 1643–7.[103] The most prominent were Charles I's lord treasurer, Francis Cottington, his dean of the chapel, Richard Steward, and one of his judges, Sir John Bankes, who lodged with Provost Tolson. There were army officers such as Sir Matthew Appleyard, Richard Conquest, and Richard Herbert; and, like several colleges, Oriel provided accommodation for a woman. One Lady Gardiner became the first woman in the history of Oriel to be entered on the college books. Several others were returning Orielenses, including ex-Provost Lewis and Sir Maurice Williams, and the college also welcomed William Smith, former warden of Wadham and once an ally of Archbishop Laud.[104] The Privy Council's executive committee met in the college, close to the king at Christ Church.

Beyond the college, like most groups and even some families, Orielenses were to be found on both sides of the conflict. Sir Robert Harley (1597) was a leading parliamentarian, William Prynne (1616) active in the defence of parliament and in the prosecution of Archbishop Laud.[105] In contrast, others joined the king and saw action, such as Francis Sandford (1602), chief engineer in the army of Arthur, Lord Capel, and William Salusbury (1599), a devoted royalist and military governor of Denbigh castle, in which he held out for five months in 1646 against a parliamentary siege until directly ordered to surrender by Charles I. Others preached up the king's cause:

---

[102] HUO iv. 691–6; Wood, *Fasti Oxonienses*, i. col. 398, ii. cols. 8, 56.

[103] *Registrum Orielense*, i. 249–53 gives 21 names, and other resident members are listed in the buttery books for 1643–7: OCA TF 1 E1/1–4. For Bankes, see HUO iv. 702. See also M. Toynbee and P. Young, *Strangers in Oxford: A Side Light on the First Civil War 1642–1646* (London, 1973), 58, 84.

[104] P. R. Newman, *Royalist Officers in England and Wales 1640–1660: A Biographical Dictionary* (New York, 1981), 3, 81, 188. Varley errs when he suggests that Lady Gardiner was the wife of Robert Gardiner, admitted *commensalis* in 1643–4, since he was only aged 16. Smith was resident in 1646–7 and not in the 1650s, as Shadwell states. Smith was accompanied by his 'most faithful servant', Richard Matthew, who later bequeathed £5 to the college: F. J. Varley, *The Siege of Oxford* (Oxford, 1932), 30; *Registrum Orielense*, i. 252–3; OCA TF 1 E1/1–14, BT 1 A/1, p. 11. Merton entertained the queen, Brasenose the duchess of Buckingham and Lord Keeper Littleton's mistress. Mordaunt Crook, *Brasenose*, 54–5.

[105] Both, however, were to oppose the execution of Charles I.

Giles Widdowes, a former fellow and rector of St Martin Oxford, was 'much valued and beloved, and his high and loyal sermons frequented, by the royal party and soldiers'. Thomas Wyatt, another former fellow and local clergyman, referred in his journal to the parliamentarians as 'the rebels' and greeted the news in 1643 of the death of John Pym, the principal opponent of Charles I in the House of Commons, with the tart comment that 'it had bin good for church and common weale if he had never bin borne'. Wyatt noted with some satisfaction that when parliamentary soldiers broke down the organ at Worcester Cathedral, 'one who did so fell and brak his limbs', a providential judgement on such sacrilegious behaviour. Sectarian excesses horrified him, such as soldiers in London ridiculing the surplice and prayer book in a procession, 'putting every leaf to their posteriors'. Based near the front line at Ducklington near Witney, at different times Wyatt had to offer quarter to parliamentarians as well as royalists.[106]

Wyatt learned of events from royalist newsbooks, which reminds us that this was also a paper war: the two sides used the press to win recruits, influence public opinion, and rebut the allegations of their opponents. Two important royalist propagandists had Oriel connections. The first was John Berkenhead, who proceeded BA and MA at Oriel before entering Archbishop Laud's service and being enticed by him to All Souls. Probably from an office in Oriel, Berkenhead edited *Mercurius Aulicus*, the official and wildly successful royalist newspaper weekly which ran from 1643 to 1645. Berkenhead was able to tap royalist intelligence at Oxford as well as finding informants in the House of Commons and the Westminster Assembly in London, and used invective and satire to press home his arguments. Parliament had to answer in kind, setting up its own newsbook, *Mercurius Britanicus*, which admitted in print that Berkenhead had done 'prodigious service' to the king, much more so than Prince Rupert had done on the battlefield. Another journalist was Bruno Ryves, lodging at Oriel, whose *Mercurius Rusticus* (1643–4) chronicled the outrages committed by parliamentary troops across the country.[107]

With limited accommodation available, intermittent plague, and the city under siege from parliamentary forces, undergraduates stayed away from Oxford and from Oriel. Eight students were admitted to the college in 1643, dropping to two in 1644 and just one in 1645. A mere handful of students were resident in 1645 and, as the royalist cause collapsed and the court dispersed, the buttery books record for May 1646 an entire community of seventeen people—the provost, eight fellows, two sojourners, William Smith

---

[106] W. J. Smith (ed.), *Calendar of Salusbury Correspondence 1553–c.1700* (Cardiff, 1954), 159–71; Wood, *Athenae Oxonienses*, iii. col. 179; Oxford, Bodleian Library MS Top. Oxon. c.378, 350, 383, 403, 405, 409; VCH *Oxfordshire*, xiii (1996), 143.

[107] P. W. Thomas, *Sir John Berkenhead 1617–1679* (Oxford, 1969), 37–8, 43–5, 57, 60, and *passim*; J. Peacey, *Politicians and Pamphleteers* (Aldershot, 2004), 189–90; ODNB s.n. Bruno Ryves. Rather amusingly, Berkenhead's reward was the chair in moral philosophy.

of Wadham, one student, and four servants.[108] At the same time, the college's finances were stretched to breaking point. Support for the king proved costly. In January 1643 the college gave 29 lbs of gilt plate and 52 lbs of white plate to be turned into coin, representing almost all the college collection of plate, and a year later paid £20 towards the fortifications of the city.[109] College audits were constantly deferred, as rent from college estates fell into arrears. Whereas total receipts for 1641–2 reached £478, by 1643–4 they had dropped to £362. Arrears began to rise, reaching £289 in 1645–6. Under such pressures, several colleges such as Balliol had to close down.[110]

In the midst of this crisis, in December 1644, Provost Tolson died. The fellowship sensibly opted for a seasoned insider when they elected John Saunders to replace him. As a former undergraduate (1599–1602) and fellow of Oriel (1602–17), Saunders had resigned his fellowship to practise as a physician, returning to academic life as principal of St Mary Hall in 1632, which he vacated to become provost. He had been a vigorous principal, stiffening academic discipline, repairing 'all chambers at his own charge' and building the hall and buttery with the chapel above in the south-east corner of the quad.[111] In 1645–6 Saunders acknowledged that, without drastic reform, the college was heading for ruin. So he adopted a series of measures to steady the college's finances, borrowing money from tenants, putting fines towards the cost of the common table, reducing the commons' allowance by half, and imposing an admission fee on *commensales*. Further savings were made on the deaths of Richard Winch, Henry Eccleston, and William Wyatt in 1646 by leaving their fellowships vacant.[112]

The same year the Civil War drew to a close and Oxford surrendered to forces led by Sir Thomas Fairfax. Parliament was determined to purge the university of its political and religious opponents, and in 1647 established a board of Visitors to ensure 'the due correction of offences, abuses, and disorders, especially of late times, committed there'. So began a cat-and-mouse game between Oriel and the parliamentary Visitors which was to continue, intermittently, until 1654. William Prynne, briefly, was amongst the Visitors. The opening salvo came in October 1647, when the Visitors demanded each head to submit all statutes and accounts relating to the

---

[108] *Registrum Orielense*, i. 248–53; OCA TF 1 E1/2–3.
[109] DR 297–300; OCA MG 2 A2; Jones, *Catalogue of Plate*, xi–xiv. The college may have also paid £70 to maintain three regiments of horse dragoons and foot; see Oxford, Bodleian Library MS Rawlinson D 912, fo. 60.
[110] DR 298–9, 301; OCA TF 1 A1/5, fos. 347^r, 352^r, 361^r; HUO iv. 720, 784–5; Hopkins, *Trinity*, 116. In 1645–7 the college withheld the stipend of John Edwards, their collector general, until 'hee brought in his arrears': OCA TF 1 A1/5, fos. 359^v, 365^r.
[111] DR 301–2; *Provosts and Fellows*, 88–9; Beddard, 'Projected Cromwellian Foundation', 159, 175–6. Two of the three commissioned by the Visitor to install Saunders were Bruno Ryves and Thomas Ryves, royalists lodging in Oriel: DR 304–5.
[112] DR 307–13.

internal government of their college. The dean, Robert Say, replied that the college could not comply, in the absence of the provost. A month later, Saunders himself declined the request, since he could not accept the authority of the Visitors, and thereby violate the 'severall oathes by me in publique and solemne manner taken', primarily to uphold the college and university statutes. Where Saunders led, most of the fellowship followed. In May 1648 they pleaded conscience as the reason why they would not cooperate, although leaving open the possibility that they might be persuaded to conform. As Arthur Acland stated: 'I shall humbly submit to this Visitation when it shall be made cleare to me that I may doe it without violation of my oathes formerly taken.' Only two of the fourteen fellows submitted immediately.[113] Expulsions followed, although when the dust had settled, Oriel escaped lightly compared to many colleges. Seven fellows were expelled, two of whom were re-admitted, presumably after they had conformed, in 1651–2. Among the survivors were Provost Saunders, John Rouse, and Robert Say, even though the latter two had been sentenced to be ejected. But the record is incomplete and it is possible a form of words was agreed on to keep them both in post.[114]

The Visitors appointed eight new fellows in 1648–9 from outside the college to fill the vacancies, and kept two fellowships vacant to help reduce the college debts. Thereafter they continued to select, or approve, the appointment of most new fellows until 1654, a sign that they did not entirely trust the college with full independence. Certainly, the provost and senior fellows were not always cooperative. In November 1648 they were reluctant to hand over the college accounts to the three new fellows appointed by the Visitors as senior and junior treasurers and what the Visitors called 'the bursar'; in 1654 the Visitors reproved the college for electing probationer fellows without permission, and then reprimanded the new provost, Robert Say, for suppressing this order and going ahead with the election of George Davenant, which was declared void. At the same time, it appears that the Visitors stood back to allow the free election of Say on the death of Provost Saunders in March 1653.[115] But we should not be too jaundiced about the rule of the Visitors. They oversaw an increase in the annual stipend of heads of the poorer colleges, so that from 1650 the provost of Oriel received an additional £92 a year. John Rouse, so nearly deprived of his fellowship in May 1648, used the Visitors' authority in October 1648 to force the college to

---

[113] M. Burrows (ed.), *The register of the Visitors of the University of Oxford, from AD 1647 to AD 1658* (Camden Society, new series, xxix, 1881), 49, 65–6, 118, 123, 537; DR 317–18; Wood, *History and Antiquities*, ii. 506, 542, 568–9, 571–2. The two who submitted were James Farren and Thomas Sheppard.

[114] Burrows (ed.), *Register*, 89, 93, 536–7; DR 315–17; HUO iv. 728–31. Sharrington Sheldon and Richard Saunders were the two re-admitted.

[115] Burrows (ed.), *Register*, cxxv, 209–11, 214, 254, 383, 386; OUA, CC Papers 1655/42, nos. 6, 10.

repay a long-standing debt of £70. One Orielensis, Thomas Weston, was given a fellowship at Brasenose by the Visitors.[116]

What was the character and impact of the thirteen fellows chosen by the Visitors in 1648–53? Six of the eight imposed in 1648–9 were Cambridge graduates, but thereafter Oxford men predominated, including two or three Orielenses.[117] The majority of these fellows were birds of passage, resigning (or in one case, dying) within three or four years of their appointment. An extreme example was Henry Lomax, who spent little time in Oxford following his admission in 1648. He served as Cromwell's chaplain in Ireland in 1649–50, and was then granted leave for two further years; his fellowship was filled by 1652.[118] But we should not assume that these outsiders never felt at home in Oriel. William Bragge, who was admitted in August 1648, made 'my loving friend' Robert Say his sole executor when he composed his will in 1652. Thomas Ofield, who may have been intruded by the Visitors in 1651–2, left legacies of 40s. to 'Robert Say, the worthy provost', 20s. to every fellow, and £20 to the college.[119]

At his death in 1653, Provost Saunders was praised for his happy and temperate rule of more than nine years, and he was the first provost to be buried in the new college chapel.[120] Certainly, by that date, the college had recovered from the dire conditions of the mid-1640s. Student admissions now matched those of the 1630s, arrears of rent had been largely recovered, all eighteen fellowships were filled by 1654, and there was sufficient income to rebuild Bartlemas almshouses, severely damaged in the Civil War, and in 1652 to reconstruct the tennis court.[121] After 1654, moreover, the parliamentary Visitors left Oriel alone. The new provost, Robert Say, had been a dogged opponent of the Visitors, and after his election presided over a period of relative peace in Oriel for the remainder of the decade. But there is evidence that the college was unreconciled to republican government and the rule of the saints. In 1650 the fellows had given money to the Scots captured at the battle of Worcester, fighting for Charles II; its students contained the highest proportion of royalist offspring of any Oxford college. Among them were John Bankes and Charles Steward, sons of two important

---

[116] Burrows (ed.), *Register*, 89, 204, 251, 268, 483, 537; Lambeth Palace Library, Arc. L.402/E16, 390–1, COMM. VIa/12, pp. 15, 109: DR 319–20, 323; *Registrum Orielense*, i. 245; Mordaunt Crook, *Brasenose*, 54.
[117] DR 315–17. The Orielenses were Charles Perrott, Robert Wolcombe, and (if he were intruded) Thomas Ofield. See *Provosts and Fellows*, 108.
[118] *Provosts and Fellows*, 107; DR 322; OCA TF 1 A1/5, fo. 375^v, A1/6 [1650–2].
[119] TNA PROB/11/291, fo. 247^v, 11/273, fo. 40^v.
[120] DR 327. His wife Dorothy remains an invisible figure, but for the gift of 'my cabinet' from one of the fellows, Richard Winch, in 1646. TNA PROB/11/203, fo. 101^v.
[121] *Registrum Orielense*, i. 200–74; Burrows (ed.), *Register*, 363; HUO iv. 707; OCA TF 1 B1/1; DR 325–6. By 1651–2 the arrears were down to £24 (OCA TF 1 A/6).

royalists who had stayed at Oriel in the Civil War.[122] In 1659 there was an unsuccessful royalist uprising in the north-west led by Sir George Booth, and Henry Carey, Viscount Falkland, tried to raise Oxfordshire. One of his leading supporters was Sir Anthony Cope of Hanwell, an Orielensis of 1649, and the conspirators in Oxford met in the provost's lodgings in Oriel.[123] Say escaped arrest, and within the year, the English Revolution had turned full circle, with the restoration of the Crown, the House of Lords, and the historic Church of England. The provost and many of the fellows could now hope to enter into their loyalist inheritance.

---

[122] OCA TF 1 A1/6 [1650–1]; HUO iv. 702, 767; *Registrum Orielense*, i. 248–9, 251, 270, 283.
[123] D. Underdown, *Royalist Conspiracy in England 1649–1660* (Hamden, Conn., 1971), 265; *Registrum Orielense*, i. 259; O. Ogle et al., *Calendar of Clarendon State Papers*, 5 vols. (Oxford, 1852–1970), iv. 387–8.

5
A Protestant College, 1574–1660

Kenneth Fincham

From 1559 the universities, and their constituent colleges, were vital allies of the state in supporting the fledgling Protestant Church of England. They were expected to promote outward conformity to the new religious order and teach its precepts to the growing body of undergraduates. At the same time, with the increasing number of graduates entering the ministry, Oxford and Cambridge in effect became Protestant seminaries from which the majority of the clergy were recruited. English Protestantism itself, however, was a dynamic not a static force. From the 1560s there was a fierce debate over the priorities and character of the new religion, as first puritans pushed for further reform and then from the 1590s their opponents began to retaliate, culminating in the counter-reformation led by Archbishop Laud in the 1630s. Further religious turmoil followed in the 1640s, as the English Revolution swept away the established Church and puritans took control, within and beyond the universities. The rule of saints in the 1650s proved to be fatally compromised by internal divisions, as puritans fragmented into competing minorities.

The impact of these developments on Oriel, and the contribution it made in return, forms the focus of this chapter. The college was slow to embrace the new religion. It never became a nursery of puritans, such as Magdalen or Brasenose, nor a home for crypto-Catholics as did Gloucester Hall. Instead, by James I's reign, Oriel was professing an unspectacular Protestant conformity, mixing obedience to the established Church with Calvinist theology, a commitment to preaching reformed doctrine, and an antipathy to the Roman Church. There were also a few more radical spirits in Oriel, both puritans and Laudians, anxious to recast religious practice and doctrine, who participated in the religious upheavals of the mid-seventeenth century. The most prominent of these was William Prynne, who became a national figure for his fiery opposition to Laudian reforms in the 1630s.

The transformation in Oriel's religious culture from Catholicism to Protestantism proved to be a protracted process, with decisive change occurring as late as the 1580s, so that the claim that the college was 'converted from popery with relative ease' is misleading.¹ In 1574 the new provost, Anthony Blencowe, inherited a youngish fellowship, all elected since the official re-establishment of Protestantism in 1559, and only one fellow old enough to have studied in Marian Oxford. William Allen, the future cardinal, had long since left Oriel along with other opponents of the new faith, but residual Catholicism remained within the college. One of Blencowe's first tasks, in April 1574, was to cite an absent fellow, William Holte, to return to Oriel, effectively a sentence of deprivation since Holte was already at the Catholic seminary of Douai, and would later become a Jesuit.² Exactly a year later, in April 1575, the college gave two fellows permission to study abroad, with the stipulation that they avoid Leuven in Belgium with its Catholic university. This concern was well founded, since one of them, Richard Barret, never returned and joined Holte at Douai. The other, John Jackman, the only survivor from Marian Oxford, might have followed suit but for the fact that he was chosen as dean that year and remained at Oxford, eventually resigning his fellowship in 1584 to work as a local physician.³ The problem persisted into the early 1580s: Stephen Rowsam, who was a student at the college in 1572 and then served as minister at St Mary the Virgin Oxford, was admitted to the Catholic College at Rheims in 1581, where he was joined in 1583 by Ralph Stanford, fellow of Oriel since 1577.⁴

At the same time, other fellows were studying reformed theology and went on to serve as preachers in the Protestant ministry. Robert Hill, fellow 1562–72, proceeded BD in 1581 and became a beneficed preacher, ending his days as archdeacon of Gloucester; another, Richard Reynolds, fellow from 1566, graduated as BD in 1577 and joined the preaching ministry in Buckinghamshire.⁵ But we know nothing of the fervour or flavour of their religious commitment. The careers of some of their contemporaries reveal a little more: John Hurlock, fellow from 1561 to 1570, dean in 1566–7, and principal of St Mary Hall 1565–70, proceeded BD in 1571, then received two Hampshire livings from Bishop Robert Horne of Winchester, who was a zealous evangelical Protestant and may have recognized in Hurlock a kindred spirit.

---

¹ HUO iii. 409–10.
² DR 167; *Provosts and Fellows*, 75.
³ DR 170; *Provosts and Fellows*, 71, 74; ODNB s.n. Richard Barret.
⁴ *Registrum Orielense*, i. 43; G. Anstruther, *Seminary Priests*, i: *Elizabethan 1558–1603* (Durham, 1968), 296–7, 330–1; *Provosts and Fellows*, 77, 199; CCEd, 'Stephen Rowsam' (Clergy ID 134029). Thomas Belson matriculated from St Mary Hall in 1582, then studied in Douai, and in 1589 was executed for treason in Oxford (ODNB s.n.). The last of these converts was Edward Catcher, who matriculated from Oriel in April 1597, curiously on the same day as the godly Robert Harley, and became a Jesuit in 1609 (*Registrum Orielense*, i. 86).
⁵ *Provosts and Fellows*, 71, 74; CCEd, 'Robert Hill' (Clergy ID 82252), 'Richard Reynolds' (132910); C. W. Foster (ed.), *State of the Church in the Reigns of Elizabeth and James I* (Lincoln Record Society, xxiii, 1926), 124.

Richard Kirby, fellow 1570–5, was beneficed in Essex and a licensed preacher, and it is suggestive that he was domestic chaplain to two bishops, John Aylmer of London and Thomas Ravis of Gloucester, who were both noted for their hostility to puritan nonconformity.[6]

In contrast to Hurlock and Kirby, Richard Pigot was a beneficed minister who retained his fellowship. Pigot was an important figure in Elizabethan Oriel. He was fellow from 1561 to 1613, senior fellow from 1601, three times dean, and principal of St Mary Hall from 1570 to 1578. His influence may have extended to religion, though Pigot never proceeded beyond MA and took up civil law in the 1590s. Certainly, his committed Calvinism emerges from the preamble to his will of 1613, where Pigot wrote of his assurance that he was one of Christ's elect and so 'to have and to enioye life everlasting'.[7] One of the students in college in the early 1570s was Thomas Holland, a St Antony exhibitioner (1569–73), who was BA in 1570, became a fellow of Balliol, and eventually a distinguished Calvinist theologian and Regius Professor of Divinity. Holland's favourite valediction was 'I commend you to the love of God, and to the hatred of popery and superstition'.[8] Clearly, then, Protestantism was making some impression on Oriel in the 1570s, but we should not exaggerate its reach. Richard Davyes (fellow 1565–83) was presented to the college living of Swainswick near Bath in 1576. Evidently Davyes had no great commitment to the work of conversion, for he was never licensed to preach by the local bishop.[9] Coleby in Lincolnshire, also in the college's gift, was granted in 1572 to William Lang, neither an Orielensis nor a graduate but at least a preaching minister, who was reported in 1576 as knowing 'but little Latin' and only 'moderately versed in sacred learning'.[10]

Greater momentum is evident from the 1580s. In his will of 1580 William Chapman, ironmonger of London and probably the brother of Henry Chapman, Dudley exhibitioner in 1564–5, left £200 to support 'two poor scholars to study divinity' at Oriel, who were to be replaced by two others when they reached the age of 30, an arrangement which Chapman intended should last 'untill the end of the world'. It was a vote of confidence in the college's

---

[6] *Provosts and Fellows*, 70, 75; CCEd, 'John Hurlock' (Clergy ID 107276) and 'Richard Kirby' (133721).

[7] *Provosts and Fellows*, 70; CCEd, 'Richard Pigot' (Clergy ID 135596); TNA PROB/11/122, fo. 28ᵛ.

[8] *Registrum Orielense*, i. 37–8; ODNB s.n.

[9] *Provosts and Fellows*, 74; CCEd, 'Richard Davyes' (Clergy ID 56436); Somerset Heritage Centre, D/D/Vc 80, fo. 21ᵛ. Davyes was near neighbours with the college tenants at Swainswick, which was not always a harmonious relationship. For over a decade there was a quarrel between the Davyes and the Prynnes, after it was alleged (inaccurately, as it turned out) that Davyes's wife Rebecca had said 'she had as leeve see a tode as to see Mrs Prinn'; Somerset Heritage Centre, D/D/Ca 220 [11 September 1620].

[10] CCEd, 'William Lang' (Clergy ID 135781); C. W. Foster, *Lincoln Episcopal Records in the Time of Thomas Cooper STP Bishop of Lincoln AD 1571 to AD 1584* (Lincoln Record Society, ii, 1912), 6, 160; Foster, *State of the Church*, 409, 424.

Protestant credentials, and the money was earmarked for poorer fellows ('*indigentes*') with an interest in theology.[11] Among these Chapman scholars were representatives of a new generation of fellows, pursuing higher degrees in theology, and they included John Charlett, fellow 1587–1603, who became BD in 1602 and DD in 1614. The three theses he defended when he took his doctorate in divinity were orthodox Calvinist teaching on grace. 'Could the elect fall from grace? No'; 'Is predestination to eternal life from God's mere grace? Yes'; and 'Whether God from his own pleasure from eternity reprobates some? Yes'. When Cadwallader Owen, fellow 1584–1602, had proceeded BD in 1603 he responded to very similar propositions.[12] A third theologian elected in the 1580s was John Day, son of the staunch Protestant and printer of the same name, who had illegally printed anti-Catholic tracts in Mary's reign and was responsible for all four Elizabethan editions of that canonical text of English Protestantism, John Foxe's *Book of Martyrs*.[13] John Day junior was a fellow for forty years (1588–1628), serving as college catechist, and vicar of St Mary's. Among the undergraduates at Oriel in the 1580s was one future influential theologian. In a college lecture in 1613 Day cited the work of Francis Mason, describing him as 'a painefull and skilfull workman in the house of God', and adding that 'I referre you the rather to him for he was sometimes of this House'. Mason had been an undergraduate at Oriel in 1583–6 before graduating BA from Brasenose, and became a champion of the reformed Church against its Catholic and puritan critics.[14] All these theologians—Charlett, Owen, Day, and Mason—also served in the parochial ministry.[15]

The office of college catechist, held by Day in 1612–13, also dated from the 1580s. The university authorities had ordered the appointment of catechists in 1579 in order to protect the young and impressionable from being seduced into Catholicism, and over the next decade many colleges complied—New College in 1580, University College in 1583, Merton in 1589, and, characteristically in the middle of the pack, Oriel in 1585.[16] Richard Wharton, a theologian and fellow from 1577 to 1626, was the first college catechist, charged with teaching the rudiments of the Christian faith to junior members. At the same time, reinforcing precept with practice, the fellowship

---

[11] OCA BT 1 I.
[12] *Provosts and Fellows*, 82–3; A. Clark (ed.), *Register of the University of Oxford*, ii (1571–1622), part 1 (Oxford Historical Society, 1887), 203, 210.
[13] See E. Evenden, *Patents, Pictures and Patronage: John Day and the Tudor Book Trade* (Aldershot, 2008). Day junior was a proud son, and occasionally drew attention to his father's work: see J. Day, *Day's Dyall* (Oxford, 1614), sig. ¶3ᵛ; J. Day, *Day's Descant on David's Psalms* (Oxford, 1620), 25, 161.
[14] *Registrum Orielense*, i. 54; Day, *Day's Dyall*, 203.
[15] CCEd, 'John Charlett' (Clergy ID 142132), 'Cadwallader Owen' (73149), 'John Day' (12112), and 'Francis Mason' (46847); and ODNB s.n. for all four.
[16] HUO iii. 326–7.

was ordered to ensure that pupils took communion regularly, which merely meant a minimum of three times a year.[17]

The labours of Wharton and his immediate successors as college catechists remain obscure, since they published nothing and left no personal papers. Only with the appointment of John Day can we examine the catechist at work, using the cycle of twelve lectures he delivered in the college chapel in 1612–13, which were subsequently printed. In them Day addressed the fundamentals of Protestantism, including the Trinity, the Creed, the Lord's Prayer, and the Thirty-Nine Articles, the Church of England's confession of faith. He did so, as he explained, 'above the pitch of catechising' and expected his undergraduate audience to be well grounded in the basic tenets of Christianity. Deploying a favourite device of James I, Day set out to defend the middle ground between the twin perils of 'popery' and 'puritanisme'. His tone was intimate, as befited a small academic society: Day mentioned personal and national tragedies—the recent deaths of his mother, Prince Henry, and Sir Thomas Bodley 'that great Mecaenas'—referred to university events, cited college customs, and praised college alumni, the exception being Cardinal William Allen, whom Day quoted but did not acknowledge as an Orielensis! Day chose to publish the lectures since the student body was constantly changing, 'some going, others comming, and every yeare some new ones' who would be able to read what their seniors had once heard, and print allowed him to support the text with numerous and detailed citations, including cross-references to some of his other writings.[18]

Day was also vicar of St Mary's, and was remembered by Anthony Wood, later in the seventeenth century, for his 'constant and painful preaching' whereby he won 'great love and respect' from both the university and the city.[19] From a number of his published sermons, preached there between 1609 and 1620, it is evident that Day was a conscientious pastor propounding a highly distinctive set of views. As Wood implied, St Mary's was no ordinary cure, combining the role of university church and an urban parish, so Day had to address his message to two separate constituencies, 'the Learned and the Unlettered', as he called them. The topics he covered were aimed first and foremost at his parishioners, and they treated the central feasts of the Christian calendar—the nativity, the passion, and the resurrection—the two sacraments retained by the English Church, and also diurnal matters of marriage, families, servants, and charity. When he moved on to expounding the Psalms, Day provided an accessible summary or 'analysis' of his argument at the start of each sermon. In conventional fashion, Day urged his congregation to take communion more often than once a year and, unusually, reproduced in print a letter he had written to a parishioner who had just received the sacrament

---

[17] DR 182.   [18] Day, *Day's Dyall*, sig. ¶2ᵛ, 1, 3, 39, 98, 131, 203, 278, 328.
[19] DR 226; A. Wood, *Athenae Oxonienses*, ii. col. 412.

for the first time, in which he outlined its purposes and enclosed some meditative readings on the Eucharist by English and foreign divines. He also supplied a preparatory prayer, to be said in private, and another as a thanksgiving after reception. Day's self-description, as 'your no lesse loving, than loved pastor', may have been quite accurate. At the same time, Day did not ignore his academic audience. Copious marginal notes were provided as 'a necessary helpe to young students', and Day printed in Latin the extracts on communion by John Calvin and his fellow Genevan Anthony Sadeel for those who 'have not themselves the books by them'.[20]

Day himself was a fervent admirer of Richard Hooker, author of the *Laws of Ecclesiastical Polity* which had appeared in the 1590s. 'The Church of England may blesse the time that ever he was borne' was Day's heartfelt view, and time and again in his sermons he cited Hooker as an authority in his understanding of the sacraments, the status of Rome as a true Church, fasting, holy days, marriage, worship, and much else.[21] We used to regard Hooker as the moderate and irenic voice of Elizabethan Protestantism, but recent scholarship has uncovered his polemical stance under the rhetoric of reasonableness, one that was both deeply hostile to puritanism, and advocated novel views of the character and priorities of the reformed Church of England. Most Calvinist conformists rather sidestepped his work, so Day's debt to Hooker is rather remarkable. But he was not alone: Hooker's memory was kept alive in his old college, Corpus Christi, by his literary executor John Spenser and by Henry Jackson, 'my worthy friend' as Day called him, who published his minor works in 1612–14.[22]

Day's antipathy to puritan practices is probably a major reason why he was drawn to Hooker. Day followed Hooker in condemning the contemporary obsession with preaching, which led prayer to be neglected. He also had sharp words about unprofitable sermons by puritan ministers, who from the pulpit attacked non-preaching bishops and fellow clergy or else discoursed learnedly about the doctrines of predestination and reprobation 'which if in a vulgar auditory they may doe good perhaps to one or two' while the rest will be 'little edified by it, if not hindred in their salvation'. Day denounced the spiritual lethargy of so many laity who 'cry out for preaching, for lecturing, for sermons' yet never practised a word of what they heard, nor

---

[20] J. Day, *Davids Desire to go to Church* (Oxford, 1612), sig. ¶4iv^r; Day, *Day's Festivals*, sig. ¶3^v, 131–3, 161–3, 168–83; J. Day, *Day's Descant*, sig. B3^r, 1–2, 32–3, 60–1, 85–6, 111–12, 148–9, 171–2, 197–8. In his will of 1628, Day bequeathed an unbound copy of the latter work 'to every householder of St Maries parish in Oxford'. TNA PROB/11/153, fo. 208^v.

[21] Day, *Day's Descant*, sig. ¶2^v; Day, *Day's Dyall*, 37, 124, 126, 289, 295; Day, *Day's Festivals*, 108, 112, 168–9, 281.

[22] P. Lake, *Anglicans and Puritans? Presbyterianism and English Conformist Thought from Whitgift to Hooker* (London, 1988), ch. 4; D. MacCulloch, 'Richard Hooker's Reputation', EHR 117 (2002), 773–90; Day, *Day's Descant*, sig. D2^v.

bothered to read the Scriptures at home.²³ Day also despised the self-regard of puritans as 'more religious then the meyny or multitude' and lambasted their strict observance of the Sabbath, teaching absurdities such as that to throw a ball or hold a wedding feast on a Sunday 'is as great a sin as to commit murder, or as if a father should take a knife and kill his child'.²⁴

Day's remarks about puritans seem to have been aimed at targets beyond the college walls. It is true that in Day's time Oriel did house two fellow commoners who later became prominent puritans, Sir Robert Harley and Sir Richard Knightley. Harley entered the college in 1597, to be tutored by Cadwallader Owen, fellow 1584–1602 and a famous disputant in his day, known affectionately as '*Sic doceo*' (thus I teach). Harley was head of the only major puritan family in conservative Herefordshire, and led a network of laity and clergy determined to evangelize the border country. Among his intimates was William Voyle BA (Oriel 1613) and curate of Llainfarwaterdine in Shropshire. Harley was elected to the Long Parliament in 1640 as a religious reformer committed to purging the Church of its popish character, and was himself a noted iconoclast, pulling down what he regarded as monuments of idolatry in Westminster Abbey as well as back home in Herefordshire: at Leintwardine, where he was patron, Harley personally broke the stained-glass windows and then threw the shards into the river Teme, as he put it, 'in imitation of King Asa 2 Chronicles 15: 16 who threw the images into the brook Kidron'.²⁵ The Knightley connection with Oriel went back to John Knightley, fellow 1513–22. Richard Knightley of Preston Capes, Northamptonshire, was admitted a fellow commoner in 1609, and afterwards became a patron of revered puritans such as John Dod and John Preston, and a member of that godly circle opposed to Charles I's non-parliamentary rule and the Laudian reform of the Church, which included William Fiennes Lord Saye and Sele, Robert Greville Lord Brooke, and John Hampden. Knightley died in 1639, but had he lived he would have probably been as prominent a parliamentarian in the 1640s as Harley. But Knightley and Harley were hardly representative of Orielenses in this period and seem to have derived their religious views from elsewhere, Harley probably from his mother rather than his tutor, and in Knightley's case from his wider family, as he inherited the mantle of puritan politician from his uncle Sir Richard.²⁶

---

²³ Day, *Davids Desire*, 51–2, 102; Day, *Day's Dyall*, 186, 213; Day, *Day's Festivals*, 124, 296, 318; Day, *Day's Descant*, 112, 128–9, 167.
²⁴ Day, *Day's Dyall*, 232–4; Day, *Day's Festivals*, sig. ¶2ᵛ, 338–9.
²⁵ *Registrum Orielense*, i. 86, 138; Wood, *Athenae Oxonienses*, iv. col. 85; BL Add. MS 70,002, fo. 168ʳ; J. Eales, *Puritans and Roundheads: The Harleys of Brampton Bryan and the Outbreak of the English Civil War* (Cambridge, 1990), 17, 29, 59, 65, 106–7, 115; A. G. Matthews, *Calamy Revised* (Oxford, 1988), 504.
²⁶ ODNB s.n. Sir Richard Knightley 1533–1615 and Richard Knightley 1593–1639; H. I. Longden (ed.), *The Visitation of the County of Northampton in the Year 1681* (Harleian

ILLUSTRATION 5.1 Sir Robert Harley (1579–1656), *commensalis* 1597–9

Oriel College, line engraving by George Vertue after Peter Oliver

The religious texts acquired for the library provide useful insights into the Protestant temper of the college. The earliest library catalogue dates only from 1625, but the benefaction book records gifts and purchases from about 1608. Sometimes the money was spent on patristic writers, such as Origen, Irenaeus, and Athanasius in 1608, but on other occasions the college strengthened its holdings in modern Protestant commentaries and polemics. In 1608–12 it bought two recent works by John Rainolds, the distinguished theologian and late president of Corpus Christi College, one against the English Catholic John Hart, a second against the claims of Cardinal Robert Bellarmine that the apocrypha were canonical texts of

Society, lxxxvii, 1935), 102–9. For Knightley ties to Oriel, see *Provosts and Fellows*, 52, 104; *Registrum Orielense*, i. 41, 122, 126.

the Old Testament; tracts by John Calvin and his disciple Beza; the two-volume *Opera* published in Geneva of William Whitaker, the most famous Cambridge Calvinist of his generation; the three-volume works of the Italian Protestant Hieronymus Zanchius, best known for his advocacy of the doctrine of absolute predestination; and the works of John Jewel, doughty defender of English Protestantism, which had just been republished under the direction of Archbishop Bancroft of Canterbury. Donations from fellows echo this interest in international Protestant scholarship against the Roman Church: Thomas Johnson, fellow 1598–1608 and a doctor of medicine, presented to the college Calvin's commentaries on the Gospels and Epistles, and *Anti-Bellarminus*, the attack on Bellarmine's teachings by the Lutheran Samuel Huber. Thomas Wyatt, fellow 1600–11 and doctor of divinity, gave Matthias Flacius's *Clavis scripturae sacrae*, a pioneering work by the controversial Lutheran in historical criticism of the Bible.[27] Their contemporary Richard Cluett, fellow 1603–16 and another doctor of divinity, preferred to donate works by Plutarch, Bonaventure, and a copy of *Piers Plowman* rather than contemporary divinity, but we can hear his evangelical accent in an unpublished sermon of his preached in October 1612. In it Cluett contrasted the centuries in which England stood in spiritual darkness under Roman yoke with the coming of the Reformation which brought freedom from 'the fetters of popery'. 'How beautifull now were the feet of them that after soe many hundreths of yeares, did by their preaching bring the glad tidings of peace and salvation to this land', and Cluett warned his audience against despising the power of preaching, and the message of preachers such as himself.[28]

By c.1600, it seems clear that Oriel was very much in the theological mainstream of the reformed Church of England, with solid Calvinists such as Richard Pigot, Cadwallader Owen, and John Charlett on the fellowship, and Richard Cluett preaching up evangelism. John Day's position seems somewhat different, as an enthusiastic disciple of Hooker, advocating views that would be popularized by Laudian reformers in the 1630s. But Day seems to have been more anti-puritan than anti-Calvinist, working within the traditional reformed theology, and with staunch Calvinist friends and patrons including Thomas Holland, Henry Jackson, and Archbishop George Abbot.[29] Nor is there any sign that Day had protégés in college who adopted his viewpoint.

---

[27] P. Morgan, *Oxford Libraries outside the Bodleian* (Oxford, 1980), 103; OCL, shelfmark D. C. V. 22; OCA, BT 1 A/1, pp. 16–19. Most of these volumes remain in the senior library, with a contemporary note on the flyleaf of their purchase or donation.
[28] OCA BT 1 A/1, p. 17; Oxford, Bodleian Library MS Rawlinson D 1016, fos. 21^v–4^r.
[29] Day, *Day's Festivals*, 25.

The college had only five livings in its gift to provide preferment to the numerous fellows and graduates hoping to build a career in the Church.[30] A college statute laid down that fellowships were only compatible with benefices worth less than 10 marks (£6 13s. 4d.) in the 'King's Book' of 1535; the statute was invoked in 1656, for example, to declare two fellowships vacant when the fellows accepted livings which exceeded this limit. On the other hand, in 1614 a new statute allowed a fellow to hold an incumbency of any value within the city of Oxford, with the intention, it seems, of retaining Richard Cluett, who had just become rector of St Aldate's, on the fellowship.[31] The only one of the five college livings worth less than 10 marks was St Mary the Virgin, which as a result was held by a succession of fellows from 1583 to the nineteenth century.[32] The close ties between the college and the incumbent came under strain only once in this period, when John Taylor, oddly presented by the Crown rather than the college, ran foul of Provost Tolson in 1625 for illegally celebrating marriages in Bartlemas chapel and for his contentious responses (*'verba quaedam brigosa'*) when summoned to explain himself. The dispute then escalated. Tolson laid charges against Taylor and then with other fellows requested the Visitor, John Williams bishop of Lincoln, to expel him from the fellowship for his open irreverence to the provost, according to the Dean's Register, although a later source claims this only amounted to a 'few indiscreet words'. Williams was impressed with Taylor, so arranged for him to resign rather than be expelled, and then nominated him to a living in his gift. Nevertheless, Taylor remained vicar of St Mary's until 1639, with his curate, John Horne, a fellow of the college.[33]

As for the other four livings in the college gift, one, Swainswick in Somerset, was regularly filled by former fellows or graduates of Oriel.[34] What is more striking is that the other three livings in the college's gift—Aberford in the West Riding, Moreton Pinkney in Northamptonshire, and Coleby in Lincolnshire—were usually conferred on others. Indeed in 1639 the college had no record of the name of the current incumbent of Coleby and had to obtain the information from Michael Wigmore, a former fellow beneficed in the area.[35] Neither Aberford nor Coleby were particularly wealthy benefices, and evidently fellows were not tempted into resignation

---

[30] *Provosts and Fellows*, 226.

[31] DR 236–7, 337–8. Cluett accordingly remained on the fellowship.

[32] *Provosts and Fellows*, 199; John Bacon, *Liber regis vel Thesaurus rerum ecclesiasticarum* (London, 1786), 787.

[33] DR 260, 266–7; J. Hacket, *Scrinia reserata* (1693), ii. 61; CCEd, 'John Taylor' (Clergy ID 17209) and 'John Horne' (13394).

[34] Thus John Rawe (1559–75) and Richard Davyes (1576–1629), both former fellows, were followed by Benjamin Tanner (1630–74), a graduate of the college. Nevertheless, in 1626, the reversion of the living had been promised to Martin Aylworth of All Souls (DR, 264).

[35] OCA, DL 14.

for them.³⁶ Yet this contrasts with the eighteenth century when all five college livings were usually held by Orielenses, even though by that date the college's patronage had more than doubled. However, the college did acquire a temporary interest in the living of Eltham in Kent, forfeit to Oxford University since its patron was a Catholic recusant, and three fellows or quondam fellows served there from 1628 to the 1640s.³⁷

Faced with this paucity of attractive college patronage, most graduates and fellows had to look elsewhere for advancement, although the friendships and connections forged at Oriel remained important. Two fellows—Thomas Wyatt and Richard Cluett—became domestic chaplains to John King, the dean of Christ Church, vice-chancellor of the university, and then bishop of London and one of James I's favourite divines, whom James labelled, rather lamely, 'the king of preachers'. Wyatt was King's first chaplain while he was vice-chancellor in 1610–11, and acquired two local livings, Ducklington and Newnham Courtenay, the latter from Ralph Fawconer, fellow 1599–1617 and patron for that turn. Cluett, as we have seen, was rector of St Aldate's, but quit the living after joining King's household in London, and received from him two livings, a canonry at St Paul's and the archdeaconry of Middlesex.³⁸ It is possible, too, that Robert Forward's decision to resign his fellowship in 1635 and move to Ireland, as chaplain to the Lord Deputy, Thomas Wentworth earl of Strafford, was influenced, perhaps even facilitated by Maurice Williams, former fellow and Strafford's favoured physician in Dublin.³⁹

Others had to struggle to make their way. Michael Wigmore was elected fellow in 1608, and twice in 1610 was admonished by Provost Blencowe, first for his rowdy drinking parties and then for frequenting taverns in the town. Perhaps in response to pressure, Wigmore resigned his fellowship the following year. He was ordained to the priesthood in 1615 and according to Anthony Wood became a 'painful and zealous preacher', but it took him another fourteen years to land his first benefice, Thoresway in Lincolnshire, despite engineering some promising opportunities for advancement.⁴⁰ In 1618 and 1620 Wigmore preached two sermons at Paul's Cross, the most famous pulpit in the kingdom, and again at York House in London before Lord Chancellor Bacon, who distributed much of the Crown's ecclesiastical

---

³⁶ OCA, DL 14; Bacon, *Liber regis*, 445, 1107. Moreton Pinkney was a perpetual curacy, and not entered in the 'King's Book'.

³⁷ Robert Forward (1628–35), Edward Witherstone (1635–6), and Richard Owen (1636–c.1646). On the first occasion, Oriel exercised the patronage: CCEd, 'Robert Forward' (Clergy ID 4057).

³⁸ Oxford, Bodleian Library MS Top. Oxon c 378, p. 228; CCEd, 'Thomas Wyatt' (Clergy ID 16131), 'Richard Cluett' (10940).

³⁹ *Provosts and Fellows*, 94, 96.

⁴⁰ DR 229, 230, 232; Wood, *Athenae Oxonienses*, ii. col. 290; CCEd, 'Michael Wigmore' (Clergy ID 105004).

patronage.⁴¹ Oriel connections may well account for both openings. The bishop of London was responsible for choosing the preachers at Paul's Cross, and it is likely that Bishop King's chaplain Richard Cluett spoke up for Wigmore, since to preach twice there in three years was exceptional, and suggests personal ties with the bishop's circle. The chance to preach before Bacon was presumably provided by Wigmore's contemporary at Oriel, William Lewis, by now provost of the college and chaplain to Bacon. It was unfortunate for Wigmore that Bacon fell from power in 1621, but it may be that his habit of courting controversy, beyond his youthful indiscretions as a fellow, hindered his career. Wigmore admitted that his first sermon at Paul's Cross, on the theme of wickedness, had been censured 'as bitter' before delivery (censuring being the responsibility of an episcopal chaplain, probably Cluett himself) and Wigmore himself omitted further passages for the printed version. Years later, in 1639, we find Wigmore complaining of 'those sparkes of discontent, latelie kindled by some insinuating colloquers' against him at Oriel.⁴² His living of Thoresway, when it finally came in 1629, was in the gift of the Crown.

That Wigmore himself never achieved higher office in the Church comes as no surprise, but it was typical of Orielenses before the Civil War, and the few that were promoted to deaneries and bishoprics usually had ties with other colleges. A notable exception was Robert Forward, son of the manciple of Oriel, successively St Antony's exhibitioner, bible-clerk, and long-serving fellow of the college (1614–35), who ended his career as dean of Dromore.⁴³ More representative was Ralph Barlow, dean of Wells 1621–31, who matriculated from the college in 1594, but took his degrees from New College and Corpus Christi. Just five bishops, four of them with Welsh secs, had Oriel connections in this period. John Hanmer, bishop of St Asaph 1624–9, matriculated from Oriel in 1592 but then moved to All Souls; Roger Mainwaring, bishop of St David's 1635–53, was a St Antony exhibitioner in 1605–7, then also migrated to All Souls; Hugh Lloyd, bishop of Llandaff 1660–7, proceeded BA and MA at Oriel before becoming a fellow of Jesus; and Henry Bridgeman, bishop of Sodor and Man 1671–82, graduated BA from Oriel and then became a fellow of Brasenose. By contrast, Humphrey Lloyd, bishop of Bangor 1673–89, started at Jesus, but took his degrees from Oriel and became a long-serving fellow from 1632 until his ejection by the parliamentary Visitors in 1648.

---

⁴¹ Michael Wigmore, *The Way of All Flesh* (London, 1619); Michael Wigmore, *The Holy Citie* (London, 1619, preached at York House); Michael Wigmore, *The Good-Adventure* (London, 1620).

⁴² Wigmore, *The Way*, sig. A2i^r; OCA, DL 14.

⁴³ *Provosts and Fellows*, 94. In a document of 1620 a 'Robert Forward' is listed as a former servant to Provost Blencowe, but this is probably a mistake for his father, Thomas: OUA, Hyp/B/5, fo. 35^r; TNA PROB/11/131, fo. 150^v.

Given that the establishment of Protestantism in Oriel coincided with the lengthy rule of Provost Blencowe, from 1574 to 1618, it is worth enquiring how much of this change can be attributed to him. Like many of his generation, Blencowe came from a Catholic background, born and bred in Cumberland in the 1540s where Protestantism was scarcely known. His religious views after going up to Oxford in 1560 remain obscure, although his steady advancement within the college and university implies that, at the very least, he outwardly conformed to the Protestant regime. Despite his longevity, Blencowe's inward faith remains a closed book: the religious preamble to his will of 1618 is unrevealing and the sixty-six books he bequeathed to the college disclose little beyond his expertise in civil law. Yet it has been observed that as provost, his closest friends included a notable number of Catholics.[44] Is it possible that he was actually some kind of crypto-Catholic and that he tolerated rather than led the reformation of Oriel's religion?

One of Blencowe's fast friends was Ralph Sheldon, a Worcestershire gentleman who was described by the Orielensis Cardinal Allen as 'good a Catholic as any in England'. For Sheldon was a notorious Catholic activist and an agent of Mary Queen of Scots during her captivity in England; he was imprisoned by the Privy Council in 1580 'for his obstinacie in relligion' and a suspect in an assassination plot against Elizabeth I in 1594. In his will of 1613 Sheldon left his 'best horse' to 'my deare and good frend' Provost Blencowe as well as a bequest to his 'good frend' Thomas Allen of Gloucester Hall, a church papist or closet Catholic.[45] Allen was also close to Blencowe, who appointed him an executor to his will. Blencowe was equally friendly with several crypto-Catholic gentry in Oxfordshire, such as Sir Christopher Brome of Holton, whose overseer he was in 1589, and Sir Michael Dormer of Ascott, to whom Blencowe left a ring in his will. In July 1608 Blencowe travelled to Spa in the Spanish Netherlands, a noted meeting place for English Catholics, and there oversaw the delivery of a jewel from 'Mrs Brome', presumably Sir Christopher's widow, into the hands of 'Mr Sheldon', probably Edward Sheldon, one of Ralph Sheldon's sons.[46]

How persuasive is this evidence? It is perilous to deduce much about an individual's religious views from the company he sometimes keeps. Catholics

---

[44] TNA PROB/11/131, fos. 150ᵛ–151ʳ; OCA BT 1 A/1, pp. 13–14; A. Davidson, 'Ralph Sheldon and the Provost of Oriel', *Worcestershire Recusant*, 21 (1973), 22–7; J. W. Blencowe, *The Blencowe Families* (n.p., 2001), 136, 141–2.

[45] E. A. B. Barnard, *The Sheldons* (Cambridge, 1936), 28–42; Davidson, 'Sheldon', 22–7; P. W. Hasler (ed.), *The House of Commons 1558–1603*, 3 vols. (London, 1981), iii. 374–5; M. Foster, 'Thomas Allen (1540–1632), Gloucester Hall and the Survival of Catholicism in Post-Reformation Oxford', *Oxoniensia*, 46 (1981), 99–128; TNA PROB/11/121, fo. 222ᵛ.

[46] TNA PROB/11/131, fo. 151ʳ, PROB/11/74, fo. 115ʳ; Foster, 'Thomas Allen', 112, 119; N. E. McClure (ed.), *The Letters of John Chamberlain*, 2 vols. (Philadelphia, 1939), i. 262, 284; BL Add. MS 72,248, fo. 63ʳ. Blencowe was to leave a bequest in his will to Edward Sheldon: TNA PROB/11/131, fo. 151ʳ.

were much less marginal in post-Reformation society than has been suggested both by Catholic martyrologists at the time and some more recent historians, and religious divisions did not usually preclude friendship. Blencowe may have known Sheldon from 1566, when Sheldon became a college tenant, and was probably drawn to him and to Allen by common intellectual interests. There was much more to Allen than his Catholic leanings: John Aubrey, a near-contemporary, described him as 'a cheerful, facetious man' whose company 'everybody loved'; he was also a celebrated mathematician and antiquary, in touch with the influential scholars of his time such as Camden, Cotton, Selden, as well as the navigational astronomer Thomas Harriot, once of St Mary Hall. Another admirer of Allen was John Rouse, fellow 1601–52 and Bodley's second librarian. Rouse commissioned a set of fine glass medallions, probably in the early 1630s, depicting Queen Henrietta Maria, Provosts Blencowe and Tolson, Sir Thomas Bodley, and Allen. Both Allen and Sheldon supported Bodley's foundation of the university library in 1602, a project in which Blencowe was also closely involved, and in 1613, when Sheldon died a relatively poor man, he left £50 to the library. Sheldon added a north aisle to his local parish church of Beoley, Worcestershire, in which he created a family mausoleum, a nice example of Catholics' attachment to their parish church even as they disparaged the Protestant services conducted within them. Sheldon commissioned verses for his parents' tomb there from Richard Eedes, the Protestant dean of Worcester and incidentally an old friend of Blencowe. Similarly, Allen had numerous Protestant friends and allies, including the Elizabethan earl of Leicester and Provost Tolson, his 'kind frend' and executor of his will in 1632.[47] Blencowe's connections tell us more about the omnipresence of Catholic networks in early modern England than they reveal about his personal faith.

Nor were Blencowe's friendships confined to Catholics. They included staunch Protestants such as John Bridges, bishop of Oxford.[48] Significantly, there is no hint in Blencowe's long career at Oxford that he was regarded by any contemporaries as a crypto-Catholic, an allegation certainly pinned on Allen. We should also recall that he was chancellor of the dioceses of Oxford and Chichester, charged with enforcing conformity on Catholic as well as Protestant nonconformists, and during the vacancy of the see of Oxford in the 1590s directly answerable to Archbishop Whitgift of Canterbury. It is

---

[47] DR 156; ODNB s.n. Thomas Allen; R. E. Poole, *Catalogue of Portraits in the Possession of the University, Colleges, City and County of Oxford*, 3 vols. (Oxford, 1912–25), ii. xxi, 107; A. Davidson, 'Catholics and Bodley', *Bodleian Library Record*, 8 (1967–72), 255–6; G. W. Wheeler (ed.), *Letters of Sir Thomas Bodley to Thomas James* (Oxford, 1926), 17, 27, 31, 40, 43, 47, 48, 59, 79, 82, 91, 94, 133, 138, 147–50, 169, 177; G. W. Wheeler (ed.), *Letters of Sir Thomas Bodley to the University of Oxford 1598–1611* (Oxford, 1927), 6 n., 10, 18, 20; Barnard, *Sheldons*, 80–1; TNA PROB/11/162, fo. 355^r.

[48] TNA, PROB/11/131, fo. 151^r.

implausible that by this time, as Protestantism became entrenched across much of the country, such important posts would be entrusted to a closet Catholic. Indeed, given the strength of recusancy in Elizabethan Oxfordshire, Blencowe's personal connections with gentry families may have been a positive asset as he could nudge them towards some form of outward conformity. His active role as provost, described in the previous chapter, makes it implausible that he was vigilant over discipline and government yet allowed others to take the lead in religion. The elimination of Roman Catholicism from Oriel, and the appointment of a succession of fellows committed to the new religion, could not have occurred without the active backing of the provost. In short, the balance of the evidence suggests that in all likelihood Blencowe was a solid Protestant, in line with the conformist temper of Oriel which he himself had helped to mould.

In the 1630s both Oxford and the wider Church of England experienced a second reformation led by William Laud, chancellor of the university and archbishop of Canterbury, who sought to combat Calvinist teaching and replace puritan practices with a Protestant beauty of holiness in the setting and performance of divine worship. In the process, fatal divisions opened up between English Protestants, as Laudians often stigmatized their opponents as schismatics while puritans accused Laud of attempting to unpick the Tudor reformation and usher in popery, and these rising tensions helped lay the ground for the puritan revolution of the 1640s. While the college as a whole quietly acquiesced in Laudian reforms, there were Orielenses who actively embraced or openly defied these changes. The most defiant of all was William Prynne, Laud's *bête noire* and, in the eyes of his supporters, a puritan martyr.

Laud had an influential voice in university affairs from the later 1620s, and in April 1630 took full control on his election as chancellor.[49] One of his first acts was to check John Tooker, MA, of Oriel, for breaching the royal moratorium of 1629 on discussing the doctrine of predestination. Tooker had preached against Calvinist teaching on grace, a view which Laud would have personally endorsed although he was obliged publicly to condemn, and Tooker readily agreed to avoid the topic in future. The following year Tooker was presented to a Hampshire living by Bishop Neile of Winchester, Laud's patron and also hostile to Calvinism, which is perhaps more than a coincidence.[50]

Later in 1630 two Orielenses, Giles Widdowes and William Prynne, crossed swords in print over the hot topics of conformity and ritualism. Widdowes was the older man, elected to a fellowship in 1610 after the Visitor

---

[49] There is no independent evidence to verify Wood's claim that the Visitor, Bishop Williams, mobilized support in the college against Laud's candidature. See A. Wood, *The History and Antiquities of the University of Oxford*, ed. J. Gutch, 2 vols. (Oxford, 1792–4), ii. 368.

[50] W. Laud, *Works*, ed. W. Scott and J. Bliss, 7 vols. (Oxford, 1847–60), v. 15; CSPD (1629–31), 260; CCEd, 'John Tooker' (Clergy ID 59874); A. Hegarty, *A Biographical Register of St John's College, Oxford 1555–1660* (OHS NS xliii, 2011), 457.

ILLUSTRATION 5.2 William Prynne (1600–69), commoner 1616–21

Oriel College

had overruled some unspecified objections against his candidature, from which he resigned in 1621, and thereafter he served as incumbent of St Martin's Carfax in Oxford. Prynne was an undergraduate at Oriel in 1616–21, but it seems that Anthony Wood was mistaken in his suggestion that Widdowes was Prynne's tutor. In their printed exchanges, Prynne stated that the two were 'fellow-collegians' and did not include himself in a reference he made to Widdowes's pupils, while Widdowes implied that his teaching role never extended beyond that of moderator when Prynne took part in a college disputation.[51] The controversy started after Widdowes had published an attack on puritan nonconformists, including a taxonomy of ten varieties of puritan, and describing them as 'the troublesome inventers of division', all

---

[51] *Provosts and Fellows*, 92–3; *Registrum Orielense*, i. 152; Wood, *Athenae Oxonienses*, iii. col. 179; G. Widdowes, *The Lawlesse Kneelesse Schismaticall Puritan* (Oxford, 1631), 10; W. Prynne, *Lame Giles his Haultings* (London, 1630), 10, 31.

of which was dismissed by Prynne as 'a confused rapsodie of vaine, idle conceits'. Widdowes retorted by condemning Prynne's opposition to bowing at the name of Jesus, notwithstanding it was a canonical duty, and revealed a professional hauteur that Prynne, a mere lawyer, would dare to meddle in the mysteries of theology being 'no publique ecclesiasticall priest' with no authority to teach. Instead, he was 'Mr Ignoramus, a young scholler, a stranger to metaphysicall divinitie', and Widdowes mocked him by reminding him of what he had learned as 'a freshman' at Oriel. In his rejoinder, Prynne did not pull his punches, portraying Widdowes as suffering from 'distractions' or bouts of mental illness, 'a poore haulting widdow in truth for braines and learning, of which hee never had two mites'.[52]

Behind this personal abuse lay real theological differences, which mirrored wider conflicts between English Protestants. Widdowes asserted the Church's authority to determine ceremonies, and advocated imagery in churches, the use of organs, and bowing to the communion table, which Prynne regarded as popish idolatry; in the 1630s at St Martin's Carfax, Widdowes created an altar at the top of the chancel, placed a depiction of the crucifixion in the east window above, and won Laud's approval for the unusual practice, in this period, of holding daily prayers in church at 6 in the morning and 8 in the evening.[53] Prynne continued to denounce in print what he saw as the corruption of religion and manners, and as a result was prosecuted by the government through Star Chamber, deprived of his degree, expelled from the university in 1634, and twice had his ears cropped. In 1637 Prynne was also branded with the initial S.L. or seditious libeller, though he chose to read it as 'stigmata laudis', a sign of praise *and* a sign of Laud. Along with his fellow defendants in 1637, Henry Burton and John Bastwick, Prynne became a puritan hero, and his journey to prison in north Wales turned into a triumphant procession.

Prynne had his revenge on Laud, after the archbishop fell from power in 1640, gathering evidence against him for his trial in 1644, and seizing and publishing his private diary. Prynne's political antennae were never very sensitive, and the diary revealed a pious and God-fearing archbishop, so that Laud actually enjoyed some regard and popularity in the last months of his life, thanks inadvertently to his inveterate opponent. Prynne always remained attached to Oriel, as tenant of the college manor of Swainswick near Bath as well as an alumnus. In 1630 he dedicated a tract in defence of

---

[52] G. Widdowes, *The Schismatical Puritan* (2nd edn., Oxford, 1631), sig. B2^r–C3^r, F3i^r; W. Prynne, *Anti-Arminianisme* (London, 1630), sig. oo*2^r; Widdowes, *Lawlesse*, 1, 10, 31; Prynne, *Lame Giles*, 1–2, 4, 11. Wood also stated that Widdowes was 'of so odd and strange parts, that few or none could be compared to him' (*Athenae Oxonienses*, iii. col. 179).

[53] Widdowes, *Schismatical Puritan*, sig. E^v–E2^r, E3i^v, F3i; Widdowes, *Lawlesse*, 89; Prynne, *Lame Giles*, 19; W. Prynne, *Canterburies Doome* (London, 1644), 72; Oxfordshire RO PAR/207/4/F1/1, p. 173, and MS Oxford Diocesan Papers c 27, fos. 266^r–72^r, 274^r–82^r.

Calvinist teaching on predestination to Provost Tolson and the fellowship as a testimony of his affection and gratitude, and in his will of 1669 promised the college 'one of each sort of my owne printed books which they yet want', potentially a landslide of a bequest as Prynne had published about 200 books and pamphlets. It appears from the library catalogue that the college declined this benefaction and acquired most of its extensive Prynniana in more recent times.[54]

Widdowes and Prynne provide two contrasting reactions to the advent of Laudianism. An Orielensis such as Richard Cluett, archdeacon of Middlesex, once chaplain to the Calvinist Bishop King of London, went with the flow, and his articles issued on visitation during the 1630s observed the new ceremonialist agenda.[55] Former Provost Lewis, too, was firmly in the Laudian camp in the 1630s.[56] William Salusbury (1599), a layman, was probably another enthusiast. In 1637 Salusbury built a remarkable private chapel at Rug, near Corwen, in north Wales. It is lavishly decorated with a magnificent painted ceiling, with four large angels projecting from the base of roof trusses, supported by carved and painted panels below, with a railed altar at the east end. Salesbury's religious views are obscure, but he was clearly comfortable with Laudian notions that church interiors should shine with the beauty of holiness, and it is a rare survival, too, as puritan iconoclasts in the 1640s and the Oxford Movement in the nineteenth century have almost obliterated the widespread remodelling of church interiors that occurred in the 1630s.[57]

We can be in no doubt as to the views of Thomas Wyatt, once a fellow and by the 1630s parson of Ducklington and Nuneham Courtenay in Oxfordshire. His private journal contains many observations on the weather and the harvest, plenty of political gossip, and reveals Wyatt to be a conformist Calvinist, suspicious of the Laudian party in the Church. Wyatt's hostility is clear from his comments on the death of various prominent Laudian bishops such as John Howson of Durham and John Bancroft of Oxford. Howson, he wrote, 'was noted to be very popish', while he gave his diocesan Bancroft a damning epitaph in 1641: 'none so bad as he before him, nor none so bad can come after him.' But Wyatt was equally opposed to the puritan agenda. He described Scottish Presbyterianism, which puritans wished to

---

[54] S. R. Gardiner (ed.), *Documents relating to the Proceedings against William Prynne in 1634 and 1637*, Camden Society n.s. xviii (1877), 97–118; Prynne, *God no impostor nor Deluder* (2nd edn., London, 1630); Morgan, *Oxford Libraries*, 101.

[55] See, for example his *Articles to be enquired of, within the Arch-deaconrie of Middlesex* (London, 1634), which includes a question (sig. B^r) on whether each minister had read the Book of Sports of 1633 from the pulpit, a requirement which many puritans tried to evade.

[56] ODNB s.n. William Lewis; Prynne, *Canterburies Doome*, 356.

[57] K. Fincham and N. Tyacke, *Altars Restored: The Changing Face of English Religious Worship, 1547–c.1700* (Oxford, 2007), ch. 6; ODNB s.n. Sir William Salesbury.

adopt in England in the early 1640s, as 'a Babilonish confusion', and subscribed to the university's petition of 1641 in favour of episcopacy.[58]

Laud proved to be a tireless reformer of the university in the 1630s, responsible for the statutes which bear his name and for a new charter confirming and extending the university's privileges. In 1637, with the suspension of his enemy Bishop Williams of Lincoln, Laud became Visitor of Oriel but was not drawn into college business. While Laud had some respect for Tolson, granting him a canonry of St Paul's in 1632, he did not regard the provost as a close ally and never chose him to be vice-chancellor. Indeed Oriel seems to have largely escaped Laud's notice: as a prisoner in the Tower in the early 1640s, with time on his hands, Laud compiled a history of his chancellorship, in which the college scarcely features. It is telling that whereas Laud often noted building projects being undertaken by the university or by individual colleges, he makes no mention of the rebuilding at Oriel in the late 1630s.[59]

Quite clearly, Oriel was no Laudian powerhouse in the 1630s, though it was prepared to countenance a statue of the Virgin and child in the centre of the new east façade, opposite the gatehouse, similar to that erected by one of Laud's chaplains above the new porch of St Mary's. The latter proved to be more controversial at the time, because it adorned a religious building, but the college statue was deemed to be unacceptable in Interregnum Oxford and was removed in 1651.[60] It is significant, too, that Orielenses played very little part in the petition of 1642 against Laud's controversial rule in the university as chancellor.[61] Oriel's conformity in the 1630s clearly did not impress Sir Robert Harley, once a fellow commoner and more recently a contributor to the college building fund, who was a prominent puritan and critic of Laud. In 1639 he sent his son Ned to Oxford, placing him not in Oriel but in the godly society of Magdalen Hall, to be tutored by Edward Perkins, a committed Calvinist and future Presbyterian.[62]

A harbinger of troubles to come in the 1640s and 1650s was the sermon preached on 1 September 1640 to the honourable artillery company in London, just days after the Scottish covenanters had invaded England, by Calybute Downing, an Orielensis who had a doctorate in civil law from Cambridge. Downing denounced the evil councillors advising Charles I, and advocated armed resistance against his regime. 'Extraordinary times…allow

---

[58] Oxford, Bodleian Library MS Top. Oxon. c 378, pp. 258, 313, 318, 320.
[59] CCEd, 'John Tolson' (Clergy ID 15685); Laud, *Works*, v. 47, 62, 84, 115, 123, 142–3, 174.
[60] HUO iv. 160; OCA TF 1 A1/6 [1651–2].
[61] HUO iv. 693; Oxford, Bodleian Library Bodley MS 594, fos. 137^r–138^r lists 93 of the signatories. They include three Orielenses (Francis Croft, George Clerke, and Richard Freeman); a fourth, identified as 'Tho Horne' of Oriel, is probably a mistake. No Thomas Horne was at Oriel, and John Horne, fellow 1617–48, was unlikely to have signed the petition.
[62] BL Add. MS 70,002, fos. 168^r, 299^r; Eales, *Puritans and Roundheads*, 26, 108; HUO iv. 209; A. G. Matthews, *Calamy Revised* (Oxford, 1988), 386–7.

extraordinary undertakings.'[63] Parliament's victories in the two Civil Wars of the 1640s unleashed a religious revolution across the country. As we have seen, the university was subject to a parliamentary visitation in 1648, followed by ejections from college fellowships and university posts. The established Church of England was largely dismantled, with the abolition of the royal supremacy, episcopacy, cathedrals, and church courts, while in the parishes, many ministers were ousted and the Book of Common Prayer banned from public worship. Puritanism itself broke into numerous rival sects, and in the 1650s there emerged a state Church of sorts, partially Presbyterian in its government, broadly Calvinist in its theology, and godly in its practices and aspirations. Like so many other societies and individuals, Oriel adjusted to these changes without ever embracing the new order.

In the mid-1640s many country clergy lost their livings on parliamentary authority either for political and religious 'malignancy', that is say, for royalism, attachment to Laudian ritual, the Book of Common Prayer, and episcopacy, or for 'scandalous' behaviour in the conduct of their ministry. Several Orielenses were among these ejected ministers, including Richard Owen, fellow 1628–38, who was removed from Eltham in Kent and the city living of St Swithin in London.[64] The charges against Owen read as primarily political: he was accused of failing to stir up his parishioners when he was obliged to read parliamentary declarations from the pulpit and, together with his friends, of 'being favourers of malignants'. Under attack, Owen turned for help to Sir Robert Harley MP, a powerful figure in Westminster politics, and once the pupil of Owen's father Cadwallader; Owen, indeed, had cultivated relations with the family as recently as the late 1630s. As he explained to Harley, his difficulties actually arose from his refusal to renounce episcopacy. We do not know if Harley took up Owen's cause, but in any event the appeal was unsuccessful, and Owen was ejected.[65]

The purges at Oxford came a little later in the decade, with the parliamentary visitation of 1648 resulting in the expulsion of seven fellows of Oriel who refused to accept its authority.[66] One of the seven was John Horne, a senior fellow elected in 1617, theologian and formerly vicar of Headington, who then retired into private life. His will of 1658 contains a remarkable list of benefactions to nearly thirty royalists and episcopalians who had suffered in the 1640s, some of whom subsequently had made their peace with the English Republic, but others who remained implacably opposed to Cromwell and to service in his state Church. Among the beneficiaries were Gilbert

---

[63] *Registrum Orielense*, i. 188; J. S. A. Adamson, *The Noble Revolt* (London, 2007), 67–9.
[64] A. G. Matthews, *Walker Revised* (Oxford, 1948), 54–5. Others were James Battye, Richard Cluett, John Gandy, William Lewis, and Thomas Wyatt (Matthews, *Walker Revised*, 42, 44–5, 112, 186, 301).
[65] BL, Add. MSS 70,002 fos. 184^r, 188^r, 219^r, and 70,004, fo. 174^r.
[66] DR 315.

Sheldon, former warden of All Souls and future archbishop of Canterbury, Richard Bayly, formerly president of St John's and nephew to Laud, George Wild, once chaplain to Laud, and Bruno Ryves, royalist journalist and dean of Chichester, as well as fellow Orielenses Richard Owen, Henry Chamberlaine, Charles Tooker, and John Berkenhead. Several clergy were also given funds to be distributed to other needful 'ministers of Christ' known to them. Such charity towards royalists and episcopalians in the 1650s was common enough, but Horne's will is striking for its lengthy list of names.[67]

Was the religious character of the college much altered by the introduction of the thirteen new fellows by the parliamentary Visitors between 1648 and 1654? This seems unlikely. Most, as we have already noted, remained on the fellowship for only three or four years. Undoubtedly, some of the thirteen were zealous evangelicals. John Eston, fellow 1648–52, left Oriel to join the preaching fraternity in the city of London, where, as he put it, he 'laid open the unsearchable riches of Christ' and published a sermon preached at a lecture or 'exercise' at St Thomas Apostle, in which he commented on that perennial puritan aspiration, the reformation of the parish clergy. He claimed that a 'dark ministry' operated in many parts of the country consisting of 'corrupt opinions and misunderstandings of the grace of God to sinners, of a loose Gospel unbecoming life', in contrast to the situation here in London:

> Having ministers like fixed stars, who by the sweet distillation of their lips teach, by an orderly and regular motion of their lives confirm, and by both enlighten many, with such orient pearls, the Churches, in some places, like a bright sky in a clear evening, sparkle and are bespangled.

Like Samuel Dix, fellow 1649–57, and Henry Long, fellow 1649–52, Eston was evidently ordained as a Presbyterian. At the Restoration, as the old order returned, the three quietly accepted episcopal orders, government by bishops, and the Prayer Book and continued to work in the parochial ministry. None was evidently a radical firebrand. In contrast, Benjamin Way (fellow 1653–5) was ejected for nonconformity in 1662 and later became a Congregationalist.[68]

The college itself trained up several Presbyterians, who were ejected for refusing to accept the Act of Uniformity of 1662. One was John Berry, who proceeded MA at Oriel in 1653, and in the same year secured a testimonial from Provost Say and five fellows certifying his learning and probity. Berry became rector of East Down in Devon, and was an active preacher in the south-west. At the Restoration, Berry was prepared to receive re-ordination by a bishop in 1661 but decided not to take the Act of Uniformity and was

---

[67] TNA PROB/11/281, fos. 209^r–10^r; K. Fincham and S. Taylor, 'Episcopalian Conformity and Nonconformity 1640–1660', in J. McElligott and D. L. Smith (eds.), *Royalists and Royalism during the Interregnum* (Manchester, 2010), 27–8.

[68] John Eston, *The Falling Stars* (London, 1653), sig. A2^v, 11; CCEd, 'John Easton' (Clergy ID 87909), 'Samuel Dix' (87786), and 'Henry Long' (126174); Matthews, *Calamy Revised*, 515.

ipso facto deprived of his living. In 1672 he was licensed as a Presbyterian at Barnstaple, and was commended by the celebrated puritan divine Richard Baxter as 'an extraordinary humble, tender-conscienced, serious, godly, able minister'.[69] A second was James Farren, first an undergraduate and then a fellow (1634–51) of Oriel, who submitted to the parliamentary Visitors in 1648, only to be removed by them from the vicarage of St Mary's the following year for reasons which remain unclear. Farren resigned his fellowship in 1651 to take a living, probably Middleton Stoney in Oxfordshire. At the Restoration, he secured his title by obtaining a presentation from the Crown in 1660, but like Berry found the Act of Uniformity to be the stumbling block, and in the autumn of 1662 was deprived of his living.[70] The fact that a number of fellows and students at Oriel in the 1640s and 1650s actively supported the puritan revolution did not, in itself, necessarily change the traditionally moderate Protestantism of the college as a whole. The treasurers' accounts for 1653–4 record the payment of 5s. 6d. to bind together the works of Henry Hammond, already revered as the principal champion of episcopalianism against its puritan and Catholic enemies. Opponents as well as supporters bought Hammond's writings, of course, but to collect together his various pamphlets into a single volume suggests commitment to his viewpoint.[71]

Out in the wider country, several Orielenses emerged in the 1640s and 1650s as supporters of religious reform. One was Edward Buckler (matriculated 1628), beneficed in Dorset and then the Isle of Wight, who became a pillar of Hampshire's godly community in the 1650s. His patron was William Sydenham, army officer and a member of Oliver Cromwell's protectorate council, and it was probably through Sydenham that Buckler served as one of Cromwell's chaplains.[72] On the other hand, very few religious sectaries attended the college. Perhaps the most influential, Robert Towne, had been active long before the Civil War. Towne had entered Oriel in 1612, proceeded BA in 1614, and was then ordained into the ministry. By the late 1620s he had become a leading Antinomian, part of an underground splinter group within English Protestantism which proclaimed that Christians were freed from the burdens of the Mosaic law and attacked conventional puritan piety, such as the strict observance of the Sabbath, for being shaped by obsessive adherence

---

[69] Matthews, *Calamy Revised*, 52; E. Calamy, *A Continuation of the Account of the Ministers, Lecturers, Masters and Fellows of Colleges, and Schoolmasters, who were ejected and silenced*, 2 vols. (London, 1727), i. 370–1.

[70] *Provosts and Fellows*, 101–2; CCEd, 'James Farren' (Clergy ID 14806).

[71] OCA TI 1 A1/6, [1653–4].

[72] Matthews, *Calamy Revised*, 84–5; E. Buckler, *God All in All: or the Highest Happines of the Saints* (London, 1655), sig. A4i^r; ODNB s.n. William Sydenham. Other examples would be Robert Bath and Humphrey Saunders who, like Buckler, were ejected for nonconformity in 1662. Matthews, *Calamy Revised*, 36, 426.

to the moral law. Towne's task was 'to oppose that Antichristian darknes and fleshly wisdome that reignes in the children of disobediences', which brought him into trouble with the ecclesiastical authorities, and he was twice imprisoned before 1640. Given that his target was puritan divinity, Towne experienced more problems thereafter, this time from the newly empowered puritans: he was condemned by the Westminster Assembly of divines, mostly Presbyterians and Independents, and in 1648 removed from his curacy by the Presbyterian classis at Bury in Lancashire. By 1655 Towne had acquired the curacy at Haworth in Yorkshire from where, unsurprisingly, he was ejected in 1660.[73]

A younger Orielensis, James Browne, was in residence from 1635, proceeded BA in 1638, and was ordained in 1638–9. Sometime in the 1640s he renounced the Church of England, and emerged by the early 1650s as a General Baptist, describing himself as 'through mercy a preacher of the faith which once he destroyed'. He regarded the traditional ministry as anti-Christian and defended separation as a requirement of Christ, advocated adult baptism, and maintained Christ's promise of salvation as open to all, just the sort of teaching on grace that John Eston condemned. For these views 'are we counted the troublers of Israel, such as turn the world upside down, ringleaders of Sects'. Browne participated in several public disputations, a distinctive feature of the religious culture of these years, including one in Ellesmere parish church in April 1656 as moderator for another Baptist, Henry Haggar, against Thomas Porter, a local Presbyterian minister, on the subject of infant baptism. From the hostile account we have of this debate, which was held in front of several thousand people and lasted five hours, Browne was not a persuasive disputant, and grew frustrated: 'it was observed, that Mr Brown for very indignation did gnash with his teeth, as if he would have bitten; and did knit his fist together, as if he would have beaten Mr Porter therewith.' The experiences of both Towne and Browne in the 1640s to 1650s testify to the ways in which puritanism often came to devour itself.[74]

In the 1650s, with Cromwell's rule looking impregnable and little prospect of an imminent return of Crown or episcopacy, a number of ejected fellows and sequestered clergy made their way back into the national Church, among them some Orielenses. Henry Chamberlaine had been expelled from the

---

[73] ODNB s.n. Robert Towne; D. Como, *Blown by the Spirit: Puritanism and the Emergence of an Antinomian Underground in pre-Civil-War England* (Stanford, Calif., 2004), 310–13 and passim; R. Towne, *A Re-assertion of Grace, or, Vindiciae Evangelii. A Vindication of the Gospell-truths, from the unjust censure and undue aspersions of Antinomians* (London, 1654), sig. A3i^v; Matthews, *Calamy Revised*, 489–90.

[74] ODNB s.n. James Brown [Browne]; J. Browne, *Scripture-Redemption freed from Men's Restrictions* (London, 1653), sig. a^r, a2^r, 1, 5, 16, 61–2; *A True and Faithfull Narrative (for substance) of a Publique Dispute between Mr Tho. Porter, & Mr Hen. Haggar; concerning Infant-Baptism* (London, 1656), sig. A3^r and passim.

fellowship in 1648, and for a time worked unofficially as a schoolmaster and unordained preacher in Shillingford, Berkshire, before obtaining formal permission to hold these posts. In 1656 he was then admitted to the vicarage of Haslingfield in Cambridgeshire having been approved by the Triers, the gatekeepers to the ministry established by Cromwell in 1654. Having outwardly conformed, Chamberlaine then resorted to Bishop Skinner of Oxford to receive episcopal ordination, although this was prohibited by parliamentary ordinance. Chamberlaine was one of hundreds priested illegally in the 1650s, but the only known Orielensis so to do.[75]

Another former fellow was Richard Owen, as we have seen ejected from his livings in the mid-1640s, who continued to live in Eltham, and operate outside official channels. He struck up a friendship with a neighbour, John Evelyn, royalist, virtuoso, and diarist. Owen was an eye-witness, it seems, to the execution of Charles I and went home to tell Evelyn of all the 'circumstances' of that day. Between 1649 and 1657 Owen acted as the Evelyn family's unofficial household chaplain at Sayes Court, preaching and using the proscribed prayer book for the rites of baptism, communion, and churching after childbirth, sometimes in the library, sometimes in the parlour, sometimes in the study, and, once, for a christening in front of neighbours and friends, in the little drawing room. In one of these sermons, in 1653, Owen offered solace for beleaguered Anglicans such as Evelyn. Preaching on the text from Luke 18, 'And shall not God avenge his own elect, which cry out day and night unto him?', Owen observed that just as God had protected the Church of England in times past from its enemies such as the Gunpowder plotters, so he would avenge his servants and deliver his Church. 'Wherfore, even at her present diminution, we should not faint, or despond, but reinforce our devotions to God...the time onely is to be to left to God...deliverance will certainly come at last.' After 1660 Evelyn came to regard the sermon as 'a kind of prophesie'.[76] Owen, too, eventually made his peace with the Cromwellian regime. In 1656 he petitioned Cromwell's council for a licence to preach, and in 1657 was admitted by the Triers to the living of North Cray in Kent.[77] Provost Say may have followed suit, if it is the case that he took a living at nearby Orpington in 1659.[78] As these examples demonstrate, by the end of the

---

[75] Matthews, *Walker Revised*, 32; CCEd, 'Henry Chamberlaine' (Clergy ID 5145); K. Fincham and S. Taylor, 'Vital Statistics: Episcopal Ordination and Ordinands in England, 1646–60', EHR 126 (2011), 319–44. Among Chamberlaine's gifts to the library were works by Richard Hooker and Lancelot Andrewes, both lionized by Laudians. See OCA BT 1 A/1, pp. 25–6; OCL shelfmarks E c 23, E f 13.

[76] BL Add. MSS 78,298, fo. 45^r and 78,364, fo. 31^r; E. S. de Beer (ed.), *The Diary of John Evelyn*, 6 vols. (Oxford, 1955), ii. 547, 552, iii. 75, 76, 79, 89, 90, 94, 144–5, 147, 195.

[77] Matthews, *Walker Revised*, 54–5; another example would be John Gandy, ejected in 1645 and back in a benefice by 1652 (Matthews, *Walker Revised*, 112).

[78] *Provosts and Fellows*, 102.

1650s, the Cromwellian Church was well stocked with clergy who were not its natural allies.

Oriel's history from 1570 to 1660, traced over the last two chapters, was largely shaped by its standing as a smallish college with limited resources. It was rarely at the forefront of major developments and tended to follow the flow rather than to direct it. Senior posts in the university habitually fell elsewhere, and only one fellow of Oriel from this period became a bishop.[79] Nevertheless, the fellowship included some influential figures beyond the walls of Oriel, notably John Rouse, for over thirty years Bodley's second librarian, who protected and advanced the interests of the university library, above all in the difficult decade of the 1640s. Another was John Day, fellow for forty years, who was an energetic teacher and conscientious pastor, preaching an idiosyncratic blend of Jacobean Calvinism and Hookerian theology. The provosts at this time emerge as men of calibre and some steel. Three of them—Blencowe, Lewis, and Tolson—supervised the complete rebuilding of the college between 1613 and 1642, an unprecedented achievement in this period.[80] Oriel was certainly no theological powerhouse, and none of the fifty of so translators of the King James Bible was a fellow of Oriel. Indeed, the ex-fellow who contributed most to religious controversies in this period was not a Protestant but a Catholic—Cardinal William Allen. That said, the college did produce a large number of learned Protestant clergy who made their mark in their localities, such as Giles Widdowes in Oxford, Bartholomew Parsons in Wiltshire, and Richard Owen in Kent.[81] The first two generations of Oriel undergraduates were later to be found in many walks of life, as MPs, lawyers, JPs, teachers, literati, court physicians, businessmen. Many Orielenses seem to have been episcopalian in religion and royalist in politics. Yet the college also bred more nonconforming, radical spirits—Harley and Prynne who attacked Laud, Towne who pushed the unpopular Antinomian ideas, Petty and Buckler who prospered in republican England. In 1660 not all Orielenses would have welcomed the restoration of the Crown and established Church.

[79] Namely Humphrey Lloyd, fellow 1631–48, and bishop of Bangor, 1673–89.
[80] The rebuilding of University College began in the 1630s, but was not completed until the late 1670s.
[81] Two of the translators, John Rainolds and Thomas Holland, were Orielenses, though both had made their name at other colleges.

6

Politics and Interest, 1660–1781

Paul Seaward

It was at Oriel that the Restoration at Oxford began: at least, it was at Oriel that the commission established by the Marquis of Hertford on 14 June 1660, two weeks after Charles II's arrival in London, for the visitation of the university began its work. About a month after this, Hertford's commission was superseded by a royal one, which was given statutory authority by the end of the year.[1] The visitation would reinstate members of the university and colleges who had been illegitimately removed from their places during the 1648 parliamentary visitation or subsequently. At Oriel, two fellows ejected in 1648—John Duncombe and Henry Chamberlaine—were restored, and Samuel Carter, an intruded fellow, was removed. A former head butler, Roger Fry, petitioned for, and obtained, his own restoration to his position, usurped by Thomas Newman in 1654.[2] Compared to the changes at other colleges, the impact of the visitation at Oriel was minimal. Oriel and Provost Say, who sat as one of the commissioners, had earned a reputation for stout royalism during the Interregnum, one of the 'Sanctuaries of Loyalty', according to the royalist propagandist and old member David Lloyd.[3] The provost and several of the fellows—George Davenant, Thomas Sheppard, John Broderwick, and George Moore—underlined their loyalty with their

---

[1] 'The Restoration Visitation of the University of Oxford and its Colleges', ed. F. J. Varley, *Camden Miscellany*, 18 (Camden Society, 3rd series, lxxix (1948)), vi–ix. For a full modern account of the visitation and the politics surrounding it, see R. A. Beddard, 'The Origin of Charles II's Visitation of the University of Oxford in 1660', *Parliamentary History*, 24 (2005), 261–94.

[2] 'The Restoration Visitation', 19, 24–5.

[3] David Lloyd, *Memoires of the lives, actions, sufferings & deaths of those noble, reverend and excellent personages that suffered* (1668), 541. See Hearne, *Collections*, ii. 331: 'David Lloyd of Oriel college has publish'd several books, some of wch he was asham'd of. One of them containing memoirs of those that sufferd for ye Cause of King Charles Ist and the chiefe Sufferers, which has been lately reprinted on one side of a Broad sheet, but much better done, & it hangs up in the Chambers of several honest Gentlemen.'

contributions to a set of celebratory verses on the Restoration.[4] Despite the favour in which he was held by the Restoration regime, Say, however, had unfortunate connections.[5] As the Christ Church student James Heath pointed out, his brother, William Say, had been one of the regicides, 'a well-practised but ill counselled Lawyer'. For Provost Say's sake, wrote Heath, 'I will speak no more of him, till Justice finde him, for he is fled'.[6]

Perhaps it was this that prevented Say from reaping the full benefit of his loyalism. Several of his fellow commissioners—Thomas Barlow, Walter Blandford, Thomas Lamplugh—scaled the heights of the Restoration Church, while Say received no senior preferment.[7] Perhaps Say's modest rewards reflected the relatively undistinguished character of Oriel's standing among the Restoration establishment. There were former Oriel members among senior figures in the Restoration Church establishment: Humphrey Lloyd[8] became dean of St Asaph in 1663 and bishop of Bangor in 1673; Henry Bridgeman[9] was appointed dean of Chester in 1660 and bishop of Sodor and Man in 1671; William Lloyd[10] was dean of Bangor from 1672 and bishop of St Asaph from 1680 and went on after the Revolution to serve the sees of Coventry and Lichfield, and Worcester. In the civil state, William Prynne[11] remained a prominent political figure after the Restoration, if no longer a very influential one; John Berkenhead[12] was a key propagandist; Sir William Scroggs[13] a Whiggish Chief Justice of the King's Bench from 1678 to 1681; John Holt[14] was Chief Justice of the King's Bench after the Revolution of 1689. But it was a meagre haul. The clergy, moreover, were in the least attractive senior positions in the Church and were (except Humphrey Lloyd) more closely identified with other colleges where they had held fellowships. The gathering of mostly ex-Oriel politicians at the college in March 1681 to attend the Oxford parliament included no very significant figures.[15] Only a

---

[4] *Britannia Rediviva* (Oxford, 1660).

[5] For the views on Say of Gilbert Sheldon, appointed bishop of London later that year and archbishop of Canterbury in 1663, see Beddard, 'The Origin of Charles II's Visitation', 264 n. 27.

[6] James Heath, *A chronicle of the late intestine war in the three kingdoms of England, Scotland and Ireland* (London, 1676), 201.

[7] He was instituted to the rectory of Marsh Gibbon, Buckinghamshire, a living in the king's gift, in September 1661 (Clergy of the Church of England database).

[8] Adm. BA, January 1630, elected fellow, October 1631 (*Provosts and Fellows*, 100).

[9] Matric. 12 October 1630; see on him and the following members of the college *Registrum Orielense*, i, s.n.

[10] Matric. 25 March 1639.

[11] Matric. 24 April 1618.

[12] Matric. 13 June 1634 (Berkinhead).

[13] Matric. 17 May 1639.

[14] Matric. 31 July 1658.

[15] Among the additional names listed in the buttery book from 18 March are the following members of one or other House: Theophilus Hastings, earl of Huntingdon; Humphrey Lloyd, bishop of Bangor; Sir Nathaniel Napier (matric. 16 March 1654, MP, Corfe Castle); Sir John Borlase (matric. 31 July 1658, MP Chipping Wycombe); Sir Thomas Putt (matric. 10 July 1661,

handful of fellows of Oriel during the Restoration were involved in activities likely to obtain for them prominent positions in the administration of Church or state. Charles Perrott[16] worked for undersecretary of state Joseph Williamson on compiling the government's newsbooks from about 1665 to 1671; George Moore[17] died in Spain in 1668 in attendance on the English ambassador, the earl of Sandwich; John Haslewood served as chaplain to the Lord Lieutenant of Ireland.[18] Of the Restoration fellowship, only John Robinson, who went to Sweden in 1677 to accompany his sister, the wife of the envoy to Stockholm, and ended up himself as English agent there, and later bishop of London and Lord Privy Seal, would secure real distinction.[19]

The lack of distinction among the Oriel fellowship is in some ways surprising. Oriel's eighteen fellows were chosen from among those who had already taken the BA degree. There were no junior, undergraduate, members on Oriel's foundation, and unlike fellowships in most colleges, Oriel fellowships were not restricted to matriculated members but open to all graduate members of the university. There were some restrictions: the four Frank fellowships were limited to men from Somerset, Devon, Wiltshire, and Dorset; the Carpenter fellowship was reserved for men from the diocese of Worcester, and there was a similar restriction for one of the primary

---

MP Honiton); Sir Francis Warre (matric. 16 October 1674, MP 1685); Sir Richard Wenman (matric. 27 June 1673, MP Brackley); Sir Robert Owen (matric. 20 April 1674, MP Merioneth); William Trenchard (matric. 7 December 1660, MP Westbury); Richard Fownes (matric. 28 February 1668, MP Corfe Castle); John Ashe (matric. 14 May 1671, MP Westbury); Scorey Barker (matric. 17 May 1667, MP Wallingford); Mr Walker (?Thomas Walker, MP Exeter); and in the following week, Sir Thomas Exton (Trinity Hall, Cambridge, 1647, MP Cambridge University). All had left by the week beginning 1 April except for Sir Robert Owen who remained until 10 April. Shadwell, *Registrum Orielense*, i. 364–6, provides a full list of the additional names.

[16] Matric. 9 April 1647, elected fellow, April 1652.

[17] Wood, *Athenae Oxonienses: an Exact History of all the Writers and Bishops who have had their Education in the most Ancient and Famous University of Oxford... The Second Volume* (1692), 283. More's absence abroad (and allowance of commons while away) is noted in the Dean's Register, OCA GOV 4 A1 at 5 August 1667, and his death at 28 July 1668.

[18] Admitted probationer, 28 January 1669. Shadwell has him as chaplain to the duke of Ormonde in 1685; Wood (*Athenae Oxonienses. the Second Volume*, 897), refers to him as chaplain to the 2nd earl of Clarendon while he was Lord Lieutenant in 1685. Ormonde lost his commission on the death of Charles II in February 1685, and Haslewood was presumably chaplain to both viceroys. Haslewood resigned his fellowship in 1694 on presentation to the prestigious living of St Olave's, Southwark. Haslewood preached the funeral sermon on the death of Charles Perrott in 1677, although no copy has been found: Wood, *Life and Times* (ii. 372). See also Wood, *Life and Times*, ii. 386 for his preaching at a visit of the duke of Ormonde in 1677. Haslewood published three sermons: *A sermon preached at St. Olave Southwark, September the 8th, 1700. Occasioned by the recantation of Dr Joh. Spire, lately a Quaker* (1700); *St. Paul, no mover of sedition: or, a brief vindication of that apostle, from the false and disingenous [sic] exposition of Mr Hoadly, in a sermon preach'd before the Lord Mayor... of London* (1706). *A sermon preach'd at the assizes held at Kingston upon Thames, on Thursday March the 13th, 1706/7* (1707).

[19] Admitted probationer fellow 18 December 1675.

fellowships, although this was disputed, as will be seen. But the relatively open nature of Oriel fellowships meant that they could be seen as a fall-back position for those in other colleges who had failed to be elected in their own societies. A member of University College in 1699 who was allegedly victimized by the master and prevented from obtaining a fellowship was told by his tutor that 'there was no living quietly for me in this college'. The tutor advised him to resign his scholarship and ask for his *decessit*, his permission to leave the college; 'and go, says he, enter your self at Oriel College, and he was pleased to add, where you need not doubt of a Fellowship'.[20]

Oriel's fellows were, as a result, drawn from a large pool: out of 137 fellows in the period 1660–1781 only 56 had matriculated at the college, around 41 per cent. Perhaps it was as a consequence of this and the fact that Oriel had only a very small number of funded undergraduate places—the Dudley exhibitions and, after 1744, the Beaufort and Ludwell exhibitions—that Oriel was a relatively elitist place. In the seventeenth century the status of 60 per cent of its fellows was given as gentleman, esquire, nobleman, baronet, or knight, as against 36 per cent at Brasenose, 37 per cent at Exeter, 41 per cent at Lincoln, 47 per cent at Magdalen, and 38 per cent at Wadham.[21] Another consequence should have been that Oriel's fellowships were relatively competitive. A paper written at Queen's in the mid-eighteenth century explained that 'Those colleges in which men are elected into fellowships without having been previously of any inferior order in the house—as at Merton and Oriel—will have it in their power to choose the most deserving; so far...as their knowledge of them shall extend. And it may fairly be supposed, that, for the sake of their own credit, and independently of every other consideration, they will generally do this.' The author though had to heavily qualify the point: 'No doubt however but that here also improper influence will sometimes find a place.'[22]

There is indeed evidence that fellowships were largely arranged affairs. It was normal for a new probationer fellow to be elected to replace a resigning fellow on the day of the resignation—which scarcely gave time for a proper competitive examination to be organized. On 7 December 1661, for example, Thomas Sheppard resigned his fellowship, and a replacement, John Holbrooke, was elected the same day.[23] The election of James Davenant in September 1661 to the place vacated by the death of his brother George ('*fratris suae charissimi*') a couple of weeks before may suggest sentiment on the part of the fellows. It could equally be evidence of a version of the system

---

[20] *A Letter to a Member of the Convocation of the University of Oxford: containing the Case of a Late Fellow Elect of University College in that University* (London, 1699), 5.
[21] HUO iv. 82.
[22] Queen's MS 456, quoted in I. G. Doolittle 'College Administration', in HUO v. 234 n. 4.
[23] OCA GOV 4 A1; see other examples at 14 November 1667, 5 March 1668, 29 March 1669.

in operation at All Souls by which fellows effectively nominated their successors on resignation. At All Souls, the practice enabled them to sell their fellowships, an abuse which Archbishop Sheldon, as its Visitor, was trying hard to stamp out.[24] An obscure row in 1673 between the provost and—ironically—James Davenant shows that the practice was rife at Oriel as well. In June that year, the Visitor, Bishop Fuller of Lincoln, established a commission consisting of the vice-chancellor, Peter Mews, the dean of Christ Church, John Fell, and the principal of Brasenose, Thomas Yates, to look into the dispute.[25] Unfortunately, their report seems not to have survived, but Fell's covering letter is suggestive enough:

> Had we suffered angry men to multiply accusations, I fear neither your Lordship, nor we should have lived long enough to see an end of them. Besides, the buying & selling of places is an odious subject, and could not be unravelld without great scandal, and that mischief which scandal draws after it.[26]

Fell's letter discussed proposals apparently originating with the fellows themselves to reform the system of elections, which the bishop was apparently working to implement, and ten days later he wrote optimistically that 'Oriel College is I think in a very good preparation to that unity which is the foundation of all industry and duty'.[27]

Before Fuller had promulgated a new set of rules, it would seem that a fresh occasion for controversy had broken out. A mandate from the king dated 28 January 1674 recommended the election of Thomas Twitty, 'willing and requireing you forthwith upon the first avoidance of a fellowship in that College to electe and admitt him...into the same'.[28] As, no doubt, was well known, a vacancy already existed through the resignation of Robert Kellway on 21 October 1673. The royal letter must have been anticipated: Twitty proceeded to a BA on 20 January 1674, qualifying him for the fellowship, just a week before it was sent. Fuller's overdue decree concerning the election of fellows is dated 24 January, four days before the date of the king's letter. In its preamble, he referred to *'execrabili nundinatione'*—the corrupt trafficking in fellowships. His letter required there to be thirteen full days between the announcement of a vacancy and the succeeding election; and that the same

---

[24] Scott Mandlebrote, 'All Souls from Civil War to Glorious Revolution', in S. J. D. Green and Peregrine Hordern (eds.), *All Souls under the Ancien Regime: Politics, Learning and the Arts, c.1600–1850* (Oxford, 2007), 72–3. For the sale of fellowships at New College, see Hearne, *Collections*, v. 100, and John Buxton and Penry Williams (eds.), *New College, Oxford* (Oxford, 1979), 52, 58.
[25] OCA GOV D4/A, Commission of Bishop Fuller, 16 June 1673. OCA GOV 2 D4/B is a draft of the commission dated (by Shadwell) 1673.
[26] OCA GOV D8/1, Fell to Fuller, 1 August [1673].
[27] OCA GOV D8/1, Fell to Fuller, 1 August and OCA GOV D8/2, Fell to Fuller, 11 August [1673].
[28] OCA GOV 4 A1, 28 January 1674.

ILLUSTRATION 6.1 Robert Say (c.1613–91), fellow 1635, provost 1653–91
Oriel College

notice be given of the day of the election by a notice fixed to the door of the chapel. Secondly, it insisted that a departing fellow should not solicit support for his successor. Third, that anyone was eligible for election who had completed the BA (*determinaverit*) before the first Sunday in Lent previous to the election. Fourth, on the day before the election there would be a public examination of the candidates by the provost, the dean, and the other officers and fellows: there had to be twelve fellows present, not including the provost. The man properly elected would be admitted to a probationer year.[29]

It is probable that the royal mandate had been solicited by the provost and some of the fellows themselves, presumably in order to circumvent Fuller's decree. Writing again to the bishop on 17 February Fell described how Oxford's establishment had been mobilized to resist Twitty's appointment: even the university's MP, the recently elected Thomas Thynne, and its chancellor, the duke of Ormonde, Fell wrote, had offered their assistance. Fuller overturned it without needing their intervention. The king issued new letters to the college stating that Fuller had explained that Twitty was not qualified, and that the precedent would 'be a great

[29] GOV 2 D5, statute of the bishop of Lincoln, 24 January 1673 [1674].

discouragement to learning, much lessen the authority of him your visitor, & prove directly prejudiciall to the good government of that college', and left the college to proceed to a new election according to its statutes, and the injunctions—presumably the new injunctions—of the Visitor.[30] Say was clearly extremely put out: he wrote to Fuller what Fell described as a 'peremptory letter' and issued threats to Thynne for misreporting him; but although Fell believed it likely that the provost had been 'a party to Twitties proceedings', he counselled the bishop to let the matter rest, as the court would not take kindly to further investigation of its own role in the matter, and especially the use of a royal mandate. 'It is below the dignity of a visitor to contest in empty words', he went on, but 'if the provost goes on with this hectoring, tis possible he may run himself so in the briers, that twill not be easy for him to get out.'[31]

Fuller's decree—important enough for All Souls to have transcribed it carefully in 1710[32]—did have an effect: at least elections thereafter are carefully minuted to show that they followed the 1674 procedures. One election in 1696 is described in more than usual detail in the Dean's Register because it proceeded less than smoothly. Two notices were fixed up on the chapel door the required thirteen days in advance of the elections, one inviting candidates to present themselves on the appointed day and the other giving notice to the fellowship to attend. On this occasion, when the fellows assembled in the common room for the fellowship examination there were fewer than the necessary twelve present, and the elections were put off for two days. When they reconvened there were still not enough fellows. So the candidates were set to work at the written exercises which formed part of the examination while urgent messages were sent to Mr Lidgould in London to return to make up the numbers. He arrived that evening and the next day the twelve fellows examined the candidates, hearing disputations in the afternoon before proceeding to the election in the evening.

Accounts of fellowship elections in the early eighteenth century suggest that the examination was only part of the process. The antiquarian, non-juror, and indefatigable diarist Thomas Hearne described the election held on 28 May 1709, probably from the report of his friend, the Oriel fellow Richard Dyer:[33]

There were three vacancies, and 9 candidates for them. There were 2 of Oriel College who stood and one of them came in, as being Pupil to one of those chiefly concerned

---

[30] OCA GOV D8/5, Fell to Fuller, 17 February [1674]; OCA GOV D8/4, Charles II to provost and fellows, 13 February 1673[4].
[31] OCA GOV D8/7, Fell to Fuller, 22 February [1674].
[32] All Souls Autograph Letters, vol. ii: the king's letters from the Dean's Register of Oriel, 1674, copied by George Cooper, notary public, 28 November 1710.
[33] Matric. 16 November 1669; admitted probationer 22 April 1674.

in the election; the 2d was of Merton and the 3rd of Wadham College. Mr Johnson an ingenious good natured modest gent of Xt Ch. stood and performed better at least as well as any; but Interest swayd (notwithstanding what was given out both before the election and since) as I have been informed by one of the college, an observer of the Transaction, but perfectly unprejudic'd (as having nothing to do in the election, one way or other) & one of the electors has himself declar'd that he was engaged sometime before the time of Tryal by a Gentleman in the country. So that both in this as well as other colleges things are manag'd by Interest, not by merits.[34]

An account of the 1715 fellowship election by one of the gentlemen commoners also suggests that fellows engaged their 'interest' for one or other candidate well before the formal examinations:

In our late election in this house for fellows in which there were 12 or 13 candidates... I believe you will be surprised to hear that Mr Ingram[35] has lost it, and that by the chief procurement of his own Tutor. There is great variety of opinions and speculations about this affair, a great many blaming Mr Ibbetson[36] for his hard usage to his pupil, but I am sorry to say Mr Ingram's management will justify his conduct in it. For Mr Ibbetson very often desired Mr Ingram to stand upon his interest, and assured him of success, he refusing to stand, his Tutor gave his vote & interest to another (I believe Walsall). Before the day of election Mr Ingram upon the desire of Mr Dering[37] changed his mind, and accepted of his interest, which was a vexation to Ibbetson who [did] not for that reason, & the obligation of his former promise, vote for him.[38]

Oriel attracted relatively little attention in late seventeenth-century Oxford: almost the only event in the college to be noticed outside it was the theft by its senior treasurer, George Barbour, of £230 of the College's money in 1679 (Wood had heard it was £500).[39] Another scandal in May the same year was hushed up, when Edmund Thorne agreed to leave the college. The reasons are unclear, although he had been formally admonished for drunkenness several years earlier, the fact recorded in the Dean's Register (it was heavily deleted subsequently).[40] The political crises of the late 1670s and 1680s seem to have made little impact on Oriel, despite the presence of parliament in 1681 and the intense pressure placed on Oxford by James II's campaign to force Magdalen to accept a Catholic president in 1687. It was perhaps even an

---

[34] Hearne, *Collections*, ii. 202. Thomas Weeksey, Charles Cotes, and William Cary were elected.
[35] Presumably George Ingram, matric. May 1711 as fellow commoner; admitted probationer fellow, 24 March 1716.
[36] Richard Ibbetson, admitted probationer fellow, 19 April 1700.
[37] Admitted probationer fellow, 16 March 1706.
[38] Oxford, Bodleian Library MS Fairfax 35, fo. 94: Henry Culpeper Fairfax to his brother, 15 October 1715. The election had taken place on 28 April. Those elected were Samuel Catherall, John Walsall, and James Yate.
[39] OCA GOV 4 A1, 26 May, 17 October 1679; Wood, *Life and Times*, ii. 451. Barbour ['George Barbone'], from Merton, was admitted a probationer fellow on 29 September 1669.
[40] OCA GOV 4 A1, 19 October 1672.

indication of Oriel's marginal status in Oxford and national politics, and also the survival of its loyalist tradition, that an Oriel fellow, Henry Gandy,[41] would become after the Revolution of 1689 one of Oxford's tiny number of non-jurors—men who were removed from their positions in Church and state because of their refusal to take the oaths of allegiance to King William III and Queen Mary II. Gandy was the son of a man who was himself an Oriel fellow before the Civil War and who had been removed from his Devon parish because of his loyalty to Charles I.[42] On the anniversary of the Restoration in 1685, shortly after the accession of James II, Henry Gandy had preached the St Mary's sermon 'much against phanaticks',[43] but there is little to explain why he would become one of the very few who found it impossible to accept the change of regime. A 'worthy honest man', according to Hearne,[44] he would become one of the newly consecrated non-juring bishops, holding to the separation from the Church of England even after the last of the bishops who had been deprived after the Revolution, Thomas Ken, finally returned to it in 1710.

Even though very few in the Oxford of 1689 directly contested the legitimacy of the Revolution, the university was at the heart of resistance to its implications. During the reign of William III, conservative dons watched in horror as the Whigs—a party they regarded as subversive of the state and especially of the Church—established their ascendancy in the administration of both; many of them regarded even Tory governments as unreliable defenders of the interests of the Church of England. As the intellectual headquarters and emotional centre of dyed-in-the-wool Toryism, Oxford was regarded by the more radical Whigs with loathing or derision and they willingly painted its resistance to themselves as a desire for the restoration of James II and his heirs. Whig and even moderate Tory administrations saw Oxford as a major problem of political management for a century after the Revolution. In a number of colleges it resulted in a struggle between a head zealous for promotion from the government, and a fellowship suspicious of his intentions and jealous of its independence. Although the battle was real enough throughout the reigns of William and Mary and Queen Anne, it was with the accession of George I and the severing of the last real link with the Stuart dynasty that it reached its climax, fought in Oriel with particular bitterness.

The old loyalist Provost Say died in November 1691, having served for thirty-eight years. His successor was Dr Royse, a fellow since 1675. Tories came to regard Royse with deep suspicion. Hearne described him as a

---

[41] Matric. 15 March 1667; admitted probationer 30 May 1671.
[42] John Gandy, matric. 10 November 1620, elected fellow 4 October 1626; John Walker, *An Attempt towards Recovering an Account of the Numbers and Sufferings of the Clergy* (London, 1714), part ii, 69.
[43] Wood, *Life and Times*, iii. 143.   [44] Hearne, *Collections*, x. 451.

'smooth Preacher and a rank Whigg',[45] a man 'of good parts, well read in Pamphletts, of great cunning and design',[46] and complained of his neglect of his, and Hearne's, *alma mater*, St Edmund Hall, and his failure to find preferment for a nephew, an Oriel man.[47] According to Hearne, Royse had been noticed preaching at St Mary's by the earl of Berkeley, who made him his chaplain; in London he got to know the prominent Whig clergyman Dr Tillotson by preaching at Lincoln's Inn. Recommended by one or other of them, he became a chaplain to William III. When Tillotson succeeeded William Sancroft as archbishop of Canterbury in 1691, Royse became his domestic chaplain, and was presented by him to the rich living of Newington in Oxfordshire. In 1694 he obtained the deanery of Bristol.

Royse had been elected provost a week after Say's death. Hearne's story was that the election was fixed by 'some of the fellows with whom Royse used to drink', who 'got a majority together at Mother Shepherds at Headington, where they agreed to choose Dr Royse, and not Mr Davenant who was always looked upon by the men of learning and integrity in the University to be the fittest for provost'.[48] Hearne later changed his opinion about Davenant, but Royse was in fact elected unanimously by the twelve fellows present on 1 December 1691—although Davenant, perhaps significantly, was not there.[49] Hearne's mentor, Dr Thomas Smith, saw Royse as the epitome of the careerist don:

formerly there was that great regard had to the Heads of Houses in both Universities that the vacant bishoprics were usually supplyed hence, but then they were men of great gravity and learning and made a considerable figure in the Church, before they came to be admitted to so great a share in the government of it: but now the chiefe qualification, as it has been since the Revolution is to be a London minister, and to be able to preach a florid Sermon at Court, and by their flattery insinuate themselves into the favour of great men and women, who have an influence on such as can dispose of Church preferments.[50]

Hearne noted with sardonic satisfaction the off-hand treatment Royse and a number of other establishment heads received when they went to see the duke of Marlborough in 1706,[51] and with outrage his refusal to accept for the college a copy of George Hickes's *Thesaurus*, the great study of ancient northern languages and cultures by another Oxford non-juror, along with

---

[45] Hearne, *Collections*, ii. 82.   [46] Hearne, *Collections*, i. 202.
[47] Presumably William Royse, servitor, of Barrington, Somerset, matric. 27 April 1700, later vicar of Winsham, Somerset.
[48] Hearne, *Collections*, i. 214.
[49] For Davenant, see Hearne, *Collections*, ii. 214, 224, v. 332, viii. 166, ix. 51, 372.
[50] Hearne, *Collections*, ii. 104, though Hearne did also report that Royse told Dr Hudson in 1705 that he would not accept the bishopric of Gloucester if it were offered him: no doubt Hearne would not have believed it.
[51] Hearne, *Collections*, i. 167, 169.

the less than generous sum that Warden Gardiner of All Souls handed over for his copy: 'such encouragers are these two brothers (in eating and drinking) of learning'.⁵² He peddled a rhyme on 'certain Whiggish gentlemen drinking at Heddington', written by 'two or three honest gentlemen of Xt Ch.'.

> There's Dunstar the Lowzy, and Royce the bouzy
> With the slye informer Rye

Dunster was the Warden of Wadham, then suffering from 'an odd distemper'; and George Rye⁵³ was a fellow of Oriel, who was reported to have informed on a fellow of Magdalen, Mr Hart, for seditious words in a sermon in St Mary's.⁵⁴

Royse's first official act recorded in the Dean's Register was the deprivation of Henry Gandy.⁵⁵ Whether it was a matter of policy, or simply a sign of the times, some of the fellows elected during his tenure suggest that the college was open to Whig and low church influences. Richard Ibbetson and Nicholas Rogers,⁵⁶ both elected in 1700, were present at the notorious Woodcock Dinner in All Souls in 1707 on the anniversary of the execution of Charles I, apparently planned as a deliberate insult to his memory. Although Ibbetson was deeply embarrassed—particularly as he was a pro-proctor—and told Hearne that he had been completely unaware of it, both of them, Hearne noted, were 'low church men', and Ibbetson, at least, was a Whig. One of the All Souls' fellows involved, Charles Talbot, was son to the bishop of Oxford, and had been an undergraduate at Oriel.⁵⁷ Hearne was outraged when Rogers at Easter that year preached a sermon which criticized the works of his mentor, another non-juror, Henry Dodwell. Talbot's sermon, he wrote, 'bears the character of being one of the worst that ever was preached in St Maries, especially upon this occasion'.⁵⁸ John Salmon, elected in 1707, was regarded by Hearne as a low church prig.⁵⁹ Much later, in 1724, after Bishop Benjamin Hoadly had become the Church's most prominent defender against the claims of the non-jurors, the disappointed St Johns fellow and Whig satirist Nicholas Amhurst masqueraded as one of Oxford's Tories to write:

> From our old track whole colleges depart,
> And preach new doctrines with *Hoadleian* art,
> Long since the *Merton Lollards* went astray,
> And *Wadham's* sons to *Oriel* led the way,

---

⁵² Hearne, *Collections*, i. 309.   ⁵³ Admitted probationer fellow, 11 April 1696.
⁵⁴ Hearne, *Collections*, ii. 104. See W. R. Ward, *Georgian Oxford* (Oxford, 1958), 30, 31, for Hart's sermon, and Hearne, *Collections*, iv. 329, for a revised opinion of Rye, but also vi. 325, for his 1719 sermon against nonconformists, which must have restored Hearne's original opinion.
⁵⁵ OCA GOV 4 A2, 5 March 1692.
⁵⁶ Admitted probationer, 20 April 1700.
⁵⁷ Hearne, *Collections*, i. 337. Talbot had matric. 25 March 1702.
⁵⁸ Hearne, *Collections*, ii. 6.
⁵⁹ Matric. 18 March 1703; admitted probationer fellow, 23 July 1707.

> *Exeter* follow'd; and in some degree,
> Scarce is a College from infection free.⁶⁰

The reference is probably to George Rye, the Wadham BA elected in 1696, the 'sly informer Rye', whom Hearne regarded as hostile to non-jurors.⁶¹ In 1721 Hearne regarded another Oriel fellow, Peter Randal, as 'a mighty Friend...of K George's, and an utter Enemy of the Nonjurors, whom he got silenc'd some Years agoe, when they met in St Marie's parish privately for their Devotion', though Randall was of much older vintage, having been elected in 1685.⁶²

Royse died in April 1708, three months or so after he suffered a stroke.⁶³ A few days after his interment in the college chapel (the sermon was preached by Ibbetson), the fellows elected George Carter. Hearne approved: Carter was 'a worthy ingenious sober Gentleman, and a good scholar',⁶⁴ who he thought might lead Oriel along a more congenial political path. Carter, for all the later abuse directed at him, proved to be an able and energetic promoter of the college in a complex political world. He sorted out the wainscoting of the hall, cajoling contributions from former members, organized the college investments through William Bromley, the university MP and linchpin of the Tory resurgence late in the reign of Queen Anne, and secured from the Tory establishment in 1713 the prize, admittedly self-interested, of letters patent, subsequently confirmed by act of parliament, annexing a prebend in Rochester Cathedral to the provostship. But Carter's determined pursuit of his own career quickly attracted sarcastic comment. The speech intended to have been given by the Terrae Filius at the Act of 1713 sneaked in a snide remark about 'calling upon the Head of O___l, Dr C___r, to vouch for his principles'.⁶⁵ Carter deftly established a relationship with the Whigs' favourite

---

⁶⁰ *Oculus Britanniae: an Heroi-Panegyrical Poem on the University of Oxford* (London, 1724).

⁶¹ Hearne, *Collections*, ii. 104, 115; iv. 329–30. Rye was admitted probationer on 11 November 1696 and resigned in 1718: he was later Regius Professor of Divinity and a canon of Christ Church. He published a massive *Treatise against the nonconfoming Nonjurors*, 2 vols. (London, 1719). Other fellows of Oriel originally from Wadham were John Lidgould, admitted probationer 16 November 1687 (resigned 3 March 1707) and Edmund Brickenden, admitted probationer 22 March 1692 (resigned 10 January 1702). Brickenden features on Wood's 1694 list of Oxford men who were *non compos mentis*: Wood, *Life and Times*, iii. 475.

⁶² Admitted probationer 3 November 1685. Hearne, *Collections*, vii. 186 (8 November 1721). The story behind the rhyme about Randal (On Peter R__dal of Oriel college: Here lies R___dal Peter, | Of Oriel, the eater. | Whom death at last has eaten: | Thus is the biter bitten | This is for a memorial | Of Peter R__dal of Oriel) is obscure. It was printed in the satirical account of the 'Poetical Club' in Nicholas Amhurst's *Terrae-Filius: or, The Secret History of the University of Oxford; in Several Essays* (London, 1726), ed. William E. Rivers (Newark, Del., 2004).

⁶³ Hearne, *Collections*, ii. 103.

⁶⁴ Hearne, *Collections*, ii. 104.

⁶⁵ *The Speech that was intended to have been spoken by the Terrae-Filius, in the Theatre at O - - - - - d, July 13. 1713* (London, 1713), 13. The Act was in the event suppressed by Vice-Chancellor Gardiner.

cleric, William Wake, perhaps when he was bishop of Lincoln and Oriel's Visitor, and kept it up following his translation to Canterbury in early 1716. In 1717, when senior Oxford Tories William Stratford and Arthur Charlett were turned out of their royal chaplaincies, Carter was one of those who replaced them. In 1719 he secured a prebend at Peterborough thanks to Wake. Carter cultivated Wake's replacement as bishop of Lincoln (and the man who would take over his role as manager of the Church on behalf of the Whigs), Edmund Gibson, bishop of Lincoln, and John Robinson, the former Oriel fellow, now distinguished diplomat, politician, and bishop of London, from whom he secured a generous benefaction for the college in February 1719.[66]

On the accession of George I in 1714, Oriel fellows, like other Oxford dons, dutifully trooped off to the quarter sessions to reassure him by swearing their allegiance, all duly recorded in the Dean's Register. Nevertheless, Whigs within Oxford and outside it questioned the genuineness of their commitment, mounted a campaign in the London press against what they alleged were the complacency, corruption, and political unreliability of the university and its colleges, and hotly demanded moves to curb their independence. Though a full-scale visitation of the university was averted in 1719, there was continuous pressure on Oxford from Whig ministers and their clerical allies to show its loyalty and divisions within Oxford on how to respond. The university made some efforts to comply, including prising one of its most notorious Jacobites, Thomas Hearne himself, from his post of sub-librarian at the Bodleian and replacing him with the library's janitor, Joseph Bowles. Bowles had helped to evict him, changing the locks on the door and listening behind it as Hearne hammered to be let in.

Ambitious heads of houses such as Carter were well aware of what was required of them. On the afternoon after the 1716 fellowship election he wrote to Archbishop Wake that:

This morning we chose three fellows. I can assure your Grace with the highest satisfaction, they are not only good scholars but also true friends to the present establishment. I have an intire confidence in them as to this particular inasmuch as those persons on whom they depend chiefly are wholly devoted to King George and his ministry.... I assure your Lordship I shall have a particular regard to men's principles & loyalty as well as their learning, than which I know I cannot give your grace a better & more agreeable instance how faithfully I am...[67]

Carter's appointment as one of the royal chaplains in February 1717 was an early reward for his commitment to the regime and the government. His

---

[66] See Carter's memorandum book, OCA PRO 1 C1 1, and the letters to Robinson (addressed as 'your E'), Gibson, and Wake, among others.
[67] OCA PRO 1 C1 1.

loyalty to the regime began to have an impact on Oriel. There was no fellowship election in 1717, but in 1718 the two successful candidates were Bowles, the new Bodleian sub-librarian, travelling rapidly from vigorous Oxford Toryism to careerist Whiggism, and Henry Brooke, eventually one of Carter's executors, who was appointed high master of Manchester Grammar School in 1727 in spite of Tory opposition.[68]

Though there is no sign of discord in 1718—the elections are recorded as being unanimous—these appointments were perhaps straws in the wind. There were no elections in 1719 or in 1720 but the July 1721 fellowship election would mark the beginning of a ten-year battle between the provost and the majority of the fellows. No less than four fellowships were available that year, those of Beckham, Randal, Walsall, and Ingram. Hearne's friend Richard Dyer regretted that his own favoured candidate, Robert Fysher from Christ Church, who, he claimed, 'appear'd to be the best Scholar', was quickly discarded.[69] Two vacancies were filled without controversy, by John Woollin from Merton and Alexander Rayner from Christ Church. But over the second two there was a dispute over the complicated issue of which candidate should be elected to which fellowship. Beckham had been one of the ten fellows on the primary foundation, while Randal had been elected to the Carpenter fellowship endowed in the fifteenth century for a candidate from the diocese of Worcester. One of the remaining candidates, the inappropriately named William Makepeace from Merton, the most Whiggish college in Oxford, was a native of the diocese of Worcester as it was in 1721; another, Robert Bernard, also from Merton, could be counted as a native of the diocese as it had been in Bishop Carpenter's time. All seemed to accept that Bernard should have a fellowship: but he was eligible for the Carpenter fellowship as well as Beckham's open fellowship. If he was appointed to the latter, it would limit the remaining vacant place to someone from Worcester diocese. The real choice was between Makepeace and a candidate from Jesus, Henry Edmunds, who did not qualify for a Carpenter fellowship. Nine fellows voted Edmunds in to Beckham's open fellowship; the provost and three others voted that it should go to Bernard. To replace Randall, nine named Bernard, and three voted with the provost for Makepeace.[70] Carter, ignoring the fact that he was in the minority, admitted Woollin, Rayner, Bernard, and Makepeace on 2 August. Henry Edmunds appealed to the Visitor, Edmund Gibson.

No one could have had much doubt about the outcome of the appeal. On 24 November, the provost communicated to the college Gibson's

[68] Matric. 16 October 1713; admitted probationer 1 May 1718; see ODNB s.n.
[69] Hearne, *Collections*, vii. 263. Hearne mentioned that Fysher was Mr Estwick's nephew. Two of Carter's draft letters to Wake refer to Estwick, which might mean that Wake supported Fysher's candidacy, but Carter did not. See OCA PRO 1 C1 1, 34, 50; and his address (Petershill, near St Paul's) is included in the address list at the back of the volume.
[70] OCA GOV 4 A2, 27 July 1721.

decision, which complicated matters further. He pointed out that the college had in 1482, following Carpenter's benefaction, decided not only that the new fellowship should go to someone from the diocese of Worcester, but also that a similar restriction should apply to one of the primary fellowships, if any suitable candidate should be found. This strengthened the case for giving Beckham's fellowship to Bernard. Makepeace was then the only candidate who fulfilled the conditions of the Carpenter fellowship.[71]

Following the election the atmosphere within the college became sulphurous. Some of the odium attached to Bowles, who was seen as a protégé of Carter's. He was blamed by Hearne for the suicide of Thomas Ward,[72] one of the fellows, in the November following the election. Since Hearne passed by no opportunity to decry the faults of his rival, this may have been unfair; nevertheless it was Richard Dyer who told him that Bowles was 'the greatest rogue in the world':

> For (says he) he was the chief Incendiary in our College, & was the occasion of Tom Ward's shooting himself. For, being great with Ward, Mr Ward intrusted him with his Secrets, all which Bowles betray'd, particularly what related to the late Business of election, which could not but much affect Ward, who thought Bowles had been a true Friend, as Mr Dyer also did once, who now is so fully satisfy'd of the contrary that he will not keep him Company, as, indeed, no-one else of any Denomination in the college will, he being, withall, look'd upon as lewd Fellow.[73]

Political tension at Oxford reached one of its many peaks a few months later, at the peculiar March 1722 election for the university's members of parliament. The moderate establishment Tory sitting members were challenged by Oxford's presiding Jacobite genius, Dr William King, the principal of Oriel's neighbour, St Mary Hall. Oriel's vote was marshalled behind the establishment candidates, although Carter himself seems not to have voted, and only eight fellows voted in all.[74] Bowles was said to have promised his vote initially to Dr King, but he is recorded as having voted for the establishment candidates, and indeed worked for them.[75]

It is not clear whether the election had anything to do with the next stage of the battles at Oriel. In late 1722, Bishop Gibson and the provost were corresponding concerning the status of two fellows—William Dering and Charles Cotes, both elected in 1709, who had failed to be ordained. Fellows

---

[71] OCA GOV 3 A 14e.
[72] Matric. 23 April 1695; admitted probationer 26 November 1702.
[73] Hearne, *Collections*, vii. 311. See also vii. 293 for the date of the suicide, 8 November 1722.
[74] On the peculiarities of the election, see Ward, *Georgian Oxford*, 124–8.
[75] Hearne, *Collections*, vii. 349. *A True copy of the Poll for Members of Parliament for the University of Oxford, Taken March the 21st 1721* [i.e. 1722], *Digested into an Alphabetical Order* (Oxford, 1722). Nicholas Rogers, who had just been presented to the recently acquired living of Ufton Nervet, and who would resign his fellowship later in the year, was the only fellow to vote for King.

were supposed to take holy orders within a reasonable time of their election, although exceptions could be made, particularly for those holding specific offices or faculty positions in medicine and law. In December 1722 the bishop wrote to Carter acknowledging that a 1612 statute permitted up to three dispensations from the requirements of ordination. Since neither Cotes nor Dering held dispensations (Carter said that he did not think either of them had 'ever applyd themselves in earnest to the study of the civil or canon Law'),[76] the bishop insisted that the college should declare the two fellowships vacant. He pointed out also that the dispensation enjoyed by Dr Whalley, to practise medicine, had been granted purely for the purpose of attending to the medical needs of the college; since Dr Whalley was currently residing in Lancashire, he could scarcely perform that function.[77]

It is conceivable that in the wake of the 1722 election, Gibson, already closely identified with Whig ministries, was pursuing some attempt to remove Tories from Oriel. Hearne wrote that both Dering and Cotes were 'honest Gentlemen'. Both were from prominent Tory families. Cotes was son of John Cotes, of Woodcote, Shropshire, who had been a Tory MP. Dering was the brother of Sir Cholmley Dering, the Tory MP for Kent who died as a result of wounds received in a duel in 1711; Cholmley's son, William Dering's nephew, would enter Oriel in 1722 as a baronet. Cotes resigned at the end of February 1723; Whalley gave up his fellowship on 18 March 1723; Dering, whom the fellows tried to save through various expedients (Dyer, who did have a dispensation, offered to resign his fellowship so that Dering could take his place), had his fellowship vacated at evening prayers in the chapel on 29 March when he failed to respond to an ultimatum from Gibson.[78] Hearne thought that the affair was promoted by Carter himself, despite the 'great kindnesses' he had received from Dering, who had been his own pupil. He explained that 'the Provost endeavours to get all to be of Bangorian principles that are of the College'.[79] In fact, their correspondence on the subject suggests that the initiative was Gibson's, who appears to have been almost as exasperated with the provost's lack of firmness as with the opposition and foot-dragging of the fellows. Carter's last letter about the affair (very carefully drafted, as all Carter's letters were) seems curiously double-edged:

I am sensible that I ought to make my acknowledgement to your Lordship in the fullest manner for your great justice moderation, resolution and wisdom in beginning carrying on and accomplishing this matter. But what I am sensible I could never duly perform, your Lordships multiplicity of business of much greater consequence excuses me from attempting.[80]

[76] OCA PRO 1 C1, 41.
[77] OCA GOV 2 A3, Bishop of Lincoln to Carter, 4 December 1722 (copy).
[78] OCA GOV 4 A2. [79] Hearne, *Collections*, viii. 60. [80] OCA GOV 2 A3.

In April 1723, within three weeks of Dering's removal from the fellowship, a new election was held. With the approval (and possibly at the instigation) of their Visitor, the fellows had instituted new rules governing fellowship elections in August the previous year, 1722. The elections would take place every year on the Friday after Easter; no place would be regarded as vacant unless it had been vacated before the Wednesday before the Sunday before Easter; no one would be accepted as a candidate unless he presented himself on the Wednesday before the election; the fellowship examination would take place on the Thursday before the election; the election would be finished before 6 p.m. on the Friday concerned; and if no election had been made the provost was to notify the Visitor within two weeks. Although Carter had suggested it to Gibson, no provision had been made for the Visitor to nominate in case no agreement was reached among the fellows.[81] At the April 1723 elections, five men were chosen for the five vacancies, including Robert Fysher, the unsuccessful candidate from Christ Church of 1721, and Henry Edmunds, the man whose election Carter had resisted in 1721.[82] All were elected by a large majority. The provost refused to admit any of them, insisting that he had a veto. The dean and the rest of the fellows admitted them instead.[83]

An appeal from the newly elected fellows to the bishop was inevitable, and this was, according to one view in Oxford, precisely what Carter had intended to precipitate: the bishop of Lincoln would void the election, confirm that the provost had a veto, and claim that in case of a dispute he could nominate fellows himself.[84] This time, though, it was a different bishop. Gibson was nominated to the diocese of London in April 1723, following the death of Robinson. His replacement, Richard Reynolds, was nominated at the end of May 1723. In the interval Carter must have sent the requisite letter to the bishop under the new statute, informing him that no

---

[81] OCA GOV 3 A14f, Statute of the bishop of Lincoln, 15 August 1722. The agreement is recorded in the Dean's Register under 15 August, OCA GOV 4 A2. See Carter's draft letter to the bishop (undated): 'I had call'd a meeting of my fellows this day upon ye matter you were pleased to mention: All of us, Dr Woodward among ye rest, came unanimously to this resolution, that I should in ye name of the society desire your Lordship to fix a particular day in the year, on which we should be obliged to fill up our vacant fellowships. We were all likewise of opinion, that the most convenient time for this purpose would be just after determinations were ended [that we might have the great choice at our elections I believe my Lord] & Tuesday in Passion week will be a day most convenient for every one's attendance. Your Lordship commanding me to suggest whatever I should think proper to be added to that which the society agreed upon. I leave it to your Lordships judgement whether it would not be of use, to insert into your injunction or decree that if on any account there should happened to be no election into the vacant fellowships on that day, that then your Lordship will fill them up your self.' OCA PRO 1 C1 1, 30: see also 32.

[82] The other successful candidates were Samuel Martin (Lincoln), James Parker (Brasenose), and Philip Pipon (Pembroke).

[83] OCA GOV 4 A2, 19 April 1723.

[84] HMC, Portland MSS, vii. 356 William Stratford to Edward Harley, 25 April 1723.

agreement had been reached concerning the election of new fellows. Shortly afterwards he wrote to Reynolds:

I [am] heartily concerned that I should give your Lordship so much Trouble, upon your first coming into your Bishopric. But I believe all that know me will do me so much justice as to say it hath been my constant end to preserve & promote peace wherever it hath been my fortune to live.[85]

The appeal was made, but naturally, Reynolds's first priority was not an Oxford dispute.[86] While the college waited for him to deal with it, Bowles made some attempt to mend fences, inviting the senior fellow, the venerable and weighty Joseph Woodward, elected in 1671,[87] to dine on a large piece of venison 'given him by some noble friend'. But having established that the 'noble friend' did not exist and that the venison had been bought at the market by the college cook, Woodward contemptuously turned it down.[88] A few days later, on 8 August, Hearne wrote that

Dr Carter, Provost of Oriel College, is justly look'd upon as a vile Man, & a sneaking Hypocrite, which last Name Mr Dyer called him to his face lately, upon account of his most scandalous behaviour in an election of Fellows...and tis observable that that pitifull, silly Rascal, Bowles, is one of those that struck in and keeps now pace with the Provost who, however, cares for Bowles no more than as a tool. This Provost is of a strange reserved temper, being afraid almost to discover his own Name, & yet he will do any thing for Interest. The President of St John's College told him well lately that he had learned some things when he was young, & some not. Says he, 'Mr Provost, you have learned the Lord's prayer, because you must ask (for the Provost will ask for any Preferment). The Creed you have not learned, because you must believe (whereas the Provost is of no Principles of Religion). The Commandments you have not learned, because you must answer (whereas this provost will not give any answer); and you have learned the French Tongue, because you must ask (it being said that he learned the French tongue that he might qualify himself to go beyond Sea, though he was disappointed, with K George, & ask of him preferment in that language, which K George understands, though he does not understand English).'[89]

A rumour circulated later that Reynolds planned to void the election, and claim a right of 'devolution'—that in the case of a dispute, the right to elect fellows would devolve on the Visitor, as it did in some other societies, such as

---

[85] OCA PRO 1 C1, 49.
[86] In addition to the five new fellows, the appeal was in the names of eight fellows: Walter Hodges, dean, Joseph Woodward, senior fellow, Richard Dyer, Samuel Catherall, Henry Brooke, John Woollin, Alexander Rayner, and Robert Bernard. There had been thirteen fellows at the election, although there is no record of who they were. Bowles and Makepeace presumably supported the provost or were neutral.
[87] Matric. 6 July 1666; admitted probationer, 21 July 1671.
[88] Hearne, *Collections*, viii. 162: the entry is of 28 January 1724, which is when Dyer told the story to Hearne. Bowles's letter, copied by Hearne, is dated 5 August.
[89] Hearne, *Collections*, viii. 104.

All Souls. He was said to have taken steps to introduce his own son into the fellowship.⁹⁰ In the meantime, Woodward and Richard Dyer signed affidavits, testifying that in their experience as fellows, going back to 1671 and 1675 respectively, the provost had never previously voted in elections except to break a tie.⁹¹

Following several postponements, in October Reynolds gave his decision on the case, chiding the college on the dispute, and, as predicted, rejecting the appeal and the validity of a fellowship election made without the provost's consent.⁹² In such circumstances, he said, 'I presume it is not unknown to you, that, of *common right*, the collation of the vacant fellowships devolves to me.' He would hold off from exercising that right for a week to see if agreement could be reached between the provost and fellows.⁹³ No agreement was reached, and on 19 November his *mandamus* was read in the college chapel requiring the college to admit his three nominees: John Coppen and John Dewe from Oriel, and one Lane, from Merton.⁹⁴ Hearne's friend Dyer read out a formal protest, and the fellows walked out: after which, wrote Hearne, 'none remained in Chapel but the Provost and his vile assistant Bowles'. Then

The provost call'd to one of the protestors to bring in the Batchelors, but, they having Protested, every one declin'd. Upon which Bowles said he would fetch them in, & thereupon went out of the Chappel, leaving the provost by himself, &, bringing them in, they were admitted by only these two, the provost & Bowles, & the legally elected Men were ejected.... After this was over, Bowles, like a poor, sorry rascal as he is, made great Rejoycings, & took the three Intruders into the Common Room at Night, where, however, no body else was with them, a thing against Custom & Practise for Batchelor Fellows to come there, by which & other proceedings he hath now

---

⁹⁰ HMC, Portland MSS vii. 369, William Stratford to Edward Harley, 3 December 1723.
⁹¹ LAO, Dioc. VV 9, The Information, or Affidavit of Jos. Woodward LLD, 27 September 1723, The Information of Richard Dyer MA, 29 September 1723.
⁹² Reynolds's decree in the case, dated 2 October 1723, is at LAO Dioc. VV 99; see also the minutes of the hearing on 24 September.
⁹³ OCA GOV 4 A2, letter dated 4 October 1723, inserted into the volume.
⁹⁴ It is not clear why only three candidates were nominated, rather than five. In a draft letter to the bishop of Lincoln following the removal of Dering, Carter had said that he had 'by the assistance of my friends found out a person every way well qualified for the fellowship appropriated to the Diocese': but since the election of Bernard and Makepeace the two fellowships now regarded as reserved for men from Worcester diocese were filled up. Bernard, over whom the argument concerning Worcester had first emerged, died on 14 November 1723, but this was months after Dering's removal: OCA PRO 1 C1 1, 47. John Coppen and John Dewe were Oriel commoners from Kent and Oxfordshire respectively. Hearne states (*Collections*, viii. 137) that Dewe had not stood in the election, so presumably Coppen and Lane had done, but had failed to be elected. Another explanation may be indicated by Reynolds's draft letter to the bishop of Bristol, which refers to Reynolds telling the provost that he 'would put in three fellows at his single recommendation, & as to ye other two, they should be such as he should have no exception to' (LAO, Dioc. VV 9, Reynolds to the bishop of Bristol (Joseph Wilcox), undated partial draft), yet this still fails to explain why the two to be nominated by the bishop without the provost's advice were not named—unless it was because, as may be implied by his unfinished letter, he could not find anyone with the satisfactory qualifications.

(as, indeed, he had sufficiently before) lost himself quite & clean, & as he is known to be an illiterate man, so now he hath the Character among all sorts of people (for even the Whiggs despise him, notwithstanding his being a tool for them) as a downright impudent Rogue.[95]

Five fellows signed the protest, and two others, Dyer and Walter Hodges, indicated their support for it.[96]

The case was followed closely by the rest of Oxford. 'If the Fellows can be well supported, this cause may make near as much noise as ever the case of Magdalen College did,' wrote Dr Stratford from Christ Church. The other bishops were concerned too. Reynolds drafted (but did not complete) a letter to one of his colleagues, justifying his actions in the case. He complained of the noise and trouble that he had undergone over the affair, despite having treated the provost and his opponents with 'all the respect they could desire, and with somewhat more than either He or they could expect'. He explained his difficulty in finding alternative candidates to put into the fellowship:

I was inclined to put in a cousin German of mine who is an excellent scholar, of an unblemisht character, and as hearty a friend to ye Governmt as either you or I, or any other of the kings friends are. But there's a gentleman at Merton, & another at Oriel, who are much depended on for characters, and they being pleas'd to say he was a Tory—I must be content to drop him. The next man was Mr Pipon, to whom I was inclin'd by ye recommendation of Mr Carteret: he said yt this young Gentleman's father or uncle was my Lord Carteret's Lieutenant in ye Government of Guernsey, That the Pipons, were ye support of ye kings interest in that Island and that if there were any doubts about him, there could be no such thing as depending on any man Living. Yet the same Gentlemen of Oxford being pleased to pronounce this candidate a Tory likewise, He was to be set aside, or I was to be held no friend to the common cause. Well! W[he]n it was apparently impossible to find a Whig at Oxford, who came not through these Gentlemen's hands, and thinking it somew[ha]t derogatory to my character as visitor....[97]

In a parallel case at University College (Carter's old college), a dispute over a mastership election also turned into an argument over the exercise of visitatorial jurisdiction. The fellows of University College may have taken their inspiration from Oriel, as they certainly did seek encouragement as their own

---

[95] Hearne, *Collections*, viii. 137.
[96] OCA GOV 4 A2, 19 November 1723. The other protestors were Joseph Woodward, Thomas Weeksey, Samuel Catherall, and Alexander Rayner. The two of the original appellants who did not sign the protest were Woollin and Bernard. Bernard died on 14 November. Thomas Weeksey signed the Protest but was not apparently one of the appellants. See also Carter's letter to Reynolds of 19 November at PRO 1 C1 1, 50, conveying the thanks of the new fellows to the bishop.
[97] The letter ends at this point: LAO, Dioc. VV 9, Reynolds to the bishop of Bristol (Joseph Wilcox), undated partial draft. Lord Carteret was secretary of state, a key ally—and rival—of Sir Robert Walpole. It is not clear from the letter whether the Pipon concerned was the same man as Philip Pipon, already elected by the fellows.

case ground more slowly.[98] Stratford's old colleague in the service of Robert Harley, earl of Oxford, Francis Gastrell bishop of Chester, helped the Oriel fellows to prepare their case.[99] By early December, they had started proceedings against the bishop in the Court of Common Pleas.[100] Hearne had a conversation with Dyer and Henry Brooke in February which shows that the fellows were ransacking the college archives to prepare a case against the bishop's visitatorial power.[101]

Before the case was heard, the death of one fellow (Bernard, the candidate of 1721) and the resignation of a second meant another election, in April 1724. This time the provost barely pretended to take part in a straightforward election. Two candidates (St John Chester and William Craster) were chosen by eight out of ten fellows (not including the provost) present.[102] Expecting the provost to refuse to admit them, Thomas Weeksey led three other fellows, the elected candidates, and their lawyer in a body to the provost's lodgings. When the provost insisted that the two were not properly elected, Weeksey asserted the rights of the fellowship and threatened that 'to recover their statuable and customary rights and liberties lately unjustly and unlawfully invaded by the said provost and his abettors they would use and pursue all lawfull ways and means to recover and maintain the same'.[103] Perhaps their *démarche* gave him pause, for it was a few days before Carter wrote to Reynolds to recount the events of the election, and to ask him to take the appropriate action:

The persons which I and my friends were willing should have succeeded were Cobb of Oriel College[104] and Edward of Magdalen Hall both qualified in respect of counties as well as learning and affection to the government. If your Lordship think it proper to put them immediately into the vacancies of Mr Bernard and Mr Evans, I must desire you would be pleased to send me your commands by Tuesday post, that I may execute them before I set out for London.[105]

Anticipating a fight he also wrote to Reynolds's son—perhaps some evidence for the story that Carter and Reynolds had planned to nominate him—about evidence in a legal challenge he now anticipated.[106]

---

[98] Robin Darwall Smith, *A History of University College, Oxford* (Oxford, 2008), 247–59.
[99] HMC Portland MSS vii. 367, Stratford to Harley, 25 October 1723; 437, Stratford to Harley, 18 May 1726; Ward, *Georgian Oxford*, 109.
[100] HMC Portland MSS vii. 369, Stratford to Harley, 3 December 1723.
[101] Hearne, *Collections*, viii. 166.
[102] OCA GOV 4 A2, 10 April 1724. Hearne plausibly reports that the two fellows in the minority were Bowles and Makepeace: Hearne, *Collections*, viii. 200.
[103] OCA GOV 4 A2, 11 April 1724.
[104] Thomas Cobb, matric. 23 May 1720, from New Romney, Kent.
[105] OCA PRO 1 C1 1, 59 (Carter's draft). The actual letter as received by Reynolds is in LAO, Dioc VV 9, dated 14 April.
[106] OCA PRO 1 C1 1, 59.

Henry Edmunds, one of the blocked probationer fellows from the previous year, led the legal challenge to the bishop. At an initial hearing in the Court of Common Pleas in Westminster Hall on 14 May he challenged the visitatorial power of the bishop on the grounds that the founder of the college had been Edward II under its initial charter of 1326, not Adam de Brome, as had normally been understood, under the statutes of May that year and December 1329; that the bishop had no overall power of visitation under the first charter; and therefore the only authority able to determine disputes relating to the governance of the college was the heir of the founder: the king.[107] Carter was alarmed by the outcome of the initial hearing, where an injunction was granted to prevent Reynolds exercising his visitatorial power until the case was determined. When he gathered from those with more experience in these matters that the court might well incline to his opponents' view he wrote to the archbishop of Canterbury: 'I need not tell your grace that if the judges pass such a sentence all that I have been doing toward the settling my college will (I am afraid) be defeated at once.'[108]

Carter, and all of the fellows, had another two years to wait for a judgement. In the meantime Hearne's great friend Richard Dyer left the college to live on his own estate in Devon. Hearne would later record that he had left because of the 'broils in the college', although the fact that he took with him Mrs Alice Wells, 'a comely maiden body of about fifty years of age', whom he later married—'and they own the marriage' he added—suggests this might have been mixed with a happier reason for his departure.[109] At last in May 1726 there was a full hearing of the case before a jury, and Edmunds won on almost every point. The jury decided that he, Fysher, Pipon, Parker, and Martin had been properly elected by a majority of the fellows without the consent of the provost; the college had been founded by Edward II; and the bishop of Lincoln had no visitatorial power.[110]

Hearne relished Carter's defeat:

This is a great confusion to the Provost, who hath not only lost his Negative by this (a thing he much insisted upon, what was never done before in the college), but hath likewise made the Bp of Lincoln loose his visitatorial power of that College, the King being at the same time, viz. when this affair for the two Appellants was decided, declared Visitor of the College. Had Carter succeeded, other Heads would have also insisted upon a Negative, & then there would have been an End of all elections. That rascal, Bowles, all along struck in with the Provost. Mr Dyer hath been so great a

---

[107] See F. J. Varley, 'The Oriel College Lawsuit, 1724–6', *Oxoniensia*, 6 (1943–4), 56–69, see 61 for the hearing. There seems to be no reliable account of the hearing itself, so this summary of the arguments is derived from the subsequent history of the case.
[108] OCA PRO 1 C1 1, 57.
[109] Hearne, *Collections*, ix. 112.
[110] Varley, 'Oriel College Lawsuit', 63–4 summarizes the copy of the proceedings and judgement incorporated into the Dean's Register, OCA GOV 4 A2.

friend in this business, that some time since I heard several of the Fellows say that, if they carried their Point against the provost, they ought to reckon Mr Dyer a Restorer of their college.[111]

Stratford, from Christ Church, saw the victory as a valuable precedent for the fellows of University College.[112] He had already likened the stand of the fellows of Oriel against their Visitor to the struggle of Magdalen against James II in 1687, and Hearne harked back to a comment made by Serjeant Wright, recorder of Oxford, in discussing a speech by Bishop Stillingfleet in the House of Lords in 1695 on the case of Exeter College. Exeter had been in dispute with its Visitor, the powerful episcopal baronet Sir John Trelawney, bishop of Exeter, over the extent of his powers, and Stillingfleet had argued that Visitors of colleges were the ultimate, and unaccountable, judges where disputes had arisen within a college. Wright had commented:

> Had King James…staid & made Popish Bishops, such of those Bishops as were visitors of any colleges might, by the Power allow'd them, by this speech (which is the foundation of the authority of deciding matters of Colleges allowe'd ever since twas spoke) bring in Popery into Colleges, by fixing upon such Fellows as they thought fit. Twas but having Heads to their Mind in Colleges, & the Fellows might be managed with ease by the Heads' pretending to a negative.[113]

Carter was advised by his counsel that it would be hopeless to appeal, and that 'all w[hi]ch I could now do out of Honour & Respect to your Lords[hi]p would be, not to admit any One of the Plaintiffs Fellow, until I had rec[eive]d a mandate from his Ma[jes]ty or one of his Courts'.[114] When, not long afterwards, Edmunds turned up at the lodgings shortly after it had been made asking when the provost 'would be so kind as to admit him and the others into the fellowships', Carter recorded that they had 'had a good deal of discourse', but that he insisted on the mandate.[115] Edmunds and his colleagues turned to the fellows themselves who on 18 July disregarded the provost and admitted them without his consent.[116] Carter seems to have tried to argue that the court had settled only the question of whether the Visitor was the king or the bishop of Lincoln, rather than the question of the propriety of the original election, and drew up a petition for presentation to the king, asking him to determine the case.[117] He certainly took further

---

[111] Hearne, *Collections*, ix. 133.
[112] HMC Portland MSS vii. 437, Stratford to Harley, 18 May 1726.
[113] Hearne, *Collections*, viii. 310. Stillingfleet's speech is in *Ecclesiastical Cases relating to the Duties and Rights of the Parochical Clergy*, included in *The Works of that Eminent and most learned Prelate, Dr Edward Stillingfleet*, 6 vols. (London, 1709–10), iii. 877–85.
[114] LAO, Dioc. VV 9, Carter to Reynolds, 17 May [1726].
[115] OCA PRO 1 C1 1, 74–5. See Darwall-Smith, *History of University College*, 255, for the supporters of Denison deploying a similar tactic in 1727 following their defeat at law.
[116] OCA GOV 4 A2, stamped paper inserted into the book, 18 July 1726.
[117] PRO 1 C1 1, 75.

legal advice, and in September 1726 forwarded it to Secretary of State Lord Townshend or Edmund Gibson (now bishop of London and the government's ecclesiastical manager). Carter had asked about an appeal to the House of Lords: he had been told that it would not succeed.[118]

In the long term, the events of 1721–6 seem to have exhausted Oriel's appetite for highly political fellowship elections. Thereafter they were rather quieter affairs: no election after 1726 up to the end of this period seems to have been (formally, at least) other than unanimous. Interest was still, of course, constantly employed on behalf of candidates. John Frewen received a recommendation in 1751 on behalf of a Mr Harrington 'a young gentleman of amiable qualifications a candidate for a fellowship at Oriel College';[119] in 1768 Samuel Johnson wrote to Thomas Apperley, a gentleman commoner at Oriel, to ask him to employ his influence in an impending Oriel fellowship election in favour of Mr Crofts.[120] Even as late as 1738, the unanimous election of George Shakerley in place of his brother, who had just resigned, suggests that the practice of a departing fellow managing to pass on a fellowship to his designated candidate persisted, despite the bishop of Lincoln's ruling of 1674.[121] Nevertheless, it is perhaps a sign that the college was taking the election exercises more seriously by 1768 that Provost Clark wrote to John Nowell, when he offered money to fund a college prize, that

> It has often been matter of concern to the residents in college, that the generality of our electors have been personally unacquainted with the literary merit of our college candidates, except so far as the temporary tryal which is frequently unfavourable to modest merit, has explained it to them.[122]

Within sixteen months of the 1726 judgement, Carter was dead. Thomas Weeksey told Hearne that his heart had been broken on losing the case, and that had he lived longer he would have resigned the provostship and gone to live in the country.[123] Hearne heard gossip, though, which scarcely suggested a broken heart, about how the provost had been known to 'keep some forward women company', and that he was a little too free with Mr Wood the surgeon's wife.[124] When the election for his successor was held in the chapel on 14 October 1727, Walter Hodges[125] received eight votes. Thomas

---

[118] BL Add. MS 36136, fos. 113–45.
[119] East Sussex Record Office, FRE 1182, W. Mundy to John Frewen, 7 November 1751. See also the letter of (probably) John Frewen senior to 'D.N.', undated, concerning his son's candidacy at Oriel, FRE 1180.
[120] *The Letters of Samuel Johnson*, ed. Bruce Redford, 5 vols. (Oxford 1992–4), i. 296–7.
[121] OCA GOV 4 A2.
[122] OCA PRO 2/36/3: Clark to William Nowell,? February 1768.
[123] Hearne, *Collections*, ix. 372.
[124] Hearne, *Collections*, ix. 356.
[125] Matric. 24 March 1711; admitted probationer 24 March 1716.

Weeksey ('who had been aiming at it for several years', wrote Hearne)[126] had seven, one of them his own, and another that of Makepeace, the man admitted in 1721 against the will and the votes of the majority of fellows, and whose continued presence in the college clearly rankled with them. Hearne pointed out sourly that Weeksey had also been supported by his *bête noire* Bowles, whom he had made his curate at St Mary's, and by Henry Brooke, another old supporter of Carter's.[127] He was also egged on by Robert Shippen, principal of Brasenose and former vice-chancellor, and William Denison, who was still clinging on to the idea that he was master of University College despite losing his case at law.[128] Dean Catherall declared Hodges ('once my own pupil', Weeksey wrote bitterly) elected.[129]

While Hodges went up to London to present himself before the Lord Chancellor for the confirmation of his election, Weeksey, 'much nettled' according to Hearne, raced off to try to have it overturned. As the chancery judgement had left it unclear who exactly was the proper authority to confirm the election of a new provost, William Craster[130] was dispatched to the bishop of Lincoln with the usual instrument for confirmation.[131] The bishop said, according to one account, that he wanted nothing further to do with the college; according to another, he mentioned a number of objections to the election which presumably came from Weeksey, who had petitioned Reynolds (from the George Inn in Holborn) at the same time as he put in his petition to the Lord Chancellor.[132] The Lord Chancellor heard Weeksey's petition on 26 October. Hearne's account of the case says that Weeksey claimed that Hodges's income—an estate said to be of £1,500 a year—was incompatible with the position of provost: no one, not Hearne and not the Lord Chancellor, had any time for this argument, and it was certainly not encompassed in King's decision on the petition.[133] The argument that was

---

[126] Hearne, *Collections*, ix. 357.

[127] In his covering note to his petition sent to the Bishop of Lincoln on 17 October 1727 Weeksey mentions Ibbetson as one of his supporters (LAO, Dioc. VV 9). Brooke's presentation to Manchester School, and the need to hold the college audit (Brooke was one of the treasurers) before he left the college, was later given by Hodges as the reason why he could not attend the bishop for the confirmation of his election: LAO, Dioc. VV 9, Hodges to Reynolds, 6 November 1727.

[128] LAO, Dioc. VV 9, Hodges to Reynolds, 6 November 1727.

[129] LAO, Dioc. VV9, Weeksey to Reynolds, 23 October 1728.

[130] Matric. 7 April 1720; elected fellow 10 April 1724; admitted probationer 18 July 1726.

[131] OCA PRO 1 A1/9. Craster's affidavit (dated April 1729) refers to his being dispatched in November, some weeks after the election. But Catherall's notice of election is dated 16 October, and the college notes on Weeksey's petition that 'to obviate any the least objection the society did immediately send one of the fellows with a proper and usual presentation under the college seal to the present bishop of Lincoln praying his Lordship to grant his usual instrument of confirmation' (OCA MEM 1 A3).

[132] i.e. the college's notes on Weeksey's petition (OCA MEM 1 A 3) and Craster's affidavit (OCA PRO 1 A1/9). Weeksey's petition to the bishop, in LAO, Dioc. VV9, is dated 17 October 1727.

[133] Hearne, *Collections*, ix. 357, 363. Presumably Weeksey would have argued that the estate would have disqualified Hodges from being a fellow, rather than provost as such.

more seriously considered, similar to one which Carter had been developing in 1726, was that four of those who had voted for Hodges—the four who had been admitted following the judgement of that year—had been admitted to their fellowships in the absence of the provost. The Lord Chancellor, however, dismissed the point and Weeksey's petition. Hodges, he said, had been 'duly elected'.[134] Hodges's return to Oxford on 1 November was supposed to be a triumph, with the bells rung and people turning out to meet him, although unfortunately he arrived home unexpectedly late.[135] Hodges's triumph was also dampened by the reaction of the bishop of Lincoln. In an exchange of letters with Reynolds, Hodges defended his decision not to visit the bishop in person to present his credentials. Reynolds's response indicated how deep the rift had become between the fellows of Oriel and its erstwhile Visitor: he had told Craster, he said to the provost,

> That if Mr Hodges or others of Oriel coll. shall visit as gentlemen or clergymen I shall receive them with ye respect due to their character but if they come to me as members of Oriel College and of the set of men who lately called me in as their domestic judge to compose their differences and then straightway accused me in ye kings courts as having made myself a judge where I had nothing to do; who by solemn act of appeal first claimed my office and interposition as their visitor and then went their way and made affidavit (if I am well informed) that I was not their visitor but an invader of ye kings rights in that very act which I had done at their earnest request and solicitation, if any of these men come to me again with fair speeches desireing my interposition in their affairs, I should doubtless be upon my guard and probably say yt I do not know that I have and certainly do not desire to have any further concern with them.[136]

Weeksey, meanwhile,

> (who is looked upon as a Rogue, & to have been altogether in the scheme of the late Provost, tho he pretended then to be otherwise) is quite now thrown by, tho perhaps he may still pretend, that there is a nullity, unless Mr Hodges be also confirmed by the Bp of Lincoln, which, however, I believe will signify just nothing.[137]

On 21 November, Weeksey told Hearne that he had no way of carrying on his battle with Hodges.[138] Even so, he continued to deny the right of Hodges to be provost and to pretend that he was provost himself, perhaps emulating the tactics used by the supporters of William Denison at University College. As Hearne predicted, he claimed that Hodges could not act as provost until he was admitted by the bishop of Lincoln; he refused to give up the Dean's Register which he had in his possession; and he made difficulties about the will of

---

[134] OCA GOV 4 A2, 26 October 1727.   [135] Hearne, *Collections*, ix. 364.
[136] LAO, Dioc. VV 9, Reynolds to Hodges, 10 November 1727.
[137] Hearne, *Collections*, ix. 363.   [138] Hearne, *Collections*, ix. 372.

Provost Carter of which he and Henry Brooke were executors.[139] Eventually, a college meeting in October 1728 found him '*contumacem, inobedientiem et intolerabilem*', as well as in possession of a benefice which, it alleged, was of greater value than was compatible with a fellowship. It declared his fellowship vacant. Naturally, Weeksey enlisted the help of the bishop of Lincoln, with whom he had continued to correspond about the provostship over the previous year;[140] and he appealed to the Lord Chancellor, laying out his argument that Hodges had needed and had failed to have himself admitted in person to the provostship by the bishop of Lincoln, apart from by proxy 'which your petitioner conceives to be absurd and inconsistent with the nature of the thing there being several oaths on this occasion to be administered'.[141]

The Lord Chancellor tried to deflect such a tiresome case. Weeksey reported to Reynolds how, shortly after he had put in his petition, the Chancellor's secretary had called him in and told him that his grievance was the result of his own stubbornness in refusing to admit that Hodges had been elected provost, 'which is in effect Rebellion against my Lord Chancellor, who swore him into his office'. Weeksey fumed about the delays of the law:

I think My Lord it is a great hardship upon me, that I should now have come to London 3 times within these 9 moneths to apply to my Lord Chancellor, and he now apparently as far from redress as ever: but I think it still a greater hardship, that I should be deprived of my fellowship by a fellow that has no right to ye Headship and by a minority of boys, at a time too, when I want the profits of it to defend myself against their arbitrary and illegal practices.[142]

Nevertheless, the Chancellor sat on the case for several more months. Surprisingly, he concluded in June 1729 that Weeksey had a point: in normal circumstances Hodges *should* have been formally presented to the bishop of Lincoln, but in this case, the election of Hodges had not been made as normal by the fellows, but as the result of the decision of the Lord Chancellor on Weeksey's original petition. Hodges had, in effect, been elected by the Visitor and needed no confirmation. In such a case, pronounced the Chancellor, 'inasmuch as this was a matter of real difficulty and not clear and evident it doth not seem reasonable to punish the petitioners past mistakes therein with the penalty due to a wilfull contempt or contumacy'.[143]

---

[139] OCA GOV 4 A2, 3, 6, 20 July, 30 September, 20, 22 October 1728. For Weeksey's pursuit of the issue of the provostship, see LAO, Dioc. VV 9, Opinion of Mr William Hawkins, 19 May 1728, Opinion of Mr Thomas Reeve, 22 August 1728, Opinion of Thomas Lutwyche, 29 August 1728, and the letters of Weeksey to Reynolds, 2 September 1728, 21 October 1728.

[140] LAO, Dioc. VV 9, Weeksey to Reynolds, 23 October 1728.

[141] OCA MEM 1 A3.

[142] LAO, Dioc. VV 9, Weeksey to Reynolds, 31 December 1728.

[143] OCA GOV 4 A2, 21 June 1729. See also Weeksey's letter to Reynolds of 24 June 1729, in LAO, Dioc. VV 9. There are further parallels with the University College case, which was determined by a visitation by commissioners on 19 April 1729, which finally decided that

It is difficult to understand the logic of this conclusion, and no subsequent election was confirmed by the bishop of Lincoln. And indeed, almost seven years later, Henry Edmunds together with a barrister called Hugh Watson discovered that the Chancellor's original decree of October 1727, which said that Hodges had been 'duly elected Provost of Oriel College', had been doctored while the papers were in the Lord Chancellor's office to suggest that there had been some defect in the election, and that Hodges had been imposed on the fellowship by the Chancellor. Edmunds certainly suspected that the government were now laying a claim to appoint in the case of a disputed election.[144] The case, though, was not then pursued any further, and no more was heard, at least over the eighteenth century, of the Chancellor claiming a power to make his own choice of provost in the case of a disputed election.

At the first fellowship election after Hodges became provost, on 28 April 1728, the fellows marked a new era by re-electing William Dering—whose fellowship had been vacated seven years before. 'Even Bowles', wrote Hearne, 'concurred with the Society in this Act, not out of an honest Principle, but because there were not enough knaves to prevent it.'[145] Weeksey, though, did not long survive his restoration by the Lord Chancellor: his fellowship was removed again—this time permanently—only a few months after the Chancellor's decision, this time on the sole grounds of his holding an incompatible benefice. In 1732, the fellows seized upon an opportunity to settle an old score when they deprived Makepeace of his fellowship, having discovered that he had been married since 1728.[146] The continued animus against Carter was detected by Shippen in their litigation over his will in 1734: 'I cannot pretend to advise your Lordship', he wrote to the bishop of Lincoln, 'what is proper to be done with such contentious people who are to use Dr Carter's money to go to Law with his best Friend.'[147]

The defeat of Carter and his allies reflected the failure of the Whigs to make inroads into Oxford's instinctive Toryism during the 1720s.[148] Oriel relaxed back into it. The college stood solidly for moderate Tory William Bromley in the 1737 by-election.[149] Hodges, 'a good scholar, & an honest man' in Hearne's view,[150] was perhaps genuinely more interested in biblical scholarship than in chasing preferment. Careful to protect the privileges of

---

Thomas Cockman was master, and removed William Denison from the fellowship on grounds of having an incompatible fellowship.

[144] OCA GOV 4 A2, 10 April 1736.
[145] Hearne, *Collections*, x. 8.
[146] OCA GOV 4 A2, 1 April 1732.
[147] LAO, Dioc. VV 9, Shippen to bishop of Lincoln, 16 December 1734.
[148] See HUO v. 114.
[149] *An Exact Account of the Poll, as it stood between The Honourable Mr Trevor, and Wm. Bromley, Esq; Candidates at the late election of a Member for the city and University of Oxford, in the Room of Dr Clarke, Deceas'd* (London, 1736 [= 1737]).
[150] Hearne, *Collections*, ix. 357.

the provostship and the position of the college, he warily minuted his letter authorizing the fellows to make the election in April 1728 while he was in the country so 'that I may not be thought to have given up any right of my office'.[151] Hodges was thought reliable enough to be made vice-chancellor for 1741–4, and was lucky enough to quit before the real difficulties in which Oxford found itself in the late 1740s.

Oriel's now straightforward Toryism and the new prominence of an Oriel man in university politics were perhaps factors in attracting the munificence of one of the country's senior Tories, the 3rd duke of Beaufort, in 1744. Beaufort had been alienated from his own college when his old school tutor, William Denison, had been pushed out of the mastership in 1729. His gift—the sum of £100 a year in perpetuity to support four undergraduate scholars from Gloucestershire, Monmouthshire, and Glamorgan, for seven years each, to be nominated by the lord of the manor of Badminton in Gloucestershire (in effect, the dukes of Beaufort and their successors)—provided Oriel with its first undergraduate exhibitions, although it was probably more valuable to the college in terms of the connection it brought with one of the most prominent noble families involved in Tory and Oxford politics.[152] The first Beaufort exhibitioner was appointed in 1747, and the college celebrated the Beaufort connection with an enormous painting of the 4th duke, now in the lobby of the common room.

The 3rd duke himself had been something of a nonentity (perhaps spoiled by the extraordinary deference of the dons at University College in the 1720s), but his successor, his brother, had connections with the Jacobite court, and serious political ambitions to lead the parliamentary Tory party in an aggressive opposition to the post-Walpole Whig government. Just as he inherited the title in February 1745 he was orchestrating a *coup d'état* within the Tories to depose their current leader, the 1st Earl Gower. The Beaufort connection may have helped to confirm the college in its current political trajectory: the parliamentary by-election of 1751 revealed, as it did in many colleges, the now highly conservative nature of Oriel's Toryism as the college voted for the ultra Tory Sir Roger Newdigate rather than the more pragmatic Robert Harley. Two fellows, though, voted for Harley: Dr Bosworth[153] and the ambitious careerist Edward Bentham,[154] who had become one of the mouthpieces of Oxford anti-Jacobitism in the late 1740s.[155] John Mulso, a

---

[151] OCA PRO 1 C2, 16 October 1731. It is not clear why Hodges wrote this three years after the event.
[152] See OCA GOV 4 A2, duke of Beaufort to Hodges, 5 March 1745, and same to same, 20 March 1745 (copies), and copy of Beaufort's will. See also OCA BT 1 C3.
[153] John Bosworth, matric. 17 December 1741; admitted probationer 20 July 1747.
[154] Admitted probationer 20 July 1731.
[155] *A True copy of the Poll taken at Oxford January 31, 1750. With several papers sent to The common rooms of the respective colleges, relating to the election of a Member of Parliament for*

ILLUSTRATION 6.2 Charles Somerset, 4th duke of Beaufort (1709–56)
Oriel College

friend and regular correspondent of the naturalist and Oriel fellow Gilbert White,[156] evidently found the strident tone of some of the fellows jarring: he complained in his letters about the 'party rage' of Charles Whiting,[157] 'not so much because we have increasing obligations to the present Family, but for a

---

the University (London, n.d.). For Bentham's careerism, see his letter from Oriel to the duke of Newcastle in British Library, Add. MS 32731, fo. 397, 25 April, 1753, and subsequent letters from Christ Church in the same correspondence. For the 1751 election, see HUO v. 125–7.

[156] Matric. 17 December. 1739; admitted probationer 20 July 1744.
[157] Admitted probationer 20 July 1736.

real Regard for the University, which is in a very low Consideration for the sake of a Parcell of fools who are a Disgrace to it in every View and are of the most contracted hearts of any Set of men that I know'. Mulso referred again in 1755 to 'the perverse party' in Oriel—presumably also referring to its ultra Tories.[158]

Hodges died in January 1757 after what had probably been a long illness. The subsequent election of Chardin Musgrave[159] is recorded as having been unanimous, but although a contest was avoided, there seem to have been preparations for one. White's friend Mulso had expected White to stand for some time before Hodges's death, and it is evident from their correspondence that he had intended to do so. James Beaver,[160] the dean, was worried enough about the arrangements for the election to seek legal advice from the Oxford lawyers James Gilpin and Sir William Blackstone concerning how long an election could be deferred under the college statutes, and to consider this at some length with other resident fellows, including Musgrave, John Frewen,[161] and Edward Bentham. They agreed amongst themselves 'That in case the election of Provost was deferred to a longer time than three days after the death of the late provost that they would not take any advantage of such delay, thinking that the publick registry of the college gives sanction to such proceedings.'[162] Mulso heard of the election shortly after it took place from Musgrave's older brother (and former gentleman commoner), Sir Philip Musgrave,[163] who complained about 'Frewen's Proceedings as not very handsom upon the Occasion, & as putting them to the Necessity of applying out of the College, when they would have had it determined there'.[164] Mulso subsequently wrote to White to wish that he had 'put yourself up from the Beginning, if anything we could have done would have given you success'.[165]

Musgrave's provostship saw Oriel clinching the Beaufort connection. The 4th duke had died in 1756, but his son, the 5th duke, came to Oriel in 1760. He helped to attract other men from prominent Tory families.[166] Musgrave's tenure also saw Oriel slide further into a firm alignment with conventional Oxford Toryism, just as George III and his ministers made moves to open the

---

[158] *The Letters to Gilbert White of Selborne from his intimate friend and contemporary The Rev. John Mulso*, ed. Rashleigh Holt-White (London, n.d.), 91: Mulso to White, 13 November 1754; 98, Mulso to White, 8 April 1755.
[159] Matric. 3 March 1740; admitted probationer 20 July 1744 (together with White).
[160] Matric. 14 January 1741; admitted probationer 20 July 1748.
[161] Admitted probationer 20 July 1739.
[162] OCA PRO 1 A1/13–16.
[163] Matric. 8 January 1733.
[164] *The Letters to Gilbert White of Selborne*, 115, Mulso to White, 24 February 1757. Musgrave was presumably hoping that the election would be settled by the resident fellows, rather than requiring the whole of the non-resident fellowship to come up.
[165] *The Letters to Gilbert White of Selborne*, 117, Mulso to White, 19 March 1757.
[166] Most obviously the son of Sir Watkin Williams Wynn, who had dominated Wales for the Tories, and who would marry the daughter of the 4th duke of Beaufort in 1769.

government to Tories, and as even Oxford began to grow weary at the survival of party sentiments which had virtually died out elsewhere. Musgrave and Oriel voted for the Tory candidate, Lord Foley, in the chancellorship election of 1762, rather than the successful ministerial candidate, Lord Lichfield.[167] Musgrave was among those who persuaded Sir Walter Bagot, a country gentleman of impeccable Tory credentials, to become the university's member of parliament at a by-election in 1762.[168] When Bagot died at the beginning of 1768—only weeks before a general election was due—there was a concerted effort to create an alliance between the independent Whig interest, represented by Charles Jenkinson, and the more pragmatic Tories. But the Tory party found a candidate—Sir William Dolben—whose popularity among Tories wrecked Jenkinson's chances. Why this election should have caused the death of Oriel's provost is unclear, but it seems that Musgrave may have been wrong-footed as negotiations went on between the Tories and Dolben, and found himself appearing to have been deeply implicated in double dealing.

Last week was likewise vacated the Headship of Oriel by the shocking suicide of Dr Musgrave Brother to Sir Philip, a Cumberland Baronet. For some Days before the Atmosphere had been remarkably warm heavy & relaxing, this, with a Constitution which must surely have been before unhing'd, & a Disappointment in electioneering matters, where he had very hotly engag'd, produc'd a Fever upon the Spirits, & in a Fit of Despondence, while a most affectionate Wife was in the Room, he thrice stab'd himself in the Throat, cut the jugular Vein & expir'd; his fond Wife turn'd around, beheld him in Agony, flew distracted into the Quadrangle crying Blood, Blood, ran into an Old Man's Room, clasp'd him about the Neck & swoon'd away.[169]

Musgrave's death would have little impact on the college's politics. His successor, John Clark,[170] the then dean, was elected unanimously (though the college worried again about the notice given for non-resident fellows).[171] The solidest support for the 5th duke of Beaufort's unsuccessful bid to become chancellor of the university in 1772 came from Oriel, and from Jesus, a college with its roots in Beaufort country on the borders of Wales.[172] A former fellow of Oriel, Thomas Nowell,[173] who had moved to the principalship of St Mary Hall, took the leading role in the expulsion of six St Edmund Hall students for attending unauthorized evangelical prayer meetings. In the same year Clark was in the forefront of those resisting the

---

[167] Ward, *Georgian Oxford*, 218–23. [168] Ward, *Georgian Oxford*, 224–5.
[169] W. Stanhope to John Stanhope, 4 February 1768, West Yorkshire Archive Service: Bradford, Sp. St. 6/1/90.
[170] Admitted probationer 20 July 1755.
[171] OCA PRO 1 A1/23–26.
[172] Ward, *Georgian Oxford*, 258.
[173] Matric. 10 May 1746; admitted probationer 20 July 1753.

removal of the requirement that all members of the university, lay as well as clerical, should subscribe to the Thirty-Nine Articles, and even dismissed his curate at Purleigh because he signed the petition for relief from it.[174] After its flirtation with Whiggism and the low Church, Oriel on the eve of its ascendancy was again a bastion of the Tory and Anglican establishment.

[174] Ward, *Georgian Oxford*, 260.

7

An Anglican Foundation

Paul Seaward

Most fellows expected their time at Oriel to be an episode in a clerical career, rather than a lifetime's vocation. Gilbert White's friend John Mulso[1] told him in 1758 that 'Fellowships are a sort of temporary Establishments for men of good Learning and small Fortunes, till their Merits or some fortunate Turn pushes them into the World, and enables them to relinquish to men under the same Predicament'.[2] White's career-long search for an adequate and untroublesome income was typical. The chief preoccupation of most fellows was to find a suitable benefice which would enable them to marry and set up home in a comfortable parsonage, which would usually mean relinquishing their fellowship. Like White, they would have to calculate whether any particular living was valuable enough, and manageable enough, to make it worth giving up Oriel.

Their calculation would depend partly on the value of the fellowship. Oriel was not a wealthy college. The 1592 assessments of each college's 'Old rents' still used in the 1660s had placed Oriel's annual income, at £200, about two-thirds of the way down the list of colleges, way below Christ Church (£2,000), Magdalen (£1,200) New College (£1,000), and All Souls (£500) and Corpus Christi (£500), and on a par with Exeter and Trinity. A rough estimate in the 1690s put Oriel's annual revenue more realistically at £600 a year, but still in the same place in the hierarchy of colleges: way below Christ Church, Magdalen, New College, All Souls, St Johns, and Merton; on a par with University, Exeter, Brasenose, and Trinity, and above Lincoln, Balliol, Jesus, Wadham, and Pembroke.[3] The basic income of the provost and fellows, their

---

[1] White: matric. 17 December 1739, elected fellow, 30 March 1744. Mulso: matric. 26 November 1740, MA 5 May 1747.

[2] *The Letters to Gilbert White of Selborne from his intimate friend and contemporary The Rev. John Mulso*, ed. Rashleigh Holt-White (London, n.d.), 137: Mulso to White, 29 November 1758.

[3] J. Gutch, *Collectanea Curiosa, or miscellaneous tracts, relating to the History and antiquities of England and Ireland*, 2 vols. (Oxford, 1781), ii. 191–5. The list is reproduced in HUO v. 273.

allowance of commons, came from the college's rents. The commons was raised in 1629 to 6s. a week for the provost and 4s. for fellows (which would theoretically produce an income of £10 8s. a year for a fellow in permanent residence). Since 1602, the fellows had also shared as a dividend the sum left over from the college rents after the commons had been distributed. Fines, paid on the renewal of college leases, were also distributed among those fellows who were present at the sealing of the lease. Another payment was made to the college's treasurers on sealing leases, although in 1729 the college decided that this, too, should be divided among the fellows, and in 1730 the stipends of the treasurers were increased to £6 for the senior, £4 for the junior, to compensate.[4] A fellow's college income therefore fluctuated with the yield from rents and fines from renewals, and his average annual income was unpredictable at the time and hard to calculate now.[5]

It might have been much higher than it actually was, if the college had been able to profit from its most valuable estate, the manor of Wadley and Wickensham. Oriel had made an unfortunate miscalculation in 1538, 'when the estates of colleges were thought to be in some danger'. It had leased the estate for seventy eight years for £58 a year to Alexander Unton, and a few weeks later extended this lease for a further fifty years at the same yearly rent. In addition, it had covenanted that Unton's heirs should have the property after the expiry of the second lease for a further eighty years at the same yearly rent, on payment of a fine of £60. In total, the estate had been alienated for 208 years. It passed through Unton's granddaughter to Sir Valentine Knightley, who held it at the time when the first lease was coming to an end. According to the college, when Knightley heard that the college was planning to dispute the validity of the second lease and the covenant, he obtained a letter from James I requiring them 'not only to suffer him quietly to enjoy the same without any disturbance from you, but also that there may be any means found to confirm and establish the estate he hath, that you do confirm and establish him in it'. As the king had only recently granted the college a charter of incorporation confirming their estates they felt unable to contest the instruction. They agreed to an act of parliament which confirmed the charter of incorporation and the leases on Wadley, although the rent was raised to £100 a year.[6]

---

[4] OCA PRO 1 C 1/5.

[5] It might be assumed that the income of an ordinary fellow from commons, dividends, and fines would amount to roughly two-thirds of that of the provost. If so, judging by Provost Clark's calculations in the late 1760s and early 1770s, a fellow probably obtained around £90–£100 a year. Income earlier in the period, before the college started to move away from the old system of reserved rents, would have been much lower than this. See East Sussex Record Office, FRE 11180, John Frewen to his father, Merton, 29 April 1735: 'Tis not yet known who will make the vacancy at Oriel. The living it seems proves a better than expected, wch makes worse for me.'

[6] This account is taken from the college's printed explanation of its case, inserted into the Dean's Register, OCA GOV 4 A2, under 14 March 1737.

In the seventeenth century the leases were passed down to Knightley's son-in-law Sir Henry Purefoy. Relations with the Purefoys seemed cordial. Sir Henry Purefoy, either the son or grandson of the man who had inherited Wadley, was admitted to Oriel in 1671.[7] In 1673, his mother, Lady Katherine Bellingham (she had remarried after her husband's death), had died in the provost's lodgings in Oriel. Sir Henry, according to Wood, died in Oxford shortly afterwards. Without children, he made Sir Willoughby Aston of Cheshire, his mother's sister's son, his heir and executor, without taking notice of his uncle, Knightley Purefoy, of Shaddleston in Buckinghamshire (one of the Shaddleston Purefoys, also Henry, was admitted to Oriel in 1719).[8] The college seems to have got along with the Astons equally well: another Willoughby Aston was admitted as a gentleman commoner in 1730 (he even took BA and MA degrees).[9]

Even so, the college was well aware of how unfortunate the leases were. Richard Saunders, the senior treasurer in 1645, noted at the back of a set of the college statutes the original terms of the leases, and calculated the number of years expired so far.[10] Wadley was a very valuable estate, 'a very fine manor belonging to Oriel Coll.', wrote Anthony Wood after visiting in 1678.[11] In 1737 the college claimed that it was worth £1,000 a year, as well as the rent from various copyhold leases, amounting to £400 a year.[12] Charging a more realistic rent for the estate had the potential to transform the college's finances. Bishop Robinson's 1719 bequest was designed to compensate for the college's low income until the end of the current lease: Robinson was 'informed that the present income of the provost and scholars commonly called fellows of the College is very small but that the same is like to be considerably augmented when a certain lease of the manors of Wadley and Wickenham . . . now held of the said College for the term of 28 years or thereabout yet to come shall determine', and therefore he left his £2,500 to be invested and the income divided among the provost and scholars 'in such proportion as the rents of the said College are now usually divided', until the lease had ended.[13]

The lease was due to end in 1747. In 1730, with about seventeen years still to run, the then lessee, Richard Aston (around the same time as his son Willoughby was sent to Oriel), asked the college to renew the lease for twenty-one years. According to the college's account of events, they told him that they would only renew on the basis of the Elizabethan legislation then in force which linked part of the rent to the price of corn. Aston rejected the offer: it would triple the rent, and mean that the total charges on the estate

---

[7] Matric. 13 November 1671.
[8] Wood, *Life and Times*, ii. 263. Matric. 13 November 1719.
[9] Matric. 7 January 1730. [10] OCA PRO 2/36/16.
[11] Wood, *Life and Times*, ii. 405.
[12] *The Case between Oriel College in Oxford, and Richard Aston Esq.*
[13] OCA GOV 4 A2, 25 February 1719.

would exceed its annual value. 'And there the matter rested without any kind of agreement, or other formal treaty with regard to any rent or fine.' According to Aston's later account of events, he was told that it was not the college's policy to renew more than fourteen years before the end of a lease, though they suggested that were he to send them an up-to-date map and valuation of the estate they might be prepared to negotiate. Aston said that he had complied with their request; but the college first quibbled over the ownership of the tithes on the estate, and then about the payment of Land Tax on the rent. In 1734, Aston took the college to court over the taxes. As a result, he claimed, it had been forced to pay the tax on the rent for the last six years and for the future too; the college retorted that the case had been dismissed, but that it had afterwards voluntarily agreed to allow Aston the Land Tax.

Aston said that the college had responded to his suit with a counter-claim for damage he had made on the estate, 'his selling timber to the value of £5000, breaking up pasture and meadow lands, never ploughed before, with many more false suggestions, and of that length, as to take up many hundred sheets of paper to answer, delivering likewise to the under tenants copies of an injunction, to prevent their ploughing, committing waste, &c. whereby the tenants were very much intimidated'. The college claimed that it had had information upon oath, that it had exhibited a short bill in chancery against him and obtained an injunction to stay waste; but that it had never taken the matter further.[14] Aston said that he had visited the college shortly afterwards and had asked 'their reason for exhibiting that long bill against him, for which, they knew in their consciences, there was no foundation'. He alleged that he had proved that the college had gained the benefit of any timber sold on the estate 'to which justification they had nothing to object, but desired he would not put in his answer, excusing themselves by saying, he had declared war first'. There were further arguments over the ownership of the tithes (worth, according to the college, a further £200 a year) and another small piece of land. Aston complained that these were manoeuvres to avoid a renewal: the college was clearly determined to extract the maximum benefit.

Aston escalated the war in 1737 by appealing to the House of Commons. In doing so, he evidently sought to take advantage of the hostility to the involvement of clerical institutions in the private property market which had been manifested in the Mortmain bill affair of the year before and the row over the lease by Queen's College of Sparsholt rectory which had emerged in the Commons the year previously.[15] A copy of the printed paper he distributed to Members was preserved in the Dean's Register. Aston argued that 'Till very lately colleges have thought themselves virtually oblig'd to renew for the usual or reasonable fines, upon application in due time.' In this case,

---

[14] See also OCA PRO 1 C1 1, under 11 April 1735.
[15] For Sparsholt rectory, see HUO v. 279.

Oriel had refused. He requested that the college should be compelled 'to accept such fine as shall be thought reasonable to have been demanded, to add seven years to his term of fourteen, to complete the usual terms of twenty one years'. Alleging that on his inheritance of the lease, he had been given assurances about the renewal of the lease on its expiry, and on the basis of those assurances, he had spent £900 improving the house on the estate, he asked that 'the Parliament will now interpose to prevent the ruin of those families who (relying upon the vertue and honour of such reverend and learned societies) have purchased upon the faith of colleges'. Oriel's paper in response argued

that the provost and fellows of this college are the only sufferers in this case, and real objects of compassion, considering the four additional fellows maintained so long upon the small share reserved from this estate; and the lowness of the present revenue occasioned by these extravagant leases: and as to Mr Aston, he, and those under whom he claims, have enjoyed this estate for near two hundred years without paying one fine to the College, and Mr Aston himself has enjoyed it about thirty-three years, and has about ten years yet to come, and will then have the aforesaid advantage of granting 400l p. ann. copyhold estates; and therefore it is humbly apprehended he is not intitled to any extraordinary interposition of the legislature in his favour.

Aston's petition was presented in the House of Commons on 15 March 1737. The names of the speakers for and against the petition, and the House's narrow vote not to commit it to a Select Committee, were also entered into the register.[16] Despite their success in fending off Aston, the college remained wary. When, a month after the vote in the Commons, some copyholders from the college estate at Dean asked to renew their leases, there was a discussion within the college about whether copyhold tenures should be allowed:

Some were against renewing any more copys, & allowing the Tenants only a Liberty of taking leases for 21 years. The Provost observd that such a proceeding seemed too violent, & might at this juncture occasion much clamour & bring an odium upon the college, especially after what had happened in Mr Aston's affair so lately. That Mr Aston might hear of this matter and join these tenants with himself in a fresh petition to the H of Commons. That he should be very sorry to have the name of this college in every one's mouth as using their tenants ill, or introductory to some bill, which may affect colleges in general. The question being put by the Provost, 5 fellows were against setting any Price for renewing the copyholds, 4 for it; the provost was likewise for it, but as the majority was not so clear, it was not agreed that any one should renew but upon 21 years leases.[17]

---

[16] Speakers listed in OCA GOV 4 A2 against the petition were: Lord Cornbury, Lord Noel Somerset, Lord Tyrconnel, Sir Robert Walpole, Sir William Wyndham, Hon. Thomas Townshend, Dr George Lee, William Shippen, and Sir William Yonge; those for it were Sir Thomas Aston, Sir Wilfred Lawson, Colonel Mordaunt, Walter Plumer, John Pollen, Robert Knight.

[17] OCA PRO 1 C1 2, 15 April 1737. See HUO v. 280–1.

Aston's failure to secure the interest of the House of Commons seems to have encouraged a settlement of the case, and the lease was renewed in 1738.[18] But there was further litigation with Richard Aston's heir over the smaller part of the estate in 1744–5, and a final settlement with the family was not reached until 1750.[19] Nevertheless, the renewal of the Wadley lease marked a change in the fortunes of the college. The fellows celebrated by agreeing to augment the weekly commons by 3s. a week for themselves and 4s. 6d. for the Provost, both payments irrespective of residence.[20]

With the increase in commons an Oriel fellowship rose in value. It perhaps resulted in fellows remaining for longer: the average period for which a fellowship was held certainly increased by about two years for fellows elected after 1740.[21] It no doubt would have altered fellows' estimates of the value of a living for which it would be worth resigning from Oriel.

Defining what sort of living would require a fellow to resign from the society—what living would be incompatible with the fellowship or an *'uberius beneficium'*—was the source of endless difficulty, in Oriel as in all other colleges. According to the statutes, any living valued at 10 marks (£6 13s. 4d.) or more would disqualify. Fellows would usually turn to the 'King's Book', the assessment of the value of livings carried out in 1535 for Henry VIII, to establish the value of the benefice. It was normal for them to inform the college on institution to a disqualifying benefice, a procedure which would usually ensure that they received the customary 'year of grace' before formally resigning, and continue to receive the emoluments of the fellowship for the following twelve months. The bishop of Lincoln regularized this practice in 1673, and specified the procedure for informing the college of institution.[22] In 1728 the college decided that it would regard all benefices which were exempt from paying the taxes of first fruits and tenths under the acts establishing Queen Anne's Bounty as compatible with a fellowship—those worth under £50 a year in the modern valuation.[23] At a college meeting on

---

[18] OCA PRO 1 C1 2, 20 July, 27 October 1738.
[19] See Hardwicke's notes on the case, British Library MS Add. 36056, fo. 117ff.; HUO v. 280 n. 2.
[20] OCA GOV 4 A2, 16 October 1739.
[21] For fellows elected between 1660 and 1739 inclusive, the average period the fellowship was held was about 14.8 years; for fellows elected between 1740 and 1780 inclusive, the average was about 16.4 years. These figures include men who apparently did not seek livings for whatever reason and men who died while still fellows.
[22] OCA GOV 2 D5.
[23] OCA GOV 4 A2, 6 July 1728: see also 19 October. OCA MEM 1 A3/13 is an undated decree that no benefice be deemed *uberius* if it were less than £8 on the King's Book or certified by the commissioners in the reign of Queen Anne not to exceed £50 a year; benefices which dated from after that time or were omitted in that valuation were to be deemed *uberius* unless the incumbent gave in a certificate from the bishop of the diocese that he is credibly informed that the reputed value of the said benefice did not exceed £80 a year, and the certificate to be entered in the college register. There is, however, no trace of this decree on the register.

21 July 1740, on the enquiry of George Shakerley (presumably on expectation of his appointment to a prebendal stall at Wells Cathedral), it extended the £50 a year rule to sinecures.[24]

The college in 1729 collected a number of examples of those who had left their fellowships on institution to an incompatible benefice: Beckham, in 1721, for a living valued in the King's Book at £11 0s. 7d.; Rogers, the same year, for a living of £11 3s. 1d.; Ingram in 1718, for a living of £17 5s. 2d.; Rye in 1716, for a living of £16 13s. 6d., and Brickenden in 1700, for one of £13 9s. 4d.[25] These were not the actual current values of benefices: most would be worth substantially more than their sixteenth-century valuations, although rising taxation had to some extent counteracted the growth in clerical incomes at the same time.[26]

Plenty of fellows were therefore able to augment their income with a living of lower value while they retained their fellowships. They might hold more than one: clergy could obtain a dispensation from the archbishop of Canterbury to hold two benefices at the same time, as long as the parishes were not more than thirty miles apart, the minister concerned spent at least two months a year in each, and employed a satisfactory curate.[27] There was no difficulty in serving as chaplain to a nobleman, and several Oriel fellows did. Fellows holding a compatible benefice with care of souls would generally live away from Oxford, on the living, unless it could be avoided. Non-resident fellows received a smaller share of commons,[28] although resident fellows were occasionally permitted a full share of commons if they were temporarily non-resident for special reasons: for example Christopher Robinson in 1738 when he went to live at the college farm in Littlemore on doctor's orders, and Charles Whiting in 1740 when he took refuge at Cowley from the smallpox.[29]

Some resident fellows could earn much more by teaching undergraduates. The college offices, occupied in rotation by fellows, produced a small stipend, although that of chaplain was often not filled. Some fellows chose to supplement their income by serving parishes in Oxford or close to it. The presentation to the vicarage of St Mary the Virgin was, of course, in the hands of the college, and in the eighteenth century was always held by a senior fellow. But there were other opportunities, albeit generally unattractive ones. In 1713, for example, John Salmon was presented by the Lord Keeper to St Peter's in the Bailey in Oxford (snatching it from under the nose of a

---

[24] OCA PRO 1 C1 2; see also OCA GOV 4 A2, 21 July 1740, 21 March 1741.
[25] OCA MEM 1 A 3.
[26] See John H. Pruett, *The Parish Clergy under the Later Stuarts: The Leicestershire Experience* (Urbana, Ill., 1978), 100–10.
[27] See W. M. Jacob, *The Clerical Profession in the Long Eighteenth Century 1680–1940* (Oxford, 2007), 95–9.
[28] Although they received the full amount of the commons added in 1739.
[29] OCA PRO 1 C1 2, 1 March 1738, 21 July 1740.

fellow of Corpus), which was 'not worth above £15 per an.' (in current, rather than sixteenth-century, values). Hearne regarded Salmon as a hair-shirted figure, 'a very starch'd white livered Republican', who

> pretends to great sanctity of Life. He drinks always water, and hath no parts nor learning. He preaches by heart, and makes horrid work of it. He catechizes the children at St Peters making them use that vile wretched catechism published by Burnett, Bishop of Sarum, with whom Salmon is said to be great.[30]

On his death a few months later of smallpox, though, Hearne was prepared to admit that Salmon 'did some good by keeping several Girls at School in Oxford at his own Charge, being commonly call'd Salmon's charity school of Girls'.[31] Hearne also heard that another Oriel fellow, George Parry, had been prepared to act as chaplain of Clifton, near Dorchester, where the tithes had fallen into the hands of a lay impropriator, and therefore was not served by a resident clergyman, 'for ten pounds or thereabouts per annum'.[32] Arrangements like these were evidently common. In October 1750 Provost Hodges was furious to discover that the only fellow in residence, Charles Whiting, who had undertaken to read prayers in the chapel during the long vacation, was also conducting services in several other local churches: having abandoned prayers in the chapel, he had commissioned the bible clerk to ring the bell anyway, 'that our neighbours might not know that we had no prayers'. That evening, Whiting came to Hodges and complained of the amount he had to do: 'I told him', wrote Hodges in a memorandum, 'that he was only blameable for undertaking more than he or any one could well perform.'[33]

In practice there was considerable confusion and room for manoeuvre in determining whether a particular benefice was compatible with a fellowship. As Provost Eveleigh noted in the 1790s, the rectory of Cholderton in the patronage of the college, charged in the King's Book £11 0s. 7d., had been regarded as incompatible, but Aberford, which he thought of greater value, had been regarded as compatible with a fellowship.[34] Thomas Weeksey had been in possession of his rectory of Llanfihangel, Cwmdu, in Breconshire for six years before the college used it in its efforts to remove him in 1729. He accepted that the benefice was more than 10 marks in the King's Book (it was

---

[30] Hearne, *Collections*, iii. 294. Admitted in perp. 23 July 1708.
[31] Hearne, *Collections*, iii. 393.
[32] Hearne, *Collections*, iii. 355. Hearne pointed out that Oriel was itself the impropriator of St Bartholomew's hospital and failed to provide a proper chaplain there.
[33] OCA CHA 2 A1/1. Hodges's annoyance with Whiting may have also been caused by what he regarded in September 1750 as his neglect in his duties as junior treasurer when he put the college seal onto an instrument giving the college's consent to the Radcliffe trustees' taking part of St Mary's churchyard: see OCA PRO C1 2, 13 December 1750.
[34] OCA MEM 1 A 3/14. I am grateful to Rob Petre for comparing this manuscript with others by Eveleigh and with the handwriting of other contemporary Oriel fellows to confirm its authorship.

valued at £19 15s.): however, he argued that in Pope Nicholas's *valor* of 1291, the valuation in normal use when the original statute was made in the reign of Henry VI, the benefice had not been valued at all, and 'is of much lower value than the generality of benefices valued in the said old valor at the rate of ten marks'. The college responded with its list of the recent occasions on which fellows had resigned fellowships for livings of lower value, and affected not to know exactly what Weeksey meant by Pope Nicholas's *valor*:

> As to the mention in the petition of an old valor, it is not certain, what the petition means but probably it may be a book of late years so called and kept in the Bodleian Library which is only a private manuscript and of no authority and appears to be a very incorrect and imperfect copy of some ancient valor, but when made is uncertain. There are in this book 3 or 4 entrys in modern hands, which probably contain the conjectures of some former proprietors of the book one begins with a query whether it was not made in the 20th of Edward the 1st another containing a quotation out of Radulphus Cestriensis giving an account that taxation was made of all beneficies the 17 of Edward the 1st by command of Pope Nicholas, which is the probable occasion of calling this book by that name.[35]

After 1728 there was continued pressure from fellows to increase the value of compatible benefices to enable them to retain their fellowships. Eveleigh suggested in the 1790s that after the rise in the value of the fellowship after 1739 fellows 'reasoned that if they were allowed to hold 10 marks before, they might now hold more, when their fellowship were so much augmented'.[36] Under the provostship of Chardin Musgrave, there was an effort to rationalize the system. William Thomas in 1760 asked whether the vicarage of Aberavon would be compatible with a fellowship: although the college appears to have decided that it was incompatible, Thomas retained both the vicarage and his fellowship.[37] In October 1763 another query from him caused the college to mount a more serious attempt to work out what it currently meant by an *uberius beneficium*, and to draw up a statute. It sent instructions to the college's steward, the recorder of Oxford, Mr Gilpin, who produced a draft agreed by the resident fellows in November.[38] The new draft would exempt all ecclesiastical benefices whose current annual post-tax value was £100 or more, whether rated in the King's Book or not, and whether or not discharged from payment of first fruits in the Queen's Bounty Act. A fellow who held freehold or copyhold lands, tithes, rents of the same value or more would normally be deemed *uberius* too.[39] The non-resident fellows were summoned for a meeting at the end of April 1764. Not surprisingly, many of them objected to making ordinary estates of this size incompatible with fellowships, arguing that the word *beneficium* in the

---

[35] OCA MEM 1 A 3/1.   [36] OCA MEM 1 A 3/14.
[37] OCA GOV 4 A2, 12 April 1760. See CCEd s.n.   [38] OCA MEM 1 A 3/3.
[39] OCA MEM 1 A 3/8.

founder's statutes referred only to ecclesiastical benefices and not secular property. The college agreed to send to the Visitor for his view,[40] though it seems also to have commissioned opinions on the subject from Gilpin and from William Blackstone, the Vinerian Professor of Law: the latter, at least, advised against extending the definition of benefice to secular property.[41] Nevertheless, the college seems to have pressed on with its attempt to produce a wider definition, and there are fresh instructions to Gilpin, dated 19 October 1764. These would retain the £100 after tax limit for an ecclesiastical benefice, although they allowed an additional £30 for the cost of a curate if a living had more than one church and could not be supplied by one person; and they still included freehold or estates for life—or any combination of these and ecclesiastical benefices.[42] But as Eveleigh noted, nothing was ultimately done. He described the position at the end of the century:

> the common opinion in the college seems to be that the valuation of the Kings books is to be neglected and the living estimated according to its real value & compared after deducting the stipend paid the curate with the averaged value of a fellowship; but when this opinion first began I cannot say.... the precise value of a fellowship has never yet been ascertained nor has any sum ever been fixed with which the real value of a tenable living is to be compared; nor any decree or statute passed to alter the old mode of proceedings.[43]

As the discussion in 1764 showed, the possession of estates other than ecclesiastical benefices was a difficult issue, for a number of fellows had significant private means.[44] Several were known for their personal wealth, including George Carter, James Davenant, Richard Dyer, and Walter Hodges (Hodges's wealth, of around £1,500 a year according to Hearne, was regarded as a good reason why he should be elected provost).[45] Hearne reported that Thomas Whalley, who resigned his fellowship in 1723, had a paternal estate of about £500 or £600 a year, and left a significant sum to the college in his will.[46] Peter Randal, on his death in 1721, was said to have left £5,000.[47] Joseph Woodward, who died in 1729 after having been a fellow for fifty-eight years, left a large private income to his niece, with whom he had lived in New Inn Hall Street.[48] Private wealth was not exactly disregarded, but, like marriage, would normally be viewed with a blind eye. Gilbert White was

---

[40] OCA MEM 1 A 3/3. [41] OCA MEM 1 A 3/11.
[42] OCA MEM 1 A 3/12. [43] OCA MEM 1 A 3/14.
[44] Though see Hearne, *Collections*, iii. 125 for examples elsewhere of real estate disqualifying from a fellowship.
[45] Hearne, *Collections*, ix. 357, 363, 372.
[46] Hearne, *Collections*, viii. 317.
[47] Hearne, *Collections*, vii. 186.
[48] Hearne, *Collections*, ix. 283. Woodward's niece married the physician and Camden Professor of History Dr Richard Frewin in 1727. It is unknown whether he was any relation to John Frewen, the fellow of Oriel admitted probationer 20 July 1739.

in some difficulty about it on the death of his father in September 1758: it was said that White had succeeded to a very large estate, and Provost Musgrave (who had recently beaten White to the provostship) wrote to him to point out that this would be inconsistent with his fellowship and his possession of a college living. White's wealth in fact seems to have been small, and Musgrave relented, sending a message to White via Mulso that 'it was in your own breast to keep or leave your Fellowship; for Nobody meant to turn You out if you did not choose it Yourself'.[49]

The right to nominate clergy to benefices lay in many hands, ecclesiastical and secular, personal and institutional. Some fellows were lucky enough to have a family living, and had simply to hold their fellowship until it became available.[50] But most would not have had such a convenient family connection, and would need to search for a suitable living from some lay or ecclesiastical patron. Some might expect to benefit from connections with those who attended the college. John Clark, in 1767, shortly before he unexpectedly became provost, was presented by Lord Leigh (admitted to the college as a nobleman in 1761, and perhaps assigned to Clark's tutorship, and made high steward in 1767) to the vicarage of Leek Wootton in Warwickshire.[51] Robert Penny must have received the vicarage of Badminton at the hands of the duke of Beaufort, who sent him a present of oysters to Oriel, and whom he attended in London.[52] One surprisingly important connection was the patronage exercised by the Hodge family, which in addition to the rectory of Shipton Moyne in Gloucestershire, held by Walter Hodges's father, Dr William Hodges, possessed the right to present to the rectory of Easton Grey. Edward Rayner was appointed rector of Easton Grey in 1733 where he succeeded Richard Weeksey, presumably a relative of Thomas Weeksey.[53] In fact, as Warden Coxed of New College told Vice-Chancellor Niblett in March 1736, patrons willing to prefer fellows of their Oxford college, rather than other friends or relations, were hard to come by: 'the difficulty of obtaining and of preserving an interest among Foreign Patrons sufficient to promote one of the members of such societies yearly is also evident and is not

---

[49] *The Letters to Gilbert White of Selborne*, 137–41.
[50] For example, Bartholomew Martyn, the son of John Martyn of Steeple Ashton, Wiltshire, presented to the living of Steeple Ashton in 1688; Bradley Whalley, son of a clergyman of Cogenhoe, Northamptonshire, who became rector of Cogenhoe in 1703, perhaps on the death of his father; Edmund Brickenden, son of a clergyman from Corton, Somerset, who became vicar of Corton Dinham in 1701; George Sandys, who became rector of Yeovilton in succession to his father in 1706. Edward Popham, appointed rector of Chilton Foliat in Wiltshire in 1779, was presumably the beneficiary of the patronage of his mother, Dorothy Popham, the widow of Francis Popham.
[51] OCA PRO 1 C1 4.
[52] W. N. Hargreaves-Mawdsley (ed.), *Woodforde at Oxford, 1759–76* (OHS, Oxford, 1969), 206.
[53] 29 April, 31 July 1740: see *London Evening Post*, 9 October 1733; 8 November 1737.

to be disproved by the experience of the largest society in Oxford [Christ Church] who are presumed not to have had a single member preferred in this manner one year with another.'[54] The livings in the hands of the state were an important source of patronage, but subject to the vagaries of politics. When Sir Robert Henley, apparently a friend of Gilbert White, was appointed Lord Keeper in 1757, White's friend Mulso expected imminent news of preferment for White, although his prospects seem to have been wrecked with the construction Henley placed on his vote in the 1759 chancellorship election.[55]

The college's own livings were therefore a crucial alternative for many fellows, although Oriel had a relatively small number of them, and none seems to have been regarded as ideal. The vicarages of St Mary's in Oxford, Aberford, in Yorkshire, and Coleby, in Lincolnshire, had been owned by the college from the foundation, or soon afterwards. The rectory of Swainswick, Somerset, had been presented by Dr Dudley in 1529, and the perpetual curacy of Moreton Pinkney, in Northamptonshire, had been purchased in 1559. Two more were acquired before 1700: the rectory of Saltfleetby St Peter, Lincolnshire, left in 1683 in the will of Dudley Hodson, a former bible clerk,[56] to be given in preference to a bible clerk of Oriel; and Cholderton, Wiltshire, left in 1693 in the will of Sir Thomas Cholwell. An estimate of 1736 valued Cholderton at £100 a year, Swainswick at £55 a year, and three others were discharged under the legislation setting up Queen Anne's Bounty—in other words, were worth less than £50 a year.[57]

In 1720 the college put together money from a number of sources to purchase more advowsons. The college resolved in 1720 to use more than £100 of the interest on the money left the college by Samuel Desmaistres,[58] and £300 each from the current fellows Richard Dyer and Thomas Whalley, to buy the advowson of the rectory of Ufton Nervet in Berkshire.[59] In his will of 30 December 1726, George Carter left £1,000 to buy a living to annex to the provostship, and most of the rest of his money to purchase one or two advowsons to be disposed by the provost to a resident fellow.[60] The college must have put this money together with sums from other sources to purchase Cromhall and Tortworth, both in Gloucestershire, from Lord Ducie in 1728 for £1,300.[61] The 1736 estimate valued Ufton at £130 and Cromhall and

---

[54] Quoted in Clarke, 'Warden Gardiner and the Church', in S. J. D. Green and Peregrine Horden (eds.), *All Souls under the Ancien Regime* (Oxford, 2007), 212.
[55] *The Letters to Gilbert White of Selborne*, 123: Mulso to White, 14 July 1757.
[56] Matric. 7 March 1663.
[57] All Souls MS 522, Paper P.
[58] See OCA GOV 4 A2, 16 November 1695, 22 September 1703.
[59] OCA GOV 4 A2, 22 June 1720. Hearne *Collections*, vii. 272 makes a slightly inaccurate report.
[60] OCA PRO 2/35/1.
[61] See Gloucestershire Archives, D340a/C20/18, Tho. Rous to Lord Ducie, 27 February 1726 [1727].

Tortworth at £130 and £140 a year respectively.⁶² Purleigh was bought in the early 1730s as the provost's living.⁶³

From the beginning of the eighteenth century Oriel fellows seem to have been resorting to the college's own livings with greater frequency. But in 1736 all of Oxford was sent into a panic as the Mortmain bill, presented in the House of Commons by the more anti-clerical end of the Whig party, threatened to close down this avenue of preferment.⁶⁴ The bill, among other things, was designed to limit the number of advowsons that each college could hold. In his efforts to coordinate opposition to the bill, Vice-Chancellor Niblett tried to establish how many advowsons each college possessed, and how they had been used. Hodges, like most other heads of houses, helped to collect information for Niblett, as well as passing on information about the broadly sympathetic views of Samuel Sandys, the Whig member for Worcestershire,⁶⁵ although he also tried to take advantage of Niblett's trips to London to ask him to run some minor errands ('3 pounds of breakfast Green Tea from the same place &c. and that you would pay his 2d subscription for Couragers History &c and after it is bound, letter'd and gilt in London, that you would be pleased to order it down hither to him').⁶⁶ Oriel responded to Niblett's circular that 'For the last 30 years viz from 1705 to 1735 there have been 40 fellows preferred or otherwise gone or taken off from the said society, of which number 4 only have in all that time gone off to a college living by the presentation of the society.'⁶⁷

The efforts of Niblett and the university's MPs meant that the Mortmain Act was much less damaging than had been feared, permitting colleges to hold up to half as many advowsons as they had fellows. It allowed Oriel to purchase one more, that of Plymtree, in 1737. It was also thought to be easily evaded. The will of Walter Hodges may have been one attempt to provide further livings for Oriel fellows without directly infringing the terms of the Act. Hodges, on his death in 1757, left the Hodges family estates (the manors of Easton Grey, Shipton Moyne, and Shipton Duffield, in Gloucestershire and Wiltshire with their advowsons) to his sister, Elizabeth Nowell, who had married a fellow of the college, William Nowell, in 1746.⁶⁸ The will provided that if there was a vacancy in either of the livings of Shipton Moyne and Easton Grey, Dr John Ratcliffe, master of Pembroke (who had married the

---

⁶² All Souls MS 522, Paper P.   ⁶³ OCA PRO 2 35 6.
⁶⁴ See W. R. Ward, *Georgian Oxford* (Oxford, 1958), 157–60, and John Clarke, 'Warden Niblett and the Mortmain Bill', in *All Souls under the Ancien Regime*, 217–32.
⁶⁵ All Souls MS 535: W. Hodges to Niblett, 21 March 1736.
⁶⁶ All Souls MS 550: Jo Mather to Niblett, 5 April 1736.
⁶⁷ All Souls MS 522, Paper O. It is not clear how the figure of four was calculated. Fellows who resigned on presentation to college livings in this period were Nicholas Rogers (Ufton Nervet, 1721); Edward Beckham (Cholderton, 1720); Henry Brooke (Tortworth, 1730). Provost Carter held Cholderton from 1709 until 1720, when he obtained another benefice.
⁶⁸ For the date of the marriage (5 October 1746) see OCA GOV 4 A2, 4 November 1746.

sister of Hodges's late wife),[69] should be presented: if he were dead or should refuse to accept, then the living concerned should be presented to the 'most deserving fellow of Oriel College'.

The college, however, was cheated of its hopes. In February 1768, eleven years after Hodges's death, William Nowell wrote to the recently elected provost, John Clark, to tell him that the living of Easton Grey was now vacant. Offering a gift of £20 to the college ('to be disposed of at your discretion in Prizes for exercises on theological Topicks by batchelors of Arts to be pronounced before the society'), he stressed that the living had been '*desired* not *willed*' by Dr Hodges to be offered first to Ratcliffe, then to a fellow of Oriel. Ratcliffe had now turned it down, and with affected graciousness, Nowell offered it 'to a Fellow of Oriel who will reside upon so small a Preferment tenable with his Fellowship'. 'My respect for Oriel engages me to make the offer, to which my regard for the Parish obliges me to annex residence: and besides the income is too small to admit of a Dividend between Rector and Curate.' He suggested a preference for Dr Bosworth, though he assumed that it would be too small for him to take, and expected another fellow to take advantage of it.[70]

Clark's even more flowery reply thanked Nowell effusively for his gift, which 'has opened a Field for emulation'. As to the living, Dr Bosworth had politely refused, 'notwithstanding the Happiness he might propose to himself of being so much in the neighbourhood of Shipton', but Clark promised to make further enquiries to find someone willing to take on the obligation of residence.[71] Eventually one did offer himself, Charles Hobbs.[72] Unfortunately, Hobbs was unwilling to offer the guarantees on which Nowell insisted. In mid-April 1765 Nowell wrote again to the provost, shortly after an unsatisfactory meeting with the candidate.

> The condition on which the small living of Easton Grey was offered to Oriel was, you know, from the beginning *Residence*. It was on this principle that some of my old Acquaintance among the senior Fellows were passed by, because it was not convenient for them to comply with it. It could not therefore be expected, that condition should be dispensed with in favour of a stranger as Mr Hobbs is to me: and if not to be dispensed with, some security for fullfilling it might reasonably be expected from an unknown person. The proper security in the case is a bond, which however odious in most cases of ecclesiastical presentations, is no way dishonourable for the purpose of residence. Which however was not intended to be so strict or illiberal as not to allow two or three months in a year for other Avocations and a liberty likewise to live near the parish till the parsonage House could be made habitable. This satisfaction Mr

---

[69] For the marriage of Hodges to Miss Ratcliffe in July/August 1742, see *London Evening Post*, 5/7 August 1742. For her death, see *London Evening Post*, 24 October 1754.
[70] OCA PRO 2/36/2.   [71] OCA PRO 2/36/3.
[72] Admitted full fellow, 10 July 1765.

Hobbs not thinking fit to give me He has just now left me without the presentation. And indeed I cannot see that it was worth his acceptance, who has a curacy not much inferiour in value which though more remote from Oxford is in his native country, and besides as I have been informed has a living in the same neighbourhood now held for him. This last circumstance made me perhaps more tenacious in requesting a bond, lest when called away to his other living this might be committed to a curate, & the income too small for one be divided between two. He is not I find in Priest's Orders, but might be ordain'd time enough to prevent a lapse: that was therefore no obstruction. But now it is certainly high time for me to fill the vacant church, which I shall do with speed.[73]

The provost and the college smelt a rat. The correspondence continued in a heavily ironic vein. 'It gives me I confess a little uneasiness on your account', Clark wrote in reply,

that, as your own inclinations so entirely coincided with Dr Hodges bequest, you have been so unhappy as totally to thwart them. The total silence in Dr Hodges bequest concerning Residence and a security for it was doubtless an omission—unless perhaps being Provost of Oriel and knowing the conditions of that society, he might not chuse to involve an Orielite in intentional perjury at least in an embarrassment between two obligations or, which is more probable being acquainted with the Piety of those he left in Trust, he might think caution in this case superfluous. If such were his Thoughts they are not disappointed in the event. But it is a matter of strange suprize to us, that Mr Hobbs, after having accepted the recommendation of the society under the terms of residence and permission of Non residence, should spurn at the demand of a security, unless we attribute it to that quick and manly sense of Honour, which animates all his actions, and fires his resentment at but a suspicion of his Integrity. . . . Indeed, indeed, my good sir, when an executor intends not to comply with the request of a testator (which request, by people of an old-fashioned turn, if equitable, has been held sacred) there seem be only two ways to evade it; the one, is more manly and open, and that is by refusing to comply except upon compulsion, the other is apparently, tho not in fact, more wary and prudent, and this is, by superadding conditions which will render the legacy unacceptable.[74]

Nowell's response was straightforwardly sarcastic:

On reading your letter I began to fear I had lost your favour & was to undergo a little of your college discipline: you had a mind, it seemed, to handel Your new rod, & to honour me with a few of the first strokes. In this apprehension I was beginning to be angry when fortunately a bystander prevented that troublesome passion from rising, by assuring me 'that I had totally mistaken the meaning of your epistle, which, tho appearing in the form of Irony, was most certainly to be understood in it's plain literal sense. For that the Provost of Oriel . . . never descended from his dignity into Banter and Ridicule.'[75]

[73] PRO 2/36/5, 15 April 1768.   [74] PRO 2/36/6, undated.
[75] OCA PRO 2/36/7, 23 June 1768.

The college, also thinking about the likelihood of Shipton Moyne becoming vacant in the near future, took advice from the senior politician and former Attorney General Charles Yorke, who told them that Nowell had no right to impose such conditions.[76] Reluctant to be party to the dispute, Nowell's nominee, Dr Wickes, had resigned by June 1769. Both sides, however, then became aware of the possible effect of the Mortmain Act on the provisions of Hodges's will. A second opinion from Yorke seemed to concede that the 1736 Act would frustrate Hodges's intention; the Nowells appear to have taken advice from the Attorney General to the same effect, given that Oriel already had its quota of advowsons. Although the college entered a caveat against the institution of a new incumbent,[77] it was withdrawn following a correspondence between the new incumbent's uncle and the provost—one which included a number of bitter reflections on Nowell's conduct.[78]

As the reluctance of fellows to volunteer for Easton Grey shows, they were not always falling over themselves to take advantage of the first available living. College livings were normally offered to the fellows by seniority. Cholderton was turned down in 1709 by the three senior fellows, and eventually taken by Provost Carter.[79] In April 1738 Aberford was turned down by all apart from the then probationer fellow, William Nowell, 'provided he signifies his resolution to take it within one month. But if he shall not think it worth his acceptance and declare it by that time, Mr Bentham's brother of Cambridge is to have it.'[80] White dithered endlessly over whether or not to accept a college living. His friend Mulso advised him in 1755 not to 'fix your Eye upon Cromwell [Cromhall] & Tortworth, or indeed upon any thing particular; for the fixt Eye will be an aking one, believe me. I have looked at Peterboro' till it now seems lost in a Mist; indeed low Spirits are great Dimmers of the Eyes, for to tell You the Truth, at present I seem to see Nothing.'[81] In 1757 he congratulated White on his presentation to Oriel's curacy at Moreton Pinkney: 'you who can make £20 go further than I can £40 have a pretty little Increase by this Curacy.'[82] In January 1765 he was surprised to hear that White was inclined to leave Oriel for 'so moderate a living at Cholderton', although he acknowledged that 'if you can be dispenced with for residing at Cholderton, any little thing added to your own Fortune would make you comfortable', and offered the information that the current bishop of Salisbury was very lenient in that respect.[83] In 1767 Mulso

---

[76] OCA PRO 2/36/8, 29 June 1768. [77] OCA PRO 1 C1 3, 17 October 1768.
[78] OCA PRO 2/36/9–15. [79] OCA GOV 4 A2, 5 September 1709.
[80] OCA PRO 1 C1 2, 13 April, 20 July 1738. Thomas Bentham was, indeed, given the living: CCEd.
[81] *The Letters to Gilbert White of Selborne*, 100: Mulso to White, Hampton, 18 September 1755.
[82] *The Letters to Gilbert White of Selborne*, 114: Mulso to White, 13 January 1757.
[83] *The Letters to Gilbert White of Selborne*, 193: Mulso to White, Hampton, 7 January 1765.

heard of the death of John Frewen, rector of Tortworth, and of the expectation that White would take it. 'I am afraid that this is not the best Living of the College: but nevertheless I think I collected by our last Confabulation, that You was inclined to secure to yourself the first Thing that fell, & get rid of your fellowship before your Fellowship get rid of you.'[84] In July 1768 White was again talking about Cholderton, and Mulso was puzzled about why he found it so difficult to make up his mind.[85] Eleven years later, Mulso was still trying to persuade White to come to a decision about Ufton Nervet, and discussed the prospects of raising its income by charging rack-rents. A little while later he responded to White's objections with remarkable patience:

I cannot but approve of your refusing Ufton upon the reasons that you give. A living is a very troublesome Charge; and there are but two Reasons for burthening Oneself wth it: 'the hope of doing real good', & 'the reasonable expectation of a large Increase of Income'. The first You could have done as well as any man, had you chosen a constant residence there; but yet there does not lie so much spirituall power and efficacy in the clergy of the Church of England now, as did formerly. The itching ears even of the Vulgar, & the republican principles of the times, make all the Members of our Church look'd upon with an Evil eye. As to the last You are the best Judge of it; but in my opinion a certain small income is better than a precarious large benefice.[86]

Dithering like this was frequently a problem as fellows tried to weigh the value of a college benefice against the possibility of receiving a better offer. In 1768 the college ordered that the first fellow who had been offered a living in the gift of the college had to make a decision within three months after the vacancy; if he turned it down, the second 'optionist' had another six weeks, and some decision had to be made within twenty-one weeks after the vacancy.[87] In May and June 1774, when James Morgan was considering whether to take Swainswick, there was presumably a possibility that Cholderton might become available shortly. Morgan asked the provost to consult the resident fellows about swapping Swainswick for Cholderton, and to allow a longer period for him to make up his mind. The college refused: others would take Swainswick under the present terms; but Morgan's seniors would take Cholderton. Morgan decided not to take Swainswick anyway.[88]

The college did what it could to make its own livings a more attractive proposition. In 1734 it considered negotiating with the commissioners of

---

[84] *The Letters to Gilbert White of Selborne*, 206: Mulso to White, Witney, 13 October 1767.
[85] *The Letters to Gilbert White of Selborne*, 212: Mulso to White, 26 July 1768.
[86] *The Letters to Gilbert White of Selborne*, 287, 288: Mulso to White, 27 September, 21 December 1779.
[87] OCA PRO 1 C1 3, 17 October 1768. See also the provisions to deal with the situation where a fellow presented to a college living decided that he wanted to give up the living and return to the college, decided at the same meeting.
[88] OCA PRO 1 C1 1.

Queen Anne's Bounty about the augmentation of Moreton Pinkney.[89] In 1738 it agreed to contribute to the repair of Cromhall parsonage house, though it refused to give anything towards Swainswick House. Around the same time it agreed to contribute £100 towards augmenting Aberford Vicarage when Lady Betty Hastings, the noted Yorkshire philanthropist, offered to give land towards the same purpose, and to make the house habitable for the residence of a minister.[90] In 1774 the college agreed to share the cost of improving the parsonage at Cromhall with the rector, the former fellow, Mr Penny.[91]

The college's custom and practice, as elsewhere, was to permit a fellow who had disqualified himself from the fellowship, either by taking an incompatible benefice or by marriage, to continue to take the emoluments of his fellowship for a further year to defray the initial costs (the first fruits tax, in particular, due on taking up a benefice) of the living. The custom had been regularized in Fuller's 1674 decree: the year's grace would be allowed, at the discretion of the college, provided that within a month of institution to a qualifying benefice the fellow concerned notified the provost of the fact by means of a formal certificate from the bishop's registrar.[92] Frequently, of course, the capture of an acceptable living was quickly followed by marriage, which would normally also lead to the surrender of the fellowship. When Edward Talbot was married in 1715, the provost wrote to him with the form of words for his resignation 'which even she cannot see you write with more joy than I shall receive it with sorrow'.[93] A number of fellows, however, managed to evade the requirement to resign on marriage, or their married status was connived at. Hearne in 1714 was unsurprised that George Parry had accepted a position as perpetual curate near Dorchester for only £10 a year, 'Mr Parry having married foolishly one that hath nothing, and thereby cut himself off from the affection and kindness of his brother (who is a baronet and a rich man) and disobliged several in the college (who nevertheless continue him in his fellowship) and being under a strait, he is forced to take up with small inconsiderable incomes.'[94] John Mulso asked Gilbert White in 1754, 'How did Whiting salve to his Conscience the holding his Fellowship six Years in Wedlock? Was this one of his indefeasible Rights?'[95]

---

[89] OCA PRO 1 C1 2, 15 October 1734. The augmentation seems to have still been proceeding in 1749: see East Sussex Record Office, FRE 1181, John Frewen to his brother, Oriel 3 January 1750: 'Morton Pinkney augmentation proves a very troublesome tedious business—cannot be completed under a 12 month longer, & obliges me to turn purchaser into the bargain.'

[90] OCA PRO 1 C1 2, 1 March 1738: see also 27 October and OCA GOV 4 A2, 1 March 1738. For Lady Elizabeth Hastings, philanthropist and benefactress of Queen's College, see ODNB s.n.

[91] OCA PRO 1 C1 1, Michaelmas Audit, 1774.

[92] OCA GOV 2 D5.

[93] OCA PRO 1 C1 1, 17. Talbot resigned 20 October 1715.

[94] Hearne, *Collections*, iii. 355. Parry was elected probationer on 23 July 1707.

[95] *The Letters to Gilbert White of Selborne*, 91: Mulso to White, 13 November 1754. The comment about indefeasible rights may indicate that Whiting was one of Oriel's Whigs.

William Makepeace was the only fellow whose fellowship was removed because he was found to be married: he was summoned to appear at a college meeting in 1732 when it was discovered that he had been married in 1728. Makepeace duly resigned at the meeting.[96] The rest of the fellowship were almost certainly looking for an excuse to remove the man who had been put in on the authority of Provost Carter eleven years before.

The provost was entitled to a higher share of commons and the other emoluments of a fellowship than the other fellows and was also entitled to marry while remaining a member of the society. They no doubt enjoyed a rather higher standard of living than other fellows: when the contents of a stone chamber under the provost's lodging, apparently used as a cess pit around the late seventeenth century, were analysed in the early 1980s, they were found to contain evidence of an exceptionally rich diet, including grapes, raspberries, wild strawberries, plums, figs, mulberries, and a walnut.[97] Commonly wealthier and more successful than the other fellows before their election, provosts had greater opportunities after it for further preferment. Royse had already caught the attention and the patronage of the earl of Berkeley and Dr Tillotson, the archbishop of Canterbury, before he became provost; after it he secured the deanery of Bristol in 1694, although Tillotson's death probably ended his hopes for promotion to a bishopric. Carter and the provostship were eventually beneficiaries from the scheme to increase the income of several college heads, which was initiated in 1711,[98] probably thanks to the intercession of a former fellow, Bishop Robinson.[99] A prebend at Rochester Cathedral was annexed in perpetuity to the provostship, although it was not until the end of the last session of parliament of the reign of Queen Anne that it was confirmed by statute[100] and not until 1719

---

[96] OCA GOV 4 A2, 1 April, 24 May 1732.

[97] Brian Durham, 'Diet of a Provost', OR (1982), 18. There is no mention of pomegranates, despite the tree referred to in the 1738 account of Oriel by 'Shepilinda' (Elizabeth Shephard): its fruit was perhaps a perquisite of the provost, for she wrote that its 'fruit is Delicious as they Tell me but I dont know that for Certain, for I had it from no one but the provost'. Bodleian MS Top. Oxon. d.287, *'Shepilinda's memoirs of the City and University of Oxford Jan^{ry} 7th 1737/8. For Dear Scrippy.'* I am grateful to Geoffrey Neate for drawing this MS to my attention and for allowing me to quote from his transcription of it.

[98] Ward, *Georgian Oxford*, 47–8.

[99] See the letter to 'Your excellency' in the Carter memorandum book, in which Carter explains how he was told by the Lord Chancellor that Oriel had the recipient to thank. OCA PRO 1 C1, 12.

[100] 12 Anne Stat. 2, c. 6: An Act for taking away Mortuaries, within the Dioceses of Bangor, Landaff, St. David's, and St. Asaph, . . . ; and for confirming several Letters Patents granted by Her Majesty, for perpetually annexing a Prebend of Gloucester to the Mastership of Pembroke College in Oxford, and a Prebend of Rochester to the Provostship of Oriel College in Oxford, and a Prebend of Norwich to the Mastership of Catherine Hall in Cambridge.

that Carter actually received the fruits of it.[101] In the meantime he was not shy of regularly putting himself forward for further promotion with the bishops—Robinson of London, Gibson of Lincoln and London, and Wake of Canterbury—with whom he regularly corresponded. 'I believe I need not acquaintt your Lordship how much my station stands in need of it,' he wrote to Gibson or Robinson; if there were to be a promotion to a bishopric which would result in numerous consequential promotions, he wondered whether 'there is Room to obtain for me any preferment, or a place amongst his majesty's chaplains I shall ever gratefully acknowledge your great favor'.[102] He asked for a prebend in the royal gift, suggesting that the earl of Sunderland would support his application: 'what makes me now mention this matter to your Lordship is that I find upon casting my eye on one of the news Papers that Dr Butler made prebendary of Canterbury is dangerously ill. I should be extremely oblig'd to your Lordship for a stall in that or any other of his Majesty's churches.' Carter obtained a canonry at St Paul's in 1714, presumably thanks to John Robinson, who had become bishop of London the year before, and was presented by Wake to a prebend at Peterborough in 1719.[103] He continued to press for more: he asked Wake for the deanery of Peterborough, although unsuccessfully.[104]

Hodges in his turn benefited from the Rochester prebend, and obtained from the dean and chapter the vicarage of Wateringbury in Kent, in 1735, replaced by the more valuable rectory of Kingsdown with Maplescombe the following year. Purleigh was bought for £1,200 by 1734 with the money left by Carter, and more than thirty years later it was annexed to the college by act of parliament.[105] Musgrave retained his rectory of Woodeaton in Oxfordshire throughout his tenure of the provostship, and added the rectory of Lamberhurst, Kent, in the gift of the dean and chapter of Rochester, shortly before his death. His successor, John Clark, kept a careful note of his preferments. After his election at Oriel in February 1768, he was installed in the Rochester prebend at the end of April; the dean and chapter presented him, as they had done Hodges, to the vicarage of Woodnesborough in Kent in July. In addition

---

[101] Instituted 21 October 1719: *Fasti Ecclesiae Anglicanae 1541–1857*, iii: *Canterbury, Rochester and Winchester dioceses* (London, 1974), 66–9. It had been widely reported that the prebend annexed to the Oriel headship would be one at Norwich (which Carter thought was the best one). See HMC Portland MSS vii. 170 (Stratford to Harley, 31 October 1713) and 171 (16 November 1713) and Carter's letters in his memorandum book, OCA PRO C 1, 12–13.

[102] OCA PRO 1 C 1, 15.

[103] *Fasti Ecclesiae Anglicanae 1541–1857*, viii: Bristol, Gloucester, Oxford, and Peterborough dioceses (London, 1996), 124–6.

[104] OCA PRO 1 C1 1, 33. Presumably in 1721, 1722, or 1725 when it changed hands.

[105] OCA PRO 2/35/6. 7 George III, c. 27, An Act for annexing the Rectory of Purleigh, in the County of Essex, to the Office of Provost of the House of the Blessed Mary the Virgin, in Oxford, commonly called Oriel College, of the Foundation of Edward the Second, of Famous Memory, sometime King of England.

to these, he was able in 1769 to take possession of the rectory of Purleigh. It was a few years before he could replace Woodnesborough with something larger in the gift of the dean and chapter: in 1775 he received the vicarage of Lamberhurst; the following year he moved to the parish which Hodges had enjoyed, Kingdown and Maplescombe.[106] In 1769, the first full year of his provostship, his income from the college amounted to £143, including commons and his share of the fines and dividend. The income from the prebend (similarly made up of fines and dividends) was nearly £168, while Woodnesborough netted Clark another £71. Purleigh was the most valuable of his holdings, bringing in £282. His total income from these sources amounted to £676 for the year. By 1776, however, with Woodnesborough swapped for Kingsdown, Clark was receiving £920 a year from the same estates.[107]

Not all fellows were in search of a clerical career. Some, evading the requirement to take holy orders either licitly or illicitly, established themselves as lawyers or doctors. Henry Edmunds, the organizer of the opposition to Carter in 1724, became an eminent civil lawyer, an expert in the law of the admiralty, practising in the court of arches.[108] Edmunds was plainly an unusual figure: Robert Shippen, the principal of Brasenose, described Edmunds in 1734 as having a particular influence on the fellowship;[109] the young and highly impressionable Elizabeth Sheppard wrote a few years later in her account of the various colleges of Oxford that 'there is no very great Curiosity in this College except Dr Edmonds D^r of Law a Man that talks as much as 3 women'.[110] Philip Foster was another civil lawyer.[111] William Hawkins, who resigned his fellowship in 1708, nevertheless continued to live in Oxford practising law and writing an abridgement of Sir Edward Coke's *Institutes* and other legal manuals, although Hearne thought he was less than successful in his Oxford practice because of the dominance there of Serjeant Wright, the recorder.[112] Henry Martyn,[113] Charles Cotes (one of those forced to resign in 1723 because he had failed to take holy

---

[106] OCA PRO 1 C1 4.
[107] OCA PRO 1 C1 4. Clark's accounts do not include the income from Leek Wootton, which he continued to hold until his death, perhaps because he did not consider this as part of the emoluments attributable to the provostship.
[108] Licensed to study civil law, OCA GOV 4 A2, 21 March 1730: published *Extracts from the several Treatises subsisting between Great Britain and other Kingdoms* (London, 1741).
[109] Lincs. RO, Dioc. VV 9, Shippen to bishop of Lincoln, 16 December 1734.
[110] Bodleian MS. Top.Oxon. d.287, 'Shepilinda's memoirs of the City and University of Oxford Jan^{ry} 7th 1737/8. For Dear Scrippy.'
[111] Admitted probationer April 1674.
[112] Hearne, *Collections*, vi. 126. Hawkins seems to have acted for Weeksey in his dispute with Hodges and the college in 1728: see Lincs. RO, Dioc. VV 9, Opinion of Mr William Hawkins, 19 May 1728, and Weeksey to the bishop of Lincoln, 31 December 1728. This may explain why the fellows resisted his appointment as an arbitrator in the case concerning the will of Dr Carter in 1734: see Lincs. RO, Dioc. VV 9, Rob. Shippen to the bishop of Lincoln, 16 December 1734.
[113] Admitted probationer July 1689.

orders), William Makepeace (Carter's nominee of 1724), Richard Head,[114] and Robert Wood[115] also combined their fellowships with legal practice. William Clarke, from Swainswick, a nephew of William Prynne, resigned his fellowship only three years after being admitted probationer, presumably as he had no intention of taking holy orders, and went to live and practise medicine, in Bath, and later in Stepney.[116] George Cowslade in 1675 was licensed to study medicine and thereby to avoid taking holy orders,[117] as was Thomas Whalley in 1717, well after he had become a practising doctor.[118]

Some fellows, while they took holy orders and searched for preferment, pursued essentially administrative careers. Charles Perrot worked for Joseph Williamson's government information service in the 1670s. The most distinguished was John Robinson, who was given licence to travel abroad in 1677,[119] two years after his election as a fellow, when he accompanied his brother-in-law in the entourage of Henry Coventry as ambassador in Stockholm, where he remained, eventually as English agent, until 1687, finally resigning his fellowship in 1686. Robinson returned to Sweden after the Revolution, spending most of his time there until 1709, and his appointment as bishop of Bristol, Lord Privy Seal and negotiator at the Treaty of Utrecht, and bishop of London in 1714. Some fellows took posts in the administration of the university: Robert Fysher was elected Bodley's librarian in 1729.[120] Henry Edmunds, the lawyer, stood for election to be keeper of the Ashmolean Museum the same year.[121] Joseph Woodward served as registrar of the vice-chancellor's court, whose 'abominable corruptions and villainies' he abhorred, according to Hearne.[122]

Besides the young men seeking preferment were older fellows who remained in or around Oriel all, or nearly all, their lives. James Davenant, who died in the college in 1716, had lived there for fifty-four years, and had been a member of the college for over sixty. He never received any ecclesiastical preferment: 'He lov'd to live at his ease, as he did. He died rich, having an estate' (he was worth £10,000 at his death, Hearne later found out).[123] Hearne's friend Richard Dyer left Oxford in 1724 to live on his Devon estate after fifty-two years as a fellow. After Hearne heard of his death in 1731, aged 77 or 78, he wrote of him that

---

[114] Admitted probationer July 1764. [115] Admitted probationer July 1772.
[116] Clarke was admitted a fellow in October 1663. See Wood, *Athenae Oxonienses*, iv. 133. He published *The natural history of Niter: or, a philosophical discourse of the nature, generation, place and artificial extraction of Niter* (London, 1670).
[117] OCA GOV 2 D6; see also OCA GOV 4 A1, 16 October 1675.
[118] OCA GOV 4 A2, 15 October 1717.
[119] OCA GOV 4 A1, 9 June 1677; see also 1 October 1678, 30 October 1679, 16 October 1680.
[120] Hearne, *Collections*, x. 207. [121] Hearne, *Collections*, x. 208.
[122] Hearne, *Collections*, x. 106. [123] Hearne, *Collections*, v. 332.

ILLUSTRATION 7.1 John Robinson (1650–1723), fellow 1675–86, bishop of London

Oriel College

He was a man of great modesty, an excellent Scholar, and admirably well skilled in Botany, in so much that there was hardly any excelled him. Bishop Fell would fain have had him to be botanick professor, but he declined it. I do not know that he ever published anything, unless it be the preface to the 3d volume of the Oxford History of Plants, and Dr Morison's life before it, tho his name be not to either. He was a very healthfull man, a great Walker, and had not he married in his old age, but lived in Oxford after his old way, he might have lived much longer & been a very great Benefactor to his college, but the broils in the college forced him to retire.[124]

Not all fellows were as unproductive in academic terms as Dyer, although the college's learned output was fairly modest. Fellows favoured in London would publish their sermons.[125] Samuel Catherall churned out lengthy

---

[124] Hearne, *Collections*, x. 362.
[125] e.g. Richard Ibbetson's *The Divinity of our Blessed Saviour prov'd from Scripture, and Antiquity. A Sermon preach'd before the University of Oxford, at St. Mary's, on the Epiphany, January. 6. 1711–12* (Oxford, 1712); George Rye's *A Sermon preach'd at the consecration of the Right Reverend Father in god, John Lord Bishop of Oxford, at the Archbishop of Canterbury's Chappel in his Grace's Palace at Lambeth, on Sunday May 15, 1715, by George Rye, BD, Chaplain to the Earl of Derby, Rector of Adwell in Oxfordshire, and Fellow of Oriel College Oxford* (London, 1715); Royse's *A Sermon Preach'd before the Queen at Windsor, September 23. 1705* (Oxford, 1705).

poems on divine and classical subjects during the 1720s, which he advertised in the London papers,[126] before going mad by 1731.[127] Hodges wrote lengthily on the book of Job and other biblical subjects, confessing that he had been influenced by the self-taught anti-Newtonian theologian and Hebrew philologist John Hutchinson.[128] Charles Whiting published a slim volume on learned authority in sacred matters.[129] Ibbetson published an edition of Marcus Aurelius, which he dedicated to Provost Carter.[130] Edward Bentham wrote popular textbooks on moral philosophy, divinity, and logic and other pedagogical tracts.[131]

Such a limited record of achievement among the fellowship suggests some truth behind Nicholas Amhurst's bitter characterization of the eighteenth-century don ('In short, I love my Bottle and my Ease; | The Tenor of a College Life I keep, | Eat thrice a Day, pun, smoke, get drunk, and sleep'). It is perhaps telling that Oriel's most distinguished eighteenth-century intellectual, the theologian and philosopher Joseph Butler, found Oxford deeply uncongenial, and despite the impact of his thought on Oriel's noetics, found little to value in the education he received at Oxford, and there is little evidence that his work had much impact on the college before Eveleigh. Yet Butler derived great benefit from the patronage and friendship of Edward Talbot, a fellow from 1712 to 1715, as did Butler's friend Thomas Secker, the future archbishop of Canterbury who, like Butler, moved from a lively dissenting milieu into successful conformity. And if one looks beneath the usual performance indicators of academic life, there is plenty of other evidence of serious intellectual life and endeavour at Oriel in the century before

---

[126] Samuel Catherall *An Essay on the Conflagration In Blank Verse* (Oxford, 1720); *A Portraiture of Socrates, extracted out of Plato, in blank verse* (Oxford, 1717); *An Epistle, humbly inscrib'd to the University of Oxford, occasion'd by the Death of the Lord bishop of Durham, Written in Imitation of Waller's Style* (Oxford, 1721); *Cato Major. A poem, upon the Model of Tully's Essay of Old Age* (London, 1725).

[127] See Surrey History Centre, Inquisition of the lunacy of the Rev Samuel Catherall, late of Oriel College, Oxford, and now of Bethnal Green, Middx, rector impropriate of Englishcomb, Somerset, and owner of other property in Montgomeryshire and Cheshire, 1731, LM/1544.

[128] *Elihu or an Enquiry into the Principal Scope and Design of the Book of Job* (London, 1750); *The Christian Plan, second edition with additions: with other theological pieces by the same author: to which is subjoined an Oration by him delivered to the University of Oxford October 5 1744* (London, printed for James Hodges, 1755); *The Christian Plan, exhibited in the Interpretation of Elohim* (Oxford, 1752).

[129] *De Doctorum Auctoritate in rebus sacris. Concio, coram Academica Oxoniensi* (Oxford, 1748).

[130] *Marci Antonini ... eorum quae ad seipsum libri xii. Recogniti & notis illustrati* (Oxford, 1704).

[131] *Reflexions upon the nature and usefulness of Logick as it has been commonly taught in the Schools* (Oxford, 1740); *An Introduction to Moral Philosophy* (Oxford, 1745); *Reflexions upon the Study of Divinity. To which are subjoined Heads of a course of Lectures* (Oxford, 1771); *An Introduction to Logick, Scholastic and Rational* (Oxford, 1773).

ILLUSTRATION 7.2 Joseph Butler (1692–1752), bishop of Durham
Oriel College: Mr Taylor of Durham, 1750–2

Eveleigh. If few fellows published, many were avid readers and accomplished scholars. Royse's library, advertised for sale at St Mary Hall in 1710, contained

most of the Fathers in Greek and Latin of the best Editions; and many of the Classick Authors, (cum Notis Variorum & in usum Delphini,) by these celebrated Printers; viz. Rob and Hen. Stephens, Wechelius, Juntas, Plantin; Sen. Elzevir, &c . . . Also a large and Valuable Collection of Ancient and Modern Physick Books. Likewise a choice Collection of Divinity, History, and Poetry, &c.[132]

John Salmon possessed a substantial library, sold in Oxford after his death;[133] Charles Whiting's library was likewise advertised for sale in 1754.[134] Hearne was impressed with Peter Randal's collection,[135] and equally taken with the

---

[132] *Bibliotheca Royseana: Or a Catalogue of Curious Books contain'd in the Library of the late Reverend Dr Geo. Royse Dean of Bristol and Provost of Oriel College in Oxford* advertised in the *Daily Courant*, 9 March 1710, issue 2613.
[133] *Daily Courant*, 3 February 1714.
[134] *London Evening Post*, 7 December 1754, issue 4225.   [135] Hearne, *Collections*, iii. 165.

ILLUSTRATION 7.3 Gilbert White (1720–93), naturalist, fellow 1744–93
Oriel College

efforts of Thomas Ward to compare the modern Book of Common Prayer with the Laudian, 1636 version ('the variations are enter'd in the margin and in leaves inserted');[136] Edward Bentham discussed Roman coins with him.[137] Many dons had wider interests: Samuel Desmaistres was one of the twenty-two members of the scientific society created in 1683;[138] Charles Perrott, 'a well bred gent and a person of a sweet nature', was an accomplished musician, who played in a circle that included Anthony Wood, meeting sometimes at Perrott's rooms in Oriel;[139] and the natural historian Gilbert White himself, unable to make up his mind about taking on a college living, teased by his friend Mulso for shooting, drinking cider, and flirting, would demonstrate how remarkable scientific and scholarly work might be supported—albeit informally—by an Oxford Anglican foundation.

[136] Hearne, *Collections*, ii. 359.
[137] Hearne, *Collections*, xi. 287, 290.
[138] Wood, *Life and Times*, iii. 76–7.
[139] Wood, *Life and Times*, i. 275.

8

A Society of Gentlemen

Paul Seaward

Oriel ranked in the late seventeenth and eighteenth centuries as one of the smaller of the university's colleges and halls. In the early 1690s it was estimated that besides its 18 fellows, Oriel had 12 exhibitioners and bible clerks and only 10 commoners, by which it meant men who were not supported in some way out of college funds. According to this reckoning, Oriel had fewer commoners than any other college except Corpus (also with ten), equal with New College and Magdalen, most of whose students were maintained on the foundation.[1] These figures are certainly misleading in terms of absolute numbers. The college's buttery books around this time show 12 commoners and 13 gentlemen commoners, who appear to have been completely ignored in the 1690s list. Buttery book enrolments, though, are themselves misleading on the number of members in each college. As Thomas Hearne wrote: 'Tis a wrong way to take the number of members of any College or Hall in Oxford from the names in the buttery books, names standing in the books very often from year to year after several of the Persons have been gone many years, nay sometimes they stand after they are dead.'[2] Certainly the buttery books from time to time include many men whose current connection with the college seems to have been tenuous. In 1681, for example, a group of peers and members of the House of Commons listed in the buttery book were in Oxford for the meeting of parliament held there at the height of the Exclusion Crisis;[3] and in the book for 1781–2, the duke of

---

[1] John Gutch, *Collectanea Curiosa, or miscellaneous tracts, relating to the History and antiquities of England and Ireland*, 2 vols. (Oxford, 1781), ii. 191–5. See HUO iv. 43 for discussion of this document. The number of servitors and servants is not recorded for each college or hall: a global number is given for the university as a whole.

[2] Hearne, *Collections*, xi. 268.

[3] The buttery book for 1680–1 contains a list of names at the beginning which is headed by earl of Londonderry (matric. 29 November 1637 as Weston, Lord Ridgeway). Copleston, in his notes on members of the college refers to a list of Independent members in 1686 in the first leaf of the buttery book 'not mentioned in the several weeks'.

Somerset, the duke of Beaufort, Viscount Dudley, the bishop of Durham, Lord Leigh, Lord Grosvenor, Viscount Wenman, Sir Mark Parsons, Sir Watkin Williams Wynn, and Sir Henry Gough were all listed, none of whom can have been currently in residence.[4]

The buttery book figures which Hearne copied down in 1733, and which provoked his remark, compared the size of each of the colleges and halls that year. They attributed 68 members to Oriel (including 18 fellows and 14 exhibitioners). However, a list of members of the college in 1731/2 contained in a commonplace book now in the Bodleian Library gives a much lower figure for the period. Apart from the provost and 16 fellows or probationer fellows, there were 2 gentlemen commoners, 9 bachelors, 11 commoners, and 3 servitors—a mere total of 42, possibly a more accurate indication of the number of men actually in residence.[5] Examination of the buttery books for 1660–1 shows that the number with expenditure recorded against their names fluctuated between 27 and 53, much lower than the number actually listed (87) with peaks at late November and early December, and (especially) in July, just before the Act, the annual culmination and celebration of the exercises required for graduation as a bachelor. But even if the absolute number of resident members of the college at any one time is difficult to establish, the picture of the relative size of the college derived from the 1690s estimate was broadly accurate. Hearne's 1733 figures also showed Oriel as the smallest of the colleges apart from Corpus and All Souls, although it was only just behind Lincoln (70) and well ahead of all of the halls. Given the decline in numbers in the halls in the eighteenth century, this suggests that the ranking in the 1690s list was correct.

Oriel was no exception to the common experience in Oxford of a steep decline in student numbers during the late seventeenth century and slow recovery during the eighteenth. The number of men recorded on the buttery books each year suggests that numbers declined from the 1660s, began to rise again around the 1720s, and had more than recovered by the 1780s. (See Table 8.1.)

These figures may be equally misleading, perhaps reflecting the tendency to retain gentlemen commoners on the college books as much as anything else. The admissions records compiled by Shadwell provide a more complex and more accurate picture. Some 1,423 men are recorded by Shadwell as having been admitted to Oriel between 1660 and 1780, an average number of

---

[4] Edward Seymour, duke of Somerset, matric. 25 February 1736; Henry, duke of Beaufort, matric. 18 October 1760; John Egerton, matric. 22 May 1740; Edward, Lord Leigh, matric. 14 July 1761; Philip Wenman, matric. 1 February 1760; Mark Parsons, matric. (Ch Ch) 22 December 1760, adm. Oriel 22 December 1763; Sir Watkin Williams Wynn, matric. 9 May 1766; Henry Gough, matric. 6 October 1767. They are, however, listed apart from the gentlemen commoners, and immediately after the fellows, so it would seem that they were not regarded as part of the normal complement of the college. See also HUO v. 197 for why the names of those not currently in residence might be maintained on the buttery book.

[5] Bodleian Library, MS Eng misc e. 25, fo. 43.

TABLE 8.1 Numbers entered on the buttery books at twenty year intervals (in the first week of each year for which figures are available)

	1660–1	1680–1	1702–3[a]	1720–1	1740–1	1760–1	1780–1
Provost	1	1	1	1	1	1	1
Fellows	18	17	17	16	18	18	18
Gentlemen commoners[b]	19	13	13	10	24	22	41
Graduates	9	5	14	14	22	28	31
Commoners	31	20	12	26	28	30	46
Servitors	8	12	13	12	6	3	0
Total	87	68	70	79	99	102	137

[a] The buttery book for 1700–1 is missing.

[b] The figure for gentlemen commoners includes those occasional visitors who may have been intended to form a separate category in the books.

admissions of just under 12 a year. Admissions peaked in 1667, reaching a figure (24) not attained again until after 1780 (although in that year 23 men were admitted). The decline in the late seventeenth century was rapid. In the ten year period 1665 to 1674, there was an average of 16.6 admissions a year. By the late 1670s admissions had dropped to 11.6 a year; in the early 1680s to 7.2. In the 1690s they were running at an average of about 5.5 a year. Numbers recovered in the eighteenth century, although never to the levels of the 1660s, and with considerable fluctuation. Admissions were up to 15.8 a year in 1715–19, but back down to 8.4 a year in the late 1720s, up to 15.4 in the early 1740s, back down to 9.2 in the early 1770s, and up to 15.6 in the late 1770s. The graph (Figure 8.1) shows three peaks in the period: in the late 1660s and early 1670s; 1710 to 1714; and 1739 to 1744, with periods of decline after each.

Oriel's admissions broadly reflect the position across the university. Oxford admissions were high in the 1660s, recovering from a slump during the 1640s, and peaked in 1666.[6] They then began to decline steeply from the mid-1670s, driven by declining confidence in the educational value of a university education and some doubts about the corrupting effect on the young of Oxford independence and Oxford politics, as well, perhaps, as by political instability.[7] (The unflattering portrait of an Oxford undergraduate and his tutor in the play published in 1697 by a former commoner of Oriel, Thomas Dilke, *The City Lady*, suggests how unfashionable an Oxford education might seem by then.[8]) University

[6] HUO iv. 34.   [7] See HUO iv. 237–8, v. 312–13.
[8] Thomas Dilke (matric. 18 March 1678) *The City Lady or Folly Reclaim'd* (London, 1697). The play is dedicated to his brother, Fisher Wentworth, who matric. 12 May 1673 as Fisher Dilke.

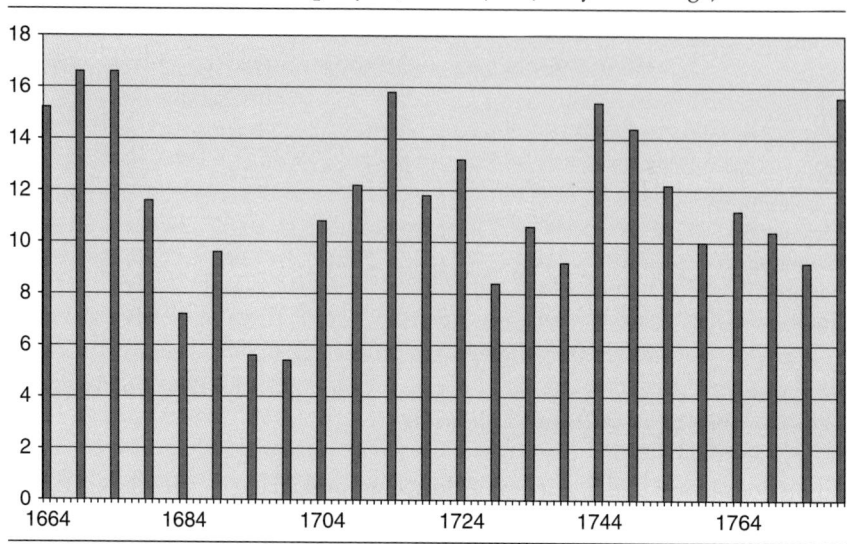

FIGURE 8.1 Oriel admissions per year, 1660–1780 (five year average)

admissions reached a nadir in the 1750s and did not recover to the levels of the 1660s until the nineteenth century.[9] But each college was different. Lincoln's admissions, for example, had fallen in the 1690s, but it was not until the 1740s that they experienced steep decline.[10] Trinity, on the other hand, fell from around 15–20 a year in the first quarter of the eighteenth century to a low of around 10 a year in the middle before returning to nearly 15 a year by its end.[11]

Specific events no doubt account for the peculiarities of Oriel's own admissions, although they are not always obvious. As elsewhere, the personality, energy, and reputation of the provost was probably a significant factor in determining the college's success in obtaining commoners or fellow commoners. One young gentleman pleading in 1763 with Sir Robert Wilmot, presumably either his guardian or the man who had taken financial responsibility for his education after the death of his father, suggested that Oriel since Chardin Musgrave had been provost 'has gained great reputation, he is a gentleman that is extremely well known here [in Bath] and so strongly recommended to my Mama and me by Mr Davenport brother to Doctor Davenport of Divinity'.[12] Provosts spent much time and energy building up

[9] HUO v. 310.
[10] Vivian Green, *The Commonwealth of Lincoln College 1427–1977* (Oxford, 1979), 638.
[11] Clare Hopkins, *Trinity: 450 Years of an Oxford College Community* (Oxford, 2005), 197.
[12] 'Mr Cope' to Sir Robt. Wilmot, 16 October 1763, Derbyshire Record Office, D3155 M/C 3399.

and maintaining close relationships with the parents of potential or actual undergraduates. George Carter, for example, wrote to one parent to ensure that the family was aware of everything necessary for her son's arrival in Oxford:

I have taken care to have every thing in a readiness for your son. Besides what he wears he must bring with him two a pair of about half a doz sheets and towels and a doz napkins and all his books. He will want a morning gown which he may buy here or at London. As for his university gown it will be best to buy it here. There are two Oxford carriers by whom you may send any things twice a week, one returns hither on Mondays and puts up at the Oxford arms in Warwick land. The other lodges at the White Swan by Holborn bridge and comes from thence early Thursday.[13]

Carter was particularly fulsome when it came to a peer, albeit a Scottish peer, thanking the dowager Lady Cameron for the honour of entrusting him with the care of her son, Lord Fairfax: 'Your ladyship may easily imagine, it is with concern and unwillingness I part with his Lordship, whose conversation and sweet temper and dayly improuvement under my eye afforded me much pleasure; But it is no less satisfaction and delighte to me that I can assure your ladyship He hath all the benefit of an university education, without the least inconvenience.'[14] Another of Carter's draft thankyou letters was presumably testament to the lasting value a provost could derive from his connections with wealthy, titled, and powerful parents of Oriel undergraduates:

My Lord perhaps your Lordship might expect that after I had tasted so long & so very fully of it, the Obrion & Margouse might have raised my gratitude to more lofty expressions for your favrs, but I leave to you to determine whether the vast difference which I find between your good wines, and those I now drink may not as much depress my thoughts at present, as the noble liquors warm'd and enlivened them.[15]

It is certainly noticeable that admissions tended to be at their lowest during the final years of any provostship, and would recover thereafter. The drop in Oriel's admissions in 1755 and 1756, for example, was probably due to the final illness of Provost Walter Hodges.[16]

Unlike the great majority of colleges, Oriel had no positions on the foundation for undergraduates. As a result Oriel would be a second choice for those who needed or expected to obtain a scholarship, and was often used as a fall-back position. James Woodforde (Parson Woodforde of the diary) had been a scholar at Winchester College. He was low down on the list of those to be translated to New College, so he enrolled and matriculated at

---

[13] OCA PRO 1 C1 1, 64.   [14] OCA PRO 1 C1 1, 8.   [15] OCA PRO 1 C1 1, 8.
[16] A rumour that the provost has died is referred to in a letter from John Mulso to Gilbert White of 10 February 1755 (*The Letters to Gilbert White of Selborne*, 96). See also references to his illnesses in Mulso's letters of 11 April 1750 and 28 March 1752 (*The Letters to Gilbert White of Selborne*, 32, 59). Hodges died on 14 January 1757.

Oriel, while he waited for a vacancy.[17] He soon afterwards heard that he had indeed obtained a scholarship, and moved across to New College, where his ascent to the fellowship was assured. It was a well-trodden path.[18] The same thing clearly happened with Magdalen: students would enrol at Oriel while they waited for a valuable demyship to become available.[19]

As a result, Oriel was probably a net exporter of students to other colleges, albeit by a small margin.[20] The college could itself poach from others. It was George Carter's aggressive recruitment from other colleges, aided and abetted by his sidekick Bowles, in fact, that provoked a minor Oxford *cause célèbre* in 1723. By accepting a student, William Seaman,[21] who wanted to migrate from Hart Hall, they upset its principal, the notoriously single-minded and talkative Dr Richard Newton, founder of Hertford College, who was still sore at the defection to Oriel of his star pupil Bowles, seven years before. Newton refused to permit Seaman to leave by granting him his *discessit*, something normally a matter of routine. Bowles, with Carter's approval, admitted him regardless, accepting the derisory fine set by the university in such circumstances. Initially, the case raised much mirth in Oxford because of speculation about the encounter between the notoriously loquacious Newton and the famously taciturn Carter.[22] A few years later, Newton published a lengthy, aggrieved, and widely ridiculed discourse about the case and also the loss of another student, Joseph Somaster, to Balliol also in 1723.[23] According to Hearne it was 'a most wretched, silly, trifling thing, in wch are many Lyes, but not so much as one curious or good Observation throughout the whole'.[24]

---

[17] 1740–1803: matriculated 17 May 1758.

[18] Anthony Sanderson (Winchester, 1742; matric. Oriel 17 September 1748; New College, 1750); Thomas Hayward (Winchester, 1745; matric. Oriel 23 February 1749; New College, 1750); Isaac Moody Bingham (Winchester, 1747; matric. Oriel, 19 October 1752; New College, 1753); Thomas Nichols (Winchester, 1748; matric. Oriel, 17 December 1754; New College, 1755); Charles Boteler (Winchester, 1750; matric. Oriel, 6 November 1755; New College, 1756); and later examples.

[19] William Walker (matric. 26 April 1722; demy, Magdalen, 1722); Edward Ventris (matric. Oriel, 30 April 1733, demy, Magdalen, 1734, fellow, Magdalen, 1737); Francis Ventris (matric. Oriel, 23 December 1740, demy, Magdalen, 1742, fellow, Magdalen, 1747); Charles Stone (matric. Oriel, 3 July 1742, demy, Magdalen, 1743); Richard Scrope (matric. Oriel, 8 April 1747; demy, Magdalen, 1748, fellow 1757); Robert Smith (matric. Oriel 11 July 1747; demy, Magdalen, 1747); Richard Paget (matric. Oriel 24 April 1747, demy, Magdalen, 1750, fellow, Magdalen, 1754); and later examples.

[20] 110 students were admitted to Oriel who had been matriculated at other colleges; 114 students who were admitted to Oriel went on to take BA degrees at other colleges. There may, of course, have been other students admitted to Oriel who moved to other colleges, but failed to take BA degrees.

[21] Matric. 21 March 1723 at Hart Hall.

[22] Hearne, *Collections*, viii. 295.

[23] *University Education, or, an explication and amendment of the statute which, under a Penalty insufficient and eluded, prohibits the admission of scholars going from one society to another without the Leave of their respective governors... on occasion of the late irregular admission of William Seaman, Commoner of Hart-Hall, into oriel College* (London, 1726).

[24] Hearne, *Collections*, ix. 113. See also Nicholas Amhurst, *Terrae Filius* (London, 1733), 371–80.

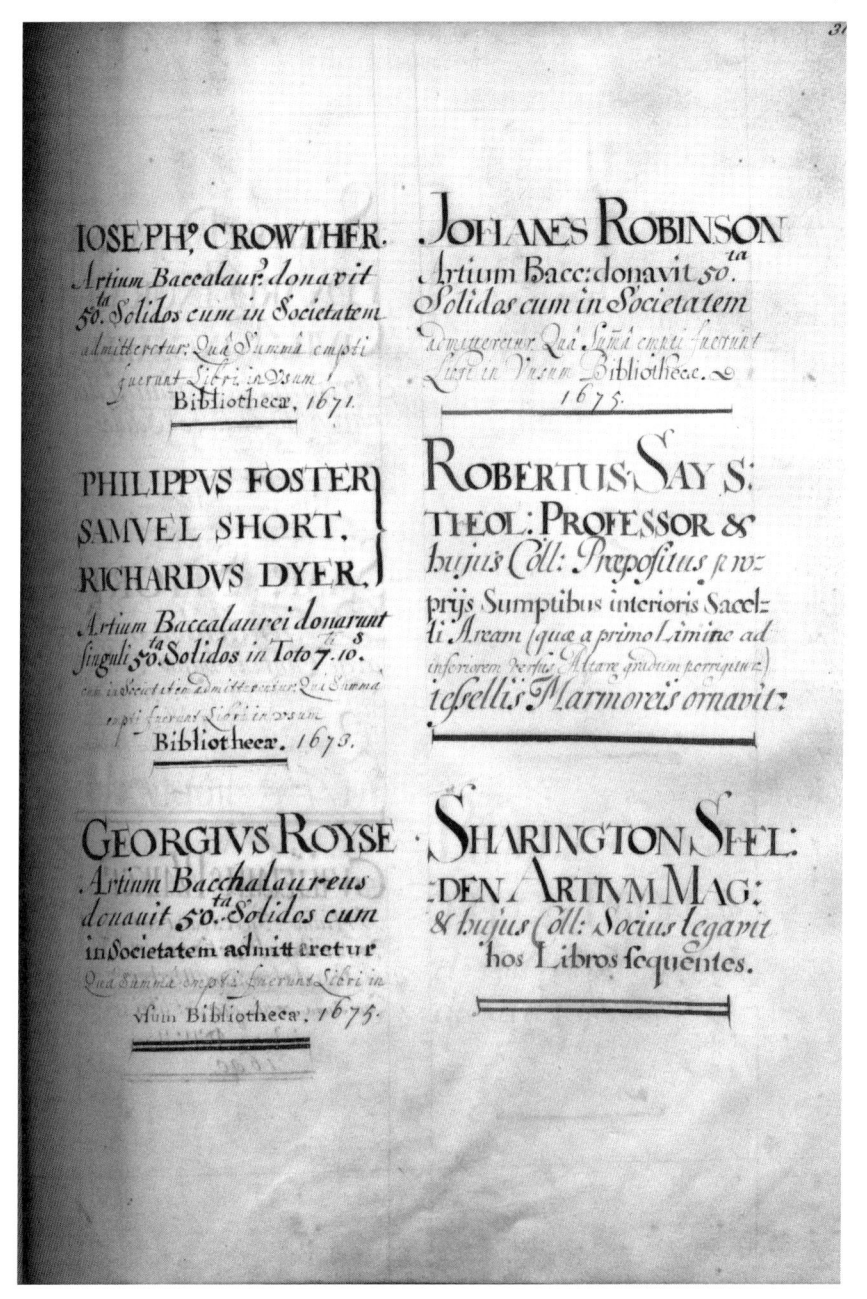

ILLUSTRATION 8.1 The benefactors' book: donations of the 1670s, *OCA*

Most undergraduates would arrive in Oxford at around 17—the average age on matriculation over the whole period is just over 17—although Thomas Apperley, a gentleman commoner, and friend of Samuel Johnson, who was admitted in 1766, was 32 at matriculation.[25] It was common, however, for undergraduates to be admitted at 16 or 15, especially earlier in the period; by the end of it more were being admitted at the age of 18. Oriel could claim a relatively elite student body. In the period 1650–89 it was one of the five colleges in which sons of peers and bishops constituted more than 3 per cent of all matriculands—although it could not, of course, hope to compete with Christ Church, the normal college for all noblemen.[26] Only two men, Henry, 5th duke of Beaufort,[27] and Edward Lord Leigh,[28] were entered on the college's books during the period as noblemen, a category which brought considerable privileges, but also exceptionally high charges.[29] They were admitted within a year of one another in 1760–1. The young Jeremy Bentham heard the bells (presumably at St Mary's) being rung at Leigh's admission.[30] Another peer, Lord Wenman, was entered more economically as a gentleman commoner in 1737.[31] Noblemen were rare birds; but a number of sons of peers or Irish or Scottish peers were admitted as gentlemen commoners.[32] Two men inherited peerages unexpectedly: Henry Bowes Howard became 4th earl of Berkshire;[33] Edward Seymour became duke of Somerset.[34] Oriel was, over the eighteenth century as a whole, second only to Christ Church and University College, and significantly ahead of Magdalen, in the number of peers and peers' sons attending.[35]

---

[25] See *The Letters of Samuel Johnson*, ed. Bruce Redford, 5 vols. (Oxford, 1992–4), i. 296–7.
[26] HUO iv. 63.
[27] Matric. 18 October 1760.
[28] Matric. 14 July 1761.
[29] HUO v. 317; see also John Jones, *Balliol College: A History* (2nd edn., Oxford, 1997), 139–40.
[30] *Correspondence of Jeremy Bentham*, ed. T. L. S. Spragge (London, 1968), i. (1752–76), 19, Jeremy Bentham to Jeremiah Bentham, 29 October 1760.
[31] Matric. 9 June 1737. Philip and Richard Wenman (see n. 32) were the grandsons of Richard Wenman, the 4th viscount (matric. 27 June 1673), who succeeded his great-uncle in the title.
[32] Sons of Scottish and Irish peers: the two sons of the 5th Lord Fairfax of Cameron, Thomas, later the 6th Lord Fairfax (matric. 14 January 1710), and Henry Culpeper Fairfax (matric. 1 March 1714); Robert Tracy, the son of the 2nd Viscount Tracy of Rathcoole (matric. 29 October 1672); James Bulkeley, the son of Viscount Bulkeley (matric. 30 April 1735); Richard Wenman, the brother of Viscount Wenman (matric. 9 February 1744; see n. 31 for his brother), Philip, the 7th viscount (matric. 1 February. 1760); the four sons of Viscount Irvine (Arthur Ingram, later 6th viscount, Henry, later 7th viscount, George, later 8th viscount, and Charles: matric. 25 June 1706, 17 May 1708, 7 June 1711, 29 April 1714). Sons of English peers: John Ward, son of 1st Viscount Dudley, and his brother William, later the 2nd and 3rd viscounts (matric. 7 February 1743 as 'Wardle', 14 March 1770 as 'Wood'); James and Robert Brudenell, the sons of the earl of Cardigan (matric. 7 April 1743 and 9 October 1744).
[33] Matric. 20 March 1703.
[34] Matric. 25 February 1736.
[35] John Cannon, *Aristocratic Century: The Peerage of Eighteenth-Century England* (Cambridge, 1987), 50.

Between 1660 and 1780, out of all of those who were admitted to the college, 5.65 per cent were described on matriculation as the sons of peers, baronets, or knights. Those whose fathers were described as armigerous or as 'esquire' constituted 25 per cent of the intake; 30 per cent were described as the sons of 'gentlemen'; 15 per cent were the sons of clergy; 10.65 per cent were the sons of plebeians, and 8 per cent the sons of paupers.[36] Over the period as a whole, the proportion of the college made up of paupers or plebeians declined considerably and the proportion of the armigerous increased, particularly after the mid-1740s. In 1660–99 the average 25 per cent armigerous was exceeded three times; over 1700–39 fourteen times; and over 1740–80 it was exceeded thirty-one times. The descriptions used in the matriculation registers were not exact, and not consistent over time: the clerical category tended to be understated, the distinction between 'esquire' and 'gentleman' was none too clear, and the category 'pauper' ceased to be used in the early eighteenth century.[37] The apparent growth in social distinction—evident in the university as a whole—may reflect an inflation in the way in which undergraduates were described as much as real growth.[38]

Nevertheless, it is difficult to overcome the impression that the college became more socially exclusive over the period. A similar trend is evident in the rank accorded to undergraduates on their admission to the college (and therefore the fees they paid). Over the period the numbers of gentlemen commoners admitted to the college rose, from an average of around 1.5 a year to about 2.5; the numbers of commoners rose too, from about 6 to 8 a year. Gentlemen commoners became a higher proportion of the college, from making up about 13 per cent of admissions in the 1660s to 24 per cent 110 years later. As everywhere else, however, the number of servitors—undergraduate positions for poor men, who would earn their keep by waiting in hall, serving in chapel, and performing other menial tasks—dwindled to almost none over the course of the eighteenth century. From the Restoration to the 1690s, at least two servitors were admitted each year. In the early eighteenth century there were years in which only one servitor was admitted; in the third quarter of the century there were often years in which none were admitted at all. In the 1660s servitors made up about 28.3 per cent of admissions; during the 1770s they constituted only about 6.4 per cent. The last man to be admitted as servitor was John Ireland, the son of a butcher from Ashburton, Devon, in 1779, who went on to be dean of Westminster in

---

[36] These percentages exclude the small number described as bishops, professors of theology, deans, and an archdeacon, and a number of doctors, who are identified as such in the matriculation registers. It therefore rather understates the clerical element among the undergraduate body, and indeed the social elite, if one were to include bishops and deans among this. For further problems with the clerical category, which may mean that it is even more understated, see HUO iv. 51.
[37] See HUO iv. 51, 54 for a discussion of the categories in the seventeenth century.
[38] HUO v. 313.

1816 and left the college £2,000 and the university £10,000 to found a professorship for the exegesis of Holy Scripture.[39]

The college's old exhibitions—the Carpenter or St Antony and Dudley exhibitions—all went to servitors. But formal appointments to these exhibitions had ceased by the second decade of the eighteenth century. The last St Antony exhibitioner recorded was in 1714;[40] the last appointment to a Dudley exhibition was also in 1714.[41] They may already have been in practice merged with the bible clerkships, as they certainly later were. Appointment to the new exhibitions created in the eighteenth century—the Robinson, Beaufort, and Ludwell exhibitions—went usually to commoners (although the Robinson exhibition was for Bachelors of Arts). In part this was almost inevitable, given the terms of the gifts: in her 1761 bequest Elizabeth Ludwell stipulated that in the nomination of exhibitioners 'my own relations to be first and principally regarded and chosen', and made no provision relating to the wealth or status of candidates. The duke of Beaufort's 1744 exhibition only required that the recipients of his charity should be 'of good character and learning' and born in the counties of Gloucester, Monmouth, or Glamorgan. Bishop John Robinson in 1718 gave preference for thirty years to his relatives, and to men educated at Charterhouse school.[42]

Oriel, not unusually for Oxford, drew the bulk of its student body from the Severn basin and the mid-south-west of the country.[43] The county which contributed the largest number of matriculands was Gloucestershire, with 155, including the cities of Bristol (25) and Gloucester (14). Next came Devon, with 98 (22 of them from Exeter); then London (94—although to this might be added the 31 from Westminster, 33 from Middlesex, and 1 from Southwark); Wiltshire (85); Somerset (75); Worcestershire (60); Kent (54); Oxfordshire (49); and Dorset (44). Only Westmorland and Northumberland seem to have been entirely unrepresented, although a number of counties contributed very few students, including Yorkshire (10), and, unsurprisingly, Cambridgeshire (1). Many of those who gave a metropolitan address on matriculating were no doubt also based in one or other county communities. A few came from further afield: 22 gave parental addresses in Ireland (although again, many of these may also have been based in one or other county in England); 12 were listed as coming from the West Indies; 8 from America; one each from the Netherlands, France, and Spain.

Family tradition and connection was naturally important in choosing a college. Many names recur throughout the period, such as the Belfields[44] and

---

[39] 1761–1842: matric. 8 December 1779; ODNB s.n.
[40] Edward Latter, matric. 9 March 1714: appointed St Antony exhibitioner 8 July 1714.
[41] John Ross, matric. 29 April 1713: appointed Dudley exhibitioner 17 March 1714.
[42] OCA GOV 4 A2, 26 June 1765; 20 March 1745; 25 February 1718.
[43] Compare the figures in HUO iv. 59.
[44] John, matric. 6 March 1688; John, Finney, Samuel, and Alan, his sons, matric. 8 March 1720, 16 November 1720, 16 July 1726, 22 March 1731; and Samuel's son Finney, matric. 29 March 1775.

the Musgraves,[45] and it would be easy to multiply examples of connections between families which sent their sons to Oriel. Some parents had a connection with the college through its estates or advowsons. Sir Henry Purefoy came to the college from Wadley in Berkshire, the college's biggest estate.[46] Richard Standish came from Moreton Pinkney in Northamptonshire, one of the college advowsons.[47] William Clarke, a commoner in 1657 and subsequently a fellow, was nephew of William Prynne, and came from Swainswick. Thomas Lodge came from Cromhall in Gloucestershire, although this was before the living was purchased by the college.[48] The first Beaufort exhibitioner, Walter Wightwick, appointed in 1747, came from Tetbury in Gloucestershire, close to Shipton Moyne, the family home of the provost, Walter Hodges, where Hodges's father had been rector.[49] Eleven men came from the city of Worcester, 6 of them described either as 'plebeian' or 'pauper', reflecting the college's old relationship with the city. Nine were from Wootton-under-Edge,[50] the same number as from the city of Oxford, which no doubt indicates some connection which had been established between the town and Oriel. It may have been to do with Evan Griffith, lecturer in the town, who was referred to by Anthony Wood as a former member of the college, although his name seems not to have been entered onto the register.[51]

Sometimes two sons would be admitted together, such as the Trott brothers, John and Edmund, sons of a baronet, who were admitted gentlemen commoners at the same time in August 1660 and matriculated together on 7 December 1660, despite the disparity in their ages (16 and 17).[52] Edward Owen and Francis Haley, both commoners, both matriculated on 15 May 1667, and

[45] Christopher, matric. 20 May 1731 at Christ Church, Philip, matric. 8 January 1733, Hans, matric. 26 October 1734, and Chardin, matric. 3 March 1743, all sons of Sir Christopher (4th baronet) of Eden Hall, Cumberland; Philip's sons John Chardin, matric. 27 January 1775 and Christopher, 16 February 1778; also the 4th baronet's grandsons Joseph (matric. 26 October 1749) and George (matric. 11 May 1758).
[46] Matric. 13 November 1671.
[47] Matric. 27 March 1673.
[48] Matric. 18 March 1713.
[49] Matric. 19 July 1746, appointed Beaufort exhibitioner 25 March 1747. *London Evening Post*, 9 October 1733, issue 919: d of Revd Mr Hodges, Minister of Shipton Moyne, near Tetbury.
[50] William Purnell, 1718; Robert Wight, 1721; Edward Hill, 1726; Richard Smith, 1746; Samuel Panting, 1754; Thomas Pearce, 1763; James Cooper, 1767; Daniel Veysie, 1772; Philip Dauncey, 1777.
[51] Wood, *Athenae Oxonienses* (1692), ii. 427.
[52] Similar cases are the Dyer brothers, William and Richard, who matriculated together on 16 November 1669, the sons of Richard Dyer, a gentleman from Malborough in Devon; and the two sons of Sir John Bridgeman, baronet, who matriculated on 25 August 1685; Nicholas and Francis Webb, the sons of John Webb, a clergyman, who matriculated on 15 December 1714; George and William Bent, sons of William Bent, gentleman, from Jacobstow, Devon, who matriculated on 13 March 1721; Robert and Thomas Mawdesley, sons of Robert Mawdesley, from Eccleston, Lancashire, who matriculated on 10 July 1724; the Loder brothers, matriculated 26 March 1743; the Morgan brothers, matriculated on 29 March 1757.

both from Eltham in Kent, one a gentleman's son, the other the son of a doctor in divinity, were presumably well known to one another. Simon Archer, gentleman commoner, and William Malins, servitor, both from Upper Tysoe, in Warwickshire, and both matriculated on 6 February 1673, were presumably also connected: Malins probably came to act as Archer's servant (Archer's brother Andrew was admitted and matriculated two months later).

The society encompassed its servants as well as its fellows and students: indeed, the line dividing the college servants from the students was porous. In 1692 Richard Adams, a servitor, was appointed porter.[53] The college servants recorded in the buttery books were a steward (*promus*), the bible clerk, cook, serving-woman (*famula*), porter (*janitor*), barber, and gardener. But there were clearly more people involved in keeping and serving the college than this. In 1660 a head butler, Roger Fry, was restored to his position, usurped by Thomas Newman in 1654.[54] The bonds of a succession of butlers—Roger Fry in 1669, Arthur Kight in 1715, Mark Morse ('gentleman') in 1734, and Thomas Webb in 1743—and of cooks—Thomas Crutch in 1675, Samuel Stockford in 1765, and Edward King in 1799—survive in the college archive.[55] Anthony Wood referred to a cook of Oriel called Williams, who had three sons born in 1692 in St Mary parish.[56] In 1773, the college decided to give a gratuity of £10 to the college butler, in recognition of his fidelity and good services to the college.[57] In 1774, during the provost's illness, the college agreed to abolish the place of college barber and to withhold the stipend, but in the succeeding October audit (when the provost returned) it was restored. The scouts or bedmakers are not recorded in the buttery books. As elsewhere, they were mostly employed personally by individual fellows and students, although the rates were set by the college, in 1768 at 7s. 6d. per quarter for commoners and 16s. for gentlemen commoners.[58] Hearne referred to 'Goody Earl a Scout';[59] a bedmaker found the body of Thomas Ward, a fellow, on his suicide in 1721;[60] and George Carter left Christian Newman 'bedmaker of Oriel College' a sum in his will.[61] A note in the buttery book for 1719–20 lists the three men who were 'To serve ye cake: Mr Dandridge upon alsaints; Mr Franklin upon xmas day and twelfth night; and Mr Thorne at Candlemas'. None of these men seem to have been servitors. Bull, who was the common room steward from at least

---

[53] Matric. 1 March 1692.
[54] 'The Restoration Visitation of the University of Oxford and its Colleges', ed. F. J. Varley, *Camden Miscellany*, xviii (Camden Society, third series, 1948), lxxix. 19, 24–5.
[55] OCA STA 1 A1/1–4; STA 1 A2/1–3.   [56] Wood, *Life and Times*, iii. 417.
[57] OCA PRO 1 C1 1, 100.   [58] HUO v. 257; OCA PRO 1 C1 3, 24 April 1767.
[59] Hearne, *Collections*, ii. 117.   [60] Hearne, *Collections*, vii. 293.
[61] OCA PRO 2 35 1.

1744 to at least the end of this period, may or may not have been identifiable with the steward listed in the buttery book.

There is little evidence available about Oriel's teaching practices, although no doubt they were very similar to what is known from other colleges. Oriel certainly held twice-termly disputations for undergraduates, for the college set out detailed rules for how they should be run at a meeting in 1708.[62] The philosopher Joseph Butler complained that he had to 'mis-spend so much time here in attending frivolous lectures and unintelligible disputations'.[63] Each student would spend much of his time (when working) under the direction of his college tutor. Thomas Dilke's 1697 play *The City Lady: Or, Folly Reclaim'd* pokes fun at the Oxford scholar Pedantry Grumble, son of a rich city merchant, and his tutor, Burgersditius Secundum (a name presumably meant to indicate a follower of city wealth). Burgersditius accompanies his pupil on a visit home to clinch a marriage with his cousin: his family can no longer understand the young Oxford scholar, now trained in disputation, and even less his bizarre tutor:

LADY GRUMBLE: (Pedantry *kneeling*) Bless my Child, thou art welcome kindly, and so are you Sir; I shall not be wanting in being Grateful, for the care you have had of my Son here.
BURGERSDITIUS: It has been, Forsooth, as well my Nocturnal as Diurnal Study, to embellish Mr Pedantry's Interiors, with the Rudiments of sound Philosophy. Hem! hem!
PEDANTRY: Lady Mother, I thank you for the last Plum-cake you sent me, dad 'twas pure good, and we was so merry at the eating of it, and had so many pretty Disputes about it,—what do you think; but we prov'd it a Sea-horse, a Crocodile, a Rhinoceros, and a Dromedary, and forty more things, till at last we prov'd it— nothing, he, he, e.
BURGERSDITIUS: Ha, ha, a, that was Wit profest, that was Wit.—I profess your Son here, Forsooth, may be call'd a Quotidian *Terrae filius.*

The identity of Dilke's tutor at Oriel is sadly unknown, and the portrayal a mockery; but it does reflect the degree to which the relationship between tutor and pupil could become as much social and paternal as pedagogical. As elsewhere, it was the prerogative of the college head to appoint tutors for undergraduates, and the tuition of individual undergraduates, no doubt especially those of greater wealth or higher social standing, were important and lucrative concerns for the provost and the teaching fellows. Chardin Musgrave wrote in 1763 to a Dr Davenport about the education of Mr Cope:

---

[62] OCA GOV 4 A2, 23 December 1708.
[63] Matric. 17 March 1715. *The Works of Bishop Butler*, ed. David E. White (Rochester, NY, 2006), 27, J. Butler to Samuel Clarke, *c.* September 1717.

as you mention some particular circumstances in the early part of Mr Cope's education, betwixt this & my coming to Bath which I propose next Month the Tutor & I shall be able to judge what more than common attention will be wanted and we will take the best method of supplying it which will partly depend upon the future intentions for the young Gentleman.[64]

George Carter described how

Mr James came to Oxford and drank a glass of wine with me on Tuesday in the evening. He breakfasted & dined with me ye next day and set out from hence in the afternoon. The librarian being fellow of my college I took care should shew several curious books in his own way in the public library.... He entered his son a commoner, but intends if he don't like that gown that he shall put on a gentleman commoners.[65]

He also recorded his thanks to the archbishop of Canterbury for

yr good opinion of me and my college in ... recommending to it a son of Sir Thomas Scawen, a gentlemen of whom I know your Grace [has] a very great esteem.... I have enquired after a room and I find the young gentleman may have a very good one. I have spoke to the person whom I design for his Tutor, a very honest worthy man of my society, and he hath promised to take a more than ordinary care of him, particularly in instructing him in such parts of learning as most useful for one that is to apply himself to the study of the common law. I can depend upon him for what he undertakes, however I shall likewise my self often strictly inquire what improvements he makes and do my utmost toward his improvement.[66]

The identity of few of Oriel's tutors is known. They included diligent Edward Bentham (lampooned by Dr King, the Jacobite principal of St Mary Hall, as the 'little tutor') who produced textbooks in English on logic and moral philosophy during his twenty years or more as a tutor before his move to Christ Church in 1754. John Clark, John Dodson, and John Eveleigh served as tutors too. But it is not clear how many fellows were involved in teaching undergraduates, or whether, as in some other colleges, a small number of the fellows did all of the teaching.[67] Fees for tutors varied depending on status: Gilbert White, a commoner matriculating in 1739, paid £6 for a 'year's tutorage',[68] but William Calley, a gentleman commoner who matriculated in January 1765, paid John Clark and John Dodson (fellow 1756–69) 50 guineas for tuition (presumably also covering the year).[69]

Tutors' fees were only a small part of the expense of Oxford life, and for very many of those attending the college, learning was a very small part of its

---

[64] Musgrave to Davenport, 8 November 1763, Derbyshire Record Office, D3155 M/C 341.
[65] OCA PRO 1 C1 1, 36. John James, matric. 23 May 1722.
[66] OCA PRO 1 C1 1, 63. Robert Scawen, matric. 25 October 1725. Scawen's father was an alderman of the City of London.
[67] See e.g. Hopkins, *Trinity*, 188.
[68] Matric. 17 December 1739: Gilbert White MSS, Oriel College Library.
[69] Compare the figures in HUO iv. 85.

charms. For young men of 16 or 17, Oxford represented an opportunity to lead an independent life for the first time, and it was one usually grasped with enthusiasm. One of the first concerns was, naturally, accommodation. Musgrave's letter of November 1763 about Cope's anticipated arrival in the college considered this in some detail:

Since I wrote to you the Duke of Beaufort has given me notice of his leaving College this month which vacates three Rooms and upon an Enquiry I find three more sets likely to be vacant soon & that some of the gentlemen who have been in Lodgings sometime have their Friends consent to stay in them by which means I may insure a set of Rooms to Mr Cope if he enters this month... If the young Gentleman comes to Oxford upon the shortest notice I will have a borrowed Room ready for him till he may have one of his own.[70]

The borrowed rooms were probably those belonging to non-resident fellows.[71] In 1735 the arrival of a group of gentlemen commoners seems to have caused problems, with a college meeting deciding to delegate to the dean and senior treasurer decisions on 'such alteration and removals as they judged proper (saving the rights of particular owners)'.[72] The Robinson and Carter buildings (built from 1720 and 1729 respectively with the gifts of the bishop and the provost) ought to have made more room available, but the high numbers admitted in the early 1730s (14 in 1731 and 1733 and 11 in 1734) combined with the tendency to provide more spacious accommodation may have limited the rooms available.

Furnishing and decorating the rooms could become expensive, although the costs were reduced by the system of 'thirdings' by which subsequent incumbents of the room paid the depreciated cost of the goods. Henry Purefoy's mother explained in 1736 how her son 16 years before had 'furnished his apartment in the new building in Oriell College Oxford with wainscot, hangings & all other goods & enjoyed them only the 2 last years he was there, & notwithstanding nothing was the worse his successor paid him but 2 thirds & by enquiry I find tis a common rule in such an occasion in other places'.[73] Gilbert White paid £4 5s. 7d. for 'thirds of my room', and in addition 6s. for '3ds of a cupboard' and 3s. for '3ds of some locks' (White, as a commoner, evidently enjoyed only a room, and not rooms).[74] Peter Harvey Lovell, a gentleman commoner who matriculated in 1777,[75] bought for his rooms in Oriel a mahogany bureau, a bedside carpet, a firescreen, a 'press

---

[70] Musgrave to Davenport, 8 November 1763, Derbyshire Record Office, D3155 M/C 3411.
[71] See HUO v. 330.
[72] OCA PRO 1 C1 2, 11 April 1735.
[73] *Purefoy Letters 1735–1753*, ed. G. Eland (London, 1931).
[74] Gilbert White MSS, Oriel College Library.
[75] Matric. 18 March 1777, son of John Lovell of Bath, Somerset, later described as of Cole Park, Wiltshire.

bedstead with folding doors', 'a line and tassel to the bell', and a 'tin coal scoop'.[76] There was rent to pay to the college as well: White had to pay £4 for his room. In 1773, at the instance of the provost, John Clark, but against the opposition of one fellow, the college increased the rent by £1.[77] It was presumably as a result of causing serious damage to his rooms that the college had to order in 1775 a repair to Mr Hare's room, for which it agreed to charge him £50.[78] In addition to the money laid out on the room and its furniture, undergraduates had to pay fees: caution money, in theory returned at the end of the period of residence; for gentlemen commoners library fees as well (ordinary commoners and servitors were not permitted to use the library). A handful of men, presumably only those who played tennis, also paid 'ball court money'. Caution money was in 1660 £10 for gentlemen commoners, £6 for commoners, and 50s. for servitors; in 1728 it was increased to £12 and £8 respectively, and £15 for noblemen.[79] There were college admission fees (£3 10s. in 1778) and the university matriculation fee (17s. 6d.).

For those privileged enough to afford it and to avoid the hard grind of diligent study, the life of an undergraduate at Oxford was liberating. The new gentleman commoner Peter Harvey Lovell wrote to his mother in March 1778 that

My gown flows in a manner now become habitual, & the Tuft of my cap depends decently on either side of it, in plain English I am very well settled in a situation which my Fathers bounty has so generously prepared for me, for which please to tender him my most sincere thanks.... With respect to the Disposal of our Time, we go to Prayers every morning at 8 o clock, then go to Breakfast, & after Breakfast to Lecture, then leisurely dispose of ourselves as we please till Dinner time about 3 o clock after which retire to the common Room (a Room to which the gentlemen Commoners & Fellows of the College only have admission) there drink a glass or two of Wine, & after setting about an Hour & half go to Prayers in the Chapel, then drink tea at our own Chambers, & sup in the common Room if we choose.[80]

Lovell's younger brother, John, who came up exactly a year later, wrote to his mother in November 1778 full of the joys of Oxford:

My bed answers very well in every Respect, but is not to be painted till the Vacation. In the Space of two or three Days last week, we had eight or nine Hundred of the Militia, part Glocestershire & part Derbyshire, come to this place on their march from Warley Common, to winter Quarters, they had amongst them 12 Baggage Waggons, & as many artillery Waggons loaded with Powder & Ball, somewhat like Herses &

---

[76] Lovell to his mother, n.d., 161/159. The same items are included in a bill from James Halse, dated 28 October 1778.
[77] OCA PRO 1 C1 1, 100.
[78] OCA PRO 1 C1 1, 14 November 1775.
[79] OCA GOV 4 A2, 19 October 1728.
[80] Wiltshire and Swindon History Centre, Lovell of Cole Park collection, 161/159.

drawn by 4 Horses, also 4 Field Pieces on Wheels; all the Officers came in on Foot, which together with a good Bands of Music formd two fine sights. I rode out Tuesday to Woodstock & about 2 or 3 Miles beyond it met with the Duke of Marlborough's Harriers, they found a Hare setting we hunted with them about an Hour & so returnd Home to Dinner… I am now perfectly well settled at a Place which my Father has so liberally provided for me & in a Rank, which my age by no means entitled me to expect.[81]

The Lovell boys' bills show the scale of expenditure incurred by the pair. Those from the tailor, Thomas Benwell & Son, record frequent pairs of breeches, and mending gowns; R. Blenkinsop, the barber, charged £3 15s. for one and a half years' hairdressing; there were also payments to Walter Walsh for hair dressing (including '16 Sunday dressings'—on Sunday students were expected to appear at chapel properly dressed) and powder and pomatum; fruit from Maria Young including apples, pears, walnuts, grapes, almonds, raisins, dried apples, oranges, oranges 'at the Musick room', 'Prstata nutts' or 'p stationery nutts' (presumably pistachios), strawberries, cherries, and raspberries, 'a pint of olives', sometimes fruit 'at the common room'. Elizabeth Collet charged £3 3s. over a quarter for washing and mending stockings, waistcoats, and shirts, E. Bull (presumably the wife or daughter of C. Bull the Common Room steward) charged 13s. 4d. for milk and cream over the course of a year and also supplied cleaning materials such as a slop pan, a hearth broom, candlesticks, and candles; Benjamin Cosier supplied a 'powney', saddle, and bridle; James Halse was the upholsterer who supplied the bureau, bed, and bedding; Nicholas Halse supplied saddle and other tack; there were hats and hose from John Parsons; shoes and shoe mending from John Floyd; tumblers, glasses, paper, pens, sugar, a tea tray, decanters, tongs, a milk boat from Couldrey; paper and books from Robert Bliss, including copies of Dionysius, Blackstone (4 volumes), Ferguson's astronomy, Xenophon, Cicero's *De officiis*, Grotius *De veritate*, Chesterfield's Letters, Buxtorf (presumably his Hebrew grammar), and Plato; Daniel Prince supplied Ainsworth's dictionary, the *Orationes* of Demosthenes, Juvenal, and paper; Ann Griffin charged for faggots, coals, and charcoals. One Campione charged 7s. 6d. for 'Three small landskips in gold and Blue frames and glass'; Stephen Haynes, glovemaker, supplied gloves (including, in December 1779, two pairs of ladies' gloves) and skin breeches; A. King supplied jelly, coffee, and rum; William Strange a tureen, twelve plates, and a Wedgwood teapot. Lovell senior would go to visit the boys at Oriel, travelling via the King's Head at Cirencester and Burford. Regular bills from Edward Brockis at the Bear Inn, in the High Street, and one from the Star at Oxford on 24 February 1781, including beds, presumably relate to his

---

[81] Wiltshire and Swindon History Centre, Lovell of Cole Park collection, 161/159, J. Lovell to his mother, Friday 20 November 1778.

visits. Brockis hired out transport as well, charging 16s. in June 1779 for a chaise to Burford.

Tutors were often entrusted by their pupils' parents not only with the education and guardianship of their children, but also their finances. Ten years before the Lovells came into residence, John Clark, tutor for William Calley, was sent money to pay Calley's bills (which included one of June 1769 for setts of tennis from John Hardway). The Lovell correspondence indicates the difficulties in which the tutor might be placed. Peter Lovell's tutor, John Eveleigh, wrote to Lovell's father in June 1778 to tell him that his son's behaviour had been 'very regular in every respect', and told him of his thirds and battels. The thirds came to £40; the battels to £18 7s. 6d.; Eveleigh had paid the thirds himself, and asked for the total to be sent 'in whatever manner is most agreeable'.[82] A year later, Eveleigh was writing again to Lovell to say that he would call in at Cole Park on his way to Devon, to collect the money owing: 'I shall have no inconsiderable bill to settle with you'. It amounted to £62 16s. 6d. for three quarters' battels and room rent, plus a year's tuition, at £42, plus other expenses.[83] In the next year's letter, in April 1780, Eveleigh referred to a 'particular order' made by the college for the regular payment of battels, as a result of which Lovell's son had asked Eveleigh to pay the arrears due from him and his brother, and to send Lovell an account. Eveleigh had also, he said, paid their wine bills, and given the younger son 5 guineas towards his upholsterers bill. As in the previous year, most of the sum due was the three quarters' battels at £38 12s. and another year's tuition, at £42. Lovell senior went up to Oxford at the end of that Trinity Term to settle the bills and pick up his sons.[84] He did not always find it easy to lay his hands on the money. Almost another year later, at the end of March 1781, Eveleigh wrote apologising for asking for money again, 'yet as the orders of the college for the payment of Battels every Quarter &, at present also, of the wine-bills every Quarter are general I cannot help sending some other accounts in addition to those which I sent before'. 'My circumstances at present', Eveleigh went on, 'are such that it is not in my Power to pay these Bills for your son & they must all be paid within a month according to an Order of the College, which extends alike to every person.' As he had not received £200 the previous summer from Lovell, he had been

---

[82] Wiltshire and Swindon History Centre, Lovell of Cole Park collection, 161/159, Eveleigh to John Lovell, 20 June 1778.

[83] Wiltshire and Swindon History Centre, Lovell of Cole Park collection, 161/159, Eveleigh to John Lovell, 24 June 1778. It is unclear whether Eveleigh was charging £42 for one or for both sons. He wrote 'tuition due at the end of Mich. Term 1778—one year—for each', but the £42 is not doubled in the total bill, and as it would appear that John only came up at Michaelmas 1778.

[84] Wiltshire and Swindon History Centre, Lovell of Cole Park collection, 161/159, John Lovell to his sons [draft], 15 June 1780.

forced to borrow that sum himself.[85] Eveleigh does seem eventually to have received his money in two instalments in May and July 1781,[86] though some of the Lovells' other bills were not paid until 1786, four years after John Lovell had taken his bachelor's degree. Although such forbearance was more likely to be paid to a gentleman commoner than to an ordinary one, tutors clearly had to be prepared to hold substantial sums of money in their hands to cover the needs of their pupils.

Some of the Lovells' bills were incurred in the common room, which was the centre of social life for part of the college. A story told of Gilbert White suggests that gentlemen commoners' access to the common room was restricted to certain times, and that they seldom made use of it:

> White, as long as his health allowed him, always attended the annual election of fellows at Oriel College, when the gentlemen commoners were allowed the use of the common room after dinner. This liberty they seldom availed themselves of, except on the occasion of Mr White's visits, for such was his happy and, indeed, inimitable manner of … telling a story that the room was always filled when he was there.[87]

However, the common room accounts, which exist from 1744, and the Lovells' bills give a rather different impression. The accounts were kept separately from those of the college, although they seem often (though not invariably) to have been kept by the senior or junior treasurer of the college, and were signed off by the dean. They show that the common room's income came from 'the schemes', a contribution from the college of about £7 each quarter, and from admission fees received from each new member. Fellows and gentlemen commoners were admitted, but not all new fellows and new gentlemen commoners are recorded as having paid.[88] The basic income paid for a stipend to Bull, the common room steward; to the same man for washing, and various sundries; for an almanac, packs of cards (frequently replaced), and dice; glasses and decanters; firewood ('billetting'); candles; a glazier's bill; an annual bill for mistletoe. There were occasional extraordinary items: Dr Plot's *Natural History of Oxfordshire*; oysters and oyster knives; maps showing the engagement in February 1744 off Toulon, a subject of great public interest throughout 1745; tobacco and pipes; carriage for the duke of Beaufort's picture in 1753. From 1762 the room subscribed to a newspaper; by 1763 it would receive the court calendar as well. In 1779 the

---

[85] Wiltshire and Swindon History Centre, Lovell of Cole Park collection, 161/159, Eveleigh to John Lovell, 28 March 1781.
[86] Wiltshire and Swindon History Centre, Lovell of Cole Park collection, 161/159, Receipts written on Eveleigh to John Cole, 28 March 1781 and separate receipt dated 12 May 1781.
[87] *Boswell's Life of Johnson*, ed. George Birkbeck Hill, revised edn. by L. F. Powell (Oxford, 1934), ii. 443.
[88] Hearne mentions (from Dyer) in 1723 that it was against the college's 'Custom & Practise' for 'Bachelor fellows' to use the common room. Hearne, *Collections*, viii. 137.

cost of newspapers suddenly doubled, and there was a subscription to the *Oxford Journal* (in 1784 the Common Room was subscribing to the *Oxford Journal*, the *Morning Chronicle*, and the *Monthly Review*).[89] The Lovells' visits to the common room were frequent. Most days there would be a 'reckoning' of between 6*d*. and 1*s*.; occasionally there would be a larger order: 6 bottles of port on 1 December 1778; 3 bottles of sherry on 7 December; 2 bottles of sherry and 6 of port on 8 March 1779; 4 bottles of port on 5 April; 3 bottles of port and 1 of sherry on 13 April; 6 bottles of port on 10 May, and so on (the days when Oriel common room would be famous for its consumption of tea were still in the future). Just before the Lovells came into residence, the diarist James Woodforde in January 1774 spent an evening in the common room with his friend and mentor Robert Penny, a fellow, one other fellow of Oriel (John Eveleigh), a gentleman commoner of Oriel, and a fellow of Wadham, where they stayed till after 11, playing whist, and eating a barrell of Colchester oysters (sent to Penny from London by the duke of Beaufort).[90] The common room was more, though, than a social institution. By 1755 it seems to have been covering the costs of probationer fellows reading in the chapel, apparently to cover the turns of fellowships that were vacant, or possibly of fellows who were absent from Oxford.

There were young women around to admire the more presentable undergraduates. One of them, the lively Elizabeth Sheppard, found in 1738 the principal attraction of Oriel to be neither its buildings ('pretty enough'), nor its pomegranate tree (whose fruit the provost attested to be delicious), but one young man in particular:

in this college shines the Gold Tuft of L^d. Wenman,[91] & the Genteel M^r. Talbot[92] & the most deserving Young Gentleman Commoner throwoly well bred Genteel & polite, without Afectaition; Modest without reserve, & Gay without Galoping Generous without extravagance in short to sum up his Character in few words as possible I will only add he is what every True English Gentleman of Fortune ought to be—his B^r is a Commoner[93] & very deserveing but Shines not quite with so Radiant a Lustre as his Elder B^r Ld Wenman I should have said more of & now will say few of our Young Nobility are so Courteous Sober & affable a Man of very solid Sense a great Oeconomist & a Good Scholar; & if he lives will make if not a great, what is much Better, & that is a good Man.[94]

---

[89] OCA SL 1 A1.

[90] *Woodforde at Oxford, 1759–76*, ed. W. N. Hargreaves-Mawdsley (Oxford, 1969), 206.

[91] For Wenman, see n. 33. 'The Gold Tuft' suggests that Sheppard believed that Wenman wore the academic dress of a nobleman, despite the fact that he was admitted to the college as a gentleman commoner: but perhaps she is using the Oxford term simply to indicate his (non-Oxford) noble status.

[92] John Talbot, matric. 5 February 1735, aged 17.

[93] Thomas Talbot, matric. 20 January 1737, aged 17.

[94] Bodleian MS. Top.Oxon. d.287, '*Shepilinda's memoirs of the City and University of Oxford Jan^{ry} 7th 1737/8. For Dear Scrippy.*' I am grateful to Geoffrey Neate for drawing this MS to my

Not all Oriel undergraduates were as charming; and less innocent pastimes than drinking and playing cards in the common room were, of course, available to those who looked for them. Wood mentioned the expulsion of an Oriel MA, Michael Smith, in August 1684 for an attempted rape.[95] Hearne recorded the assault on New Year's Eve 1723 on Mr Allen, a barber of St Clements, by three gentlemen commoners of Queen's and one from Oriel 'for no manner of reason, only for hindering his maid (whom he had sent forth on an errand) from being abused by them'.[96] Some of Hearne's allegations about undergraduate dissoluteness may be exaggerated: his description of another Oriel gentleman commoner, William Talbot, who matriculated in 1674, as 'most remarkably and scandalously idle and debauched', during his career at Oxford, where he 'minded no studies of learning, but was a compleat Rake, and indeed he had very little of religion to his dying day' was no doubt politically motivated: Talbot later became dean of Worcester and bishop successively of Oxford and Durham, his elevation to the deanship, Hearne remarked, on the interest of the Whig duke of Shrewsbury after the removal of the non-juror George Hickes.[97] Hearne's animus against him possibly related to Talbot's son as well, who, a fellow commoner of Oriel, became a fellow of All Souls, and was involved in the notorious Woodcock dinner at All Souls (a deliberate insult to the memory of Charles I) in 1707.[98]

The most serious incident of undergraduate mayhem in eighteenth-century Oxford was in fact political in origin, and Oriel was closely involved. After the accession of George I, Oriel men were prominent members of the Constitution Club, the Whig society based at New College 'consisting of a few Masters and some undergraduate Scholars, about 17 in all', which, against the grain in Oxford, aimed to celebrate and protect the Hanoverian succession.[99] Their provocative plans to light a bonfire in the street outside the King's Head Tavern in the High Street on 28 May 1715, King George I's birthday, set off rioting over two days. William Dering, senior proctor and a fellow of Oriel, tried to disperse the crowd, and sent the members of the Club on their way. According to the published report by Richard Rawlinson, when they got to New College and were safely protected behind the college gate, 'they shot off several Blunderbusses, and other Fire-Arms, at a venture

---

attention, for allowing me to quote from his transcription, and for other information about Elizabeth Sheppard.

[95] Wood, *Life and Times*, 107.
[96] Hearne, *Collections*, ix. 390.
[97] Matric. 28 March 1674. Hearne, *Collections*, x. 72.
[98] Hearne, *Collections*, i. 337. Charles Talbot, matric. 25 March 1702, later Lord Chancellor.
[99] Richard Rawlinson, *A Full and Impartial Account of the Oxford Riots* (London, 1715), lists 8 Oriel men, members of the Constitution Club, who were cited to appear before the vice-chancellor's court after the riots: [Thomas] Hamilton, Yeoman [John Yeamans], Harle [unidentified], [Thomas] Hales, [Henry] Hadley, Francis Button, Sayer [George Sawyer], Charles Ingram.

among the People, some of which they wounded, and others had very providential Escapes'.¹⁰⁰ One of those firing was Thomas Hamilton, an Oriel gentleman commoner and son of the physician to Queen Anne.¹⁰¹ More shots were fired that night from the windows of Hart Hall and Oriel; and on the following night, the anniversary of the Restoration in 1660, Oxford's Tories created a counter-demonstration. After destroying the Quaker meeting House near St John's, part of the mob moved on to Oriel Square,

> where one Mr Charles Ing__m,¹⁰² Brother to the Lord Ir__in, having collected a great Number of his own Party into a Room, which they called the Guard-Room, and which was replenished with Guns, Pistols, Powder, and Ball, which they made sufficient Use of, without any Provocation. As soon as the People came near the College, the Fire-Arms were immediately discharged, and a Person wounded in the Groin, which gave just Grounds to the injur'd People, to demand Justice; this was required at the College-Gate but denied; and had not the Provost and Fellows came down, and one of the People interposed, 'till Justice was promised on the Offenders, the college might have been pulled down to the Ground, and the People De-Witted.¹⁰³

Henry Culpeper Fairfax,¹⁰⁴ a gentleman commoner, gave his version of the events at Oriel in a letter to his brother 5 months after the riots. After the rioters' failure to get at the constitutioners at New College, he wrote, 'their whole design was then turn'd against Oriel being, as they said, the Harbour for such Rogues, but we were oblig'd for our safety to Mr Ge: Ingram¹⁰⁵ who discharg'd a gun out of his window, as did Du Bois,¹⁰⁶ which dispersed the mob.'¹⁰⁷ It is unclear whether it was Charles or George Ingram who fired out of the window (it could have been either, although the fact that the senior proctor, William Dering, supported George Ingram's bid for a fellowship the same year makes it more likely to have been Charles). The incident provoked a crisis in the university's relationship with the government, and was the background to the imposition of a military garrison on the city later in the year, after the beginning of the Jacobite rebellion. The members of the Constitution Club were cited before the vice-chancellor's court, although

---

¹⁰⁰ Rawlinson, *A Full and Impartial Account*, 3. See also the account in HMC Portland MSS, vii. 223.
¹⁰¹ Matric. 20 October 1713.
¹⁰² Charles Ingram, gentleman commoner, matric. 29 April 1714.
¹⁰³ Rawlinson, *A Full and Impartial Account*, 5–6. 'De Witted' is presumably an allusion to the fate of Jan and Cornelius De Witt, lynched by a mob in The Hague in 1672.
¹⁰⁴ Matric. 1 March 1714. His brother was Thomas, 6th Lord Fairfax, who matric. 14 January 1710. Henry Fairfax was elected a fellow of the Royal Society in 1727.
¹⁰⁵ Gentleman commoner, matric. 7 June 1711, BA 23 April 1714, el. fellow, 23 March 1716.
¹⁰⁶ Charles Du Bois, commoner, matric. 10 October 1712.
¹⁰⁷ Bodleian Library MS Fairfax 35, fo. 94: Henry Culpeper Fairfax to brother, 15 October 1715.

they received the lightest of punishments.[108] There was no obvious consequence for Oriel, unless the small number of gentlemen commoners admitted in the years after the riot (1 each in 1716, 1717, and 1718 after the peak of 5 in 1715) was related. The stabbing of a commoner of Oriel in 1717 by another undergraduate was also attributed to 'the same spirit of Faction' which 'still reigns among some of the Collegians of Oxford as usual'. According to the London papers, one 'Eves[109] of Oriel College', 'making too free with his Majesty's Character in a way very unbecoming him, was mildly reprov'd for his Impudence by one Mr Stafford of the same College, whereupon Eves Stabb'd him with a Penknife'. Stafford died a little while later,[110] but Eves, to Hearne's indignation, was acquitted a year later for want of evidence.[111]

There is little evidence of further political trouble in Oriel among the undergraduate body, even in 1748, when a drunken declaration of allegiance to the Pretender by two undergraduates from St Mary Hall and Balliol escalated into a government prosecution of the vice-chancellor.[112] Edward Bentham's response to those events, his *Letter to a young gentleman of Oxford*, was a loyalist tract preaching obedience to the government to undergraduates, an 'Antidote in Print for the Use of his Pupils, whenever an Attempt should be made to tamper with their Principles, and withdraw them from their Obedience to the Laws of the Land': Bentham claimed it was not occasioned by 'the late treasonable Disturbance in Oxford', but he wrote 'with a view however to this, as well as the Affair with which he was himself more particularly concerned', but what this might have been is not known.[113] Life after Oriel

The university's requirements for taking the BA degree included 4 years' or 16 terms' residence, although this could be reduced through various expedients (including dispensations for those of particularly high status). The period between matriculation and the award of the degree in Oriel over the period was commonly around three and a half years.[114] Many men,

---

[108] Ward, *Georgian Oxford*, 88. A letter from Nicholas Rogers, fellow of Oriel, of 17 July 1715, to Hamilton's father informs him of the citation to the vice-chancellor's court. Gloucestershire Archives, D1571/F75

[109] Henry Eve, matric. 11 February 1716.

[110] *Weekly Journal or British Gazetteer*, 20 July 1717.

[111] *Original Weekly Journal*, 15 March 1718. Hearne, *Collections*, vi. 71, 155. No student called Stafford appears to have been admitted at Oriel sufficiently close to 1717 to make him likely to be the victim. Hearne said the assailant was 'Bull', not Eve, though since George Bull (matric. 17 March 1717) died in 1717 and was buried at Great St Mary's he is more likely to have been the victim. He also says that the assailant was convicted of manslaughter.

[112] See Ward, *Georgian Oxford*, 170–1; HUO v. 125.

[113] Edward Bentham, *A Letter to a Young Gentleman of Oxford* (London, 1749), advertisement. See Ward, *Georgian Oxford*, 171–3 for the controversy sparked by the *Letter*.

[114] HUO iv. 89–91, v. 470.

particularly those not intending to take their degrees, would have spent much less time in college than this might suggest. Some failed to stay the distance, for certainly earlier in the period, deaths among the undergraduate and graduate population were common. Wood regularly records them. In November 1660 John Smith, a gentleman commoner, died at the house of 'one Daye a Tailor in St Aldate's parish'.[115] John Stone was buried in the college chapel in March 1673. In 1676 a fever epidemic in Oxford carried off one Oriel man.[116]

Of all those admitted to the college in the period, just over half proceeded to the bachelor of arts degree. Another 32 took the 'Law line', the BCL degree, sometimes because of its reputation as an easier option, although all but one of them did so after 1700, and most of them were after 1740.[117] Gentlemen commoners, naturally, were the least likely to take a degree: of 234 gentlemen commoners admitted over the period only 26 took BA degrees, and 3 the BCL.[118] A number of the most exalted (many of them the sons of peers or baronets) received honorary MA degrees, although this seems to have been very uncommon before the 1740s, and many did not bother.[119] Perhaps the fuss concerned was not always to the taste of those grand enough already, and exposed the honorand to possible ridicule. Hearne remarked on the award of the degree to Sir Edward Dering in 1725, that when Thomas Weeksey presented him at convocation 'he spoke much of the antiquity of Sir Edward's family, making it famous even in the Saxon times, which is false, & speaking much of Sir Edward's beauty, which is also false, at least it was fulsome, Sir Edward being not beautiful.'[120] About 42 per cent of commoners went on to take their BA degrees. Naturally, servitors were the most likely to do so: about 74 per cent of them took BA degrees: none of them took the BCL.[121]

A letter to Lord Fairfax in 1713 discussed his leaving the university at the end of July, and suggested that he should consult with the provost 'what is most proper to be given at leaving college', and that he should 'do what is handsome'. It was assumed that Fairfax would donate his caution money to the college; to 'treat the whole Hall' could not be avoided.[122] Many gentlemen commoners, and some commoners too, gave pieces of silver, much of it specifically for the use of the provost. Fairfax, in the end, decided on a

---

[115] Wood, *Life and Times*, i. 338.   [116] Wood, *Life and Times*, ii. 359.
[117] HUO iv. 562, v. 487.
[118] For the unusualness of a gentlemen commoner taking a BA, see HUO iv. 234. Cf. also HUO v. 371 for comparative figures from other colleges, which suggests that Oriel's proportion of gentlemen commoners proceeding to a degree was quite high.
[119] Neither the duke of Beaufort nor the duke of Somerset were made MA by creation.
[120] Hearne, *Collections*, ix. 71.
[121] See, again, HUO v. 371 for comparative figures.
[122] Fairfax MS 35, fo. 86, ? to Fairfax, 25 February 1713.

FIGURE 8.2 Oriel clerical and legal careers, 1660–1779

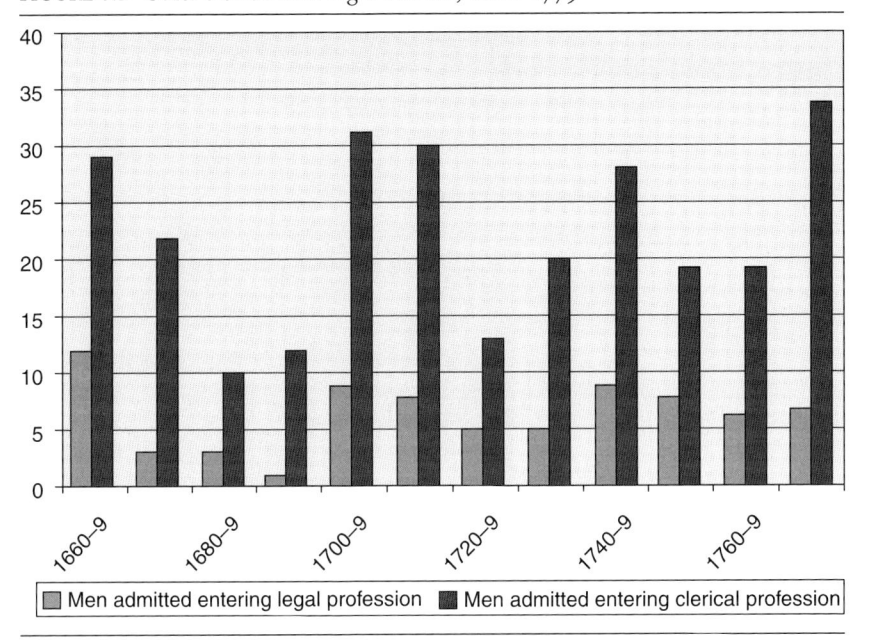

tankard, as did George Sawyer, who had joined the previous year. William Calley gave a coffee pot for the use of the provost and 6 spoons.[123] Sir Edward Dering gave a punch bowl in 1724; Sir Watkin Williams Wynn gave a silver soup tureen for the common room in 1771, but also 4 candlesticks for the provost. Dennis Hampson gave trees in 1670. The Lovells, however, seem not to have been donors.

The Church and the law, naturally, were the normal destinations for those Oriel leavers who needed to earn their living. The numbers of those entering either profession fluctuated during the period in much the same way as the numbers admitted to the college fluctuated, but there is a noticeable increase in the number of men admitted to the college in the first two decades of the eighteenth century who would go into the Church (see Figure 8.2)

Seventy-eight Oriel men were called to the bar; 155 were entered at one of the Inns of Court without, apparently, taking steps to enter the legal profession. Although it was normal for a man to be entered into one of the Inns sometime after they were admitted at Oxford, it was not uncommon for

[123] OCA PRO 1 C1 4.

ILLUSTRATION 8.2 Joseph Warton (1722–1800), literary critic, commoner 1740–4
Oriel College

admission to Oriel and an Inn to take place at roughly the same time, and from the 1720s quite common for men to be admitted to one of the Inns a year or so before admission to Oxford. About a third of those entering the Inns of Court were gentlemen commoners; the remainder were commoners. For most, the Inns of Court represented a short episode in a gentleman's education, rather than a chance to train for a vocation. A handful of those who were called to the bar attained real distinction in the law. Charles Talbot preceded the more celebrated Lord Hardwicke as Lord Chancellor in 1733–7; Robert Tracy was a judge in the Court of Common Pleas (and adjudicated on the college's case in 1726).

Around 268, almost 19 per cent, entered the clerical profession, usually as parish clergy. Some of them became schoolmasters. Hearne wrote of James Ellis who kept a private school at Thistleworth 'purely for grounding young gentlemen, noblemen's sons or gentlemen of some rank, in classick learning, and fitting them for the University, in which faculty he is of considerable repute'.[124] William Purnell became high master of Manchester Grammar

[124] Hearne, *Collections*, ii. 9: matric. 10 November 1676.

School in 1749.[125] Joseph Warton was head master of Winchester for 27 years.[126] A few Oriel men reached the highest levels of the Church. William Talbot, Charles Talbot's father, became dean of Worcester, 1691–1715, bishop of Oxford, 1699–1715, of Salisbury, 1715–21, and Durham, 1721–30.[127] Edward Willes, in part through his loyal service as decipherer to the king, became dean of Lincoln, 1730–43, bishop of St David's, 1742–3, and Bath and Wells, 1743–73.[128] The philosopher Joseph Butler, whose career benefited from the patronage of the Talbot family (Edward Talbot, Charles's brother, a fellow from 1712 to 1715, was his friend and mentor), became bishop of Bristol (1738–50) and dean of St Paul's (1740–50), and later bishop of Durham (1750–2). John Egerton became successively bishop of Bangor (1756–68), Coventry (1768–71), and Durham (1771–87).[129] William Buller became dean of Exeter (1784–90), dean of Canterbury (1790–2), and bishop of Exeter (1792–6).[130]

A remarkable number of Oriel men became members of parliament over the period.[131] Thomas Master, who was returned for Gloucestershire in 1788

---

[125] Henry Brooke, fellow, 1718–31, was also master of Manchester Grammar from 1727 to 1749.

[126] Matric. 16 January 1740.

[127] Matric. 28 March 1674. Talbot displaced the prominent non-juror George Hickes as dean of Worcester.

[128] Matric. 16 April 1709. For the difficulty Willes found himself in, in taking his DD degree in 1726, as a result of his work in deciphering the letters of Francis Atterbury, Jacobite bishop of Rochester, see Nicholas Amhurst, *Terrae-Filius: or, The Secret History of the university of Oxford; in Several Essays*, ed. William E. Rivers (Newark, 2004), 75. See also Hearne, *Collections*, vi. 293 for his marriage in Merton Chapel to Mrs Jenny White, daughter of Alderman White of Oxford, and the judgement that both White and Willes were 'constitutioners, as they are call'd' and 'very great Whigs'.

[129] Matric. 22 May 1740.

[130] Matric. 10 April 1753.

[131] They are with dates of matriculation William Trenchard, 7 December 1660; John Blencowe, 24 May 1661; Thomas Putt, 10 July 1661; Edmund Prideaux, 10 April 1663; Scorey Barker, 17 May 1667; John Ashe, 24 May 1671; Richard Wenman, 27 June 1673; William Selwyn, 11 April 1674; Robert Owen, 20 April 1674; Sir Francis Warre, 10 April 1674; William Drake, 4 June 1675; John Monk, 20 October 1676; Orlando Bridgeman 13 February 1688; John Belfield, 6 March 1688; John Cope (no matriculation date); William Bromley, 10 April 1701; John Fleetwood, 23 March 1702; Joseph Ashe, 4 March 1702; Arthur Ingram, 25 June 1706; George Chafin, 12 July 1707; Henry Ingram, 17 May 1708; John Dodd, 2 July 1709; Thomas Hales, 15 December 1711; John Owen, 10 October 1715; Sir Edward Dering, 31 January 1722; Thomas Chester, 10 July 1713; Sir Robert Austin, 10 October 1715; Francis Gwyn, 4 July 1717; Kelland Courtenay, 10 June 1724; Paulett St John (no matriculation date); Willoughby Aston, 7 January 1730; Philip Musgrave, 8 January 1733; James Bulkeley, 30 April 1735; Philip Jennings, 7 November 1739; John Ward, 7 February 1743; James Brudenell, 6 April 1743; Robert Brudenell, 19 October 1744; Sir John St Aubyn, 19 October 1744; William Hamilton, 4 March 1745 (Chancellor of the Exchequer in Ireland); Richard Grosvenor, 25 October 1748; Robert Waller, 11 June 1751; Thomas Grosvenor, 27 June 1751; Clement Tudway, 12 November 1751; John Pugh Pryse, 16 June 1756; James Long, 2 November 1756; George Musgrave, 11 May 1758; Philip Wenman, 1 February 1760; Thomas Master, 22 May 1761; Sir Watkin Williams Wynn, 9 May 1766; John Morshead, 15 May 1766; Henry Gough, 6 October 1767; John Keane, 21 March 1776; John Inglett, 28 October 1775.

on the Beaufort interest, had been admitted a gentleman commoner in 1761, the same year as Beaufort, although, as a Gloucestershire man, his connections with Beaufort were no doubt much older. But few of Oriel's MPs could be said to have had distinguished political careers. 'He is not celebrated for a peculiar attention to his parliamentary duties,' the *Public Ledger* remarked about Sir James Long, MP for Wiltshire seats from the 1760s to the 1790s, and the comment could stand for many of them.[132] John Morshead's career was wrecked by a gambling addiction (despite having 'a most amiable disposition and the strictest honour in all his engagements').[133] Even Sir Watkin Williams Wynn, scion of the most powerful Tory dynasty in eighteenth-century Wales, closely linked to the Beauforts (he married the 4th duke's daughter), and MP successively for Shropshire and Denbighshire in the 1770s and 1780s, took more interest in art, drama, and politics than in his political career. A few—Philip Jennings, MP for Totnes from the late 1760s to the late 1780s and before that a lieutenant colonel in the Horse Guards, and George Musgrave—had reputations, but never built political careers. The one Oriel politician who did have a significant political career in the period was William Hamilton—the clever son of a barrister who sat in the Irish parliament in the 1760s and for various seats in England from 1754 to 1796, ending up as Chancellor of the Exchequer in Ireland. A patron of Burke and a friend of Samuel Johnson, William Pitt, and the prince of Wales, he was regarded as a brilliant failure, 'single speech' Hamilton, who never opened his mouth in the House of Commons after 1765.[134]

Oriel's inability to produce successful brilliance in the eighteenth century may have had something to do with the elite status of many of its members. Oriel, a gentlemanly college, but without the connection with the great schools such as Magdalen, Christ Church, or New College possessed, specialized in wealthy squires rather than brittle geniuses. Typical, perhaps of the sort of contented gentleman whom Oriel turned out was the Mr Sawyer described by Hearne, who in 1728 was having Bittlesden Abbey, in Buckinghamshire demolished and a new house built in its place: 'a gentleman of about 26 years of age, as yet unmarried, a Whig, and formerly Gentleman commoner of Oriel College. I am told he is a good-natured man, & tho he is much addicted to his sports, yet reads pretty much at intervals.'[135]

---

[132] *History of Parliament: The House of Commons, 1754–1790*, iii. 53.
[133] *History of Parliament: The House of Commons, 1754–1790*, iii. 169.
[134] *History of Parliament: The House of Commons, 1754–1790*, ii. 573.
[135] Hearne, *Collections*, x. 75: perhaps Henry Sayer, matric. 7 August 1722.

9

Eveleigh and Copleston

The Pre-Eminence of Oriel

Ernest Nicholson

During the early decades of the nineteenth century, Oriel was acknowledged to be foremost, both academically and intellectually, among the colleges of Oxford. This ascendancy of Oriel, as it has been termed,[1] began as a result of initiatives taken by John Eveleigh (provost 1781–1814) and reached new heights under his successor, Edward Copleston (provost 1814–28), when the Oriel common room was deemed to be the intellectual power house of the university. The esteem in which the college was held survived the lustre of these early decades; when it had faded, and pre-eminence had passed to other colleges, a fellowship at Oriel remained among the most coveted in the university. Together with Balliol, the college was the favoured destination for parents seeking to gain entry for their sons at Oxford. Mark Pattison, who had to take his place on a waiting list for admission to Oriel, which he gained in 1832, records that '[i]n the matter of tuition there were two colleges whose repute stood higher than that of any—viz. Oriel and Balliol', adding what his friend Lord Conyers had, from his undergraduate point of view, commented to him about these two colleges: 'We call those the two prison-houses.' Pattison continues: 'I was eager to doom myself to either of the prisons. And it was clear that the choice was restricted to these two.'[2] A few years earlier William Wilberforce, preferring Oxford for his three younger sons rather than Cambridge, where he had been an undergraduate at St John's, secured places for them at Oriel.[3]

---

[1] See K. C. Turpin, 'The Ascendancy of Oriel', in HUO vi. 183–92.
[2] Mark Pattison, *Memoirs* (London, 1885), 23. Pattison was elected to a fellowship at Lincoln College in 1839 and was rector 1861–84.
[3] Wilberforce's eldest son, also William, had fecklessly squandered his time at Cambridge; doubtless this, in addition to his own recollections of dissipated undergraduate life at Cambridge, decided his choice of Oxford and Oriel for his remaining three sons. He met Edward

In office Eveleigh faced very different historical circumstances from those that were to confront Copleston. For most of Eveleigh's thirty-three years as provost, Britain was either bracing itself for war or was actually at war with France. A few months after Copleston succeeded him in December 1814, the final defeat of Napoleon at Waterloo brought peace, and a new and far-reaching political agenda which shortly after Copleston left office, early in 1828, led to a series of reforms which marked the end of Britain's *ancien régime*. These reforms evoked deep divisions of opinion in Oxford, and not least in Oriel. The Act of Catholic Emancipation (1829), supported by some, evoked fury in others, further fuelled by subsequent legislation to reform the Church of Ireland. The Irish Temporalities Act (1833), considered by many an act of national apostasy, provoked the agitation later termed the Oxford Movement. The constitutional reforms of these years stirred up a prolonged period of debate, never less than acrimonious and often bitter, about reform of the university and its colleges.

Eveleigh, and the generation of heads of houses to which he belonged, saw as one of their most urgent tasks the maintenance and survival of the established order: the interdependence of Church and state, of religion and civil government, which they held to be the very sinews of society.[4] They viewed 'enthusiasm', which fostered schism and sectarianism and possibly sedition, as a major threat to which, they believed, the young men in their care were more than ever exposed. An equally potent threat took the form of the philosophical sceptics' challenge to revealed religion, a challenge that had found mordant expression in Edward Gibbon's *Decline and Fall of the Roman Empire* (1776–8), with a notoriously scathing depiction of Christianity in chapters 15 and 16. It was expressed even more provocatively in the philosophical writings of the Scottish philosopher David Hume. Apprehension about where such thinking would lead was soon confirmed by the violence and bloodshed of revolutionary France, which Edmund Burke had predicted in his *Reflections on the Revolution in France* (1790), attributing it in particular to the abandonment of religion inspired by the pervasive anti-Christian influence of the French *philosophes*. Even Gibbon was

---

Hawkins, already a fellow of Oriel, on a coach from London to Oxford in 1815; Hawkins had just returned from Paris in flight from Napoleon, and Wilberforce was on his way to interview a tutor at Nuneham Courtenay, Edward Garrard Marsh, for his sons Robert and Samuel. A friendship between Wilberforce and Hawkins developed from this chance meeting which eventually determined Wilberforce's choice of Oriel for his sons: Robert Wilberforce matriculated in 1820, Samuel in 1823, and Henry in 1826. See J. W. Burgon, *Lives of Twelve Good Men* (London, 1888), i. 390–1.

[4] For this see, for example, E. R. Norman, *Church and Society in England 1770–1970: A Historical Study* (Oxford, 1976), ch. 1, 'Christian Social Teaching at the End of the Eighteenth Century'; and J. C. D. Clark, *English Society 1688–1832: Ideology, Social Structure and Political Practice during the Ancien Régime* (Cambridge, 1985), esp. 'Introduction: The Nature of the Old Order'.

ultimately persuaded by Burke's argument that the unrelenting attack of the French intellectual elite upon religion and the national Church led directly to revolution.[5]

The university's newly instituted Bampton Lectures, the first series of which was delivered in 1780, and which were especially intended for undergraduates, became an occasion for defending established religion both against the assault of Hume and against the sceptics and the influence of 'enthusiasm' with its attendant perils.[6] This general theme is summed up in an opening statement of one of the earliest of the Bampton lecturers, George Croft, formerly fellow of University College, in the first of his sermons, 'The Use and Abuse of Reason' (1786): 'The pride of Philosophy has too highly exalted reason, the mock humility of Enthusiasm has debased it.' He devoted his sermons to 'a Vindication of the Church of England against the objections of the principal Sects'.[7] Earlier, in the first series of the sermons, James Bandinel, fellow of Jesus College and public orator of the university, had lectured on the Christian revelation as alone the justified claimant to the title of divine truth, and lamented schism and heresy that divides, and had appealed for unity within the Church of England.[8] Joseph White, who was among the most learned orientalists of his time, offered in 1784 a comparison of Islam and Christianity, and took the opportunity to respond to Gibbon's unflattering comparison of Christianity with some of the virtues of Islam:

We are by no means insensible to the merits of our historian; but at the same time we know and lament his eagerness to throw a veil over the deformities of the Heathen theology, to decorate with all the splendour of panegyric the tolerant spirit of its votaries, to degrade by disingenuous insinuation, or by sarcastic satire, the importance of revelation, to exhibit in the most offensive features of distortion the weakness and the follies of its friends, and to varnish over the cruelties, and exalt the wisdom of its merciless and unrelenting enemies.[9]

---

[5] See Edward Gibbon, *Memoirs of my Life and Writings*, first published 1796, reference here to the bicentenary edition by A. O. J. Cockshut and Stephen Constantine (Keele, 1994), 214: 'I beg leave to subscribe my assent to Mr Burke's creed on the revolution in France. I admire his eloquence, I approve his politics, I adore his chivalry, and I can almost excuse his reverence for church establishments. I have sometimes thought of writing a dialogue of the dead, in which Lucian, Erasmus, and Voltaire should mutually acknowledge the danger of exposing an old superstition to the contempt of the blind and fanatic multitude.' See D. Womersley, 'Gibbon, Edward (1737–1794)', ODNB.

[6] The sermons were endowed by the will of John Bampton (1689–1751), canon of Salisbury, 'to confirm and establish the Christian Faith and to confute all schismatics and heretics', and they were to be delivered annually.

[7] *Eight Sermons Preached before the University of Oxford* (Oxford, 1786), 4, 3.

[8] *Eight Sermons Preached before the University of Oxford* (Oxford, 1780).

[9] *A Comparison of Mahometism and Christianity in their History, their Evidence, and their Effects, in Nine Sermons* (Oxford, 1784), 145. Joseph White (1746–1814) was Laudian Professor of Arabic (1774–88), Regius Professor of Hebrew (1804–14). See David Paterson, 'Hebrew Studies', HUO v. 535–50.

Eveleigh's own Bampton Lectures, delivered in 1792, were a comprehensive exposition of the history and substance of Christian revelation, and a defence of its credibility in the face of 'an adventurous and sceptical philosophy'.[10] Among Bampton preachers of the time, none was more persistent or passionate than Eveleigh in his comments on Hume, whom he regarded, together with Gibbon, as among the most malign assailants of Christian revelation.

We are not well informed of Eveleigh's life; one writer has said that we know no more about Eveleigh than we do of Methuselah.[11] He left no memoirs or diary, and surviving correspondence is less than sparse. He was born on 22 February 1748 at Winkleigh, Devon, the eldest of the three sons of the rector, John Eveleigh (1716?–1770), and his wife Martha. He matriculated from Wadham College in May 1766, was Goodrich and Pigott exhibitioner (1766), scholar (September 1767), and again Goodrich exhibitioner (1767 and 1769), and Hody exhibitioner (1767 to 1770). He graduated BA (January 1770) and was elected fellow of Oriel in March; he proceeded MA in November 1772, BD in November 1782, and DD in May 1783. We know nothing of him during his years as a fellow other than that he was dean of the college in 1775, and vicar of St Mary the Virgin (the university church and an Oriel living) from 1778 until elected provost in succession to John Clark (5 December 1781). As provost of Oriel he was *ex officio* canon of Rochester. No longer subject to the statute binding fellows to celibacy, he married Dorothy, daughter of William Sanford (c.1711–1783), sometime fellow of All Souls. Eveleigh died suddenly after a short illness at Oxford on 10 December 1814, and was buried in St Mary the Virgin.

Much more can be gathered about him, however, from four significant undertakings, both in Oriel and in the university at large, in which as provost he was involved, and in some of which he was the prime mover. They ensured that his name was 'still remembered with veneration in Oxford' even in the closing years of the nineteenth century.[12] These were, in chronological order, the building of the college's new library following the bequest of Edward, Lord Leigh (1786); his Bampton Lectures (1792), which are a neglected source of information on his learning, and which shed light upon two further projects: the election of a Devon man, Edward Copleston (Corpus Christi), in 1795 to a Franks fellowship formally intended that year for Wiltshire candidates, affirming that academic and intellectual criteria were paramount in elections to fellowship; and Eveleigh's role as primary promoter of the

---

[10] *A View of our Religion... Eight Sermons Preached before the University of Oxford in the Year MDCCXCII* (Oxford, 1792), 2.

[11] See ODNB s.n. Eveleigh, and Anon, 'Oriel Worthies. II: John Eveleigh', OR (March 1920), 132–3.

[12] Burgon, *Lives*, i. 383.

examination statute of 1800, the foundation stone of modern Oxford, which established the right of any undergraduate who so desired to compete for honours in the BA examination.

The building of a new library in the second quadrangle, made necessary by Lord Leigh's bequest, was the first major task to land upon Eveleigh's desk, and his handling of it indicates foresight, native shrewdness, and efficiency. He responded creatively to a gift of singular value to the college, which however called for expenditure well beyond its normal resources, with an appeal for substantial funding to the college alumni.[13] Edward, 5th Baron Leigh of Stoneleigh Abbey near Kenilworth in Warwickshire, had been an Oriel undergraduate, entering as a nobleman commoner in 1761, and becoming master of arts, as custom required of noblemen, in February 1764. In 1767, at only 25, he was made high steward of the university, with the degree of DCL by diploma. In the same year he made his will, bequeathing his library to the college: a magnificent collection, assembled by Leigh himself, with numerous rarities, but mostly of the current and the previous century.[14] He then succumbed to severe mental illness: in 1774 he was declared 'a lunatic of unsound mind', under the guardianship of his sister Mary and his uncle William, Lord Craven. Only a deeply poignant and anguished prayer composed by his sister, probably in 1775, throws light on his later years: it reveals the alarming nature of his illness, with a propensity to violence to himself and others and the affliction of 'frightful imaginations'.[15] He died on 26 May 1786. Being unmarried and without direct heirs, his benefaction took effect; the will was proved on 22 July 1786.

The pace with which Eveleigh advanced the project indicates that the college had long been aware of the will and had given thought to the housing of the books; the existing library, in the north-east corner of the first quadrangle between the provost's lodgings and the hall, would have been far too small. Probably the high steward's early death had been anticipated. Early in March 1787, less than eight months after probate, an appeal to old members was launched; the fashionable architect James Wyatt, who had recently designed Christ Church's neighbouring Canterbury Gate, had already been commissioned as architect of the new building and had produced drawings. An estimate of the cost of the building had also been calculated, and the college had already transferred £200 from the library fund for the purpose, with a further £300 from the common room fund. The arrangement indicates

---

[13] See F. J. Varley, 'Lord Leigh's Benefactions', OR (1943), 215–16; Antony Dale, 'The Building of The Library', OR (1951), 13–18.

[14] For the assembly and character of the collection, with additional information about Leigh himself and his illness, see M. Purcell, '"A Lunatic of Unsound Mind": Edward, Lord Leigh (1742–86) and the Refounding of the Oriel College Library', *Bodleian Library Record*, 17 (2001), 246–60.

[15] Purcell, '"A Lunatic of Unsound Mind"', 249.

that the common room, which was adjacent to the existing library, would also be sited in the new building, making it the first purpose-built common room in Oxford.

It is a mark of Eveleigh's perspicacity in raising funds for such a project that, before launching the public appeal, he saw to it that the provost and fellows had themselves contributed donations: he himself gave £100 and later made a further gift of the same amount, and each fellow was asked to subscribe £20. The appeal to former fellows and to old members was made in a personal letter from Eveleigh dated 12 March 1787.[16] He wrote to each:

Sir,
I take the liberty of requesting your favourable attention for the following circumstances. The late Lord Leigh having bequeathed to Oriel College his very extensive and valuable collection of Books, we find ourselves under the necessity of building a new Room for their reception, our present Library being very inconveniently situated, and not large enough to admit the addition of his Lordship's benefaction. We intend to build the New Library in the College Garden; and as we wish to do it in a substantial and handsome manner, we cannot estimate the expense of it at less than £3,000. We have no fund for the purpose, and we are obliged to depend for the Execution of our design upon private Contribution. Such a Contribution the present Members of the Foundation have begun among themselves, and we have reason to think it will amount to nearly £1000.

Having oftentimes experienced distinguished marks of regard from the Gentlemen who formerly honored us with their Residence among us, we are encouraged to ask for their generous assistance on the present Occasion.
  I am Sir, your most obedient Servant
    John Eveleigh

Henry, 5th duke of Beaufort, who had matriculated at Oriel in 1760, proffered a generous hand in the fund-raising, writing to the provost:[17]

Sir
The Gentlemen whose Names are on the enclosed Card and myself thinking that a public Meeting may greatly promote the Design of Oriel College in Building a new Library we have advertised one in the London Papers. If you and any of the present Fellows will favour us with your Company it may be very conducive to the Purpose of the Meeting particularly if you can explain to us the Plan and the probable expense of it.
  I am Sir
    Yr. most obt. Humble Servant
      BEAUFORT
Grosvenor Square
May 10.87.
  I have by this Post sent to Mr Jackson to insert the enclosed in his Journal next Saturday.

---

[16] OCA FB 3 E1/2.   [17] OCA FB 3 E1/3.

The card referred to, which served as the advertisement sent to Mr Jackson, and which would also have been sent by Beaufort to Orielenses, friends, and colleagues, stated[18]

Oriel College OXFORD
The Duke of Beaufort, Earl Grosvenor, Viscount Dudley And Ward, Sir Watkin Williams Wynne, and many other Noblemen and Gentlemen who have been, or are now, Members of this College, intend to dine together, at the *St. Alban's Tavern* on *Thursday*, 24th May, when a Proposal will be made for a Contribution towards building a new Library in the said College.

The Company of all such as are well-wishers to this Proposal, is earnestly requested, and they are hereby desired to send their Names to the Bar of *St. Alban's Tavern* by *Tuesday*, 22nd Day of May.

Dinner will be on the Table at Half past 4 o'clock.

We have no information about the meeting and who attended it. But its remarkable success is reflected in a list containing the name of Beaufort and known friends of his, with their generous gifts.[19] Eveleigh kept a record of the donations.[20] It was audited and signed on 21 April 1797 by Daniel Veysie (dean), George Cooke (senior treasurer), and John Woolcombe (junior treasurer), and the total was confirmed as £3,313 15s., including the donations from the provost and fellows, the subscriptions from the library and common room funds, as well as from former fellows, and old members. Two odd sums of money from 'others' (£86 1s. 11d. and 7s. 6d.) are mentioned in this same audit, as well as sums of £524 and of £50, which had evidently been received as contributions due to the new Library from the annual revenue accruing to the junior treasurer's fund.[21] According to this audit, the total amount available from donations, from the contributions from the library and common room funds, and from the junior treasurer's annual revenues, was £3,974 4s. 5d. The audit also records the cost of the library to have been £5,961 12s. 10¾d.

In 1789 the college already knew that the initial estimate which Eveleigh had mentioned in his appeal to old members was well short of what was required, and to this end in October it borrowed £1,000 from the college's caution bag, this sum to be repaid over a number of years from the junior treasurer's book.[22] At the Michaelmas Audit of 1790 it was agreed that a further sum of £1,000 should be borrowed by the sale of stock, this sum also to be repaid with interest over a number of years.[23] Additional costs, one for

---

[18] OCA FB E1/1. [19] See OCA FB 3 E1/4: Accounts and subscribers.
[20] OCA FB 3 E1/6: State of J. Eveleigh's Library Account.
[21] The note (OCA FB 3 E1/6) states simply 'from [James] Landon', who had been junior treasurer in 1789, and 'from [George] Richards', who had been junior treasurer in 1792.
[22] OCA TF 1 A10/3: Provost's bag book and TF 1 A10/4: College bag book.
[23] OCA TF 1 A9/1: Audit memoranda.

£87 6s. 6d. in 1801 for slater's work carried out by Wyatt at the library and the college's stables,[24] and one in 1806 for decorating the senior common room,[25] were presumably paid out of current funds. It took longer to make ready the library itself, and the common rooms, than perhaps had been anticipated. It was not until 1795 that the common rooms were furnished and some remaining 'work done in the same'; the installation in the larger room of the chimneypiece, designed by Richard Westmacott I (bap. 1746–d. 1808), followed in 1796.[26] The library was not ready to receive the books, both the Leigh collection and those in the old library, until 1795, when a sum of £1 16s. 6d. was paid for their removal there.

In 1806, in a letter to James Henry Leigh of Adlestrop, father of the 1st Lord Leigh of the second creation, who had just inherited the estate from Mary Leigh and had contested Edward Leigh's will,[27] Joseph Hill, the latter's receiver, who had helped him to assemble the collection of books, wrote that he had always regretted the legacy to Oriel 'so expensive to that Society, and probably of so little use to them'.[28] There is no evidence of any such regret on the part of the provost and fellows; on receiving the books and the various items that came with them, Eveleigh wrote with manifest delight to Mary Leigh that 'the Collection is large and valuable beyond the high Opinion which we had formed of it'.[29] That costs mounted beyond the early estimates induced no loss of nerve, and no long-term financial burden resulted from the project. There is a careful annual record of the repayment of the two sums of £1,000 borrowed respectively from the caution bag and the college bag, the repayment to the latter being complete in 1805, and to the former in 1808. This was sooner than anticipated, the final and still substantial sums being paid off with something of a flourish: £250 to the college bag, and £150 in 1807 and again in 1808 to the caution bag. The financial soundness of the college is underlined by the prompt undertaking of the renovation and refurbishment, for the purposes of accommodation, of the premises previously occupied by the library and the common room. The work began in 1796, when £400 was borrowed from the caution bag; repayment was made in three tranches, in 1797, 1800, and 1802.

The expenditure upon the library throws light on an incident of 1791 which brought some opprobrium upon the college. In that year a first

---

[24] OCA FB 3 E1/7.   [25] OCA FB 3 F1/1.
[26] It was not until 1800 that a carpet, probably for the larger of the two rooms, was purchased. The purchase of another for the smaller room had to wait a further seven years and cost more. For details of the furnishing of the common room and its cost, see G. N. Clark, 'Antiquities of the Oriel Common Room', OR (1925), 304–8.
[27] As Purcell points out ('"A Lunatic of Unsound Mind"', 246), Lord Leigh's will was complex, giving rise to legal wrangling well into the nineteenth century.
[28] See Purcell, '"A Lunatic of Unsound Mind"', 256.
[29] Cited in Purcell, '"A Lunatic of Unsound Mind"', 256.

wave of refugee Roman Catholic clergy fled to England from mounting violence in revolutionary France. The university spontaneously launched an appeal to help them, convocation itself making a donation, followed by contributions from individual colleges, including heads of houses and members. The record of donations has the note 'Oriel makes a shabby figure'.[30] Since the college's accounts make no mention of a response to the appeal, we must assume that Oriel made no donation. Perhaps the reason for the college's absence from the list of contributors was financial caution, arising from the ongoing costs of the new library: a prudent anticipation, as necessary then as today, that costs would outrun estimates, with an eye also on further outgoings to prepare the former premises of the library and common room for new use. There would certainly have been no antipathy, and no theological or ideological scruples to the appeal, on the part of Eveleigh and the fellows; and at the Easter Audit of 1796 it was agreed to donate 18 guineas 'towards the relief of the distressed French Emigrants'.[31] Eveleigh and his colleagues may well have made additional private contributions; but of this there is no record.

Joseph Hill's comment that Lord Leigh's library would be of little use to the college was ill informed and wide of the mark; it substantially enlarged and modernized Oriel's holdings, to the great benefit of the fellows, who in Oriel as elsewhere were the principal users of the library. Perhaps Hill thought Oxford dons read only works on theology and classical antiquity; the Leigh collection, besides holdings in these subjects, contained a wide range of secular and modern literature. The members of the Oriel common room had more eclectic reading interests than Hill imagined, however, as their borrowing from the library demonstrates. Besides theology, the interests of the fellowship included law, medicine, history, literature, and notably political economy, which was now emerging as a separate subject of enquiry. Henry Beeke, elected in 1776 from Corpus Christi, fellow until 1789, Regius Professor of Modern History (1801–13), and dean of Bristol (1813–37), is said to have been the first to teach political economy at Oxford, lecturing in Oriel hall. He contributed significantly to the debate on income tax (recently instituted by William Pitt), notably in *Observations on the produce of the income tax, and on its proportion to the whole income of Great Britain.*[32] He

---

[30] L. G. Mitchell, 'Politics and Revolution 1772–1800', HUO v. 188–9.

[31] OCA TF 1 A9/1, 21; and see Eveleigh's remarks on 'our Christian brethren' in his Bampton Lectures *Eight Sermons Preached before the University of Oxford in the Year MDCCXCII* (Oxford, 1792), 176–7.

[32] Henry Beeke, *Observations* (London, 1799, reprinted and expanded 1800). On the contribution of fellows of Oriel, including Beeke, Copleston, Davison, and Whately, to the emerging study of political economy, see Boyd Hilton, *The Age of Atonement: The Influence of Evangelicalism on Social and Economic Thought, 1795–1865* (Oxford, 1988); A. M. C. Waterman, *Revolution, Economics and Religion: Christian Political Economy, 1798–1833* (Cambridge, 1991).

regularly advised Nicholas Vansittart, Chancellor of the Exchequer (1812–23).[33] He was known also for his interest in botanical studies and geology.[34] George Richards, elected from Trinity in 1790, was Bampton lecturer in 1800 (*The Divine Origin of Prophecy*) but gained a wider reputation as a poet and writer on poetry. A friend of Charles Lamb, he ended his career as rector of the fashionable parish of St Martin-in-the-Fields (1825–37).[35] John Mayo, elected from Brasenose 1784, was Harveian Orator in 1795 and Physician-in-ordinary to Caroline, princess of Wales. Christopher (later Sir Christopher) Pegge, elected from Christ Church 1788, was later to become Lee's reader in anatomy and subsequently Regius Professor of Medicine (1801–22). John Warren, elected from St John's 1791, was later a barrister and charity commissioner; in 1790 he was awarded the English Essay Prize for his *General Knowledge; its real nature and the advantages to be derived from it*.[36]

No one would have more appreciated Leigh's wide-ranging collection than Eveleigh himself, whose breadth of learning and scholarship, virtually neglected in later appraisals, was much admired by his contemporaries; it shaped the initiatives in college and university in which he took a lead. A few months after his death, the proctor's valedictory address of 1815 contained a tribute to him, written at the request of the proctor by the pre-eminently learned Dr Martin Routh, president of Magdalen:

So within the space of a few months a redoubtable and holy man has been taken from our midst, the Provost of Oriel, who combining learning both sacred and secular with Hebrew scholarship, not only expounded elegantly Holy Scripture but sturdily defended orthodox teaching.[37]

Eveleigh's only substantial publication was his series of Bampton Lectures, delivered and published in 1792.[38] Unusually, Eveleigh like Joseph White before him gave his eight sermons a title and, uniquely, dedicated them in an affectionate inscription to the undergraduates of the university, describing himself as 'their faithful friend and servant'. Beside their commitment to the well-being of undergraduates, the lectures suggest that Eveleigh's mind, in the face of the mounting scepticism which many believed had brought about

---

[33] According to Rannie, *Oriel*, 162, 'tradition credited Beeke with the suggestion' of this tax. On Beeke's contribution see Hilton, *The Age of Atonement*, 41–2; Waterman, *Revolution, Economics and Religion*, 184, 191, 204, 275.

[34] See N. A. Rupke, 'Oxford's Scientific Awakening and the Role of Geology', HUO vi. 553.

[35] See ODNB s.n. George Richards; *The Divine Origin of Prophecy* (Oxford, 1800).

[36] See ODNB on Mayo and Pegge; on Warren see *Provosts and Fellows*, 152.

[37] Rannie, *Oriel College*, 179.

[38] They were published under the title *A View of our Religion, with regard to its Substance, with regard to its History, with regard to the Arguments by which it is Confirmed, and with regard to the Objections by which it is Opposed*. A second edition of 1794 had four additional sermons; and the third of 1814 appeared in two volumes. He had earlier published *The Doctrine of the Holy Trinity* (1791) and a few separate sermons.

the chaos and violence of revolutionary France, was already turning to means of enhancing their learning and scholarship, especially among the ordinands, to combat more effectively the intellectual challenges of the time. As his later initiatives imply, both the colleges and the university should be redeployed to equip them for the task.

The general title of the lectures already indicates their scope. They were published as a book of eight chapters, with numerous footnotes, and offered a compendious overview of the origins and history of Christianity. Some chapters focused on the 'evidences' of Christian revelation, against the non-revelatory religion of deism widely influential in the eighteenth century; against the atheism found in more recent radical writings; and against philosophical scepticism, especially in the works of Hume, with many comments on Gibbon's 'sarcasms', as Eveleigh described them. It is likely that he always intended the published work to be a *vade mecum* for Oxford men intending ordination, whose task would be to teach; this is supported by the appearance of a second edition in 1794 and a third in 1814, and by the unusual addition of extensive footnotes, providing compendious information which could not be transmitted in the original sermons, to the published text.[39] The volume displays Eveleigh's wide learning in theology and secular disciplines, which Routh would later extol. He was at home both in biblical scholarship and in the literature of classical antiquity, and was a knowledgeable Hebrew scholar.[40] He had an imposing command of the writings of the church fathers, and he provided a sure-footed brief history of Christendom, including the schism between East and West; on the Reformation he cites the works of the major continental reformers, frequently referring to Erasmus, whom he admiringly portrays as its intellectual forebear. After a tour of the erratic course of the English Reformation through the reigns of Henry VIII, Edward VI, Mary, and Elizabeth I, he salutes Hooker's formulation of the Church of England's teaching.

His secular references are of interest. Gibbon and Hume, his special *bêtes noires*, are cited frequently. Rabelais and Montaigne make an appearance, as do Voltaire and Rousseau (*Emile, or On Education*), Jonathan Swift's *Miscellanies*, Samuel Johnson's *Dictionary of the English Language*, and Joseph Addison's *Spectator*. There are references to Thomas Warton's *History of English Poetry*, the Scottish historian William Robertson's *History of America*, Pierre Marie François de Pagès's *Travels round the World*; Constantin

---

[39] Joseph White appended seventy-five pages of 'Notes and Authorities', much of which, however, would have been well above the heads of undergraduates, whilst its extensive Arabic quotations were intended only for a small number of experts in Islamic literature. The most expansive notes ('end notes') are those provided by Edward Nares in 1805.

[40] He was fully conversant with the work on the Hebrew Bible and Hebrew poetry of Benjamin Kennicott (1718–83) and Robert Lowth (1710–87), two of the most celebrated Hebraists of the century. He ventured a new interpretation of Psalm 87, which is one of the most problematic in the Psalter. See his *A Sermon preached before the University of Oxford, November 24, 1805, in which is proposed a new interpretation of the lxxxviith Psalm* (Oxford, 1806).

François de Chassebœuf, comte de Volney's *Travels through Syria and Egypt*; Georges Louis Le Clerc, comte de Buffon's multi-volume *Natural History*; Henry Home, Lord Kames's *Essays on the Principles of Morality and Natural Religion*; Sir William Hamilton's *Observations on the Volcanoes of the two Sicilies*; James Cook and James King's *Captain Cook's Third and Last voyage to the Pacific Ocean*; Samuel Stanhope Smith's *Essay on the Causes of Variety of Complexion and Figure in the Human Species*; and Chambers's *Cyclopaedia, or An Universal Dictionary of Arts and Sciences*.[41] All this indicates wide reading and, more specifically, an assiduous endeavour on Eveleigh's part in seeking authority for the arguments he makes, whether against his adversaries or in support of inherited biblical and theological teaching.

Edward Gibbon remarked of Oxford that its government was 'in the hands of clergy, an order whose manners are remote from the present world, and whose eyes are dazzled by the light of philosophy'.[42] Some support for this might be derived from a recent survey which finds that none of Hume's works made its way into Oxford's libraries, including Oriel's, until the nineteenth century.[43] Writers such as Eveleigh, however, among other sources, show that Hume's works were soon well known in the common rooms of Oxford. Were their eyes, then, 'dazzled' by his philosophy?

It is the case that Eveleigh was not versed in technical philosophy, and one looks in vain among publishing Oxford academics of the time for anything approaching philosophical thinking and analysis. There was no parallel, for example, to the strong engagement in philosophical discourse to be found in the Scottish universities and led by figures such as Thomas Reid and Dugald Stewart, leading lights of the Scottish Enlightenment and widely respected on the Continent. There was no philosophical void, however, such as Gibbon's

---

[41] Rousseau, English translation (London, 1767), from *Émile, ou de l'éducation* (Amsterdam, 1762); Thomas Warton, *History of English Poetry*, 3 vols. (London, 1774–81); William Robertson, *History of America* (London, 1777); Pierre-Marie François de Pagès, English translation (London, 1791–2) from *Voyage autour du monde* (Paris, 1782); Constantin François de Chassebœuf, English translation (Dublin, 1788), from *Voyage en Syrie et en Égypt* (Paris, 1787); Georges Louis le Clerc, comte de Buffon, English translation (London, 1791) from *Histoire naturelle*, 15 vols. (Paris, 1749–67); Henry Home, Lord Kames, *Essays on the Principles of Morality* (Edinburgh, 1751); Sir William Hamilton, *Campi Phlegraei: Observations on Volcanoes* (Naples, 1776–9); Cook and King, *Captain Cook's Third and Last Voyage to the Pacific* (London, 1784); Smith, *Essay on the Causes of Variety of Complexion* (Philadelphia, 1787); E. Chambers, *Cyclopaedia* (London, 1728).

[42] Edward Gibbon, *Memoirs*, 79–80. That he was here referring to the condition of Oxford at the time of writing the *Memoirs* is clear from the context: he commented on both Oxford and Cambridge, their monopoly of public instruction, which induces a spirit that is 'narrow, lazy, and oppressive', the costliness of what they offer, and their 'slow and sullen reluctance' to introduce reforms. He added that 'so deeply are they rooted in law and prejudice, that even the omnipotence of parliament would shrink from an inquiry into the state and abuses of the two universities' (*Memoirs*, 80).

[43] See J. Yolton, 'Schoolmen, Logic and Philosophy', in Sutherland and Mitchell, HUO v. 591; and in the same volume I. G. Philip, 'Libraries and the University Press', 740 n. 2.

remark implies. Against scepticism, the leading apologetic precept in Eveleigh's defence of Christian revelation was his conviction of its reasonableness, of the *rational probability* of its claim to truth; and there is no doubting the source of such an approach, the work of an earlier Orielensis: Butler's *Analogy of Religion*, 'a work', Eveleigh wrote, 'which can never be recommended with too much earnestness to the Christian philosopher'. His statement that 'it is by no means the design of Providence...to force us into action by any more persuasive motives, than *rational probabilities*'[44] reflects Butler's principle, already stated in the introduction to *The Analogy*, that 'for us probability is the very guide to life'; that is, as in everyday life we make decisions on the basis of evidence yielded by a range of experiences and observations that support and confirm each other and warrant a desired action, so also what is required for reasonable belief in religion is not certainty but *probability*.[45]

There was more to Eveleigh's attack on scepticism, however, than an engagement in theological and philosophical debate and controversy. For him much more was at stake, and a note on the historical context of his Bampton Lectures is necessary, if we are to grasp this. Butler wrote the *Analogy* against deism, which emerged in the seventeenth century and gained influential support during the early decades of the eighteenth. It was not a 'school' or unified movement, but the different expressions of it shared the conviction that what can be known of God can be known through reason alone ('natural theology'), and that the claims made in the name of revealed religion that went beyond what the human mind could naturally discern of the Creator are irrational and dispensable. Significantly, such heterodoxy was believed to carry radical political implications, for a rejection of revelation 'was a way of asserting that human reason could of itself attain access to all necessary religious truth; by inference, man would be self-sufficient, too, in the lesser sphere of politics. The sanction of custom, and, more important, divine sanctions via revelation for any particular regime were all called in doubt. Deism was the most generalised intellectual solvent of its time.'[46] That is, 'infidelity' was only an easy step away from disloyalty and from an agenda for dismantling or overthrowing the established order of society. Though deism had gone into eclipse before the middle of the century—the *Analogy* was among its most effective critiques—it re-emerged at the hands of political radicals, most effectively so in the writings of Thomas Paine, and continued during the revolutionary 1790s and their aftermath of war.[47] In this atmosphere, Eveleigh and the other Bampton lecturers of the age saw it

---

[44] Eveleigh, *A View of our Religion*, 246, 245 (emphasis added).
[45] Joseph Butler, *The Analogy of Religion, Natural and Revealed, to the Constitution and Course of Nature* (London, 1736).
[46] See Clark, *English Society 1688–1832*, 326.
[47] For this see Clark, *English Society*, esp. ch. 4 'The Religious Origins of Disaffection, 1688–1800'; on Paine, 385–96.

as a solemn duty to defend what they believed to be the truths of revelation against all 'infidel' claims, especially those advanced by Hume, and so to uphold the bond between Church and state, which they held to be the divinely willed ground of civic society.

The influence of Butler's *Analogy* can be detected, whether in direct citations or references or underlying the argument, in several of the Bampton lecture series during these years, and it is to this time that we can trace the emergence of the standing attained by the *Analogy* at Oxford and retained well into the nineteenth century.[48] It was the favoured philosophical text of the Oriel Noetics and a mainstay of their apologetics, and it was one of their number, Renn Dickson Hampden, who in his influential work *An Essay on the Philosophical Evidence of Christianity* (1827) both modelled his thought upon Butler's analogical method and at the same time elucidated the more obscure parts of the *Analogy*. It was also Hampden, with the support of Richard Whately, who in 1832 secured a place for the *Analogy* as a set book in 'Greats' alongside Aristotle's *Ethics*.[49] Whately's earlier ironic *Historic Doubts relative to Napoleon Buonaparte* (1819), directed against Hume's *Essay on Miracles*, was itself based on a form of Butler's argument concerning miracles.[50]

An additional philosophical treatise, however, lay behind Eveleigh's dismissive treatment of Hume, whose thinking he dubbed 'scepticism' and 'metaphysical sophistry', the questioning behind it 'perverse', the resulting philosophy 'delusive', which his listeners and readers were invited to reject as lacking all credibility. Eveleigh considered Hume's central propositions as decisively refuted at length by a philosophical work which, though now largely forgotten, was at that time widely valued, and whose author, described by Eveleigh as 'an admired writer', Oxford had signally honoured.[51] Eveleigh and his contemporaries at the university were conversant with the critique of

---

[48] In Hoppner's portrait of Eveleigh in the Common Room, Eveleigh's right hand rests firmly upon Butler's *Analogy*, which stands upright upon a table signalling its pillar-like significance for Eveleigh, with the title on the spine prominently displayed in commendation to the viewer. On the reception of Butler in both Oxford and Cambridge in the nineteenth century, see Hilton, *The Age of Atonement*, 170–83.

[49] R. D. Hampden, *An essay on the Philosophical Evidence of Christianity* (London, 1827). The *Analogy* held sway until mid-century—its critics and detractors, who included Matthew Arnold, Pattison, and Benjamin Jowett, dubbed it 'the Oxford Koran'—when Kant and Hegel had become much more a focus of attention, and by the mid-1850s it was no longer on the list of required books for Schools. For the eclipse of Butler, see Hilton, *The Age of Atonement*, 337–9.

[50] R. Whately, *Historic Doubts relative to Napoleon Buonaparte* (London, 1819). Employing Hume's distinction in his *Essay on Miracles* between the worth of experience as against testimony, Whately argued that, since we can now have no direct *experience* of Buonaparte, much doubt can be raised as to whether a historical figure of that name could in reality ever have existed, such are the remarkable achievements that *testimony* attributes to him. Butler, in discussing the credibility of miracles, had similarly argued that there was a presumption against the historicity of Caesar. See Richard Brent, *Liberal Anglican Politics: Whiggery, Religion, and Reform (1830–1841)* (Oxford, 1987), 153–4.

[51] Eveleigh, *A View of our Religion*, 235.

Hume's leading philosophical tenets by his fellow Scottish philosophers, but most notably by James Beattie (1735–1803), professor of moral philosophy and logic at Marischal College, Aberdeen, in his widely fêted *Essay on the Nature and Immutability of Truth, in Opposition to Scepticism and Sophistry* (1770).[52] The *Essay* is a long engagement with the philosophy of Descartes, Malebranche, Locke, Berkeley, and especially Hume, the main subject of Beattie's critique, with a discussion of Hume's questioning of the common belief in the relationship between cause and effect, a critique of the philosophical theme of the non-existence of matter, and considerations of liberty and necessity, and of the belief that human actions are determined by free will and choice and not by necessity, that morality depends upon our exercise of free will, and that virtue arises from this—all topics alluded to by Eveleigh.

Beattie's *Essay* was a popular presentation of the 'common sense' philosophy of his more distinguished colleague, Thomas Reid (1710–96), professor (regent) at King's College Aberdeen and co-member of the Aberdeen Philosophical Society, whose best-known work, *Inquiry into the Human Mind, on the Principles of Common Sense*, was generally deemed an astute critique of Hume's philosophy.[53] Reid was especially concerned to refute Hume's sceptical proposals, which he viewed as subversive of any grounds for belief in the existence of the external world, the self, God, and morality. His work however is nowhere mentioned in Eveleigh's Bampton Lectures. Beattie's *Essay* was much more widely read: it went through fourteen further editions before 1800, was translated into French, Dutch, and German, and earned him celebrity status in London intellectual circles. Its reviews, one of them probably by Burke, were wholly favourable; Dr Johnson considered it had confuted Hume.[54] It also gained Beattie an annual pension of £200 from a grateful George III. Such was the impact of the *Essay* at Oxford that in 1773 the university conferred upon him an honorary DCL.[55]

---

[52] James Beattie, *Essay on the Nature and Immutability of Truth* (Edinburgh, 1770). On Beattie see Sir William Forbes, *An Account of the Life and Writings of James Beattie*, republished from the 1806 edition with a new introduction by Roger J. Robinson (London, 1996). Robinson's introduction offers a modern critique of Beattie's work and contribution. Eveleigh also refers to Beattie's *Evidences of the Christian Religion; briefly and plainly stated* (Edinburgh, 1786), which was written for a more popular readership.

[53] Thomas Reid, *Inquiry into the Human Mind* (Edinburgh, 1764). For the meaning of 'common sense' in this context, see Paul Wood's article on Thomas Reid ODNB. Cf. Robinson's introduction to Forbes, *James Beattie*, xii–xix.

[54] For the reception of the *Essay*, see Robinson's introduction to Forbes, *James Beattie*, xxviii–xxxiv, and xxxv for Johnson's opinion: 'Boswell: Then Hume is not the worse for Beattie's attack? Johnson: He is, because Beattie has confuted him.'

[55] The episode, like the *Essay*, has been long forgotten among historians of the university, but since it underlines the esteem in which Beattie was held among Oxford academics, it is worth recounting here. The formal proposer that a DCL by diploma be conferred upon Beattie was made by William Markham, then bishop of Chester and dean of Christ Church. The conferment of the degree was arranged for the day of the installation of Lord North as chancellor of the university on 9 July 1773. Farcically, at an advanced stage in the arrangements, someone pointed

All of this suggests that, far from being 'dazzled by the light of philosophy', Eveleigh and his Oxford contemporaries, who defended revelation in Butler's terms and drew upon Beattie's attack on Hume,[56] were at home with Enlightenment ideas. Eveleigh was indeed familiar with the new, secular learning of his time, and with works directly inspired by it; and he applauded the discoveries of its seventeenth-century begetters, Newton and Boyle, who 'enlighten the present age'.[57] As already noted, he had read the works of the comte de Buffon, who believed that nature had a history much older than Genesis suggested, and who speculated that species could change over time; and of Samuel Stanhope Smith, who argued for the monogenesis of the human species against a separate origin of its different races; and of Sir William Hamilton, whose study of volcanoes convinced him of a geological age of the earth inconsistent with the Bible. Among other authors cited, William Robertson belongs with Hume and Gibbon as one of the three British Enlightenment historians; Lord Kames, a supporter of Hume—and an admirer of Butler— wrote a history of the stages of human development very different from the Bible's, and argued in his *Essays* that morality was determined by the human constitution and not by any faculty of free choice. *Chambers' Cyclopaedia*, first published in 1728, was an initiative of the Scottish Enlightenment and in turn directly inspired the *philosophes* Diderot and d'Alembert to produce the *Encyclopédie*. Aware from such literature of the spirit of enquiry of the age,

out that since a degree by diploma conferred upon the honorand all the rights and privileges of the university, it could not be conferred upon Beattie, who as a Presbyterian could not be a member of the university! It was hurriedly agreed, however, to confer the degree *honoris causa* upon Beattie, who had been alerted to the difficulty. Beattie was now re-summoned by Markham, who informed him 'that though the success of a diploma-degree in laws seemed doubtful, (notwithstanding that all the heads of houses in the university were as favourable as could be wished) an honorary-degree did not seem liable to any hazard', and that he should travel without delay to Oxford. There were fifteen honorands on this occasion, among them Sir Joshua Reynolds. Beattie's biographer, writing from an eye-witness account, narrates that only Reynolds and Beattie were the subjects of *encomia* (by Robert Vansittart, Regius Professor of Civil Law, who was on that occasion public orator), and that the applause for Beattie was 'remarkably loud'. Sir Joshua Reynolds subsequently painted an allegorical portrait of Beattie under the title *The Triumph of Truth with the Portrait of a Gentleman*. See Forbes, *James Beattie*, 264–7.

[56] Beattie's deep animosity towards Hume—among other comments, he described *The Treatise on Human Nature* as a 'vile effusion'—brought down severe criticism upon him from some of his Scottish colleagues, especially from his more distinguished contemporary Dugald Stewart. See Robinson's introduction to Forbes, *James Beattie*, xxxiv. Hume, who on principle never responded publicly to the reception of his writings, is said to have commented on Beattie's *Essay* 'Truth! There is no truth in it; it is a horrible large lie in octavo'. See E. Campbell Mossner, *The Life of David Hume* (Oxford, 1954), 581.

[57] *A View of our Religion*, 268. Similarly, Edward Nares wrote of the age as claiming 'to be regarded as an enlightened age', *A View of the Evidences of Christianity at the Close of the pretended Age of Reason* (Oxford, 1805), 513. The use of the description 'enlightened' by Eveleigh and Nares should not be taken, however, to indicate that they were aware of a single 'Enlightenment', as represented by the German word *Aufklärung*, French *Lumières*, Italian *Illuminismo*. The English term 'the Enlightenment' was evidently not coined until the mid-nineteenth century. See Clark's note, *English Society*, 9–10.

Eveleigh and his colleagues were not, however, prepared to affirm 'reason' as being alone the guide to truth. Their *ne plus ultra* was revelation, and any aspects of the new thinking that were irreconcilable with revelation must be intrinsically erroneous. Though among the more learned of his Oxford peers, Eveleigh did not differ from them in this respect: revelation was an assured and immutable *credendum*, and they regarded as one of their most important tasks its defence against 'the pride of philosophy'. That entailed, just as urgently, the defence of the established order of society.

Their stance was hardened by the radical thinkers of the 1790s, among them Thomas Paine, Mary Wollstonecraft, and William Godwin. In one of the most erudite series of Bampton Lectures of the time, Edward Nares, while commending the new learning and discoveries that 'have distinguished the age we live in', the progress of which should be contemplated 'with admiration and delight', as also the 'spirit of research and enquiry' and the 'insatiable curiosity' that moved it, still insisted upon the sovereignty of revelation: 'In religion and morality there is no deficiency; no room for improvement, no want of the aid and support of human philosophy... Let us never then be induced to abandon this great light, to follow after the phantoms of a disputatious philosophy.'[58] Thus, though Hume's works and other contemporary philosophical writings were read at Oxford, philosophical thinking and analysis were not 'domesticated' there, as they were in the universities of Scotland. To respond to Hume's scepticism, Oxford divines summoned Beattie's *Essay* to their aid and returned to Butler's *Analogy*, now launched anew by Eveleigh and others as Oxford's own philosophical text. It became dominant from the 1820s. Mark Pattison recorded that it was not until the 1850s that Kant's philosophy penetrated Oxford, introduced by Henry Mansel (1820–71).[59] Later still, Benjamin Jowett lectured on Hegel.[60]

---

[58] Edward Nares, *A View of the Evidences of Christianity* (Oxford, 1805), 474–6. Nares was a fellow of Merton and later Regius Professor of Modern History (1813–35).

[59] Pattison, *Memoirs*, 166. There is an early allusion to Kant—the earliest reference I have come across in Oxford publications—by William Finch in his Bampton Lectures of 1797, *The Objections of Infidel Historians and Other Writers Against Christianity* (Oxford, 1797), 164, noting 'Professor Kant's German mode of natural religion recently introduced', but without citing any of Kant's works. The reference is so cursory that it seems unlikely that Finch had read any of Kant, but may have read an English report of it; for Kant's reception in Great Britain see R. Wellek, *Immanuel Kant in England 1793–1838* (Princeton, 1931), ch. 1. Taking a characteristic sideswipe at new trends in philosophical thinking and teaching in Oxford in the second half of the nineteenth century, including 'idealist' philosophy associated with T. H. Green, Charles Neate, then senior fellow of Oriel, wrote that students in Oxford had 'been led or driven away from the fair and fertile fields of ancient Literature to batten upon that most barren of all moors, stripped as it is of its Grecian verdure, the Republic of Plato, and the adjacent bottomless bogs of German Philosophy, on which no blade of wholesome grass ever grew'! (*The Universities Reform Bill* (Oxford, 1876), 7).

[60] On the continuing influence and relevance of Butler's thinking, notably his moral philosophy, in the latter half of the nineteenth century, see Jane Garnett, 'Bishop Butler and the *Zeitgeist*: Butler and the Development of Christian Moral Philosophy in Victorian Britain', in C. Cunliffe

Burgon records John Keble's memory of Eveleigh, in a letter of 1855: 'He was Provost when I was elected fellow [1811]. I had known him as long as I can remember anyone. He was, I verily believe, a man to bring down a blessing on any society of which he was a member.'[61] The blessing will have included the reforms which Eveleigh's cultivation of new academic standards initiated, and which gave rise to the high intellectual quality of the Oriel common room in the early nineteenth century. Its ethos was caught by the contemporary term *noetic*, a word of Greek derivation meaning 'intellectual', which was applied (by whom originally is unknown) to some fellows and members of the common room, known for their rigorous and audacious debate of issues of current concern.[62] Though they were most distinctive in Copleston's time, there is no doubt that their convergence in Oriel derived from Eveleigh's policy on elections to fellowships. The decisive move was the election of Edward Copleston to a fellowship in 1795. The fellowship was a Franks fellowship restricted to candidates from Wiltshire. When the candidates were examined, however, none of them was considered worthy of election. Edward Copleston of Corpus Christi, who had been awarded the Chancellor's Prize for Latin Verse in 1793 and had graduated BA in January 1795, was reputed as an intellectual high flyer and an eminently desirable appointment to the fellowship, to which he was invited to accept election although, as a Devon man, he had not been a candidate. Interviewed by the dean, Daniel Veysie, Copleston at first declined, since one of the Wiltshire candidates was a friend of his, but being informed that there was no question of any of them being elected, he accepted and was elected that morning, 10 April 1795.[63] He had turned 19 on 2 February.

Unusually for an Oxford college at that time, Oriel's fellowships had never been restricted to members of the college or to any particular school or diocese; in practice, most of the fellows had long been elected from other colleges. Only the four Franks fellowships were restricted (one each to Wiltshire, Somerset, Devon, and Dorset). Richard Whately, writing on Copleston's election, stated that the rules governing elections to fellowships in Oxford colleges required that, in the first instance, a college would seek to appoint a duly qualified candidate from the stipulated school, county, or

---

(ed.), *Joseph Butler's Moral and Religious Thought: Tercentenary Essays* (Oxford, 1992), 63–96, and in the same volume (7–28) David Brown, 'Butler and Deism'. See the impressive study by B. Tennant, *Conscience, Consciousness and Ethics in Joseph Butler's Philosophy and Ministry* (Woodbridge, 2011).

[61] Burgon, *Lives*, i. 383.

[62] See Brock, 'The Oxford of Peel and Gladstone, 1800–1833', 48 n. 271, and Richard Brent, 'Note: The Oriel Noetics', in HUO vi. 73–6.

[63] 'At eight in the morning', wrote Whately, 'he had not the slightest expectation of anything unusual; and at noon, he was probationary Fellow of Oriel College'; Richard Whately, *Remains of the Late Edward Copleston D.D. Bishop of LLandaff* (London, 1854), 5.

diocese, but that, should no eligible candidate be found, the fellowship would then be thrown open to free competition. The benefactor's wish to encourage learning would then be fulfilled.[64] But he went on to say that, in practice, a candidate from the designated location or institution was elected, however deficient in the qualifications required. At Oriel, however, 'it was the practice to adhere strictly to the Founder's designs', with the result that in this case, since none of the Wiltshire candidates proved electable, and since the following day was fixed by statute for an election, the decision to invite Copleston was unanimously agreed.

Although Whately is correct about the election of Copleston, his implication that its procedure was historic practice at Oriel is questionable. Although, for unknown reasons, the Somerset fellowship had been held by men from elsewhere from 1500 to 1521, and the Dorset fellowship from 1524 to 1645, since then candidates from the designated shires had always been elected. All Copleston's predecessors since 1658 had been Wiltshire men.[65] Oriel's practice had not differed from that of other colleges, and therefore, contrary to Whately's claim, Copleston's election to this fellowship was a clear break with custom. What lay behind it? It is unlikely that it was done on the spur of the moment, prompted by a clutch of unelectable candidates; a break with Oxford's long-established practice must have called for deliberation, and for assurance that there was no breach of the founder's intention. Nor, apparently, did it follow a run of bad elections to the Franks fellowships; none of their recent holders seems to have been less than moderately distinguished, being worthy, and in some cases learned clergymen. Further, it offered no general opportunity for a transformation of the college's fortunes, since fourteen of the eighteen fellowships were already open. The most likely explanation is that in 1795 the college introduced a more searching means of discerning intellectual gifts and scholarly potential in candidates for fellowship, distinct from the mere accumulation of knowledge.

Mark Pattison, who tried without success to gain a fellowship at his old college, wrote that examinations for an Oriel fellowship 'were conducted upon the principle of ascertaining, not what a man had read, but what he was like. The prizes or classes which a candidate might bring with him to the competition were wholly disregarded by the electors, who looked at his papers unbiased by opinion outside'; that is, the verdict of university examiners, if not set aside, was never a primary consideration.[66] Thus the double firsts achieved by John Keble, Edward Hawkins, and others, would have availed them little in the eyes of the Oriel fellowship examiners, while candidates such as Richard Whately, John Henry Newman, Hurrell Froude,

---

[64] Whately, *Remains*, 3–6.
[65] See Sir David Ross, 'Oriel Fellowships', OR 1953, 11–16.
[66] Pattison, *Memoirs*, 77–8.

and Thomas Mozley, none of whom was placed in the first class in the honour school list, had the opportunity to persuade the provost and fellows that such results concealed rather than revealed their true intellectual potential. Pattison added that the word which best expresses what the examiners looked for was *originality*. Richard Church, the classic historian of the Oxford Movement, who was elected a fellow in 1838, provided additional commentary from his own experience, both as candidate and examiner:

> The Oriel common-room was rather proud of its seemingly easy and commonplace and unpretending tests of a man's skill in languages and habits and power of thinking for himself. They did not care if he had read much so that he came up to their standard of good Latin, good Greek, good English, and good sense... The two papers which were almost invariably the guide to the first decision were the English into Latin and the English Essay. It was very seldom that men who were clearly first in these did not maintain their superiority throughout the rest of the examination, and no man who failed in these had much chance of retrieving himself... A good deal of weight was attached to *vivâ voce*... It was thought to be a good test of the way in which a man met difficulties, and whether he faced them fairly or tried to evade them.[67]

The method was evidently peculiar to Oriel. If Whately implied a stricture on the neglect of other colleges in their elections to closed fellowships, it does not appear that there was any general discussion of the matter in Oxford, in contrast to the long deliberation and general agreement on the examination statute in 1800. Copleston's election seems to have been conducted on a procedure decided upon entirely in Oriel. It can hardly be doubted that Eveleigh was its architect, since it is wholly of a piece with his dedication to scholarship and learning. Equally, given the number of fellows who shared a wide range of intellectual interests with him, the change must have been discussed in the Oriel common room, which at this time differed in its serious tone from the laxness and idleness commonly (if perhaps not entirely fairly) attributed to the general run of Oxford common rooms.[68] The intention of the reform, to identify and attract outstanding intellectual talent in the university, is consistent with Eveleigh's later leading role in drawing up the examination statute of 1800 and its amendment in 1807, which, by instituting an honours list in the examination for bachelor of arts, encouraged a serious aspiration to excellence. In addition, it gave focus to the role of the fellows both in fostering scholarship and in bringing on the intellectually talented. The condition of Oxford on both counts had been a topic of debate

---

[67] R. W. Church, letter to H. P. Liddon, in Liddon, *The Life of Edward Bouverie Pusey*, ed. J. O. Johnston and R. J. Wilson, 4 vols. (London, 1893–7), 66–9.
[68] Besides Beeke, Richards, Mayo, and Warren, Daniel Veysie should be noted. Elected 1776, he was Bampton lecturer in 1795 (*The Doctrine of Atonement*, Oxford, 1795) and published a number of other scholarly works on New Testament topics, including contemporary trends in the study of the composition of Mark's Gospel.

throughout the eighteenth century, in which more or less radical reforms, including a call for government action, had been proposed. They included a limitation on the tenure of fellowships, their laicization, a requirement that fellows be resident instead of pursuing careers outside Oxford, and that when resident they should engage in serious academic pursuits, not merely wait for a college living to fall vacant.[69] Eveleigh's reforms answered many of the critics' strictures.

High church Tory that he was, however, in the midst of war with revolutionary France, where the old order of society had collapsed, and where the new order had systematically subverted religion, Eveleigh clearly had in mind the need to fortify established English society by means of a better-trained and more dynamic university cadre. He strove for a new intellectual elite, more rigorously imbued with 'the elements of religion, and the doctrinal articles'—the only novelty among the subjects laid down for examination in the statute[70]—that would be capable of defending Christian revelation and the claims of the existing order of Church and state, and of exposing the causes and dangers of schism, the peril of 'enthusiasm', the growth of dissent, scepticism, and the subversion of piety. He was motivated by an urgent need for vigorous engagement in a mounting war of ideas that had gathered momentum in the 1790s, through the publication and popular dissemination of such radical works as Thomas Paine's *Rights of Man: being an Answer to Mr Burke's Attack on the French Revolution*, his *Age of Reason*, the Jacobin intellectual William Godwin's *Enquiry concerning Political Justice, and its Influence on General Virtue and Happiness*—and a volley of other books and pamphlets.[71]

---

[69] For this, see especially V. H. H. Green, 'Reformers and Reform in the University', HUO v. 607–37.
[70] Green, 'Reformers and Reform in the University', HUO v. 626.
[71] Paine, *Rights of Man* (London, 1792); *The Age of Reason* (Paris, 1794); Godwin, *Enquiry concerning Political Justice* (London, 1793). On Godwin see Waterman, *Revolution, Economics and Religion*, esp. ch. 2. The topics of the annual Bampton Lectures, appointed by the heads of houses, are a sure barometer of issues of current concern in the university. In 1805, for example, Edward Nares delivered one of the most erudite and intensively written series, *A View of the Evidences of Christianity at the Close of the Pretended Age of Reason* (Oxford, 1805), containing 280 closely printed pages of detailed notes, some of them of essay length, combating a wide range of 'infidel', deistic, social, and political radicals as well as sceptical writers, past and present, including Hume and Gibbon, of course, as well as French *encylopédistes*, and more recent publications by Paine and Godwin; Mary Wollstonecraft's *A Historical and Moral View of the French Revolution* (London, 1794); Joseph Priestley, especially *Free Discussion of the Doctrines of Materialism and Philosophical Necessity* (London, 1778), the result and deposit of a debate between him and his friend and co-political radical Richard Price; Erasmus Darwin, *Zoonomia* (Dublin, 1796–1800); Robert Fellowes, *Religion Without Cant* (London, 1801), and new and daring views on the non-Mosaic authorship of the Pentateuch by the Scottish Roman Catholic theologian Alexander Geddes, *The holy Bible, or the books accounted sacred by the Jews and Christians*, 2 vols. (London, 1792–7) and *Critical remarks on the Hebrew Scriptures* (London, 1800), and works by German scholars sharing a similar approach to that of Geddes, such as J. G. Eichhorn. 'Enthusiasm' and the schism it brought or threatened, likewise remained an issue

ILLUSTRATION 9.1 Richard Mant (1776–1848), fellow 1798–1805
Oriel College

In an often quoted vignette penned by Tuckwell, Edward Copleston is described as 'a majestic figure... monarch in his day alike of Oriel and of Oxford, dethroner of uncreating Chaos, supreme for twenty years over the new *saeclorum ordo*'.[72] On taking up his fellowship, he soon proved to be the exceptionally talented young man that his dramatic election promised. During his probationary year as a fellow he was awarded the Chancellor's much coveted English Prize, his *Essay on Agriculture* attracting a letter of congratulations from Sir John Sinclair, President of the Board of Agriculture.[73] Eveleigh appointed him a college tutor in October 1797, 'the

---

of continuing preoccupation, as in George Nott's series *Religious Enthusiasm Considered* (Oxford, 1802), and Thomas Le Mesurier's *The nature and guilt of schism considered* (London, 1808).

[72] Tuckwell, *Pre-Tractarian Oxford* (London, 1909), 17.
[73] *Essay on Agriculture* (Oxford, 1796).

beginning of the great tutorial period at Oriel'.[74] In the same year, at the alarming prospect of a French invasion, he became captain of a college volunteer corps, and was considered the ablest officer and 'tightest drill' in the university, skills born of his well-known physical strength and remarkable stamina. He was renowned as a daring rider and remarkable long-distance walker, frequently making the journey to London on foot, on one occasion, as he records in his diary for 12 January 1799, being 'robbed by two mounted highwaymen, on my return to Oxford with Mr Woolcombe and Mr Mant [both fellows of Oriel], between Uxbridge and Beaconsfield'.[75] In another entry, on 6 July 1798, he records: 'Walked from Oxford to [his parents' home in] Offwell [in Devon] with my brother—to Marlborough in one day.'[76]

He rapidly established himself as among the most accomplished tutors in Oxford, lecturing to small tutorial classes. Richard Whately, who came up as an undergraduate in 1805 and later was himself a legendary tutor, is recorded as having declared, 'I would limp upstairs upon one leg to attend a lecture of Copleston.'[77] Eveleigh received Copleston's strong support in his drive to introduce an honours list in the BA examination, eventually agreed in 1800. They disagreed only at the final vote in convocation, when Copleston led a party who argued passionately that passmen, as well as honours candidates, should be placed on the list of successful candidates. He was wholeheartedly committed to the new system, however, and in 1801 volunteered with five other Oriel fellows to conduct, without remuneration, the first examinations under the new statute: a mark both of his leadership and of the general support which Eveleigh's initiative had in Oriel. Debate about the new statute continued for several years: the Hebdomadal Board set up a committee in 1804, which reported in 1806. The statute was amended twice in 1807, and a second statute was passed in 1808, by which candidates awarded first and second class honours were listed. In the 1809 reissue of the 1807 statute, the second class was divided into two, in effect creating three classes.[78]

A year after his appointment as a tutor, Copleston took his turn as junior treasurer and, according to custom, served as senior treasurer in 1799. More unusually, he served again as senior treasurer in 1800, as junior treasurer for a second time in 1804, and once more as senior treasurer in 1805, holding office until 1810. An entry in his diary for 1806 records that, by means of various astute financial arrangements relating to the college's estate revenue, 'the income of the college has been trebled, all its debts liquidated, and the estates

---

[74] Rannie, *Oriel College*, 164.
[75] See W. J. Copleston, *Memoir of Edward Copleston, D.D. Bishop of Llandaff* (London, 1851), 7.
[76] Copleston, *Memoir*, 6.
[77] See Tuckwell, *Pre-Tractarian Oxford*, 54.
[78] For these and other details see Green, 'Reformers and Reform', HUO v. 626–8.

better tenanted'.⁷⁹ We do not know precisely what debts these were, but in 1805 the substantial sum of £250 owing to the college bag for the library fund was summarily paid off. The remaining debt to the caution bag for the same purpose must have been liquidated, owing to the healthy increase in the revenues which Copleston's financial acumen had effected.

While he was enhancing the college's revenues, Copleston was also the professor of poetry, being elected for the customary ten-year tenure in 1802, at the age of 26. The lectures, which were published in Latin under the rather plain title *Academic Lectures Delivered at Oxford*, were much admired in their time, though only of historical interest today.⁸⁰ His high esteem in Oxford was crowned, however, by his celebrated defence of the university against the attack, pursued in several issues of the *Edinburgh Review* in 1808–9, on both the sufficiency of its undergraduate curriculum—Oxford tutors, it was claimed, 'confine themselves to the safe and elegant imbecility of classical learning'—and the quality of its scholarship; the authors ridiculed a recent edition of Strabo's *Geographica* by the University Press as a 'ponderous monument of operose ignorance and vain expense'. Though the articles in the *Edinburgh Review* were printed anonymously in the usual way, three writers were known to be involved.⁸¹ Their claims were mercilessly exposed by Copleston as ignorant of what was currently taught at Oxford, in his *A reply to the Calumnies of the Edinburgh Review against Oxford* (1810).⁸² Their charge, for example, that in the teaching of mathematics at Oxford 'the dictates of Aristotle' were 'still listened to as infallible decrees' was crassly misinformed, since for more than a century the *Physics* of Aristotle had not been set in Oxford's curriculum, and it ignored the new honour school of mathematics.⁸³ He pointed out that they were ignorant of the part played by divinity and logic in college studies, that they knew nothing of the provision of professorial lectures in astronomy, chemistry, mineralogy, botany, and anatomy, or of the lectures given each term by the professor of poetry and the professor of modern history, or of those, albeit

---

⁷⁹ See Copleston, *Memoir*, 19. The entry is confusing, since it states that he had 'continued six years in the office', contrary to usual practice of an annual new appointee of this office, and that this enabled him to introduce his 'plan'. We must presume that by 'six years' he was referring to his first year as junior treasurer (1798) and his first two years as senior treasurer (1799, 1800) together with his further year as junior treasurer (1804) and the first two years (1805, 1806) of his longer stint as senior treasurer from 1805–10. At any rate, it is evident that by the time he wrote this entry, the measures which had been implemented had already met with marked success.

⁸⁰ *Praelectiones academicae habitae oxonii* (Oxford, 1813; 2nd edn., Oxford, 1828).

⁸¹ The writers were John Playfair (1808), Richard Payne Knight (1809), and Sydney Smith (1809), all three combining in a 'Joint "Rejoinder" to a "Reply", etc.' in 1810 to Copleston's *A reply* of 1810.

⁸² The first 'reply', which comprised 190 pages, was followed in 1810 by *A second reply to the Edinburgh review* (118 pages) in response to the 'Rejoinder' by the three authors to his 'Reply', and by a brief *Third reply* in 1811.

⁸³ Copleston, *Reply* (2nd edn., Oxford, 1810), 10.

less in demand, of the professors of Anglo-Saxon and Oriental studies for interested students. In response to the comment that 'a set of lectures upon political economy would be discouraged in Oxford, probably despised, probably not permitted', he drew attention to the well-known lectures on this subject by Henry Beeke, Regius Professor of Modern History.[84] As for the Press's recent edition of Strabo (1807), it was not the work of an Oxford academic but of Thomas Falconer, a physician at Bath, who had never been a member of the university, and who had inherited material for it from an uncle.[85]

The core of Copleston's *Reply* was a defence of Oxford's conviction that classical studies, accompanied by instruction in logic and mathematics, formed the best basis of a university education, the main purpose of which was the cultivation, training, and disciplining of young minds, who would thus be prepared for whatever profession they should choose: if 'this liberal instruction [in classical literature] be first provided, and if the intellect be duly prepared by correct logic and pure mathematical science, there is no analysis, which the business of life may afterwards call upon him to investigate, beyond the reach of a moderate understanding. The habit of discrimination, the power of stating a question distinctly, and of arguing with perspicuity, are of much greater importance than the hasty acquisition of miscellaneous knowledge', which is 'much more easily attained by a well-disciplined mind, after he enters into life, than the other studies upon which we lay the greatest stress'.[86]

There were echoes in all this of the recent debate on the new examination statute, in which some members of convocation advocated the broadening of the curriculum. Edward Tatham, the rector of Lincoln, was their most outspoken advocate, assailing the conservative nature of the proposals and calling for radical reform that would modernize the curriculum:

An University is the seat of *Universal Learning* increasing and to be increased, from the nature of men and things, with the lapse of time...its *Discipline* should accordingly be *adapted to the Increase or Advancement of Learning improving and to be improved according to the times*, otherwise it may occupy young-men in studies that are obsolete and in errors that are exploded.[87]

---

[84] Copleston, *Reply*, 154.
[85] *Strabonis Rerum Geographicarum Libri xvii*, ed. Thomas Falconer (Oxford, 1807). Copleston devoted his longest chapter to this issue (31–103), correcting a number of misapprehensions of the *Edinburgh Review* articles, and not least their unlearned criticism of Falconer's Latin in the preface to the edition of Strabo.
[86] Copleston, *Reply*, 176–7.
[87] E. Tatham, *An Address to the Members of Convocation at Large on the Proposed Statute on Examination* (Oxford, 1807), 1. On this debate see Green, 'Reformers and Reform', HUO v. 628–32.

Copleston's view of a university education prevailed overwhelmingly against Tatham's, and, indeed, formed the core of Newman's famous lectures later in the century, published as *The Idea of a University* in 1873. Tatham's cantankerous and pugnacious nature discredited him in Oxford and lost him what slight following he might have had. His view of what a university should be raised a question, however, that would come increasingly to the forefront in the prolonged debates on reform of the university after 1850. The effect of Copleston's victory over the 'calumnies' of the *Edinburgh Review* was virtually to set in stone Oxford's focus, primarily upon classical literature and secondarily on mathematics, as the most substantial content of the curriculum. This emphasis was already receiving an unexpected boost from the introduction of honours, the gradually growing appeal of which brought about such concentration on the examination syllabus that unexamined parts of the prescribed course were neglected, including the professorial lectures in astronomy, chemistry, mineralogy, botany, anatomy, political economy, and history, attendance at which markedly declined.[88] The view expressed by Copleston in his *Reply*, that the natural sciences were, in curricular terms, of only secondary significance, was that of all but a few in Oxford. 'They are taught', he wrote, 'and esteemed and encouraged here: but we do not deny that they are the subordinate, and not the leading business of education.' It required arduous work on the part of such leading figures in modern science at Oxford as Charles Daubeny, Baden Powell of Oriel, Henry Acland, and especially the Royal Commission of 1850, before science subjects began to acquire a proper place in Oxford's undergraduate curriculum.[89]

Copleston's robust response to the writers of the articles in the *Edinburgh Review* brought him a congratulatory letter from the chancellor, Lord Grenville, and in January 1815 the university marked its gratitude by conferring upon him its highest honour, a DD by diploma. Later that year, the proctor, in his end-of-year address to convocation, after citing President Routh's tribute to Eveleigh, recorded Routh's comment on his successor as provost, whom he described, with an obvious allusion to Copleston's response to the *Edinburgh Review*, as 'a great ornament and protector of our academy, who carries the support of all, and needs neither my own endorsement nor that of any other person'. Eveleigh died unexpectedly on Saturday 10 December 1814 after a short illness. Copleston as dean was in charge of arrangements

---

[88] See W. R. Ward, *Victorian Oxford* (London, 1965), 16; M. G. Brock, 'The Oxford of Peel and Gladstone, 1800–1833', HUO vi. 18–22.

[89] Copleston, *Reply*, 177. See T. W. Heyck, *The Transformation of Intellectual Life in Victorian England* (London, 1982), esp. ch. 3 'The Worlds of Science and the Universities'; Pietro Corsi, *Science and Religion: Baden Powell and the Anglican Debate, 1800–1860* (Cambridge, 1988), see esp. ch. 9 'Science and Academic Politics at Oxford: 1825–35'; N. A. Rupke, 'Oxford's Scientific Awakening and the Role of Geology', in HUO vi. 543–62; Robert Fox, 'The University Museum and Oxford Science, 1850–1880', HUO vi. 641–91.

for the funeral, dispatching letters to non-resident fellows and taking in hand the statutory requirements for the election of a successor.[90] The funeral took place on Friday 16 December at St Mary's, where Eveleigh was interred in the Adam de Brome Chapel. In a notice of his death placed in the local newspapers Copleston wrote:

Yesterday were interred in St Mary's Church the remains of the Rev[d] John Eveleigh DD late Provost of Oriel College in this University—who died at his Lodgings in the College on the 10th instant, after a few days illness, in the 67th year of his age—A firm trust in God, an earnest but mild zeal for his service, and a boundless charity towards all men, were the well-known characteristics of this excellent man. Besides these virtues he was also distinguished by a strong sense of public duty and by a steady resolution in doing whatever his conscience directed. He was followed to the grave by his nearest relations, and by the members of the College over which he had presided three-and-thirty years, who loved and revered him as a Father, and among whom his memory will never cease to be honoured.

It is an indication of the esteem in which Copleston stood among the fellows that, as he records, 'within a day or two after the funeral' all the fellows had been in touch with him, and that 'as their opinions coincided in the choice of a successor, they signed a form of address to the Rev'd Edward Copleston, Dean of the College, requesting him to accept the office'. They wrote: 'The undersigned fellows of the college, in discharge of the solemn duty imposed upon them by their recent public loss, are induced, by their regard to your distinguished qualifications for such a trust, to request you will allow yourself to be put in nomination by them as their Provost, and to accept their cordial and unanimous suffrages to that effect.'[91]

The following Thursday, 22 December, was agreed for the election, and the previous day fixed for giving formal notice of the vacancy. Copleston's address to the fellows on Wednesday 21 December contained the following tribute to Eveleigh:

We have lost in our late Provost, not only a bright example of piety, worth, and benevolence, but each one of us has lost a friend, while the college has lost an experienced and conscientious Governor—one who conducted its concerns for three-and-thirty years with singular uprightness and fidelity, and who preserved its harmony uninterrupted, even among differences of opinion, by his own candour and invariable mildness of temper. In every question that divided the Society, it was

---

[90] Copleston wrote a twelve-page memorandum (OCA/PRO 1 A1/37: Election of a Provost 1814) of the arrangements, which fell to him to put in place, and their execution during the fortnight following Eveleigh's death.

[91] It was signed by Edward Holwell, William Bishop, John Davison, William James, Richard Whately, James Tyler, William Barter, Edward Rudd, John Keble, Thomas Mayo, William Tinney, Richard Burdon, Willingham Franklin, Charles Grey, and Edward Hawkins. One fellowship lay vacant at the time, and one fellow, Thomas Davies, was absent, the total number of fellows being eighteen.

evident to all that his sole endeavour was to discharge his conscience. There was no mixture of pride, of obstinacy, of love of power; no impatience of opposition; no separate interest or selfish motive ever intruded into his dealings with us. He displayed at all times a respect for the judgment of others, a readiness to compare opinions, and a liberal disposition to concede whenever he thought his conscience not involved in the support of his own judgment.

Copleston was elected at the meeting of the fellows convened in the chapel at 10.00 a.m. the following day, and shortly after 11 o'clock, with carriages waiting at the main gate, to make use of as much of the daylight as possible on one of the shortest days of the year, the provost-elect, accompanied by four fellows (John Davison, William Tinney, William James, James Tyler), travelled to London where, the following morning, Copleston duly took the oaths of allegiance and supremacy, and the oath of observance of the college statutes, before the Lord Chancellor, Lord Eldon, acting on behalf of the Visitor, at Lincoln's Inn. They returned to Oriel the same day, where in the evening Copleston was formally installed according to the usual procedures: a ceremonial entry of the new provost at the main gate and a procession to the chapel, where the Lord Chancellor's completion of the electoral process was confirmed. There followed a college meeting, at which Davison was appointed dean in succession to Copleston. One can only admire the sheer stamina, especially of Copleston and those who accompanied him over two days of travelling, much of it outside daylight hours. On the following Sunday, Christmas Day, Copleston wrote out his account of the preceding fortnight's events.

Years of social and political change lay ahead for Copleston and his colleagues, and at an even faster rate than during the previous generation of revolution and war. In June 1815 convocation, sending congratulatory greetings to the Prince Regent on the victory of Waterloo, repeated its pledge to instil in undergraduates the Christian principles on which the established order of society depended.[92] This was no mere conventional sentiment, in the face of the revolutionary ideology which had undermined and destroyed France's *ancien régime*. Since the 1790s radical religious, political, and social ideas had spread widely, and the influence of the Church in the rapidly expanding urban conglomerations had been eroded.[93] The bond between Church and state on which traditional English 'hegemonic'[94] society stood,

---

[92] Convocation undertook 'to impress upon the youth committed to our care...those Christian principles, which are the only sure foundation of public and private virtue, [and] in a more especial manner...to inculcate...obedience to civil authority, not merely as a social, but as a religious obligation'. See M. G. Brock, Introduction to HUO vi. 1.

[93] On the changed and changing situation, see Clark, *English Society*, esp. section 5 'The Old Order on the Eve of its Demise: Slow Erosion'.

[94] For this term and others characterizing English society in 'the long eighteenth century', see Clark, *English Society*, introduction.

and to which dissenters and Catholics implicitly consented, was now under unprecedented strain. In 1820 Godfrey Faussett, formerly fellow of Magdalen and future Lady Margaret Professor of Divinity, spoke in his Bampton Lectures of 'the increasing defections from our Church' and 'the indifference with which such defections are regarded', and of the 'listless apathy, the blind security, and latitudinarian spirit of these alarming times', and he warned of 'the rising tide of encroachment which threatens to overwhelm us' and of 'our situation as an Ecclesiastical Establishment...becoming extremely critical'.[95] He was referring, among other matters, to the renewed calls for repeal of the Test and Corporation Acts and, consequently, for Catholic emancipation.

Dissenters were no longer willing to put up with mere annual suspension of the Test Act, which legally excluded them from public office, and they demanded its repeal. But the repeal of the Act had obvious implications for the position of Roman Catholics, legally excluded from parliament. Fear of rebellion in Ireland, where some six million Catholics were taxed and tithed by the small resident Anglican ascendancy, was heightened by the memory of the rising of 1798 and gave added impetus to the debate about Catholic emancipation. Social unrest and agitation for repeal gained such momentum that by the time Copleston was leaving Oriel for the see of Llandaff, in January 1828, legislation was in the making that would transform Britain's old 'confessional' society. The repeal of the Test and Corporation Acts (1828), Catholic Emancipation (1829), and the Reform Act (1832) brought the 'long eighteenth century' to an end and ushered in the modern pluralist state.[96] Copleston took up office as these discontents were becoming acute, and the underlying social, political, intellectual, and religious transformation of Britain which they signalled formed the background to the thinking of the Noetics, who dominated the Oriel common room in his time.

More immediate for Copleston in the opening months of 1815, however, were two domestic projects: the expansion and renovation of the provost's lodgings and the provision of much needed additional college accommodation, in a period that had brought a marked increase in student applications, not least to Oriel. They were twin projects from the outset, since the extension of the lodgings involved incorporating part of the ground floor of the Carter Building, while the extension of the Robinson Building, on the east side of the quadrangle, would more than compensate for the loss, by

---

[95] *The Claims of the Established Church To Exclusive Attachment and Support, and the Dangers which menace her from Schism and Indifference considered* (Oxford, 1820), 18. His series was a passionate endeavour 'to demonstrate the unreasonableness of separation from that pure branch of the Church of Christ which is established in this country; to assert her claims to our undivided attachment; and to point out the dangers which menace her from the latitudinarian spirit of the times'.

[96] See Clark, *English Society*, esp. section 6 'The End of the Protestant Constitution'.

providing an additional fifteen rooms. Originally built in 1632 as four rooms on three floors, the lodgings had already been extended about 1730 by incorporating what had hitherto been student accommodation in the adjoining staircase VI, in the west range of the first quadrangle.[97] This included what is now the dining room (originally a set of two rooms) and bedrooms above it on the first floor. Copleston evidently lost no time in commissioning the London architect Henry Hakewill (1771–1830), who had a brilliant reputation, to advise him and execute the task. We can infer that Hakewill visited the lodgings relatively early in 1815, since letters making observations and proposals on various suggestions, evidently already discussed on site, were sent by him to Copleston on 23 and 27 March, followed by a further letter on 26 April.[98] Drawings offering varying designs were ready by April, followed by another in May, when a contract was signed.[99] The correspondence that survives consists only of some letters from Hakewill to Copleston.[100] It suggests that at one stage Copleston proposed locating a newly designed drawing room on the site of the first floor bedrooms, which overlook Oriel Square, and redesigning the 'old drawing room', which occupied part of the present drawing room, for use as a bedroom. Hakewill tactfully steered him away from this in favour of developing 'the old drawing room' on account of its aspect—the altogether more pleasing view of the Wyatt Library and the second quadrangle—rather than making a new one over the 'Eating Room', where it would be 'to the west and in some measure overlooked by the rooms of Christ Church'.[101] Hakewill also built the fine large projecting bay window that is such an attractive feature of the drawing room, thus enhancing its pleasing aspect.[102] For proportion, he raised the ceiling of the room, reducing the height of the rooms above.[103]

On the ground floor, the two sets of rooms of the Carter Building (Staircase IX) were annexed, the set nearest to the lodgings being reconstructed as a study in the form of a delightful Georgian library, with book cases similar to those in the library at Lamport Hall, Northamptonshire, which Hakewill

---

[97] I am indebted for some of the information that follows to a brief outline of the history of the lodgings drawn up some years ago with the help of David Sturdy for the use of visitors to the lodgings.

[98] OCA FB 3 B3/10: letters and estimates for building works on the Provost's Lodgings 1815–16.

[99] OCA FB 3 B3/11: plans of proposed alterations to the Provost's Lodgings by Henry Hakewill.

[100] It is possible, however, that these were the only letters and that they were in part responding, after due reflection, to ideas and preferences expressed by Copleston when Hakewill was on site surveying the lodgings.

[101] Hakewill to Copleston, 27 March 1815. Though today the Wyatt Building is commonly regarded as the most eye-catching of Oriel's buildings, it was not at all popular in the time of Copleston, who perhaps shared this view. Fortunately Hakewill's suggestion for the location of the drawing room prevailed.

[102] Hakewill to Copleston, 26 April 1815.   [103] Hakewill to Copleston, 27 March 1815.

installed in 1819. On top of the bookcases, and already envisaged in the drawings, were four busts (Newton, Shakespeare, Aristotle, and Homer), so characteristic of Georgian libraries. A newly constructed entrance hall, with a grand staircase to the first floor leading to the drawing room, joined the lodgings with the Carter Building. Hakewill also completely redesigned the dining room, the elaborate cornice, with matching mahogany doors, a gently curved fireplace recess, and the fine Regency grate and the whole atmosphere of which are of this time. One of the most masterly features of Hakewill's plan was the construction of a corridor running from the entrance hall past the dining room and on, round to the Jacobean staircase at the east end of the house, thus joining the disparate parts of the lodgings together, just as if they were planned as a whole, instead of being tacked on at random, as in fact they were, over nearly two centuries. The arches and niches in this corridor, and the coat-cupboards disguised as pilasters, further illustrate Hakewill's architectural flair. He also constructed a corridor, from the vestibule of the entrance hall northwards along the interior west side (the Oriel Street side) of the Carter Building, to provide easy access to the lodgings for the provost's butler, for whom a room at the further end of the building was reconstructed as an office. We can identify Copleston's butler, who doubled as secretary to the provost, as William Palmer, who had served Eveleigh too, holding office from 1784 to 1824. Palmer was the butler who, on Copleston's instructions, brought the news of Newman's election to him at his rooms in Trinity as he played his violin. A fine portrait of Palmer, a dignified figure proudly holding the Founder's Cup, hangs appropriately in the lodgings. Hakewill's imaginative design, coupled with his skill and ingenuity, yielded a grand, spacious residence, reflecting the standing of the nineteenth-century heads of houses. The cost of the renovations, which were carried out over the period 1815–17, was shared between Copleston and the college, Copleston contributing £1,194 11s. 5½d., and the college donating £1,000.[104] The sum contributed by Copleston evidently included Hakewill's fee for his work on the lodgings, which is not separately recorded. Hakewill was at the same time commissioned by the college to advise on, and draw up a plan for, the construction of eight sets of rooms to be erected at the back of the Robinson Building, for which he submitted a design and estimate in June 1817. The building was completed by the following year at a cost of £1,803 0s. 8d. His brief from the college also included the construction of seven sets of rooms

---

[104] OCA FB 3 B3/7: note in Provost Copleston's hand of moneys paid for 'Improvements in the Provost's Lodging'. In recording the second tranche of £450 from the college in 1818, Copleston (OCA/TF 1 A10/3: Provost's bag book) writes, 'Towards alterations in the Provost Lodgings (including Bookcases in the Study, but exclusive of the Bath) being, together with £500 paid by the College last year, the moiety of the whole expense.' A further £50 was donated by the college in 1820.

'adjoining the Old Library staircase' (staircase VII). It was completed in 1819 at a cost of £2,098 14s. 8¾d., for the work, with Hakewill's fee of £338 3s. 8d.

Tuckwell narrates an anecdote that, when Copleston was leaving hall on the day of his election as a fellow, another fellow 'besought him to recollect always that he owed his preferment to merit alone, and never to forget the principle on which his fellowship was won'.[105] The reminder was understandable, when election to Oxford fellowships was determined more on personal and social grounds than by intellectual merit. Neither social standing, nor regional affiliation, nor what he described as 'the quackery of the schools' was ever admitted by Copleston as a relevant consideration in elections.[106] Copleston's election as a fellow was the first of a series of elections over subsequent years which shaped the illustrious Oriel common room of the early nineteenth century. During Eveleigh's provostship he was joined by John Davison, elected from Christ Church in 1800: he was noted at the time for his *Discourses on Prophecy* (1824), championing the superiority of revealed religion over the 'deficiency' of what can be derived from natural religion, and arguing for the progressive nature of revelation. He contributed to current discussion of the Poor Laws (*Considerations on the Poor Laws*, 1817), and in an open letter to Canning was critical of the abrupt abolition of tax on imported silk, as detrimental to domestic silk manufacturing (*Some Points in the Question of the Silk Trade Stated: in a letter Addressed to the Right Hon. George Canning, M.P.*, 1826).[107]

Richard Whately, elected in 1811, had entered Oriel in 1805, where he formed a lifelong friendship with Copleston, whose college lectures rescued him from a mediocre tutor. He was one of the most independent and clear sighted intellects of his time, a brilliant and influential tutor; of his character as mentor Mozley wrote in later years:

> ...it would not be possible to describe now the terror his presence was sure to infuse among all who wished things to remain much as they were in their own lifetime. Instead of being comforted and built up in the good old fashion, they were told they were altogether wrong, and must first retrace all their steps and undo all they had been

---

[105] Tuckwell, *Pre-Tractarian Oxford*, 25, and see 21, where he gives the name of the other fellow as Williams. If this is so, and if the story can be relied upon, this Williams would have been William Williams, a Wiltshire man, who was Copleston's immediate predecessor in the Franks fellowship. There is no record, however, of Williams having been an archdeacon, as Tuckwell claims.

[106] In a letter to Hawkins in 1843 he wrote: 'Every election to a fellowship which tends to discourage the narrow and almost technical *routine* of public examinations, I consider as an important triumph. You remember Newman himself was an example. He was not even a good classical scholar, yet in mind and powers of composition, and in taste and knowledge, he was decidedly superior to some competitors who were a class above him in the schools.' See Copleston, *Memoir*, 188.

[107] John Davison, *Discourses on Prophecy* (London, 1824); *Consideration on the Poor Laws* (Oxford, 1817); [Anon.], *Some Points in the Question of the Silk Trade* (London, 1826).

doing. What was worse, the efficacy of the cure which had become necessary consisted in the hearers thinking it out for themselves.[108]

He was a formative influence upon the development of Newman at Oriel, who wrote of Whately that he 'opened my eyes, and taught me to think and to use my reason', and 'taught me to see with my own eyes and to walk with my own feet'.[109] In the 1820s, when Copleston became more engaged in public affairs, Whately became the leader of the Noetic group at Oriel, which by then was the most influential intellectual movement in Oxford.[110] He was elected Drummond Professor of Political Economy (1830–2) in succession to one of the foremost political economists of the century, his former private pupil Nassau Senior (1790–1864). Whately's own contribution to political economy was valued in its day.[111] He would later found and endow the chair of political economy at Trinity College, Dublin. He accepted the invitation to be archbishop of Dublin (1832–63), among the least attractive and the most challenging of sees, through a sense of duty.[112] He was the architect of Ireland's national education system.[113] John Keble, elected from Corpus Christi in 1811, the same year as Whately, was a future leader of the Oxford Movement. His *Christian Year* (1827) was among the most widely read books of the nineteenth century; his name is one of the most hallowed in the history of Anglicanism. Newman, upon becoming a fellow, trembled with awe to meet him.[114] Edward Hawkins, elected from St John's in 1813, took one of the earliest double firsts in the new final honour school in classics and mathematics. His renowned sermon on Scripture and tradition, preached before the university in 1818, had a profound influence upon Newman as an undergraduate.[115] When Newman came to Oriel as a fellow in 1822, Hawkins was the prime influence in his evolution away from Calvinism.

---

[108] Mozley, *Reminiscences*, 19.
[109] J. H. Newman, *Apologia pro vita sua*, ed. Ian Ker (London, 1994), 31.
[110] For a succinct but admirably comprehensive overview of his life and career, both at Oxford and in Ireland, see Richard Brent, 'Richard Whately (1787–1863)', in ODNB. The main biography remains that by E. Jane Whately, *Life and Correspondence of Richard Whately, D.D.*, 2 vols. (London, 1866).
[111] See Hilton, *The Age of Atonement, passim*; Waterman, *Revolution, Economics and Religion*, esp. 204–15.
[112] See Tuckwell, *Pre-Tractarian Oxford*, 69–73. On Whately after Oriel, see Chapter 12.
[113] See Richard Clarke, *Richard Whately: The Unharmonious Blacksmith*, Church of Ireland Historical Society (Dublin, 2002); D. H. Akenson, *A Protestant in Purgatory: Richard Whately, Archbishop of Dublin* (Hamden, Conn., 1981).
[114] In a letter to a friend soon after the day he was elected a fellow of Oriel and was summoned to meet the provost and fellows in the Tower Room over the front gate to receive their congratulations, Newman wrote: 'I bore it till Keble took my hand, and then felt so abashed and unworthy of the honour done to me, that I seemed desirous of quite sinking into the ground' (*Apologia*, 16).
[115] *A Dissertation upon the Use and Importance of Unauthoritative Tradition* (Oxford, 1819); Newman, *Apologia*, 29–30.

This talented body was reinforced in Copleston's time. In 1815 Renn Dickson Hampden and Thomas Arnold were elected; Hampden had entered Oriel in 1810, was Davison's tutorial pupil, and took a double first in classics and mathematics. He was professor of moral philosophy (1834–6) and Regius Professor of Divinity from 1836 to 1848, when he became bishop of Hereford (1848–68); his first book, *An Essay on the Philosophical Evidence of Christianity* (1827), reveals an analytical, philosophical mind unmatched by any of his peers. He can, indeed, be described as Oxford's first professor of philosophical theology; his own Bampton series, published as *The Scholastic Philosophy Considered in its Relation to Christian Theology*, was the subject of bitter controversy following his appointment as Regius Professor.[116] Thomas Arnold, elected from Corpus Christi, was one of the leading liberal thinkers of the nineteenth century, a future Regius Professor of Modern History (1841–2), and the legendary headmaster of Rugby; Provost Hawkins, supporting his candidature for the headmastership, wrote: 'If you appoint Mr Arnold he will change the face of education all through the public schools of England.' In 1822 John Henry Newman of Trinity was elected: one of the most penetrating minds of his time, he was leader, with Keble and Froude, of the Oxford Movement; England's most famous convert to the Roman Catholic Church (1845), he became a cardinal in 1879. His thought has exercised a powerful influence upon the Roman Catholic Church in the twentieth century and upon the ecumenical movement throughout the churches generally. Edward Bouverie Pusey was elected from Christ Church in 1823: deeply learned among his peers, he was leader of the Oxford Movement after Newman, Regius Professor of Hebrew, and a canon of Christ Church (1828–82), and a formidable figure in university politics virtually until his death in 1882. Newman referred to him as ὁ μέγας, The Great Man. Richard Hurrell Froude, an Oriel undergraduate elected in 1826, was a key figure in Newman's life, a forceful influence upon him as upon Keble, and the catalyst of the Oxford Movement. He died prematurely in 1836, one 'who lived but to die', as Mozley poignantly put it.[117] Robert Wilberforce, second son of William Wilberforce, entered Oriel in 1820, obtained a first in both classics and mathematics, and was elected fellow in 1823. Strongly influenced by Keble, he moved from his evangelical upbringing to the high Anglican tradition; later he identified himself with the new movement led by Froude, Keble, and Newman, and, after the latter's conversion to Roman Catholicism, he became the leading theological voice of the Oxford Movement. Early in the 1850s, however, he suffered a period of

---

[116] Renn Dickson Hampden, *An Essay on the Philosophical Evidence of Christianity* (London, 1827); *The Scholastic Philosophy considered in its Relation to Christian Theology* (Oxford, 1833).
[117] Mozley, *Reminiscences*, 18.

anguish over the authority of the Church of England, and in 1854 followed his close friend Henry (later Cardinal) Manning, as well as Newman and his own younger brother Henry, into the Roman Catholic Church.

Others elected during these years pursued successful careers in law, politics, the university world, and the Church. They included Robert Ingham, elected in 1816, QC in 1851, MP for South Shields (1832–41, 1852–68) and Recorder of Berwick-on-Tweed; John Awdry, elected from Christ Church in 1819, Chief Justice of Bombay (1839–41), and one of the executive commissioners appointed to redraft university and college statutes after the Royal Commission of 1850; and Henry Jenkyns, elected from Corpus Christi in 1818, later professor, first of Greek (1833–41) and subsequently of divinity (1841–78), at Durham University, and editor of Cranmer's *Remains*, with its strongly Protestant preface. Joseph Dornford matriculated at Trinity College, Cambridge, in 1809 at the age of 15, left in 1811 and fought as a volunteer in the Peninsular War, entered Wadham in 1813, and was elected fellow of Oriel in 1819. In 1820 he climbed Mont Blanc. Richard Jelf, elected from Christ Church in 1821, became principal of King's College, London (1844–68). Samuel Rickards, an Oriel undergraduate elected in 1819, was a source of wise counsel to fellow clergy during the ecclesiastical turmoil of the time. He fortunately possessed a duplicate manuscript of Keble's *Christian Year*, from which the text was printed when Keble's own copy was lost. Not everyone elected under the presiding eye of Copleston turned out to be well chosen: Hartley Coleridge, son of Samuel Taylor Coleridge and himself in later life a poet and writer, was elected in April 1819, but was not given tenure in 1820, on account of his 'sottishness' and general nonconformity to college life. The protests of his father, who came to Oriel to remonstrate personally with Copleston on the matter, were to no avail.

There were three others, who, though not fellows, were members of the common room and were counted among the Noetics. The mathematician and physicist Baden Powell, who entered Oriel as an undergraduate in 1815 and was a pupil of Whately, became a fellow of the Royal Society in 1824, and was elected Savilian Professor of Geometry in 1827. In his earlier career he contributed to the response to scepticism.[118] Over time, however, especially in the 1850s, in a series of publications, he moved away from his earlier, religiously conservative apologetic to a more radically liberal stance: he denied the reality of miracles, commented favourably on Darwin's theory of evolution, and contributed an essay, 'On the study of the evidences of Christianity', to the controversial volume *Essays and Reviews* (1860), whose seven essayists were dubbed the *Septem contra Christum*, and which finally alienated Whately from him.[119] Samuel Hinds entered Queen's College in

---

[118] See especially Corsi, *Science and Religion*, part I.
[119] Corsi, *Science and Religion*, esp. part III.

ILLUSTRATION 9.2 Baden Powell (1796–1860), fellow 1808–11
Oriel College

1811, and became a private pupil of Whately, who in 1827 as principal of St Alban Hall appointed him vice-principal. He followed Whately to Dublin as his chaplain, and was later dean of Carlisle (1848–9) and bishop of Norwich (1849–57), chairing in 1850 the Royal Commission on the university. Joseph Blanco White, a Spanish Catholic who converted to Anglicanism, settled in England, and opposed Catholic emancipation.[120] On the proposal of Copleston, the university conferred on him the degree of MA by diploma in 1826, and he took up residence in Oxford, becoming an honorary member of Oriel. He too was influenced by Whately and, abandoning his earlier opinion, sided with his mentor in favour of emancipation in the divisive argument over the question in the Oriel common room. He subsequently voted for Peel's re-election as the university's MP. He followed Whately to Dublin in 1832 but returned to England in 1835 as his opinions veered toward Unitarianism.[121]

---

[120] J. Blanco White, *Practical and Internal Evidence against Catholicism* (London, 1825).
[121] See Martin Murphy, *Blanco White: Self-Banished Spaniard* (New Haven, 1989).

This audacious common room cast its reputation over the university at large. 'Its most prominent talkers, preachers, and writers seemed to be always undermining, if not actually demolishing, received traditions and institutions; and whether they were preaching from the university pulpit, or arguing in common room, or issuing pamphlets on passing occasions, even faithful and self-reliant men felt the ground shaking under them. The new Oriel sect was declared to be Noetic...and when a fellow of the College presented himself in the social gatherings of another society, he was sure to be reminded of his pretence to intellectual superiority.'[122]

They formed no united school of thought; they were not a coordinated movement with a coherent programme, and it is anachronistic to anticipate, in the 1820s, the divisions and groupings that were to characterize Victorian church life.[123] Mark Pattison recalled them as 'men having an individual stamp. There was the widest diversity of opinion, and a fermentation of thought maintained among them, which was as a stimulating leaven in the mass of university torpor.' '[A]t bottom', he continued, 'their intellectual effort went to sound and probe the sources of the thought and feeling of their age. Thus this effort was a truly philosophical effort, inasmuch as it sought to pass by the war of opinion to the causes of opinion.' They saw their task as 'assisting at the resuscitation of religious sentiment, at the attempt to re-unite Christianity with the thoughts of the age'.[124]

The leading figures, the Noetics proper, were Copleston, Davison, Whately, Hawkins, Hampden, Thomas Arnold, Baden Powell, Blanco White, and Hinds. The differences of emphasis in their views were held in check by their harmonious collaboration in the tasks of combating scepticism and unbelief, which had gained ground in recent years, and of addressing growing dissent and indifference.[125] They maintained that the political and the religious nation were coterminous, but they firmly rejected the idea that the Church was merely a pillar of the secular order of society.[126] They

---

[122] Mozley, *Reminiscences*, i. 19.
[123] On the origin and emergence of these groupings and parties, see Peter Nockles, *The Oxford Movement in Context: Anglican High Churchmanship 1760–1857* (Cambridge, 1994), especially his historiographical introduction.
[124] Mark Pattison, 'Philosophy at Oxford', *Mind*, 1 (January 1876), 82–97, cf. 83, 84.
[125] Butler's *Analogy* was their philosophical text and they made full use also of William Paley's popular apologetic works *A view of the Evidences of Christianity* (London, 1794) and *Natural Theology* (London, 1802). Samuel Hinds, *An Inquiry into the Proofs, Nature, and Extent of Inspiration, and into the Authority of Scripture* (Oxford, 1831) sought to meet head-on 'the advance of free-thinking and scepticism'; Baden Powell defended revelation against Unitarian deism in his *Rational Religion Examined: Or, Remarks on the Pretensions of Unitarianism; Especially as compared with those Systems which professedly discard Reason* (London, 1826). The latter was a scientist's defence of revelation, directed against deism. Richard Whately's *Essay on Some of the Peculiarities of the Christian Religion* (Oxford, 1825) was concerned with growing indifference to Christianity.
[126] The anonymously published pamphlet *Letters on the Church by an Episcopalian* (London, 1826), which was probably written by Whately (see Newman, *Apologia*, 32), forcibly argued for

saw an urgent need to 'Christianize' potentially secular subjects, such as political economy; they engaged in a bold appeal against 'party spirit' and its resulting schismatic tendency, and for religious unity. That appeal was expressed, for example, in Whately's Bampton Lectures, *The Use and Abuse of Party Feeling in Matters of Religion* (1822), and in Arnold's bold call, in his *Principles of Church Reform* (1833), for a national Church into which all citizens, under a new ethos of brotherly toleration, would be shepherded.[127] The Noetics therefore, as Pattison put it, tried to 're-unite Christianity with the thoughts of the age': to meet new intellectual and social challenges and the mounting religious diversity which current constitutional reform was designed to accommodate. Their attempt was the fount of a liberal theological way of thinking that would become a leading feature of Anglican tradition.[128] In Oriel itself, constitutional reform precipitated a decisive new departure in the common room and the emergence of a movement of a quite different temper, that would have momentous, and permanent, consequences for the future of the Church of England. In the university, it provoked new calls for internal reform, though Oxford's own *ancien régime* was not swept away until after the mid-century.

While the common room was coalescing round the Noetics, Copleston was recruiting a talented body of undergraduates. With room for about sixty in college, the numbers admitted ranged between eleven in 1815 and twenty-nine in 1821, with an average of seventeen or eighteen. Copleston's Oriel was, as Mark Pattison observed, 'eminently a gentlemen's college': Eveleigh had already admitted Lord North's nephew Henry Verney (1790), later 8th Lord Willoughby de Broke, and the two sons of his secretary, William and George Brummell (1794), the latter to be notorious as Beau Brummell. Richard, Earl Temple (1815), would be a profligate duke of Buckingham, Lord Harry Vane (1821) a sober duke of Cleveland. Several would achieve high office, owing little, to all appearance, to the Oriel phase of their progress. James, Lord Fitzharris (1825), remembered leaving at the earliest opportunity consistent with a degree; as earl of Malmesbury he was twice Foreign Secretary in the

---

the sovereign independence of the Church from the state, coming close to support for disestablishment, though Whately never subsequently argued for this. His anti-Erastianism was a strong influence in the development of Newman's thought (*Apologia*, 32).

[127] Contributions by both Copleston and Whately in the emerging field of political economy call for special mention here, notably the former's letters to Peel in 1819 (*A Letter to the Right Hon. Robert Peel, MP for the University of Oxford, on the Pernicious Effects of a Variable Standard of Value, especially as it regards the Condition of the Lower Orders and the poor Laws* and *A Second Letter to the Right Hon. Robert Peel, MP for the University of Oxford, On the Causes of the Increase of Pauperism, and on the Poor Laws*, Oxford, 1819), and Whately's *Introductory Lectures in Political Economy* (London, 1831), which went into several editions. See alsoWhately, *The Use and Abuse of Party Feeling* (Oxford, 1822) and Arnold, *Principles of Church Reform* (London, 1833).

[128] See now especially Brent, *Liberal Anglican Politics*.

RICHARD GRENVILLE PLANTAGENET NUGENT TEMPLE, MARQUIS OF CHANDOS.

ILLUSTRATION 9.3 Richard Temple (1797–1861), 2nd duke of Buckingham, nobleman commoner 1815–18
National Portrait Gallery: Robert Cooper after Anne Mee, 1821

ILLUSTRATION 9.4 Sir George Grey (1799–1882), statesman, commoner 1817–21
Oriel College

Derby administrations.[129] Others however owed their future eminence in large part to their privileged membership of a select body, among them Charles Wood (1817), who gained a first in classics and mathematics, and later became a notable Whig Chancellor of the Exchequer (1846–52), and the

---

[129] James Howard Harris, earl of Malmesbury, *Memoirs of an ex-Minister* (London, 1885), i. 14. See, for Pattison's remark, his *Memoirs* (London, 1885), 69.

ILLUSTRATION 9.5 Charles Wood (1800–85), 1st viscount Halifax, commoner 1818–21

National Portrait Gallery

1st Viscount Halifax; and George Grey (1817), who with a first in classics and an evangelical conscience was a long-serving Home Secretary (1846–52 and 1861–6). A number achieved eminence in the university and the Church, some of them from long-standing Oriel families like the Froude brothers, others recruited by Copleston like the Wilberforces. Something of their life at Oriel can be seen in the surviving extracts from the diary of William Hale (1813), later archdeacon of London.[130] He came up from Charterhouse in April 1813 and was given rooms at the top of staircase I; he judged Oriel 'the most comfortable college' in Oxford. He was assigned to John Davison, whom he found agreeable. Hale was amused to find the previous occupant of his rooms had left a mixed collection of books: 'Homer, Odyssey, the Bible in

---

[130] OCL, Oriel Letters, ii. 137, and see letters to him from his contemporary John James Strutt, ii. 126 and 128.

duodecimo, Euclid, Sporting Anecdotes, Prayer Book, General Stud Book, Eveleigh's Sermons, 2 vols.' His friends included the talented Henry Riddell Moody (1811), John James Strutt, later Lord Rayleigh (1814), and Temple. The two latter were members of the Oriel Book Club, of which Hale was secretary, evidently a discussion group. His interests were not confined to the classics: he attended a lecture on comparative anatomy, with a dissection, and joined a 'Geologizing Party' led by William Buckland, and including all the Oriel resident fellows, to 'examine the various strata... between Oxford and Shotover Hill'. Clearly the broad interests of the Noetics influenced the junior members of the college, among them Hale's younger contemporary Baden Powell.

Copleston left Oriel just before the constitutional reforms of the late 1820s took place, at a time when, for all its disputatiousness and 'logomachy', as Pattison called it, the Oriel common room remained a harmonious forum of debate.[131] The year 1826 had marked the fifth centenary of the founding of the college, and the main occasion of commemoration and celebration was held on 15 June. Copleston recorded in his diary:

Preached at the commemoration service in St. Mary's Church. Presided at dinner in the library. One hundred and forty guests. The whole passed off extremely well.

A few weeks later we read this entry:

July 24. Received Lord Liverpool's letter offering me the deanery of Chester.

The appointment was to be held in plurality with the provostship of Oriel and with Copleston's *ex officio* appointment as a canon of Rochester. He was installed at Chester on 5 September. The tenure was short, however, for on 30 November 1827 he received a letter from Lord Goderich offering him the see of Llandaff; the deanship of St Paul's was later included with this appointment. Some months earlier he had been passed over for the bishopric of Oxford, when Charles Lloyd, who had been Peel's tutor at Christ Church, was appointed. Copleston's biographer comments that his 'course had been so independent, and his opinions so little accommodated to those of persons in power, that his preferment seemed to be no very probable contingency'.[132] Whatever may have been the reasons for his overdue preferment—a friend wrote to him that 'no man ever owed his promotion more entirely to his own abilities, industry, and character'[133]—he gladly accepted, was consecrated at Lambeth Palace on 13 January, and on 14 February took his seat in the House of Lords, where he was immediately involved in the historic debate that led to the repeal of the Test and Corporation Acts.

In his farewell letter to the dean and fellows, which was accompanied by his formal resignation, Copleston wrote:

---

[131] Pattison, 'Philosophy at Oxford', 84.   [132] Copleston, *Memoir*, 109.
[133] Copleston, *Memoir*, 110. See also Richard Brent's comments in ODNB s.n. Copleston.

ILLUSTRATION 9.6 James Harris (1807–89), 3rd earl of Malmesbury, nobleman commoner 1825–8

Oriel College, engraving by G. Zobel after J. G. Middleton, 1852

It is now more than thirty years that Oriel has been the scene of nearly all my labours and pursuits, my cares and anxieties, my intellectual and social enjoyments. The place is endeared to me by the strongest ties of a personal and local kind. It has been the parent of my dearest friendships, as well as of my purest pleasure... The government of the college has, indeed, been rendered comparatively a light burden, by the vigilance and energy by which all its officers have maintained its discipline, by the unanimity which has pervaded the resident members, and by the kind, frank, and cordial intercourse which has subsisted between them and myself. From such a scene, and from such connexions, I cannot withdraw unmoved. Yet I am supported by the confident hope that there will be no loss of private friendship, and that frequent opportunities will arise of renewing that personal intercourse which must now for a time be suspended. It is no light consolation, also, to feel assured that the society will continue to flourish as it has hitherto done. There are no marks of degeneracy visible—no symptoms of decrepitude or decay.

The clear sense of the harmony of the common room that comes through here is confirmed by Copleston's note in his diary two years earlier, on the

ILLUSTRATION 9.7 William Palmer, the college butler
Oriel College

occasion of the Candlemas Gaudy on 2 February 1826, which inaugurated the quincentenary celebrations:

Feb. 2. Completed my fiftieth year, the college its five hundredth. Dined in hall. The society in a very flourishing state, and in excellent discipline. The fellows united, and the most cordial harmony subsisting.

It was a harmony that would not survive the turbulent political circumstances of 1828–9. After the repeal of the Test and Corporation Acts, the Act of Catholic Emancipation in 1829 made a breach between Newman, who with Keble, Froude, and others, opposed emancipation, and Whately, who with Hawkins, Hampden, and others, supported it. Following the Irish Temporalities Act (1833), which was the immediate occasion of the Oxford Movement, division deepened, both in Oriel and in the university at large; and new proposals for university reform produced further acrimony. The controversies that now began would mark the most significant passage in the emergence of modern Oxford.

10

Oriel and Religion, 1800–1833

Peter Nockles

'When I contemplated so many young men, all communicants at the altar, worshipping in an audible and reverent manner, the God of Heaven, and pouring out their prayers and praises with one voice, through Jesus Christ, I could hardly believe myself on earth.'[1]

This awe-struck observation in November 1823 from Philander Chase, a visiting bishop of the Protestant Episcopal Church of the United States, while he was briefly residing in Oriel as the guest of the provost, Edward Copleston, gives a rosy, if not flattering, account of devout religious observance during a communion service in the college chapel. Such observations, however, can be notoriously subjective, and more negative impressions of religious observance and practice in contemporary Oxford colleges, Oriel included, can be cited.[2]

---

[1] Bishop P. Chase to T. Wiggin, 18 November 1823, *Bishop Chase's Reminiscences: An Autobiography*, 2 vols. (Boston, 1848), i. 221. As bishop of Ohio, Chase was on a fund-raising visit to England to raise subscriptions among Church of England dignitaries for his impoverished American diocese. This was the context for Provost Copleston's invitation for him to visit Oriel. Oriel also played host to the visit of another American bishop, a rival to Chase for English subscriptions, a pronounced high churchman, John Henry Hobart, bishop of New York. It was Copleston who initiated the invitation, which was sent via a leading high churchman, J. H. Spry. J. H. Spry to Bishop J. H. Hobart, 26 January 1824, *The Posthumous Works of the Late Right Reverend John Henry Hobart, Bishop of the Protestant Episcopal Church in the State of New York. With a Memoir by the Rev. William Berens*, 3 vols. (New York, 1833), i. 291. John Henry Newman unflatteringly described Bishop Hobart at a dinner in Oriel organized by the provost: J. H. Newman to Jemima Newman, 8 March 1824, LDN, i. ed. I. Ker and T. Gornall (Oxford, 1978), 173. It was a measure of Oriel's standing under Copleston that the college should have had such a high profile in ecclesiastical affairs and in receiving distinguished ecclesiastical visitors.

[2] For examples, see John Henry Newman's and Isaac Williams's comments on low standards of observance in Trinity College chapel and on saints' days in the university church of St Mary the Virgin respectively, see *The Autobiography of Isaac Williams, B.D. Fellow and Tutor of Trinity College... Edited by his Brother-in-law the Ven. Sir George Prevost* (London, 1892), 52–3. See also the comment of Elizabeth Grant, niece of James Griffith, master of University College (1808–21), after she visited the college in 1810: 'The religion of Oxford appeared in those days to consist in honouring the King and his ministers, and in perpetually popping in and out of chapel. All the Saints' days and all the eves of Saints' days were kept holy. Every morning and every

John Campbell Colquhoun (1803–70), an evangelically minded gentleman commoner of Oriel, went so far in 1822 as to address the heads of houses of the university on the evils of profanation and impiety attendant upon enforcement of compulsory chapel attendance for undergraduates.[3] Colquhoun's strictures on a system whereby undergraduates might go straight to chapel after carousing over wine seem to have been inspired by his Oriel experience. A few years later John Henry Newman, then a young fellow of Oriel who was only slowly moving away from his early evangelicalism, privately aired similar complaints over what he later characterized as a 'lax traditional system' in the college,[4] as well as of a lack of sufficient 'direct religious instruction' in the tuition at Oriel[5]. However, Colquhoun was comprehensively answered and rebutted by Edward Hawkins.[6] Such impressions have been used by later historians to convey a picture of contemporary university religion as essentially arid.[7] Yet it would be invidious to build claims of Oriel's superiority or laxity in this respect on anecdotal evidence alone; the higher standards of a later generation, shared by evangelicals and Tractarians alike, make retrospective accounts of collegiate religious practice problematic, if not anachronistic. Impressions of the religious character of an Oxford college should not anyway be confined to the formulaic and statutory observances maintained within its chapel.

A better index of religious activity might be provided by evidence of how well the college fulfilled its statutory obligations by way of religious

---

evening there were prayers in every College chapel, lengthened on Wednesdays and Fridays by the addition of the Litany. My Uncle attended the morning prayers regularly.' She also recorded University College undergraduate attitudes to chapel attendance: 'The Chapel going was felt to be an "uncommon bore", and was shirked as much as possible.' E. Grant, *Memoirs of a Highland Lady*, ed. A. Tod, 2 vols. (Edinburgh, 1992), i. 161–2. I owe this latter reference to Robin Darwall-Smith. For another testimony to the low level of attendance at prayers in the university church of St Mary in this period, see *The Life of the Rev. Joseph Blanco White. Written by Himself. Edited by John Hamilton Thom*, 3 vols. (London, 1845), i. 288.

[3] [J. C. Colquhoun], *An Appeal to the Heads of the University of Oxford by an Undergraduate* (London, 1822). Colquhoun matriculated in 1820, took a first class in classics, and graduated in 1823. See *Registrum Orielense*, ii. 350. Colquhoun was MP for Dumbartonshire 1833–4, Kilmarnock 1837–42, and Newcastle-under-Lyme 1842–7. He became a prominent Protestant evangelical churchman and anti-Catholic, anti-Tractarian, and later anti-ritualist polemicist. He was a regular platform speaker in that great metropolitan citadel of pan-evangelicalism in the 1830s and 1840s, Exeter Hall, and was president of the Church Association in the 1860s. He was the author of *Ireland. Popery and Priestcraft: The Cause of her Misery and Crime* (London, 1836). See also the negative testimony as to the lack of religious instruction in Oriel, from a former fellow, R. B. Sanderson, whose outlook was albeit coloured by his later rejection of the Church of England in favour of Protestant dissent.

[4] J. H. Newman to Frederic Rogers, Lord Blachford, 22 October 1884, LDN, xxx. ed. C. S. Dessain and T. Gornall (Oxford, 1976), 409.

[5] Diary entry for 7 May 1826, LDN, i. ed. I. Ker and T. Gornall (Oxford, 1975), 286.

[6] [E. Hawkins], *An Appeal to the Author of 'An Appeal to the Heads of the University of Oxford' upon compulsory attendance at the Communion, by a Graduate* (Oxford, 1822).

[7] V. H. H. Green, *Oxford Common Room: A Study of Lincoln College and Mark Pattison* (London, 1957), 99–101.

instruction to its junior body. Here again objective evidence is not easy to uncover, though much evidence for revived tutorial methods as a medium for inculcating particular religious ideas will emerge in our discussion of John Henry Newman, and of Oriel between 1826 and 1832 as the seed-bed of the future Oxford Movement. Moreover, there are tantalizing glimpses of the college's emphasis on undergraduate religious instruction in the pre-Tractarian era. Oriel undergraduates were required to attend and take notes on university sermons.[8] The *Censor Theologicus* was enjoined to check these notes, and more informal and private note-taking evidently occurred. In a typical entry for 17 May 1814, the Oriel undergraduate William Hale wrote: 'We have an exercise to do every Sunday which consists of sermon notes—to give a short epitome of the sermon at St Mary's. Last Sunday Van Mildert preached the Bampton Lectures considerably longer than an hour, the text, "rightly dividing the Word of truth" and I managed to bring in the heads of the sermon in my memory. I find it a most useful exercise to the head.'[9]

Another benchmark of collegiate religious practice was the relative seriousness with which fellows fulfilled their pastoral obligations when taking up college livings. In the present chapter, however, these considerations and the minutiae of formal religious practice will be secondary to the theological controversies which arose within the college itself and which ultimately divided it, and to the broader religious influences brought to bear by the fellows on their pupils and through them on the wider national arena. These influences were felt as much through personal contact, sermons, and theological publications as through tutorials and lectures, though the tutorial system would become a powerful engine of personal religious influence and the inspiration for a wider religious movement. The wider impact of religious ideas born within Oriel is as significant as the damaging division within the college itself: the long-running conflict between Newman and Hawkins in 'a house divided', with its fellows often locked in bitter theological combat. This broader theme is as intrinsic a part of the college's history as, in the words of an earlier Oriel historian, 'a record of the jealousies, the squabbles and the scandals for which the life of a small society gives so melancholy an opportunity'.[10] However, while genuine theological and academic principles were at stake and divisive, personality and human foibles had their place, and served to exacerbate doctrinal controversy.

The history of Oriel in this period is inseparable from that of the Oxford Movement, of which the college was notoriously the birthplace and *dramatis*

---

[8] See W. Tuckwell, *Pre-Tractarian Oxford: A Reminiscence of the Oriel 'Noetics'* (London, 1909), 152.
[9] 'Extract from the Diary of William Hale', OCL, Oriel Letters ii, fo. 137. William H. Hale (1795–1870), matriculated Oriel 1813, BA 1817, domestic chaplain to Charles James Blomfield, bishop of Chester (later London), prebendary of St Paul's 1829–40, archdeacon of London.
[10] G. C. Richards, 'The Provosts and Fellows of Oriel College, Oxford', OR (June 1923), 139.

scena. As Thomas Mozley found, to write a history of the one was to write a history of the other.[11] For as another historian of the college observed, the two were linked not merely because Oriel was to become the citadel of the Oxford Movement, but because the movement was nurtured by 'sources inherent in the particular college system'.[12] In short, the Oxford Movement would be a product of what might be called Oriel's 'tutorial movement'. The religious as well as the intellectual and academic character of Oriel was an important component of the college's era of ascendancy in Oxford. This chapter will explore the various competing elements in the college's religious character, and how far those elements served to shape, promote, and eventually inhibit and retard its pre-eminence, and continued to operate in the era of its gradual relative decline and eclipse.

The prevailing religious orthodoxy within the University of Oxford in the early part of this era has been described as 'high and dry', or more opprobriously 'port and prejudice' or 'two-bottle orthodoxy'. It is noteworthy that the main force of religious zeal in the Church of England over the preceding half-century, evangelicalism, was poorly represented and rather despised in Oxford, outside St Edmund Hall under the principalship of John Hill.[13] For a time in the late 1820s and early 1830s a Calvinist evangelical fellow of Exeter, Henry Bellenden Bulteel, aided by J. C. Philpot of Worcester, was stirring up theological passions and bringing down on himself the censures of the university authorities.[14] Oriel was largely immune from the Bulteelite stirs.[15] Provost Hawkins preached from the university pulpit of St Mary's in

---

[11] T. Mozley, *Reminiscences of Oriel College and the Oxford Movement*, 2 vols. (London, 1882).

[12] Rannie, *Oriel*, 155.

[13] See P. B. Nockles, 'Lost Causes and...Impossible Loyalties: The Oxford Movement & the University', HUO vi. 195–267. Newman later wrote of evangelicalism as 'a form of Protestantism which never flourished in Oxford. Mr Hill of Edmund Hall, Symons of Wadham, Bulteel of Exeter, and one or two more were members of that school', Newman to J. C. Fisher, 17 November 1877, LDN, xxviii. 269. Thomas Mozley, albeit a chronicler notoriously unsympathetic to evangelicalism, stated that it was 'difficult to convey an idea of the very low position it had in the university', Mozley, *Reminiscences*, i. 23.

[14] Bulteel castigated Oxford's heads of colleges for granting college testimonials for ordination candidates to 'men notorious for nothing so much in their day as profaneness, debauchery, and all kinds of riotous living' while withholding them sometimes from men of 'piety, honesty, and sobriety' for no other reason that they were Calvinistic evangelicals. H. Bulteel, *A Sermon on 1. Corinthians II. 12 preached before the University of Oxford, at St Mary's on Sunday February 4, 1831* (Oxford, 1831), 46–7. For Bulteel, see T. C. F. Stunt, *From Awakening to Secession: Radical Evangelicals in Switzerland and Britain 1815–35* (Edinburgh, 2000). For Philpot, see R. Sharp, 'A Worcester Seceder', *Worcester College Record* (1997), 41–7; Nockles, '"Floreat Vigornia": Worcester College & the Oxford Movement', *Worcester College Record* (2007), 69–71.

[15] Charles Lancelot Lee Brenton was a rare 'Bulteelite' exception. After returning to Oriel from a short spell of pastoral duty, Brenton seceded from the Church of England in December 1831 in the wake of Bulteel's own secession and 'set up a new sect, of no very peculiar or distinctive character'. Thomas Mozley was convinced that Brenton 'was mad when he came back to college', causing embarrassment in the common room—'he took the lead of the conversation, and conducted arguments in a voice that shook the building', Mozley, *Reminiscences*, ii. 114–20.

1831 against the antinomianism implicit in Bulteel's doctrine.[16] Although one of her former fellows, after turning dissenter, assailed the Church of England in the mid-1830s as a 'Mark of the Beast' as ascribed in the book of Revelation,[17] Oriel remained conspicuous for its relative lack of representatives of the evangelical tradition.[18] The young Samuel Wilberforce, one of the three Oriel sons of the famous evangelical William Wilberforce, made the point clearly in a letter to his father on going up to Oriel in 1823 (for 'religious' read 'evangelical'): 'At Oriel there are perhaps above two or three men whom you can call really religious...the men generally who are most religious belong (I believe) to Wadham or St Edmund Hall and are very low by birth and equally vulgar in manners, feelings and conduct.' He went on to describe the religious and moral character of his contemporaries at Oriel, observing that there were 'a great proportion of moral, hopeful, good sort of men', as well as a minority of 'men occasionally perhaps actually immoral but who would not obtrude their actions and dispositions on their acquaintances if they were differently disposed'.[19] On the other hand, pre-Tractarian Oriel could also count few representatives of the 'high and dry' church tradition, or of the more devotional, overtly sacramental and liturgical form of high churchmanship, rooted in the early fathers and Caroline divines, which characterized Magdalen and its long-lived president, Martin Routh (1755–1854).[20] In contrast, the religious outlook of the Oriel fellowship was detached from, if not opposed to, both these prevailing orthodoxies: 'equal bigotries' in Whately's trenchant phrase.[21]

The rise within Oriel of a vigorous school of intellectual religious enquiry, the Noetics, has already been described. This school came to dominate the common room by the 1820s, under the leadership of the college's energetic provost, Edward Copleston; it included such figures as Richard Whately, Edward Hawkins, John Davison, Baden Powell, Renn Dickson Hampden,

---

See *The Seceders (1829–1869): The Story of a Spiritual Awakening as Told in the Letters of Joseph Charles Philpot, M.A. and of William Tiptaft, M.A. With an Introduction by J. H. Philpot* (London, 1931), 93–5.

[16] E. Hawkins, *A Sermon upon the Way of Salvation, preached in the chapel of Oriel College, Oxford, February 27, 1831* (Oxford, 1831), esp. 8.

[17] See R. B. Sanderson, *The Church of England identified, on the authority of her own historians chiefly, with the Second Beast, as ascribed in the Book of Revelation, Chapter XIII, verses 11–18* (London, 1836). Sanderson (p. iv) was especially critical of Oxford and by implication Oriel 'as a place of religious instruction, where, if a man be really religious at all, he must be so in spite of the place'.

[18] Exceptions included the gentleman commoner John Colquhoun (1820) and, at a later date, Edward Arthur Litton, fellow 1836–43.

[19] Cited in D. Newsome, *The Parting of Friends: A Study of the Wilberforces and Henry Manning* (London, 1966), 73.

[20] R. Darwall-Smith, 'The Monks of Magdalen 1688–1854', in L. W. B. Brockliss (ed.), *Magdalen College Oxford: A History* (Oxford, 2008), 339–40.

[21] Mozley, *Reminiscences*, i. 23.

Joseph Blanco White, Thomas Arnold, and Samuel Hinds. Whately and Hawkins led the way in practising the Socratic method of improving thought by constant questioning; florid and inaccurate expression was discouraged and exposed.[22] The common room, in a memorable phrase, was said to have 'stunk of logic'.[23] But while the Noetics represented a unity of intellectual purpose and gave rise to a keen interplay of ideas in the common room, it would be misleading to portray them as a distinct theological party bound together in mutual doctrinal agreement. Blanco White, who on his admission to the common room in 1815 described the college as 'one of the most distinguished bodies of the University',[24] remarked that the common room 'united a set of men, who, for talents and manners, were most desirable as friends and daily companions'.[25] Moreover, it was characterized by social and religious harmony as much as by intellectual brilliance, even if at least one newcomer from Christ Church in the late 1820s, George Anthony Denison, found it to be 'a curious place at that time' and its members, contrary to received wisdom, to be 'stiff, and starched, and afraid of one another'. His experience of coldness and distance belied the common room's acknowledged reputation for 'freedom of intercourse'.[26] Denison, who had social pretensions of his own and thus different expectations, clearly felt alienated from the earnest intellectual club-like atmosphere. If the ever mischievous Thomas Mozley in his dotage is to be believed, Denison wanted to refurbish the common room both socially and materially in the style of a fashionable West End club or drawing room.[27] For Denison, the Oriel common room, with its prominent teapot, 'was as dull a place socially as I can remember anywhere'.[28]

---

[22] H. P. Liddon, *Life of Edward Bouverie Pusey*, 4 vols. (London, 1894), i. 58. After his election in 1826, Hurrell Froude complained that in the common room the fellows were forever 'taking up each other's expressions and cavilling at the slightest inaccuracy of language'. *Remains of Richard Hurrell Froude* [ed. J. H. Newman and John Keble], 4 vols. (Derby, 1838–9), 177. On the Noetics see R. Brent, 'The Oriel Noetics', HUO vi. 72–6.

[23] The expressive phrase was used by the Oxford clerical annalist William Tuckwell. W. Tuckwell, *Reminiscences of Oxford* (London, 1900), 17.

[24] *Life of Joseph Blanco White*, ed. Thom, iii. 136.

[25] *Life of Joseph Blanco White*, ed. Thom, iii. 136.

[26] G. A. Denison, *Notes of my Life, 1805–1878* (Oxford, 1878), 50; J. Coombs, *George Anthony Denison: The Firebrand* (Oxford, 1984), 13. George Anthony Denison (1805–96) was a fellow of Oriel 1828–38 when he became vicar of Broadwindsor, Dorset. He was a college tutor from 1830 to 1836 and college treasurer 1836–8. He later became archdeacon of Taunton and a very prominent high churchman famous for being a protagonist in a eucharistic controversy which divided the Church of England in the mid-1850s. See ODNB s.n.

[27] According to the indiscreet recollection of Mozley, 'Denison's fastidiousness was often tried, sometimes severely. He did his best to make the society of the common room such as even a Samuel Wilberforce or a Lord Dudley could have walked into fresh from a West-End drawing room without offence to his taste': Mozley, *Reminiscences*, ii. 97. William Tuckwell was no less unflattering about Denison: 'The historian of the century, if he recalls Denison at all, will speak of him as the high-bred aristocrat, relic of a class extinct.' Tuckwell, *Reminiscences of Oxford*, 196. See also G. C. Richards, 'The Oriel Common Room in 1833', OR (January 1933), 238.

[28] Denison, *Notes of my Life*, 50.

Although, as the example of Denison shows, some were clearly impervious to the intellectual élan and opportunities which the common room provided, the ideal of harmony and consensus was relentlessly espoused. In fact, the dangers of promoting a religious party spirit was a regular Noetic refrain. In 1822, Whately devoted his Bampton Lectures to the subject.[29] Copleston was no less alive to the incipient danger, touching on the theme in his sermon preached before the college at the 500th anniversary commemoration in 1826. With almost prophetic insight as to what was to come (though at the time it was delivered with a backward glance to recent divisions between Calvinists and Arminians over free will and predestination, the seventeenth of the Thirty-Nine Articles[30]) Copleston warned that theological controversy could produce an 'excess of zeal which knows no bounds' and obscure one's primary religious duties.[31]

A similar emphasis on the inherent moral evils of party spirit would be evident in the writings of Thomas Arnold, elected fellow of Oriel in 1815, who would become, in 1828, Rugby School's most famous headmaster. Arnold, who would be part of the Noetic coterie for a season, remained a lifelong friend and correspondent of Whately and Hawkins.[32] He wrote feelingly, as early as 1833 when he was already being denounced 'in the University pulpit at Oxford...almost by name', of 'the reproach and suspicion of cold friendship and zealous enmity' which would always be the portion of those who strove to 'follow no party but Christ's'.[33] Above all, the Noetics stood against a narrow ecclesiasticism; 'fanaticism' was a term of regular reproach in their vocabulary. Theirs was an ideal which survived the vicissitudes of the *odium theologicum* that would divide Oriel in the 1830s and 1840s, and which Provost Hawkins boldly restated from the university pulpit in 1855 and again as late as 1871.[34] It was a stand which had been tested to destruction, in and out of Oriel, in the intervening decades.

---

[29] R. Whately, *On the Use and Abuse of Party-Feeling in Matters of Religion. Eight Sermons Preached before the University of Oxford in the Year MDCCCXXII* (Oxford, 1822).

[30] According to Whately, Copleston 'though not adopting, himself, the theory of the Calvinists or the Arminians, he was not for excluding either from the Church, or from its Ministry; nor did he speak (as some on each side are too apt to do) as if there were not at least something plausible to be urged by each'. R. Whately (ed.), *Remains of the late Edward Copleston, D.D. Bishop of Llandaff. With an Introduction containing some reminiscences of his life* (London, 1854), 83. Copleston had taken a moderate position on the Arminian–Calvinist controversy in his *Inquiry into the Doctrines of Necessity and Predestination* (London, 1821).

[31] E. Copleston, *A Sermon, preached before the members of Oriel College, upon the Commemoration Festival, held June 15, 1826, to celebrate the completion of five hundred years from the foundation of the College* (Oxford, 1826), 10.

[32] Educated at Corpus Christi College, Oxford, Arnold was only a fellow from 1815 to 1821, when he married, and never took rooms in Oriel, continuing to reside at Corpus.

[33] A. P. Stanley, *The Life and Correspondence of Thomas Arnold, D.D.*, 2 vols. (London, 1844), i. 295.

[34] E. Hawkins, *Christian Unity: A Sermon preached before the University of Oxford, on Quinquagesema Sunday, February 18, 1855* (Oxford, 1855); and *The Duty of weighing the*

Noetic influence was not narrowly restricted to the college alone or confined to matters of religion. However, their role as religious thinkers and prophets concerns us here. While individual writers varied their emphasis, the Noetics and especially Copleston are best understood as orthodox apologists for rational Christianity and Revelation in general, and the Church of England in particular, against heterodoxy, infidelity, Protestant dissent, and Romanism; and as 'free-thinking' or independent in their methodology and approach but not in their conclusions. Thomas Mozley famously characterized the Oriel Noetics as 'consumed by a morbid intellectual restlessness', only too ready 'to impose certain opinions and expressions when the opportunity offered itself', and seeming 'to be always demolishing, received traditions and institutions', so that 'even faithful and self-reliant men felt the ground shaking under them'.[35] However, their orthodoxy, not least that of Copleston, was never in doubt.[36] The truths of Christianity were defended and grounded on a clear philosophical basis. Significantly, Origen against Celsus was one of Copleston's favourite books, and he encouraged Hampden to produce a new English translation and edition of that ancient classic of Christian apologetic.[37] One of Copleston's Bosworth Lectures (popularly known as 'Bossies') on the Christian Church, delivered in Oriel chapel under the will of a college benefaction, espoused the '"high" theological creed of pre-tractarian days, with an insistence on the Church as a divinely appointed society, visible and universal, holding spiritual authority and governed by officers tracing descent from the Apostles in a long chain of historical succession'.[38]

Although not an unbiased witness, given his later tortured religious history, the Anglicized Spanish poet and journalist refugee from persecution, Joseph Blanco White,[39] who first entered Oriel in 1815 and in 1826 became

---

relative importance of questions, especially of religious questions. A Sermon preached before the University of Oxford, on the 29th June, 1871 (Oxford, 1871), esp. 12.

[35] Mozley, *Reminiscences*, i. 19–20.

[36] Copleston has been represented as combining 'something of the temper, though not the doctrinal conclusions, of the liberal rationalists of the previous century', W. R. Ward, *Victorian Oxford* (London, 1965), 17. This verdict does not quite do justice to the depth and texture of Copleston's orthodox Anglican churchmanship. In truth, his religious temper was probably closer to that of the early and mid-eighteenth-century Anglican apologists against deism and Socinianism. In 1814 he even described himself as a 'high churchman': W. J. Copleston, *Memoir of Edward Copleston, D.D. Bishop of Llandaff* (London, 1851), 47. Moreover, a rigid and old fashioned high churchman, John Hume Spry of Oriel, regarded Copleston as a friend: Spry to Bishop J. H. Hobart, 26 January 1824, *Posthumous Works of the late Right Reverend John Henry Hobart*, i. 291.

[37] E. Copleston to R. D. Hampden, n.d., H. Hampden (ed.), *Some Memorials of Renn Dickson Hampden, Bishop of Hereford* (London, 1871), 18.

[38] W. Tuckwell, *Pre-Tractarian Oxford: A Reminiscence of the Oriel 'Noetics'* (London, 1909), 'Copleston', 44.

[39] Joseph Blanco White (1775–1841) was born in Seville, ordained a priest in 1808, but abandoned first the priesthood and then Christianity. He settled in England in 1810 and became

an honorary member of the college and MA of Oxford at Copleston's instigation, long thereafter remaining under Whately's protection, later described his new-found friends as 'though orthodox enough to remain within the Church, were continually struggling against the mental barriers by which she protects her power'.[40] Blanco White owed his new-found standing in Oxford to his opposition to Catholic emancipation; he dedicated his anti-Catholic treatise, *Practical and Internal Evidence against Catholicism* (1826), to Copleston in recognition of 'the friendly intercourse with which you have honored me'.[41] Copleston, White intimated, had read most of the manuscript.[42] Moreover, the influences and interaction cut both ways. Whately gave a generously fulsome dedication of his own *Errors of Romanism* (1831) to Blanco White: 'I am indebted to you for such an insight into the peculiarities of the Church of Rome as I could never have gained from anyone who was not originally, or from anyone who still continued to be a member of that Church.'[43] Loyalty to his Noetic friends in Oriel common room for a time kept Blanco White's incipient heterodoxy in check, while his services to the anti-Catholic cause in the debates over emancipation and his anti-evangelical instincts earned him a certain grudging respect from Oxford's high church party. Blanco White was full of praise for Hawkins's sermon against Bulteel, delivered in Oriel chapel in 1831; he obsequiously acknowledged to Hawkins that his sermon would 'be a most useful manual to the undergraduate where they might constantly find the true principles of an essential part of the Christian doctrine, not usually stated in the clear light you have placed it. It would be the best and most convincing answer to the charge that the Church of England and especially the University have swerved from their scriptural professions of faith.'[44]

However, as we shall see, Blanco White was to become an acute embarrassment to the Noetics as the years passed: Whately and others would have cause to regret the extent of their connection with him. In particular, Hampden and Whately (whom Blanco White followed to Dublin on Whately's elevation to the archbishopric of Dublin in 1831) would later be damaged by association as the theological pendulum swung decisively against them in the 1830s. For Blanco White, always at the margins of Christian belief, it was his

---

a political journalist and protégé of Lord Holland before retiring to Oxford and Oriel. For the best study of Blanco White, see M. Murphy, *Blanco White: Self-Banished Spaniard* (London, 1989), esp. ch. 11: 'Dear Oriel'.

[40] Thom (ed.), *Life of Joseph Blanco White*, i. 206.

[41] J. Blanco White, *Practical and Internal Evidence against Catholicism, with occasional strictures on Mr Butler's 'Book of the Roman Catholic Church': in six letters, addressed to the impartial among the Roman Catholics of Great Britain and Ireland* (2nd edn., London, 1826), v.

[42] White, *Practical and Internal Evidence*, iv.

[43] R. Whately, *The Errors of Romanism traced to their Origin in Human Nature* (Oxford, 1831), vi.

[44] J. Blanco White to E. Hawkins, 27 February 1831, OCL, Oriel Letters, i. 96.

perception of his Noetic patrons as tolerant liberal churchmen which almost alone made Oxford congenial for him. He clearly had his own personal reasons for understating the orthodoxy for which the Noetics could rightly lay claim.[45]

Typical specimens of the Noetic genre of apologetic included Whately's one-time pupil Baden Powell's *Rational Religion Examined* (1826), which compared the Unitarian and 'Romish' religious systems as both equally irrational and unphilosophical;[46] John Davison's *Discourses on Prophecy* (1824);[47] and another of Whately's pupils Samuel Hinds's *History of the Rise and Early Progress of Christianity* (1828) and *Inquiry into the Proofs, Nature, and Extent of Inspiration and into the Authority of Scripture* (1831).[48] There were, however, strict limits to the freedom of religious enquiry championed by the Noetics. In his sermon of 1831, Hinds maintained that intellectual enquiry needed to be informed by religious knowledge and theological learning, arguing that intellectual scepticism was often the result of the vacuum created by a failure to exercise the intellect sufficiently on religious subjects, so as to match the attention readily given to the acquisition of purely secular knowledge.[49] Copleston later warned against

---

[45] Nonetheless, this perception needs to be qualified by Pietro Corsi's suggestion, on the evidence of Whately's marginal comments on a sermon of Blanco White's preached at St Mary's in 1827, that Blanco White's anti-dogmatism might have been confirmed or strengthened, not checked, by his Noetic friends: P. Corsi, *Science and Religion: Baden Powell and the Anglican Debate, 1800–1860* (Cambridge, 1988), 99.

[46] B. Powell, *Rational Religion Examined; or remarks on the pretences of Unitarianism; especially as compared with those systems which professedly discard Reason* (London, 1826). A mathematician and physicist, Baden Powell entered Oriel in 1815. Tutored by Whately, he became a fellow of the Royal Society in 1824, and was appointed Savilian Professor of Geometry in 1827. For a comprehensive study of Baden Powell's thought, emphasizing the Oriel context and connections, see Corsi, *Science and Religion*.

[47] John Davison (1777–1834) was a fellow of Oriel (1798–1818). He was a college tutor from 1810 until 1817, dean 1813–17, prebendary of St Paul's (1824) and Worcester (1825). See his *Remains and Occasional Publications of the late Rev. John Davison, B.D. formerly Fellow of Oriel College, Oxford. Author of 'Discourses on Prophecy'* (Oxford, 1840). According to Whately, Davison's stiff and difficult prose style hindered his literary influence. R. Whately to R. D. Hampden, 18 December 1834, OCA 'Hampden Controversy' Box i, no. 15a. On the other hand, the Tractarian Newman, while acknowledging his 'stiffness', regarded Davison as 'a man of the cast of Hooker and Butler' but that, owing to the constraints imposed by the limited religious horizons of pre-Tractarian Oxford, was 'confined pretty much to the contemplation of the first principles of Christian doctrine'. J. H. Newman, 'John Davison, Fellow of Oriel' [April 1840], *Essays: Critical and Historical*, 2 vols. (London, 1881), i. 376. In a later letter Newman wrote of Davison: 'He was our greatest light, more so than Whately, Arnold, Keble, Pusey, or Copleston', and that he had 'ever delighted in his writings—and don't know whether to be glad or sorry that he did not live into the Puseyite movement'. Newman to W. Walker, 27 February 1856, LDN xvii. 161.

[48] Hinds had been an undergraduate at Queen's, but he was privately tutored by Whately who made him vice-principal under himself of St Alban Hall in 1827. He went on to become bishop of Norwich (1849–57).

[49] S. Hinds, *An Inquiry into the Proofs, Nature, and Extent of Inspiration, and into the Authority of Scripture* (Oxford, 1831), 4–5.

'that false liberality in religious matters, which treats the truths of revelation as if they were things of indifference or of a conventional nature, or at best, matters of speculation merely, to be received or rejected according to our own pleasure, like the various hypotheses and theories about which men of leisure may dispute, but not binding upon the conscience, or of any real moment to an enlarged and enlightened mind'.[50]

While Richard Whately can be regarded as the *éminence grise* among the Oriel Noetics[51] and a larger than life and 'bear-like' presence[52] capable of overawing the rest of the Oriel common room,[53] in many ways their inspiration and mouthpiece was Copleston himself. Copleston as tutor acted as the formative influence on the young Whately when he arrived at Oriel in 1805. One of Whately's earliest pieces of religious apologetic, his *Historic Doubts Relative to Napoleon Buonaparte* (1819), a satirical parody of the philosophical principles of David Hume as displayed in Hume's *Essay on Miracles*, owed its inspiration and even final execution to Copleston's guiding hand. As Whately later recalled: 'I remember conversing with him on the subject of an article in the "Edinburgh Review", eulogizing Hume's "Essay on Miracles"; and we were observing to one another how easy it would be, on Hume's principles, to throw doubt on the history of the wonderful events that had recently occurred in Europe. I put down on paper the substance of our conversation, and showed it to him: when he told me he had just been thinking of doing the very thing himself.'[54]

It was Copleston who initially suggested that Whately should satirize Hume's doctrine of evidence by first giving a plausible account of Hume's position but then rendering it ridiculous: 'by extending, restating, and generalizing the position until the absurdity of its implications when taken together becomes devastatingly apparent'.[55] Whately dedicated his Bampton Lectures (1822) and *Elements of Logic* (1826) to Copleston, who became

---

[50] E. Copleston, 'False Liberality', *False Liberality, and the Power of the Keys. Two Sermons preached 15 November 1840, at St Paul's Church, Newport, on the Opening of an enlarged Popish chapel in that Town* (London, 1841), 9.

[51] Having entered Oriel in 1805 and won the English Essay Prize in 1810, Whately was elected a fellow in 1811, and in 1825 became principal of St Alban Hall. He became archbishop of Dublin in 1831, dying in office in 1863.

[52] Whately was known as the 'White Bear' from 'his blunt, gruff manner, combining with a habit which he had of attiring himself in a white coat and a white hat, and being usually attended by a white dog': T. Hamilton, 'Archbishop Whately', *New Biographical Series*, no. 8 (London, 1891), 3.

[53] According to Samuel Wilberforce, bishop of Oxford 1845–69, who matriculated at Oriel in 1823, Whately had a 'powerful and somewhat rude intellect': S. Wilberforce, 'Dr Newman's Apologia', *Essays contributed to the 'Quarterly Review' by Samuel Wilberforce, D.D.*, 2 vols. (London, 1874), i. 343.

[54] Whately (ed.), *Remains of the Late Edward Copleston*, 83–4.

[55] R. Whately, *Historic Doubts relative to Napoleon Buonaparte* [1819]. *Edited & with a Critical Introduction and Notes by Ralph E. Pomeroy* (London, 1985), xxix.

godfather to Whately's daughter. Whately later made clear that he was indebted to Copleston not only for his role in this youthful work, but for his other publications in his Oxford years, and even many works subsequently published. Such publications, Whately explained, 'may be regarded as so far Bishop Copleston's, that though he is not responsible for any part of them—since I always decided according to my own conviction—they were submitted, wholly or in great part, to him before publication, and are indebted to him for any important suggestions and corrections'.[56] If a latitudinarian or even Erastian tendency can be found within the ranks of the Noetics, it was well exemplified in the writings of Thomas Arnold. Arnold insisted on the 'essential character of Christ's Church' not being confined within 'the peculiarities of any one particular denomination',[57] and rejected a 'false distinction' between the secular and the spiritual, laity and clergy.[58] For Arnold, the Church had no independent governing authority. However, this theological line was not typical of Oriel Noeticism.

Noetic theologizing was certainly capable of a 'high church' tendency, and tended to be anti-evangelical because of a perception of the 'unreasonableness' or irrationality of the evangelical system and even for its apparent undervaluing of the efficacy of purely sacramental grace. A few examples can suffice. In his *Remarks on Baptismal Regeneration* (1816), John Davison obliquely touched on a theme that later would be taken much further by Tractarian controversialists: that in exposing the 'excesses' of 'Romanist' notions of the sacraments, the Reformers may have 'driven the reform into the opposite extreme, that of stripping the two sacraments, that really were real, too much of their spiritual nature'.[59] One of Whately's notable publications, *Letters of an Episcopalian* (1826), can be construed no less in support of a 'high church' position. The evidence of Copleston's handiwork in this work is more problematic than in other writings of Whately. This was partly because the pamphlet's actual authorship, though initially ascribed to Whately,[60] later came to be doubted not only because its original anonymity

---

[56] Whately (ed.), *Remains of the Late Edward Copleston*, 83.

[57] T. Arnold, *Fragments on Church and State: written in 1827–1840; and published as appendices to the First Edition of the 'Fragment on the Church'* (London, 1845), 60.

[58] T. Arnold, *Fragment on the Church* (London, 1844), 19.

[59] J. Davison, 'Remarks on Baptismal Regeneration: originally published in the Quarterly Review for July 1816', *Remains and Occasional Publications of the Late Rev John Davison*, 301.

[60] On its publication, Newman was one of the few to doubt Whately's authorship, but as Newman later recorded: 'I found the belief of Oxford in the affirmative to be too strong for me; rightly or wrongly I yielded to the general voice; and I never heard, then or since, of any disclaimer on the part of Dr Whately.' J. H. Newman, *Apologia pro vita sua* (1st edn., London, 1864), 70. According to William Tuckwell, it was a work which Whately 'neither owned nor disclaimed, but which nobody doubted to be his'. Tuckwell, *Pre-Tractarian Oxford: A Reminiscence of the Oriel 'Noetics'*, 'Whately', 67. Corsi concludes that 'a careful internal analysis of the text confirms that Whately was the author of the Episcopalian pamphlet'. Corsi, *Science and Religion*, 87.

had been maintained but because its views—which supported a 'high church' doctrine of the Church's divine origin and authority as akin to that of the Jewish theocracy[61] and of its essential independence from the state—did not seem at all to accord with later perceptions of Whately's 'low church' theology.[62] In this work, Whately challenged latitudinarian or 'low church' notions of the Church's constitution as merely a voluntary organization of believers, lamenting the excesses of the Protestant reaction against the pretensions of 'the Romish hierarchy' as evidence of the frailty of human nature in falling 'from one extreme into another'. With a side-swipe against Protestant dissenters and 'irregular' Anglican evangelicals, Whately argued that '"the Church" (that is, the Catholic or Universal Church), certainly is not, as some seem to regard it, merely a collective name for all who happen to agree in certain opinions, like the names of "Cartesian" or "Newtonian", but is a society, or, body-corporate (if I may use such an expression), of divine institution'.[63] On the other hand, Whately did not restrict his definition of the Church to bodies comprising an episcopal system of church government as a strict high churchman might have done. Moreover, there were limits to church authority, as presented by Whately: the Church could not impose articles of belief not warranted by Scripture, though it could regulate rites and ceremonies left undetermined by Holy Writ.[64] To his later dismay, however, Whately's reflections on the limitations of a church establishment due to the restrictions consequent upon the state connection,[65] and his essentially anti-Erastian conception of church policy and cautious advocacy of disestablishment without dis-endowment, would strike a chord with the Tractarians in the following years.[66]

The most explicit trope of high church theological principle in Noetic apologetic was to be found in a remarkable sermon on Tradition preached by

---

[61] [R. Whately], *Letters on the Church. By an Episcopalian* (London, 1826), 60.
[62] Many decades later, Newman even had to remind Hawkins (when he had raised a doubt as to Whately's authorship) that 'the general impression in Oxford was that the book was Whately's', and that it was his own 'uninterrupted memory since 1826' that 'you at that date led me to ascribe them to Whately—that you then thought them his yourself—that Dornford thought you thought so': Newman to Hawkins, 24 March 1869, OCA, Hawkins Papers, Letter Book, iii. 376. Newman's reference was to Joseph Dornford (1794–1868), fellow of Oriel from 1819 and tutor from 1831. Thomas Mozley later maintained that Whately always had more respect for 'the old High Church, for it was learned and cultivated' than he had for evangelicalism, because 'it could appeal to something more than those incommunicable sensations which it is impossible to reason upon'. Mozley, *Reminiscences*, i. 23.
[63] [Whately], *Letters on the Church*, 1.
[64] [Whately], *Letters on the Church*, 63.
[65] Whately used the analogy of the human body to describe the relation between the Church and its establishment, arguing that the Church's establishment condition rendered it 'somewhat feeble in muscle'. *Letters on the Church*, 164.
[66] On this issue, see also Y. Brilioth, *The Anglican Revival: Studies in the Oxford Movement* (London, 1925), 84.

Edward Hawkins in St Mary's in 1818.[67] Hawkins argued that in the early Church a system of oral instruction was traditionally transmitted which, though verified by Scripture and thus in itself unauthoritative, had been indispensable for supplying the fullness of revelation that was not otherwise communicable in a systematic form. While accepting that Hawkins's position was quite distinct from a Roman Catholic advocacy of tradition as in itself authoritative, low church critics assailed 'this new pretension of tradition' for appearing to derogate from the sufficiency of Holy Scripture.[68] Significantly, much to the later embarrassment of Hawkins himself and of his Noetic allies, his sermon would serve as an inspiration for the Tractarians, and the published version made 'a most serious impression' on Newman in particular.[69] Whately cited it no less approvingly in his *Letters*.[70] He adopted Hawkins's argument 'that the New Testament Scriptures are evidently not calculated, nor could have been intended, to convey to hearers, the elements of the Christian faith, all the books of which it consists having been written for the use of Christian converts, and that therefore it must have been the intention of Jesus Christ that the Church He established should have the office of drawing out and settling its order, with a view to instruction in the truths of the Gospel, referring to the inspired writers for the proofs of every thing they advanced'.[71] Whately immediately distanced this position from 'the error of the Romanist' which advanced 'their claim of authority for their tradition, independent of Scripture'.[72] Nonetheless, in private correspondence with Hawkins, in an argument directed against the individualism inherent in the evangelical way of salvation, Whately argued 'that individual Christians have no life in them unless they continue branches of the true Vine as members of the Body of Christ'. He emphasized that the Church was 'the appointed channel through which grace is conveyed'.[73]

Another Noetic, John Davison, while not critical of Hawkins, was careful to argue that it was only prior to the rise of the written Scripture that tradition had necessarily had an authority as the record of faith. Thereafter, tradition only had a secondary use as evidence as to whether the ancient Church had the faith of particular doctrines later enshrined in Scripture.[74]

---

[67] E. Hawkins, *Dissertation upon the Use and Importance of Unauthoritative Tradition* (Oxford, 1819).
[68] G. Miller, *An Historical View of the Plea of Tradition: as maintained in the Church of Rome; with strictures on 'A Discourse upon the use and importance of Unauthoritative Tradition'* (London, 1826), 75, 78–9.
[69] Newman, *Apologia pro vita sua*, 66.
[70] [Whately], *Letters on the Church*, 67.
[71] [Whately], *Letters on the Church*, 67–8.
[72] [Whately], *Letters on the Church*, 68.
[73] Whately to Hawkins, 3 September 1830, OCA Hawkins Papers, Letter Book, ii. 179.
[74] J. Davison, 'An Inquiry into the Origin and Intent of Primitive Sacrifice, and the Scripture Evidence respecting it' [1825], *Remains and Occasional Publications*, 139–40.

On the other hand, Hawkins's exposition of tradition was in line with a high church tradition of teaching on the subject[75] and was later plausibly claimed by Tractarians in support of their own position.[76] By the mid-1830s, with Whately and Thomas Arnold both locked in theological combat with Newman and his Oriel disciples, Oxford's theological climate had altered beyond recognition. With the benefit of a hindsight shaped by the rise of the Tractarians, they both privately blamed Hawkins for having 'contributed to their mischief by his unhappy sermon on Tradition'.[77] Hawkins accepted the criticism and determined upon revising his sermon so as to rebut what he came to regard as unfair inferences being drawn from it.[78]

The prominent Noetic Renn Dickson Hampden was no less engaged in philosophical apologetic for Christian orthodoxy.[79] His *Essay on the Philosophical Evidence of Christianity* (1827), which elucidated Bishop Butler's analogical arguments for Christianity, was to prove highly influential, and seems to have even been intended as a companion to and modernization of Butler's *Analogy of Religion* (1736). At the root of Hampden's apologetic lay a determination to highlight the difference between revealed truth and the theological language in which it was clothed, a view which Hampden shared with Thomas Arnold.[80] Hampden gave an uncontentious spiritual expression of this theological position in his *Parochial Sermons* (1828) in which he insisted on the unity of Christian faith and Christian holiness behind the obscuring layers of speculative theology and inappropriate philosophical categorization.[81] Hampden's growing interest in scholastic theology stemmed from a perception that scholasticism had been a source of a later confusion between the 'facts' of Revelation and the theories of philosophical theology. Although he could claim the sanction of Bishop Butler, Hampden's later working out of the practical implications of this approach in his Bampton Lectures, *The Scholastic Philosophy considered in its relation to Christian Theology* (1832), was to render him notorious as a theological *bête noire* of the Oriel Tractarians, Newman especially. Hampden maintained, like Hinds in his *History of the Rise and Early Progress of Christianity*, that metaphysical speculations and technical language had obscured the word of Scripture. One might draw the implication that creeds and articles were symbols of scriptural truth rather than enjoying the authority of revelation.

---

[75] See J.-L. Quantin, *The Church of England Christian Antiquity: The Construction of a Confessional Identity in the 17th Century* (Oxford, 2009), esp. ch. 6: 'The Case for Tradition', 327–95.
[76] Keble to Hawkins, 26 July 1840, OCL, Hawkins Papers, Letter Book, viii. 762.
[77] Arnold to Whately, 4 May 1836, OCL, Hawkins Papers, Letter Book, ii. 34.
[78] Hawkins to Whately, 11 September 1836, OCL, Hawkins Papers, Letter Book, ii. 218.
[79] See *Some Memorials of Renn Dickson Hampden*, 16–18.
[80] Arnold to Hampden, 17 May 1835, OCL, 'Hampden Controversy' Letter Book.
[81] *Some Memorials of Renn Dickson Hampden*, 20.

Yet, as we shall see, there was to be a considerable time-lag before Newman and his friends made their outraged response to Hampden's Bampton Lectures. That reaction would have to wait for the religious battle-lines in Oriel to emerge more clearly and can be explained by other factors, not only theological. It is indicative of the greater degree of theological consensus in Oxford in the 1820s that Hampden should have been for a time (1825–6) editor of the high church journal *The Christian Remembrancer*, in which such high church doctrines as baptismal regeneration and priestly absolution were expounded.[82] It has even been claimed that he 'served as a pillar of orthodoxy in church journalism'.[83] Like Baden Powell, Hampden had close connections with the then influential 'Hackney Phalanx' group of high churchmen who had first established the journal in 1819, and was curate to the father figure of the 'Phalanx', Henry Handley Norris (1771–1850), at Hackney parish church.[84]

It was into this intellectually vibrant, Noetic-dominated society that the future leader of the Oxford Movement, the young John Henry Newman, entered as a fellow on 12 April 1822, proudly proclaiming to his mother that he had become 'a member of "the School of Speculative Philosophy in England" to use the words of the Edinburgh Review'.[85] Newman's religious and intellectual development from youthful evangelicalism on a long spiritual journey into the Roman Catholic Church in 1845 via high church Anglicanism was to owe much to Oriel and, in particular, to his mentors among its Noetic fellows, Whately and Hawkins. Intellectually and psychologically, they were the making of him. They found Newman to be shy and reserved, with a powerful sense of 'spiritual solitariness' shaped partly by his then Calvinistic religious beliefs, when he entered the college. They drew him out and formed him for the future.

Newman's Oriel Noetic mentors gradually weaned him away from the moderate Calvinistic evangelicalism which he had embraced under the earlier tutelage of Walter Mayers and Thomas Scott of Aston Sandford. As he recorded in his *Apologia*, from the moment when he entered Oriel in 1822: 'I came under very different influences from those to which I had been hitherto subjected.'[86] The intellectual and theological as well as personal

---

[82] [H. W. Wilberforce], 'Dr Hampden and Anglicanism', *Dublin Review*, 17/33 (July 1871), 102.

[83] Ward, *Victorian Oxford*, 93.

[84] Corsi, *Religion and Science*, 9–20; R. Brent, *Liberal Anglican Politics: Whiggery, Religion and Reform* (Oxford, 1987), 148–9. For the 'Hackney Phalanx' and its influence, see P. B. Nockles, *The Oxford Movement in Context: Anglican High Churchmanship 1760–1857* (Cambridge, 1994); C. Dewey, *The Passing of Barchester: A Real Life Version of Trollope* (London, 1991), ch. 8.

[85] J. H. Newman to Mrs Newman, 16 April 1822, LDN i. 135. In the same letter, Newman observed: 'I have, whenever I wish, the advice and direction of the first men in Oxford.'

[86] Newman, *Apologia*, 64.

influence of Hawkins was immediate and profound, and would give a bitter taste to the later breach when it eventually came. In 1824 Newman became curate of St Clement's, across Magdalen Bridge, while Hawkins had become vicar of St Mary's in 1823. During the summers of 1824 and 1825 they were often the only two to dine in Hall, spending much time together; time spent in theological discussion. Given the history of their later relations, it was to be ironic, as Mozley noted, that 'from the first he loved and admired the man with whom eventually he lived most in collision, Edward Hawkins'.[87]

In his *Apologia*, Newman recorded that it was Hawkins 'who taught me to anticipate that, before many years were over, there would be an attack made upon the books and canon of Scripture'.[88] Newman proceeded to highlight the way in which his reading of the printed version of Hawkins's famous sermon on tradition and its core argument that the sacred text of Scripture was never intended to teach doctrine had a long-term influence on him in the direction of Catholicism, even though, as Newman admitted, Hawkins did 'not go one step, I think, beyond the high Anglican doctrine, nay he does not reach it'. Hawkins's view that the truths of Christianity were to be learned from the Church's formularies (her creeds and catechism), which Newman was convinced Whately held too, dealt a fatal blow to the principle on which the evangelical-dominated Bible Society was founded. It was not long before Newman withdrew from membership of its Oxford branch, marking an early step in his gradual retreat from evangelicalism.[89] It was a retreat prompted by Newman's reaction against the excesses of the type of radical evangelicalism in Oxford associated with Henry Bulteel, and also by Newman's personal conflict with the views of his own brother Charles. But it was aided by Oriel influences, such as Hawkins's criticism of a draft of an early sermon to be preached at St Clement's, in which Newman in quasi-Calvinistic fashion had sharply separated the 'sheep' from the 'goats', saints from sinners. Hawkins's critique helped implant in Newman's mind the importance of the doctrine of baptismal regeneration, whereby rebirth or renovation was conferred by the rite itself on the infant and was not necessarily predicated on a later conversion or adult will to convert. The influence of another Oriel fellow, William James (1787–1861), in imparting to Newman the doctrine of an apostolical succession of bishops, would prove to be another milestone in his evolution towards the uncompromising high churchmanship of the future Oxford Movement.[90] He also owed much to another contemporary Oriel fellow, the high churchman Samuel Rickards,

---

[87] Mozley, *Reminiscences of Oriel College and the Oxford Movement*, i. 29.
[88] Newman, *Apologia*, 65.
[89] Newman, *Apologia*, 66.
[90] Newman, *Apologia*, 67. James, who became vicar of Cobham, Surrey, was a proponent of high church views of the sacraments in sermons preached before the university in the 1820s. See W. James, *The Benefit and Necessity of the Christian Sacraments, and the Perpetual Obligations*

continuing to correspond with him long after Rickards had taken up the Oriel living of Stowlangtoft, Suffolk.[91] Moreover, Blanco White, for all his later heterodoxy (he was already moving in the direction of unitarianism while at Oriel), was not only on friendly terms with Newman as a kindred spirit with a shared love of music and playing the violin, but he did much to educate Newman, Froude, and Henry Wilberforce in Roman Catholic liturgical lore, and in the Breviary; an education which Newman would put to good use as the Oxford Movement evolved.[92]

The impact of Whately's *Letters of an Episcopalian* on the impressionable Newman—in being the first to teach him 'the existence of the Church'[93]—was another step along that path. However, Whately's greatest influence on Newman was his training him in the weapons of disputation, weapons which he would later turn to such brilliant use against the very theological liberalism with which Whately's name came to be associated. Newman himself recognized as much. As he explained to his mentor in a revealing letter: 'Much as I owe to Oriel, in the way of mental improvement, to none, as I think, do I owe so much as to you. I know who it was that first gave me heart to look about me after my election, and taught me to think correctly, and (strange office for an instructor) to rely upon myself.'[94] In short, Whately was 'the first person who opened my mind...gave it ideas and principles to cogitate upon'.[95] Whately used Newman, as he did others, as an intellectual anvil on which he thrashed out his own ideas.[96] The intellectual closeness of the relationship ripened during their period of greatest intimacy between 1825 and 1828 when Newman was Whately's vice-principal at St Alban Hall, a hall whose hitherto low academic standing earned it the nickname 'Botany Bay'. Newman worked closely with Whately to overturn this reputation. Their close relationship was also illustrated by the assistance which the young Newman provided to his mentor's influential *Elements of Logic*, first published in 1827, and which Whately fulsomely recognized in his preface.[97] Newman was almost embarrassed by the extravagance of

---

of the Moral Law...*considered in Four Sermons, Preached before the University of Oxford* (London, 1830).

[91] See *A Selection from the Sermons of the late Rev Samuel Rickards, MA Rector of Stowlangtoft, and formerly Fellow of Oriel College, Oxford* (London, 1866).

[92] Tuckwell, *Pre-Tractarian Oxford*, 239.

[93] Newman also claimed that it was Whately who fixed 'in him those anti-Erastian views of Church polity, which were one of the most prominent features of the Tractarian movement', *Apologia*, 69.

[94] Newman to Whately, 14 November 1826, LDN i. 307.

[95] Newman to W. Monsell, 10 October 1852, LDN xv. 176.

[96] H. Tristram (ed.), *John Henry Newman: Autobiographical Writings* (London, 1956), 67.

[97] Whately singled out for special mention, 'the Rev. J. Newman, Fellow of Oriel College, who actually composed a considerable portion of the work as it now stands, from manuscripts not designed for publication, and who is the original author of several'. R. Whately, *Elements of*

Whately's published notice of him in a way which bore the seed of their future painful parting of the ways. When he examined many years later their correspondence with each other at this formative time, Newman alighted on the prophetic significance of the phrase in the letter above, 'to rely upon myself'.[98]

A key moment in Newman's dawning self-knowledge and new-found sense of self-reliance, associated with a feeling of alienation from his Noetic friends, was prompted by the critical reaction to a sermon which he preached in Oriel chapel at Easter 1827. Newman aimed to explain the ante-Nicene doctrine of the Trinity but laid himself open to charges of systematizing beyond Scripture, if not of rationalizing: even Whately criticized his former pupil of Arianizing. Newman himself came to regret the sermon as 'a specimen of a certain disdain for antiquity which had been growing on me now for several years'.[99] He now drew back from the brink and struck out on a new course. For in truth, as Whately himself had prophetically warned Newman, his mentor had become 'dangerous' to know and lean upon.[100] Other crucial formative influences within Oriel, which had for some time been competing for Newman's attention, now pulled him in a very different direction from that previously set by his Noetic mentors. As Newman made clear in his *Apologia*, it was two other Oriel figures who stood outside the Noetic camp, John Keble (1792–1866) and Richard Hurrell Froude (1803–36), who helped rescue him from the proud liberal intellectualism to which he felt he was in danger of succumbing under Noetic influence.[101] Newman's contact with another young Oriel fellow, Edward Bouverie Pusey (1800–82), later one of the leading lights in the Oxford Movement, also left its mark. They each represented a new and very different school in the college from that of the hitherto dominant Noetics. It is in this emerging school, as much as in the Noetics, that Oriel's reputation as the cradle of the future Oxford Movement rests.

While the origin of the Oxford Movement was undoubtedly underpinned by the renewal of the study of logic and rhetoric through Whately's influence in Oriel, there was something lacking. Oriel was the home of incessant but informal criticism and enquiry but, as Pusey's biographer Liddon observed,

---

Logic. Comprising the substance of the article in the Encyclopaedia Metropolitana with additions, etc. (London, 1827), vi–vii.

[98] J. H. Newman, [Memorandum] 10 November 1860, LDN i. 307.

[99] Newman, *Apologia*, 72–3.

[100] 'I am not sure you are wise in your ambition to be *known* as a friend of mine: it is likely, as far as it has any effect, to have a dangerous effect; as I am not now reckoned a safe man, and my reputation, I warn you, is not at all likely to improve.' Whately to Newman, 20 November 1826, LDN i. 303.

[101] Newman conceded that he had begun 'to prefer intellectual excellence to moral'. Newman, *Apologia*, 14.

this emphasis had the danger of making individual capacities or accomplishments an absolute rule of excellence.[102] In a prescient phrase of one of Newman's favourite Oriel pupils, Samuel Francis Wood, Whately's writings and teaching had 'sharpened and disciplined the intellect' but they had done so 'without giving it matter to feed upon'.[103] John Keble, his pupil Hurrell Froude, and eventually Newman himself would fill this lacuna and 'speak to' their generation in a way which struck a deep religious chord. On the other hand, the influence of Pusey, at this time still somewhat liberal in his churchmanship and away in Germany from 1826 to 1828 and thereafter based at Christ Church as Regius Professor of Hebrew, was more indirect and slower in coming to fruition. After Pusey became a fellow in 1823, he and Newman enjoyed an intellectual and emotional companionship, conversing on religious topics on regular walks together, Pusey even on one occasion making a form of religious confession to Newman.[104] While awed by Pusey's piety, Newman at first worried that it did not conform to his own evangelical ideal, confiding to his journal the comment: 'That Pusey is Thine, O Lord, how can I doubt?... Yet I fear he is prejudiced against Thy children.'[105] Shy and retiring even by Newman's early standards as well as otherworldly, Pusey was never an active player in the intellectual jousting that characterized the Oriel common room, though he was not unmarked by the mental thoroughness and exactness of the Noetics. Henry Woodgate, an undergraduate and later fellow of St John's, was another lifelong friend whom Newman first got to know in the mid-1820s, and who, as a regular visitor to Oriel, became, like Newman, one of Whately's 'anvils'.[106]

John Keble was the first name which Newman had heard spoken of with reverence, not merely admiration, when he had initially come up to Oxford. An undergraduate and fellow at Corpus Christi from 1806 to 1811, Keble had then become a fellow of Oriel. From 1818 to 1823 his influence as a college tutor on an impressionable group of pupils which included Froude (who came up in 1821 and took a double second in 1824), and Robert Wilberforce, both of Oriel, and Isaac Williams of Trinity, was to be profound: all three were invited by Keble to the first of a series of reading parties at his curacy at Southrop during the long vacation of 1823. This reading party might be regarded as the germ of the future Tractarian circle. The group, under Keble's tutelage, would lay the religious and moral, as distinct from

---

[102] H. P. Liddon, 'Oriel Society', *Life of Edward Bouverie Pusey*, 4 vols. (4th edn., London, 1894), i. 59.
[103] [S. F. Wood], 'Revival of Primitive Doctrine [1840]', Pereiro, *Ethos and the Oxford Movement*, appendix II, 253.
[104] Newman, *Autobiographical Writings*, 76.
[105] Newman, *Autobiographical Writings*, 191.
[106] S. Gilley, *Newman and his Age* (London, 1990), 55.

ILLUSTRATION 10.1 John Keble (1792–1866), fellow 1811–35

Oriel College, after George Richmond, 1863

the purely intellectual, foundations of what was to become the Oxford Movement.

Having returned to his father's parish of Fairford and the curacy of Southrop in 1823, Keble was no longer resident during Newman's formative years in the college. Unlike Newman, Keble found the atmosphere of Oriel common room uncongenial and in sermons and personal influence set his face against its intellectualism: in the words of Keble's pupil Isaac Williams, 'the Keble school' in 'opposition to the Oriel or Whatleian, set ethos above intellect'.[107] Williams himself later described how his own sermons, under Keble's influence and in contradiction of 'the intellectual Oriel school', were 'especially directed against the pride of intellect and the dangers of theory and mere knowledge in religion'.[108] Keble's deep sense of pastoral calling was

---

[107] *Autobiography of Isaac Williams*, 46.
[108] *Autobiography of Isaac Williams*, 45–6. According to an acute observer and leading Oriel son of the Oxford Movement, Keble: 'was a man who, with a very vigorous and keen intellect, capable of making him a formidable disputant if he had been so minded, may be said not to have cared for his intellect...Goodness was to him the one object of desire and reverence'. R. W. Church, 'Coleridge's Memoir of Keble' [*Saturday Review*, 20 March 1869], *Occasional*

such that he had only undertaken the tutorial office in Oriel and among private pupils 'as a species of pastoral care', otherwise questioning whether 'a clergyman ought to leave a cure of souls for it'.[109] Keble acted upon his conviction that the search for truth was inseparable from the pursuit of moral integrity, if not holiness. Lack of moral rectitude or a bad ethos biased the mind towards religious error and intellectual pride. On the other hand, moral qualities and the assistance of the Holy Spirit were more important than intellectual powers in discerning religious truth.[110] In fact, the virtuous had a predisposition towards discerning religious truth.[111] The role of a good tutor thus was even more about imparting moral and religious precepts and example than in inculcating 'head' knowledge and intellectual or logical proficiency. Keble himself had a vigorous and keen intellect but as it was later said of him by one who got to know him well, 'he used it at need, but he distrusted and undervalued it as an object and help. Goodness was to him the one object of desire and reverence.'[112]

Keble based his tutorial and catechetical ideal upon his understanding of Aristotle's *Nicomachean Ethics*: a text that was enshrined in the Oxford syllabus which Keble utilized in Oriel and during the reading parties at Southrop.[113] Keble also drew on Bishop Butler in a very different way from that of Hampden. He reapplied the ideas of analogy and probability which Bishop Butler had used in his defence of Christianity against deism, unbelief, and critics of Revelation into new and uncharted territory—in the defence of orthodoxy against heresy and as a guide to deciding upon the rival claims of religious denominations and even church parties. Keble's *Christian Year* (1827), a devotional classic of poetry that would influence generations, signalled the rise of a religious temper and ethos that stood apart from both the dominant Noeticism within Oriel and the popular evangelicalism without. Keble was an especial harbinger and foreshadower of what would become characteristic Oxford Movement teaching: he stood for the principles of reverence for sacred things, the ancient doctrine of reserve in communicating religious knowledge, as well as personal self-effacement

---

Papers, 2 vols. (London, 1897), ii. 299. According to the same observer, although Keble was repelled by Whately's 'boldness and independent thought' and 'self-sufficiency and intellectual display', even Keble was affected by Whately's influence 'of which he showed the traces to the last'. Church, *Occasional Papers*, ii. 298.

[109] J. Keble to J. T. Coleridge, 29 January 1818, *A Memoir of the Rev. John Keble, M.A. Late Vicar of Hursley. By the Right Hon. Sir J.T. Coleridge, D.C.L.* (3rd edn., London, 1870), 73.

[110] J. Keble, 'Favour Shown to Implicit Faith' (1822), *Sermons Academical and Occasional* (Oxford, 1847), 4.

[111] Keble, 'Implicit Faith Reconciled with Free Enquiry' (1823), *Sermons Academical and Occasional*, 44–5.

[112] Church, *Occasional Papers*, 299.

[113] *Autobiography of Isaac Williams*, 21.

and humility.[114] He rejected both the dialectical showiness of Noeticism and the over-familiarity in references to sacred things characteristic of the evangelical school. In *The Christian Year*, Keble became the siren voice of a new 'music' within the Church of England and Oxford. Orthodoxy had become poetical, while no longer could 'serious religion' be identified exclusively with evangelicalism.

For Newman, the religious truths learned from Keble's writings were similar to those which he had already absorbed from reading Bishop Butler—he had begun to read the *Analogy of Religion* in June 1825, and identified with Butler's arguments against unbelief, that God communicated in mysterious ways, and used the model of working through Nature. His debt to Butler's famous Rolls Chapel sermons on conscience found eloquent expression in one of Newman's most impressive university sermons, delivered in April 1830, 'The Influence of Natural and Revealed Religion Respectively', in which Newman argued that while the ability to discriminate between right and wrong actions was open to all, Christian and heathen alike, moral and religious truth in their fullness could only be communicated by 'a personal presence'.[115] Newman later reflected that he further recast this Butlerian approach 'in the creative mind of my new master', John Keble, namely 'the Sacramental system; that is, the doctrine that material phenomena are both the types and instruments of real things unseen'; and that it was not merely probability that made one intellectually certain but that it was 'faith and love which it give to probability a force which it has not in itself'.[116] Newman was to owe still more to Keble's combative favourite pupil Hurrell Froude.

It was Keble's friendship with, and formative influence upon, his pupil Froude that was to be crucial in the slow genesis of religious temper and ideals that would emerge in the Oxford Movement. Here was a young man who soon became infused with notions entirely antipathetic to the characteristic Noetic nostrums and who was prepared to challenge them and their holders: as Thomas Mozley observed, 'Woe to anyone who dropped in his hearing such phrases as the dark ages, superstition, bigotry, right of private judgment, enlightenment, march of mind or progress.'[117] According to Isaac Williams,

---

[114] For a study of the Tractarian understanding of the *disciplina arcanae* practised in the early Church and doctrine of reserve, see P. Selby, *The Principle of Reserve in the Writings of John Henry Cardinal Newman* (Oxford, 1975).

[115] Gilley, *Newman and his Age*, 83.

[116] Newman, *Apologia*, 77–9. Newman acknowledged Keble's overarching influence upon him just a month after his conversion: 'To you I owe it, humanly speaking, that I am what and where I am. Others have helped me in various ways, but no one can I name but you, who has had any part in setting my face in that special direction which has led me to my present inestimable gain', Newman to Keble, 14 November 1845, LDN xi. 34. Newman recalled that when he was nearly dead with fever in Sicily in May 1833 'I compared myself to Keble, and felt that I was merely developing his, not my, convictions': Newman, *Autobiographical Writings*, 125.

[117] Mozley, *Reminiscences*, i. 226.

while Froude was 'naturally inclined to speculation' and if left to nature might have felt at home in the 'Oriel or Whatleian' school, he was 'himself entirely of the Keble school', absorbing the concept of ethos from Keble and further refining it so as to postulate an ever closer correlation between right faith and moral probity, orthodoxy and sound ethos and character.[118] Troubled for a time over the damnatory clauses in the Athanasian Creed insofar as they seemed to render opinions in themselves the object of divine wrath, Froude's unease was resolved by his conclusion that the condemned opinions must involve something moral for which man, according to the free will granted him, ought to be responsible.[119] Habitual immoral behaviour and practice ultimately blinded man to religious truth and reality.

Froude, however, was no mere passive legatee of Keble's religious influence. He, like Robert Wilberforce, was elected a fellow of Oriel in 1826, and thereafter increasingly became a source of direct religious influence on others, both undergraduates and other fellows. Like his mentor Keble, he regarded the tutorial office as much as a medium of pastoral and religious supervision as of academic instruction. Newman, who also became a tutor in 1826, had himself come under Froude's influence by then, but he was not alone. Newman insisted that Froude in turn reacted upon Keble himself as well as having been formed by him.[120]

Like Isaac Williams and the Keble family group in Gloucestershire, Froude at first associated Newman with Whately and the Noetic circle.[121] However, as Whately's influence on Newman waned, so did Froude's increase, and this in itself drew Newman further away from Whately. For Froude not only served as a conduit for Keble's religious influence on Newman and helped Keble and Newman to understand each other, but gave a startling and often provocative expression to Keble's ideas, and circulated them to a wider audience. While Whately and other Noetics were alienated, Newman was captivated not only by Froude's playfulness, gentleness, and versatility of mind, but by his religious ideas and personal asceticism. Newman was impressed by Froude's emphasis on self-denial and mortification and his uncompromising vision of sanctity and the pursuit of holiness. Froude instanced what some have claimed to be a 'morbid' spirit of self-denial and self-analysis in a penitential journal which he kept during his

---

[118] Williams, *Autobiography*, 46.

[119] See H. Froude, 'Occasional Thoughts. "On the Connexion between a Right Faith and Right Practice on the *Ethos* of Heresy"', *Remains of Richard Hurrell Froude* [ed. J. Keble and J. H. Newman], 2 vols. (Derby, 1838–9), i. 114–17. For development of the argument for Froude's role as a proponent of the concept of ethos as a foundation stone of the Oxford Movement, see J. Pereiro, *Ethos and the Oxford Movement: At the Heart of Tractarianism* (Oxford, 2008), 99–101.

[120] Newman, *Apologia*, 84.

[121] P. Brendon, *Hurrell Froude and the Oxford Movement* (London, 1974), 102.

Oriel years. Newman's identification with Froude's ascetical spirit would be exemplified in his decision to edit and publish (along with Keble) extracts from the journal in a posthumous two-volume collection, *The Remains of Richard Hurrell Froude* (1838–9). Newman was also susceptible to Froude's uncompromising anti-Erastianism. As Newman later noted, Froude 'delighted in the notion of a hierarchical system, of sacerdotal power and of full ecclesiastical liberty'. For Froude built upon and much extended Whately's idea, expressed in his *Letters of an Episcopalian*, that the Church had an independent status as a great and sacred corporate body with a right to govern itself. Froude explored points which Whately had eschewed or left unsaid, such as in what the internal life of the Church consisted, and precisely what doctrines it should teach. Under the influence of the classes on the liturgy conducted in 1825–6 by Charles Lloyd (1784–1829), Regius Professor of Divinity (soon to become bishop of Oxford), which he attended with Newman and Robert Wilberforce, Froude drew on the Book of Common Prayer and the sources on which it was modelled.[122] However, unlike other contemporaries imbibing high church notions, Froude's ecclesiastical *beau idéal* became the Church of the Middle Ages rather than the Church of antiquity. Newman was also struck by Froude's 'high severe idea of the intrinsic excellence of Virginity; and he considered the Blessed Virgin its great pattern'.[123] In all this, Froude was running well ahead of his spiritual mentor, John Keble.

Newman himself would follow Froude's lead gradually and haltingly, coming in later years to make his own various doctrines, principles, and practices—the value of penance, mortification, and celibacy, the Real Presence in the Eucharist, admiration for the Church of Rome, denigration of the Reformation and the Reformers—which Froude had already embraced by the mid-1820s, albeit in an undeveloped form. Newman was explicit as to the extent of his religious debt to Froude, later conceding: 'It is difficult to enumerate the precise additions to my theological creed which I derived from a friend to whom I owe so much.'[124] It would seem, as James Pereiro has convincingly argued, that Newman's own increasing emphasis on the correlation between error or unbelief and a bad ethos owed much to both Keble's and Froude's influence.[125] In his own private correspondence with

---

[122] Lloyd delivered a series of lectures from 1823–9 in his capacity as Regius Professor. For his influence on Newman, Pusey, Keble, and Froude, see E. S. Ffoulkes, *A History of the Church of St Mary the Virgin: The University Church* (London, 1902), 404–5. As early as 1824, Lloyd had proposed that Newman 'compose a work for him for the use of students in divinity, containing such miscellaneous information as is only to be found in Latin'. Newman, *Autobiographical Writings*, 197.
[123] Newman, *Apologia*, 84–5.
[124] Newman, *Apologia*, 87.
[125] Pereiro, *Ethos and the Oxford Movement: At the Heart of Tractarianism*, esp. 104–10.

his wayward brother Charles in the mid-1820s, Newman had concluded that rejection of Christianity or indeed heresy arose from a fault of the heart, not the intellect; in short, that unbelief stemmed from pride or sensuality.[126] It was an understanding which would underpin Newman's new-found mistrust of Noeticism and help sharpen the rift, both theological and personal, that would emerge between the two groups within Oriel in the ensuing years: a rift foreshadowed by Froude's growing irritation at what he regarded as the liberal theological opinions being sported in the Oriel common room; an irritation expressed in a private note wherein he stated that he 'abandoned the Noetick School' before the long vacation of 1827.[127] However, while it was to be a divide which had theological roots, it would be issues of college and university politics that would bring the divide to the surface and mark the definitive commencement of hostilities in Oriel.

There was still no hint of real religious conflict in Oriel, however, at the time of the election of a provost early in 1828 in succession to Copleston. On the contrary, an increasingly fragile theological consensus prevailed, partly because Oriel had not yet taken sides on the Test and Corporation Bills aimed at rescinding the exclusion of dissenters from parliament. The college continued to give united support to the annual anti-Catholic petition by the university. Blanco White's book against Catholicism thus pleased many and confirmed his position in Oriel.[128] Even Keble gave it a cautious welcome, though found it 'too vehement to be very convincing' and open to the common fault of laying 'on the religion itself the faults of those professing it'. Moreover, Williams's later analysis of a theological breach within Oriel by the mid-1820s between 'the school of Keble' and 'school of Whately' may have been with hindsight overstated and dated too early. When Froude was elected to an Oriel fellowship in 1826, Keble had taken pride in 'the Southrop interest' having prevailed but wished that Whately or Davison had still been resident in college so as 'to take him in hand'—'he would make a capital pupil for either of them'.[129] Moreover, had the future religious battle-lines already been clear at the time of Copleston's elevation, then Newman would surely have supported Keble as a candidate for the vacant provostship. Hurrell Froude urged Keble's claims, arguing that he would 'bring in a new world; that donnishness and humbug would be no more in the College, nor the pride of talent, nor an ignoble secular ambition'. Newman was unmoved, and backed Hawkins as the more practical man of business, remarking: 'that if an Angel's place was vacant, he should look towards Keble, but that they were

---

[126] Newman, 'Memorandum on Revelation—January 2 1830', LDN ii. 281–2.
[127] Brendon, *Hurrell Froude*, 77.
[128] Corsi, *Science and Religion: Baden Powell and the Anglican Debate*, 91.
[129] J. Keble to J. T. Coleridge, 3 April 1826, Bodleian Library MS Eng. Lett. d.134, fos. 184–5.

only electing a Provost.'[130] Newman himself conceded that after his election, Hawkins initially supported him and his two fellow tutors Froude and Robert Wilberforce, in enforcing discipline and in their measures of 'purification of the College'.[131] Tensions, however, soon surfaced, eventually finding expression in differences between the provost and the tutors (Newman, Robert Wilberforce, and Hurrell Froude) in what became known as Oriel's tutorial controversy.

To understand the tutorial dispute in Oriel, one has to recognize Newman's strictly religious understanding, shared by Froude and Robert Wilberforce, of the tutorial office; an understanding which Wilberforce and Froude had first learned from Keble. It was Keble's Southrop reading parties which provided the characteristics for the tutorial method which Newman sought to put into practice in Oriel[132] from January 1826 until June 1832 when he finally relinquished the office, the provost having closed off his supply of new pupils from June 1830. Religious and moral as well as academic standards needed to be raised and this underpinned Newman's determination to reduce the numbers and influence of the sometimes profligate and worldly gentlemen commoners for whom Oxford was little more than a 'finishing school', and for whom a degree did not matter. For Newman, as for Froude and Robert Wilberforce, the role of a college tutor involved far more than the imparting of knowledge or preparation of pupils for examinations. The tutorial office had an inherent spiritual and pastoral dimension, and was part of one's ordination vow. Years later, he described his model of pastoral care over undergraduate pupils at Oriel: 'With such youths he cultivated relations, not only of intimacy, but of friendship, and almost of equality, putting off, as much as might be, the martinet manner then in fashion with College Tutors, and seeking their society in outdoor exercises, on evenings, and in Vacations.'[133]

It is possible to discern some religious and pastoral benchmarks of Newman's success as a tutor. In a recent study covering the period 1821–31, in which Newman acted as first a private and then a college tutor, Philippe Lefebvre has shown that in Oriel's undergraduate population, the number of men of family and fortune (the gentlemen commoners) declined, as did the number of undergraduates who failed to take a degree (with fewer gentlemen commoners among them), while the number of undergraduates gaining honours increased, together with the number of future clergy among them. Lefebvre shows, from evidence in Newman's autobiographical memoirs as well as from his published correspondence, that Newman had a clear

---

[130] Newman, *Autobiographical Writings*, 91.
[131] Newman, *Autobiographical Writings*, 92.
[132] Pereiro, *Ethos and the Oxford Movement*, 86.
[133] Newman, *Autobiographical Writings*, 90.

ILLUSTRATION 10.2 James Endell Tyler (1789–1851), fellow 1812–28
Oriel College

conception of the evils in the existing system, one of which was the preponderance of the gentlemen commoners.[134] His disapproval of them diverged sharply from the attitude of Provost Copleston and Dean Tyler. Thomas Mozley waspishly observed of Tyler that it was commonly held that he 'had cared for gold tufts and silk gowns more than for the college generally' and that his 'especial fondness was reserved for the Gentlemen Commoners'.[135] Tyler had left the college in 1826 to become vicar of St Giles, Holborn, but he would not have applauded Newman's sense of triumph expressed in a letter to his friend and former Oriel fellow, Samuel Rickards, in February 1829,

---

[134] P. Lefebvre, 'The Student Population at Oriel College and Newman's Pupils (1821–1833)', Annexe 1.A., 'John Henry Newman tuteur: Tradition, rupture, développement (1826–31)' (unpublished dissertation, Université de Paris III, 2004), 105–15.

[135] Mozley, *Reminiscences*, i. 82. Newman privately accused Tyler of 'tuft and silk courting'. Newman to S. Rickards, 19 March 1827, LDN ii. 8. In the same letter, Newman observed: 'we get on better for Tyler's absence—the evil which tuft and silk courting has been to the college, is best seen by the effect of its being withdrawn.'

outlining the 'innovations' which he had introduced into the college over the preceding year: these included the marked diminution (by over half) of the number of gentlemen commoners, as well as the rejection of unprepared candidates and the refusal of testimonials to unworthy candidates. Newman was able to inform Rickards, who had only resigned his fellowship for a college living two years earlier, that 'the college is so altered that you would hardly know it'.[136]

The rift between Newman and Hawkins over tutorial practice and policy has been analysed by this author elsewhere.[137] The dispute partly stemmed from the provost's perception that in rearranging college tuition to foster a closer relation between undergraduate and tutor, in accord with the particular gifts of each undergraduate, Newman and Froude were encouraging favouritism. Both sides believed in a religious dimension to the tutorial office and in the religious mission of the college; Newman and the other tutors merely took this consideration further and interpreted it in a different way. The provost was insistent that pastoral concerns, important as they were, should not overshadow the place of teaching, or of college custom and order. Hawkins also took a somewhat laxer line on the issue of testimonials for holy orders and of administering the sacrament to undergraduates,[138] and resisted Newman's attempt to dispense with the custom of gentlemen commoners dining with the fellows. However, more than a merely personal conflict of wills was at stake:[139] the root of Hawkins's misgivings lay in the nature and direction of Newman's personal religious influence on his pupils. The former provost, Copleston, shared these misgivings, commenting to Hawkins as early as 1830: 'From what you say of Newman's religious views, I fear he is impractical. His notion of dangers to church and state I cannot understand. For even under the system we wish to continue religious instruction is part of the class lectures, and in private it is part of each tutor's business with his own pupils.'[140]

---

[136] Newman to Rickards, 6 February 1829, LDN ii. 117–18. As Newman explained to Rickards, the main change was that 'bad men are thrown into very large classes…and thus time saved for the better sort who were put into very small lectures, and principally with their own tutors, quite familiarly and chattingly'.

[137] Nockles, 'Oriel and the Making of John Henry Newman: His Mission as College Tutor', OR (2008), 44–51.

[138] Newman was concerned about the lax or unprepared spiritual state in which undergraduates might take the sacrament in the college chapel. See Newman to H. Jenkyns, 30 September 1832, LDN iii. 98. Henry Jenkyns (fellow 1818–35) was a classical scholar and one of Oriel's few high churchmen of the old school. In the wake of Newman's dismissal as a tutor, Jenkyns would persuade the Cambridge high churchman Hugh James Rose to invite Newman to contribute to his new 'Theological Library' the work which was eventually published as *The Arians of the Fourth Century*. In 1833 Jenkyns would be the first professor of Greek at the new University of Durham.

[139] Nockles, 'Oriel and the Making of John Henry Newman', 48. Cf. [G. C. Richards], 'The Oriel Common Room in 1833', OR (January 1933), 237.

[140] Cited in Rannie, *Oriel*, 202.

Although the shape of the three tutors' religious views was not yet clear or fully formed, Hawkins sensed the danger of concentrating tuition in the hands of unchecked and potentially unsound teachers. Given the later theological development of the three tutors, even Thomas Mozley conceded that the provost 'seemed to be justified by the event in not virtually resigning the education of his college into Newman's hands'.[141] Incipient religious differences rendered the disagreement insurmountable. Newman resigned his last two pupils into Hawkins's hands at Easter 1831, and Froude and Wilberforce followed in the Long Vacation. The potential for future division and strife was also heightened by Hawkins's decision to call on Renn Dickson Hampden, now a married former fellow residing in Oxford, to plug the gaps left thereby. The tuition controversy and its outcome would cast a long shadow over the religious condition as well as the academic state of the college in the following decade. The seeds of the waning of Oriel's academic ascendancy had been sown.

The evidence of Lefebvre's study shows that concerns of religious orthodoxy and the cultivation of moral habits were a high priority for Newman, alongside that of academic achievement. The care which Newman took over his pupils as individuals whom he took into his confidence is clear from the manuscript memorandum books on them which he kept; a record which extended to moral formation and to spiritual as well as intellectual progress. A sample entry dated 'Easter 1826', for a particular favourite, his future brother-in-law Thomas Mozley, is revealing: 'very promising—clear & elegant mind—hopeful in religion, a good scholar.'[142] Newman's successes with his pupils may have attracted jealousy, though, as in the case of James Howard Harris, 3rd earl of Malmesbury, and Charles Murray, he had his 'failures' among the gentlemen commoners.[143] One reason for suspicion, as Lefebvre suggests, and as Copleston and Hawkins clearly feared, may have been that he regarded his tutorial office as a way of preparing some of his chosen pupils for the defence of the Church in the future trials which he evidently already foresaw.[144] If so, this was prophetic. Certainly, the names of many of Newman's and Froude's pupils reads like a roll-call of Tractarian followers in the 1830s: Henry Wilberforce, Thomas Mozley,

---

[141] Mozley, *Reminiscences*, i. 233.

[142] [J. H. Newman], 'Memorandum Book about [Oriel] College Pupils', Newman Archives, Birmingham Oratory Library MS A6.15. I am grateful to Monsieur Lefebvre for allowing me to consult his photocopies from a microfilm version in Yale University Library.

[143] James Howard Harris (matriculated 1825) wrote critically of Newman's alleged inability to keep tutorial discipline during Harris's time as Newman's pupil in 1826–7. *Memoirs of an Ex-Minister: An Autobiography. By the Rt Hon the Earl of Malmesbury*, 2 vols. (3rd edn., London, 1884), i. 18. However, Malmesbury's claims and version of events was rebutted by other contemporary pupils such as Frederic Rogers, besides Newman himself. On this episode, see Nockles, 'Newman and Oxford', in *John Henry Newman in his Time* (Oxford, 2007), 31.

[144] Lefebvre, 'Student Population at Oriel College'.

ILLUSTRATION 10.3 Joseph Blanco White (1775–1841)

National Portrait Gallery: Joseph Slater, 1812

Charles Marriott, Samuel Wood, Frederic Rogers, Sir George Prevost, Charles Page Eden, Robert Francis Wilson, John Frederic Christie, and many others. If Newman was training his pupils for a future trial of the Church, when that time came in 1833 many of them were indeed at their posts and ready to enter the fray. Thomas Mozley, who knew his brother-in-law so well, later highlighted Newman's sense of destiny and future expectations for his Oriel pupils and later disciples: 'Newman looked out inquiringly, expectantly, and believingly for the special powers and intentions of his younger friends. They generally agreed that his fault lay in believing and expecting rather too much of them. He would easily accept a promise, and interpret silence itself favourably.'[145]

Oriel's tutorial dispute also needs to be viewed in the light of an episode of wider significance in the university's history, the impact of which had profound religious repercussions for Oriel: the attempted re-election to parliament of Sir Robert Peel in 1829. Oxford's rejection of Peel as its member after he had voted for Catholic emancipation, resigned his seat, and stood for

---

[145] Mozley, *Reminiscences*, i. 208.

re-election was the real catalyst of the theological realignment that would now divide the college. The university election of 1829 drew Newman and Hawkins apart, marking the decisive parting of the ways between the Noetics and the future Tractarians. Blanco White, always acutely sensitive, instinctively recognized that the polarized positions which his Oriel friends took up on the issue were the dawn of what he called a 'mental revolution', the harbinger of tractarianism.[146] He rightly recognized that its consequences in Oriel went far deeper than differences over the merits of making concessions over the Catholic claims. Before the election, in Oriel as in Oxford generally, ideological differences in the college had been submerged by the strength of personal bonds and a broader sense of the common ground. Oriel Noeticism had always been more a frame of mind and religious temper than a distinctively liberal theological creed. As we have seen, it encompassed many shades of opinion, some of them markedly 'high church'. Blanco White had felt at home in this climate. The Oriel Noetics seemed to have the future before them, their intellectual supremacy within the university still largely unquestioned.

The Noetics, notably Whately, had for some time been supporters of Catholic emancipation and thus were not in tune with prevailing Tory high church anti-emancipationist sentiment. Newman, under Whately's influence, had himself supported Catholic emancipation and voted against the anti-Catholic petitions of 1827 and 1828. In 1829, he professed indifference on the emancipation question itself, but took a vigorous stand against Peel on other grounds, projecting the deeper values which he had imbibed from Keble and Froude, and which he had made his own. So he hailed the university's rejection of Peel as a 'glorious victory' for 'the independence of the Church and of Oxford' in equal measure.[147] For Newman, the episode fuelled the potent image of Oxford as a 'place set apart' to witness to a degenerate age and nation. His imagination was given full rein. Walking along the 'old road from Oxford' to visit his mother and sister at Horspath, he recalled 'King Charles and his Bishop [Laud] seemed to rise before him'.[148] On the other hand, Newman's erstwhile Noetic mentors were cast as suspect in their loyalty to Church and university, allies of a hostile spirit of latitudinarianism and 'indifferentism' by which both were threatened. He rejoiced in a victory over the 'rank and talent' of the university, a triumph for moral principles over political expediency.[149] The language of Newman's own anonymous pamphlet in the contest and his private correspondence at the time presaged

---

[146] *Life of Joseph Blanco White*, ed. Thom, iii. 131.
[147] Newman to Mrs Newman, 1 March 1829, A. Mozley (ed.), *Letters and Correspondence of John Henry Newman during his Life in the English Church* (London, 1891), i. 202.
[148] Newman to J. W. Bowden, 16 January 1830, LDN i. 189.
[149] Newman to Mrs Newman, 1 March 1829, Mozley, *Letters*, i. 202.

ILLUSTRATION 10.4 Richard Jelf (1798–1871), fellow 1821–30
Oriel College

the coming era of religious conflict within and without the walls of Oriel. For their part, the Oriel Noetics were bruised by the unexpected experience of defeat; Peel's rejection was a psychological body-blow from which they never recovered. Dismayed by the popular passions roused by the election, they increasingly turned to their London Whig parliamentary friends in a way that would only isolate them and heighten their unpopularity among the rising Tractarian generation in the 1830s. Whately, like the other Noetics, conspicuously failed to grasp the depth of feeling and principle that would set his erstwhile friends on a new course. In short, the rift with Newman would become personal, and the religious climate in Oriel would turn sour and embittered. In Oriel, as in the wider university, the moral initiative was passing to Newman and his followers and away from the increasingly discredited Noetics.

On the other hand, by challenging the Noetics on an important point of principle, and defending the rights both of university and Church against what they regarded as the 'insolence' of the self-styled 'talent' of Oxford, Newman and his friends were riding with rather than initiating a reaction against the Noetic hegemony. A later generation would need reminding that until at least 1829 the real opponents of the Noetics were neither the future Tractarians nor even the evangelicals, but what Newman described as the 'old unspiritual high-and-dry, then in possession of the high places in Oxford'.[150] This dominant group may not have held sway in Oriel, but it had some notable representatives among non-residents, notably John Hume Spry, a London high churchman linked to the 'Hackney Phalanx' and an Oriel master of arts who had been close to Provost Copleston. One sign that the earlier rapprochement between the Oriel Noetics and 'Hackney Phalanx' was truly over was Spry's complaint in December 1829 to the prominent 'Hackney' high churchman Henry Handley Norris about the damage wrought by 'Dr Whately's books'; he deplored Whately's 'sophistical attempts to destroy the Christian Priesthood', a surprising and significant charge, given Newman's own acknowledged debt to the author's *Letters of an Episcopalian*. In an angry tone, Spry declared himself 'sick of Oriel and its writers', and condemned Whately as the 'mouthpiece and indefatigable supporter of a party in the Church which promises to do more harm to her doctrine and discipline than all the Calvinism, or dissent, or evangelism of the last century has effected'.[151]

In the light of such criticism Whately naturally assumed that Newman in turning against him must be allying himself with the 'two-bottle orthodox' and the 'high and dry' of popular caricature, under-represented as they were in Oriel. He took mischievous pleasure as principal of St Alban Hall in seating the fastidious Newman in the company of 'a set of the least intellectual men in Oxford to dinner, and men most fond of port'. As Newman recalled, Whately afterwards 'asked me if I was proud of my friends'.[152] Of course, Newman and his disciples saw things differently. Their stand was only incidentally at one with that of Spry and his school. Their action in the Peel election and their attempt to revolutionize tuition within Oriel signified a much deeper point of departure from the old religious consensus within the college. They had taken a first crucial step in establishing the moral and religious influence which they would enjoy in and out of Oriel in the subsequent decade. Crucially, Newman's and Froude's relinquishment of

---

[150] Newman, *Autobiographical Writings*, 73.
[151] J. H. Spry to H. H. Norris, 11 December 1829, Bodleian Library, MS Eng Lett. c.789, fos. 200–1.
[152] Newman, *Apologia*, 73.

the Oriel tuition freed them to pursue a broader vision and initiate a wider religious movement. Isaac Williams later reflected that 'their course had, as yet, been chiefly academical; but now, released from college affairs, their thoughts were more open to the state of the Church'.[153] This somewhat overstates the extent of an undoubted shift in focus; it was more a change of emphasis than a completely new direction.

In truth, Newman together with his friends and incipient Oriel disciples never ceased to be preoccupied with college affairs; but they had for some time been coming to perceive a state of crisis in the Church as a whole, a situation which had to be urgently addressed by a return to 'apostolical' principles, the faith and practice of antiquity. This evolution owed much to Newman's own intense course of reading in the early fathers, based, as Kenneth Parker has convincingly shown, from the evidence of its register, on works borrowed from the college library as well as on books in his own possession.[154] Newman's course of reading had begun as early as 1826, when he had agreed to write an article for Edward Smedley for the *Encyclopaedia metropolitana*, and had eventually borne fruit in his influential theological treatise *The Arians of the Fourth Century* (1833).[155] For Newman, what happened at Oxford and Oriel was bound up with the wider cause of the Church at large, and was related to his view of the early Church that was being shaped by his immersion in patristic literature. Newman's patristic studies at Oriel directly led him into making analogies between what he regarded as the heresies and dangers threatening the contemporary Church of England and those which had once assailed the early Church.[156]

The religious and academic fortunes of Oriel remained a matter of acute concern for Newman, even when he was searching for 'kindly light in the encircling gloom' on his Mediterranean journey in 1832–3. He remained hopeful that Oriel fellowship elections would be made from among the stock of his former pupils, whom he would soon enlist as 'Apostolicals'. He had hardly recovered from his near-fatal fever in Sicily in April 1833 when he had news of the election of his disciple and former pupil Frederic Rogers to an Oriel fellowship,[157] about which he was inevitably in

---

[153] *Autobiography of Isaac Williams*, 47.
[154] See K. Parker, 'John Henry Newman and the Oriel College Library: A New Lens on the Life and Work of an Oriel Fellow' (forthcoming).
[155] As Newman explained to his sister Jemima in 1826, perhaps with a touch of exaggeration: writing the article 'would consequently involve a reading of all the Fathers—200 volumes at least—(you saw some good stout gentlemen in Oriel Library)...' Newman to Jemima Newman, 1 May 1826, LDN i. 285.
[156] S. Thomas, *Newman and Heresy: The Anglican Years* (Cambridge, 1991), esp. parts i and ii.
[157] 'As to the Oriel election, I first saw the news of it in a *Galignani* at Palermo, and on seeing that Rogers was elected, I kissed the paper rapturously.' J. H. Newman to F. Rogers, 5 June 1833, A. Mozley, *Letters of Newman*, i. 404. Rogers, who had been one of Newman's favoured undergraduate pupils, became one of his closest Oriel friends. It was later said of him: 'there

ILLUSTRATION 10.5 Edward Bouverie Pusey (1800–82), fellow 1823–9
Keble College

suspense.¹⁵⁸ The election seemed to bode well for the religious plans which Newman envisaged for Oriel¹⁵⁹ as much as for the Church of England as a whole.

The future Oxford Movement had been conceived in Oriel. Long before 14 July 1833, when John Keble preached his famous sermon on 'National

was no one who was a closer friend than Rogers, no one in whom Mr Newman had such trust, none whose judgment he so valued, no one in whose companionship he so delighted'. R. W. Church, 'Lord Blachford' [*Guardian*, 27 November 1889], *Occasional Papers*, 2 vols. (London, 1897), ii. 485.

¹⁵⁸ 'I am of course very anxious about the election, and shall pay the penalty of not being present by being kept in suspense about the result (I suppose) a good month.' Newman to H. Jenkyns, 7 April 1833, LDN iii. 238.

¹⁵⁹ Newman retained high aspirations for a return to the original religious spirit behind Oriel's fourteenth-century founders and benefactors with current practice being brought more into line with college statutes, e.g. prayers for founders, and the idea of a resident body of celibate fellows engaged in advanced theological study as well as teaching rather than being lured away into parochial work. A. D. Culler, *The Imperial Intellect: A Study of Newman's Educational Ideal* (New Haven, 1955), 90.

ILLUSTRATION 10.6 The Oriel Teapot: emblem of Noetic temperance
Oriel College

Apostasy' from the pulpit of St Mary's, the event normally seen as the formal beginning of the movement, the ground had been laid and prepared, not only in Oriel lectures but in the pulpit of St Mary's, where Newman had been vicar since 1828. The impact of the Oxford Movement in and out of Oriel is the subject of another chapter.

11
A House Divided
Oriel in the Era of the Oxford Movement, 1833–1860

Peter Nockles

While Newman regarded 14 July 1833, the day of Keble's 'National Apostasy' sermon, as 'the start of the Oxford Movement', the event was hardly noticed by contemporaries;[1] Newman's university sermon of 22 January 1832, 'Personal Influence the Means of Propagating the Truth', has a better claim to be the movement's true beginning.[2] The core of the Oxford Movement lay in the personal loyalty and affection between Newman, Froude, and Keble. Although the strict historical reliability and objectivity of Newman's *Apologia* has been recently called into question, Newman's emphasis in that work on the principle of 'personality' as a distinguishing mark of the Oxford Movement was faithful to its inspiration.[3] A religious movement required 'a common history, common memories, an intercourse of mind with mind in the past, and a progress and increase in that intercourse in the present'.[4] Newman's Oriel friends and disciples and the ethos which they created in the college provided precisely these core ingredients: the common room literally provided the physical space for the earliest conferences in the summer of 1833 of the movement's leading protagonists, Newman, Keble, Froude, and at this early stage William Palmer of Worcester College, with the first meetings between Palmer and Froude at the start of the long vacation.[5]

---

[1] J. H. Newman, *Apologia pro vita sua* (London, 1864), 100. Sir John Taylor Coleridge considered it too abstruse for a sermon: BL MS Add. 86183, J. T. Coleridge to J. Keble, 31 August 1833. J. H. Rigg, a Methodist historian of the Oxford Movement, called it a 'solemn but feeble threnody': J. H. Rigg, *Oxford High Anglicanism and its Chief Leaders* (London, 1895), 19–20.

[2] H. Tristram (ed.), *John Henry Newman: Autobiographical Writings* (London, 1956), 119; Gilley, *Newman and his Age*, 112.

[3] See F. M. Turner, *John Henry Newman and the Challenge to Evangelical Religion* (London, 2002).

[4] Newman, *Apologia*, 108.

[5] W. Palmer, *A Narrative of Events connected with the publications of the 'Tracts for the Times'* (London, 1843), 6–7.

ILLUSTRATION 11.1 John Henry Newman (1801–90), fellow 1822–45, cardinal

Oriel College: George Richmond, 1844

The Oxford Movement was as much a call to holy living as a reassertion of the authority and independence of the Church. Newman's preaching and published sermons, and the Tracts for the Times launched with Keble and Froude in 1833, enabled Newman's personal religious influence to spread far beyond Oriel. The forty-six early Tracts (1833–6) on priesthood, apostolic succession of bishops, sacramental grace, tradition, and the authority of the Church were a 'call to arms' *ad clerum*. But Newman's preaching had the greater immediate impact in Oxford.

The principal occasion for Newman's preaching was the Sunday afternoon service at St Mary's, initiated by Edward Hawkins. It soon drew undergraduates from all colleges, who 'were never in the same room as Newman, and never exchanged a word with him'.[6] Supported by his curate, Isaac Williams of Trinity[7], Newman revived the disused daily services of matins and

---

[6] Mozley, *Reminiscences of Oriel College and the Oxford Movement*, i. 239.
[7] Although Williams was never formally attached to the college he spent most of his formative years in the company of friends at Oriel. See ODNB s.n. Isaac Williams.

ILLUSTRATION 11.2 Newman at St Mary's
Oriel College

evensong and Sunday Holy Communion,[8] and introduced evening lectures in the Adam de Brome Chapel. Some heads of houses altered the dinner hour so that undergraduates could attend Newman's sermons, changing it back as they became more controversial. Personal testimonies of the power of his preaching abound, notably that of Matthew Arnold: 'Who could resist the charm of that spiritual apparition, gliding in the dim afternoon light through the aisles of St Mary's, rising into the pulpit, and then, in the most entrancing of voices, breaking the silences with words and thoughts which were a religious music—subtle, sweet, mournful.'[9] Its spiritual beauty and depth, with its emphasis on reserve in contrast to popular evangelical preaching, eluded others, including an American visitor who found him 'cold...as an icicle'.[10] It was 'marked by the strong instinctive shrinking, which was one of

---

[8] Newman told Mark Pattison that: 'Morning daily prayers began the day after St Peter's Day, 1834.' M. Pattison, *Memoirs* (London, 1885), 201; M. Ward, *Young Mr Newman* (London, 1948), 314.

[9] M. Arnold, *Discourses in America* (London, 1885), 139–40.

[10] Cited in J. Bertram, *Newman's Oxford: The Places and Buildings Associated with the Blessed John Henry Newman during his Years in Oxford 1816–1846* (Oxford, 2010), 32.

the most remarkable and certain marks of the beginning of the Oxford Movement from anything like personal display, any conscious aiming at the ornamental and brilliant, any show of gifts or courting of popular applause'.[11] The secret of his power was his psychological insight into the state of the souls of his congregation, his asceticism and latent severity, and the challenging spiritual content of his message. It was a personal impact: 'heart speaks to heart'.

Although Whately later claimed that they enshrined 'a preference for the Latin ecclesiastical system', Newman's sermons were not theologically controversial, and indeed his progress from evangelicalism had been initiated by his Noetic mentors, and his debt to Joseph Butler and reading of Aristotle's *Ethics* instilled by Keble in the Oriel lecture room, as his Oriel disciple Samuel Francis Wood pointed out.[12] He rejected a religious ethos which exalted private judgement and lacked a sense of awe and reserve. As a leading evangelical, John Hill, vice-principal of St Edmund Hall, sourly noted: 'St Peter's Day. Newman preached a miserable sermon at St Mary's, more calculated to produce Scepticism than any other feelings—on the province of reason in theology—on implicit & explicit faith, etc. etc.'[13] He persuaded numerous undergraduates from evangelical backgrounds into tractarianism, notably R. W. Church, who first came under Newman's spell at an afternoon sermon, the turning point of his life, in April 1836.[14] It was not surprising that his influence was mistrusted and feared. It was vividly remembered by former undergraduates who were eventually sceptical of religion, like Mark Pattison or Arthur Hugh Clough, or who became opponents of the Tractarians, such as Edward Woolcombe.[15] Newman's impression on Samuel Wilberforce (Oriel 1823–6), in spite of his influence on other members of the family, was more ambiguous. Wilberforce retained vestiges of his inherited evangelicalism when he moved towards moderate high churchmanship. Always inclined more to the practical than the speculative side of theology, he was critical of Pusey's stern teaching on post-baptismal sin and Newman's uncompromising call to holiness: '[I] read several of Newman's new volume of sermons...their

---

[11] R. W. Church, 'Newman's *Parochial Sermons*' [*Saturday Review*, 5 June 1869], *Occasional Papers*, 2 vols. (London, 1897), ii. 449–50.
[12] [R. Whately], *The Controversy between Tract No. XC and the Oxford Tutors* (London, 1841), 6; J. A. Froude, 'The Oxford Counter-Reformation', *Short Studies*, iv. 283; James Pereiro, '*Ethos' and the Oxford Movement* (Oxford, 2008), 103.
[13] John Hill's Diary, Bodleian Library MS St Edmund Hall 67/13, fo. 12, 29 June 1840.
[14] M. C. Church (ed.), *Life and Letters of Dean Church* (London, 1885), 14, 17.
[15] Mark Pattison, *Memoirs*, 163, 170–3; V. H. H. Green, *Oxford Common Room: A Study of Lincoln College and Mark Pattison* (London, 1957), 941; H. S. Jones, *Intellect and Character in Victorian England: Mark Pattison and the Invention of the Don* (Cambridge, 2007), 27–33; F. Nolan, 'A Study of Mark Pattison's Religious Experience 1813–1850' (D.Phil. thesis, University of Oxford, 1978); A. H. Clough to J. N. Simplinson, 6 January 1838, F. L. Mulhauser (ed.), *Correspondence of Arthur Hugh Clough*, 2 vols. (Oxford, 1957), i. 66; E. C. Woolcombe to Newman, 27 February 1878, LDN xxviii. 322.

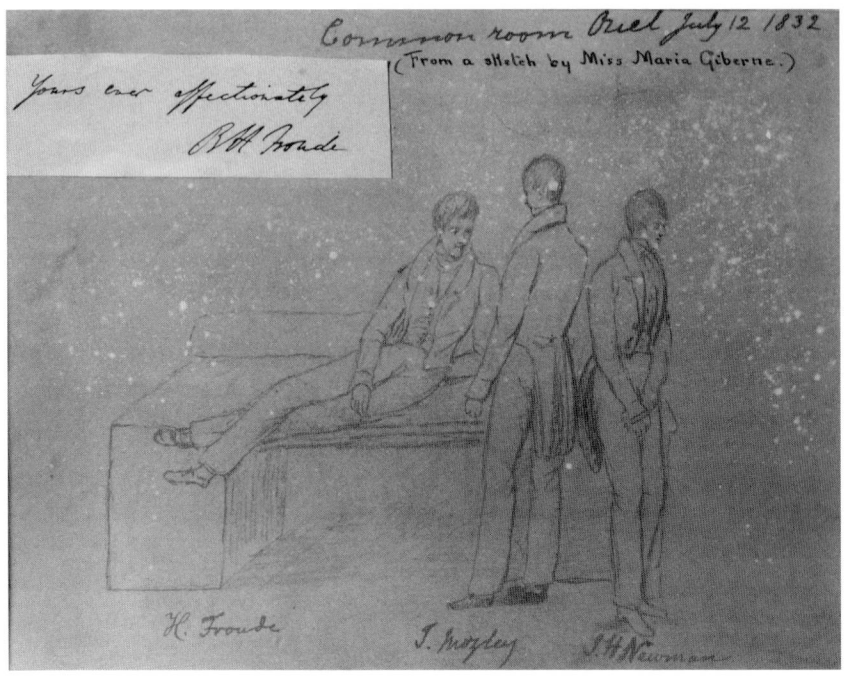

ILLUSTRATION 11.3 Hurrell Froude, Thomas Mozley, and Newman in the common room

Oriel College, after Maria Giberne

tone and standard magnificent, for holiness and separateness from the world, but I think too little evangelic.'[16] George Grey and Charles Wood, Oriel men now Whig ministers, attended one of his sermons out of curiosity in 1837, but their impressions are not recorded.[17]

Newman had had a preponderant personal influence on younger fellows of Oriel such as John Frederic Christie (elected 1829) since the late 1820s, and he continued to attract recruits: Charles Marriott of Exeter and Frederic Rogers of Oriel (elected 1833) would be keen Tractarians.[18] Even more stalwart was Thomas Mozley (elected 1829) who distributed the Tracts for the Times in Northamptonshire in 1833–4; he later married Newman's sister Harriett and

---

[16] A. R. Ashwell (ed.), *Life of the Rt. Rev. Samuel Wilberforce*, 3 vols. (London, 1880), i. 142.
[17] J. B. Mozley to M. Mozley, 29 March 1837, *Letters of the Rev. J. B. Mozley, D.D.*, ed. A. Mozley (London, 1885), 65.
[18] On Marriott see J. W. Burgon, 'Charles Marriott: The Man of Saintly Life', *Lives of Twelve Good Men*, 2 vols. (4th edn., London, 1899), i. 305; ODNB s.n.; he was part author of Tract 78. On Rogers, later Lord Blachford, ODNB s.n.; on Christie, a contributor to the high church *British Critic*, see Newman to H. J. Rose, 17 March 1834, LDN iv. 207.

retired to Cholderton.[19] The older generation of fellows, however, was unconvinced. Though there were no representatives in Oriel of the numerous and hostile 'two bottle orthodox' party of easygoing heads of houses and fellows,[20] the Noetics were unsympathetic. Newman initially remained on good terms with ex-Provost Copleston. As late as March 1835 Edward Copleston was asking his nephew William Copleston to convey his gratitude to Newman for his gift of a copy of Newman's pamphlet on suffragan bishops: 'I have a great personal regard for Newman, which I hope is in some degree reciprocated; yet I can scarcely imagine that our opinions on matters of academical and ecclesiastical concern do not exactly coincide.'[21] Other Noetics had a sharper sense of the emerging division; Hampden and Arnold were particularly outspoken. Hampden observed on the appearance of the Tracts, 'these gentlemen without even knowing it, have passed the Rubicon: they do not see that they are already Romanists'.[22] Arnold regarded the Tracts as a provocative attempt to rally the clergy to oppose the Whig government's church reforms, complaining to the still circumspect provost, 'you do not seem to me to apprehend the drift of these Tracts, nor the point of comparison between these and St Paul's adversaries'; there was nothing more 'schismatical and anarchical: in Elizabeth's time it would have been reckoned treasonable'.[23] Whately was no less condemnatory of 'the protestant-papists at Oxford', criticizing Newman's sermons as 'very little different from Romanism, except in not placing the Pope at Rome'.[24] The antagonism was reciprocated: Newman avoided Whately during the archbishop's visit in 1834, as he honestly avowed, provoking a pained response.[25] He had already reacted sharply when Hawkins accepted a bust of Whately for the college, telling him that he 'believed a strong feeling against such a measure would be found to exist in some quarters'. The provost had 'laughed at the notion', saying he 'too disagreed with Whately but what then? What was that to do with taking or refusing a bust. Whately was a distinguished member of the college.' Unmoved, Newman informed Keble, 'who was furious' and threatened to write to Whately himself unless the bust was declined. The bust finally

---

[19] ODNB s.n.
[20] On the epithet see Newman to J. C. Fisher, 17 November 1877, LDN xxviii. 270.
[21] E. Copleston to W. J. Copleston, 24 March 1835, W. J. Copleston, *Memoir of Edward Copleston*, 160.
[22] H. Hampden (ed.), *Some Memorials of Renn Dickson Hampden* (London, 1871), 32.
[23] Arnold to Hawkins, 14 April 1834, Stanley, *Life and Correspondence of Thomas Arnold D.D.*, 2 vols. (London, 1844), i. 376.
[24] OCL Hawkins Papers, Letterbook 3, 211, Whately to Hawkins, 20 July 1833; 214, 25 October 1835.
[25] Whately to Newman, 25 October 1834, E. J. Whately (ed.), *Life and Correspondence of Richard Whately D.D. Lord Archbishop of Dublin* (3rd edn., London, 1875), 112–13; Newman to Whately, 28 October 1834, Whately (ed.), *Life and Correspondence*, 113–14; Whately to Newman, October (no date) 1834, Whately (ed.), *Life and Correspondence*, 118.

ILLUSTRATION 11.4 Renn Dickson Hampden (1793–1868), fellow 1815–18
Oriel College: Sir Daniel Macnee, 1867

arrived at Oriel, but was ignominiously confined to the provost's lodgings.[26] It is still there.

Newman's relations with Hampden also deteriorated after he was 'floored' in his ambition for the chair of moral philosophy by the election of Hampden. The reverse was keenly felt: 'I have met my conqueror and departed,' as he confided to Henry Wilberforce.[27] Hampden lacked the urbanity of the common room at that time. As Thomas Mozley remembered

> Dr Hampden, when he reappeared in Oxford at the age of thirty-six, was one of the most unprepossessing of men. He was not so much repulsive as utterly unattractive. There was a certain stolidity about him that contrasted with the bright, vivacious, and singularly loveable figures with whom the eyes of Oriel men were then familiarized. Even the less agreeable men had life, candour, and not a little humour... Someone said of him that he stood before you like a milestone, and brayed at you like a jackass.[28]

---

[26] Newman to R. H. Froude, 14 June 1834, LDN iv. 272.
[27] Newman commented: 'I was so sure of being elected Moral Philosophy Professor that I wished the title inserted in my title page to my Sermons.' LDN iv. 201.
[28] Mozley, *Reminiscences*, i. 380.

As Mozley explained, some slight and civil acknowledgement was conventional between acquaintances, but Hampden demanded more:

> Hampden, not quite certain whether he was to be cut or recognized, looked for a very marked recognition, which some men doubtless found it not easy to give. Others met the emergency by doing what Hampden evidently looked for, and then he took it rather amiss when they gave their votes in Convocation to incapacitate him from his chief functions.[29]

Arnold too came under Newman's censure. His throw-away remark in Rome to Anthony Grant, an Anglican clergyman, 'but is [Arnold] a Christian?', was reported back to the headmaster, who responded indignantly.[30] For his part, Arnold recognized that Newman used the word 'Christian' in 'a sense of his own'; he had nothing personal against Newman but only 'to that party to which he has attached himself' which, he claimed, imputed unscrupulously 'to those who differ from them all sorts of unworthy motives'.[31] Newman was even offended by the former fellow James Endell Tyler, who returned a sermon intended for a collection to be published by the SPCK without giving a reason: Newman's sarcastic response, though not sent, was preserved among his papers.[32]

Underlying the wounded pride and personality clashes which beset Oriel in the early 1830s was a deep-seated divergence of theological principle, with profound implications for the nature of the university. The Tractarians, the most dynamic element in the fellowship, confronted the older and now scattered generation of Noetics, still bound to the college by their old association. While Newman and his colleagues were expounding the spiritual authority and independence of the Church in the Tracts for the Times, Thomas Arnold was asserting a contrary latitudinarian ecclesiology in his *Principles of Church Reform* (1833), advocating an established national Church on the basis of a communion among the denominations worshipping separately in their parish church.[33] As Newman satirized it:

---

[29] Mozley, *Reminiscences*, i. 381.
[30] Newman to Grant, 16 November 1833, LDN iv. 106.
[31] Arnold to Grant, 11 November 1833, LDN iv. 108.
[32] Newman to Hurrell Froude, 13 November 1833, LDN iv. 100; Newman to Tyler, 12 December 1833, LDN v. 139; Rogers prevailed on him not to send it. Newman later confessed to his ferocity to Tyler, but excused it: 'can one begin a movement in cold blood?', LDN iv. 139 n. (7 August 1860). Newman satirized Tyler's apparent tendency to be to be all things to all men for which he invented the expression 'to Tylerise'. As he told Froude, 'I used to say, with reference to the Catholic Question, that Hawkins was on neither side, and Tyler on both', Newman to Froude, 14 June 1834, LDN iv. 272.
[33] Arnold maintained that 'all articles, creeds, and prayers for public use', ought to be framed 'so as to provide the least possible disagreement without sacrificing in our own parochial worship, the expression of such feelings as are essential to our own edification', T. Arnold, *Principles of Church Reform* (London, 1833), 38, 79.

If I understand it right, all sects (the Church inclusive) are to hold their meetings in the parish churches, though not at the same hour of course. He excludes Quakers and Roman Catholics, yet even with this exclusion, surely there will be too many sects in some places for one day. This strikes me as a radical defect in his plan. If I might propose an amendment, I should say pass an Act to oblige some persuasions to change the Sunday. If you have two Sundays in the week, you could accommodate any probable number of sects, and in this way you would get over Whately's objections against the Evangelical party and others; make them keep Sunday on Saturday.[34]

For Arnold, priesthood, apostolic succession, and the sacraments, doctrines dear to the Tractarians, were only a species of idolatry, 'the worst and earliest form of Antichrist'.[35] Two radical and incompatible ecclesiologies, both nurtured in the same small college, would now collide in the public arena, driving the Oriel common room into irreconcilable division.

The first public challenge to the Anglican character of Oxford came in 1834, with the bill to abrogate religious tests and admit dissenters to the university, which passed the House of Commons but was defeated in the Lords. This provoked a declaration against any future attempt to modify subscription, signed by 1,900 members of convocation and over 1,050 undergraduates. The Oriel Tractarians were naturally signatories; the Noetics were more divided. Baden Powell rejected it, publishing his *Reasons for not Joining in the Declaration*. Hampden however signed, his concerns allayed by the generalized wording of the document.[36] But his controversial *Observations on Religious Dissent* (1834) showed where he really stood: advocating the admission of dissenters and abolition of all doctrinal tests, he made a distinction between 'religion' or divine revelation and 'theological opinion', suggesting that Christians were in broad agreement over the former and that only human interpretations of Divine Word caused Christians to differ over the latter.[37] Arnold agreed: 'Your view of the difference between Christian Truth and Theological opinion is one which I have long cherished.'[38] Both tempered their relativism in practice, expecting dissenters at Oxford to conform to existing religious practice and attend college services.[39] Baden Powell was

---

[34] Newman to R. F Wilson, 18 March 1833, LDN iii. 257–8. Robert Francis Wilson (1810–83), Oriel 1827–31. He was close to Keble, whose *Letters of Spiritual Counsel and Guidance by the Late Rev. J. Keble MA* he edited (Oxford, 1875).
[35] T. Arnold, *Fragment on the Church* (London, 1844), 19; J. B. Mozley, 'Dr Arnold', *Essays Historical and Theological*, 2 vols. (London, 1878), ii. 33–5.
[36] His signature caused Christie to regret that the declaration was not more unambiguous: Lambeth Palace Library, MS 2837, fo. 13, J. F. Christie to W. Palmer of Magdalen, 11 May 1834.
[37] R. D. Hampden, *Observations on Religious Dissent with particular reference to the use of religious tests in the University* (2nd edn., Oxford, 1834), 18.
[38] OCL 'Hampden Controversy', i, no. 16, Arnold to Hampden, 17 May 1835.
[39] Hampden, *Observations on Religious Dissent*, 34, 85; Arnold to Hampden, 17 May 1835: 'I an inclined to open the University to all Dissenters—not that I would admit any man to my college who would object to attend my religious worship and instruction—but because I conceive tests are purely injurious.'

more uncompromising: he wondered whether Hampden's 'claim for the maintenance of the university as exclusively a Church of England institution' was 'quite consistent with those opinions which he has expressed in previous publications'.[40] Nonetheless, he supported Hampden's contention that the university, and by implication the college, was 'not the Church' but 'a literary society' and only 'incidentally a society of church members'.[41]

Newman dreaded giving Hampden publicity, but felt obliged to write a sharp letter to him, pointing out 'that by its appearance the first step has been taken towards interrupting that peace and mutual good understanding, which has prevailed so long in this place, and which if once seriously disturbed will be succeeded by dissensions the more intractable because justified in the minds of those who resist innovation by a feeling of imperative duty'.[42] He would now find himself in conflict with the provost, who supported a proposal in the Hebdomadal Board to replace subscription with a form of declaration, which was however defeated in convocation. The provost insisted, against Newman and Pusey, that no relaxation of principles was involved in the measure; only a change of form, so as 'to clear our system from objections'.[43] But on this question the Noetics were again divided: ex-Provost Copleston was still more conservative than Hawkins.[44] For Pusey, subscription was a mark of submission to church authority, a bar to latitudinarianism as much as to heterodoxy; the provost's scheme would alter 'the character of our church'.[45] Equally, it would undermine the principle of a college where instruction flowed from the personal relationship of tutor and pupil; the example of Cambridge, where dissenters were permitted to matriculate, did not signify because its colleges were larger and many junior members lived out. The religious basis of Newman's tutorial method would be threatened:

The students are required to attend chapel, morning and evening (as the rule) and the Lord's Supper terminally. Each tutor knows his pupils personally, with more or less

---

[40] [Baden Powell], 'University Education without Religious Distinctions', *Quarterly Journal of Education* (July 1835), 9.
[41] [Baden Powell], 'University Education without Religious Distinctions', 38.
[42] Newman to Hampden, 28 November 1834, LDN iv. 371. In draft, though not in the version sent to Hampden, Newman observed that Hampden's views led to 'formal Socinianism'.
[43] [E. Hawkins], *Oxford Matriculation Statutes: answers to the 'Questions Addressed to Members of Convocation' by a Bachelor of Divinity, with brief notes upon church authority* (Oxford, 1835), 16–17.
[44] 'As to the admission of Dissenters I am not so liberal or so bold as you are. My hope is that they will never be admitted except on the same terms as at Cambridge—compliance with the whole routine of college discipline.' OCL Hawkins Papers, Letter Book 14, no. 1338, Copleston to Hawkins, 15 November 1837.
[45] [E. B. Pusey], *Subscription to the Thirty-Nine Articles; Questions Respectfully Addressed to Members of Convocation on the declaration Proposed as a Substitute for the Subscription to the Thirty-Nine Articles, by a Bachelor of Divinity, with Answers by a Resident Member of Convocation, and Brief Notes Upon those Answers by a Bachelor of Divinity* (Oxford, 1835), 6–7.

intimacy according to the disposition of each party, etc, but still, in many cases, with an intimacy bordering on friendship. The tutor is often the means of forming his pupils' minds, of setting up a standard of thought and judgment in his society, and that, of course, in accordance with, or rather based upon, the doctrines of the Church. Now consider what can be more different than the respective tempers, or ethos, of dissent and churchmanship,—the one founded on reverence; the other, on boldness and self-will...How can a tutor do anything for pupils whose first element of character differs from that of the Church?...will it not of necessity follow, that dissenting pupils will demand dissenting tutors?[46]

Newman continued:

are dissenting pupils to go to our college chapels or not?...Is it not a tyranny of conscience to oblige men to attend upon those forms which they disown? Is it allowable to recognize a kind of hypocrisy? Will it 'satisfy' the dissenting faction to force such a measure of discipline? On the other hand, are we to recognize the presence of persons in our college who live without this decent worship? Will it be possible, for any long time, to insist upon attendance in the case of church pupils, when their companions do not attend?[47]

The debate was taken a stage further by an anonymous pamphlet, soon understood to be by Henry Wilberforce, but of which Newman was effectively at least part-author, in the form of a letter to the archbishop of Canterbury.[48] Wilberforce echoed Newman's description of his practice as a tutor at Oriel: undergraduates were to be trained up

in pure and uncalculating loyalty to the church...to regard as the sacred ark wherein the truth has been preserved...not as sceptical disputants, who would investigate for themselves a new road to the shrine of truth; but as humble and teachable disciples, labouring to ascertain what has been the Church's faith and practice.[49]

---

[46] Newman to H. J. Rose, editor of the *British Magazine*, 17 March 1834, LDN iv. 209.
[47] LDN iv. 211.
[48] [H. Wilberforce], *The Foundations of the Faith Assailed at Oxford; a Letter to His Grace the Archbishop of Canterbury...Visitor of the University, with Particular Reference to the Changes in its Constitution now under Consideration* (London, 1835). See the reluctant Wilberforce's comment to Newman: 'I should not at all mind putting my name [to it] (so strongly do I feel) but that...The pamphlet being really yours, it is hardly sincere...', Wilberforce to Newman, LDN v. 65. Wilberforce's candid admission to Hampden of his authorship of the pamphlet only prompted Hampden to complain bitterly that a man could 'show a heart so little touched with the tenderness of the Gospel towards a brother Christian and a member of the same college', Hampden to Wilberforce, 22 May 1835, LDN v. 74. See Turner, *John Henry Newman*, 252. Newman rejected these personal considerations, citing 'a duty (but that I have not done) under certain circumstances to denounce individuals, when they become organs, representatives, and sanctions of a system', Newman to James Stephen, 27 February 1835, LDN v. 32. He had originally suggested the still more provocative title of *Socinianism in Oxford*, under which epithet Arnold, Hinds, Whately, Hampden, and Nassau Senior were to be arrayed, Newman to H. W. Wilberforce, 23 March 1835, LDN v. 50–2, 53–6, 63–4.
[49] *Foundations of the Faith Assailed at Oxford*, 3–6.

He proceeded to assail a 'spirit of innovation', in effect an indictment of the Noetic principles which Arnold and Hampden were now carrying to new lengths: they spoke for a party possessed of an

> unequivocal disposition to modify our system by a series of liberal changes, tending to make knowledge, rather than moral discipline, the object of our studies, and to cultivate rather the habit of bold and irreverent inquiry.[50]

He concentrated his attack on Hampden's *Observations on Dissent*, which he claimed by implication went 'far beyond the errors of Socinus and Crellius'.[51] The pamphlet's strictures on Hampden created uproar among the Noetics.

Hampden himself, already angry at the damage to his reputation caused by Pusey's pamphlets in particular, demanded an apology for misrepresentation of his religious position. Newman was well aware that he was the main object of Hampden's wrath, confiding to a friend: 'I really do believe were it not for the restraint of society etc., he could take a knife and stick me in the fifth rib.'[52] The absent Hurrell Froude wrote to strengthen Newman's resolve, sarcastically commenting on his account of Hampden's frenzy 'if there was not something so shocking in a clergyman's professing a wish to fight a duel, there is a commendable originality in the motive, i.e. to prove himself a Christian'.[53] Hampden sought to draw Newman out from his cover behind Wilberforce, complaining 'it is but right that society should have its eye on persons who can so unfeelingly scatter their venom under a mask; that at least one may not mistake them for friends'.[54] Newman made matters worse in the summer of 1835 when he and Pusey collected together all the Oxford pamphlets in defence of subscription, and added a controversial introduction and postscript which highlighted Henry Wilberforce's allegations of Socinianism. Hampden's furious letter to Newman gave full vent to his aggrieved feelings: 'you have been among the "crafty firsts" who have sent their "silly seconds" to fight their mean and cowardly battles by their trumpery publications ... You have sent out to the public what you knew to be untrue ...'[55] Newman's replied that he could not 'enter into the details' of the matter 'without doing violence to his own feelings of self-respect'.[56]

Whately threw the weight of his own authority behind Hampden, regarding him as 'a man of sound views, who will keep aloof from all party'. He even sounded Hampden out as to whether he might accept a bishopric

---

[50] *Foundations of the Faith Assailed at Oxford*, 8–9.
[51] *Foundations of the Faith Assailed at Oxford*, 13–15.
[52] Newman to S. L. Pope, 28 June 1835, LDN v. 86.
[53] Froude to Newman, 2 July 1835, LDN v. 97.
[54] Hampden to Wilberforce, 20 May 1835, LDN v. 73–4.
[55] Hampden to Newman, 23 June 1835, LDN v. 83.
[56] Newman to Hampden, 24 June 1835, LDN v. 84.

if offered one.[57] He later reflected: 'the "faith"...whose "foundations" [Hampden] was accused of assailing (and he did assail them very powerfully), is manifestly not that of the Church, but that of those nominal members of it who studiously inculcate doctrines utterly opposed to its fundamental principles.'[58] Provost Hawkins meanwhile sought to mediate by seeking Pusey's partial retraction, though hampered by his association with the Noetics. Arnold teased him on his discomfiture:

> I sincerely congratulate you on being honoured with the abuse of...in company with Whately, Hampden, and myself; and perhaps I feel some malicious satisfaction that you should be thus...forced into the boat with us, while you perhaps are thinking us not very desirable companions.[59]

Whately told him that he found 'allusions to me, which are to be felt by you' in Tractarian pamphlets, and complained that Newman had written 'as if I were another Judas'.[60] The public controversies of 1834–5 had destroyed the harmony of Oriel.

The subscription dispute made Hampden the leading antagonist of the Oxford Movement, whose Bampton Lectures (1832) and other writings were in consequence scrutinized for heterodoxy by his opponents.[61] It was not surprising therefore that his appointment as Regius Professor of Divinity in February 1836 was highly controversial. The Prime Minister, Lord Melbourne, had preferred his Whig friends' advice to that of Archbishop Howley, whose list of six included Newman and Pusey; on Whately's recommendation, confirmed by Copleston, he had settled on Hampden, 'a safe man' and a solid scholar. His appointment united old high churchmen, evangelicals, and Tractarians in furious opposition, and a motion to require the Hebdomadal Council to examine his theological writings was promoted in convocation. In Oriel it alienated even moderate opinion, including the dean, William James Copleston, who wrote outspokenly to Hampden that he had 'been conscientiously obliged to join the ranks of those who thus declare war against your published theological opinions'.[62] Twenty Oriel men signed the requisition to the Hebdomadal Council. The opponents of Hampden met in the Corpus Christi common room with Vaughan Thomas of Corpus in the chair. Newman was the driving force, drawing up an anonymous pamphlet, *Elucidations of Dr Hampden's Theological Statements*, drawing largely on his Bampton

---

[57] OCL 'Hampden Controversy', i, no. 17, Whately to Hampden, 16 October 1835.

[58] R. Whately, *Statements and Reflections Respecting the Church and the Universities, being an Answer to an Inquiry made by some of the Clergy of the Diocese concerning the Movement connected with the Appointment of the Bishop of Hereford* (Dublin, 1848), 33.

[59] Arnold to Hawkins, 27 May 1835, Stanley, *Life of Arnold*, i. 362. The ellipsis probably referred to Pusey.

[60] OCL Hawkins Papers, Letter Book 3, no. 211, Whately to Hawkins, 9 June 1835.

[61] H. Hampden, *Memorials of Renn Dickson Hampden*, vi.

[62] OCL 'Hampden Controversy', no. 14, W. J. Copleston to Hampden, 24 February 1836.

Lectures and associating their rationalist tendency with the suspicious influence of Blanco White.[63] The Noetics regarded reference to the lectures as a pretext. Baden Powell pointed out that they had not prevented Hampden's appointment to be principal of St Mary Hall or election to the chair of moral philosophy; 'the peculiar theology' of the Tractarians explained 'the vehement appeals and fearful denunciations in which its votaries indulge, [which] must appear more like the reveries of visionaries and the hallucinations of fanatics than the sober deliberations of academical divines'.[64] Blanco White, himself now effectively a Unitarian, lamented that his old friend Newman seemed to be acting in the spirit of the Spanish Inquisition, informing the provost that he now regarded Newman and Froude as 'very remarkable instances of the poisonous nature of bigotry'. Constrained by his old friendship, he felt unable to write against them, but speculated on their state of mind:

When people have advanced to that stage of mental disease (I do not know a milder word in the circumstances of the case) in which the ultimate ground of argument is an act of the will, it is most distressing to attempt any thing like reasoning. Newman, I am convinced, is in that state; and I remember to have perceived the first symptoms while I was at Oxford. He had drawn into the same cause the more lively mind of poor Froude, who seemed to me at times to laugh at the extravagance of the conclusions into which he found himself compelled by logical consistency.[65]

Like Newman he saw Oriel's divisions in personal terms. He wrote to Hawkins, 'however changed the college may be, I shall never lose the agreeable and interesting recollection of my companionship with you. You are to me Oriel—the Oriel which I shall ever love.'[66] But he was aware of his own compromised position: his support of Baden Powell's defence of Hampden was likely to do Powell harm.[67]

Other Noetics were less tender. Hampden himself was indignant that his orthodoxy was impugned: 'never was any member of our Church more falsely charged with Socinianism than I have been.'[68] Arnold entered the fray with relish: he assured Hampden that he would be writing 'an article on your persecution and on the Judaizing Christians your persecutors in the next Edinburgh Review'.[69] Provocatively entitled 'The Oxford *Malignants*

---

[63] [J. H. Newman], *Elucidations of Dr Hampden's Theological Statements* (Oxford, 1836); Mozley, *Reminiscences*, i. 352–3.
[64] Baden Powell, *Remarks on a letter from the Rev. H.A. Woodgate to Viscount Melbourne, Relative to the Appointment of Dr Hampden* (Oxford, 1836), 3–4.
[65] OCL Letter Book 2, no. 109, Blanco White to Hawkins, 9 May 1836.
[66] OCL Letter Book 2, no. 108, Blanco White to Hawkins, 11 April 1836.
[67] J. Blanco White, 24 August 1839, J. H. Thom (ed.), *Life of the Rev. Joseph Blanco White written by himself, with portions of his correspondence*, 3 vols. (London, 1845), iii. 8.
[68] OCA MPP/H 2/7, Hampden to J.W. Mackie, 3 March 1836.
[69] OCL 'Hampden Controversy' i, no. 3, Arnold to Hampden, 28 March 1836.

and Dr Hampden', it deplored Hampden's critics for exhibiting 'the character, not of error, but of moral wickedness'.[70] He called a pamphlet of Pusey 'the last seal of the perfect triumph of the lowest fanaticism over a noble nature'.[71] But his protégé at Rugby, the Balliol undergraduate Arthur Stanley, who hero-worshipped his former headmaster, lamented his inability to judge the work of minds wholly different from his own. Convinced that Arnold and Newman were much closer spiritually than their theological views suggested, he regretted Arnold's article as likely to 'make the breach...irreparable'.[72] Arnold himself later recognized his common ground with Newman.[73]

A constant trope of the Noetics was the inquisitorial nature of the proceedings against Hampden.[74] Baden Powell drew a cartoon, entitled *The Procession of the Grand Auto da Fe Celebrated at Oxford in 1836*.[75] Whately's Dublin chaplain Charles Dickinson's spoof *Pastoral Epistle of His Holiness the Pope to some Members of the University of Oxford* called the Tractarians the pope's 'beloved children' and 'our Missionaries'.[76] More seriously, Whately focused on their unconstitutional and subversive character, noting the irony that 'those who are emphatically styled high-churchmen, who declaim the most loudly against schism', went to 'the greatest lengths in schismatical proceedings'. Proceedings should be instituted by regular ecclesiastical authority, 'not by any individual or any number of individuals taking upon themselves to be accuser, judge, jury, and executioner, all in one; and by their own self-constituted authority, to denounce and stigmatize a brother-clergyman'.[77]

---

[70] [T. Arnold], 'The Oxford *Malignants* and Dr Hampden', *Edinburgh Review*, 63 (April 1836), 238.

[71] OCL 'Hampden Controversy', no. 2, T. Arnold to R. D. Hampden, 17 February 1836.

[72] R. E. Prothero, *The Life and Correspondence of Arthur Penrhyn Stanley, D.D. Late Dean of Westminster*, 2 vols. (4th edn., London, 1894), i. 162.

[73] Arnold made a remarkable admission to the provost in 1840, when he took issue with him for repeating the common assumption that 'Newman is one extreme and I another'. As Arnold explained: 'the truth is, that in our views of the importance of the Church, Newman and I are pretty much agreed, and therefore I stand as widely aloof as he can do from the language of "religion being an affair between God and a man's conscience".' Arnold to Hawkins, 4 December 1840, Stanley, *Life of Arnold*, i. 241.

[74] On Nassau Senior's account of 'the *auto-da-fe* at Oxford' see H. Hampden, *Memorials of Renn Dickson Hampden*, 66–8; *State of Parties in Oxford* (Oxford, 1836), 41–2; *The Oxford Persecution of 1836, extracts from the public journals, in defence of the present Regius Professor of Divinity, and his appointment to that chair, and in condemnation of the proceedings at Oxford subsequent to that appointment* (Oxford, 1836).

[75] For a detailed explanatory study of the iconography of this cartoon, see D. B. Roberts, 'The Church Militant', Magdalen College Occasional Paper no. 8 (Oxford, 2013).

[76] [C. Dickinson], *A Pastoral Epistle from His Holiness the Pope to Some Members of the University of Oxford* (Oxford, 1836), 34–5. Baden Powell was clearly in on the joke and incorporates an image of 'the pope's nuncio bearing the pastoral Epistle' in his cartoon.

[77] OCL 'Hampden Controversy', i, no. 20, Whately to Copleston, 21 November 1836 (copy).

The Noetics were, as usual, themselves not united. Hampden claimed the approval of the late John Davison for the Bampton Lectures, but his widow was doubtful.[78] Copleston and Hawkins were far more measured than were Arnold or Whately in assessment of Hampden's writings. Copleston cautioned Hampden against his use of ambiguous language: 'I apprehend that your phrase matters of fact, has led to much of this misrepresentation. I observe you oppose this phrase to the word doctrine "strictly so to speak", etc. Now this is a phraseology which seems to me objectionable.' He urged Hampden to reply to Newman, but did not object to the Hebdomadal Board examining Hampden's writings in accord with 'their general superintendence that concerns the well being of the University'.[79] Hawkins, under pressure from Keble to distance himself from 'Whately's school', was still more critical of the Bampton Lectures, remarking to Whately, 'as you may be aware from what I said to you when I had read his Bampton Lectures, that I am far from approving of all he had written, and think indeed that there are many things very rash and contentious in his writings, and, as they stand, unsound'.[80] Hampden's Inaugural Lecture 'had pretty well silenced the cry against his personal faith' and should 'expose some of the absurd fallacies and blunders in the extracts and propositions said to be maintained by him'.[81] On the Hebdomadal Board Hawkins attempted to mitigate the formal proceedings instituted against Hampden, acting as his ally and friendly interpreter. He did not however ultimately carry the day on the board, and on 5 May 1836, on the second attempt and after a proctorial veto, convocation deprived the Regius Professor of the power to appoint select preachers and the right to sit among the judges of heresy cases.

Hampden was unrepentant. He reissued his Bampton Lectures with a new introduction, in which he asserted against his critics, 'I see no reason, from what they have alleged, for changing a single opinion, or retracting a single statement. Nor indeed, in that posture of mind in which they applied themselves to the work of criticism, were they likely to discover any real objections.'[82] With Newman in mind, he derided them for failure to understand him and relying on hearsay and garbled statements: 'It is not only true that men condemn what they do not understand, but that they are disabled

---

[78] Thomas Mozley did not regard them as a legitimate offspring of 'the old Oriel school'. Hampden could only produce Davison's polite acknowledgement of them as evidence of approval, Mozley, *Reminiscences*, i. 355, 371.
[79] OCL Hawkins Papers, Letter Book 1, no. 4a, Copleston to Hampden, 18 February 1836.
[80] OCL Hawkins Papers, Letter Book 8, no. 761, Keble to Hawkins, 7 March 1837; Letter Book 5, no. 413, Hawkins to Whately, 18 February 1836.
[81] OCL Hawkins Papers, Letter Book 5, no. 416, Hawkins to Whately, 31 March 1836.
[82] R. D. Hampden, *Introduction to the Second Edition of the Bampton Lectures of the Year 1832* (London, 1837), 3.

from understanding what they have been taught to condemn.'[83] He had reason for confidence, having been worsted only by a temporary alliance of evangelicals and traditional high churchmen with the Tractarians.

The Hampden affair further embittered the Oriel common room. The provost's attempt to present himself as a force for harmony did not ring true: as James Mozley reported to his sister Anne, after one of the provost's sermons on the subject, 'he observed that it was a disgusting habit in persons finding fault with other people's theology. Nothing tended so much to make the mind narrow and bitter. They had much better be employing themselves in some active and useful way. This is laughable enough as coming from the Provost, who has been doing nothing less but objecting all his life.'[84] Hawkins cannot have welcomed the spread of Tractarian religious practices in the college, including fasting, self-denial, and personal asceticism. They had originated during the tutorship of Newman and Hurrell Froude; the ascetic influence of Froude in particular lasted long after he had gone out of residence and then died (28 February 1836). Its moral legacy was profound, notably on Samuel Francis Wood, now a barrister.[85] Newman and Keble later published Froude's *Remains*, alienating the old high churchmen for good.[86] In his absence, Newman led by silent and self-effacing example. His rooms were linked to an adjoining large closet above the chapel door which had become a lumber room. Newman turned it to his private religious use. As Thomas Mozley recalled, 'Newman fitted it up as a prophet's chamber, and there, night after night in the Long Vacation of 1835, offered up his prayers for himself and the Church. Returning to college late one night I found that, even in the gateway, I could not only hear the voice of prayer, but could even distinguish the words.'[87]

Every fellowship election appeared to strengthen the Tractarian hold on the college, notably that of Richard William Church of Wadham (1838). Church, later reckoned the paradigm of all that was noble about the Oxford Movement, had been introduced to Keble and Newman by Charles Marriott in 1835, and would become one of Newman's closest Oriel friends.[88] But outside the college a reaction was gathering force. Oriel men were encountering

---

[83] Hampden, *Introduction to the Second Edition*, 4.
[84] J. B. Mozley to A. Mozley, 26 November 1836, *Letters of the Rev. J. B. Mozley*, 61.
[85] He may have influenced Newman's idea of the development of doctrine. See Pereiro, *Ethos and the Oxford Movement*, 9–13, 141–63.
[86] J. H. Newman and J. Keble (eds.), *The Remains of the late Reverend Richard Hurrell Froude* (London, 1838–9); P. Brendon, *Hurrell Froude and the Oxford Movement* (London, 1974), 180.
[87] Mozley, *Reminiscences*, i. 396.
[88] ODNB s.n. Mark Pattison commented on Church's election: 'I presume that Church was Newman's candidate, though so accomplished a scholar as the Dean need not have required any party push. I have always looked upon Church as the type of the Oriel fellow,' also observing that there was 'such a moral beauty about Church that they could not help taking him'. Pattison, *Memoirs*, 163.

ILLUSTRATION 11.5 Charles Marriott (1811–58), fellow 1833–58
Oriel College

difficulty in fellowship elections to other colleges.[89] The polarization of parties alienated some younger fellows: Henry Vaughan (elected 1835) noted, 'there is no mean between Newmanism on the one hand and extremes far beyond anything of Arnold's on the other'.[90] He chose the latter extreme. Pusey and Newman responded by renting a house in St Aldates in the summer of 1837 for their disciples, nicknamed the *Coenobitium* or *Monasterio*, where they could live ascetically and study patristics, and contribute to Pusey's *Library of the Fathers*; Pattison, James Mozley, and Albany Christie (Oriel 1835–9, and fellow 1840–5) were among the Oriel residents. As James Mozley put it, rather prematurely, 'my chances being over, I can of course afford to be cool and courageous in the matter'.[91]

In 1838 a new controversy on the relation of Scripture to tradition as sources of faith arose, with Oriel partisans again in the lead. Keble's *Primitive Tradition recognized in Holy Scripture* (1837) provided the stimulus.

---

[89] 'It had become clear that association with the writers of *Tracts for the Times* was a bar to election to a Fellowship in most Colleges,' *Letters of the Rev. J. B. Mozley*, 107; Pattison, *Memoirs*, 182–3.

[90] W. G. Ward to A. H. Clough, 23 July 1838, F. L. Mulhauser (ed.), *The Correspondence of Arthur Hugh Clough*, 2 vols. (Oxford, 1957), i. 53.

[91] J. B. Mozley to A. Mozley, *Letters of the Rev. J. B. Mozley*, 78. He was elected a fellow of Magdalen in 1840.

This time Hawkins provided some support for the Tractarians with his sermon *The Duty of Private Judgment* (1838). Newman wrote to Marriott, 'the Provost has printed a Sermon (a very good one) on the duty of private judgment and is writing a book'.[92] Hampden seized the opportunity to placate the evangelical party in a lecture on tradition, in which he presented the Tractarians as a threat to scriptural orthodoxy.[93] Baden Powell took a different view, rejecting both tradition and biblical literalism, though he rested Christian doctrine 'solely in the New Testament'.[94] Whately was more pugnacious:

The term 'Apostolical' is perpetually in the mouths of those who the most completely set at naught the principles which the Apostles have laid down for our guidance in the inspired writings, and who virtually nullify these by blending with them the traditions of uninspired men.[95]

Hawkins, embarrassed by Tractarian reliance on his sermon on tradition in 1818, used his 1840 Bampton Lectures to strike a middle path, reasserting the old Anglican balance on tradition and Scripture, and censuring by implication both Tractarian excess, the ultra-latitudinarian position of Baden Powell, and the biblical literalism of Hampden.[96]

The debate on tradition was mild, however, in comparison with the storm unleashed by the publication of Newman's notorious Tract 90, *Remarks on Certain Passages in the Thirty-Nine Articles*, on 27 February 1841. Newman ambitiously set out to demonstrate, using all the powers of dialectic honed by his Noetic training, that, though drafted 'in an un-catholic age', the Articles were 'patient' of a 'catholic' sense.[97] The reaction in Oxford was hostile, and was exacerbated by the campaign of a resident clergyman, Charles Portales Golightly, to expose what he saw as the Romanizing tendency of the Tract. Golightly had been an undergraduate of Oriel (1824–8)

---

[92] Newman to Marriott, 8 January 1839, LDN vii. 10.

[93] R. D. Hampden, *Lecture on Tradition, Read before the University in the Divinity School, Oxford, on Thursday, March 7th 1838, with additions* (Oxford, 1839).

[94] Baden Powell, *Tradition Unveiled; or, an exposition of the pretensions and tendency of authoritative teaching in the Church* (Oxford, 1839); *A Supplement to Tradition Unveiled* (London, 1841); *The Protestant's Warning and Safeguard in the Present Times. The substance of a Sermon, Preached before the Mayor and Corporation of Oxford* (Oxford, 1841); P. Corsi, *Science and Religion: Baden Powell and the Anglican Debate, 1800–1860* (Cambridge, 1988), 197.

[95] R. Whately, *The Kingdom of Christ delineated, in two essays on Our Lord's own account of His Person and of the Nature of His Kingdom, and on the Constitution, Power, and Authority of a Christian Church as Appointed by Himself* (London, 1841), 226.

[96] E. Hawkins, *An Enquiry into the Connected Use of the Principal Means of Attaining Christian Truth* (Oxford, 1840), 38 ff., 55 ff. The provost emphasized that his Bamptons were a conscious repudiation of the Tractarian theory of tradition, OCA Hawkins Papers, Letter Book 5, no. 422, Hawkins to Whately, 28 September 1840. See also his sermon, *The Nature and Obligation of Apostolic Order: A Sermon preached before the University of Oxford, May 24, 1842* (London, 1842).

[97] [J. H. Newman], *Remarks on Certain Passages in the Thirty-Nine Articles* (Tracts for the Times, No. 90; 1841), 4, 82–3.

and a pupil of Newman, whose private means precluded an Oxford fellowship.[98] Having taken orders, he settled in Oxford and was well placed for an active part in the Tractarian controversies. He had supported the campaign against Hampden in active alliance with the Tractarians, and was on friendly terms with Charles Marriott and James Mozley.[99] Newman had offered to put him in charge of his new chapel at Littlemore, but after he had disagreed with Pusey on sin after baptism in a sermon, the offer was withdrawn. Newman was not forgiven. Thereafter Golightly found Newman's views on justification and on the Reformation in general objectionable, as he did Newman's practice at Holy Communion.[100] His single-minded campaign against Tract 90 was one of several high-profile religious crusades which he undertook in a long career of ecclesiastical agitation.[101] His tactic was to bring Tract 90 to the attention of as many people as possible in the hope that the university authorities or the bishops would pronounce against it. Newman's Oriel friends were alarmed. As Church informed Rogers, Golightly

> became a purchaser of No. 90 to such an amount that Parker [the bookseller] could hardly supply him, and sent his copies to all the Bishops, etc. In the course of a week he had got the agitation into a satisfactory state, and his efforts were redoubled...The row, which has been prodigious, they say, has made Golly a great man.[102]

Throughout 1841 a torrent of pamphlets on Tract 90 poured from the press, Golightly's *Strictures on No. 90*, in which he questioned Newman's 'honesty and fair play', being one of the first and longest contributions.[103]

Newman himself had not been prepared for the controversy which Tract 90 provoked. He was aware that Golightly had fanned it: 'Golightly...is the Tony-Fire-the-Faggot of the affair, and would be pleased to know that I felt him to be so.'[104] The latter sought Oriel allies, notably—and unsuccessfully—Charles Page Eden.[105] Pusey, aware that Golightly was fuelled by 'a secret grudge or dislike of Newman', sought its origins from his time in Oriel: 'whether it be owing to your having been annoyed in the Oriel Common Room, or to whatever other ground, certain it is, that while you speak kindly of myself, you speak very differently of him, who is every way

---

[98] ODNB s.n.; *Registrum Orielense*, ii. 368; A. Atherstone, *Oxford's Protestant Spy: The Controversial Career of Charles Golightly* (Milton Keynes, 2007). The young Golightly greatly admired his tutor and was close to Newman's sisters.

[99] See C. P. Golightly, *Brief Observations upon Dr Hampden's Inaugural Lecture* (Oxford, 1836); Birmingham Oratory Archives, Thomas Mozley Papers, Golightly to J. B. Mozley, 16 January 1834.

[100] C. P. Golightly, *A Letter to the Bishop of Oxford* (London, 1840), 2, 12–14.

[101] Atherstone, *Oxford's Protestant Spy*, 86–96.

[102] Church to Rogers, 14 March 1841, LDN viii. 109–10.

[103] C. P. Golightly, *Strictures on No. 90* (Oxford, 1841), 18.

[104] Newman to A. P. Perceval, 12 March 1841, LDN viii. 68–9. The reference is to a character in Sir Walter Scott's *Kenilworth*.

[105] Atherstone, *Oxford's Protestant Spy*, 91.

ILLUSTRATION 11.6 Frederic Rogers, Lord Blachford (1811–89), fellow 1833–45
Oriel College

far my superior.'[106] But several resident fellows, Rogers, Marriott, Church, and John Frederic Christie, as well as the non-resident Keble, rallied to his side, while Newman addressed an explanatory letter to a former fellow, William Richard Jelf.[107] Jelf however was not a wholehearted protagonist of Newman. Now a canon of Christ Church, he had played a moderating role in the Tractarian controversies, supporting especially his close friend and former classmate Pusey. He had been alarmed by 'certain parts of Tract 90' and had only consented to Newman's use of his name in the explanatory letter out of regard for Pusey and with great reluctance, 'and then only on the express understanding that I was to retain my own judgment and free agency

---

[106] Lambeth Palace Library, MS 1808, fo. 242, Pusey to Golightly, 23 October 1841.
[107] J. F. Christie to Newman, 23 March 1841, LDN vii. 117; [J. H. Newman], *A Letter Addressed to the Rev. R. W. Jelf D.D. Canon of Christ Church, in Explanation of No. 90, in the Series called the Tracts for the Times. By the Author* (Oxford, 1841).

ILLUSTRATION 11.7 Richard William Church (1815–90), fellow 1838–54
Oriel College

entire'.¹⁰⁸ But while deploring 'the prevailing excitement', he maintained that the Tractarian movement represented an inevitable and healthy reaction to 'the low and superficial teaching of the last age'.¹⁰⁹

Of much greater consequence for the college was the reaction of the provost, who had responsibilities both as a member of the Hebdomadal Council, which objected to Tract 90 for explaining 'away the sense of the Articles', and as a college head obliged to exact subscription to them.¹¹⁰ Abandoning the middle way, he could now proceed against the Oriel Tractarians. As Church reported to Newman, 'Golly has struck up a great intimacy with the Provost, whom he has propemped twice to his lodgings, and whom he patronizes most kindly. The first consequence to the Provost of his new alliance was the loss of his breakfast owing to G's pertinacious prosing.'¹¹¹ The provost was determined to make repudiation of Newman's interpretation of the Articles the litmus test of theological orthodoxy and

---

¹⁰⁸ Jelf to an unknown correspondent, 7 March 1842 (letter in private possession).
¹⁰⁹ See R. W. Jelf, *The Via Media: or the Church of England our Providential Path between Romanism and Dissent. A Sermon preached in the University of Oxford in Christ Church Cathedral, on Sunday January 25th 1842* (Oxford, 1842), 6.
¹¹⁰ Hawkins to Newman, 14 March 1841, LDN vii. 73.
¹¹¹ Church to Newman, 11 March 1841, LDN vii. 66.

eligibility for college office and preferment. Church's refusal to disavow Tract 90 prompted the provost reluctantly to remove him from his Oriel tutorship. According to Rogers, when Church informed Hawkins that he agreed with Tract 90,

> The Provost said first he was a young man and did not know his own mind, which would have left things in a very uncomfortable position for Church as leaving it in the Provost's power to keep him (on trial) just as long as it was convenient, and then push him off on the plea of being incorrigible, but since that he has had a talk in which he proposed Church's keeping the tutorship but not lecturing on the Articles. This Church declined on the ground of the statute granted by the Heads of Houses, which makes it the duty of tutors to teach the Articles. Then the Provost proposed laying it before the Vice-Chancellor. This Church also declined; it being perfectly clear how the Vice-Chancellor would give it (against Church) and the Provost being perfectly competent to act by himself. So that the only effect would have been forcing from a University authority a strong judgment against No. 90.[112]

Inconvenient as it was for the provost to lose the gifted Church as a tutor, it was on these grounds inevitable.

The provost pursued his policy consistently, delaying his testimonial for Charles Page Eden, who succeeded Newman as vicar of St Mary's in 1843. He confronted Eden at a college meeting, demanding to know whether he subscribed the Articles 'under the explanations suggested in Tract XC'. Eden pointedly refused to answer, leaving the provost to complain, 'when I am desirous to express my opinion of a person's fitness for a situation, I believe I am entitled to ask him any question which I may think necessary for my satisfaction'. Eden refused to accept a testimonial on that basis, and Hawkins backed down, finding himself able to 'sign the testimonial without scruple' but regretting 'that your own openness had not saved me altogether from this difficulty'.[113] He applied the same criterion for ordination testimonials, notably in the case of Albany Christie, whom he already suspected of Romanizing tendencies. Christie's sentiments had been denounced by one colleague, Henry Shepheard, and his edition of Ambrose on virginity criticized by another, William Copleston.[114] The provost made a note of 'his idea

---

[112] F. Rogers to S. Rogers, 27 June 1841, *Letters of Frederic Lord Blachford*, 105.
[113] OCL Hawkins Papers, Letter book 1, no. 78, Hawkins to Eden, 20 October 1843; no. 83, Eden to Hawkins, 23 October 1843; no. 84, Hawkins to Eden, 21 October 1843.
[114] Shepheard related Christie's positive opinion on the Gallican service, and noted Newman's influence. OCL Hawkins Papers, Letter Book 1, no. 11, Shepheard to Hawkins, 1 April 1841; no. 12, 23 April 1841. W. J. Copleston feared for the college's reputation, OCL Hawkins Papers, Letter Book 1, no. 8, W. J. Copleston to Hawkins, 18 November 1843. See A. J. Christie, *On Holy Virginity: with a Brief Account of the Life of St Ambrose* (Oxford, 1843). Christie reported his interview with Hawkins on this book: 'The Provost spoke to me very seriously about St. Ambrose. I said as little as I could as you had forewarned me. He attacked St. Ambrose as much as he rebuked me. Two of his expressions were that "St Ambrose was a very foolish ignorant fellow": and that the early Christians were "entirely ignorant of the interpretation of Scripture".

of taking pupils to pass the Long Vacation in France and attend a Roman Catholic mass, his intention not to read the state service for 5th November and yet conceal such intention from the Bishop, his turning to the east and intoning the service'. This was more than enough to deny him a testimonial.[115] Christie then sought a medical career, but the provost made an issue of his absence, and the correspondence concluded with an ill-tempered exchange of letters.[116] In the event, the provost was justified (and Newman himself came to hope he would not subscribe to the Articles): Christie joined the Roman communion, and became a Jesuit.[117]

The provost's tests had the backing of his predecessor, who regretted the passing of a more relaxed age, but was determined to confront the 'heresy' of Tractarianism. The Oriel Tractarians were aware of, and reciprocated, Copleston's antagonism, having objected in 1841 to his portrait being hung in hall. Copleston had been pained by the episode: 'Thirteen years of my absence (just the period of my Provost-ship) ought to have prepared me for the change of disposition in so changeable a body. Yet I am surprised at it more perhaps than I ought to have been—for I had imagined that there were other grounds for placing a memorial of me than mere personal regard.'[118] Now, anxious that Oriel should 'regain its credit for sound opinions in religion', he was glad that Hawkins was making rejection of Tract 90 the touchstone of 'eligibility to office in college'.[119] He wondered about 'the disposition of the majority of your Fellows, and whether you think they would support you in decisive measures for the suppression of this heresy within your society'.[120] He thought mere suspicion should be enough for the provost to refuse a testimonial: 'If you suspect, why should you recommend? I would seriously avoid recommendation, in such a case, even though I might be able to say that I have not seen or heard that he has held anything contrary to the doctrine or discipline of the established church.'[121]

So inquisitorial a stance did not however convince every member of convocation. Sir John Taylor Coleridge, a judge of Queen's Bench and friend

---

He told me too that I ought to be aware of my own advantages over them in this respect.' [Christie] to Newman, 19 January 1844, LDN x. 93. Christie's authorship can be established from the context though the signature has been cut away.

[115] OCL Hawkins Papers, Letter Book 1, no. 19, MS Notes by Hawkins on Christie, 1841, 1844. See R. G. Clarke, *In Memoriam. A Short Sketch of Father Albany Christie of the Society of Jesus* (London, [1893]).

[116] OCL Hawkins Papers, Letter Book 1, no. 15, Christie to Hawkins, 22 January 1845: 'I believe that your great conscientiousness is scrupulosity'; no. 16, Hawkins to Christie, 10 March 1845: 'I think I ought to tell you that the letter itself was an improper one...it is unbecoming of you to censure me for the discharge of an official duty.'

[117] Newman to Pusey, 12 October 1844, LDN x. 362.

[118] OCL Hawkins Papers, Letter Book 9, no. 864, Copleston to Hawkins, 8 December 1841.

[119] OCL Hawkins Papers, Letter Book 5, no. 406, Copleston to Hawkins, 10 April 1843.

[120] OCL Hawkins Papers, Letter Book 5, no. 404, Copleston to Hawkins, 26 September 1843.

[121] OCL Hawkins Papers, Letter Book 1, no. 40, Copleston to Hawkins, 26 November 1845.

of several Tractarians, bluntly warned Hawkins of its consequences: 'Our Church is a strong church but a wide church. Do not tempt the inconsiderate, the unstable, the wrong headed to think that they have no alternative but to break bounds, to jump over the hedge that separates them from other pastures.' He objected 'to the justice and expediency of any doctrinal test imposed on Tutors—if on them, why not on Professors, Heads of Houses etc. The same reason applies, it may be in different degrees, to all. And suppose the Fellows of a college should elect for their head, a man statutably qualified, or the Crown should appoint a Professor statutably qualified, and either refused the Test, what would you do?'[122] The provost indignantly insisted that he was only doing his conscientious duty 'to the university and my college, and all parents who may wish to send their sons to Oriel', that he preferred to appoint 'those who go into no extreme views of any kind', that he was of 'no party' himself, was even-handed against 'error' from opposite quarters, and was no 'enemy of peace'.[123] The judge was doubtless concerned for the prospects of his Tractarian son Henry James Coleridge, who was nevertheless elected a fellow of Oriel in 1845.[124]

Newman himself responded to the growing hostility of the Oxford establishment by retreating to Littlemore for ever longer periods. He was aware that even before the publication of Tract 90 the university authorities disliked the effect of his preaching, and conceded that 'I am leading my hearers, to the Primitive Church if you will, but not to the Church of England.'[125] He would have liked to give up St Mary's, while keeping its dependency, Littlemore, but 'the Provost would not hear of the separation of the living'.[126] In September 1843 he resigned as vicar of St Mary's without this concession. He took little part in the many passages of arms between the Tractarians and their opponents after 1841: the attempt of Isaac Williams to be elected professor of poetry, the campaign to restore Hampden's powers as Regius Professor, and the challenge to Benjamin Symons, warden of Wadham, when his turn to be vice-chancellor came up. He was inactive in the storm which arose over Pusey's sermon on the Eucharist in 1843, in which Hawkins, as

---

[122] OCL Hawkins Papers, Letter Book 11, no. 1087, J. T. Coleridge to Hawkins, 13 January 1844.

[123] OCL Hawkins Papers, Letter Book 11, no. 1088, Hawkins to J. T. Coleridge, 16 January 1844.

[124] *Provosts and Fellows*, 176. The college continued to take Tractarian candidates seriously: George Moberly narrowly missed a fellowship in 1843. Coleridge Papers, BL MS Add. 85931, H. J. Coleridge to Sir J. T. Coleridge, 7 May 1843.

[125] Newman to Keble, 26 October 1840, LDN vii. 417. Newman accurately gauged their attitude: the vice-chancellor reported to the chancellor that Newman was making his parish pulpit 'an organ for propagating his views among those who are educating for the church', A. T. Gilbert to the duke of Wellington, 26 December 1839, Southampton University Library, Wellington Papers MS 2.250/65.

[126] Newman to Mrs William Froude, 9 April 1844, G. H. Harper, *Cardinal Newman and William Froude, FRS: A Correspondence* (Baltimore, 1933), 43.

one of the six doctors who examined the case, played an ambiguous part and all but quarrelled with Pusey.[127] In all these conflicts the other Oriel Tractarians were vocal, and time did not appease Thomas Mozley's indignation over the treatment of Pusey.[128]

Newman was absent again from the dramatic denouement of the university's proceedings against the Tractarians at the convocation meeting of 13 February 1845. The Hebdomadal Board had proposed a new statute to restrict permissible interpretations of the Articles, and though liberal opposition had aborted the plan, the board put forward three motions, the first two condemning propositions published by the extreme Tractarian W. G. Ward of Balliol and depriving him of his degrees, and the third condemning Tract 90. The two first were carried by majorities. The third motion, which Hawkins firmly supported, had the blessing of Copleston, who remarked that not 'even Newman could devise an evasion'.[129] Many others deprecated it, notably William Gladstone, who wrote to Hawkins in defence of Newman.[130] Marriott, Rogers, and Eden all recorded their dissent in print.[131] As Eden pointed out, Newman had largely withdrawn from his college and church functions, rendering the motion vindictive.[132] Copleston himself was jeered by the more boisterous Oriel undergraduates and younger masters of arts when he took his place in the Sheldonian Theatre. In the event the motion was defeated by the intervention of the two proctors, one of whom was Church, with a resounding cry of *non placet*. The ambiguous verdict of convocation marked the end of the university's proceedings against the Tractarians. Newman's only comment from his studied distance was to liken the Hebdomadal Council's action to 'scattering the ashes of the dead'.[133]

Newman was growing apart from his Oriel world. He no longer held any college office, and his thoughts of accepting the provostship if Hawkins were promoted, once lively, had long evaporated.[134] The newly elected Arthur

---

[127] OCL Hawkins Papers, Letter Book 11, no. 1029, Hawkins to Pusey, 4 June 1843, no. 1030, Pusey to Hawkins, 22 September 1843, no. 1051, Hawkins to Pusey, 26 September 1843, where the provost claimed that he had no part in bringing a charge against the sermon, and that it was 'against his judgment that it was brought at all'.

[128] Mozley, *Reminiscences*, ii. 252.

[129] OCL Hawkins Papers, Letter Book 1, no. 58, Copleston to Hawkins, 22 November 1844.

[130] OCA Gladstone–Hawkins Correspondence, no. 1, Gladstone to Hawkins, 6 February 1845; no. 66, Hawkins to Gladstone, 8 February 1845.

[131] See F. Rogers, *A Short Appeal to Members of Convocation upon the Proposed Censure of No. 90* (London, 1845).

[132] C. P. Eden, *To the Hon. and Right Rev. the Lord Bishop of Oxford*, Oriel College, Oxford, February 6, 1845, 1–2.

[133] Newman to Mrs John Mozley, 10 February 1845, LDN x. 542. Newman commented to another correspondent: 'the matter now going on has not given me a moment's pain, nay, or interest', Newman to Charles Miller, 11 February 1845, LDN x. 545.

[134] Rogers had been especially warm to the prospect: Rogers to Newman, 18 August 1836, G. Marindin (ed.), *Letters of Frederic Lord Blachford* (London, 1896), 34. J. W. Burgon (fellow 1846–76) had good reason to suggest that Hawkins was not made a bishop for fear of Newman's

Hugh Clough's account of the fellows in residence in 1842 conveyed a sense of division: on one hand, the evangelical Edward Litton; Henry Vaughan and Clough himself, increasingly sceptical former disciples of Arnold; and the 'high and dry' James Fraser;[135] on the other the Tractarians, Church, Marriott, Rogers, and Eden. Clough and Fraser noted that intellectual activity in the college was limited to current theological controversies.[136] The common room was no longer the cauldron of intellectual debate which it had been in the 1820s. Newman felt isolated: 'For some years, as is natural, I have felt I am out of place at Oxford, as customs are. Everyone about is my junior'... 'I do fancy I am getting changed, and find myself out of place. Everything seems to say to me. "This is not your home". The college seems strange to me, and even the college servants seem to look as if I were getting strange to them.'[137] His relations with the provost were cold. Newman always disliked an atmosphere of artificial constraint in social relations and found the glacial attitude of Hawkins a trial. He recalled an instance of it during the Candlemas Gaudy of 1842 at which his old *bête noire* Thomas Arnold was present. As senior fellow standing in for the dean, he sat between Arnold and the provost in hall, and in common room he looked after their distinguished guest. Deeply rooted theological differences and misunderstandings between them might have created *froideur*. To his own surprise, they got on very well, warming to each other; Newman found Arnold 'natural and easy'. The contrast was 'very marked between Arnold and the Provost', Hawkins being 'so dry and unbending and seeming to shrink from whatever I said'.[138]

Newman's influence within Oriel remained strong. Church and Marriott contributed to his controversial series of *Lives of the English Saints*.[139] Moreover, he remained visible in the college. Mozley recalled that though by then he was rarely seen in Hall, 'he gave receptions every Tuesday evening in the common room, largely attended by both the college and out-college

succession; see J. W. Burgon, 'Edward Hawkins: The Great Provost', *Lives of Twelve Good Men*, 2 vols. (4th edn., London, 1889), i. 424.

[135] According to Matthew Arnold, 'Fraser rather represented the high-and-dry church in Common Room with an admixture of the world—so far at least as pleasure in riding and sport may be called worldly—of the ascetic and speculative side, nothing.' Cited in T. Hughes, *James Fraser. Second Bishop of Manchester: A Memoir 1818–1885* (London, 1887), 31.

[136] Clough to J. P. Gell, 17 April 1842, *Letters and Remains of Arthur Hugh Clough* (London, 1865), 53; James Fraser, *The Lancashire People's Bishop* (Manchester, 1891), 2.

[137] Newman to Mrs J. Mozley, 15 February 1842, LDN vii. 463 and 13 August 1844, LDN x. 312.

[138] Newman to Mrs J. Mozley, 31 October 1844, LDN x. 378–9. He added: 'At last the Provost and Arnold got up to go, and I held out my hand, which he [Arnold] took, and we parted. I never saw him again. He died the June after.'

[139] In his life of St Wilfrid, the eighth-century bishop of York, even Church could write: 'To look Romeward is a Catholic instinct, seemingly implanted in us for the safety of the faith.' [R. W. Church], 'St Wilfrid, Bishop of York', *Lives of the English Saints* (London, 1844), 4.

men'.[140] A close examination of the college's buttery books has shown that Newman's physical withdrawal from Oriel was much more gradual than has been supposed. The continued regularity of his visits to the college suggests that they were not merely to do duty at St Mary's, since they continued well after his resignation; he visited the college on a Sunday throughout the first half of 1844, attending both the Candlemas and Shrove Monday Gaudies.[141] It would seem that he visited his close friends among the fellowship, Church, Marriott, J. F. Christie, and (when resident) Albany Christie. He hoped to vote for Marriott as a candidate for provost if Hawkins had been elevated to a bishopric, and to help elect fellowship candidates with Tractarian sympathies.

In the *Apologia* Newman would accuse the 'liberals' of Oxford—the Oriel Noetics—of driving him from the university.[142] His statement is supported by their private remarks: Whately expressed the hope, after Tract 90 was published, that if 'the authorities were to proceed with spirit and consistency they would expel Newman from the University'.[143] Late in 1844 Copleston was still complaining about 'the supineness of the Academical body' in tolerating tractarianism.[144] Newman confided to Elizabeth Bowden: 'I verily believe that the Provost will not let me rest in peace long, even if I do not retire from the fellowship myself. I am disposed to think he would not let me vote in an Election. One of his tests the other day to one of our fellows who proposed to take orders was "Whether he thought me an ill-used man".'[145] A few months later he told Henry Wilberforce, 'Whately and Hawkins have both used opprobrious language about me, till I begin to think of myself really deceitful and double dealing, as they said.'[146] Even Samuel Wilberforce, who was elevated to the see of Oxford in 1845, advocated proceeding against the Tractarians, recommending Golightly to prosecute Pusey in the vice-chancellor's court.[147]

More painfully, in his last Anglican years, Newman and his Oriel friends began to separate. The closest, Church and Marriott, stood by him. But in April 1843 Frederic Rogers refused to give advice on Newman's projected

---

[140] Mozley, *Reminiscences*, i. 416.
[141] C. S. Emden, *Oriel Papers* (Oxford, 1948), 168–75.
[142] Newman, *Apologia*, 329.
[143] OCL 'Hampden Controversy', 1, no. 23, Whately to Hampden, 27 March 1841.
[144] OCL Hawkins Papers, Letter Book 1, no. 57, Copleston to Hawkins, 13 November 1844. Copleston was scathing about the few temporizers in Oxford, referring to the fellows of Exeter as 'political rats': Letter Book 1, no. 40, Copleston to Hawkins, 26 November 1845.
[145] Newman to E. Bowden, 16 November 1844, LDN x. 412.
[146] Newman to H. W. Wilberforce, 27 April 1845, LDN x. 641–2.
[147] Lambeth Palace Library, Golightly Papers, MS 1811, fo. 181, S. Wilberforce to C. P. Golightly, 16 January 1846. Newman was never intimate with him, alone among the Wilberforce brothers, as he later recalled, Newman to A. R. Ashwell, 30 March 1876, LDN xxviii. 46.

resignation of St Mary's, explaining regretfully that while he appreciated Newman's friendship and influence he wished no longer to occupy a 'place in a movement which I feel is tending to a secession from England to Rome', and doubted whether he and Newman could remain on their 'former terms'.[148] Charles Page Eden, Newman's successor at St Mary's and always a less reliable Tractarian, had refused to bow to the provost's request that he should condemn Tract 90, and publicly opposed its censure in convocation in February 1845, but he now kept his distance in college. Newman observed: 'Eden who has come near enough to know me, has shown no tenderness, no real respect, no gratitude.'[149] It was ironic that of all his Oriel colleagues it should have been Blanco White, no longer a Christian of any kind and a fierce anti-Catholic, who had continued to speak of him with affection.[150] But Newman himself had withdrawn from his Oriel friends. He told John Frederic Christie that he had become 'useless as a child of Adam de Brome', since he was no longer fulfilling college offices and had become a stranger to undergraduates. Christie pleaded: 'Is really a life of study and devotion now unsuitable to a child of Adam de Brome? Can you ever affirm that there is any one fellow who fulfils more nearly what Adam de Brome's own notion of a fellow would be than yourself, except indeed in this one point that you have latterly shut yourself up much at Littlemore.' Christie, like so many others in Oriel, owed everything to Newman as teacher and religious mentor, but wished that 'you would not treat us as aliens to you'.[151]

Newman's Oriel ties were the last of his Anglican links to be broken, and may even have delayed his departure from the Church of England. He resigned his fellowship on 3 October 1845; the provost received and accepted his letter on 6 October, and he joined the Roman communion on 9 October, followed shortly afterwards by Albany Christie. He left behind him a community acutely aware of the loss, but determined to go on. As Charles Marriott wrote, 'it is strange and painful to feel going on without Newman, but we are going on at a rate that at once encourages and alarms me'.[152] Henry James Coleridge, who took up an Oriel fellowship in Michaelmas 1845, had a similar sense of desolation. His father recorded in his diary for Sunday 19 October: 'Henry left us on Friday morning... very much out of spirits, even to tears, at the prospect before him there.'[153] Even James Fraser, no Tractarian, wrote,

---

[148] Rogers to Newman, n.d. (after 5 April 1843), LDN ix. 302.
[149] Newman to H. W. Wilberforce, 27 April 1845, LDN x. 641–2.
[150] Newman to H. W. Wilberforce, 27 April 1845, LDN x. 641–2.
[151] J. F. Christie to Newman, 17 November 1844, LDN x. 419.
[152] OCL Hawkins Papers, Letter book 11, no. 1072, Marriott to Sir J. T. Coleridge, 10 October 1845.
[153] British Library, Coleridge Papers, MS Add. 86047, 'Diary of Sir John Taylor Coleridge', entry for 19 October 1845.

His departure from among us is much felt—even by those who differed from his views—where his urbanity and manners, not less than his exalted intellect and eminent piety, had much endeared him. There may be a few who are foolish, or shortsighted, or malicious enough, to rejoice in it, but I am happy to say they are but few. The general feeling is one of deep regret, not unaccompanied by anxious queries, 'What is to become of the Church of England?'

Fraser made clear that personally being 'so far below Mr Newman in all those spiritual graces and intellectual gifts' he felt himself to be 'quite incompetent to pass judgment on his act'.[154] The Noetics were relieved at Newman's departure, believing that a poison had been removed from the college. Whately, conceding the Noetic training of the Oriel converts, later remarked, 'argumentative powers, indeed, and learning, several of them possess in a high degree, but those advantages they think themselves bound to lay aside, and to disparage, in all that pertains to religion'.[155] The provost wrote kindly but without any instinctive understanding of their action both to Newman and Albany Christie, hoping they would avoid 'the worst errors of the Church of Rome'.[156]

Hawkins was vigilant in exposing potential Romanizing tendencies in the college, forcing Frederick Neve, an Oriel pupil of Newman, to declare his intentions while still deliberating on conversion. He wrote, 'if you suppose that I am acting against the law it is open to you to get your name inserted into the books of some other college or Hall within three months from this day, if any Head of House will receive your name, and then your privilege will be preserved'.[157] Henry Coleridge was equally suspect. He had been schooled by his father how to handle the provost, being warned to beware 'of the Provost's one-sided bigotry in religious matters' and to abstain from even reading Tract 90.[158] He took the advice, reporting that during his fellowship interview he 'was not very roughly handled by him'. He had pleaded theological ignorance of the Tract 90 controversy and escaped lightly with the provost's acid comment: 'You have a very great deal to learn.'[159] However,

---

[154] J. Fraser to Mrs Helen Fraser, 19 October 1845, T. Hughes, *James Fraser*, 40. Fraser could not resist informing his mother that owing to Newman's departure, he now stood ninth or 'half way up the ladder' in terms of seniority in the list of fellows.

[155] R. Whately, *Conversions and Persecutions. A Charge delivered at the Triennial Visitation of the Province of Dublin in the Year 1853* (London, 1853), 6–7.

[156] Hawkins to Newman, 6 October 1845, LDN x. 782; OCL Hawkins Papers, Letter Book 8, no. 708, Hawkins to A. J. Christie, 14 October 1845; no. 710, Hawkins to A. J. Christie, 25 October 1845.

[157] OCL Hawkins Papers, Letter Book 8, no. 714, Hawkins to Neve, 23 December 1845. Frederick Robert Neve (1807–86) entered Oriel in 1824 and joined the Roman communion in 1845, later becoming rector of the English College in Rome. See W. G. Gorman, *Converts to Rome* (London, 1910), 210.

[158] BL MS Add. 85887, J. T. Coleridge to H. J. Coleridge, 14 February 1845.

[159] BL MS Add. 85931, H. J. Coleridge to J. T. Coleridge, 8 March 1845.

Henry's religious doubts eventually provoked the provost to withhold his ordination testimonial.[160] Sir John Taylor Coleridge was equally anxious, but laid the blame 'at the door of the repulsive scrupulosity & pugnaciousness of the Provost'. Henry eventually agreed to take orders and accept a curacy; Sir John Coleridge went on, 'after a quarrel with the Provost of Oriel, [Henry] was given testimonials and ordained deacon in Exeter Cathedral on 3 June 1849, by Bishop Phillpotts'.[161] But Henry's doubts only grew, proving a bitter trial for both his father and the provost. He was converted in 1852 and joined the Society of Jesus.

For others there were mixed emotions. Burgon, not yet a fellow but a friend of several, wrote to Newman in June 1845

To some it will be cruel mockery and insult. To others cool indifference. Some, will feel invited to follow on. Others will feel adrift, and think themselves at liberty to wander where they please. Many must be quite confounded—nay who must not be? And many down their heads in silence. Many must think they have been deceived. More will think, and grieve to think that you have only deceived yourself. Others, who followed timidly, will now hurry back to their old ways.[162]

Only a minority of members of Oriel would follow Newman to Rome, and very few, as Isaac Williams observed, who had been his colleagues.[163] Marriott, Rogers, and Church remained to uphold his Tractarian legacy and the principles of the Church of England as a *Via Media*, striving to separate the 'revival' from 'Romanizing' trends, but nonetheless remained under the provost's suspicion.[164] In the provost's eyes, the self-denying and otherworldly Marriott was tainted by his old association with Newman. As late as 1857 an irascible Hawkins was chiding Marriott as vicar for allowing the chancel of St Mary's to be dressed with flowers, an innovation which made him 'still more alarmed about you than I was before'. The provost explained that 'such things at this time will revive all the fears and suspicions of the

---

[160] On 17 December 1848 Sir John Coleridge noted in his diary that Henry 'has difficulty with the condemnatory parts of the Articles and the Provost I suspect will refuse his testimonials'. See T. T. Toohey, *Piety and the Professions: Sir John Taylor Coleridge and his Sons* (London, 1987), 227.

[161] British Library, Coleridge Papers, MS Add. 86162, Sir J. T. Coleridge to C. Dyson, 11 September 1848.

[162] Burgon to J. H. Newman, 27 June 1845, LDN x. 718. Newman commented wryly on this letter: 'Mr Burgon has sent me a sermon, very well meant. It should have been in verse.' Newman to J. D. Dalgairns, 29 June 1845, LDN x. 721.

[163] *Autobiography of Isaac Williams, B.D. Fellow and Tutor of Trinity College, Oxford. Edited by his brother-in-law, the Ven. Sir George Prevost, late Archdeacon of Gloucester* (London, 1892), 121–2.

[164] See C. Marriott, *Five Sermons on the Principles of Faith and Church Authority* (Littlemore, 1850); and C. Marriott, *True Cause of Insult and Dishonour to the Church of England. A Sermon, preached in the parish of St Mary the Virgin, Oxford, on Sunday, January 6, 1851* (Littlemore, 1851), 17.

parishioners, as well as raise new suspicions about your college'.[165] Newman's friendship with Church in particular endured, while a renewed understanding was reached with Rogers after a period of coolness. Church was probably summing up his own view when he later wrote of Rogers's attitude to Newman's conversion: 'He recognized that the error, deplorable as he thought it, was the mistake of a lofty and unselfish soul; and in the light of the popular outcry against him he came forward...to take his old friend's part and rebuke the clamor.'[166]

It was Marriott's premature death in 1858, rather than Newman's departure for Rome, which marked the effective passing of Tractarian ascendancy in Oriel. Further anti-Tractarian blasts from Whately, Hawkins, and sometimes Tyler were an index of its persistence.[167] Whately complained that the elevation of his protégé Samuel Hinds to the see of Norwich had been opposed 'by Keble and Marriott of our college...even the talk of such a thing brings division and contempt on our Church'.[168] Hawkins fixed particularly on the advanced Tractarian teaching of the quondam fellow Robert Wilberforce.[169] Both of them hoped to preserve the anti-Tractarian repute of Copleston after his death in 1849: Whately feared that the projected memoir by his nephew, the sometime ally of Newman William Copleston, would underplay this aspect, but Hawkins tried to reassure him; Whately, unconvinced, published his own account of Copleston.[170] Hawkins himself was embarrassed by the Romanizing repute of Oriel in some Protestant circles and did what he could to correct the impression.[171]

In an era of university reform and pervasive theological liberalism, the Oriel Tractarians and others who had known Newman in college were left to 'wander where they pleased'. Arthur Hugh Clough's scruples over subscribing the Articles prompted his gradual loss of faith, causing the provost much trouble and alarm, especially as he had been a star pupil of Arnold at Rugby; he eventually resigned the 'bondage in Egypt' of an Oriel fellowship in

---

[165] OCL Hawkins Papers, Letter Book 8, no. 794. Hawkins to Marriott, 15 June 1857.
[166] Church, 'Lord Blachford', *Occasional Papers* (London, 1897), ii. 486.
[167] See J. E. Tyler, *The Worship of the Blessed Virgin Mary in the Church of Rome contrary to Holy Scripture, and to the Faith and Practice of the Church of Christ through the first five centuries* (London, 1844), and *Primitive Christian Worship: or, the evidence of Holy Scripture and the Church, against the Invocation of Saints and Angels, and the Blessed Virgin Mary* (London, 1847).
[168] OCL Hawkins Papers, Letter Book 12, no. 1115, Whately to Hawkins, 6 November 1849.
[169] See E. Hawkins, *Sermons on Scriptural Types and Sacraments, preached before the University of Oxford, with reflections upon some recent theories* (London, 1851).
[170] OCL Hawkins Papers, Letter Book 3, no. 292, Hawkins to Whately, 22 December 1849; no. 297, Whately to Hawkins, 4 November 1850. See R. Whately (ed.), *Remains of the late Edward Copleston, D.D. Bishop of Llandaff. With an introduction containing some reminiscences of his life* (London, 1854); W. J. Copleston, *A Memoir of Edward Copleston, Bishop of Llandaff* (London, 1851).
[171] OCA PRO 2/4/6.

1849.[172] Mark Pattison bitterly repudiated his Tractarian past.[173] William Froude, Hurrell's younger brother who had come up to Oriel in 1828 and who after a Tractarian phase became a successful engineer and scientist, lost his faith in later life but retained a lifelong affection for Newman. He wrote to the provost

> I now look back with wonder and not without humiliation at the heat and vehemence with which I joined in the fray, conscious as I ought to have been that I was taking part in a movement, not which my own judgment imperiously drove me into, but which the exigencies of partisan warfare seemed to require...I do not reproach myself for simply taking a side and giving vote on questions of which I knew I did not see the bottom or in a true sense of the word exercised my judgment, but for taking sides with such vehemence and heat; when although my real reason for taking it (indeed my avowed reason) was only that I gave my adhesion to those good men who were its leaders. I could not but admit that many whom I knew to be good men were leaders on the other.[174]

The youngest Froude brother, James Anthony, had always been more independent since he came up to Oriel in 1835. He respected Newman and paid tribute to his power of spiritual insight, and even contributed a life of St Neot to Newman's *Lives of the English Saints*.[175] As Hurrell's youngest brother, however, he was in an awkward position, carrying higher expectations of friendship and allegiance to Newman than he was able to meet. He declined the offer of his brother's rooms and rarely attended Newman's parties, holding the Tractarian party at arm's length. According to Thomas Mozley, he was in Oriel but not of it.[176] As a fellow of Exeter (1842–9), he became ever bolder in his liberal Protestant views, sharing the intellectual doubts of his friend Clough, which he expressed in a semi-autobiographical novel, *The Nemesis of Faith*, which was condemned by Whately and Hampden and burned by the sub-rector.[177] In later life, while paying tribute to Newman, he regarded the Oxford Movement, not as a betrayal of Protestantism, nor an affront to rational Christianity, but as quite beside the point:

---

[172] Clough to Thomas Arnold junior, 31 January 1848, *Prose Remains of Arthur Hugh Clough. With a selection from his letters and a Memoit. Edited by his wife* (London, 1888), 120.

[173] Pattison rejoiced in his 'deliverance from the nightmare which had oppressed Oxford for fifteen years', Pattison, *Memoirs*, 236. Church, noting his morose temperament, later remarked that many would not 'easily pardon the lengths of dislike and bitterness to which in after life Pattison allowed himself to be carried against the cause which once had his hearty allegiance'; Church, *Occasional Papers*, ii. 352.

[174] OCL Hawkins Papers, Letter Book 1, no. 66, W. Froude to Hawkins, 8 August 1855. Froude's wife Catherine came under Newman's spiritual influence and eventually joined the Roman communion. Harper, *Cardinal Newman and William Froude*, 3–5; *Registrum Orielense*, ii. 391.

[175] J. A. Froude, *The Nemesis of Faith* (London, 1849), 144; 'The Oxford Counter-Reformation', *Short Studies*, iv. 274, 282.

[176] Mozley, *Reminiscences*, ii. 30, 31. [177] ODNB s.n.

ILLUSTRATION 11.8 James Anthony Froude (1818–94), commoner 1835–40, fellow 1892–4

Oriel College

The excitement was unnecessary. The sun was not extinguished because a cloud passed over its face. Custom, tradition, conservative instinct, and natural reverence for the truth handed down to it, would have sufficed more than amply to meet such danger as then existed.[178]

James Mozley completely dissociated himself from his old mentor. He published a series of articles in the *Christian Remembrancer*, explaining away Newman's conversion, which Newman regarded as betrayal of confidence.[179] He evidently never forgave Newman for abandoning the Church of England. There was no lingering bitterness on Newman's part. Looking back many decades later, he described James Mozley as 'a very able and remarkable man, who tried might and main, as no one else did, to keep me in the Church of England, and was much disgusted when he could not'.[180] Mozley finally broke with the Oriel Tractarians over baptismal regeneration.[181]

[178] Froude, 'The Oxford Counter-Reformation', iv. 245.
[179] ODNB s.n.
[180] Newman to Mrs F. R. Wood, 13 January 1878, LDN xxvii. 301.
[181] See J. Mozley, *The Primitive Doctrine of Baptismal Regeneration* (London, 1856).

Other fellows had always been untouched by Newman's influence, among them George Anthony Denison (fellow 1828–38), whom the provost had made a tutor in 1830 with responsibility for pupils withdrawn from Newman's and Froude's care. By the 1850s he had nevertheless become an extreme high churchman and had been condemned by the archbishop of Canterbury for a 'Romanizing' sermon on the Eucharist. He later explained that in the 1830s Newman was 'much more in earnest than I was'.[182] Joseph Dornford (fellow 1816–32), another eccentric colleague, had supported Hawkins in his contest with the tutors, but became a passionate admirer of Newman's writings only after leaving Oriel.[183] Edward Arthur Litton, elected fellow in 1836, though an avowed evangelical, took no part in college controversies, but his *Church of Christ*, published in 1851, was a comprehensive rebuttal of high church teaching on the constitution of the church and sacramental grace.[184] Even then his main concern was the challenge of unbelief, to which he believed the Tractarians had contributed by their exaggerated notions of the Church.[185] Newman's Noetic opponents too were apt, in Burgon's phrase, to 'wander where they pleased' after 1845. Baden Powell became the spokesman for extreme credal relativism:

> Every individual believer may be equally bound to maintain his conscientious adherence to those tenets of whose truth he is convinced. But all this may be done, and therefore ought to be done, without intolerance, or arrogantly assuming the offence of judging or condemning the opposite parties.

Truth might be 'one' but 'it must necessarily be received in endless diversity among mankind'.[186] He then went further, denying in his *Christianity Without Judaism* that there was unequivocal rational evidence for Christianity: a parting of the ways with Whately and Hampden, whom he now regarded as 'behind the age'. His contribution to *Essays and Reviews* in 1860 decisively rejected the Noetic legacy of natural theology, and included a critique of Whately's *Historic Doubts Relative to Napoleon Buonaparte*, which he now regarded as of little apologetic value, witty but ineffectual.[187] In response, Hampden used Noetic arguments to refute Baden Powell's 'mythical

---

[182] G. A. Denison, *Notes of my Life, 1805–1878* (Oxford, 1878), 49–50, 67–8; H. P. Denison, *George Anthony Denison* ('Heroes of the Catholic Revival', no. 25) (London, 1909), 6.
[183] Mozley, *Reminiscences*, ii. 70.
[184] E. A. Litton, *The Church of Christ, in its idea, attributes, and ministry: with a particular reference to the controversy on the subject between Romanists and Protestants* (London, 1851), esp. vi.
[185] Litton, *Intellectual Religionism. A Sermon preached before the University of Oxford, at St Mary's, on Sunday, March 28, 1852* (Oxford, 1853), 7.
[186] Baden Powell, *Free Inquiry in Theology, the basis of truth and of liberality* (Oxford, 1848), 67, 69.
[187] Baden Powell, 'On the Study of the Evidences of Christianity', *Essays and Reviews* (London, 1860), 158. Corsi, *Baden Powell*, 219–20.

ILLUSTRATION 11.9 James Fraser (1818–85), fellow 1840–61
Oriel College

interpretation of Scripture',[188] while Whately denounced the change of mind of his former pupil on the subject of miracles. It was a decisive shift in the intellectual focus of mid-nineteenth-century Britain. Baden Powell was accused of joining 'the infidel party', and saved from almost certain prosecution only by his sudden death in June 1860.[189]

By the mid-1850s the call in Oriel for an end to theological party strife had become insistent. The provost, Charles Page Eden, and James Fraser all focused on this theme.[190] In a series of sermons preached before the university and dedicated to the provost, owing 'much to the influence of his teaching', James Fraser appeared to allude directly to his own experience as a fellow:

---

[188] ODNB s.n. Hampden.   [189] Corsi, *Baden Powell*, 195, 224, 217.
[190] Hawkins, *Christian Unity. A Sermon preached before the University of Oxford, on Quinquagesima Sunday, February 18, 1855* (Oxford, 1855); Eden, Sermon XV: 'Unity in the Church, How to be Sought' (Preached before the University, in Act Term, 1855), *Sermons Preached at St Mary's in Oxford* (London, 1855).

We should begin to feel that we have long exhausted the spectacle of 'a house divided against itself'. We ought to be able to see that there are other points of view from which religious questions may be regarded, other aims with which means of practical usefulness may be advocated, than what are so invidiously and offensively called either Tractarian or Evangelical. All really good earnest hearts among us are yearning for peace. All simple minds are trying to grasp their way out of the mass of perplexity produced by our bitter controversies and endless discussions.[191]

Echoing an old Noetic refrain, Fraser castigated party spirit as playing into the hands of unbelievers.[192] This call for peace did not extend to turning a blind eye to the complete abandonment of religious belief. The liberalizing tendency culminated in *Essays and Reviews* in 1860, with Oriel protagonists on both sides of the argument. Besides Baden Powell, Mark Pattison contributed an essay, while Thomas Hughes (Oriel 1841–5) attacked the dishonesty of attempts to silence the essayists.[193] But Jelf, one of their most searching critics, moved its formal condemnation in the Church's house of convocation.[194] Litton and Burgon composed treatises on Scripture by way of response.[195] Even Hampden weighed in and made a determined effort, despite his own 'persecution' for heterodoxy, to have the authors prosecuted.[196]

The Tractarian controversy had raged most fiercely in Oriel. As one observer remarked:

It is our object, to appeal to anyone who was acquainted with the inner life of the Oxford religious world twenty and five-and-twenty years ago, whether two very opposite, and now very prominent, parties in the English Church, are not the development of private discussions and every-day conversations within the walls of Oriel common-room.[197]

The ferocity had taken its toll, though at first the damage was not apparent. Undergraduate devotions had increased: on a sample Sunday, 28 January 1866, a third of the undergraduates had been to a parochial church service as

---

[191] James Fraser, *Six Sermons preached before the University of Oxford* (Oxford, 1855), ix, xxxii.
[192] *Six Sermons*, iii, 'Christian Manliness' (preached 20 February 1853), xix.
[193] T. Hughes, *A Layman's Faith* (London, 1868), 6–7.
[194] R. W. Jelf, *Specific evidence of unsoundness in the volume entitled 'Essays and Reviews', submitted to the Lower House of Convocation, February 26th, 1861, on moving an address to the Upper House with a view to Synodical Censure* (Oxford, 1861).
[195] E. A. Litton, *A Guide to the Study of Holy Scripture* (London, 1861). Burgon's sermon 'Inspiration and Interpretation' represented his response. His concern over the unbelief of a new generation of Oriel undergraduates led him to institute Sunday evening bible classes in the early 1860s. E. M. Goulburn, *John William Burgon, late Dean of Chichester: A biography with extracts from his life and letters*, 2 vols. (London, 1892), ii. 260–1.
[196] I. Ellis, *Seven Against Christ: A Study of 'Essays and Reviews'* (London, 1980), 163–4.
[197] *Christian Remembrancer*, 23, 'Memoir of Bishop Copleston' (January 1852), 18.

ILLUSTRATION 11.10 Charles Neate (1806–79), fellow 1828–79

Oriel College

well as to college chapel.¹⁹⁸ This was not only due to Tractarian influence: Arnold and the example of Rugby had played its part. But in other ways the price of conflict was high. The Noetics noted the intellectual decline. As Whately observed to the provost when Matthew Arnold was elected, 'what an interesting thing that M. Arnold should have been elected just thirty years after his father! Would that the college was now what it was then!'¹⁹⁹ He had regretted as early as 1838 the 'blight which had fallen on the literary reputation of the college ... I feel as if I were beholding, not only the dead face of an old friend, but his mouldering and decaying corpse.'²⁰⁰ Once the Tractarian ascendancy in Oriel was established, Whately resolved 'to efface the memory of Oxford and of his Oxford friends generally from his mind, and to be as if he had never been at that university'.²⁰¹ This partial perspective was challenged by Keble as early as 1830: as Hurrell Froude noted, 'Keble is very angry to find the College calumniated in all quarters as rapidly on the

---

¹⁹⁸ J. W. Burgon, *The Oxford Sunday: A Letter to Mr Sandford, in reply* (Oxford, 1866), 13–14.
¹⁹⁹ Whately to Hawkins, 20 April 1845, *Life and Correspondence of Richard Whately*, 236.
²⁰⁰ Cited in Tuckwell, *Pre-Tractarian Oxford*, 83.
²⁰¹ Mozley, *Reminiscences*, i. 369.

ILLUSTRATION 11.11 The Procession of the Grand Auto da Fé, 1836 (detail): Hampden in front, the Tractarians behind

OCA, Cartoon by Baden Powell, 1836

decline—He thinks that this notion has set about by old Cop[leston]'s part—and that what Hawkins is at is to brush us up and set the College on its old ground.'[202] But there is other, less subjective evidence of decline. Mark Pattison and James Anthony Froude, both undergraduates in the 1830s, believed the Tractarians had diverted their energies from the 'true business' of a college. As Froude put it, his contemporaries 'divided into parties, and the measure with which they estimated one another's abilities was not knowledge or industry, but the opinions which they severally held'.[203] Their opponents were equally to blame: as Thomas Hughes put it, 'the battle which was raging in the Church and University round Tract XC interested Provost and Fellows far more deeply than the ordinary routine work of the college, and that work suffered accordingly'.[204] Oriel's divisions were sharper than elsewhere, though Tractarian zealotry was equally strong in other colleges; but the emollient Plumptre of University College and Routh of Magdalen coped with it better than the inflexible Hawkins.[205] As Hughes argued, 'a man of wide sympathies and the power of guiding...others' might

---

[202] Froude to Newman, 1 August 1830, LDN ii. 259.
[203] Froude, 'The Oxford Counter-Reformation', iv. 255.
[204] Hughes, *James Fraser*, 24.
[205] R. Darwall-Smith, *A History of University College, Oxford* (Oxford, 2008), 359.

ILLUSTRATION 11.12 'Ye Provost and his Satellites', c.1849: Provost, D. P. Chase, Charles Marriott, George Buckle, C. P. Chretien, Charles Daman, *OCA*

have turned the powerful materials of Oriel 'to the best account... but such a man in those years was not forthcoming'.[206]

With time, the old antagonisms began to heal. By 1860, Newman himself conceded that he had sometime provoked Hawkins and 'might have acted more generously to a man whom he owed much'. He lamented 'the painful state of our relations between 1829 (February) and 1845 when I became a Catholic... a state of constant bickerings... of coldness, dryness and donnishness on his part, and of provoking insubordination and petulance on mine. We differed in our views materially, and he, always mounting his horse, irritated and made me recoil from him.' Reading over the provost's letters, Newman concluded, 'It is plain... that I had angered and alienated him. He is, when not frigid, hot (or rather always frigid in manner, often hot in thought). But I doubt not, if I would see my own letters, I should be very ashamed of them.'[207] In 1876 he was dismayed when Pusey maintained that he 'had lived to regret the part he had taken in Hawkins's election to the Oriel Provostship', and that Hawkins's rule

---

[206] Hughes, *James Fraser*, 24.
[207] Newman, Memorandum on Edward Hawkins, 15 July 1860, LDN ii. 202–3.

had been 'the sorrow of our lives'.[208] For Newman, Hawkins's election as provost in 1828 and his own subsequent removal as a tutor were providential. Otherwise he might never have emerged as leader of the Oxford Movement.[209] He carefully collected old correspondence to retain 'the records of misunderstandings or personal collisions, as mine with Golightly... Hampden etc', but insisted that by so doing he was 'not implying that I was always right, and my correspondent wrong'.[210] He manifestly wished to bury the quarrels, not least with the provost. Hawkins was absent from the consecration of Keble College chapel in 1876, when the mention of Newman's name 'raised a very hearty cheer';[211] but relations between Newman and Hawkins had nonetheless mellowed. Newman noted that the provost replied 'kindly' to his own 'lines of condolment' sent after Copleston's death in 1849; and thereafter he was the recipient of further 'very kind letters from Hawkins', though the provost could still answer the gift of his book on university education with 'a sharp word of criticism, or rather he lectured me on some provoking passage'.[212] He remained on friendly terms with James Endell Tyler, and was deeply affected by his death in 1851.[213] While his rift with Whately and Hampden was never healed in their lifetime, Newman at least made his peace with Whately's daughter Elizabeth and Hampden's daughter Henrietta when they published the correspondence of their respective fathers in the mid-1860s and early 1870s. Newman wrote to express his satisfaction to Hampden's daughter at her *Memorials* of her late father in which he was 'kindly mentioned'.[214]

Church too after 1870 had a more detached perspective on the old controversies, seeing them now as 'a story of friends fighting in the dark, having the same great cause at heart, and yet fatally misunderstanding one another'.[215] The provost had 'brought to the weariness and disappointments of old age an increasing gentleness and kindliness of spirit, which is one of the rarest

---

[208] H. P. Liddon, *Life of Edward Bouverie Pusey*, 4 vols. (London, 1893–7), i. 139.

[209] In 1844 Newman remarked to Catherine Froude that had Keble been elected provost 'we should never have been dismissed from the Tuition, we (K, R.H.F. and I) should never have turned our minds so keenly to other subjects, not a Tract would have been written. I should have gone on with Mathematics (which I was bent on doing and did...). I should have gone on with Niebuhr and Aristotle', Newman to Catherine Froude, 4 April 1844, LDN x. 191–2.

[210] Newman, 'Memorandum: Letters from Friends. Correspondence with Friends...from 1828 to 1836', LDN i. 128–9.

[211] In his account of the occasion for Newman's benefit, H. P. Liddon explained Hawkins's absence on the grounds of 'old age' combined 'perhaps with some faint traces of his old feelings about the Tractarian School'. Liddon to Newman, 12 May 1876, LDN xxxii. 59.

[212] Newman, 'Memorandum on Edward Hawkins', 202; Newman to Ambrose St John, 4 January 1853, LDN xv. 243.

[213] Newman to Hawkins, 9 October 1851, LDN xiv. 380. In response, the provost thanked Newman 'for your kind letter which I was sincerely pleased to receive'. Hawkins to Newman, 11 October 1851, LDN xiv. 381.

[214] Newman to H. Hampden, 26 March 1871, LDN xxv. 336.

[215] OCL Hawkins Papers, Letterbook 13, no. 1255, R. W. Church to Miss Hawkins, 16 January 1886.

tokens and rewards of persistent and genuine self-discipline'. Church remarked that 'no one probably guided with such clear and self-possessed purpose that policy of extreme measures, which contributed to bring about, if it did not cause, the break-up of 1845' and that 'a hard hitter like the Provost of Oriel must often have left behind the remembrance of his blows'; but Hawkins was not among the worldly heads of houses sunk in 'port and prejudice' which were often the butt of Tractarian satire. 'No one who ever knew him can doubt the constant presence in all his thoughts of the greatness of things unseen.'[216] Preparing for a biography of the provost, never completed, Church observed, 'I am very much struck by the deep pervading religious tone of the letters, as contrasted with the more purely intellectual character of Archbishop Whately and Bishop Copleston.'[217] He was closer in spirit to his Tractarian opponents than either side realized at the time.

Church was impatient with the liberal consensus that Tractarian partisanship had diverted Oriel from its true path: if Keble and Hurrell Froude were 'narrow', Arnold and Whately were equally narrow. They may have 'differed widely as to what was false doctrine, but they did not differ much as to there being such a thing'; narrowness that arose from a harsh temper was quite compatible with 'the widest theoretical latitude'.[218] J. A. Froude disagreed, contrasting Newman's combination of intellectual breadth and doctrinal certitude with the 'limitations' of John Keble who 'had looked into no lines of thought but his own'.[219] Newman and Arnold were both possessed of religious zeal and had a high view of the tutorial office; and Arnold's zeal unwittingly prepared star pupils such as Arthur Hugh Clough for Newman's abiding religious influence.[220] Arnold himself had made clear that he was no doctrinal relativist; he and Newman were at one in their conviction that objective religious truth mattered.[221] Thrown into each other's company in Oriel when Arnold came up to give his lectures on modern history, they warmed to each other.[222] Arnold was 'a man whom he had always separated from the people he was with, always respected, often defended'. He only lamented that Arnold 'from accident...got a notion that I was a firebrand and presumably hostile to him. There is no doubt he was surprised and thrown out on finding that I did not seem to be what he had fancied. He told Stanley that it would not do to meet me often.'[223]

---

[216] R. W. Church, 'Retirement of the Provost of Oriel' [*Guardian*, 4 November 1874], *Occasional Papers*, ii. 347–50.
[217] OCL Hawkins Papers, Letter Book 13, no. 1255, Church to Miss Hawkins, 16 January 1886.
[218] Church, 'Coleridge's Memoir of Keble', *Occasional Papers*, ii. 306–7.
[219] Froude, 'The Oxford Counter-Reformation', iv. 280.
[220] Walter Bagehot, 'Mr Clough's Poems', *National Review* (October 1862), in *Arthur Hugh Clough: The Critical Heritage*, ed. M. Thorpe (London, 1972), 168.
[221] Arnold to Hawkins, 4 December 1840, Stanley, *Life of Arnold*, i. 241.
[222] Mozley, *Reminiscences*, ii. 54.
[223] Newman to Mrs J. Mozley, 31 October 1844, LDN x. 379.

Personal chemistry could not remove theological differences. Newman maintained that Arnold and Hampden unleashed forces of which they were unaware. Twenty years later Hampden would finally see the consequences in *Essays and Reviews* and in the spread of unbelief in Oxford. The Noetics were not liberals. Indeed the Tractarians looked upon agnosticism with more equanimity, as J. A. Froude saw: 'Intellectually, the controversies to which I had listened unsettled me. Difficulties had been suggested which I need not have heard of, but out of which some road or other had now to be looked for.' The Tractarians 'provoked the storm' of a reaction of unbelief but 'had no spell which would allay it. They did not try to allay it. They used it for their own cause.'[224] Nonetheless the 'personality' which Newman in the *Apologia* deemed to be at the core of the Oxford Movement reasserted itself eventually against differences of principle. For a long time Oriel seemed anxious to disown its Tractarian past; no Oriel representative was present at the opening of Keble College chapel in 1876.[225] It was Trinity which gave Newman an honorary fellowship in 1877; Church wryly noted Oriel's failure to do so.[226] But Newman explained,

My affections have ever been with my first college, though I have more and more intimately personal Oriel friends. There was too much painful at Oriel, to allow of its remembrances being sweet…hence I rejoice that it is Trinity, not Oriel, that has honoured me.[227]

Oriel was now anxious to make amends. Provost Monro, himself a convinced liberal, sent him a tribute on behalf of the college on 20 February 1890 congratulating him on what he wrongly thought was his ninetieth birthday:

Few of us now here can look back to the time when your work still lay in this place but your name and that work have passed into the traditions of the college, and the story of that period is almost as familiar to us as if it were within our own memory. Knowing the deep affection which you bear to this college, I feel that you will allow me to say this.[228]

Oriel had learnt to be proud of Newman. After half a century, the ghosts of religious division had been finally laid to rest.

---

[224] Froude, 'The Oxford Counter-Reformation', iv. 311, 332.
[225] 'But explain to me why there was no representative of Oriel there?' Newman to Liddon, 10 May 1876, LDN xxvii. 59.
[226] Church to Newman, 22 December 1877, LDN xxviii. 284 n. 2.
[227] Newman to Lord Emly, 26 December 1877, LDN xxviii. 290.
[228] OCL Hawkins Papers, Letter Book 7, no. 696, Monro to Newman, 20 February 1890.

12

Oriel to Oliver Twist

Noetics and Tractarians at Large

Simon Skinner

In the volume on 'Nineteenth-Century Oxford' in the definitive *History of the University of Oxford* series, published in 1997, only two colleges were thought to merit dedicated chapters: 'Balliol: From Obscurity to Pre-eminence'; and 'The Ascendancy of Oriel'.[1] Balliol succeeded in the second half of the nineteenth century, in its academic distinction, reformist impulses, and consequent nourishment of an influential mandarin caste, to Oriel's position in the first half; but the latter's role as a font of avant-garde thought has been little appreciated outside a specialized historiography. Historians of the university have acknowledged Oriel's institutional pre-eminence at the time, and historians of religion have explored the theological significance of the Noetic and Tractarian schools in late Hanoverian Oriel, but the much wider diffusion of their influence on politics, on economics, and on social thought have not been properly comprehended. When Thomas Mozley, undergraduate at Oriel (1825–8) and fellow (1829–37), came in the 1880s to publish his memoirs, it would not have seemed odd or parochial to contemporaries that he should have called them *Reminiscences, Chiefly of Oriel College*.[2] To write about Oriel, it was implied, was to write about no ordinary Oxford college.

The pivotal role played by Provost John Eveleigh in creating the precedent of open competition and election on intellectual merit, which helped to elevate Oxford's reputation from eighteenth-century Gibbonian caricature, has already been described. These reforms were to lead to greater rigour in university examinations, with the new examination statute enacted in 1800: in 1814 Eveleigh was hailed as 'one of the most strenuous originators of the

---

[1] Respectively J. H. Jones and K. C. Turpin, in HUO vi. 174–82, 183–92.
[2] T. Mozley, *Reminiscences, Chiefly of Oriel College and the Oxford Movement*, 2 vols. (London, 1882).

present system of classes and honours' by his own successor as provost, Edward Copleston.³ The more immediate consequence was the establishment of Oriel as Oxford's intellectually pre-eminent college. 'With Eveleigh', the *History of the University* rightly pronounced, 'began the sequence of events which led to Oriel's years of great distinction',⁴ under a cadre of scholars notable for their writing and teaching in theology and political economy, and consequently wide intellectual influence. Donald Akenson has nicely characterized the Oriel of these years as 'an early Bloomsbury, the most fashionable intellectual circle' of its time.⁵ Mozley, the student and confidant of Newman who would later be a noted journalist and man of letters, recalled that 'Oriel College at that time contained some of the most distinguished personages, the most vigorous minds, and the most attractive characters in Oxford. From the Provost, Dr Coplestone [*sic*], to the youngest undergraduate they had been carefully selected, for to get a son into Oriel was a great thing in those days'. He added that 'its most prominent talkers, preachers, and writers seemed to be always undermining, if not actually demolishing, received traditions and institutions; and whether they were preaching from the University pulpit, or arguing in common room, or issuing pamphlets on passing occasions, even faithful and self-reliant men felt the ground shaking under them. The new Oriel sect was declared to be Noetic.'⁶

'Noetic', a term only recently established in the historical lexicon, plainly enjoyed colloquial currency in the 1820s: Samuel Wilberforce wrote of 'the Noetick School' in a letter of 1827.⁷ Deriving from the Greek, it is perhaps best rendered as 'intellectuals' or 'reasoners': 'noesis' is the fourth and last stage of human intelligence in Plato's *Republic*. The term appears to have been popularized in Mozley's *Reminiscences*, featuring also in the *Church Times* and in an essay (reviewing Mozley) by Mark Pattison in *Academy* in the same year. Pattison's own much reissued *Memoirs* of 1885, the Revd William Tuckwell's *Reminiscences of Oxford* of 1900 (referring to 'the Noetic school...provoking by their political and ecclesiastical liberalism the great revolt of the Newmania') and especially Tuckwell's later *Pre-Tractarian Oxford: A Reminiscence of the Oriel 'Noetics'* of 1909, all served to canonize the term.⁸ Tuckwell's characterization of Oriel's clerical freethinkers is typical of a literature which, insofar as it noticed the Noetics, did so in terms of

---

³ W. J. Copleston, *Memoir of Edward Copleston, D.D., Bishop of Llandaff, with Selections from his Diary and Correspondence* (London, 1851), 28.

⁴ Turpin, 'The Ascendancy of Oriel', 183.

⁵ D. H. Akenson, *A Protestant in Purgatory: Richard Whately, Archbishop of Dublin* (Hamden, Conn., 1981), xii.

⁶ Mozley, *Reminiscences*, i. 18–19.

⁷ S. Wilberforce to H. Froude, 9 October 1827, and quoted in P. Brendon, *Hurrell Froude and the Oxford Movement* (London, 1974), 77.

⁸ W. Tuckwell, *Reminiscences* (London, 1900) and *Pre-Tractarian Oxford* (London, 1909).

their ephemeral role as *agents provocateurs* of the Oxford Movement, whose own literature is of course voluminous. More recently, however, scholars have begun to pay closer attention to Noetic thought in its own right. Boyd Hilton's *Corn, Cash, Commerce* of 1977 recovered the authentic intellectual importance of Oriel's coterie of what he dubbed 'christian economists', in contradistinction to the classical political economy hitherto associated with Adam Smith and David Ricardo.[9] Richard Brent's *Liberal Anglican Politics: Whiggery, Religion, and Reform 1830–1841* recovered the degree to which Noetic thought also influenced the 'philosophy in office' in the 1830s,[10] and in particular, as Peter Mandler has shown, the watershed of social legislation, the Poor Law Amendment Act (or 'New Poor Law') of 1834.[11] Oriel was not, of course, unique in its gestation of a liberal theology and a new patristic scholarship which sought to meet the challenges of dissent and rationalism on surer ground than that occupied by the Burkean Anglicans of the eighteenth century. They had their Cambridge analogue, for example, in a trinity of 'Trinity liberals': the Arabist Thomas Musgrave, later dean of Bristol and bishop of Hereford, and then archbishop of York;[12] the Germanist Julius Hare, rector of Hurstmonceaux, Sussex, intimate of John Sterling and Baron Bunsen;[13] and Connop Thirlwall, commentator on Schleiermacher, collaborator with Hare, and a stalwart proponent of pluralism, who was made bishop of St David's by Lord Melbourne in 1840.[14]

---

[9] A. B. Hilton, *Corn, Cash, Commerce: The Economic Policies of the Tory Governments 1815–1830* (Oxford, 1977).

[10] R. Brent, *Liberal Anglican Politics: Whiggery, Religion, and Reform 1830–1841* (Oxford, 1987) and A. M. C. Waterman, *Revolution, Economics and Religion: Christian Political Economy, 1798–1833* (Cambridge, 1991) were important contributions; see also Waterman, 'The Ideological Alliance of Political Economy and Christian Theology, 1798–1833', *Journal of Ecclesiastical History*, 34 (1983), 231–44; Brent, 'God's Providence: Liberal Political Economy as Natural Theology at Oxford 1825–1862', in M. Bentley (ed.), *Public and Private Doctrine: Essays in British History Presented to Maurice Cowling* (Cambridge, 1993), 85–107; Hilton, 'Whiggery, Religion and Social Reform: The Case of Lord Morpeth', *Historical Journal*, 37 (1994), 829–59; and P. Corsi, *Science and Religion: Baden Powell and the Anglican Debate, 1800–1860* (Cambridge, 1988).

[11] P. Mandler, 'Tories and Paupers: Christian Political Economy and the Making of the New Poor Law', *Historical Journal*, 33 (1990), 81–103; and his contribution to 'The Making of the New Poor Law Redivivus' in *Past & Present*, 117 (1987), 131–57.

[12] Thomas Musgrave (1788–1860), fellow of Trinity College, Cambridge (1812–37), professor of Arabic at Cambridge (1821–37), dean of Bristol and bishop of Hereford (1837–47), and archbishop of York (1847–60).

[13] Julius Hare (1795–1855), fellow of Trinity 1818, classical lecturer 1822; joint author of *Guesses at Truth* (London, 1827); he published translations (with notes) of Niebuhr's *History of Rome* with Connop Thirlwall (Cambridge, 1828–32), among other German works; *The Victory of Faith* (Cambridge, 1840), *The Mission of the Comforter* (London, 1846), plus vindications of Niebuhr, Luther, and *Miscellaneous Pamphlets on Church Questions* (Cambridge, 1855).

[14] Connop Thirlwall (1797–1875), fellow of Trinity 1818; published work on Schleiermacher's *Critical Essay on the Gospel of St Luke* (London, 1825); and *Letters on the Admission of Dissenters to Academical Degrees* (Cambridge, 1834), deprecating the inclusion of religious teaching in Cambridge, and was then obliged to resign college appointments; given living of

ILLUSTRATION 12.1 Nassau Senior (1790–1864), economist associate of the Noetics
National Portrait Gallery: engraving after Henry Wyndham Phillips

But at Oxford, Copleston was the effective founder of a new school of Anglican apologetics which, as its principal historian Richard Brent has put it, 'sought to provide a defence of Christianity on the ground of its reasonableness against the onslaughts of deists and Unitarians...to shore up Anglicanism by ensuring that the ancient universities were educationally capable of producing clergymen competent of defending the Church of England' against intensifying intellectual assault.[15] Copleston was a college tutor from 1799 and one of the six Oriel fellows who conducted the first university examinations under the reform statute of 1800. He sustained Provost Eveleigh's opening up of college scholarships and fellowships; developed the tutorial system which was the basis of Oriel's rising academic reputation; and encouraged changes to the Oxford curriculum, accommodating the study of logic and of the natural and social sciences, an important conduit therefore for the thought of the Scottish Enlightenment to *ancien régime* Oxford.[16] Tuckwell later recalled him as 'monarch in his day alike of Oriel and Oxford, dethroner of uncreating Chaos, supreme for twenty years over the new *saeclorum ordo*'.[17] Copleston's own theological commentary was exiguous and derivative,[18] and his real importance lies partly in the enormous purchase of his writing on political economy—which is explored below—and partly in the intellectual distinction and cohesion of his circle. This circle of fellows and common room members, John Davison, Richard Whately, Edward Hawkins, Baden Powell, Renn Dickson Hampden, Thomas Arnold, Blanco White, Samuel Hinds, and others, has been described in a previous chapter. The political economist Nassau Senior was another of Copleston's protégés and an intimate of Whately. Senior had matriculated at Magdalen in 1806; frustrated by his poor examination performance, he hired Whately (only three years his senior) as a private tutor, after which he secured a first in classics and a fellowship at Magdalen. In 1825 Senior was appointed Oxford's first Drummond Professor of Political Economy. He became a lifelong friend of Whately, to whose *Elements of Logic* (1826) Senior furnished an appendix defining 'ambiguous terms in political economy'; Whately himself succeeded Senior as Drummond Professor in 1830.[19] As the great economist Joseph Schumpeter observed, he 'formed Senior, whose whole approach

---

Kirkby Underdale by Brougham; completed *History of Greece* (London, 1835–44); supported the abolition of Jewish disabilities, 1848, and the disestablishment of the Church of Ireland, 1869.

[15] R. Brent, 'Whately, Richard (1787–1863)', ODNB s.n.

[16] R. Brent, 'Copleston, Edward (1776–1849)', ODNB s.n.; P. Corsi, 'The Heritage of Dugald Stewart: Oxford Philosophy and the Method of Political Economy', *Nuncius, Annali di Storia della Scienza*, 2 (1987), 89–144.

[17] Tuckwell, *Pre-Tractarian Oxford*, 17.

[18] See his *An Enquiry into the Doctrines of Necessity and Predestination* (London, 1821), which drew on Joseph Butler's famous *Analogy of Religion* (1736).

[19] P. Deane, 'Senior, Nassau William (1790–1864)', ODNB s.n.

betrays Whately's influence'.[20] Small wonder that due to this remarkable constellation, as Newman was to recall, 'Oriel, from the time of Dr Copleston to Dr Hampden, had had a name far and wide for liberality of thought; it had received a formal recognition from the Edinburgh Review...as the school of speculative philosophy in England'. It was a school, Newman added portentously, 'too different from mine for us to remain long on one line'.[21]

If the religious and political significance of the Noetics has until recently been underestimated, this was partly because later liberal narratives of the nineteenth century were more concerned with a simple genealogy of Victorian agnosticism than with so complex a theological organism as the Noetic body of thought.[22] But it is chiefly because they were overshadowed by the high-church reaction of the 1830s and 1840s which in part they provoked. Although Oriel is indelibly associated with, and much of posterity intoxicated by, the Oxford Movement, Oriel's early nineteenth-century distinction was established by the school which preceded it. The two schools were neither strictly contemporary nor, at least initially, crudely antithetical. Newman was to recall that the Oriel fellowship into which he was inducted in 1822—Whately's '*clientela*'—was 'neither high Church nor low Church' but a 'new school' whose real enemies were 'the old unspiritual high-and-dry, then in possession of the high places of Oxford';[23] this was a demonology which had much to commend itself also to nascent Tractarianism, and was of a piece with Hurrell Froude's notorious disdain for the 'smug parsons' or 'Zs' of the previous generation of churchmen.[24] And in the *Apologia*, Newman was to record his personal and intellectual debt to individual Noetics in startling terms. Hawkins, Newman wrote, was 'of great service to my mind', doctrinally leading him 'to give up my remaining Calvinism, and to receive the doctrine of Baptismal Regeneration'; Hawkins taught him to anticipate the intellectual assaults of the age on 'the books and the canon of Scripture' and to move beyond bibliocentrism to 'the doctrine of Tradition', while Blanco White too led Newman 'to have freer views on the subject of inspiration than were usual in the Church of England at the time'. Newman, arrestingly, wrote of Hawkins: 'I can say with a full heart that I love him, and have never ceased to love him.'[25] Newman also recalled Whately's 'great kindness', for example in making Newman his vice-principal of Alban Hall in 1825. Whately, he wrote, 'opened my mind, and taught me to think and to

---

[20] J. Schumpeter, *History of Economic Analysis* (London, 1954), 483–4.
[21] Newman, *Apologia*, 167, 141.   [22] Brent, 'Note: The Oriel Noetics', 72.
[23] Newman, *Apologia*, 145; Newman, *Autobiographical Writings*, 73.
[24] *Remains of the Late Reverend Richard Hurrell Froude, M.A., Fellow of Oriel College, Oxford*, ed. J. H. Newman and J. Keble, 4 vols. (vols. i–ii, London, 1838; vols. iii–iv, Derby, 1839), i. 429, 329.
[25] Newman, *Apologia*, 137–8.

use my reason'; just as Hawkins had led Newman from a low churchmanship to one founded on the Church's tradition, so Whately's role was 'to fix in me those anti-Erastian views of Church polity, which were one of the most prominent features of the Tractarian movement'.[26]

In the reform climate of the 1830s the fissures between the Noetic and Tractarian tectonic plates were prised open. The animosities over Catholic emancipation, Newman's conception of the tutorial role, and the matriculation and Hampden controversies, were exacerbated by the tendentious journalism of the *British Critic*, where Hurrell Froude's review of Blanco White's *Observations on Heresy and Orthodoxy* (1835) polemically construed the work as the logical outcome of liberal Protestantism in order to cast doubt, by association, on the orthodoxy of Whately and Hampden.[27] The violence of the rupture is usually represented as an episode in university politics, and as a symptom of the intensification of the war between church parties. But Oxford's debates resonated in the wider political and intellectual register of the nation; the issues were constantly debated in parliament, the staple of regular commentary in the new daily newspapers and the kernel of myriad pamphlet wars. Oriel, the storm centre of Oxford's turmoil, was therefore the node of a nationwide *odium theologicum*. But it is vital to understand that the odium was not confined to theological questions. 'These early Victorian clerics', as Richard Brent has written specifically of the Oriel Noetics, 'were not nice observers of those academic distinctions which now separate one discipline from another': any account of their 'promethean activities', as is obvious from a glimpse of their scholarly attainments, entails 'the study of theology, political economy, history, philosophy, philology, classics, and the natural sciences'.[28] It was in a convergence of the first two of these fields, however—what Whately's own *Introductory Lectures on Political Economy* of 1831 called the 'connexion of Political-Economy with Natural-Theology'[29]—that Prometheus would be unbound, and that the Noetic ethos was to find the most tenacious purchase.

In 1798 Thomas Malthus had postulated in his famous *Essay on the Principle of Population* that scarcity and therefore misery were ineradicable because population, capable of increasing exponentially, would always outrun the means of subsistence, which was only capable of increasing

---

[26] Newman, *Apologia* 137–8, 141–2.
[27] See for example R. H. Froude's review of White's *Observations on Heresy and Orthodoxy* (1835) in the *British Critic*, 19 (January 1836), 204–25; this piece, orchestrated by Newman, was the very first Tractarian submission to the *Critic*: S. A. Skinner, *Tractarians and the 'Condition of England': The Social and Political Thought of the Oxford Movement* (Oxford, 2004), 38 n. 44.
[28] Brent, *Liberal Anglican Politics*, 144.
[29] R. Whately, *Introductory Lectures on Political Economy, being part of a course delivered in Easter Term, MDCCCXXXI* (London, 1831), xiv.

arithmetically.³⁰ How, therefore, were these divergent lines on the graph to be reconciled? The answer was what he notoriously called the providential 'Checks to Population' of disease, pestilence, war, and ultimately famine. Malthus's tract was deeply influential at a time of giddying population growth: in the two decades after the first census, between 1801 and 1821, the population of Britain increased by over a third, from 10.5 to 14.1 million. In consequence, poor rates almost doubled, from £4.3 million p.a. in 1803 to £7.9 million in 1818. Malthus's tract therefore enjoyed obvious empirical purchase: although he had actually extrapolated his conjectures from the previous quarter-century of the United States, it now seemed prophetic in his own country. 'Gentlemen who have been looking into the cause of this distress', Whately told a juvenile audience in his *Village Conversations* of 1831, 'have found it to be brought about by the immense increase in population.'³¹ But Malthus's theorems—or, often enough, bastardized versions of them—were not just empirically compelling, they were ideologically convincing: their political context was as decisive to their reception as their demographic basis. As Andrew Waterman has observed, 'the ideological purpose of Christian Political Economy was to refute Jacobinism and to justify the ancien regime.'³² Malthus's arguments, that is to say, were congenial to a propertied order anxious to frame a response to radical political demands in the aftermath of the French Revolution, for they could be deployed to demonstrate that the social optimism of the British Jacobins— polemicists such as Thomas Paine and William Cobbett, orators such as Henry Hunt, and theorists such as Thomas Spence—was fundamentally misplaced: organic social improvement was ultimately unattainable; the poor will always be with us; poverty, famine, and disease were ineradicable; this mortal life was a vale of tears. Malthusianism was a powerful social bromide, therefore, which ideologically reinforced the judicial repression— Pitt's 'reign of Terror'—already confronting radicals in the Napoleonic era.

In Britain the wider response to the Jacobin disciples of the French Enlightenment had of course largely been framed in religious language, often by the clergy of the universities and notably by Eveleigh himself.³³ Malthus, too, was a clergyman, a Surrey curate when he wrote the *Essay*. In affording the conservatives of the revolutionary epoch an expedient eschatological rejoinder to radical utopianism, Malthus would also bequeath a

---

³⁰ T. Malthus, *An Essay on the Principle of Population, as it Affects the Future Improvement of Society. With Remarks on the Speculations of Mr Godwin, M. Condorcet, and Other Writers* (London, 1798).

³¹ [Whately], *Village Conversations in Hard Times* (London, 1831), i. 37.

³² Waterman, *Revolution, Economics and Religion*, 255.

³³ See in general J. C. D. Clark, *English Society 1688–1832: Ideology, Social Structure and Political Practice During the Ancien Regime* (Cambridge, 1984), and for a thematic study R. Hole, *Pulpits, Politics and Public Order in England, 1760–1832* (Cambridge, 2004).

theological hangover to his clerical brethren in the post-Jacobin generation: how this dismally pessimistic world-view might be reconciled with the existence of a benevolent Creator; how, in other words, a cosmic order of famine and pestilence could possibly have been divinely intended. This was the problem of theodicy with which theologians had wrestled since the time of Augustine, and it was one to which the Noetics sought to furnish an answer in their own time. There were, of course, other notable voices in this dialogue between theology and economics: Malthus's own first edition, as John Pullen has noted, conjectured that 'the pressure of population on the food supply was providentially ordained by God as a stimulus to human development ("the growth of mind")',[34] and in revised later editions Malthus was anxious to assert that he had 'never felt any difficulty in reconciling to the goodness of the Deity the necessity of practising the virtue of moral restraint in a state allowed to be a state of discipline and trial'.[35] Other contributors were the evangelical John Bird Sumner, later archbishop of Canterbury,[36] and in Scotland Thomas Chalmers, who became a celebrated proponent to a worldwide readership of the reconcilability of Christianity with the fashionable precepts of political economy.[37]

But Oriel was the single most important tributary of that stream of clerical political thought in the early nineteenth century now designated 'Christian economics'. The Noetics sought, through their confident adoption of a system of logic, to accommodate Malthusianism in a thoroughly modern application of theodicy to social organization. They argued that a Malthusian cosmos was part of God's design. How might the inevitable scarcity of the means of subsistence be reconciled with a good God? The answer: contained in his system were the necessary checks and spurs to good conduct. If man was to avoid ecological catastrophe he must be moral. Shortages were a clever contrivance of the Almighty, to ensure that in competing for the crumbs men were forced to be hard working, virtuous, and sexually abstinent. For the middle classes, limited wealth might then correlate with virtue, thrift, and industry; for the labouring classes, limited food might correlate with hard work, mobility, and sexual self-restraint. That was to explain the moral appeal of an unregulated economy: it created an arena of trial which

---

[34] J. M. Pullen, 'Malthus' Theological Ideas and their Influence on his Principle of Population', *History of Political Economy*, 12 (1981), 39–54; J. M. Pullen, 'Malthus, (Thomas) Robert (1766–1834)', ODNB s.n.

[35] Malthus, *Essay* (5th edn., London, 1817), iii. 423; Waterman, *Revolution, Economics and Religion*, 146–7, 172.

[36] For Sumner's thought and writing see esp. Waterman, *Revolution, Economics and Religion*, 150–70.

[37] For Chalmers see esp. Hilton, *Corn, Cash, Commerce*, 308–13; Hilton, 'Chalmers as Political Economist', in A. C. Cheyne (ed.), *The Practical and the Pious: Essays on Thomas Chalmers (1780–1847)* (Edinburgh, 1985), 141–56; Waterman, *Revolution, Economics and Religion*, 222–9.

maximized individual responsibility and therefore inculcated good habits. 'Fear of debt would make the middle classes moral, as fear of death from hunger elevated the poor.'[38] Christian economics gave a subtle but hugely significant twist to orthodox political economy as expounded by Adam Smith and David Ricardo, whose premises had been positive, optimistic, and econometric. As Boyd Hilton has stressed, the Christian economics of the 1820s was preoccupied less with the growth of the economy than with the growth of morality; pessimistic about shortages and privation, it was optimistic about the moral consequences. As Whately was to put it, 'If good boys have a larger slice of cake than the rest, this does not indeed increase the amount of cake, but it may increase good conduct.'[39] Moral arguments for the market are a modern political commonplace in the West, from Gladstone's prim insistence on exchequer probity as 'the new morality',[40] through colonial rhetoric such as Sir John Bowring's dictum that 'Jesus Christ is free trade, and free trade is Jesus Christ',[41] to the 'greed-is-good' sado-capitalism of Thatcherism and Reaganomics in the 1980s.[42] No coterie did more to establish the nexus of political economy and personal morality in British intellectual life than the Noetics. And in due course, no group more loudly protested the perceived consequences of the dismal science than the Tractarians.

Noetic ideas were diffused far beyond the tutor's study and the lecture hall, which themselves were places of influence on future statesmen: Copleston 'taught' economics to Sir Robert Peel, and tutored the politicians William, Lord Lyttelton, and John Ward, earl of Dudley.[43] Among Oriel students was a cadre of young gentlemen from landed parliamentary families, notably George Grey and Charles Wood, who would influence government policy for a generation.[44] Noetics and Tractarians also mobilized over the broadest polemical front: pamphlets, periodical articles and journalistic initiatives, school textbooks, published sermons, fiction both for adults and children, and even poetry. But if Noetics appeared increasingly besieged by Tractarianism's numbers and noise, they enjoyed a third, crucial means of influence: the systematic ecclesiastical and academic patronage of sympathetic Whig and conservative governments throughout the years of conflict: 'friends in high places', as Whately called them in 1831.[45] Reinforcing

---

[38] Hilton, *Corn, Cash, Commerce*, 311.
[39] E. J. Whately, *Life and Correspondence of Richard Whately, D.D.*, 2 vols. (London, 1866), i. 77.
[40] H. C. G. Matthew, *Gladstone 1809–1874* (Oxford, 1986), 76.
[41] D. Todd, 'John Bowring and the Global Dissemination of Free Trade', *Historical Journal*, 51 (2008), 385.
[42] A phrase made famous by the character of Gordon Gekko, a corporate trader, in the 1987 film *Wall Street*.
[43] S. Rashid, 'Edward Copleston, Robert Peel, and Cash Payments', *History of Political Economy*, 15 (1983), 251 n. 6.
[44] B. Gordon, *Political Economy in Parliament 1819–1823* (London, 1976), 108.
[45] [Whately], *Village Conversations*, i. 36.

pedagogy and polemic with patronage, the Noetics held an advantage which gave them a circumference out of proportion to their numbers. Both parties therefore took their fundamental disagreements from the high table and the library to a national arena, not just over church reform, but over those attitudes to wealth and poverty which were such contested territory in Victorian Britain.

Interest in political economy was not unprecedented in Oriel: Edward Copleston had composed a prize essay on agriculture early in his career, while Henry Beeke, fellow from 1775, had written about the income tax and had been consulted by Pitt and Vansittart.[46] John Davison, one of Noeticism's earliest luminaries, wrote in the *Quarterly Review* in the 1810s, where he attacked the high-church *British Critic*, and supported Copleston's defence of Oxford's reforms against the attacks of the *Edinburgh Review*;[47] he also published *Remarks on the Property Tax* in 1816, issued pamphlets in support of popular education and Irish conciliation, and *Some Points on the Question of the Silk Trade* in 1826.[48] His influential *Considerations on the Poor Laws* (1817) proved the most enduring of his 'reasonings on public morals, as affected by the Criminal Laws of a country, by its Institutions for the relief of the Poor, and by its mode of carrying into effect discoveries in (what is called) Political Economy'.[49] Davison's civic virtues were acknowledged by the Prime Minister, Lord Liverpool, who awarded him a lucrative prebend at St Paul's in 1824, and then at Worcester in 1826.

Copleston's prominent role in the university rapidly gained him entry to the Whig and the liberal-Tory political worlds. He became a frequent visitor to Dropmore, the Buckinghamshire house of the pro-Catholic Lord Grenville, chancellor of the university 1810–34, as well as to Althorp, the home of the 2nd Earl Spencer, also pro-Catholic, a bibliophile, and father of Lord Althorp, subsequently 3rd earl, who was leader of the Commons and Chancellor of the Exchequer at the formation of the reform ministry in 1830.[50] Copleston's famous open letters on bullionism to Sir Robert Peel in 1819, the first on *The Pernicious Effects of a Variable Standard of Value, Especially as it Regards the Condition of the Lower Orders and the Poor Laws*, and the second *On the Increase of Pauperism, and on the Poor Laws*, in Andrew Waterman's words, 'measure the high-water mark of Christian Political

---

[46] E. Copleston, *Essay on Agriculture* (Oxford, 1796). H. Beeke, *Observations on the Produce of the Income Tax* (London, 1799); Waterman, *Revolution, Economics and Religion*, 184.
[47] *Some Account of a Recent Work Entitled 'Elements of general knowledge'* (Oxford, 1804); 'Review of Replies', in *Remains and Occasional Publications of the Late Rev. John Davison, B. D.* (Oxford, 1841), 347–406.
[48] Davison, *Remarks on the Property Tax, as connected with a standing army in time of peace* (Burnham, 1816); *Religious and moral education recommended* (Newcastle, 1825); and *Considerations on the piety, or religious principle of conciliatory measures towards Ireland* (Oxford, 1829).
[49] Davison, *Remains*, xii.
[50] Copleston, *Memoir*, 20; Tuckwell, *Pre-Tractarian Oxford*, 48.

Economy'.[51] They were praised in parliament and in *The Times'* editorials, and are credited with converting Peel's mind on the return to the gold standard in 1819.[52] Copleston subsequently became what has been dubbed a 'clerical counsellor' to the Liverpool administrations throughout the 1820s;[53] he met with Alexander Baring, the banker and political adviser (who sent his eldest son to Oriel), was elected to the Alfred Club, an elite salon of metropolitan political economists, and wrote a series of widely noticed publications on educational reform (in response to attacks on Oxford in the *Edinburgh Review*), and on political economy and the gold standard.[54] He was duly showered with church preferment: the deanery of Chester, the famously plum deanery of St Paul's, and finally in 1828 the see of Llandaff. As a bishop Copleston helped to frame the form of declaration which was to replace the Test and Corporation Acts and which was adopted by the government in its repeal legislation of 1828.[55] The liberal Anglican project to reconcile dissenters with the Church was here to find direct legislative expression. In the Lords, Copleston voted in favour of Catholic emancipation in 1829 and, after some vacillation, the Reform Bill.

Thomas Arnold, too, argued for Catholic emancipation and parliamentary reform through an energetic print campaign. He issued a pamphlet *On the Christian Duty of Conceding the Roman Catholic Claims* (1829), and in 1831, during the reform agitation, co-edited with his nephew, the Whately protégé and later diplomat John Ward, the pro-reform *Englishman's Register*, endeavouring 'to Christianize liberals and tories alike in the hope of engendering mutual respect and sympathy between them in the cause of social justice'. At the paper's close Arnold addressed a series of letters on 'the social condition of the operative classes' to the *Sheffield Courant* in 1831–2.[56] The Noetic case for the relaxation of the Church's formularies in order to accommodate Protestant dissent was sustained by his famous *Principles of Church Reform* of 1833, which provoked Keble to break off personal relations and Newman to question his very Christianity; in keeping with the *Principles*, Arnold was one of the founding fellows of the Whig-founded, undenominational University of London in 1836. Arnold was another notable beneficiary of government patronage, being made Regius Professor of Modern History at Oxford by Peel in 1841, just before his early death a year later. Hampden too had served an apprenticeship in journalism as editor of the *Christian Remembrancer* in

---

[51] Waterman, *Revolution, Economics and Religion*, 195.
[52] Rashid, 'Edward Copleston', 249–59.
[53] Hilton, *Corn, Cash, Commerce*, 79, 94; Copleston, *Memoir*, 86, 105.
[54] E. Copleston, *A reply to the calumnies of the Edinburgh Review against Oxford* (Oxford, 1810), with second and third replies 1810–11; *An Examination of the Currency Question* (London, 1830).
[55] N. Gash, *Mr Secretary Peel: The Life of Sir Robert Peel to 1830* (London, 1961), 464–5.
[56] A. J. H. Reeve, 'Arnold, Thomas (1795–1842)', ODNB s.n.

1825–6. His *Observations on Religious Dissent* of 1834, which argued for the abolition of subscription to the Thirty-Nine Articles at matriculation in Oxford, was therefore arguing for the university what Arnold had argued for the nation. Like Copleston, Hampden graduated from pamphleteering to political engagement, helping Lord Radnor draft a bill for the admission of dissenters to Oxford which was defeated in the Lords in 1835; and advising the Melbourne ministries (1834–41) on university reform, and on the formulation of the 1840 'Deans and Chapters Act', which raided cathedral revenues in order to augment the stipends of the Church's poorer livings. In patronage terms, Hampden was the poster child for enlightened Whig goading of *ancien régime* Oxford and high Anglicans generally; his nomination to the chair of divinity by Melbourne in 1836, and to the see of Hereford in 1847 by Russell, were the occasions of splenetic high-church protest.[57]

Blanco White also took the Noetic ethos into the realms of public discourse. In the late 1820s, with the Tory *Quarterly Review* and the radical *Westminster Gazette* having undergone changes of editor, Nassau Senior judged the moment opportune for a journal which would 'bridge the gap between the academic world of Oxford and the political world of London', and recruited White, who enjoyed extensive literary contacts at home and on the Continent, as the founding editor of what they christened the *London Review*. The *Review*, drawing on contributions from 'Senior's circle of London friends, Broad Churchmen and advocates of social reform' such as Edwin Chadwick,[58] soon failed, but White's metropolitanism had deeper roots. In August 1815 Lord Holland had engaged him as tutor to his son Henry, and at Holland House, the social epicentre of the Whig world, White came to know Sydney Smith, Lord John Russell, and Thomas Malthus himself,[59] while as 'part of the Holland House ménage, Blanco did the round of the great Whig houses', meeting Dugald Stewart, the Scottish Enlightenment mathematician and philosopher, in Scotland. White left Holland House in 1817 but remained as much in London as Oxford, serving as tutor to Senior's son and residing in Kensington in the late 1820s.[60]

In the almost conjoined persons of Whately and Senior, Noeticism was to find its most direct and extensive legislative application; as a clerical contemporary put it in 1832, 'they have got a new-fangled system of their own ready cut & dried which they would like to force down the throat of

---

[57] Brent, 'Hampden, Renn Dickson (1793–1868)', ODNB s.n.
[58] M. Murphy, *Blanco White* (London, 1989), 145–6; S. L. Levy, *Nassau W. Senior 1790–1864: Critical Essayist, Classical Economist and Adviser of Governments* (Newton Abbot, 1970), 60–4.
[59] Holland House dinner-books, BL Add. MSS 51951–3.
[60] Murphy, *Blanco White*, 101, 151.

England & Ireland'.[61] Senior's writings on political economy in the *Quarterly Review* in the early 1820s had drawn him to the approving notices of David Ricardo and James Mill, who in 1823 proposed Senior for membership of the Political Economy Club frequented by the avant-garde of the academic, political, and commercial worlds.[62] 'For most of the next four decades', as his biographer Phyllis Deane has put it, 'Senior participated actively at the club's meetings, where current problems of economic theory and policy were regularly debated by prominent economists, bankers, businessmen, civil servants, and parliamentarians.'[63] He was appointed to Oxford's first Drummond chair in political economy in 1825, publishing much of his lecture material in the *Outline of the Science of Political Economy* (1836). After the Whigs' assumption of office in 1830 Senior commenced decades as 'a one-man government think-tank',[64] preparing a report for the Home Office on the laws relating to trade unions (which informed his 1841 *Report on the Condition of the Handloom Weavers*); he was the presiding voice on the Royal Commission on the Poor Laws in 1832, and advised Home Secretary Russell on Irish Poor Law reform in 1836; he addressed *Letters on the Factory Act as it Affects the Cotton Manufacture* to the president of the Board of Trade before serving on a Royal Commission on the condition of unemployed weavers in 1837; and two decades on, he was still in harness on a Royal Commission on popular education in 1857.[65]

Senior's tutor and mentor Richard Whately was literally born into the political classes, in the London house of his maternal uncle William Plumer, the second-generation MP for Hertfordshire and a wealthy, dedicated Foxite Whig, while his paternal uncle Thomas Whately had been Grenville's Secretary to the Treasury and party manager in the Commons in the 1760s.[66] Whately published his Oxford *Introductory Lectures on Political-Economy* (1831), which ran through multiple editions, and succeeded his protégé Senior as Drummond Professor of Political Economy in 1829. The 1830s were the years of Whately's greatest political influence, exercised from his see of Dublin: as his biographer Donald Akenson has written, 'Bishops are as central to Irish history as are cabinet members to the history of most western political democracies.'[67] Whately advised Lord Melbourne on ecclesiastical

---

[61] Whewell Papers, Trinity College, Cambridge, Add. MS c.52/51, R. Jones to W. Whewell, 21 March 1832, quoted in H. Maas, '"A Hard Battle to Fight": Natural Theology and the Dismal Science, 1820–50', *History of Political Economy*, 40 (2008), 144.

[62] K. Tribe, 'Founders of the Political Economy Club (act. 1821–1829)', ODNB <http://www.oxforddnb.com/view/theme/95369>.

[63] P. Deane, 'Senior, Nassau William (1790–1864)', ODNB s.n.

[64] Murphy, *Blanco White*, 152.

[65] ODNB s.n. Senior.

[66] Brent, 'Whately, Richard (1787–1863)', ODNB s.n.; R. T. Cornish, 'Whately, Thomas (1726–72)', ODNB s.n.

[67] Akenson, *A Protestant in Purgatory*, xi.

appointments and Lord Duncannon on Irish matters, played a leading role in drafting Irish tithes measures, and served as *ex officio* Lord Justice in the absence of the Lord Lieutenant. At Senior's urging he was appointed to chair the Royal Commission on the Irish Poor Law, and acted in support of the Whig national education scheme of non-denominational instruction.[68] His migration to Dublin gave Whately a further field in which to sow the seeds of a Christian economics. In 1832 he founded the chair of political economy at Trinity College, Dublin, as 'part of a more extensive educational offensive on the part of Whately in the dissemination of political economy in Ireland'.[69] It still bears his name. The offensive continued with the foundation in 1845 of the undenominational Queen's Colleges—to their sectarian opponents, 'the godless colleges'—in Belfast, Cork, and Galway, all of which had chairs in political economy; and in 1847, during the famine, of the Dublin Statistical Society, which aimed at 'promoting the study of Statistical and Economical Science'. Whately was president from 1847 until his death in 1863.[70] As Tom Boylan and Tadhg Foley have recently observed, 'the founders of the Society included the academic, administrative, and professional elite of Irish society', a major 'component in Whately's organizational armoury for the dissemination of political economy in Ireland, a dissemination that was to be comprehensive in both scope and scale, extending from the apex of the educational system at university level through the learned society, and down to the national school system'. For, in addition to his university and statistical initiatives, Whately 'used his position as a Commissioner of the Board of National Education, emerging as its "invisible president",[71] to have political economy included in the curriculum of the national schools'.[72] Whately wrote and compiled the school textbooks himself as the sort of introduction to political economy which he thought Copleston had failed to provide: its principles, he declared, should 'be explained even to the ploughman, and made clear to the comprehension of children'.[73] His *Easy Lessons on Money Matters: For the Use of Young People* of 1833 duly became the prescribed text for the national schools in Ireland; it was then adapted for

---

[68] ODNB s.n. Whately.
[69] T. Boylan and T. Foley (eds.), *Irish Political Economy*, 4 vols. (London, 2003), i. 2, 15–16.
[70] Whately, quoted in R. D. Collison Black, *The Statistical and Social Inquiry Society of Ireland: Centenary Volume 1847–1947* (Dublin, 1947), 1.
[71] D. H. Akenson, *The Irish Educational Experiment: The National System of Education in the Nineteenth Century* (London, 1970), 117.
[72] Boylan and Foley (eds.), *Irish Political Economy*, i. 2, 15–16; M. E. Daly, *The Spirit of Earnest Inquiry: The Statistical and Social Inquiry Society of Ireland 1847–1997* (Dublin, 1997); N. Vance, 'Improving Ireland: Richard Whately, Theology, and Political Economy', in S. Collini, R. Whatmore, and B. Young (eds.), *Economy, Polity, Society: British Intellectual History 1750–1950* (Cambridge, 2000), 196–8.
[73] Whately, 'Report of the Address on the Conclusion of the First Session of the Dublin Statistical Society', *Transactions of the Dublin Statistical Society*, 1 (Dublin, 1847–9), 7.

English schools in the 1840s and 1850s, with nearly two million in use by 1859. Moreover, it was circulated by the Society for the Propagation of Christian Knowledge to children throughout the world. Still in print in its twentieth edition in the 1870s, it was extensively translated, including into Japanese and Maori. This made Whately, in the sober judgement of more than one historian, 'the most widely read economist of the first half of the nineteenth century'.[74]

Whately did not just export Noetic ideas to Ireland. He had an ancestral interest in colonial affairs: his paternal family had been prominent in the settlement of New England, and his Grenvillite uncle and patron Thomas Whately had been responsible for colonial policy in the mid-1760s; the new township of Whately, Massachusetts was named in his honour in 1771. Richard Whately himself had pressed the merits of emigration in response to social problems—as distinct from transportation, which he deprecated as injurious to colonies—in an article, 'Emigration to Canada', in the *Quarterly Review* as early as 1820,[75] in his anonymous fiction, *Village Conversations in Hard Times* of 1831, and again in an influential pamphlet, *Thoughts on Secondary Punishments... and Some Observations on Colonization*, addressed to Grey in 1832.[76] He was a prominent member of the National Colonization Society (NCS) established in 1830 to propagate the ideas of Edward Gibbon Wakefield in favour of 'systematic colonization', 'to theorize colonization by means of the new science of political economy, and to introduce the market mechanism into dealings in colonial lands'.[77] Whately also established the first Irish branch of the Society for the Propagation of the Gospel in Foreign Parts (SPG).

But Noetic colonial influence was not confined to Whately's global readership. His pupil Samuel Hinds was born in Barbados to an early settler family, and after Oxford had returned to the West Indies in 1822 as a missionary for the Society for the Conversion of Negroes, and then as principal of Codrington College in Barbados, which had been established by the SPG. Like Blanco White and intermittently Senior, Hinds followed Whately to Dublin in 1831, serving as his domestic chaplain and 'first subaltern', and then rejoining him in 1843 when appointed to a prebend of St Patrick's Cathedral, becoming again one of Whately's chaplains. Hinds's own ecclesiastical trajectory typified the

---

[74] Mandler, 'Tories and Paupers', 103; J. M. Goldstrom, 'Richard Whately and Political Economy in School Books, 1833–80', *Irish Historical Studies*, 16 (1966), 100–34; Boylan and Foley, *Political Economy and Colonial Ireland: The Propagation and Ideological Function of Economic Discourse in the Nineteenth Century* (London, 1992), 67; W. D. Sockwell, *Popularizing Classical Economics: Henry Brougham and William Ellis* (Basingstoke, 1994), 101–2.

[75] Gordon, *Political Economy in Parliament*, 202 n. 30.

[76] [Whately], *Village Conversations*, i. 36–41, ii. 5–60; Akenson, *A Protestant in Purgatory*, 49–50, 116–19.

[77] Boylan and Foley (eds.), *Irish Political Economy*, iv. 7.

official favour enjoyed by Noetics: he was appointed chaplain to the Lord Lieutenant of Ireland in 1846, was presented by the Crown to the deanery of Carlisle in 1848, and a year later nominated by Russell to the see of Norwich.[78] Hinds like Whately was an advocate of the NCS's programme of 'systematic colonization'. Although of course the missionary endeavour itself was not new—the SPG had been founded in 1701, and the major denominations soon had their parallel initiatives—Hinds was, as Hilary Carey has put it, 'one of the first Anglican clergymen to...give systematic colonisation a religious twist'; to see emigration, that is, 'not just as a solution to a social problem, but an opportunity to create Christian communities throughout the British world'.[79] As Carey has shown in her recent study of the role of religion in British colonialism, *God's Empire*, Hinds was a pivotal figure in the movement for 'Christian colonization', preaching and writing on the topical question of New Zealand's colonization in particular.[80] He issued a gazetteer to New Zealand in 1838; interestingly, this was co-authored with the Orielensis Sir Richard Bourke who, nominated by the Whig ministry as governor of New South Wales (1831–7), oversaw controversial church acts which extended public monies to denominations in proportion to their numbers, emulating the education clauses of the Whigs' Factory Act (1833).[81] Hinds was the only clergyman on the committee of the New Zealand Association, founded in May 1837, which included the Oriel MP William Bingham Baring,[82] and William Hutt MP, educated at St Mary Hall;[83] he is thought to have penned the chapter on 'Religious Establishment' in the Association's prospectus,[84] which made the striking declaration that in the distribution of 'colonial funds, no preference should be given to any one denomination of Christians'.[85] Here again, one encounters Noetic connections at every turn: Baring's father was close to Copleston, while the secretary of the New Zealand Colonization Company, who collated the prospectus, was John Ward, Thomas Arnold's nephew and journalistic collaborator, and a

---

[78] Akenson, *A Protestant in Purgatory*, 84–5.

[79] H. Carey, *God's Empire: Religion and Colonialism in the British World, c.1801–1908* (Oxford, 2011), 312.

[80] S. Hinds and R. Bourke, *The Latest Official Documents Relating to New Zealand, with Introductory Observations by S. Hinds* (London, 1838); Carey, *God's Empire*, 314.

[81] H. M. Stephens, 'Bourke, Sir Richard (1777–1855)', rev. Hazel King, ODNB s.n.

[82] Baring (1799–1864) graduated BA in classics in 1821, and held various parliamentary seats (1826–48) before succeeding as the 2nd Lord Ashburton. He was secretary to the Board of Control under Peel (1841–5) and paymaster-general until 1846: K. D. Reynolds, 'Baring, Harriet Mary, Lady Ashburton (1805–57)', ODNB s.n.

[83] Hutt (1801–82), at St Mary Hall in 1820, MP for Hull and then Gateshead (1832–74), was active in free trade and colonial questions, a commissioner for the foundation of South Australia, and instrumental in the annexation of New Zealand: G. C. Boase, 'Hutt, Sir William (1801–82)', rev. H. C. G. Matthew, ODNB s.n.

[84] Carey, *God's Empire*, 314; P. Temple, *A Sort of Conscience: The Wakefields* (Auckland, 2002), 418.

[85] *The British Colonization of New Zealand; Being an Account of the Principles, Objects, and Plans of the New Zealand Association* (London, 1837), 68.

Whately protégé.[86] This argument for the concurrent endowment of New Zealand's religious establishments was an obvious affirmation of liberal Anglican principles. In 1838 Hinds pressed the case for New Zealand's Christian colonization in a lengthy testimony to the Select Committee of the Lords set up to report on its prospects.[87] 'What the Savage wants', Hinds declared, 'is to have before his Eyes the Example of a civilized and Christian Community.'[88] As Carey has put it, he was 'capturing the spirit of the age in which emigrants, having been derided as those with no stake in the British nation, were to be lauded as the creators of a new, moral and Christian empire overseas'. Hinds's name is on the first of the four plaques commemorating the Christian founders of the settlement in the porch of Christchurch Cathedral.[89] It was not therefore at random that Whately's *Easy Lessons on Money Matters* was translated into Maori. It was in a literal, global sense that Whately had pronounced: 'the world must be governed, has been governed, and will be governed by Political Economists.'[90]

In no field did the Christian economics find more trenchant application, or provoke fiercer denunciation, than that of the Poor Laws. Under the stimulus not only of Malthus, but of direct engagement with the problem of pauperism in parishes—John Davison's at Washington in County Durham, or Whately's at Halesworth in Suffolk—Noetics rained fire and sulphur on the old, pre-1834 Poor Law. It had been a natural Christian impulse to care for the incapable, the diseased, orphaned, and widowed. But since the 1790s relief had been extended to others 'capable of industry and prudence' so that, as John Davison wrote in his *Considerations on the Poor Laws* of 1817, they now acted 'to discourage or hinder good habits of character'. He duly urged the abolition of outdoor relief for the able-bodied, since this only nourished dependency: 'There is poison', Davison wrote, 'in the alms of their mistaken charity.'[91] The *Considerations* were widely noticed, procured positive reviews in both the Whig *Edinburgh Review* and the Tory *Quarterly Review*, and inspired 'a rash of local experiments in Poor Law' reform made possible by a parliamentary act of 1817.[92] Copleston, citing Malthus in his second public letter to Robert Peel, *On the Causes of the Increase of*

---

[86] A. W. Ward, 'Ward, John (1805–1890)', rev. H. C. G. Matthew, ODNB s.n.

[87] *Report from the Select Committee of the House of Lords, Appointed to Inquire into the Present State of the Islands of New Zealand, and the Expediency of Regulating the Settlement of British Subjects Therein* (London, 1838); Hinds's testimony is at 124–46.

[88] *Report from the Select Committee*, 131. See also Carey, *God's Empire*, 315, and P. Moon, *Fatal Frontiers: A New History of New Zealand in the Decade before the Treaty* (London, 2006), 139–42.

[89] Carey, *God's Empire*, 316, 311.

[90] Whately, 'Report of the Address', 7.

[91] Mandler, 'Tories and Paupers', 90; Davison, *Considerations*, 64.

[92] 'Poor-Laws', *Edinburgh Review*, 34 (January 1820), 91–108; 'On the Poor Laws', *Quarterly Review*, 18 (January 1818), 259–308; Mandler, 'Tories and Paupers', 93.

Pauperism, and on the Poor Laws of 1819, stated that the Poor Laws had propagated 'the most erroneous notions of the duty of Government' and affirmed that 'the absurd notion also of a *right* to a full supply of wheaten bread must be steadily denied'.[93] Readers were given a foretaste of the letters by a striking inscription at the bottom of the title page: '*Laissez nous faire*'. Whately's own impact, characteristically, was practical as well as literary. In Oxford, he joined a local society which provided morning meals to indigent travellers through the city, and took his turn in the society's Carfax office where, suspecting that beards were used as a disguise by serial beggars, he gave bearded supplicants 'the choice of shaving off their facial hair or going without breakfast'. When marriage necessitated leaving his fellowship he went to the family living of Halesworth, where as a parish clergyman (1822–5) he could practise what he had heard preached in the Oriel common room. He immediately had privately printed 'a two-page broadside letter' to the local Poor Law guardians, the directors of the House of Industry at Bulcamp, denouncing existing levels of relief as 'a bounty to idleness',[94] became one of the directors of the local Poor Law union, and duly abolished relief for the able-bodied on the grounds of what he strikingly called the 'benefits trap': as Brent has put it, 'a labourer had little incentive to seek employment if local wages were no more than the level of local relief'.[95] At the same time Whately's brother Thomas, installed in another family living at Cookham in Berkshire, established Poor Law reforms which were 'to be hailed as a model by the royal commission'.

The Noetics had reached for themselves and framed the principle of 'less eligibility' which the Poor Law Amendment Act of 1834 was to enshrine.[96] The deserving poor—orphans and widows—could be distinguished from the undeserving, able-bodied poor, from whom outdoor relief would be withdrawn as a spur to seeking work. The 'New Poor Law' duly introduced the deterrent workhouse: the so-called *bastilles*, which spawned anti-Poor Law riots in the northern manufacturing districts, the political protest of Chartism, and the literary protest of *Oliver Twist*. Nassau Senior played an instrumental role on the Royal Commission established by the Whigs to frame the new legislation, as Phyllis Deane has put it: 'from drafting the questionnaires circulated to all English parishes and identifying the relevant facts to be gathered by the twenty-six assistant (regional) commissioners...to writing the final report, published in 1834. Senior then acted as midwife to the Poor Law Amendment Act by careful explication and justification of the

---

[93] Copleston, *Second Letter to the Right Hon. Robert Peel*, 25, 97.
[94] [Whately], *Letter to the Directors of the House of Industry at Bulcamp* (Halesworth, 1823); Akenson, *A Protestant in Purgatory*, 124, 50–1.
[95] Vance, 'Improving Ireland', 199–200; Brent, 'Whately, Richard', in ODNB s.n.
[96] Mandler, 'Tories and Paupers', 96 n. 65, 91.

commission's recommendations to the lord chancellor and other cabinet ministers, and by continuously advising on the details of the consequent legislation as the bill went through parliament.'[97] Nor do the Noetic tentacles end there. Needing a third cleric, but with Whately in Ireland and John Davison considered too old, the commission alighted on an Oriel man, Henry Bishop, a relatively obscure figure but, significantly, a younger brother of William Bishop, Copleston's colleague as tutor; an old friend of Blanco White, a student of Whately in the early 1810s, and a lodger at Senior's house in Hyde Park Gate, he was engaged to Whately's sister-in-law. Moreover, Senior appointed to serve as secretary of the commission George Taylor, an advocate of Noetic views in the *Quarterly Review*. Peter Mandler's analysis of the Noetic stranglehold on the commission further discloses that at least ten of the roving assistant commissioners were close friends or students of Whately and Senior. Even when the parliamentary bill came to be formally drafted, the technical job fell to a hitherto obscure lawyer, John Meadows White, who had facilitated Whately's Poor Law reforms in Suffolk in the early 1820s and was recommended by him to Senior.[98] Blanco White did his part in cheerleading for his London host, defending the embryonic legislation from its conservative critics in 'The Bill of Belial: A Political Allegory' in the *New Monthly Magazine* in 1833.[99] Senior's daughter-in-law Jane even became the first woman inspector of workhouses and pauper schools. The New Poor Law, which swept away the haphazard paternalism of the old eighteenth-century system, and which represented the quintessence of the new Christian economics, was therefore covered in Oriel's fingerprints.

At the other end of this axis, of course, was Whately in Dublin. Senior had visited and extensively reported on Irish pauperism in 1819, and stayed with Whately in 1831 when asked by Lord Howick to report on the Irish Poor Laws; the resulting *Letter to Lord Howick* avowed the imprudence of outdoor relief at a time of rising pauperism.[100] In 1833 Whately superintended the inquiry into the Irish Poor Law at Senior's suggestion, with one of his brothers-in-law appointed an assistant. Though not all of his proposals were adopted, the commission did reject parochial employment and outdoor relief for Irish labourers since, as Whately told the Lords in 1836, 'we cannot recommend a system which offers bounties on improvidence'.[101] Confronted even with the Irish Famine and a million deaths from starvation, Whately refused to deviate from Christian economic doctrine, insisting to the Lords in

---

[97] Deane, 'Senior, Nassau William', ODNB s.n.
[98] Mandler, 'Tories and Paupers', 97–9, 101 n. 88.
[99] White, 'The Bill of Belial: A Political Allegory', *New Monthly Magazine*, 37 (1833), 412–17; Murphy, *Blanco White*, 152.
[100] Vance, 'Improving Ireland', 200–1; Senior, *A Letter to Lord Howick on a Legal Provision for the Irish Poor* (London, 1831).
[101] *Parl. Deb.* 3rd ser. 91 (March 1847), col. 431.

1847 that 'the only mode of relieving Ireland—unless we wait for the operation of famine and pestilence—from that now superabundant population which presents an insuperable obstacle to its ultimate improvement' was his old panacea of an 'organized and vigorous system of emigration'.[102] As Norman Vance has observed, 'Ireland has never forgiven Whately for opposing outdoor relief during the Famine when it might have saved lives and brought short-term alleviation of distress'.[103] Whately was not alone: his old tutor, Copleston, also saw in the Irish Famine 'a providential message of the truth of Malthusianism'.[104]

In the face of this recovery of Noetic social attitudes, it ought to be remembered that the mission to discourage pauperism systematically could coexist with great personal sympathy and generosity. John Davison worked tirelessly during the cholera outbreak of 1832, wrote furiously to Canning to protest the 'agonising misery' suffered by the silk workers, and was remembered for his 'deep, uncompromising, generous care for the Poor'.[105] As a bishop Copleston donated his entire episcopal income to diocesan charities.[106] Whately too, during the Irish Famine, offered as much additional paid employment in his own grounds as he could afford, a mini-experiment in the sort of public works programme which the commission had repudiated. But it was typical that Whately's gesture was governed by 'scientific principles': he assured the Lords that he took care to pay Irish labourers at just below the market rate in order not 'to draw them off from profitable employment'.[107] In 1832, when Senior was drafting his own royal commission material, Whately had written to him: 'Pray suggest, in your report on paupers, that any female receiving relief should have her hair cut off ... A good head of hair will fetch from 5s. to 10s., which would be perhaps a fortnight's maintenance.'[108] Then and now, such comments lent Christian economics a hideous aspect. Nobody did more to shine a light on it than their Tractarian critics.

The reaction to Noetic rationalism and Christian economics began at home. As we have seen, its focus was the defence of the Church, and its occasion the campaign of Keble, Hurrell Froude, and Newman against the re-election of the Noetics' patron Peel in February 1829. Keble had long found the intellectual atmosphere of the common room uncongenial, and had retired to his father's parish at Fairford. His immensely popular book of religious poetry, *The Christian Year*, which was first published in 1827 and

---

[102] Whately, *Substance of a Speech Delivered in the House of Lords, on Friday, the 26th of March, 1847, on the Motion for a Committee on Irish Poor Laws* (London, 1847), 35.
[103] Vance, 'Improving Ireland', 202.
[104] Brent, 'Copleston, Edward', ODNB s.n.
[105] Davison, *Remains*, ix, xii. 651.
[106] Waterman, *Revolution, Economics and Religion*, 193.
[107] Vance, 'Improving Ireland', 202; Whately, *Substance of a Speech*, 12–13.
[108] *Life and Correspondence of Richard Whately*, i. 163.

went through ninety-five editions even before his death, introduced a note of Wordsworthian romanticism into Oriel, which was taken up by a younger generation alienated by Noetic austerity. Denied the same entrée into the liberal-Tory and Whig governing circles as the Noetics, these younger fellows sought to compensate by an appeal to popular sentiment: 'we must *look to the people*', Newman declared in the *British Magazine* in 1833.[109] The medium of this appeal was print: their very moniker, of course, is owed to the *Tracts for the Times* on which Newman and his circle embarked in 1833, the same year as Keble's published *Assize Sermon*, the anti-Erastian call to arms from which Newman himself always dated the movement.[110] Tractarians duly mobilized on the broadest possible polemical front, at first primarily on religious issues, but by a natural extension of their theology of the Incarnation ranging into the same fields of social policy which Davison, Copleston, and Whately had cultivated.

Alongside their authorship of the *Tracts*, Froude, Newman, Keble, and Pusey wrote for the high church *British Magazine* in the early 1830s, though Newman felt the tactical necessity of an autonomous periodical voice: 'what these men want', he wrote of his Oxford circle in late 1837, 'is, an organ...we want all subjects treated on one and the same principle or basis—not the contributions of a board of men, who do not know each other, pared down into harmony by an external Editor.'[111] The following year he successfully manoeuvred for the editorship of the *British Critic*, a quarterly which was rapidly established as the Tractarians' house magazine, packed with commentary on theological, political, and social questions. After an unceremonious cull of older high-church reviewers, a roll-call of Oriel contributors was installed, with Froude, Newman, Keble, and Pusey only the best known.[112] Others included S. F. Wood, Newman's devoted pupil and later a barrister before his early death in 1843; John F. Christie, elected fellow at the same time as Thomas Mozley in 1829; Frederic Rogers, later as Lord Blachford the first civil servant to be ennobled, student and then fellow of Oriel from 1833 and lifelong intimate of Newman and Froude, and later a co-founder of *The Guardian* newspaper in succession to the *Critic*;[113] and Charles Marriott, fellow from 1833 and then dean, whose social concerns later found expression in a commercial scheme at Oxford named the Universal Purveyor, an attempt to regulate the quality and price of daily essentials.[114] They also included a distinguished brace of brothers: the Wilberforces—sons of the great slavery campaigner

---

[109] *British Magazine*, 4 (October 1833), 422.   [110] Newman, *Apologia*, 162.
[111] LDN vi. 170, Newman to Churton, 21 November 1837.
[112] S. A. Skinner, 'Newman, the Tractarians and the *British Critic*', *Journal of Ecclesiastical History*, 50 (1999), 716–59.
[113] H. C. G. Matthew, 'Rogers, Frederic, Baron Blachford (1811–1889)', ODNB s.n.
[114] J. W. Burgon, *Lives of Twelve Good Men*, 2 vols. (London, 1888); i. 296–373; J. H. Overton, 'Marriott, Charles (1811–1858)', rev. K. E. Macnab, ODNB s.n.

ILLUSTRATION 12.2 Thomas Mozley (1806–93), fellow 1829–37
Oriel College

Willliam Wilberforce, both of them converts to Rome in the early 1850s—and the Mozleys. Robert Wilberforce, undergraduate at Oriel (1820–4) and fellow (1826–33), an intimate of Keble and Newman, proved a trenchant reviewer especially on educational matters; his brother Henry was student, pupil, and thereafter close friend of Newman at Oriel from 1826, and president of the Oxford Union. James Bowling Mozley was an undergraduate at Oriel (1830–4), and since his brother Thomas was fellow he enjoyed instant access to Tractarianism's inner sanctum. Unable to secure an Oriel fellowship due to a reluctance to have two brothers on the foundation, he served as Newman's curate at St Mary's and became one of his most intimate friends before finally securing a fellowship at Magdalen in 1840. Later a journalist and theologian of distinction, Mozley attained the regius chair of divinity; at his death R. W. Church, the Oxford Movement's first chronicler, judged James Mozley, after Newman, 'the most forcible and impressive of the Oxford writers'.[115]

[115] R. W. Church, *The Oxford Movement: Twelve Years 1833–1845* (London, 1891), 337.

The most important of Newman's recruits to the *British Critic*, however, was James's brother Thomas. Thomas Mozley matriculated at Oriel in 1825, was tutored by Newman, and elected to a fellowship (succeeding Pusey) in 1829. Although Mozley was already a friend of Newman's and an enthusiastic distributor of the *Tracts*, his ties with the movement were consummated by marriage to Newman's elder sister Harriett in 1836, on which he resigned his fellowship and accepted the college living of Cholderton in Wiltshire. It was the polemical brio of a pseudonymous pamphlet of Mozley's in 1838, denouncing the intrusion of the Poor Law Commissioners into the Church's management of education, which alerted Newman to his potential as a reviewer.[116] In 1841 he succeeded Newman as editor of the *Critic*, and by the time of its closure in 1843 he had written over thirty lacerating articles on such subjects as the 'Religious State of the Manufacturing Poor', 'Agricultural Labour and Wages', and Chartism.[117] It is a measure of the contemporary regard in which Mozley was held that at the demise of the *Critic* Mozley began a long association with *The Times*, for which he wrote leading articles almost daily until 1886. A great favourite of John Walter III, proprietor from 1847 and an undergraduate admirer of Newman, Mozley was much the best paid of its leader writers and a stalwart at *The Times* during the long and influential editorship of John Thadeus Delane.[118] The anonymity of Mozley's prodigious periodical and newspaper journalism has cost him a much wider reputation as a Victorian man of letters.[119] Under Newman's and then his own editorships, the *British Critic* propagated, more than any other journal, a coruscating critique of the commercial spirit and of the economic model deployed to justify it.

As Christopher Dawson recognized at the outset of his celebrated essay on *The Spirit of the Oxford Movement* in 1933, 'its hostility to Liberalism was due, at least in part, to its dissatisfaction with a social system which seemed dedicated to the service of Mammon'.[120] For the movement's writers on social questions 'the love of money' was, indeed, 'the root of all evil'.[121] Newman protested 'an intense, sleepless, restless, never-wearied, never-satisfied, pursuit of Mammon' in a sermon of 1836, 'Doing Glory to God in Pursuits of the World', which, one commentator holds, 'bristles with prophetic, proto-

---

[116] *A Dissection of the Queries on the Amount of Religious Instruction and Education, Circulated by Lord John Russell, Through the Poor Law Commissioners* (Salisbury, 1838). It was signed 'By a Clergyman of South Wilts.'.

[117] E. R. Houghton, 'The *British Critic* and the Oxford Movement', *Studies in Bibliography*, 16 (Virginia, 1963), 119–37; Mozley, *Reminiscences*, ii. 216, 219; Skinner, *Tractarians and the 'Condition of England'*, 36–65.

[118] G. E. Buckle, S. Morison, I. McDonald, et al. (eds.), *The History of The Times*, ii: *The Tradition Established, 1841–1884* (London, 1939), 124–6.

[119] S. A. Skinner, 'Mozley, Thomas (1806–93)', ODNB s.n.

[120] C. Dawson, *The Spirit of the Oxford Movement, and Newman's Place in History* (London, 2001), xi.

[121] J. H. Newman, *Parochial and Plain Sermons*, 8 vols. (London, 1873), ii. 349; 1 Timothy 6: 10.

Marxist scorn'.[122] Mozley mourned that 'covetousness and competition' affected the minds of every class.[123] Henry Wilberforce, preaching on the occasion of a church restoration in Southampton in 1839, professed disgust that 'at a time when funds in abundance are supplied for every work which tends only to the temporal prosperity and splendour of your town; they should be wanting only for that which is to show forth among you the glory of God'.[124] In his recent survey of *Morality and the Market in Victorian Britain*, G. R. Searle recognized the intensifying problem for churchmen of how 'Christ's teaching, with its stern warnings about material wealth as the source of corruption, could be made compatible, if at all, with contemporary social and economic arrangements'.[125] For Tractarians, it could not.

In no area did Newman's takeover of the *British Critic* change the tone of the review more dramatically than that of political economy. The pre-Tractarian *Critic* had cheerfully subscribed to the Noetic venture of reconciling political economy and Christianity: a reviewer of April 1837, for example, addressing the subject of 'Social Improvement in connexion with the Church', insisted that there was 'the closest agreement... between the precepts of the Bible, and the truths which the great science of social economy is eliciting day by day'. 'Religion and human knowledge are joint as well as gigantic levellers in the improvement of society', he wrote, looking forward to the day when religion 'shall step forward, and demand the homage of humanity, with the Bible in her right hand, and the volume of human knowledge in her left!', a juxtaposition distasteful in the extreme to Tractarians. The reviewer was by no means insensitive to social conditions: 'vice and ignorance', he continued, 'turbulence and discontent, seem to cluster and congregate, as by a natural attraction, amidst the congregated masses of the poor.' The reviewer's palliative, however, was not the Christian charity and alms-giving to be enjoined by later Tractarian reviewers as the fundamental duty of churchmen: 'alleviation', he concluded, should come rather in the form of 'judicious advice in the plain and practical details of social and domestic economy'. Utilitarian principles were 'in many respects enlightened', and Christianity itself could be sanctioned in terms of utilitarian criteria: 'It is' after all, the pre-Tractarian *Critic* declared, 'the very essence of Christianity to promote the highest good of mankind; to secure the greatest happiness of the species at large'.[126]

---

[122] D. Goslee, *Romanticism and the Anglican Newman* (Athens, Oh., 1996), 198.

[123] [T. Mozley], 'Lord John Manners' *Plea for National Holy Days*', *British Critic*, 33 (April 1843), 433.

[124] H. W. Wilberforce, *The Building of the House of God. A Sermon, Preached in the Church of All Saints, Southampton, on Tuesday, August 13, 1839, at the Rebuilding of the Ancient Church of St. Lawrence* (Southampton, [1839]), 5–6.

[125] G. R. Searle, *Morality and the Market in Victorian Britain* (Oxford, 1998), viii.

[126] 'Social Improvement in Connexion with the Church', *British Critic*, 21 (April 1837), 502, 503, 508, 513, 497.

For Tractarian critics, 'political economy', 'laissez-faire', 'utilitarianism', and 'Benthamism', were interchangeable. On this broad canvas, a trilogy of articles by the London lawyer and social commentator Samuel Bosanquet, published in the *Critic* under Newman and Mozley, constitutes the most sustained and vitriolic assault on political economy in general and the Poor Laws in particular within the commentary.[127] Political economy was, Bosanquet shrieked, the 'national ensign and watchword', it meant no more than 'money-getting': it was 'shallow, conceited, exclusive, tyrannical'.[128] Political economy was the 'theory of the day, and one of a great name has said it, and a few examples have proved it, and it suits our convenience greatly... It matters not that some people die in the streets.' Political economists, he raged, 'make war with the poor', for 'it is so very economical and makes a convenient amount of charity go so far, to give only to those who are proved to be starving without any fault or weakness of their own'.[129] Political economy was, in the summary words of a pamphlet by Philip Pusey MP which was first exhorted and then rapturously endorsed by his brother Edward, 'very like individual stinginess'.[130]

Many of the Tractarian novels penned by William Gresley and F. E. Paget and encouraged by Keble and Pusey in order to compete in the growing early Victorian market were devoted to this theme, such as one of Paget's longest and best-known novels, *The Warden of Berkingholt; or, Rich and Poor*, of 1843. In it, Paget made explicit the connection between the selfishness of the rich and contemporary enthusiasm for political economy, insisting on the absolute irreconcilability of political economy and Christianity. The villain of *The Warden of Berkingholt* is Mr Livingstone, chairman of the Board of Guardians, anti-mendicant *Edinburgh Reviewer*, prospective Whig parliamentary candidate, and therefore comprehensive demon. Introducing him, Paget's narrator records that he used the village children as unpaid servants on the grounds that regular employment was doing them moral good. Paget observed, in lines which almost anticipated Whately's later Irish experiments: 'as there is no amount of cruelty and severity towards our fellow-creatures which may not be proved to be meritorious upon some received principle of political economy, that gentleman made use of his politico-economical opinions as a stalking horse, and saved his own pocket considerably.'[131] A later

---

[127] 'Pauperism and Alms-giving', *British Critic*, 28 (July 1840), 195–257; 'Private Alms and Poor-law Relief', *British Critic*, 28 (October 1840), 441–70; 'The Age of Unbelief', *British Critic*, 31 (January 1842), 91–123.

[128] 'The Age of Unbelief', 101, 105.

[129] 'Pauperism and Alms-giving', 207, 227.

[130] P. H. Pusey, *The Poor in Scotland; Compiled From the Evidence Taken before the Scotch Poor-Law Commission* (London, 1844). The pamphlet was reprinted from an article in the *Christian Remembrancer* of October 1844. The Scottish act was passed in 1845.

[131] F. E. Paget, *The Warden of Berkingholt; or, Rich and Poor* (Oxford, 1843), 12.

dialogue between Mr Livingstone and the eponymous warden, the saintly Dr Clinton, explicitly juxtaposes the maxims of political economy with Christianity. Mr Livingstone, for example, asserts that it is better to allow one person to suffer than to encourage 'a thousand mendicants in their idle habits, by injudicious liberality', and therefore accuses the warden of the Berkingholt almshouse of presiding 'over an establishment for the encouragement of pauperism'. In defence of the almshouse's statutory provision of dole for anyone who seeks it at the gate, and of a now unfunded hall of refectory for sixty out-pensioners, the warden says that the founders' 'principle was that of simple, unqualified obedience to the command of Scripture that we shall feed the hungry and clothe the naked'.[132] Bosanquet too juxtaposed utilitarian and scriptural maxims in Newman's *Critic* in July 1840 to show that political economy defied Jesus's command that 'Thou shalt open thine hand unto thy brother, thy poor, and to thy needy in thy land'.[133]

This antithesis between the dismal science and the sacred was realized, as Sydney Checkland and more recently Richard Brent have pointed out, within Oxford's university politics, where the fledgling discipline of political economy faced unrelenting Tractarian antagonism. This was acted out in a succession of partisan elections to the Drummond chair of political economy as significant, if not as well known, as those over the regius chair of divinity and the poetry professorship.[134] When the Malthusian Whig Herman Merivale was elected to the Drummond chair in March 1837, Keble commented drolly to Newman that it was 'the right thing on the principle of *non-sancta non-sanctis*'.[135] Tractarian commentators were fond of pointing out that, measured by the empiricism which the political economists boasted, no observer of the condition of England could doubt which of these opposites was the proper therapy. The warden of Berkingholt's first dialogue with Mr Livingstone closes with an impassioned denunciation of the follies of the political economists and their rejection of 'ancestral wisdom'. Turning to their purest legislative expression, Dr Clinton protests that 'Pauperism you have not checked: the poor rates tell us that. Mendicancy you have not checked':

Every measure of niggardly, pinching economy, which the heads of misers could devise, every ingenious refinement of cruelty which can hurt a poor man's feelings, or can brand his poverty as a crime, have been carried out under the regulations of the new Poor Law, with the intention of proving that it is in the power of 'fire-new'

---

[132] Paget, *Warden of Berkingholt*, 64–5, 67.
[133] 'Pauperism and Alms-giving', 242–9; Deuteronomy 15: 11.
[134] S. Checkland, 'The Advent of Academic Economics in England', *The Manchester School of Economic and Social Studies*, 19 (1951), 67–9; R. Brent, 'God's Providence: Liberal Political Economy as Natural Theology at Oxford 1825–1862', in M. Bentley (ed.), *Public and Private Doctrine: Essays in British History Presented to Maurice Cowling* (Cambridge, 1993), 89–94.
[135] Keble College Archives, NP 1/A/45, Keble to Newman, 4 March 1837; Brent, 'God's Providence', 88.

theories of Political economy to accomplish, what God has declared shall *never* come to pass,—namely, that the poor shall cease from the land ... It has had a fair trial: and what is the result?'[136]

In the *Critic*, Bosanquet too argued that the most cursory survey of the state of the nation demonstrated the manifest failure of the prescriptions of political economy: 'give these up at once, the conclusions of a worldly wisdom,' he pleaded, 'and the products of scientific calculation, seeing their results, and their signal failure'.[137] A later number of the *Critic* attempted to explain why despite manifold evidences of its failure 'human reason' had 'gained ascendancy over revelation and faith, in England'.[138] This was a consequence of the very breakdown in social relations attendant on commercialism: 'It is far easier to sit at home and read returns, and reports, and evidence on oath, and figures, and statistics, and to work out problems of society by a table or machine, mathematically certain and demonstrable, and squaring all to a fraction, than to pry into dirty courts and lanes, and dismal rooms and cellars, full of vermin, and filth and infection, and to converse with the low-minded, the vulgar, the dying, the drunken, the discontented, the miserable.'[139] Thus it was that the political economy promulgated by Copleston as a providential 'system of *rewards* and *punishments*', and by Whately as the workings of 'a wise providence', came to be designated, in a review edited by their colleagues Newman and Mozley, 'the philosophy of Antichrist'.[140]

The starting point for many Tractarian critics of political economy was their polemical indictment of the Whig ministry in the course of the 1830s, and in particular of the New Poor Law. By contrast, just as pre-Tractarian commentators in the *Critic* had been far from hostile to political economy, so they evaluated its statutory expression in often approving terms. One wrote in April 1832 of the 'heaving and restless ocean of pauperism' by which 'we are imminently menaced' and insisted on the necessity of legislation to reform the Poor Laws; another in the same issue scoffed at the notion that the clergy themselves could be expected to alleviate the burden.[141] Two years later reviewers wrote in terms of the social utility, as opposed to the social injustice, of Senior's New Poor Law. One wrote with an air of *hauteur* that without the legislation of 1834 'the labourers', 'our peasantry', were 'likely to become sources of disgrace, and danger, and perpetual disturbance', and saluted the Noetic prescription—the abolition of outdoor relief in favour of a deterrent workhouse—'as an effectual remedy'.[142] Just as Newman's assumption of the editorship in 1838 was reflected in dramatic shifts in the

---

[136] Paget, *Warden of Berkingholt*, 65, 67–8.
[137] 'Pauperism and Alms-giving', 242.   [138] 'The Age of Unbelief', 100.
[139] 'Pauperism and Alms-giving', 201–2.   [140] 'Pauperism and Alms-giving', 227.
[141] 'Divine Visitations', *British Critic*, 11 (April 1832), 381; 'The Church and its Endowments', *British Critic*, 11 (April 1832), 332.
[142] 'The Poor Laws', *British Critic*, 15 (April 1834), 225–6, 221.

Critic's tone on such subjects as establishment, Thomas Chalmers, and political economy, so it was with pauperism and the Poor Laws.

Tractarian criticism of the New Poor Law centred on three main aspects: the first its enshrinement of the maxims of political economy, the second its adoption of the principle of centralization and therefore encroachment on clerical prerogatives, and the third its institution of the workhouse. The first was that the revision to the law had made the provision of poor relief a tax rather than a charity. The levying of a rate was not itself new, of course, but the terms in which the 1834 Act was justified seemed to Tractarians to mark a shift away from the latter, and the *British Critic* fastened onto this aspect of the law at length. Its basic iniquity was that the supersession of private charity by public provision encouraged the avarice of the propertied and further insulated them from the lower classes. As Bosanquet put it in the *Critic* in October 1840: 'There can be no stronger symptom of the growing harshness and unchristian state of feeling towards the poor, than the opinion now both hinted at and affirmed—that the legal provision for the poor ought to be a substitute for private charity: that the one interferes with the other. There is none more erroneous... We assert that the *private charity ought to supersede the public provision*.'[143] Pusey made the same point in a sermon of the mid-1830s, mourning that 'Recent changes have turned the compulsory provision for the poor into a measure of restriction and police', and warning that 'to save ourselves at the expense of the poor... would be a nation's curse'.[144] In passing the new legislation, the Whigs had capitulated to the delicacy and financial self-interest of newly enfranchised middle-class ratepayers. Poor relief was no longer an administered charity, but a tax, 'and as being a tax, it is considered that it may be lawfully economised as much as possible; nay, that it is a virtue to economise it... So the motive and habit are always present to dispose us to make our contribution small and niggardly.' Thus, concluded Bosanquet, 'we are at war with the poor'.[145] Where Tractarians held that the Church commanded Christians to give up at least a tenth of their incomes for the relief of the destitute, the 1834 regime positively encouraged the principle of economy. The Tractarian *Critic*'s response was emphatic: 'Economy, economy: the savings of expenses: money! money! We abhor the selfish idea.'[146]

The second main aspect of Tractarian criticism of the New Poor Law was its undiscriminating character. This, of course, was a consequence of its dependence on the principle of centralization which was a cardinal Noetic principle. The only object of the law, the *Critic* complained, was to remedy

---

[143] 'Private Alms and Poor-law Relief', 441.
[144] E. B. Pusey, *Parochial Sermons*, 3 vols. (Oxford, 1848–83; revised edn., 1886), iii. 143.
[145] 'Private Alms and Poor-law Relief', 451.
[146] 'The Age of Unbelief', 119; 'Private Alms and Poor-law Relief', 456.

'the inconvenience of the rich'; it was 'wholly without regard to the condition or necessities of the poor and of the lower classes'.[147] Poor relief was now to be undertaken by agencies far too remote to differentiate between the various claimants on its pinched resources: 'Being based in luxury and disdain, and a selfish sensibility, we persecute the whole herd of beggars, not to distinguish and punish the impostors, but to get rid of a NUISANCE.' It was 'the union of parishes into districts' by Senior's assistant commissioners which had depersonalized poor relief and consigned without discrimination vast numbers to indoor relief.[148] In an article on 'The Poor Laws' in 1834 the pre-Tractarian *British Critic* had adduced 'most satisfactory' instances of the unions;[149] under Newman and Mozley the *Critic* insisted on their disbandment and the restoration of the parish clergyman as the determinant of relief. Outdoor relief would be orchestrated at the parochial level, and admission to a refugial rather than deterrent poor-house scrutinized on the basis of a pastoral knowledge which no guardian could ever equal. Thomas Mozley's very first publication was a pamphlet of 1838 attacking the intrusion of the Poor Law Commissioners into parochial affairs. 'Let the relief of the out-door poor by the guardians of unions be given up', said the *Critic*, 'and let it be restored to the parishes.'[150]

In their vigorous promotion of the machinery of the parish, the necessity of almsgiving, and the restoration of the offertory, the Tractarians were shifting the debate from the proper responsibilities of the poor to that of the proper responsibilities of the rich. In an article of 1832 the pre-Tractarian *British Critic* had ridiculed the notion that the Church might assume the burdens of pauperism itself. 'Support the Christian poor out of the revenues of the Church!' it spluttered: 'Why, can anything be required, in order to expose the prodigious absurdity of such a proposition?'[151] Eight years later Newman's *Critic* solemnly avowed that it was the Christian duty of parishioners to relieve the poor and to pay the poor-rates on top if the state insisted.[152] 'From the beginning,' wrote Henry Wilberforce in his *The Parochial System* of 1838, the very treatise under review in the *Critic*, 'the Church relieved her own poor, she might do so again. We begin a wrong course when we leave the poor in Christ to the fortuitous exercise of benevolence, and to the dole of a legal pittance. The benevolence of Christians should be wise, well-ordered, discriminating, and bountiful. Such are the alms of the Church.'[153] Moreover,

---

[147] 'Pauperism and Alms-giving', 203.
[148] 'Private Alms and Poor-law Relief', 449, 446, 454–5.
[149] 'The Poor Laws', 215.
[150] 'Private Alms and Poor-law Relief', 460–1.
[151] 'The Church and its Endowments', *British Critic*, 11 (April 1832), 332.
[152] 'Private Alms and Poor-law Relief', 456–7.
[153] [H. W. Wilberforce], *The Parochial System: An Appeal to English Churchmen* (London, 1838), 40–1.

'Under the church's auspices, even the reviled workhouses might be redeemed, converted into poorhouses again, and not workhouses... welcome asylums and refuges for real distress and destitution'.[154]

For the third Tractarian criticism of the New Poor Law was the deterrent workhouse. The earliest major broadside, foreseeably, was an article by Thomas Mozley in the *Critic* of October 1839. In the course of a litany of indictments of the Whig administration, culminating in an attack on Lord John Russell's letters to Lords Lieutenant approving the arming of private citizens in the face of Chartist agitation, Mozley fastened onto the widespread popular opprobrium in which the workhouses were held. By their act of 1834, the Whigs had, Mozley said, 'shut up all who wanted bread, like so many lepers, in certain piles of brick, to which the poor have given a name more expressive of their own antipathies, than of the benevolent intentions of the founders'[155]—that is, the 'bastilles'. Throughout his own *Critic* contributions, Samuel Bosanquet railed against the 'Bastille' as a standing monument to political economy and the workhouse test itself as 'abhorrent'.[156] In a later issue, Mozley protested that 'the poor are thrust out of sight into living graves'. 'There is no grace, no religion', he wrote in October 1842, 'in any single stage of the collection or application of the poor-rate.'[157] The difference between the generations was, in fact, caught in miniature within the Mozley family itself. In 1834 the pre-Tractarian *Critic* had explicitly commended various local workhouse experiments, adducing amongst others the efforts of the 'Rev. Thomas Whateley' [sic]—Richard Whately's brother—and a 'Mr Mosley [sic]', who had effected 'a considerable improvement' by his 'fixed determination to oppose the allowance system'.[158] This was none other than Mozley's father, Henry Mozley, the Derby-based bookseller and printer, who had used Sturges Bourne's Select Vestries Act of 1819 to establish an 'Inconvenient'—i.e. deterrent—workhouse and to withdraw relief from the ablebodied. Thomas Mozley later recalled the St Werburgh's workhouse as 'a vile hole' and said of his father's earlier role as overseer of the poor at Gainsborough in 1826: 'I think I was a little disgusted, and thought my father had better have let it alone.'[159]

If Tractarian reviewers identified the workhouse as the grim terminus of Christian economics, the novelists were able to illustrate their horror of the Poor Laws in lurid colours and at greater length. In a scene in Paget's novel

---

[154] 'Private Alms and Poor-law Relief', 460–1.
[155] [T. Mozley], 'Armed Associations for the Protection of Life and Property', *British Critic*, 26 (October 1839), 427.
[156] 'Private Alms and Poor-law Relief', 455.
[157] [T. Mozley], 'Pews', *British Critic*, 32 (October 1842), 494.
[158] 'The Poor Laws', 215.
[159] T. Mozley, *Reminiscences, Chiefly of Towns, Villages and Schools*, 2 vols. (London, 1885), ii. 60–7.

on the theme, *The Warden of Berkingholt*, the kindly Dr Clinton stumbles upon a weeping refugee from the Berkingholt workhouse who faints in his arms as she exclaims, 'I will never go back there again...do have mercy upon me...I'll do anything to earn my livelihood...if you will save me from that man.'[160] 'That man', it transpires, is the sinister Venham, master of the Berkingholt workhouse, a powerful Tractarian reworking of Dickens's Mr Bumble,[161] who has beaten Allen for breaking two dishes. The workhouse, we are told, has already claimed the lives of both her parents, while her elder brother drowned himself in order to escape Venham's persecution. When, later in the book, the Clintons succeed in drawing Venham's character to the notice of the Board of Guardians and he is dismissed, Paget cannot forbear to add: 'But he is a clever fellow, has friends at Somerset House, and as it is known that he has discovered a very nutritive preparation of glue and saw dust, which is quite as palatable, quite as wholesome, and a hundred-fold cheaper than any "cheap food" yet placed on the Work-house dietaries, he may be looked upon as a rising man, and will probably live to be a Poor Law Commissioner himself.'[162]

Tractarians' parochial experiences occasionally demonstrated that such representations were not altogether melodramatic. 'Under the New Poor Law', Thomas Mozley was to recall in his *Reminiscences*, 'some of my poor parishioners, in spite of my remonstrances, were hurried off to Andover Union, there quickly to rot and die. It was the workhouse in which the aged paupers, set to break the horse bones from Mr Assheton Smith's dog-kennels, first gnawed and sucked them.' Mozley added: 'The flavour of the bones I know, for I often passed them on the way to Andover. It was not pleasant.'[163] It was the Andover workhouse scandal of 1845–6, broken by *The Times* and pursued by its proprietor John Walter, and matching in horror anything concocted in Tractarian fiction, which was to impel the termination of the Poor Law Commission in 1847.[164] That Thomas Mozley had joined *The Times* as a leader writer in 1844, and that the paper issued a celebrated succession of thunderous leaders on the Andover scandal a year later, are unlikely to have been coincidental.

The Christian economics of the Noetics, which Copleston and his colleagues developed not only on the basis of statistical tables but in the light of a high ideal of personal responsibility, had justified the classical Victorian assumption that wealth correlated with virtue, poverty with indolence and moral failing.

---

[160] Paget, *Warden of Berkingholt*, 91.
[161] *The Adventures of Oliver Twist* appeared in 1837 and 1838, five years before the publication of *Warden of Berkingholt*.
[162] Paget, *Warden of Berkingholt*, 119–20.
[163] Mozley, *Reminiscences*, ii. 172.
[164] I. Anstruther, *The Scandal of the Andover Workhouse* (London, 1973), 19–23, 27, 33, 101–2, 106–8, 139–40, 144–5.

The Methodist banker Mr Bulstrode in George Eliot's *Middlemarch* infers that he must be good because he is prosperous; the poor, by contrast, were idle, or feckless, or sexually incontinent, and deserved to starve. That assumption informed the principle of less eligibility enshrined in the New Poor Law and the workhouses of *Oliver Twist*; it could be found in the classic manual of Victorian values, *Self-Help*, by Samuel Smiles, published in 1859, and in the high-Victorian dictum of the Charity Organisation Society (COS, founded 1869) that to aid was to injure. The Tractarians' rejection of these consequentialist maxims was absolute. Newman's *Critic* inveighed against the notion that poverty was accountable to 'worthless character' or 'individual fault', that 'no one in this rich and prosperous country *can* be in distress, unless they are either fools or idle', and savaged the sanctimonious Noetic chorus which insisted that 'your distress is all your own fault, and I should only be encouraging you and making you worse by now relieving you'.[165] Thomas Mozley, with an eye on the New Poor Law, similarly lamented in the *Critic* that 'poverty is treated as a sin or leprosy, to be restrained to a prison or a lazaretto'.[166] In asserting that vice was the consequence and not cause of poverty, the paternalism to which Tractarians subscribed in some ways constituted a counter-cultural bridge between eighteenth-century notions of the rights of labour, and twentieth-century arguments premised on environmental explanations of poverty. Many other paternalistic commentators, including William Cobbett, Thomas Carlyle, Benjamin Disraeli, Charles Dickens, and John Ruskin, shared this diagnosis though none, of course, the Tractarians' rigorously Anglican and clerical prescription.

Neither Christian economist nor Christian paternalist visions of poverty and wealth could endure. Weakening religious profession, declining birth rates, diminishing economic efficiency relative to Germany and the United States, and Boer War generals lamenting the 'physical deterioration' of recruits all created a *fin de siècle* anxiety over 'national efficiency'. Perhaps above all, the social surveys of Charles Booth, Henry Mayhew, and Seebohm Rowntree, in statistically demonstrating the scale of poverty in the Victorian slum, disclosed the existence of an underclass generated not by moral deficiency but inherited circumstances. This, late Victorians and Edwardians realized, was on a scale with which it was far beyond the scope of voluntary philanthropy—churches, chapels, and the charity of the affluent—to deal. This plainly posited the need for state intervention, which was of course the origin of twentieth-century welfare. But Oriel's intimate connection with social policy and the Poor Laws in particular did not end with the passing of a Noetic–Tractarian dialectic. Indeed these developments were nicely captured in the person of Lancelot Ridley Phelps, undergraduate at Oriel

---

[165] 'Pauperism and Alms-giving', 204, 220.   [166] 'Pews', 494.

(1872–6), fellow (1877–1914), and ultimately provost (1914–29), through whom the college would maintain substantial official influence in the field of social policy. Phelps was one of Oxford's most prominent Liberal figures for five decades, a supporter of university extension and the settlement movement, active in the National Church Reform Movement, stalwart member of the Political Economy Club, the Social Science Club, the Tutors' Club (founded by Thomas Arnold), the (University Reform) Club, and the Oxford Economic Society, diehard free trader and member of the Committee of the Trade League of the University, City, and County of Oxford, and a founder of the *Economic Review*.[167] Noting that—in some respects like his Noetic predecessors—Phelps 'never became a specialist in any academic subject' but 'was an excellent and popular lecturer on classics and on political economy', the ODNB pronounced that he 'probably had as wide and deep an influence as any Oxford tutor of his time...In particular, his lectures on economics to Indian Civil Service probationers influenced many who became distinguished civil servants; and in later years he had an equally great influence on the members of the Sudan civil service.'[168] Phelps's influence was not confined to the rising generation of colonial mandarins, but had civic and national dimensions. In the town itself, as Tony Howe has noted, 'Phelps devoted a vast amount of time to Oxford's poorest citizens', a mainstay of both the Oxford Cottage Improvement Society, a town–gown initiative of 1865, and the Oxford branch of the COS, whose quintessentially Victorian doctrines we have already encountered. Phelps became a Poor Law Guardian in 1880 and Chairman of the Guardians in 1912, later serving on the public assistance committee. 'No prominent member of the university', in the estimate of one obituarist, 'probably has ever taken so large a share in City affairs'.[169]

Phelps was a broad churchman theologically and a Liberal in his politics.[170] If his sympathy for the cooperative movement or Home Rule stamps him as a man of his own time and no simple Noetic redivivus, Phelps's attitudes to the poor were most certainly of a recognizably Christian-economist hue. In a pamphlet (published by the COS) of 1887, *Poor Law and Charity*, Phelps sternly distinguished between poverty ('the absence of comforts') and pauperism ('the absence of necessaries'), arguing that poverty should be relieved by charity but that pauperism was the remit of the Poor Law and required a

---

[167] A. Kadish, *The Oxford Economists in the Late Nineteenth Century* (Oxford, 1982), 23, 27–8, 34, 43, 177–8, 185–6, 193, 275.

[168] D. Ross, 'Phelps, Lancelot Ridley (1853–1936)', rev. M. C. Curthoys, ODNB s.n.; OR (1937–9); H. S. Furniss, *Memoirs of Sixty Years* (London, 1931), 52.

[169] A. C. Howe, 'Intellect and Civic Responsibility: Dons and Citizens in Nineteenth-Century Oxford', in R. C. Whiting (ed.), *Oxford: Studies in the History of a University Town Since 1800* (Manchester, 1993), 28–9.

[170] Kadish, *Oxford Economists*, 78, 192.

deterrent workhouse regime. The hair-peddling Whately himself might have authored Phelps's exhortation 'to keep clearly in view the large teachings of experience and of reason amidst a cloud of detail and a mist of sentiment', as he set out resolutely the folly of extending out-relief to the sick ('you discourage people from making any provision from themselves'), the old ('certainty of a public pension, when the day of work is over, [is] fraught with great evils'), and the widowed ('out-relief cripples energy, it teaches a person to earn just so much as will enable her to keep relief, and no more').[171] He duly chastised the preceding generation of the Oxford Guardians for their undiscriminating largesse and presided over reductions in the scale of outdoor relief which would have had his Oriel forebears beaming with doctrinaire gratification: by 1898 the Oxford Guardians were dispensing out-relief to 17 per cent of the paupers with whom they dealt, compared with 65 per cent in 1872.[172] Like so many of the Noetics, 'The Phelper' was therefore someone in whom great personal charity could coexist with a 'doctrinal rigidity', proscribing any scheme which deviated from resolutely individualist prescriptions.[173]

Local practice therefore fortified received morality when it came to Phelps's wider influence in national debates over poor relief. Just as Noetic schemes earlier in the century had been transmitted directly from the academy to Whitehall, so in his day Phelps was to play a direct role in the formation of public policy. A member of the Royal Commission on the Poor Laws of 1905–9, along with a number of other COS lobbyists such as Helen Bosanquet, Phelps influenced and helped to draft the famous 'Majority Report', which bracingly insisted, in defiance of escalating contemporary conviction, that poverty was a moral condition and that 'self-caused poverty is a crime', that the Poor Law should be retained, and that Boards of Guardians dispensed excessive outdoor relief.[174] At the onset of the Great Depression the near-octogenarian Phelps was still to be found dedicating himself to public policy and pauperism: on leaving the provost's lodgings in 1929 he spent two years in the chair of a Home Office departmental committee on the relief of the casual poor, raging at the dying of the moral-individualist light.[175]

Just as Phelps's gospel was being read to the university, the city, and ultimately the nation, so it provoked opposition. Though confident that he was the natural successor to Thorold Rogers in the Drummond chair of political economy in 1890, he was passed over in favour of Francis

---

[171] L. R. Phelps, *Poor Law and Charity* (Oxford, [1887]), 5, 6–7, 8–10.

[172] 'Parish Government and Poor-Relief', in A. Crossley and C. R. Elrington (eds.), *A History of the County of Oxford*, iv: *The City of Oxford* (London, 1979), 342–50; 'A Note on Pauperism in Oxford', in Phelps, *Poor Law and Charity*, 14–15.

[173] Howe, 'Intellect and Civic Responsibility', 29.

[174] J. Harris, *Private Lives, Public Spirit: Britain 1870–1914* (London, 1994), 240.

[175] Ross, 'Phelps, Lancelot Ridley (1853–1936)', rev. M. C. Curthoys, ODNB s.n.

Edgeworth of Balliol, one of a generation of younger, more austerely mathematical and technical Oxford economists who disdained Phelps's 'preach and teach' methods and his investigative emphasis on moral factors.[176] On the local stage Phelps found himself at loggerheads with Oxford's MP, the Conservative brewer A. W. Hall, who led civic opposition from the late 1880s to the Guardians' insistence on the workhouse test;[177] in 1900 town and gown antipathy to 'the Phelpsian doctrine' found expression in a 'Committee for Securing in Oxford Out-Relief for the Deserving and Aged Poor in Suitable Cases', backed by leading townsmen such as the builder T. H. Kingerlee, and clergymen, including the Oxford branch of the Christian Social Union.[178] In 1902 a number of dons pressed for the redrawing of the Poor Law boundaries with the overt aim of marginalizing Phelpsian austerity.[179] At the level of national policy, it was a measure of growing opposition to Poor Law orthodoxy that Beatrice and Sidney Webb's dissident 'Minority Report' of the Royal Commission of 1905–9 excoriated the old Poor Law, and attributed poverty to 'social disorganization' rather than moral deficiency; in its insistence on the necessity of an apparatus of interventionist and insurance-funded state and municipal provision, it anticipated many of the features of modern British welfarism.[180] In the next generation, the Minority Report, embodying a new conception of mass citizenship and marking the transition from the 'atomism' of the early Victorian era to a new 'organic' age, secured a political consensus:[181] with a nice irony, the old, Oriel-engendered Poor Law was formally wound up in 1929, Phelps's last year as provost. The diagnosis of its myriad Victorian paternalist critics had prevailed: poverty was to be attributed to environmental rather than moral factors. Of course, the ensuing assumption of responsibility for their remedy by a universal welfare state, rather than a national welfare church, represented as signal a defeat for the Tractarian as for the Noetic prescription.

Noetic economics, therefore, came to be perceived as unjust, and paternalist remedies as inadequate; the welfare state of the twentieth century would supersede both. But in the preceding century, the ideas which emanated from the Oriel common room had been central both to the rise of laissez-faire

[176] Kadish, *Oxford Economists*, 192–7, 200–2, 214; Kadish, *Historians, Economists and Economic History* (London, 1989), 67.
[177] 'Parish Government and Poor-Relief', 349; OCL, Phelps Papers, Hall to Phelps, 26 June, 11 and 27 July 1887.
[178] T. H. Kingerlee, *Letter to Heads and Bursars of Colleges who elect Guardians to the Oxford Union* (Oxford, 1900).
[179] W. S. Holdsworth, W. H. Hughes, and W. M. Merry, *Poor Law Administration in Oxford* (Oxford, 1902); Howe, 'Intellect and Civic Responsibility', 30.
[180] Its acknowledged architect, Balliol's William Beveridge, served as a researcher for the Webbs on the Minority Report and was to claim that 'the Beveridge Report stemmed from what all of us had imbibed from the Webbs': Beveridge, *Power and Influence* (London, 1953), 86.
[181] Harris, *Private Lives, Public Spirit*, 241.

attitudes and to their counter-culture. In its intellectual influence Oriel before 1850 is comparable with Balliol after that date; but Balliol was associated with a single ethos, whereas Oriel, remarkably, nourished two increasingly diverse and ultimately antithetical schools of thought. Beyond their immediate pedagogical influence and clerical homiletics, through their wider polemics and active organization—and for Noetics, consistent government patronage—Noetics and Tractarians were not only quarrelling theologians, but social and political thinkers with a nationwide and sometimes imperial purchase. For a long stretch of that half-century, therefore, the Oriel common room has some claim to be the most intellectually vital place in the English-speaking world.

13

Hawkins, Monro, and University Reform

Ernest Nicholson

Edward Hawkins was born in February 1789 and died in November 1882 at almost 94. He took a double first in classics and mathematics at St John's in 1811 and became a fellow of Oriel in 1813. He was elected provost in succession to Edward Copleston in January 1828 and remained so for fifty-five years, though the last eight, from 1874 until his death, were spent at Rochester, where he was *ex officio* a canon of the cathedral. David Monro, a fellow since 1859, was appointed vice-provost to oversee the running of the college during these final years of Hawkins's life.

It is a measure of Hawkins's longevity that he was born some months before the French Revolution, and that he lived into late Victorian England, dying just five years before the queen's Golden Jubilee. He left no journal, but at the end of his long life he must have had a sense of being overwhelmed by radical change on a wide front. Nowhere was such change more manifest, and more troubling for Hawkins, than in the university. He found himself living into 'an iron time of doubts, disputes, distractions, and fears' and his originally liberal disposition, which had been shaped among the robustly questioning and hard-thinking Noetics of the Oriel common room of his younger years, was abandoned in an endeavour to stem the tide of change.

Hawkins had been placed first among three fellows elected in 1813.[1] He had originally hoped to pursue a career at the Bar, but following the premature death in 1806 of his father (also Edward) he took upon himself, as eldest son of the family and at the young age of 17, the responsibility for providing for his widowed mother Margaret, who lived until 1859, and her family of nine other

---

[1] The others were Orielenses, Thomas Mayo, FRCP, FRS who had a distinguished medical career, and Richard Burdon, awarded the English Verse Prize for his poem *The Parthenon* (1811) and the English Essay Prize for his essay on *A Comparative Estimate of the English Literature of the Seventeenth and Eighteenth Centuries* (1814). See *Provosts and Fellows*, 162.

children (three sisters and five brothers the youngest of whom was a mere six months old). In these altered circumstances, an Oxford fellowship provided a more secure source of income than a young lawyer's precarious livelihood could offer.[2] When Hawkins was elected, the college had already acquired a distinguished academic reputation under the able and energetic leadership of Provost Eveleigh, and was attracting as fellows some of the most promising young minds in the university. He had been preceded in 1811 by the election of John Keble, who had proved himself a brilliant young scholar of Corpus, and who a year earlier than Hawkins had taken a double first in classics and mathematics, had additionally won the Chancellor's English Essay and the Latin Essay Prizes in 1812, and was already an examiner in the Schools in 1813. In 1828 Keble would be Hawkins's rival for election as provost following the resignation of Copleston. Richard Whately, who had entered Oriel in 1805, had also been elected in 1811, and Hawkins, at this stage of his life on the 'progressive' wing of thought, found in Whately and Copleston kindred spirits to his own, and readily associated himself with them. He was joined in 1815 by the election of two further intellectually talented and like-minded colleagues with whom he enjoyed an enduring friendship, Renn Dickson Hampden and Thomas Arnold.

A year after his election, Hawkins accepted appointment as private tutor to James William, Viscount Caulfeild, in France in 1814,[3] no doubt as a welcome supplement to his college stipend in meeting his responsibility to his mother and siblings, but fled Paris on 20 March 1815, the day that Napoleon re-entered the city. Upon his return to Oxford, Hawkins devoted himself to extending his learning in divinity, and soon acquired a reputation as an able and learned preacher: Newman described him as 'a very striking preacher', and perceptive theological thinker.[4] His sermon on Scripture and tradition, preached before the university in May 1818, had a profound influence upon the young Newman, at that time an undergraduate at Trinity.[5] Later, Hawkins expanded his thinking on the topic in his Bampton Lectures delivered in 1840.[6] In 1847, consequently, he was invited to accept appointment as the first occupant of the new chair of the exegesis of Holy Scripture, endowed by the will of John Ireland, a chair which he held until 1861.[7] Hawkins's

---

[2] See W. Tuckwell, *Pre-Tractarian Oxford: A Reminiscence of the Oriel 'Noetics'* (London, 1909), 151.

[3] OCL, Oriel Letters 1295, Lord Charlemont to Hawkins, 14 July 1814.

[4] Mark Pattison, *Memoirs* (London, 1885) 84, comments that 'Hawkins was in those days an effective preacher; in any one of his sermons there was matter enough for two, and his manner in the pulpit was peculiarly impressive.'

[5] *A Dissertation upon the use and importance of unauthoritative Tradition* (Oxford, 1819); Newman, *Apologia pro vita sua*, ed. Ian Ker (London, 1994), 29–30.

[6] They were published under the title *An inquiry into the connected uses of the principal means of attaining Christian Truth* (Oxford, 1840).

[7] John Ireland entered Oriel as a bible clerk in 1779 and was dean of Westminster from 1815 until his death in 1842.

scholarship had further extended to a four-volume edition of Milton's poetic works, providing an edited collation of older commentaries to which he added some of his own observations.[8]

He became a tutor at Oriel in 1819 and remained so with great effect until 1828. He was appointed vicar of St Mary's (the university church and an Oriel living) in 1823, where he instituted the Sunday afternoon sermon made famous by his successor Newman, vicar from 1828. At that time Hawkins had a predominant influence upon Newman, especially after 1824 when pastoral duties kept them both (Newman was then curate of St Clements) in Oxford during vacations, often alone in the college. In spite of the circumstances which would drive them far apart, not without mutual animosity, a letter from Newman to Mrs Hawkins in response to one from her to him telling him of her husband's death reflects the early bond between them, and the debt Newman felt:

> Birmingham.
> Nov. 21 1882.
>
> Your dear husband has never been out [of] my mind of late years... I have followed his life year after year as I have not be able to follow that of others, because I knew just how many years he was older than I am, and how many days his birthday was from mine. These standing reminders of him personally sprang out of the kindness and benefits done to me by him close upon sixty years ago, when he was Vicar of St. Mary's and I held my first curacy at St. Clement's. Then during two Long Vacations, we were day after day in the Common Room all by ourselves, and in Ch. Ch. Meadow. He used to say that he should not live past forty, and he has reached, in the event, his great age. I never shall forget to pray for him, till I too go, and have entered his name in my Obituary book... May God be with you, and make up to you by His grace this supreme desolation.
> Most truly yours,
> John H. Card. Newman.[9]

Hawkins was exact in his scholarship, and business-like, efficient, and practical in administration. These qualities, and the standing he had achieved in the university, made him an obvious candidate for election as provost in 1828. Keble, regarded as 'the first man in the university', was the other candidate, but was not viewed as a serious rival when it came to matters of discipline in the college, or in the administrative tasks that a head of house was expected to undertake both in college and in the university. Upon learning that half the fellowship favoured Hawkins, Keble withdrew and Hawkins was duly elected on 31 January.

---

[8] *The Poetical Works of John Milton with notes of various authors principally from the editions of Thomas Newton D.D., Charles Demster, M.A. and Thomas Warton B.D. to which is prefaced Newton's Life of Milton*, 4 vols. (Oxford, 1824).

[9] OCL, Oriel Letters 1016, Newman to Mrs Hawkins, 21 November 1882.

Hawkins had the misfortune, however, that momentous constitutional changes in national life and in Oxford brought about, from his first year of office, deep divisions in his college: the repeal of the Test and Corporation Acts, the Act of Catholic Emancipation and the parliamentary Reform Act of 1832, followed by the abolition of the redundant bishoprics of the Church of Ireland by the Irish Temporalities Act, 1833. This last measure, seen by some as a national outrage, was the catalyst of the Tractarian Movement, or Oxford Movement. Inspired and led by Keble, Hurrell Froude, and Newman, it became a significant force in the university for decades to come. All this ensured that Hawkins had no honeymoon period as provost. A common room which just a few years earlier Copleston had described as 'united, and the most cordial harmony subsisting', was now divided. Reform precipitated still more change, secularism, pluralism of belief, tolerance of non-belief. Most of Hawkins's many years in office were spent in adjusting to continual change, unrelenting turmoil in the university, perennial and frequently bitter controversy, and to a series of reforms from which emerged a collegiate university approximating in most, though not in all essentials to what Oxford is today. Without the resisters as well as the reformers, however, matters might well have emerged differently from so prolonged a period of *Sturm und Drang*. In all of this, Hawkins himself and several fellows of Oriel played significant and often mutually antagonistic roles. Oriel, like other colleges, was a battle ground.

Though Hawkins was a strong and commanding personality, tenacious in any undertaking, thorough in organization and administration, shrewd and always well prepared in committee and on the Hebdomadal Board, in which he soon established himself as a leading figure, such assets were outmatched by flaws in his character that intruded themselves more and more into his relations both with colleagues and with undergraduates. Dean Burgon gave him the title of 'the great provost'.[10] The epithet requires much qualification; he was his own worst enemy. Over-jealous of his authority, he became intolerably autocratic in his management of the college, determined not just to reign but to rule. William Tuckwell, who knew him in his later years and wrote admiringly of his undiminished energy and 'unwearied intelligence', also wrote thus of him:

Sharp and shrewd and practical, his mind wanted largeness: a master of detail, he was deficient in grasp, and lived amongst minutiae until his accuracy became pettiness, his conscientiousness scrupulosity, his over-exactness destructive of sentiment and warmth. He had neither the unchallengeable lordliness of Copleston, on whom as Provost he professed to model himself, nor the analytic, logical, all comprehending

---

[10] J. Burgon, 'Edward Hawkins: The Great Provost', in his *Lives of Twelve Good Men*, i (London, 1888), 374–465.

certitude of Whately, nor the crusading contagious vehemence of Arnold...his virtues leaned to the side of failings. They were therefore troublesome to those around him; he would needs take into his keeping not only his own but his neighbour's conscience, insisting on what you ought to think, as well as on what you ought to do.[11]

He failed to take constructive initiatives in the development of the college, and his strong disapproval of the ideas of Newman, Robert Wilberforce, and Hurrell Froude for the tutorship of their pupils led to their resignation in 1831. He made energetic moves to supply their place by lecturing himself and engaging Renn Dickson Hampden, formerly a fellow of Oriel, to assist him, but the college never quite recovered from their loss.[12] Mark Pattison referred to the dismissal of Newman, Wilberforce, and Froude as tutors as marking the beginning of the decline of Oriel's academic pre-eminence attained under Hawkins's two predecessors.[13]

In the wake of Newman's resignation the undergraduates of the 1830s were in the care of the former soldier Joseph Dornford, W. J. Copleston, nephew of the former provost, and George Anthony Denison: 'three inefficients' as Pattison unkindly described them.[14] With Clement Greswell (tutor 1832–40) they kept the teaching establishment going through the turbulent Tractarian years. College lectures must have been livelier when they were succeeded by R. W. Church (tutor 1839–42), James Fraser (1842–7), who was especially popular among undergraduates as a tutor, and Arthur Hugh Clough (1844–8), and perhaps in the 1850s by John Earle (1852–6), an energetic literary scholar who combined his tutorship with the Rawlinson chair of Anglo-Saxon. Some of the Greats men may have gone to another fellow, Alexander Grant,[15] who was only a private tutor but who was the first to treat Aristotle's *Ethics* historically: 'a candid, but always encouraging, critic of essays' who anticipated the tutorial system in its modern form.[16]

---

[11] Tuckwell, *Pre-Tractarian Oxford*, 162. On Copleston as his model, see his address after election to the fellows, when, referring to Copleston's expression of debt to the example of his predecessor, John Eveleigh, he wrote of his predecessor: 'His own example, I trust, will still do service through the medium of his Successor...' (OCA, PRO 1 A1/67). Hawkins's stern demeanour impaired his relationship with undergraduates. D. P. Chase, who entered Oriel in 1839 and was a fellow of the college from 1842 until his death in 1902, wrote of his student days that he 'hated to have anything to do with [Hawkins]: there was nothing genial in his manner to us, though I have no doubt that he felt a real responsibility for our well-being', adding, however, what many others also recorded, that when he became a fellow Hawkins at a personal and private level always showed great kindness to him (OCL, Oriel Letters 1262, Chase to Greenhill, 6 January 1890).

[12] See K. C. Turpin, 'The Ascendancy of Oriel', HUO vi. 188–90, who suggests that the three tutors 'were pressing for a scheme which would increase their influence on the religious views of the ablest students', adding that 'Hawkins's reluctance to sanction that is understandable'.

[13] Pattison, *Memoirs*, 88.

[14] Mozley was slightly kinder (*Reminiscences*, ii. 58, 92–8, 408–9, but remarked that after Keble, Dornford was 'a sad let-down'.

[15] Elected 1849 from Balliol, he later became vice-chancellor of Bombay University (1863–8), then principal of Edinburgh University (1868–84).

[16] M. C. Curthoys, 'The Colleges in the New Era', in HUO vii. 134.

ILLUSTRATION 13.1 George Anthony Denison (1805–96), fellow 1828–39

National Portrait Gallery

In 1863 David Binning Monro was appointed tutor and was credited with raising the tutorial standard, just as its modern form was developing from the college lecture or class. The undergraduates whom they taught were also gradually changing. The gentlemen of Copleston's era were still admitted, if in smaller numbers, and accordingly fewer graduates of the college achieved public eminence. The last to rise, not quite effortlessly, in the manner of Malmesbury and George Grey were Gathorne Hardy (1833), a future Conservative Home Secretary and Secretary for India, and John Spencer-Churchill, marquess of Blandford (1840), who as duke of Marlborough was an educational reformer and Lord President of the Council (1867–8). George Goschen (1850) was the harbinger of a new kind of public man. Son of a merchant banker of Saxon origin, he had to make his way, striving for and achieving first class honours and the presidency of the Oxford Union; his expertise on foreign exchange was honed at Oxford, and eventually bore fruit in his service as Chancellor of the Exchequer (1887–92). The common calling of his contemporaries, however, had changed very little from the clerical career followed by their predecessors in the previous century. A significant minority went on to learn law at the Inns of Court, or simply to follow the avocation of a gentleman in the country. Among the clergy Edward King (1848) stands out, not so much for academic distinction as for his personal qualities. A disciple of Charles Marriott, he was admonished by Hawkins for over-strict attendance at chapel; but he lacked the rigorism of some Tractarians, finding inspiration in Butler's *Analogy* and (perhaps under Grant's influence) Aristotle's *Ethics*. As Regius Professor of Pastoral Theology (1873–85) and bishop of Lincoln (1885–1910) his distinctive combination of ritualism and active pastoral care shows the enduring effect on him of the Oriel of 1848. In 1935 his position in the succession of saints of the see was recognized in the diocese of Lincoln.[17] In the academic year 1848–9 among Oriel men whose careers are known, the majority (52.3 per cent) followed a clerical career, slightly lower than the university average.[18] In this respect Oriel, like the rest of Oxford, would wait until after the mid-century to feel the effects of radical change.

At the Oxford which Edward Hawkins entered in 1807 all members, senior and junior, were required to subscribe to the Thirty-Nine Articles of Religion of the Church of England, and to take an oath upon the Act of Supremacy. All the heads of houses with the exception of Merton were in holy orders, and all fellows after a probationary period were required to be ordained. They must also be celibate, vacating their fellowships upon marriage. Election to fellowships was restricted: as late as 1850 only twenty-two fellowships were genuinely open, twelve at Oriel and ten at Balliol, leaving in excess of 500 restricted in some way. The undergraduate curriculum was confined to the pass degree or to honours in classics and mathematics. Only a small number of fellows taught these courses, perhaps 20 per cent of the total, though as demand grew these were supplemented by 'coaches' who could be hired for a fee. Fellows who did not teach collected their emoluments, and mainly spent their time preparing themselves for a career at the Bar or for ordination, or putting in their time until a parish living became available. The great majority of fellows pursued a career in the Church, making the university a kind of Anglican seminary, though it provided no formal training by way of preparation for ordination and ministry.

The professoriate was minimally endowed and staffed. There were twenty-five professors (twenty-four at Cambridge). The rewards were meagre, and their lectures, though often stipulated by tutors for their pupils, were not compulsory. For undergraduates, the examinations to be passed were the

---

[17] See ODNB s.n.
[18] Figures derived from *Registrum Orielense*, ii. 473–7. For the university figures see M. C. Curthoys, 'The Careers of Oxford Men', HUO vi. 482, fig. 14.3.

focus of their academic endeavours, and the teaching or, indeed, 'cramming' provided by tutors and 'coaches' was more to the purpose than the lectures of professors. When Baden Powell of Oriel became Savilian Professor of Geometry in 1827, Edward Copleston advised him not to trouble himself about lecturing, counselling instead that the 'credit of the University will be chiefly consulted by such philosophical essays and scientific researches as form your principal employment'.[19] Science, though destined to become part of Victorian high culture, had at best only a marginal place in the education of Oxford students.[20]

Oxford's anomalies and deficiencies were manifold, and in a rapidly changing nation it was bound to become gradually more peripheral to the evolving needs of society. It gave no lead, and made little contribution, to learning and letters; science and developing technology were seen as activities that properly belonged to provincial industrial towns. The Royal Institution, founded in 1799, and the British Association for the Advancement of Science, established in 1831, were the initiatives of extra-mural individuals supported by wealthy patrons and employing men such as the gifted Michael Faraday. The university's narrowly conceived curriculum made no provision for careers in the professions, including the Church, since no training in theological ideas or changing pastoral requirements was offered to the many graduates who entered the Church's ministry. There were no courses in law, and medicine could only be taken up after graduation. Indeed, any education aimed at training young men for particular careers was considered unworthy of what the university should properly provide. A classical education, on the other hand, Copleston declared, whilst not preparing a student for 'any of the employments of life...enriches and ennobles all'.[21] In short, as the 1850 commissioners had to point out, the connection that once existed between the university and the learned professions had been gradually severed.[22]

Further, subscription to the Thirty-Nine Articles, which had defined the traditional role of the university in the national Church, continued to be imposed, although the civil disabilities of dissenters had gradually been attenuated even before the repeal of the Test and Corporation Acts in 1828.[23] 'Subscription meant what it said, and the *remnants* of the establishmentarian

---

[19] W. J. Copleston, *Memoir of Edward Copleston, D.D. Bishop of Llandaff* (London, 1851), 114–15.
[20] For this see especially T. W. Heyck, *The Transfiguration of Intellectual Life in Victorian England* (London, 1962), esp. chs. 3, 4, 5. Among distinguished Oxford scientists were William Buckland, professor of mineralogy and geology, Charles Daubeny, professor of chemistry, Baden Powell, and H. W. Acland who became Lee's reader in anatomy in 1846.
[21] Edward Copleston, *A Reply to the Calumnies of the Edinburgh Review, Containing an Account of Studies Pursued at that University* (Oxford, 1810), 133–4.
[22] *Report of Her Majesty's Commissioners appointed to inquire into the State, Discipline, Studies, and Revenues of the University and Colleges of Oxford* (London, 1852), 70–1.
[23] For this see H. C. G. Matthew, 'Noetics, Tractarians, and the Reform of the University of Oxford in the Nineteenth Century', *History of Universities*, 9 (1990), 195–225.

constitution defined the character of the University in a way that... they had in considerable measure largely ceased to do in wider English civil society.'[24] The resulting anomaly was that Oxford remained a confessional university in an increasingly non-confessional state. Oxford was even more restrictive than Cambridge, which had abandoned subscription at matriculation and graduation. It became, indeed, the most controversial and passionately contested issue of university reform, and it is a measure of Oxford's resistance that, although some concessions were secured as a result of parliamentary action, it was not until 1871 that subscription was finally ended.

With the Reform Act of 1832, 'the great bill for giving everybody everything' or for 'making everybody equal', and the dominance of the Whigs in government, the universities became an obvious target for dissenters, and especially subscription.[25] In April 1834 a bill to abolish it was introduced by George Wood, succeeded with a large majority in the Commons, but was defeated in the Lords, the duke of Wellington, the new chancellor of the university, playing a leading role.[26] But Wellington was already advising the heads of houses that it was better to begin taking action for the riddance of various abuses and obsolete statutes, among them subscription, before government did it for them. He found it perplexing and embarrassing, debating the issue in the Lords, that Oxford was out of step with Cambridge, which had abolished subscription at entrance and for the BA degree without any of the supposed ill effects, and that it was imposed on young matriculands who could not be expected to understand it. Corresponding with Edward Cardwell, principal of St Alban Hall and vice-chancellor, he wrote in irritation that the heads did not know 'what was passing in the world'.[27] The Hebdomadal Board in response to the chancellor proposed substituting a declaration instead of subscription at matriculation, and asked Hawkins to draft it as a simple test of conformity to the Church of England, and thus not an abrogation of principle but only a change of form. In drafting it Hawkins was influenced by a pamphlet from the pen of the principal of St Mary Hall, his friend Renn Dickson Hampden, who argued both theologically and practically for replacing subscription but retaining the governance of the university within the Church of England.[28] The proposal was withdrawn

---

[24] Matthew, 'Noetics, Tractarians', 197.

[25] I owe the reference to Asa Briggs, *The Age of Improvement* (London, 1959), 260, who cites for its source Samuel Warren, *Ten Thousand a Year* (1841). It is estimated that in 1834, when a first serious attempt was made in parliament to abolish subscription, upwards of thirty pamphlets on the admission of dissenters to the universities were published. The classic narrative of the history of the long crusade to abolish subscription is Lewis Campbell's *On the Nationalisation of the Old English Universities* (London, 1901).

[26] *Parl. Deb* 3rd ser. xxii. 902–4, 17 April 1834. Wood was a unitarian and MP for South Lancashire.

[27] See *The Prime Ministers' Papers: Wellington. Political Correspondence*, i: *1833–November 1834*, ed. J. Brooke and J. Gandy (HMSO, 1975), 714–15: Cardwell to Wellington, 3 November 1834. *Wellington. Political Correspondence*, i. 726: Wellington to Cardwell, 5 November 1834.

[28] R. D. Hampden, *Observations on Religious Dissent* (Oxford, 1834).

but was revived in 1835 when a fresh attempt at parliamentary abolition of the test was undertaken. Once again, however, parliamentary action failed, while in Oxford itself the Tractarians defeated the proposal for a declaration of conformity, at once humiliating the Hebdomadal Board and rebuffing the chancellor himself.

During these years the scope of the debate for reform was widened by an attack upon the university that trenchantly depicted it as failing to deliver to the nation what a national university should, and had originally been intended to deliver. It came from the pen of Sir William Hamilton, Scottish philosopher and academic, in a series of articles in 1831–5 in the *Edinburgh Review*, a journal not unknown for its broadsides on Oxford in the early nineteenth century. Hamilton's essays however were no mere lampoon by someone ill disposed towards Oxford. He wrote as a former Snell exhibitioner at Balliol who had achieved a first in literae humaniores in 1810, with an examination performance whose erudition is said to have astonished his examiners. Here was a powerful and biting critique, 'a splendid piece of reasoned invective',[29] which provoked immediate debate, and contributed significantly to the proposals made in the Report of the Royal Commission of 1850. Hamilton's analysis was all the more telling for being simple: Oxford was, he declared, '[o]f all academical institutions at once the most imperfect and the most perfectible'. What Oxford had become, as compared with what the university was historically and lawfully intended to be, was a result of a 'flagrant usurpation' on the part of the colleges and 'obtained through perjury and only tolerated from neglect'. The original distinction between the university proper and the colleges had been abandoned: the former

original and essential, is founded controlled and privileged by public authority, for the advantage of the state. The latter, accessory and contingent, are created regulated and endowed by private munificence, for the interest of certain favoured individuals... The university as a national establishment is necessarily open to lieges in general: the colleges as private institutions, might universally do as some have actually done—close their gates upon all except their foundation members... If the university ceases to perform its functions, it ceases to exist; and the privileges accorded by the nation to the system of public education legally organised in the university, cannot—without the consent of the nation—far less without the consent of the academical legislature—be lawfully transferred to the system of private education precariously organised in colleges, and over which neither the State nor the University have any control. They have, however, been unlawfully usurped.[30]

In short, the colleges had subsumed the university. Thus '[a]t one stroke [Hamilton] required the present system to prove its innocence, established

---

[29] Campbell, *Nationalisation of the Old English Universities*, 39.
[30] *Edinburgh Review*, 53 (1831), 386.

the right of the state to intervene, and disposed of the university test. The university as a teaching body had been displaced by the colleges, and in Hamilton's view the substitute was contemptible.'[31] '*As at present organized*', he wrote, 'it is a doubtful problem whether the tutorial system ought not to be abated as a nuisance.'[32] Scathing though he was about the present state of affairs, however, he argued on the other hand that 'a tutorial system in subordination to a professorial (which Oxford formerly enjoyed) we regard as affording the condition of an absolutely perfect university'.

Hardening attitudes in Oxford towards reform that might diminish its Anglican ethos and its educational principles persuaded reformers in and out of the university that its internal enactment was impossible, and that change would only come with direct government action. Hampden, who had hitherto opposed such a suggestion, now supported it. The idea of a royal commission, raised in the 1830s and reinforced by the failure of further parliamentary bills, was finally accepted in 1850 by Lord John Russell's government, on the motion of the Unitarian James Heywood (MP for North Lancashire) to establish a Commission of Inquiry into the English and Irish universities, 'with a view to assist in the adaptation of those important institutions to the requirements of modern times'.[33]

The Royal Commission of 1850 and the Act of 1854 was the watershed between the ancient university and modern Oxford. Inevitably, there was the strongest possible opposition within Oxford, not least from Hawkins, who maintained that the university had been continuously reforming itself since 1800. In a letter to Gladstone in April 1850 he wrote scathingly of 'those individuals who last year and at present have urged the premier to send a commission to Oxford, who have scarcely any of them (I think of the list of names annexed to a memorial to Lord John Russell in 1849) any practical acquaintance with our system'.[34] An open letter to Russell by a member of convocation roused Hawkins to comment further to Gladstone and in terms reminiscent of Copleston's defence of Oxford education forty years or so earlier:[35]

You will of course have observed that Education in this writer's view, and probably in Mr Heywood's, I fear also in Ld. John Russell's, means the mere *acquisition of knowledge*. Of course we could not convey all knowledge in three years. But we

---

[31] W. R. Ward, *Victorian Oxford* (London, 1965), 83.
[32] *Edinburgh Review*, 53 (1831), 397–8.
[33] *Parl. Deb.* 3rd ser. cx. 691–7, 23 April 1850.
[34] BL Add. MS 44206 fo. 29, Hawkins to Gladstone, 30 April 1850.
[35] See BL Add. MS 44206 fo. 29, Hawkins to Gladstone, 30 April 1850. The author of the open letter was C. A. Row (Pembroke), headmaster of the Royal Free Grammar School, Mansfield: *Letter to the Right Hon. Lord J. Russell on the constitutional defects of the University and Colleges of Oxford with suggestions for a Royal Commission of inquiry into the Universities by a member of the Oxford Convocation* (London, 1850).

can strengthen and exercise the *faculties of the mind*, which is therefore our principal aim. Knowledge (of many things) will best be acquired afterwards. The external world, says the letter, has changed around us, and modern science has made large advance. Be it so, but the youthful mind and its faculties are just what they were 1,000 years ago, and in many cases the *old* studies are still the best for the improvement of the mind. Ancient History better than modern, Euclid than Chemistry.

Russell instructed the commission to make proposals for coordinating the professorial and tutorial systems to cope with the two new honour schools of natural sciences, and law and modern history, and for reforming college statutes to the same end, while keeping founders' intentions in mind. It was not to consider the larger question of the admission of dissenters.[36] In the debate that ensued, Gladstone, one of the university's two members of parliament, questioned the legality of what was being proposed, declaring also that it was untimely and unnecessary.[37] The university's legal objections were unsuccessful, but the Hebdomadal Board offered passive opposition, and no head of house responded to the commission's questionnaire on colleges, though in some cases individual officers and fellows provided information. Hawkins wrote a brief acknowledgement of a letter received from the commissioners and similarly acknowledged tersely two from A. P. Stanley, a former fellow of University College, and their secretary. Nothing further was sent from Oriel, not even a copy of the statutes, as the commissioners noted. They recommended that the college should endow twelve scholarships tenable, as in other colleges, for five years, adding the observation that the 'College...does not obtain such success in the Examination Schools as might be expected from the character of those from whom its Fellows are taken'.[38]

If the Hebdomadal Board and the heads of houses maintained their self-defeating failure to cooperate, many individual professors and fellows did respond. The field was thus left effectively to the reforming activists. Among the most ardent and extreme of these was the Regius Professor of Modern History (1848–58), Henry Halford Vaughan, who had been a fellow of Oriel from 1835 until 1842, when he refused to take orders and was deprived of his fellowship.[39] Vaughan's plan was to secularize the university completely, and to govern it through an oligarchy mostly comprising lay professors, with many more lay fellowships and redistributed college endowments. Though Vaughan's reforming friends, notably Benjamin Jowett, A. P. Stanley, and Mark Pattison, did not endorse all of this, he was not alone in his call for a revived and expanded professoriate, a main feature of Sir William Hamilton's

---

[36] *Parl. Deb.* 3rd ser. cx. 747–55, 23 April 1850.
[37] *Parl. Deb* 3rd ser. cxii. 1495–1513, 18 July 1850.
[38] *Report of Her Majesty's Commissioners* (London, 1852), 200.
[39] He resigned his chair when Oriel in endowing it insisted that its incumbent reside in Oxford.

essays on reform. In 1852 the commission itself 'adumbrated a centralised university run predominantly by professors and faculties, with a much higher emphasis on research, on the Scottish/German model'.[40]

It was only when the commission reported that the Hebdomadal Board was finally stirred to issue its own recommendations, which were published in 1853.[41] More constructive and influential was the evidence and proposals by the Tutors' Committee, whose Association sprang into action at a meeting in the Oriel common room on 8 November 1852, convening twice weekly thereafter.[42] The tutors issued four reports on university extension, the constitution of the university, the professorial and tutorial systems, and college statutes.[43] Their reasoned arguments and recommendations were a rallying ground for moderate opinion. The tutors desired greater recognition for the professors, but opposed the commissioners' recommendation that they should dominate the governance of the university:

> We by no means desire so entire a revolution... the Tutors and the Resident Masters of Arts, intimately connected as they are with the working and daily life of Colleges, are on the whole the best body to give a tone and colouring to the character and teaching of Oxford... Let us further be allowed to add, that if coming improvements are likely to raise our professors, they are equally likely to raise our Tutors and Resident Fellows... In the prospect of a larger body of Resident Fellows of increased qualifications and with additional educational employment, we see a further reason for assigning to this class an important place in the government of the University.[44]

---

[40] Colin Matthew, 'Gladstone and the University of Oxford', *Oxford Magazine*, 2nd Week, Michaelmas Term 1999, 4. See also Lawrence Goldman, 'University Reform and the Idea of a University in Victorian Britain', in *The Idea of a University in Historical Perspective* (*Reviews in Higher Education*, No. 84, November 2005), 19–31.

[41] *Report and Evidence upon the Recommendations of Her Majesty's Commissioners for Inquiring into the State of the University of Oxford* (Oxford, 1 December 1853). Gladstone viewed this report as containing little of value in its recommendations, but much that was useful in the evidence it offered: BL Add. MS 44291 fo. 69, Gladstone to Russell, 14 November 1853. On the other hand, the *Report and Evidence* did not lack a certain amount of colour, some of it provided by the vice-chancellor himself, Dr Cotton, provost of Worcester College, who, in apocalyptic tone, wrote (*Evidence*, 388): 'Vast indeed is the importance of permitting Oxford to retain its present position as a place of education for the Church of England. When we contemplate the wide regions of the earth, penetrated by rays of light issuing from the Church of England, and consider the immense tracks of country which they may yet illuminate, we cannot but see the unspeakable importance of maintaining the truth unalloyed in Oxford, as a pure source of light, whence radiation through our Church and our Colonies, and our Missionary Stations, may enlighten in ever advancing extent the dark places of the earth.'

[42] See Ward, *Victorian Oxford*, 180–4; A. J. Engel, *From Clergyman to Don: The Rise of the Academic Profession in Nineteenth-Century Oxford* (Oxford, 1983), 43–9.

[43] Three fellows of Oriel were committee members actively involved in drawing up and publishing the Reports: Charles Marriott (for Reports 1, 3, 4), Richard Church (1), and Charles Neate (2).

[44] Tutors' Association Report No. 2: *Recommendations Respecting The Constitution of the University of Oxford as Adopted by the Tutors' Association April 1853* (Oxford, 1853), 50–1.

They further rejected the proposal to allow the professors to direct teaching:

> To give to [a professor] *ex officio* authority to control the opinions and dictate the teaching of a body, some of whom may be as competent to lecture to him as he to them, would spread among our ablest instructors a sense of degradation...which would greatly diminish their interest in their occupation, might in some cases deprive the University of their services altogether, and in its general operation would destroy the independence of thought among the equal members of an intellectual republic, to make way for the energetic rule of an official despotism.[45]

Accordingly, they resisted a restructured governing board in which the professors would predominate: 'as it is in no way desirable that the instruction of the Professors should ever become the main instruction of the place, so it seems unfit that its dispensers should have the chief influence in University legislation.'[46] On all these counts, in the framing of the Oxford University Act (1854), the Tutors' Association won its battle, which was crucial to the regeneration of the collegiate university in preference to the 'Scottish/German model'. It further inaugurated an emerging career structure for fellows who wished to pursue an academic vocation.[47] The result was a new and enhanced status for college tutors in Oxford, and the consequent decline in the authority of heads of houses in university and college government.

Gladstone drafted and then revised the bill, eventually delegating much of the detail to executive commissioners. In Oxford, both liberal and conservative opinion welcomed this. Though he too welcomed the revision, Hawkins's comments were decidedly acid when he wrote to thank Gladstone for a copy of the revised bill:

> I should thank you also for what seem to me great improvements in this copy of the Bill, but that I suspect what appears to me improvements you think the very reverse. All this, of course, (the whole history of the Bill, I mean) I deeply regret. Indeed I have wondered how a Graduate of our University pledged to observe the privileges of the University could be instrumental in what seemed to me so needless an invasion of our privileges. But I have no doubt you think you are doing us good...P.S. What can make you wish to take away the Vice-Chancellor's veto in Convocation? It is never used but for the *public convenience*.[48]

This evoked a reply from Gladstone:

> Thank you sincerely for the kind expression of your belief that I have not willingly been engaged in doing mischief to Oxford. The position is a painful one and my several duties are I will not say difficult to combine in themselves, but difficult so to

---

[45] Report No. 3: *Recommendations Respecting the Relation of the Professorial and Tutorial Systems as Adopted by the Tutors' Association, November 1853* (Oxford, 1853), 77–8.
[46] *Recommendations Respecting the Constitution of the University of Oxford*, 42.
[47] For this see especially Engel, *From Clergyman to Don*.
[48] BL Add. MS 44206 fo. 138, Hawkins to Gladstone, 17 June 1854.

combine that their harmony shall be visible especially when my own infirmities are taken into view. Though the work is full of interest I am for many reasons glad to think it is near an end.[49]

The question of the admission of dissenters remained outside the scope of the bill; but at the report stage, James Heywood moved a clause abolishing all declarations and oaths at matriculation. This was carried by a majority of ninety-one; a further clause to admit dissenters to degrees in arts, law, and medicine was lost by only nine votes.[50] Gladstone had earlier warned that the introduction of such provisions into the bill 'would doom the measure itself to the bottomless pit, and would not bring the Dissenters one inch nearer the object which they desire to attain'.[51] He opposed Heywood's motion. In subsequent negotiations with Heywood and his supporters, however, it emerged that they would be satisfied with the abolition of subscription at matriculation and at admission to the degree of bachelor of arts. If, for a radical like John Bright, MP for Manchester, this did not go far enough,[52] it satisfied moderate opinion. The argument from the analogy of Cambridge was compelling, and before the bill left the House of Commons the Test had been abolished, as at Cambridge, for matriculation and the bachelor's degree. This concession, hard won though it was, made little immediate difference, since colleges could still impose religious obligations upon dissenters seeking admission, and upon candidates for fellowship: the executive commission agreed that colleges could require a declaration of conformity to the liturgy of the Church of England. Such an arrangement, it was argued, would avoid a test 'which scrutinizes conscience as opposed to outward conduct' and which thus gives 'the minimum of security with the maximum of offence'.[53] A dissenter who was willing to conform to the liturgy of the Church of England for the sake of gaining admission, or election to a fellowship, faced no formal test of subscription.[54] This was the sort of arrangement that Hawkins had urged upon the university more than twenty years earlier. Now, it could no longer stem the tide. Pusey, the tireless leader of the church party, realized that the university could not be saved for the Church of England; he wrote gloomily to Keble in 1854 that 'the talent of young Oxford is all liberal', and following the Oxford University Act believed that from now onwards he was carrying out a retreat.[55]

---

[49] BL Add. MS 44206 fo. 140, Gladstone to Hawkins, 19 June 1854.
[50] *Parl. Deb* 3rd ser. cxxxiv. 585, 590, 22 June 1854.
[51] BL Add. MS 44318 fo. 27, Gladstone to Stanley, 3 April 1854.
[52] He described the bill as 'pusillanimous and tinkering' and 'insulting...to one half the population of the country' (*Parl. Deb.* 3rd ser. cxxxii. 983, April 1854).
[53] BL Add. MS 44303 fo. 121, Goldwin Smith to Gladstone, 27 March 1857.
[54] For this see C. Harvie, 'Reform and Expansion, 1854–1871', in Brock and Curthoys, HUO vi. 701.
[55] See I. Ellis, 'Pusey and University Reform', in P. Butler (ed.), *Pusey Rediscovered* (London, 1983), 310.

By this stage of the century another significant trend that was to have far-reaching effects on Victorian society was emerging and establishing itself—erosion of religious belief. The now familiar word 'agnosticism' was coined by T. H. Huxley in 1869,[56] and in the final years of the century the philosopher Andrew Seth Pringle-Pattison recorded that the most characteristic attitudes of the later nineteenth century were 'evolutionism and agnosticism'. But doubt and unbelief were in growth much earlier, and a university that required a solemn affirmation of religious belief from its members would sooner or later have to come to terms with this feature of emerging modernity. Erosion of belief had manifold sources: the discoveries of science, notably of geology, and the rise of radical historical criticism of the biblical texts. Mary Ann Evans, before she wrote under her pseudonym George Eliot, made her own contribution to the changing times by her translation and anonymous publication in 1846 of David Friedrich Strauss's *Leben Jesu*, gazing up from time to time, it is said, to a statue of the risen Christ as she did so. Strauss's book subjected the Gospels to a mythical interpretation, leaving little of a historical Jesus. Perhaps more than any other single work from German biblical scholarship at this time, Strauss's book evoked the rise of a deep mistrust of German biblical and theological scholarship in England that was to endure until the final decades of the century. More immediately, it accelerated the progress of doubt; among its readers was Arthur Hugh Clough, a Balliol graduate who became a fellow of Oriel in 1842, but who in 1848 had to resign because of his loss of faith.

It is hard to imagine that Hawkins, who was Dean Ireland Professor of Exegesis (1847–61), did not know of Strauss's *Life of Jesus*; but his uncomprehending, if kindly, attempts to lead Clough back to the fold of faith imply his ignorance of the work. Uninformed about these new grounds for unbelief, he was insensitive to the intensity of doubt and anguish, the 'eternal note of sadness', it brought for growing numbers. The poem *On Dover Beach*, from which this phrase is taken, was written by Clough's friend and colleague at Oriel, Matthew Arnold, and more than any other writing of the time (it may have been written in 1851, though published in 1857) it captured the sense of loss that collapse of belief carried for increasing numbers of his generation, including Clough, whom years later he would memorialize in *Thyrsis* (1866). It is a poem of 'reflective sadness':

> The Sea of Faith was once, too, at the full, and round earth's shore
> Lay like the folds of a bright girdle unfurl'd.
> But now I only hear

---

[56] For a convenient description of the rise of agnosticism in Great Britain in the nineteenth century see James C. Livingston, 'British Agnosticism', in Ninian Smart, John Clayton, Steven T. Katz, and Patrick Sherry (eds.), *Nineteenth Century Religious Thought in the West*, ii (Cambridge, 1985), 231–70.

> Its melancholy, long, withdrawing roar,
> Retreating, to the breath
> Of the night-wind, down the vast edges drear
> And naked shingles of the world.

This 'haunting evocation of bleak absence', as these lines have been described, expressed the emptiness left by the loss of faith for a growing number of Arnold's generation, both within and outside his college.[57]

At every stage of Clough's journey into doubt, Hawkins was impressively patient with him, expressing concern, when Clough pondered resigning his fellowship, that he should not hurry into a decision. In pastoral mode he also cautioned him against mere 'speculation', which could be vague and uncontrolled and lead to nothing more than a 'general scepticism', a temptation which, as Hawkins perceived, would suit Clough's temperament only too well. He added, in Noetic mode, that he was 'not saying a word against full and fair enquiry', which is a purposeful, directed, and disciplined act of the mind.[58] As one of Clough's recent biographers has noted, however, for all his kindness Hawkins

> had no sympathetic insight into Clough's mind in the sense of understanding what, intellectually, the trouble was all about. Secure in his own learned but old-fashioned faith, he was as remote from the men of Clough's mental climate as if he lived in an intellectual antipodes... He was trying to combat the new scepticism with the intellectual weapons of half a century back. Eight months later, after Clough had burnt his boats by resigning his fellowship, Hawkins wrote to him almost in the tone of tutor[59] to student recommending him a *course of serious study* with a view to his getting a firm hold of the *elementary principles* [Hawkins' emphases] of Religion, recommending him books—Paley's *Natural Theology*, Butler's *Analogy*, Lardner's *Credibility of the Gospel History*, and half a dozen more. Their arguments were conclusive to him, but how did he expect eighteenth-century arguments, most of which were directed to altogether different aspects of the subject, to satisfy a young man who had just steeped himself in the most modern German Higher Criticism? And this is what Clough had been doing.[60]

In the year following Clough's resignation, James Anthony Froude, the brother of Hurrell Froude and a former undergraduate at Oriel, published

---

[57] Stefan Collini, *Arnold* (Oxford, 1988), 40. In his thematically linked poem *Stanzas from the Grande Chartreuse* (probably composed in 1852), Arnold wrote of himself as 'Wandering between two worlds, one dead the other powerless to be born...', perhaps here, Collini suggests (41), 'taking a perverse pleasure in his stranded state' and in fact contrasting himself and the growing number as belonging to the coming era, in contrast to the monks of the Grande Chartreuse, who belong to a dying age.

[58] For these observations see K. Chorley, *Arthur Hugh Clough: The Uncommitted Mind* (Oxford, 1962), 97 ff.

[59] OCL, Oriel Letters 737, Hawkins to Clough, 20 November 1848.

[60] Chorley, *Clough*, 98–9.

ILLUSTRATION 13.2 John William Burgon (1813–88), fellow 1846–76
Oriel College

ILLUSTRATION 13.3 Arthur Hugh Clough (1819–61), fellow 1842–9
Oriel College, after Samuel Rouse, 1860

ILLUSTRATION 13.4 Edward King (1829–1910), commoner 1848–51, bishop of Lincoln
Oriel College, engraving by T. L. Atkinson after George Richmond

ILLUSTRATION 13.5 Samuel Wilberforce (1805–73), commoner 1823–6, bishop of Winchester
Oriel College

his novel *The Nemesis of Faith*. It cost him his fellowship at Exeter, where the sub-rector publicly burned the book, while the rector himself and the Visitor, the bishop of Exeter, began proceedings to deprive Froude of his degree: an outcome which he escaped by promptly resigning.

Troubling though it was to individuals, at mid-century unbelief was not yet on a scale that would rock the orthodox ship. Nevertheless, both Clough and Froude, each brilliant in his own way, were harbingers of a new intellectual pluralism, which would within thirty years breach the confines which a closed clerical society sought to maintain. Clough by then had escaped them by suicide; but Froude, who left Exeter College in ignominy in 1849, was elected an honorary fellow in 1882; ten years later, he returned to Oriel as the Regius Professor of Modern History, in the rapid *bouleversement* of opinion which Hawkins had had to witness. In the meantime, even after 1850 there was a price to be paid for 'full and fair enquiry'. Benjamin Jowett of Balliol, who in 1855 had published a controversial commentary on Paul's Epistle to the Romans, was required to appear before the vice-chancellor to subscribe anew to the Thirty-Nine Articles. Six years later he and six others—*the Septem contra Christum* of their conservative critics—published *Essays and Reviews*, for which Pusey attempted to arraign him before the chancellor's court. They were the last efforts to impose orthodoxy in Oxford: in June 1860, Samuel Wilberforce, now bishop of Oxford, and Thomas Henry Huxley had debated, in the new University Museum, the issues raised by Charles Darwin's *Origin of Species*. After this public exhibition of unorthodox ideas, further suppression was impossible.

In Oriel, the implications of the new declaration of conformity were soon tested. Heads were now required to convene not less than two stated college meetings a year, at which decisions would be passed by a simple majority and no longer subject to a veto by the head of house.[61] Voting now became normal, and Hawkins frequently found himself outvoted, to his discomfort, on issues which throughout earlier years he would have achieved by virtual diktat. His personal memoranda of college meetings reveal his frustration; they show, equally, 'how difficult his opposition and passion for detailed objection must have made college meetings'.[62] A measure of the change that was taking place and of the frustration it induced in Hawkins is provided by the celebrated case of James Bryce, whose brilliant career would make him Regius Professor of Civil Law, member of parliament, and British ambassador to Washington.[63] Born in Ulster into a strongly Presbyterian family which

---

[61] On the reconstitution of governing bodies and the new-found influence and role of fellows, see M. C. Curthoys, 'The Colleges in the New Era', in Brock and Curthoys, HUO vii. 115–57; Engel, *From Clergyman to Don*, ch. 2, 'The Rise of the Tutors 1854–76'.
[62] See K. C. Turpin, 'The Ascendancy of Oriel', HUO vi. 192.
[63] See H. A. L. Fisher, *James Bryce (Viscount Bryce of Dechmont, O.M.)*, 2 vols. (London, 1927).

moved to Scotland when he was 8, his exceptional intellectual ability had already been displayed at Glasgow University. In 1857 he applied to Trinity, where, ranked first of twenty-seven candidates for a scholarship, he was told by the president that scholars were required not only to attend chapel but also to sign the Articles. Bryce resisted the condition: willing to attend chapel and to say grace at dinner, he could not in conscience sign the Articles or take Holy Communion. He wrote to his parents: 'I think it likely that if asked to sign at Trinity, I shall be told it is merely a form, but to me that would not make it less wrong to do it. From the moment I heard of it, I determined not for a thousand times the honour and the money to do it.'[64] He succeeded, and with the support of the younger fellows was awarded the scholarship. He wrote again to his parents: '[Trinity] will of course never venture to put this test... again when it has once been broken through, and the affair has been a good deal talked of in Oxford, and produced, I hope, rather a good effect altogether.'[65] The episode certainly indicated the effectiveness of the Act of 1854, and the leading role of the tutors and the corresponding decline of the prerogative of heads of houses: as D. P. Chase of Oriel later remarked, 'democratic rule was substituted for a (rather unlimited) monarchy'.[66]

A further trial of character lay ahead for Bryce. Taking a first both in Greats and in the new honour school of law and modern history in 1861, and receiving a number of prizes and awards in the process, it was suggested that he enter for a still much coveted fellowship by examination at Oriel. He expressed some reluctance, writing to his parents that Oriel 'is not a pleasant College to reside at—its head is specially disagreeable and would doubtless vote against me on the score of the Articles. However he is always outvoted anyway and probably could do me very little harm afterwards.'[67] On balance, he decided to compete. Hawkins's memoranda reveal the outcome. At the college meeting of 6 April 1862, and in the knowledge that Bryce would be a candidate in the fellowship examination, there was some discussion under the heading 'Qualifications of candidates—church membership'. It was agreed that Bryce would be accepted as a candidate 'conforming' under the arrangement agreed by the Commission Executive Committee.[68] At the meeting of 9 April, it was further agreed to enquire of Sir John Awdry as to what the college could require of a dissenter 'conforming'.[69]

---

[64] The episode and the correspondence with his parents at the time are described in Fisher, *Bryce*, i, ch. 3; see 38.
[65] Fisher, *Bryce*, i. 43.
[66] OCL, Oriel Letters, 1262, Chase to Greenhill, 6 January 1890.
[67] Fisher, *Bryce*, i. 55.
[68] OCA/GOV 4 B1/1/7 1861–7: Notes on College Meetings and memoranda by Edward Hawkins.
[69] J. W. Awdry, former fellow of Oriel, elected 1819 from Christ Church. He was a distinguished barrister and from 1839 to 1841 was Chief Justice of Bombay; he had been one of the Executive Committee set up by the Royal Commission to frame college statutes.

Then at the meeting of 21 April, Hawkins showed Bryce the relevant paragraph of the Ordinance governing the admission of dissenters, and informed him that the college had a legal opinion to the effect that 'conforming' required participation in Holy Communion, and that the college's own statutes required a present intention on the part of candidates to that effect; but Bryce was not at this stage required to declare his intention. He was elected to the fellowship on 25 April, the first year being probationary. But on 6 April 1863, when he was admitted 'actual fellow with the usual oaths and declaration', Hawkins recorded in his memorandum of the college meeting: 'Js B had never partaken of the Lord's Supper at Oriel during his probationary year—having been advised to the contrary—[saying that he] "c[oul]d not receive it here at present"—this after repeated remonstrances from [the] Provost', adding as a question 'will he take it here by and by?'[70] Whatever Hawkins may have wished to happen 'by and by', however, he was powerless to impose this condition upon Bryce.[71] The latter never did conform, and refused to take the MA degree, which still required subscription, proceeding directly in due course to the doctorate in civil law. The case of James Bryce's election to a fellowship vividly illustrates how painful Hawkins felt the current changes to be, and how unrelenting he was in his opposition to them.

A year later (10 June 1864) Bryce was among a large number of alumni of Oxford and Cambridge who met at the Freemasons' Tavern, Great Queen Street, near Lincoln's Inn, to make a concerted effort to complete what, in their view, the 1854 Act had left unfinished. Fellows of Oriel and distinguished Orielenses were present in force, including Charles Neate, (fellow 1828–79), MP for Oxford (1863–8) and former Drummond Professor of Political Economy (1857–62); the barrister Edward Poste (fellow 1846–1902); Edward Vansittart Neale (Oriel 1827), a founding figure in the cooperative movement; George Goschen (Oriel 1850), MP (1863–1900) and future Chancellor of the Exchequer and chancellor of the university; Thomas Hughes QC (Oriel 1842), county court judge and author of *Tom Brown's Schooldays*; and another barrister, Robert Wright (fellow 1861–80).[72] Their initiative induced further reform in the Oxford colleges, notably in Oriel. At the Easter Audit meeting in April 1865, Wright, no doubt with the purpose of bringing the matter of 'conformity' to a head in the college, moved a motion 'to allow persons not

---

[70] OCA/GOV 4 B1/1/7 1861–7.

[71] That only Hawkins and three fellows (Francis Harrison the dean, Chase, and Charles Neate) were present, and that no vote was taken, indicates that confirmation of Bryce in his fellowship was regarded as a settled matter among the fellows, *pace* Hawkins's discomfiture, which can be assumed from his memorandum to have been voiced to those present.

[72] Wright went on to be Junior Counsel to the Treasury and a Judge of Queen's Bench Division (1890–1904). He became an honorary fellow of the college in 1882, and was knighted in 1891. There is a portrait of him by the well-known Spanish Basque painter Ignacio Zuloaga (1870–1945) in the large senior common room.

PLATE 1 Edward Copleston (1776–1849), fellow 1795, provost 1814–28
Oriel College: Sir Thomas Phillips, 1820

PLATE 2 Richard Whately (1787–1863), fellow 1811–22
Oriel College

PLATE 3 Thomas Arnold (1795–1842), fellow 1815–20
Oriel College

PLATE 4 Edward Hawkins (1789–1882), fellow 1813, provost 1828–82
Oriel College: Sir Francis Grant, 1854

PLATE 5 Matthew Arnold (1822–88), fellow 1845–53
Oriel College

PLATE 6 David Binning Monro (1836–1905), fellow 1859, provost 1882–1905
Oriel College: Sir William Quiller Orchardson, 1897

PLATE 7 Cecil John Rhodes (1853–1902), commoner 1873–81
Oriel College

PLATE 8 Charles Lancelot Shadwell (1840–1919), fellow 1864, provost 1905–14
Oriel College

PLATE 9 James Bryce (1838–1922), Viscount Bryce of Dechmont, fellow 1862–93
Oriel College

PLATE 10 Lancelot Ridley Phelps (1853–1936), fellow 1877, provost 1914–29
Oriel College: Briton Rivière, 1916

PLATE 11 The Dean Estate Map (detail), *OCA*

PLATE 12 Sir David Ross (1877–1971), fellow 1902, provost 1929–47
Oriel College

members of the Church of England to enter their names for admission to the college... and to make such relaxations of discipline in their favour as may be necessary'. The motion was passed decisively by ten votes to two, only Hawkins and Burgon opposing, with one abstention (Neate).[73] The surmise is warranted that Hawkins's irate note afterwards[74] on this item on the agenda not only reveals his private frustration following the defeat, but implies the argumentative tone and obstructive content of his opposition in the meeting.[75] His cause was lost: the last vestiges of subscription were abolished in 1871.

The decisive support for Wright's motion shows that the fellowship in 1865, including its senior members, was predominantly reformist. Besides Neate, Poste, and Bryce, who had attended the meeting at the Freemasons' Tavern, the fellows who voted for it were Drummond Percy Chase (Oriel 1839, fellow 1842–1902), and principal of St Mary Hall (1857–1902),[76] the barrister James Hooper (fellow 1848–85), Henry Parker (fellow 1851–85), Francis Harrison the dean (fellow 1852–66), Henry Crucknell (Oriel 1848, fellow 1853–81), David Monro (fellow 1859–82, Hawkins's successor as provost 1882–1905, and vice-chancellor 1901–4), and Lancelot Shadwell (fellow 1864–1905 and provost 1905–14). They were soon joined by kindred spirits, William Stubbs, the Regius Professor of Modern History (1866–84), who was elected a professorial fellow in 1867, Francis Henry Hall (fellow 1873–1918), the classical scholar John Cook Wilson (fellow 1874–96); John King (fellow 1876–1907), and Lancelot Ridley Phelps (Oriel 1872; fellow 1877–1914 and provost 1914–29). Hawkins was consistently supported only by the theologian John William Burgon (fellow 1846–76, vicar of St Mary's (1863–76), and then dean of Chichester), a traditionalist reckoned to be one of the most reactionary men of his time.[77]

---

[73] That Neate, who was personally pro-reform, abstained was probably because, as MP for the university, he considered it proper to remain neutral on an issue which continued to be so divisive throughout the colleges.

[74] Following the meeting, Wright wrote to Hawkins objecting to certificates of baptism being mentioned in the advertisement for entrance scholarships. In his note of the meeting, Hawkins drew the conclusion that 'by persons not members of the Church of England' Wright had meant that 'persons not members of the Church of Christ' should be admitted—'Jews, Turks, unbelievers, Heretics, of any or no Religious Profession'.

[75] Chase, who loyally stood by Hawkins 'to the best of my power, to the last' during these years of change, commented also: 'In old days he was thought a Liberal, but the stream of innovation left him where he had always been, and I suppose the more rapid thought him an Obstructive': OCL, Oriel Letters 1262, Chase to Greenhill, 6 January 1890.

[76] Chase is described as 'a don of the old school, courteous, gentle, kindly, brimming over with quiet fun and quaint Oxford anecdotes'. See Andrew Clark's entry as revised by M. C. Curthoys in ODNB.

[77] Burgon remained throughout firmly opposed to the abolition of the religious tests. Upon the election of Eleanor Elizabeth Smith to the first Oxford school board in 1870, he preached a sermon entitled 'Woman's Place', in which he deplored the appearance of women on public bodies and argued that their place, like Sarah's, was 'in the tent' (Gen. 18: 9). The admission of women to university examinations in 1884 inspired a further sermon, subsequently published

Hawkins himself yielded nothing to the spirit of reform at Oriel, but in October 1874 and in his eighty-sixth year he himself brought about further change when he petitioned the Visitor for permission to reside permanently at his canonry house at Rochester, and to appoint a vice-provost to manage the college in his absence.[78] On 17 November, in accordance with the Act of 1854, the fellows chose by vote three names to submit to the Lord Chancellor: in the order of the support they received, they were David Monro, A. G. Butler the dean, and Lancelot Shadwell. The Lord Chancellor replied on 5 December appointing Monro: the first vice-provost to be appointed in Oriel, and Hawkins's eventual successor. Like Bryce, Monro had come to Oxford from Glasgow, and had distinguished himself as a classical scholar at Balliol. Elected fellow of Oriel in 1859, he was made a tutor in 1863, where he notably raised the standard of tuition, and laid the basis of his future high repute as a philologist and Homeric scholar. A bachelor, he lived out of college, leaving the provost's lodgings to be occupied by the dean. His liberal sympathies, shown in his vote on Wright's motion, were in accord with those of most of the fellows and would eventually restore a spirit of harmony in the fellowship. Meanwhile, the vice-provost and the fellows lost no time in further reform of the college statutes. On 16 March 1875 it was resolved that the vice-provost should write to the Lord Chancellor and the Home Secretary 'with a view to obtaining their assistance in the separation of the clerical preferments now annexed to the Provostship and in establishing the eligibility of laymen to hold the office of Provost'. The only dissentient voice was Burgon's.[79] Lord Cairns responded through Henry Graham, his principal secretary, that the matter lay outside the powers exercised by the Visitor and that he did 'not at present see how any change could be effected by the power of the Visitor or by any authority short of an Act of Parliament'.[80] Monro replied, stating that what the college sought was the Lord Chancellor's opinion as to the grounds proposed for requesting such a change in the statutes, and whether the college could count upon his support in parliament.[81] The principal secretary wrote back, rather pointedly:

The Lord Chancellor desires me to say that it would not be proper for him as a single member of the Government to express any opinion on the merits of your proposal; but, if you will be so good as to put in writing the details of the arrangement which

under the title *To Educate Young Women Like Young Men and with Young Men: A Thing Inexpedient and Immodest.* See ODNB s.n.

[78] OCL, Oriel Letters 1288 and 1289, Hawkins to the Lord Chancellor, Lord Cairns, 3 October 1874 with petition. He explained that his 'general strength and active powers' had declined, and was especially concerned at 'the growing failure' of his sight.
[79] OCA/GOV 4 B/2/1 1874–8.
[80] OCL, Oriel Letters 616, Graham to Monro, 29 March 1875.
[81] OCL, Oriel Letters 617, Monro to Lord Cairns, 9 April 1875. This is a draft of the letter approved at a college meeting.

you would propose as to the Headship of the College and the Ecclesiastical Preferments at present annexed to it, the Lord Chancellor would communicate it to the Provost, and then lay the proposal, with any observations which the Provost may desire to make on it, before the Cabinet.[82]

There the correspondence ended. It is clear that Monro desired to avoid any involvement of Hawkins with the Cabinet on the matter.[83]

Meanwhile, however, Lord Salisbury, the chancellor of Oxford and Secretary for India, was in process of securing government agreement to establish a new royal commission, the Selborne Commission, the legislation for which went through parliament in 1876–7.[84] It was intended to expand the professoriate and other academic posts and to enhance the provision for university libraries, museums, and scientific apparatus, with funding derived from college revenues. Salisbury laid special emphasis upon research, since 'the mere duty of communicating knowledge to others does not fulfil all the functions of an University, and that the best Universities in former times have been those in which the instructors, in addition to imparting learning, were engaged in adding new stores to the already acquired accumulation of knowledge'. The colleges were explicitly included in this proposal, which 'provides that college revenues may be applied to the maintenance and benefit of persons of known ability and learning, who may be engaged in study or research in the realms of art and science in the University'.[85]

On 6 April 1877, during the progress of the bill through the legislature, a committee comprising the vice-provost, Bryce, and King was appointed to monitor its progress 'with a view of carrying out the objects of which the college had already expressed its desire of obtaining'.[86] A significant reform was achieved when George Goschen, at the college's request, tabled an amendment on 14 June providing for the severance of the canonry at Rochester from the office of provost.[87] This was passed without a division. There

---

[82] OCL, Oriel Letters 618, Graham to Monro, 15 April 1875. It is possible that Cairns may have considered that Monro, a layman, whom he had appointed vice-provost a few months earlier, had a vested interest in such a change of statute. Monro was acting, however, on instructions following a decisive vote requesting him to do so. The desire to laicize the office of provost was also wholly of a piece with the move to laicize fellowships (see below), whilst the urgency was no doubt occasioned by a natural anxiety to have the necessary measures in place before the now very elderly Hawkins died.

[83] There would have been no doubting what Hawkins's observations to the Lord Chancellor on this matter would have been, since, in that same year, he published his own protestation against any suggestion of laicization of the provostship in his *Notices concerning the design, history, and present state of Oriel College, with respect to the ecclesiastical character of the institution and of the Provostship* (Rochester, 1875).

[84] On the work of this commission see Christopher Harvie, 'From the Cleveland Commission to the Statutes of 1882', HUO vi. 67–95; Ward, *Victorian Oxford*, 300–16.

[85] *Parl. Deb.* 3rd ser. ccxxvii. 791–803, 24 February 1876.

[86] OCA/GOV 4 B1/2/1 1874–8.

[87] *Parl. Deb.* 3rd ser. ccxxxiv. 1802, 14 June 1877.

was no mention in Goschen's amendment of the laicization of the provostship, but the intention was manifest, and on 1 June 1878 it was agreed by the college to draw up 'a statute to be submitted to the commissioners on the basis of removing the clerical restriction from the Headship', which was followed in October by a petition submitted to the commissioners to include in their proposals 'that from the time of the severance of the Canonry at Rochester from the Provostship the person elected would not be required to be in Holy Orders'. It had further been agreed on 1 June that another statute be submitted to the commissioners to annex the canonry to endow a new chair in theology. What emerged from this was the establishment of the Oriel Professorship of the Interpretation of Holy Scripture, the holder of which would be *ex officio* a canon of Rochester.[88] At a college meeting on 8 June it was agreed to seek an association with a new chair in physics proposed by the commissioners or, failing this, with the projected new chair in pure mathematics, but neither of these chairs was established at this time, both of them, with others, being casualties of the loss of college income from the mounting agricultural depression of those years.[89] At the same meeting, finally, it was agreed 'that the qualification of Holy Orders should not continue to be necessary for Fellowship'.[90]

The college, it is clear, was firmly resolved to make these changes, although the Selborne Commission, sympathetic to Oxford's clerical tradition and generally conservative in inclination,[91] left the question to individual colleges' decision. Some colleges, including Oriel, changed their statutes on these matters; others did not. Jowett, now the master of Balliol, wrote to Charles Roundell, MP for Grantham, that the principle adopted by the commissioners 'has a tendency to divide the University into clerical and anti-clerical colleges' and that 'a great national institution should not be left to this sort of caprice', adding that the 'attempt to maintain Clerical Restrictions is an anachronism in the present state of Oxford opinion'.[92] All remaining clerical restrictions were abolished by a resolution of the Commons in 1881, on a petition of a strong body of Oxford opinion presented by

---

[88] See Ernest Nicholson, *Interpreting the Old Testament: A Century of the Oriel Professorship* (Oxford, 1981).

[89] Of the new chairs projected by the commission, only five had been established by the end of the century. See J. Howarth, 'The Self-Governing University, 1882–1914', Brock and Curthoys, HUO vii. 610–11; Engel, *From Clergyman to Don*, ch. v 'The Agricultural Depression and the Fate of the 1877 Commission's Plan'.

[90] OCA/GOV 4 B1/2/1 1874–8.

[91] One indication of this is that Burgon was at first included among the commissioners, but was dropped between the abandonment of the first bill and the introduction of a second. Jowett, in the letter referred to below, complained that in cases where colleges were divided on the issue of clerical fellowships, 'the commissioners appear to throw their weight into the clerical scale'.

[92] Jowett to Roundell, 6 July 1880. See E. Abbott and L. Campbell, *Letters of Benjamin Jowett, M.A. Master of Balliol College Oxford* (London, 1899), 39–40.

Roundell, subject only to making provision for chapel services and religious instruction of the undergraduates.[93]

Provost Hawkins died on 18 November 1882, three months short of his ninety-fourth birthday. In his letter of condolence to Mrs Hawkins, Monro wrote: 'one cannot help the feeling that we of the present generation have seen a mere fraction of such a life as the Provost's.'[94] This is more than an allusion to longevity: Hawkins had lived through momentous constitutional, social, and cultural changes, which had dissolved the bond of Church and state and created a pluralist and secular society. In this light Hawkins's intransigence in the face of reform, and his irritation at and obstructiveness to its advance, is understandable; and frequent as were his disagreements with the fellows and the occasions when they overruled him, there is no evidence to indicate any rancour towards him. At the college meeting of 14 March 1883 at which plans for alterations to the chapel were discussed, Monro, who had been elected provost in the previous December, and the fellows resolved to commission a stained-glass window to be installed at the east end as a memorial to him.[95]

Monro was already preoccupied as acting provost with more pressing domestic issues than university reform, some of which would outlast him. The future of St Mary Hall was high on the agenda from as early as 17 March 1875, when a committee was appointed to consider the proposal for its union with the college.[96] The proposed annexation had the full support of Principal Chase: the university's independent halls had gradually lost their appeal and were considered to be in terminal decline. Since 1868 undergraduates had been permitted to live in lodgings, at a generally cheaper rate than the halls could offer, while benefiting from the rising standard of college teaching. Chase, giving evidence to the Selborne commissioners on 24 October 1877, referred to the inferior academic reputation the halls had in the university, commenting that 'with very rare exceptions no man ever enters at a hall who can gain admission into or remain at a college', and adding that 'endowment cannot reasonably be expected; a man inclined to such liberality would not be likely to bestow it where it must necessarily produce the minimum of good'.[97] In the case of St Mary Hall, he told the commissioners, 'I have always thought that the proper thing to do with it would be to merge it in Oriel'.[98]

---

[93] For these events see Campbell, *Nationalisation of the Old English Universities*, ch. x.
[94] OCL, Oriel Letters 1277, Monro to Mrs Hawkins, 20 November 1882.
[95] OCA/GOV 4 B1/2/3 1882–7. Arthur Butler was charged with raising subscriptions, and kept a careful record of the donors.
[96] OCA/GOV 4 B1/2/1 1874–8.
[97] *University of Oxford Commission. Part I, Evidence* (London, 1881), Q615, 37–8.
[98] *Evidence*, Q674, 40–1.

The college already had a merger in mind. At a meeting in March 1876, the committee, to which Chase was now co-opted, was instructed to prepare a scheme for submission to the commissioners, and following further consultations with the chancellor and vice-chancellor, Chase was enjoined to prepare a draft statute. At a special college meeting on 15 June 1878 it was unanimously agreed to apply to the commission to make statutory provision for the unification of St Mary Hall with Oriel upon the next vacancy in the principalship.[99] Following the death of Chase in 1902, St Mary Hall was united with the college under the commission's Statute of 1882.

The demise of the halls was but one outcome of other changes in the colleges during these years, some of them the result of developments that had already been taking place and some of them legislated by the commissioners in the 1877 Act. The end of the fellowship without teaching duties—the 'prize fellowship' won by written examination—was among the latter.[100] The commissioners had designed that Oriel should gradually reduce the number of fellows to twelve, through natural wastage, leaving only 'official' fellows with a college office, tutors, and professors. The small group of tutors, among whom Monro had himself recently been a leader, were correspondingly more central to college affairs. In his acting provostship his principal colleagues were Arthur Gray Butler, fellow since 1856 and a former headmaster of Haileybury, and Lancelot Shadwell, who was lecturer in law and history (1865–75). Colleges were beginning to join forces to secure effective teaching: Shadwell would be a lecturer at Christ Church and Lincoln, and Oriel employed four lecturers, two of them, including the church historian Mandell Creighton, fellows of Merton. A tutorial alliance with Lincoln was made in the 1880s, when a tutorial team of Butler, Francis Henry Hall (Modern History), John Richard King, and John Cook Wilson (Philosophy) was afforced by lecturers, including the internationally renowned ancient historian William Warde Fowler and several other fellows of Lincoln. The intercollegiate system of public lectures was another enduring innovation of the period. Overwhelmingly the tutors taught in the school of literae humaniores, leaving lecturers to do the bulk of the work in history, law, mathematics, and theology. Butler, Hall, and King continued as a team into the 1890s, joined by Lancelot Ridley Phelps, an Oriel undergraduate (1872–6) and fellow (elected 1877), in 1893. Hall was tutor for thirty-nine years (1875–1914); in his later years he was joined by George Richards (tutor 1897–1928), David Ross (1903–29), and Marcus Tod (assistant tutor 1905–14, tutor 1914–47). All four provosts from 1882 to 1946, therefore, had served as tutors. In their hands the method of teaching gradually changed from the college lectures, really classes for small groups, of the early nineteenth

---

[99] OCA/GOV 4 B1/2/1 1874–8.   [100] See Engel, *From Clergyman to Don*, 257–62.

century to individual tuition, the 'private hour' which had previously only been offered by hired coaches.[101] The tutorial was now the principal occupation of those fellows who as lecturers or tutors had taken on the onerous task of undergraduate instruction.

The beneficiaries of this desirable but time-consuming system were the undergraduate members of the college. They too had evolved. Their numbers were higher than before, though not overwhelmingly so: twenty-six were admitted in 1888, twenty-nine in 1898. Most of them, in the last two decades of the nineteenth century, were from professional backgrounds and had been educated at a wide variety of public schools; the sons of clergy were a much diminished body. The mixture was modified by the election of scholars from a broader social range, including Harold Idris Bell (1897), future keeper of manuscripts in the British Museum and one of the founders of papyrology, who was recruited from Nottingham High School, and by the Neale scholars, sons of members of the Co-operative Union, through a benefaction in memory of Edward Vansittart Neale (1827). The category of gentlemen commoners or *commensales* had been abolished by the college in 1865; the last were William Wildman Kettlewell (1863), later high sheriff of Somerset (1899), and Hugh John Ellis Nanney (1864); the former's son Henry was admitted as a commoner in 1895. Few of the Oriel men of Monro's time became gentlemen of leisure; the largest contingent took holy orders, with substantial numbers going to the Bar and into the Indian Civil Service and the colonial service. The range of subjects studied had changed less. In the class of 1888, four of the twenty-six went down without a degree, eight read a pass degree, six passed through the final honour school of literae humaniores, five that of modern history, two jurisprudence, and one theology. The class of 1898 was little different. Twelve went down without a degree, six read pass degrees, eight classics, two jurisprudence, and one theology. There were two firsts in 1888, one in classics and one in history, and two again, both in classics, in 1898. These statistics minimize somewhat the predominance of classics, as several men read classical moderations before a final honour degree in another school. The overall impression is of a college now close to the average in Oxford. The intellectual, as well as the social distinction of the college in Copleston's time had faded away.[102]

A more serious and persistent problem for the college throughout these years was the severe effect upon annual endowment income of the agricultural depression. The problem was already emerging in the earlier 1870s, even as the Cleveland commissioners were making their calculations—which would be adopted by the Selborne commissioners—of future college income.

---

[101] Curthoys, 'The Colleges in the New Era', 133–4.
[102] The information in this paragraph is derived mostly from Shadwell, *Registrum Orielense*, ii.

ILLUSTRATION 13.6 Harry Vane (1803–91), 4th duke of Cleveland, *commensalis* 1821–4

National Portrait Gallery, after Frederick Sargent

ILLUSTRATION 13.7 John Spencer-Churchill (1822–83), 7th duke of Marlborough, nobleman commoner 1840–3

National Portrait Gallery

ILLUSTRATION 13.8 Gathorne Gathorne-Hardy (1814–96), 1st earl of Cranbrook, commoner 1832–6

National Portrait Gallery: George Richmond, 1857

ILLUSTRATION 13.9 George Goschen (1831–1907), 1st Viscount Goschen, commoner 1850–3

National Portrait Gallery, c.1868

Opinion is divided on the general severity of the depression.[103] There is no doubt, however, that Oriel was soon affected and among Oxford colleges especially hard hit. From December 1878 there were requests from tenants for remission of rent, frequently repeated from 1879 to 1895 and again in 1901, 1903, and 1905. The effects of the college's sharply depleted income are seen in repeated decisions to suspend fellowships as they fell vacant, recorded in 1881, 1885, 1886, 1888, 1889, 1893, 1895, 1900, 1901, and 1902.[104] Even with this saving, the emoluments of fellows were correspondingly reduced, according to one report by nearly one half.[105] The severe shortfall in annual endowment income had a more lasting effect upon the college's financial well-being than could reasonably have been anticipated.

Amid these gloomy circumstances, the record of college meetings, as well as correspondence and contemporary testimony, attests that Monro's Oriel enjoyed a degree of harmony and collegiality that was a far cry from the disputatious decades of the mid-century. The congenial atmosphere was largely attributable to Monro himself, who was described by Phelps, his successor but one as provost, as 'one who ruled in a wise and liberal spirit', and in whom 'a sound judgement and a rare grasp of principle were linked to fine courtesy and warmth of heart'.[106] The mood was well illustrated by the letter which James Bryce wrote to the provost in October 1894 upon being invited to accept election to an honorary fellowship:[107]

My Dear Provost
There is nothing I should feel to be a greater honour than to be connected afresh with Oriel as an honorary fellow; and should the college so favour me, I should accept the tie and the distinction with the most sincere pleasure, feeling indebted every day of life to Oriel and those whom I have known there in a thousand ways.
James Bryce.

Among Monro's unofficial notes of college meetings in the later 1870s are lists of students who, as university statutes now permitted, were granted leave to live in lodgings in town. Among these names is that of Cecil Rhodes. He had been admitted on 13 October 1873 at the beginning of what was to be Hawkins's final full academic year of residence at Oriel.[108] The well-known story that Rhodes had first sought admission to University College, whose master turned him down, sending him on to Hawkins at Oriel, is unlikely to

---

[103] See J. P. D. Dunbabin, 'Finance and Property', in HUO vi. 375–437, and Engel, *From Clergyman to Don*, 97–9 and ch. v 'The Agricultural Depression and the Fate of the 1877 Commission's Plan'.
[104] OCA GOV 4 B1/2/2, 4 B1/2/3, 4B1/2/4.
[105] See Ward, *Victorian Oxford*, 306 citing the *Guardian* 1880, 1829.
[106] See the entry on Monro in ODNB, originally by L. R. Phelps and revised by Richard Smail.
[107] OCL, Oriel Letters 693, Bryce to Monro, 17 October 1894.
[108] See G. N. Clark, *Cecil Rhodes and his College* (Oxford, 1953).

be true: the more plausible explanation of Rhodes's choice of college was his friendship with a relative of Provost Hawkins, Henry Caesar Hawkins, who lived in Natal. After one term's residence Rhodes, probably through lack of funds, returned to South Africa for two and half years, and came back to Oxford for six terms from 1876 to 1878. He formed a friendship with the dean, Arthur Butler, who later claimed to have persuaded the fellows to keep Rhodes's name on the books at the next interruption of his studies; but it may have been Rhodes himself who needed persuading.[109] The next three years were spent in South Africa; he then returned to Oriel for Michaelmas Term 1881, already a rich man and a member of the Cape parliament, for the final term before his degree, which he took on 17 December. His residence in King Edward Street during the term is marked by a commemorative plaque.

Rhodes's friendship with Butler was significant enough to be acknowledged in the seating plan for the Gaudy at the college on 21 June 1899, following the conferment of an honorary DCL upon Rhodes at Encaenia that day. The university had agreed seven years earlier to confer the degree, but Rhodes was unable to return to Oxford to receive it, and the occasion had to wait until 1899. In the meantime, in South Africa the abortive 'Jameson raid' took place in early January 1896, and the ill repute which Rhodes incurred for his involvement in it raised a serious threat that the conferment of the degree would be vetoed by the proctors at Encaenia. When it became known, however, that Lord Kitchener, the victor at the battle of Omdurman in 1898, who was also to be honoured at that Encaenia, would withdraw if such action was taken against Rhodes, and that the duke of York (later George V) would also absent himself, the occasion went off without incident.

At dinner at Oriel that evening, while Rhodes was seated beside Butler, he enquired about the financial difficulties which were widely known to have severely diminished the college's resources. Butler, who at a later time gave an account of the conversation, told him of 'the general impoverishment' of the college, 'dwelling in some detail' on the 'great losses, owing to the agricultural depression', of the suspension of fellowships through lack of funding and of the 'much diminished' value of fellowships:

At last, he said pointedly: 'How much would be needed to put the College right, to restore it to its full dignity and efficiency?' I said it would want a large sum. He then said: 'Would £100,000 be sufficient? I am going... to make my will in London during the next few days.'[110]

---

[109] Clark, *Cecil Rhodes*, 5.
[110] The letter, dated 18 October 1903 to W. J. Lewis, who had at the time been a non-resident fellow of Oriel and professor of mineralogy at Cambridge, is reproduced in Clark, *Cecil Rhodes*, 10–11.

On the following morning and with Rhodes's agreement, Butler reported the conversation confidentially to the provost who 'drew up a full account of our wants, giving the exact figures of wants I had already stated, and this, with some further hints from Shadwell (whom I took the liberty to consult confidentially) substantially to the same effect, I enclosed to Rhodes'. That was Rhodes's last visit to Oriel. He died on 26 March 1902 at the age of 49. The payment of his bequest to Oriel was reported at a college meeting on 23 April 1903.[111]

In his will Rhodes bequeathed to the college £100,000, prescribing that of this sum, £40,000 was for the erection of a building on the north side of St Mary quadrangle, and additionally to provide an investment fund that would cover the loss to revenue from the rented properties on the High Street frontage of the existing building. A further £40,000 was to augment the endowment of the fellowships. Of the remainder, £10,000 was to endow the high table, and £10,000 to maintain the college buildings. Each of these sums was separately invested, that for the building being subdivided into a Rhodes Building Fund (£22,500) and a Loss of Income Fund (£17,500).[112]

The transaction, however, has received a bad press from subsequent commentators. The charge levelled against Monro and Shadwell, who supplied what Butler refers to as the 'exact figures' for addressing the college's needs, is that these figures were inaccurate, especially in underestimating severely the loss of income from the rented properties on the High Street frontage of the old range of buildings.[113] By 1919, only eight years or so after the opening of the Rhodes Building, the college's auditors 'reported that financially the College was worse off as a result of the Rhodes Building'.[114] More generally, the response of the college to Rhodes was held to be 'pedestrian in its objectives', its main purpose 'restoration rather than advancement'.[115] There was 'no suggestion that the College should attempt in any respect to do more than it had done in the past', and it has been claimed that the part of Rhodes's will relating to Oriel reflects 'the anxieties of the dons and their comparatively unenterprising attitude to the future' and 'stands in sharp contrast with the part relating to the altogether new and revolutionary idea of the Rhodes scholarships, which was Rhodes's own'.[116]

Perhaps behind the charge of financial ineptitude levelled against Monro and Shadwell was the memory of Rhodes's own words in his will, in which he describes the 'College authorities' as living 'secluded from the world' and 'like children as to commercial matters', whom he goes on to advise to consult his

---

[111] OCA GOV 4 A5: 23 April 1903 and OCA 4 B1/2/5: 23 April 1903.
[112] OCA GOV 4 A5: 23–4 April 1903.
[113] Clark, *Cecil Rhodes*, 13–14, citing a letter dated 14 July 1948 from L. L. Price, who was senior treasurer from 1889 to 1918.
[114] See Eric Vallis, 'Oriel's Estates and Interests in Land, 1324–1991', OR (1991), 33.
[115] Paul Winby, 'The Rhodes Bequest', OR (1994), 36–7.
[116] Clark, *Cecil Rhodes*, 12.

trustees in London as to the investment of the various funds provided in his will.[117] The college duly consulted the trustees, but its rejection of their advice was itself proof that Rhodes's opinion of their financial acumen was wide of the mark. The trustees advised the college to purchase the De Beers Company, founded by Rhodes, which, it seems, the benefaction would have made possible. At the time this would have been a hazardously speculative investment, and the fate of the college would have been unpredictable. To apply so large a sum to a single investment was contrary to good practice.[118] Further, for several years De Beers paid no dividend. The prudence of the college officers in declining what the trustees suggested was, in the circumstances, fully justified.[119]

The charge of miscalculating the projected loss of income from the properties demolished to make way for the Rhodes Building, alleged as the prime cause of the deficit reported by the auditors in 1919, is equally unjustified, or at best an oversimplification. The minutes of college meetings during the years of planning the building reveal a far more complex series of events and decisions that led to the eventual shortfall: none of them can justly impugn the due diligence of Monro or Shadwell, or the fellows who acted with them. In October 1904 Basil Champneys was appointed architect for the new building, with instructions in the first instance to produce 'a general report as to the mode of laying out the ground, including the question of building a new Provost's house'.[120] The minutes of college meetings reveal from the outset a vigilant caution about the cost, further reflected in the changes in design called for, not always successfully, by the fellows. At a meeting in February 1905 a sum not exceeding £15,000 was set aside for the building.[121] Their unease about costs was heightened by Champneys's preliminary proposals, discussed at the same meeting. They immediately objected to his incorporation of a large, open arcade on the High Street frontage, raising the same objection in April, when it was agreed, with a view to maximizing the potential of the new building, 'that no plan for the new buildings on the High St site will be satisfactory to the College that does not provide for the utilisation of *the entire space* [emphasis added] for either residential College or professional purposes'.[122] It was agreed at the same meeting that as 'the

---

[117] In his letter to Clark (see *Cecil Rhodes*, 14), Price, referring to these remarks of Rhodes, said that Shadwell had told him that Rhodes, contrary to his comment in the will, had paid tribute to the financial competence of Oriel, complaining that while he was 'plagued in London with requests for financial "tips"', he 'rejoiced in immunity at Oriel in that matter'.

[118] As noted above, the different accounts were themselves separately invested.

[119] The senior treasurer, Price, mentions this in his letter to Clark.

[120] OCA GOV 4 A5: 12 October 1904.

[121] OCA GOV 4 A5: 15 February 1905.

[122] OCA GOV 4 A5: 27 and 28 April 1905. The comment about using 'the entire space' clearly had in mind the largish space allocated to the open arcade on the High Street frontage, as set out in Champneys's first proposal. For an artist's impression of the High Street frontage and the inbuilt arcade see H. Colvin, *Unbuilt Oxford* (New Haven, 1983), 156.

College still feel the necessity of limiting the expense', Mr Champneys be asked 'to consider the possibility of economy by utilising the existing buildings', though a note is added that this was to be put to him in an informal manner and not as an option on which the college had settled. Due diligence is in evidence again in a decision at a meeting in May to consult Messrs Field and Castle, the college's land and estates agents in Merton Street, 'as to the loss of capital involved in pulling down the houses in the High St on the site of the proposed new buildings'—presumably to update the figure provided by Monro and Shadwell in 1899. In November, again probably with the cost of the building in mind, it was resolved to abandon the inclusion of new lodgings for the provost in the new building, and to consult Champneys on the modernization of the existing lodgings.

In October 1906 the architect was asked to draw up a revised design of the Rhodes Building. He persisted however with his original concept of the building, into which he now incorporated an archway through the middle, a feature to which the college perennially objected, without ultimate success.[123] In December the college reaffirmed that the cost of the building should not exceed £15,000.[124] In June 1907, however, after detailed discussion of the revised design, it was agreed to revise this figure upwards, and the provost was instructed 'to inform Mr Champneys that the *maximum* sum to be spent on the Buildings should be £20,000, inclusive of lighting, heating, and architect's and Surveyor's fees', a sum still within the original amount set aside for this purpose.[125] Further discussions with Champneys on details of the building culminated in an acrimonious confrontation between the newly appointed building committee and the architect, which was reported at a college meeting in March 1909.[126] Eventually, on 5 June it was agreed with Champneys to draw up a contract to the sum of £17,822 18s. 2d. with the builders Woodridge & Simpson, 'to be settled by the Provost and Treasurer; and a guarantee to be required'.[127] When the completed accounts for the building were brought by the treasurer to the college at its meetings on 9 and 10 October 1912, they amounted to £23,136, comprising £19,965 for the builder, including the cost of the new approach 'from the Back Quadrangle into St Mary's Quadrangle', not included in the contract, a payment of £1,440 to the sculptor, and the architect's fee of £1,731. The treasurer reported that this sum exceeded the amount in the Building Fund by £3,305. It was agreed on his proposal to provide this shortfall from the Loss of Income Fund.[128] The cost was not much more

---

[123] See OCA GOV 4 A6: 9 and 10 October 1907.
[124] OCA GOV 4 A6: 5 December 1906.
[125] OCA GOV 4 A6: 7 June 1907.   [126] OCA GOV 4 A6: 3 March 1909.
[127] OCA GOV 4 A6: 5 June 1909.   [128] OCA GOV 4 A6: 9 and 10 October 1912.

than the sum initially allocated for this purpose. But it substantially exceeded what was available in the Building Fund.

The college minutes reveal that only a few months after receipt of the benefaction, it was agreed that the annual income from the Rhodes Building Fund and its associated Loss of Income Fund should be applied to the repayment of college debt.[129] It was not until the end of 1907 that this order was rescinded. At the stated general meeting in April of that year, Shadwell gave notice that at the next stated general meeting (October) 'he would propose the repayment by the College to the Rhodes Building Fund of the moneys paid thereout since 1903 to the reduction of College debt'.[130] In October it was agreed, on a motion of the treasurer, 'to discontinue, as from the end of the year 1907, the application of the income of the Rhodes Building Fund and the Loss of Income Fund to the repayment of College Debt' under the college order of 14 October 1903.[131] There is no reference here to *repayment* of the monies appropriated from these funds, as Shadwell's motion evidently intended; the treasurer's proposal was adopted instead. In 1912, when the treasurer reported the shortfall in the Building Fund, the sum to make this up was charged not to the college but to the Loss of Income Fund, which, already deprived of four years of accrued interest, was thus further depleted.

It emerges from all this that at an early stage the college determined that the sum of £40,000, including the sum of £17,500 for loss of income, was more than sufficient for the purposes for which this total was intended, and thus considered it as financially feasible to deploy the income of these funds to repay college debt. The heavy weight of debt which the agricultural depression had engendered left the college in effect dependent, for a time, on the Rhodes Building Fund and the Loss of Income Fund to make ends meet. So when it was resolved to discontinue appropriating the income of these funds, the college was unable to reimburse them as Shadwell had intended—a further indication of straitened financial circumstances.[132] By then it was acknowledged that the cost of the building would exceed its budget. The college's protracted and rather laboured engagement with Champneys's proposals, from early 1905 until 1910 when the building work proper began, exacerbated by Champneys's unwillingness to meet some of their wishes, must have contributed to the overrun the fellows had laboured so diligently to

---

[129] OCA GOV 4 A5: 14 October 1903.   [130] OCA GOV 4 A6: 25 and 26 April 1907.
[131] OCA GOV 4 A6: 9 October 1907.
[132] A further indication of this is the college's expression of regret (OCA GOV 4 A6: 9 and 10 October 1907) at its 'inability to contribute' to a new professorship of engineering, with which it had been invited by the vice-chancellor to associate itself. That the decision followed due deliberation, which was reserved for a stated general meeting, and was not an impromptu polite refusal, indicates that the college at that time was not uninterested in attempting 'to do more than it had done in the past' and was far from displaying an 'unenterprising attitude to the future', as Clark concluded.

avoid.¹³³ Shadwell's notice of motion in April 1907 must have been put forward when he realized that the depleted Building Fund could not meet the actual cost of the building. In consequence on 1 June the college raised the available sum to £20,000. So the analysis of the auditors in 1919 that 'financially the College was worse off as a result of the Rhodes Building' was superficial. Had the college not had to cope—struggle is an apter word—with severe debt during the early years of the century, neither the cost of the Rhodes Building nor the loss of rental income would have strained resources.

Would the continuing stringency of college finances have been avoided if Butler, or Monro, had been less modest in estimating the college's needs in response to Rhodes? The latter's affection for Oriel, and his whole-hearted readiness to reinstate its financial well-being, may justify the claim that an opportunity to ask for a larger sum than the rough and ready figure he mentioned was missed.¹³⁴ It was after all rather less than 2 per cent of his estate of £6,000,000 upon his death. In fact Monro's 'full account of our wants' was evidently drawn up with Rhodes's own figure of £100,000 in mind, when he would probably have increased the sum, had he been asked. For all that, however, the sum was very substantial, indeed unprecedented at the time. Faced with such a generous figure, Monro's response is fully understandable, whatever hindsight may suggest.

In all this the outcome of the entire episode is not to be overlooked. The Rhodes Building remains an enduring memorial to the college's greatest benefactor of modern times, and one of the university's most far-sighted. The statues on the quadrangle side, Adam de Brome, Joseph Butler, John Henry Newman, and Thomas Arundel, are a reminder to passing generations of Orielenses of a spiritual ancestry that spans seven centuries, and of the many others who have been at the college before them, leaving more than their names after them in Oxford and in England and the world. On the High Street frontage, the statue of Rhodes himself looks out upon the university whose advantages his munificence has extended to many thousands of young people from diverse nations, races, and cultures who, bearing the proud title of Rhodes scholar, have sought the benefits of one of the world's great seats of education and learning, and who in turn have contributed so significantly to its academic, intellectual, and collegial life and well-being, to the enrichment of Oxford's unique *genius loci*.

---

¹³³ G. C. Richards, a fellow of the college at the time, later wrote: 'My sole experience of an R.A. led me to think that he can be a very obstinate and unreasonable man, if ever he is thwarted by those who have invited his services': *An Oxonian Looks Back: 1885–1945* (Oxford, 1960), 14.

¹³⁴ In his letter to Lewis cited above Butler wrote that 'Rhodes dwelt, at least twice in our conversation, on his wish to restore "the full dignity and efficiency of the College"'.

14
Oriel and the Wider World

Alexander Morrison

> To conclude, *Guiana* is a Countrey that hath yet her Maydenhead, neuer sackt, turned, nor wrought, the face of the earth hath not beene torne, nor the vertue and salt of the soyle spent by manurance, the graues haue not been opened for gold, the mines not broken with sledges, nor their Images puld down out of their temples. It hath neuer been entred by any armie of strength, and neuer conquered or possesed by any Christian Prince.
>
> Sir Walter Raleigh, *The Discoverie of Guiana* (1596)[1]

There is a curious opposing symmetry in the careers of what are arguably Oriel's two most famous sons, both of whom made their names overseas. Raleigh and Rhodes each sought gold and dominion, but whilst the former was executed, disgraced, bankrupt, and disappointed, the latter would not only enjoy fabulous riches and great political power during his short life, but would have his name perpetuated in that of an African colony for over seventy years after his death, whilst the trust he established and the scholarships it funds endure to this day. Conversely Raleigh's reputation has fared rather better than that of Rhodes in recent years, partly because the schemes of colonization and plunder he proposed never came to fruition, but perhaps also because in his *History of the World* and *Discoverie of Guiana* he left a written legacy far more substantial than anything produced by Rhodes.

These two characters have something else in common: in neither case can we honestly claim to know of any profound influence which their education at Oriel had on their intellectual development and subsequent careers. We know almost nothing of Raleigh's time at Oriel save that he matriculated in 1572 as 'Rawley, W.', and that he borrowed a gown from a relation who was also there.[2] Perhaps it was at Oxford that he acquired some of that knowledge of

---

[1] Sir Walter Raleigh, 'The Discoverie of the Large, rich and bewtiful empyre of Guiana', in Joyce Lorimer (ed.), *Sir Walter Ralegh's Discoverie of Guiana* (London, 2006), 211.
[2] See *Registrum Orielense*, i. 42; 'Sir Walter Raleigh at Oriel', *Oriel Record*, 3/3 (April 1919), 80–3; Cecil Emden, 'Sir Walter Raleigh: His Friends at Oriel', *Oriel Papers* (Oxford, 1948), 9–21.

ancient history which he would later work into *The History of the World*. He is also supposed to have been taught mathematics by Thomas Harriot of St Mary Hall, who would later accompany Sir Richard Grenville as a navigator: it is hard to say much more.³ In the case of Rhodes we are, of course, much better informed, and there seems little doubt that he held Oriel in considerable affection, as having been prepared to admit him after his rejection by University College, and to allow him to spread his residence over seven years before he finally obtained his pass degree.⁴ That he remembered the college generously in his will (albeit in notoriously patronizing terms, so far as the fellowship was concerned) is proof enough of this.⁵ In the same document he expressed clearly what he thought most important about Oxford: namely that it was a residential university, stating that it was this consideration which impelled him to make his gigantic bequest there rather than to one of the Scottish universities where more practical subjects with greater relevance to his aims had more prominence in the curriculum.⁶ However, Rhodes was 20 when he came up in 1873, and had already amassed a considerable fortune during the two years he had spent in South Africa: his path in life was clear. The reason it took him seven years to complete his degree was because he spent most of his time looking after his burgeoning mining empire on the Rand, and his interest was always in acquiring the social imprimatur of a spell at Oxford, rather than in any intellectual content.⁷ As one of his contemporaries recalled:

I remember him [Rhodes] well. We matriculated at the same time, but few of his contemporaries ever imagined that he would attain to such colossal greatness as he subsequently achieved. We did not conceive that this delicate and somewhat lackadaisical young man should ever play the most striking part in the history of modern British Imperial development.... Some of us remember too, that when he returned from his first visit to South Africa, and had 'struck diamonds', he used to carry some of the precious stones in a little box in his waistcoat pocket. On one occasion when he condescended to attend a lecture, which proved uninteresting to him, he pulled out his box and shewed the gems to his friends, and then it was upset, and diamonds were scattered on the floor, and the lecturer looked up and asking what was the cause of the disturbance received the reply, 'it is only Rhodes and his diamonds.'⁸

Oriel cannot really claim to have spawned or fostered either Rhodes's business acumen or his empire-building. This was something he learned in

---

³ Richard Symonds, 'Oxford & Empire', HUO vii. 689.
⁴ On Rhodes's Oxford career and connections see Philip Ziegler, *Legacy: Cecil Rhodes, the Rhodes Trust and Rhodes Scholarships* (New Haven, 2008).
⁵ 'And finally as the College authorities live secluded from the world, and so are like children as to commercial matters, I would advise them to consult my Trustees as to the investment of those various funds [£100,000]', 'Will of Mr Cecil Rhodes', *The Times*, 5 April 1902.
⁶ 'Colonial Scholarships at Oxford', *Morning Post*, 5 April 1902.
⁷ Shula Marks and Stanley Trapido, 'Rhodes, Cecil John (1853–1902)', ODNB s.n.
⁸ P. H. Ditchfield, 'Famous Men of Oriel College', OR (March 1910), 163–4.

the harsher world of the Rand, and Oriel can take neither blame nor credit for his wider African legacy.

In light of what these examples tell us, I do not propose in this chapter simply to provide a check-list of the great and the good who, after passing through Oriel, went on to serve abroad, or indeed to try to record exhaustively all those who came to Oriel from overseas. Most colleges in Oxford can boast such lists, often stretching back many centuries, and with a few exceptions (such as Balliol's connection with India) there is nothing particularly distinctive about them, no suggestion that the specific character or intellectual atmosphere of a college attracted more students from overseas, or impelled more of its graduates to seek their fortunes there.[9] Much more interesting is the question of whether knowledge acquired at Oriel would later be employed elsewhere, whether we can trace intellectual currents from their origin in the senior common room to their expression and application in Punjab, Rhodesia, or the West Indies. Equally fascinating are the international networks of friendship, solidarity, and support which were forged between fellows of the college, and amongst undergraduates with each other and with their tutors. It is only in more recent times that it becomes possible to look at these connections, which, overwhelmingly, took place within the framework of the British Empire. Accordingly although, as the example of Raleigh shows, the history of Oriel and the wider world begins when Britain began to expand overseas, and although by no means all the college's overseas links were those of empire, it is the latter, and in particular the nineteenth and early twentieth centuries, which will occupy the central place in this chapter.

Sir John Seeley famously observed in 1883 that the 'general drift or goal of English history', since at least the late sixteenth century, was 'the extension of the English name into other countries of the globe, the foundation of Greater Britain'.[10] His plea to place imperialism and 'expansion' at the heart of English (we would now say British) history was adopted with enthusiasm in Oxford, and in many ways had already been anticipated there. Apart from Rhodes Oriel also played host to three of the nineteenth century's more important imperial thinkers, namely Goldwin Smith, Regius Professor of Modern History from 1858 to 1865, his pupil James Bryce, Lord Bryce, and his competitor for the chair and eventual successor in 1892–4, James Anthony Froude.[11] Remarkable figures though they were, no great intellectual consistency can be found between the views of these three on empire and Britain's place in the world, but they were often linked in unexpected ways. Smith was perhaps the

---

[9] As the diplomat Sir Cecil Spring-Rice (1859–1918) is supposed to have said to his old tutor at Balliol, 'one might as well talk of the P. & O. boats breeding Viceroys as of Eton breeding Governor-Generals: it was the only line for them to go by.' My thanks to S. J. D. Green for suggesting this comparison.

[10] Sir John Seeley, *The Expansion of England* (London, 1883), 8–9.

[11] Symonds, 'Oxford and Empire', 694, 696–7.

original 'Little Englander', writing of the possibility that 'owing to the multitude of her useless dependencies, and the consequent dispersion and exhaustion of her forces, the power of England is beginning to decline'.[12]

Smith would continue to advocate the separation of colonial dependencies from Britain for the rest of his career, although he made a reluctant exception in the case of India, where he felt that despite the inherent evils of foreign rule, Britain's intentions and influence had on the whole been good.[13] While Goldwin Smith's historical contributions were slight, he played an important role in the campaign for university reform, and as a mentor for a generation of young radicals, many of whom would go on to political careers of a kind which eluded him.[14] He himself, after spending two years at the then newly founded Cornell University (he became an admirer of American republicanism, though not of other aspects of its mass democratic culture), would in 1871 settle in Toronto, where he exercised a substantial (if occasionally controversial) influence over the nascent intellectual life of Canada.[15]

Goldwin Smith had written a highly critical review of J. A. Froude's *History of England* when it appeared in 1858, and the views of the two men also differed profoundly on the question of empire. This was with the notable exception of Ireland, where both men opposed Home Rule. In Goldwin Smith's case this was purely on grounds of national security, but Froude, who was an undergraduate at Oriel from 1835 to 1840, had a genuine belief in the benefits of Anglo-Saxon and Protestant settlement, and in the maintenance of empire.[16] He firmly rejected the liberal view, exemplified by Goldwin Smith, that most of Britain's colonies were no more than encumbrances to be shed as quickly as possible, famously writing that

so far as our own colonies are concerned it is clear that the abandonment by the mother country of all pretence to interfere in their internal management has removed the only cause which could possibly have created a desire for independence. We cannot, even if we wish it ourselves, shake off connections who cost us nothing and themselves refuse to be divided. Politicians may quarrel; the democracies have refused

---

[12] Goldwin Smith, *The Empire: A Series of Letters published in the 'Daily News' in 1862, 1863* (Oxford, 1863), x.

[13] Goldwin Smith, 'British Empire in India', *North American Review*, 183/598, 7 September 1906, 338–48.

[14] One judgement was that 'His chief weaknesses as a historian [were] a complete disregard of painstaking research into primary sources and a habit of violent partisanship', Elisabeth Wallace, 'Goldwin Smith on History', *Journal of Modern History*, 26 (1954), 220–32.

[15] Christopher A. Kent, 'Smith, Goldwin (1823–1910)', ODNB s.n.

[16] J. A. Froude, *The English in Ireland in the Eighteenth Century*, 3 vols. (London, 1874); Goldwin Smith, *Irish History and Irish Character* (London, 1862). See further D. McCartney, 'James Anthony Froude and Ireland: A Historiographical Controversy of the Nineteenth Century', *Historical Studies*, 8 (1971), 171–90.

to quarrel; and the result of the wide extension of the suffrage throughout the Empire has been to show that being one the British people everywhere intend to remain one.[17]

Instead Froude was an eloquent advocate of the imperial federation of the Anglo-Saxon peoples, arguing that colonies should be used to absorb surplus population, tying them closer to the mother country and producing a more energetic race of agricultural colonists who would help to maintain Britain's position of power in the world against the rising challenge of the United States.[18] His advocacy of representative institutions, however, only extended to white inhabitants of the empire, and not even to all of them. Notoriously he argued for the withdrawal from the West Indies of such limited concessions to self-government as existed:

If you choose to take a race like the Irish or like the negroes whom you have forced into an unwilling subjection and have not treated when in that condition with perfect justice—if you take such a race, strike the fetters off them, and arm them at once with all the powers and privileges of loyal citizens, you ought not to be surprised if they attribute your concessions to fear, and if they turn again and rend you.[19]

Elsewhere Froude was still more explicit about the need to maintain an authoritarian system of government akin to that in India (which he greatly admired) in any area with a population 'the enormous majority of whom are of an inferior race'.[20] With his evident disdain for the people and places he visited and his romantic Toryism, he would appear to have little in common with that pragmatic Liberal and 'eager traveller in many lands' James, Viscount Bryce, fellow of Oriel from 1862 to 1889, and Regius Professor of Civil Law for much of that period.[21] The latter exemplifies the mixture of literary history and active politics so characteristic of late nineteenth-century Britain, although arguably he never entirely fulfilled his ambitions as a politician. He did not become Foreign Secretary in the Liberal government of 1905, losing out to the less well-travelled but cannier Grey, and instead the summit of his career came as ambassador in Washington from 1907 to 1913.[22] As a scholar he enjoyed greater distinction, becoming well known as the leading British interpreter of American politics and society, producing numerous works on the subject over his long career.[23] His interests spanned the globe, however: as he himself said in 1914, on thanking Rudyard Kipling

---

[17] J. A. Froude, *The English in the West Indies or The Bow of Ulysses* (London, 1888), 2–3.
[18] A. F. Pollard, 'Froude, James Anthony (1818–1894)', rev. William Thomas, ODNB s.n.
[19] Froude, *The English in the West Indies*, 208–9.
[20] Froude, *The English in the West Indies*, 286–7.
[21] Ernest Barker, 'Lord Bryce', EHR 37 (1922), 221.
[22] Keith Robbins, 'History and Politics: The Career of James Bryce', *Journal of Contemporary History*, 7 (1972), 37–52.
[23] His *magnum opus* was *The American Commonwealth*, 2 vols. (London, 1888).

for an address to the Royal Geographical Society, he had 'a love for the Earth's surface, a desire to see every part of the Earth's surface, be it more beautiful or less beautiful'.[24] Bryce was an indefatigable traveller, visiting every continent apart from Antarctica, and, like many of his Oxford contemporaries, a keen mountaineer. He combined both enthusiasms while still a fellow of Oriel when he climbed Mount Ararat, the end point of a journey which took him through Russia from Kazan down the Volga, and then from Saratov via the Black Sea steppes to Transcaucasia, resulting in what was probably his best-known book of travels. Although Bryce compared the relations between the Russian state and its Muslim subjects favourably with the situation in British India or French Algeria, he considered the Russian regime to be cumbersome and backward.[25] On his return Bryce became well known as a champion of the Armenians under Ottoman rule, maintaining a voluminous correspondence which ranged from lengthy descriptions of oppression, famine, and suffering by Nerses, the Armenian orthodox Patriarch of Constantinople, to begging letters from impecunious students.[26] Bryce's writings on eastern Anatolia and its inhabitants indicated clearly his preference for a form of progressive, developmental imperialism in place of supposedly 'stagnant' oriental rule, as he remarked that 'it is a sort of race between Persia and Turkey which shall govern the worst, and which shall do the least for the countries under their control'.[27]

Bryce was strongly influenced as an undergraduate by Goldwin Smith's high-minded radical Liberalism, reminiscing in his letters to him about 'all that I have been privileged to learn from you through your voice and your books, ever since I went to your lectures in the hall of University College', and the two men subsequently overlapped in Oriel senior common room for four years.[28] They corresponded from Smith's departure from Oriel for Cornell in 1866 until his death in 1910. At first this was only intermittent, but the outbreak of the Boer War produced a flurry of letters in which they denounced the origins and conduct of the war, and deplored the popular imperial fervour which it had produced. 'Who could believe that a nation which has a hereditary House of Lords, and a State Church, and which holds in bondage three hundred millions of Hindoos, was crusading for political and religious equality in the Transvaal? . . . This tidal wave of jingoism seems

---

[24] Viscount Bryce and Rudyard Kipling, 'Some Aspects of Travel: Discussion', *Geographical Journal*, 43 (1914), 376.
[25] James Bryce, *Transcaucasia and Ararat: Being Notes of a Vacation Tour in the Autumn of 1876* (London, 1878), 117–20.
[26] Bodleian Library MS Bryce 191, 134, Nerses to Bryce, 16 January 1880; MS Bryce 192, 163–4, Gregory Alexandrian to Bryce, 15 October 1884.
[27] James Bryce, 'Armenia and Mount Ararat', *Proceedings of the Royal Geographical Society of London*, 22 (1877–8), 171.
[28] Bodleian Library MS Bryce 17, 188, Bryce to Goldwin Smith, 19 November 1904 (copy).

to have been set flowing by a sort of satiety of civilization. I shall not live to see it ebb, but you will.'[29]

Bryce's respect and affection for Smith are clear, and he shared many of his views, most notably a powerful dislike of the Ottoman Empire (echoing Gladstone's concern with the Christian victims of Turkish atrocities in Bulgaria and Armenia), of Joseph Chamberlain and 'jingoism', and of Froude, of whom Bryce wrote in response to an article on the latter by Smith in the *Atlantic Monthly* that 'what made his presence always so odious to me was the impression he conveyed not only of absolute indifference to truth but of a love of cruelty'.[30] Nevertheless it is not clear that Bryce can be regarded as Smith's political disciple. Where Smith opposed Home Rule for Ireland and argued for the severance of formal ties with the Dominions, Bryce supported the former and was one of the earliest politicians to advocate a form of imperial federation amongst the white dominions of the empire. However much they would both have resisted the comparison, Goldwin Smith and Bryce alike shared with Froude the belief, typical of all but a tiny minority of intellectuals at the time, that the despotic rule of Europeans was beneficial in regions 'where we deem that this native population is not qualified by its racial characteristics and by its state of education and enlightenment to work self-governing institutions'.[31] In one of his later works Bryce provided a more comprehensive justification for this inequality of rights between metropole and colony which was central to nineteenth-century Liberal imperialism.

> The truth is that, though a few intelligent men, educated in European ideas, complain of the despotic power of the Anglo-Indian bureaucracy, the people of India generally do not wish to govern themselves. Their traditions, their habits, their ideas, are all the other way, and dispose them to accept submissively any rule which is strong and which neither disturbs their religion and customs nor lays too heavy imposts upon them.
>
> Here let an interesting contrast be noted. The Roman Emperors were despots at home in Italy almost as much, and ultimately quite as much, as in the provinces. The English govern their own country on democratic, India on absolutist principles. The inconsistency is patent but inevitable. It affords an easy theme for declamation when any arbitrary act of the Indian administration gives rise to complaints, and it may fairly be used as the foundation for an argument that a people which enjoys freedom at home is specially bound to deal justly with and considerately with those subjects to whom she refuses a like freedom. But every one admits in his heart that it is impossible to ignore the differences which make one group of races unfit for the institutions which have given energy and contentment to another more favourably placed.[32]

---

[29] Bodleian Library MS Bryce 16, 108, Goldwin Smith to Bryce, 3 December 1899.
[30] Bodleian Library MS Bryce 17, 194, Bryce to Goldwin Smith, 16 June 1906 (copy).
[31] James Bryce, 'Some Difficulties in Colonial Government Encountered by Great Britain and how they have been Met', *Annals of the American Academy of Political and Social Science*, 30 (1907), 19.
[32] James Bryce, 'The Ancient Roman Empire and the British Empire in India', in *The Roman and the British Empires* (Oxford, 1914), 31–2.

The language is more measured, but in this, if in no other way, Bryce's political vision of empire resembled Froude's, in that it was based upon the permanent exclusion of the majority of its inhabitants from any say in the way they were governed, on the grounds of race.

Thus Oriel played its part in developing the ideologies of nineteenth-century imperialism, but it is still not clear whether, even in these prominent cases, the intellectual atmosphere of the college had a great deal to do with this. It seems unlikely that Oriel would have been a congenial environment for Goldwin Smith, though Bryce may have secured him common room rights, and Oriel made him an honorary fellow in 1867, having rejected him for a fellowship in 1846. As one of the first 'railway dons', he was more active at the Athenaeum than in Oxford. Froude's early exposure to the Tractarians at Oriel produced a strong negative reaction which governed much of his subsequent career, but his specifically imperial interests were developed during his travels in Ireland, South Africa, Australasia, and the West Indies in the 1870s and 1880s, in between his brief periods in the college. Only in the case of Bryce do we have a man who successfully straddled academic and political life during his twenty-seven years of fellowship, and in his relationship with Goldwin Smith we can see that at least some of his thinking on empire and the wider world had its origins in Oriel senior common room.

Leaving aside such prominent intellectual examples, what part did Orielenses play in Seeley's grand drama of expansion—was the creation of 'Greater Britain' reflected in the origins and destinations of the college's members? The early seventeenth century saw not only the foundation of the first successful Virginian settlement at Jamestown, but also the granting of the first Charter to the East India Company. In these tough, buccaneering, mercantile early years of British expansion, when trade was dominant and the majority of overseas settlers in the Americas and the West Indies were indentured labourers, the products of the English universities played only a very minor role, Raleigh of course excepted. However, the early years of the *Registrum Orielense* do yield a number of names of Orielenses whom we know to have pursued careers abroad. Among Raleigh's near contemporaries we find John Lane, who took his BA in 1564 and 'travelled with Father Parsons the Jesuit, became a Jesuit, and died in great sanctity in the University of Complutum (Alcala) in Spain, 1578'; Edward Unton, who took his BA in 1573 and was 'killed in Portugal, 1589, while serving in the expedition under Sir John Norris and Sir Francis Drake, for the restoration of Don Antonio to the kingdom'; together with his brother Henry, who also took his BA in 1573 and was ambassador to the king of France in 1591 and 1595 before dying overseas.[33] Between 1665 and 1737 nine American students matriculated at

---

[33] *Registrum Orielense*, I, no. 1, 33, 41–2.

Oriel, of whom eight were Virginians. All were from Middlesex County, and four of them were Robinsons, related to John Robinson, bishop of London, who paid for a range of buildings in the second quadrangle. From 1775 to 1800 there were another seven Oriel students from America.[34] In the nineteenth century the number of students from overseas matriculating gradually increased, although statistically they remained fairly insignificant until the influx of the Rhodes scholars after 1903 (see Table 14.1);[35] moreover almost all of them were British and educated at public schools. In 1819 there was just one matriculand born overseas, Jonathan Blenman Cobham from Barbados, who made his career as a clergyman in Britain. In 1828–9 there was none, but in 1838–9 there was a sudden increase to eight, a remarkable 18 per cent of the total, from Malta, Canada, Jamaica, Nagpur, Saint-Omer,[36] Florence, Mauritius, and Barbados, although all had Anglo-Saxon names and most had careers in Britain. This seems to have been an unusual peak, as in 1848–9 there were three, one the son of an English merchant from Rio de Janeiro, one from Calcutta, and one an American from Cincinnati. By 1878–9 the proportion of overseas matriculands had fallen, with two from Calcutta and one a German from St Petersburg. This only rose marginally in 1888–9, although that year saw a strengthening of Oriel's South African connection with the admission of Allan Webb, the son of the bishop of Grahamstown,[37] and Arthur Scanlen, the son of Sir Thomas Scanlen, a prominent lawyer and member of parliament for the Cape Colony, who would later be responsible for drafting much of the earliest legislation of the new colony of Rhodesia, at the invitation of his erstwhile protégé, Rhodes himself.[38] By 1898–9 this had increased to six, or 9 per cent of the total, with two West Indians, one from Calcutta, one who lived in Biarritz, and two Germans. Nevertheless, there was no very visible upward trend. (See Table 14.1.)

By the late eighteenth century a growing number of Orielenses had begun to make their careers overseas. This export of Oxford graduates was intimately linked with the growth and consolidation of empire, but until the middle of the nineteenth century the overwhelming majority of university graduates who made careers in Britain's colonies were churchmen, whether missionaries or incumbents in the new dioceses and parishes which were being created in ever larger numbers east of Suez. As M. C. Curthoys has observed, it was not until the latter half of the nineteenth century that the

---

[34] Cecil Emden, 'Virginians at Oriel 1665–1737', *Oriel Papers*, 77–82.
[35] Oriel's initial share of Rhodes scholars was a generous 11, but Balliol had 17. E. T. Williams, 'The Rhodes Scholars', HUO vii. 722.
[36] This was Drummond Percy Chase, son of an army paymaster from Northamptonshire, elected fellow in 1842 and the last principal of St Mary Hall. Andrew Clark, 'Chase, Drummond Percy (1820–1902)', rev. M. C. Curthoys, ODNB s.n.
[37] G. S. Woods, 'Webb, Allan Becher (1839–1907)', rev. Lynn Milne, ODNB s.n.
[38] Basil T. Hone, 'Scanlen, Sir Thomas Charles (1834–1912)', ODNB s.n.

TABLE 14.1 Orielenses born overseas (*Registrum Orielense*, ii)

Year	1818/9	1828/9	1838/9	1848/9	1858/9	1868/9	1878/9	1888/9	1898/9
Total matriculands	46	37	44	39	47	36	56	51	69
No. born overseas	1	0	8	3	4	4	3	4	6
Percentage	2%	0%	18%	8%	8.5%	11%	5%	8%	9%

ancient universities began to play a prominent role in preparing men for other forms of public life. In the 1850s and 1860s Oxford's role in this respect seemed, if anything, to be diminishing. Before 1850 a majority of undergraduates who matriculated took holy orders, and among those who took degrees the figure was 75 per cent. Very few entered the lay professions or government service.[39] The first signs of a significant change came after 1854, when the introduction of competitive examinations for the Indian Civil Service and the gradual elimination of patronage as the basis of appointments to the East India Company's civil service saw its 'capture' by university graduates, overwhelmingly from Oxford and Cambridge.[40] Oxford men gained a third of Indian appointments offered for competition between 1855 and 1859, and during the first fourteen years of the system they accounted for the largest number of recruits. However, the proportion of graduates entering the Home Civil Service remained small (not least because it adopted competitive examinations much later), and the proportion of ordinands fell more slowly than is often realized. The 'shift to the professions' only really began in the 1870s, and the relative decline in the ecclesiastical character of Oxford graduates came only in the 1890s. Even in 1897 18 per cent of them took holy orders, making them the single largest group.[41] Accordingly, although the Indian and colonial civil services were dominated by Oxford and Cambridge graduates at least during the period from 1890 to 1914, and careers in the empire represented about 20 per cent of the University Appointments Committee's placements by the latter year, the clerical element remained important well into the inter-war period.

The broad picture of changing career paths of Oxford graduates, and the university's intimate connection with empire, has long been clear. Oriel largely conformed to those Oxford trends: from 1877, when over half of those who graduated from the college took holy orders, the proportion of

---

[39] M. C. Curthoys, 'The Careers of Oxford Men', HUO vi. 482–3.
[40] C. J. Dewey, 'The Education of a Ruling Caste: The Indian Civil Service in the Era of Competitive Examination', EHR 88 (1973), 263–5.
[41] Curthoys, 'The Careers of Oxford Men', 489–90, 503.

clergy declined to 32 per cent in 1887, 27 per cent in 1895, and 22 per cent in 1896.[42] While Shadwell's register is not comprehensive when it comes to the careers of non-clerical Oriel graduates, those whose careers he describes were fairly evenly divided between the Bar, the army, and the home, Indian, and colonial civil services.

The *Oriel Record* contained regular lists of Orielenses who had taken up overseas postings, news of their honours and achievements, and occasionally accounts of their experiences. The very first issue, in 1909, noted that P. C. Lyon, Chief Secretary to the Government of Eastern Bengal, had been made CIE and was a member of the Legislative Council, that H. G. Stokes ICS was Officiating Assistant Secretary in the Home Department, Government of India, that R. E. Holland of the ICS Political Department was HM Consul and Political Agent at Muscat, H. J. Anderson Inspector of Schools in the Cape Colony, and that G. Garlick was now professor of philosophy at the Aligarh Muslim University in the NW Provinces of India. 'In addition to the above, R. B. Smith has left to take up his appointment in the Civil Service of India, R. K. Winter, T. F. Sandford and G. A. Fuller-Maitland have received similar appointments in the Soudan, Rhodesia and British East Africa; A. Wimbush and V. N. Forbes have entered the Indian Forest Service.'[43] The issue also contained a fulsome article by D. R. Seth-Smith on the bright prospects for European settlement in British East Africa.[44] This indicates a lively interest in empire which was typical of Edwardian Oxford, and which would be maintained well into the 1930s. The activities of a regular stream of colonial bishops and clergymen, district commissioners and assistant under-secretaries, were enshrined in the pages of the *Record*, overwhelmingly within the framework of the empire, with occasional intriguing exceptions—'Mr Michaelopoulos, who has returned to Oxford to complete his work in Honour Moderations, is, we understand, not only a scholar of Oriel, but Assistant Governor of Smyrna'[45]—presumably a short-lived appointment, given the disastrous failure of the Greek *Megali Idea*. Of the 193 subscribers to the *Oriel Record* in 1921, twenty-six, or 13.5 per cent, were working overseas, in regions as diverse as Mesopotamia, Zanzibar, Assam, and Connecticut.[46] Among these was Oriel's only genuine proconsular figure of this period, Robert Chalmers, Baron Chalmers, who rose from humble beginnings to be governor of Ceylon from 1913 to 1919, and who was also the editor of a number of important Buddhist texts.[47] Pockets of Orielenses

---

[42] *Registrum Orielense*, ii. [43] OR (February 1909), 3.
[44] D. R. Seth-Smith, 'British East Africa', OR 1/1 (February 1909), 31–3.
[45] OR (March 1920), 129–30.
[46] 'List of Subscribers', OR (March 1921), 25–8.
[47] G. C. Peden, 'Chalmers, Robert, Baron Chalmers (1858–1938)', ODNB s.n.

existed all over the world. One of the densest concentrations, appropriately enough, was in Johannesburg and Cape Town:

> In or near these two centres are a great many of the old Oriel men now in South Africa. At Cape Town the *doyen* of them is Professor William Ritchie, a year junior to the Provost, who is the senior professor of Capetown University. The first Rhodes Scholar, Frank Reid, is a rising barrister; his brother Norman, the Rugby full-back, is a solicitor. H. J. Anderson is chief inspector of training colleges for the Cape Province, and is contemplating the formation of an Oriel Society in South Africa. H. A. Thomson is a Cowley Father, and is at present stationed at Capetown. Dallas and Shacksnovis are also there: the latter writes most Saturdays in the *Cape Argus*. W. M. Smail is professor at Rhodes University College, Grahamstown: A. Wagner is lecturer at the University of Johannesburg, and R. McKerron is professor there. K. McLachlan, of the Community of the Resurrection, is teaching at St John's College, a public school at Johannesburg, and F. F. C. Lewis is at Diocesan College, Rondebosch. I was lucky enough to meet J. S. Lister, who is a Presbyterian minister in the eastern part of the Cape Province: he does more without sight than most men do with their eyes to help them. At Bloemfontein I was kindly entertained by Mr Justice McGregor, whose daughter is entered for Somerville in October. Time and weather—it was very hot, and we have no conception of an African sun—prevented me from going to the Transkei, or I should have seen L. W. Mallward, now Dean of Umtata, and I had to abandon the idea of Rhodesia and seeing Godfrey King. Unfortunately I was unable to meet C. T. Blakeway in Johannesburg where he is an advocate in a large practice.[48]

However, with the notable exception of a strong link with the Sudan Political Service, the college was not remarkable in the extent or proportion of its overseas links: it is remarkable, however, in having somehow preserved in its archive a source which allows us to explore those links in extraordinary detail. As Richard Symonds has observed, 'the most comprehensive impression of how Oxford men viewed their work in the I.C.S., colonial and other services of the Empire may be found in the remarkable correspondence of Phelps of Oriel between 1877 and 1936.'[49]

The Reverend Lancelot Ridley Phelps (1853–1936, fellow 1877, provost 1914–29) was second only to Jowett as a mentor and guide for undergraduates who would go on to imperial careers. This was partly in his role as tutor to, at a conservative estimate, a third of Oriel's undergraduate body at any one time, but also because, as the university's most popular lecturer on political economy, he taught most of the ICS probationers when they were following their preliminary course of instruction at Oxford.[50] His personal enthusiasm for the college's imperial mission is revealed in (presumably unwelcome) observations in some of his occasional letters to Bryce: at the

---

[48] 'Oriel in South Africa', OR 4/13 (June 1927), 394.
[49] Richard Symonds, *Oxford and Empire* (London, 1986), 199.
[50] David Ross, 'Phelps, Lancelot Ridley (1853–1936)', rev. M. C. Curthoys, ODNB s.n.

1899 Gaudy 'Rhodes made a remarkably fine speech, which I need not say struck a chord', while in 1914 'the late Bishop of Natal, Baynes, was good on the Imperial mission of Oriel as centre of the Rhodes Trust'.[51] Anecdotes concerning 'The Phelper' abounded—a hugely bearded man who wore a straw hat in winter, lunched daily off a rice pudding, and under whose window undergraduates would gather in the mornings to hear him say, 'Be a man, Phelps, be a man!' before he entered his cold bath.[52] Many were also invited to the reading parties which he organized at High Force, on the Tees, and his influence upon them was profound, long-lasting, and commemorated in what must be the largest collection of letters of its kind anywhere in Oxford.[53] As his obituary in the *Oriel Record* put it:

It is hardly too much to say that for generation after generation of Oriel men, Phelps *was* the College.... what Phelps achieved is most of all bound up with his friendships and his influence in the lives of other people. Of this he was probably conscious himself, for he used to keep every letter he received, explaining that if his life were ever written, his biographer would best understand him from his effect on the outlook of others. His own correspondence was vast; and he did not scribble notes, he wrote letters, in the style of the epistolary age, not even excluding the long esses. All through the war he poured out his letters to members of Oriel on all the fronts; they came as regularly as the rations and were quite as eagerly looked for. These were the link between us and the College, between us and the sane enduring world.[54]

As Arnold Forster wrote from the SS *City of Benares* on his way back to the Sudan in 1910, 'Why are you so good a correspondent? You make one feel most frightfully ashamed...'[55] It is not clear whether Phelps only wrote to former pupils serving overseas, or whether he only kept those letters from far afield, but the collection today consists of seven boxes of letters from India, two from Africa, and one from 'miscellaneous' imperial possessions such as the West Indies, Hong Kong, and South-East Asia, containing hundreds and hundreds of replies to the letters he poured out across the world. The predominance of Indian correspondence is partly because service there was far more prestigious than anywhere else in the empire and attracted many more Oxford graduates, but also reflects the fact that many of the letters are not necessarily from Orielenses, but also from Old Carthusians (Phelps was an

---

[51] Bodleian Library MS Bryce 188, 157, Phelps to Bryce, 24 June 1899; 174, Phelps to Bryce 28 June 1914.
[52] This last expression has entered into legend—so much so that it has been used by philosophers as a classic example of self-exhortation to do that which one already knows to be right: J. D. Mabbott, 'True and False in Morals', *Proceedings of the Aristotelian Society*, ns 49 (1948–9), 139–40. See further C. J. Martin, 'Arthur Edwin Boycott. 1877–1938', *Obituary Notices of Fellows of the Royal Society*, 2/7 (January 1939), 562.
[53] They occupy ten large boxes in the Oriel Archives, OCA PRO 2/44/1, *Phelps Letters*.
[54] F. R. Barry, 'L.R.P.' OR (January 1937), 161–2.
[55] OCA PRO 2/44/1 Africa i. 157–60, Forster to Phelps, 12 August 1910.

OC himself and a governor of Charterhouse) and above all from the many ICS probationers whom he had taught political economy. The African letters are almost all from Orielenses, and in particular from individuals in the Sudan, where with Phelps's encouragement a remarkably close link emerged between the college and the Sudan Political Service. The Indian and African letters also cover somewhat different timespans, owing to the relatively late development of a significant British presence in Africa. The earliest African letters (from the Cape, unsurprisingly) date from 1897, while Phelps was already receiving letters from India in 1883, just six years after he was elected a fellow. In many ways it is the African correspondence which is most interesting. This is partly because almost all of it comes from Orielenses, but also because the African letters cover a broader cross-section of colonial life, including teachers, planters, soldiers, merchants, lawyers, and bankers as well as civil servants. Sadly it is impossible to do real justice to this remarkable collection within the constraints of this chapter, but as an insight into the mentality of Orielenses serving overseas, and of the links forged at the college which continued to bind them to each other and to their old tutor, it deserves some detailed analysis.

The letters vary widely in content and length, but not in the affection which they express for the college, and for Phelps himself, whose habits and eccentricities are frequently described with fond nostalgia: 'Do you still smoke 17 different pipes in succession?' enquired R. F. McCall from Johannesburg in 1929.[56] Correspondents kept him updated not only on their professional careers, but also their personal lives, indeed the two are often hard to separate. One such was E. Saxon, who wrote from Sokoto in northern Nigeria to tell Phelps that he had fallen in love, meant to get married, and consequently felt he had to resign from the service.[57] Certain themes recur frequently: enquiries as to the college's sporting record, requests for intellectual advice and assistance, and political debate and commentary. While Phelps himself was at the radical end of the spectrum of liberal opinion (he was best known as an active social reformer and a member of the Royal Commission on the Poor Laws), the opinions expressed by his students were normally conservative, not to say reactionary. As A. R. Wise wrote from Kenya after the Labour party first formed a coalition government in 1924:

I am afraid that I am unable to share your regret that there is too much blue and not enough red in our present government but I am entirely with you in regarding the political experiment with misgiving though possibly from a different cause. However it is best that Labour should have its first innings on a wicket so sticky that they depend solely on the charity of the bowler for its duration and success.[58]

[56] OCA PRO 2/44/1 Africa ii. 291, McCall to Phelps, 1 November 1929.
[57] OCA PRO 2/44/1 Africa ii. 459–64, Saxon to Phelps, 29 March 1920.
[58] OCA PRO 2/44/1 Africa ii. 592–8, Wise to Phelps, 22 March 1924.

Some of them made direct connections with what they had learnt from Phelps on the subject of political economy and Poor Law reform. L. M. Heaney wrote from Government House, Dar es Salaam, in 1932

> I came out here two years ago with some qualms as I thought empire building might be over strenuous and rather tedious. I have been agreeably surprised...As I remember our Sunday afternoon walks to Cowley Road workhouse, I note that there is over here no Poor Law problem! No one need starve for in most places a native can find a fellow tribesman whose duty it is to maintain him and give him shelter. The European government will, I suppose, eventually destroy this happy state of affairs by its gospel of hard work and by placing the native's domestic economy on a cash basis, giving him money for his labour, and making him eventually perhaps a 'wage slave'. But that is as yet hundreds of years away.[59]

Some wrote just one letter, others continued to correspond for years, or wrote again after lengthy intervals: Phelps's election as provost in 1914 brought a shower of congratulatory epistles in which his old students also brought him up to date with their latest movements; he answered every one of them individually. Leonard Frederick Morshead was perhaps Phelps's most prolific correspondent: he wrote him twenty-one letters from India between 1890 and 1924, including one from Bhagalpur in which he asked for Phelps's verdict on Kipling's *Departmental Ditties*, which he had been reading with great enjoyment.[60] Sir John Hose, a former probationer who had a distinguished career in the ICS, was not far behind with nineteen letters between 1887 and 1912.[61] Alongside correspondence from students and clerical colleagues there were occasional letters from proud or anxious mothers, of which the most peculiar was undoubtedly that from Winifred Warner in South Africa, who appears to have been suffering from a form of religious mania, sending a letter full of heavy underlinings which attributed messiah-like qualities to her son Hugh.[62] Hugh himself, a member of the first Eight whose own letters to Phelps were bluff and cheery, would no doubt have been mortified by this.[63] A striking aspect of much of the early correspondence, when Phelps was still a relatively young man, is the irreverence and familiarity with which his former students felt they could address him.

---

[59] OCA PRO 2/44/1 Africa i. 238–41, Heaney to Phelps, 21 January 1932.
[60] OCA PRO 2/44/1 India i. 458–63, Morshead to Phelps, 21 September 1890. For Morshead's other letters see India i. 379–83, 608–13, 664–9; India ii. 129–34, 237–9; India iii. 87–94, 97–102, 109–12, 132–5, 151–7, 177–80, 202; India iv. 10–13, 48–53, 162–6, 232–5, 274–9, 336–43, 408–11, 423–6; India vi. 87, 129; India vii. 23–7.
[61] OCA PRO 2/44/1. For Hose's letters see India i. 47–54, 78–81, 120–5, 139–48, 183–6, 250–3, 337–342, 420, 676–9; India ii. 85–9, 185–90, 374–9, 486–93; India iii. 32–5, 167–72; India iv. 14–17; India v. 240, 113, 118–21, 158–61.
[62] OCA PRO 2/44/1 Africa ii. 547–8, Winifred Warner to Phelps, 18 July 1925.
[63] OCA PRO 2/44/1 Africa ii. 541–2, Hugh Warner to Phelps, 21 July 1924.

In 1887 A. R. Bonas wrote from Satara in the Central Provinces of British India that

> I've had no pig-sticking as yet, & am not likely to have any hereabouts, as there is no country for pig near here;…I stayed in Bombay a week with some friends of my people, & had a rattling time. Tennis every morning & most evenings; visits to the bazaar, the Yacht Club & other places where the Bombay loafer most does congregate; sitting about reading all day in the verandah, smoking splendid cigars at about four rupees per hundred (think of that, weeds at 6/- per hundred!, which would cost 40/- in England). Of course it's all Indian tobacco.[64]

Similarly in 1905, writing from the Sudan Club in Khartoum, W. H. Evans (who would die in an air crash in 1913 and whose letters Phelps consequently kept separately), felt no embarrassment at recalling an encounter with Dr Shadwell, Phelps's predecessor as provost,

> Very many thanks for your letter which reached me on Nov 6th at the precise hour of 7.35 and helped to divert my attention from bad fish & smelly kidneys…I am glad that they made Mr or Dr Shadwell Provost because he once gave me a dinner that I shall take long to forget: but at the same time I owe him a grudge on account of that same dinner. I arrived rather early and sat down very shy to talk to him HE said 'Do you know Reynolds of Oriel'! I said no, not remembering that I had as a matter of fact met him. He said 'Don't know Reynolds!' Then as an afterthought 'oh! Well, of course you wouldn't be in quite the best set in the College.'[65]

He followed this up by offering to send Phelps a Rhinoceros-hide whip. Denis Gye clearly thought Phelps would be interested to learn that 'I find that I am unique in Egypt in one respect if no other; namely that I continue to smoke American tobacco and have never taken to the Egyptian cigarette. I roll my own cigarettes. However I have now returned vigorously to pipe smoking and have routed out my old Oxford meerschaums.'[66] The pre-First World War letters are rife with observations of this kind, trivial in themselves, but offering insights into both the social mores of the time and the close bond which existed between Phelps and many of his former pupils.

A darker but unsurprising side of the letters is their commonplace, casual, and persistent racism. This ranged from the patronizing of non-Europeans as 'children' to full-blooded biological determinism. 'The native is a beast', wrote John Hose from Gorakhpur in 1888, and such sentiments were not unusual.[67] Forty-five years later W. S. Baldock wrote from Tanganyika that 'The native mind is not a pleasant thing to study & none of the finer thoughts are known or understood by them. Many of them suffer from physical

---

[64] OCA PRO 2/44/1 India i. 33–42, Bonas to Phelps, 4 March 1887.
[65] OCA MPP/E 8/1, *Letters from W H B Evans*, 9 November 1905.
[66] OCA PRO 2/44/1 Africa i. 203, Gye to Phelps, 21 February 1907.
[67] OCA PRO 2/44/1 India i. 125*v*, Hose to Phelps, 10 June 1888.

deformities...'[68] The following year A. R. Wise chose to devote most of his letter from the Nairobi Club in neighbouring Kenya to a vitriolic disquisition on 'the worst races of the Indian Empire' who flocked to the colony, describing them as 'naturally dirty', 'untruthful', and 'cowardly'; 'When actually face to face with an officer, he cringes to such an extent as almost to make one physically sick.'[69] Such views were quite common amongst Orielenses who had settled in African colonies, though tempered in the case of those races considered more 'martial' (such as the Masai) by a respect for their supposedly greater physical courage.[70] The milder but unconsciously patronizing attitude of Oswald Bosanquet (later resident at Indore and Bhopal) was perhaps more typical of most civil servants:

> You ask what is the general opinion about the Imperial service and the changes in our service out here. I think men don't object to it much. Certainly they don't mind the natives being put into higher posts. The native B.A. of the present day is not a bad creature. Of course socially he is worth less. His talk is limited to 'shop'. All native officials who come & call on one talk 'shop'. Of course, it is the only interest we at present have in common.... People are pretty agreed that it won't do to put the natives into the higher executive posts such as Collectors: they will do very well as judges, as they are almost entirely as honest as Englishmen & law is a thing they can thoroughly understand.[71]

Bosanquet could accept educated Indians participating (to a limited extent) in a modern civil service and legal system, but in Africa there was a widespread assumption amongst British officials that the natives were still too underdeveloped for such responsibilities, and that instead they would benefit from a more paternalistic, devolved approach. S. J. Hogben, an education officer in Sokoto in northern Nigeria, wrote in 1921 that

> The natives here are dear old things but always half asleep and at least 3000 years behind us in civilisation. Nothing worries them, and nothing will persuade them that a job of work is worth doing properly. They are quite happy with their modest wants and ambitions: I wonder what good our 'bettering' will do—we profess a desire to make them better Hausas and to raise their standard of living.[72]

According to another Nigerian Orielensis, Duncan Stewart, Hogben was the man 'who taught the sons of the Emir of Katouma to play polo, and to play it

---

[68] OCA PRO 2/44/1 Africa i. 17–20, Baldock to Phelps, 31 May 1923.
[69] OCA PRO 2/44/1 Africa ii. 592–8, Wise to Phelps, 22 March 1924.
[70] Although W. S. Baldock wrote that 'the Masai are a picturesque people that wander about with 8 foot spears & a few skins, otherwise the Masai are a very degraded type...' OCA PRO 2/44/1 Africa i. 17–20, Baldock to Phelps, 31 May 1923. On the peculiarities of British 'Martial Race' theory see David Omissi, *The Sepoy and the Raj: The Indian Army 1860–1940* (Basingstoke, 1994), 10–46.
[71] OCA PRO 2/44/1 India i. 103ᵛ–104, Bosanquet to Phelps, 13 May 1888.
[72] OCA PRO 2/44/1 Africa i. 249–50, Hogben to Phelps, 21 November 1921.

so well'.[73] The anecdote reveals Frederick Lugard's ideal of Indirect Rule in action, and it was another recurring theme in Phelps's correspondence, as District Officers sang the praises of a system which (so they believed) helped to clothe alien rule in local colours, and to preserve both social stability and the best aspects of local culture.[74] Francis Wilkinson wrote from Katsina in Kano Province of northern Nigeria that

> Just here we have about the most enlightened Emir in Nigeria. He has been to England twice and to Mecca once. He knows very well which side his bread is buttered, and got the medal for meritorious service for First Class Chiefs... So there's no trouble about enforcing our rule.[75]

Writing from Darfur in the Sudan, John Mackrell was still more explicit about the need to preserve as much as possible of what he saw as traditional 'tribal discipline':

> It is this tribal discipline which the Government regards as the key to the peaceful development of the whole country. For tribes who have lost their tribal soul, there is small chance of salvation. The people are idle, irreligious, discontented and without self-respect. They have no unity and no leader. They readily absorb the undesirable parts of European civilisation, and learn to despise the honourable customs of their fathers.
>
> To the tribe which has preserved its tribal discipline intact, all things are possible. Its characteristics are an integrity and straightforwardness, which make easy its dealings with other sincere people.
>
> It is the aim of the Government to consolidate the position of the great tribal heads, and to pursue a policy of gradual devolution of its powers on these chiefs. Darfur was, until the entry of the Government, ruled by a Sultan, who was compelled to struggle continuously to keep the five or six great tribes under his personal control. These tribes had their own hereditary chiefs, who looked on the Sultan as foreigner and a usurper of their powers and privileges. Their resistance to his rule was stiffened by barbarity and oppression. With the coming of the present Government they were not slow to appreciate the great improvement of their lot. The pacification of the country, accomplished with very little fighting, brought a security to person and property which had never before been known. The removal of the Sultan also strengthened the position of these half-dozen big tribal heads, to whom the people now looked as their natural leaders. Very soon, the Government was able to give them some official recognition... we shall see everything that is best in their traditional government, operating in a state of security which it could never have known without our

---

[73] OCA PRO 2/44/1 Africa ii. 489–91, Stewart to Phelps, 4 June 1929.

[74] For the classic statement of the theory of indirect rule see Frederick Dealtry Lugard, *The Dual Mandate in British Tropical Africa* (London, 1922). Lugard took the princely states of India as a model for his system of indirect rule through the Muslim emirs of northern Nigeria; for a contemporary academic exploration of the idea see Margery Perham, 'Some Problems of Indirect Rule in Africa', *Journal of the Royal African Society*, 34 (1935), 1–23.

[75] OCA PRO 2/44/1 Africa ii. 575–6, Wilkinson to Phelps, 12 January 1925.

intervention. What a reward if we see Darfur enjoy a Golden Age as a result of our labours!⁷⁶

Mackrell's conviction that colonial rule was benevolent and paternalistic is hardly surprising, but what is striking is the degree to which he presents it as 'restoring' earlier rights. It is a fundamentally conservative vision, and a far cry from the developmental or 'civilizing' idea of colonial rule.⁷⁷ An earlier generation of Sudanese administrators was less sentimental: W. B. Evans, for whom Phelps seems to have had a particular affection, wrote in 1906 that 'We boast at home of our justice, clemency, equal rights for inhabitants etc, but the only thing that exists is justice untempered with mercy.'⁷⁸ Two years later he complained from Kassala in the Sudan that:

> One reads of brutal floggings in the Daily Mail if you allow it inside your house but you are not told at the same time that the black is about as insensible to the lash as a brick wall and that in many places it has fallen into disuse because it is such a futile form of punishment. Any man who says that the black is the equal of the white is a fool, and anyone who acts on that hypothesis is a criminal.⁷⁹

None of this suggests that Oriel can have been a terribly welcoming place for non-white students in the decades leading up to the Second World War. By the 1920s the college had admitted a number of Indian students, as the *Oriel Record* rather coldly observed: 'we note the addition to the college of three Indian students, to whom, we have no doubt, a hearty welcome has been given. But Freshmen, of whatever nationality, must not expect to be at once "hand and glove" [*sic*] with everybody in the College.'⁸⁰

It seems likely that Phelps's own welcome was rather warmer than this suggested, and that he did not share the more extreme racist sentiments in some of the letters he received. In the 1920s he received a number of letters from Indian students who appeared to remember him with much affection. In 1924 Srinivasa Raghunatha Rao, an Orielensis who worked for the Forestry Department in Guntur, wrote that

> There are three or four Oriel men in this presidency. Mr C. R. Armstrong who is on the same Railway as my brother, was good enough to invite me to tea when I was in Madras in July. He made v. kind enquiries about all the Dons and his college. Sir Arthur Knapp whom you know intimately I am happy to say is in excellent health & at the head of my department. Whenever I meet him, he makes kind enquiries about you.

---

⁷⁶ OCA PRO 2/44/1 Africa ii. 307–17, Mackrell to Phelps, 11 September 1930.
⁷⁷ It thus chimes well with David Cannadine's contention that in most colonies the British saw the restoration, preservation, and fossilization of supposedly 'traditional' hierarchies as a key aim of their rule, and the best guarantor of stability. David Cannadine, *Ornamentalism: How the British Saw their Empire* (London, 2001), 58–70.
⁷⁸ OCA MPP/E 8/1, Evans to Phelps, 24 February 1906.
⁷⁹ OCA MPP/E 8/1, Evans to Phelps, 27 January 1908.
⁸⁰ OR (March 1921), 5.

I was very pleased to hear of Sen getting a first and to hear of the successes of Ghose, & Imam. Though it is only about ten months since I left England, I wish I could get back there this minute![81]

Arguably a keen sense of class hierarchy and social privilege was at least as important a theme as race in the Phelps correspondence. In Denis Gye's letters from Egypt uneasiness at the effects of foreign birth and climate on those of English descent mingled with a straightforward sense of superior upbringing:[82]

Now the agents of the National Bank are mostly recruited from Levantines; i.e. Englishmen born in Beyrout or Smyrna, and they don't seem to have the same healthy characteristics of sport and cleanliness. If there is any truth in the adage that Cleanliness is next to Godliness, I can only suppose that my fellow lodger is on the extreme borders of heathendom!

When I first arrived I found everything in an extreme state of dirt, so much so that even my native cook (native cooks are not as a rule over-particular) objected to using such a kitchen. However I took the law into my own hands and now things are more presentable. I do not complain, except in cases in which my own personal comfort is threatened, as it is unpleasant to have rows with a man you are compelled to live with. When, however, I counted 14 consecutive days during which he had not had a bath, I enquired with some sarcasm if he had given up baths altogether. He replied quite casually 'No, only now it is too cold!'... I have lately made the pleasant discovery that he keeps no tooth-brush. I believe that these Levantine people object to Englishmen who have been born at home because they are so stuck up. I think that it is not a case of where you were born but of how you were brought up.[83]

Gye himself, however, could have fallen foul of the prejudices of many of his fellow Orielenses because he worked in commerce rather than administration, a 'box-wallah'.[84] It was one of the great paradoxes of the British Empire that, whilst it was founded on commerce and, fundamentally, as a money-making enterprise, the 'prefects' who emerged from the public schools and ancient universities to run it were supposed to have a contempt for the apparent crassness and materialism of the commercial bourgeoisie inculcated in them from the earliest days of their schooling.[85] In practice there were limits to this: large numbers of public schoolboys would enter the more

---

[81] OCA PRO 2/44/1 India vii. 43–4, Rao to Phelps, 8 December 1924.
[82] On changing ideas of the effect of climate on national or racial character in the nineteenth century see Mark Harrison, *Climates and Constitutions: Health, Race, Environment and British Imperialism in India, 1600–1850* (Delhi, 1999).
[83] OCA PRO 2/44/1 Africa i. 203, Gye to Phelps, 21 February 1907.
[84] On the often bitter political divisions which existed between the official and non-official British in India (where this contemptuous term was coined) see Alexander Morrison, 'White Todas: The Politics of Race and Class amongst European Settlers on the Nilgiri Hills ca.1860–1914', *Journal of Imperial & Commonwealth History*, 32 (2004), 54–85.
[85] Bernard Porter, *The Absent-Minded Imperialists: Empire, Society and Culture in Britain* (Oxford, 2004), 61.

'gentlemanly' branches of capitalism, most notably banking (as did Gye). By the late nineteenth century financial, landed, professional, and service interests would increasingly be blended within the ruling elite of the British Empire.[86] Nevertheless, the rhetorical hostility towards 'vulgar commerce' remained. Phelps's lectures in political economy seem to have done nothing to dispel this most characteristic of imperial prejudices, and indeed if one letter is to be believed, he shared them: 'I never forget your disgust', wrote J. C. Penney of the Cairo City Police in 1927, 'when Lagden (I think it was) gave up being an administrator and became a brewer!'[87] From the Sudan M. H. V. Fleming condemned 'the counter-jumping Imperialism which Wells wrote against in "Joan and Peter"':[88] for him it was a nobler calling, whose purpose was civilization rather than the sordid business of trade, something also visible in R. K. Winter's wistful remark that 'The Red Sea used to be a delectable Province, but is now made hideous by vulgar commerce—since Manchester discovered how good is our cotton.'[89] For T. Sandford, fighting an uphill battle to protect African mineworkers from excessive exploitation by the settlers of Northern Rhodesia, Phelps's letters 'bring, as it were, a breath of fresh air into this atmosphere of money-grubbing and materialism'.[90] His critique of white settlers was highly characteristic of the British Empire's 'Guardians', a mixture of high-minded but condescending humanitarianism and class prejudice: 'The class of settler is not very high in many cases & their one idea seems to be to do down their boys... I cannot tell you what a heart breaking job it is sometimes on a station like this with many settlers in the district. If only they were men of education matters would be easier, but 75 per cent are absolute adventurers from their youth.'[91] However, in Kenya (which attracted a rather better class of settler than Northern Rhodesia) Orielenses were to be found on both sides of the divide. Arthur Walford, a member of the education department of the Kenyan Civil Service, bemoaned the failure of the 1932 Kenya land commission to redress the wrongs done to the Kikuyu and other tribes and protect their land from further encroachment by European settlers, but also wondered what the opinion of H. E. Schwartze, another Kenyan Orielensis, would be. 'After all he too is a member of a public school & a University, but also an unofficial member of Legislative Council & spokesman for the settlers... it is incidents

---

[86] P. J. Cain and A. G. Hopkins, *British Imperialism, Innovation and Expansion 1688–1914* (London, 1993), 29–37, 116–31.
[87] OCA PRO 2/44/1 Africa ii. 378, Penney to Phelps, n.d. [early 1927].
[88] OCA PRO 2/44/1 Africa i. 149–152, Fleming to Phelps, 13 April 1930. He is referring to a passage in H. G. Wells, *Joan and Peter: The Story of an Education* (London, 1918), 222–5, in which one of the protagonists denounces the supposedly 'Teutonised' New Imperialism espoused by Joseph Chamberlain.
[89] OCA PRO 2/44/1 Africa ii. 591, Winter to Phelps, 26 March 1925.
[90] OCA PRO 2/44/I Africa ii. 438–43, Sandford to Phelps, 18 February 1910.
[91] OCA PRO 2/44/1 Africa ii. 448–50, Sandford to Phelps, 15 February 1911.

such as this which seem to make the ultimate surrender of the Empire inevitable, if not desirable.'[92] Perhaps conscious that Phelps might regard him as *déclassé* because he was not in public service, J. Harper made a point of stressing the pedigree which a public school and Oxford education supposedly conferred when he wrote from Kenya defending the white settlers against metropolitan attacks: 'assuming you have noticed—which I hope you have not—the gratuitous and malignant slanders lately directed against this Colony (which, ironically, is peopled almost exclusively by public school and varsity men—a class less likely to merit these slanders than any in the history of the Empire)—I am sure you will have discounted them at their value.'[93]

Another major group of overseas Orielenses were the missionaries and churchmen, although it is striking how few of the overseas letters are from Phelps's fellow clergymen. It is perhaps a reflection of how far he was from sharing in the proselytizing impulse that R. F. McNeile in Cairo appeared to feel no embarrassment in writing to him of missionaries that 'Lord Cromer made it a rule never to have one of the breed inside his house—unless they inserted themselves—even at formal functions for fear of raising a Pan-Islamic cry!! . . . I have not yet been here sufficiently long to be seriously tarred with the brush of aggressive piety.'[94]

Nevertheless, Oriel continued to play an important role in missionary enterprise well into the twentieth century. In 1920 the *Oriel Record*'s editorial proudly proclaimed,

Our frontispiece is from a photograph of the Oriel Bishops at the recent Lambeth Conference. From left to right they are as follows:
The Right Rev. A. Hamilton Baynes, late Bishop of Natal
The Right Rev. A. J. May, Bishop of North Rhodesia.
The Most Rev. E. A. Parry, Archbishop of the West Indies
The Right Rev. A. J. Doull, Bishop of Kootenay, Canada.
The Right Rev. G. W. Kennion, Bishop of Bath and Wells.
The Right Rev. E. D. Shaw, Bishop of Buckingham.
The Right Rev. Gilbert White, Bishop of Willochra, Australia.[95]

Of these, Alston May of the Universities Mission to Central Africa was the most interesting figure. As bishop of Northern Rhodesia from 1914 until his death in 1940 he wielded a considerable degree of political influence, which

---

[92] OCA PRO 2/44/1 Africa ii. 534–8, Walford to Phelps, 22 January 1933; see Michael S. Coray, 'The Kenya Land Commission and the Kikuyu of Kiambu', *Agricultural History*, 52 (1978), 179–93; David Anderson, *Histories of the Hanged: Britain's Dirty War in Kenya and the End of Empire* (London, 2005), 10.
[93] OCA PRO 2/44/1 Africa i. 226–7, Harper to Phelps, 14 March 1927.
[94] OCA PRO 2/44/1 Africa ii. 318–19, McNeile to Phelps, 1 January 1903.
[95] OR (September 1920), 153.

he exercised above all in efforts to protect the native population from the worst excesses of exploitation by Northern Rhodesia's white settlers and miners. He had a reputation for remarkable energy and austerity: until 1927 he toured his vast diocese almost entirely on foot, later switching to bicycle or motor-van and sleeping on a camp-bed.[96] He wrote regularly to Phelps, mingling questions of religious and African politics with news of other Orielenses in the colony:

> The only Oriel man I have seen lately is Tom Sandford, who is now engaged in the hard and thankless task of holding the scales of justice even i.e. between Black & White, in the mining camp of Broken Hill. Every part of the world has its own special problem today: but I do believe that Africa's colour problem is the stiffest of them all. Here we have got on pretty well up to now: but a big mining development is upon us, which means an invasion of South African men and manners. Alas![97]

Along with the insights the Phelps correspondence gives us into the mentality of different elements of colonial society, what is perhaps most striking is what it reveals about the informal networks that bound the empire's rulers together. With the exception of those who had served in the First World War, most colonial officials and businessmen took up their first posts so young that the only links they had beyond their families were those of school or college. Shared memories, nostalgia, and anecdote were the glue that held these networks together, often with a profound impact on the administration of colonies and on patterns of recruitment and settlement. Orielenses wrote to Phelps to find out what their contemporaries were doing, and to report what they knew. During the First World War the martial activities of the living mingled with the melancholy lists of the dead, though sometimes in unexpected ways. While on leave from the East African front W. G. Edwards wrote to ask '...what happened to Deneke with whom I digged for of course he was partly German. Also Von Polier, I am afraid he is fighting tho' I trust for his sake against the Russians.'[98] Equally Phelps enquired assiduously after news of other Orielenses abroad, and was rarely disappointed. L. M. Heaney wrote from Dar es Salaam, 'You enquire of Orielenses. There are not many in Tanganyika—two Baldocks, one in the Forests, one on a Coffee estate; H. R. Herring of the red face, who is also in the Forests; and Kenneth Dobson, who came out to the administration last August. W. F. Baldock is stationed in Dar es Salaam so he is the old Oriel man whom I see most often. He is the local expert at "squash" and cricket.'[99]

---

[96] Bengt Sundkler and Christopher Steed, *A History of the Church in Africa* (Cambridge, 2000), 788; John Weller, 'The Influence on National Affairs of Bishop Alston May 1914–1940', in T. O. Ranger and John Weller (eds.), *Themes in the Christian History of Central Africa* (Berkeley, Calif., 1975), 195–212.
[97] OCA PRO 2/44/1 Africa ii. 343–4, May to Phelps, 14 June 1925.
[98] OCA PRO 2/44/1 Africa i. 109–10, Edwards to Phelps, 29 January 1915.
[99] OCA PRO 2/44/1 Africa i. 238–41, Heaney to Phelps, 21 January 1932.

J. Harper responded to a similar query from Kenya that 'The colony is infested with Oriel men. Offhand I can think of Seldon, Gerald Edwards, Vidal, Schwartze, Donald Seth-Smith, Grieve. Two of my contemporaries, John Hughes and Pitt died here and Philip Newbold who was a settler was killed in the war.'[100] E. R. W. Gillmor wrote from Nigeria that 'Two more Oriel men have recently come out to Nigeria in addition to Hogben & Scott. Gott came about 3 months ago—I suppose it is the same one—& is I think in the Secretariat at Lagos, & quite recently Backhouse was appointed to this Province. Curious that he should have come to my part of the world.'[101] But often such concentrations were far from accidental—one Oriel man would recommend another, or encourage him to apply, and if they could think of no one suitable they would write to Phelps, who acted as an informal recruiter for the ICS, the Sudan Political Service (SPS), and the Colonial Civil Service. When R. M. Hansard's superior asked him to find a man to fill a junior inspectorship in the survey department at Cairo, he wrote to Phelps to ask if he could suggest an Orielensis. 'He wants a man who is mathematical, not necessarily of the highest order, who is keen on things geographical, and above all, a man who is a gentleman. I am writing to you, for you if anyone can help me.'[102]

The development of an 'Oriel network' was clearest in the case of the Sudan Political Service, where a connection grew up which was perhaps the closest equivalent any other Oxford College has had to Balliol's with ICS. It began with the appointment of W. H. B. Evans in the very first batch of civilian administrators in 1904, and was clearly encouraged by Phelps, who was frequently thanked for having found new men for the service. Robert Collins estimated that at one time no less than 10 per cent of those serving in the Sudan Political Service were Oriel men, and while that figure is slightly exaggerated the college's contribution was still remarkable.[103] A. H. M. Kirk-Greene's examination of the social and educational profile of the Sudan Political Service demonstrated that there was a certain amount of truth in the old aphorism that the Sudan was 'a land of blacks ruled by Blues', although the Service's officers combined considerable intellectual ability with their sporting qualities. His study revealed the remarkable dominance of a few public schools (Winchester provided 30 officers, and Eton 21, out of a total of 331) of Oxford (180) and within Oxford of a few colleges. Oriel provided no fewer than sixteen members of the Service between 1899 and 1952, second only to New College and equal with Magdalen, both of them much larger.[104]

---

[100] OCA PRO 2/44/1 Africa i. 226–7, Harper to Phelps, 14 March 1927.
[101] OCA PRO 2/44/1 Africa i. 189–91, Gillmor to Phelps, 18 February 1925.
[102] OCA PRO 2/44/1 Africa i. 224–5, Hansard to Phelps, 29 November 1911.
[103] Robert O. Collins, 'The Sudan Political Service: A Portrait of the Imperialists', *African Affairs*, 71 (1972), 296 n. 8.
[104] A. H. M. Kirk-Greene, 'The Sudan Political Service: A Profile in the Sociology of Imperialism', *International Journal of African Historical Studies*, 15 (1982), 21–2, 38–9.

The letters they wrote to Phelps reveal them to be a tightly knit group, proud of both their sporting and their intellectual qualifications, often larding their correspondence with classical allusions. In between making uncomplimentary remarks about the native population of Halfa in the Sudan and mentioning an encounter with Cecil Rhodes's brother, Reginald Winter remarked that 'Naturally, being on the border, they are a motley crowd—varying from colonists from the Southern Sudan to the unstable Hellene, whose character and habits are deplorable. When first I read the notices to passengers on the public ferries at Khartoum, "$απαγορενειδι$ $αυπγεως$ $το$ $πτνειν$ $επι$ $του$ $στρωματος$"[105] it struck me that such a caution was rather a come-down for the descendants of the occupants of the Salaminian galleys—(and moreover I hope my Greek is not entirely ungrammatical—one forgets the little classical lore that one ever imbibed in the hopeless groping among the maze of Arabic idiom.)'[106] They kept in touch with each other and met as often as their remote postings would allow, celebrating the college's (and Oxford's) successes and doing all they could maintain SPS recruitment from Oriel. J. K. Richardson wrote to Phelps in 1922 from Gordon College in Khartoum, saying

> As the latest batch of Oxonians arrived in this country yesterday & all seem very charming, I feel I must write & rebuke you for sending no Oriel men this year, in which rebuke Williams wishes to share.
> Next August, however, the Gordon College will want another man in my place, as I am to go out to the provinces. I wonder if you know a likely man. We want one of the same calibre as those chosen for the political service; the pay & social position is the same & after a few years we go out to the political service for a period of 4 or 5 years.... 'A gentleman' is essential, about a 2nd Class in schools & if possible one who plays a little soccer. I feel that Oriel can supply the man we want & make up the deficiencies this year.[107]

In 1927 G. R. Bredin wrote with satisfaction that 'I hear the Cambridge candidates for the Sudan Political were a very poor collection this year. The Oxford ones were, I believe very good; I hope that Oriel, to quote your own words in your speech at the Gaudy in 1925 "still holds a monopoly in the administration of the Sudan."'[108] That this was still not so far from the truth three years later is reflected in a letter written from El Fasher, Darfur Province, Sudan:

> On my arrival here the first thing to greet me was a message from yourself delivered to me by Mackrell who is working with me in the district. He is getting into the work

---

[105] 'It is strictly forbidden to spit on the mattresses' (my thanks to Peter Thonemann for this translation).
[106] OCA PRO 2/44/1 Africa ii. 587–8, Winter to Phelps, 17 March 1909.
[107] OCA PRO 2/44/1 Africa ii. 411–12, Richardson to Phelps, 30 November 1922.
[108] OCA PRO 2/44/1 Africa i. 48–9, Bredin to Phelps, 7 July 1927.

quickly and will do well. Ewen Campbell is in the next district to the North of me and I am hoping to see him in a day or two. It will be the first time I have met him since we did our final Arabic exam together in 1923. I saw Newbold last May. He has just been made Deputy Governor of Kassala Province and is in charge of the Red Sea Coast and hinterland from the Egyptian border down to Port Sudan.

Winter and Penney I left behind me in the Secretariat when I left Khartoum. Arnold Forster you have probably seen within the last month as he has been home trying for a job at Magdalen. Williams is still in the Gordon College at Khartoum. He is now a travelling inspector of the Education Dept. and goes around reporting on the schools. Morrison and Wordsworth are in Dongola Province and I have not seen either of them for some time.

This province (Darfur) was administered from 1924 to 1926 by Bence-Pembroke, of whom I remember you used to say that 'his smile was a college asset!'

A census recently held of the members of the Political Service by Colleges brought Oriel out well at the head of the list and I hear the good work is still being carried on, as the latest batch of recruits is said to include three from Oriel.[109]

In 1932 the *Oriel Record* celebrated the Sudanese connection with an article which traced its history from the recruitment of W. H. B. Evans in 1904 to the appointment of Douglas Newbold as governor of Kordofan,[110] and in 1936, after Phelps's death, the Sudanese Orielenses affirmed their ties to each other and to the college with a dinner, the culinary reality of which would have had a very hard time living up to the magnificent drollery of a menu that only made sense to the initiated:

Memories of Oriel remain green despite the burning sun of the Sudan. On March 14th ten Orielenses (four were unable to be present) sat down at Khartoum before the following menu: Pamplemousses Manciple; Consomme High Table; Filet de Barbue Phelper, Sauce Randan; Dindonneau Regnante Carolo, saucisses Oxonienses, Legumes Rhodes, Pommes Rosses, Sauce Hardy Norseman; Glaces aux Oranges Adam de Brome, Crème Bartlemas, Gaufrettes R.K.; Savori Skimmery; Fruits Roi Eduard; Café Black Prince.[111]

The nostalgia revealed in this list of familiar names, combined with a certain delight at the contrast between damp Oxford memories and 'savage' colonial surroundings, is a recurring hallmark of the Phelps letters. In 1915 A. W. Facer, atypical of most of Phelps's correspondents in that he was a scientist, wrote from Sinoia in Southern Rhodesia (where he had taken up a temporary war service vacancy in the Rhodesian civil service after being rejected by the military because of poor sight):

I sit in a small round thatched hut, which shudders, creaks and groans in the strain of a tropical hurricane. Thunder claps and lightning flashes shake the earth and rend the sky. A huge tree just outside has just been rent with wind or lightning, and its top—

---

[109] OCA PRO 2/44/1 Africa i. 53–6, Bredin to Phelps, 19 January 1930.
[110] D.M.H.E., 'Ex Africa', OR 5/9 (June 1932), 202–4.   [111] OR (June 1936), 103.

Orielenses in the Sudan, 1936.

	Oriel
R. K. WINTER	1907
J. C. PENNEY	1912
J. N. RICHARDSON	1912
D. NEWBOLD	1913
G. R. F. BREDIN	1919
E. CAMPBELL	1919
C. W. WILLIAMS	1919
J. HYND	1922
J. E. C. MACKRELL	1924
M. C. WORDSWORTH	1924
J. K. K. MORRISON	1925
T. H. B. MYNORS	1925
J. C. N. DONALD	1926
D. M. H. EVANS	1926

Orielenses Bibite

Air: Tannenbaum.

BRIGHTEST Gem in learning's crown,
What power can bring thy great name down?
Mighty men have been of yore,
Where we too soon shall be no more,
New voices sing as ours before, ORIELENSES BIBITE.

Come passmen, classmen, ploughmen, all,
To this first toast your minds recall;
Drink, drink to those whose lightest sighs
Are dearer far than learning's prize,
To blushing cheeks and sparkling eyes—ORIELENSES BIBITE.

Come oarsmen from the river-side,
The "Hardy Norseman's" stalwart pride,
Let arms be strong and hearts be true,
To keep the flag with stripes of blue,
Where Head of all it floats anew. ORIELENSES BIBITE.

Victorious may we still be found,
On football field or cricket ground;
And still at every year records,
May Oriel's sons be seen at Lords.
So to our blues 'midst loudest chords, ORIELENSES BIBITE.

Come ye who burn the midnight oil,
Forget for once your constant toil;
No Dons your joyous mirth shall blame,
For in the First we'll see your name,
And so you'll raise old Oriel fame. ORIELENSES BIBITE.

Come Oriel men with one accord
Join hands around this festive board.
United may we ever be,
In all our work and revelry,
So drink this toast to three times three. ORIELENSES BIBITE.

Menu.

Pamplemousses Manciple

Consomme High Table

Filet de Barbue Phelper
Sauce Randan

Dindonneau Regnante Carolo
Saussisses Oxonienses
Legumes Rhodes
Pommes Rosses
Sauce Hardy Norseman

Glace aux Oranges Adam de Brome
Creme Bartlemas
Gaufrettes R. K.

Savori Skimmery

Fruits Roi Eduard

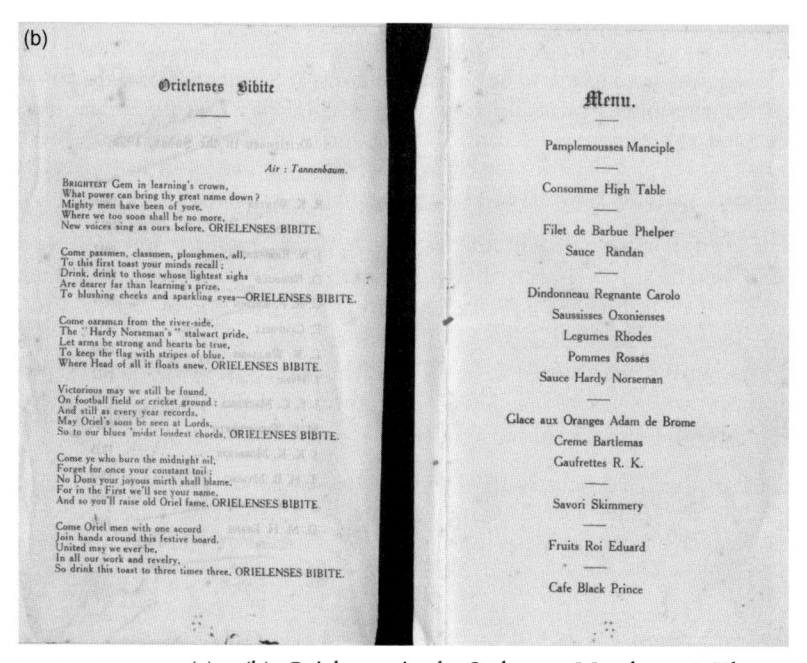

Cafe Black Prince

ILLUSTRATION 14.1 (a) & (b) Orielenses in the Sudan, 14 March 1936: Khartoum dinner menu card, *OCA*

falling with a huge crash—just missed my hut. Insects of all sizes and colours, scared or shaken from the roof, scurry round my feet—(one has just dropped down the neck of my shirt)—and my dog whines piteously in the corner. Yet these things are all to me as though they were not, for the 'Oriel Record' lies open before me, and my thoughts of yearning, of pleasant and sacred reminiscence, and of sad regret are there.[112]

He went on to list the names of those killed recorded in its pages. For T. Sandford, writing from Northern Rhodesia, it was the reading parties at High Force which were the most treasured memory:

Oh those magic names! Mickle Fell—High Cup Nick—the cave. To think that I am allowing myself to be boiled alive—for unlike the sandy Sudan, we have a wet heat here—and my very backbone weakened in a land where we see naught but trees of stunted growth, sometimes walking miles in such a case and when we find a hill we look down on miles and miles of the atoms of nature struggling for supremacy, when I might be gazing in rapt amazement at the beetling crags and raging torrents of snow clad Teesdale, drinking in health and British doggedness on the steeple of all the dale, Mickle Fell.[113]

W. H. B. Evans, Phelps's first Sudanese correspondent, perhaps summed up best what the letters meant to their recipients when he wrote, 'Many thanks for your letter. It smelt of running streams, of heather and of an exquisite undercut of beef, and made me long to be with you.'[114] Nostalgia also expressed itself in the sharing of old Oxford jokes 'I suppose there is no chance of their pulling down Keble?',[115] A. R. Wise enquired from Kenya in 1924. Sometimes this could be taken to what seem like unhealthy extremes. G. W. James, working for the Colonial Service in Sierra Leone, wrote in 1920 from Batkanu that 'In the large wooden bungalow in which we are at present living 3 of my predecessors have died during the past 6 years...the Oriel arms decorate my bungalow verandah wherever I may happen to be.'[116] Five years later he wrote, 'At Kennam I have a mud house (not bad as mud houses go, but with no furniture except my own touring kit), which I have christened "Oriel Cottage", affixing a shield with the arms at the front door. I feel that I am part and parcel of the College which has done so much for me, and anything that can keep its memory before me I gladly do. People have remarked that I seem to have a perfect mania for Oriel and all things of Oriel: it is true, and I am not ashamed of it. I am devoted to the old foundation.'[117] And three years later in Moyamba

[112] OCA PRO 2/44/1 Africa i. 117–24, Facer to Phelps, 29 November 1915.
[113] OCA PRO 2/44/1 Africa i. 438–43, Sandford to Phelps, 18 February 1910.
[114] OCA MPP/E 8/1, Evans to Phelps, 16 April 1911.
[115] OCA PRO 2/44/1 Africa ii. 592–8, Wise to Phelps, 22 March 1924.
[116] OCA PRO 2/44/1 Africa i. 263–5, James to Phelps, 3 October 1920.
[117] OCA PRO 2/44/1 Africa i. 266, James to Phelps, 10 July 1925.

My thoughts are never very far from Oriel, and, as I write, I am faced, at my bungalow table, by a picture of the front quadrangle, framed for nothing for me by one of the Fathers at the Roman Catholic Mission in Moyamba. Flanking it are pictures of the High Street, opposite Queen's, and of Oxford from the top of Magdalen Tower. On a screen facing the front door, our visitors are faced by the old original Oriel shield—now alas! A little battered and worn by frequent journeyings—which I had in my first term as a freshman. So even you would not feel 'not at home' in at least one spot in Moyamba.[118]

The picture which emerges from the Phelps letters and other sources on Oriel's overseas and imperial links is of a college conscious of its imperial connections and fiercely proud of them. Phelps himself had clearly approved of Rhodes, and must have relished a letter from the Cape Town barrister Frank Reid, the first Rhodes scholar (and by this date a selector for the South African cricket team):

I am so bucked with my photos of the Rhodes Memorial that I feel I must send you some. One of them (No. 1)—the silhouette view of G. F. Watts 'Physical Energy'— you may be inclined to have reproduced in the 'Oriel Record'.... Oriel is prominent hereabouts—still more so at the moment, for a horse of that name has just won the race of the South African year![119]

There were moments of doubt, however, particularly in the letters of Tom Sandford from Northern Rhodesia, where even before the First World War he deplored the exploitation of black miners, the vulgarity, casual violence, and cruelty of colonial life, 'But of all the rottenest places on the earth let me commend you to Broken Hill'; he even allowed himself some veiled criticisms of Rhodes himself, and 'his principle of England the chosen ruler of the earth.'[120]

But what are we doing for the good of the native [?] We are teaching him a hotch-potch of native & English law; we teach him that he is dirt before the white man, in general that the laws and the white man are things to be respected, wholesome so far as it goes. But we make no attempt as far as I can see to teach him to rule himself speaking of the race as a whole. We have taken away everything from the chiefs bar the name, even their influence and we start at the beginning again.... I need not mince matters; but I may tell you that I was horrified, and am so still, at the general behaviour of the white man, official & civil, when away from the restraints of civilisation.[121]

Sandford's are amongst the most intelligent, and prescient, of all the letters in the Phelps collection, for he was one of the very rare correspondents who reflected intelligently both on the brutality and fragility of colonialism, and who even before the First World War questioned how long it could survive. Phelps's death in 1936 marked the end of an era in more ways than one: while

---

[118] OCA PRO 2/44/1 Africa i. 271–2, James to Phelps, 21 February 1928.
[119] OCA PRO 2/44/1 Africa ii. 388–90, Reid to Phelps, 6 June 1924.
[120] OCA PRO 2/44/1 Africa ii. 434–7, Sandford to Phelps, 11 February 1909.
[121] OCA PRO 2/44/1 Africa ii. 444–7, Sandford to Phelps, 14 August 1910.

ILLUSTRATION 14.2 The Oriel bishops, 1930, *OCA*

		Alexander John Doull	Mark Carpenter-Garnier	
		Kootenay	Colombo	
A. J. M. May	A. H. Baynes		E. D. Shaw	P. H. Eliot
Northern Rhodesia	Natal		Buckingham	Buckingham

E. A. L. Moore (Travancore and Cochin) absent

Oriel lost the core of its institutional memory, and thousands of former students a much-loved tutor, the empire lost the node of one of its more important networks. Increasingly attention would turn to events on the Continent, and hints of the coming cataclysm could be found surprisingly early in the pages of the *Oriel Record*, in a report from Guy Wint, an exchange student in Berlin: 'Today the National Socialists think they see in Hitler the third great leader [after Frederick and Bismarck]. Thus, on the one hand, there are untrained politicians, and on the other intolerant subjects looking for a demi-god.'[122] The British Empire's contribution to the war effort was gigantic (although until recently often unacknowledged), but the strain also hastened its dissolution.[123] Although anxieties about local

---

[122] F. Guy Wint, 'Oriel and Berlin', OR 5/9 (June 1932), 213.
[123] See Ashley Jackson, *The British Empire and the Second World War* (London, 2006).

nationalism are visible in some of the letters Phelps received in the 1920s and 1930s, probably none of his correspondents could have envisaged so swift a retreat from Britain's imperial possessions and responsibilities as took place in the twenty or so years after the Second World War, effectively ending Oriel's (and Oxford's) role as a nursery for colonial administrators. Whilst Oriel's international links increased greatly in the post-war period, it would be on terms of increasing equality and reciprocity. Ever larger numbers of students came to the college from overseas, but not only from the anglophone world of the empire and Commonwealth. Orielenses continued to make careers abroad, but increasingly they did so without any particular political privileges or power. The change was embodied in the figure of Hugh Lambrick ICS (1904–82), an Orielensis who apart from a brief stint as District Magistrate of Sholapur in the Bombay Presidency 1937–9[124] served in Sind from 1927 until Indian independence cut short his administrative career, whereupon he returned to Oriel as a research fellow. Lambrick produced a series of scholarly works on the ancient and modern history of the province he had administered for twenty years, winning the Royal Asiatic Society's Burton medal in 1978, but he always seems to have harboured a certain regret and resentment at the enforced end to a career he had clearly loved.[125]

With hindsight we can now see what an extraordinary period Phelps's life and correspondence covered—the high point of Britain's reach and influence in the world, reflected in a vast collection of letters collected by a single, rather eccentric clergyman at Oriel. Their significance goes well beyond the history of Oriel, for they demonstrate clearly the importance of educational and institutional culture in constituting the imaginative fabric of the British Empire. Phelps's unusually assiduous correspondence has preserved in paper a small corner of an imperial network that was typical not only of Oxford and Cambridge colleges and public schools, but of many less prominent educational institutions at the time. On leaving the college these very young men carried the ideas they had imbibed there overseas, where they might then spend the next forty or fifty years with only short stints of leave. As Lambrick wrote when reminiscing about his own career:

Who were those district officers? So far as the European element goes, they were men who came out to India at the age of twenty-two or twenty-three direct from British

---

[124] Manjiri Kamat, 'Disciplining Sholapur: The Industrial City and its Workers in the Period of the Congress Ministry, 1937–1939', *Modern Asian Studies*, 44 (2010), 100.

[125] H. T. Lambrick, 'Prospects for a United India after the Cessation of British Rule as these Appeared in Sind 1930–46', in C. H. Philips and M. D. Wainwright, *The Partition of India: Policies and Perspectives* (London, 1970), 516; his best-known works were *Sir Charles Napier and Sind* (Oxford, 1952); *The Terrorist—Translated and Edited from the Sindhi* (London, 1972); and *Sind before the Muslim Conquest* (Hyderabad, 1973).

universities. Their ideas about politics and administration were liable to be derived from Plato's *Republic*, Aristotle, the works of Hobbes and Rousseau, and Burke's speeches. For the most part they arrived in India completely innocent of politics and administration from the practical point of view.[126]

Under these circumstances the friendships, connections, and intellectual relationships forged at school or college were often the only link these men had with their contemporaries at home. The shared memories, attitudes, and beliefs could span continents, and last for an entire lifetime.

---

[126] Lambrick, 'Prospects for a United India after the Cessation of British Rule', 505.

15

The Estates of Oriel, 1324–1920

†*Ralph Evans and J. P. D. Dunbabin*[1]

Many, perhaps most, of the students of medieval Oxford were lodged, and to an extent taught, in halls; and in establishing what became Oriel Adam de Brome began by acquiring two halls, Perilous Hall, soon to be joined by Kettel Hall, in Candych (roughly, the modern Broad Street), and the newly built 'Tackley's Inn'. Perilous and Kettel Halls were always meant to pay rent. Tackley's Inn was originally intended to house de Brome's scholars behind the shops built into its High Street front. But when James of Spain, a senior chancery clerk and associate of de Brome, transferred to the college his life-interest in La Oriole (formerly Seneschal Hall) on the south-west corner of its present site, the scholars became established there in 1329. So the whole of Tackley's Inn was let: by the mid-fifteenth century it had been subdivided into two, Bulkeley Hall, and a tavern exploiting the still extant Gothic wine-cellar. This was rented at between £2 and £3 p.a.; but Oriel regarded it proprietorially as *taberna nostra*, and used it for entertainment connected with striking deals and for socialization with important tenants—in 1516 one shilling and eight pence was spent on 'drinking with Master Unton' (the tenant of Oriel's Wadley manor) who stayed two days 'at our tavern', while a little later he was supplied with wine and his wife and servants with dinner.[2]

De Brome also transferred to his new college, via the king, the rectory of St Mary the Virgin in Oxford, of which he was the incumbent, with its property in Oxford and the tithes of Littlemore, some three miles south of Oxford, along with a messuage and half acre of land there.[3] In 1328 the college received

---

[1] The authors gratefully acknowledge the generous permission of the Trustees of the Imperial War Museum to quote from the papers of Sir Henry Tizard.

[2] W. A. Pantin, 'Tackley's Inn, Oxford', OR (June 1941), 139–55, cf. 139–43, and *Oxoniensia*, 7 (1942), 80–92, cf. 80–3. Perilous Hall was sold to Trinity for £104 in 1736, Kettel Hall for £3,200 in 1883.

[3] For the foundation and early endowment of the college see Chapter 1. E Vallis, 'The Estates of Oriel', OR (1991), 32–57 is an extremely helpful listing, by a former treasurer, of the college's

the hospital of St Bartholomew in the parish of Headington, which, besides its economic value, provided a refuge during periodic outbreaks of plague; unfortunately it also occasioned recurrent friction with the city of Oxford.[4] The hospital's property included six acres next to its site, arable in the fields of Headington (and a few acres in Cowley and Iffley), tenements and land in the suburb of St Clement's, several tenements in Oxford itself, and six acres of meadow in St Giles (reduced by the 1829 Enclosure award, and exchanged in 1861 for four acres in Iffley). During the fourteenth and fifteenth centuries the college acquired several further properties in the city, including dwellings, shops, and academic halls; many of the latter were incorporated into the college's site—some more or less immediately and some much later—but others continued to yield rent into the nineteenth century.[5] However by the late fifteenth century Oxford tenements, and halls, were in decline; so it is fortunate that Oriel could turn increasingly to its agricultural estates.

A variety of such lands to the east of Oxford were received in 1328: Stowford farm in Stanton St John, three and a half miles from the college (later gifts increased its area to some 120 acres), two acres of meadow at Waterperry, eight miles away, later known as Oriel lake, and twenty acres of woodland, later known as Oriel Wood, at Boarstall (in Buckinghamshire but only ten miles from the college).[6] Other properties were more distant. In 1328 Adam de Brome gave the valuable rectory of Coleby near Lincoln. In 1324 he had acquired the advowson of the church of Aberford, between Pontefract and Wetherby in the West Riding of Yorkshire, and in 1332 it was appropriated to Oriel. The revenues of the appropriated churches of Littlemore, Coleby, and Aberford, based essentially on their tithes, were

properties with a summary description of their nature, their dates of acquisition, and their disposal.

[4] The medieval dispute related to the city's liability to make Oriel an annual payment in support of the hospital's almsmen, and over whether the city or Oriel should select these. Litigation in 1520–4 and 1534–6 was finally resolved by the Lord Chancellor's compromise award. Trouble returned in the mid-nineteenth century, and still more the 1890s when (in a situation much like that of Trollope's *The Warden*) the city contended that Oriel had appropriated the growth in the value of the hospital's estates, but virtually nullified the charity by leaving the almsmen's stipend at the statutory 9*d.* a week. Oriel's defence, 'a masterly monument to Shadwell's erudition', was purely legalistic. In 1900 the Charity Commissioners effected a compromise: Oriel made over some £2,400 of stocks to the Oxford Municipal Charities, but gained absolute title to Bartlemas and its lands—Anthony Wood, *Survey of the Antiquities of the City of Oxford*, ed. Andrew Clark (OHS 1890), 511–13; R. E. Bagnall-Wild, 'The Treasurer's Report—Bartlemas', OR (1962), 12.

[5] Besides the halls already mentioned, Vallis lists Bradwell Hall (sold to the university in 1866 for £1,796), St Thomas Hall (demolished in 1872 to create King Edward Street), Magna Scola, Bedel Hall, St Mary Hall, and Martin Hall (all now incorporated into the main college site), Maiden and St Edward Halls; 'Estates of Oriel', 37–40, 57.

[6] On the properties in Oxfordshire see too the articles on Cowley, Headington, Littlemore, Stanton St John, and Waterperry in VCH *Oxford*, v (1957), 76–96, 157–68, 206–14, 282–93, 295–309.

broadly similar in value, and were much greater than those of the college's smaller properties close to Oxford.

In assembling an estate a founder and his college were constrained both by the depth of their pockets and by what was then on the market. The founder's network of contacts, and knowledge of what property might be available on advantageous terms, was an important factor. So too could be royal favour, which might give access to properties not otherwise attainable. In choosing between the estates that were available geographical location must have been a significant consideration. A property's value had to be weighed against the difficulties of administration imposed by its distance from the college. The high potential yield of Oriel's appropriated churches in Yorkshire and Lincolnshire justified the possible problems of dealing with remote lessees and the long overland transfer of cash. Even in the period before the Black Death in the mid-fourteenth century, when many manors were not leased out but managed directly, colleges did not normally get the bulk of their foodstuffs from their estates; instead the estates' profits would be used to buy provisions more locally. It could however be convenient to have estates close at hand, like Oriel's to the east of Oxford, from which timber or other supplies might be drawn. Properties like Stowford farm or Boarstall would have seemed much less appealing had they been situated in some other part of the country.

In the fifteenth century the college acquired two groups of properties in Berkshire and west Oxfordshire that were both valuable and close to Oxford. The manor of Wadley, with some 400 acres, just east of Faringdon in Berkshire (now Oxfordshire), was bought in 1440 with a legacy of £1,000 from John Frank, Master of the Rolls from 1423 to 1438. It proved in some ways problematic: a nearby abbey petitioned the Crown for its restitution; Wadley occasioned some six years of legal pleadings in the Exchequer; and it was, for political reasons, briefly taken into the king's hands after Edward IV's accession in 1461. Wadley was to fund four new fellowships (with a south-western preference in their recruitment); its value to Oriel was enhanced in 1478 when the former provost John Hals, bishop of Lichfield, acquired the very large manor of Littleworth, immediately to its north, which passed first to feoffees and then in 1483 to the college. In 1476 Oriel received by the bequest of another former provost, John Carpenter, bishop of Worcester, the adjacent manors of Dean and Chalford in west Oxfordshire, which together contained some 850 acres and were intended to support one of the original fellowships plus a new one (both to be filled by men from Worcester diocese). Chalford was then sheep country, and the late fifteenth century seems to have seen the 'Depopulation perhaps by enclosure' (in Scots, the 'clearance') of two small villages.[7] The college later bought two additional yardlands there; rent from

---

[7] We have no precise date for this. Lessees in 1480 were 'bound to maintain fences etc. of "the said pastures and closes"', though this could have been merely archaic; a lease of 1536 described

these first appears in the treasurers' account for 1611–12, and continued to be accounted separately from the manor of Chalford. In the 1630s they yielded a fixed annual rent of £20, at a time when the combined rent of the manors of Dean and Chalford was about £60, plus £4 10s. for land that was formerly wooded (also accounted separately).[8]

In his lifetime Carpenter had given the college not only Bedel Hall, received in 1455 and soon incorporated in its site, but in addition, in 1451, the manors of East Hall and Valence in Dagenham. However Oriel immediately demised this Essex property to the hospital of St Antony in Threadneedle Street, London (of which Carpenter had been master), in return for an annuity of 25 marks (£16.67), for the support of nine exhibitioners who were to live in Bedel Hall. In 1475 Edward IV granted custody of the hospital, with responsibility for the annuity, to the dean and chapter of Windsor. But it was only in 1504–5 that the annuity was first paid, and then at the reduced rate of £10.40; this payment continued until 1919, when it was commuted for a lump sum.[9] Demising the Dagenham manors was perhaps the most unfortunate estates decision Oriel ever made, since it meant that the college would not profit from the area's twentieth-century development.

The geographical distribution of Oriel's estates was both confirmed and extended by the acquisition in the sixteenth century of several valuable properties, some of which supported fellowships. In 1504 William Smyth, bishop of Lincoln, a former vice-chancellor of the university who was shortly to be a generous benefactor of Lincoln College and a co-founder of Brasenose, gave part of a manor at Shenington (near Banbury but until 1844 in Gloucestershire) which he had bought for £300; its revenues funded the Smyth fellowship, and also supplemented the emoluments of the provost, fellows, and officers. Further purchases were made, notably in 1565 and 1775–80; and after the 1780 enclosure Oriel's 1,481 acres accounted for over 90 per cent of the village.[10] By 1582 Oriel held a small piece (*iuger*) of the arable land

---

the estate as 'the college's pasture called Chalford and Nether Chalford' (K. J. Allison, M. W. Beresford, and J. G. Hunt, *The Deserted Villages of Oxfordshire* (University of Leicester, Department of English Local History Occasional Paper xvii, 1965)). Chalford (which is unfortunately not yet covered by the *Victoria County History*) was not cited to the 1517 Enclosure Commissioners. But Oriel's lessee at Dean was presented as having converted to pasture 40 acres of arable and of so handling that and 100 acres of pasture that four residents had had to leave; and the lessee of Stanton St John had also converted 40 arable acres to pasture (I. S. Leadam (ed.), *The Domesday of Inclosures 1517–1518*, 2 vols. (London, 1897), i. 355, 361). Leadam's calculations (43) suggested that the lessees and tenants of ecclesiastical houses were the people most likely to effect such depopulating enclosures.

[8] See the article on the parish of Great Faringdon (including Faringdon, Wadley, Wickensham, Littleworth, Thrupp) in VCH *Berkshire*, iv (1924), 489–99, ODNB s.n. [Halse] and Carpenter; OCA TF 1/A1/5, treasurers' accounts 1582–1649.

[9] R. E. Bagnall-Wild, 'Oriel's Agricultural Property', OR (1964), 12; article on manors in the parish of Dagenham in VCH *Essex*, v (1966), 267–81.

[10] VCH *Oxfordshire*, ix (1969), 139–47.

in Headington that contained a quarry, apparently distinct from the property of the hospital of St Bartholomew. A tenement in Burford, Oxfordshire, with three pieces (*iugera*) of land in its fields (treated as appurtenances of Shenington), and a tiny plot, the site of a former barn, at Faringdon, were acquired at an unknown date (they were sold off in 1807). In 1525 Richard Dudley, who had once been senior treasurer, gave the manor of Swainswick, which he had bought for £420. It contained about 550 acres in a steep north–south valley to the east of Bath, and supported the two Dudley fellows and the Dudley exhibitioners—though on Dudley's death his family threatened legal proceedings, and election of the fellows had to be temporarily suspended. By 1564 the rectory (more precisely five-sixths of the rectory) of Eltham in Kent, very close to London, had been added; its revenue was perhaps half that of Coleby. By contrast the appropriated church of Moreton Pinkney (some thirty-five miles north-east of Oxford in Northamptonshire), which was acquired in 1559, yielded twice as much as Coleby and remained the college's most profitable rectory. A further clutch of properties were located in Wiltshire, between those in Somerset and Berkshire. Ryles farm in Leigh Delamere, six miles north-west of Chippenham, came to Oriel at an unknown date before 1582; in 1794 it contained four separate farms with a combined area of 227 acres. By 1565 the college held land in adjacent Sevington and smallholdings in nearby Castle Combe, as well as pasture at Christian Malford, six miles or so to the east. These properties were, however, sold in 1810 and 1799 respectively to enable Oriel to redeem Land Tax on other holdings.[11]

The college's landholding was not extended significantly until the mid-eighteenth century, though there were one or two small short-term additions and some more important acquisitions in places where Oriel already held an estate. In 1740 a farm of 181 acres at Stadhampton, eight miles south-east of Oxford, was purchased. And by the bequest of Elizabeth Ludwell, the sister of George Carter, provost from 1708 to 1727, a farm at Throwley near Faversham in Kent was received in 1761 to endow exhibitions. This was exchanged in 1815 for another property in Kent, Bilham Farm, with 169 acres between Sevington and Smeeth just to the south-east of Ashford; its revenues were received by a trust administered by the college, and do not appear in the treasurers' accounts. About the same time the proceeds of the sale of houses in Oxford financed the purchase of a 189-acre farm at Charlton-on-Otmoor, nine miles north-east of Oxford. In 1827 Oriel bought the rich advowson of Twerton, just west of Bath, and soon added a garden there. This was sold in 1837 for the construction of the 'new road called in the vulgar tongue "Rail-way"'; but it was later replaced with cottage properties in the same village. With the advowson of North Wraxall in Wiltshire the college

---

[11] ODNB s.n. Smith [Smyth], William; article on Shenington in VCH *Oxfordshire*, ix (1969), 139–50; OCA TF 1/A1/5, treasurers' accounts 1582–1649.

acquired in 1859 an acre and a half of garden that it let to the rector. Subsequent decades saw a considerable adjustment in Oriel's portfolio of Oxford houses: sales from 1866 to 1883 amounted to at least £15,086, while between 1875 and 1906 the college bought £26,578 worth of property in its more immediate vicinity.[12] There was change, too, in relation to the estates. In the past, Oxford and Cambridge colleges had been permitted to sell land only in special circumstances or for the redemption of their Land Taxes, but in 1856–8 they acquired full powers. Using these, Oriel bought, between 1874 and 1890, some 148 acres at Shenington and 11 at Littleworth, and sold 220 acres at Chalford, 104 elsewhere in Oxfordshire, 14 acres at Swainswick, and 6 at Twerton: a net reduction of some 185 acres. Thereafter there was little change before the First World War, the chief development being the sale of Oriel Wood.[13] So at the start of 1919 the college's estates were still recognizably those of the sixteenth century; at the end of the year it abruptly decided to sell most of them, a decision implemented in 1920–1 with considerable speed and success.

Oriel's lands were very far from continuous. But a cluster of properties, large and small, was to be found in an arc running from the northern half of Oxfordshire and adjacent parts of Northamptonshire and Buckinghamshire, through north Berkshire and north Wiltshire, to the north-east corner of Somerset. The places at either end, Moreton Pinkney and Swainswick, were only eighty miles apart. In addition (besides an annuity from property in Essex not administered directly by the college) there was a farm in east Kent and appropriated churches in Yorkshire, Lincolnshire, and north-west Kent.[14] Thus the college possessed both urban tenements in Oxford and rural properties. These latter ranged from valuable rectories through large estates and manors with varied internal structures to tiny properties, and embraced tithe, arable, meadow, woodland, and quarries. How they could best be exploited varied with time and place.

The estate records preserved in Oriel form an extremely rich archival deposit, only a few seams of which have been mined for this chapter.

---

[12] Figures in Vallis, 'Estates of Oriel'; but Oriel told the Cleveland Commission that £5,520 of its bond holdings came from its 1872 'Sale of houses in Oxford' PP 1873 xxxvii part 2, 311, whereas Vallis records, for that year, only the sale of 116 High Street for £2,500.

[13] Vallis, 'Estates of Oriel'. For the act permitting the exchange of the farm in Throwley for Bilham Farm see L. L. Shadwell (ed.), *Enactments in Parliament Specially Concerning the Universities of Oxford and Cambridge*, 4 vols. (OHS lviii–lxi, 1912), iv, appendix iii, 325 (54 Geo III cap. 20). For North Wraxall and for the purchases and sales of the later nineteenth century, see L. L Price, 'The Recent Depression in Agriculture as Shown in the Accounts of an Oxford College, 1876–90', *Journal of the Royal Statistical Society*, 65 (1892), table I, 7, 11, and 'The Estates of the Colleges of Oxford and their Management', *The Surveyors' Institution Transactions*, 45 (1912–13), 560.

[14] See maps of 'Oriel's estates and land interests, 1324 to 1991, and of the major land holdings (Wadley and Littleworth, Dean and Chalford, Shenington, and Swainswick), below, pp. 499–504, derived from Vallis, 'Estates of Oriel', 50–5.

Systematic investigation of this large and well-catalogued collection would require a substantial volume. Subjects mentioned in passing here, like the college's role in enclosure or the surveying of its estates, certainly merit fuller attention; the value of its detailed records for the study of particular places has been shown by the excellent article on Shenington in the *Victoria County History*. What is now offered is more by way of an overview, illustrated with specific examples. Its principal source is the fine series of accounts of the college's treasurers, which survive in the archive for the years 1409–15 and 1450–1525, and then in an unbroken sequence (as the 'Style') from the accounting year 1582–3 to 1927. Five-year samples have been taken every fifty years, starting in 1582–3, with the years 35–6 and 85–6 of each century used for detailed comparison. Information of a kind not recorded in the accounts has been drawn from a selection of other documents in the archive, notably the records of fines taken and leases granted between 1726 and 1866.[15] The Cleveland Commission on 'the Property and Income of the Universities of Oxford and Cambridge, and of...[their] Colleges and Halls' (the most detailed listing ever made), the Oxford college accounts (published annually since 1883), and the analyses published by Langford Lovell Price, treasurer of Oriel, have also supplied valuable information.[16]

During the sixteenth and early seventeenth century rising population pushed up the price of agricultural produce, while greater productivity was bringing down the real costs of agricultural production, and agricultural wages did not increase as fast as prices.[17] A concern to ensure that corporate landlords should share in the benefits of this process lay behind legislation in the parliaments of 1571 and 1572 to control the length of leases, and the colleges of Oxford, Cambridge, Winchester, and Eton were the specific beneficiaries of the Corn Rent Act of 1576.[18] In the fifteenth century colleges, unlike some other ecclesiastical landlords, had mostly let their non-urban

---

[15] OCA TF1/A1/5, treasurers' accounts 1583–1649; TF1/A1/6, 1650–1727; TF1/A1/8, 1728–64; TF1/A1/9, 1765–95; TF1/A1/10, 1796–1829; TF1/A1/11, 1830–65; TF1/A1/12, 1866–90; TF1/A1/13, 1866–1908, TF1/A1/14, 1909–27; fine books, TF1/B4/1, 1726–57, TF1/B4/2, 1757–74, TF1/B4/3, 1765–1807, TF1/B4/4, 1774–1823, and Est A2/B2, 1775–1866.

[16] PP 1873 xxxvii parts 1 and 2; [University of Oxford], *Abstracts of the Accounts of the Curators of the University Chest..., together with the Accounts of the Colleges* (Oxford, 1884 ff.), hereafter *Accounts of the Colleges*; Price, 'The Recent Depression in Agriculture', his follow-up articles on the accounts of the colleges collectively, *Jl. of the Royal Statistical Society*, 55 (1892), 58 (1895), 67 (1904), and 'The Estates of the Colleges of Oxford', *Surveyors' Institution Transactions*, 45 (1912–13).

[17] P. Bowden, 'Agricultural Prices, Farm Profits, and Rents', in J. I. Thirsk (ed.), *The Agrarian History of England and Wales 1500–1640* (Cambridge, 1967), 674.

[18] 13 Eliz. I cap 10, 14 Eliz. I cap 11, 18 Eliz. I cap 6, *Enactments*, i. 176–7, 188–91. This legislation is conveniently explained in G. E. Aylmer, 'The Economics and Finances of the Colleges and University c1530–1640', in HUO iii. 534–6. See too J. P. D. Dunbabin, 'College Estates and Wealth 1660–1815', in HUO v. 270; Bowden, 'Agricultural Prices, Farm Profits, and Rents', 687.

properties on short leases, normally for terms of ten years or less. Such terms lengthened from the start of the next century. Between 1532 and 1568 Balliol leased some of its properties for terms of thirty-one, fifty-one, sixty-three, and seventy years. At Magdalen, perhaps between 1561 and 1591, a system of 'beneficial' leases was introduced, whereby leases for terms as long as ninety-nine years at relatively low annual rents were balanced by very high entry fines.[19] Leaving aside for the moment the fact that these fines came to be divided between the individual fellows rather than paid into the common funds of the society, the obvious dangers were that colleges would lose the opportunity to renegotiate rents to match changing conditions, and that the real value of fixed rents would be eroded by inflation. The measures of 1571–2 limited to forty years the maximum term for which a college's urban property could be leased, that for rural property to twenty-one years or three lives.

The length of Oriel's leases, too, increased during the sixteenth century. Thomas Peniston had a lease of Dean and Chalford for the eight years from 1536 to 1544, having probably been in occupation since 1534 when he paid a fine of £66 13s. 4d. But in 1560 the reversion of Dean and Chalford was granted to John Gore, a former fellow, for a term of twenty-one years; in 1564 Thomas Badnoll took Littleworth for sixty years, and Moreton Pinkney was leased for twenty-one years. In 1565 Eltham rectory was leased for forty years; and the college allowed Provost Marbeck's brother a similar lease of Dean and Chalford, though this was, at the instance of the earl of Leicester, superseded the following year by a sixty-year lease to Ralph Sheldon for an entry fine of £266 13s. 4d.[20] However, like other colleges Oriel seems to have observed the restrictions on the length of leases imposed by the legislation of 1571–2, both immediately and in succeeding centuries. In 1595 the college's lands in Castle Combe and Sevington were leased for twenty-one years to Anthony Brewer, then a bible clerk in the college, in succession to his father; in 1601 the same properties were granted to Brewer for three lives. In 1606 the rectory of Coleby was leased to John Dackam, armiger, for three lives; Littleworth was granted in 1624 to Sir William Curten for twenty-one years.[21] It was twenty-one years rather than three lives that became the standard term in leases of Oriel's rural estates. And forty years emerged as the normal term for leases of its urban properties, though in fact much shorter terms (commonly twenty years) were usual before 1571. It also became normal at Oriel, as elsewhere, to grant a lease for twenty-one years, but to renew it and take a new fine after seven years (strictly speaking, to comply with the legislation,

---

[19] T. A. R. Evans and R. J. Faith, 'College Estates and University Finances 1350–1500', in HUO ii. 678–82; G. D. Duncan, 'The Property of Balliol College c1500–c1640', appendix I to Aylmer, 'Economics and Finances', HUO iii. 567–8; for Magdalen see H. E. Salter (ed.), *A Cartulary of the Hospital of St John the Baptist*, 3 vols. (OHS lxvi, lxviii, lxix, 1914–16), iii. 333–4.
[20] DR 68, 100, 102–3, 146, 150, 154, 155, 156.
[21] DR 206–7, 215, 288.

the old lease was not renewed but a new one created). Leases of urban properties might be renewed after fourteen years.[22]

The provisions of the Corn Rent Act of 1576 were more complex. When a new lease of a college's property was made, one third of the old rent was to be paid either in wheat and malt, or as its cash equivalent. If, as became normal, this reserved portion of the rent was actually paid in cash, it was expressed first as quantities of wheat or malt based on prices specified in the act (10*d*. for a bushel of wheat and 7½*d*. for a bushel of malt) and then converted back to cash according to the current Oxford market price for college purposes.[23] The consequent increase in the value of the reserved third, termed the increment of corn rent or just the corn rent, provided a measure of protection against inflation. Whenever the rent of a property was payable, it had to be recalculated against the current price of wheat and malt. Such calculations are indeed preserved in the Oriel treasurers' accounts. Soon after 1576, in the accounting year 1582–3, John Southby renewed his lease of Monksmill at Wadley, at an annual rent divided into two instalments of 30*s*.; in that year corn rent was calculated only on the second instalment, presumably the first after the renewal. In 1583–4 corn rent was calculated separately for each instalment. The first was payable at Michaelmas 1583, and one third of that 30*s*. was reckoned to be 'paid as 5 bushels (modii) of wheat at 10*d* the bushel and 8 bushels of malt at 7½*d* the bushel, which wheat and malt were sold for 26*s*, that is the wheat at 2*s* 4*d* the bushel and the malt at 18*d* the bushel'. A similar calculation was made for the 30*s*. payable at Lady Day 1584, based on current prices of 2*s*. 2*d*. for wheat and 18*d*. for malt, giving a total of 25*s*. rather than 26*s*. for the revalued reserved third. Thus the corn rent took the total from a nominal £3 to £4 11*s*., an increase of 52 per cent. The rent actually received from a property could of course vary significantly from year to year with fluctuations in the price of corn. Receipts from Monksmill in the following seven years until Southby's death in 1590–1 were £4 12*s*., £5 18*s*., £7 3*s*. 4*d*., £4 10*s*., £4 12*s*., £5 4*s*. 8*d*., and £5 4*s*. 8*d*. again. As further new leases were granted after 1576 corn rents spread across the college's properties, and several such calculations had to be made each year. Corn rents did not become quite universal. They applied to leasehold for set terms but not to copyhold, nor probably to tenure at will; rectories were sometimes leased for fixed cash sums; and at Swainswick in Somerset, where all lessees were paying corn rent in the later eighteenth century, most rents had by the 1830s been converted to fixed cash payments.

It is hard to know exactly how the college found lessees for its properties, and what kind of bargaining might have preceded the grant of a lease.

---

[22] Dunbabin, 'College Estates 1660–1815', 270, 284; *Enactments*, i. 190. The Dean's Register includes leases of various Oxford properties before 1571.

[23] Oxford corn market prices were still being reported to the Committee of College Estates Bursars in 1996, though by then only for traditional reasons.

The college agreed in 1542 to grant a twenty-year lease of Coleby, after the expiry of the current lease, to whomever the king might nominate; the role of the earl of Leicester in securing a lease for a client in 1566 has already been mentioned; and John Dackam owed his 1606 lease of Coleby (for a fine of 200 marks) to the backing of Robert Cecil earl of Salisbury, at a time when Oriel needed powerful friends in view of its dispute with the lessee of Wadley. External patronage and pressure may well have been at work at other times without leaving a trace in the records. In the sixteenth century Oriel sometimes leased its properties to former fellows or the relatives or associates of the provost or current fellows. In 1522 Stowford was leased to Provost James More and his assign, Robert Gough, for ten years, or longer should he wish; the rent was to be 30s. if the provost held the property himself, 40s. if it was taken by Gough. On the same day a five-year lease of Littlemore was given in reversion to William Freeman, who resigned his fellowship to marry, and much later became president of the College of Physicians. It was agreed in 1533 that Robert James should have a five-year lease of Stowford when he resigned his fellowship; he was no longer a fellow in 1541, when the reversion was confirmed, and his term as lessee of Stowford ended in 1549. The John Griffith DCL who leased Eltham for forty years from 1565 was probably the former fellow of that name. John Belley, provost from 1566 to 1574, secured the lease of Swainswick for his brother in 1568; in 1585, no longer provost, he became the lessee of Coleby.[24]

Equally there might often have been an influential local family, like the Untons at Wadley, with some expectation of being offered the lease, and the college may have had little scope, or indeed reason, for bypassing such natural lessees. Many lessees of Oriel's larger properties were described as gentleman, esquire, armiger, knight, or baronet. They included Sir William Hill at Dean and Chalford, Sir Henry Purefoy, Bt., and Sir Willoughby Aston, Bt., at Wadley in the 1680s; Sir Edward Gascoigne, Bt., at Aberford and Sir John Boyce at Bartlemas in the 1730s. Thomas Scrope at Coleby, John Mander at Littleworth, Charles Pye at Wadley, and William Sanford at Swainswick in the 1780s were all styled armiger, as were Thomas Evans at Dean and Charles Bourchier at Littleworth in the 1830s. Even lessees of smaller properties included Sir John Curson, Bt., at Waterperry in the 1630s and 1680s and John Aubrey, armiger, at Oriel Wood in the 1780s.

William Roper, the son of John Roper, attorney-general to Henry VIII and the son-in-law of Sir Thomas More, owned the estate of Well Hall in Eltham and several manors elsewhere in Kent. According to Daniel Lysons, writing in the late eighteenth century, and perhaps not entirely accurately, Roper bought the rectory of Eltham about 1550 and then sold it to Oriel on

---

[24] DR 120 (1542), 156 (1566); 57, 58, 94, 116, 129, 155, 158, 160; 233 (1606).

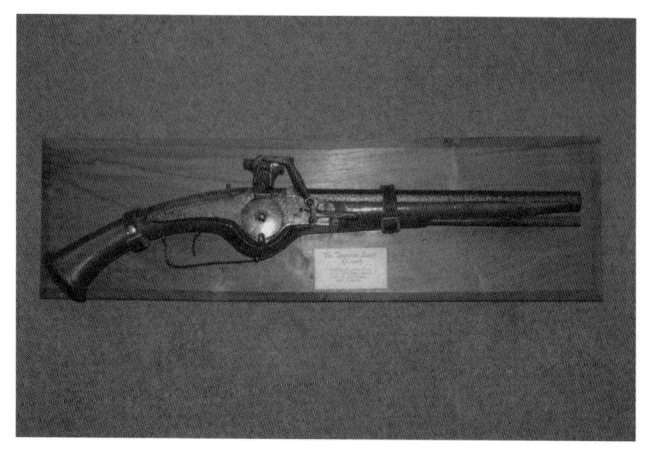

ILLUSTRATION 15.1 The Treasurers' Pistol for protection against highwaymen
Oriel College

condition that it should be leased back periodically to his heirs for terms of three lives or twenty-one years at an annual rent of £14 with a fine of £100 on each renewal. On Anthony Roper's death the trustees of his under-age son failed to renew the lease and the college granted it to Christopher Comport, gentleman, of Eltham. It subsequently passed to Comport's daughter and heir Alice, wife of Sir Thomas Fitch, to Alice, daughter and heir of Sir Comport Fitch, Bt. (died 1720) and wife of Sir John Barker, Bt., whose son Sir John Fitch Barker died without issue in 1766 and left his interest in the rectory to Robert Nassau esquire; the lease was then purchased by John Green.[25] This succession from the later sixteenth to the later eighteenth century illustrates how changes in the lessees' surname can conceal continuity of tenure within a family over a long period.

Individual holdings within some of the college's estates might be valuable enough to command high fines and require a lessee of substance. This was particularly true when previous leases had expired, enabling the college to grant—and charge for—a full new twenty-one-year lease. Thus at Shenington, though the rent of one property (formerly Ashworth's) was only some £9 p.a., in 1760 its twenty-one-year lease to Mr Hewens commanded a fine of

---

[25] D. Lysons, *The Environs of London*, 4 vols. (London, 1792–6), iv. 394–421; but cf. Vallis, 'Estates of Oriel', 41, who suggests that the college's share (five-sixths of the tithes) had been bought by the provost from Roper's predecessor Walter Hendley and transferred to the college by 1564. See too ODNB s.n. Roper, William and Fitch, Sir Thomas. Anthony Roper appears in the treasurers' accounts in the 1630s, Sir Thomas Fitch in the 1680s, and Lady Fitch, widow, in the 1730s; the executors of Lady Barker are succeeded by Lady Ann Green in the 1780s; a John Green was still the lessee in the 1830s.

£440, not so much less than the £600 Sir Willoughby Aston had paid in the previous year for the renewal (after seven years) of the very valuable manor of Wadley. Similarly in 1792 the Revd Edward Hughes paid £750 for a twenty-one-year lease of lands (formerly Goodchild's) that had previously been rack-rented; and when a holding at Swainswick 'fell into the hands of the college by the death of Mr Burton' in 1771, Oriel next year secured from the Revd James Morgan a fine of £840 for a new lease.[26] Usually the status of lessees is not apparent in the college's estate records. It might be expected that most tenants of sub-manorial tenements would be prosperous husbandmen. But leased lands were very frequently sub-let, often in combination with holdings of other ownerships. Perhaps for this reason, we encounter several small lessees of gentry status, like Lady Dochen at Shenington in the 1630s or Lady Lee at Dean, Lady Elizabeth Townsend at Shenington, and Thomas Kington, armiger, at Swainswick in the 1830s. Clergymen who leased holdings within a manor included John Townsend and Joseph Davie at Shenington, Peter Gunning (who held four separate holdings, the leases of some at least of which he had inherited) and James Morgan at Swainswick in the 1780s, J. P. Maude at Swainswick in the 1830s, and J. Earle, W. S. Vale, and H. R. Wilkins at Swainswick in the later nineteenth century. The college's sub-manorial holdings and urban tenements may often have been attractive to a range of potential lessees, giving it some room for bargaining, though the details are rarely recorded. Martin Boswell agreed to pay a fine of £192 to take a house in St Mary Hall Lane in Oxford for forty years from Michaelmas 1782, but proved unable to find the money and had to forfeit the contract after paying the rent for the year 1782–3; the lease was taken from Michaelmas 1783 by Edward Rusbridge at a fine of £170.[27]

The value of a property or group of properties might remain stable for long periods, but it could also change dramatically, either absolutely or in relation to the estate as a whole. In 1585–6 the four rectories of Aberford in Yorkshire, Coleby in Lincolnshire, Moreton Pinkney in Northamptonshire, and Eltham in Kent brought in £49, some 20 per cent of the college's current estate rental of £252 (all subtotals are here rounded to the nearest pound). Rents from the town of Oxford provided £41 (16 per cent), rural properties in Oxfordshire, together with Oriel Wood in Buckinghamshire, yielded £58 (23 per cent), the estates in Berkshire £66 (26 per cent), those in Wiltshire just £6 (2 per cent), and in Somerset £21 (8 per cent); the annuity from the Essex lands was fixed at £10 (4 per cent). The total of occasional income from estates, payments beyond the current year's rent, varied greatly from year to year. In 1585–6 it was unusually high at £49, made up from sales of wood

---

[26] OCA TF 1 A9/1, fine book 1757–74, unpaginated.
[27] OCA EST/A2/B2, register of leases 1765–1807 (foliation ends after fo. 51), fos. 49–51 and unnumbered folios.

from Bartlemas and Stowford, a few rents paid in advance of the next year, a fine of £10 from the lessee of Aberford, and £13 6s. 8d. in part payment of a fine by the lessee of Coleby. The college's non-estate income was also liable to wide fluctuation and came this year from such sources as payments relating to the church of St Mary in Oxford, the goods of a deceased brother of St Bartholomew's hospital, the fixed fee farm of £19 for that hospital from the corporation of Oxford, and the admission fees of commoners.

Fifty years later, in the accounting year 1635–6, the relative value of the various groups of properties had changed only slightly, but the total annual rental had risen from £252 to £466. Such a change was by no means unusual in this period, when the greater profits to be made from agriculture allowed landlords to ask for much higher rents. Landed families in various parts of England doubled or trebled their rental income between the 1580s and 1630s. Specific local factors might hold back a landowner's ability to raise rents, and colleges in particular may have been more inclined to extract high entry fines than to raise rents. The rents paid by Balliol's lessees changed hardly at all between the 1540s and 1640. But Balliol seems atypical: if there was no great increase in colleges' revenues from 1540 to 1580, and indeed some houses found themselves in occasional financial difficulty, there was generally a substantial increase between the 1580s or 1590s and 1640.[28] This was the case at Oriel. It happened, however, in an era that has been termed the 'Great Inflation'; and though finding an appropriate index is not unproblematic, some allowance must be made for this. Contemporaries recognized the centrality of grain prices, and if we apply these as a crude deflator, there had been hardly any gain;[29] if, instead, we use Phelps-Brown and Hopkins's indices of the prices of 'Composite Unit of Consumables', the gain would seem to have been of the order of 10 per cent. (See Table 15.1.)

As Oriel's rents in the town of Oxford had increased from £41 in 1585–6 only to £46 in 1635–6 and the annuity for the Essex lands was constant at £10.40, their proportion of the total had fallen to 10 per cent and 2 per cent respectively. The shares of Berkshire (25 per cent), Wiltshire (4 per cent) and Somerset (7 per cent) had hardly changed, since their absolute levels had risen more or less in line with the overall growth of the college's rents. But the yield of the four churches outside Oxfordshire had more than doubled, to £110. So they now accounted for 24 per cent of the annual rental. The rental of the Oxfordshire estates had swelled most of all, to £136, much more than

---

[28] Bowden in *Agrarian History of England*, iv. 690–1; Duncan, 'Balliol', HUO iii. 563–6; Aylmer, 'Economics and Finances', HUO iii. 532–3.

[29] If adjusted by the ratio of 'all grains' prices in the 1630s to those of the 1580s, the £466 of 1635–6 would have been worth only £267.48 half a century before, if by the ratio of 'all agricultural products' only £262.36—*The Agrarian History of England and Wales*, iv, 1500–1640, tables 8 and 13. On the difficulty of assessing inflation in this period see Aylmer, 'Economics and Finances', 546–7.

TABLE 15.1 Rental, 1585–6 to 1735–6[a]

Sample year		Nominal value in pounds	Value in 1736 pounds
1585–86	Current estate rental	252	386
1635–36	Total annual rental	466	424
1685–86	Money rental excluding money paid for arrears	457	441
1735–36	Total current rental	473	473

[a] The conversion into 1736 pounds has been made using the indexes of the price of composite unit of consumables in southern England in H. Phelps-Brown and Sheila V. Hopkins, 'Seven Centuries of the Price of Consumables', *Economica*, 92 (November 1956), 312–73, which draws in part on the accounts of colleges and hospitals in south-east England.

twice the figure fifty years earlier, and formed 29 per cent of the new total. In all, estate revenue accounted for 93 per cent of the treasurers' gross income (net of arrears) of £481.

Non-rental estate income in 1635–6 amounted to just £15, derived from sales of wood and pasture and heriots from copyhold tenants. The sale of pasture at Bartlemas provided a steady £2 in this period. The provision of bundles of firewood to the college from Stowford and Bartlemas appears in the accounts as internal sales for sums of between £1 and £3. These were distinguished from other sales of firewood at Bartlemas for £4 2s. in 1635–6. Entire trees at Bartlemas and Stowford were sold in 1633–4 for £3 and £1 15s. respectively. Income from heriots on those manors where the college had copyhold tenants was by its nature irregular, but provided £11 from Swainswick and Shenington in 1633–4, £9 5s. from Dean and Swainswick in 1634–5, £7 12s. from Swainswick and Shenington in 1635–6, and £1 13s. 4d. from Dean in 1636–7; by contrast no heriot fell due in 1632–3. Income from heriots had been recorded in the accounts of the 1580s, but income from pasture and timber was then all but absent.

It was of course the change in rents paid by lessees that had caused the massive rise in estate income since the 1580s. In most cases a new lease at a higher rent had been issued in the intervening period, but when the lease included corn rent the precise sum received each year also varied with the price of corn. In 1585–6 Thomas Bucktrout rendered £13 18s. for the rectory of Aberford in Yorkshire. This seems to have been the first year of a new lease for he also paid an entry fine of £10. In 1582–3 and 1583–4 he had paid just £7 13s. 4d., presumably with no corn rent. Under his new lease the variability of corn rent could make his total as low as £11 8s. 8½d. in 1589–90 or as high as £15 10s. 6½d. in 1590–1. By 1635–6 Sir Thomas Bland was paying £20 6s. 2½d. for Aberford, again with some annual fluctuation reflecting the price of corn. Wadley had from 1539 been leased for £58 a year, but in

1606 Oriel managed (as we shall see below) to increase this to £100. In the 1580s the adjacent manor of Littleworth was let to Thomas Badnoll for £2 6s. 8d., and the lease passed to Henry Badnoll at the same fixed rent. Littleworth was held in the 1630s by Sir William Curten for a corn rent that produced £6–7. The mill at Wadley called Monksmill was held in the 1580s by John Southby at a rent that yielded £3 18s. in 1585–6. It passed briefly to his widow in 1591–2 and then to Francis Young with no significant change in rent. But in 1635–6 it was held by George Purefoy, who then paid £8 2s. 6d. Thus the Berkshire estates that had returned £66 in 1585–6 produced £115 in 1635–6.

In other properties the constituent units leased out might change. In 1585–6 Richard Grimes, the college's bailiff at Shenington, accounted for £13 4s. 8d. from three-quarters of the college's land—described as demesne but evidently occupied by copyhold tenants—while John Grimes paid £4 2s. 6½d. for the other quarter. In addition Nicholas Durram owed a rent of 2s., the vicar an annual payment of just 2d., and, this year for the first time, John Wilmot a rent of 3s. 4d., making a total from Shenington of £17 12s. 8½d. Fifty years later the bailiff, John Grimes, was returning a steady £14 8s. 9½d. p.a. from the tenants of lands and cottages, not much more than in 1585–6. But five lessees, Lady Dochen, Martin Meake, William Palmer, Richard Grimes, and John Wilmot, were each paying rents that, though varying with the price of corn, fell within a band between £1 5s. and £3 10s., Meake and Palmer apparently holding equal shares of a single divided property. More generally Oriel seems to have had there:

1619 14 copyholders	6 leaseholders	
1737 6 copyholders	3 leaseholders	6 cottagers
1760 6 copyholders	8 leaseholders	6 cottagers

After enclosure in 1780, Oriel had seven lessees, and by 1813 fifteen, with a number of copyholders converting to leasehold when extending or renewing their terms.[30]

If Oriel's money rental had nearly doubled between 1585–6 and 1635–6, fifty years on again, in 1685–6, it had at £457 (or £475 including arrears from Swainswick) changed remarkably little in money terms, and risen only slightly in terms of the Phelps-Brown–Hopkins index. The yield of the Somerset lands had risen from £33 to £41, that is from 7 to 9 per cent of the total, while the share of the other regions had changed by 1 per cent at most. In all, estate income represented 89 per cent of the college's income. As to non-estate income, by the later seventeenth century the college was receiving a modest but fairly stable income from St Mary's,

---

[30] VCH *Oxfordshire*, ix. 143, 145–6.

the university church. In the 1680s oblations were fixed at £3 7s. 6d., and there were payments relating to graduations (in 1685–6 £4 11s. 6d. was received from bachelors determining in the faculty of arts and 12s. from doctors). The college was also receiving quite significant amounts from internal payments. In this year the treasurers accounted for £7 and £9 15s. under the heads respectively of rent for rooms and presentations. Payments by probationary fellows called refection fees (refectiones) amounted to £15.

A source of income that occurs sporadically in the accounts is the sale of timber. Wood is of course a slow maturing crop, and timber sales were a welcome but very occasional source of income. Each college found its own way of allocating such irregular profits. At All Souls a decree of 1619 made it clear that the proceeds were to go mainly into the college's funds, though the individuals involved in securing the sale were to receive a small share. Conversely at Emmanuel College, Cambridge, all income from timber sales was from early in the seventeenth century divided among the fellows along with fines, and the same was probably true of Corpus Christi College, Oxford, from the 1540s.[31] In 1638 the Visitor of Magdalen reproved its fellows for dishonestly felling more trees than they needed for repairs in order to increase their dividend. During the Civil Wars the loss of some regular sources of income and the imposition of extraordinary expenses drove colleges to sell off more timber than they might normally have thought prudent: in 1643, in order to meet wartime costs, Oriel raised nearly £280 from the sale of wood. New College was said to have felled a huge number of trees at Stanton St John, near Oriel's property of Stowford, in 1649, and All Souls made substantial wood sales, averaging some £225 in the twelve years for which figures survive between 1646–6 and 1659–60.[32]

Through the eighteenth century All Souls, Wadham, and, more especially, New College received a considerable, if irregular, income from the sale of wood.[33] Oriel's estates did not include much woodland, and the most important holding, the 20-acre Oriel Wood, was leased out like any other

---

[31] Aylmer, 'Economics and Finances', HUO iii. 528–9 (All Souls); S. Bendall, 'Estate Management and Finances 1584–1719', in S. Bendall, C. Brooke, and P. Collinson, *A History of Emmanuel College, Cambridge* (Woodbridge, 1999), 174 (Emmanuel); Duncan, 'Accounts of Corpus Christi', HUO iii. 577–8. For the management by Queens' College, Cambridge, of its timber see J. Twigg, *A History of Queens' College, Cambridge, 1448–1986* (Woodbridge, 1987), 113–14.

[32] J. Twigg, 'College Finances, 1640–1660', in HUO iv. 789–91; DR 309. For its early seventeenth-century rebuilding Oriel had used its own wood (and stone), authorized a £100 sale of timber, and sold fallen trees at Wadley for £143.33 (DR 204 (1606), 248–9 (1619), 255 (1621)).

[33] Their average annual takings in the 1730s were £5, £68, and £659 respectively, in the 1810s £507, £636, and £3,010—Dunbabin, 'College Estates 1660–1815', HUO v. 289 and table 10.4.

property.³⁴ Ordinarily when estates were leased, the standing timber remained the landlord's property. Oriel sought to exploit this in 1637, when (in order to rebuild the college) it resolved to require the loan of a year's rent from all its tenants, with the threat that, were this refused, timber of equivalent value on their lands would be felled.³⁵ More conventionally, we find occasional sales of wood (£31 in 1583–4, but usually much less) from Bartlemas and Stowford in the treasurers' accounts of the 1580s and of the 1630s, and from Dean and Chalford and Swainswick in the 1780s (as much as £48 in 1785–6). But the fine books show that in the intervening period the proceeds of wood sales were generally divided between the fellows, not paid into the college's common funds: in 1733 £2 for cutting trees at Swainswick was thus divided, as was, in 1740, another £100 for timber felled there. John Quatermain of Cowley gave £5 for seven ash trees at Bartlemas in February 1747, and the sale of large trees from Oriel Wood yielded £46 6s. 6d. at Michaelmas 1750, £21 4s. in June 1757 and £43 10s. at Lady Day 1764. When a lessee was due to pay eleven guineas in 1761 for rather over 2½ acres of woodland at Swainswick, he was allowed one for 'mounding', which suggests some measure of active oversight by the college. And the lease book records that in 1773–4 the college's coppice at Swainswick was cut and sold for £22, while in 1775 Thomas Child, the lessee of Castle Combe in Wiltshire, paid £80 11s. for timber. This was the last sale recorded in the fine books. In the 1780s timber sales were again passing through the treasurers' accounts, though later they seem to have been diverted to the college bag (one of the college's cash funds). Annual receipts for timber averaged £124.50 between 1856 and 1870, but 89 per cent of this was accounted for by takings in 1856 and 1870.³⁶ It was perhaps because this revenue was so very occasional that it was not treated in a consistent manner.

Managing the estates must have required much unquantifiable time and effort on the part of the provost, some fellows, and the college's servants. The 1536 lease of Dean and Chalford bound the lessee, twice a year on two days' notice, to find food and drink for the provost and three companions, plus fodder for their horses, for two days and one night; by the eighteenth century the number to be entertained had risen to five, and the later leases usually included a clause specifying that, during their stay, 'the Provost and Fellows should have the use of the parlour and two good beds and bedchambers'.³⁷

---

³⁴ In 1785 the fine was calculated on the basis that, when coppiced every nine years, its wood should be worth £120; but prices might be lower 'shd the Oxford Canal take place'. Another 20-acre wood (at Spelsbury, near Dean) was said in 1871 never to be let, but its underwood 'was cut and sold periodically, and timber cut by the college' (PP 1873 xxxvii part 2, 315).
³⁵ DR 286–7.
³⁶ PP 1873 xxxvii part 2, 321.
³⁷ M. D. Lobel, *The History of Dean and Chalford* (Oxfordshire Records Society xvii, 1935), 71, 148. However fishing as well as business was the reason for some of these visits.

But specific charges are hard to detect in the accounts. In 1685–6 the evident costs of running the estates amount to barely £16, or 3 per cent of gross receipts. This includes the regular £6 13*s.* 4*d.* paid to Nathaniel Clarke, the vicar of Coleby; £1 5*s.* 1*d.* was paid to discharge the tithes of Lockmead; quitrents for certain Oxford properties, including 4*s.* to University College for the provost's stable, totalled £1 18*s.* 6*d.*, and the fixed annual allowance of £4 to feed the provost's horses is here considered an estate expense. The treasurers themselves got £1 6*s.* 8*d.* as their stipends, plus various more or less customary allowances including 2*s.* 6*d.* for writing the treasurers' account and 4*d.* for parchment and ink, while the steward received a stipend of £1 and the bailiffs of Dean and of Shenington 5*s.* and 9*s.* 4*d.* respectively. In some years a particular property gave rise to specific costs. Thus Mr Forward was paid 4*s.* 6*d.* and Mr Wilmot 3*s.* 6*d.* for their visits to Shenington in 1632–3; two years later John Edmunds received £2 in respect of college business at Dean; in 1636–7 Mr Hornie was reimbursed £3 7*s.* in connection with a lawsuit about Stowford, while an attorney was paid no less than £14.[38] From time to time fellows were appointed to attend manorial courts. Thus on 16 July 1519 William Freeman and William Rose were assigned to the court of Dean; on 17 October 1552 the college decreed that the provost, the dean, William Collinge, and John Edwardes should before next Michaelmas hold courts at Dean and Shenington, where they were to deal with all matters that appeared to affect the college's rights; and on 10 July 1587 it was decided that a court should be held at Swainswick, with Richard Pigot chosen to accompany the provost. The treasurer's accounts duly record that in 1586–7 the provost and Mr Pigot went to Swainswick, at a cost of £1 14*s.* 4*d.*; the provost returned two years later with the dean, incurring similar costs. In 1650 a scale of daily allowances for travelling on college business was established: 11*s.* for the provost and his servant, 7*s.* for a fellow, 6*s.* for the steward.[39] But even the larger sums of this kind seem slight when set against the college's rental income.

Over time the system naturally evolved. By the 1730s the treasurers' share of the fees for sealing leases and copyholds had been commuted to £6 p.a. for the senior and £4 p.a. for the junior treasurer;[40] and in the 1780s they were also receiving poundage on butter (worth £4 5*s.* 9½*d.* each in 1785–6). More

---

[38] Bagnall-Wild, 'Oriel's Agricultural Property', 12, observes that a 'striking feature' of Oriel's records 'is the considerable number of law suits about property'. In 1524, when Cardinal Wolsey made an award over Bartlemas in Oriel's favour, the Dean's Register advised avoiding the Court of the Exchequer should Oxford ever revive the dispute, 'as I believe we should never have got any of the holding's rent had we continued our case there' (DR 60).

[39] DR 49, 134, 191, 325.

[40] Fees were charged for sealing leases and copyholds: in the 1730s £2 was commonly paid for the treasurers, £1 3*s.* 6*d.* to the steward, 2*s.* 6*d.* each to the bible clerk and the servant (probably the treasurers' assistant), making a total of £3 8*s.* 6*d.*; for small copyholds this occasionally exceeded the fine charged. For a licence to alienate (that is to pass on/sell the lease/copyhold) a further half sealing fee of £1 14*s.* 3*d.* was added. The treasurers' fees were in fact paid into the

significantly Oriel had been among the earliest colleges to open a London bank account (with Hoare's in 1719), presumably chiefly for its security of deposit, and in 1799 an Oxford account (with 'Messrs. Fletcher & Parsons').[41] But continuities were far more marked. The identifiable costs of running the estate in 1785–6 can be put at about 3 per cent of gross receipts, much as they had been a century earlier. This calculation includes the formal remuneration of the treasurers, the steward's stipend of £10, and the customary £4 for feeding the provost's horses (unchanged since the 1580s). In 1785–6, the treasurers and steward were also refunded £2.98 for expenses incurred on college business (£12.98 in 1784–5, £4.98 in 1786–7). The treasurers were assisted by a servant named Lyne who was paid a guinea a year. Thomas Calcott, bailiff of Dean, received two guineas, and James Combe, bailiff of Wadley, five. John Plumb, bailiff of Shenington, was paid 15s., plus 6s. in respect of the obligation to attend the court of Tewkesbury. William Palmer was paid for attendance at courts in the local parishes of St Mary Magdalen, St Giles, St Clement, and Headington, 6d. for each. And a man named Budd was paid 5s. each year for looking after Oriel Wood, even though the property was held by a lessee. Quitrents in Oxford amounted to £1 18s. 10d. In the 1730s the cost of writing college letters (6d. in 1686–7) varied between one and six shillings, but by the 1780s there was a fixed annual allowance of a shilling.

The rents of the broadest sample of colleges conveniently available increased by a third between 1689–90 and 1739–40.[42] But in 1735–6 Oriel's estate income looked very much as it had fifty or a hundred years before. Total current rental was £473, almost exactly the same as the £457 of 1685–6—a gain of 7 per cent according to the Phelps-Brown–Hopkins index. Once more the share of the various regions had changed by at most 1 or 2 per cent. Estate income other than current rental at first sight seems higher, at £58. But of this, £46 represented arrears of rent, suggesting that delays in payment had become a serious issue. In the 1630s late payment of rent by the college's lessees and manorial bailiffs appears to have been negligible, but by the 1680s a few lessees were failing to pay on time, though payment was not long delayed. The rounded total of rent defaults (defalcata) at the close of the accounting year at Michaelmas 1683, 1684, 1685, 1686, and 1687 was £20, £1, £18, £16, and £11. Strangely the rent of Moreton Pinkney,

---

college's funds, and it is only these that appear in the treasurers' accounts to indicate the granting or renewal of a lease or some other such transaction.

[41] Audit Memoranda (OCA TF 1 A 9/1), November 1799; Donald Adamson, 'Child's Bank and Oxford University in the Eighteenth Century', *Three Banks Review*, 136 (1982), 45–52. Unlike e.g. All Souls, Oriel had few properties in places where it would have been safer to deposit the rents directly into a London bank; but a London account may have been a good place to receive large fine payments from wealthy or upper-class lessees.

[42] All Souls, Balliol, BNC, CCC, Ch.Ch., Lincoln, New, St John's, and Wadham—Dunbabin, 'College Estates 1660–1815', HUO v. 275.

£50 in full, was between three and five shillings short each year. Thomas Sylvester defaulted in the payment of half or all of his 10s. annual rent for land at Burford in three of these years, and in two Daniel Grimes produced only half of his rent of about £3 for a tenement at Shenington. More substantially Mr Blake, who owed more than £30 for land at Swainswick, held back between £14 and £18 in three of these years; in one year this was said to be for lands and cottages that were decayed (debilis), and it is possible that Blake was finding it hard to get tenants for them. And in 1686–7 the municipality of Oxford failed to pay half its fee farm of £19 on time. With the possible exception in some years of the slight underpayment from Moreton Pinkney, these defaults were made good in the following accounting year.

By the 1730s there was more late payment, and in a few cases the delays were longer. The total of rents unpaid at the end of one accounting year could be around £20, £50, or even £80, but they were largely paid off in the next. Indeed by this time the accounts had separate sections for defaults of the current and earlier years. Most lessees paid on time, while a handful more or less persistently fell behind; those who did so were more often the holders of small than of large properties. At Michaelmas 1733 some £27 of rent was overdue, mostly for the current year. Current rents were outstanding from Oriel Wood, the plot at Faringdon, both tenants at Burford, the lessees of all the properties in Wiltshire, that of Monksmill, and some but not all of the tenants at Shenington, among whom John Grimes owed £14 8s. 9d. Those who owed rent for part or all of earlier years included the bailiff of Shenington, who had not paid £7 1s. 2d. for the half year to Lady Day 1732. In the following four years it was these properties, sometimes with the addition of Littleworth, Dean, Wadley, and Swainswick, that generated arrears. Most often a late payment for one year was received in the next. Thus the half year's rent of £50 that Richard Aston failed to deliver for Wadley in 1733–4 (perhaps as a by-product of the dispute over the renewal of his leases) swelled that year's total of defaults to more than £80, but was received in the following year. By contrast the lessee of Ryles farm paid his rent for 1732–3 and 1733–4 a year late, but then stopped paying at all, so that by Michaelmas 1737 three years' rent (£18.75) was outstanding. John Gunning, who leased holdings at Swainswick, failed to pay in 1733–4, paid in full in the next two years, but did not pay in 1736–7, ending that year with arrears of £5 3s. 10½d. By the same date John Hawten, a tenant at Shenington, was no fewer than seven years in arrears and owed the college £7 18s. 10¾d.

Later in the century arrears became more common. Tenants at Moreton Pinkney, Coleby, Dean, Littleworth, Faringdon, Christian Malford, Shenington, Burford, Oriel Wood, Stadhampton, Cowley, Bartlemas, and Swainswick failed to pay part or all of their current rents on time in one or more of the five years between 1782–3 and 1786–7. But the number of rents more than one year overdue was low, and had been entirely eliminated by

Michaelmas 1785. In 1785–6 some £92 of arrears were paid off, and at the end of the year only £21 7s. 10d. of the current year's rents were outstanding; a year later the figure was just £14 14s. 11d. Nevertheless Oriel resolved at the Easter audit 1786 'That the names of the College Tenants who have not paid their rent & arrears before Mids[ummer] day be regularly given into the College Steward, who will be directed to proceed against them'.[43] Whatever the circumstances that made it difficult for particular lessees to pay their rents in these years, Oriel may have worked hard to contain the arrears to the extent that it did.

Not all the income from college estates passed through the main corporate accounts, significant amounts being instead divided between the head and fellows individually. Arrangements differed between the various Oxford and Cambridge colleges, but in the later sixteenth and seventeenth century it became normal for at least part of the entry fines paid by lessees taking up or renewing leases to be so divided. Even within a single college this system may have emerged somewhat erratically, rather than being introduced definitively at a single date. At Emmanuel in Cambridge there was contention over the division of fines, reflecting the importance of this source of income to its fellows. In 1592 it was decided to divide all fines between the master and fellows, who were in return to give up their claim on the rent of the bake-house and brew-house. In addition the college's small income from corn rents was divided for the first time in 1610, and the proceeds of sales of wood in 1611. In 1621, however, it was agreed that only a quarter of fines should be divided among the fellows. This rule was confirmed in 1634, but was soon modified so that all fines of less than £10 and a quarter of the higher fines were shared out. The fellows of Emmanuel also received the fees paid by lessees, three-quarters of corn rent, all money from sales of timber, and even a share of increased rents.[44] Fines were certainly being divided at New College by 1567, at All Souls by 1592, and at Queen's by 1628. And a document of the 1620s or 1630s records that the share of fines going to the college rather than directly to the head and fellows was three-quarters at Jesus, two-thirds at All Souls and Queen's, half at Merton and New College, a third at Trinity, a quarter at Magdalen, a fifth at Corpus Christi, and a ninth at Brasenose. Oriel, like Balliol, University College, Exeter, Lincoln, Christ Church, St John's, Pembroke, and Wadham, is not mentioned.[45] But it had decreed in 1555 that the fines should be paid only to those present at the sealing of the leases in question and to those who were then ill but within the college premises. Occasionally, but only occasionally, fines might be diverted to other purposes: in the 1580s and 1590s a few entry fines found their way

---

[43] Audit Memoranda, OCA TF A 9/1, 10.   [44] Bendall, *Emmanuel College*, 172–5.
[45] Aylmer, 'Economics and Finances', HUO iii. 527–8; Duncan, 'Accounts of Corpus Christi', HUO iii. 568–9, 577–8; Bendall, *Emmanuel College*, 172.

without explanation into the treasurers' accounts; in 1636–8 the large fine (£700) for the reversion of the Littleworth lease was earmarked for college rebuilding; and during the Civil War it was decided in November 1645 that, in the light of the shortfall in revenue, £70.67 of fines should be assigned to the support of the common table, on the understanding that the distribution should be made 'if and when' (*quandocunque*) the rents were received.[46]

It is not until the comparatively late date of 1726 that we have a systematic record, in the fine books, of their amount and disposal. These books note the name of the lessee, the property leased, the starting date and length of the term, and the fine paid (though not the rent payable). But they are really records of how the fines (and initially also the fees charged for sealing the new leases) were distributed. Equal shares are assigned to the provost and a list of named fellows (typically numbering around fifteen); in the early records the fellow or his proxy signs against his name to confirm that he has received his share. The provost receives exactly the same share as the other fellows; by contrast, he got a slightly larger share at the annual dividend in November.[47] Generally the full amount of the fine is divided—sometimes the arithmetic is easy, sometimes not: in 1784–5 Thomas Calcott's fine of £26 1s. for a yardland and a half at Dean was split into sixteen portions of £1 12s. 6¾d.[48] Very occasionally part of a fine was set aside for college purposes. When Mr Trollope took a lease of Dean and Chalford to begin at Lady Day 1733, his fine was no less than £1,920. The provost and fellows received £100 each, and £120 was 'Laid aside by an Order of the College for Publick use' (though it does not appear in the treasurers' accounts); and on the lease's next renewal (for £350) £30 was assigned 'to defray the expence of surveying the estate'. In 1734–5 Sir Edward Gascoigne paid £33 16s. for the tithes of Aberford for twenty-one years from Michaelmas 1728; of this, two guineas were used as a fee for a legal opinion about the tithes. In 1782–3, when the butcher Stafford Shellord leased for three lives a slaughterhouse in a holding at Shenington, his fine of £6 4s. 9d. was not divided at all but set against the costs of enclosing that holding; and of a £750 fine for another Shenington holding in 1792, £398 was applied 'to the discharge of the remainder of the Debt incurred by the inclosure of this Estate'. Similarly of the £132 8s. received for the conversion of a copyhold at Dean to leasehold in 1784–5, forty guineas was not shared out but allocated to the costs of enclosure there.[49]

---

[46] DR 139 (1555), 284–5 and 287–8 (Littleworth), 308–9 (1645).

[47] This derived from the surplus in certain other funds, occasional miscellaneous items like the 2s. 3d. for old iron included in November 1783, and money from a bequest by John Robinson, bishop of London; in 1783 the provost's dividend was £7 13s. 4½d., that of each fellow £5 2s. 3d. On Robinson and his benefactions see ODNB s.n. Robinson, John.

[48] OCA TF1/B4/1–3, books of fines 1726–57, 1757–74, 1774–1886.

[49] OCA TF/B4/1, fine book 1726–57, 44, 61 (Dean and Chalford, Aberford); OCA TF/B4/3, fine book 1774–1866 (unfoliated), under 1782–3 (Shenington); OCA EST/A2/B2, register of leases 1765–1807, fo. 40 (Shenington, St Giles), unnumbered folio (Dean).

Fines were also payable when copyhold tenure (customary tenure proved by a copy of the relevant entry in the manorial court roll) was renewed, or when a life was added to a copyhold. The college's earliest fine book records that a court was held at Dean on 30 March 1727 at which 'Mr Bishop and Sturdy's copy were filled'. Next day Bishop paid a fine of £40 for one copyhold half-yardland and Sturdy £16 for another. In 1731–2 the tenant of Dean mill paid £25 to add his son's life to his copyhold; and at a court held at Dean in January 1738 John Freeman paid a fine of £30 for a yardland and a half in copyhold. Later a number of Dean copyholds were converted into leaseholds, either at the option of the tenants when renewing or through the decision of the college when copyholds fell in. The process could generate substantial fines: William Gibbs paid £168 to convert the copyhold tenure of two yardlands into a twenty-one-year lease from Michaelmas 1775, Thomas Cowling £126 18s. to do the same with a yardland and a half; and Elizabeth Walker paid a fine of £90 8s. when she leased Freeman's former copyhold for twenty-one years from Michaelmas 1784.[50] Similarly at Shenington, as we have seen, the number of leaseholders rose and that of copyholders fell.[51]

Not every college estate improved over time. The rectory of Aberford in Yorkshire had become one of Oriel's more valuable properties in 1585–6 when its rent nearly doubled to some £14 (including corn rent). It was held for about £22 yearly in the 1630s by Sir Thomas Bland, whose seat was at Kippax, eight miles from Aberford. But the rent failed to keep pace with inflation. Perhaps the college had difficulty in bargaining with distant gentry families, for the rent had actually fallen back to £15–£18 by the 1730s, when the tithes were in the hands of Sir Edward Gascoigne of Parlington in Aberford, a member of a prominent West Riding family. The tithes were leased briefly by Henry Ingram, Viscount Irvine, who in 1756 paid the same fine of £33 16s. as had Sir Edward Gascoigne in 1728, 1742, and 1749. The Ingrams had estates and influence centred on Whitkirk in Yorkshire and Horsham in Sussex, but their fortunes were declining. Like his brother Arthur, whom he succeeded in 1736, but unlike their two elder brothers

---

[50] OCA TF/B4/1, Fine book 1726–57, fos. 7–8, 39, 82; OCA EST/A2/B2, register of leases 1765–1807, under 1775–6; OCA TF/B4/3, fine book 1774–1866, under 1784–5.

[51] Such changes could only be effected where the college retained control of the manor court. Where this was in the hands of the lessee, there was always the danger that he might in effect appropriate copyholds by adding new lives, or by regranting them, when they fell in, to family members. For a case (East Walton, Norfolk) where this operated very much to Christ Church's disadvantage, see Dunbabin, 'College Estates 1660–1815', HUO v. 302–4. In the 1730s Oriel feared that Richard Aston would take some such steps to appropriate the benefits of copyholds worth collectively some £400 p.a. To guard against such dangers, Oriel was, by 1759, inserting into leases comprising manors a standard clause reserving to itself the right of entry in order to hold manor courts (to Sir Willoughby Aston, OCA DLL 3, unsorted correspondence, 17 October 1759). In 1784 Oriel resolved to hold a court there while it revalued the Wadley holdings, and in 1789 to hold 'Courts Leet and Courts Baron' at all its manors over the course of the ensuing year (OCA TF 1 A9/1, Audit Memoranda).

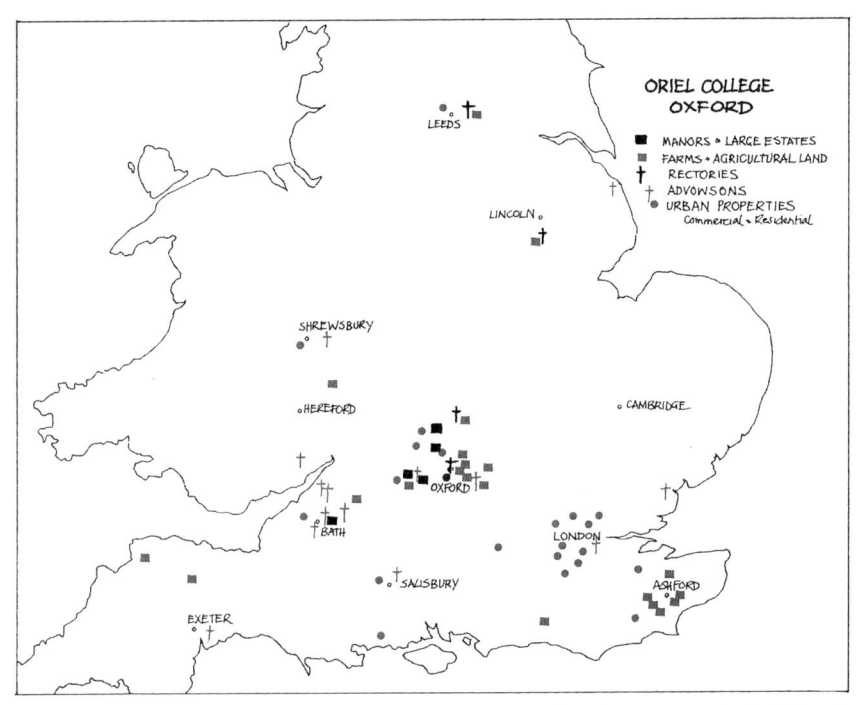

MAP 1 Oriel's estates and land interests, 1324–1991, showing properties held both before and after 1920, *OCA*

who had been fellow commoners at Christ's College in Cambridge, Henry Ingram was an Oriel man (MA 1712), and this no doubt influenced the college's transfer to him of the Aberford lease. Henry died in 1761 and the title passed first to his brother George, who had also been an undergraduate at Oriel (MA 1717), and then to their nephew Charles, not a graduate of either university, who renewed the lease in 1763 for a fine of £42 2s. 6d. Whether because the Ingrams' link with Oriel had been lost or for some other reason, it was another Sir Thomas Gascoigne who took the lease from 1770 for the same fine; but in the 1780s he was paying only £25 or so in rent.[52] The lease was again up for renewal at Michaelmas 1784; but the college had finally had enough, and the fellows determined that Gascoigne's lease should be allowed to run out, as they were considering granting it to the vicar. (Oriel could not end the lease before the expiry of its full term, but was not obliged

---

[52] It is sceptically noted against the record of the 1770 fine that 'In discount of the Rent of Beckay alone [Gascoigne] charges the A[rch]. B[ishop]. Of York with 45£ which he says he pays to O.C.': OCA TF B4/2.

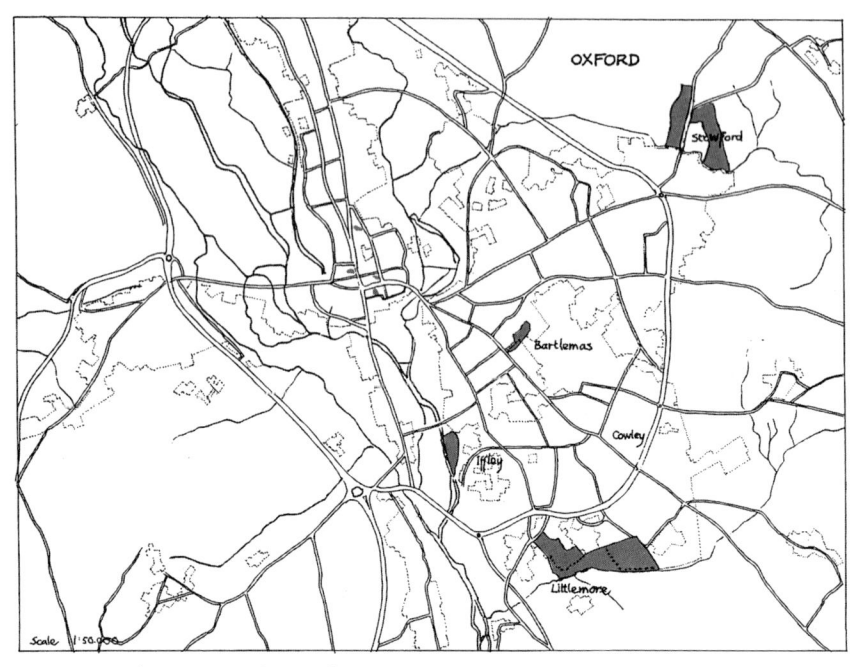

MAP 2 Oriel estates in the Oxford region, *OCA*

to grant a fresh term.) However the fellows were not prepared to forgo the renewal fine; instead they agreed that it should be taken out of college funds, and £65 17s. from the college bag was divided between the provost and fellows. No further fine was received for Aberford. The same device had been employed when the lease of Coleby held by Thomas Scrope, armiger, came up for renewal in 1777. It was noted in the register of leases that 'the college resolved not to renew with Mr Scrope but paid the fine [of £126] and fees out of the college stock'. At Michaelmas 1784, when seven years of Scrope's lease remained, another fine of £126 was taken from the college bag and shared out.[53] Other colleges too adopted this expedient.

---

[53] See J. Burke, *A genealogical and heraldic dictionary of the landed gentry of Great Britain and Ireland*, 4th edn. (London, 1863), 112–13 (Bland of Kippax Park), 536 (Gascoigne of Parlington); G. E. C[ockayne], *The complete peerage of England, Scotland, Ireland, Great Britain, and the United Kingdom*, 14 vols. in 15 (2nd edn. London, 1910–98), vii. 71–5 (Irvine, Irwin, or Irwing); ODNB s.n. Gascoigne, Sir Thomas, 2nd baronet (1596–1686); ODNB s.n. Ingram, Frances, Viscountess Irwin (1734?–1807), online edn. January 2008; OCA EST/A2/B2, register of leases 1765–1807, unpaginated; OCA TF/B4/1–3, fine books 1726–57, 1757–74, 1774–1866, unpaginated.

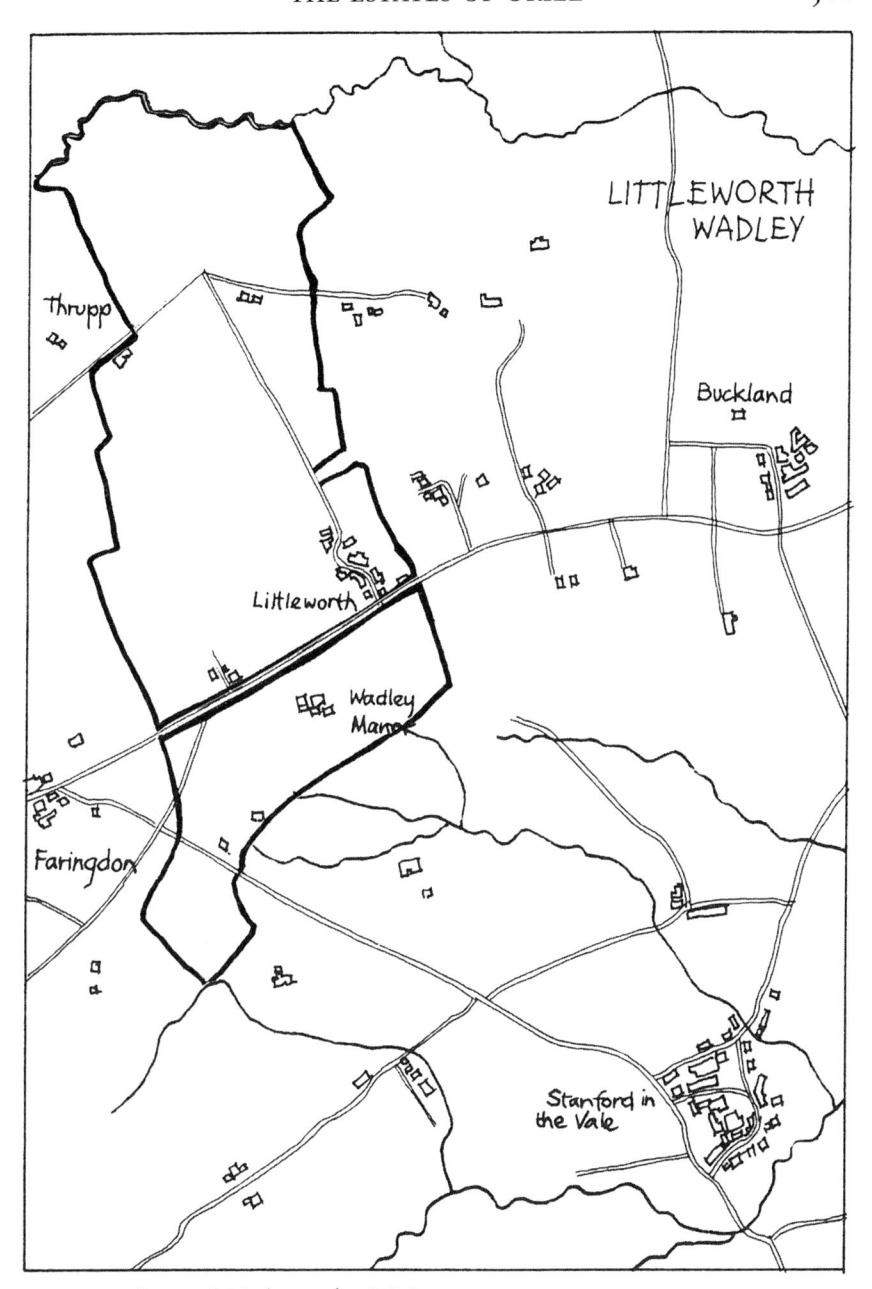

MAP 3 Wadley and Littleworth, *OCA*

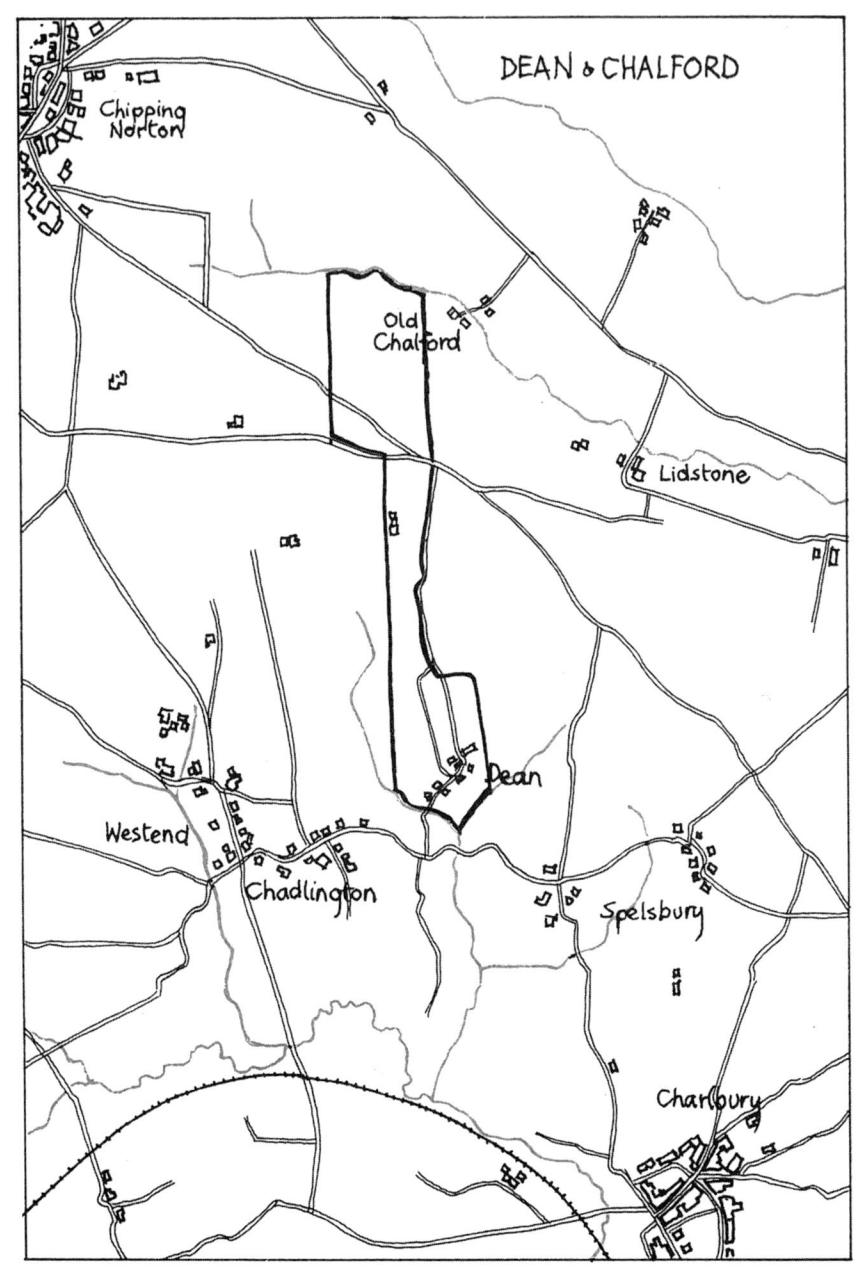

MAP 4 Dean and Chalford, *OCA*

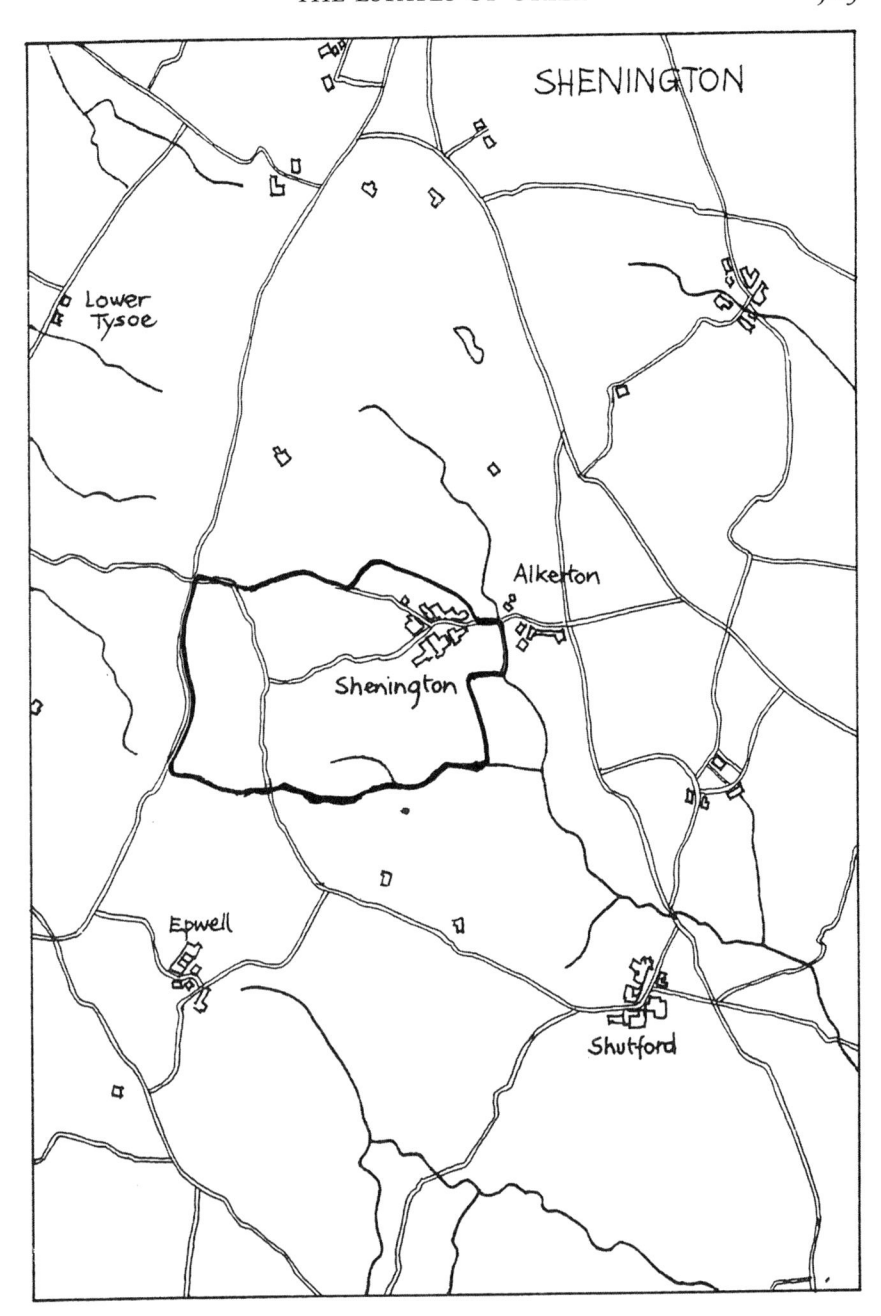

MAP 5 Shenington, *OCA*

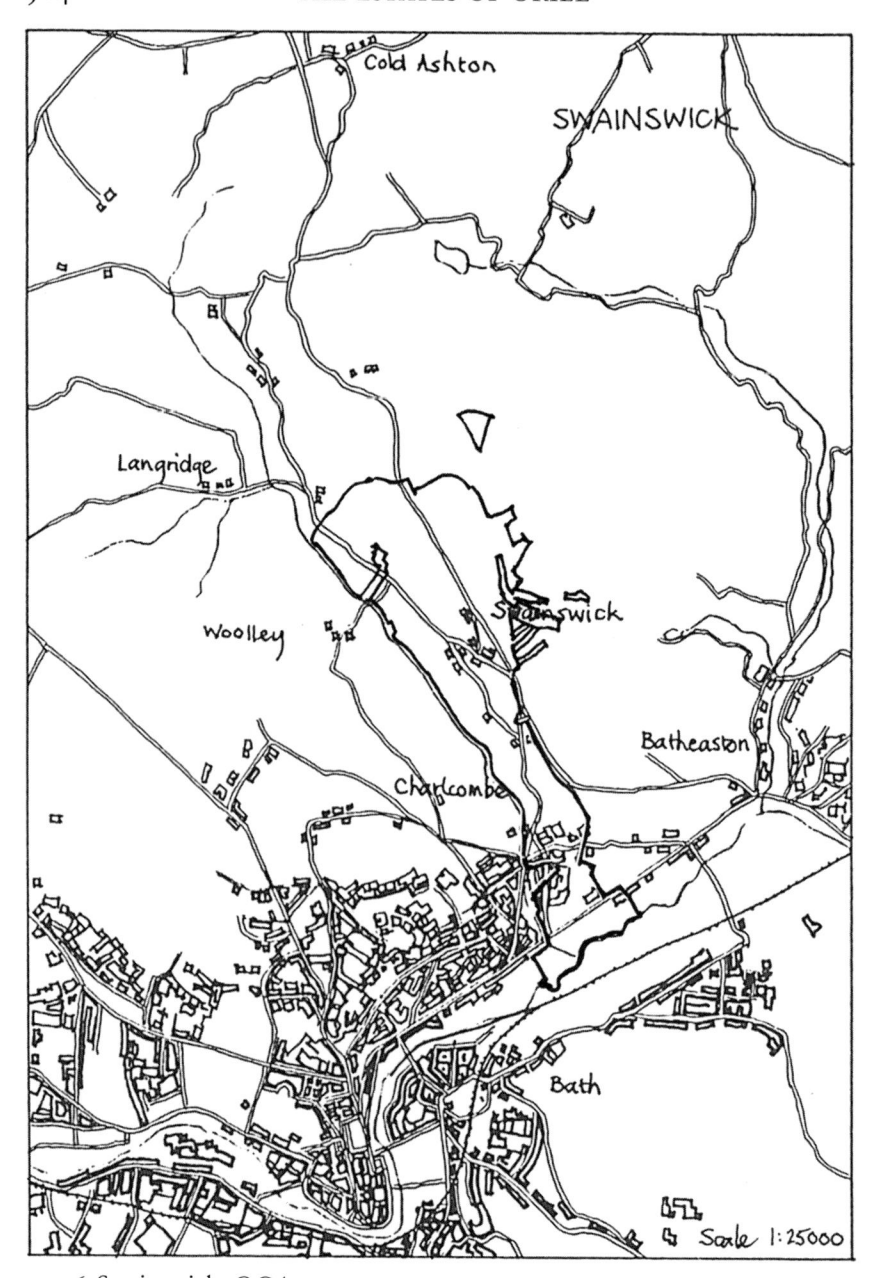

MAP 6 Swainswick, *OCA*

There could also be difficulties in the renewal of the leases of smaller properties. When the Revd Peter Gunning renewed his lease of a 10-acre holding at Swainswick from Michaelmas 1775, he was evidently late in paying the fine of £27 9s. 9d.; Oriel was displeased but agreed to regularize the transaction retrospectively: 'The College being offended at Mr Gunning would not sett the Fine at the proper Time, though afterwards they thought proper to date the Lease back.' In the 1760s William Hopkins had been renewing his lease for lands at Shenington regularly every seven years. But the fine involved was rising, and for the new lease from Michaelmas 1776 Oriel asked £37 11s. 7½d. Hopkins seems initially to have refused; he later accepted the college's terms, but one lease book noted that the fine was too high. Puzzlingly in 1780–1, with only four years of the lease elapsed, a new fine of £12 was set for a twenty-one-year extension; but in 1782 it was recorded that, although the fine had been divided and the fees distributed, Hopkins had never paid them, and they had had to be covered by a withdrawal from the college bag. In 1787–8, with the more usual seven years elapsed, the fine of £37 11s. 2½d. was sought and apparently received. But it was noted that Hopkins had not paid 'a chief Rent due to the College...for a bit of free land at Shenington from the time of the [1780] Inclosure'. The question was posed 'whether refusing to renew at Michaelmas 1793 would not be the best means of compelling the payment'. It was subsequently added that the rent had been paid; and in 1794–5 Hopkins was, for a fine of £17 2s. 6d., given a lease for the rather odd period of seventeen years. This was followed three years later by one for twenty-one years for £39 12s. 2d., and thereafter the usual cycle resumed.

In Charles II's time it was normal for Oxford colleges, when renewing a twenty-one-year lease after seven years, to set the entry fine at one year's clear annual value of the estate, net of the rent payable to the college. In the 1750s this commonly rose to a year and a quarter's clear annual value, as, for example, at Brasenose in 1752 or 1753 and at New College in 1759. New College increased its rate to one and a half years' value in 1774, Trinity in 1777, Brasenose in 1786, Balliol in the 1780s, and Christ Church only in 1811.[54] Oriel began the process considerably earlier, at least in principle. Its first surviving fine book records that at Michaelmas 1726 it was resolved that in future no less than one and a quarter years' purchase—that is one and a quarter times the annual value net of the reserved rent and certain other burdens—was to be taken for leases of twenty-one years and at least a year and a half for leases of lives or for adding a third life to a lease.[55] This was

---

[54] Dunbabin, 'College Estates 1660–1815', HUO v. 277.
[55] Rather cryptically it was also resolved that at Dean and Chalford Oriel would insist on two years' purchase for adding a third life, three years' for a second and third life, and three and a half years' purchase for three lives. This may have related to copyholds, where the bases of

reaffirmed on 17 October 1740 (the date of the annual audit of the treasurers' accounts): for estates worth over £20 p.a. whose reserved rent was less than a fifth of their real annual value, the renewal fine for seven years was to be a year and a quarter (which quarter 'shall be applied to publick [college] use' rather than divided). Then on 20 April 1775 it was decided that 'in setting of Fines for the future instead of a year and a Quarter's rent (*deductis deducandis*), a year and a half shall be taken', except on estates where the reserved rents exceeded a sixth of the annual value, and also on those recently purchased or converted from copyhold to leasehold on the basis of a new survey and higher valuation.[56] Fines for renewing leases after a longer period than seven years, or for wholly new twenty-one-year leases, naturally ran higher—in the 1780s we find fines of twelve, and in the 1790s of thirteen years' purchase for new leases.

In practice, circumstances altered cases. Thus in 1772 the fine for adding two lives to a Shenington copyhold 'was set so low in consideration of the late tenant's poverty'. In a particularly sensitive context, Oriel claimed in 1759 only to be asking one year's income 'upon what we suppose to be a fair Valuation, an indulgence peculiar to Wadley', to the problems of which we refer below.[57] In 1766 the fine for the manor of Swainswick was set £10 too low through miscalculation; in 1785 a small fine for a house and land in Cowley was not raised, in recognition of the money the lessee had spent on repairing it; and in 1778 it was noted (without explanation) that three fines had been set at 1½, two at 1¼ years' clear value.

Local knowledge could be very useful. In 1786 a plea for reduction in a fine 'on acc[oun]t of the Swanswick new Road' was refused since the lessee had not allowed his sub-tenant any such reduction. Usually the valuation used to set a fine is not known, but occasionally the complex calculations are recorded in the college's fine and lease books. These confirm that Oriel was in fact determining its fines by taking an adjusted annual value of the estate, net both of true quitrents and of the rent received by the college, and multiplying it by one and a quarter or one and a half. When John Mander renewed his lease of Littleworth for twenty-one years from Michaelmas 1783 it was noted in the register of leases that the renewal fine seven years earlier

---

calculation seem to have been different—in 1770–1 the record of a fine for the granting of copyhold for three lives was deleted with the explanation that 'This grant did not take place because the fine demanded by the College was not 2 years' copy-rent, or 13s. 4d., but 2 years rack rent of the house.'

[56] The reserved rent (in Oriel's parlance 'quitrent') to be deducted from the annual value for these calculations was to be based on the average price of corn for the previous seven years. The decisions of 1726 and 1740 are recorded on a sheet tipped in, upside down, at the back of the fine book for 1726–57; for the ruling of 1775 see provost's fine book 1774–1883, 2.

[57] Oriel's 26 September and 17 October 1759 replies to Sir Willoughby Aston, rejecting his claim that the fine should be lower given the size of the poor rates he had in practice to pay on the properties of several copyholders in his manor; see OCA DLL 3, unsorted correspondence.

had been £220 4s. 6d., based on a valuation of £164 9s. 2d. p.a., a rent of £15 12s. 10d. (the grain prices used to set the corn rent are given) and an unspecified quitrent paid by Mander to Sir Robert Throgmorton. For the 1783 renewal it was observed that Mander was letting the estate for just £160 and the fine was therefore reduced by one and a half times the difference between this and the previous valuation, which brought it down to £213 10s. 9d. It was further noted that 'in strictness of calculation' the reduction should have been less, as the average prices of wheat and malt over the seven years to Lady Day 1783 would have reduced the rent to £13 16s. 6½d., so that the net value on which the fine was based would have been slightly higher.[58] At Littleworth the college seems to have had reliable information about the true value of its estate, but it sometimes had to work with figures that were known to be unrealistic. When George Clarke paid £531 15s. for a lease of the Swainswick manor farm from Lady Day 1794, a full explanation was provided. The valuation was largely based on what were evidently only estimates. About 200 acres lay near the village and were occupied by Mr Hooper; they were worth, 'one with another', about £1 yearly, or £200 in all. Presumably the college had failed to discover what Hooper was paying Clarke for this land. A further 53 acres were nearby at Lambridge, and it was known that, more than 30 were let for £4 per acre; all were valued 'one with another very low at £3 per Acre', making £159. The house, garden, and appurtenances at Lambridge were valued at £30, but were said to be 'worth very considerably more'. When an average rent of the preceding seven years of £34 10s. was deducted, the value was £354 10s., which multiplied by one and a half gave the fine of £531 15s.[59]

Such knowledge may have been slow to reach Oxford. Mr Reynolds paid a fine of £3 6s. 6d. for the lease of the college's small close at Faringdon from 1792. In 1796 it was noted that the bailiff of Wadley had estimated the close's annual value as £4 4s., and that several people had made offers on that basis. When Reynolds renewed in 1799 the fine was £6, close to one and a half times the bailiff's estimate, and almost double the previous fine. On occasion official valuations could be used, as when Mrs Walker's fine for the manor farm at Dean was set at £240 16s. 4½d. in 1794 on the basis of the 'quality price' estimated by the enclosure commissioners, or when the fine for the conversion of a copyhold at Dean to leasehold in 1784–5 took account of the commissioners' valuation. Obtaining new valuations could be expensive, but must often have been worthwhile. When Dr Leyborn paid a fine of £350 to

---

[58] OCA EST/A2/B2, register of leases 1765–1807, 1783–4, unnumbered fo. (Hayes); fos. 50ᵛ–51 (Littleworth). In 1776 the fine had been reduced from £223 4s. 6d. to £220 4s. 6d. by the refund of a quitrent of £3 paid or 'said to be paid' by Mander to Throgmorton: OCA TF 1 B4/4, provost's fine book 1774–1883, 8.
[59] OCA TF/B4/1, fine book 1726–57, 41; OCA TF 1 B4/4 provost's fine book 1774–1883, 58–9.

TABLE 15.2 Rents and fines, 1735–6 to 1835–6[a]

Sample year		Nominal value in pounds	Value in 1786 pounds
1735–36	Total estate income, excluding arrears	485	
	Average annual fine income, 1730–1 to 1739–40	436	
	Total	921	1,434
1785–86	Estate income, excluding net receipts for arrears	1,180	
	Average annual fine receipts, 1780–1 to 1789–90	822	
	Total	2,002	2,002
1835–6	Rents	3,859	
	Average annual fine receipts, 1830–1 to 1839–40	936	
	Total	4,795	3,400

[a] Conversion of the 1735–36 total into 1786 pounds has been made using the Phelps-Brown and Hopkins index; that of the 1835–6 total back into 1786 pounds was done by the <safalra.com/other/historical-uk-inflation-price-conversion/tool>, which derives from Jim O'Donoghue, Louise Golding, and Grahame Allen, 'Consumer Price Inflation since 1750', *Economic Trends*, 604 (March 2004), Office for National Statistics. This is itself largely based on the Phelps-Brown and Hopkins index for the period before 1850; for 1850–70, it uses the Retail Price Index produced by G. H. Wood from Board of Trade material on wholesale and retail prices and on Cooperative Society records; and thereafter, C. H. Feinstein's estimates of consumer expenditure, *Statistical Tables of the National Income, Expenditure and Output of the United Kingdom, 1855–1965* (Cambridge, 1976).

take a new lease of Dean and Chalford from 1740, the college set aside £30 to defray the cost of surveying the estate. In 1771 a Swainswick holding 'fell into the hands of the College by the death of Mr Burton'. It was therefore easy to have it revalued, and to grant an entirely new twenty-one-year lease with a fine to match (£840). Most of this was divided among the fellows, constituting something of a windfall, but the college paid £52 as the cost of a valuation (and £60 to buy out Gunning's interest in the down at Swainswick). Perhaps new valuations should have been secured more often.[60] (See Table 15.2.)

---

[60] OCA TF 1 B4/4, provost's fine book 1774–1883, 54, 55, 1799–1800, unnumbered page (Faringdon); 59 (Dean 1794); OCA EST/A2/B2, register of leases 1765–1807, unnumbered folio, 1784–5 (Dean); OCA TF/B4/1, fine book 1726–57, unnumbered page (Dean and Chalford 1740); OCA TF/B4/3, fine book 1767–74, unnumbered page (Swainswick 1772). Cf. S. Bendall, *Emmanuel College*, 367–9; Dunbabin, 'College Estates 1660–1815', HUO v. 282–5.

Though fines were directly divided between the provost and fellows rather than going into the college accounts, they represented an important part of estate incomes—indeed in the eighteenth century one more important to Oriel than its easiest comparator, the combined fines of All Souls, Lincoln, New College, and Wadham to those colleges. As Oriel's fines are recorded only from 1726, they could not feature in our earlier comparisons of the college's estate income over time, but they must be included in subsequent surveys. They were, however, very 'lumpy' items, with many or large fines received in some years, few or small ones in others. To reduce the impact of this volatility, our comparisons will be of the decennial averages[61] of the fines received together with (as before) Oriel's rents in given years at fifty-year intervals. Total estate income (excluding arrears) in the treasurers' account for 1735–6 was £485, and the annual average of the fines received between 1730–1 and 1739–40 (November to November) was £436, together making £921. By 1785–6 estate income (excluding net repayment of arrears) was £1,180 and the decennial average of fines £822, together making £2,002—an increase in money terms of 117 per cent, though only of 40 per cent if we adjust by the Phelps-Brown–Hopkins index.[62] The 143 per cent rise in Oriel's rents far outstripped that of our broader sample of colleges (40 per cent between 1739–40 and 1789–90), while the decennial average of Oriel's fines increased by 89 per cent as compared with 62 per cent for those of All Souls, Brasenose, Lincoln, New College, and Wadham.[63]

The gain in rents was far from uniform across Oriel's estates. In the fifty years to 1785–6 income from the four appropriated churches had (in money terms) risen by just 45 per cent, as the rent of Moreton Pinkney, the most valuable, had been unchanged at £50 for more than 150 years. The yield of the estates in Wiltshire had increased by 33 per cent, in Somerset by 66 per cent, and from rural properties in Oxfordshire by 74 per cent, boosted by the purchase in 1740 of Stadhampton (which returned some £22 in 1785–6). By contrast rents in the town of Oxford had grown by 177 per cent, and income from the college's Berkshire estates had risen by a notable 320 per cent (from £119 in 1735–6 to £500 in 1785–6), so that it accounted for 42 per cent of all current rental.

The principal change was in the manor of Wadley, whose tangled history illustrates many of the problems of early modern college estate management. In 1538, Oriel later claimed, colleges had feared that the Reformation might

---

[61] Even decennial averages only reduce, not eliminate, volatility. For fines due at seven-year intervals will have been paid twice in some decades, once only in others; and when new twenty-one-year leases were granted, their fines were much higher than those for ordinary renewals.

[62] The estate income figures used in this chapter for 1585–6 to 1735–6 are those extracted from the accounts by T. A. R. Evans, those for 1785–6 and 1835–6 are J. P. D. Dunbabin's; so there may be minor inconsistencies between them in the interpretation of certain items in the accounts.

[63] Dunbabin, 'College Estates 1660–1815', HUO v. 276.

lead to the confiscation of their property. Oriel had accordingly first granted the tenant of Wadley a new lease continuing his existing rent for seventy-eight years, then covenanted that this lease should be followed by one for fifty years and thereafter, on payment of a £60 fine, by another for eighty years. This secured the college its rent of £58 p.a. for the foreseeable future, and hopefully also gave a leading local family an interest in the preservation of college property. But after James I had confirmed Oriel's charter and title in 1603, the college proposed to contest the validity of the promise of the fifty- and eighty-year leases. The tenant, Sir Valentine Knightley, moved quickly to secure royal protection, and James abruptly ordered the college to 'suffer' Knightley 'quietly to enjoy his lease' and to take steps to 'confirm and establish him in it'. Oriel, though, also had advocates at court, like Henry Howard, earl of Northampton. The upshot (presumably after negotiations with Knightley) was the passage in 1606 of a private act of parliament enshrining a compromise: Oriel's charter of incorporation was confirmed, but so were all Knightley's leases; and in return for an increase of his rent to £100 p.a., he was to enjoy them without payment of 'any fine or other consideration'.[64] So matters rested until the eighteenth century, with the lessees (in Oriel's jaundiced view) paying only £100 p.a. for an estate worth at least seven times as much.

Then in 1712 the manor house needed major rebuilding. Before undertaking this, the current lessee, Sir Richard Aston, sought and obtained assurances that Oriel would grant a new lease when the old one expired. In 1730 he approached the college for a renewal, and was encouraged to provide a survey and valuation of the lands in question. But relations soon turned sour. The first dispute came over the ownership of the local tithes, which, in effect, both he and Oriel claimed; over this, Aston made good his case. There followed a wrangle over whether he or Oriel were liable to pay the Land Tax, and in 1734 Aston took the issue to the courts. This, he later wrote, 'highly exasperated the Society', which, stating that Aston 'had declared war first', responded by seeking £5,000 damages for past timber felling and other waste on the estate. The upshot was referral of the Land Tax question to arbitration, and an award in Aston's favour (albeit with Oriel's liability for the past constrained by the statute of limitations). But the real issue concerned some 60 acres known as the 'Park Pieces': Oriel claimed, and Aston denied, that these were included in the Monks Mill copyhold that Aston held from the college in addition to his lease of Wadley manor; the question turned on the interpretation of a 1657 enclosure award. To pressure Aston on this, Oriel refused to renew the lease of the manor. Aston countered by petitioning the House of Commons to intervene (as it had occasionally done in the 1660s); he recited his version of the

[64] 3 Jac. I c. 9; Shadwell, *Enactments in Parliament*, i. 236–4.

dispute, stressed the £900 he had, on assurance of future renewal, spent on rebuilding the manor house, and asked for action 'to prevent the Ruin of those Families, who (relying on the Vertue and Honour of such Reverend and Learned Societies,) have purchased [leases] upon the Faith of Colleges'. Oriel counter-petitioned. But at a time of strong anti-clericalism, Aston had touched a nerve. In the Commons debate of March 1737, six people spoke for Aston, nine (including Sir Robert Walpole) against; the motion to refer Aston's case to a committee was defeated only by 119 to 101.[65]

This seems to have encouraged compromise. For in 1738 Aston was granted a new lease for Wadley manor, without fine but with a £250 p.a. increase in the rent. Debate continued as to what its fine should be on next renewal, but in 1739 a settlement appeared to have been reached, and Oriel received congratulations from John Potter, the archbishop of Canterbury.[66] In 1745 a £300 fine was taken, on the understanding that next time it should be £581. That did not, however, resolve the question of the ownership of the Park Pieces, which occasioned prolonged litigation in Chancery, followed eventually by another compromise: in 1750 on receiving £100 from Oriel, Sir Willoughby and Elizabeth Aston formally acknowledged its ownership of the Pieces, and both these and Monks Mill were granted them without fine for three lives. Sir Willoughby continued to question the appropriateness of a £581 fine for the manor, but it was taken in 1752, followed by £600 in 1759. Oriel, however, regarded this as an exceptional concession representing, roughly, one year's clear value; and for the rest of the century, after poverty had forced Aston to sell the lease to Charles Pye, the fine rose steadily to £1,230 in 1787 and 1794.[67] By the 1780s Pye was in addition paying a corn rent that yielded £446.98 in 1785–6.

Gratifying as rising fines were, it was well understood that landlords' incomes were reduced by the system of beneficial leases. In economic terms the basic rents remained low, while the lump sum fines that offset them were, as advance payments, heavily discounted; in the later eighteenth century measurement of the discount stimulated the publication of compound interest tables. Two factors chiefly inhibited change. One was the fear that refusal to renew leases might provoke a dangerous political backlash, whereas (as President Routh of Magdalen put it) 'the old system of leases interested so many persons of weight and position in the protection of

---

[65] Aston's petition, Oriel's counter-petition, and the relevant passage from the Journals of the House of Commons, 15 March 1736–7, are bound into OCA GOV 4 A2/A, the Dean's Register vol. ii, s.a. 1737; OCA DLL 2 and DLL 3, unsorted papers. See also P. Langford, 'Tories and Jacobites', HUO v. 115–18 and Dunbabin, 'College Estates 1660–1815', HUO v. 278–80.

[66] OCA DLL 3, 8 May 1739. His concluding sentence, 'If in any Thing hereafter I may be serviceable, you will, I hope, on all occasions command', suggests, though it does not prove, that he may have had a hand in the negotiations.

[67] OCA TF/B4/1–3, Fine Books, and OCA DLL 2–3, Wadley papers.

college property'. The other was the fact that colleges were, in the language of the day, 'flux societies'; so the fellows who, to run out a lease, forwent fines after seven and fourteen years might well have left Oxford before it fell in and a full commercial rent could be charged. Nevertheless some steps were taken in this direction. As early as the 1750s Balliol was refusing to renew the leases on much of its property. From 1794 Pitt put an end to the analogous system of letting Crown lands, as part of his general financial reforms. And in the 1810s Jesus seems to have largely stopped taking fines, though the great majority of colleges continued to do so.[68]

Oriel began running out leases quite early: it resolved in 1776 not to renew that of the rectory of Coleby, in 1784 that of Aberford. But it did not do so consistently: in 1789 it decided that a Shenington property that had come into hand and been rack-rented 'should be sold upon a lease for 21 years', with £448 'of the purchase money [fine] applied to the liquidation of the [enclosure] Debt at present on the Estate'.[69] In 1806, however, we encounter something more definite. For Edward Copleston noted in his diary:

Obtained the consent of the college to a plan for improving the revenues, by borrowing fines [from internal college 'bags'] instead of taking them from lessees at renewals, and increasing the reserved rents instead.

N.B. Being continued six years in the office [of Senior Treasurer, 1805–10], contrary to the usual system of electing for one year only, succeeded in establishing this plan, by means of which the income of the college has been trebled, all the debts liquidated, and the estates better tenanted.[70]

That this trebled Oriel's income seems unlikely. But the fine books do show that many, though certainly not all, fines were commuted for 'additional rent', with the provost and fellows being compensated from internal funds. In 1806–7 £368 was received in cash, with £354.55 taken from college bags to compensate for the remainder; and it is noted that at one Swainswick property 'an addition was made to the reserved rent of 2 qu[a]r[ter]s of wheat & £9 a year', at another of '1 Q[uarte]r of Wheat per ann'. The policy was continued in subsequent years, though the fine books give no details of the 'additional' rents: from 1807–8 to 1811–12 £3,963 was taken in cash (with £1,000 not divided but assigned to the college bag), and £4,846 taken from college bags for division among the fellowship. The splits did not always represent policy: in 1809–10 £657 of the £890 that came from college bags did so only because 'Mr Hall refuses the terms offered by the College for his

---

[68] Dunbabin, 'College Estates 1660–1815', HUO v. 281; Dunbabin, 'Finance and Property', HUO vi. 377, 380.
[69] OCA TF 1 A9/1, Audit Memoranda. A fine of £750 was secured in 1792, with £398 now sufficing to cover the debt.
[70] William James Copleston, *Memoirs of Edward Copleston, D.D., Bishop of Llandaff* (London, 1851), 19.

renewal of the Lease of Chalford.' There could, too, be marked shifts from year to year, no doubt reflecting both college politics and changing perceptions of the external economic environment. In the two years 1813–15, of the £2,826 divided, £2,301 came from college bags, but in the next three years these contributed only £146 of the £4,206 divided; the pendulum then swung some, but not all, of the way back towards taking the fines internally from the bags.

All this makes the true position quite hard to determine from the fine books. And the 'Style' was also becoming a less comprehensive guide to Oriel's overall financial position. For there was much flow from one independent bag to another. At the Michaelmas 1789 audit it was decided to sell £1,200 of Consols and repay £1,000 'of the debt due from the College Bag to the Caution Bag'; this was then to lend £1,000 to the New Library, to be repaid with £60 p.a. from the junior treasurer's book plus 'the money due on account of the new road at Swanwick ... when [if?] it falls in to the College'. Ten years later it was noted that 'the surplus arising from the Rectory of Coleby is now paid into the College Bag' (which had financed the fines forgone in running out the lease), and that this should therefore pay £50 p.a. to increase the value of the living. In October 1804 it was decided that the rent reductions allowed to Oriel's tenants for their payment of the Property Tax should be 'charged on the Chapel Book'. And in 1826 the 'New Houses Account' was set up to cover the costs of looking after the college's Oxford houses as they came out of beneficial lease into hand; it was to receive half their rents, the other half still going into the Style via the account of the Collector Redituum.[71] Also some of the entries in the Style itself were becoming anachronistic. Thus in the years after 1799 a number of small properties were sold to finance the redemption of the Land Tax on other Oriel holdings, but in 1835–6 they were still entered in the Style as yielding £144, though this probably now represented an internal transfer from the Land Tax bag. Similarly £14.78 appears from the 'Old South Sea annuities', though they had been sold to finance the building of a road.

This must reduce confidence in our snapshot of Oriel's financial position in the 1830s. But further progress does seem to have been made during the previous half-century. In 1835–6 rents appear as £3,859, more than three times their 1785–6 level, though the decennial average of cash fines received was, at £936, only slightly up. The combined total of £4,795 represented a rise of 140 per cent in money terms, or perhaps 70 per cent in real terms.[72] Comparisons with other colleges are not easy, partly because, in the early nineteenth century, their policies on fines differed very widely, with corresponding effects

---

[71] OCA TF 1 A9/1, Audit Memoranda.
[72] As adjusted by the Safalra historical UK inflation converter, for which see the footnote to Table 15.2.

on their rents. However the rise in Oriel's fines seems not unlike that in those of the combination of All Souls, Brasenose, Lincoln, New College, and Wadham, though the growth in its rents was higher (227 per cent to 138 per cent).[73]

In percentage terms it was the rise in Oriel's Somerset rents that was the most notable. The college's holdings at Swainswick had been slow to change, looking in the 1730s very much as they had done in the 1580s. But fifty years later, whether from the conversion of copyholds to more commercial leases or from the subdivision of existing leasehold tenements, both the number of leases and the total rent received had risen. This process then accelerated into the nineteenth century, and by the 1830s the college had twenty-two leasehold tenements at Swainswick, with some lessees holding more than one tenement. Holdings varied greatly in size, Joseph Cottle paying £2.63 for his lease, plus a shilling for a plot besides the public highway, but Philip John Miles and Thomas Kington paying £57.50 jointly, Eleazor Pickwick £73.98, and Samuel and William Slack £87. Between 1735–6 and 1835–6 the value of the main estate at Swainswick had risen by just a quarter, in round figures from £26 to £32, but that of the entire property had increased elevenfold, from £40 to £452. The details remain unclear, but it appears that this had been achieved essentially by converting copyholds that fell into the college's hand to leasehold at market rates, and by raising the rents when leases were renewed. Any reduction in the rentable value of the core estate, which rose more slowly than most of the college's properties, was more than offset by the large rents received from the new leaseholds.

There were similar developments, too, in the more important Wadley, Wickensham, Littleworth complex in Berkshire. Together these had paid £489 in 1785–6. The year 1794–5 brought the spinning off from the joint holding of 'Wadley and Wickensham' of a new property, Wickensham, with surprisingly little reduction of the Wadley rent. By 1805–6 the overall complex yielded £720. Five years later the total was £2,080. This transformation was due partly to the rise of Wickensham's rent from £183 to £317 and the near doubling of that of Wadley manor from £448 to £866; these increases were presumably related to the forgoing of the 1808–9 fines for both properties in return for 'additional rent'. But 1809 had also seen the emergence in 1809 of three new large holdings in Littleworth; together with a number of other much smaller properties, these took the total for Littleworth and Thrupp from £63.51 in 1805–6 to £866.08 in 1810–11. After which the Style's receipts for the complex showed no major changes over the next three decades despite the forgoing of the Wickensham fines in 1822–3 and 1829–30, but only a general downwards drift linked to that of corn prices.

---

[73] Dunbabin, 'College Estates 1660–1815', HUO v. 276, and 'Finance and Property', HUO vi. 380–1, with a little extrapolation.

The audit of all these rents was a considerable occasion. In October 1842 the senior treasurer, R. W. Church, wrote that

> For four mortal days we have been at it, living on accounts (and sandwiches) from ten to near six, with nothing but ledgers and account books...meeting one's eye—nothing to amuse one but corn rents and money rents, consols and reduced annuities, sums in long addition and long division, practice and interest—all of us in our gowns and all our work a good part in Latin.

So far, so traditional.

> But oh! The miseries entailed upon unhappy Treasurers...by the [recently reintroduced] income tax, especially if they are unlucky enough to have Provosts [Hawkins] to do business with, who like making the most of whatever business falls in their way, and spin it out as long as it will last...I should like to roast Sir R. Peel with all the returns made about his Tax.[74]

Such audits continued throughout this period. Those of 1849, the Easter audit in 1850, and the October audit in 1852 all discussed the desirability of 'bringing the College property more nearly to the state of Rackrent tenures, instead of Beneficial Leases'. A paper on the subject (published in 1853 as *Observations on College Leases*) was commissioned from the barrister and economist Charles Neate, who had recently served as senior treasurer. Finally the Easter 1853 audit resolved to start making the changeover 'with certain exceptions (chiefly those on which there are Houses other than mere Farm Houses.)'.[75]

This meant much more estate work. For under the system of beneficial leases, the college had, in effect, delegated the role of landlord, often for generations, to the lessees of at least the larger holdings. Now it would have to deal directly with the occupiers, usually on a year-to-year basis since very few of them wanted long leases on the Scottish model. And during the changeover, business might be particularly demanding. For where the beneficial leases were being run out, the lessees had little incentive to spend money on repairs; and it was often claimed in the mid-nineteenth century that one could therefore tell college property by its dilapidated state. On taking over, colleges were anxious to remedy this; and, in an era when capital-intensive ('high') farming was in vogue, they were often attracted by the idea of upgrading their estates and so attracting a better class of tenant farmers who would pay higher rents. It was, too, a time of dawning susceptibility as to the deplorable condition of so many rural cottages. Many fellows will have shared in this feeling; and anyway it was important, for reasons of public

---

[74] Letters quoted by R. E. Bagnall-Wild, 'Some Treasurers of Oriel', OR (1967), 22–3. The accounts' language was switched to English with effect from 1859.
[75] Charles Neate, *Observations on College Leases* (Oxford, 1853); OCA TF 1 A9/1, Audit Memoranda, Easter 1853.

relations in an age of reform, that colleges should not leave themselves vulnerable to exposures of bad housing conditions on their estates. Accordingly we find Oriel buying back one of its copyholds, where the 'cottage accommodation' was 'very inadequate and at an exorbitant rent', 'in order to get rid of the nuisance and the scandal'. A similar impulse led it in 1872, in relation to its Oxford houses, to the very Victorian response of demolishing 'several old tenements' and laying out in their place 'a new street lined with houses of a higher class': namely, King Edward Street, erected on building leases by the new tenants.[76] In 1858 parliament empowered colleges to borrow for such purposes (and in 1860 also to compensate their fellows for fines forgone); and in 1859 Oriel resolved to borrow £12,200 'For the Wadley enclosure and the consequent improvements on the property', 'For the purchase of the remainder of the Wadley lease' and for that of two other leases, and for cottages and buildings on Bayliss Farm. In 1867 it put the next decade's expenditure 'upon the expiration of beneficial leases' at at least £12,000, plus £3,000 to 'complete the improvements in labourers' dwellings, now for some years carried on'; but this was soon exceeded. By 1872 a total of £25,823 had been borrowed for such purposes (plus £10,100 to compensate fellows for fines forgone), and by 1886 £52,525 (though of this £10,325 had come from internal college funds).[77]

Greater activism led, unsurprisingly, to changes in the way the estates were managed. Previously the office of senior treasurer had rotated around the fellows: Newman (1829–31) was said to have been very rapid and always accurate with the accounts, but there is at least a college tradition that Keble (1820–2) once added the current day's date into them. Drummond Chase, however, held the senior treasurership from 1849 to 1874 with only one brief intermission—a development with parallels in other colleges. He was succeeded by Charles Lancelot Shadwell, who served until 1887 when he had to resign his fellowship on acquiring 'too well paid a benefice'. Perhaps on Shadwell's advice, Oriel then looked outside to choose a professional, Langford Lovell Price, whose fellowship clearly derived from his office. Questions of estate policy had always been put to the fellows, both at the big biennial meetings linked to the audits and at the regular meetings of residents: in 1834 Newman accused Provost Hawkins of blocking discussion on more contentious issues by instead taking meetings through 'all the posts, barndoor fowls, and chimney pots' on the estates.[78] This involvement continued throughout

---

[76] PP 1873 xxxvii part 1, 67.

[77] In 1872 Oriel had, in Shenington, Dean, Littleworth, and Wickensham, 21 'tied' cottages let with its farms, and 43 let directly to the occupiers. PP 1873 xxxvii part 2, 294, 311, 315; OCA TF 1 A9/1, Audit Memoranda, Easter 1859; *Accounts of the Colleges*, 1885–6.

[78] Newman to Froude, 14 June 1834, LDN iv. 272, quoted in K. C. Turpin, 'The Ascendancy of Oriel', HUO vi. 191. But Hawkins was a fusspot, so it may have resulted from incompetence, not strategy.

the period, as the governing body minutes make clear. But day-to-day matters, the Cleveland Commission was told, were handled largely by the senior treasurer and the 'agent', both of whom, Oxford being 'easily accessible by railways', received a number of business visits from college tenants. For this, for rent collection, and for attending college meetings when appropriate, the agent received a retainer of £50 p.a., making further charges for visits to value college properties or to plan and supervise repairs and new buildings. Bath solicitors collected the rents of the nearby beneficial leases, and bailiffs (paid four pounds or four guineas a year) those of cottages and copyholders at Dean, Shenington, and Wadley/Littleworth 'where the college is lord of the manors'. But rack-rents were collected by the agent, sometimes accompanied by the treasurer who found this a good opportunity to inspect the properties. Fellows might come too (at college expense), but were said rarely to do so—though in 1859 Charles Neate was chosen to act as Oriel's 'agent in the Wadley Enclosure'.[79]

From the eighteenth century, Bagnall-Wild writes, the college bag had been 'used as a reserve which to some extent stabilised the dividend from year to year'. By the nineteenth century its chief sources of income, besides ad hoc college contributions when money was plentiful, had become internal room rents, Oriel's tithe receipts, redeemed Land Tax, and the increase of rents 'by buying up leases' (only the previous average receipts being divided among the fellows). The general rationale, the Cleveland Commission was later told, was that the college bag was assigned certain sources of income,

it being always agreed that these should not be divided. The fund had to bear certain definite expenses (among these were augmentation of [college] benefices... payments to schools... and charities of all kinds, donations to public purposes, and to all other purposes connected to duty as landowners), and all expenses of repairs [for both the College buildings and those on the estates], management of property, except [Oxford rack-rent] houses. The object being to arrive, without perpetually raising questions, at the sum which should be paid as dividend to the provost and fellows.

It was chiefly from this source, too, though also on occasion from other bags, that fellows were compensated when fines were not paid or not taken. But, we learn, the balance 'soon melted away under the expenses' of systematically running out leases after 1853, leaving the college bag only a rather cumbersome accounting device. The upshot was the development of the new, and more complete, 'Senior Treasurer's Statement of Account'—the Cleveland Commission printed the account for 1870–1. And this became the main focus for Oriel's financial business, though from 1883 it was

---

[79] PP 1873 xxxvii part 2, 311; OCA TF 1 A9/1, Audit Memoranda, October 1855 and 7 April 1859. Oriel had also, in 1853, agreed 'to appoint an Architect to superintend all repairs in the College or in houses in Oxford'.

supplemented by the returns in the format the University Commissioners imposed on all colleges.[80]

For our next snapshot of Oriel's financial progress, we therefore have a number of accounts to choose from. In 1835–6 rents had been some £3,859, which with the decennial average of fines received gave a total of £4,795. In 1870–1 a similar calculation from the Style gives us rents of £10,314, though receipts from fines will have been right down.[81] Alternatively we can take the Cleveland Commission's calculation, for lands, rent-charges, tithes, and house property 'after deducting fixed charges', of £11,951, or that of the senior treasurer's Statement for gross receipts from estates, houses, and tithes of £12,239.[82] Since prices were, if anything, lower in 1871 than in 1836 these gains were real.

But the picture was to prove less rosy than they suggest. For only a proportion of the gross rents was actually available for college use. This is shown most clearly in the accounting format chosen by the Cleveland Commission and continued in the statutory Accounts of the Colleges. Against the gross rents had to be set 'repairs and improvements on estates' (£2,925), and management, legal costs, insurance, rates, and taxes (£1,234, though half of this represented part of the costs of securing a private act of parliament). Charitable contributions mostly linked to the estates—subscriptions and donations, and the augmentation of benefices—accounted for £1,128; and interest on, plus repayment of, estate and fine loans took another £1,799. Not all these outgoings were new. Schemes for the augmentation of benefices had been discussed in the Audit Memoranda since the eighteenth century; it was hard to build up the living of Coleby to the point where any fellow would be prepared to take it. And in the 1830s the college bag had been much used for contributions to schools and other charities. But rates and taxes were rising. And by taking its estates into hand, the college was assuming many 'landlord' functions hitherto fulfilled by its larger lessees. These included local charitable obligations, but more especially the provision (and insuring) of buildings and other fixed capital for their tenant farmers. Like other colleges, Oriel entered enthusiastically into this role, and borrowed to do so; the 1870–1 'repairs and improvements' were more than covered by the £3,068 estate loan then taken out. But such loans had to be repaid. The expectation was that it could be done out of the rent increases

---

[80] PP 1873 xxxvii part 2, 306; OCA TF A9/1, Audit Memoranda, Easter 1785; Bagnall-Wild, 'Some Treasurers of Oriel', 21, and 'A Century of Change 1826–1926', OR (1969), 21.

[81] Wadley manor paid £735 in 1872, £700 in 1879, £600 in 1886 (Price, 'The Recent Depression in Agriculture... 1876–90', 20), but there will have been few other large fines.

[82] To give greater continuity with the Style's format, £921, the 1872 value of the canonry of Rochester annexed to the provostship (Vallis, 'The Estates of Oriel', 42), is here deducted: PP 1873 xxxvi part 1, 65–7, part 2, 311–12; the dates of the Cleveland Commission's accounting year may differ from those of the senior treasurer's Statement.

proceeding from the improved 'high' farming, but this was to be severely tested by the so-called 'Great Depression' of agriculture in the last quarter of the nineteenth century. Historians have shown that the depression was in fact patchy, hitting different types of farming at different dates and to a different extent. Oriel's estates, a mixture of arable and pasture, were perhaps average for southern England, neither escaping the pressure of the times nor experiencing the disaster of finding that no tenant would take them. Price, the treasurer, used its accounts, and those of the other Oxford colleges, to chart the fortunes of agriculture in a series of papers: all useful, but weakened by the fact that, although he was an economist, Price made no allowance for the changing value of money.[83]

Price used rents as his measure of the depression, and had no difficulty in establishing that the money paid had fallen considerably, 1879 being a particularly bad year. In theory the proper response to these pressures was to move from arable to pasture (livestock prices being affected later, and on the whole less, than those of corn); and Oriel went some way through building, fencing, and draining to help tenants to do so: which Price in 1892 saw as one reason why expenditure on repairs had remained roughly constant.[84] Other and quicker responses to a farmer's hardship, all then expected of a good landlord, were to acquiesce in the delayed payment of rent and/or to concede temporary abatements or (ideally) permanent reductions. Price's first paper shows that both abatements and arrears shot up in 1878–90, with actual receipts from landed estates (other than the trust property in Kent) in 1879 of only £7,209 as compared to £10,739 in the peak year of 1877–8. There was some recovery, and repayment of arrears, in the early 1880s, followed by another bad patch in the middle of the decade; and in 1890 receipts were only £7,570.[85] Unfortunately Price's later papers do not continue these figures, though the depression that he hoped in 1892 had ended returned later in the decade, with Oriel's landed estate rental (including the Kent property) reaching its nadir in 1897 at £6,930, as compared to the £10,659 of 1877–8.[86]

But though these 'agricultural estates' furnished the bulk of Oriel's external income, they did not provide it all. We should, therefore, broaden our examination, using—again with Price—the statutory College Accounts when they become available in 1883 to give a sharper picture. (See Table 15.3.)

---

[83] That this was only very rarely noticed in the discussions that followed their delivery is a sign of the then general prevalence of 'money illusion'.
[84] Price, 'The Recent Depression', 35. However it dipped in the 1890s, then rose in the twentieth century.
[85] Price, 'The Recent Depression', esp. 25–6. The apparent nadir was the £6,688 of 1887, but this was largely the result of an accounting arrangement 'due to the final settlement of the affairs of an outgoing tenant' whose difficulties really stemmed from 1879.
[86] Price, 'The Estates of the Colleges', table 7; the 1877–8 receipts had been increased by repayment of arrears.

TABLE 15.3 (a) Oriel's agricultural estate rental (including Kent)

1877–8 (*in 1883 pounds*) £10,659 (£10,000)	1883 £9,016

(b) Oriel's gross and net external receipts in current pounds (1883 pounds in brackets)

	1883	1892	1902	1912
Receipts				
Lands	7,965	7,257	6,621	6,853
Houses	1,459	1,815	2,258	1,772
Tithes (including tithes for the provost)	1,870	1,505	1,176	1,317
Total estates (including misc. sums not noted above)	11,560	10,713	10,215	10,046
Dividends	329	90	17	17
Total external receipts	11,889	10,803	10,232	10,063
External expenditure				
Loans: interest and repayment	2,654	2,054	1,300	958
Repairs, taxes, and other external expenditure (including charitable donations)	3,576	4,021	5,076	4,953
Total external expenditure	6,230	6,075	6,376	5,911
Net external income	5,659	4,728 (4,900)	3,876 (3,900)	4,152 (3,900)

This confirms the decline in Oriel's external income, which was the more disappointing in that the Cleveland Commission had anticipated an increase of £1,512 p.a. by 1895.[87] Initially things had gone well: Price says the agricultural rental peaked in 1877–8. But then they went downhill. In fact the fall from the Cleveland Commission's £11,951 (perhaps £12,000 in 1883 pounds) to the 1883 gross estates income of £11,560 had not been great. But the fall in external receipts then continued until the turn of the century. Between 1902 and 1912 there was some agricultural recovery and hence increase in income from Lands and Tithes. It was apparently more than

[87] A much smaller increase, of course, than for those colleges that had been slower to run out their beneficial leases; PP 1873 xxxvii part 1, 65. The increase that never came through sounds like the 'deficiency in the College revenue of some £1,500 per annum whereby the Fellowships are impoverished and the status of the College is diminished' to which Cecil Rhodes referred in his will.

offset by lower takings from Houses; but this will have reflected the loss from those demolished to make way for the new Rhodes Building, for which the college was compensated (though some fellows thought inadequately) on another account. In terms of external expenditure, the chief development was the steady repayment of debt and fall of debt charges. Overall net external income on this account was slightly higher in 1912 than in 1902. Correcting for the changing value of money, the position was unchanged; but if we then factor in the benefits of Cecil Rhodes's will (£40,000 to construct a new building and compensate the college for income from the houses that building destroyed, £10,000 as a college building repair fund, £40,000 to increase the incomes of the resident fellows, and £10,000 to support 'the dignity and comfort of the High Table'[88]), Oriel's position had certainly improved.

More important, though, in the long run was the composition of its external income. This came chiefly from 'Lands', and in money terms it fell until the turn of the century and then broadly flat-lined. For since Oriel had already run out most of its beneficial leases by 1871, it could not derive much more from this source. Tithes were linked to the price of corn over the last seven years, which meant that they were outside the college's control except insofar as they were granted away to augment benefices.[89] As to the third main source of external income, 'Houses', these did indeed improve until the twentieth century. But Oriel's estates were not well sited to enable it to join in the suburban building boom that compensated many colleges for the shortfalls in agricultural rents and made some—most notably Magdalen—enormously wealthy. In this context Oriel may, in 1861, have been mistaken in exchanging its 3¾ acres in St Giles's fields for land in Iffley. It did, however, have some hopes of Swainswick, where in 1871, it was looking to run out two beneficial leases 'in expectation of letting the land on building leases'.[90] But nothing much ever came of this.

Of course not all was doom and gloom. By 1912 Oriel had paid off most of its debt. It had attracted a useful legacy from Cecil Rhodes. And internal college income had increased. A rough calculation suggests that in terms of overall net revenue Oriel moved from equal thirteenth place among the colleges in 1871 to equal tenth in 1920, in those of income per resident undergraduate from sixth to equal twelfth.[91] But it depended heavily on agricultural rents that basically flat-lined; it was, as Price said, 'not customary for English land-lords to raise the rents of sitting tenants'.[92] So if inflation

---

[88] These investments, being made through the Rhodes Trustees, seem not to appear directly in the accounts.
[89] The chief change was the passage of liability to pay tithe from the tenants to the college, sometimes by way of individual rent reduction, but after 1891 universally by act of parliament.
[90] PP 1873 xxxvi part 2, 294.
[91] Dunbabin, 'Finance since 1914', HUO viii. 657.
[92] Price, 'The Estates of the Colleges and their Management', 563.

took off, there would be trouble. And of course it did: the Retail Price Index more than doubled between 1913 and 1919.

During the war the college suffered a strange half shut-down existence. In 1919 there was much re-examination of its workings, with committees on future tutorial arrangements and payments, on the Rhodes Benefaction payments to the Resident Fellows Fund, and on the pay of the female domestic staff. Among those much involved was the chemistry fellow Henry Tizard, who came back from high-powered scientific administrative war service in April and was promptly made senior common room steward. 'I found the wine in a shocking state...We had to pour the contents of some dozens of bottles of vintage Burgundy down the sink, because they were all "corked".' He soon set about more important matters.[93] Oriel's accounts showed 'Lands' as producing only £35 more in 1918 than in 1914, 'Houses' less (since the wartime absence of undergraduates had led to rent reductions); only 'Tithes' were buoyant, up by a third in response to the rise in grain prices—and this was almost cancelled out by the corresponding rise in Oriel's tithe payments. But the only recommendations in the college Auditor's Report of March 1919 were that the wartime reductions on Oxford house rents 'should now cease', and that the £420 agency costs of the estates should be reduced. Oriel had in fact been approached by London land-agents seeking to 'purchase estates'. The first offer of November 1915 was rejected; that of March 1918 to buy Wadley and Littleworth for £50,600 was put to the April 'stated' meeting and declined, with a further resolution taken next month 'on general ground to decline an offer to purchase'. It was, admittedly, agreed in April 1919 to accept the tenant's offer for Bilham Farm in Kent, and in June, on receiving an offer to buy the Dean estate, to get 'a valuation of the College property in Dene and Chalford'. But equally Oriel decided in July to bid up to £1,500 (in the event unsuccessfully) for Lower Farm, Shenington, a village where it had had ideas of establishing a tree nursery and of possible iron-stone quarrying in conjunction with New College, and where it was discussing water supply and housing with the local authorities.[94]

Tizard saw things differently. 'Farmers', he correctly recollected, 'had become prosperous during the war, and the price of land rose considerably. Government stocks on the other hand had depreciated. The price of 4 per cent Funding Loan was at one time as low as 66.'[95] Tizard's biography says

---

[93] On Tizard, who was knighted in 1937, see ODNB s.n.; Imperial War Museum, Papers of Sir Henry Tizard, HTT 713: unfinished typescript autobiography, 117. Tizard's folder of Oriel papers (HTT 3) contains reports from the internal reform committees here mentioned, and is the source of subsequent references to 1919–20 Oriel papers where no other reference is given.

[94] OCA GOV 4 A7–8, college minutes.

[95] Autobiography, 123. Farmers seem to have been the chief beneficiaries of the pre-war agricultural revival: C. O' Gráda, in R. Flood and Donald McCloskey (eds.), *The Economic History of Britain since 1700*, ii (Cambridge, 1981), 177; more anecdotally A. G. Street writes of

'he pressed on his seniors with persuasive argument' the idea of selling land and buying stocks, presumably initially in private discussions.[96] In August the Treasurer, P. C. Lyon (who had succeeded the conservative Price only a year earlier), asked Tizard whether he wanted anything included on the agenda of the October stated meeting; and when this was finalized on 8 September it included, as a new item, Tizard's motion 'That the College consider the advisability of selling the whole or part of its estates.'

In Tizard's papers, enclosed within the college auditors' 'Statement of the Senior Treasurer's Accounts for the Years 1909–18', are his manuscript notes for the speech he gave either to the meeting of 8 October 1919 or to its sequel on 12 November:

Shortage of funds   Increase of repairs
How can income be increased
40% gross income goes back in agency & other ways
Value of land about 20 years purchase gross rent
    5% on this (Funding Loan) = £7000   Increase income £3000
Capital increase = ¼ in 40–70 years = £35,000
Imposs. to increase rent except v. slowly—but repairs will be double
Sentimental reasons inadequate
Work of [Asquith] Commission [on Oxford and Cambridge Universities]—either compulsory sale, or pooling of estates
    ? sentimental reasons
Propose that Treasurer be authorised to make enquiries for tenants on general [illegible—? basis] that 25 years purchase be accepted

Among other scribbled notes are '£50,600 Littleworth & Wadley', presumably a reference to the offer rejected in 1918.

Those influenced by the 'sentimental reasons' would have included Provost Phelps, who was very much a countryman at heart: he kept the fleece of 'the famous ram "Oriel"' (bred at Wadley) by his bedside, and one of his 'post-war projects' had been 'that each of the "college ladies" [presumably fellows' wives] should take charge of one of the college properties, and supply the want of a resident land-owner's wife'. But he considered Tizard's proposal with an open mind, and, once convinced, 'used all his energy in putting it through'.[97] In October the governing body considered Tizard's motion and asked the treasurer to submit 'a report on the capital value of the

---

his own farming experience, in an area of Wiltshire not unlike the places where Oriel had property, that after the war 'we all had money to burn', 'farmers tumbled over each other in their eagerness to get farms', and social and motoring diversions abounded—'I did all these things, paid the interest on the borrowed capital, and paid off about five hundred pounds per annum for a year or so immediately after the War'; A. G. Street, *Farmer's Glory* (London, 1933), 223, 225, 228.

[96] Ronald W. Clark, *Tizard* (London, 1965), 49.
[97] G. N. Clark, 'Provost Phelps and the College Estates', OR (1937), 212–13.

several estates' to 'a special general meeting'. This 'Valuation of certain landed properties' gave a gross rental of £6,953 and a value of £154,550, or, on average, twenty-two years' purchase, and it promised the production of more detailed accounts at the 12 November meeting.[98] The meeting itself decided to authorize the treasurer to negotiate, and the regular fortnightly governing body meetings to conclude, 'the sale of the College Estates'. Tenants were to be given the first option to purchase, and, as a first step, they were to be invited to dinner in December.[99]

The sales were pushed through with remarkable speed. Any lingering hesitation was addressed by W. A. Craigie and Tizard in their March 1920 Auditors' Report, where they noted that in 1919 estate expenditure had absorbed £7,056 of the £8,235 gross rents from land and houses.[100] By Michaelmas 1921 property worth £159,365 had been sold at slightly above valuation, mostly to sitting tenants,[101] with sale of a further £3,245 agreed. So only some £23,390 worth remained, chiefly the mansion house and related lands at Wadley which were still on beneficial lease.[102] The money raised was mostly invested in Trustee Security stocks yielding, on average, rather over 5 per cent. And 'to commemorate their long, and now severed, association with the College', Provost Phelps saw to the establishment of parish rooms in Swainswick, Littleworth, and Shenington. 'These three village halls', G. N. Clark wrote, 'are Phelps' special monuments.'[103]

At a technical level, the estate sales and re-investment in stocks had been admirably conducted, catching the land boom at the peak of the market and re-investing before the yield on stocks began to fall from August 1921. Though no other college sold so high a proportion of its lands, Oriel was, of course, not alone—Cambridge land sales in 1918–20 totalled over £525,000 (the largest vendor being King's), Oxford's probably over £332,000.[104] The Asquith Commission thought this an admirable development. Other college bursars did not: in March 1920 the 'Committee of Estates Bursars' produced a slew of contrary arguments, notably the proposition that land was a much

---

[98] Imperial War Museum HTT 3, typescript in the Tizard papers.
[99] OCA GOV 4 A7–8, college minutes, 8 and 9 October, 12 and 26 November 1919.
[100] The full picture was not quite so gloomy—tithes and quitrents had contributed £1,393 and timber sales £1,005; but Oriel's external income did not cover the deficit on its internal expenditure.
[101] Once land prices had fallen Oriel encountered some criticism for having encouraged its 'trusting tenants' to buy at the top of the market, often with borrowed money (Oriel itself lent its Dean buyers over half the purchase price at 5% interest).
[102] In 1922 Wadley's lessee refused the £12,000 price Oriel had asked, and in 1932 it was eventually sold to someone else for £10,750—Bagnall-Wild, 'Oriel's Agricultural Property', 15.
[103] OCA TF 2/D2/3, P. C. Lyon, 'Report on the Sale of Landed Property belonging to Oriel College in the Years 1920 and 1921', 3 April 1922; Clark, 'Provost Phelps and the College Estates', 213.
[104] PP 1920 x, 358, 366, Royal Commission on Oxford and Cambridge Universities; figures for Peterhouse's small and Exeter's appreciable takings are not given.

better store of value than money—it had appreciated twentyfold since Queen Elizabeth's day—and that it also carried with it the possibility of 'windfall' gains—'Probably all the richest colleges have benefited largely by the development of building land...etc., which would not have affected the selling price of their estates 100 years ago.' Over different time horizons, both the Asquith Commission and the estates bursars were right. Towards the end of the 1920s, when land prices had fallen and lower interest rates had increased the price of stocks, Tizard himself advised Oriel to sell these and buy 'land and property in provincial towns'; some such purchases were made in the 1930s, but Tizard regretted that the college did not do more.[105]

---

[105] Report of the Royal Commission's 'Estates Committee', May 1921 PP 1920 x. 218–21, which did address the danger of monetary depreciation by advising colleges to spend only two-thirds of their increased income from land sales and re-invest the remainder as a hedge against 'depreciation'; memorandum from the Estates Bursars committee (Balliol, Merton, Queen's, All Souls, Magdalen, Christ Church, Jesus), *Royal Commission..., Appendices to the Report of the Commissioners* (HMSO, 1922), 38–9; Tizard, Autobiography, 124.

16

Property and Investments, 1920–1990

Wilf Stephenson

> Blest spot! Where childlike learning sits
> Remote from worldly cares,
> And leaves to skilled financiers its
> Pecuniary affairs

Having been reminded of A. D. Godley's lines in 'Ode on a Distant Prospect of Oriel College' inspired by Cecil Rhodes's will, Provost Clark lamented in his valedictory Provost's Notes of 1957:[1] 'We wish we could!' Others, considering the management of the college's financial affairs over most of the twentieth century, might comment, perhaps unfairly, for particularly after 1974 financiers had been closely involved: 'We wish they had'!

The decision in 1919 to sell the college's historic landed estates was one of the most significant moments in the history of Oriel's finances. Its short-term impact is clear: income increased and funds were released to carry out much-needed repairs to buildings as well as to complete the acquisition of the properties forming the Island Site. Three new fellows were recruited, a substantial increase of the fellowship as it was before and during the Great War. The longer-term consequences are much less certain. Would the college now rank nearer to All Souls and Christ Church or to Worcester and St Peter's had the estates been retained? An external review of the college's financial management carried out for the provost at the end of the century considered that 'Oriel is one of the poorer colleges in Oxford but has the most expensive taste'. This may seem unfair when the facts are examined, but perhaps it does give one clue as to why the college has struggled to build reserves comparable to many of the older Oxford colleges. A series of dedicated treasurers each brought his own particular skills and experience to managing the finances in the face of substantial challenges; in 1967 the

---

[1] OR (1957), 6–7.

treasurer commented in the *Oriel Record* that 'Walter Maye, Senior Treasurer 1519 to 1521 was admonished for striking another fellow, a temptation many other treasurers have possibly found hard to resist'.[2] They were supported by a series of long-serving college clerks or accountants, including C. F. Horn (1930–69), C. Brindle (1969–92), and N. J. Pearson (1992–2009). In spite of all their efforts, the college was in great financial difficulties by the early 1970s, followed by a period of gradual restoration and recovery.

Provost Ross described L. L. Price, treasurer from 1888 to 1918, as good and careful though perhaps not very enterprising. He credited Henry Tizard with the plan to sell the major estates and thereby almost to double the college's income.[3] At the time Tizard was a 34-year-old fellow and lecturer in chemistry, not on the face of it the best-qualified member of the college to drive such a radical change, but a man with substantial experience of the commercial world through his service in the Great War. Oriel was not alone in making such a decision. Balliol and five other colleges made substantial disposals of land during the 1920s, as did twelve Cambridge colleges. The Auditors' Report of 1919, written by Tizard and W. A. Craigie, commented that in 1918 estate expenditure had absorbed £7,056 of the £8,235 gross rents from land and houses, leaving a return of only 1 per cent of the capital value.[4] It was acknowledged that this was an exceptional year for expenditure, as works delayed by the war were carried out. More than anything else, the very low net return shows why the sales were such a success in the short term: the college's spending was restricted to income. No account could be taken of movements in capital value, even though the timing of the sale was chosen for precisely that reason. Removal of the expenses that went with ownership of estates turned the gross income into net income available to spend.

In 1918 P. C. Lyon had taken over as treasurer on Price's retirement. Having matriculated at Oriel in 1881, he had enjoyed a long career in the Indian Civil Service as Chief Secretary of East Bengal, Member and Vice-President of the Viceroy's Legislative Council, and Vice-President of the Legislative and Executive Councils of Bengal. He was perhaps not well placed to challenge the persuasive arguments put forward by Tizard, and he readily took on the task of implementing the sales. The support of Provost Phelps was important, particularly in handling critics who took the college to task either for selling to the tenants at too high a price, or for spoiling the market by selling too cheaply, as G. N. Clark noted.[5] In 1920 the Asquith Commission estimated that by re-investing the proceeds of land sales at 5 per cent, colleges more than doubled net receipts, noted that Oriel, Oxford's most active seller, believed that it had tripled them. The commission's favourable view of land

---

[2] R. E. Bagnall-Wild, 'Some Treasurers of Oriel', OR (1967), 21.
[3] OR (1957), 21.   [4] OR (1964), 14.
[5] G. N. Clark, 'Provost Phelps and the College Estates', OR (1937), 211–14, cf. 212.

sales alarmed the Oxford bursars, who feared that they would be pressed into further sales. The Estates Bursars Committee commented: 'the [colleges] can find no investment likely, in the long run, to be more remunerative than land. There is the appreciation in value and windfalls of various kinds... probably all the richest colleges have benefitted largely by the development of building land...'. They also feared more drastic consequences for, if their endowments consisted only of 'stocks and securities', it 'could be argued that the colleges were, in effect... glorified hostels... that they ought to be brought under central management of some University Delegacy... and that the Tutors and Lecturers of the Colleges should become Recognised Teachers of the University and be appointed thereby. The College system would thus be destroyed... It may also be remarked that confiscation of stocks and securities is a simpler matter than that of lands.'[6] The commission did not accept all the arguments of the bursars but recognized that some land should be retained. However, it concluded that some colleges had 'largely profited by the advantageous opportunity, and more could have done so'. So there was significant external endorsement of the bold steps taken by Oriel's governing body.

In 1919 local estate management mainly concerned conversion of pasture at Bartlemas into a new cricket and football ground. The Amalgamated Clubs, rather than the college, carried out the work, which was partially funded by a 'munificent gift' from Dr Shadwell. Unfortunately this was insufficient to cover the full cost of the works, over £2,000. The college lent almost £1,000, at an interest rate of 5 per cent, and an appeal to old members for funds for help in building a pavilion was planned. However, an appeal for a War Memorial Scholarship Fund had already been launched so this had to be postponed. The fund was opened in 1920, and the first cricket match at the new ground, against BNC, took place on 14 May. In 1921 the appeal continued and it was reported in the *Oriel Record* that the undergraduates had contributed nearly £400, while the savings held by the Amalgamated Clubs had contributed for £500 towards the total cost. It was noted that 'but for the fall in the value of securities this contribution might have been twice as much'.[7]

In 1922 Lyon was granted a year's leave to visit India, and W. A. Craigie was appointed acting treasurer. A year later the provost commented: 'We are glad to welcome Mr Lyon back to England and the College; he has resumed his duties after a year's absence during which Mr Craigie has been an efficient guardian of the College finances.'[8] He had overseen extensive building works and significant expenditure on fabric repairs. Lyon was the last treasurer to

---

[6] Memorandum of the Committee of Oxford Estates Bursars to Asquith Commission, *Royal Commission...Appendices to the Report of the Commissioners* (1922), 38–9, cited J. P. D. Dunbabin, HUO viii. 659.
[7] OR (September 1921).
[8] OR (December 1923).

keep the accounts in the old style.⁹ Their form had been little changed since 1410. Two sets of accounts were maintained, the senior treasurer's showing the corporate revenues and the junior treasurer's showing internal revenue and expenditure. Neither was in the format that had been prescribed by the University Commissioners in 1882, and the treasurer was obliged to recast them each year in the required form. A committee had been asked to review the college's financial arrangements; it reported in September 1921, recommending that the formally separate offices of the senior and junior treasurers should be abolished, and the distinction between their accounts should cease, as most of the estates had been sold and the dividend system for payment of fellows had lapsed. The London bank accounts held at Messrs Hoare's should be closed now that the Old Bank was part of Barclays. Further, it proposed significant increases in charges to undergraduates, since costs had risen by 25 per cent during the war.¹⁰ The new format of accounts did not show capital values of the college's investments, whether in one of the many trusts or in the college reserves.¹¹ As investments consisted of loan stock and property, the main indicator of the financial state of the college is the aggregate net income from investments, which in 1920 was £6,323. By 1925 this had increased to £14,048, and by 1929 the income received by the trust funds showed a significant increase to £16,481.

A review of payments to servants in 1920 helps to put this income in context. A kitchen clerk was appointed on wages of £1 a week plus meals. It was reported that the bursars had agreed that bedmakers' pay should be £3 a week, with some on a higher rate of £3 10s. This amounted to about £182 a year; at Oriel they were paid £98 a year plus between £30 and £45 in gratuities. It was recommended that an assistant porter's pay should be increased from £145 a year to £160 a year and the Head Boot Black's from £117 to £130 a year. By contrast, the Committee on the Emoluments of the Provost in 1929 reported that the late provost's emoluments consisted of:

2 fellowships @£300	£600
Provost's stipend	£400
Purleigh Tithe average income	£475
Repayment of income tax	£300
Total	£1,775

---

⁹ R. E. Bagnall-Wild, OR (1967), 24.
¹⁰ OCA, Report of Committee on Finance and Accounts, 14 September 1921.
¹¹ What are now called the unrestricted reserves or endowment.

The amount provided for in the statutes was £1,275. Having reviewed the relative position of the college in the university, and taking into account expenses associated with the lodgings and the rise in the cost of living, the committee concluded that the provost's emoluments should be supplemented by an entertainment allowance of £300. This was slightly below the average of a sample of colleges but was the same as that paid by St John's.

In April 1928 Lyon wrote a paper for the governing body reviewing the finances since the sale of the estates and answering criticism in the auditors' report on the 1927 accounts.[12] As well as providing a very informative account of finances during this period, it gives some insight into the position of the treasurer, who was about to retire. The capital generated from the sales of the estates was invested at an average interest rate of 5.75 per cent, giving the significant increase in income described above. However, considerable arrears of repairs and maintenance work had accumulated during the war. At the same time prices and wages had increased, so the cost of running the college had risen 'to a figure far in excess of pre-war expenditure'. The number of fellows had also risen, from seven in 1913 to twelve in 1927. As an indication of the increase in costs, Lyon's figures show that expenditure on fellows had risen by 200 per cent and that on scholars and exhibitioners by over 90 per cent. The wages bill for college servants had also risen by 75 per cent. Expenditure on new buildings, repairs, and improvements between 1920 and the end of 1927 totalled £31,025 after deducting the contributions made by gifts and legacies. This included £9,400 on building new kitchens, boiler rooms, offices, and other facilities in the angle between the hall and the chapel. The new kitchens were equipped with up-to-date plant, electric lifts, and a cold store. Other expenditure during this period included £1,400 on the celebrations for the sexcentenary (about £70,000 in 2012 money using the RPI), as well as a further £400 to publish two volumes of commemorative records. Most of the investment revenue was derived from dividends on stocks held by the Ministry of Agriculture and Fisheries on behalf of the college. The ministry was willing to allow transfers of capital to land or properties that would generate income, but where the expenditure was not directly remunerative the college was required to replace the principal within ten years. As a result, any advances spent on repairs or new buildings were treated as loans which had to be repaid according to a fixed schedule. The college took a very conservative approach to the treatment of this expenditure, so that funds spent on improvements to investment properties at Bartlemas and in King Edward Street and on redemption of tithe payments were replaced even though they generated new income or eliminated future expenditure. Lyon explained that while this policy was sound, it placed limits

---

[12] OCA, P. C. Lyon: 'Note by the Treasurer on the College Accounts and Report of the College Auditors' for the year 1927.

on the college's ability to build up a separate reserve. In the three years after the decision to sell the estates the college repaid debts of £6,719, of which £2,700 had been borrowed 'internally' from the Caution Money Fund. However, between 1923 and 1927 the college had taken out loans from the funds held by the ministry totalling £24,100, resulting in annual payments of £2,333, of which £1,033 represented payments out of revenue for new investments.

The Royal Commission had commented on the policy of exchanging investments in land for stocks and shares, and accordingly the college had decided in 1923 to establish a reserve fund to safeguard against depreciation in the value of the new investments. In spite of the constraints of higher expenditures and loan payments, between 1923 and 1926 £2,000 a year was paid into the reserve; in 1927 this was merged with the old 'College Bag', the name being passed to the new combined fund, formally called 'The College Bag (General Reserve Fund)'. However, the pressures of expenditure towards the end of 1927 created an operating deficit of £300 and forced the abandonment of the contributions. As Lyon explained, 'instead of reporting my inability to make the payment, I thought it best to carry out the orders of the College and to explain the facts at the Stated General Meeting in April, 1928 when the accounts for 1927 would be presented.' He proposed that the grant made to the fund in 1927 be recalled. By that time the College Bag had about £10,500 invested, generating an income of £200 a year. However, most of the investments accumulated compound interest, and he projected a value of £17,500 after ten years; this he believed should prove more than adequate to meet any depreciation in the value of the college's securities that could be reasonably anticipated. Lyon concluded that the deficit in the accounts was due first to a general increase in running costs not covered by increases in charges: 'the fact is that we have not raised our charges sufficiently since the war to meet increased cost of services which they are supposed to meet', secondly to the conservative policy adopted on the loans, and thirdly to having tried to save a larger sum than was possible in the circumstances. The auditors had called for an investigation to find economies and Lyon recommended that this be left until his successor had settled in. However, he believed that an investigation of costs and charges would be fruitful and that charges could be increased 'without endangering our reputation as one of the least expensive Colleges in the University'. A budget estimate would also prove beneficial and would be much easier with more normal patterns of expenditure. The idea that major expenditures should be planned and budgeted for a year in advance does not seem to have been considered. Finally, a further adjustment to the form of accounts was required to make them comply with the revised stipulations of the university. This would be fully implemented for the 1929 accounts.

The college did not follow Lyon's recommendation to leave the review of costs to his successor. A committee on possible economies on internal expenditure and cost of services was appointed, which reported at the end of June 1928. It was recommended to fix the charge for dinner at high table and to take care that the cost did not exceed this sum, and to raise establishment charges from £10 to £12 a term, and room rents by 25 per cent. The election of a treasurer proved no easy matter: 'the standard set by Mr Lyon...was so high, the number of candidates so embarrassingly large (126)...the choice of the College fell on Mr Cecil Stuart Emden DFC, Assistant Chief Clerk in the Solicitor's Department of the Treasury.'[13] Emden had been something of a war hero. He had been severely wounded, having lost a leg while serving with the British Expeditionary Force and having been further injured in action with the Balloon Corps. Apart from his administrative and financial skills, the committee considered it a substantial advantage that he would reside in college. This was a difficult time to arrive at Oriel. In spite of the tight financial situation, Lyon had been highly regarded, having successfully completed the sales of most of the estates at better than anticipated prices. The auditors' report for 1928 expressed concern about the financial situation.[14] They believed that the outlook up to the end of 1931 called for 'the most rigid economies in all departments' and saw little prospect for improvement until the end of 1933: 'the utmost that can be hoped for in these five years 1929–1933 is some diminution in the accumulated deficit (at present over £2500) on the Revenue account...' The following year there had been some improvement in the situation, attributed both to economies and to increased income particularly from room rents, but the need for retrenchment remained.[15] The improvement in the operating accounts continued and, in addition to repaying capital borrowed from the funds held for the college by the Ministry of Agriculture (mainly to finance the building of new kitchens), £350 was invested in a new capital fund in 1930. By 1932 the financial position had strengthened to the extent that the auditors could recommend the establishment of a New Building Fund in preparation for building new lodgings for the provost and converting the existing lodgings into undergraduates' rooms.[16]

By 1930 the only significant land holding retained by the college was the major part of Wadley Manor, consisting of 387 acres of agricultural land together with a manor house, farmhouse, and farm buildings. The disposal of this had been delayed initially by legal difficulties. A sale was finally agreed in 1932 for £10,750, compared to the price of £12,000 offered to the sitting tenant in 1922. In 1931 it had been decided to return to investment in agricultural land, now viewed as an investment asset to be held as part of a portfolio which might be traded from time to time, depending on the relative

---

[13] OCA, Report of the Committee on election of a Treasurer, 1928.
[14] OCA, Auditors' Report, 1928.
[15] OCA, Auditors' Report, 1929.   [16] OCA, Auditors' Report, 1932.

attraction of different asset classes. Wadley Manor was considered unsuitable as it included a manor house of considerable size,[17] which might make re-letting difficult and would require substantial expenditure on modernization and repairs. So when Wadley was sold, some stocks were sold in addition, and the Gaines estate on the borders of Worcestershire and Herefordshire was acquired; this was a highly regarded estate, consisting of three farms totalling 380 acres in good farming and fruit-growing country.

In 1932 a significant investment was also made in urban property with the purchase of the Midland Bank in Oxford Street, London, for £25,202. This was let on a long lease with a valuable reversion in 2004. Further acquisitions of high street properties were made during the 1930s. Shops at 20–2 and 46 High Street, Sutton, Surrey, were bought in 1933 for £6,736. An office and warehouse at 70–1 Wells Street and 86 Margaret Street, London, were bought for £12,045 in 1934. The National Provincial Bank at 29 Boars Lane, Leeds, was bought in 1935 for £26,637 and a shop at 57 Christchurch Road, Bournemouth, was bought in 1936 for £18,460. Urban property was also sold during this period in Aberford, Yorkshire, realizing £1,450. Local loans stock was sold in anticipation of falling interest rates. The proceeds were used to fund the property purchases and invested in Dominion, Colonial, and Corporation Stocks.[18] Overall assets remained divided between fixed income securities and property. By early 1937 it was recommended that the policy of increasing the proportion of investment in real property should cease.[19] By that time about one-third of the net income of the college was derived from rents and two-thirds from stocks and shares. The internal auditors, W. A. Pantin and D. L. Hammick, commented that it was becoming increasingly difficult to find satisfactory property investments, and that a reasonable yield from investment in 'trustee' stocks and shares was now to be expected.

The net income from investments had increased, but even though less had been spent on the buildings after the post-war activity of the previous decade, expenditure had grown faster. In Oxford further improvements were made at Bartlemas with the construction of eight lawn tennis courts alongside the sports ground. Provost Phelps contributed to planting of the wood where in 1926 a cypress had been planted to mark Oriel's sexcentenary. Although repair and maintenance work had been restricted, essential works continued. In 1931 several beam ends on the Merton Street façade were found to have been attacked by death-watch beetle and similar problems were found the following year on the Oriel Street front when refacing work was being carried out. Expenditure was funded from the operating budget, from a building reserve fund, and by borrowing.

---

[17] Letter from the treasurer to the Ministry of Agriculture and Fisheries, quoted in OR (1964).
[18] OCA, Auditors' Report (1934).   [19] OCA, Auditors' Report (1936).

In 1933 the Royal Commission on the Tithe Rent Charge recommended the reduction of the tithe to 8.44 per cent below par and the subsequent commutation of tithes on terms regarded as disadvantageous. This had a relatively small impact on Oriel, although it marked a further break with the college's historic estates. However, the provost's stipend had been largely paid from the Purleigh tithe and with its replacement with gilt-edged stock in 1936 other arrangements had to be made. It was time for some longer-term planning. Reports on the various funds maintained by the college, among them the Tuition Fund, the Pension Fund, the Rhodes Reserve Fellows Fund, and the Rhodes 'C' Fund show that the college was aware that prudent management of its limited resources demanded a longer view. In 1933 the report on the Rhodes 'C' Fund included projected income and expenditure from 1934 to 1942. Growth in expenditure was expected to exceed growth in income, and if the trend had been projected to 1944 the fund would have gone into deficit. The report on the fund made in 1945 noted that this deficit had not come about, but only because savings had been made by the vacancy in N. M. Tod's fellowship and the absence of several fellows on war service. Although the savings had been re-invested, thus boosting income, a deficit was expected in 1946 or 1947. Perhaps this longer perspective moved the college in 1944 to recognize the contributions of its former treasurers L. L. Price and Percy Lyon, by electing them to emeritus fellowships.

In 1941, in Emden's absence on war service, J. W. Gough was appointed acting treasurer with a stipend of £50 a term, with the provost continuing to supervise planting in the quadrangles, and in 1946 Gough succeeded as treasurer when Emden retired from his fellowship.[20] The war did not prevent activity in the property market. In 1941 a bequest of a house and land in Surrey was received from G. W. James. The previous year the 373 acres of Huish Barton Farm near Barnstaple were purchased for £15,500 and the 278 acres of Stone Farm, Longcot, near Faringdon for £12,500, followed in 1947 by Western Farm, Oakford, Devon, although the drawback of low income from agricultural land had returned. Alongside these purchases, further retail and commercial properties were acquired. Shops were purchased at 39–41 High Street, Aylesbury, for £17,491 in 1940; at 150–2 High Street, Slough, for £11,867 in 1944; at 333–5 Holdenhurst Road, Bournemouth, for £7,240 in 1947; at 334–46 High Street, Dorking, for £9,875 in 1947; at 157 High Street, Staines, for £8,243 in 1947; and at 67 The Mardol, Shrewsbury, for £11,000 in 1949. The property at 57 Christchurch Road, Bournemouth, was sold in 1948. Unlike the agricultural properties, expenses were low. This active approach to management of the portfolio resulted in an improvement to income, as commercial property rents offered a better yield than stocks or

---

[20] OR (April 1946), Provost's Notes, 5.

agricultural land. At Bartlemas much of the land was let for allotment gardens during the Second World War, the hockey pitch thus divided until the end of the decade and the paddock up to the present day, to the detriment of college assets. In 1945 the City Corporation offered to acquire part of this land for the construction of a nursery school; but the treasurer was able to persuade the authorities to accept a plot of land located at the bottom of the garden of Bartlemas Cottage instead. In 1942 the acting treasurer was authorized to sell the college's holdings of 4 per cent Consolidated Stock and 4 per cent Funding Loan Stock, and to use the proceeds to purchase debenture stocks of Electricity Supply companies as they became available. It was also proposed that the same stocks held in the name of the Agriculture Ministry should be sold and the proceeds invested in three per cent, Savings Bonds but this was deferred pending the outcome of the possible purchase of property in the High Street and Bear Lane, Oxford.

The restrictions that obliged all Oxford colleges to invest the proceeds of land sales in a narrow range of trustee investments were eased by the University and Colleges (Trusts) Act of 1943. This permitted the formation of trust pools with powers of investment to be approved by the Privy Council. Doubt over whether the changes extended to permitting investment in equities were resolved first by Queen's College, whose scheme to this effect was approved in December 1945.[21] However, Oriel did not rush to invest in equities, preferring to take the advice of its alumnus G. P. S. Macpherson (1921), appointed an additional member of the Finance Committee in 1950. The active management of the college's property assets was now complemented by a more active approach to other investments.

Property investment had mixed results. In 1951 Western Farm, acquired four years previously, was sold for £11,000, a gain on the purchase price of only £695 after the college had spent some £2,350 on improvements. Other agricultural investments were much more successful: most of the Gaines estate was sold during the 1950s, realizing good capital gains. A total of £18,050 was received in three sales making up about two-thirds of the asset. This gave a return of approximately 230 per cent over a twenty-five-year period, in addition to the small net income from rents. The sales proceeds were largely invested in equities.

Current conditions however required new expenditure, in particular the lecture rooms planned in Oriel Square. The ebb and flow of student numbers was commented on frequently, particularly when this was severely disrupted and had a significant impact on the college's income. Following a return to a full complement after the war, in Trinity Term 1951 numbers had fallen to 209, down by 34; as the provost remarked, 'this is the level we think desirable

---

[21] J. P. D. Dunbabin, 'Finance Since 1914', HUO viii. 670.

for the College, though it is expected that we shall have to exceed it for financial reasons'. There was a need to increase income to cover costs of teaching by generating greater fees. The following year Clark returned to the theme: 'like other colleges we find we cannot meet the perpetually rising costs of our buildings and services without adding to our income from fees and it is neither possible nor desirable to raise our fees and charges sufficiently to keep pace with the rise in costs. We have made enormous economies, but we have resisted the temptation to cut down the amount of tuition which we give to our undergraduates. Compared to other colleges of similar size and revenues we have a large number of fellows engaged in teaching.'[22] To fund the new lecture rooms the treasurer was enjoined to apply for a larger than planned loan from the Common University Fund; it had been intended to borrow £11,000 and to sell stock to meet the balance of costs, but the secretary to the University Chest wrote suggesting that the college borrow £20,000 at 2 per cent and retain stock on which it might expect an income of 3–4 per cent. The 1 margin on £9,000 would make a substantial contribution to the cost of a 2 per cent loan of £11,000.

In 1951 Gough reverted to his tutorial fellowship and Hugh Lambrick (Oriel 1926), formerly of the Indian Civil Service and Special Commissioner for Sind, was appointed treasurer, combining the post with a research fellowship to study Indian history and politics; he gave up office for a senior research fellowship in 1955, to be succeeded in 1956 by Brigadier R. E. Bagnall-Wild. During the interregnum the treasurer's responsibilities were shared; Professor Ian Ramsey looked after investments and Kenneth Turpin domestic matters, and the former treasurer C. S. Emden was honoured with an emeritus fellowship. Bagnall-Wild had been a distinguished officer who contributed notably to the logistics of the Eighth Army in North Africa. He took genially to the dual role of governing with argumentative colleagues and executing their decisions: 'his clear and informative expositions did much to educate them on finance, and he supervised a long-deferred programme of repairs to the fabric.'[23]

Although the operating account had shown a surplus in most years since the war, the underlying financial position was a cause for concern. As Bagnall-Wild wrote in his report on the years 1946–55, 'the "Gods of the Copy Book, Headings" as Kipling called them, are apt to speak in clichés, and if I am right, we have in recent years, in common with many individuals, corporations, and the nation as a whole, sinned against these gods.'[24] He pointed out the cumulative deficit of about £30,000 for the period, and the decline in the value of the investments, including capitalized rentals, from £754,000 to

[22] OR (1951), Provost's Notes, 8; OR (1952), Provost's Notes, 11.
[23] Obituary, *The Times*, 17 March 1975.
[24] R. E. Bagnall-Wild, Treasurer's Report (to the governing body) 1956.

£735,000. Some of this was explained by the expenditure of sums set aside for deferred repairs, new works, and general purposes; but he had inherited a long list of further repairs 'deferred for financial reasons'. In addition, the college had incurred debts to build the new lecture rooms, and 'to add to our bravery we have committed ourselves to borrowing another £7,000 from the future to build a new and fairly luxurious boathouse'. He congratulated the acting senior and junior treasurers for the measures already taken to deal with the problem: costs had been reviewed, savings made, repairs deferred, and various dues and charges increased. Income from the endowment had been increased by 'good management and wise speculation'. The switch of investment from gilts to equities, though a little late, had helped. He anticipated a more active investment policy, balancing risk with protecting the college from inflation, and noted that a switch back to gilts when the time came would need to be made with greater speed than 'we displayed in climbing onto the bandwagon of the boom in equities'. Following this analysis, measures were taken to improve the situation by the launch of the Oriel College Endowment Fund. The funds raised were mainly invested, with a proportion used for the new boathouse instead of borrowing as had been anticipated. The college's essential repair work was covered by a grant from the university's Historic Buildings Appeal. As a result, in spite of financial constraints it was possible to make significant progress in restoring and updating the buildings. In 1961 it was reported that the average cost of catching up with repairs deferred since 1939 had been £3,500 a year over the period 1956–61.[25] This was in addition to approximately £6,000 a year spent on routine repairs and minor new works. The treasurer predicted that at this rate of progress the backlog would have been caught up in another six years.

The financial and domestic administration of the college came under increasing strain in the early 1960s. In 1966 Bagnall-Wild asked whether there should now be three treasurers, for estates, investments, and domestic affairs, each with a professional training in his sphere. The increase in paperwork required by a larger college, and more particularly by PAYE, graduated pensions, National Insurance, contracts of service, and the demands of government and university authorities, was extremely onerous. He concluded that the college was too small to afford such a luxury and that there would be difficulties of coordination, and fell back on the concept of a full-time treasurer with professional advisers.[26] This system continued until the mid-1970s, when it was gradually modified until, by 1986, a treasurer, an estates bursar, and a domestic bursar, the first two offices part-time, were in place.

Oriel's position relative to the other colleges is well documented in evidence gathered by the Franks Commission. The college sat on the edge of

[25] OR (1961), 11.   [26] OR (1967), 25.

TABLE 16.1 Endowment income of selected Oxford colleges, 1964

Selected colleges	Agricultural rents	Urban rents	Dividends and interest	Total	For external purposes	Gross endowment income available
Christ Church	101,575	79,968	119,782	301,325	25,213	276,112
St John's	51,404	131,504	48,410	231,318	0	231,318
Magdalen	63,032	67,664	57,150	187,846	1,765	186,081
Brasenose	25,289	24,954	68,990	119,233	113	119,120
Corpus Christi	53,579	2,774	45,724	102,077	0	102,077
Trinity	13,788	6,249	51,887	71,924	70	71,854
Lincoln	9,582	27,574	31,271	68,427	0	68,427
Wadham	15,182	20,001	23,507	58,690	0	58,690
Oriel	2,464	23,209	31,355	57,028	365	56,663
Exeter	14,116	5,109	23,608	42,833	113	42,720
Pembroke	1,973	3,388	31,491	36,852	0	36,853
Hertford	0	0	13,808	13,808	0	13,808

Note: Adapted from the *Report of the Franks Commission of Inquiry*, 1966, i. 290

financial respectability, its endowment income being just above the level at which payments from the richer colleges through the college contributions system would be available (Table 16.1).

The table overstates the true contribution of property, taking no account of its costs. Oriel received only £2,464 in agricultural rents, just over 4 per cent of its endowment income. Christ Church derived over a third of its gross endowment income from this source, Corpus Christi over half, and Wadham, the college with endowment income most closely comparable with Oriel's, over a quarter. By contrast, Oriel obtained over 40 per cent of its endowment income from urban property and St John's well over half.

The final and the most informative annual reports by Bagnall-Wild were issued after the implementation of the Franks Report's new format for college accounts (which the treasurer found less useful), with the financial year conforming to the academic calendar. In 1967–8 there was a modest overall surplus of £2,800, which was regarded as a good result although it masked some continuing unsatisfactory trends in the underlying accounts. There was an unexpectedly large deficit on the internal account, which covered catering and accommodation, for two familiar reasons: charges for board and lodging were too low, and expenditure on building repairs and maintenance was too high. An additional factor, improbably attributed to the provost's turn as vice-chancellor, was the low level of conference income. The value of the endowment was estimated at about £1.1 million, split between £400,000 in property and £700,000 in other investments. The non-property investments were split between fixed income stocks (45 per cent) and equities (55 per cent). The value of the investments had appreciated by 15 per cent during the year, but this was not regarded as a good result. As Macpherson commented, 'the percentage gain appears small, the large gain in equities offset by languishing gilts. The latter, however, may well improve substantially in 1969/70.'[27] The following year the treasurer reported that he had revalued the property assets at £700,000, though if offered for sale it would be difficult to find purchasers. The market value of the other investments fell sharply. Messrs Kleinwort Benson valued the portfolio at £667,495, including more than £50,000 given by Sir Weldon Dalrymple-Champneys and others. Nevertheless, the portfolio had outperformed the stock market, suffering a fall of 11 per cent compared to the FTSE index's 17 per cent. Significant investments were made in improvements to properties and the lease of 8 King Edward Street was bought. Thus a fall in dividends was more than compensated for by an increase in rents. Bagnall-Wild concluded his final report, 'although it has a number of unsatisfactory features, the general financial picture of the College is far rosier than it was fourteen years ago, and it is with some pride that I sign off after a most enjoyable spell of duty to Oriel.'[28] It is now clear that behind this improvement in the financial position there were warning signs; but in 1969 and the following years the college undertook some major projects, including the construction of a new senior common room, the Champneys Room, and the installation of central heating over much of the site. Meanwhile, inflation began to accelerate and the stock market continued to fall.

Bagnall-Wild retired in 1970 and Derek Shorthouse was appointed to succeed him. Shorthouse spent only three years at the college, struggling with a very difficult financial situation. Stringent economies were imposed, and charges raised; fixed-price building contracts for the new works were negotiated, successfully controlling their costs. A house was purchased at 4 Alfred Street with accommodation for up to six graduate students. The contribution from the endowment to the college's operating costs, which had oscillated for most of the century, apart from the war years, between 30 per cent and 50 per cent, fell sharply to 20 per cent and lower, as costs escalated, rents remained flat, and dividends fell. The deficit and the overdraft increased dramatically. As Graham Vincent Smith observed, 'when I was elected in 1968 the College was embarked on a building programme funded on hope: hope of a successful appeal. We were hit hard by the 70s

---

[27] OCA, R. E. Bagnall-Wild, Treasurer's Report (1967–70).
[28] OCA, R. E. Bagnall-Wild, Treasurer's Report (1968/9).

crash, so hard that the bank required guarantors for the College payroll. George Moody and Jeffrey Bonas took on this responsibility.'[29] The generous guarantors were both alumni of the college. In response to these problems, it was agreed in 1972 to establish a separate charity to raise funds, incorporated under the chairmanship of George Moody. By the following year the college had set out its development objectives, which were priced at approximately £1,050,000. This sum would provide three new tutorial fellowships, two junior research fellowships, and the internal renovation of many college buildings. The Rhodes Trust contributed £25,000 towards renovation of buildings in the St Mary's Quadrangle, above all the Rhodes Building.

On Shorthouse's departure in July 1973 the treasurer's duties were divided between the vice-provost, Professor Hedley Sparks, and Ben Brown, who acted as domestic bursar, while a successor was recruited. Eric Vallis, a chartered surveyor, took office in January 1974. Vallis's appointment turned out to be inspired: he combined great expertise in property investment with a willingness to take an entrepreneurial approach to investment in the stock market. He commented many years later, in a private memo to Sir Zelman Cowen, 'at that time the College's financial position was extremely serious—more so than perhaps anyone other than myself appreciated at the time... it is salutary to remember that informal discussions among Estates Bursars were taking place in 1974 as to what steps might have to be taken to rescue Oriel.'[30] From this low ebb, the steady recovery in the financial position of the college began. There was some good fortune, notably, as Vallis pointed out, the timely reversion of the building leases in King Edward Street, which with the good return from the retail properties in the High Street considerably improved the investment income.[31] An investment sub-committee was formed towards the end of 1974. In addition to the treasurer, the members were Leslie Chater, senior partner of Spencer Thornton stockbrokers, Patrick Pirie-Gordon, an Oriel alumnus and director and manager of Holt's Bank in Whitehall, Norman Leyland, managing director of National and Commercial Development Capital Ltd and investment bursar of BNC, and Eric Barratt, senior partner of Tansley Witt, chartered accountants. In March 1976 the performance of the investment portfolio since January 1975 was considered 'very satisfactory by comparison with movements of the Financial Times Industrial Ordinary Share Index over the same period'.[32] A trading strategy had been adopted and capital gains approaching £100,000, on a starting value of approximately £200,000, had been achieved in little over a year. The achievement had not been without risk, and Vallis gave much credit to Pirie-Gordon:

---

[29] OCA, G. Vincent Smith, valedictory comments to the governing body, June 2008.
[30] OCA, E. A. Vallis, memorandum to the provost, 11 March 1987.
[31] E. A. Vallis, 'The Estates of Oriel', OR (1991), 33.
[32] OCA, Finance and Estates Committee minutes, 17 March 1977.

'a new bank account was opened to deal with capital monies at Holt's branch in Whitehall. Pat Pirie Gordon was General Manger of the Branch...under the new banking arrangements and as part of the capital restructuring we obtained very flexible overdraft facilities relatively unsecured which gave the Investment Committee the resources with which to operate a trading policy without which it would not have been possible to rebuild the portfolio.'

In 1972 Oxford City Council had identified the sports ground at Bartlemas as the site for a new East Oxford Middle School, and offered the college £1million for it.[33] The offer was declined; but the possibility of selling the sports ground for development remained under consideration. The treasurer had negotiated the acquisition from the Donnington Trust of land adjoining a small site at Iffley that the college had owned since the middle of the nineteenth century, with the aim of developing a new sports ground, large enough to contemplate sharing it with Lincoln. The whole site had been a city refuse tip until the early 1960s, but with suitable covering and levelling was deemed suitable. Plans were prepared for sports pitches and a pavilion. Had the plans come to fruition, up to £110,000 of capital could have been released for investment. Interest costs incurred as a result of the purchase of the Iffley land would have been eliminated and the costs of sports ground upkeep halved, together generating an annual benefit of £20,000. Early in 1977 the treasurer was urged to conclude the sale of Bartlemas to the City Council, even if the replacement ground would not be ready for some years, as the addition to the endowment would transform the income of the college. However, little progress was made.

By 1977, of the target set in 1970 for building works of £860,000, £402,000 had been raised or pledged. The building programme included the improvement of rooms on all college staircases, a new library reading room and book stack, and the installation of central heating; it omitted work on the Island Site, allowing no potential for additional income from student rents. The overdraft had reached £300,000 by the end of 1974, with an annual interest bill of almost £40,000; interest rates were rising rapidly and the stock market falling, reaching its lowest point early in 1975. Furthermore, as Eric Vallis commented, the property market was almost non-existent.[34] Building work had to be stopped in 1975, leaving staircases I–IV, the Rhodes Building, the hall, and the chapel undone. However, development priorities changed and in 1976 a building survey started with Oriel Street and was extended to the whole college, with the aim of considering areas for new development that could be funded under the terms of a bequest from Edgar O'Brien.

The serious deficits of 1973–6 had been the result of interest charges, cost inflation, amortization charges to replace assets sold to fund the building

---

[33] OCA, Finance and Estates Committee FP/86/1: E. A. Vallis, 'Bartlemas', 24 March 1986.
[34] OCA, E. A. Vallis, paper to governing body, 22 September 1977.

programme, and loss of income from the assets sold. By 1976–7 a surplus was achieved, attributed by the treasurer to strict budgetary control and better estate and investment management. On the other hand, more assets had been sold to reduce the outstanding debt, further reducing endowment income amid falling interest rates. Income from fees and charges was expected to rise at most in line with inflation, but that was very unlikely to apply to endowment income. A large increase in the return from rents, interest, or dividends would only be obtained by sacrificing capital growth. A switch of the entire portfolio to fixed interest securities would have almost doubled dividend and interest income, but at the cost of a falling real value of capital. In marked contrast to the situation in 1919, this was fully recognized. It was also noted that out of an endowment value of £2.7 million in July 1977, £752,000 was employed in residential and recreational accommodation for members of the college from which no income was obtained. The true value of the endowment was therefore over a quarter lower than reported in the accounts.

A new building and maintenance programme was costed at £1.4 million. This included expenditure of £300,000 on refurbishment of the remaining staircases on the main site, including the Rhodes Building, improvements to the hall, the library, and the senior common room service areas. Alterations and improvements to the Oriel Street houses and the proposed conversion of the Oriel Square lecture rooms for residential use were costed at £400,000. New building work costed at £700,000 included a new middle common room in the north-east corner of the second quadrangle, conversion of the old tennis court in the Island Site, and the proposed closure of Oriel Street and its integration into the college. The treasurer proposed a financial plan to fund it: a renewed effort to realize the value of the Bartlemas estate, retaining the land fronting the Cowley Road, the sale of all college houses, use of the O'Brien bequest, sale of a half share in the land acquired at Iffley to Lincoln, and a new appeal to make up the total required.

Throughout this period of financial strain the college had continued a policy of active management of its property. In the three years from January 1974, investment properties in Slough, Staines, Shrewsbury, Aylesbury, Bournemouth, and Sutton were sold, yielding £126,000. In Oxford five college properties were sold, some to the fellows occupying them, yielding £60,000. The proceeds were used to pay off debt, to fund loans to fellows, and to buy more properties for college use, and the balance invested in the Charities Property Unit Trust and other investment assets. The overall effect was to withdraw about £50,000 from income-producing investment property. But by the end of the decade the college's financial position was much healthier; the overall improvement had come both from growth in the endowment and close attention to costs. Expenditure grew at an annualized rate of about 14 per cent, while income grew by 25 per cent for most of the decade. However, in 1978 the internal auditors, Gordon Macpherson and

Professor Alec Turnbull, warned that the position was actually unstable and would be very difficult to maintain in the future.[35] The problem was much the same as before: heavy commitments had been made to building and repairs which were very much dependent on income. Endowment income at the time was particularly unstable: 37.5 per cent being derived from stock market trading. The auditors anticipated that the college would soon be under severe financial strain again, stressing the need to reconcile the requirement for high yield investment returns with the stability of investments to insure against stock market fluctuations.

In spite of these warnings, progress was steady during the first half of the 1980s, and by the end of 1985 it was felt that the direct management of the investment portfolio had run its course and the investment sub-committee would now advise rather than manage the funds. The portfolio had grown from a net value of just over £200,000 in 1975 to £3.25 million. After deducting new money, £1.4 million from fund-raising and property sales, the increase in value was almost £1.7 million, a gain of 809 per cent, compared to growth in the FTSE over the same period of 384 per cent, and of the Retail Price Index of 167 per cent. During the next year the investments were placed with third-party fund managers, including Sarasin Compagnie. Their performance in 1986 was good and in a strong market a gain of 33 per cent was recorded in the first six months of the year, to take the value to over £4 million. By July 1987 the portfolio peaked at £5.3 million.

In 1986 Vallis decided to give up his financial responsibilities and concentrate on property and his own historical research in it. He took the post of estates bursar and senior research fellow, and Eric Barratt was appointed treasurer, combining the role with his work in London; domestic management had been in the enterprising hands of the bursar, Brigadier Hugh Browne, since 1978. Eric Barratt was responsible for one of the most profitable investments the college made in the twentieth century, the so-called South London Estate. This was not the remnant of a medieval holding in modern Clapham and Wandsworth but a portfolio of retail, residential, and commercial investment properties assembled by a private investor, Dick Southwood, with the help of a very shrewd local property agent, Ron Brown. Appropriately, Southwood had been a distinguished oarsman at Thames Rowing Club, where many Oriel crews had trained, and the winner of a gold medal at the 1936 Olympic Games. Just over £900,000 was withdrawn from the investment funds for the purchase of three companies: Land Estates and Property Limited, Trinity Park Limited, and Farranlea Limited, at a small discount to net asset value. The projected yield of the combined portfolio was up to 10 per cent. In 1988 and 1989 a number of other transactions were completed. Sales of

---

[35] OCA, Internal Auditors' Report, 1977–8.

properties in Kent, Oxford, and London yielded £500,000, and retail properties were bought in Moreton-in-the-Marsh and Tenterden. Two properties were also acquired by a gift and a legacy. The switch into urban property was timely. By the end of January 1988 the portfolio value had fallen to £3.1 million, a loss in value of 23 per cent, slightly better than the FTSE All Share Index which fell 24 per cent. The treasurer reported the following month, 'we are slowly recovering our losses'. By the middle of 1989, when Patrick Pirie-Gordon stood down from the Investment Advisory Committee after fifteen years' service, the portfolio was still valued at £3.1 million, of which £2.4 million was invested in equities and £700,000 was held in cash. But between December 1987 and December 1990 the college's stock market investments performed extremely well relative to the market, recording growth of about 19 per cent in a period when the FTSE All Share Index fell by 19 per cent.

In addition to the acquisition of the urban properties, the college had returned to agricultural property. In 1979 it had accepted a recommendation that up to £1 million be invested in agricultural land and to seek a suitable farm or small estate. However, the market strengthened and yields fell to between 2.5 per cent and 3.5 per cent, while the stock market continued to be strong. Wisely, no purchase was made. But by the end of 1984 the treasurer considered that the time was ripe for a return to the agricultural market. A property with a number of farm buildings was sought with a view to capital appreciation from rental growth, and capital generation by the sale of houses and parcels of land for development; two appropriate adjoining farms were acquired, Dowle Street Farm and Frith Farm near Ashford in Kent. The policy bucked the trend: by 1988–9 thirteen Oxford colleges had no income from agricultural land, though only Balliol and Hertford of the older colleges were among them. While Oriel's agricultural property contributed less than 2 per cent to the gross endowment income, over 75 per cent in total came from real estate investment. Plans to develop its site at Bartlemas were less successful. A few years earlier Bartlemas House, Farm House, and Cottage had been sold to raise capital for the development of the Island Site, and in 1985 the Oxford District plan designated the sports ground as suitable for housing development. A number of schemes for disposing of it to the City Council were considered, among them one to acquire land at South Hinksey for a new sports field on a better site than Iffley Field. The value of the Bartlemas site was now estimated at £2 million, which would have generated a net gain for the endowment of £1.3 million after developing an alternative sports ground. The plan, however, and the college's own planning applications for the site, came to nothing as the Council's priorities changed.

An enterprising and successful period of fund-raising to endow fellowships and finance the building programme was punctuated in 1990 by a setback. About £5 million had been raised in gifts and pledges, including promises of almost £1.3 million by a benefactor whose group went into liquidation when only £200,000 had been received, and as a consequence a loan of £600,000 to fund building work could not be repaid as planned. In spite of this, by the end of 1990 the value of the college's endowment had reached £20.7 million. Most of this continued to be invested in property, with only £500,000 invested in equities and £1.4 million held as cash or fixed deposits. This disposition of assets seemed likely to continue. Eric Vallis retired as estates bursar in 1993 and was succeeded by one of Oxford's leading property professionals, James Offen. His substantial contribution, the acquisition of the site of Nazareth House, is recorded in another chapter; in addition to this, he expanded the agricultural portfolio with the purchase of Dynes Farm and Frid Farm near Bethersden in Kent. Seventy years after the college decided to sell its estates, the endowments were again almost entirely dependent on land and buildings, although now of a very different complexion.

In conclusion, in 1920 income from investments held by Oriel or by trusts contributed about 40 per cent of the college's gross operating budget, excluding catering. Figure 16.1 shows the contribution for the years from 1920 to 1990. It grew fairly steadily until the end of the 1930s, apart from a brief drop in 1928, and reached over 60 per cent during the Second World War, when revenues from tuition and student rents were very low and only partly replaced by government compensation payments. Post-war increases in student numbers and prices reduced the total endowment contribution to around 30 per cent in the early 1950s, but by 1960 it was almost exactly the same proportion of expenditure as in 1920. A period of complacency ensued during the 1960s, when fees and charges failed to keep up with inflation, and investments were made to generate income at the expense of maintaining capital value. The crisis years of the early 1970s cut the income available and the college was forced to increase charges and cut costs, resulting in a sharp fall in the proportion of expenditure funded by the remaining endowment. As the endowment income recovered from the mid-1970s, boosted by trading on the stock market and rapid growth in property rents, first from the King Edward Street buildings and then from the new South London estate, it was able to contribute 38 per cent of the budget by 1990.

Oxford and Cambridge colleges were severely restricted to a limited range of Trustee investments other than land and buildings until the 1943 Act, with results that had appalled Cecil Rhodes. However, while most colleges followed similar paths, J. M. Keynes was able to transform a fund for King's College, Cambridge, to which the restrictions did not apply, from £30,000 to £410,000. As a proxy for proper asset allocation values, Figure 16.2 shows the contribution of property rents to Oriel's endowment income. These rents fell from 65 per cent in 1918 to nil, but soon returned to 20 per cent by the late 1920s. After a steady increase, disposals of properties in the late 1940s and early 1950s as the college started to build up an equity portfolio reduced the

FIGURE 16.1 Proportion of expenditure funded by endowments 1920–90

proportion, but it soon grew again to over 40 per cent, hovering around this level until the 1970s when it first grew and then fell due to disposals to fund the building programme. At the end of the period the contribution of the South London estate, along with rising rents in Oxford, took the college's dependence on income from property back to the level last seen in 1920.

In 1920 the Oxford colleges collectively had an income almost three times that of the university, whose income did not exceed that of the colleges until the 1950s, with the rapid growth of public funding. Table 16.2 shows the relative income and expenditure per resident student of a number of colleges against a base of Pembroke. Oriel's position is remarkably stable considering

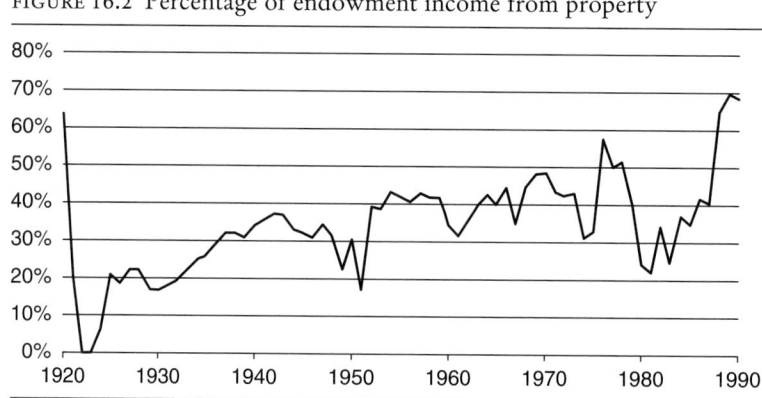

FIGURE 16.2 Percentage of endowment income from property

TABLE 16.2 Total income or expenditure, and income or expenditure per resident student: Oriel and selected Oxford colleges, 1920–88

	1920		1954		1970/71		1987/8	
Magdalen	4.7	3.7	2.4	1.8	1.9	1.8	1.6	1.4
St John's	2.2	1.8	1.7	1.6	1.6	1.6	2.3	2.0
Corpus Christi	1.2	2.2	1.0	1.5	1.0	1.6	1.1	1.6
Christ Church	4.0	1.9	3.4	2.0	2.3	1.8	2.1	1.8
Brasenose	1.9	1.7	1.6	1.1	1.5	1.3	1.3	1.3
Trinity	1.3	1.4	1.1	1.1	1.1	1.6	1.1	1.4
Exeter	1.5	1.3	0.9	0.7	1.0	1.2	1.1	1.2
Oriel	**1.5**	**1.3**	**1.4**	**1.2**	**1.1**	**1.3**	**1.1**	**1.2**
Lincoln	1.1	1.0	1.0	0.8	1.0	1.2	1.2	1.4
Pembroke	1.0	1.0	1.0	1.0	1.0	1.0	1.0	1.0
Hertford	0.7	0.9	0.7	0.7	0.7	0.9	1.0	1.0
Wadham	0.9	0.9	1.2	0.8	1.1	1.6	1.9	1.0

Note: Adapted from J. P. D. Dunbabin, HUO viii. 657.

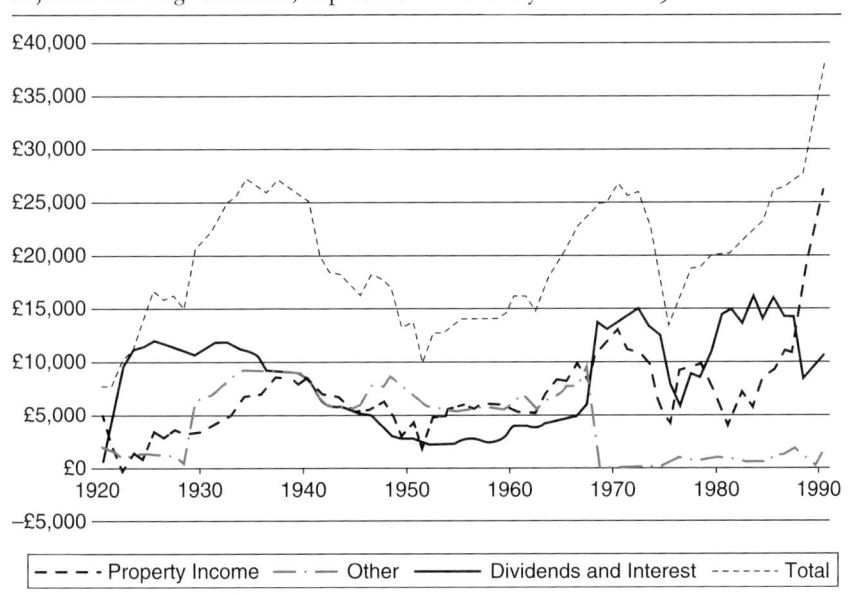

FIGURE 16.3. The sources and fluctuations of Oriel's endowment income adjusted for wage inflation, expressed in monetary values of 1920

events within the college. This contrasts with Magdalen and Christ Church, whose relative position fell significantly; there are substantial variances both in endowment income and in the dependence of colleges on internal income, money paid by or on behalf of students for tuition, accommodation, food, and other charges.

What was the effect of the sale of Oriel's estates and subsequent financial decisions? Overall, it is possible to conclude that the sale of the estates and re-investment, largely in government stocks and bonds, in the 1920s had a positive effect on college finances for at least forty years. In 1964 Bagnall-Wild wrote that the short-term advantages of the sale were obvious and the medium-term advantage was one of timing. The value of agricultural land had fallen from the time of the main sales to the end of the 1930s. It did not rise above £30 per acre until the inflation of the war. Meanwhile, the price of securities had continued to rise, with yields falling and not returning to 5 per cent or more until after 1945. Bagnall-Wild concluded that 'the timing of the sale was as good as it could be':[36] it enabled the college to weather the worst effects of the depression of the 1930s, at which time the opportunity was taken to re-invest in agricultural land. However, it was reported in 1987 that one of the Oxfordshire estates sold in 1921 for £4,650 was valued at over £1 million: growth in value well in excess of that achieved by the college since the 1920s.

What was achieved between 1920 and 1970, and how Oriel might have fared had the sales not taken place, are questions that need to be considered carefully. The college was able to grow and the fellowship to increase. Oriel now owned the whole Island Site, after five centuries of piecemeal acquisition; the kitchens and common room facilities were rebuilt or improved. While inflation remained relatively low, a tight budget could be sustained. However, in spite of surges of expenditure on repairs and some modest updating of the college's buildings, few resources were available to improve accommodation and other facilities. The financial difficulties of the 1970s seem to be largely attributable to the coincidence of a period of high inflation, which substantially reduced the real value of the endowment, and over-ambitious plans to improve the deteriorating facilities. Even then bold financial management, active fund-raising, and an innovative approach to building enabled the Island Site to be transformed into comfortable student accommodation. This achievement, together with the acquisition of Nazareth House, put the college well to the fore in Oxford in the provision of both private and communal accommodation. While the value of the college's ancient endowment might be higher in 2013 had the estates not been sold, it is very unlikely that the overall value of its assets would have matched its current level.

---

[36] Bagnall-Wild in OR (1964).

17
The Buildings of Oriel

Matthew Bool

Alumni of Oriel and many others are well acquainted with its existing three quadrangles, the Island Site, and James Mellon Hall. But all of them have in the course of seven centuries been modified and rebuilt more than once, and the physical evolution of the college is, inevitably, less well known. It is not a story of great architecture and important architects: with the exception of James Wyatt's Leigh Library and arguably Basil Champneys' Rhodes Building, college buildings have generally been designed and modified as utilitarian structures for residential and commercial use. From the fourteenth to the twentieth centuries, they follow the traditions of vernacular architecture, put up by local builders and craftsmen such as Robert Carow in the fifteenth century, perhaps Timothy Strong in the seventeenth, William Townesend in the eighteenth, and Richard Ward in the twentieth. What follows is an attempt to trace the development of these buildings in accordance with the changing needs of the college community.

The earliest building used by the fellows of Oriel was the rectory house of St Mary's church on the High Street, where they resided from 1326 to 1329; it was then used as an academic hall, St Mary Hall, in the ownership of the college. It is likely that the High Street range of five or six shops with solars above was the probably timber-framed structure recorded there in 1397, which was still standing, though much altered, until its demolition to make room for the Rhodes Building in 1909–11. The hall behind, with its accommodation at the northern end of Oriel Street, was built in stone; the hall survived into the 1660s, but the chambers, where the rector and later the fellows must have lived, collapsed in the 1440s and were then rebuilt.[1]

---

[1] W. A. Pantin, 'The Halls and Schools of Medieval Oxford', in R. W. Southern et al. (eds.), *Oxford Studies Presented to Daniel Callus* (Oxford, OHS, 1964), 31–100, see 41–3. For the shops in 1397 see OCR 443.

Soon after the foundation in 1324, Tackley's Inn on the High Street to the west of Oriel Street was acquired by Adam de Brome for the maintenance of his scholars. Though in part rebuilt, its substance is still standing, the college's oldest building, and, as a purpose-built residence for scholars, the oldest university building in Oxford.[2] It contains arguably the best preserved domestic crypt or vaulted cellar in the city, a fine, if restored, fourteenth-century window, and a good sixteenth-century roof. It is one of the very few surviving examples of an academic hall in which undergraduates and graduates, until the sixteenth century, would have been resident.

Both St Mary Hall and Tackley's Inn are discussed below. But the main part of the college site was acquired between 1329 and 1392. Most of the front quadrangle was occupied by a property called La Oriole, which was the college's first home after the St Mary's rectory house. A large house dating to the late twelfth century, La Oriole stood at the corner of Shidyerd Street (now Oriel Square) and Merton Street; with a back gate into Magpie Lane at the north-east; the first mention of the name is the grant of the reversion of La Oriole to the provost and scholars in 1327. James of Spain, a kinsman of Queen Eleanor, appears to have been the occupant, but he surrendered it to the college in 1329 together with a small strip of land to the east fronting Merton Street which was previously known as Domus Zacharie.[3] The other property which formed part of the front quadrangle was Martin Hall. This would have occupied the south-east corner, where the chapel and part of the hall fronting on to Merton Street and Magpie Lane currently stand. Until 1503, Martin Hall had its own principal, and was leased to Oriel in 1503 by St Frideswide's Priory at a rental of 18s. 8d. and then 5s. 4d. in 1510, until it was purchased by the college in or after 1559; there are numerous references to rooms and lectures in Martin Hall in the Dean's Register from 1516 to 1543.[4]

According to Anthony Wood, on what authority is not stated, only the south and west sides of the future quadrangle were standing in 1329, and building on the north and east followed the acquisition of the adjacent properties, so that it became 'a quadrangular pile' about the end of Edward III's reign; and even then the north and east ranges were a mix of buildings, 'some of stone and others of timber and plaister'.[5] If this information is reliable, the piecemeal development parallels that of most of Oxford's medieval colleges. Our earliest view of the quadrangle is provided by the

---

[2] Pantin, 'Halls and Schools', 38–41 and 'Tackley's Inn', OR (1941), 139–55.
[3] H. E. Salter, *Survey of Oxford*, 2 vols. (Oxford, OHS, 1960–9), i. 207; Anon., 'The Site of the College', OR (1966), 24.
[4] 'The Site of the College', 24.
[5] Anthony Wood, *History and Antiquities of the Colleges and Halls of Oxford*, ed. John Gutch (Oxford, 1786), 130.

Bereblock plate of 1566.⁶ As depicted there, it may have conformed to the shape of La Oriole as it was in 1329, but Wood's account of its gradual formation is confirmed by occasional references in the early deeds. The first surviving treasurers' accounts record the construction of a vaulted gateway with a room above it in 1410 and 1411, which is perhaps the gate shown by Bereblock, on the west range and rather to the south side of the present gate.⁷ The first chapel was probably built about 1373 by the benefaction of Richard, the 3rd Fitzalan earl of Arundel, whose son Thomas was then a sojourner. According to Wood, he had 'begun and pretty well carried on' a chapel, 'but being not in a capacity to see the work ended, because taken off by civil affairs, his son, Thomas Arundel, Bishop of Ely sometime a student in this house finished it and made it complete for use'.⁸ The chapel was on the north range next to the garden.⁹ However a new chapel was built in the middle of the south range shortly before 1437, when a licence was granted for mass there; this is the chapel shown in Bereblock's drawing. Wood describes the windows being emblazoned with the arms of Fitzalan, Warenne, Lancaster, Buckingham, France and England, Beauchamp, Bohun, Maltravers, Thomas Holland earl of Kent, Mortimer, and Ferrars. Under the south window were the inscriptions (which must have been transferred from the older chapel): *Rex Edwardus Fundator Collegii Beatae Mariae Oxoniae*, and *Richardus Comes Arundelliae et Thomas Filius Ejus Episcopus Eliensis Istam Capellam Construi Fecerunt*.¹⁰ The panel of fragments of sixteenth-century glass, now in the window of the ante-chapel, with a figure of St Margaret with her book, cross-staff, and dragon, was presumably put together from remnants of this chapel. The only other possible survival from it is a Gothic door, placed on the Merton Street side of the south range behind the stairs of staircase III, and later incorporated in the seventeenth-century rebuilding.

The site of the earliest library is unknown; perhaps it was already in the east range, where a library was constructed or remodelled shortly before 1449, with the help of Thomas Gascoigne; it stood on the first floor, on the site of the present hall.¹¹ Bereblock depicts a row of transomed windows on the west side, doubtless repeated on the east. By 1487 and presumably much earlier there was a treasurers' house used for the audit and sometimes for college meetings; as it was 'the old treasury' in 1631–2, still standing after the

---

⁶ On the building of the original quadrangle see W. A. Pantin, 'Oriel College', VCH *Oxford*, iii (1954), 126–8, which the following pararaphs largely follow.
⁷ OCA TF 1 A1/1, 77 (1410–11).
⁸ Wood, *Colleges and Halls*, 133. The chapel 'already built or about to be built' had a licence for the celebration of mass on 22 March 1373 (OCR 29–30).
⁹ OCR 491.
¹⁰ The consecration in 1420 cited by Salter, OCR vi, from LAO Bishop's Register XVI, Reg. Fleming, fo. 213ʳ, refers to Queen's, not Oriel; for the licence of 3 December 1437 see OCR 61. Wood, *Colleges and Halls*, 134.
¹¹ DR 370.

rebuilding of the south and west ranges, it must have been either in the north range, perhaps to the east of the hall and kitchen, or somewhere in the east range.[12] The earliest hall, still called 'the old hall' in 1605-6, and therefore in a different position from the hall then in use, was approached at a corner of the quadrangle, perhaps the south-west corner abutting the chapel consecrated after 1437.[13] At some date before 1449, it must have been replaced by another hall in the north range, with a window on the north and another at the end, presumably the west end; this is first mentioned in reference to Gascoigne's room, 'an upper room at the end of the hall next to the street'; it was panelled in 1457-8.[14] It had a large closet (*cipharium*), presumably at the east end, spacious enough for college meetings in 1507 and later.[15]

This hall was rebuilt about 1535 during the provostship of Thomas Ware. In November 1531, an order was made that the college should 'proceed to the building of a common hall', and that the provost and the treasurers should arrange the matter with the workmen so as to disturb the college as little as possible. After the collection of the necessary funds, the provost was authorized, in January 1535, to make a contract with the masons and the carpenter, with the advice of Thomas Heritage, a former fellow and currently a surveyor of the King's Works at Westminster. Sufficient money had not been collected and in December 1535 two fellows, Alexander Ryshton and John Smyth, prepared begging letters for the building fund to be sent to former fellows.[16] As depicted by Bereblock it stood on the north side of the quadrangle, approximately where the existing provost's lodgings stand, ending with a large west window looking on to the street and an oriel window at the north-west corner. The screens must have been at the east end, with a large porch shown projecting into the quadrangle, and, further east, the kitchen, indicated by the three large chimneys. The hall was panelled to half the height of the walls in 1593-4. On its outer wall, in the quadrangle, there was, by 1608, a sundial.[17]

Within the medieval quadrangle, chambers for the fellows and lodgers were generally called by their occupants' names. It is possible to determine that there were chambers at the end of the hall in 1449, large and small chambers in the garden in 1482, and two chambers in Martin Hall in

---

[12] *Domus thesauriorum* in OCA TF 1 A1/3, 101 (1487-8); a college meeting summoned *in auditorium siue staurum* (1574, DR 165); another *in domum publicis calculis atque computationibus destinatam* (1588, DR 195).

[13] OCA TF 1 A1/2, 198 (1463-4): *aula antiqua iuxta cameram magistri Spryngbet*; OCA TF 1 A1/5 (Style, 1583-1649), fo. 35ᵛ (1588-9).

[14] DR 369-70; for windows, OCA TF 1 A1/3, 220 (1492-3), TF 1 A1/3, 248 (1493-4); for panelling, TF 1 A1/2, 98, 105 (1457-8), TF 1 A1/2, 128 (1459-60).

[15] DR 15, 59, 71, 72, 90.

[16] DR 86, 99, 102. On Heritage see H. M. Colvin, *History of the King's Works*, 6 vols. (London, 1963-82), iii. 15, 20-2.

[17] OCA TF 1 A1/5 (Style 1583-1649), fo. 58ʳ (1593-4); Pantin, 'Oriel College', VCH *Oxfordshire*, iii. 127.

1524.[18] The chambers would have been on two floors with cock-lofts and arranged in pairs with staircases between them. Each chamber had one or more studies (one for each occupant) and wood-houses. It is probable that bachelors and lodgers would have shared a room, but it would seem that each fellow master of arts had his own room, possibly shared with his scholar.[19] The provost's lodgings were in the south-east corner of the quadrangle next to the chapel with perhaps a small garden to the north of Martin Hall.[20]

While the front quadrangle evolved out of one large property with some appurtenances, the area which formed the middle or garden quadrangle comprised many different plots. They were acquired by the college, clearly following a plan to join with St Mary Hall, in stages following the foundation. Using Salter's survey, it is possible to determine their situation and the order in which they were acquired. On the Oriel Street frontage, the properties from south to north were known as Aungevyn's, Wyght's, Bookbynder's, Spalding's, Stodle's, Magna Scola, and Stylyngton's.[21] On the Magpie Lane frontage also from south to north, Hore's (also known as Torner's and Winter's), Picard's (also known as Tymberhouse), and a tenement of St Frideswide's.[22] Aungevyn's was the southernmost section of the quadrangle; it was acquired from Ralf Aungevyn by Richard de Overton, Brome's former colleague and trustee, in 1333 and passed to the college in 1362.[23] Wyght's, once known as Adam Faber's, had been made over by Simon Wyght's widow Joan and her second husband Thomas de Legh in 1340 to a chantry in the church of St Michael at the Southgate. But the endowments of the chantry proved inadequate, and Thomas son of Thomas de Legh in 1357 agreed that the property should be given to Oriel, on condition that masses were said daily in St Mary's for his family.[24] Adam the Bookbinder died in 1349 and left his tenement to St Mary's, which the college as rector took over. Spalding's and Stodle's may have been one property: Spalding's was acquired by three fellows acting as trustees, Walter de Wandesford, Adam de Plumpton, and John Colyntre, from William de Bergueny, skinner, in 1362, and passed to the college in 1376; Stodle's was bought from John de Stodle by the same trustees in the same year, and similarly granted to the college in 1376. Magna Scola was a toft, a vacant plot once built over, acquired by the provost and two fellows from Henry Iarpomuylle and his wife in 1364 and granted to the college in 1392. Stylyngton's was acquired in 1363 from John de Stylyngton and his wife and made over to Oriel by 1380.[25]

---

[18] DR 370; OCA TF 1 A1/3, 1; DR 61–2.
[19] Pantin, 'Oriel College', VCH *Oxford*, iii. 127.
[20] F. J. Varley, 'The Provost's Lodgings at Oriel College', OR (April 1946), 15.
[21] Salter, *Survey*, i. 208–10.   [22] Salter, *Survey*, i. 206–7.
[23] OCR 124–5.   [24] OCR 125–31.
[25] OCR 131 (Bookbinder's); 131–2 (Spalding's); 132–4 (Stodle's); 134–5 (Magna Scola); 135–6 (Stylyngton's).

The plan also encompassed the Magpie Lane properties. The house at the south-east corner of the quadrangle was once two plots, known as Torner's and Winter's, names in use in the college records until 1397. It was another property of Legh's chantry and passed to Oriel with Wyght's in 1357. Picard's had at some time a building known as Tymber house; it was acquired as a toft 46 feet long and 13 feet wide in 1362 by three fellows acting as trustees, John Middelton, Walter Wandesford, and John Colyntre, from Thomas son of Nicholas de Forsthulle, and was granted to the college in 1392. Finally, the tenement of St Frideswide's was rented for 2s. p.a., according to the college accounts for 1409–10, and was described as a garden. It is not known when or how Oriel came to own this plot instead of renting it, but it was probably exchanged at some time between 1410 and 1450 for some property which the college had acquired in St Ebbe's in 1394.[26]

By the end of the first century of Oriel, the college had acquired (or in the case of one plot, rented), the whole of the future middle quadrangle as well as the front quadrangle, but it was not until the eighteenth century that the provost and fellows started to build there. For the intervening period, it was their garden, as had perhaps been planned since the 1350s or even earlier. Loggan's view probably gives a fair representation of its layout. College records indicate that the fellows employed a gardener whose duty was to attend to the college garden as well as the gardens of St Mary Hall and Bartlemas. The garden contained an arbour as well as fruit and flowers and there are references to a raised walk, seats, benches, and a sundial. The perimeter wall was of undressed stone and abutted Oriel Street, St Mary Hall, and Magpie Lane. A ball-court was constructed against the east wall in 1598, and when the new provost's lodgings were built in 1613–14, it is likely that a portion of the garden was set apart for his private use.[27]

The beginning of the seventeenth century saw a dramatic change in the existing edifice of the front quadrangle, as it was completely rebuilt between 1620 and 1642. This action followed a general period of rebuilding across the university, during which time a number of the early colleges and others less well endowed, financially dependent as they were on an ever-increasing body of fee-paying commoners, began to respond to the need to rebuild or extend.[28] The more recent foundations such as Christ Church, Brasenose, and Jesus were also stirred into building activity, while extensive work began at the newly founded Wadham College through the benefaction of Nicholas

---

[26] OCR 142–4 (Torner's and Winter's); 144 (Picard's); 145 (St Frideswide's tenement).

[27] OCA TF 1 A1/2, 266 (1466–7); TF 1 A1/5, Style 1583–1649, fo. 108ᵛ, 1603–4 (gardener); fo. 26ᵛ, 1586–7 and fo. 180ʳ, 1613–14 (arbour); TF 1 A1/6, Style 1649–95, fo. [8ʳ, unfoliated], 1649–50 (raised walk); TF 1 A1/5, fo. 317ʳ, 1636–7 (benches); fo. 286ᵛ, 1630–1 (sundial); fo. 13ʳ, 1583–4 (wall); fo. 83ʳ, 1597–8 (ball-court); fo. 201ʳ, 1616–17 (provost's garden). See F. J. Varley, 'The College Garden', OR (1946), 6–8, and Pantin, 'Oriel College', VCH Oxford, iii. 127.

[28] John Newman, 'The Architectural Setting', HUO iv. 134.

ILLUSTRATION 17.1 Agas's map of Oxford, 1578 (detail showing Oriel and St Mary Hall)
Bodleian Library

and Dorothy Wadham. The style of architecture at Wadham clearly influenced other colleges, including Exeter and Oriel, who by the 1620s were busy with their own building projects.

At Oriel, unfortunately, the building accounts were kept separately from the general accounts and have since been lost. But the first plans towards reconstruction can be dated to 8 December 1608. On this date timber sales of up to £100 from college lands were authorized to raise money to rebuild the front part of the college, which by this stage was becoming ruinous.[29] However, the college delayed for a decade, and it was not until it received Provost Blencowe's bequest of £1,300 in 1618 that the building process was set in motion.[30] Even then further funds were required to complete the west

[29] DR 224, cited Newman, 'The Architectural Setting', HUO iv. 136.
[30] Newman, 'The Architectural Setting', HUO iv. 142.

and south ranges, allegedly requiring Blencowe's successor, William Lewis, to send out to eminent members of the college 'letters, elegant, in a winning persuasive way'.[31] In October 1636, when the college resolved to complete the rebuilding, a benefactors' book was opened and contributions were solicited from former fellows and fellow commoners. William Lewis contributed £100, and Provost Tolson, eventually, £1,150.[32] Between 1637 and 1641 the college strained to collect its resources: trees on college farms were felled, admission fees for fellows and others were diverted to building, Littleworth was leased, presentations to livings were offered for sale, and plate given by non-contributors was ordered to be sold.[33] Such measures ensured that the momentum of building was maintained until the project was completed.

The main period of building occurred between 1620 and 1642, though it had been preceded, about 1613, by the erection of the new provost's lodgings in the south-west corner of the garden, as shown in Loggan's view, which remained in use until its demolition to construct the Carter Building in 1729. The front quadrangle's significance in architectural history is as a fine

ILLUSTRATION 17.2 The first quadrangle: south and west sides, built 1620–2
Douglas Hamilton photograph

---

[31] Wood, *Colleges and Halls*, 527 n. 65, quoted Newman, 'The Architectural Setting', HUO iv. 142; but Wood was probably attributing Provost Tolson's appeal of the 1630s to his predecessor, as argued in Chapter 4.
[32] DR, 251, 285.   [33] Newman, 'The Architectural Setting', HUO iv. 143.

ILLUSTRATION 17.3 The first quadrangle: north and east sides, built 1637–42
Douglas Hamilton photograph

example of vernacular Gothic craftsmanship, still practised vigorously throughout Oxford during the seventeenth century; both in planning and style it was rebuilt by men who still had a fifteenth-century conception of how a college should be designed and how it should look.

Because funds could not be raised quickly, the front quadrangle was built in two sections: first, the mainly residential west or gate side and the south side, followed later by the construction of the north and east ranges. There is no firm evidence to confirm the identity of the architect. Since there are similarities between the front quadrangle and the slightly earlier quadrangle constructed at Wadham, it has been reasonably suggested that the surveyor of the Wadham building was also employed here. It is also possible that the mason responsible for the numerous curved gables within the front quadrangle was the Cotswold master mason Timothy Strong. It is known that Strong was working in Oxfordshire at roughly the same time as the front quadrangle of Oriel was being rebuilt: in 1632–3 he worked on Cornbury House near Charlbury for Henry Danvers earl of Danby, to the designs of Nicholas Stone; and in 1634 he and his sons carried out work on the

Canterbury quadrangle at St John's College, Oxford.[34] A comparison of the gables at Oriel with those on the gatehouse of Stanway House near Tewkesbury, probably built by Strong in the same year, also reveals some similarities.[35] However, in the absence of positive evidence any link must remain speculative.

The west and south fronts of the college were rebuilt in 1620–2, their original appearance being much as Loggan depicted it about 1675.[36] A short battlemented tower stands over the gate, with an elaborate oriel window on its lower floor. The great gates beneath still survive, the upper panels delicately carved with vine leaves, oak leaves, roses, and thistles, and adorned with coats of arms. The gatehouse was designed with a stone fan-vault with round central panels asserting the college's royal identity, in cartouches of its arms and those of James I. The room on the first floor immediately above was probably intended as the bursary. It may have been used for college meetings, and by the early nineteenth century was the place of the written examination of candidates for fellowships.

The east range opposite the gate was built between 1637 and 1642. It was intended, perhaps following the example of Wadham, to accommodate the college hall and its services, and next to it a new chapel. The more or less symmetrical façade is therefore rather strained, since the orderly arrangement of doors and windows conceals dissimilar parts behind. The oriel window of the hall on the left, with the door to the kitchen below, was balanced by a false oriel to the right above the door to the chapel, while the louvre or smoke-vent of the hall was repeated by the chapel's bell-turret. The line of three hall windows on the left was continued by three similar windows on the right, which actually cover a staircase, two floors, and a corner of the ante-chapel.[37] In the centre a porch was erected, whose pierced parapet forms the words *regnante carolo* in capitals. It was completely rebuilt, however, in 1897. Oriel's royal foundation and Marian dedication was repeated above the porch, in canopied niches with the figures of two kings, representing Edward II and either James I or Charles I. Above them in another niche a figure of the Blessed Virgin and Child was placed. Perhaps the influence or at least approval of William Laud, archbishop of Canterbury and chancellor of the university, can be detected in this return to the college's ancient patronal imagery. The statue of the Virgin was removed in 1651 under Oxford's puritan regime, but replaced in 1674.

---

[34] H. Colvin, *A Biographical Dictionary of British Architects 1600–1840* (3rd edn., London, 1995), 934.
[35] D. Verey, *The Buildings of England: Gloucestershire: The Cotswolds* (London, 1970), 416.
[36] The following details owe much to the description in [D. E. R. Watt], *Oriel College* (Oxford University Archaeological Society guide, Oxford, 1960), 10–12.
[37] [Watt], *Oriel College*, 11.

The chapel too was designed on Laudian principles. In accordance with his policy of restoring altars and 'the beauty of holiness', and with his own achievements at St John's as an example, Laud as chancellor facilitated the refurbishment of college chapels to a state of ordered elegance, as he set about with equal firmness to clear the university's secular functions from the university church of St Mary, a process only completed when Wren's Sheldonian Theatre was opened in 1669.[38] In Oriel, the present arrangement was probably not achieved until after 1660. An ante-chapel was separated from the chapel proper by an oak screen, divided into three bays by two Ionic columns. When the door of this screen was closed, it had a circular opening in its top half, flanked by oval openings on each side. Within the chapel, the panelling above the stalls with its perspective arches and pediments continued the theme of restrained order. On either side of the door were stalls with hexagonal canopies supported by slender shafts, intended for the provost and his deputy. The design of the carved communion rails echoes the oval openings in the screen. The bronze eagle lectern presented in 1654 during the puritan interregnum by Nathaniel Napier, a commoner of the college, was probably not intended to be a controversial statement. A painted window, illustrating the Presentation in the Temple, was inserted at the east end (later removed to the ante-chapel) in 1767. It was painted by William Peckitt, who was noted for his work in New College chapel and York Minster.[39] The original shape of the chapel was altered by T. G. Jackson in 1884, to incorporate more seating space; the screen was moved back into its present position, leaving only a narrow portion of the ante-chapel.[40] The great carved case, made in 1716 for Christopher Schrider's organ at St Mary Abbots, Kensington, was placed in the gallery above at the same time, rendering unusable the space within the projecting window which John Henry Newman had employed as an oratory. In 1987 an new organ was built within the existing case by J. W. Walker and Sons, in the course of which the oratory was restored and dedicated to Newman.[41] Through the munificence of Norma, Lady Dalrymple-Champneys, a new stained-glass window in memory of Newman, designed by Vivienne Haig and realized by Douglas Hogg, was installed in 2001.

The entry to the hall is by a series of steps which form part of the central porch. The hall itself is a well-lit space of limited size with its original open-timber hammer beam roof. The original fireplace was in the centre of the floor, with an open louvre above which is now glazed. It was probably panelled from the beginning; the panelling was renewed in 1710, some of which is still in the buttery at the south end. It was replaced by Gothic

---

[38] Newman, 'Architectural Setting', 137.   [39] [Watt], *Oriel College*, 11.
[40] N. Pevsner and J. Sherwood, *The Buildings of England: Oxfordshire* (London, 1974), 178.
[41] John Harper, 'New Wine in an Old Cask: The Organ at Oriel College, Oxford', OR (1989), 22–5.

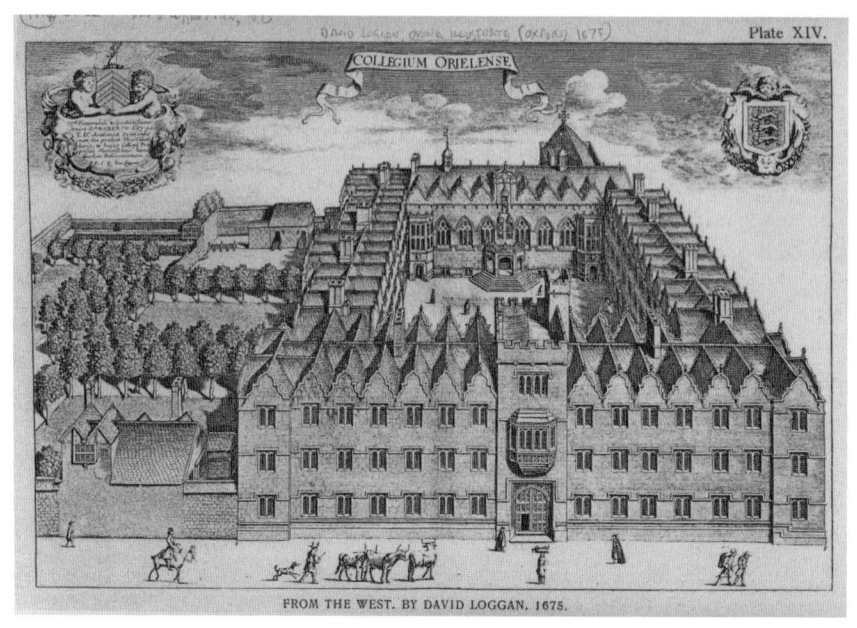

ILLUSTRATION 17.4 Oriel in David Loggan's view, 1675
David Loggan, Oxonia Illustrata (*Oxford 1675*)

ILLUSTRATION 17.5 St Mary Hall in David Loggan's view, 1675
David Loggan, Oxonia Illustrata (*Oxford 1675*)

panelling during the nineteenth century, perhaps when a new fireplace, now covered up, was built in the east wall, and again in 1911, when it was designed by Sir Ninian Comper (1864–1960), along with the screen. Comper was trained as an architect by Bodley and Garner, and in stained glass by C. E. Kempe. By the 1890s he was the best-known designer of church furnishings in England, creating complete schemes, and his expertise is clearly visible in the work he completed for Oriel.[42] The modern heraldic glass in the windows displays the arms of a large number of benefactors and distinguished members of the college; three of the main windows are the work of Comper, which can be identified by his strawberry motif signature in the bottom right hand corner.[43]

The north range contained the provost's lodgings, and a narrow passage led to the garden. A further staircase in the corner of the north and east ranges, now staircase VII, led to a fellows' common room (so designated in the plan of 1733), currently known as the Box, and to the library, relocated to the second floor of the north range to the east of the lodgings. The design of the eastern range is in marked contrast to the plainer style of the sets of rooms which surround the other sides of the quadrangle. The most original feature of these staircases is that they are generally arranged in a square design, in contrast to those at Wadham. As originally planned the first and second floors were probably occupied by fellows, and the rooms on the ground floor shared by undergraduates.[44] Above the doorways into the quadrangle, cartouches were placed bearing the arms of the benefactors and provosts contributing to the rebuilding. The deterioration of the local Oxfordshire stone has necessitated partial refacing of the walls and ornamental features during the twentieth century.

As the eighteenth century dawned, Oxford remained a great centre of architectural activity. While the university commissioned large and elaborate projects during this period, notably the Clarendon Building and the Radcliffe Camera, individual colleges were equally busy, engaging in a variety of schemes which sought to remedy the problems of inadequate accommodation. In most colleges there was limited space, with students having to share rooms with their tutors. However, the growing social status of the university meant that the medieval practice of 'chumming' was no longer tolerable for fellows and undergraduates, who would have regarded themselves as gentlemen. Consequently, much of the new building during this period was designed to cater for the influx of gentlemen commoners, who demanded and were willing to pay for individual accommodation.

---

[42] P. San Casciani, 'Short Report on Stained Glass Windows in the West Wall of the Dining Hall', August 2000, OCA FB 2 C1/7.
[43] I owe information on the heraldry in the hall to the kind help of John Whitehead.
[44] Pantin, 'Oriel College', VCH *Oxford*, iii. 128.

The response to this new requirement at Oriel during this period led to the development of the middle quadrangle around the garden, which largely disappeared as a consequence of the building works.[45] Its first fruit was the Robinson Building on the east side of the quadrangle, built about 1720. An inscription over the door states that John Robinson, formerly fellow and then envoy extraordinary to Sweden and currently bishop of London (1713–23), commissioned this building at the suggestion of his wife; the inscription ends with an Old Norse maxim in runic characters (an incident of his scholarly activities in Sweden), 'man is the increase of mould'.[46] This *memento mori*, doubtless incomprehensible to its first inhabitants, bears no relation to the building itself; it was designed and built by William Townesend, arguably the most successful member of the great Townesend family of master masons who lived and worked in Oxford throughout the eighteenth century.[47] Townesend was heavily involved in many collegiate and university projects, among them the Clarendon Building and the Radcliffe Camera. As Hearne noted, Townesend 'hath a hand in all the Buildings in Oxford, and gets a vast deal of

ILLUSTRATION 17.6 The Robinson Building (1720), built by William Townesend
Douglas Hamilton photograph

---

[45] Varley, 'The College Garden', 8–10.   [46] [Watt], *Oriel College*, 12.
[47] Colvin, *Dictionary*, 986.

ILLUSTRATION 17.7 The Carter Building (1729) with Henry Hakewill's extension (1815–17) *OCA, Stephen Humphries photo*

Money that way'.[48] It is likely on stylistic grounds that he also built the Carter Building, on the west side of the garden, in 1729, the result of a generous benefaction by Provost George Carter. Carter had died on 29 January 1727, leaving instructions that '800£ be laid out towards rebuilding the back lodgings equal in extent of ground to Bishop Robinson's new building for the sole use and benefit of the Provost of the said College'.[49] In addition, Carter gave the college 'such books of mine as my Executors shall think proper to put into it'.[50] The cost of the new building, together with the work done in the library (amounting to £54 4s. 4d.) in order to receive Dr Carter's books, was £1,113 7s. 3d.[51]

As twin blocks these two buildings, each containing six sets comprising one large and two small rooms, stood detached in the garden for nearly a hundred

---

[48] T. Hearne, *Records and Collections*, ed. C. E. Doble et al., 11 vols. (Oxford, OHS, 1884–1918), vii. 247. For a full list of William Townesend's architectural works see Colvin, *Dictionary*, 985–7.
[49] OCA TF 1 A10/1, Provost Carter's will in *The Account of the College, Dr Carters Mrs Ludwells and the Benefaction Bags*, 12.
[50] Provost Carter's will, 10.   [51] Provost Carter's will, 15.

years.[52] Erected in a traditional Jacobean style, they incorporate various architectural elements of the front quadrangle. This is most clearly apparent in the gables, here repeated with a uniform pattern and shape. Placed alongside Townesend's other architectural commissions, the Robinson and Carter buildings illustrate his flexibility as a draughtsman and mason; he was experienced in several architectural styles, including Palladio's and Vanbrugh's, but in deference to the adjacent buildings chose a more conservative manner in Oriel.[53]

In 1818–19 the Robinson and Carter buildings were joined to the main quadrangle. Eight sets of rooms, on four floors, were added to the side of the Robinson Building, at a cost of £1,803, and seven sets on four floors were constructed 'adjoining the old library staircase', staircase VII, thus joining up the Robinson Building with the front quadrangle.[54] These extensions followed the remodelling of the provost's lodgings from 1815 to 1817 by Henry Hakewill, who was architect to the Radcliffe Trustees and to the Benchers of the Middle Temple.[55] In this project Hakewill added the entrance hall and staircase on the north-west, and the south ground-floor room of the Carter Building was fitted up as the provost's study.

Since 1819 the only significant architectural modification of these ranges was the building of the Champneys Room in 1969–70, by gutting and extending one of Hakewill's additional sets. The need for a new public room had been felt for some time, and the opportunity came by the generosity of Sir Weldon Dalrymple-Champneys, Bt., who sought a suitable home for his family portraits. It was designed by Geoffrey Beard of Oxford Architects' Partnership as an irregular rectangle, its eastern wall aligned with Magpie Lane and its large window overlooking Kybald Street. A small garden made use of its flat roof. The conversion of the fine room overlooking the quadrangle into fellows' lavatories was less successful, and was reversed in 1996–7, when the lavatories were relocated to the ground floor and the room redesigned as a small public space, the Benefactors' Room. The Champneys Room itself after several decorative plans was given a new floor and repainted in 2005–6.[56]

Hakewill's remodelling of the provost's lodgings, however, followed Oriel's most important architectural commission of the eighteenth century, the erection of the Leigh Library, or senior library as it is currently known. In 1786 the college received a large and valuable bequest of books from Edward Lord Leigh of Stoneleigh Abbey in Warwickshire; it was resolved to build a new library at the end of the old garden to accommodate them, in the words

---

[52] Pantin, 'Oriel College', VCH iii. 129.   [53] Colvin, *Dictionary*, 985.
[54] Pantin, 'Oriel College', VCH iii. 129.   [55] Colvin, *Dictionary*, 444–6.
[56] On the Champneys Room plans see the sketch in OCA FB 3 G1/1, and unaccessioned papers.

ILLUSTRATION 17.8 The Leigh Library: designed by James Wyatt (1791)
OCA, Stephen Humphries photograph

of Provost John Eveleigh, 'in a substantial and handsome manner', with common rooms beneath.⁵⁷ Though built only sixty years after the earlier blocks in this quadrangle, it is quite different in style. It was designed by James Wyatt, an architect whose work stimulated a range of opinions in and after his lifetime. Horace Walpole described his buildings as 'the invention of a genius'; A. W. Pugin (thinking of his alterations to churches) castigated '[t]his monster of architectural depravity—this pest of cathedral architecture'. As John Martin Robinson remarks, the legend of 'Wyatt the destroyer' has had a baneful influence. His building was not admired in Victorian Oriel; its qualities have been more appreciated in the twentieth century, and are now generally recognized as by far the most distinguished building in Oriel.⁵⁸

The Leigh Library was begun in 1788 and was ready to receive the books in 1795. It was Wyatt's third major project at Oxford. Wyatt had a very extensive connection with Oxford, his work in the city spanning the period from 1773 to 1809, during which time he built in eight colleges and completed the

---

⁵⁷ OCA FB 3 E1/2, Eveleigh's form letter soliciting funds, 12 March 1787.
⁵⁸ J. M. Robinson, *The Wyatts: An Architectural Dynasty* (Oxford, 1979), 56.

Radcliffe Observatory.[59] By the time Wyatt was appointed to build the library he was at the height of his fashionable career, and his selection as architect may well be the result of his having designed the Canterbury gate of Christ Church opposite the front of Oriel.[60] An elevation and section dated 1787 and signed by Wyatt survives.[61] There is also an undated estimate addressed to 'the Rev. Mr Beck' (presumably the dean, Henry Beeke) and submitted by Edward Edge of the city of Oxford.[62] Edge was to build the 'shell or carcase of the said new Library'.[63]

According to the accounts kept by Provost Eveleigh, payments amounting to £261 4s. were made to Wyatt; in addition, £191 6s. was granted 'for slate and self'. This refers to the method of roof-slating invented and patented by Wyatt, with which the library (and the provost's stable) was roofed. It consisted of slate slabs over which fillets of slate, bedded in putty or cement, were screwed down, giving the roof a regular appearance; but the method was soon abandoned owing to the constant dislodgement of the putty. These payments, apart from the proportion paid for patent rights, no doubt represented Wyatt's usual commission of 5 per cent on the total outlay. He was also paid £20 for work done in the provost's lodgings.[64]

The Leigh Library is a simple, dignified building of fine proportions. Even if it is not 'the most perfect piece of architecture in Oxford' as one contemporary, James Dallaway, described its exterior (while deploring its situation), it is certainly one of the best additions made to the architecture of the city during the eighteenth century.[65] The front of this two-storeyed building has a rusticated ground floor with five round-headed windows set in arcading and a similar doorway at each end. This ground floor forms a podium on which stand eight engaged Ionic columns, rising the whole height of the building above to support the entablature. These divide the façade into seven bays, which echo the seven gables of the Robinson and Carter buildings. The whole front is faced with various kinds of Cotswold stone.

The library extends above both the two common rooms on the ground floor: an elegant, rather plain room, with the whole wall space from floor to ceiling on three sides occupied by unornamented bookshelves. The east end of the room forms an apse, the main architectural features of note consisting of two green scagliola columns, which separate this apse from the remainder of the room; Dallaway considered the columns too highly

---

[59] These were Christ Church, Worcester, Oriel, New College, Brasenose, Merton, Magdalen, and Balliol. See Colvin, *Dictionary*, 1111. His attempts at a Gothic style at New College and Magdalen were less successful, perhaps, than his classical buildings.
[60] A. Dale, 'The Building of the Library', OR (1951), 13.
[61] OCA FB 3 E2/1.   [62] OCA FB 3 E1/5. Dale, 'Building of the Library', 13.
[63] Dale, 'Building of the Library', 14.   [64] OCA FB 3 E1/6, 1789–1801.
[65] James Dallaway, *Anecdotes of the Arts in England* (London, 1800), 120, in part quoted in A. Dale, *James Wyatt* (Oxford, 1956), 85.

ILLUSTRATION 17.9 The proposed 'infill' of the north-east corner of the garden quadrangle, 1947
Oriel College

ornamented for the plainness of the apse. An iron gallery runs around three sides of the library about two-thirds of the way up the walls. This leads at the west end to a small room above the main staircase, which is known as the Cedar Room, although it is actually panelled in oak. There is an oral tradition in the college that this panelling came from the east end of New College chapel, where Wyatt was working at the time when the library was built. But unlike his practice at the Radcliffe Observatory, Wyatt did not design any furniture for the library. The interior of the library has seen various changes since its construction. 'Considerable improvements' were made in 1931–4 'in its appearance, in the accommodation for reading, and in the arrangement and repair of books'.[66] At this stage the twenty seats for reading were added as well as the placement of a celestial and a terrestrial globe in the middle of the room. On 7 March 1949 the roof of the library caught fire and was burned out. Only minor damage was suffered by the main structure, and in little more than a year the building had been restored along the old lines; regular use of the library was resumed at the beginning of Michaelmas Term, 1950.[67]

[66] Anon., 'The Library', OR (June 1934), 370.
[67] R. Robinson, 'The Fire in the Senior Library', OR (1949), 8–9; and 'The Restoration of the Senior Library', OR (1951), 10–12. The damage to the books took longer to repair.

The two common rooms below were the first in Oxford to be built for that purpose, one oblong and the other more or less square. Their furniture was not bought until 1795. The chimneypiece in the east common room was designed by Richard Westmacott and cost £48 5s. 2d.[68] In 1970 the common rooms were restored on an eighteenth-century decorative plan, on the advice of John Fowler, and at the instigation of Hugh Trevor-Roper, the acting steward of Common Room, and are now among the most elegant public rooms in Oxford.

The eighteenth and early nineteenth centuries therefore witnessed a dramatic period of architectural growth within the college. The Robinson and Carter buildings add character, while the Leigh Library fulfils Provost Eveleigh's hope for the construction of a handsome new building. By the end of this period little was left of the ancient garden, beyond a fragment of the old raised terrace in the north-east corner. Today the garden consists of the fellows' lawn with a range of small flowerbeds and borders against the old walls, a simple arrangement which complements a well-styled quadrangle. A proposal to build a neo-classical addition in this corner in 1947 came to nothing.

The remainder of the college site had been in principle separate from the quadrangle and adjacent garden of Oriel. Since the provost and fellows moved out in or after 1329, it was known as St Mary Hall, one of the longest lived of the medieval academic halls. In practice it was an integral part of the establishment, occupied by undergraduate scholars ruled by an Oriel fellow as principal. In the sixteenth century it became a more independent institution; at the injunction of the Visitor, the communicating door between the hall and the Oriel garden was blocked up.[69] The principals of St Mary Hall continued however to be fellows of Oriel until 1656. Plans to convert the hall into a separate college during Cromwell's rule did not survive the Restoration.[70] Thereafter it was an academic hall with its own domestic life until, under the Oxford and Cambridge Act's provisions of 1877, it was eventually united to Oriel upon the death of Principal Chase in 1902.[71]

The hall's buildings were therefore designed to maintain a separate institutional existence. The nucleus of the community was the 'manse' or rectory house of St Mary's Church, consisting of six shops on the High Street and chambers above, with a hall lying behind to the south. This hall survived as the refectory of St Mary's, perhaps so used until the building of the later hall in 1639–40. This site was afterwards occupied by the principal's house and is

---

[68] Dallaway, *Anecdotes*, 85.
[69] *Statutes of the College of Oxford*, i, Oriel, 39. I am grateful to Mrs Elizabeth Boardman for this reference.
[70] For a full discussion see: F. J. Varley, 'Oliver Cromwell and St. Mary Hall', OR (June 1939), 15–16; R. A. Beddard, 'A Cromwellian Project for St. Mary Hall', OR (1998), 45–65.
[71] Pantin, 'Oriel College', VCH *Oxfordshire*, iii. 130.

now in part staircase XV in the Rhodes Building; the rest was at the northwest corner of the present quadrangle. The western range of the hall along Oriel Street became ruinous about 1446. When the college asked Bishop Carpenter for a benefaction towards its rebuilding, his answer was not only to agree to subvent the cost, but to acquire from the university the adjacent property to the south, Bedel Hall, and merge the two halls into one large society. The south-west corner of the hall quadrangle (now staircase X) has never been rebuilt entirely since the fifteenth century, and may have contained a range of chambers built when it was united with St Mary Hall; the ground floor, with its stone outer walls, timber-framed partitions, and straight steep staircase, is probably the surviving remnant.[72] The exact position of Bedel Hall has been a matter for conjecture, but it must have extended from the northern boundary of the Oriel garden to the southern wall of St Mary Hall, more or less where staircases X and XVII now stand.[73]

As depicted in Loggan's view of 1675, the fifteenth-century west and south-west ranges have two storeys and an attic (with large dormer windows added). Williams's plan shows the disposition of chambers and studies in 1733. The room on the first floor of the south range nearest the hall has large transomed windows in Loggan's depiction, which suggests an important room, perhaps the library. The eastern range of the modern quadrangle had been acquired piecemeal by Oriel during the fifteenth century and was probably a garden attached to the hall, but the northern part of it must have been built over later, since Wood mentions 'certain chambers on the east side, some of which were pulled down an. 1664'.[74]

At the end of the sixteenth century the principal's lodgings were built on the east side of the quadrangle where staircase XII now stands; it is shown as a tall gabled range in Loggan's view. In 1639–40 the hall and buttery with a chapel above, later the junior common room and junior library, were built in the south-east corner of the quadrangle. This is the only example in Oxford of such a plan. It is a high structure, with imposing wide windows, built in the current vernacular Oxford style.[75] Little has been done since to modify it, apart from converting the chapel into part of the library, adding a writing room to the former hall in 1936, after its conversion to the junior common room, and placing the memorial to the fallen of the First World War in the screens passage; and, in 2012, incorporating the whole into the library.

In 1743 the old principal's lodgings were replaced by a timber-framed and rendered seven-bay house at the behest of Principal King; the stone building

---

[72] OCA FB 101/13, Conservation Survey Report, 26.
[73] For the most convincing reconstruction see Pantin, 'Halls and Schools', 42–3.
[74] Wood, *Colleges and Halls*, 674.
[75] Wood, *Colleges and Halls*, 674. Wood attributes the cost of it partly to Principal John Saunders, later provost of Oriel, and partly to benefactors.

shown on this site in Williams's plate of 1733 as *pars imperfecta* must have been an early and doubtless too expensive plan. The house that was put up was known originally as 'Dr King's house' and later as the 'Dolls' house'; it contained six sets of rooms. It is surprising that an Oxford residential building should be constructed in so rustic a style at this late date; whatever the financial constraints which precluded a stone structure, its elegant rendering of an early eighteenth-century façade in traditional materials adds character to the quadrangle. The Oxford Almanack for 1746 shows a potential project for rebuilding the whole quadrangle, except for the hall and chapel, in this style.[76]

The rebuilding of this side of the hall had been possible because between 1712 and 1719 the north-western corner, including the fourteenth-century refectory, had become the site of a new principal's lodging. In the late eighteenth and early nineteenth centuries the whole of the western half of the quadrangle underwent major work. Between 1776 and 1791, under Principal Nowell, a second floor was added to the south-west corner of the quadrangle; new windows were constructed in the ground and first floors, and other internal improvements made.[77] This was followed in 1826 by the reconstruction of the remainder of the range. The architect was Daniel Robertson. He began his work at Oriel in 1826, alternating it with several commissions in Oxford, most notably the design of the new University Press building on Walton Street, for whose handsome Graeco-Roman façade he was responsible. He also restored the Gothic front at All Souls, in addition to work at Wadham and St John's as well as to St Clement's Church and to Kennington Church in Berkshire.[78] As a piece of architecture, the ornate romantic style of this range, typical of the Gothic Revival, provides an interesting contrast with the more sober traditional Gothic craftsmanship of the front quadrangle and the Robinson and Carter buildings. Two oriel windows, one of six, the other of four lights, were placed asymmetrically within the range, 'the best example in Oxford of pre-archaeological gothic'.[79] The heraldic stained glass in the six-light oriel window (room 5 of staircase XV) was produced by Thomas Willement (1786–1871), who was Heraldic Artist to George IV, and later Artist in Stained Glass to Queen Victoria.[80]

---

[76] Conservation Report, 26: Williams's drawing of principal's house and its successor.
[77] OCA SMH 1 A1, Liber Aulae Beati Virginis Mariae, fos. 33ʳ, 41ʳ; Pantin, 'Oriel College', VCH iii. 131.
[78] A full list of all architectural works by Daniel Robertson can be found in Colvin, *Dictionary*, 822–3.
[79] Nicholas Pevsner and Janet Sherwood, *The Buildings of England: Oxfordshire* (London, 1974), 180.
[80] For more information on Thomas Willement see Thomas Woodcock and John Martin Robinson, *The Oxford Guide to Heraldry* (Oxford, 1988), 181–2. See also C. Wainwright, *The Romantic Interior* (New Haven, 1989). For more information on the stained-glass windows within the college, see Casciani, 'Short Report on the Stained Glass', OCA FB 2 C1/7.

ILLUSTRATION 17.10 Pre-archaeological Gothic: Daniel Robertson's improvements to St Mary Hall, 1826

OCA, Stephen Humphries photograph

Finally, about 1833 Principal Hampden rebuilt the principal's house at his own expense along with three adjoining sets of rooms for scholars on the north side of the quadrangle. This was constructed in a Gothic style to complement the western range, as can be seen in the view taken by Hollis, before it was demolished and replaced by the Rhodes Building.[81]

The most recent architectural work to have been completed within the north range of the St Mary quadrangle is, of course, the Rhodes Building. This was erected from summer 1909 to 1911 on the strength of a large bequest from Cecil Rhodes; it replaced most of the current lodgings of the principal as well as the shops along the High Street (nos. 95, 96, 97, 98, 99, 100, and 101). Rhodes had died in 1902, leaving £100,000 to the college of which £40,000 should be discharged for the 'erection of an extension to the High Street of the College Buildings' and the remainder of that sum to be held as a fund to make good 'the loss to the College revenue caused by pulling down of the houses to make room for the said new College buildings'.[82] Rhodes's bequest was alleged by the senior treasurer, L. L. Price, to be of smaller financial benefit than expected: 'the loss to the College from the disappearance of the rents of the shops and lodging houses on the site of the new Rhodes Building was considerably underestimated.' In fact the shortfall was largely due to the application of some of the interest on the Rhodes Fund to the repayment of college debts. The Rhodes Building was not therefore the only criterion of its value to Oriel.[83] Independently of its cost, it made a dramatic and permanent change in St Mary's quadrangle to the fabric of the college.

The architect of the Rhodes Building was Basil Champneys, one of a group of architects, including T. G. Jackson, George Gilbert Scott junior, G. F. Bodley, and T. Garner, who were active within Oxford during the last quarter of the nineteenth century. There was much competition among them; contemporary comments indicate that there was a particularly keen rivalry between Champneys and Jackson, the latter clearly being Oxford's favoured architect who completed works at several colleges and above all at the Examination Schools, the building which established Jackson's reputation in Oxford.[84] Champneys, an equally competent architect, was an accomplished designer in a distinctive late Gothic manner, as is clearly visible in his work at New College (1885 onwards), Mansfield (1887–9), and Merton

---

[81] OCA FB 5 B3/1–2.

[82] Will of Cecil Rhodes, quoted in G. N. Clark, 'Cecil Rhodes and his College', OR (1980), 22–3.

[83] Letter from L. L. Price (senior treasurer 1888–1918) to G. N. Clark, 14 July 1948, quoted in Clark, 'Cecil Rhodes and his College', 23; Brian Escott Cox, 'A Hundred Years of the Rhodes Building: Its Creation and a Reappraisal', OR (2011), 49–63; OR (2012), 37–42. The author is grateful to Mr Cox for an early sight of this article.

[84] On Jackson see William Whyte, *Oxford Jackson: Architecture, Education, Status and Style, 1835–1924* (Oxford, 2006), in whose judgement (226) the Rhodes Building is 'an almost wholly Jacksonian edifice'.

THE BUILDINGS OF ORIEL 573

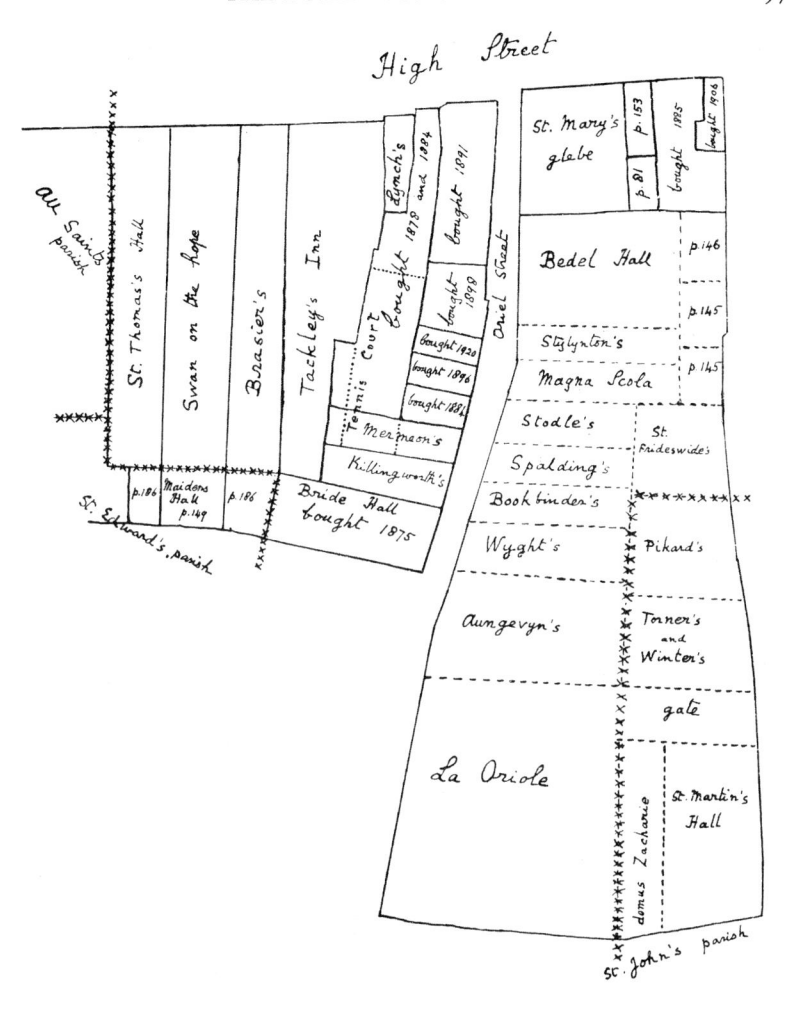

Site of the College

PLAN 1 The college site
Oriel College

(1904–10); he had developed his own variety of Jacobean styling which manifested itself at the Indian Institute (1883–96), Somerville Library (1902–4), and the warden's lodgings at Merton (1908). The Rhodes Building, designed by Champneys and put up by John Woodridge and George William Simpson, of Woodridge and Simpson Builders and Contractors, was the last monument of the Jacobean Revival in Oxford.

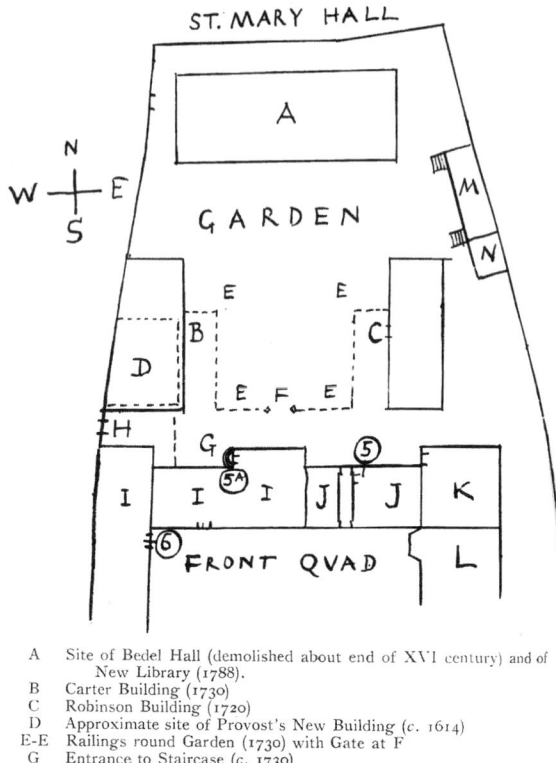

```
                    ST. MARY HALL

                   ┌─────────────┐
                   │      A      │
          N        │             │
       W ─┼─ E     │   GARDEN    │  ┌─┐M
          S        │             │  │ │
                   │    E   E    │  └─┘N
                   │  ┌─┐ ┌─┐    │
                   │D │B│ │C│    │
                   │  └─┘ └─┘    │
                   │   E F E     │
                   │ H  G    ⑤   │
                   │ I  I⑤ᴬI J J K│
                   │ ⑥ FRONT QUAD L│
                   └─────────────┘
```

A   Site of Bedel Hall (demolished about end of XVI century) and of New Library (1788).
B   Carter Building (1730)
C   Robinson Building (1720)
D   Approximate site of Provost's New Building (c. 1614)
E-E Railings round Garden (1730) with Gate at F
G   Entrance to Staircase (c. 1730)
H   Gate (1730)
I-I Present position of Provost's Lodgings
J-J Old Library (on second floor)
K   Old Common Room
L   Hall
M   Raised Walk
N   Ball Court (1598)
(5)-(6) Staircases

PLAN 2 The college garden and its new buildings, c.1730, OCA

The architect's first proposal in December 1904 was based to some extent on suggestions made by the college, and included an arcaded loggia, which would open the quadrangle to the High Street. By the following February the college had decided that the loggia would take up too much space, and Champneys submitted a revised plan on 26 April 1905, largely replacing the loggia with lecture rooms; he proposed a domed central feature and balustraded parapet. The left hand block and much of the centre was to constitute new lodgings for the provost, and the five windows on the first floor above the arcade were to light a gallery within it. These plans were evidently not considered by the governing body, and in the summer the death of Provost

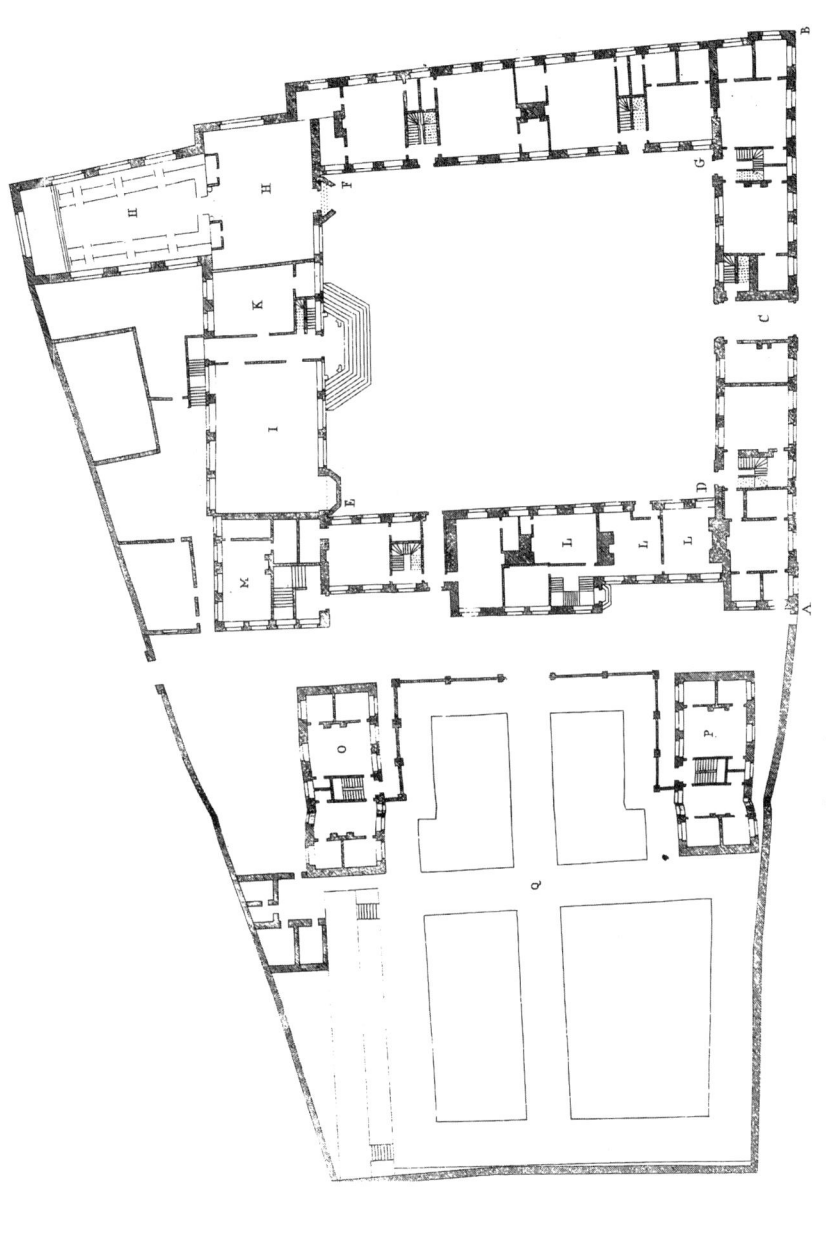

PLAN 3   William Williams's plan of Oriel, 1733
W. Williams, Oxonia Depicta (Oxford 1733)

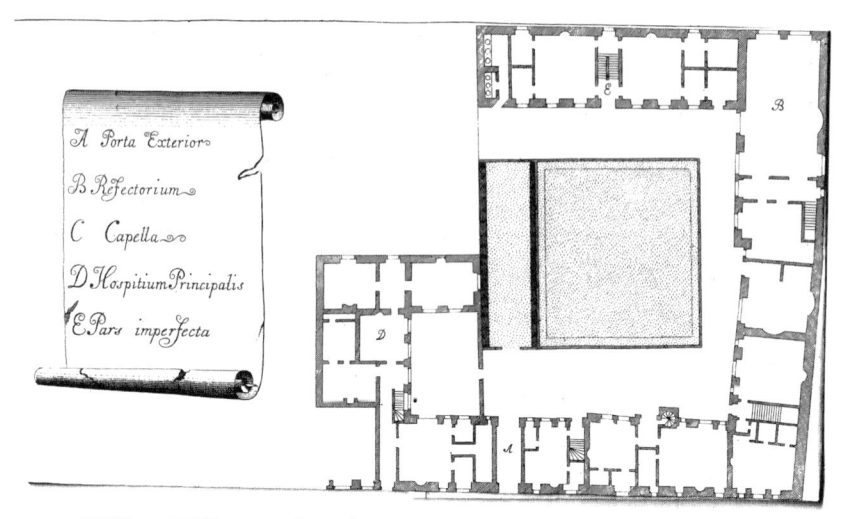

PLAN 4 William Williams's plan of St Mary Hall, 1733
W. Williams, Oxonia Depicta (Oxford 1733)

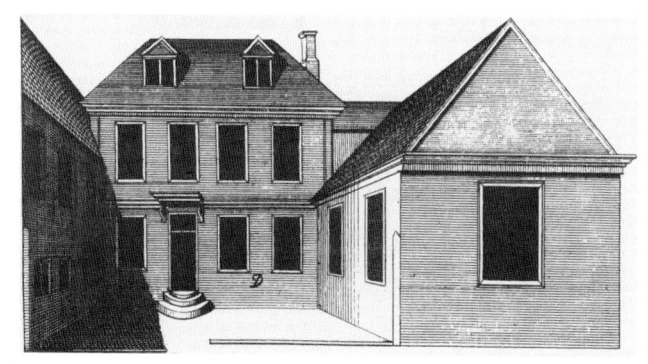

PLAN 5 The principal's lodgings, St Mary Hall, 1733
W. Williams, Oxonia Depicta (Oxford 1733)

Monro and the election of C. L. Shadwell prompted a review of the college's requirements. In November 1905 it was decided to retain the existing provost's lodgings, and to ask that the design proposed by Champneys should include detailing 'more in accordance with the style which has become traditional in Oxford'. After a long delay, in October 1906 Champneys was asked to make a new design in the style of the first quadrangle, without a gate into the High Street. He demurred on architectural grounds, emphasizing the

PLAN 6 The proposed rebuilding of St Mary Hall, 1746

Oxford Almanack, 1746, by permission of the Secretary to the Delegates of Oxford University Press

pivotal position of the site on the High Street, and his new plan and elevation retained the symmetry of his previous design. College opinion was divided, and at a special meeting on 2 March 1907 J. R. King, supported by G. C. Richards, proposed a motion which effectively rejected the plan. It attracted no other support, and the alternative motion of the dean, F. H. Hall, that Champneys be asked to submit an alternative and more traditional elevation, was adopted. The further modification submitted by the architect was accepted at a college meeting on 10 October. With a few alterations of detail this plan was executed in 1909–11. The heavily rusticated ground floor of the Rhodes Building and the inner and outer elevations with their statues effectively preserved Champneys's concept; the gables recall the design of the front quadrangle, in response to the fellows' regard for college tradition. It was to be the last addition of substance to the architecture of the High Street.[85]

It is unfortunate that the standard account of these transactions was written many years later by Richards, who was one of the minority hostile to the whole concept in 1907 and whose memory was far from perfect in

---

[85] On the various plans see Cox, 'A Hundred Years of the Rhodes Building', to which this account is heavily indebted. The plan of 26 April 1905 (OCA FB 5 E 2/1) is reproduced in Howard Colvin, *Unbuilt Oxford* (New Haven, 1983), 156.

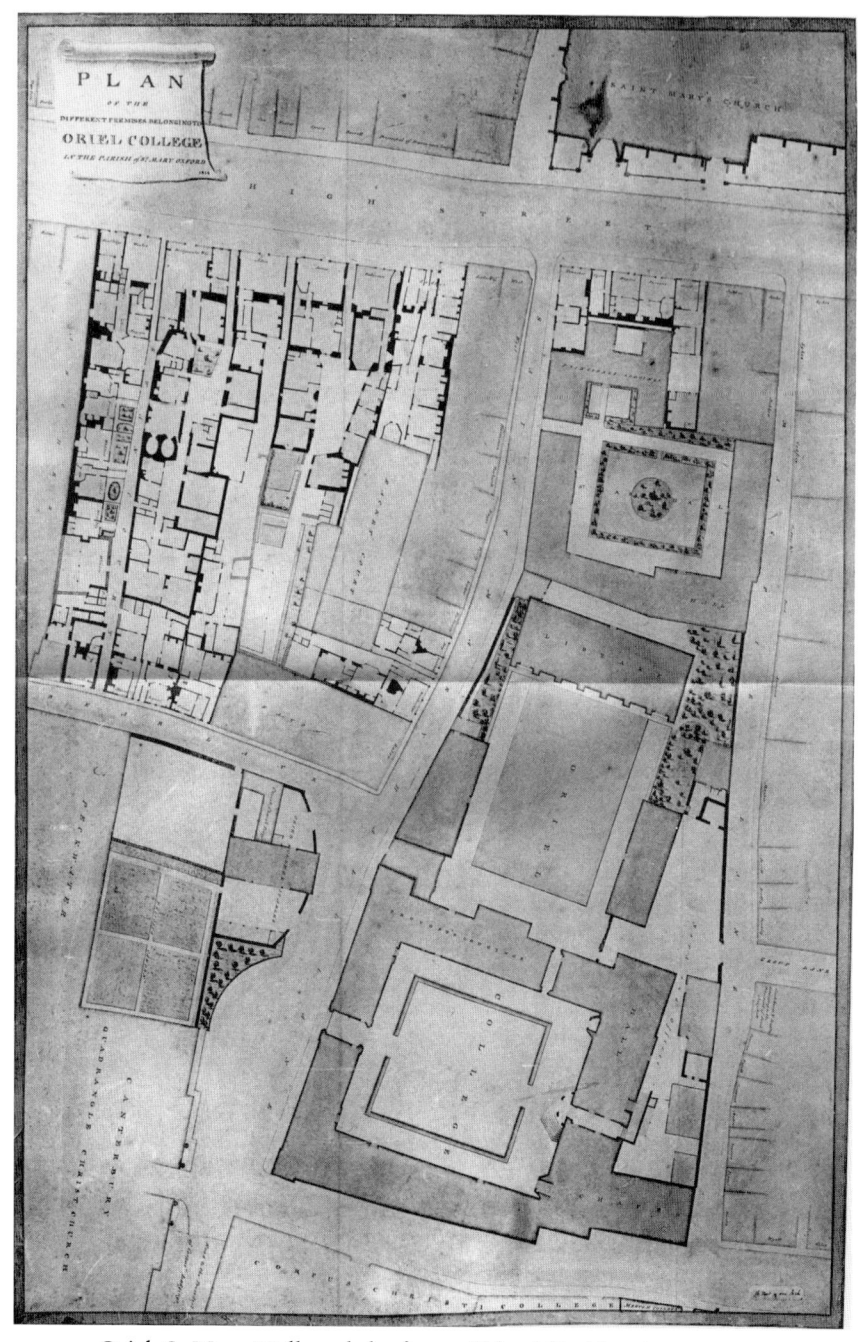

PLAN 7 Oriel, St Mary Hall, and the future 'Island Site' in 1814
Oriel College

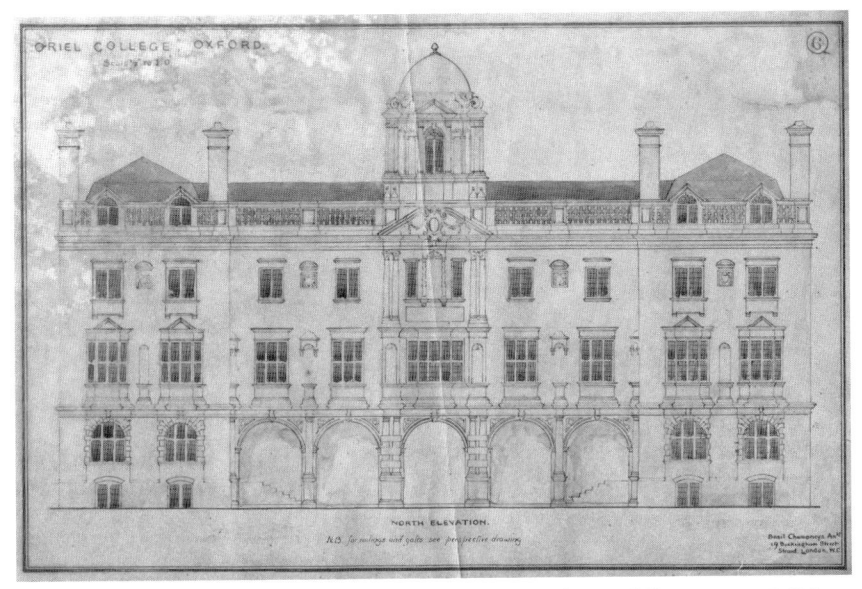

PLAN 8 Sir Basil Champneys' first plan for the Rhodes Building, 1905, *OCA*

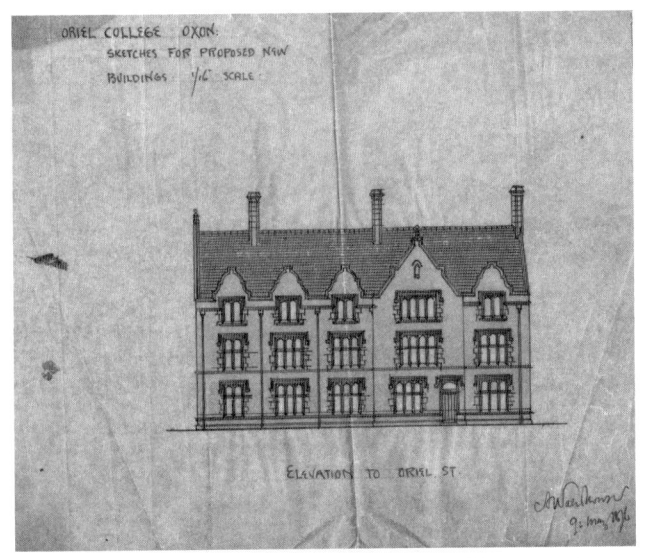

PLAN 9 Alfred Waterhouse's first plan for a new building on the north side of Oriel Square, 1876, *OCA*

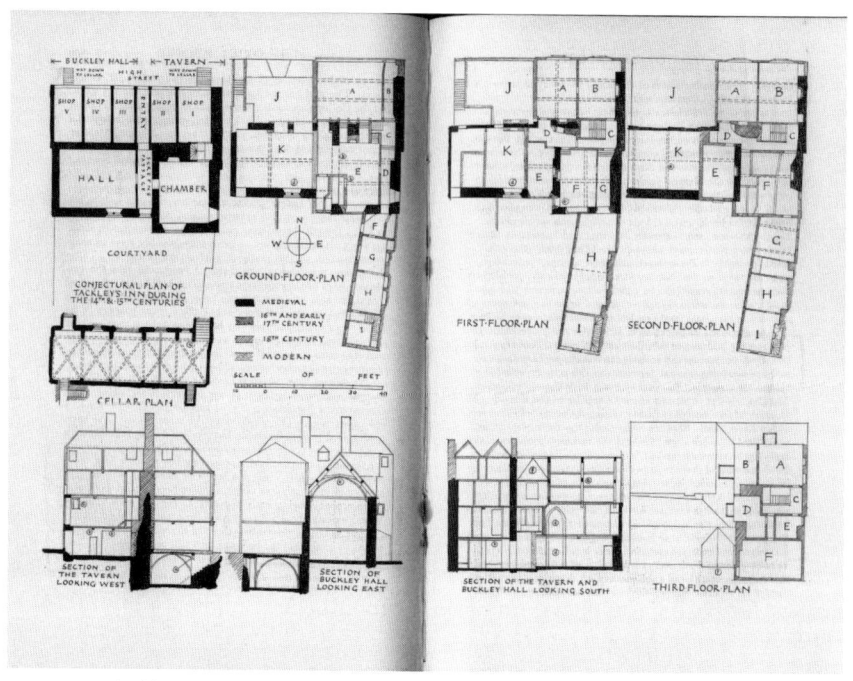

PLAN 10 Tackley's Inn: plan and elevation of the original building
W. A. Pantin

1945, when he wrote his memoirs. In his version, Champneys's second scheme had 'a portico open to the street with a gateway we did not want'. The scheme was rejected, '[b]ut he would only give us a modification of this', and it is this scheme which formed the final design. He added:

It appeared that he [Basil Champneys] had designed a figure of Cecil Rhodes for the highest niche overlooking the High. I pointed out to him that if he placed Rhodes above the two Kings, it would certainly excite unfavourable comment, which he could avoid by transferring the Kings to the wings. He agreed that it was as I said, but took no action. The inner façade has a certain dignity which the exterior lacks, but the rustication of the ground floor is quite unnecessary, and most people would say of the frontage that the architect was determined to have something totally different from Sir T. G. Jackson's High Street front of Brasenose. It is different, but immeasurably inferior. My sole experience of an R. A. led me to think that he can be a very obstinate and unreasonable man, if ever he is thwarted by those who have invited his services.[86]

[86] G. C. Richards, *An Oxonian Looks Back, 1885–1945* (Washington, DC, 1960), 21–2.

Richards was inaccurate on the course of the negotiations, and rather unfair to the memory of Basil Champneys. But the Rhodes Building was not much admired in the following decades. Evelyn Waugh included it in a list of modern Oxford horrors.[87] The college was nevertheless proud of the benefaction and the building. As Provost Shadwell put it after its completion, the Rhodes Building 'stand[s] as the visible monument of the generosity and loyalty of Cecil John Rhodes'.[88] It was officially opened on 28 September 1911 and in the 1912 issue of the *Oriel Record* there was a poem to commemorate the occasion.[89] The façade has not been modified since, except to erect, in the archway which leads towards the High Street, the memorial for the Second World War. The building has been better appreciated in the twenty-first century than it was in its immediate aftermath. In January 2011 it was upgraded to a Grade II* Listed Building.

The only other significant building in the St Mary quadrangle has been invisible; the successive infilling of the space between the Leigh Library and the modern library established in the south range, to create stacks and reading rooms, and the building of an archive store above them. The first extension was made at first- and second-floor levels by the Oxford Architects' Partnership in 1971–4, and the second stack, on the ground floor, in 1987–8. Finally in 1993–6 the archives, which had been kept in a cellar under the treasurer's office in unsatisfactory conditions, were removed to a new store above the library stacks equipped for modern standards of conservation, with a small but elegant archive reading room, an improvement made possible by the generosity of the Bernard Sunley Foundation. The library complex was thus developed as a contiguous block, stretching over the whole space between the middle and St Mary's quadrangles.[90]

In addition to the three main quadrangles, Oriel gradually acquired the whole of the block bounded by the High Street, Oriel Street, Oriel Square, and King Edward Street. Before King Edward Street was driven through it, it was merely the eastern extension of a much larger block stretching to Alfred Street. The area as presently defined, approximately one acre of land, contains some of the college's oldest property, but was not entirely in the college's possession until 1920 with the purchase of 6 Oriel Street. It gradually came to be conceived as a unity, as is implied in the term 'Island Site', employed of it in

---

[87] 'A very small expenditure on dynamite should be enough to rid us for ever of...the High Street front of Oriel': Evelyn Waugh, 28 February 1930, in *The Letters of Evelyn Waugh*, ed. Mark Amory (London, 1980), 49.
[88] C. L. Shadwell, 'Oriel New Buildings', OR (March 1912), 14.
[89] By C. S. Harington, OR (March 1912), 14–15.   [90] OCA FB 5 D1 5–9.

college parlance, perhaps from the latter part of the nineteenth century.[91] Over the centuries, the policy of the college had been to acquire piecemeal the properties which comprised it, if necessary disposing of outlying Oxford property in its place. The High Street frontage here was intersected by several alleyways along which were numerous small properties, houses, shops, trade workshops, gardens, and inns. Along the High Street, Tackley's Inn (now 106 and 107 High Street) had been acquired by Adam of Brome in 1324; Braziers (now 108 High Street and part of King Edward Street) and the Swan on the Hoop, an inn now part of King Edward Street, in 1369; and St Thomas Hall or Boar's Head, now 109 and 110 High Street, in 1361.[92] They were evidently acquired to be rented, however, not for any projected college use. The same was true of Kylyngworth's in Shidyerd Street, now 12 and 11 Oriel Street, acquired by Provost Daventry in 1367, and Mermyon's next to it (10 and 9 Oriel Street), which the college obtained in 1486; and of Lynch's, 105 High Street, left to Oriel by a former fellow, William Lynch, in 1513. All these properties were leased to local tradesmen and householders.[93]

The remaining properties on the Island Site were acquired after the making of King Edward Street: the old tennis court behind 104 High Street in 1878; 104 High Street itself in 1884, and 102–3 High Street, with 1–2 Oriel Street, in 1891; 7 Oriel Street in 1896; 4–5 Oriel Street in 1898; and finally, 6 Oriel Street in 1920.[94] Many of these premises were still rented out, but some of the upper floors provided digs for Oriel men. In contrast to the spirit of earlier acquisitions, these later purchases are clear evidence that in the late nineteenth century the college saw the whole site as a unity. Although it was not immediately feasible to develop the entire site or even a part of it for direct college use, the potential for an overall plan was carefully preserved. It was only in the last quarter of the twentieth century that a plan was evolved and realized.

The unity of the Island Site was, of course, a consequence of the project to drive a street from the High Street to Bear Lane. On this, however, college records are rather reticent; records of college meetings on the subject and architects' proposals do not survive. There are rentals and leases for the affected properties before and after the street was built, but the college bag accounts for 1872–4 are not extant. There is some correspondence of Dr Drummond Chase, the senior treasurer, with tenants and neighbours, including Lincoln College, and with the agent, Francis Field, but it is not revealing on the college's intentions. However a letter from Field of 30 March 1872, considered by the Local Board on 17 April, shows that the college proposed

---

[91] Eric Vallis, 'The Island Site and Oriel's Other Oxford Properties', OR (1989), 28–36, cf. 28.
[92] OCR 163–97; Vallis, 'The Island Site and Oriel's Other Oxford Properties', 28, 30.
[93] OCR 200–6, 212–16.   [94] OCR 209–13, 207–9.

ILLUSTRATION 17.11 Projected lodgings for the provost on the south-west corner of King Edward Street, 1874, *OCA*

to build a road between the High Street and Bear Lane and to give up this new street for use by the public; the implication is that both sides of the street would be developed for intensive commercial use. The building plans were to be subject to the board's approval. Presumably the college was permitted to name the new street after its founder.

Oriel spent over £1,000 on this project in the years 1875–9, and an unknown but probably comparable amount in 1872–4; the seventeen lots were disposed of at premiums which must have balanced the college expenditure, on ninety-nine-year building leases at ground rents for a total sum of £645 p.a.; the 1870 rental for the demolished properties was just under £450 p.a.[95] Frederick Codd was responsible for the elevations and presumably made the design for a large part of the street, perhaps the whole of it; the plan was executed by

---

[95] R. E. Bagnall-Wild, '"The Island Site" and King Edward Street', OR (1963), 10–19, cf. 14; Oxfordshire Record Office, Oxford City Archives R5.5 (minutes of the Local Board), 240. For relevant letters of Dr Chase see OCA WB 2 (unsorted correspondence).

the builders Fisher and Hobdell.[96] The further idea of building a new lodging for the provost on the western side at the junction with Bear Lane was entertained for a time; a plan and drawing survives, submitted by the firm of W. F. McCarthy of London SW and dated August 1874. Not even the most enthusiastic devotee of Victorian architecture can regret the college's decision not to execute this plan.[97] The antiquary J. C. Buckler gave his opinion on the whole project unequivocally: '... and I regret very much that for the sake of Swan Court, the finest range in the High Street is to be destroyed by a street which leads to nothing; it will open to view the blank and lofty wall of Christ Church. It is a *builders plan*, and will be more profitable to him than to the College.'[98] It is at best an undistinguished example of Victorian urban architecture, built in an unattractive yellow brick and with few details of any interest. Its only virtue was the considerable accretion of commercial space.

The building of King Edward Street made some adjustments to the southern edge of the Island Site inevitable. Some small tenements attached to their northern neighbours on the High Street were demolished; only one was let separately, the Bird in Hand public house. On the east was a larger property, Bride Hall, later 14 and 15 Oriel Street. In 1346 Bride Hall belonged to the monastery of Godstow. The land was acquired by Lincoln in 1622 and was sold to Oriel in 1875 for £4,462.[99] A thin 75-square-yard segment to the south was acquired from Christ Church in 1876. In Loggan's view of 1674 Bride Hall was a garden between two ranges aligned from north to south; the western range was a stable. The eastern range seems to have been rebuilt in a style similar to and perhaps contemporaneous with the other properties in Oriel Street, built in the 1720s. Even before this property was acquired by the college, an ambitious plan had been formed to build there a new range of college accommodation, for which designs were sought from the London architect Alfred Waterhouse, already well known in Oxford for his work at Balliol. This was a much more attractive proposition, but it proved somewhat too expensive and was abandoned.[100] What remains of the existing range was converted by the college in 1951 to new lecture rooms, fellows' garage, and flats.[101] In 1985 it was decided to move the middle common room from its location 'in a very depressing, dark, long, narrow room in number 5 Oriel Street' to the large lecture room.[102] This change of use has provided an

---

[96] On Codd, at this time City Surveyor and a pupil of William Wilkinson, the architect of the Randolph Hotel, see Andrew Saint, 'Three Oxford Architects', *Oxoniensia*, 35 (1970), 53–102, see 85, and Geoffrey Tyack, *Oxford: An Architectural Guide* (Oxford, 1998), 244.

[97] OCA FB 6 D1/1. See OCA TF 1 A10/5, College Bag accounts 1853–92 (unpaginated), 1876: £51 10s. paid to McCarthy.

[98] Buckler to Chase, 31 October 1870, OCA WB 2 (unsorted correspondence).

[99] Salter, *Survey*, i. 213, 257; for the deeds, OCR 197–200.

[100] OCA FB 6 G1/1, plans and correspondence with Waterhouse, 1876–8.

[101] Bagnall-Wild, '"The Island Site" and King Edward Street', 15.

[102] Graham Vincent-Smith, 'Notes on the Island Site', OR (1985), 16.

elegant common room with fine Georgian windows reaching to the floor and a splendid view over Oriel Square. The segment obtained in 1876 provides parking spaces and a small patch of lawn.

This segment had been exchanged with Christ Church for 480 square yards of what was then the garden and stables of the provost of Oriel, situated partly in the rectangle of grass now belonging to Christ Church just north of Canterbury Gate. Oriel had acquired this site in two parts, Marre's tenement in 1358 and St Edward Hall in 1485, the latter a property of University College and by then a garden.[103] Though Oriel thus lost more land than it gained, the garden, overlooked from the back of Peckwater, was doubtless now unattractive, and the object of the transaction was, according to the Ledger of the Deeds, the altruistic aim of 'improving the alignment of the highway'.[104] In effect it allowed the city to create Canterbury Square, later Oriel Square (actually an irregular quadrilateral), from the narrow confines of Oriel Street, with its intangible but real benefits of space and light.

The Island Site thus delineated was progressively acquired by deliberate policy in the next fifty years. The steadily increasing pressure for more residential space, and sporadic attempts to find a new site for the provost's lodgings, made its exploitation ever more urgent. A further sixty years, however, were to elapse before it could be developed as a whole. A plan to clear the centre of the site to build a new lodging for the provost was considered in the 1930s, and another for a new quadrangle there in the 1950s, but nothing was done. In 1963 the treasurer, Brigadier Bagnall-Wild, stated what was probably the majority view of the fellows, that 'I have little doubt that most of the existing buildings on the island site have outlived their life, or nearly so, and that a property group could with profit demolish the whole site and build a skyscraper in its place. Personally I would deplore such action on sentimental grounds, but such grounds are suspect.'[105] Any action of this kind would however have been opposed by W. A. Pantin, a pioneer of the study of vernacular architecture, and by the late 1970s, when the advent of a new bursar with experience of military engineering, Brigadier Hugh Browne, made a new plan feasible, planning laws would have made the inevitable demolition highly dubious. This was the complex problem which the bursar and his colleagues needed to confront.

Palliative action to ease the problem of accommodation was taken in 1973 with the acquisition of 4 Alfred Street, a mid-Victorian house on the site of part of the medieval Bear Inn, and in 1977 by the lease (converted to purchase of the freehold in 1997) of 3 Magpie Lane, a late eighteenth-century house

---

[103] Salter, *Survey*, i. 214–15; OCR 217–21.
[104] Bagnall-Wild, '"The Island Site" and King Edward Street', 15; OCR 216–17.
[105] Bagnall-Wild, '"The Island Site" and King Edward Street', 16.

built where Lion Hall had once stood.[106] But decisive action was only taken in 1982. The first step was the establishment of a working group, the Island Site Committee, which would meet under the chairmanship of the provost (first Sir Zelman Cowen and then Ernest Nicholson) almost every week, term and vacation, until the mid-1990s. Several fellows played an active part in it at various stages: besides Hugh Browne, Eric Vallis the treasurer, Robert Beddard, Bill Parry, Graham Vincent-Smith, Jeremy Catto, Michael Williams, and later Brigadier Mike Stephens, who succeeded Hugh Browne as bursar in 1989, and Douglas Hamilton. They began with no overarching plan; the law, and their own inclination which was sympathetic to current notions of conservation, effectively committed them to renovation of the existing buildings. They therefore dispensed with an architect, abandoning any prospect of endowing the site with a structure of the kind fashionable in the 1970s. They relied instead on the tried expertise of the Oxford builder Richard Ward, who was appointed Clerk of Works and who undertook with his firm the entire realization of the committee's designs; on the calculations of the structural engineer Ian Howdill, the detailed drawings of Bert Tighe, and the indispensable advice of the City Council's Conservation Officer, John Ashdown. These experts more than made up for the lack of an architect.

Two ideas, however, gave shape to the work of renovation. The first was Graham Vincent-Smith's. If the houses in Oriel Street and the High Street opened only onto an alleyway which could be made between the tennis court building and the street frontage, they could be treated as traditional college staircases, looking inwards to a further (if eccentrically shaped) quadrangle. The second was conceived by Hugh Browne and Jeremy Catto. If a tunnel could be made between the main college site and the alleyway behind Oriel Street, this new quadrangle could be fully integrated into the existing college and treated as a contiguous extension. The first concept was easy to execute and its advantages were obvious. The second was technically more difficult to realize because of the services running below Oriel Street, but was successfully brought to completion in 1985–6. In addition, it was determined that a high standard of accommodation, with en-suite facilities either individual or shared between two rooms, was in the long term more economical. It was possible by ingenious adaptation and especially by the use of the capacious chimney stacks of eighteenth-century houses to reconcile this with the requirements of conservation. These developments commanded the general approval of both university and city, and were regarded as a model of good practice in the treatment of old buildings. As an editorial in the *Daily Telegraph* commented, 'In Oriel, the latest development is bucking the

---

[106] On the site of the Alfred Street house see Salter, *Survey*, i. 175–6; on that of 3 Magpie Lane, Salter, *Survey*, i. 186–7, 202. On Oriel's purchase of both, see OCA 12.D.3 (unaccessioned papers).

modernist trend. A small, bourgeois medieval courtyard is being slowly and carefully restored so that every room is a different shape and character. An old street lamp lights the scene, and a tunnel bored through ancient foundations connects this almost Italian side-street with the rest of the college... The secret? In this home of lost causes, no architect has been employed.'[107]

The Island Site comprised several ancient properties. Of these the most venerable was 106–7 High Street, Tackley's Inn. This house was built between 1291 and 1300 by Roger le Mareschal, parson of Tackley in Oxfordshire.[108] It was evidently intended to be an academic hall from the beginning, perhaps under Roger as the principal, but he transferred it to Adam de Brome, for the maintenance of his college, in 1324.[109] Its essential structure has survived until the present. Tackley's Inn was functionally divided into two parts. The northern part adjoined the street, consisting of a row of five shops, with five solars above and a cellar of five bays below, for commercial use. Behind these buildings to the south and reached by a passage or 'entry' between the shops was a hall and inner chambers which were let as an academic hall, 'to inhabit after the manner of scholars'.[110] The college rental for 1363 indicates that the southern part or hall was let, at a rent of £4 13s. 4d., to a canon, perhaps as an academic hall for Augustinian canons. As to the northern part of the street, the vaulted cellar under the shops was let as a tavern or wine vault, together with the easternmost shop. The other four shops were let to three other tenants.[111]

By 1442 and probably several years earlier the property had been reorganized into eastern and western portions, divided by the entry. The western part was an academic hall, leased from 1438 to 1458 by the grammar-master Richard Bulkeley or Buckley (and hence later known sometimes as Buckley Hall), but in 1436, 1461, and 1462 occupied by principals who were fellows of Oriel and perhaps therefore used as an annexe to St Mary Hall.[112] The eastern portion was known as the Tavern, *taberna nostra*, rented out at commercial rates but often in use for college purposes. It consisted of the eastern chamber to the rear and what had been the two easternmost shops in front, together with the whole of the cellar, which extended under the

---

[107] Sir Zelman Cowen, 'Provost's Notes', OR (1988), 11; *Daily Telegraph*, editorial, 1 August 1985.
[108] Pantin, 'Halls and Schools', 38–40, with a plan and section, 39.
[109] For the deeds and leases concerning Tackley's Inn, see OCR 163–9; Pantin, 'Tackley's Inn', OR (June 1941), 140.
[110] Pantin, 'Tackley's Inn', 140. In the deed of 6 December 1324 the property was assigned to the college as a residence, but in the foundation charter the property is granted *ad scolarium ipsius sustentacionem*, for their maintenance (OCR 4), while the statutes of January 1326 assigned the rectory of St Mary's for their residence, *pro inhabitacione sua* (OCR 12).
[111] OCR 382; Pantin, 'Tackley's Inn', 141.
[112] OCR 308–9; *Registrum Cancellarii*, ed. H. E. Salter, 2 vols. (Oxford, OHS, 1932), i. 21, ii. 55, 88; Pantin, 'Tackley's Inn', 141–2.

western portion as well as under the Tavern. It was here, apparently, that a contract to copy a book was agreed in 1425, 'in a certain upper chamber in the house commonly known as Tackley's Inn, at the east end of the hall'.[113] Around 1500 the college tavern was frequently used, as the treasurers' accounts show, for college entertainment; its tenant from 1483 to 1503 was William Lynch, a former fellow and a physician to Henry VII, who must have been at least partly an absentee; perhaps his wife was the real tavern-keeper.[114] But in 1549 the whole property was let as one to Garbrand Harkes, a bookseller known to bibliographers for his rescue of numerous medieval manuscripts. In Mary's reign it was a 'receptacle for the chiefest Protestants', who worshipped in the cellar. But the two halves were seen as separate messuages, 107 and 106 High Street; they were again let individually in 1817. The latter property was resumed by the college in 1974.[115]

The structure of Tackley's Inn and its several alterations has been much studied.[116] The vaulted cellar and the large hall with its splayed window are among the best-preserved physical remains of Oxford academic halls. After the property was divided into eastern and western halves, the roof of Buckley Hall on the west was reconstructed by the Oxford master carpenter Robert Carow in 1512–14.[117] This roof too has survived. The Tavern on the east was more directly under college supervision, and developed into a large house, with eight hearths, as opposed to two in Buckley Hall, in the hearth tax returns of 1665. Originally consisting of two chambers, one above the other, at the back, and two shops with rooms above in front, it was organized as a single dwelling with a central chimney stack and a staircase next to it. As the treasurers' accounts indicate, this was probably effected in 1465–6.[118] A wing on the south-east corner was added, perhaps about 1700. The range of shops

---

[113] OCR 309; London, British Library MS Harley 862, fo. 18ʳ, *in quadam alta camera infra domum vulgariter nuncupatum Tackle ys ynne ad finem aule orientalem*. On college use of the Tavern see Pantin, 'Tackley's Inn', 142–4.

[114] Pantin, 'Tackley's Inn', 142–4; BRUO ii. 1189.

[115] OCR 166–9. The Harkes family continued to rent it in the seventeenth century; during the mid-century tenancy of Tobias Harkes, a doctor of physic, it was used to conduct anatomies on executed criminals; see Robert G. Frank, *Harvey and the Oxford Physiologists* (London, 1980), 52–3, citing [Richard Watkins], *Newes from the dead. Or a true and exact narrative of the miraculous deliverance of Anne Greene* (2nd edn., Oxford, 1651), 1–8; see Anon. 'Back from the Dead at Tackley's Inn, formerly Buckley Hall, 1650', OR (1989), 37. On the Harkes family's tenancy see Pantin, 'Tackley's Inn', 144–5.

[116] Pantin, 'Tackley's Inn' and 'Halls and Schools'; Julian Munby, 'Tackley's Inn: New Discoveries, 1986–8', OR (1988), 24–6; Hugh Browne, 'Tackley's Inn; A New Phase', OR (1988) 28–30.

[117] A beam uncovered in the 1986 restoration of 106 High Street was been dated by dendrochronology to 1514; see Munby, 'Tackley's Inn: New Discoveries', 26–8. On Robert Carow see E. M. J[ope], 'Some Mediaeval Craftsmen of the Building Trade Connected with the College', OR (1946), 7–11.

[118] OCA TF 1 A1/2, 231.

ILLUSTRATION 17.12 Tackley's Inn restored: the east front, 1989
Oriel College

at the front were rebuilt from 1514 to 1516, and again probably in the early eighteenth century, on a timber-framed structure.[119]

By 1974 the state of 106 High Street was becoming ruinous. Its restoration, which began in 1986, was a major challenge for the college.[120] The committee was resolved to restore, so far as possible, the shape and character of each room, and to extend the range of Georgian windows; it was required in addition to reproduce the existing stairwell. On the top floor, an additional room with a dormer window was made, and on the second floor, the thirteenth-century chamber was recreated by clearing away the internal partitions. On the first floor, its counterpart with a new window based on the southern window of Buckley Hall was also restored. The fifteenth-century chimney was uncovered in the process. The entrance to Tackley's was removed from the High Street to the south-eastern corner where a new external double staircase

[119] Pantin, 'Tackley's Inn', 152–3.
[120] For further details on the nature of the renovation see Hugh Browne, 'Tackley's Inn; A New Phase', 28–30.

has been created in the courtyard of 104 High Street, and connected to the rest of the Island Site by a passage through the tennis court building. As part of the renovation, the committee had the opportunity of exposing and repointing the fine stone walls where they survive. In five rooms, sixteenth-century fireplaces were uncovered, several with the original herring-bone, fire-scorched backing. These were carefully restored. Where new windows were needed, they were constructed in the style of Georgian sash windows with low sills and are of generous proportions.[121]

The other ancient house which substantially survives is at the southern end of Oriel Street. Now staircases XVIII, XIX, and XX, and up to 1985 11 and 12 Oriel Street, it was known from the fourteenth century, after an early tenant, as Kylyngworth's. After the mid-fourteenth-century depopulation of Oxford the adjoining plots were vacant lots or gardens; Kylyngworth's continued to be occupied as a house standing alone, until, in the seventeenth century, the street frontage of Oriel Street was once more built up.[122] Kylyngworth's had been connected with Oriel since 1367, when William Daventry, the fourth provost, acquired it from Peter de Kylyngworth (or Kenilworth), though it was not a college property until granted by Daventry's trustee in 1392. It was acquired to provide income, and let to various townsmen, including James Edmonds, Esquire Bedel of the university (1535), and Garbrand Harkes, the bookseller tenant of Tackley's Inn (1565). By 1881 it was occupied by the Oriel porter and used to provide accommodation for undergraduates.[123] The house was a typical fourteenth-century town house, with a street frontage and a long back wing. Nothing remains of this house, except perhaps part of the stone walls of the wing. This (and perhaps the whole house) was rebuilt about 1600; the section at the front which now survives was put up, this time as two houses, between 1724 and 1738. In the seventeenth century the principal rooms were in the back wing, with a prospect over a small courtyard to the north which was sharply curtailed with the extension of the tennis court about 1683; it was perhaps for this reason that the front of the house was remodelled shortly afterwards.[124]

The front part of the house is virtually identical in plan and elevation with the adjoining house to the north (Mermyon's, nos. 9–10 Oriel Street), an

[121] Browne, 'Tackley's Inn; A New Phase', 29.
[122] W. A. Pantin, 'Kylyngworth's', OR (January 1944), 246–53.
[123] OCR 202–4; Pantin, 'Kylyngworth's', 248–9.
[124] Pantin, 'Kylyngworth's' gives a full description of the house. A two-light mullioned window in the north wall on the first floor was completely plastered over, inside and out, before work started on renovating Kylyngworth's in 1984. It contains very old glass tinted blue and green, stabilized by a central wooden post attached to the 'corners' by leather thongs. There are also traces of a large window, now blocked, on the ground floor; this was probably a mullioned window which lost its light when the tennis court was extended.

Oriel property since 1486. Mermyon's was then a garden; it was still a garden in 1608, but the street frontage had evidently been built over by 1651. It had lost most of its rear area to an extension of the tennis court behind the range by 1683, and it is likely that the college rebuilt the street frontage between 1724 and 1738, together with that of Kylyngworth's, as part of a unified plan for a row of shops.[125] The front part of Kylyngworth's appears to have been built as two houses, with two spiral staircases in the back corners. The northern staircase has been modified on the ground floor to accommodate the passage; the ground floor section of its southern counterpart was removed after 1814, but survives in the cellar below and the floors above. Each of the two 'houses' contained a single room, about twelve feet wide, on each floor, looking onto the street. Like Mermyon's, it had a large central chimney stack, with angle fireplaces. Both houses are good examples of a timber-framed structure built along solid traditional lines, with old-fashioned stop-chamfered beams; a concession to eighteenth-century taste was made in the elegant façade by the large three-light sash windows with entablatures, on the first and second floors.[126] The 1814 plan shows that the ground floor was then a shop, with a shop-front like that which survives in Mermyon's.[127] The survey of 1772[128] and the plan of 1814 show the premises used as one house, with one shop below, whereas nos. 9–10 was then shown as two houses, with two shops.[129]

The early eighteenth-century rebuilding of these properties seems to have followed and imitated a similar project undertaken about 1720 by the Oxford apothecary William Ives, who had bought 103 and 102 High Street with 1 and 2 Oriel Street (apparently already incorporated into 102 High Street). He seems to have acquired in addition 3–4 Oriel Street, and perhaps in a separate transaction the open ground of 5–6 Oriel Street; all these properties were rebuilt, though not as a single range. Though there is no surviving evidence on the eighteenth-century ownership of 7–8 Oriel Street, the linking pediment from nos. 5 to 8 seems to imply that Ives owned or leased these houses too.[130] Like Kylyngworth's and Mermyon's, Ives's new shops were timber-framed, with fireplaces angled in large central chimneys shared between two houses, and modern sash windows on the street; perhaps the college employed his builder for its own development. All these properties came into college possession between 1891 and 1920. The uniformity of style enabled

---

[125] On the dates see the leases for these two years, OCR 206.
[126] Pantin, 'Kylyngworth's', 252.
[127] See part of plan, OCR 528.
[128] *Surveys and Tokens*, 16 (St. Mary Hall Lane) cited in Pantin, 'Kylyngworth's', 253.
[129] Pantin, 'Kylyngworth's', 253; OCR 214–15.
[130] Loggan's plan of 1674 seems to show 3–4 and 7–8 as houses, while 5–6 is a vacant lot. On the properties of William Ives see OCR 207–10. Nos. 5–6 had been two cottages in 1480 and a stable in 1572 and 1651; see Salter, *Survey*, i. 213 and OCR 214–15.

their restoration in 1984–91 to proceed on similar lines: the entrances were moved from the street to the passage made behind them, along the side of the former tennis court, and showers and lavatories were fitted into the large chimney stacks. In this way the structure of these houses was preserved and adapted to modern college conditions.

Kylyngworth's and the houses on Oriel Street were rebuilt through the munificence of three benefactors. The first was the late Edgar O'Brien (Oriel 1920), who expressed the wish that his benefaction be used for 'a single project of a permanent nature designed to enrich the beauty and usefulness of the college'. At a ceremony in July 1985, the whole site was named the O'Brien quadrangle in his memory.[131] The second was William Nelson Turpin (Oriel 1947), with his wife Nancy Bisell Turpin, through whose generosity 6 and 7 Oriel Street were restored. The third was the late Leopold Muller (1902–88), by whose munificence 4 Oriel Street was renewed.

The third substantial property in the Island Site occupied a section of the High Street front and the whole of its centre: 104–5 High Street, originally one tenement, and the tennis court belonging to no. 104 behind them. No. 105 was left to Oriel in 1513; its only original feature is the stone-lined cellar, while the house above was rebuilt in the seventeenth century and its principal room, on the first floor, panelled in the early eighteenth century.[132] No. 104 High Street passed from the chantry of St Thomas to the haberdasher Henry Milward who had it in 1572; he was probably responsible for rebuilding its middle range and for furnishing its principal room on the first floor with an elegant moulded plaster ceiling. It too has an early cellar of which the west wall is probably medieval.[133] In the garden behind it either Milward or a predecessor had by 1572 erected a 'tennis-play' or real tennis court. It remained in use until about 1833; Charles I and his nephew Prince Rupert played here in 1642. From 1836 to about 1860 it was the Theatre Royal. Briefly reinstated as a tennis court (Edward prince of Wales received instruction in the game here as an undergraduate), it was by 1868 a billiard room. The college acquired it in 1878, and 104 High Street in 1884.[134]

The conversion of the old tennis court itself monopolized the construction schedule from 1991 until 1994. An initial architect's concept for the project was commissioned but rejected by the committee, which elected to proceed along the now tried, if unconventional Oriel plan. First, the Oxford Archaeological Unit carefully excavated the top layers of earth and monitored the deeper excavations as they occurred. This was followed by exploration of the footings of the existing construction. Test holes quickly showed the need for

---

[131] Sir Zelman Cowen, 'The Provost's Notes', OR (1985), 9.
[132] Royal Commission on Historical Monuments, *The City of Oxford* (London, 1939), 164.
[133] Royal Commission on Historical Monuments, *The City of Oxford*, 164; OCR 214.
[134] OCR 212–14 for the leases.

ILLUSTRATION 17.13 The entrance to the Harris Building, 1993
Douglas Hamilton photograph

extensive foundation work.¹³⁵ The decision was therefore taken to build extensive foundations for what was effectively a new structure within the existing walls. A hundred steel-coated concrete piles were sunk into the underlying clay, on which were cast reinforced concrete pile caps connected by reinforced concrete ground beams which carried the weight of the stone walls.

This was the most expensive project within the Island Site development. It was funded by the generosity of Sir Philip Harris, later Lord Harris of Peckham, and named the Harris Building in memory of his father Captain Charles William Harris. It was opened by the Prime Minister, John Major, on 10 August 1993, the culmination of the whole Island Site scheme, and a public recognition of its innovative reconciliation of the demands of conservation of ancient buildings with the needs of modern college accommodation, which the college could offer to 290 students by 1996. Whether its eventual form fulfilled the plan conceived more than a century earlier by Vice-Provost

---

[135] See Greg Campbell and Brian Durham, 'The Real Tennis Court Archaeological Investigations: An Interim Report', OR (1990), 39–43, and Brian Durham, 'The Real Tennis Court Archaeological Investigations Second Interim Report', OR (1991), 67–8.

Monro and the senior treasurer Dr Chase is impossible to say. But it certainly gave renewed life to the acre of the city they effectively added to Oriel.

The need to house all its junior members, however, was increasingly obvious to Oriel as it was to other colleges by the 1990s, in the light of decreasing alternative accommodation in Oxford. In 1996 it was calculated that a further seventy rooms were needed to reach this goal.[136] The policy of coping with the surplus through individual houses bought for the purpose provided only a short-term solution and so the college sought to acquire and develop an area of land for the housing of its students in a relatively central location. James Offen, who had succeeded Eric Vallis in his role as estates bursar, tried to persuade the City Council to sell land to Oriel in the Bulldog Yard, St Aldates, on the site of the medieval Hinxey Hall, a site which would have provided space for thirty to forty student rooms within 200 yards of the college. This was not, ultimately, successful; but shortly afterwards the opportunity arose to acquire Nazareth House, across the Cherwell on the corner of Cowley Road and Rectory Road, half a mile from the college. On this site, with some restoration and some new building, it would be possible to accommodate a hundred students. Oriel took possession of it in September 1995.

The Poor Sisters of Nazareth had acquired the site in 1875, when they arrived in Oxford. At this stage it was an elegant private house of the early nineteenth century, standing in a garden of about three-quarters of an acre. Originally known as Charnwood Lodge, it was renamed Larmenier House after an early member of the Order. Two buildings were erected (1876–8): the larger, by F. W. Tasker, contained a kitchen, refectory, and various offices at ground level and a chapel above. The second was a stable block with a common room and bedroom upstairs. At the turn of the century, a large wing was added at right angles to, and detached from, the chapel block, designed by the well-known Victorian architect Edward Goldie. This building contained three large rooms at each of the ground, first, and second floor levels, which enabled the nuns to open an orphanage. Outbuildings were constructed, and four terraced houses in Rectory Road were bought. After the need for the orphanage ceased, the large rooms in the Goldie wing were partitioned to form six bedrooms on each level. A lift was installed, and it became a nursing home for the elderly. But by 1995, the task of caring for the patients had become too much for the now older and smaller body of nuns.[137]

This project was made possible by the munificence of James Mellon (Oriel 1975) who generously donated the funds for the central residential block, and of David Paterson (Oriel 1963), who was the benefactor of the sports

---

[136] Mike Stephens, 'Building in Oriel: The End of an Era', OR (1996), 78.
[137] James Offen, 'Nazareth House', OR (1996), 80.

ILLUSTRATION 17.14 The James Mellon Building, 2000
Oriel College

facilities, together with numerous other alumni of the college who sponsored particular named rooms. The college employed the local architect Phillip Pryce and Hopgood and Sons, builders, to convert Goldie's building, which provided forty rooms by Michaelmas Term 1996. The next stage was the demolition of the stable block, the central section, and the outbuildings of Nazareth House to create a site for a new four-storey block of student rooms, and in a separate building, a new weights room and squash court. They were designed by the firm of David Morley, architects, and built in 1999–2000. It was appropriate that the enterprise which at least for the foreseeable future satisfied the needs of the college as to residential space should have been sustained by its own members, whose predecessors had rebuilt St Mary Hall in the 1450s and the front quadrangle in the 1630s, and had funded the Rhodes Building in the first decade of the twentieth century. It was equally appropriate that it should have been inaugurated by the descendant of Edward II the founder, Oriel's Visitor HM Queen Elizabeth II, on 8 November 2000.[138]

Oriel's buildings, from St Mary Hall and Tackley's Inn in 1324 to James Mellon Hall at the turn of the twenty-first century, were designed, or

[138] Ernest Nicholson, 'The Provost's Notes', OR (1999), 11.

ILLUSTRATION 17.15 The Provost's Mouse, 2004
Sue Morris

adapted, to accommodate the needs of study and teaching in the sparest possible way. Provost Eveleigh's desire for a handsome library was fulfilled, but Wyatt's edifice was a unique ornament, which as a public and not a residential space underlined the dignity of learning. The original ideas of a Reginald Pecock, a Thomas Harriot, or a John Henry Newman did not require grandeur—indeed all of them, especially the last, are likely to have repudiated it as a distraction. The traditional quadrangular architecture of Oxford, interpreted variously in successive eras, and put up generally by the craftsmen and builders of the city, has proved repeatedly to answer better than any alternative to the enduring needs of the college.

18

Oriel and Sport

Clive Cheesman

In 1792, near the end of his life, Gilbert White wrote, 'Though I have long ceased to be a sportsman, yet I still love a dog; and am attended daily by a beautiful spaniel...who amuses me in my walks by sometimes springing a pheasant or partridge...'[1] But a sportsman he had certainly been fifty years before, as an Oriel undergraduate. From his second year onwards, his account books record sums spent on guns, horses, and dogs; expenses that, in contemporary terminology, would have been classified under the general rubric 'sport'.[2]

The fact is that before the mid-nineteenth century (and later, according to context) 'sport' had a very different meaning from the one we usually give it now, referring instead to country pursuits of a more or less aristocratic character. A sportsman was a man who, for private amusement, hunted, or shot, or fished. The principal word for the activities we now group together as sport was simply 'games'; if the need was felt to distinguish those that required physical exertion from less energetic ones such as chess, bridge, or billiards, the term used was 'athletics'. The latter word could still be used for sport in general at the start of the twentieth century, its ancient connotations perhaps resonating in a university where classics still dominated. It also perhaps—on occasion—expressed a faint hint of dismissiveness.[3]

This is more than a point of vocabulary. This chapter attempts to trace, as if it were a unitary and enduring phenomenon, a disparate and evolving set of activities. It is not even clear that sport as we understand it has existed or had a recognizable counterpart in every age, and certainly organized sport in Oxford is really a creature of the nineteenth century. It may seem strange that an apparent universal of human experience (which is what sport is presented as nowadays) should have clear and recent origins, but without a crucial nineteenth-century phase of evolution and codification competitive games as

---

[1] Quoted by Emden, *Oriel Papers*, 132.   [2] Emden, *Oriel Papers*, 131.
[3] Thus *Registrum Orielense*, xi–xii.

Oxford knows them now would scarcely exist, and would certainly not be truly college activities. Nonetheless, they stretch far back into the Oxford past as personal or private activities, with inevitable impact on college life, manners, and morals. It would be wholly wrong to start a history of Oriel sport in the nineteenth century; its prehistory too must be examined.

In the medieval and early modern academic world, there was little desire to distinguish among pastimes that seemed equally irrelevant to education, equally threatening to order and discipline. In the universities of northern Europe, it has been said, there was a general desire 'to inhibit organized levity'.[4] Thus our earliest references to student sport in Oxford, the texts of college and hall statutes, proscribe games of all sorts, whether energetic or sedentary, aristocratic or banausic. Chess was forbidden by statute at Queen's in 1340; dice, chess, gambling, and the keeping of pets including hawks, dogs, and ferrets at New College in 1400. Equivalent provisions do not survive for Oriel, but it may be assumed that similar rules were in force. These inhibitions show that such sports were popular; and some competitive and energetic pastimes, it came to be recognized, might actually benefit study. Chess was not among the pursuits banned by the All Souls statutes of 1443.[5] In 1517 Corpus Christi allowed 'handball' (*pila manualis*) in the college garden for the sake of bodily and mental health. This could refer to 'palm play', *jeu de paume* or simply 'paume', which could designate a racketless cognate of tennis, played face to face with or without a net, or the ancestor of the various forms of fives, played against a wall. The aularian statutes of 1483–90 (which applied to St Mary Hall) had forbidden this activity along with an interesting range of others:

Item, that no-one play at dice or board games or engage in handball, two-handed sword or buckler play or any other game of dishonourable character, tending to a breach of the peace or deleterious to study. Penalty, for each offence: 4d.[6]

The prohibition of sword and buckler play (reaffirmed in the seventeenth century)[7] is understandable; 'a form of fencing much cultivated in London, where instruction in it could be had...it made a natural school for highwaymen.'[8] But the reality was that to the west, east, and south of the city were fields where not only the townsfolk but the student body would repair for

---

[4] Alan B. Cobban, *The Medieval Universities: Oxford and Cambridge to c.1500* (Aldershot, 1988), 36.
[5] Cobban, *The Medieval Universities*, 36, citing a 'growing tolerance of chess in the fifteenth century'.
[6] SA 576.4-7: Item, quod nullus ludum alearum, tabellarum vel ad pilam manualem, artemve gladii bimanualis seu bokelarie aut aliquem alium ludum inhonestum pacis perturbativum, studii subtractivum, exerceat, sub pena tociens quociens iiijd.
[7] SA 589.31-3: artemve gladiatoriam vel alia quaecunque arma.
[8] J. I. Catto, 'Citizens, Scholars and Masters', HUO i. 151–92 at 183-4.

competitive play and exercise, and it was gradually understood that it was impossible and counterproductive to try and prevent it. More than that, games might favour study by exercising the body and directing youthful energies away from turpitude and into harmless channels.⁹ The aularian statutes quoted above encouraged principals to send students to some appropriate spot for outdoor recreation. One fellow of Oriel went further still: Thomas Cogan (fellow 1563–75) found authority in Galen for the benefits of tennis:¹⁰

...above all other kindes of exercises, Galen most commendeth the play with the little ball, which we call Tenise... chiefly for that it doth exercise all parts of the body alike... wherefore those founders of Colleges are highly to be praysed, that have erected Tenyse courtes for the exercyse of their Scholers: and I counsaile all students as much as they may to use that pastime.

The reference is to Galen's short treatise *De pilae parvae exercitio*, in which the great physician of antiquity specifically recommended exercise with a small ball on the grounds that it worked the whole body, upper and lower, and developed coordination of the eye and hand.¹¹ In fact the essay takes for granted the holistic benefits of physical activity in general; it was therefore unlikely to persuade any hardline anti-athletes among Cogan's contemporaries that tennis courts were suitable objects of college expenditure. Furthermore it is obvious that Galen was not writing about tennis as known in the late sixteenth century: he explicitly refers to a form of ball play that required no equipment other than the ball itself (in particular no nets) and hence could be easily pursued by the poorest. Perhaps he was recommending an ancient version of *pila manualis*; perhaps it was a simple game of catch.

Nonetheless tennis—the variety now known as 'real' tennis, but itself also called 'paume'—was popular among Oxford students in the early modern period, and represents the first continuous form of sporting activity available to them. The city was well supplied with courts—some were indeed provided by colleges, as Cogan recommended, while others, including the best known, were commercial enterprises in premises rented (often from colleges, of

---

⁹ On permitted and prohibited early modern recreations elsewhere, see John Twigg, 'Student Sports, and their Context, in Seventeenth-Century Cambridge', *International Journal of the History of Sport*, 13/2 (1996), 80–95.

¹⁰ T. Cogan, *The Haven of Health* (London, 1589), 3–4. On Cogan, see Emden, *Oriel Papers*, 22–8.

¹¹ Galen, *De pilae parvae exercitio* in *Claudii Galeni opera omnia*, ed. K. G. Kühn, 20 vols. (Leipzig, 1821–33), viii. 899–910; E. Wenkebach, *Sudhoffs Archiv für Geschichte der Medizin*, 31 (1938), 258–72. The treatise was popular in the Renaissance; R. J. Durling, *Journal of the Warburg and Courtauld Institutes*, 24 (1961), 230–305, lists seven editions or translations, stating (at 243) that this may reflect publishers' preference for short works; but the apparent relevance of the work to contemporary leisure tastes may also be a factor.

course) by private operators.¹² The 'Oriel' tennis court was one of the latter, and therefore in strict terms lies outside the scope of a college history. But it was on college property, close at hand to the undergraduate body, and must have been a feature of college life for Orielenses throughout its long history. The first mention of the court, which was apparently constructed over part of the garden of a tenement on the High Street, is in a lease of an adjacent property in 1572, referring to the neighbouring 'tennis play'.¹³ It was operated by a series of tradesmen known as 'paumiers' (*palmarii*, to use the possibly tongue-in-cheek neo-Latin), some of whom have left physical trace of their existence in the form of trade tokens bearing their names and trade marks. Thomas Woods, the court's lessee in the 1650s, also leased the adjacent Oriel tenements of 104 and 105 High Street, where he ran a tavern called the Salutation; not only were his tokens struck with the image of a tennis racket, but the wine bottles he served bore a design showing two players competing in a roundel studded with tennis balls.¹⁴

Undoubtedly the establishment was patronized in this period by a mixture of town and gown, but its social high point came when the Civil War drove the king to take up residence in Oxford with his court; it is to the antiquary Anthony Wood that we owe the well-known report of Charles I and Prince Rupert playing there at Christmas 1642, and even interrupting a game to consider matters of state.¹⁵ But as a strictly commercial operation the court was starkly exposed to the whims of fashion. Its fortunes were clearly mixed in the eighteenth century, and it was already in decline in 1813 when the freehold was purchased by Thomas Hardaway, corn dealer, for £1,000.

By the early nineteenth century, as we shall see, other sports were competing for students' time, but there was still fashionable participation in tennis, and Oriel men were part of it. Charles Wordsworth, the great Christ Church all-rounder of the late 1820s, recalled, 'At tennis, the men with whom I played most were three Gentleman Commoners of Oriel—the college nearest "Sabin's" (the best) tennis court.'¹⁶ The three—all prominent college figures—were Francis Trench, Edmund Head, and the Hon. Charles Murray, who won for three

---

¹² Jeremy Potter, *Tennis and Oxford* (Oxford, 1994). Chapter 8 (67–76) is a good account of the Oriel Street court, though it regularly misunderstands leases of adjacent properties (naming the court as a boundary marker) as leases of the court itself.

¹³ OCR 201-2. The surviving fabric of the court was investigated by the Oxford Archaeological Unit in 1990–1; reports in OR 1990, 39–43, and 1991, 67–8; also *Post-medieval Archaeology*, 25 (1991), 169–70.

¹⁴ A surviving bottle is Ashmolean Museum, Oxford, AN1896–1908M68; for an image, see <http://britisharchaeology.ashmus.ox.ac.uk/highlights/bottlesandseals.html>. For a token issued by Thomas Burnham, lessee from 1663, also showing a tennis racket, see Potter, *Tennis and Oxford*, plate facing 56.

¹⁵ A. Wood, *Life and Times*, ed. A. Clark, i (Oxford, 1891), 75.

¹⁶ Charles Wordsworth, *Annals of my Early Life 1806–1846* (London, 1891), 60–1; cf. 'A Chapter of Autobiography', *Fortnightly Review*, 34/199 (July 1883), 50–71 at 64.

consecutive years (and hence retained) the silver racquet offered to the best player in the university.[17] Tellingly, however, the court Wordsworth refers to is not the court in Oriel Street, for all that he says Oriel was the closest college. William Sabin was tenant of the Merton court (and brother-in-law of the keeper of yet another commercial court in Blue Boar Lane). When Queen Adelaide visited Oxford in 1835, it was at Sabin's that two of her princely nephews played a game,[18] and it is Sabin's that, alone among the old tennis courts of Oxford, survives today. Much like modern stadia, commercial courts were used for a variety of paying events, from theatrical shows to boxing matches, which did not necessarily reflect on their viability.[19] But competition for the dwindling real tennis market was stiff, and the Oriel court was perhaps unfortunate in having as its keeper from 1838 James Russell ('Duck-leg Jem'), a convivial and respected figure but a poor businessman. Despite Russell having the honour of giving a lesson to the undergraduate prince of Wales there in 1859,[20] the court's days were numbered. After a stint as a playhouse (the 'Theatre Royal Oriel Street') it is recorded as a billiards hall in 1868,[21] and in 1878 the college bought it back for £1,800.[22] It spent the twentieth century subdivided and put to a variety of purposes, some of them connected with sport: it housed the college's 'multigym' weights machine and ergometer in the 1980s, while another part was (somewhat ironically) the table tennis room. Conversion of the structure into the Harris Lecture Theatre in the 1990s was a kindness, allowing proper archaeology on the site, and recognizing the inescapable fact that Oriel's special relationship with real tennis, always a tenuous and commercial one, was now over.[23]

The only other early Oxford game that remained prominent, without radically changing form, into the nineteenth century and beyond was cricket; so central a place was it to have in later student sport that it makes sense to deal with it below. Bowls, fencing, and archery are of course followed to this day, but are hardly the staple activities they once were.[24] Nor are they carried on in the name of the college—though bowls remains a popular pastime on

---

[17] Sir H. Maxwell, *The Hon. Sir Charles Murray, K.C.B.: A Memoir* (Edinburgh, 1898), 60.
[18] *Jackson's Oxford Journal*, 24 October 1835.
[19] A hot-air balloon was exhibited to the public at the Oriel court during Commem in 1823 (*Jackson's Oxford Journal*, 17 May 1823). An attempt to display a live elephant in the Blue Boar Lane court was foiled by the doors being too small to admit the animal; it was shown instead at the Wheatsheaf inn; *Jackson's Oxford Journal*, 16 April 1831.
[20] *Jackson's Oxford Journal*, 29 October 1859. A contemporary illustration of the lesson is reproduced by Potter (*Tennis and Oxford*, facing 57) and appears as the frontispiece to OR (1995).
[21] When conveyed in 1876 it contained four rooms with full-size tables; OCR 213.
[22] OCR 213.
[23] Oriel's only real tennis blue seems to be Peter Seabrook who played in 1974 and 1975 with Alan Lovell of Jesus, his former Winchester pairs partner.
[24] Archery is still, rather surprisingly, bracketed with cricket as a prominent outdoor sport in ch. xi of Cuthbert Bede, *The Adventures of Mr Verdant Green* (London, 1853).

the lawns of the front quad. The college sporting revolution of the nineteenth century grew not out of these ancient pursuits but rather out of more general inclinations towards physical recreation. Student recreation had always included strenuous or even dangerous activity, as shown by the two Orielenses who drowned swimming between Sandford and Nuneham in 1781.[25] With the dawn of the nineteenth century it more often assumes the aspect of a challenge, either a purely internal and personal test or something undertaken more publicly, perhaps as a wager. The simplest activity in this category was the long walk. Even in an age of walking, a great distance covered in a short space of time might be a point of pride or admiration, worthy of record, like the prodigious walks undertaken by Provost Copleston. The Oriel undergraduate who, in August 1838, hiked the tough 16-mile route from Inveraray to Dalmally in 165 minutes was engaging in the same tradition.[26]

The better-off might undertake similar challenges mounted. On one renowned occasion in the later 1820s two Oriel undergraduates, 'gated' for minor misdemeanours, publicly undertook to ride to London and back in a day. The two were Lord Edward Thynne, later a prominent aristocratic rake, with a seat in the Commons and a spectacularly disastrous personal life, and Charles Murray, the champion tennis player, and certainly the most unusually accomplished fellow of All Souls to come from Oriel; he later spent time in North America living with Pawnees before returning to an appointment at court and a distinguished diplomatic career.[27] After lunching and dining in the metropolis and attending the first act of a play, the pair sped back to Oxford, arriving to the plaudits of their friends three minutes before the college gates closed at midnight. Equestrian feats of this sort were undoubtedly part of an enduring tradition of conspicuously costly daredevilry, deplored by authority.[28] They were allied to the exploits and expenses of 'sport' in the older sense of the hunting field, which continued to be disapproved as a socially divisive, dangerous distraction that got undergraduates into debt. As Francis Trench recorded of Copleston in the same decade, 'a red coat was his abhorrence; and he discouraged the favourite pursuit of hunting by all possible means'.[29] The reality was that, at this time, when the reputation of Oriel's common room stood at its height, the college was also known for the ample resources and gentlemanly pursuits of some, at

---

[25] William Buncombe and Joseph Smith, *Morning Herald*, 1 June 1781.
[26] *Bell's Life*, 2 September 1838. The 'gallant pedestrian' (named only as 'Mr N____') had previously walked from Inveraray to Glasgow (62 miles) in under 14 hours.
[27] Maxwell, *Murray*, 58–9. On Thynne, see *History of Parliament 1820–32*, vii. 434–5.
[28] G. V. Cox, *Recollections of Oxford* (London, 1870), 33–5, implicitly recognizing the shared source of the 'match again time' and the organized sport of a later day.
[29] 'Notes from Oriel Hall, about 1827', *Macmillan's Magazine*, 13/74 (December 1865), 157–62 at 157.

least, of its undergraduate members,[30] and for years afterwards Oriel was a good college background for a huntsman.[31] However the challenge of racing to London and back on a horse is not wholly disconnected from the first stirrings of organized athletic activities. There were points of intersection between these showy exploits, less costly personal challenges undertaken on foot, and other pursuits of a more leisurely kind. The competitive, sometimes combative, spirit to which undergraduates (even the noble ones)[32] are liable was enough to make these areas of overlap into fertile ground for the germination of college sport.

Several vivid descriptions of early Victorian undergraduate life at Oriel, and the role of sport in it, were written by Thomas Hughes, the apostle of muscular Christianity, who went up to the college in 1841. He was the middle of three brothers to enter the college in the early years of that decade, sons of a father who had distinguished himself academically there in the Copleston era. The best known of Hughes's versions is the lightly fictionalized though heavily moralized *Tom Brown at Oxford*, the sequel to his more famous account of life at Arnold's Rugby, *Tom Brown's Schooldays*. But he dealt with the subject in other places too, such as the laudatory memoir he wrote of his elder brother George and a similar biography of James Fraser, bishop of Manchester, who was a fellow of Oriel when the Hughes brothers were there.[33] Hughes represents Oriel as at a low ebb academically: like others such as Mark Pattison, he felt that the bitter but abstruse religious controversies of the 1830s and 1840s, in which Oriel's common room had played such a prominent part, had led to a decline in the quality of teaching. 'With the exception of Christ Church, there was at this juncture probably no college in Oxford less addicted to reading for the Schools, or indeed to intellectual work of any kind.'[34] It was, by contrast, a place full of sport: three-quarters of the undergraduates cared for little else. This sport was not, however, the traditional fare of country pursuits. Although the college had a high number of wealthy gentlemen commoners (a woefully high number, he and others thought), whose chief amusements were to be found on the hunting field, the activities that delighted the majority and in which the

---

[30] 'Maxim II: Never, if you can avoid it, become a member of a *small* college, "alio nomine", a *raffish* one. If by holding back two years you can get into Oriel, Christ-Church, Brazen-Nose, St. John's, or the like, don't be in a hurry to go to College.' Anon., 'Maxims and Confessions by a Rusticated Oxonian', *Literary Lounger* (August 1826), 359–64 at 362. 'Raffish' at this point still meant 'mean, lowly, pertaining to the riff-raff'.

[31] 'Nimrod', 'The Life of a Sportsman', *New Sporting Magazine*, 2/8 (August 1841), 73–81 at 75.

[32] Two Oriel noblemen (along with some Christ Church 'tufts') were said to have been sent down for taking part in town-and-gown street fights in March 1826: *John Bull*, 20 March 1826; subsequently denied, *John Bull*, 27 March.

[33] Thomas Hughes, *Memoir of a Brother* (London, 1873), 59–87; *James Fraser, Second Bishop of Manchester: A Memoir 1818–1885* (London, 1887), 24–54.

[34] Hughes, *James Fraser*, 25–6.

ILLUSTRATION 18.1 The Oriel eight at Hall's Boat House, c.1860
Magdalen College Archives

college excelled were cricket, rowing, and boxing. The last of these was still, to a large extent, a spectator sport, dabbled in by undergraduates but practised by professionals: Oriel 'almost supported a retired prize-fighter who had been known in the ring as the "Flying Tailor"... and cordially welcomed any stray pugilist who might be training in the neighbourhood and in need of a pound or two'. These professionals were paid to spar and fight full-scale matches in college, sometimes in undergraduate rooms, and might be recruited to support the student cause in town/gown disturbances.[35] But this was sport at arm's length, so to speak, and cultivated as rough entertainment or as something to bet on; awkward social and ethical difficulties could arise if the rough entertainers were themselves undergraduates.[36]

---

[35] Hughes, *James Fraser*, 26. Cf. the story of the 'Putney Pet' in *Verdant Green*, part 2, chs. iii and iv.
[36] *Tom Brown at Oxford*, 70–2.

ILLUSTRATION 18.2 A muscular Christian: Thomas Hughes, commoner 1841–5

Oriel College

In other athletic pursuits, however, important changes had taken place. To an extent they mirrored the same era's conscious attempts to codify and regulate the educational side of university activity, with honours degrees ranking candidates by class first awarded in 1800, and the beginnings of demarcated degree subjects or schools in 1807. In a not dissimilar process, various hitherto indistinct or haphazard forms of physical exercise, competitive or otherwise, were gelling into clear 'sports' with recognized competitions. Cricket exemplifies this process to some extent, though it was already a full-blooded sport with a long history. For years it had been played by Oxonians as an adjunct to the dinners of the Bullingdon Club, largely because (like boxing) it provided something to bet on, though (again like boxing) it had a difficult relationship with the questions of professional involvement and financial reward. By the end of the Georgian era it was rapidly gaining in respectability as a pastime for boys at schools and men at university to play by themselves.[37] But the classic example of early nineteenth-century invention and codification is that of rowing: its development out of a simple leisure pursuit

[37] D. Birley, *A Social History of English Cricket* (London, 1999), 46–51.

ILLUSTRATION 18.3 Francis Henry Hall, fellow 1873–1923
Oriel College

delineates precisely the way that a sport could arise through the spirit of challenge and competition described above.

As recounted in 1900 by W. E. Sherwood in his work on the subject,[38] the details of early rowing in Oxford are hard to uncover; members of the university presumably sought leisure and amusement on the Isis and Cherwell from a very early date, but there is little record of it. Rivers were highways, often quite unpleasant in and around cities, and passage upon them was the prerogative of the professional waterman. One London waterman did try to spread awareness of the beauty and amenity of England's rivers, including those of Oxford: John Taylor, known as the 'Water Poet', who lodged in Oriel in 1625.[39] Taylor undertook many aquatic challenges as

---

[38] W. E. Sherwood, *Oxford Rowing* (Oxford, 1900), a work of formidable research and voluminous data, still often treated as authoritative, despite its inadequate citation of sources.

[39] *Taylor on Thame Isis: or The description of the two famous riuers of Thame and Isis, who being conioyned or combined together, are called Thamisis, or Thames* (London, 1632); ODNB s.n. He signs *The fearefull summer, or, Londons calamity, the countries courtesy, and both their*

publicity stunts or just to provide material for his writing. Professional watermen certainly raced among themselves from the late seventeenth century if not earlier; Doggett's Coat and Badge Race, founded in 1715, is a remarkable survival from this era.[40] Gentry might watch such events, bet on them, or even arrange them; the mock-Venetian Ranelagh 'regatta' of 1775 included a race; and, if young and energetic, they might hire craft for leisure use, but they did not as yet compete. At the end of the eighteenth century Oxford undergraduates were still rowing or sailing in leisurely fashion to Nuneham or Sandford in boats of diverse character, rented from boatmen in the town,[41] much as the Westminster schoolboy William Hickey had hired a skiff to scull around Chelsea Reach in the 1750s.[42] In Mark Pattison's day there were forms of boating that still retained this leisurely, companionable character,[43] which, of course, still survives at Oxford in punting.

In the early nineteenth century, however, the town boatmen began to offer multi-oared boats for hire: not just pairs, but fours, sixes, and finally eights; the occasional instance of a ten is recorded. Used for excursions by undergraduates—often groups of school friends, rather than members of the same college—these vessels' first recommendation was their increased capacity for food, drink, and other comforts. In 1805, G. V. Cox of New College recalled, six-oared boats frequently went to Nuneham, manned by ad hoc crews. He himself formed part of a crew that adopted a uniform mode of dress—the first, he thought, to do so. But there was still no thought of racing.[44]

Crewed boats like this were to remain capacious and be laden with picnic cargo for many years afterwards.[45] But they also introduced the elements of power and speed, making boating an inevitable arena for the personal or group challenge akin to the walking and riding exploits discussed above. Such challenges might take the classic form of a match against time, as when Viscount Newry in August 1822 won a large wager by rowing in a six with five servants from Oxford to Westminster in eighteen hours.[46] But it is clear that crews were racing side by side on the broad waters of the Tideway from early in the century, and Westminster boys and Etonians, who seem to have

---

misery (Oxford, 1625), his account of the metropolitan plague that drove him to Oxford, as 'Io. Taylor of Oriell Colledge in Oxon'.

[40] E. Halladay, *Rowing in England: A Social History: The Amateur Debate* (Manchester, 1990), 7–9; N. Wigglesworth, *The Social History of English Rowing* (London, 1992), 23–5.

[41] L. M. Quiller Couch (ed.), *Reminiscences of Oxford by Oxford Men 1559–1850* (Oxford, 1892), 199–201; cf. the experiences of T. F. Dibdin and Robert Southey, in Sherwood, *Oxford Rowing*, 1–3.

[42] Wigglesworth, *Social History*, 16.

[43] 'We were together almost every day, walking, skiffing, teaing': Pattison, *Memoirs*, 51.

[44] G. V. Cox, *Recollections of Oxford* (London, 1870), 57–8.

[45] Cf. the well-known Lady Margaret Boat Club 'tin panthermanticon' used in the 1820s: R. H. Foster et al., *The History of the Lady Margaret Boat Club 1825–1926* (Cambridge, 1926), 3.

[46] *Morning Chronicle*, 17 August 1822.

owned their boats collectively rather than hiring them, were soon doing the same. Sherwood gives the classic (though somewhat speculative) account of how, on the narrower stream of the Isis, racing in the form of a pursuit might have developed as crews returning from excursions to Nuneham filed out of Iffley lock. In 1815 he records such a race between eights from Brasenose and Jesus, and this year has accordingly (if rather arbitrarily) become the canonical year for the start of bumps racing in Oxford, with Brasenose as the first Head of the River. Other classes of boats were racing too, among them fours. In February 1817, W. F. de Ros of Christ Church (subsequently Lord de Ros) took delivery of a four-oar of his own and raced it; one account, nominating de Ros as the real father of the sport at Oxford, records that his crew included an Orielensis who had been at Westminster with him.[47] If the names of the four given by Sherwood are correct, this can only have been Walker King, a king's scholar of Westminster who came up to Oriel in 1816 and could thereby claim to be the college's first known competitive oarsman.[48] Nonetheless it was the competition between eight-oars that was to become the prestige event.

Both rowing and cricket made good their claim to solidity as parts of educational life when certain high-profile contests were established. The key steps were taken in remarkably quick succession. A cricket match between Eton and Harrow was first successfully organized in 1822.[49] Some of the participants in that encounter wished to create an analogous experience when at university a few years later: hence the first Oxford and Cambridge match, played at Lords in 1827. In 1829, a boat race was held between the universities for the first time, at Henley, after more than a decade of college races of various sorts on the Isis.[50] A bit of prosopography helps to understand the timing: Charles Wordsworth, whom we encountered as a Christ Church real tennis player, and Charles Merivale of St John's, Cambridge, had played in the Harrow XI against Eton and were instrumental in setting up the university cricket fixture. They also took the lead in arranging the first Boat Race, and were indeed both highly successful competitors for the academic prizes that the new age had to offer (as was Merivale's brother Herman, who was at Oriel under Copleston and was the first holder of the

---

[47] W. K. R. Bedford, 'University Rowing Fifty Years Ago', *Badminton Magazine*, 4/22 (May 1897), 587–604 at 587–8. De Ros's diaries have been traced: *Christ Church Matters*, 29 (Hilary 2012), 16–17. He anticipated the interest shown by later oarsmen in the details of the Greek trireme: cf. his 'On Ancient Galleys, and the Arrangement of their Oars and Rowers', *Proceedings of the Royal Irish Academy*, 9 (1864–6), 32–9.
[48] Sherwood, *Oxford Rowing*, 8. Walker King was son of the bishop of Rochester, where he was himself archdeacon, and father of Edward King, bishop of Lincoln.
[49] Birley, *Social History*, 68–9.
[50] G. G. T. Treherne and J. H. D. Goldie, *Record of the University Boat Race 1829–1883* (new edn., London, 1884), 3–11; C. Dodd, *The Oxford & Cambridge Boat Race* (London, 1983), 15–20.

Ireland Scholarship). Wordsworth himself pointed to the fact that he was up at Oxford but lived in Cambridge as a key factor in the organizing role he took;[51] Merivale's links with both places were doubtless also relevant.

It was a case of talented and energetic young men with the right connections seeking to reproduce at university what had been for them, as for many others, a significant feature of school life. If Wordsworth, Merivale, and their close associates had not taken the lead, others would have done. Their success certainly owes something to their prominence in diverse fields of endeavour, in virtue of which they were well-known and widely respected figures. Although the idea of university contests met opposition in some quarters,[52] men like these gave the enterprise a not entirely trivial character. Both Merivale and Wordsworth—future churchmen of distinction and gravity—attributed organized sport a role in their personal development, and noted its unifying role in a university where matters of doctrine, politics, or ethics were inclined to divide.[53] But their support for 'athletics' was moderate and restrained, and they remained at least in part men of the pre-sport age, ready to find improvement, relaxation, or diversion in any form of physical activity and not setting too much store by it. A far more outspoken and very influential *apologia* for organized sport in the educational context was to be formulated by Thomas Hughes, on the direct basis of his experiences at Oriel a few years later.

Thomas Hughes was an idealist, subsequently a campaigning Christian Socialist with a romantic view of national history, and the concomitant tendency to interpret the past in line with his ideals. He had firm views not only on what British manhood should or could be like, but on what it *really was like*, if it only had unfettered freedom to express itself. Inert, cloistered dons and plush, sybaritic gentlemen commoners represented not the norm, but degradations of the genuine, full-blooded article. Hughes held that physical activity, to which he optimistically believed British youth would always be drawn, was the most natural expression of true manliness. Sport was the imposition of morality on physical activity; this moral element was the factor that made it a lesson for life; but it was the channelling of a natural impulse.[54] The label of muscular Christian, which he took from Charles Kingsley, and which provided a chapter heading in *Tom Brown at Oxford*, was one that Hughes wore proudly to the end of his days.

---

[51] Wordsworth, *Annals of my Early Life*, 57 n. 2. His father was master of Trinity College, Cambridge.

[52] Dodd, *Boat Race*, 15–16. In a similar way successive headmasters of Harrow had attempted to prohibit cricket matches against Eton and Winchester: Wordsworth, *Annals*, 10–11.

[53] Wordsworth, *Annals*, 9–14, 48, 55–62; C. Merivale, *Autobiography*, ed. J. Merivale (London, 1899), 67–9, 73, 75–6, 79.

[54] On these elements in Hughes's thought, see Asa Briggs, *Victorian People* (rev. edn., London, 1965), 148–75, esp. 158–62.

These lessons Hughes's alter ego, Tom Brown, had learnt with difficulty at Rugby. At Oriel, they needed to be learned over again, and the environment made it still more of a struggle. At Rugby there had been an example on high: Thomas Arnold. Arnold had not himself been interested in athletic competition, though he did at least bestir himself to watch from the touchline. But it was the application of Arnold's ethic of selfless struggle to competitive physical activity that Hughes identifies as the origin and defining characteristic of true, morally beneficial sport. At Oriel, by contrast, the dons were distinguished not merely for a lack of interest in what so occupied the attention of their charges, but a positive dislike of it. None of them participated in sport directly,

...nor was any one of them ever seen on the river bank at the races, or on Cowley Marsh at a cricket match... All the tutors were in orders, and none of them, so far as was known, had ever used their legs except for a mild constitutional, or their arms for anything beyond handling editions of the classics and the fathers, and writing elegant prose or verse in the dead languages.[55]

The venom is a little surprising, but Hughes wrote in different voices in different contexts. It is clear, however, that he felt Oriel had lost its way, whether measured by the ethical and social standards he felt Rugby had given him, or by the academic criteria of his father's generation. It was the achievement of 'Tom Brown', and an appropriate act of *pietas* to his former headmaster, to restore at least in part the college's fibre by way of sport conducted selflessly, in a spirit that elided social and economic difference and unified the various parties of Oriel. Fortunately Oxford offered the perfect sport for this, namely rowing. By the time the Hughes brothers came up to Oriel, the bumps races from Iffley were a regular part of the Oxford scene, though they did not yet form a recognizable 'Eights Week' and there is no doubt that viewing eights races in Oxford before 1850 in terms of what came later lends them a spurious unity and uniformity. Eights were raced any time between early May and mid-June, and the contests were frequently strung out over many 'nights', not necessarily consecutive; as late as 1844 races were held in early March as well as mid-May. In 1823 races were apparently an eagerly anticipated element in Commemoration, after the end of the summer term,[56] though in the event only two crews raced; the same year saw a dispute over watermen rowing in crews, resolved in favour of their exclusion.[57] From 1825 races started above the lock rather than in it, and it was further resolved that crews should be drawn from one college only. Increasing numbers of colleges were soon competing: seven in 1836, twelve the following year, fourteen in

---

[55] Hughes, *James Fraser*, 25–6.   [56] *Morning Post*, 7 June 1823.
[57] Sherwood, *Oxford Rowing*, 10–11, not classing the single race as an instalment of the Eights.

ILLUSTRATION 18.4 College sports day, 1903, *OCA*

1840. Second crews, known disparagingly as torpids, were boated in inferior craft as early as the 1820s; from 1838, separate races were laid on for such crews, often interspersed between the ones for senior boats. In 1852 these races were detached altogether and held in Hilary Term, where they remain.

According to Sherwood's data Oriel eights competed in 1828, 1836,[58] and 1839,[59] thereafter being a nearly permanent presence (the exceptional years being 1848, 1852, and 1854–5).[60] Torpid crews were entered with regularity almost from the outset, scoring early successes. Yet we do not know the origins of the boat club. The oldest documentary evidence on the subject that Sherwood could find is still the earliest known, a volume of extracts made in 1850 from 'the former account book' covering the era 1842 to 1849.[61] It is far

---

[58] *Jackson's Oxford Journal*, 4 and 11 June 1836.
[59] *Jackson's Oxford Journal*, 8 June 1839.
[60] Sherwood, *Oxford Rowing*, 109–41. St Mary Hall was to enter crews in 1867–71, 1873–6, 1878–81, 1883, and 1891–3, finishing above Oriel in 1868, 1879, and 1880.
[61] OCA SL C 5 A1/1: 'Acts of the Oriel Crew from 1842 to Decr. 1849 (copied from the former account book)'.

ILLUSTRATION 18.5 The bump supper, March 1908, *OCA*

from the detailed record one would like, but it does start with the enviable opening line, '1842: In this year Oriel was Head of the river.' The central figure in this chapter of events was Thomas Hughes's elder brother George, who had gone up to Oriel from Rugby in early 1840 with a reputation as a good classicist and cricketer, and a recommendation from his father to pursue athletic activity of the old, eclectic (and not necessarily competitive) sort.[62] He kept up his cricket seriously enough to play for the university. But he also took up rowing, sitting in the Oriel eight of 1841 and sufficiently impressing Fletcher Menzies, the inspiring, reforming president of the still young Oxford University Boat Club, to be chosen by him as a partner in a pair and then for the 1842 university crew which would race Cambridge in London on 11 June. Thomas was initially rather baffled and disappointed by this change in his elder brother's athletic tastes, but on arrival at Oriel, of course, he too was won over to the virtues of the new sport, and joined the Boat Club in its assault on the headship. At the start of the 1842 races, held

---

[62] 'I applaud, and κυδίζε [= κύδιστε?], and clap you on the back for rowing: row, box, fence, and walk with all possible sturdiness.' Hughes, *Memoir of a Brother*, 61.

over seven nights between 11 and 27 May, the headship was held by University College, stroked by Fletcher Menzies. There had been much advance speculation however that they were destined to fall,[63] and so it proved when Trinity bumped them in the very first race. Meanwhile, however, Oriel—with George Hughes at stroke—were rising, and bumped Trinity to go head on 23 May. The often quoted account of the race given by Thomas Hughes in *Tom Brown at Oxford* remains an excellent description of a bump.[64] In the novel Oriel masquerades under the name of 'St Ambrose', Trinity under that of 'Oriel':

> Tom had an atom of go still left in the back of his head... In another six strokes the gap is lessened and St. Ambrose has crept up to ten feet, and now to five... 'A bump, a bump!' shout the St. Ambrosians on shore. 'Row on, row on', screams Miller. He has not yet felt the electric shock, and knows he will miss his bump if the young ones slacken for a moment... A bump now, and no mistake; the bow of the St. Ambrose boat jams the oar of the Oriel stroke, and the two boats pass the winning post... So near a shave was it.

The headship was not the only aquatic glory in this period, either for Oriel or for George Hughes personally. On 11 June he and another of the head crew, G. D. Bourne (progenitor of a family of Oxford oarsmen), duly won their 'blues' in Oxford's six-length victory over Cambridge. Rowing with William Wilberforce, also of the Oriel eight, Hughes won the university pair-oar competition, beating a second Oriel pair in the final.[65] The following year, in 1843, Hughes and Fletcher Menzies were again the stern pair in an Oxford crew entered in the Grand Challenge Cup at Henley; on the eve of the final, against a crew from Cambridge, Menzies was struck by illness. By a new rule substitution was forbidden; so Hughes stroked the crew as a seven-oar and won a victory that would go down in rowing history. The race, known inevitably as *septem contra Camum*, excited delirious scenes among the spectators and was said by one observer to have been 'the event which really popularised boating at Oxford'.[66] Though Oriel did not retain the headship for a second year the college continued a leading light in Oxford rowing throughout the 1840s. Two more blues were won: William Buckle in 1845 and Charles Steward in 1849, a year in which there were two Boat Races and an Oriel eight entered the Grand Challenge Cup at Henley.

In Thomas Hughes's account, of course, there was more to the headship than the rapidly fading laurels of an aquatic victory. It was the vindication of the unifying and selfless approach to college life that sport encouraged. This is seen clearly in the case of the most interesting character in the book:

---

[63] Press comment and forecasts began in *Bell's Life* and *Jackson's Oxford Journal* in early May.
[64] *Tom Brown at Oxford*, 140–1.
[65] Account Book, cit. Sherwood, *Oxford Rowing*, 214.
[66] W. Tuckwell, *Reminiscences of Oxford* (London, 1901), 113–14.

Hardy, a poor student of good family, occupying the archaic grade of 'servitor', and thereby required to carry out certain menial tasks in college in return for free rooms. (In reality Oriel no longer had servitors, though it had bible clerks as near equivalents.) A fine boxer and still finer oarsman, he had to study hard to justify the expense of his degree; he was older than the other undergraduates; and he disliked and was embarrassed by their juvenile extravagance and profligacy. Hot-tempered and reclusive he kept apart from them, and they from him; he rowed alone. But Brown fosters a gradual rapprochement, another oarsman's illness during the bumps races brings Hardy into the crew as a substitute, where his contribution is instrumental in the victory.

Of central and symbolic importance to Thomas Hughes was the role of his elder brother. George Hughes was to proceed to a second class in Greats in 1844, a brief career at Doctor's Commons, and longer years as a minor country gentleman near Uffington in Berkshire. In his younger brother's account he is represented as an unsullied type of open honesty and nobility of character coupled with physical prowess: the good squire, conscious of and obedient to his Christian and social responsibilities.[67] As in the case of the servitor Hardy, hierarchical distinctions—including those of birth—remain an important part of the set-up, but should be used for the common good. *Concordia ordinum* required *ordines*, but all ranks could pull together. The rowing metaphor is no accident. Thomas Hughes wished to present sport at Oriel as potentially democratic and unifying; tending to the improvement of the college spirit and inimical not to study, with which, in fact, it shared many aims, but rather to luxury and the abuse of privilege. Other than recognizing the evident idealism of this position, and remembering Hughes's ability to reinterpret the past, it is hard to assess how far his account matches reality. It is true that only one gentleman commoner can be identified in the crews that raced for Oriel in Hughes's day (H. M. Hamersley, who rowed 3 in the 1843 eight). All other recorded competitors were commoners, save Owen Williams (bow man in the head crew of 1842) who was, like the fictional Hardy, a bible clerk. With regard to study, however, the picture is less flattering. The sample is very small for reliable conclusions, but of the 22 identified members of the Boat Club in this era, 15 (two-thirds) took their degrees and only 4 (under a fifth) did so with honours. In this they seem to compare unfavourably with their contemporaries: of all 102 Orielenses who matriculated in the years 1839 to 1843 inclusive, 76 (three-quarters) took degrees, 32 (a third) being classmen.[68]

---

[67] Cf. the thinly veiled portrait of him in his thirties in Hughes's novel *The Scouring of the White Horse* (1859).
[68] Shadwell, *Registrum*, 436–56. Undergraduates dying while in residence have been omitted, but those taking up scholarships in other colleges included.

In some senses, though, rowing was definitively set as the community sporting activity of the college. Although, in May 1848, the subscription for membership of the Boat Club was £2, not a negligible sum, it was found convenient for the club treasurer to enter the names of *all* college freshmen in his register each year, in anticipation of large numbers joining.[69] The club was already looking forward to the day when membership, even if inactive, could be seen as the default option. College competitions, designed both for recruitment and instruction in racing, proliferated: in 1861 a gift of four silver oars and a silver rudder was received from John Eveleigh Wyndham, an undergraduate of 1832 and father of a freshman that year. Wyndham senior was grandson of Provost Eveleigh, and had been born in the lodgings.[70] The prize, offered for college fours for many years, and still recalled (if in name only) as the title of the competition for novice eights, represents the confluence of the old and new worlds of Oriel.

The introduction of newly codified sports, initially a trickle, was by the fourth quarter of the nineteenth century a rising tide.[71] Most notably, two species of football emerged from the old, indistinct mass of large-pitch team ball games with their countless, finely distinguished local manifestations. One, introduced at Oxford in 1869, was the form originating at and named after Rugby School; it was still particularly cultivated there and at Marlborough College (after 1851, to all intents, Rugby's daughter foundation).[72] The other was the no-hands variety codified in 1863 by the Football Association on the basis of the conventions used by Eton, Harrow, Charterhouse, and Cambridge; it was formally adopted at Oxford in 1871–2.[73] By the end of the century lawn tennis, hockey, golf, swimming, water polo, lacrosse, badminton, and ice hockey were all played in the university. Steeplechase and cross-country running developed as specific forms of athletics. Boxing, previously cultivated by undergraduates as a spectator sport, or conducted by professional proxy, became an arena for direct participation. Old forms of sword play and singlestick were replaced or subsumed by the reformed variety of fencing. Though not all these sports were played at every college, or in the name of the colleges, they were all available to undergraduates, and in many of them there was an intercollegiate tournament (usually known as

---

[69] Account Book.
[70] Shadwell, *Registrum*, 407.
[71] On this phase generally, see H. S. Jones, 'University and College Sport', HUO vii. 517–43.
[72] Jones, 'University and College Sport', 523–4: Oxford University Rugby Football Club was founded in 1869; until 1876 the captain, secretary, and one committee member had to be Rugbeians, and all Rugbeians and Marlburians at Oxford were expected to join.
[73] C. Weir, *The History of the Oxford University Association Football Club 1872–1998* (Harefield, 1998), 8–11. The Oxford club was founded in 1871 according to the FA code of 1863, with the exception of the latter's rule 6 (the offside rule); this was adopted a year later to allow Oxford to join the FA and enter its challenge cup—which it won in 1873.

'cuppers'). A few of them, particularly the older ones that were also carried on at schools, assumed a new centrality in Oxford life.

Closely associated with this phase at Oriel was Francis Henry Hall, fellow from 1873 to his death in 1923, and dean from 1882 to 1915. As a scholar of Corpus, Hall had taken firsts in mods and Greats and steered the university crew in three Boat Races, as well as an Oxford four in a famous match against Harvard over the Boat Race course.[74] Known initially as 'Little Hall', for his preternaturally boyish looks and slight figure, but growing considerably more corpulent with time (in later life he claimed to have doubled his coxing weight of 8 stone), Hall watched over, supported, and—from 1909, as founding editor of the *Oriel Record*—gave a wry commentary on Oriel sport in all its forms. When an amalgamated club subscription fund was created in 1889 (on a model first introduced at Balliol) to support the various sporting clubs according to their needs, Hall was the obvious choice of treasurer;[75] and when, right at the end of his life, in 1920, an appeal was raised for the new cricket pavilion at Bartlemas, it was Hall who administered it.[76] Irascible and sometimes difficult as a colleague, he tended to deploy his acute capacities and often scathing wit in favour of the status quo. As a bachelor don living in, he represented something of a link with a bygone age in both collegiate and sporting terms (his third Boat Race, in 1872, had been the last rowed on fixed seats). But several generations of sporting undergraduates had reason to be grateful to his benign supervision of their finances.[77]

In Hall's day, Oriel was a cricket and football college. In fact it might be said to have been *the* cricket and football college. In regards to cricket, the phenomenon was noted by contemporaries,[78] recorded in the press in the aftermath of the war,[79] and more recently subject to analysis and comment in the *Oriel Record*.[80] Certainly the college provided great numbers of Oxford cricketers (thirty-one players in the period 1880–1914, winning seventy-five blues between them—19 per cent of the total available), commencing with

---

[74] For an account see Dodd, *Boat Race*, 181–94.

[75] For the general move to this model, see Jones, HUO vii. 528–30. In 1913, Hall contrasted the success of the new regime (under which the total annual budget for all sports was nearly £600) with the old approach whereby individual clubs inevitably ran up large liabilities (e.g. the Boat Club's debt of £357 in 1863): OR (September 1914), 172–3. In 1923 the overall sports budget had grown to £1,000.

[76] OR (September 1920), 157.

[77] See the tributes paid at his death, OR (June 1923), 125–35.

[78] E. Peake, OR (January 1938), 287: the 1881 varsity match, in which Peake was among five Orielenses playing for Oxford, was described as Oriel v. Cambridge.

[79] *The Times*, 5 July 1919, 6 ('Cricket reminiscences: Mr A. H. Evans and Oriel College'; unsigned but by P. F. Warner).

[80] R. Hathway, 'Oriel and the Golden Age of Cricket', OR (1992), 24–6.

the great A. H. Evans, who played every year from 1878 to 1881.[81] In 1887 Oriel was able to field a team containing six blues,[82] and in the years that followed many Orielenses became prominent amateurs in the county championship, establishing themselves as central figures in what is often called cricket's 'Golden Age'. Among them were men such as L. C. N. and R. C. H. Palairet, blues in 1890–4 and subsequently openers for Somerset; V. T. Hill (blue 1892) and G. Fowler (1888), both also Somerset batsmen; K. J. Key (1884–7), long-standing captain of Surrey; B. J. T. Bosanquet (1898–1900), Middlesex all-rounder and deviser of the googly; and of course the most eminent (if not necessarily the best) cricketer ever produced by Oriel, P. F. (later Sir Pelham) Warner—a blue in 1895, captain of Middlesex and England, and president of MCC.

This was a time when the relative standard of the university sides was high. Kingsmill Key's 281 for Oxford against Middlesex at Chiswick in 1887 (still a university record) contributed to a stand of 340 for the seventh wicket, then a record first-class partnership for *any* wicket.[83] Middlesex, it has to be recalled, was a team of gentlemen amateurs, much like the universities themselves. A modicum of caution is necessary when assessing the achievements of this era, characterized as it was by a large number of cricketers who were, simultaneously and subsequently, cricket writers.[84] These multi-taskers were mostly amateurs; indeed, writing weekly columns and a book or two a year was one of the permitted ways a 'gentleman' might earn a crust from the game. An important upshot was that the concept of the Golden Age, and the features that made it golden, were largely established and delineated by those who figured in it. Since some of them also naturally gravitated into the administration of the game, through service as selectors and on MCC committees, they were perfectly placed to create and manage not only cricket's present and future but the terms in which these were assessed against its past. The prime example was Pelham Warner himself, 'the ultimate establishment man' and 'the most assiduous and influential of the player-scribblers'.[85]

Accordingly, there is a slight inevitability about the role accorded university-bred amateurs (Oriel men prominent among them) in traditional accounts of pre-Great-War cricket. The Palairet brothers—emblematic of Edwardian cricketing 'amateurs in the cavalier mode'[86]—were held up as paragons for

---

[81] Of whom Andrew Lang wrote, 'But all our hearts are in the University match, and mine, for one, has been broken year by year since Mr. Evans left Oriel'; 'Cricket Gossip', *Longman's Magazine*, 4/20 (June 1884), 147.

[82] OR (September 1914), 174.

[83] Oxford, batting first and scoring 555, won by an innings and 229 runs. Key was one of four Orielenses in the side.

[84] Birley, *Social History*, 187.

[85] Birley, *Social History*, 168–9 (citing C. B. Fry's assessment of him as 'an imperturbably accomplished school batsman' and the archetypal 'pavilion magnate'), 187.

[86] Birley, *Social History*, 177.

ILLUSTRATION 18.6 P. F. Warner (Sir Pelham Warner), commoner 1892–6, batting, 1905

National Portrait Gallery

their stylish play. Lionel, the elder, was said in his obituary to be 'generally regarded as the most beautiful batsman of all time'.[87] Bernard Bosanquet's death notice claimed that 'No man probably has in his time had so important and lasting an influence on the game of cricket.'[88] The googly—possibly

---

[87] *The Times*, 29 March 1933, 6: 'During a period when grace of style and accuracy of stroke were regarded as even more important in a batsman's stroke than making runs,' the obituary continues (perpetuating a classic piece of 'Golden Age' mythology on the way), 'Lionel Palairet stood out as the most attractive cricketer in England.'

[88] *The Times*, 13 October 1936, 21.

ILLUSTRATION 18.7 The Minnows Cricket Club, 1907, *OCA*

practised while at Oriel,[89] but originating much earlier and only perfected and unleashed in the 1901 county championship[90]—is still sometimes known as a 'bosie'. Warner certainly had reason to be grateful to it since it played a major part in Middlesex's surprise victory in the 1903 county championship and in England's victorious 1903–4 tour of Australia, both under Warner's captaincy. Warner, of course, was almost certainly the author of the obituaries just quoted; we tend unwittingly to look at Golden Age cricket through his eyes. The Oriel link mattered to him, even if not everyone else considered it of great moment,[91] and it may have influenced his decision-making on occasion. In 1919 a rare first-class appearance by the Orielensis A. J. Evans (like his father A. H. Evans a four-times blue, in 1909–12) prompted Warner to pen a nostalgic appreciation

---

[89] Hathway, OR (1992), 24.
[90] Nicolas Bosanquet (brother), letter to *The Times*, 14 October 1936, 15; obituary, 14 October 1936.
[91] *The Athenaeum*, 16 April 1920, 508, reviewing Warner's *Cricket Reminiscences*: 'What is the use of filling half a page with the names of Oriel men who have secured cricket blues?'

of the college's pre-war contribution,[92] and two years later he selected Evans for MCC against the touring Australians at Lord's, where a creditable score led to his selection for England in the second test.[93] It is less certain that the Oriel connection was an operative factor in 1932 when Warner, now chairman of the selectors, took Richard Palairet to help him manage the England touring team in Australia—though it was noted in the *Guardian* by Neville Cardus, who enjoyed such details.[94] This was the team captained by Douglas Jardine, and the series the one made infamous by England's 'leg-theory' or 'bodyline' bowling, and by the MCC's protestations (in part informed by the manager's disingenuous assurances) that no such strategy could have been countenanced.

In association football, Oriel was if anything more successful still. Though there was only one Orielensis among the thirty-five original members of the university football club in November 1871,[95] others soon followed in large numbers. In the early days, many came from Winchester (a school with its own code of football, not successfully transplanted to Oxford),[96] but subsequently the main sources were other footballing schools such as Repton, Malvern, Shrewsbury, and Charterhouse, the latter a major provider of Oriel undergraduates in general. By no means unusual was the year 1897: Oriel provided four blues, three from Charterhouse (half of the total number of Carthusians in the team) and one from Shrewsbury.[97] When football 'cuppers' were introduced in 1882 it is not surprising to find that Oriel dominated, winning twelve times down to 1914, a fact that F. H. Hall noted with quiet satisfaction.[98] Most eminent of Charterhouse and Oriel footballers was Charles Wreford-Brown. Narrowly missing a cricket blue through illness,[99] he won two for soccer, in 1888 and 1889, the latter as captain. An early and long-standing member of the Corinthians, he was capped four times for England in the 1890s, twice captaining the side, and almost achieved a form of celebrity in the early days of popular coverage of

---

[92] *The Times*, 5 July 1919, 6.
[93] Evans (a renowned escaper as a Great War POW in Germany and Turkey) had turned out for the Old Oriel eleven against the college's current side; OR (September 1921), 32–3, suggested this had helped him get back into form. In the test match he flopped and never played at that level again.
[94] *Manchester Guardian*, 7 July 1932, 4.
[95] J. H. Bridges (1870); he was to play in the FA cup semi-final of 1873 but was not selected for the final. Wyndham Merewether (also 1870) was the only other Orielensis elected before the club joined the Football Association in 1872. Both were Wykehamists. Weir, *Oxford Football*, 8–12.
[96] Jones, HUO vii. 523–4; S. Bailey, 'Living Sports History: Football at Winchester, Eton and Harrow', *The Sports Historian*, 15 (1995), 34–53.
[97] Also in this side was B. O. Corbett of St Mary Hall, who later played outside left for the Corinthians (whose first club history he wrote) and, in 1893, for England. *The Times*, 11 December 1967, 10.
[98] OR (March 1914), 137.
[99] He did however play four matches for Gloucestershire under W. G. Grace's captaincy, and toured North America in 1891 with Lord Hawke's eleven.

the sport.[100] The inevitable shift into administration followed and for nearly five decades he was Oxford's representative at the Football Association, also serving as FA vice-president and a long-term member and ultimately chairman of its international selection committee.[101] In many ways, Wreford-Brown was (*mutatis mutandis*) a benign footballing equivalent of P. F. Warner in the cricket sphere. It was no chance that both sports should have, at or near the top, men who had been at Oriel in the 1880s and 1890s. But football and cricket developed along very different lines in the twentieth century. While men like Warner managed to shield the flame of amateurism and ensure that the public school and university contribution to first-class cricket remained an essential part of the game, its image, and its authorized history, the footballing world represented by Wreford-Brown was virtually extinct by 1914, and is now forgotten.

By some unfortunate chance for most of F. H. Hall's time as fellow, dean, and chief supporter of sport at Oriel, the college was far from distinguished in his own sport, rowing. Rannie apologized for treating it first: 'For the sake of chronological accuracy we must begin with boating, though it is hardly of the river that one thinks when one speaks of the recent athletic fame of the college.'[102] From time to time an Oriel oarsman won a blue,[103] and in some years an Oriel eight or torpid surged up the chart with a prodigious number of bumps, though this tended to reflect the low position in which a previous year's ebbing fortunes had deposited it.[104] The headship of Thomas Hughes's day was a distant memory, plaintively recalled in the words of *Orielenses Bibite*. In 1873, the year that Hall arrived, fresh from his coxing triumphs with the university, Oriel attained fourth place in Torpids; but an eight sent to compete at the Royal Regatta that summer (one of only two occasions an Oriel crew raced there in the six decades from 1849) was described as 'about the worst crew seen at Henley for some years'.[105] It is not that interest in trying the sport out was lacking. T. D. Raikes (member of a distinguished rowing family) came up from Radley in 1868 and recorded that 'the number

---

[100] A full-page illustrated interview appeared in the boys' magazine *Chums* no. 217 (17 November 1897), 198.
[101] *The Times*, 27 November 1951, 8. He was also 'one of our best amateur chess players' (*The Times*, 30 November 1951, 8).
[102] Rannie, *Oriel*, 234.
[103] E. F. Henley (Sherborne, blue 1865–6, highly regarded by the great 'Guts' Woodgate, doyen of Oxford rowing in that era); J. S. Sinclair (Repton, 1874); Thomas Etherington-Smith (Repton, 1900–1).
[104] Thus the 1874 eight made eight bumps (virtually the same crew sank back down the following year); and the 1879 torpid made six in five nights—frankly assessed by H. W. Seton-Karr, the crew's stroke, OR (June 1923), 146–7. For an attempt to make sense of the essentially patternless vicissitudes, OR (September 1922), 102–4.
[105] *Baily's Magazine*, 1 August 1873, 46. In 1885 an eight was entered for the Ladies' Plate.

of boating men was fairly large for so small a college'.[106] Races were sometimes staged between crews raised from arbitrary groupings such as scholars and commoners, or occupants of First and Second Quads. In 1892 forty men received the rudimentary rowing instruction known as tubbing, contrasting with twelve in the much larger college of 1922.[107] In many ways Oriel exemplified the 'integrative' aspect of Oxford rowing described by H. S. Jones in the university history. As Jones put it, rowing 'was no mere extension of public-school sport: on the contrary, it had a particular appeal to many who had been undistinguished athletes at school, for, unlike cricket, it was a sport in which someone who took it up from scratch at Oxford could, given strength and health, achieve Torpid standard at least.'[108] Other considerations might play a part. Edward Peake, coming up to Oriel from the non-rowing school Marlborough in 1880, and 'never attracted much to rowing', nonetheless took it up 'with the idea that it might fit in better with "reading"', and went on to stroke a winning four (presumably a Wyndhams boat). His only further participation was in the purely ceremonial, though perilous, processional rowing of Commemoration.[109] Rowing was part of the Oriel experience for a wide range of men from the Scottish minister Lord Balfour of Burleigh (Boat Club captain 'in 1870 or 1871')[110] to Dr E. H. Fellowes, canon of Windsor and eminent music scholar (winner of a trial cap and captain 1893). Admittedly Fellowes himself blamed lack of interest for the college's poor showing on the river. In 1933 he recalled that 'Most of the College were cricketers in those days, and it was difficult to get a crew at all to row', pointing out that the whole undergraduate body barely amounted to eighty.[111] This is striking because we have seen how many men were coaxed down to the river for tubbing in his time. Converting this broad 'grass-roots' participation into serious commitment was evidently another matter. Hall himself regarded increasing specialization in sport as the problem. In 1913 he wrote a lament on 'the effects of the diffusion of its [the college's] energies over too wide a field':

There is, perhaps, something to be said for the view that every man should play at the game he likes best, so long as it is regarded merely as a question of play, but it is clear that a small college of little over a hundred members cannot hope to turn out successful teams in seven different departments of sport... The specialisation, indeed, which is so rapidly transforming the intellectual work of the University, shews itself even in sport. A man comes up already labelled a golfer, a hockey-player, or runner, and, having obtained a certain proficiency in one pursuit, will not take the trouble to learn a new one. That hits rowing particularly hard, as we do not get ready-made oarsmen.

---

[106] OR (September 1924), 247.
[107] OR (September 1922), 103.
[108] Jones, HUO vii. 521.
[109] OR (January 1938), 289.
[110] OR (September 1921), 36.
[111] OR (September 1933), 311.

ILLUSTRATION 18.8 College barge with swimmers, 1908, *OCA*

There followed a critique of the 'new style' in rowing.[112]

Nonetheless, and despite these unreliable foundations, Oriel rowing did occasionally show hints of future greatness. After an absence of twenty-four years, a crew entered Henley in 1909 and reached the final of the Thames Cup (the junior of the two competitions for club or college eights) where it lost to Wadham, who narrowly avoided being impeded by a kite advertisement dropping into the river just ahead of them. Not everyone was mentally prepared for the aquatic renaissance. At a bump supper in 1911 L. R. Phelps (soon to become provost) delivered 'a felicitous speech, dwelling chiefly on the cricket reputation of the college, and of Mr. L. H. Palairet in particular'.[113] Perhaps galled by this, an Oriel eight was once again entered for the Thames Cup in 1912 and, this time, won it.[114] Hall was right that Oriel did not receive many ready-made oarsmen; not one of its small crop of blues had

---

[112] OR (March 1913), 68–9.   [113] OR (March 1912), 35–6.
[114] Sir T. Cook, *Henley Races* (Oxford, 1919), 297: 'The Thames Cup was won by Oriel somewhat unexpectedly, but they thoroughly deserved the medals for their long rowing and steady workmanship.'

rowed at school. Rowing may have been a briefly intriguing pastime to a wide range of undergraduates precisely because of its difference from the various team and ball games they knew (perhaps knew and hated) from school. It may have been integrative, but it did not necessarily produce champions. It was also true that the proliferation of sports and the notion that even a small college should enter for all of them placed a strain on human resources. The same individuals could, however, shine in more than one arena. Richard Palairet was a football blue in 1891. Bernard Bosanquet threw the hammer for Oxford (it is not recorded whether his action was orthodox). A. J. Evans found time to be president of the university golf club and win a blue in racquets. One of Oriel's last pre-war cricket blues, R. O. Lagden, also represented the university at rugby, hockey, and racquets, and won the shot putt and hammer at the college sports in 1910 (not to mention being president of the JCR and commanding the Oriel contingent in the OTC). On a broader level, the undergraduate body as a whole was clearly able to transfer its skills and enthusiasm, registering successes not only in cricket and football but in hockey (the college reached the final of cuppers every year from 1909 to 1912, winning convincingly on the last two occasions) and golf (winning 'with ease' in 1911 and 1912). The popularity of golf and the remoteness of the links was the explanation given for the presence of twenty motorbikes in Oriel in March 1914. At any rate, it was the explanation that Hall received when he enquired about a topic that exercised him greatly.[115] Lawn tennis was another integrative activity: in 1912 there were forty-nine entries for the college singles tournament, and fifty-four for the doubles, the cricket ground being given over to six courts to host the matches. E. H. Fellowes, again, was a keen player, captaining the college six in the same year he led the Boat Club. Appropriately, it was to be a chance remark by a fellow player in a tennis tournament that would direct him towards his lifetime's work in the study of early English madrigals.[116]

By 1914 the college needed a new place to play its games. For some years, together with University College and Pembroke, Oriel had held a lease on the Old Magdalen ground, where once the university played cricket, but this was inadequate for the ever-growing volume of activity, and in any case University College was now detaching itself from the arrangement.[117] Other things were changing too. At the start of the war Hall gave up his deanship, his tutorial duties ('the College having no further need of his services', he wrote), and the editorship of the *Oriel Record*. Soon after, Shadwell was succeeded by Phelps as provost. The college was swiftly

---

[115] OR (March 1914), 138. [116] *Musical Times*, 1308 (February 1952), 59.
[117] It had acquired a new ground off the Abingdon Road in 1910, building a pavilion there to the design of Clough Williams Ellis; this opened in 1914. R. Darwall-Smith, *A History of University College Oxford* (Oxford, 2008), 430.

depopulated and sport more or less suspended. By mid-March 1915 Phelps was writing to the parents of R. O. Lagden, the great all-rounder of 1910, recently killed at Ypres.

The period 1875 to 1914 is often identified as the age in which the 'cult' of athleticism held sway most powerfully in British education, and specifically in Oxford and Cambridge.[118] The argument is that the later nineteenth century saw a vast increase in the public school sector, whose homogeneous, sports-mad products filled up the previously more diverse universities, so that undergraduate life became simply an opportunity to extend schoolboy activities, attitudes, and values. Athleticism was positively inculcated by school authorities; and despite a few dissenting voices, the universities at least offered no hindrance to it and in many ways assisted or even encouraged it. The result was a particular form of elite masculine culture, with sport at its heart. The period is contrasted more or less sharply with what went before and came after, the years following the Great War seeing an irreversible rupture. The 'new' undergraduate of the inter-war period—especially at Oxford—found Edwardian models of behaviour hopelessly, insufferably outdated;[119] this was especially so at Oxford, with its supposedly new, supposedly decadent ideal of the 'aesthete'.[120]

This picture needs, at least, considerable refinement. H. S. Jones has argued in more than one place that the treatment of university sporting culture as a mere continuation of the school variety ignores the sense of a fresh start and new opportunities that many undergraduates had (and have) on arriving at university.[121] Oriel's nineteenth-century oarsmen, we have seen, had only exceptionally been school oarsmen. Similarly open to question is the idea of the breach after the Great War. Strong evidence of unchanged priorities is seen in the swift re-establishment of college and university sport from 1919; despite the exigencies of shorter degree courses and the wider horizons that returning servicemen must have had, time was found for organized sport. The epitome of the approach was Oriel's Miles Howell, who had originally matriculated in 1913 and gained football and cricket blues before serving in the Lancashire Regiment throughout the war, in which he was wounded and

---

[118] J. A. Mangan, *Athleticism in the Victorian and Edwardian Public School* (Cambridge, 1981); J. A. Mangan, 'Oars and the Man: Pleasure and Purpose in Victorian and Edwardian Cambridge', *International Journal of the History of Sport*, 1 (1984), 245–71.

[119] S. Levsen, 'Constructing Elite Identities: University Students, Military Masculinity and the Consequences of the Great War in Britain and Germany', *Past & Present*, 198 (2008), 147–83. The claim for a functioning militaristic component in the pre-war cult of sport is not successfully established. On the 'insufferable ideal', cf. Noel Annan, *Our Age* (London, 1990), ch. 2.

[120] Levsen, 'Constructing Elite Identities', citing *Cambridge Gownsman*, 15 October 1925, 11, 13; 4 December 1926, 1; 14 May 1927, 12. The possibility of interpreting such pieces as specimens of very traditional anti-Oxonian spirit is not discussed.

[121] HUO vii. 521–4; M. C. Curthoys and H. S. Jones, 'Oxford Athleticism 1815–1914: A Reappraisal', *History of Education*, 24 (1995), 305–17.

lost a younger brother. On his return to Oxford he became a leading figure in the revival of both sports, playing a major personal part in Oxford's victory in the varsity cricket match in 1919. When he graduated in 1920 the *Oriel Record* noted:

Both the University and the College have suffered a great loss in the departure of Miles Howell. To the former, as Captain both of the Cricket Club and the Association Football Club, he did good service in starting things again, and in turning out two good teams against Cambridge. His services to the College were equally valuable, and to him and to other *revenants* from pre-war days it is largely due that the various activities of the College, social and athletic, have been resumed with so much energy and so little friction.[122]

Howell went on to play football for the Corinthians (winning five amateur caps for England) and occasional cricket for Surrey, though, as *Wisden* noted, in doing so he usually took the place of an experienced professional whose absence could perhaps be ill afforded.[123] A brilliant fielder of trim, athletic build who always played in spectacles, he represented continuity with the 'Golden Age' and was able to impart its values to the new undergraduate generation.

It was not only at these exalted levels that Oriel sport was quick to resume. The 1920 tennis tournament attracted an even larger entry than in pre-war days, and—it is surely not unconnected—Oriel won tennis cuppers the same year. The cricket team lost its cuppers final only in the most unfortunate of ways, the last wicket falling to a brilliant run-out by the Magdalen substitute just twelve runs short of victory; the substitute was an Orielensis, loaned to the opposition to enable them to get a team together.[124] Nor was the 'new' undergraduate averse to the older sort of personal, slightly lunatic athletic challenge: the 1920 long vacation saw an unannounced attempt by Maurice Braddell, a member of the Oriel eight, to row across the Channel with a Sandhurst cadet friend. Setting off from Folkestone and telling their families they were heading for Dymchurch, the pair made for France; eight miles out, encountering heavy seas, they took refuge on the Varne light vessel and, after a few days during which they were presumed lost, they were returned to dry land.[125] The college authorities participated in the resumption of pre-war priorities too. During the war a new sports ground at Bartlemas had been created. The first cricket match took place there on 14 May 1920, but the project was not over: increasingly desperate appeals were made by Hall

---

[122] OR (March 1920), 127.   [123] *Wisden* 1976.   [124] OR (September 1920), 158.
[125] *The Times*, 1 September 1920, 7; a wry commentary in OR (September 1920), 156. Braddell was later an actor in silent films, understudy to Noel Coward in the original production of *Private Lives*, a playwright and a picture restorer, and had leading parts in the Andy Warhol/Paul Morrissey movies *Flesh* (1968) and *Women in Revolt* (1971). For a profile, see J. Lardner, *New Yorker*, 13 January 1986, 33.

through the *Oriel Record* for funding to construct a proper pavilion.[126] The funds were eventually vouchsafed and the building's completion was announced in Michaelmas 1922, it being confidently predicted that it would play a central part in college life.[127]

All-rounders like Miles Howell might be explained as a Golden Age hangover; yet many new matriculands aspired to the model he exemplified. Chief among them were two whose all-round brilliance was to earn lasting renown: G. P. S. MacPherson and J. M. Peterson. To quote the recollections of a contemporary,

> I daresay people are tired of being told that in 1925 the Captains of both the University football teams, rugger and soccer, were Scholars of Oriel, and that they both got Firsts in Greats after previously obtaining Firsts in Mods. So I shall add that both were splendid cricketers—MacPherson also distinguished on the running track—and, Peterson particularly, were active in College societies.[128]

In the event Peterson did not captain the university side against Cambridge.[129] MacPherson, on the other hand, captained not only the university but also the Scotland rugby fifteen, while still an undergraduate, winning all his matches in that position. He and Peterson had both come up in 1921; others in the same intake included W. V. Cavill, who played in the university freshmen's fifteen, but then switched to football and won a blue before taking a first in modern languages;[130] H. M. Ward-Clarke, who won a blue as goalkeeper for the university football eleven; and three others who got into the freshers' fifteen and trialled for the university.

As indicated above, there were many other activities available to undergraduates. The passage just quoted refers to the many thriving and oversubscribed college societies; these were groups convening to read and discuss papers written by members, usually on intellectual topics distinct from their degree subjects. Membership of these societies and high-level sport were in no way inconsistent; both were viewed, by some at least, as worthwhile activities for a serious undergraduate. Other forms of college participation overlapped too: Peterson was JCR secretary in 1922–3; and the previous year H. P. Marshall was both captain of cricket and JCR president, as well as being selected as reserve for the England rugby fifteen. The presence of sportsmen of this calibre does not necessarily lead to the success of the relevant college teams, but in fact football and cricket results were still very encouraging. The

---

[126] Especially OR (September 1921), 30. [127] *OR* 4/4 (September 1922), 97.
[128] OR (1970), 30–3 at 31–2.
[129] Peterson was due to play as captain in the varsity match in December, but it was postponed and by the time it was played, unhappy with his performance, he had deselected himself from both the team and the captaincy. Weir, *Oxford Football*, 43.
[130] On the use of Cavill's bequest for the construction of a new pavilion and squash court at Bartlemas, OR (1960), 5–6; OR (1962), 13.

ILLUSTRATION 18.9 'The last stroke': Oriel rowing over Head, 1933, *OCA*

year 1924 brought victory in the football league (the competition played in Michaelmas Term, while the college's best players were committed to the university) and in spring 1926 football cuppers was won, being celebrated with a 'bump supper' and a bonfire lit by the provost.[131]

It was however some time before the college's immediately pre-war rowing form was re-established. There was clearly disappointment at this. An apologetic tone suffuses the Boat Club reports of the 1920s and a lengthy and somewhat incomprehensible account in the *Oriel Record* attempts to account for the college's defeat in the first round of the Thames Cup at Henley in 1923.[132] The sport remained popular and continued to draw in many without previous rowing experience or other athletic achievements: one of the best-known Oriel oarsmen of the 1920s was not a noted sportsman but A. J. P. Taylor,

---

[131] OR (June 1926), 347–8.
[132] OR (1923), 192–4 ('There are no doubt many old and present members of the College who read with dismay and astonishment in the daily papers of what must at first sight have appeared to be the totally unexpected failure of the Oriel Eight...').

ILLUSTRATION 18.10 Oriel four racing at Henley, early 1930s, *OCA*

the future historian, who stroked the second torpid in 1926,[133] a fact he recalled with satisfaction.[134] In the 1930s things changed. With J. H. Page of Thames Rowing Club as head coach, a concerted effort to raise standards over three years took the college from the middle of the second division to the summer headship. The final bump, on Magdalen, was clinched with what one of the coaching team described as 'one of the loveliest pieces of rowing I have ever seen'.[135]

By leaning over Weir's Bridge it was possible to follow every stroke: from a distance the crew seemed like a single sculler—the blades so perfectly together that never once, in forty strokes, was the delusion broken, and those forty strokes fell into an even minute.

Celebrations were unconfined: 'there was the usual shooting off of blank cartridges, and Oriel supporters dived into the river to welcome the crew.'[136] E. H. Fellowes, the 1893 Boat Club captain, ran alongside the victors from

---

[133] OR (June 1926), 350. [134] A. J. P. Taylor, *A Personal History* (London, 1983), 79.
[135] R. C. Sheriff, OR (1933), 295–8. [136] *Manchester Guardian*, 25 May 1933, 3.

the Long Bridges to the barge, and on returning to his canon's house in Windsor Castle was moved to write to the *Record*: 'Like all Oriel men, I am feeling a wonderful happiness at our being Head of the River this evening.'[137]

To general surprise Oriel retained the headship in 1934 and held it for a further two years, losing it in 1937 largely because a car accident early in the summer term had put three of the crew out of action. Elements in the success included the wholehearted adoption of the training and technical doctrines of Steve Fairbairn, the guru-like Australian-born coach whose methods were imbibed by Page at Thames. A regular, gruelling winter training programme was adopted and became the norm for the entire decade, including an annual row down to Putney, where the first eight would be joined by the seconds and race crews from the Tideway clubs before rowing back to Oxford after a fortnight.[138]

By 1937 Oriel had established a rowing reputation that was undiminished even by the loss of the headship. The ever-partisan Fellowes again put pen to paper, on this occasion writing to *The Times* to point out how remarkable the college's success had been.[139] More disinterested observers found much to admire too. Commenting on a general Oxford rowing revival, the *Guardian* wrote, 'Throughout all colleges there is now the spirit which only Oriel men possessed in the recent past—a spirit of determination, one which takes rowing not as an exercise but as an art.'[140] Having won the headship with mostly home-grown material, Oriel was now providing oarsmen for Oxford's effort to end a long and increasingly humiliating series of defeats by Cambridge. Bryan Hodgson, a member of the 1936 head crew, became Oriel's first blue since 1901 when he stroked Oxford to victories in 1937 and 1938. Several others won trial caps; among them George Whalley, George Huse, and Christopher Pepys were chiefly notable. Together with Hodgson these men formed a four that won the Visitors' Cup at Henley in 1938, setting a record time for that competition which lasted until 1952 and was faster than all but one of the times ever recorded in the Stewards' Cup, the Henley event for international class fours. *The Times* commented on their final:

They rowed in unpaced at 36 [strokes a minute], about 150 yards ahead, and it seems fairly plain that they were a long way the fastest English four ever seen at Henley, even in the Stewards' Cup. Hodgson stroked them superbly, they were long, smooth, perfectly balanced, and very quick in. Individually they may not have been as polished as Leander, but it was very satisfactory that Huse, one of the soundest and hardest working oarsmen who ever failed to get a Blue at Oxford, should be thus rewarded for his fine rowing at No. 3.[141]

---

[137] OR (1933), 311.
[138] J. H. Page, OR (1934), 371–4; (1935), 12–15.   [139] *The Times*, 27 May 1937, 17.
[140] *Manchester Guardian*, 1 June 1937, 4.   [141] *The Times*, 4 July 1938, 8.

In the event Huse got his blue in 1939. It was, however, to be some time before the headship was Oriel's again.

One legacy of this era outlasted the war and remains to this day: the badge of the tortoise, the college's mascot. Both the mascots known to have lived in Oriel were held in affectionate regard by sportsmen. The bulldog Bill, reputedly left behind by a departing undergraduate, frequented Oriel and neighbouring establishments for many years at the end of the nineteenth century, taking a long-suffering, perhaps even unwitting, part in the boisterous sporting life of a generation; when he died in 1898 it was a day of general mourning.[142] In the twentieth century a similar—and possibly even less conscious—role was played by the Oriel tortoise, the first introduced by F. H. Hall, another acquired in the mid-1920s. Other colleges have had tortoises, of course, but a particular attachment is attested by the well-known episode of the 1938 birth announcement in *The Times*, and the possible association between the tortoise's parturitions and the bumps made by the first eight.[143] At any rate, the 'Tortoise Club' has long been the name for the association of former members of senior crews, and a simplified plan view of a tortoise, its shell marked by two concentric white circles, has been used as an informal Boat Club emblem since the 1930s.[144]

Once again the intervention of war does not seem to have deflected the general appetite for sport within the college. The second half of the century certainly shows it becoming more varied and specialist. In 1950 the *Oriel Record* contained just four reports: rowing, rugby, cricket, and squash rackets. The presence of squash, reflecting a successful year in the new intercollegiate league and the selection of the captain as a blue,[145] was an early indication of the post-war multiplication and diversification of college sporting activity. The absence of football, on the other hand, doubtless reflects no more than standard student inefficiency and ineptitude in report-writing. Rowing, cricket, rugby, and football have continued to occupy a more or less central position, but they do so as the nucleus of a growing body of competitive pursuits—competing, that is, amongst themselves for the time of the students who pursue them. The 1980 *Record* reported on ten sports (rowing, rugby, hockey, athletics, cross-country, squash, table-tennis, tennis, cricket, and badminton). By the late 1990s, fitful coverage had been extended to such sports as lacrosse, rugby league, swimming, water polo, netball, basketball,

---

[142] 'Oriel Bill', *Country Life*, 4 June 1898, 682–3, with photographs of Bill in various forms of sports kit.

[143] OR (1992), 27; OR (1993), 38; cf. *The Times*, 12 April 1986, 12. On the animal's inscrutability, see the epitaph by Provost Clark, OR (1991), 28.

[144] Formally granted on 20 April 2009 by the College of Arms to Oriel as a badge for the use of the Boat Club, the Tortoise Club, and the Oriel Society: <www.college-of-arms.gov.uk/Newsletter/021.htm>.

[145] L. J. Verney. Four others played for the 'Squirrels', the university second five.

boxing, korfball, American football, and trampolining—an interesting mixture of old and new, mainstream and specialist, supplemented by competitive but not necessarily athletic activities like pool, darts, and bridge. It is unwise to take the *Oriel Record* as a precise record of the array of sports participated in by college members; the rise of student numbers accounts for some of the diversity. But the overall trend is unmistakable. Though competing for time in the busy student's schedule, the different sports were not necessarily antagonistic in any other sense. All-rounders in the mould of Peterson and MacPherson may have been progressively rarer, but there remained even in the latter twentieth century a considerable participation overlap, with many of the less well-subscribed activities sustained by a few pluralists. And some talented all-rounders did emerge; cricket and football skills frequently coincided, as of old, one of the more recent examples being the Nottinghamshire batsman Mark Crawley who won blues in both sports in three consecutive years between 1986 and 1989.[146]

The presence of individual talent, as before the war, did not mean success at college level. The time at Oriel of Ewen Fergusson (rugby blue 1952–3, winning five caps for Scotland) did not coincide with a period of greatness on the part of the college team, though he played for it as often as he could. But even a small plurality of talent—two or three sportsmen of university standard—can germinate something. Thus, a decade after Fergusson, the presence of R. B. Britton and (until he was rusticated) W. G. Campbell, both playing for the university, had a beneficial effect on Oriel rugby.[147] Similarly, the very bright talents of Maurice Manasseh (cricket blue 1964–5; Middlesex 1960–8)[148] and Ted Fillary (cricket and hockey blues 1963–5; subsequently a Kent batsman) elevated the expectations and the standing of the college eleven, and undoubtedly played a part in the popularity of the sport throughout Oriel in this era. The potential relationship between individual talent and college success is clearly seen in the case of Oriel football in the mid- and late 1980s. Sixteen blues in the six varsity matches between 1984 and 1989 went to Orielenses—over a fifth of the seventy-eight awarded. Several of these players came from schools with a distinguished record of football blues such as Manchester Grammar School or Queen Elizabeth's Grammar School, Blackburn, while others were drawn from a wider range. The undoubted doyen of the era at Oriel was Graham Box, who played in all

---

[146] Crawley, older brother of John, the Cambridge, Lancashire, Hampshire, and England batsman, won a fourth football blue in 1989 as a Keble undergraduate, having been rusticated by Oriel (or 'suspended for a string of yellow cards in chemistry'): OR (1990), 83.

[147] *The Times*, 13 February 1964, 4; 17 February 1964, 7.

[148] For surprise in the national press at the failure to select him in his first year, OR (1962), 8; for his 'agonizing' completion of a century in the 1964 match (against a Cambridge side captained by Mike Brearley): *The Times*, 11 July 1964, 4.

three of his undergraduate years (captaining the side in 1985).[149] Box was also known for championing the introduction of minority sport (whence the nickname 'Korf'), and together with his successor as Oriel captain, Dave Hunter, he contributed to a notable period of success at college level, especially 1984–5 when the league, cuppers, and the intercollegiate five-a-side trophy were all won. Three and sometimes four elevens were often fielded, one going by the programmatic name of Partisan Oriel.[150]

Oriel was consistently solid in many sports. Cricket has known moments of glory, such as a famous cuppers victory in 1987,[151] as have hockey and badminton, which both reported overall victories in 1988. The college rarely failed to pull together a decent athletics team, often with genuine talent on the track supplemented by oarsmen doing impromptu duty in the field events. A small stream of boxing talent has run from Jeffrey Bonas in 1964–5,[152] by way of Alex Mehta (blues in 1992–4 and 1996)[153] to Edward Cartwright, whose welterweight victory in 1999 earned the memorable headline 'Para biffs Doris'.[154] The most headline-grabbing story of Oriel sport in recent years, however, has been rowing. On paper the Boat Club should have performed well in the years immediately after 1945 but, despite the presence of three-times blue Graham Fisk and victory in the 1949 Autumn Fours, Oriel crews mostly under-performed and the club's active management shrank. The college also reverted to its usual invisibility at varsity level: after Fisk's third Boat Race in 1950 no Orielensis was awarded a rowing blue until 1974. In the 1960s, two colleges without strong rowing histories came to dominate within OUBC: of the ninety blues awarded in 1961–70, St Edmund Hall accounts for sixteen, while Keble took thirty-eight (42 per cent of those available). Together with Christ Church, these colleges also dominated bumps racing. However the simple statistics mean little in isolation. Oxford rowing in the third quarter of the century was not, in the wider context, very good. Amalgamated results from 1951–60 Boat Races put Cambridge just over thirty lengths ahead; the following decade saw this stretch to over forty-one, and the extremely heavy defeats of the first half of the 1970s meant that by 1975 the Oxford deficit since mid-century was well over seventy lengths. Unsurprisingly, as recounted by Daniel Topolski (then taking over as OUBC chief coach), the general public impression was that 'Oxford always lose the Boat Race', with rather plaintive cries that Light

---

[149] Returning as a postgraduate at St Antony's he again played in the 1993 match (in which he secured a 1–1 draw by scoring a goal at each end) and was in the Oxford eleven that went on to win the British Universities' championship that year. Weir, *Oxford Football*, 120–1.
[150] See *Guardian*, 13 December 1986, 14.
[151] OR (1987), 42–3.
[152] OR (1965), 10.
[153] OR (1996), 43; *The Times*, 7 March 1996, 39.
[154] *Observer*, 14 March 1999, C14. Cartwright was a university cadet and probationary 2nd Lt. in the Parachute Regiment; Doris was the surname of his opponent.

Blue dominance was unsporting and needed to be addressed by a change in the rules.[155] Rowing was changing at international and national level, and the universities were readjusting themselves painfully and at different speeds to the new climate; college rowing was in the process becoming less significant. But some colleges managed to participate in and keep up with improving standards longer than others, and Oriel was the one that did so with most notable success.

Certainly the 'look' of college rowing at Oxford underwent a great change with the loss of the barges and the transition to boathouses in the late 1950s and early 1960s. The history of the Oriel barges is of some interest.[156] Like several other colleges Oriel acquired its first barge from a London livery company, specifically the Goldsmiths' Company. Apparently purchased in the period 1843–50, it was *in situ* and in use by 1858 when an entry in the Boat Club accounts refers to 'repair to lock on barge'. The Goldsmiths' barge was replaced in 1892 with a new vessel built by Salter's to the design of the architect T. G. Jackson. Costing £600, it closely followed the design of its predecessor and was Jackson's first attempt at a boat; his drawings are held in the Royal Academy, the only surviving designs for a college barge. Regular upkeep and occasional refurbishment were of course required. In 1911 Hall recorded:

> The Barge has been done up, and looks resplendent. It was perhaps premature to re-gild the images of Victory, but we may observe that they have not yet set the laurel wreaths on their heads, but only hold them poised in readiness for the proper time, when it comes.[157]

Further repairs and embellishment took place in 1921–2 in memory of E. F. Henley, Oriel's blue of the 1860s, who had recently died; this work cost £400.[158] Other repairs must have been carried out in subsequent years but the overall trend was clearly towards dilapidation. A printed insert in the 1954 *Oriel Record* announced the barge's demise: 'She was on the point of sinking, and on being taken out of the water and examined by experts it was evident that the entire hull had deteriorated beyond the possibility of repair.' The resulting death sentence was executed on the slipway of Salter's where the vessel had been built sixty years earlier.

It was not only a question of the barge's decayed state. There was growing dissatisfaction with the long-standing system whereby college oarsmen showered, changed, and loafed in one location, while the boats they rowed were stored elsewhere (usually the university boathouse) and ferried back

---

[155] D. Topolski, *Boat Race: The Oxford Revival* (London, 1984).
[156] Clare Sherriff, *The Oxford College Barges: Their History and Architecture* (London, 2003), 27–35 ('The Colleges who purchased the livery barges: the Oriel College barges').
[157] OR (September 1911), 178.   [158] OR (April 1922), 60.

and forth by a waterman. Already in 1949 Oriel had entered a scheme for a joint boathouse with Queen's and Lincoln. On the break-up of the barge a successful planning application was made; with support from the College Endowment Fund, the building was complete and ready for use at Eights Week 1957, an outcome classed as a miracle by Provost Clark.[159] Environment is important and arguably little has done more to detach the contemporary experience of Eights Week from that of earlier generations than the replacement of college barges by a long and dusty promenade of vaguely modernist boathouses. Although its roof and balcony make an excellent grandstand during racing, the fond hopes that the new building would take over its predecessor's social functions at other times were not fulfilled, notwithstanding the careful transfer of the figures of winged Victory from the barge to the upper rooms. Few would choose to linger in that desolate and sometimes squalid location. Its role is for most of the year limited to its principal purpose, that of housing boats.

Nonetheless, since they started to take to the water from the boathouse, rather than the barge, Oriel's crews have achieved unprecedented success. The phase began quietly. In 1962, an Oriel crew entirely lacking in senior university oarsmen made four bumps to take it to the top of Division II; four more bumps followed the next year, when a star-studded Keble crew went head to general acclaim and already anachronistic talk of entering the Grand Challenge Cup at Henley;[160] and four more in 1964. The last four bumps required two years but the headship was finally taken from St Edmund Hall in 1966. Factors in this remarkable rise included the coaching of the elderly J. H. Page, Christopher Pepys (by now a bishop), and the college boatman Len Andrews who concentrated on giving the crews a blistering pace off the start; the adoption of the new design of oar known as the 'spade'; and the stroking of the Radleian Jonathan Close-Brooks from 1964 to 1966. The headship was not retained in 1967, but Oriel was never again out of the top four in Summer Eights. It was clear that the college could expect to compete at the top and that Keble, St Edmund Hall, and Christ Church were vulnerable.

In the last three decades of the century, as Oxford finally managed to turn things around in the Boat Race, the college's record was without parallel. Oriel 'heralded their arrival as a rowing force' in Michaelmas 1975 with victory in the Autumn Fours.[161] The following summer, a decade after Close-Brooks's crew won the headship, Oriel regained it. They lost it again in 1977, then won it back on the first day of racing in 1978 and held it without break until 1985. The title returned to the college for three years in 1987, for three more from 1992, and from 1996 to the end of the century it remained there. In the closing quarter of the twentieth century, there were only six

---

[159] OR (1957), 6.   [160] *The Times*, 1 June 1963, 2.   [161] Topolski, *Boat Race*, 129.

ILLUSTRATION 18.11 Soccer cuppers, 1908, *OCA*

years in which Oriel was not Head of the River, and the college was never out of the top three. Even more striking was the generation-long domination of Torpids, which had been a serious competition since the Second World War if not before, and was often regarded as a surer index of a college's strength in the sport than the summer races. On 2 March 1972 the Oriel first torpid bumped Balliol to go head. Not only did it remain there for the rest of the 1970s and throughout the 1980s, but it was very nearly joined at the top by the second torpid, which rose to fourth position overall in 1985 and third in 1988, being clearly faster than all other college first boats on at least the former occasion. Oriel was eventually deprived of the headship of Torpids in 1991, just before racing began, by the imposition of four 'technical bumps' for embarking on a training outing at Godstow when the river was closed. It was won back in 1993 and held until 1999, meaning that only three out of the last twenty-five years of the century did not see Oriel as victors in Torpids. It would be futile to pretend that every Oriel head crew (in Eights or Torpids) was the fastest on the river. In some years they clearly were not, and there were several in which they survived at the top by the skin of their teeth. However there were some remarkably fast crews, sometimes made up of men with stellar rowing backgrounds but quite often not; the years 1979–81 and

ILLUSTRATION 18.12 Coxless four, 1937, *OCA*

1987–9 were periods of particular talent. Dominance of Torpids in the 1980s was particularly strong, with crews having time to salute the boathouse as they went past many lengths clear, initially with square-blades rowing, subsequently with a brief easy-oar.

One of the contrasts with earlier periods of success was the way that Oriel and Oxford successes were now closely intertwined. The college had many great individual oarsmen, many of them intimately associated with the revival of Oxford's rowing fortunes in the Topolski era. To cite a few only, Paul Wright, Graham Innes, Nicholas Burgess, David Beak, Phil Head, Chris Mahoney, Nicholas Conington, Nicholas Holland, and Chris Long were all significant names in Oxford rowing and indeed beyond: most notably Mahoney, who won an Olympic silver in the British eight while still an undergraduate in 1980. Among the others there were some who did not pursue the blue that might have been within their grasp, and there was a view in OUBC at certain times that Oriel withheld its best oarsmen from the squad;[162] the Oriel view was that

[162] Topolski, *Boat Race*, 192.

ILLUSTRATION 18.13 Coxless four, winners of University Fours, 1949, *OCA*

Oxford started winning again when it started selecting Oriel men for the Blue Boat. It was not only for the ease of finding a place to pull up in the OUBC van that the university squad assembled in Oriel Square before departing for afternoon training at Wallingford or Radley.

Nor is it really a paradox that the college played a prominent part in Oxford's painful transition to the post-Topolski era. In the 'mutiny' year of 1987 Oriel was often popularly identified as the locus of dissent,[163] but the college still had three blues in the crew that won that extraordinary race, in Tony Ward, Richard Hull, and Peter Gish. The American world champion, Dan Lyons, one of those who stepped aside from the university crew in the dispute, did not disdain to row in the Oriel torpid, and was a mainstay of the exceptionally fast summer eight that regained the headship that summer. In the sequel the Oriel presence in the Blue Boat and Isis did not diminish. If it was no surprise that the British international Terry Dillon or junior world

---

[163] D. Topolski and P. Robinson, *True Blue: The Oxford Boat Race Mutiny* (London, 1989), esp. 107, 200, 215.

ILLUSTRATION 18.14 Head of the River, 1976, *OCA*

champion Peter Bridge won blues, many others were school first eight oarsmen who blossomed in the competitive college environment and were thereby emboldened to trial for a blue: one case, sadly cut short, was that of John Hebbes, who died while training with the university squad in late February 1992.[164]

The presence of top-level oarsmen such as these did not seem to discourage novices from taking up the sport. By the 1970s 'Wyndhams' were fulfilling the role of an entry-level competition for freshmen, and it was not unusual for there to be five or six eights entered, the winners receiving tankards often provided by benefactors, among them George Moody, the stroke of the 1935 head crew. The Wyndhams experience was not necessarily pleasant or even enlightening: early morning outings on an increasingly dark and cold Isis, in ancient and heavy clinker eights, constituted a rude introduction to the sport. But participation in this integrative rite was still at the end of the century understood as bestowing membership of the Boat Club and (at least when space permitted) the right to attend bump suppers. This inclusive approach

[164] OR (1992), 9, 74–5.

meant that huge proportions of the college at any given time were in the Boat Club: admittedly not, in many cases, in the same way that they might be members of other, smaller clubs in which membership meant continuing participation; but at times the Boat Club had the aspect of the college in arms. By the mid-1980s as many as sixteen eights might be entered for the bumps races, including the full gamut of 'rugby' eights, 'schools' eights, and 'beer' eights. One of the latter, formed around 1977 as 'Robin and the Seven Hoods', was to endure as the pattern and model of a hard-drinking crew, making multiple bumps in the lower divisions with facility and maintaining a strong association with the Bear Inn.[165] The Hoods' song, composed in 1982, has become general Boat Club property and is added to from time to time to record episodes of note. At the core of the social side of this extended Boat Club world was the bump supper, celebrated in this era only when a headship had been won. Presided over by the provost, proceedings followed a familiar form, concluding with the burning of an antiquated and decaying eight brought back from the riverside after the races. In origin merely a sport-specific equivalent of the bonfires that have long marked sporting and other successes at Oxford,[166] the burning boat, by its long and attenuated physical form, must have always invited leaping. This, in turn, must always have led to injuries, but one incident after the Torpids bump supper in 1986 prompted the imposition of a ban on jumping—though boats have continued to be burnt.

Even though public interest in internal Oxford affairs (and hence media coverage of them) was rapidly diminishing from the 1960s on, Oriel's dominance in rowing did attract considerable attention at large. By the end of the century broadsheets were no longer very concerned to report college bumps races in detail, but the practice lasted long enough into the reign of the modern sub-editor to produce striking headlines, vaguely inspired by the more pedestrian reports of the correspondents: to quote three examples from *The Times* in the early 1980s, 'Only a Shipwreck can deny Oriel their Crown', 'On the Oriel Express', and 'Dominance of Oriel Underlined'.[167] Oriel and rowing (and in a broader sense general sporting heartiness) became associated in public consciousness, resulting in many casual stereotypes or commonplaces. In a classic piece of scene-setting from a successful example of mid-1990s 'chick-lit' with an Oxford theme, 'a crowd of drunk, upper-class rugby players and Oriel boaties had turned up and were cheering every sexist innuendo to the rafters'.[168] Note the asymmetry: the rugby players are not attributed to any college, but the boaties are explicitly ascribed to Oriel.

---

[165] David Wigg-Wolf, personal information.   [166] Emden, *Oriel Papers*, 206–9.
[167] *The Times*, 27 May 1981, 9; 26 February 1983, 20; 4 March 1985, 19.
[168] Louise Bagshawe (subsequently Louise Mensch MP), *Career Girls* (London, 1995), 40; cf. other remarks at 13 and 26–7.

It was natural that when, in the 1980s, Hollywood decided to make an Oxford movie with a rowing theme, it did so in and around Oriel. The film that resulted, *Oxford Blues*, has at least the merit of using real locations, including the Boat Club captain's room. Extras included many members of the college's senior boats, even in the toe-curling scenes where the 'Oriel Bluejackets' (apparently the senior boat club as the doctrinally hardline oligarchs of the college, a sort of cross between the Tortoise Club and the Taliban) preside over formal hall. Interestingly one of the themes of the plot is the aversion felt by the central character (Nick De Angelo, played by Rob Lowe) to joining the college eight, though he is well up to the standard required. Like the servitor Hardy in *Tom Brown at Oxford* so long before, De Angelo prefers to row alone; like Hardy he is ultimately persuaded to join the eight, thereby finding redemption and making peace with himself. The film, which also imposed on OUBC for assistance with its not very nail-biting rowing scenes,[169] was understandably not a critical success.[170] It did not, however, sink quite without trace; a slightly later generation of under-graduates gave it the send-up it deserved in the form of *Oriel Blues*, a movie made with the Boat Club coaching video camera in which race scenes were shot in bank tubs and the Bluejackets were replaced by the Oriel Bin Liners—dressed in accordance with their name.

In the closed, perhaps claustrophobic, environment of college rowing, unprecedented success can sometimes breed envy. The palpable fact that Oriel head crews were sometimes not the fastest on the river was occasionally produced as if it were an *arcanum* of the sport that somehow undermined their achievement.[171] It has sometimes been assumed that Oriel deliberately selected oarsmen at entry;[172] a strange misrepresentation of the possibilities of the Oxford admissions procedure. Nonetheless, so distinct a phenomenon as Oriel's rowing success needs some explanation. It is not something that can be traced back far into the college's history, beginning no earlier than the early 1960s. There is no evidence that its boat club was better organized or funded than others. Freshmen with elite rowing backgrounds clearly have played a part. The input from Hampton School from the mid-1970s was significant: the 1981 first eight had four Hampton oarsmen (three of them blues, one in Isis) in addition to the cox. One of the earliest Hampton and Oriel blues, Paul Wright, later became a master at

---

[169] Topolski, *Boat Race*, 257–8.
[170] P. French, *Observer*, 19 October 1986, 25 ('bad enough to be enjoyable, and always funny except when making jokes'; the Bluejackets look 'as if they did their sixth form at Borstal').
[171] For instance, *The Times*, 7 March 1991, 32.
[172] M. Blandford-Baker, *Upon the Elysian Stream: 150 Years of Magdalen College Boat Club, Oxford* (Oxford, 2008), 236: 'Seemingly actively recruiting oarsmen, and graduate entry medical students in particular, they [Oriel] have dominated the top of Division I of both Torpids and Eights for longer than any other college would care to remember.'

Eton; either his presence there, or a more general schoolboy desire to follow success, may account for the relatively plentiful supply of rowing Etonians in the early and mid-1990s. But beside ready-made talent, numerous Wyndhams oarsmen made the first eight and some went even further. The success of the second and third eights could only rarely be put down to schoolboy oarsmen. The pervasive nature of Boat Club membership, the broad participation in lower crews, in particular forms of support and celebration, amount to something approaching a 'culture' that played a large part in the experience of many Orielenses of the era and, in more or less distorted form, characterized the college in others' eyes. This was not, of course, universally regarded with satisfaction. Within Oriel many non-rowing sportsmen felt excluded; many others felt entirely frustrated.[173]

It was partly this sense of exclusion that led some to hope that the arrival of women in 1985 would change Oriel's culture and diminish the hold that 'boatiness' had over the college.[174] Participants in that culture are recorded as fearing the arrival of women for the same reason.[175] In the event, any immediate change was hard to discern. Twenty-two women entered the college in 1985; eighteen signed up to row in the first term, enabling the formation of two novice eights.[176] Women's crews competed at once in Torpids and Eights, rising briskly up the divisions to find an appropriate level near the top of both competitions. In other sports Oriel women were equally quick to participate: as early as 1986–7 a college sports team was captained by a woman (table tennis, by Laura Goldsmith).[177] An amalgamated sports fund was introduced for women's clubs in 1992–3 and by the mid-1990s the college was fielding cuppers-winning sides in women's rugby, football, and hockey.[178] If the combination of manifold sporting prowess with academic or political eminence seen in former ages seemed by now to elude the men, Oriel's women could still exhibit it.[179] The provost who initiated the new epoch was able to conclude:

---

[173] Robert Barrington for instance wrote 'in the same week that the College gave £700 to the Boat Club for a new boat, it took me half an hour's fierce debate in the JCR to squeeze a £40 grant for a concert', OR (1986), 51.

[174] John Foot, personal information.

[175] *Tatler*, 279/8 (September 1984), 101: 'Shattered by the news that women were to be admitted to Oriel, the egg-heads chanted "No women! No women!" as they performed their traditional leap over the burning boat.'

[176] OR (1986), 52.

[177] For an interesting non-sportswoman's view of the era, see Susanna Phillippo, OR (1996), 37–8.

[178] OR (1993), 108–10; OR (1994), 110.

[179] Thus Laura Hawksworth, member of the first eight in its early years and JCR president, with firsts in mods and Greats; and Mary Lenton, captain of the cuppers-winning hockey side of 1993 and winner of a national essay prize on democracy.

Fears of irreparable change in the character of a traditional college with a strong rowing tradition were dissipated; if anything, many of the women took on the coloration of the historical college.[180]

In fact, neither of the polarized views of what would or did happen on the admission of women is tenable. Certainly it failed to satisfy the hopes of those who wanted to see an end to the culture of rowing or more generally the cult of athleticism.[181] On the other hand it is improbable that, viewed over a longer period, it has had no effect on the culture of the college. The difficulty is in ascribing to it any particular change. Even the fifteen years from 1985 to the end of the century would be quite sufficient for entirely unconnected cultural changes to unfold and substantially modify the role of sport in college life.

The attitude of the fellows has had some weight. It would be tempting to plot a line from Thomas Cogan in the sixteenth century to F. H. Hall in the early twentieth, and conclude that Oriel's dons were not merely indulgent of sport but propagated it by deliberate policy. It is true that provosts and deans have increasingly rejected the anti-sporting style of the dons excoriated by Hughes, instead emulating or outdoing Dr Arnold by going down to the river or out to Bartlemas, writing appreciative comments on sporting successes in the *Record*, and attending bump suppers and other celebrations. Some have participated with gusto. There is enough eye-witness testimony of Provost Turpin's demeanour and conduct at bump suppers to put his vicarious pleasure in a good food fight beyond doubt. Turpin's successor Zelman Cowen also writes of enjoying the bump supper experience, and performed his duties with aplomb.[182] Provost Phelps lit a bonfire in 1926; the same office was regularly performed by the college bursar at bump suppers of the 1980s. Dons have continued into recent years to coach college crews, the much appreciated work of Bill Parry and Jonathan Barnes being the most recent in a long tradition, and as in some other colleges have often themselves turned out on the river or playing field. But it is a far cry from this to the notion of any particularly indulgent attitude towards sport. Provosts who cheerfully presided over bump suppers could evince great dissatisfaction if sporting success coincided with poor academic results, despite the lack of any correlation between the two.[183] Boat Club captains do not enjoy immunity

---

[180] Z. Cowen, *A Public Life* (Carlton, Victoria, 2006), 337.

[181] 'There were those who said that having women in the College would be "civilising". So far, this has not reached the Chapel on Monday afternoons; the College still votes with its Adidas feet', Robert Barrington, OR (1987), 40.

[182] Cowen, *A Public Life*, 339–40.

[183] Thus Cowen, OR (1988), 10: 'It does the College no good at all to be seen as virtually unchallenged on the river, and as very good in other sports and, at the same time, to perform so poorly in the Examination Schools.' Oriel had been 24th in the Norrington Table; the following year (with the same or better sporting results) it was 9th.

from the requirement to show evidence of academic work, and several have been rusticated or banned from the river—including one who went on to receive a congratulatory first in finals. Even in the heyday of college support, its main proponent in Oriel, F. H. Hall, was ambivalent. Hall may have taken quiet delight in athletic victories, and believed that it was right that the college should manage the finances of undergraduate sport so that all could participate, and nobody fall into debt. But in 1911 he wrote:

> Let us hope that in time the Public Schools will wake up to the knowledge that a man has as good a chance of doing well in the Schools at Oriel as at any other College. At present they seem to regard us as an Athletic College only. Perhaps the Authorities there read only the Sporting Intelligence in the Newspapers? We must admit that the name of Oriel does sometimes occur in those columns.[184]

The notion of facilitating entry for candidates who were good at games was anathema to him. In a barbed aside, he congratulated E. D. Shaw, a former fellow whose son, at Brasenose, had just won his cricket blue: 'We feel inclined to add "*Utinam noster esses*"; but we are not as fortunate as B.N.C.; we have no scholarships for all-round excellence.'[185]

The attitude of Hall's contemporary Shadwell was similarly complex. By birth he was not unfamiliar with the role sport played for many students: among his uncles, one had rowed for Cambridge in 1839, while another had coxed Oxford in 1842 and the seven-oar stroked by George Hughes at Henley the following year. Provost Shadwell recognized that the growth of organized sport had done much 'to obliterate social divisions, and to strengthen the sense of common membership':

> Whatever other results it may have, for good or harm, it has certainly created a new core of sentiment; by identifying the whole body with the success or disgrace of its representatives on the cricket field or the river, it has helped to stimulate College patriotism. It has also had much to do in establishing those easier and more friendly relations between undergraduates and dons which contrast so strikingly with the traditions of the past.

This was evidently something Shadwell valued. But there remains something cool or distant in his reference to 'athletic competition', and his comment that in former ages pursuits such as cricket and hockey had been 'given up, along with bird-nesting and hoop-driving, on coming to the University'.[186] From the perspective of the provost's lodgings the benefits and blessings of sport, whether amounting to a culture or even a cult for its student devotees, must always be seen in the wider and fuller context of college life.

---

[184] OR (September 1911), 177.   [185] OR (March 1912), 36.
[186] Shadwell, *Registrum Orielense*, xi.

19
Science at Oriel

Robert Fox

Such evidence as we have of scientific or mathematical activity in Oriel before the sixteenth century is sparse. It is possible that some early members of the college participated in the debates of the Merton school, the distinguished circle of mathematicians and astronomers that rose to prominence at about the time of Oriel's foundation. One who did so was Richard Kilvington, an early fellow of Oriel and eventual benefactor of the college library, who went on to public prominence in the king's service from the late 1330s, and was appointed dean of St Paul's in 1354. Kilvington's writings, probably arising from university disputations and refined in his lectures, were marked by a 'confident and argumentative spirit' that distinguished him as a leading contributor to the 'new physics' of the fourteenth century.[1] Modern editions of his best-known work, the *Sophismata*, give an impression both of versatility (which extended to significant commentaries on Aristotle's *Physics* and *De generatione et corruptione*) and of originality informed by a solid base in mathematical logic.[2]

Another Mertonian with Oriel connections was Simon Bredon, a fellow of Merton in the 1330s and 1340s. A wealthy man who prospered after leaving Merton through his practice of medicine, Bredon bequeathed an astrolabe and a small number of manuscripts to Oriel in his will of 1368.[3] The bequest does not indicate a particularly close association with the college, since Bredon also left manuscripts and instruments to Balliol (his original college), University College, Queen's, and Exeter, as well as to Merton. Nevertheless, the astrolabe, now on permanent loan to the Museum of the History of

---

[1] See Chapter 1, 'The Foundation'.
[2] *Ricardi de Kilvington Sophismata*, ed. N. Kretzmann and B. Kretzmann (Oxford, 1990) and *The Sophismata of Richard Kilvington: Translation and Commentary by Norman Kretzmann, Barbara Ensign Kretzmann* (Cambridge, 1990), esp. the introduction, xvii–xxxiv.
[3] R. T. Gunther, *Early Science in Oxford*, 15 vols. (OHS, Oxford, 1923–67), ii. 52–5 and BRUO i. 257–8.

ILLUSTRATION 19.1 The Oriel Astrolabe, bequeathed by Simon Bredon 1372
Oxford Museum of the History of Science

Science in Oxford, would have been seen as an important gift, and it is certainly of great historic interest. It is unusual for its large size and for the fact that its single plate (341mm in diameter), which forms the main body of the instrument, is projected for the latitude of Oxford.[4] The signs of wear and the thinness of the metal suggest that the astrolabe was designed and (at least for some time) treated as a working instrument rather than a luxury object for display. It would almost certainly have been used by Bredon himself, possibly for the astrological calculations that formed part of his medical procedures, and it may well have been made to order under Bredon's supervision.

What use was made of the astrolabe in Oriel, following Bredon's death in 1372, is hard to ascertain. But, in the absence of any known association between members of Oriel and what remained of the Merton school, it seems unlikely that use extended beyond occasional demonstrations of the principles of the instrument. In fact, instances of Orielenses who pursued science of any kind from then until well into the sixteenth century are rare.

---

[4] Museum of the History of Science, Oxford: inventory no. 47,901. On the astrolabe, see Gunther, *Early Science in Oxford*, ii. 206–7.

The only notable exception is Henry Kayll, a fellow who was briefly provost in 1421–2. Kayll read and annotated a number of mathematical manuscripts, including the college's copy of Euclid's *Geometry*, showing a serious engagement with three-dimensional geometry, which arose from a primary interest in astronomy. His intention, though, was probably to assist those teaching difficult mathematical texts in the arts faculty rather than to make any original contribution. His limitations as a mathematician are suggested by his comment that he had only understood Theodosius of Tripoli's treatise on spheres 'with great labour'.

In this relatively low level of scientific activity, the college was reflecting trends within the university as a whole. Although the Merton school had its successors in Oxford, its creative phase ceased after the mid-fourteenth century. The dominant preoccupations of fifteenth-century Oxford thinkers were pastoral and historical theology, not physics and mathematics. As the humanist learning of the Renaissance made its mark on Oxford progressively through the sixteenth century, one result was a new seriousness that came to characterize teachers and students alike. Science, however, was at best an incidental beneficiary of this change. The growing number of aspiring parents who sent their sons to Oxford did so to provide them with a grounding in the scholarly disciplines of rhetoric, classical grammar, and dialectics, essentially those of the *trivium*, rather than in the mathematical and scientific studies of the *quadrivium*, which tended increasingly to be pursued by students who had already passed the hurdle of the BA. Nevertheless, in a university and college system that underwent unprecedented expansion between the early 1550s and the 1580s, resourceful students who wished to venture beyond the prescribed syllabus into the realms of mathematics and natural philosophy could find encouragement and guidance, usually through informal coteries of enthusiasts. Outstanding among those who did so was Thomas Harriot, a student at St Mary Hall who went on to become the foremost English mathematician of his day and a prominent figure in the circles of Sir Walter Raleigh (who had been at Oriel as a gentleman commoner in 1572) and Henry Percy, 9th earl of Northumberland.[5] Harriot was one of the thirteen recent arrivals whom the principal of St Mary Hall, Richard Pigot, presented for matriculation in December 1577, and one of three members of that group who went on to graduate BA, in his case at Easter 1580. Brought up in Oxfordshire, quite possibly in Oxford itself, he belonged to the university's growing number of 'plebeian' students, most of them from modest backgrounds and with their

---

[5] John W. Shirley, *Thomas Harriot: A Biography* (Oxford, 1983), esp. ch. 2, 'Harriot at Oxford, 1560–1580', 38–69. There is also much biographical information in the two volumes of essays based on the Thomas Harriot Lectures that have been delivered annually in Oriel since 1990: Robert Fox (ed.), *Thomas Harriot: An Elizabethan Man of Science* (Aldershot, 2000) and *Thomas Harriot and his World: Mathematics, Exploration, and Natural Philosophy in Early Modern England* (Farnham, 2012).

sights generally set on careers in the Church or as grammar-school masters. We know little about Harriot's experiences as a student, and we can only speculate about the influences that drew him to mathematics and science. He certainly did not neglect the core studies that left him adept in philosophical and religious argument and a conspicuously accomplished Latinist and 'good Grecian'.[6] But the foundations of the work in navigation, astronomy, and cartography for which he is best known owed little to the formal curriculum and virtually everything to the associations he established with contemporaries and older scholars in the university.

The most important of Harriot's contacts was probably with Richard Hakluyt, his senior by eight years. Hakluyt had taken his BA at Christ Church in 1574 and his MA in 1577. He had already resolved to devote himself to geography and exploration by the time he arrived at the university, and it was almost certainly on these subjects that he delivered his public lectures as a regent-master between 1577 and 1579. Harriot may well have attended the lectures and so established the friendship with Hakluyt that helps to explain his subsequent move into the world of practical mathematics. Another likely source of encouragement was Thomas Allen, a senior figure almost twenty years older than Harriot. By the late 1570s, Allen had moved on from his original college, Trinity, to lead an intensely scholarly life, probably as a recusant, at Gloucester Hall, a post-dissolution descendant of the monastic Gloucester College. Allen's interest in astronomy and other sciences and his fine library and instruments made him a magnet for the ambitious young mathematicians of Oxford of whom Harriot (who may have been his pupil at one time) and Hakluyt were typical. It is probable that Robert Hues, an undergraduate at St Mary Hall during Harriot's first year there, who later published a frequently reissued treatise on terrestrial and celestial globes, also frequented this world.[7] Hues's interests and career had much in common with Harriot's. Like Harriot, he knew Raleigh, and he cast his treatise on globes, despite its publication in Latin, as a primer of geography and positional astronomy for navigators and others interested in the practical aspects of voyages of discovery. The book, in fact, drew heavily on his own experiences at sea: he circumnavigated the world with an expedition mounted by Thomas Cavendish from 1586 to 1588, and undertook other adventurous voyages, including one on which he observed the Southern Cross and other stars in the southern hemisphere. Although the extent of the contact between Hues and Harriot at St Mary Hall is unknown, it is certain that the two men knew each other well in later life: they were both

---

[6] Charles Fantazzi, 'Harriot's Latin', in Fox (ed.), *Thomas Harriot and his World*, 231–6.
[7] On Hues (1553–1632) see ODNB s.n. His treatise on globes first appeared as Robert Hues, *Tractatus de globis et eorum usu, accommodatus iis qui Londini editi sunt Anno 1593, sumptibus Gulielmi Sandersoni cuius Londinensis, conscriptus a Roberto Hues* (London, 1594).

members of the Percy circle, and Hues even served as an executor of Harriot's will.

Harriot's mathematical gifts and the contacts he established in Oxford made London a natural destination once he had taken his degree. There, not only Hakluyt but also Pigot, who had been a fellow of Oriel during Raleigh's time in the college in the early 1570s, would have been well placed to ease Harriot's entry into the circle of Raleigh and others with economically motivated colonial aspirations. By the winter of 1583–4, Harriot was offering classes in Raleigh's London house on navigation and navigational instruments for a group of seamen preparing for Raleigh's exploration of the New World, and in April 1585 he sailed from Plymouth with the expedition, under Sir Richard Grenville, that attempted to establish a colony on the coast of North Carolina (then part of the larger terrain of Virginia). Although the attempt was abandoned after less than a year, Raleigh (who had not accompanied the expedition) was resolved to pursue his ambitions. Harriot's *Briefe and true report of the new found land of Virginia*, an account of the land and the Algonkian people he had seen and managed to converse with in 1585–6, was probably written at Raleigh's request as a way of attracting investors and settlers.[8] But the failure of a second attempt to establish a colony at Roanoke in 1587, the threat of the Spanish Armada in the following year, and Queen Elizabeth's mounting suspicion of Raleigh all played their part in putting an end to further transatlantic ventures.

Harriot never returned to America, and as Raleigh's star waned, it was his new patron, Percy, who maintained him from the mid-1590s until his death in 1621. In these years, Harriot devoted himself more intensively than ever to science and mathematics, mainly optics and algebra. In the summer of 1609 he made observations with a telescope several weeks before Galileo and went on to use the instrument in mapping the lunar surface and observing sunspots, the phases of Venus, and the motions of the satellites of Jupiter. In Percy's circle, he seems to have acquired the reputation of a daring speculator, mainly through his discussions of atomism and its philosophical and theological implications. His talents, though, were less those of a natural philosopher than of a mathematically gifted problem-solver, apparently with little interest in publishing. A projected work of practical mathematics and astronomy, *Arcticon*, has been lost (apart from a few surviving notes), and his work on equations was only published after his death, in a volume, *Artis analyticae praxis* (1631), that friends and executors prepared from his disordered manuscripts.[9] Through no fault of Harriot's, *Praxis* was a flawed

---

[8] Thomas Harriot, *A Briefe and true report of the new found land of Virginia* (London, 1588).

[9] The *Praxis* is now available in an annotated translation: *Thomas Harriot's Artis analyticae praxis: An English Translation with Commentary*, ed. and trans. Muriel Seltman and Robert Goulding (New York, 2007).

production. It perpetuated the author's name, but without doing justice to his originality. Another, shorter treatise on triangular numbers also did little for his immediate reputation, remaining in manuscript and virtually unknown until the recent edition by Janet Beery and Jacqueline Stedall.[10]

Through the sixteenth, seventeenth, and eighteenth centuries, such scientific presence as there was at Oriel and St Mary Hall owed much to medical men who studied or held fellowships in the college. William Rose (sometimes Ross) and Thomas Cogan (also Cogyn or Coggin), elected to fellowships in 1512 and 1563 respectively, were typical of a number of Oriel men who used their time as fellows to study medicine.[11] Rose achieved distinction as a member of the team, working in Padua under the general direction of Giovanni Baptista Opizzoni, that prepared the Aldine *editio princeps* of Galen (1525),[12] while Cogan went on to become a long-serving master of Manchester Grammar School and physician in Manchester.[13] Later in the sixteenth century Matthew Lister, who entered Oriel in 1588 and became a fellow in 1591, likewise made his name in medicine after leaving the college. The MD that he took at Basel in about 1603 and his election as a fellow of the Royal College of Physicians in 1607 helped to set him on a distinguished career in court circles, where he served as physician to James I and Queen Anne and worked with Theodore de Mayerne as a leading champion of Paracelsian chemical remedies and of measures to improve public health in the city of London.[14]

Two of the sixteenth-century fellows with scientific interests left their mark in Oriel through gifts of medical books to the college library. Cogan's gift included not only a five-volume Latin edition of Galen's works of 1562 (which survives) but also Vesalius's *De humani corporis fabrica* of 1543 (which does not). But the largest sixteenth-century benefaction of scientific interest was the bequest by John Jackman, a fellow who served as dean of the college from 1571 to 1573 and again in 1581–2, before proceeding bachelor of medicine and marrying in 1584.[15] Despite the obligatory resignation of his fellowship following his marriage, Jackman maintained close contacts with Oriel, practising in premises in the High Street leased to him by the college and doing so with apparent success until his death (and burial in St Mary's) in 1600. Jackman's bequest, of thirty-eight volumes (almost all of which have survived), included a first edition of Agricola's *De re metallica* (Basel, 1556)

---

[10] Janet Beery and Jacqueline A. Stedall, *Thomas Harriot's Doctrine of Triangular Numbers: The 'Magisteria magna'* (Zurich, 2009).

[11] *Provosts and Fellows*, 50–1, 71.

[12] Vivian Nutton, *John Caius and the Manuscripts of Galen*, published as *Proceedings of the Cambridge Philosophical Society*, supplementary volume 13 (1987), 38–9.

[13] ODNB s.n. Cogan. His recommendations on the diet of students, given in his *The Haven of Health* (1584), are discussed in Emden, *Oriel Papers*, 22–8.

[14] ODNB s.n. Lister (*c.*1571–1656).   [15] *Provosts and Fellows*, 71.

ILLUSTRATION 19.2 Specimens from Richard Dyer's cabinet of fossils, seeds, and other material, bequeathed to Oriel in 1730

Oxford Museum of the History of Science

and, in a choice collection of botanical works, an edition with coloured woodcuts of Jean Ruel's Latin translation of Dioscorides's *De medicinali materia* (Frankfurt, 1543), Rembert Dodoens's *Stirpium historiae* (Antwerp, 1583), and an early edition of William Turner's *Herbal* (Collen, 1568).[16]

A rare example of someone who used his fellowship not only for obtaining a medical degree and licence to practise but also to pursue sustained independent scientific work was Richard Dyer. Elected within weeks of graduating BA, in 1673, Dyer remained a fellow until, in 1729, the college's internal disputes towards the end of George Carter's time as provost led him to retire to his native Devon.[17] A quiet disposition deprived Dyer of the celebrity he deserved. It is typical of him that he allowed his important contributions to Robert Morison's posthumously published *Plantarum historiae universalis oxoniensis pars tertia* (1699) to appear without acknowledgement.[18]

---

[16] The volumes bequeathed by Jackman are recorded in the Donations Book, bound as *Benefactorum nomina*, fo. 14, OCA BT 1 A/1.

[17] Rannie, *Oriel*, 132–3.

[18] Rannie states that Dyer not only contributed to the book but also wrote a life of Morison, conceivably the six-page unsigned 'Vita Roberti Morisoni M.D.' in Robert Morison, *Plantarum historiae universalis oxoniensis pars tertia seu herbarum distributio nova, per tabulas cognationis & affinitatis ex libro naturae observata & detecta*, ed. Jacob Bobart (Oxford, 1699), unpaginated.

Within Oxford, however, his qualities were fully recognized. The Jacobite antiquary Thomas Hearne regarded him with respect and affection as a close friend, while Edward Lhuyd, the assistant keeper and later keeper of the Ashmolean Museum, drew on his meticulous studies of fossil shells in preparing the classified list of fossils that he published as *Lithophylacii britannici ichnographia* in 1699. Evidence of this association with Lhuyd, who praised Dyer as 'a very good friend' and 'a very curious and ingenious gentleman', survives in Lhuyd's correspondence.[19] The Museum of the History of Science also possesses a small oak cabinet belonging to Dyer in which there are still fossils, seeds, and other small specimens wrapped in pieces of paper bearing Lhuyd's handwriting.[20] Dyer would certainly have graced the university's chair of botany, a post that John Fell hoped he might take. But, with characteristic modesty, Dyer declined to be nominated. By the time of his death in 1730, at the age of almost 80, he had still published nothing under his own name.

Later in the eighteenth century, several other fellows maintained more or less serious scientific interests. Among them was Henry Beeke, who became a fellow in 1775, soon after taking his BA at Corpus, and retained his fellowship until his appointment as dean of Bristol in 1813. Although Beeke is chiefly remembered for his writings on taxation and finance and his twelve years as Regius Professor of Modern History (1801–13), he performed some botanical work, and his reputation as a geologist is still acknowledged in the name of the mineral beekite, originally found near Torbay in Devon, his native county.[21] Among Beeke's contemporaries as a fellow, though only briefly, was Christopher Pegge, the future Dr Lee's reader in anatomy and Regius Professor of Medicine.[22] After taking his BA at Christ Church, Pegge was elected to an Oriel fellowship in 1788. In the two years he spent at Oriel, he laid the foundations of his medical career by taking the degree of BM and beginning to practise medicine in Oxford, probably with an eye on the Dr Lee's readership that was to take him back to Christ Church in 1790. In a career that saw him elected a fellow of the Royal Society in 1795 and knighted in 1799, Pegge remained a prominent figure in and beyond Oxford, despite his rather lax conduct of his duties and a studiedly old-fashioned manner that made him, for many, a somewhat absurd figure. Although he evidently saw Christ Church as his main college,

---

Rannie may well be correct, although there is nothing in the Morison volume to suggest that Dyer wrote it.

[19] Lhuyd to Martin Lister, 16 July and November 1693?, in Gunther, *Early Science in Oxford*, xiv. 197 and 209.

[20] Museum of the History of Science, Oxford: inventory no. 51916. Oriel transferred the cabinet on permanent loan to the Lewis Evans Collection in 1931, a transfer acknowledged by the curator of the collection, Robert Gunther. See OCA MG 3 A1.

[21] ODNB s.n. Beeke (1751–1817).   [22] ODNB s.n. Pegge (1765–1822).

he showed some gratitude to Oriel by a bequest of £20 that came to the college on his death in 1822.

The contributions of Beeke and Pegge are too slight to sustain any case for a significant Oriel tradition in science in the eighteenth century; Beeke's engagement with natural history was intermittent, and Pegge wrote nothing. Among Oriel's fellows, however, one scientific vocation stands out: that of Gilbert White. The son of a prominent justice of the peace in Selborne, Hampshire, White went up to Oriel in April 1740, graduated BA in June 1743, and became a fellow in the following year, maintaining term-time residence until 1748.[23] Despite an evident taste for travel (mainly to visit far-flung friends and family and to meet the demands of a succession of curacies, most of them in the area of Selborne), he remained a well-known, if frequently absent member of the Oriel fellowship, and was the college's choice as junior proctor for the year 1752–3. In 1757 he could even present himself as a plausible candidate to succeed Walter Hodges as provost. To his considerable disappointment, his candidature failed, and following the election of Chardin Musgrave, his interests turned increasingly to Selborne and The Wakes, his old family home there. The fruits of the next thirty-five years, most of which White spent in Selborne with periods as curate-in-charge there and curacies elsewhere, are well known. They included not only the *Natural History and Antiquities of Selborne*, but also brief contributions to the *Philosophical Transactions of the Royal Society*, in the form of letters to his friend Daines Barrington, and the posthumous work *A Naturalist's Calendar*, prepared by another friend, Dr John Aikin, from the diaries and notebooks that White kept from 1751 until his death in 1793.[24] Although White's world remained an extensive one, it always had a place for Oxford. His scientific life had begun at Oriel, when he made his earliest observations, mainly while hunting, as an undergraduate. And even after his decision to live permanently at The Wakes, his skill as a conversationalist and a fount of knowledge of horticultural techniques and the flora and fauna of his garden made his an intriguing, if not universally popular presence in the common room during his occasional visits to Oxford.[25] The eighteenth-century Orielenses who achieved eminence in science or medicine tended to do so after leaving Oxford and with no obvious debt to their time in the college.

---

[23] On White's scientific interests, Paul G. M. Foster, *Gilbert White and his Records: A Scientific Biography* (London, 1988) is especially helpful. On his association with Oriel, see ODNB s.n.; Richard Mabey, *Gilbert White: A Biography of the Author of the Natural History of Selborne* (London, 1986), esp. 34–49, 62–4, and 73–6; and the three informative chapters on White in Emden, *Oriel Papers*, 112–32.

[24] *The Natural History and Antiquities of Selborne* (London, 1789); *A Naturalist's Calendar, with Observations in Various Branches of Natural History. Extracted from the Papers of the late Rev. Gilbert White* (London, 1795).

[25] Rannie, *Oriel*, 121.

The career of William Cadogan, who graduated BA at Oriel in 1731, illustrates the point. His most important medical qualification was the MD that he took at Leiden in 1737, and it was while practising as a physician in Bristol and London that he rose to national eminence. By the time he took the medical degrees of BM and DM at Oxford in 1755, he was already a fellow of the Royal Society and a noted authority on the nursing and early care of children (for whom he favoured loose, light clothing) and a champion of the benefits of putting babies to the breast as early as possible. In this, Cadogan swam resolutely against the tide of contemporary medical opinion, as he also did in the treatment of his gout-ridden older patients. In his *Dissertation on the Gout, and all Chronic Diseases* (1771), he presented gout as a consequence of excess and indolence for which exercise and an austere diet were the best remedies.[26] Criticism of this view, which broke with the common belief of the day that gout was a hereditary disorder, was inevitable, and it came from conservatively inclined patients and fellow-practitioners alike. Samuel Johnson, who knew the agonies of gout, or what he believed to be gout, at first hand, found Cadogan's *Dissertation on the Gout* 'a good book in general, but a foolish one in particulars'.[27] Among physicians, a typical voice was that of William Carter, an undergraduate contemporary of Cadogan at Oriel who combined a fellowship of the college from 1735 until the mid-1750s with a successful practice as a physician in Canterbury. In his *A Free and Candid Examination of Dr Cadogan's Dissertation on the Gout, and Chronic Diseases* (1772) Carter mounted a resolutely conservative case against Cadogan's attack on traditional teaching about gout and other inflammatory disorders.

More eminent than Cadogan, though even more of a bird of passage, was the Scottish surgeon and anatomist John Hunter, whose sombre portrait has hung in the former dining hall of St Mary Hall, now part of the modern library, for many years. The portrait hangs there to commemorate Hunter's brief period of residence as an undergraduate at St Mary Hall in 1755. Some years before this, Hunter had moved from the family home near Glasgow to London to work with his elder brother William, also a physician, and it was William who encouraged John to go to Oxford to acquire the literary cultivation that education in Scotland had failed to provide.[28] John duly entered St Mary Hall in June 1755, at the age of 27, but moved back to London barely two months later. His memories of Oxford betray a mixture of bitterness and amusement. 'They wanted to make an old woman of me; or

---

[26] Roy Porter and G. S. Rousseau, *Gout: The Patrician Malady* (New Haven, 1998), ch. 7.
[27] Emden, *Oriel Papers*, 98.
[28] In addition to general biographical sources, such as S. Roodhouse Gloyne, *John Hunter* (Edinburgh, 1950) and ODNB s.n., see Henry Viets, 'A Note on John Hunter at Oxford', *Boston Medical and Surgical Journal*, 182/22 (27 May 1920), 545–7.

that I should stuff Latin and Greek at the University', he recalled some years later.[29] If that was the intention, his stay was a failure. The brusque uncultivated Hunter did not fit in at Oxford. But even without the veneer of polite learning that the university might have imparted, his career eventually blossomed. Having formally qualified as a surgeon through service in the Seven Years War, he finally accumulated positions in London commensurate with his gifts. Appointments as surgeon-extraordinary to the king and surgeon-general of the army, a teaching position at St George's Hospital, and a lucrative surgical practice in Leicester Fields, the present Leicester Square, took him to the summit of his profession. They brought him the income he needed in accumulating the vast collection of anatomical specimens, the future Hunterian Museum, for which he is now chiefly remembered, and the final accolade of burial (albeit more than half a century after his death) in Westminster Abbey.

The eighteenth century ended on an unexpectedly high note for science at Oriel, when the college's holdings of scientific books and instruments were significantly enriched through the bequest of Edward, 5th Baron Leigh. After matriculating at Oriel in 1761 and receiving his MA in 1764, Leigh had gone on to become an unusually youthful High Steward of the University (at the age of 25, in 1767) and the possessor of one of the most important country house libraries of the day, at Stoneleigh Abbey, near Coventry. Between 1760 and 1767 Leigh spent at least £1,000 on books and unknown sums on scientific instruments, furniture, and pictures.[30] His collections were set to grow still further and would have done so had it not been for the insanity that inhibited his collecting and led to his withdrawal from public view from the later 1760s. Nevertheless, the books and other items that came to Oriel on Leigh's death in 1786 bear witness to a pattern of discriminating cosmopolitan tastes that embraced not only a liking for fine bindings and richly illuminated works on theology, antiquities, and architecture but also serious scientific interests. Notable among the books now in the senior library are long runs of both the *Mémoires* and the *Histoire de l'Académie royale des sciences* (recording the proceedings of the French Academy of Sciences from its foundation in 1666) and the six finely illustrated volumes of the *Machines et inventions approuvées par l'Académie royale des sciences, depuis son établissement jusqu'à présent* (1735). The instruments in the Leigh bequest seem generally to have been less remarkable. But the spherical electrical machine (almost certainly the 'Lectrifyng apparatus' in Leigh's own inventory) is a good example of the work of the London instrument-maker Edward Nairne,[31] and the mechanical models, microscopes, and other apparatus were likewise bought from the best makers of the day.

---

[29] Quoted from a letter to Sir Anthony Carlisle, in Gloyne, *John Hunter*, 23.

[30] Mark Purcell, '"A lunatick of unsound mind": Edward, Lord Leigh (1742–86) and the Refounding of Oriel College Library', *Bodleian Library Record*, 17 (April–October 2001), 246–60.

[31] The machine is now in the Museum of the History of Science, on loan from the college: inventory no. 83045 (with accessory at 87610).

It remains an open question how much, if at all, the scientific books and instruments bequeathed by Leigh were used by either fellows or undergraduates. But such use as was made of them was probably short-lived. Advances in science and a rising tide of nineteenth-century textbooks better adapted to student needs soon rendered the books obsolete, and the instruments suffered a similar fate, eventually passing on loan to the newly founded Lewis Evans Collection (the future Museum of the History of Science) in 1924.[32] Leigh's name, though, was not forgotten in the history of Oxford science. He left an enduring mark through an auxiliary bequest of £1,000, to be administered jointly by the vice-chancellor and the provost of Oriel.[33] The income from this sum was to be made available for the purchase of models and apparatus for use in 'mathematical' lectures of the kind that James Bradley (as Savilian Professor of Astronomy from 1721 to 1763) and Nathaniel Bliss (who held the Savilian chair of geometry from 1742 to 1765) had given during Leigh's undergraduate days. As soon as the £1,000 was released, on Leigh's death, the current Savilian Professor of Astronomy, Thomas Hornsby, began drawing on what appears to have been a scrupulously managed fund, and thereafter the teaching of physics in the university continued to benefit significantly until well into the twentieth century. Between 1810 and 1913, the successive holders of the readership (later professorship) in experimental philosophy— Stephen Peter Rigaud, Robert Walker, and Robert Clifton—all regularly received assistance. Although pressure on the fund increased with rising prices and the creation of the new Wykeham chair of physics in 1900, sums of between £200 and £400 were still being disbursed in most years between the First and Second World Wars.[34]

During the first half of the nineteenth century, the main weakness of science in Oxford remained its absence from university examinations, except for the 'mixed mathematics', mainly elementary mechanics and geometrical optics, that was required in the mathematical part of the syllabus under the examination statute of 1800. Despite this handicap, science came slowly to assume a more prominent place in university life. To achieve this success, its

---

[32] I am grateful to Mr A. V. Simcock, archivist of the Museum of the History of Science, for information (compiled from the first Accessions Register of the Lewis Evans Collection) about this loan of instruments, which included the Oriel astrolabe referred to earlier. Mr Simcock has also drawn my attention to a fine terrestrial globe by John Senex, which the college lent to the museum in 1931 (Museum of the History of Science: inventory no. 28920). It is conceivable that this globe too was in Lord Leigh's collection, although there is nothing in the records of either the museum or the college to suggest that this was the case. All the other instruments that Leigh is known to have acquired date from some decades after 1718, the date on the globe.

[33] Records of the bequest and payments made from the fund and into it (as interest on the capital) are in OCA BT 1W.

[34] Jack Morrell, 'Research in Physics at the Clarendon Laboratory, Oxford, 1919–1939', *Historical Studies in the Physical and Biological Sciences*, 22 part 2, 263–307, table 1 (270) and the same table in Morrell, 'The Lindemann Era', in Robert Fox and Graeme Gooday (eds.), *Physics in Oxford: Laboratories, Learning, and College Life* (Oxford, 2005), 233–66 (237).

champions (essentially the holders of the university's seventeen professorships and readerships in scientific disciplines[35]) had to fight against religious and arts-based conservatism that persisted even after the creation of the new school of natural science in 1850. But they fought tenaciously, stimulating what Nicolaas Rupke has identified as a 'scientific awakening' that took root early in the century, long before the victory of 1850 was achieved.[36] The awakening was most strikingly reflected in the popularity of the lectures of the Revd William Buckland, canon of Christ Church and reader in mineralogy from 1813 and in geology from 1818 until his death in 1856. In the 1820s and early 1830s, Buckland drew large audiences to the Ashmolean Museum building in Broad Street to hear his interpretations of earth history, always rooted in field-work though with an underlying insistence on the evidence of design in a divinely planned creation. The tide of interest in Buckland's lectures made its mark in Oriel, as it did in most colleges. At least two undergraduates were captivated, to the point of becoming pupils of Buckland and going on to distinction as geologists themselves. Robert Austen (later Godwin-Austen) attended Buckland's lectures during his undergraduate days (1826–30).[37] He then took advantage of the wealth of his own family and that of his wife to begin studies of the geology of southern England that led to his election as a fellow of the Royal Society in 1849 and the award of the Wollaston medal, the highest honour of the Geological Society of London, in 1862. A slightly younger contemporary, Hugh Edwin Strickland, who was an undergraduate at Oriel during Austen's time, was no less marked by Buckland's teaching. Like Austen, he could draw on a private family income to secure the leisure and resources that a serious engagement in geology required.[38] His work, based on extensive travels in southern Europe and Asia, was more wide-ranging than Austen's, and in 1850 Strickland (now living in Oxford) was a natural choice when the university appointed him as deputy reader in geology to act during Buckland's protracted declining years. In due course, he might well have succeeded Buckland had he not been killed by a train while examining strata in a railway cutting in 1853, three years before Buckland eventually died.

Although Austen and Strickland were exceptional in the intensity of their scientific vocations, they were certainly not the only undergraduates to have serious interests in science. Recalling Oriel contemporaries in his undergraduate years between 1825 and 1828 and his years as a fellow from 1829, Tom Mozley mentioned Edward Denison, the future bishop of Salisbury, as 'a man of science' and the brothers Robert, Samuel, and Henry Wilberforce

---

[35] The holders are conveniently listed for the period 1800–50 in Nicolaas A. Rupke, 'Oxford's Scientific Awakening and the Role of Geology', in HUO vi. 543–62 (544–5).
[36] Rupke, 'Oxford's Scientific Awakening', 560–2.
[37] ODNB s.n. Austen (1808–84).   [38] ODNB s.n. Strickland (1811–53).

as having 'a strong leaning to science'.[39] All three Wilberforces, in fact, took honours in both classics and mathematics, Robert gaining firsts in both schools in 1823 and Samuel following with a first in mathematics (and a second in classics) in 1826. As a fellow and tutor in Oriel (from 1826), Robert was typical of the younger, modern-minded dons who were attracted by Buckland's lectures, and Mozley recalled accompanying him to hear Buckland on several occasions.[40] None of Mozley's scientifically inclined acquaintances, however, could match William Froude, the second of the three Froude brothers who passed through Oriel in the 1820s and 1830s. Froude went on to distinction as an innovative railway and marine engineer, recognized by his election to the Royal Society in 1870. These later achievements owed at least something to foundations laid in his four years as an undergraduate between 1828 and 1832. Described by his older contemporary Mozley as 'the chemist as well as the mechanist of the college', Froude acquired the reputation of an eccentric for the experiments, including the preparation and administration of laughing gas, that he performed in his rooms in the front quadrangle (above those of Newman, a tutor and friend with whom he later corresponded on theological matters, despite his own growing agnosticism).[41] According to Mozley, the experiments left their mark on the walls, which were stained from Froude's window-sill down to the ground with rivulets of sulphuric acid.

Despite his streak of individualism, Froude does not appear to have found his undergraduate studies uncongenial. He took a first in mathematics along with a third in classics in the same term in 1832. In mathematics, he would have encountered tutors, Robert Wilberforce among them, who were well able to cope with even the most gifted students, including those seeking honours. Except in mixed mathematics, however, his scientific knowledge would have gone unexamined and unrewarded in the Schools. To critical outsiders as well as to the gathering lobby of professors and readers in the scientific subjects within Oxford, the marginalization of science was an intolerable anachronism. William Hamilton's scathing attack on Oxford ('of all academical institutions, at once the most imperfect and the most perfectible') in two articles in the *Edinburgh Review* in 1831 made the point indirectly, as similar attacks in the same journal had done twenty years before.[42] A main cause of Oxford's 'corruption' lay, for Hamilton, in

---

[39] Thomas Mozley, *Reminiscences chiefly of Oriel College and the Oxford Movement*, 2 vols. (London, 1882), ii. 432.
[40] Mozley, *Reminiscences*, ii. 429.
[41] Mozley, *Reminiscences*, ii. 14–15. On Froude at Oriel, see also David K. Brown, *The Way of a Ship in the Midst of the Sea: The Life and Work of William Froude* (Penzance, 2006), 7–9.
[42] William Hamilton, 'On the State of the English Universities, with More Especial Reference to Oxford (June, 1831)', and 'On the State of the English Universities, with More Especial Reference to Oxford. (Supplemental)', in Hamilton, *Discussions on Philosophy and Literature,*

the weak position of the university's professors and readers, who purveyed such scientific instruction as was available. Their interests, as Hamilton had it, were constantly outweighed by those of the college-based tutors; it was the tutors who taught the undergraduate curriculum, and they were happy to see the syllabus remain unchanged, as were most heads of houses.

Of those who protested within the university, no one spoke more forcefully than Baden Powell, who took a first in mathematics at Oriel in 1817 before going on to a clerical career and finally returning to Oxford in 1827 as Savilian Professor of Geometry. As professor, Powell never attracted more than a tiny handful of students, in some terms none at all. Hence he spoke with particular feeling when he made the case for a strengthening of the position of professorial lectures in the uncompromising introductory lecture to his course in Easter Term 1832. Published with extensive explanatory notes as *The Present State and Future Prospects of Mathematical and Physical Studies in the University of Oxford*, Powell's statement bore on more than just attendance at lectures.[43] Here and in other writings in his early years in the Savilian chair, he championed the case for a university curriculum that would reflect the full range of a liberal education, one that Powell saw as necessarily including a significant scientific and mathematical component.[44] To that end, and with a critical eye on the lack of seriousness in undergraduate life, he advocated measures that would not only open the syllabus to compulsory elements of science and mathematics but also, no less crucially, provide incentives for mathematically able candidates to seek honours rather than taking the easier route, involving only a limited amount of mathematics, to a pass degree. Essential to his cause was the maintenance of a separate class list prepared by an independent board of examiners in mathematics. As Powell argued, a single undifferentiated board necessarily worked against the interests of mathematics by making it easy for a poor performance in the mathematical part of the syllabus to be at least partially overlooked. Innocuous though the issues may seem in retrospect, the conflict went to the heart of the purposes of a university education, and it divided Oxford opinion at a time when those purposes and the examining procedures that underlay them were engendering fierce debate.

Within Oriel, Powell's arguments probably encountered indifference rather than opposition; this would certainly have been the response of Keble, who (in

---

Education and University Reform. Chiefly from the Edinburgh Review; corrected, vindicated, enlarged, in notes and appendices (London, 1852), 386–434 and 435–63, esp. (for the quoted passage) 387. On the earlier attacks in the *Edinburgh Review*, see Chapter 9.

[43] *The Present State and Future Prospects of Mathematical and Physical Studies in the University of Oxford, considered in a Public Lecture, introductory to his usual course, in Easter Term MDCCCXXXII by the Rev. Baden Powell* (Oxford, 1832).

[44] On Powell as a reformer, see Pietro Corsi, *Science and Religion: Baden Powell and the Anglican Debate, 1800–1860* (Cambridge, 1988), 106–23.

Mozley's words) believed in letting science 'go its way', and Newman, who 'abstained from science', despite an interest in mathematics that he evidently regretted abandoning after he relinquished his tutorship.[45] But the vehemence of his advocacy had the more damaging effect of alienating some of the reform-minded moderates he was seeking to win over. Two years before the publication of Powell's pamphlet of 1832, Robert Wilberforce had already elaborated his conception of mathematics as 'an instrument of Education' rather than as a 'Science' and declared his related opposition to the idea of a separate board of mathematical examiners.[46] His argument was that Euclidean geometry, which occupied most of the mathematical syllabus, cultivated the mind's logical faculties, whereas modern practical mathematics, such as might be used by a 'banker's clerk' or a 'sailor in astronomy', fostered a mechanical and hence inferior form of dexterity.[47] For this reason, as Wilberforce believed, mathematical study in the Oxford tradition fell properly within the province of literae humaniores. Faced with Wilberforce's intransigence, Powell might have expected support from the ranks of the Oriel Noetics, with whom he had much in common both theologically and on key questions of university reform. But he received only sympathy tempered by reservations. Within the Noetic camp, Copleston's considered caution bore special weight. The unease at an extension of the mathematical content of the curriculum that he had elaborated in 1810 in response to the earlier spate of attacks in the *Edinburgh Review* remained as strong as ever, growing as it did from a characteristic Noetic fear that the advance of mathematics would threaten (as Powell intended it should) the position of logic.[48] In Copleston's conception of a liberal education logic, buttressed by precisely the kind of mathematics that Wilberforce too saw as a proper element in the syllabus, should always have pride of place.[49] And that was a place to be defended tenaciously against the snares of reforms that risked opening the door to 'the hasty acquisition of miscellaneous knowledge'.[50] The sciences and other modern subjects, such as political economy, had their place in the university, though as 'the subordinate, and not the leading business of education'.[51] They were proper material only for mature minds that had first been well disciplined in the traditional subjects.

---

[45] Mozley, *Reminiscences*, ii. 430; Newman to Mrs William Froude, 4 April 1844, LDN x. 191–2.

[46] [Robert Isaac Wilberforce], *Considerations respecting the Most Effectual Means of Encouraging Mathematics in Oxford* (Oxford, 1830), 8. This is an unsigned pamphlet that Powell plausibly attributed to Wilberforce. The copy in the Bodleian Library (Baden Powell 31 [32]) is annotated with waspish comments and caricatures by Powell.

[47] [Wilberforce], *Considerations*, 9.

[48] Edward Copleston, *A Reply to the Calumnies of the Edinburgh Review against Oxford. Containing an Account of Studies pursued in that University* (Oxford, 1810), esp. 175–8.

[49] Corsi, *Science and Religion*, 108–10.

[50] Copleston, *Reply to the Calumnies*, 176.

[51] Copleston, *Reply to the Calumnies*, 177.

Through the early 1830s, the tide of Oxford opinion began to run strongly against Powell's cause, and by 1835 he bitterly admitted defeat. Thereafter, until his death in 1860, he remained supportive of the lobby of professors and readers, led by Charles Daubeny (in chemistry, botany, and rural economy), Henry Acland (in medicine), and Robert Walker (in experimental philosophy), whose more cautious advocacy eventually bore fruit in the founding of the new school of natural science in 1850. But in these years he retreated from front-line advocacy and turned his energies increasingly to his own research, mainly on light and radiant heat, and to the emerging broad church movement. Within that movement, whose style of biblical criticism and clear-eyed scrutiny of the interface between faith and reason sat easily with his own long-held beliefs, he found a setting in which he could draw to good effect on his experience as both a scientist and a Christian apologist. In arguing that the improbability of the Gospel miracles represented a difficulty rather than a resource for believers in an age of advancing scientific naturalism, he took a position characteristic of his own and the broad church's liberalism.[52] It is not hard to imagine that he would have relished an engagement in the Darwinian debate that was just beginning at the time of his death. His endorsement of 'the grand principle of the self-evolving powers of nature', which he perceived as essential to the argument of the *Origin of Species*, would have set him firmly on Darwin's side.[53]

The passing of the new examination statutes in 1850 marked a watershed in Oxford science. But while the professors and readers in the scientific and mathematical disciplines felt that a crucial victory had been won, they recognized that the creation of the school of natural science did not in itself place the sciences on an equal footing with the still dominant studies of literae humaniores. The statutes now required that all candidates for a degree should be examined in a largely classical first public examination by Moderators, before proceeding to a second public examination in two schools, normally two years later. It was a mark of the limited nature of the reform that one of these two schools had to be literae humaniores; it was only after taking at least a pass in this school that candidates were allowed to be examined in their second school, which could be either Mathematics, Natural Science, or the other new school, Law and Modern History. An amendment in 1860 eased these requirements by making it possible for candidates who gained at least third class honours in any of the four schools to take their BA without being examined in literae humaniores. Even now, however, the hurdle of classical attainment remained high, since access to the second

---

[52] Baden Powell, 'On the Study of the Evidences of Christianity', in *Essays and Reviews* (London, 1860), 94–144. For commentaries, see Corsi, *Science and Religion*, 209–24 and John Hedley Brooke, *Science and Religion: Some Historical Perspectives* (Cambridge, 1991), 273–4.

[53] Powell, 'Evidences of Christianity', 139.

public examination was still limited to candidates who had taken a pass or honours in moderations. There was not, and was not intended to be, any way of avoiding a significant engagement with Greek and Latin language, literature, and philosophy. For the majority of professors in the sciences, the classical requirements were irksome. But it was not until 1886 that scientists' criticisms of moderations bore fruit in the disciplinary emancipation that came with the establishment of the preliminary examination in natural science as the normal first examination for candidates in the school of natural science.[54]

Despite the constraints, the school of natural science got off to a promising, if unspectacular start.[55] By the late 1850s and early 1860s, an average of eleven candidates a year were taking honours, with rather more than twice that number gaining a pass. By the early 1870s, the number of honours candidates had risen a little to about fifteen a year, while those taking a pass had all but disappeared. By comparison with literae humaniores, in which as many as a hundred a year took honours and roughly twice that number a pass, these were small cohorts. Nevertheless, science had at last established a toe-hold in the undergraduate curriculum. An important further early advance was the inauguration of the University Museum on Parks Road in 1860. This eased the chronic shortage of space for the housing of the university's dispersed scientific collections and allowed the various sciences to be taught under one roof, so fulfilling the ideal of the essential unity of the scientific disciplines, to which Daubeny and Acland in particular attached great importance. The cost of the Museum, which exceeded £80,000, provoked objections among those who believed that the money would have been better spent on opening Oxford to poorer students and educating young men who would go on to the Anglican ministry. But slowly the case for laboratories and other facilities for the sciences won the day. In 1872, the new Clarendon Laboratory, built at a cost of £10,300, allowed physics to move from its already inadequate quarters in the University Museum, and a second physics laboratory was opened in 1910. By then, a new observatory (built in the Parks in 1875), a major extension of the chemistry laboratory (in the late 1870s), and a new laboratory for physiology (in 1884) had all borne witness to the university's resolve to remain abreast of the rapidly developing world of science education, both in Britain and internationally.

[54] M. C. Curthoys, 'The Examination System', in HUO vi. 339–74, esp. 352–6.
[55] On the early history of the school of natural science and the buildings and other facilities that were instituted to support it, see Robert Fox, 'The University Museum and Oxford Science, 1850–1880', in HUO vi. 641–91. Two essential studies of Oxford science in the later nineteenth century are Janet Howarth, 'Science Education in Late Victorian Oxford: A Curious Case of Failure?', *English Historical Review*, 102 (1987), 334–71 and '"Oxford for Arts": The Natural Sciences, 1880–1914', in HUO vii. 457–97.

The growth of what later became known as the Science Area between 1860 and the First World War did not win universal approval. Indeed, it caused anxiety even among those who were sympathetic to the cause of science. The cost of laboratories, equipment, and auxiliary staff exposed science to criticism by those used to book-based disciplines. And there was constant concern about the seeming remoteness of science from college life. Did it follow that science should be allowed to develop independently of the tutorial-based system of the colleges? Or was there some way in which it might be integrated and made to work with rather than against Oxford's traditional forms of teaching? One response was for colleges to provide teaching laboratories of their own, and by the 1860s Magdalen, Balliol, and (in a building constructed for anatomical teaching in the eighteenth century) Christ Church all offered laboratory facilities for their undergraduates as for some other colleges. Beginning in 1879, collaboration between Balliol and Trinity led to the establishment of the joint Balliol–Trinity Laboratories for teaching and research in both chemistry and physics (with a particular strength in physical chemistry), and Trinity added a 'Millard laboratory and workshop for experimental mechanics and engineering' in 1885. Queen's (1900) and Jesus (1907) followed suit with laboratories that became particularly noted for organic chemistry and physical chemistry respectively, and other, short-lived initiatives were realized at Exeter and Keble.[56]

Unlike these colleges, Oriel seems never to have contemplated the establishment of a laboratory, and such provision as it made for undergraduates in the sciences was minimal. This is unsurprising, since the incentives to engage more seriously with science were slight. For two decades after the creation of the school of natural science, only a trickle of candidates passed through the college, and that trickle soon dwindled. The one fellow with any understanding of the sciences, Francis Harrison, who was appointed to his fellowship and a college lectureship in mathematics in 1852, could have offered only the most elementary scientific guidance.[57] Harrison, though, was an able mathematician. After taking a first in mathematics (and a third in classics) at Queen's in 1850, he went on to win the university's senior mathematical scholarship in 1852 and so gained a modest stipend for two years of advanced study. In Oriel, as a fellow, lecturer, and (from 1860) tutor, he was both a respected teacher and a visible presence, especially during his years as a legendarily vigilant dean from 1859 until his departure from the college in 1867. His mathematical knowledge would certainly have been enough to sustain Oriel's outstanding undergraduate

---

[56] The history of college laboratories in physics and engineering is well treated in Simcock, 'Laboratories and Physics in Oxford Colleges, 1848–1947' and 'Mechanical Physicists, the Millard Laboratory, and the Transition from Physics to Engineering', in Robert Fox and Graeme Gooday (eds.), *Physics in Oxford: Laboratories, Learning, and College Life* (Oxford, 2005), 119–68 and 169–208.

[57] W. J. Lewis, 'Francis Harrison', OR (September 1912), 40–5.

ILLUSTRATION 19.3 Francis Harrison (1829–1912), fellow 1852–66, tutor in mathematics

Oriel College

scientist of this period, Thomas Heathcote Gerald Wyndham, who took a first in natural science in 1865 and went on to a fellowship at Merton and, in 1873, to the university's Aldrichian demonstratorship in chemistry.[58] But in science Wyndham would have had to look beyond the college, to the lectures provided in the University Museum, where he eventually lectured himself and did important work in petrology (before his premature death in 1876). For an aspiring scientist of Wyndham's calibre, in fact, Oriel would not have been a natural destination, and it may be assumed that he only chose the college because of its association with Provost Eveleigh, his great-grandfather.

Soon after Harrison left Oriel for the college living of North Wraxall in Wiltshire and a life of pastoral duties, local antiquarianism, and an occasional involvement in mathematics (as an Oxford examiner and the writer of textbooks), the college made a seemingly bold commitment to science by electing its first scientific fellow, William James Lewis. But the appointment

[58] Fox, 'University Museum and Oxford Science', 675 n.

heralded a false dawn, and the provision for science teaching did not significantly improve. Lewis, a friend and briefly a pupil of Harrison, came to Oriel from Jesus immediately after an undergraduate career marked by firsts in both mathematics (1868) and natural science (1869). It was a distinguished record, crowned in 1871 by the award of the university's senior mathematical scholarship, which Harrison had won almost twenty years earlier. Oriel, though, derived little benefit from a career that began so promisingly, except for the mathematical exhibition that Lewis founded towards the end of his life in honour of Harrison.[59] He retained his fellowship until his death in 1926. Yet for most of his fifty-seven years as a fellow he invested his main energies in Cambridge, where he was deputy to the professor of mineralogy from 1879 and became professor himself in 1881. Despite a frail constitution that led to his being 'ordered south' each year to avoid the English winter, Lewis was not inactive as a scientist: he published a substantial textbook of crystallography and papers that earned him election to the Royal Society in 1909. Yet there is no evidence that he ever taught at Oriel or that he did more on his occasional visits to the college than attend the half-yearly meeting of fellows. By the time he died, in the rooms in Trinity College, Cambridge that had been his home for many years, few Orielenses (as Phelps observed in his obituary) would have known, or even known of him.[60]

By any standards, the nineteenth century ended on a sombre note for science in Oriel. The college's decision of 1878 to seek an association with a proposed new chair of physics or, failing that, one in pure mathematics was a sign of good will towards the sciences, but it came to nothing; the Selborne Commission's proposal for the creation of the chairs was not implemented until much later, the physics chair only being established, as the Wykeham chair at New College, in 1900. This left the absentee Lewis the only fellow with serious scientific interests. Not surprisingly, in the thirty years from 1870 just ten candidates from Oriel took honours in the school of natural science (with another two from St Mary Hall) out of a total of 901 who did so in the university as a whole. When one of these candidates, Arthur Edwin Boycott, a future FRS and eminent pathologist and naturalist, arrived to read for the School (specializing in physiology) in 1894, he was the only undergraduate scientist in the college and was assigned to Phelps as his tutor, apparently on the grounds that Phelps's interest in political economy marked him as modern and hence less remote from science than other fellows.[61] In the Mathematical School, the pattern of neglect was similar: over the same period, just four Orielenses (out of a total of

---

[59] For some fragmentary records concerning the Francis Harrison exhibition (or scholarship, as it was called when funds allowed), see OCA BT 1 R/1 and TF 2 B1/7.
[60] Lancelot Ridley Phelps, 'W. J. Lewis, F.R.S.', OR (June 1926), 341–2.
[61] C. J. Martin, 'Arthur Edwin Boycott 1877–1938', *Obituary Notices of Fellows of the Royal Society*, 2 (1936–9), 561–71 (561–2).

459 for the whole university) took honours, and once Harrison had gone, no mathematical lecturer or fellow was appointed to succeed him. These figures set Oriel firmly among the small group of colleges (including Brasenose, Corpus, Lincoln, St Edmund Hall, Worcester, and the women's colleges) from which science was virtually absent at the turn of the century (although Worcester did do something to develop a modest mathematical tradition). The contrast with the leading science colleges (Christ Church, Trinity, New College, Keble, and Magdalen) and the body of unattached non-collegiate students was stark and it became increasingly so as the total number of candidates in the school of natural science grew after 1900.

Following the lean years of 1870–1900, the appearance of thirteen Oriel men among those taking honours in the school of natural science between 1903 and 1909 has to be seen as a significant mark of gathering interest. So too does the governing body's serious consideration of a proposal that it should seek an association with the new professorship of engineering science in 1907.[62] The expression of regret at the financial constraints that prevented acceptance of the proposal seems to have been genuine. Four years later any lingering uncertainty about the college's readiness to provide for the sciences was removed, with the appointment of Henry Tizard to its first tutorship in natural science. Tizard embodied the more outward-looking, research-oriented spirit that began to transform Oxford science generally in the new century. After firsts in mathematical moderations (in 1905) and chemistry (1908) at Magdalen, he had spent a semester in the laboratory of Walther Nernst at the University of Berlin, followed by two years of research and teaching as a Senior Demy back at Magdalen.[63] His years as a tutor at Oriel were cut short by the war, in which he showed courage as a test pilot and rose to a senior position in the research arm of the Ministry of Munitions, and afterwards he returned to the college only briefly. In 1920 he resigned his tutorship and fellowship on his appointment as university reader in chemical thermodynamics and soon moved on to a distinguished career in public life, first as assistant secretary (later secretary) of the Department of Scientific and Industrial Research, and then as rector of Imperial College in London from 1929 to 1942.

Despite the brevity of his time at Oriel, Tizard laid firm foundations, and it is a gauge of changing attitudes that he was replaced immediately. The background of his successor, Dalziel Llewellyn Hammick, was not unlike Tizard's. After taking a first in chemistry in 1908, at Magdalen, Hammick too had spent a year in Germany, at Otto Dimroth's laboratory in Munich, where

---

[62] OCA GOV 4 A6: 9 and 10, 10 October 1907.
[63] ODNB s.n. Tizard's years in Oxford are treated in some detail in Ronald W. Clark, *Tizard* (London, 1965), 9–22.

ILLUSTRATION 19.4 Dalziel Llewellyn Hammick (1887–1966), fellow 1920–52
Oriel College

he became doctor of philosophy in 1910.[64] But he had a more natural profile as a teacher than Tizard. By the time of his election as fellow and tutor in 1921, he had taught for ten years, first at Gresham's School, Holt, and then at Winchester College, and once at Oriel he stayed for the rest of his career. Even after his formal retirement in 1952, he continued giving tutorials and retained a college lectureship at Corpus until 1958. Hammick saw himself as first and foremost a college man and tutor in the traditional mould. His tutorials covered all areas of chemistry, and in his research he moved freely across the boundaries between organic and physical chemistry, showing a versatility that gave him a distinctive position in the rather compartmentalized world of Oxford chemistry. He published mainly on rates of organic reaction, which had long been something of an Oxford speciality. Within this general area, a series of papers on the mechanism of decarboxylation reactions, including some written in collaboration with Ben Brown, his eventual successor at Oriel, attracted particular attention. Recognition of his research came rather late in his career. But in 1952, when he was in his mid-sixties, he

---

[64] E. J. Bowen, 'Dalziel Llewellyn Hammick 1887–1966', *Biographical Memoirs of Fellows of the Royal Society*, 13 (1967), 107–24. Also the unsigned obituary in *The Times*, 18 October 1966, reproduced (with some additional reminiscences) in OR (1967), 31–3.

ILLUSTRATION 19.5 Kenneth James Franklin (1897–1966), fellow 1924–47
Oriel College

was elected a fellow of the Royal Society. For many years, the 'Hammick reaction', described as part of this work in a paper co-authored with P. Dyson in 1937, remained a staple element of courses in organic chemistry and it continues to be listed in the Merck Index.

In 1924, three years after its election of Hammick, the college made a second crucial appointment, of Kenneth James Franklin as fellow and tutor in physiology. Franklin resembled Hammick in the breadth and refinement of his intellectual profile.[65] Although he read physiology, he had come up to Hertford as a classical scholar, and he retained his linguistic and historical interests throughout his career, publishing translations of Richard Lower's *De corde* and William Harvey's *De motu cordis*, a biography of Harvey, and a number of other historical books and articles.[66] Like Hammick, Franklin

[65] Ivan De Burgh Daly and R. G. Macbeth, 'Kenneth James Franklin 1897–1966', in *Biographical Memoirs of Fellows of the Royal Society*, 14 (1968), 223–42. See also the unsigned obituary in *The Times*, 9 May 1966, reproduced, with an extensive obituary by R. G. Macbeth, in OR (1966), 49–52.

[66] *De corde by Richard Lower. With introduction and translation by K. J. Franklin*, published as volume ix of Gunther, *Early Science in Oxford* (Oxford, 1932); William Harvey, *Movement of the Heart and Blood in Animals: An Anatomical Essay. Translated from the original Latin by Kenneth J. Franklin* (Oxford, 1957); and Kenneth James Franklin, *William Harvey: Englishman. 1578–1657* (London, 1961).

valued his association with Oriel, and he remained prominent in college life for over twenty years. As librarian from 1931 to 1947, he left his mark as an advocate of the refurbishment of the library and of the decision to make the senior library available as a reading room for undergraduates. He was also a key figure in the growth of pharmacology at Oxford. Under a quietly effective professor, J. A. Gunn, he held a university demonstratorship in pharmacology from 1925, publishing prolifically on veins and foetal and renal circulation. His failure to secure the chair of pharmacology when Gunn resigned in 1937 in order to devote himself to the directorship of Oxford's newly founded Nuffield Institute for Medical Research disappointed Franklin. But he remained close to Gunn, as assistant director of the Nuffield Institute, and continued to serve the Oxford Medical School, notably as dean from 1934 to 1938 and then as acting dean through the difficult war years. For someone so attached to Oxford and to Oriel, the decision to leave for the chair of physiology at St Bartholomew's Hospital (where he had completed his medical studies in the early 1920s) in 1947 cannot have been easy. Nevertheless, his time at Barts, though largely devoted to administrative duties and ended by premature retirement on health grounds at the age of 62 in 1958, brought its rewards, including his election to the Royal Society in 1955.

Throughout the inter-war years, Hammick and Franklin shouldered the college's tutorial work in science. In Oriel as elsewhere in the university, theirs were the dominant sciences in terms of undergraduate numbers. Between 1918 and 1939, thirty-four candidates from Oriel took honours in chemistry, while fifty-one (many of them taught by Hammick early in their undergraduate careers, as well as by Franklin) did so in physiology. In sharp contrast, the other sciences attracted only a trickle of honours candidates: seven in engineering science in the same period, six each in zoology and botany, and five in physics. The significance of such figures has to be judged in the light of the small number of undergraduates in these disciplines within the university as a whole: the total of those taking honours in physics rarely exceeded twenty a year in the 1930s or ten in engineering science. But no such qualification can account for Oriel's almost complete withdrawal from mathematics. While the mathematical school was much smaller than Natural Science, the absence of any Oriel name from the class lists in mathematics between 1898 and 1922 betrayed a lack of commitment to the subject that lasted until well after the Second World War.

In its choice of the two disciplines in which it had tutorial fellows, Oriel was typical of the smaller, less wealthy colleges. Across the university, in fact, chemistry and physiology (in which medical students took a BA before going on to their clinical years) were the sciences in which teaching was in greatest demand and in which tutorial fellowships (fifteen in chemistry and eight in physiology in 1939) were most numerous. Oriel was also typical in using college lectureships as an economical way of catering for the occasional undergraduates wishing to read other sciences. At various times lecturers in zoology, agriculture and forestry, and geology helped to keep the science flag flying, and in these smaller disciplines the teaching that the college provided adequately met the limited demand. Often enough the college's lecturers went on to distinguished academic careers elsewhere, and in one of the smaller disciplines, botany, a long-term lectureship brought to Oriel a leading figure in Oxford science, William Owen James. From 1931 to 1959 teaching in botany was provided by James, a college lecturer who never held a fellowship in Oxford despite over thirty years in his main posts as a departmental and then university demonstrator and finally reader in the department of botany.[67] James was one of many scientists in Oxford at the time who had no choice but to pursue their careers on the fringes of college life, despite holding permanent university demonstratorships (lectureships in all but name) and winning considerable reputations within and beyond Oxford. James's was just such a case. He was a painstaking lecturer and had a particularly good record as a teacher at the postgraduate level. In research his record was outstanding. His work in plant physiology earned him a fellowship of the Royal Society in 1952 and seven years later a chair and headship of the botany department at Imperial College.

Despite the growing distinction of the work performed in the university's laboratories during the 1920s and 1930s, it took the war to arouse a concerted sense that the secondary position of science and mathematics in all but a few colleges had to be addressed.[68] By 1945, the old tag 'Oxford for arts, Cambridge for science' still circulated. But it was losing its plausibility. The university's strength in scientific research had been recognized by the award of Nobel Prizes to two professors, Frederick Soddy in 1921 and Charles Sherrington in 1932; and five others who held university or college posts in 1939 (Howard Florey, Ernst Chain, Robert Robinson, Cyril Hinshelwood, and Dorothy Hodgkin) were similarly honoured after 1945. Moreover, there could be no denying that Oxford science had a conspicuously good war. The development of penicillin for clinical use owed much to the collaboration between Florey, Chain, and E. P. Abraham in the Dunn School of Pathology and organic chemists in the Dyson Perrins Laboratory. Elsewhere in the

---

[67] A. R. Clapham and J. L. Harley, 'William Owen James 1900–1978', in *Biographical Memoirs of Fellows of the Royal Society*, 25 (1979), 337–64 and ODNB s.n.

[68] Jack Morrell has argued convincingly for the primacy of research in raising the standing of science in inter-war Oxford, despite the continuing weakness of the scientific disciplines within the colleges. The theme runs through his *Science at Oxford 1914–1939: Transforming an Arts University* (Oxford, 1997) and, with special reference to physics, his chapter 'The Lindemann Era' in Fox and Gooday, *Physics in Oxford*, 233–66. The impact of the war on science emerges strongly from several chapters in HUO viii; see especially John Roche, 'The Non-Medical Sciences, 1939–1970' and Charles Webster, 'Medicine', 251–89 and 317–43.

Science Area, physical and inorganic chemists made major contributions to the preparation of more effective charcoal for use in the British service respirator,[69] and the biochemistry department developed British Anti-Lewisite, a much-needed antidote to Lewisite, a blister agent capable of causing extreme pain and tissue damage.[70] In physics, the new Clarendon Laboratory, completed in 1940 but still not fully commissioned for undergraduate teaching, became the setting for two highly secret programmes of research: one, the code-named Tube Alloys Project, for developing gaseous diffusion techniques for the separation of the isotope $U235$ for deployment in an atomic bomb, the other a pioneering radar project (to which John Sanders, later Oriel's first fellow and tutor in physics, contributed towards the end of the war, as a member of the Clarendon-based Admiralty Research Group).

Contributions of such effectiveness to the war effort left the principal of Brasenose, William Stallybrass, with a declining number of sympathizers when he asserted, in council shortly before his death in 1948, that the expansion of the sciences 'had got to stop'.[71] An eminent academic lawyer (who had held a college lectureship at Oriel, in addition to his Brasenose fellowship, for most of the inter-war period), Stallybrass believed that the life of scientists, with their recondite, technical research pursued in costly university laboratories, unfitted them to be good college men. But such an opinion now found echoes only in the most conservative circles. Between 1950 and 1960, with the tide running strongly against such arts-based prejudice and with the professorial big guns of the Science Area campaigning relentlessly for their disciplines, colleges transformed their engagement with science through the admission of increased numbers of undergraduates in the scientific disciplines and investment in new tutorial fellowships to cope with them. Chemistry and physiology, the most popular of the pre-war sciences, were among the leading beneficiaries. But growth in the 'poor relations' of the 1930s was even more striking. The number of honours candidates in physics rose from 59 in 1950 to 141 ten years later. And whereas just five colleges had tutorial fellows in physics in 1950 (Magdalen, Christ Church, St John's, Jesus, and Wadham, in addition to New College and Brasenose, which had senior research fellows), by 1962 only four of the twenty-eight undergraduate colleges (Trinity, Somerville, St Hilda's, and St Anne's) were without at least one tutorial fellow in the subject. Engineering science

---

[69] J. S. Rowlinson, 'The Wartime Work of Hinshelwood and his Colleagues', *Notes and Records of the Royal Society of London*, 68 (2004), 161–75.

[70] Margery G. Ord and Lloyd A. Stocken, *The Oxford Biochemistry Department 1920–2006* (Oxford, 2006), 13–17. For a more detailed account, see the unpublished memoir by the same authors: 'BAL: A Chemist's Tale from the Second World War', Bodleian Library, Oxford MS Eng. c. 7203.

[71] Quoted in Roche, 'The Non-Medical Sciences', 286.

expanded less spectacularly and from a smaller pre-war base. Yet numbers taking honours rose from twenty-nine in 1950 to forty-one in 1960, and sixty-two in 1970 (in addition to twenty or so reading for the joint school in Engineering Science and Economics), an expansion proportionately comparable with that in physics. Although this all happened a little later than in physics, it had similar consequences for the integration of engineers in college life. The number of colleges with tutorial fellowships in engineering stood at three in 1961. By the early 1970s it had risen to about twenty, a pattern of expansion that has continued ever since to cope with a present entry of between 160 and 180 undergraduates a year in engineering science and the joint honour school in engineering, economics, and management.

Although Oriel was never a pacemaker, it played its part in the improved post-war provision for science. When Franklin departed for London in 1947, he was replaced immediately by Graham Weddell as tutorial fellow and lecturer (subsequently reader) in human anatomy. A specialist in mammalian nerve tissue, Weddell had built a distinguished career on his early training and research at Barts, where he graduated in 1933, followed by two years as a Commonwealth Fund Fellow in the USA between 1935 and 1937 and subsequent war service in the RAMC, part of which he spent at the neurosurgical unit in Oxford, working under Hugh Cairns.[72] During his Oriel years, Weddell remained active in research, focused mainly on the relations between leprosy and peripheral nerve damage. However, he never allowed research to diminish his enjoyment of college life, and when he advanced from his readership to the chair of human anatomy in 1973, he obtained special dispensation to hold the post at Oriel rather than at Hertford, the college to which, as professor, he should have migrated. An additional attraction for Weddell would have been the college's association with the Nuffield professorship of obstetrics and gynaecology from the chair's establishment in 1937. In Weddell's time the chair was held by a succession of distinguished professors: John Chassar Moir, John Stallworthy, and Alexander Turnbull. Following Turnbull's death in 1990, David Barlow, who was the professor until his appointment as executive dean and professor of reproductive medicine at Glasgow in 2004, maintained the tradition, providing a significant link between the college and the university's faculty of clinical medicine.

By the time Franklin left, Hammick's departure too was on the horizon; the statutory retirement age of 67 meant that he would be gone by 1952. The seriousness with which the college considered the question of Hammick's replacement was a sign of the changing times within and beyond Oriel. A number of fellows, supported by Provost Ross, evidently regarded the

---

[72] Simon Miller, 'In memoriam. Professor Graham Weddell', *Journal of Anatomy*, 173 (1990), 189–91. See also Colin McDougall's obituary of Weddell in *The Independent*, 14 April 1990, reproduced (with an additional notice by Kenneth Turpin) in OR (1990), 75–7.

choice of a successor as a matter of the highest priority. They sought the advice of Alexander Todd, a Glasgow graduate who had proceeded doctor of philosophy at Oriel in 1933 and gone on to a chair of organic chemistry at Cambridge, and Robert Robinson, still (after almost a quarter of a century in his Oxford chair) at the peak of his influence as Waynflete Professor of Chemistry and head of the Dyson Perrins Laboratory.[73] Todd and Robinson recommended that Hammick, a man they both admired, should be invited to continue teaching after his retirement, and in 1952 a three-year extension was agreed upon, with a view to the appointment of a successor who would begin college duties in Michaelmas Term 1955. An essential condition for the appointment was the availability of a departmental demonstratorship, which would provide a substantial part of the salary, and it was the unexpected availability of such a post in 1954 that prompted the college to implement its plan a year early.

The choice of both the university and the college fell on Ben Brown, the son of a south Yorkshire mining family who had come up to Oriel from Mexborough Grammar School in 1943.[74] A first in chemistry in 1947 had led to a Bishop Fraser graduate scholarship at Oriel and doctoral research in organic chemistry under Hammick, who had supervised his Part II thesis and with whom Brown wrote fourteen papers in the *Journal of the Chemical Society*, mainly on heterocyclic compounds. In 1950 Brown moved to Cambridge, where he held a senior studentship of the Royal Commission for the Exhibition of 1951 (working under Todd) and a research fellowship at Trinity Hall. In Cambridge, Brown built on the success he had enjoyed not only as a chemist but also as a footballer; he was selected for Great Britain in the 1952 Olympic Games and capped on seven occasions between 1951 and 1954 for the England amateur eleven. All this time, he remained firmly in Oriel's sights (as also in Robinson's), and when he accepted the awaited departmental demonstratorship in the Dyson Perrins Laboratory in 1954, the college elected him to the tutorial fellowship he was to hold, along with a university demonstratorship, from 1955 until his death in 1992.

Brown's appointment confirmed a tide of support for science in Oriel that led, in 1956, to the appointment of the college's first tutorial fellow in physics, John Sanders, a wartime graduate of Hertford who had worked in the Clarendon Laboratory for some years as a university demonstrator since becoming doctor of philosophy there in 1949.[75] The appointment stimulated an enlargement of the college's entry in physics (in which only twenty-six

---

[73] A plentiful correspondence concerning the succession following Hammick's retirement is in OCA CO 1 A2/Ben Brown.

[74] J. H. Mellanby, 'Ben Brown', with an extract from Kenneth Turpin's address at the memorial service for Brown, 14 November 1992, OR (1993), 86–9.

[75] Colin Webb, 'John Sanders', OR (2006), 96–8.

Orielenses had taken honours between 1918 and 1956), and the subject prospered. Following a period of sabbatical leave at Bell Labs, where he encountered the first Optical Maser in the autumn of 1958, Sanders established laser research as a leading speciality of the Clarendon Laboratory and headed a group there with a worldwide reputation. But through all this he remained a devoted undergraduate tutor and an effective champion of his subject within Oriel. By 1961, the growth in student numbers had helped to justify a further appointment, of W. E. (Bill) Parry, who had taken both his first degree and doctorate of philosophy at Queen's and now came as a fellow and tutor in theoretical physics, soon redefined as applied mathematics and theoretical physics. The redesignation of the fellowship was appropriate. It reflected the breadth of Parry's research interests, initially in many body theory and later in the application of geometrical methods in theoretical physics, including string theory. It also conveyed the breadth of his teaching within the college, to both mathematicians and physicists. The college's offering in physics was further strengthened by the arrival of Alan Segar, a university lecturer in nuclear physics with strong links with CERN in Geneva, who was elected to a fellowship in 1970 and stayed for almost thirty years, latterly as Rhodes fellow and tutor in physics. With Sanders, Parry, and Segar in post, physics continued to thrive. By the time they retired (Sanders in 1991, Parry in 1996, Segar in 2000), an average of six undergraduates a year were entering to read the subject, a figure that has remained at about that level ever since.

The 1950s and 1960s marked a turning point for science, as the decades in which the scientific disciplines finally established deep roots at the heart of college life as well as in the university as a whole. From the start, Oriel's policy with regard to science was one of consolidation, allied to cautious expansion. Following the decision to extend the provision for physics by Parry's appointment in 1961, a second tutorial fellowship in chemistry was created three years later. The first holder of the fellowship, Ian Beattie, who arrived from a readership at King's College London, only stayed two years before moving on to a chair at the University of Southampton. But his successor Keith Prout, a leading figure in Oxford's long-established chemical crystallography group, remained a fellow and tutor until his retirement, with the title of professor, in 2001. At about the same time, the college took its first steps in disciplines in which it had not previously had permanent tutorial positions. The arrival of Donald Walsh, initially as a college lecturer in engineering science in 1961 and then, in 1964, as Oriel's first fellow and tutor in the subject, marked the college as distinctly forward-looking. In 1956, when Walsh arrived in Oxford from industry on a three-year research fellowship, the department of engineering science, in which he worked, had only eight university and departmental demonstratorships, and it was not until 1959 that St Edmund Hall became the first college to appoint a tutorial fellow in the subject.[76] At Oriel, Walsh, a specialist in electronic devices and vacuum techniques, laid the foundations for a strong college tradition in engineering: in his years as tutor, the number of undergraduates reading engineering science rose from barely one a year to four or five.

A similar new departure occurred in mathematics. In the 1960s, after some years in which the subject had been catered for by stipendiary lectureships, the college confirmed its commitment to mathematics as a major undergraduate discipline. From 1961, the subject was taught, in its more applied aspects, by Parry, complemented in other areas by tutorial arrangements with other colleges. Then in 1966 the college created its first formally designated tutorial fellowship in mathematics. In the event, the first holder of the fellowship, Robert Elliot, soon left for a research post at the University of Hull. But his successor Graham Vincent-Smith, who was appointed as fellow and tutor in 1968 two years after completing a doctorate at Merton in the field of functional analysis, remained in post until he retired, as Philip and Pauline Harris Fellow, in 2008.

Since the 1960s, the expansion of science in the university has continued at an accelerating pace. As the proportion of undergraduates reading scientific subjects or mathematics rose from 20 per cent in 1939 to 35 per cent in 1950 and finally to almost half in 2000, the growth in numbers and the proliferation of new honour schools put unprecedented pressure on colleges. Oriel has responded to the challenge by immediately replacing fellows who have retired and, where possible, creating a second or even a third tutorial position in the leading disciplines. Geoffrey Raisman replaced Graham Weddell in 1973 and was himself succeeded two years later by Gordon Macpherson, a specialist in cell biology and immunology working at the Sir William Dunn School of Pathology, who remained as tutorial fellow in medicine and latterly as reader in experimental pathology and Turnbull fellow until his retirement in 2008. In physics Andrew Boothroyd, a specialist in condensed matter physics, moved from Cambridge to succeed John Sanders in 1991, and Elizabeth Winstanley, subsequently professor of mathematical physics at the University of Sheffield, succeeded Parry in 1996. In engineering science too the college has acted without delay as vacancies have occurred. When Donald Walsh retired in 1981, he was replaced by Ian Postlethwaite, a graduate of Imperial College who had done his doctorate at Cambridge. Following Postlethwaite's departure for a chair at the University of Leicester in 1987, he too was replaced, and subsequent vacancies in that fellowship and in a second tutorial position, created in 1991, have been filled promptly. It is a mark of the college's success in attracting external funding that both

---

[76] Donald Walsh, 'Engineering at Oriel', OR (2007), 48–9.

engineering fellowships are now endowed, with Douglas Hamilton holding the Emmott fellowship and John Huber the Tube Investments fellowship.

Among new disciplines that have established themselves in recent years are biochemistry and computer science. After a long history of catering for the subject through college lectureships and teaching arrangements with other colleges, Oriel appointed its first tutorial fellow in biochemistry, John Heath, in 1987. When Heath went on to a chair at the University of Birmingham in 1995, he was replaced by Lynne Cox, and a second tutorial fellowship was created in 2008. Computer science at Oriel became established in a similar way, with the familiar pattern of stipendiary lectureships giving way to a more permanent arrangement in 1994, when Michael Spivey, a specialist in programming languages, was appointed as the college's first tutorial fellow in computation, as the subject was called at the time. Like the engineering and some other fellowships, Spivey's post is endowed, in his case as the Misys and Andersen fellowship.

The arrival of new disciplines and the creation of additional tutorial positions in existing subjects have had inevitable consequences for the size and character of the fellowship in Oriel as in other colleges. Allied to these trends has been the growth of more fluid communities of lecturers and postdoctoral fellows with fixed-term early career posts in laboratories and colleges carrying a variety of teaching responsibilities and supporting research in an ever-widening range of specialities. The increase in numbers has left its inevitable mark on SCRs, which have found themselves, as in Oriel, in need of more space and facilities. Other changes, though, have been even more profound. As Robert Williams has observed with respect to chemistry, the competing demands of collegiate communities and the wider academic world have drawn many fellows 'out of the arms of a college and teaching' and into a closer involvement in laboratory-based or institute-based research financed by the university and external funding agencies.[77] Although such a tension already existed on a small scale in the nineteenth century, it has come to assume ever greater intensity in recent years.[78] To an unprecedented degree, fellows now have had to balance the time they devote to college duties against the often conflicting pressures of research groups and funding agencies calling for an ever greater flow of publications in their discipline's most prestigious journals.

With so many changes still in train, it is difficult to gauge how colleges will fare in the long run. What effect will the Higher Education Funding Council's Research Excellence Framework and other mechanisms for the

---

[77] Robert J. Williams, 'Recent Times, 1945–2005: A School of World Renown', in Williams, Allan Chapman, and John S. Rowlinson (eds.), *Chemistry at Oxford: A History from 1600 to 2005* (Cambridge, 2009), 195–291, esp. 198.
[78] Williams, 'Recent Times, 1945–2005', 202–3.

monitoring of research have on college life? And, with disciplines themselves and procedures for funding them both in flux, how easy will it be for colleges to retain the prominence they have traditionally had in Oxford? Such questions are especially relevant to the sciences. Oriel now finds itself with over a third of its fellows and of its undergraduates in scientific disciplines; among its large and rapidly expanding community of graduate students, the proportion is even higher, comfortably over 40 per cent in 2011. Compare these figures with the balance in the early 1960s, when only a fifth of the college's tutorial fellowships and a similar proportion of undergraduates were in science, and when the community of graduate students in all subjects was tiny, easily accommodated in the first, modest MCR at the foot of staircase II. In a sense, science has been a constant presence in the college since the fourteenth century. In the last fifty years, however, it has assumed a quite new visibility. While external influences in the university and the wider world of learning have done much to fashion the process, what has happened could still have been impeded by unreceptive policies within the college. But, especially since the 1980s and despite its status as one of the smaller colleges, Oriel has played its part, in certain areas a leading part, in the trends that have seen Oxford and its colleges transformed in their academic profile and priorities.

20

Government, Oxford, and Oriel, 1914–1990

John Stevenson

It is easy to romanticize the Oriel and the Oxford of which it was a part on the eve of the Great War. The sense of an Edwardian summer brought abruptly to an end by the cataclysm of the First World War and a world that would be changed for ever more is hard to escape. As with most deeply rooted 'myths' it is one which contains much truth amidst some exaggeration. Oriel College in 1914 was still a substantially independent body within a university which could regard itself as occupying a relatively sequestered place within the British polity, largely untrammelled by state or national concerns. One of the college's more famous alumni, A. J. P. Taylor (1924), looking back from the 1960s, somewhat wistfully suggested in his *English History, 1914–45*: 'Until August 1914, a sensible, law abiding Englishman could pass through life and hardly notice the existence of the state, beyond the post office and the policeman.'[1] It was a pardonable view to take, but even before the outbreak of the First World War the introduction of old age pensions, national insurance, heavier death duties, and wage boards demonstrated that this world was passing. Its passing, however, was to be greatly affected by the outbreak of war in 1914.

The Great War was to have both immediate and longer-term impacts. On the face of it, some of the short-term consequences, dramatic as they were at the time, notably the huge disruption of pre-war academic life in Oxford, were quickly repaired as college and university life revived after the peace. The tragic loss of Orielenses in the war, while memorialized and never to be forgotten, was quickly replaced by a return to normality as college rolls were replenished by returning servicemen and fresh generations spared the experience of the trenches. The war also had longer-term effects, many of them

---

[1] A. J. P. Taylor, *English History, 1914–45* (Oxford, 1965), 1.

perhaps only accelerating trends which would have manifested themselves in any event, but which became more insistent as a result of the war. As a result the war brought to the fore concerns which, in varying degrees, were to dominate the wider history of the college over the course of the twentieth century and into the twenty-first. Not least, the war had profound economic effects, in which changed post-war conditions encouraged a reappraisal and radical overhaul of college finances. Financial concerns would never be far from the minds of provosts and fellows in the future. The demands of war also precipitated government scrutiny of the university in the post-war Asquith Commission. An increasing recognition of a wider social responsibility foreshadowed issues that would come to affect Oriel as a college and its relationship both with the university and society at large. Questions about university and college finances, the relationship of the colleges to the university, the issue of admissions policy and selection to college places, the position of women within the university, the appropriateness and balance of the subjects taught, the place of the colleges and Oxford within the educational structure of the country as a whole were to be raised and, in practice, never to go away.

There was little inkling of what was to come. The editor of the recently founded *Oriel Record* remarked in September 1913: 'The Editor must not be blamed if this is a dull number. When "nothing happens" there is nothing to "record". Our subscribers in distant parts of the Empire have shown no great eagerness to send us their impressions and experiences, and our poets have, alas! left us.'[2] It was the past rather than the future which preoccupied the *Record* even into 1914, reflecting on the changes at Oriel in the century since 1813. The number of undergraduates in residence in 1914 was 132, more than double than a century earlier when all undergraduates and fellows lived in college and the college occupied only two quadrangles. The *Record* noted that the college must have been 'very full'. Oriel was now not only larger in terms of numbers but also more spacious with the recent formal acquisition of St Mary Hall and the completion of the 'New Buildings', the Rhodes Building, in September 1911. In 1814 Oriel was the fifth largest college; only Christ Church had numbers which ran into treble figures at 219 undergraduates; but Oriel had now fallen back into the middle rank. The university was larger too, with 4,025 undergraduates, compared with 1,047; there were 62 professors and 57 university readers and lecturers compared with only 22 a century earlier. In effect, in numerical terms, the university and several of its constituent parts had grown faster than Oriel over the preceding century, though the college was now in physical terms larger than it had ever been. The acquisition of St Mary Hall provided not

---

[2] OR (September 1913), 1.

only the opportunity to reconstruct the High Street frontage, but also to extend the library by converting the former chapel of St Mary Hall into an undergraduate library, connected to the senior library and now available for the use of 'the whole College'.[3]

As in the rest of the country, there was no premonition in the first part of 1914 of the impending cataclysm. At its April meeting the governing body authorized a college ball to be held in June 1914, and the only disturbance to routine activities appeared to be the mounting wave of strikes, which gave the first six months of the year the highest total of work days ever lost. Fears of a 'Triple Alliance' of miners, railwaymen, and transport workers which could paralyse the country were the talk of the spring and summer months of 1914. The college was not untouched by these alarms. In April the governing body authorized the treasurer to carry out the painting of the external woodwork during the long vacation, 'unless the imminence of labour disputes should render postponement desirable'.[4] There were other, even more important domestic preoccupations, notably the resignation of Provost Shadwell. The minutes of the April meeting contained a warm tribute to his services to the college, signed by the dean: 'The Fellows cannot forget that your work as Provost has been but the culmination of a long period—extending over more than fifty years of service to the College, as Fellow, Lecturer, Treasurer, and Provost. The debt in particular which the College owes you for your skilful management of its finances at a civilised period, your services as one of the College commissioners in drafting the new statutes, your preparation and publication of a register of the College, and the work which you have carried on for many years in making its old records available for the use of posterity—is inestimable.' Further thanks were added for 'your many very generous gifts for various College purposes... and the purchase of a cricket ground'. Finally the provost was thanked for maintaining 'in so exemplary a way the dignity of this high office which you are now vacating without any breach in those cordial relations between the Head and the Fellows which is so essential to the welfare of the College'.[5]

The summer term of 1914 ended traditionally with examinations, the college ball, and Encaenia. The last was notable because the majority of those receiving honorary doctorates were Germans. Among others, Richard Strauss received a doctorate in music and a doctorate in civil law was conferred on the German ambassador. Fatefully, this Encaenia celebrated the profound contribution of German culture to European art and science, and the growing internationalization of the community of scholarship and learning just at the point when those ties were to be savagely interrupted.

---

[3] OR (October 1914), 177–8.
[4] OCA GOV 4/A/7, Governing Body Minutes, meeting of 23/4 April 1914, 16.
[5] Governing Body Minutes, meeting of 23/4 April 1914, 29.

Oxford's links with Germany were close, with a steady stream of scholars seeking postgraduate experience at the prestigious German universities. Henry Tizard came to his fellowship at Oriel in 1911, the same year as he published a translation of the *Theoretische Chemie* of Walter Nernst, the scholar under whom he had worked during a winter semester in Berlin in 1908. The traffic was two-way: under the terms of the Rhodes Trust up to fifteen German Rhodes scholars were recruited to Oxford each year, usually spending two years at the university. As selection was in the Kaiser's personal gift, most of those who came to Oxford were from the nobility or other prominent families. The first of Oriel's pre-war cohort of German Rhodes scholars was Count Schwerin von Krosigk, who attended from 1905 to 1907, reading for a diploma in economics. He rowed for the college and was 'universally popular'. Later he was to achieve high office as long-serving Finance Minister in Nazi Germany.[6]

The war broke out on 4 August in the midst of the long vacation, so that most undergraduates and many fellows were away from Oriel during the first rush to enlist in August and September. While some enlisted from home, those in residence could join up by applying to the Oxford University Officer Training Corps (OTC) headquarters, particularly conveniently sited for Oriel men at 9 Alfred Street. Indeed on 2 August the OTC wrote to all its past and current members suggesting that they return to Oxford in the event of war. Nobody, however, had anticipated the fervour and scale of patriotic enthusiasm which overwhelmed the country in these two months. As John Keegan put it: 'It is the story of a spontaneous and genuinely popular mass movement which has no counterpart in the modern English-speaking world and perhaps could have none outside its own time and place: a time of intense, almost mystical patriotism...'[7] Patriotic fervour and Field Marshal Kitchener's call for 'the first hundred thousand' volunteers produced a huge response in which three-quarters of a million men flocked to the colours. In Oxford applicants for commissions threatened to overwhelm completely the pre-war machinery, with queues snaking down Alfred Street and onto the High. An undergraduate at Balliol, Harold Macmillan, summed up the mood of many: 'The general view was that it would be over by Christmas. Our major anxiety was by hook or by crook not to miss it.' To cope with the flood the vice-chancellor, T. B. Strong, dean of Christ Church, set up an ad hoc committee to process applications, chaired by himself, on which a pro-proctor and the assistant registrar also sat. Beginning a long stint of interviewing in early August, they had processed around two thousand

---

[6] J. M. Winter, 'Oxford and the First World War', in HUO viii. 3; for Tizard, see ODNB s.n.; for a brief outline of Schwerin von Krosigk's career, see his *Memoiren* (Stuttgart, 1977), and R. Wistrich, *Who's Who in Nazi Germany* (New York, 1982), 283.

[7] John Keegan, *The Face of Battle* (London, 1976), 217.

applicants by late September.[8] Younger fellows flocked to the colours too, Henry Tizard had sailed to Australia in July to attend the annual meeting of the British Association. News of the outbreak of war reached the ship as it approached Australia, and although the meeting went ahead, Tizard sailed back immediately at its conclusion to enlist. By October he had begun war service in the Royal Garrison Artillery at Portsmouth. The future fellow and provost G. N. Clark, in 1914 a prize fellow at All Souls and former member of the OTC, was commissioned when war broke out into the first battalion of the Post Office Rifles.[9]

In consequence the university was being drained of its life blood, the undergraduates. Oriel was particularly heavily affected. Whereas four colleges still had half their resident undergraduates at the end of the year, of 132 Oriel men in residence in 1913, 116 were in uniform by Christmas 1914. Ominously, at its meeting on 4 November the governing body already had to consider what its policy was towards placing memorials to individual undergraduates in the college chapel and had decided, in effect, that a collective memorial would be needed.[10] Although some flow of undergraduates continued into 1915, by the beginning of the academic year 1915–16 approximately half the scholars of most colleges were listed as away on military service. Oriel continued to contribute very heavily. As the *Oriel Record* for September 1915 noted: 'Starting, last Michaelmas, with thirty-five in residence, we have steadily and relentlessly diminished. One man after another has obtained a commission through the O.T.C. or found other war-work, and by the end of the Summer we found ourselves a dauntless fifteen.'[11] The process was inexorable, not only were existing undergraduates joining up, but also the supply of undergraduates from the schools was being choked off as pupils reaching the age to go to university were being recruited directly into the armed forces. By 1916 there were only 550 undergraduates in residence in the whole university, in 1917 there were 460, and in 1918 there were 369; those who were left behind were those men unfit for military service, foreign students, and women.

It was the last which added a hitherto unique addition to Oriel's experience and it came indirectly, what the *Record* remembered as 'the Great Revolution...the Amazonian invasion'. As they emptied, the university's buildings and colleges became targets for government requisitioning, and by 1915 several had been co-opted for military use. Colleges such as New College, Brasenose, and Christ Church were called on to provide billets for

---

[8] J. M. Winter, 'Oxford and the First World War', 8; J. Stevenson, *British Society, 1914–45* (London, 1984), 49–50.
[9] For Clark, see ODNB s.n.
[10] OCA GOV 4/A/7 Governing Body Minutes, 4 November 1914, 34.
[11] OR (September 1915), 238–9.

troops and cadets, while the Examination Schools had been cleared of desks and chairs and converted into a hospital complete with a mortuary in the basement. As casualties mounted the demand for hospital accommodation soared, and Somerville's position next door to the Radcliffe Infirmary made it a prime candidate for further accommodation. At the end of Hilary Term 1915 the Somerville Council was alerted to the possibility of requisition and the arrival of the Administrator of the Southern General Hospital on Sunday, 28 March to make a full inspection left little doubt that Somerville would have to seek temporary accommodation for the duration of the war. Somerville's treasurer had unofficially sounded out the provost about the possibility of renting the St Mary Hall quadrangle which now stood virtually empty. Events moved quickly; arrangements were made for the principal and bursar of Somerville to visit Oriel on Monday morning, and a formal application by Somerville was considered by a special meeting of the provost and fellows of Oriel the following day. By that evening a letter had been written and received agreeing to the occupation of the quadrangle by Somerville for the duration of the war and three months afterwards, 'except only the Junior Library and coal cellar'.[12] The 'Revolution' was accomplished, the *Record* noted, 'bloodlessly': 'Some people thought it was the millennium, others that was "the beginning of the end" (was there ever an event which wasn't that?). What happened was really very simple...The ladies knocked, and the male doors were opened. Mr Tod and the Treasurer chivalrously retired, the J.C.R. became a dining-hall, the bathrooms reeled back into kitchen ranges, and the thing was done. Mrs Grundy was appeased by two massive walls of brick in the passages between the quads. We are glad indeed that it was possible.' According to the Somerville version the 'fortifications' were installed 'to allay the Provost's expressed fears of the possibility of any "Pyramus and Thisbe" incidents', though no record exists of this concern from the Oriel side. More prosaically, the occupation earned the college £400 p.a. in rent and payments for all gas, electricity, and water consumed, a useful addition to college finances as other sources dwindled.[13]

The way Oriel as a community maintained itself during the war and the story of its 'cohabitation' with Somerville belong to another chapter, as does its record of service and its tragic toll of loss. But the ending of the war brought with it profound consequences for the nation as a whole, consequences which Oxford and Oriel could not escape. One was financial, for the ending of the war brought to a head economic problems which had been developing for some time for the university and its colleges. College incomes had been diminished for several decades before the war by the depression in

---

[12] P. Adams, *Somerville for Women: An Oxford College, 1879–1993* (Oxford, 1996), 87–90; OCA GOV 4/A/7, Governing Body Minutes, 30 March 1915, 66.
[13] OR (September 1915), 239; Adams, *Somerville for Women*, 89.

agricultural prices, caused by the vast inflows of cheap food from America and the colonies which reduced college rental incomes and made land a relatively poor return compared to other investments. Even before 1914 'smart' money was being directed by some landowners towards better investments in government stock or general equities. Oxford colleges had hitherto proved relatively conservative in their approach to investments, but losses of tuition fees and wartime inflation had taken their toll. Moreover the university's revenues were proving totally insufficient to maintain the expansion of its facilities, particularly in the area of scientific research. If the war had proved anything it was the growing importance of science which had played a critical part in the Allied victory. The enormous advances in metallurgy, engineering, electronics, chemistry, physics, and almost every branch of technology had left a permanent imprint on the intellectual culture of the country and upon the demands placed upon its higher educational institutions. Oriel had its own exponent of these developments in Henry Tizard, who was quickly plucked from mundane training duties with the Royal Garrison Artillery at Portsmouth to work as an experimental equipment officer on a range of technical issues with the Royal Flying Corps, including the development of bombsights, testing new aircraft, and experiments with aviation fuels. When the Royal Air Force was established in 1918 he was appointed assistant controller of research and experiments at the newly created Air Ministry. The transition of Tizard from Oriel don to test pilot within a matter of months, and by the end of the war, aged 33, to a position at the cutting edge of research in one of the most dramatic fields of scientific and technological developments, spoke volumes for the impact of war in emphasizing the role of science in the modern world. But there were relatively few Tizards about and the war had highlighted an issue which was current even before the Great War's unprecedented demands, namely that Great Britain was falling behind countries such as Germany and the United States in scientific and technological education. The war gave these fears fresh urgency. The government set up a committee to inquire into the position of natural science in the educational system of Great Britain and its report in 1918 recommended the removal of Greek as a necessary subject in Oxford's preliminary examinations, a 'large expenditure of public money...to equip the universities for their work in pure and in applied science', and increased grants from public funds to permit substantial reduction of their fees, thereby widening access to the ancient universities. These concerns were matched by the problems the university itself recognized it had in funding the expanding area of scientific research. In June 1919 the vice-chancellor was authorized to apply for assistance from the government. It was a momentous step and one which many felt threatened the independence of the university and ultimately the colleges, but it was one, rehearsing arguments that would echo through the decades thereafter, which recognized that without government support the university could not remain a centre of academic excellence across a broad range of disciplines. Oxford, it was felt by the majority who voted for the decree—126 votes to 88—needed to be adequately represented in the expanding fields of science, medicine, and technology.[14]

Fears of loss of independence, however, were sharpened by the conditions placed upon the granting of monies from the University Grants Commission, for any government grant was dependent upon the university's readiness to collaborate with an inquiry into its resources. The commission, headed by H. H. Asquith, the former liberal Prime Minister, conjured up many fears. A formidable head of steam was building up in the immediate aftermath of the war for a more democratic and egalitarian society from which education was unlikely to be excluded. The Fourth Reform Act of 1918 had brought universal male suffrage for the first time, and votes for women over 30, trebling the size of the electorate. War memorials currently being set up in every village, town, place of learning, or employment were testament to the scale of sacrifice involved in winning the war. The nation's resources had been strained up to and almost beyond their limits. Manpower barrels had been scraped, trade unions appeased and expanded greatly in numbers, and women given a vastly expanded role in industry and other walks of life for which the vote was seen by many of them as only partial recompense. Promises of 'homes for heroes' and a 'fit land for heroes to live in' had been instrumental in bringing the Lloyd George coalition government to power in the General Election. Whatever disillusion was to spread about these promises later, in 1919 a group of ambitious young ministers were beginning to grapple with the implementation of 'reconstruction' in an atmosphere in which the war had decisively altered how some people regarded the proper functioning of the state and what it could and should achieve. The later master of University College, William Beveridge, believed that the country had learnt as much in the four years of war about the 'art of government' as it had about the 'art of flying'. The president of the Board of Education, H. A. L. Fisher, a New College classicist turned historian and now MP for the Combined Universities, was also a former vice-chancellor of Sheffield University and familiar with civic universities somewhat more directly integrated with the needs of the state, industry, and business. He was determined to reform the universities and had become 'convinced that Oxford and Cambridge could not continue to discharge their functions or to cope with the developing requirements of applied science without help from

---

[14] For a summary of these general developments see V. H. H. Green, 'The University and the Nation', in J. Prest (ed.), *The Illustrated History of Oxford University* (Oxford, 1993), 72; for the genesis of the Asquith Commission, see J. Prest, 'The Asquith Commission, 1919–1922', in HUO viii. 27–9.

the state'.[15] Thus the Asquith Commission was set up in an atmosphere ripe—too ripe some thought—with possibilities for radical reform. As the university historian has noted: 'The Asquith Commission was confronted with the demands of organised labour for a place in the university sun, and for an end to the monopoly of higher education by purchase. The commissioners spent a great deal of time discussing ways and means of lowering the costs of a college education...'[16] There was care to represent the views of the four women's colleges through a women's representative, Emily Penrose of Somerville, and of the Workers' Educational Association, through Albert Mansbridge, the son of a Battersea carpenter. As well as canvassing the views of the university and the colleges, outside bodies such as the Labour Party, the Co-operative Union, the WEA, the Headmasters' Conference, and The National Union of Teachers submitted views. When interrogated, some of these bodies were not only implicitly critical of the university's present arrangements but in practice were calling for radical change. Complaints about different and confusing entrance examinations from the headmasters and headmistresses were the least of it, representatives of organized labour called for free university education, the pooling of college estates and investments into a single fund, and for continuous state control over Oxford and Cambridge. Faced with such radical proposals not for nothing did the *Oriel Record* express worries about the future of the college system, and fears that some of 'the reforms suggested would tend to reduce the colleges to the position of mere boarding houses'.[17]

In the event, the findings of the Commission were conservative in tone. Critically, they left the collegiate structure of the university largely intact and the autonomy of colleges only marginally diminished. Science received its first grant of £30,000, rising to £60,000 in 1923–4, and reaching £110,000 on the eve of the Second World War. Plans were laid for fifteen acres in the Parks to be allocated for new science buildings, so that practical instruction in chemistry and physics could be provided in modern laboratories belonging to the university, as was already the case in Cambridge. Here, a significant corner had been turned, the commissioners recognizing that 'there could be no greater or more disastrous mistake than for the State to encourage or permit the development of Oxford as a "Humanities" and Cambridge as a "Science" university'. The place of science at Oxford was assured and science undergraduates and dons remained, even with the new university laboratories, integrated in the collegiate structure. No hard decisions were taken about the respective powers of faculties as opposed to colleges, permitting the colleges to retain their traditionally powerful position. University-appointed

---

[15] Prest, 'Asquith Commission', 29–30.
[16] Green, 'University and Nation', in Prest (ed.), *Illustrated History*, 72.
[17] Prest, 'Asquith Commission', 35–6; OR (September 1920), 163.

professors were to be given a place in a college and tutors appointed by colleges would become university lecturers. Apart from some state provision for pensions, little was changed in the staffing position of Oxford; college-controlled appointments effectively provided the backbone of the university's teaching provision. Claims for fairer access to the university only went so far as to recommend the institution of a university entrance examination and provision for the university to send undergraduates down for idleness. State scholarships could now provide a route for a few able people of any background to attend the university, but paying the going rate for residence in college. Nor was Oriel's temporary wartime experiment in co-residence to be taken up on a permanent scale; single-sex women's colleges were to be sustained and offered a grant for ten years to ease their financial situation, but with the added suggestion that the number of women students should remain limited. Neither co-residence nor numerical equality were on the agenda.[18]

If the last point only reinforced the view that faced with big problems the Asquith Commission made only 'tentative steps towards their conclusion', the commission effectively shaped the university's future and that of its constituent colleges for decades to come, not least by declining some of the more radical proposals being canvassed. But within the evolutionary model adopted those steps were deliberate. The number of science graduates would double by 1939 and their place within college and university life grow in importance compared to the pre-1914 world. The university's decision in 1920 to allow women to matriculate for degrees, taken independently of the commission, and the financial support for the women's colleges ensured that female representation within the university was assured. Other developments represented partial modernization. Convocation had decided to drop compulsory Greek, admissions requirements were tightened up, and statutory retirement ages for fellows, heads of houses, and professors introduced. Academic matters were not entirely neglected with the introduction, after much discussion, of the new degree of 'modern Greats', philosophy, politics, and economics. The decision to set up a Committee of Advanced Studies to promote graduate studies for the newly instituted D.Phil. degree marked an attempt by Oxford to catch up with German and American universities in the provision of advanced research in arts and sciences, setting in train developments which would grow through subsequent decades.

Oriel found itself in the vanguard of one of the major upheavals consequent upon the war and the Asquith Commission, namely the sale of its landed estates. The wider remit of university reform taken on by the Asquith Commission, and the consequences thereof, obscured its original object, which was to examine the financial resources of the university in response to its

[18] Prest, 'Asquith Commission', HUO viii. 40–2.

claim for public funding for the sciences. This in itself caused considerable concern amongst some university circles who feared that the more radical voices making their claims in post-war Britain would point to the Oxford colleges' extensive ownership of land, question whether they were fit and proper landlords at the same time as they were claiming public funds, and force their sale. A committee of Oxford bursars defended land as a basis for college finances because, they contended, 'no investment was likely, in the long run, to be as remunerative as land'. Moreover it gave them a measure of independence unlikely to be matched by other kinds of investments. If their endowments consisted only of 'stocks and securities' it could be argued 'that the colleges were, in effect...glorified hostels...that they ought to be under the central management of some University Delegacy...and that the Tutors and Lecturers of the Colleges should become Recognised Teachers of the University and be appointed thereby...the College system would thus be destroyed', they concluded. But these fears were set aside as landowners of every kind, private, corporate, and collegiate, took advantage of the relatively favourable conditions created by the First World War to bring to an end centuries of estate management and, in recent years, relatively poor returns. Tenants and farmers had profited from high wartime prices and were in a position to pay higher prices per acre than for many years, but landowners, including the Oxford colleges, had often been unable or unwilling to raise rents to match the new prosperity. The result was a deluge of land sales: half a million acres were on sale by the summer of 1919, and a million sold by the end of the year. As *The Times* claimed in 1920, 'England is changing hands...'. The *Estates Gazette* concluded that by 1921 something of the order of a quarter of England had been sold, the largest and most rapid transfer of land since the dissolution of the monasteries, and possibly since the Norman Conquest.[19]

Among Oxford colleges, seven of which took part in this avalanche of disposals, Oriel was not only a participant but was in the lead as the most active seller. Sales started in April 1919 with the authorization in November at a special college meeting to commence negotiations for the sale of all estates outside Oxford with existing tenants to be offered an opportunity to purchase. According to a report compiled in April 1922 by the treasurer, the estimate for proceeds of £150,000 was substantially exceeded, with a final anticipated total of £185,900 (approximately equal to £18 million today). Invested in 5 per cent government stock, the proceeds yielded an investment income of £9,200 p.a. A calculation based on the past ten years' external income by the treasurer showed that taking into the account the heavy outgoings on landed property, amounting to over 40 per cent of

---

[19] J. P. Dunbabin, 'Finance since 1914', in HUO viii. 656–9; for the national background see Stevenson, *British Society*, 332–4.

the value of their rents, the college was £6,000 a year better off under the new arrangements, approximately doubling its net income.[20]

While noting the considerable increase in income, the *Record* also recognized that it was the end of an era. It was pleased to note that much of the land had been bought by existing tenants:

But the old days when the Fellows of the College had the privilege of the first shootings over the College land, and exercised it, have gone for ever, as have the cheery entertainments in the College Hall when the tenants came up to pay their rents, and were regaled with the College 'strong beer'—hence called 'Farmers' Joy'— punch, clay pipes, &c., to say nothing of many speeches in which the College present belauded the tenants, and the tenants reciprocated the compliment. Gone, too, are the biennial pilgrimages to Bath, when such of the Fellows as pleased went down to collect their rents and hold a Court at the Manor of Swainswick. Formerly the Fellows used to go on horseback, and a formidable pair of pistols is, or was, preserved in the Treasury, which were carried on these occasions for the protection of the Treasurer and his rents.[21]

The end of an era indeed. In being at the forefront in selling its estates, the college had taken a bold step, one which undoubtedly in the short term eased post-war financial pressures. With the benefit of hindsight it was a decision which could be criticized as the development boom after the Second World War greatly inflated land values and cast the disposals in a new light. One of the estates sold for £4,650 in 1921 was valued at over £1 million in 1987, a multiple well above the general rate of inflation. But these new receipts allowed the college to enter the inter-war years with a degree of confidence. Gloom had been expressed in the darkest days of the war by the *Record* that 'with high prices and heavy taxation parents may have less to spend on the education of their sons' and to expect 'more Americans and foreigners, and the research student who does not intend to take the ordinary degree'. These were prophetic words, but the university soon began to fill up again after the cessation of hostilities.[22] There were already 1,357 undergraduates in residence by February 1919 and 5,689 in residence by 1920. By March 1921 Oriel was declared to be 'full to overflowing' with 165 up, of whom 65 were in lodgings 'some of them as far out as Summertown'.[23]

With the war over and the modest reforms of the Asquith Commission being assimilated, there were few great external interruptions to the tenor of college life in the inter-war years. Some excitement, however, was caused when the affairs of the outside world erupted in the 1926 General Strike. The

---

[20] OCA GOV 5/A1: Reports, 1903–47, No. 13, April 1922, 1–4; Dunbabin, 'Finance since 1914', 659; E. Vallis, 'Oriel's Estates and Interests in Land, 1324–1991', OR (1991), 32–57.
[21] OR (March 1921), 4.
[22] OR (October 1917), 372; Dunbabin, 'Finance since 1914', HUO viii. 659.
[23] OR (March 1921), 3.

majority of undergraduates offered enthusiastic support for the government in what was widely seen as a national emergency when the TUC called out millions of trade unionists in support of the miners' dispute with the coal-owners. A. J. P. Taylor, then in his second year, recalled: 'It was August 1914 all over again. One of the departing heroes even said to me, "I wonder if I shall ever come back again" quite in the spirit of Rupert Brooke.' The college authorities were supportive; on 5 May the governing body decided that any undergraduate wishing to be enrolled for government service must first register with the dean, but would be granted leave of absence 'for so long as required'.[24] The *Record* welcomed it as 'a pleasing interlude in the somewhat jaded activities of ordinary life', commenting that: 'Certainly the hundred and twenty odd Oriel men who had dispersed to various fields returned with a jingling of coins and an air of satisfaction which proved conclusively that their time had not been wasted.' The Oriel undergraduates found themselves deployed in three ways. One section were formed into a group of Oriel Special Constables, another worked at the Oxfordshire milk dump at Aynho, while a third group were deployed in London at Hays Wharf, helping to move vital supplies. Although the majority of the undergraduates threw themselves into the fray on the government's side, not all did. According to his later testimony, Taylor was one of the relatively few undergraduates whose sympathies led him to seek to help the strikers and sought 'permission' from the dean to go down. The dean, J. W. C. Wand, later bishop of London, was perplexed but enlightened: 'others have gone down to do their duty. I suppose you are entitled to do what you think is yours.'[25]

Outside events, international, national, or at university level, did little to disturb the procession of Oriel's academic, sporting, and domestic affairs during the inter-war years. But the college could hardly regard itself as cut off from the outside world through the influence of its members beyond the college walls. The worsening economic crisis which followed the Wall Street crash in 1929 was registered with the election of six Oriel men as MPs in the General Election which followed the formation of a National Government in the summer of 1931.[26] The *Record* in 1932 also boasted ten bishops of the Church of England, and was moved to the larger claim that Oriel men were dominant in the government of Nigeria and the Sudan and active in central and southern Africa, North America, and India.[27] The progress of other college men nearer to home was noted; the *Record* duly marked the elevation of Count Schwerin von Krosigk to the position of Finance Minister in the German government in June 1932, a post he was to retain until 1945, succeeding Ribbentrop as Foreign Minister in the closing days of the Nazi

---

[24] Taylor, *Personal History*, 102.
[25] OR (June 1926), 328–30; Taylor, *Personal History*, 103.
[26] OR (January 1932), 172.   [27] OR (January 1933), 270.

regime.²⁸ Nobody could foresee such events, but harbingers of a troubled future were conveyed in the reports of visits and residence abroad by Oriel men in the pages of the *Record*. In May 1934 Germany was reported to be in the grip of 'a spiritual revolution', the unemployed put to work, and 'winter help' offered to those in hardship. Another reported the transformation of Florence under fascist rule, seen in its new 'squat modernistic' railway station and ban on the sounding of horns, enforced by notices on every street corner that 'Disciplina' means 'Silenzio' and ten lire fines. Uniforms were much in evidence and a fascist organization ran all non-academic activities for university students. The Soviet Union in 1935 was found to have no bath plugs but evinced 'an atmosphere of haste and impermanence', a quickened 'tempo of living... which seeks to introduce the spirit of the Five Year Plan in Four'. The USSR had much of interest: 'In organised planning, she has given the world an unparalleled example. In the field of judicial administration there is no country which cannot learn something from her... there is probably no country in the world where the law is more closely related to justice... In their treatment of women... their system is in advance of most nations.' But the correspondent also noted a great emphasis on military preparations and a new *realpolitik*: 'The ideals have shifted here; for the moment revolution abroad is merely a means for securing the safety of Soviet frontiers, instead of an end in itself.'²⁹

The Oriel which entered the Second World War was still substantially recognizable as that which had seen its members go to war twenty-five years earlier. Although there were more undergraduates in residence, 193 compared with 132 in 1913, the physical appearance of the college was largely unchanged. Expansion in undergraduate numbers had been accommodated by doubling up in the larger sets and more undergraduates living out. More reading spaces had been made available in the library, with seats now for twenty readers.³⁰ The fellowship had expanded, partly on the basis of the increase in funds made available from the land sales after the Great War. Fellows now numbered seventeen and there were ten lecturers to assist in teaching. Externally, there was little change in the appearance of the college, apart from minor alterations and refurbishments. The most noticeable to someone entering the college in 1939, compared with 1914, was the new layout of the first quad, paved and grassed the previous year, replacing the gravel familiar to earlier generations.

The experience of the college in the Second World War was to repeat many of the features of the First but with significant variations. For one thing,

---

[28] OR (June 1933), 281.
[29] OR (June 1934), 375–9 (Germany); OR (January 1935), 419–21 (USSR); OR (June 1935), 18–20 (Italy).
[30] OR (June 1934), 370.

European war did not burst out of a cloudless sky as it had in August 1914. Preparations for war began well before it was declared. In January 1939 an Air Raid Precautions Committee was set up: in response, the windows of the hall were taped up and sandbags put around the arch outside. Two rooms were designated as indoor shelters and an attempt was made to secure an outdoor shelter in Merton Fields with other colleges. A first aid kit was acquired, and thirty or forty tin hats for use by college personnel. On 1 March the college was informed that the university had put colleges at the disposal of the government in the event of war. The threat of bombing meant the dispersal of government offices from London to safer towns and cities, of which Oxford was one.[31] In effect the college was put on alert that its premises could be requisitioned for whatever purposes the government might wish. Moreover, the introduction of conscription via the Military Training Act in spring 1939 was a signal that the 'total' mobilization of manpower and resources only painfully reached towards the end of the Great War was to be introduced from the outset. Although there was no enthusiastic rush to the recruiting stations comparable to 1914, many offered themselves for military service voluntarily before conscription took its inevitable toll. By the beginning of 1940, the number of undergraduates in residence was down to 132. Of the 193 in residence the summer of 1939, no less than 115 offered themselves for military service and 'at least' 89 were serving in Her Majesty's forces by early 1940. A core of 52 foreign students, civil servants, and students in reserved subjects, such as medicine, remained to be taught with those freshmen to come still too young for military service. By Hilary Term 1940 the college took on a increasingly disused aspect. Although there were 132 undergraduates on the books, only 22 undergraduates were actually living in college, 43 were in Hertford, and the rest were in lodgings; the greater part of the college was empty, reserved for occupation by whomsoever the government chose to send it. By November the college still had about the same number of undergraduates on the books, but was expected to go down to 80 or 90 during 1941. In fact Oriel was never to plumb the depths of the Great War, when at one point there were only seven undergraduates. While the Middle and St Mary Hall quadrangles were beginning to be occupied by various government departments, a semblance of academic life was maintained with as many as 84 undergraduates in Trinity Term 1943, 45 of them in their first year.[32] Thereafter about half of those in residence were 'probationers' who came up, free of normal entrance requirements, for six months before being drafted into one of the fighting services. Their short courses, in which military training was combined with part-time study, bore little relationship to the pre-war honours curriculum. But these

[31] OCA GOV 4/A/9, Governing Body Minutes, meeting of 11 January 1939, 260.
[32] OR (January 1940), 55; OR (January 1944), 239.

service 'cadets' were matriculated, were housed in the college or digs, and lived under academic discipline. Many were to return after the war to undertake a full degree course. The register of college members engaged in the war had reached 318 by the middle of the war and 14 college servants were also in the services. By then six fellows were in various forms of war work; in compensation, in 1941 General de Gaulle had been elected a member of common room.[33]

The college housed a variety of tenants, including the Prison Service. It also provided rest periods for tired Auxiliary Fire Service workers from London and 'oldish Blitzed men' from Bristol. Oriel's other principal tenants of the Middle and St Mary Hall quadrangles, the Ministry of Aircraft Production and the British Council, remained right up to beginning of Michaelmas Term 1945, but vacated them in time for a relatively rapid return to more normal numbers; 115 undergraduates in Michaelmas 1945 and 142 by Hilary Term 1946.[34] If the college had seen a less grievous diminution in its tutorial numbers than in the Great War, it had also suffered a smaller, but still heavy price in the loss of lives. The War Memorial at the High Street entrance to the college bore the names of seventy-two members of the college who died on active service. If Oriel and the university had feared a repeat of the terrible blood-letting of 1914–18, there was the additional fear of huge damage and casualties by bombing. In light of the Blitz on London and other major cities from September 1941, there was much to dread. Although other 'historic' cities, such as Bath, York, and Exeter, were not to escape heavy damage, some of them in the deliberately designed 'Baedeker Raids' against cultural targets in retaliation for British bombing of German cities, Oxford escaped. A system of fire-watching was, however, maintained by the college in cooperation with its temporary residents throughout the war. Its 'zeal and efficiency' under Kenneth Franklin and Billy Pantin was proved when the library was nearly burnt down on New Year's Eve 1943 not through enemy bombs but by a defective flue. The alert was quickly given and what might have proved a great tragedy was confined to a small fire. The structure of the library was saved and the bulk of the books removed by the combined efforts of dons and undergraduates from Oriel and other colleges. Ironically, wartime precautions saved the library from the more severe consequences of a similar fire in the peaceful conditions of 1949.[35]

The war too had wider repercussions with which Oxford and ultimately the college would be affected. Wartime collectivism had given birth to a more

---

[33] OR (January 1942), 173.   [34] OR (January 1942), 174; OR (April 1946), 3–4.
[35] OR (June 1941), 133–4 noted that the varied inhabitants of all three quadrangles were 'pretty well co-ordinated' for fire-fighting and fire-watching and that 'roof-climbing has ceased to have the charm of the forbidden', though undergraduates have 'shown themselves very willing to do it as a patriotic duty'. For the fire, see OR (January 1944), 239.

democratic and egalitarian spirit of which the Butler Education Act of 1944 and the Attlee government's creation of a welfare state were the most obvious manifestations. No less important was the growing recognition that science had played a vital part in winning the war, enhancing its prestige both in the country and in the universities. Oriel was particularly proud of its connections through Tizard in the wartime scientific effort and its involvement in medicine; Provost Ross noted that the growth of medical studies was one of the 'most remarkable' features of recent Oxford history, much of it owing to Lord Nuffield's benefactions, and doubted 'if any college is taking so large a part in this as Oriel'.[36] Although there was no equivalent to the Asquith Commission which had followed the Great War, similar influences were at work. Free secondary education for all and the provision of grants for university education opened the way for wider access to Oxford. Meanwhile the college breathed a sigh of relief on obtaining the full possession of its buildings and the resumption of something like normal conditions. But in welcoming two new members of the senior common room with experience of university administration, the new provost, G. N. Clark, noted ruefully the changed circumstances in which the college was now operating in having to find its way in a minefield of new regulations and negotiate with goverment departments on a wide range of issues, covering almost every aspect of the college's activities, ranging from the intake of students to permission to undertake building work.[37]

Nonetheless, by Trinity Term 1948 there were 253 undergraduates on the college list and the *Record* noted with some satisfaction that there were more applications than vacancies. By 1949 numbers had climbed still further to 263 and admissions looked healthy, though the future was now recognized as dependent on decisions about university grants by the Minister of Education. Moreover, as another sign of the times, conscription was reported as 'creating havoc' with entrance examination arrangements.[38] Havoc of a different kind was in the offing, however, when having survived the ravages war largely unscathed, a fire broke out in the library late in the afternoon of the last Monday of full term, 7 March 1949. Prompt action saved a greater disaster than might have occurred. As soon as smoke was seen rising from the roof of the library and the alarm raised 'a horde of undergraduates descended like locusts upon the two Senior Common Rooms and within what appeared to be seconds, and cannot have been more than ten minutes, they had removed furniture, pictures, books, carpets and every object thy could lay their hands on'. The damage, however, was substantial and the loss of books serious. Thirty early modern editions were lost as well as two of the three leaves of

---

[36] OR (January 1942), 172–3.   [37] OR (1948), 7–8.   [38] OR (1948), 8–9; (1949), 7.

the fourteenth-century list of the college's books. In addition, the flames consumed Gilbert White's spectacles and walking stick. With the largest number of undergraduates it had ever had, temporary library facilities had to be arranged urgently. Fortunately Merton College offered its facilities and Blackwell's offered a ground floor room in Oriel Street as a temporary book store with further storage in the New Bodleian. The final reckoning of losses did not come until 1957 when the last of the insurance money was spent. The total loss of books was 311; 3,405 were repaired, 617 not repaired but hidden away, and another thousand were less badly damaged.[39]

As the college moved into the world of austerity and the straitened circumstances of Attlee's Britain, there was a growing need to do everything possible to shore up college finances. Conferences were being admitted as early as the long vacation of 1946 and three were organized for 1947 for the Easter and long vacations, while German prisoners were housed for a week in January. Threats of another kind came from the proposals aired in wartime and, later, crystallized in Thomas Sharpe's *Oxford Replanned* (1948) to relieve the pressure on Oxford's chronic traffic problem by driving an inner ring road through Christ Church Meadow. Provost Phelps had lamented in 1935 that 'the roar of traffic in the main streets is in painful contrast to the peace of the old days'.[40] The so-called 'Merton Mall' was designed to relieve pressure on the High Street. Faced, however, with a choice between the thunder of traffic on the High Street and the preservation of the Meadow, the governing body saw 'many objections' to the Mall, later making it clear to the City Council that 'it preferred an intermediate ring road to an inner relief road'. The problem of the danger traffic on the High Street posed to pedestrians could be accommodated by 'a subway...across the High Street near St. Mary's Church'. The battle over the Christ Church Meadow Road was one of the most protracted and bitterly contested environmental and planning sagas of the post-war era, not finally concluded until the Meadow scheme was abandoned in the mid-1960s after concerted pressure from colleges, the university, and prominent persons both within and outside Oxford.[41]

The post-war years were to see increasing pressures on collegiate life. One was numbers. The immediate years after the war saw a flood of returning ex-servicemen coinciding with the provisions for the public funding of the universities. Student numbers had risen from 4,163 in 1923–4 to just over 5,000 on the eve of the Second World War. After 1945 numbers rose rapidly to 7,323 in 1949–50 and to nearly 11,000 by 1970–1. Oriel shared in this

---

[39] OR (1949), 8–9; OR (1951), 10–11; OR (1957), 7–8.
[40] *Oxford Magazine*, 9 May 1935, 568.
[41] OCA, Governing Body Minute Book, 1941–57, 15 May 1946, 140; 7 March 1951, 208, for the Meadow scheme see R. C. Whiting, 'University and Locality', in HUO viii. 568–75.

expansion, from approximately 150 undergraduates in the mid-1920s, to 192 on the eve of the Second World War, and 263 in 1949–50. The strain was beginning to tell both on teaching resources and on accommodation. The number of fellows in 1951 was eighteen, only one more than in 1939, while shortage of lodgings for undergraduates in college could only partly be met by further dividing traditional 'sets' into bedsitters, soon to become the norm of college accommodation. The shortage of accommodation in Oxford generally—at the height of the post-war housing shortage—and subsequently the difficulties of finding undergraduate 'digs' in a still rapidly expanding Oxford forced Oriel, like other colleges, to extend the search for extra rooms and ultimately think about new buildings whether on site or elsewhere in Oxford. The problem was apparent when post-war restrictions on the supply of building materials compromised the ability of the college to reach the numbers it desired. The *Record* reported in 1950 that the college had been forced to admit twenty fewer undergraduates than the previous year; 'We hope that the numbers may fall still lower, so that the strain on our accommodation and teaching resources may be relieved; but like other Oxford Colleges, we find that in the interests of our finances we have to keep them above the old level. We are making considerable progress with preparations for a rearrangement of the buildings on the opposite side of Oriel Street, which is to give us more undergraduate rooms, better lecture rooms, and more revenue...' Unfortunately the programme was frustrated: 'the officials in the various Ministries have got to work and seen to it that nothing much can happen before this time next year.' Elsewhere, however, work went on apace. The library repairs were nearly completed, the chapel redecorated, the porters' lodge remodelled, and 'various reforms made in baths and heating apparatus'. But, putting all in perspective, the War Memorial at the High Street entrance was also completed. Those commemorated, seventy-two in all, would have appreciated Provost Clark's summation that amidst austerity 'Although everyone is hard at it, the place is full of life'.[42]

The library was ready to be brought back into full use by Michaelmas Term 1950, but tensions between a desirable size for the college numbers and its financial needs were openly expressed in the *Record* for 1951. Numbers had fallen back to 209: 'about the level we think desirable for the College, though it is to be expected that we shall have to exceed it somewhat for financial reasons.' It was no surprise then to find the college fuller in 1952, at 220 and further increase expected: 'Like other colleges we find that we cannot meet the perpetually increasing costs of our buildings and services without adding to our income from fees.' Worries that increasing numbers might be compromising Oxford's traditional tutorial system were already

---

[42] OR (1950), 8–9.

being voiced in the press but were firmly rebutted: 'Some of the newspapers have said in recent years that the Oxford tutorial system has been abandoned, or has broken down, but, so far as Oriel is concerned, there is no foundation whatsoever for such statements.'[43] Expansion into the houses in Oriel Street took numbers back up to 241 by 1954 and an appeal launched the following year had amongst its principal objectives the development of the Oriel Street site, as well as 'maintenance and improvement of college buildings', increased funding for fellowships, and the boathouse. The kind of pressure the college was increasingly coming under was revealed in 1958 when the governing body noted the University Grants Commission's support for additional residential accommodation to which the college responded by aiming to provide 177 sets. A target number of approximately 270 undergraduates was thought 'right' for the college, balancing finances, teaching resources, and 'available accommodation'.[44] Oxford began to sprout new buildings and quadrangles. Wadham, St John's, and St Edmund Hall had substantial new buildings by the end of the 1950s and the 1960s saw new college building on an unprecedented scale. Oriel remained for the time being content with its expansion into Oriel Street but proposals for a new quadrangle on the Island Site were already being aired by the early 1960s, though not to be fully realized until later. Expansion and refurbishment of college accommodation went on apace as colleges competed for conference trade and sought to catch up with new standards of plumbing, heating, and wiring. Many undergraduates continued to live out, in Oriel and elsewhere, over 40 per cent as late as 1968. Dedicated 'digs', often with meals provided, were becoming a thing of the past, however, and in 1970 the university abandoned its rule that junior members living out should occupy only approved accommodation. Increasingly, undergraduates, and a growing body of graduates, rented houses and flats wherever they could find them, giving a new freedom to 'living out' but also bringing the need for student accommodation directly into competition with the rest of the inhabitants of the city. The rising cost of housing in Oxford as well as the need to provide for further expansion set all colleges, Oriel included, on the path of providing as much college accommodation as possible. For Oriel this was to mean the full development of the Island Site into a fourth quadrangle and the purchase of the Rectory Road building, with the stated objective by the early twenty-first century of housing all undergraduates in college accommodation. By that time (2005) the undergraduate target number was 280, in fact only seventeen more that in the post-war 'bulge'. The difference now was to be that Oriel would be able to house its students for the whole of their undergraduate career.

---

[43] OR (1952), 11.
[44] Governing Body Minute Book, 1957–64, 5 May 1958, 20; OR (1958), 7.

What in another context would be called 'the wind of change' was also sweeping through other aspects of the university and affecting how the college operated. The Second World War had enormously increased the prestige of science and engineering. By the 1950s popular war films celebrated the achievements of men like Barnes-Wallis of the 'bouncing bomb' used in the 'Dambuster' raid, and 'Spitfire' Mitchell. No one growing up in post-war Britain could ignore the importance of war-winning developments like radar, jet-propulsion, antibiotics, and nuclear physics, and the increasing confidence of scientists to reshape the world about them. These influenced new generations of schoolmasters and their pupils and, in turn, demand for university places. As a result, science became more prominent at Oxford, as elsewhere in the university sector. At Oriel scientists made up approximately a sixth of undergraduates by the mid-1950s, reaching almost a quarter in 1959. By 1961 an expansion of provision of science at the college was anticipated by the *Record*, noting the larger number of people reading science subjects and the need for the appointment of more science fellows. True to its word, new fellowships in engineering and chemistry were created in 1964.[45]

In another direction, the changing shape of the university post-war saw an enormous expansion in graduate studies, both in numbers and in importance. In 1938–9 there had been 536 postgraduates studying in the whole university, making up only 11 per cent of all students. By 1964–5 there were 2,153, almost a quarter of the student body. Although some of the expansion was absorbed by the newly created graduate colleges, such as Nuffield and St Anthony's, many were attached to undergraduate colleges where they added a new dimension to the college community. Usually older, sometimes married, and more frequently from overseas than the general run of undergraduates, colleges offered them a 'home' in Oxford though many had supervisors elsewhere in the university or in departments. For many with no experience of Oxford, it was easy to feel somewhat semi-detached from colleges which were primarily devoted to undergraduate teaching, a view which the Franks Commission of the mid-1960s confirmed. Colleges began to adjust to this growing body slowly, but the first middle common room was established at Lincoln in 1958 and was followed quickly by other colleges, including Oriel which set up its middle common room in Oriel Street providing facilities parallel to those in the junior common room The importance of this development was emphasized by the conclusions of the Franks Commission which envisaged Oxford growing by the 1980s to accommodate 13,000 students, including up to 4,000 postgraduates, a target realized by 1986–7, most of whom continued to belong to the traditional undergraduate colleges. Although regarded by some as an unsatisfactory compromise, the

[45] OR (1961), 5–6; OR (1964), 6.

Franks Commission set the pattern that the expansion of graduate numbers in Oxford would continue to be grafted onto the traditional collegiate structure. In 1967 Oriel formally decided to hold steady the number of undergraduates but increase the number of graduates by twenty.[46] For Oriel, as in other colleges, this also meant the continued expansion of facilities for the graduate body and growing attention to providing accommodation for graduate students, including those who were married. A new and much more spacious middle common room was established in Oriel Square in 1983. The housing of graduates and their educational welfare were to become as important matters for the college's concern as those of its undergraduates.[47]

Much more visible than these changes in the composition of the student body was the changing external appearance of the college in common with the rest of Oxford as the fruits of the Historic Buildings Appeal, launched in 1957, funded the long overdue repair and refurbishment of the stonework of the colleges and university buildings. In a protracted and huge process of 'systematic refacing', the face of Oxford was literally changed as ivy was removed and stonework cleaned, axed back, or refaced, replacing decaying Headington stone and the soot of generations of coal fires with new stonework, much of it from the Clipsham quarries in Rutland. Where necessary sculpture and detailed stonework was recarved, most famously in the new 'emperors' heads' for the Sheldonian forecourt. The *Record* noted in 1961 that the process at Oriel was well under way. The statues of the kings in the front quad were renovated and the middle quadrangle repaved.[48] Combined with the clean air acts which had banished smoke from thousands of Oxford chimneys, several dozen of them in Oriel and Oriel Street, the college that emerged from this process would have astonished earlier generations with its pristine stonework and crisp new carving. Against blue skies Oriel, like the rest of Oxford, was taking on a picturesque look far removed from the blackened stonework and ivy- and creeper-covered walls of the past. Lighter was now preferred to darker, emphasized in Oriel by the substitution of white paint for bursarial green and brown.

The treasurer that year put this dramatic refurbishment into the context of the changing fortunes of the college's buildings over the course of the twentieth century, identifying three phases of neglect followed by three periods of renewal. The first phase was the period of the 'agricultural depression' from the late nineteenth century when shortage of revenues

---

[46] For graduate development in general, see Thomas, 'College Life, 1945–1970', in HUO viii. 210–11; OR (1967), 9; OR (1968), 7–8.
[47] OCA, Governing Body Minute Book, 1985–93, 2 December 1987, 140; 2 November 1988, 189.
[48] OR (1961), 6–7.

from the college estates enforced stringency, but was transformed by the Rhodes bequest and the construction of the building named after him. The First World War brought further economy and enforced neglect, but was followed by the revivifying effect of the sale of the college estates on its finances. The Second World War and the austerity years that followed marked a new deterioration in the college's fortunes, but the appeal of 1955 allowed the beginning of a new phase of repair work, assisted by the university-wide Historic Buildings Appeal launched in 1957. The college by the early 1960s was spending £3,500 p.a. in catching up on past neglect and £6,000 on current repair work.[49] In practice, the programme of refurbishment which was embarked upon marked what was to become a permanent feature of college life. Growing demands upon college facilities for the comfort of undergraduates, graduates, dons, and conferences, the greater resources brought by an expanding university sector, and generous gifts and endowments by old members, set in train an almost continuous process of renewal and expansion. At Oriel, besides cleaning and repaving, an additional senior common room, the Champneys Room, was built on a refurbished staircase in 1970. Oxford was conscious of being in competition with a generation of 'new' universities, as well as Cambridge, and colleges were in gentlemanly competition with each other in attracting students and conferences. Although there would still be periods of slowdown and retrenchment due to economic circumstances and changes in government funding, the phases of 'neglect' now lay in the past and represented at most pauses in a continuous process of upgrading.

Elsewhere Oriel reflected trends that were changing other aspects of admissions. The increasing importance of the government's financial support to universities, including Oxford and Cambridge, and a recognition that Oxford needed to demonstrate that it was genuinely meritocratic and not simply a preserve of the elite, brought about a series of university-wide changes which affected all colleges. Entrance requirements were altered to widen access to Oxford on all counts, attempting to accommodate more candidates in the sciences, and in some of the newly fashionable social sciences, and to open up an admissions system which seemed heavily weighted in favour of the public and grammar schools. In 1960 a maths or science subject was made an acceptable alternative to Greek or Latin as an entrance requirement. Attempts were made to ease entry from the grammar schools by permitting candidates to apply before A-Level, making the traditional 'third year in the sixth' unnecessary. By the mid-1960s, almost 40 per cent of male undergraduates came from maintained schools. Admissions procedures were increasingly regularized, with the colleges organized into

[49] OR (1961), 9–12.

groups and interviews normally conducted by tutors in the subject instead of, as commonly in the not too distant past, solely by the head of house. Pressures upon Oxford to become fully representative in its intake became the greater as comprehensivization accelerated in the 1960s and 1970s to embrace something of the order of 90 per cent of all secondary school pupils. Criticism of the admissions system became a frequent refrain in the press as colleges and university struggled to meet often conflicting demands for 'fairness'. Admissions policy was bound up with the issue of academic standards: by the 1960s it was becoming recognized in Oxford generally that a good flow of applicants from maintained schools seemed a necessary component of academic success, as well as politically desirable.[50] Within Oxford the issue was sharpened by the publication from 1964 of the Norrington Table, a league table of colleges' academic performance based upon a total calculated from the performance of their undergraduates in finals. Publicly scoffed at, but privately scrutinized, it highlighted what had been discussed before its publication: the divergence in academic performance between colleges. With every reason to be proud of its academic reputation, in 1969 Provost Turpin announced in the *Record* that the college's academic standing ranked first of its most pressing concerns, followed by the need to modernize its buildings and to increase undergraduate 'participation'. He noted that the college finals results showed improvement but not as fast as elsewhere. The recommendation was to increase the range of schools sending applicants to the college and to make efforts to foster academic endeavour. To attract more applicants the college was drawing up a prospectus and organizing a schoolteachers' conference.[51] Regular open days for prospective undergraduates followed. It was a course to which Oriel, like other colleges, would devote considerable attention over the next decades, supplementing the regular and more informal contacts upon which Oriel and other colleges had always depended.

Widening of access was a relatively uncontentious matter in an expanding university sector in which Oxford and colleges could not justify the receipt of government funds on any other basis than a consciously 'fair' and meritocratic system of admissions. College moves to widen access and to improve the quality of undergraduates brought the question of the admission of women to male colleges into sharper focus. Despite a small increase in the absolute number of women students in Oxford, they remained a minority in Oxford, making up about one in five of the undergraduate body from the 1920s. Unless the existing women's colleges could be massively expanded, it was bound to be difficult to alter the sex-ratio amongst Oxford undergraduates and admit more women, and achieve a balance more in line with

[50] Keith Thomas, 'College Life, 1945–70', in HUO viii. 213.
[51] OR (1969), 9.

that of other British universities. 'Fairness' to those well-qualified women denied an opportunity to study at Oxford, the creation of a mixed-sex environment increasingly common at other universities, and a raising of the general quality of undergraduates were all arguments being adduced in favour of a change by colleges to co-residence by the late 1960s, and a number of men's colleges began actively discussing it. In Oriel the issue was first raised in governing body in February 1970, but discussion was adjourned until later in the year by which time other colleges had been consulted. At a meeting in November a straw poll revealed that there was substantial but not overwhelming support for altering the statutes to admit women.[52] Undergraduate opinion had already expressed itself in a resolution to the provost questioning the continuation of restrictions on the hours women were permitted to be in college. The provost replied that no decision would be taken on women's hours until the issue of admitting women undergraduates had been resolved. The substantive deliberation came the following year, following the report of a working party submitted in June. When a special meeting was convened in November the proposal to remove the prohibition on the admission of women failed to obtain the necessary two-thirds majority to amend the statutes.[53]

Oriel was not alone in being cautious in its approach to co-residence. In the event only five men's colleges changed their statutes in 1972 to allow the admission of a restricted number of women as undergraduates and graduates. A moratorium was effectively put in place while the university insisted that other colleges postpone further decisions until what was regarded as an 'experiment' had been scrutinized in a review to be held in 1977. It was quickly apparent that the majority of colleges, men's and women's, would follow suit given the opportunity. They had noted 'the speed with which a change in patterns of schooling was producing a similar change throughout British Higher Education. The switch to comprehensive schools had made the mixed secondary school the norm.'[54] Competition for the best undergraduates applying to university, academic competition between colleges, as well as a need to increase representation from the state sector persuaded many that co-residence was the only way forward. Moreover, the period of review coincided with the passage of the Sex Discrimination Act (1975) which, as well as allowing educational institutions the facility to remove single-sex restriction from any gift or bequest over twenty-five years old (of which the Rhodes Trust was the first to take advantage), made it problematic

---

[52] OCA, Governing Body Minute Book, 1964–70, 11 February 1970, 182; Governing Body Minute Book, 1970–7, 11 November 1970, 10.

[53] OCA, Governing Body Minute Book, 1970–7, 2 December 1970, 13; 16 June 1971, 31; 24 November 1971, 42–3.

[54] M. Brock, 'The University since 1970', in HUO viii. 748.

for the university to impose on colleges further 'controlled experiments'. The university's reviewing committee admitted as much, but expressed the hope that colleges would show some 'restraint' and that applicants to Oxford would retain a choice between single-sex and mixed colleges.

Across the university events moved swiftly and with little sign of restraint. Almost all colleges quickly altered their statutes to admit women: within twelve years (1973–85) the percentage of women nearly doubled amongst the undergraduate body. Oriel's governing body still lacked the requisite two-thirds majority to alter its statutes, but reacted in other ways to the changing demands of widening admissions and accommodating undergraduate opinion on co-residence. A more active policy of recruitment was ordained and women's hours extended.[55] In 1981 a proposal to combine with a single-sex women's college was seriously entertained, involving a joint fellowship and student body with Somerville.[56] These proposals came to nothing, though seriously discussed, and by 1984 Oriel's position as the only single-sex men's college was arousing fears that it projected a negative image, causing the college to lose ground in competition for the best applicants. One member of governing body summed up the situation colourfully in the debate at a Special Meeting on 23 May when he suggested that the college was in danger of being 'seen as an old-fashioned, overly sporting institution caught up in a sort of "Brideshead time-warp"'. The necessary two-thirds majority was obtained at that meeting and a week later the practical arrangements were made for admitting women as graduates and undergraduates more or less forthwith.[57] The context in which this decision was taken was clearly revealed when the tutor for admissions announced that a new undergraduate prospectus would be prepared, to go out to over 4,000 schools, and that 2,000 copies of a graduate prospectus would be available.[58]

Ten years later, when the first women undergraduates were recording their experiences of being the first members of Oriel and their subsequent careers and achievements being noted as a matter of routine, the ground, as ever, was shifting to place fresh demands upon college resources. The full development of the Island Site and of the Oriel Street houses promised the 'fourth quadrangle' mooted since the 1960s and the ability to house the great majority of its undergraduates. But no sooner were those plans afoot than the college noted that it was unable to house as many of its graduate students as other similarly sized colleges. By 1988 the desire to provide accommodation for all undergraduates and all first year graduates was noted by the

---

[55] Brock, 'The University since 1970', 749; OCA, Governing Body Minute Book, 1970–7, 10 March 1971, 32; Governing Body Minute Book, 1977–85, 18 January 1978, 16.
[56] OCA, Governing Body Minute Book, 1977–85, 11 February 1981, 115; 10 June 1981, 128.
[57] OCA, Governing Body Minute Book, 1977–85, 23 May 1984, 248–50; 30 May 1984, 256.
[58] OCA, Governing Body Minute Book, 1977–85, 13 February 1985, 290; Governing Body Minute Book, 1985–93, 10 July 1985, 3.

governing body, reaffirmed in 1990 and leading to further fund-raising for what would eventually be the new building in Rectory Road.[59] An increase in the number of undergraduates 'housed' in college, from 230 in 1990 to 290 in 1996, was still 70 short of what was deemed to be required for undergraduate and postgraduate requirements. The new building at Rectory Road, opened in 2000, gave the college the ability to offer all undergraduates accommodation for three- or four-year courses. Graduates could be housed for at least two years, a necessary condition, together with the new middle common room, for making the college attractive to this increasingly important group. A policy of integrating graduate studies into the general academic structure of the college was developed in consequence: in 2005 the *Oriel News* in 2005 stated that though the undergraduate body was to be maintained at about 280 students, the college was developing plans for 'a larger and stronger graduate infrastructure...in any particular subject we aim, typically, to have one or two fellows researching and teaching, a junior research fellow, a graduate teaching assistant, perhaps a postdoctoral position, and an increasing number of graduate scholarships'.[60]

By the end of the first decade of the twenty-first century, Oriel had survived as a bustling, vibrant institution more than a hundred years of almost unprecedented upheaval and change. In the Edwardian era, the college was still suffering the effects of the great agricultural depression of the late nineteenth century which diminished its income and limited any expansion. However, Rhodes's generous bequest permitted the planning and construction of the new building named after him, and completed the integration of St Mary Hall into the college. But two world wars, the Great Depression, and post-war austerity posed completely unforeseen and unprecedented challenges. The virtual suspension of normal academic activity in the Great War was unprecedented since the Civil War, but nothing could compare with the scale of losses incurred by Orielenses and recorded on its War Memorial. Yet the return to peace brought no relief from economic uncertainties for a modestly endowed college entering the troubled post-war economic climate. These were met boldly. Oriel's foremost place amongst Oxford colleges in the sale of its agricultural estates from 1920 secured, at least for a time, its economic future. Although their sale broke connections that went back centuries, according to at least one authoritative account, without their sale the college might not have survived the 1930s.[61] The Second World War brought an even greater and more invasive effect upon the college, but, though grievous enough, it inflicted lower casualties, and in the event more of its normal life persisted than during the Great War. The dilapidations of

---

[59] OCA, Governing Body Minutes (Minute Book, 1985–93), Meeting of 2 December 1987, 140; Meeting of 2 November 1988, 189.
[60] *Oriel News*, 2005, 2.   [61] OR (1981), 47–8.

wartime and the rigours of post-war austerity posed fresh dilemmas, but the new challenge was to meet the demands of an expanding university sector in which colleges, while competing for the best available students, had to justify the income which they received from the taxpayer. The story of Oriel from the 1950s, increasing numbers, the rise of science, the widening of access, co-residence, the development of graduate studies, and the provision of full residential accommodation with improved facilities of every kind, was a testament to the efforts of successive provosts and governing bodies, building on the foundations laid earlier in the century to harness the college's resources, and on the unprecedented generosity of benefactors, to keep it in the forefront of the academic life of the university.

If the story was one of new challenges boldly met, it was also one of continuities. On the face of it what was remarkable about the Oriel at the beginning of the twenty-first century was what had been preserved, amid so much that had altered. Fears voiced at the time of the Asquith Commission, that once government funding was accepted the colleges might simply become halls of residence, had not been fulfilled. Critically, colleges had been able to maintain considerable autonomy within the university, and so to be flexible enough to meet the new demands placed upon them. Although dependent on the university and the Higher Education sector in general, and ultimately on the government for a large part of its funding, Oriel like other colleges had retained control over its own financial affairs and above all over its vital fund-raising actvities. Throughout the twentieth century and into the next, there would be a natural tension between the university and the colleges, a tension in constant flux, but a relation in which the independence of action of colleges remained a fundamental feature. Colleges had expanded and evolved to meet changed conditions: although science and medicine had required the provision of university-level facilities, scientists had not been hived off to a separate quarter of the university, but integrated within the colleges. The desire to increase the number of women attending Oxford was met not by the proliferation of women's colleges, but by adopting co-residence. Similarly, although the growth of the graduate sector saw the creation of distinct graduate colleges, many graduates chose to be attached to undergraduate colleges and were increasingly welcomed there.

But what was more distinctive to Oriel was the maintenance of a college that was still a real community, if not as intimate as once it was. Its population had increased on all levels, but not as radically, nor as recently, as might appear. Oriel's undergraduate numbers had risen substantially from the end of the Great War to the period after the Second World War, from approximately 150 to 250 or more, but the target number of undergraduates in 2005, at 280, was only twenty more than those on the books in 1960. Moreover what could not be foreseen was the energy and the ingenuity with which Oriel was able to increase the proportion living in or close to the college.

Although most colleges, including Oriel, developed at least one building at some distance from the main site, Oriel's development of the Island Site meant that a very large proportion of undergraduates were living within a two-minute amble to the lodge, and virtually all junior members within the fifteen-minute range. Oriel had not only survived through wars, depressions, and radical changes in university education which many felt would have overwhelmed the college known to Provost Shadwell and Provost Phelps; far from merely surviving, she had flourished.

21

The College Community, 1905–1950

John Stevenson

When Charles Lancelot Shadwell was appointed provost in 1905 the college was, as so often in its history, electing one of its own. Educated at Westminster and Christ Church, he had been a fellow of Oriel from 1864 to 1898, lecturer in jurisprudence from 1865 to 1875, and in 1898 made an honorary fellow. Devoted to his adopted college, his period as its treasurer, from 1874 to 1887, was notable for the care and ability with which he managed the college properties. Indeed his affection for Oriel has been said to have amounted 'almost to religious fervour'. Of the college's history, traditions, and muniments he was described as an 'indefatigable' explorer. The results were shown in the *Registrum Orielense, 1500–1900*, an invaluable reference point on all college members. His interests in the earlier history of Oriel were so profound and absorbing that he found the 'day before yesterday' somewhat less absorbing than its early history. As a result his chapter in Andrew Clark's *Colleges of Oxford* (1891) dwelt at length with 'the remote original foundation, forgotten benefactors, recondite incidents, and obscure earlier developments of the college', but passed over in two brief sentences the days of Arnold and Newman, and all that had happened since the Oxford Movement. As provost, however, he brought the same 'intense loyalty' he had shown as treasurer, as well as 'a stately presence', as well as dispensing 'magnificent hospitality'.[1]

But the most substantial monument of Shadwell's period as provost was the largest building project undertaken in the college since the end of the eighteenth century, the Rhodes Building. Oriel's ability to consider such a project came from the bequest of £100,000 from Cecil Rhodes. At the time of the bequest the greatest proportion of the college's external income, as with almost all Oxford colleges, came from rents from landed property and tithes. Their value had deteriorated during the great depression in agriculture of the

[1] ODNB s.n.

ILLUSTRATION 21.1 The Rhodes Building, opening ceremony, September 1911, OCA

late nineteenth century, trapping institutions like Oriel in a position of static or declining revenues and making Edwardian prosperity something of a misnomer. Rhodes's generosity offered an opportunity to build in otherwise unpropitious financial circumstances. Rhodes earmarked £40,000 for a building in the St Mary quadrangle to front onto the High Street, while the remainder of the bequest would be endowment to compensate for the college's loss of rents from the shops and lodging houses that the new building would replace. As with many building projects, the progress of the design was not entirely smooth. The architect, Basil Champneys, was a prestigious figure, with Mansfield College, the Indian Institute, the John Rylands Library in Manchester, and St Albans Quadrangle of Merton among his most prominent academic commissions. His initial designs had to be modified and the resulting building was something of a compromise between the college's needs and the ambitious designs of one of the most accomplished late Victorian and Edwardian architects. Although somewhat controversial, and latterly subject to criticism from such pundits as Evelyn Waugh, the new building was officially opened in September 1911 and the ceremony recorded by a photograph in the newly established *Oriel Record*, the first piece of college building that could be celebrated in this way.[2] Whatever its architectural merits, there was no doubt that the new building triumphantly completed the third quad, as well as providing much needed new staircases and sets. Although the original intention to provide new lodgings for the provost in the new building was abandoned, it offered spacious new rooms, and the grand frontage onto the High Street envisaged by the benefactor. The Rhodes Building was, therefore, a significant landmark in the evolution of the college: the last piece of extensive new building for college use before the redevelopment of the Island Site seventy years later. For many generations of Oriel undergraduates in the twentieth century, the college they knew had been completed by the Rhodes Building, just before the Great War.

The college to which Provost Shadwell devoted himself was in many respects still a remarkably intimate institution. It had not grown as quickly as some others and even with the new Rhodes Building remained one of the smaller in physical extent. The governing body in 1900 numbered 11, and in the early part of the twentieth century the number of undergraduates hovered around 120. The junior members reflected the typical make-up of the general Oxford undergraduate body at the time, drawn from a relatively circumscribed group of well-known public schools. Shadwell's labours compiling the *Registrum* provide an invaluable insight into the make-up of the undergraduate body at the turn of the century. Of the thirty-eight undergraduates admitted in 1899, twenty-two came from just seven schools with Charterhouse at six, and Rugby and Winchester at four each, leading the list. There was, however, a sprinkling of undergraduates from a somewhat different background: in 1899 there were four Scottish university graduates, and even before the introduction of the Rhodes scholarships, Ferdinand Springer, a German undergraduate from Berlin.[3] But not only did the great majority of the undergraduates share a similar background; a very high proportion were from families with Oriel connections, stretching back sometimes for centuries. Shadwell's *Registrum* reveals that approximately half of the matriculands in 1900 had had forebears at the college. Indeed since it was only possible to trace surnames in the *Registrum*, there may have been many more connections through a collateral line, among the extensive 'cousinhoods' of late Victorian and Edwardian Britain. Certain family names—Davies, Williams, Gilbert, Varley, and Blencowe—recurred, some going back to the early

---

[2] A sketch of the High Street frontage was carried as the frontispiece of OR (March 1910); the photograph appeared in OR (March 1912). For Champneys's other work see A. Stuart Gray, *Edwardian Architecture: A Biographical Dictionary* (Ware, 1988), 139–51.

[3] *Registrum Orielense*, ii. 728–33.

eighteenth century, and many more had more recent predecessors.[4] But there were many new names and only second generation Oriel men, the products of the burgeoning public schools of the nineteenth century. With the sprinkling of Scottish university graduates and the occasional German, soon to be afforced by a regular stream of Rhodes scholars from America, Germany, and the colonies, the undergraduate body was both intimate and varied.

Almost inevitably the era before the Great War has been seen as a period of calm before the storm that was to burst in 1914. Viewed in its own terms, however, it was a period of great vitality for the college, with the largest benefaction of its history and a fine new building affording an impressive High Street frontage. Indeed, there was no torpor in Edwardian Oriel, academically, socially, or in sport, as can be demonstrated in the class lists and activities of Oriel undergraduates and dons. Looking back from the mid-1920s and measuring the number of firsts taken by the college out of the total awarded, the *Record* traced an upswing in academic performance from the turn of the century: 'About 1899 an improvement began, and this was maintained up to the outbreak of the European War. In and immediately after the war our successes dwindle away almost to nothing; but that is a matter for pride rather than regret, and since the war we have taken a higher relative position than the College has held since the decade 1832–41.' From 1892 to 1901 Oriel had only 22 out of a total of 1,150 Firsts awarded, 1.9 per cent, but in 1902–14 it was 55 out of 1,584, 3.5 per cent. Moreover, using a modified version of the later Norrington Table, the compiler of the statistics suggested that the improvement in academic performance had been general and showed 'fairly continuous progress'.[5] A serious moral purpose was also shown in Oriel's involvement from 1903 in the south London borough of Bermondsey, where five clubs were set up for boys and men by Oxford colleges. Part of the settlement movement pioneered at Toynbee Hall in Whitechapel to enable resident graduates from the universities to work amongst the residents of deprived areas of the great cities, the clubs provided a varied menu of educational classes and sports—boxing was a particular favourite. The university settlements attracted as young men some of the most prominent figures in public life in the twentieth century, including William Beveridge, Clement Attlee, and Lord Woolton. Oriel contributed a steady stream of committed recruits to social service in the slums well into the inter-war years, most of whom spent a few months there before taking up a full-time job.[6]

Vitality of another kind was shown by the founding of the *Record* in 1909. Several Cambridge colleges and a number of public schools already had magazines. It was launched by the Revd Francis Hall, fellow from 1873 to

---

[4] *Registrum Orielense*, ii. [5] OR (December 1925), 297–8.
[6] OR (June 1926), 327–8.

1923 and dean from 1882 to 1915, who was prepared to meet the expenses of the venture out of his own pocket. His editorial for the first edition in February 1909 was both philosophical and practical. He reflected on the paradox of the impermanence and continuity of Oxford:

> One generation succeeds another with bewildering rapidity. Every October Term sees the old staircases roused from their Long Vacation torpor by a fresh influx of vigorous young life, and every Summer Term brings with it the sadness of parting and the necessity of saying 'Good bye'. The old buildings are there, the old rooms, the old furniture, but otherwise the only permanent elements in the College seem to be the Dons (who hardly count) and the Porter at the Lodge. Three short years, and those who have gone in and out together, and have formed friendships of the highest and truest kind, are compelled to separate perhaps for ever. They go out into the busy world, and except for some chance meeting, now and then, at long, long intervals, disappear entirely from view.

And yet, as he noted:

> the life of a College has a real permanence, a real continuity... Though we are gone, the College goes on. The same vigorous life pulses through it from term to term, from year to year. Men such as we were now fill our places. What the College was to us, that it is now to them. As we laboured for it, fought for it, showed ourselves jealous of its good name, so do they.

He articulated the idea of a continuing college community, even before the Great War sharply increased sensitivity to thoughts of Orielenses past and present. Highlighted by Provost Shadwell's immense labours detailing the undergraduates of the past, and reinforced subsequently by the founding of the Oriel Society in the years after the war, the *Record* provided the vehicle, as its founder put it:

> ...of knitting together the different generations of Oriel men, of recovering what scattered traces it may be possible to collect of the after-career of those who have 'gone down' of enabling them in their turn to know what kind of life their successors are leading, and how the old College is faring in their hands...[7]

Although the retirement of Francis Hall in 1914 carried the threat that the *Record* might cease after only six years of existence, intimated in the editorial for the issue of October 1914, it was carried forward, fortuitously as it happened, for as we know, it was now being read not only in rectory and common room, club and counting house, but in depots, garrisons, trenches, and ward rooms.[8]

A record of the life in the 'old college' before 1914 can be constructed from various sources. Visually, old photographs show that the main difference that generations later than the 1960s would have noticed were the

[7] OR (February 1909), Editorial.   [8] OR (October 1914), Editorial.

creeper-covered walls and the stonework blackened (and still being blackened) by coal-smoke, all removed by the great cleaning and refacing which gave the college, and Oxford in general, its present, more pristine appearance. However, the layout of the college's major facilities, once the Rhodes Building was completed, would have been broadly familiar, though the space under the hall occupied by the beer cellar from the 1950s was still in use as kitchens. Between eighty to ninety undergraduates lived in, with the reminder in digs. Hall and chapel loomed large in their lives. Undergraduates had to 'do' forty-two chapel attendances per term unless 'professed atheists' (a category which appears to have included all non-Anglicans!) recorded or 'pricked' by the 'SCR man' who attended in a top hat and frock coat. Undergraduate attendance at Sunday chapel was more or less expected, usually as a supplement to attending the university church. If the soul was well catered for by compulsory chapel attendance, the body was expected to dine five nights a week in hall, laid out with four tables, for scholars, seniors, second years and freshmen. A scout brought a cooked breakfast and set the fire for undergraduates each morning and the standard college lunch or 'commons', brought to one's rooms, typically consisted of a quarter of a cottage loaf, four marks of butter, and half a pint of beer. The college gates were locked at 9.00 p.m. on the last chime from Tom Tower.[9] As so often, it was a stranger to Oxford and its ways who recorded something of the daily routine or at least a version of it in the Edwardian college. Karl Alexander von Muller, a Rhodes scholar, opened his day at 7.30 a.m. with 'the usual cold bath', dispensed from chapel attendance as a Roman Catholic, followed by a stroll in Christ Church Meadow. It was then common for parties of four or five to meet at 8.30 or 8.45 for breakfast in one another's rooms, the host providing the tea or coffee and the scout bringing a first course of 'fish, ham and eggs, chicken or kidneys', then buttered toast and 'the delicious orange marmalade', followed by 'pipes and cigarettes'. Breakfast was leisurely, lasting until mid-morning when the time came for what later came to be called 'tutorials' and lectures. With academic work finished by 1.00 p.m., a light lunch of 'commons' was followed by 'the most important business of the day'—sport. Von Muller, used to a different age range at the German universities, found his fellow undergraduates 'undoubtedly less educated than the German students, on the average two or three years younger'. He continued: 'They seemed to have little intellectual interest in anything that was not English and factual. But when all is said, they were more natural, more wholesome, more unspoilt.'[10]

[9] See OR (1948), 14–15, account of career of Albert Annetts, 1868–1918.
[10] OR (1952), 20–31.

The provost, dean, the fellows and more than four score undergraduates who lived in were supported by a small army of porters, scouts, kitchen staff, and college servants. Prior to 1914 the head of house presided over many of the functions later taken on by professional bursars and treasurers; for example, the provost was involved in almost all appointments of college servants and personally appointed scouts to the staircase for which they became responsible. There they provided all the services that in a private household or 'digs' of the time would be provided by their landladies. Fires had to be raked out, set, and kept supplied with coal; hot water provided for shaving and washing where, as in most of the colleges, there was no hot water on tap. Meals were provided in rooms as required and rooms cleaned. Dons and undergraduates expected to be able to dine and entertain in their rooms with scouts supplying all the duties normally carried out by servants for middle- and upper-class households of the time. For many scouts and college servants the attractions of college service were security and identification with an institution of which many were intensely proud, often becoming lifelong employees. To take only two examples amongst many others, Albert Annetts, the 'common room man', who kept the register of chapel attendance before 1914 had joined the college in 1868, retired in 1918, and died aged 96 in 1948. The head cook, Mr M. J. Gillett, who retired in 1951 had been recruited under Provost Shadwell and only interrupted his fifty years employment by the college for military service in the Great War. The head porter, the senior common room man, and the head cook were major figures in the college community, each responsible for their own section of the staff, while individual scouts had considerable autonomy over 'their' staircase and its inhabitants The smooth functioning of the Edwardian college depended, however, on some of its less visible personnel, the milkman who daily brought the milk from the college farm at Bartlemas, the shoe-cleaning boy who went round every morning to clean the boots, shoes, football and cricket boots—and hunting boots too when required—left out for him, the common room boy on £40 a year, and the buttery assistant on 7s. 6d. a week. Even for the humblest, wages were supplemented by a right to 'commons', half a 2lb. loaf and eight marks of butter, twice a day. For scouts there were gratuities from students and dons, while by 1914 the college also organized staff sports and the provost gave the staff dinner twice a year. College housing was available for the senior members of staff and it was not an unrealistic expectation that vacancies as they turned up might be filled by family members. Women were already employed to make beds and husband and wife teams in college service contributed to a close-knit environment, run rather like a contemporary great country house, and which offered considerable advantages to all parties. Attachment and loyalty to a prestigious institution, security, and the prospect of advancing up a hierarchy of college positions were the compensations for relatively modest pay, long hours, and arduous duties.[11]

On to this relatively settled community the Great War broke in August 1914 with unprecedented effect. As we have seen earlier, the most direct effect of the war was that it not only took away existing undergraduates and dons but also diverted the supply of potential freshmen into the armed forces. Michaelmas Term 1914 opened with only thirty-five undergraduates in residence, a number which steadily dwindled to a mere fifteen by the end of summer term of 1915. Ominously, the first casualties were being notified and the war was beginning to mean something more than a mere inconvenience. The *Record* for September 1915 reported that: 'In the last issue we were at the opening of the new experience. There was every temptation to be depressed, and the future was dismally unapparent. The *Record* therefore hurled defiance at difficulty and did what it could to strengthen resolution. Now we have had twelve months of it, and it is possible to take some kind of survey. Chastened, it may be, but still unsubdued, and more convinced than ever of the usefulness of holding on. There is much, in fact, to inspire and nerve us.'[12] But as well as coming to terms with the new realities of a nation at war, the college was adjusting to major changes in its leading figures. Francis Hall, founder of the *Record*, retired as dean, of whom it was said, 'thirty-five generations have known him as The Dean, and the same number as Counsellor and Friend'. To his 'shrewd and tactful administration' was attributed 'the great position of Oriel in the University'. He continued to reside in college, as was the norm for retired fellows. As dean he had also been, as was unique to Oriel, vice-provost; these functions were now split between Charles Firth, the Regius Professor of Modern History, who took on the titular position, while decanal duties and discipline were taken up by the chaplain, Frank Barry.[13] Even more significant in the life of the college was the retirement due to ill health in 1914 of Provost Shadwell, to the well-earned tributes of the fellows. His successor, Lancelot Ridley Phelps, was elected in December 1914. Few provosts have taken over their responsibilities at such an unpropitious and in some respects tragic moment in the college's history; few were to achieve his almost legendary status in college memory and folklore.

In Phelps's obituary notice, his successor, Provost Ross, pointed out that as scholar (1871–7), fellow (1877–1914), provost (1914–29), and honorary fellow (1929–36), Phelps had a longer and more intimate connection with the college than anyone since Hawkins, and his connection was more complete than that of Hawkins, who had been an undergraduate of another college. That and the affection he inspired led to Ross's warm tribute: 'To

[11] OR (1951), 9: Mr Gillett.   [12] OR (September 1915), 238.
[13] OR (September 1915), 238.

all living Orielenses Phelps was the completest epitome of all that the College stands for, and his death will be felt to be the end of an epoch in its history.'[14] Certainly the recollections of 'the Phelper', as he became universally known, stretched well back into the previous century. As he recalled himself at his eightieth birthday celebrations, he was admitted to Oriel by a provost, Hawkins, who as a young fellow had barely escaped being trapped in Paris when Napoleon returned from exile on Elba during the 'Hundred Days' in 1815 and to the end of his days referred to Australia as 'New Holland'. He remembered Gladstone's visit at the height of the Home Rule crisis, his sole concern to discuss the finer points of Homeric scholarship with Provost Monro.[15] The son of a country rector, he was admitted a scholar in 1872, obtaining seconds in classical moderations and literae humaniores, then studied for two semesters in Leipzig and Göttingen. In 1877 he was elected to a fellowship and ordained a deacon in 1879 and a priest in 1896. He combined lectures on classics with an interest in the Poor Law. He earned a considerable reputation as a lecturer in economics, especially for his series on political economy to Indian Civil Service probationers in residence in Oxford, and as an exacting tutor, who 'brought to life many a sleeping mind'. As a college tutor he was responsible for the general supervision of a third of the undergraduates and was a friend to many more. He entertained undergraduates to high table, talked to them on numerous occasions not least on his many vigorous walks about Oxford, and took them on reading parties to High Force on the Tees. His concern for and friendship with undergraduates was extensive and remarkable, maintained even after they had gone down by an extensive correspondence. His college obituary regarded this as in many ways his greatest contribution to the life of the community: 'what Phelps achieved is most of all bound up with his friendships and his influence in the lives of other people.'[16] His academic interests were acknowledged to be wide rather than specialized or research-based, belonging to an earlier tradition which nonetheless took academic work seriously. As lecturer, tutor for twenty-one years, vice-principal of St Mary Hall, and steward of the common room he was a pivotal figure in college life, renowned both for his hospitality and for being, as many believed, the best conversationalist in Oxford. Indeed, his recreations were described as 'riding, walking and talking'.[17]

But although he was to live in college rooms for half a century, made sincere acknowledgement of his enjoyment of the life of a still relatively small fellowship, and could appear in later life the very model of the eccentric college don, never happier than when in the senior common room after hall 'his proper throne-room and audience chamber', Phelps had an important

---

[14] OR (January 1937), 157. [15] OR (January 1934), 343–6.
[16] OR (January 1937), 162. [17] OR (January 1937), 163–4; OR (December 1923), 171–2.

life outside the college. His academic interests and Christian convictions gave him a deep interest in contemporary social questions, especially those of poverty and vagrancy, publishing a pamphlet, *Poor Law and Charity*, as early as 1887. An active member of the Charity Organization Society, the most important coordinating body for philanthropic activity at the turn of the century, he was a keen supporter of the university extension movement which encouraged graduates to take up voluntary work in the slums, and a member of the executive committee of the Toynbee Hall Settlement in the East End. For many years an Oxford city councillor and latterly an alderman, he was a leading figure in the Oxford Cottage Improvement Society, a member of the Oxford board of guardians from 1880, and its chairman from 1912. Moreover, when a clash appeared to occur between his passionate devotion to the college and these wider concerns, he chose the latter. Thus when Provost Monro died unexpectedly in Switzerland in 1905 and Phelps thought that he might be a candidate, he expressed himself as being keener to serve on the prestigious Royal Commission which was to be appointed to investigate the operation of the Poor Laws, the principal source of 'welfare' available in Edwardian Britain. Starting in December 1905, Phelps was part of an eighteen-strong commission which met every Monday and Tuesday for two years, eventually submitting two reports in 1909. During that time he was committed to an exhaustive investigation of the operation of Poor Law Unions throughout the United Kingdom, visiting workhouses as far afield as Liverpool, a city he described as a 'curious mixture of squalor and magnificence', Hexham, Manchester, the Orkneys, Cardiff, and London. Before he set off for Ireland, he wondered, 'should one inform one's Insurance Company?' Among his fellow commissioners was Beatrice Webb, the Fabian socialist, who Phelps thought 'the cleverest person on the Committee'. Her principles he thought sound, but 'quite impractical'. Phelps signed both majority reports when they were submitted in 1909. During his time on the Royal Commission Phelps continued to take parties of undergraduates to High Force, but only finally returned to Oriel in August 1907.[18]

If Phelps's work on the Royal Commission and his continuing involvement with the practical problems of the administration of the Poor Law in Oxford gave the lie to the later image of him as primarily an engaging example of Oxford eccentricity, nothing could have prepared him for what his term as provost was to hold for him as the Great War broke in all its force over his beloved college. He began his provostship in what was a rapidly diminishing college as the demands of military service took away fellows, undergraduates, and staff. Oriel had the distinction of the highest rate of enlistment of any college, representing approximately three-quarters of those

---

[18] OR (1959), 15-21.

in residence in 1913. Enlistment included some who had matriculated as early as 1875 and a number who had been admitted to the college but had not had time to matriculate before they joined the forces. Indeed, in the first months of the war, the enlistment rate was even more dramatic: up to the end of November 1914, almost 88 per cent of those in residence in October 1914 had joined the armed forces. The 'rush to the colours' at the outbreak of the war was a widespread and general phenomenon in which Oxford undergraduates were in the lead. But even within this great patriotic wave of support, Oriel's position was exceptional: with differing rates of enlistment from college to college, Oriel headed the table in those early weeks. This high rate of enlistment was in part a consequence of the close-knit, predominantly public school entry of the college, for throughout Oxford, as the university historian has remarked, 'the higher the public school intake of a college the greater the rush to the colours'. Military connections via family and locality, school traditions, and the rise of Officer Training Corps in many schools and Oxford itself the years before the war all tended to make military service entirely natural in the wave of enthusiasm which greeted the outbreak of war for many of the undergraduates who came to Oriel in the years up to 1914.[19] The rapid outflow of young men contributed to Phelps's earliest major step as provost, the agreement with Somerville College to lease the St Mary Hall quadrangle for the duration of the war. From there Somerville could operate as a self-contained unit with their own porter's lodge, protected by 'two massive walls of brick' in the connecting passages to the middle quadrangle to prevent any unwelcome intercourse between the sexes. Thereafter, as the *Record* put it: 'Within the two quads left us we have lived our life. There have been slight changes and adjustments for altered times, but no essential breach of continuity.' By the summer term of 1915, there were only fifteen undergraduates in residence though thirty were expected in October. Nonetheless, college life was maintained though 'the reports of Clubs and Societies... are rather intensive than extensive':

The Arnold has debated, and the Literary Society has read papers, remarkable for rareness and elevation. There have been nets and tennis courts on the Ground, and some have been observed to use them. Two Firsts in Schools, a University Prize, and the highest percentage of military service of all the Colleges in Oxford. That is the skeleton narrative of events.[20]

Moreover even as war raged, thoughts about the future were being entertained. Early in 1915 the first plans were mooted for a new cricket ground at Bartlemas using funds bequeathed by Provost Shadwell, the old ground

---

[19] *Oxford Magazine*, 4 December 1914, 120–1; J. M. Winter, 'Oxford and the First World War', HUO viii. 19.
[20] OR (September 1915), 239–40.

having been relinquished for agricultural use. The release of funds from the provost's gift of £1,000 was sanctioned in November of that year, and by 1917 turf was being set aside to lay down as soon as the land could be drained and levelled, when the end of the war would make labour available. Moreover it was also a matter of pride for the college that the Amalgamated Clubs remained solvent, while those of other colleges had gone bankrupt. A substantial credit balance from before the war and readiness of the remaining members of Oriel to continue to pay subscriptions, even though they received practically nothing in return—the cricket ground having been given up and the college barge no longer in use.[21]

The war threw up unexpected challenges for the college. One consequence of the reduction in the number of undergraduates was that the gratuities to which college staff were accustomed were drastically reduced and in March 1915 it was resolved to compensate the bedmakers and female servants for their loss. Economies elsewhere were becoming the order of the day: the college 'went dry' following the example set by the king, gaudies were discontinued, and high table funds diverted to general college purposes for the duration of the war. The introduction of conscription made three of the college servants liable to call up, the under cook, butler, and under butler. It was a sign of the replacement of male with female labour throughout Britain under the pressure of war that the college resolved to engage a female cook to fill one of the gaps. Fear of Zeppelin raids in January 1917, provoked by raids on London and the east coast, led to a renewal of insurance premiums to cover the college, its contents, and the chancel of St Mary the Virgin, for which Oriel was responsible, against damage by enemy bombing.[22] By 1917 various 'voluntary rationing' and then more coercive government measures made college life increasingly austere. The weekly allowance for all members of college on 12 February 1917 was set at 2½ lbs. of meat, 4 lbs. of bread, and ¾ lb. of sugar; a week later meat was removed from breakfast and lunch, Tuesdays and Fridays declared meatless days, and tea was only to be served with oatcake or oatmeal biscuits.[23] Austerity was tightened still further in April when non-residents were only allowed to dine on meatless days, now extended to include Sundays. Gas and electricity consumption was also reduced on orders from the Board of Trade, resulting in electric lights being banned from undergraduate bedrooms and gas in servants' rooms being discontinued.[24] In December 1917 it was recognized that wartime inflation required a 25 per cent advance in wages given to

---

[21] OR (March 1917), 335–6.
[22] OCA Governing Body Minutes 4 A 7, 3 March 1915, 60; 17 May 1916, 140; 20 January 1917, 160.
[23] OCA Governing Body Minutes 4 A 7, 12 February 1917, 164; meeting 19 February, 166.
[24] OCA Governing Body Minutes 4 A 7, 6 April 1917, 191.

all college staff.²⁵ Moreover, given the increasing restrictions on food supplies, by February 1918 the college was forced to abandon the traditional provision of 'commons' to the college servants and replace it with an allowance of 9*d*. a day in compensation. The food situation was becoming sufficiently severe for a portion of the 'sacred ground' of the Parks to be given over to allotments for members of the university and their families. Nearer still, strange sights were to be seen when a portion of Merton Meadow was broken up where, according to the *Record*, 'Heads and Tutors of Colleges and their wives may be met, spade and potato-fork on shoulder, going to dig there'.²⁶ By Hilary Term 1918 Oriel was a mere shadow of its pre-war self, reduced to fourteen undergraduates, four of them invalided out of the forces, four unfit for active service, and five too young for commissions and still in training with the OTC. The teaching body consisted of three tutors, one of whom was a university lecturer, with tutors at other colleges filling in any gaps.²⁷

The provost presided over a nearly empty kingdom, but he maintained contact with former college members through his vast correspondence, especially to those serving in the armed forces. His obituary recorded:

...he did not scribble notes, he wrote long letters, in the style of the epistolary age, not even excluding the long esses. All through the War he poured out his letters to members of Oriel on all the fronts; they came as regularly as the rations and were quite as eagerly looked for. These were the link between us and the College, between us and the sane enduring world.²⁸

With over 700 Oriel men in the forces during the Great War this was a considerable burden, which Phelps took on willingly. But few provosts, perhaps only his successor in the Second World War, can have had the unenviable task of writing so many letters of condolence to the relatives of those who died on active service, many of whom he knew intimately. His obituarist pulled no punches when he wrote of Phelps that 'Those who were near him in 1914 realised how bitterly he suffered; and though he held on gaily and gallantly, he was hurt in the depths of his soul and these scars were never completely healed.'²⁹ Indeed, some of his correspondence must have made almost unbearable reading for him, as families grappled with the loss of loved ones or, perhaps even worse, uncertainty about their fate. It was, perhaps, a little consolation that some took the opportunity to record the affection in which Phelps was held. One parent wrote: 'He often spoke to me in his Oxford days of his walks and talks with and devotion to you and I feel that what you have written is a true and beautiful epitaph... No parents had

---

²⁵ OCA Governing Body Minutes 4 A 7, 12 December 1917, 200.
²⁶ OCA Governing Body Minutes 4 A 7, 16 February 1918, 195; OR (March 1917), 336.
²⁷ OR (March 1918), 2.   ²⁸ OR (January 1937), 162.   ²⁹ OR (January 1937), 162.

a nobler son.'³⁰ Others reported the current state of play with family members. One family had already lost one son when they wrote to Phelps in March 1915, hoping that Kenneth, who had come to the college in 1912 and was now serving with the Lincolnshire Regiment, 'will be back shortly under your care'. Another son Henry, who had matriculated in 1908, they reported 'has been in the trenches since Xmas with in the Essex Regiment. He has been hit twice but not really wounded.' Kenneth was killed six months later in August 1915 and Henry the following year in July 1916.³¹ Phelps was often to find himself in the position of a kind of clearing house, passing on information from his numerous correspondents to grieving relatives. Later in the year, another parent wrote: 'How can I thank you for your kind and understanding letter and your promptitude in forwarding the details of our dear boys death... we have another son fighting in Flanders before Ypres.'³² Amidst these tragedies, former undergraduates continued to turn to Phelps for advice or assistance. H. Napier wrote from the Bermondsey Mission in March 1915, having been rejected by the Medical Board for active service. Though he intended to continue his work at the mission he asked Phelps for advice on what to take up as a daytime job. The dilemma was clearly resolved as he eventually did join the forces and survived the war, serving in the Queen's Westminsters.³³ One asked him to send a letter of 'comfort' to the parents of a nephew killed in action. Another asked the provost whether he would visit his adjutant, lying wounded in Somerville: 'he is only twenty-one.' 'I am myself going strong so far,' wrote the latter and only recently matriculated (1910) correspondent, who would end the war as Brigadier-General Hunt on the General Staff, with an MC and bar.³⁴

But it was not only Phelps's correspondence and no doubt that of other fellows and tutors which helped to knit together 'Oriel at war'. The *Record*, intended for much happier circumstances, came into its own as a link between the scattered members of the college. The Orielenses in early 1918 on the Western Front, in Italy, Salonika, Mesopotamia, or the Fleet, might have forgiven the somewhat peremptory editorial from Francis Hall, requesting that 'Subscribers who are away on Military Service would materially assist the Editor if they would inform him to what address they would wish their copies forwarded' and were reminded to send in their subscriptions for 1918–19.³⁵ The *Record*, however, made grim reading in the last years

---

³⁰ OCL, Phelps letters, 1915, G. Lagden to Phelps, 13 March 1915.
³¹ OCL, Phelps letters, 1915, H. G. Peake to Phelps, 26 March 1915.
³² OCL, Phelps letters, 1915, C. Phillips-Jones to Phelps, 28 June 1915.
³³ OCL, Phelps letters, 1915, H. Napier to Phelps, 26 March 1915.
³⁴ OCL, Phelps letters, 1916, L. Pullan to Phelps, 6 January 1916; the subject of the letter was C. E. A. Pullan who had matriculated in 1913, killed on 30 December 1915; E. Hunt to Phelps, 31 July 1916.
³⁵ OR (March 1918), 1.

of the war, carrying poignant notices of casualties, many of them in families who had long-standing connections with the college, amongst whom were numbered brothers, fathers, and in some cases grandfathers. Lt. W. L. O. Parker of the 11th Hussars, attached to the Royal Flying Corps, who was reported missing and subsequently killed in October 1917, had entered Oriel from Eton in 1913 and took his commission on the outbreak of war. His brother had been at the college from 1904 to 1907, served in the war, and survived it; their father had been at Oriel from 1872 to 1875, himself the son of John Oxley Parker who had come up to Oriel in 1829.[36] Nor, of course, were the college staff immune. The loss was reported in March 1917 of Mr Sidney Smith, the college butler, who had volunteered and was a lance-corporal in the Oxfordshire and Buckinghamshire Light Infantry. He had joined the college as the butler's clerk, and 'was a good cricketer, a keen volunteer, an ardent politician on the Liberal side, and a good musician'.[37] It was little wonder that when the end of the war came in November 1918 it was greeted by celebrations amongst the few who remained to make them; discreetly reported the following spring:

> It is astonishing how myths spring up. A ridiculous story has got about, and has actually found credence, that on the evening of the day on which the Armistice was declared, a sound as of the popping of corks was distinctly heard in Hall. Some people have even the hardihood to assert that the strains of 'God save the King' were heard floating on the wintry air. This is simply absurd, for no one has ever heard of singing in Hall during dinner. Such things 'do not happen.' The whole thing probably originated in the fact that the Provost did make a few well-chosen remarks in celebration of the happy event, and it has been foolishly inferred that the King's health was drunk; an impossible supposition, for, as all the world knows, Oriel was a 'dry' college during the war, and you cannot drink the King's health in water.[38]

In the great tragedy of war in which over three-quarters of a million members of the British armed forces lost their lives, Oxford and Oriel suffered particularly heavy casualties. The idea of a 'lost generation' which cast such a shadow over the inter-war years was rooted in the belief of the loss of the brightest and the best, of those most willing to serve and represented in the volunteers who had flocked to the colours in the great wave of patriotic fervour which had gripped the country in the first months of the war. The Oxford undergraduates who had flooded into the armed forces in the early months of the war epitomized that tragedy. With the highest participation rates of all the Oxford colleges in the war, it was inevitable that Oriel paid a terrible price. Of the 725 members of the college who served in the war, 162 died, many more, never counted, were wounded, some very

---

[36] OR (March 1918), 8–10. [37] OR (March 1917), 336.
[38] OR (April 1919), 73.

seriously. The death toll represented just over 22 per cent of those who had served, second only to Corpus Christi in its scale, and significantly higher than the average for the university as a whole, at just over 18 per cent. As in the university and country at large however, the losses were disproportionately amongst the younger age group, the junior officer class, falling most heavily upon those who had matriculated between 1910 and 1914 where mortality rose almost to three in every ten of those who served. In addition there were eighteen deaths amongst those who had been admitted to the college but had not had an opportunity to matriculate. As the university historian has remarked of Oxford's high casualty rate: 'The younger the cohort the greater risk of death, which rises from 9 per cent for those aged 40 in 1914 to 19 per cent of those aged 30 and to 31 per cent for those aged 19 or 20 at the outbreak of the war. The disproportionately heavy losses at younger ages is the distinctive feature of Oxford's lost generation.' This helps to explain why the college had such a heavy casualty rate even amongst Oxford colleges as a whole. Oriel's exceptionally heavy enlistment at the outbreak of the war from existing and prospective undergraduates, their overwhelming tendency to serve as officers rather than in the ranks, their concentration in the army and Royal Flying Corps rather than the navy, where casualty rates were much lower, all contributed to the scale of the losses. Oriel had supplied no less than thirty-nine chaplains to the forces, some of whom also became casualties, but at a lower rate than of the army as a whole, concentrating the mortality rate still further amongst those in active front-line service.[39]

Amid these appalling losses, there was also recognition of the distinction with which so many had served. The Roll of Service published in the *Record* not only recorded those who had lost their lives, but also the many decorations they had earned Amongst the prospective undergraduates was Oriel's sole VC, T. R. Colyer-Fergusson, who was killed as a captain in the Northamptonshire Regiment on 31 July 1917. Seven others were awarded the Croix de Guerre, thirty-five were awarded the Distinguished Service Order and bars, ninety-three were awarded the Military Cross and bars, and there were over two hundred mentions in dispatches. War service also saw members of the college awarded two CBEs, twenty OBEs, ten MBEs, and fifteen were awarded decorations or orders by allied states.[40] Thoughts about commemorating the war dead were raised and set side while the war was still being fought, then postponed again after the armistice until the spring of 1919. Initial proposals for a memorial building in the second quad or using the gateway through to the High Street (used eventually for the Second World War memorial), were supplanted by the war memorial placed on the

---

[39] Winter, 'Oxford and the First World War', HUO viii. 18–24.
[40] OR (March 1920), 128.

ORIEL COLLEGE

1896 Adair, H. S. (Serving Aug. 4, 1914). Maj. Cheshire Regt. (Lt.-Col.). G.S.O. 2 (G.S.O. 1). France and Belgium. *D.S.O.*, Jan. 1, 1918. *D.* France, 1916 twice, 1917 twice.

1878 Adams, Rev. W. J. (Serving Aug. 4, 1914). Chaplain to the Forces (4th Class), attd. R.A. v.d. *D.* § Mar. 1918.

1907 Agar, W., B.A. (Oct. 1916). Capt. R.A.M.C., attd. 27th C.C.S. Mesopotamia, India, Salonika.

1894 Aitchison, Rev. W., M.A. (Apr. 2, 1917). Chaplain to the Forces (4th Class).

Aitken, J. M. (Apr. 1917). 2nd Lt. R.F.A. France, 1918. Died on Oct. 12, 1918, of wounds received in action near Le Cateau.

1881 Allan, J. B., B.C.L., M.A. (Sept. 17, 1915). Lt. R.N.V.R. Egypt.
1897 Allen, H. I., B.A. (Mar. 1, 1915). Lt., Technical Officer, R.A.F.
1892 Allen, R. W., M.A. (Sept. 2, 1914). Capt. 8th Hussars, Res. of Officers.
1919 Amacker, D. M. (June, 1917). Sergt. Interpreters' Corps, Divl. H. Q. 42nd Div., afterwards 1st Lt. H. Q. 1st Army, U.S. Army. France, 1918.

1898 **Amphlett, R. F.**, B.A. (July 21, 1916). 2nd Lt. 8th Worcestershire Regt. France, 1916–17. Killed in action at Hardecourt on Apr. 6, 1917.

1911 **Anderson, J. M.** (Dec. 18, 1914). Lt. 3rd, attd. 2nd, R. Scots. France and Belgium. Killed in action in Belgium on June 19, 1915.

1899 Anderson, N., B.A. (June 1, 1916). Capt. 5th London Regt. (London Rifle Brigade). D.A.A.G. France. *O.B.E.* (Mil.). *D.* France, 1918 twice.

1913 Andrew, W. M., M.A. (Apr. 18, 1915). Lt. 9th Highland L.I. France. (Prisoner of War.)

1914 Andrewes, G. L. (Nov. 1, 1915). 2nd Lt. 10th Suffolk Regt. Lt. Labour Corps (Capt. and Adjt.).

1889 **Andrews, M. P.**, M.A. (Serving Aug. 4, 1914). Capt. 4th W. Riding Regt. France. *D.* France, 1915. Killed in action on Aug. 14, 1915.

1920 Ardagh-Walter, P. F. (Jan. 24, 1918). 2nd Lt. 62nd Batt., R.G.A. France, Germany, 1918–19.

1898 Arkwright, B. H. G. (Mobilized Oct. 1914). Capt. 1/1st Derbyshire Yeomanry. Bde. Maj. Cavalry Bde., B.S.F. Egypt, The Balkans. *D.* Egypt, 1915.

1909 Arkwright,* C. G., B.A. (Dec. 1914). Capt. 4th Northumberland Fusiliers (Maj.). France. *M.C.*, Jan. 1, 1917. *D.* France, 1916.

1909 Arkwright,* C. H. (May 7, 1915). Capt. R.F.A. (T.F.).

1910 Armitage,* K. L. F., B.A. (Aug. 12, 1914). 2nd Lt. 9th R. Warwickshire Regt., afterwards Capt. 2/21st Punjabis (Lt.-Col. i/c 30th Punjabis). India, 1914–16 and from 1917; E. Africa, 1916–17. *D.* E. Africa, 1917.

1905 Armstrong, E. M., B.Sc. (1917). U.S. Medical Res. Corps.

ILLUSTRATION 21.2 First World War: Roll of Service
Oriel College

wall of the Old Buttery in the passageway between the second and third quadrangles. As significant for the future, a fund was opened for scholarships and exhibitions to be devoted in the first instance to the sons of those who had fallen in the war.[41]

By Hilary Term 1919 undergraduates began to reappear in Oxford as the forces demobilized. Austerity was being rapidly set aside and a sense of returning normality confirmed with notice of a college dance and plans for a dinner for all ex-servicemen.[42] Somerville remained in possession of the St Mary Quadrangle, however, because the War Office dragged its feet over the evacuation of Somerville's own building, much to the chagrin of both colleges. The original agreement was that Somerville would regain its buildings within two months, and vacate Oriel within three months of the end of the war. That timetable looked increasingly unrealistic, and although Phelps gave private assurances that the quadrangle would not be required until the beginning of Michaelmas Term 1919, there was beginning to be considerable anxiety on Somerville's part that they might become homeless. Fortunately the War Office issued the order to begin evacuating Somerville the day after a meeting on 7 February of the principal of Somerville, Miss Penrose, with the director of the Army Medical Service, though it was clear that Somerville would have to remain as Oriel's tenants into the summer. In a way that had not been the case when the first two quadrangles of Oriel had been virtually uninhabited, there was now much more a sense of cohabitation of the same site with consequences which might have been foreseen and suspected by both Provost Phelps and Principal Penrose. A relatively benign event was held in Trinity Term with a joint debate between the Somerville and Oriel debating societies, reported as a celebration 'of the connection between the two institutions which have for four years been bound together like the Siamese twins, each institution possessing its independent organisation, but bound to the other by a physical bond'.[43] But something of what was to come was contained in the slightly discrepant view recorded by a Somervillian: 'If Oriel's manners left something to be desired, it was, in the circumstances, excusable', describing the occasion as 'more of a rag than a debate'.[44]

With returning undergraduates, many of them ex-servicemen, it is clear that a somewhat more boisterous atmosphere had entered, or re-entered, college life. Not only had undergraduates come back, but so also had the occasions for celebrating success on the river. One such on Thursday 19 June 1919 was to enter the folklore of both Oriel and Somerville as the night of

---

[41] OCA, Governing Body Minutes 4 A 7, 23 April 1919, 23.
[42] OCA, Governing Body Minutes 4 A 7, 11 June 1919, 30.
[43] Pauline Adams, *Somerville for Women: An Oxford College, 1879–1993* (Oxford, 1996), 98–9.
[44] Adams, *Somerville for Women*, 99.

'the Oriel Raid' or 'the Pickaxe Incident'. It was a hot summer night and several of Somerville's 'Young Ladies' had decided to drag their bedding onto the grass of the St Mary quadrangle preparatory to sleeping there. Towards midnight, all remained calm, until there were growing sounds of revelry from Oriel. Alarmed, the young women hastily returned to their rooms and it soon became apparent that following their revelry some members of Oriel sought an unsolicited return to the St Mary quadrangle by breaking through the wall. A breach was made, and by the time the Somerville porter was alerted to the commotion 'a number of somewhat inebriated young men had crawled through the hole they had made and were dancing triumphantly round the pickaxe by means of which they had effected their entry and which they had cast to the ground in the middle of the quad'. The first Somerville don on the scene was the classics tutor, Miss Lorimer, who had hitherto been conscientiously working into the night with her dictionaries. Her command, 'Gentlemen have the courtesy to return to your own quarters,' was sufficient to rout the revellers who retreated through the hole they had made. Thereupon Miss Lorimer returned to her books. The porter now reported the incident to Principal Penrose who immediately dressed and roused her secretary, Vera Farnell, from sleep with the words 'There are men in the quad. Please get up and come with me.' Within minutes the principal and her secretary had arrived at the scene of the Oriel incursion, just in time to meet the Oriel porter who was asked to summon the provost. While he was doing so, the principal repelled the threat of a fresh wave of invaders whose scufflings and hubbub could be heard from the other side. A dishevelled form which appeared at her feet and made an attempt to struggle to its feet was commanded to 'Kindly keep to your own side'. His reply, 'Which ish my side?', accompanied by an unwise and ungentlemanly dig in the principal's ribs, led to a firm 'That' and his being propelled backwards from whence he came. When Provost Phelps appeared a somewhat surreal conversation took place through the hole in the wall. Invited to come through to talk to the principal, Phelps declined, assuring her that 'the men have quietened down now' and suggesting he go and ensure that 'all is quiet'. On his departure, the principal was faced with something of a dilemma: the hole in the wall remained, assurances that 'the men' were 'quiet' were clearly not trusted, and much of the night remained for further nefarious incursions. It was determined to guard the breach in the wall through the night, the principal taking the first 'watch' followed by successive tutors. An armchair was rolled up to the hole, coffee and cushions provided, and sentry duties began, the students having being sent back to bed. The night passed peacefully, without a sound from the once raucous Oriel side. The 'men' indeed were now quiet. In 1979 the copy of the *Oxford Book of English Verse* with which Miss Penrose had whiled away her vigil was presented to Somerville library. In the following days there were a flurry of apologetic letters from Oriel: 'It is difficult', wrote

ILLUSTRATION 21.3 Sir Henry Tizard (1885–1959), fellow 1911–20

Magdalen College

the provost, 'to find words which are adequate to express our regret for the deplorable incident of last night.' The classics tutor, Marcus Tod, wrote that he would have preferred the college less success on the river than that its celebrations should imperil its good name. The president of the junior common room chimed in with his regrets for what had been done 'in a thoughtless spirit'. Principal Penrose reciprocated appropriately, and cordial relations were restored. The end of Somerville's sojourn was marked by the presentation of a clock to the Oriel JCR both as a momento of their stay and as thanks for the college's hospitality.[45]

With Somerville's return to its own premises in Michaelmas Term 1919, Oriel finally could be said to have put behind it the disruptions of war. The college was filling up but there was a consciousness of change in the air, and concern what the effects would be on Oxford and the life of the colleges. Writing in the mid-1930s, Phelps reflected on those times:

When peace came, a slender body of survivors returned. They were granted degrees on special terms, but it was long before the Class list filled up. There was a gap in the

[45] Adams, *Somerville for Women*, 101–4.

history of Oxford. The traditions of the place were forgotten or unknown. The society had to be refound and a new atmosphere created... Oxford had to make a fresh start. It was a great opportunity for revising the customs obtaining in undergraduate life, to revive the good and bury the bad. But agreement on such lines is not easy to come by; meetings were held to discuss various possibilities. But the actual result was negligible. More and more the life of Oxford reverted to type.[46]

As indicated by the provost, radical changes were largely eschewed by the Asquith Commission which investigated Oxford after the war, so that college life was allowed to begin to pick up where it had left off. The year 1919 saw work begun on the new cricket and football grounds at Bartlemas, using the bequest of Provost Shadwell and funds from the Amalgamated Clubs. Societies were springing back into existence, the Literary Society and Arnold Society revived, the latter debating 'that the Labour advance to power constituted a menace to the country's best interests'. The Plantagenet Society was also resuscitated and also one 'the proceedings of which are shrouded in mystery, the *raison d'être* of which seems to be the reading of original work of poetry and prose contributed by its members'. Changes were in the air in politics both at home and abroad. The *Record* reported that notices posted up in college showed a marked increase in interest taken in political and social questions, in particular 'we have had notices of the Labour Club and its meetings... with thirteen reasons why we should join the Labour Club'. On which it somewhat tartly opined: 'We have been waiting patiently for the appearance on the Boards of twenty-six reasons why we should *not*, but so far they have not been forthcoming. We ought perhaps to be glad to see an increased appreciation of the claims of "Labour"—for, after all what is a college but a Labour Club!' There was also 'an unprecedented number of College, or as it is now the fashion to call them, J.C.R. meetings... The College is clearly "finding itself" gradually.'[47] Sport was in full swing by Michaelmas 1919 with reports on rowing, association football, rugby, and hockey carried in the *Record* for the following term. Although the number of old members returning that term was 'a little disappointing', it was also reported that there 'has been no lack of others in their place'.[48]

In its first post-war terms, the college contained a mixed and varied company, if not in background, then in experience. The new entry was still overwhelmingly public school and it was a matter of note when one school was represented heavily and another absent from the freshmen lists. But a yawning gulf must often have existed between the returning ex-servicemen some of whom had seen years of war, often in the front line, and the fresh-faced youths who had just escaped the call-up, some of them having already

---

[46] *Oxford Magazine*, 9 May 1935, 566.
[47] OR (April 1919), 73; OR (March 1920), 128; OR (September 1920), 157.
[48] OR (April 1919), 71; OR (March 1920).

presented themselves for a preliminary medical examination. Among the former were two of what were to become Oriel's most famous literati of the age, Walter Carruthers Sellar and Robert Julian Yeatman, authors of *1066 and All That*, which was serialized in *Punch* in the autumn of 1930, before its publication. Both had served in the war before matriculating at Oriel to read modern history on the same day in April 1919. Their experiences speak volumes for those who returned from active service to the college in months after the armistice. Sellar left Fettes as head boy in 1917 to become second lieutenant in the King's Own Scottish Borderers, suffering wounds that continued to undermine his health during his Oriel years, forcing him to take an aegrotat degree in 1922. Yeatman left Marlborough in 1914 to join the Royal Field Artillery; commissioned lieutenant in 1915, he was awarded an MC a year later. He also suffered severe wounds. According to one account 'he had been one of four men in a hole in no-man's-land when a shell landed in it. One was killed, one was terribly maimed, one driven mad, and Julian was the fourth.' His wounds, described as 'leaving him perforated like a colander', were such that he was warned never to fall on the ball in rugby. It was advice he ignored and played both for Oriel and the varsity 'A' (precursors to the Greyhounds), before taking a second in modern history in the same year as his later co-author.[49]

By March 1920 there were 160 undergraduates in residence, a number which, it was thought, 'has never been equalled and will probably never be exceeded'. A large number of undergraduates were in lodgings and 'in one or two cases a single sitting room has been occupied by two men' and the gallery in hall pressed into service to avoid the necessity of two sittings for dinner. There was some anxiety that this increase in numbers could mean a loss. In spite of its vicissitudes the 'lean years' of the war had shown a positive side: 'Never was the ideal of the College as a happy family, "everyone knowing everyone", so fully realised. We would impress upon present members of the College that it *is* a worthy ideal, and that every individual member of the College may, and should, do his best to promote such realisation of it as is possible under present circumstances.'[50] Moreover as well as greater numbers, there was also greater variety. To a regular trickle of Rhodes scholars from the Dominions three Indian students were added in 1921 to whom, the *Record* trusted, 'a hearty welcome has been given', taking the opportunity to reflect on the realities of a growing roll of undergraduates for the college community:

...Freshmen, of whatever nationality, must not expect to be at once 'hand and glove' with everybody in the College. Men associate together either because they come from the same school, or because they have similar trusts and pursuits, or because they are

---

[49] ODNB s.n.; OR 1971, 11. [50] OR (March 1920), 127–8.

brought together in sports and games. That 'everyone should know everyone' is no doubt a desirable ideal for a College, but even in a College of moderate size like Oriel it must, we fear, remain an ideal only.[51]

Clearly, on many fronts Oriel was going through an expansive phase after the travails of war. However carefree the image of post-war Oxford, fixed for ever by the pages of Waugh's *Brideshead Revisited*, there was a solid financial underpinning to the expanding Oriel community that entered the 1920s. In the last months of the war, the college was the recipient of several benefactions, a classics scholarship founded by Mr John Varley, a legacy of £1,000 from Mr A. F. Blackwell, and a gift from Professor W. J. Lewis for an exhibition in mathematics. These were important for, as was noted, as Oriel was 'not one of the richer Colleges, and is particularly deficient in comparison with most of the other Colleges in emoluments for Scholarships such benefactions are extremely valuable...'.[52] To them were added the scholarships founded to commemorate the Orielenses which had died in the war, but in addition the most dramatic increase in the college's income came through the sale of its estates, and the investment of the funds received in stocks and shares. Pushed through with the determined support of Provost Phelps who, though a man who had enjoyed both hunting and shooting on the college estates, now saw that their sale was advantageous to Oriel and accepted the advice to sell, on a scale greater than any other college. He also saw to it that virtually all the proceeds were invested in the educational enhancement of the college through new fellowships and scholarships. Although often regarded as a figure belonging an earlier age, Phelps in the early 1920s was directing an expanding college with a large increase in undergraduates, new fellowships, and new subjects.

Nonetheless, Phelps effortlessly acquired, some said decided to acquire, an aura of eccentricity. His long white beard, black straw hat, and clerical garb were only part of a persona which attracted to itself all manner of stories, many apocryphal, but others genuine. His habit of repeating phrases was one of his more famous, which A. J. P. Taylor believed was a trick by which he made even the most trivial remarks sound impressive, recording the story that when his own tutor, Stanley Cohn, became a fellow Phelps greeted him by saying, 'A very close election, Mr Cohn—elected by one vote and it wasn't mine, it wasn't mine.' By no means an uncritical commentator on the Oriel to which he came as an undergraduate in 1925, nor indeed of Phelps himself, Taylor regarded him as 'one of the few justifications for Oxford's existence'. It was 'with a little exaggeration', according to Taylor, that Phelps described himself as the 'titular head of the Labour Party in Oxford', though

[51] OR (March 1921), 5.   [52] OR (March 1918), 2.

his political position was probably nearer to that of a Gladstonian Liberal.[53] But whatever his precise position in the political spectrum, Phelps brought some quite distinct qualities to his position as provost. As for many years chairman of the Oxford Board of Guardians, he knew most of the Oxford tramps by name, who when met on his regular perambulations about Oxford were greeted warmly and always asked how they were accommodated.[54] But he was equally warm to undergraduates, including Taylor, whom he invited several times for lunch and to accompany him on long walks. Undergraduates were entertained to tea in rotation or seized upon to accompany him on his walks, and more than one of that generation attested to Phelps's pains to get to know people personally. He held 'Collections' at the beginning of each Michaelmas Term at which undergraduates accounted for their doings in the long vacation. Walking and conversation remained his principal recreations, walks on which 'his conversation was varied and unceasing', so much so that in 1923 the story got about that the provost was ill: 'Enquiries happily elicited that the rumours had no foundation and further research discovered its origins in the statement of a friend that he had seen the Provost and a companion returning from a Sunday afternoon walk and the companion was walking abreast of him and appeared to be doing most of the talking.'[55] The 'Phelps experience' could begin early, as he interviewed almost all prospective undergraduates. On being demobbed from the Royal Artillery, S. Thompson gave his account of his interview in the spring of 1919. Met at the door of the provost's lodgings by Phelps himself, the interview began in the hall: '"Come in my dear sir; and where do you come from, I mean". "From the Isle of Wight, Sir", I replied. "And have you read the *Silence of Dean Maitland*, the *Silence of Dean Maitland*, I mean?". "Not yet, Sir". "But you will, but you will—that's good, that's good, that's good. But you will"— these phrases were repeated ad infinitum, until they gradually faded away. We indulged in various pleasantries for a short while, till he closed the conversation by telling me the date of the following Michaelmas Term. I should say in parenthesis he took no notice at all of my father throughout the interview.'[56]

In spite of anxiety that the threads of continuity in college life were being lost, much of what had been familiar in undergraduate life before the war was being restored as the college filled up with fresh generations untouched by the Great War, so that in many respects undergraduate life in the inter-war years carried on in apparently seamless continuity, albeit with many less apparent changes. Alan Taylor as an undergraduate in the mid-1920s, like Reggie Burton as a young fellow in the early 1930s, still had a scout come to

---

[53] A. J. P. Taylor, *A Personal History* (London, 1984), 86–7.
[54] Taylor, *A Personal History*, 86; OR (1981), 19.
[55] OR (1991), 29; OR (December 1923), 171–2. [56] OR (1991), 29–31.

lay the fire in the morning, bringing a small jug of hot water for shaving and bringing a cooked breakfast. Oriel also maintained 'commons', cheese, bread, and beer for lunch and brought to one's rooms, where some other colleges were already serving breakfast and lunch communally. At dinner scholars still had a separate table down the centre of the hall, which with the chapel continued to form a centre to communal life in the college. Fifty chapel attendances a term were expected as late as the 1920s and gowns were compulsory for hall, chapel, lectures, and tutorials, as well as in the streets of Oxford. The college gate shut at 9.30 p.m. and a small gate fine had to be paid for admittance up to midnight. Entry after that meant an interview with the dean and a fine, or scaling the walls. The JCR in the 1920s was described by one contemporary as being like a gentleman's club in miniature, Taylor claiming that he was too shy to enter it until his place in the college eight gave him the confidence to do so: 'The shyness was quite unnecessary. No one noticed me one way or another.'[57] As ever it was left to individuals to shape their own time at Oriel according to their inclinations and their means. Taylor was active in left-wing politics, one of the few undergraduates to actively support the TUC during the General Strike, while most of his college contemporaries were volunteering to keep essential services running; but he also stroked a college eight, attended the Playhouse repertory theatre weekly, occasionally attended poets' parties, espying from afar luminaries such as Auden and Stephen Spender, enjoyed driving fast cars 'when my father gave me one', and shared his good taste in wine and cigars with close friends. Those who could entertained in their rooms, up to six being permissible without consulting the dean, communal breakfasts and lunches being popular for those who could afford them. Affordability, according to one undergraduate of the 1920s, was about £250 a year, on which it was possible to live reasonably well in Oxford and 'cut a dash', entertain friends for breakfast, go to the theatre in evening dress, join the Union, and buy books; 'You could do everything practically but hunt.'[58] Many at the time referred to the distinction between 'aesthetes' and 'hearties'. The former, according to Taylor, 'wore fancy clothes and spoke in affected tones' while the latter 'were athletes or would-be athletes much given to wrecking the rooms of those they disliked'.[59] In practice, both reflected something of the exuberance of fresh generations released from the threat of war and from some of the restrictions of Victorian and Edwardian convention. The arts were becoming more self-consciously an important component in Oxford life and that of many undergraduates, while sport remained a major part of

---

[57] Taylor, *Personal History*, 88.
[58] Taylor, *Personal History*, 92–5; OR (1981), 19–22.
[59] Taylor, *Personal History*, 95. More generally see B. Harrison, 'College Life, 1918–1939', in HUO viii. 98–9.

ILLUSTRATION 21.4 The second eight, 1926: A. J. P. Taylor seated in the centre of the second row, J. I. M. Stewart (Michael Innes) at his feet, *OCA*

college and university life. Association football appeared all the rage in the Oriel of the 1920s, naturally perhaps for a college that in that decade had no great success to boast on the river. As ever, a few zealots took to the extremes, while many more took in something of everything they found about them. 'Oxford bags' of 22 inches circumference below the knee were not confined to aesthetes, and while Taylor claimed he had no one he welcomed with 'My dear' one of his closest friends, Theodore Yates, 'cast himself as a distinguished elderly man. He walked with a silverheaded ebony cane and he did not walk much. He stayed in bed until midday, dined every evening at the George and sat up half the night drinking whisky.'[60] The so-called division seems in Oriel to have been mitigated by what many attest as the generally friendly atmosphere promoted by Provost Phelps and the college's still modest scale, 'a place in which it was very easy to make friends' according to at least one witness.[61]

[60] Taylor, *Personal History*, 96. [61] OR (1981), 22.

College life continued to develop under its own momentum as a sense of normality returned. Intellectual activity was not spurned as new societies were founded, including a philosophical society, the Whately. External events intruded in the first part of Trinity Term 1926 with the calling of the General Strike in May and the large rush of undergraduate volunteers, some 120 from Oriel alone, to act as Special Constables, as bus and train drivers, and man essential food depots in London and elsewhere. A few, Taylor included, threw their support behind the strikers.[62] The General Strike, however, was only a short-lived interruption to a term which had special significance in the history of the college. On Friday 18 June 1926, Commemoration Day, Provost Phelps lit a bonfire in the first quad (then ungrassed) to inaugurate part of the events for Oriel's sexcentenary. They were, appropriately, on an unprecedented scale, an elaborate celebration of Oriel's past and present, bringing together the largest number of college members ever seen. Invitations were sent out to over 1,200 known Orielenses around the world out of the 2,109 admitted to the college since 1850. Telegrams were exchanged with the king, as Visitor. On 17 June a dinner was held in hall for 150 old members; lunch in the quad was attended the next day by 318 members of the college and 158 ladies, followed by a tea party for 1,000 guests. The sexcentenary dinner on Friday was attended by the provost, twelve fellows, and all bachelors of arts and undergraduates in residence. The college's copy of the Shakespeare First Folio was put on special exhibition and three weeks later, after term was over, all seventy-two college servants were taken on an outing. The college's founding and history were also a subject of an article by the provost in the December issue of the *Record*.[63]

In 1929 Phelps resigned as provost, not it should be said into complete retirement, for as well as becoming an honorary fellow he served in 1929–30 as chairman of a Home Office committee on the relief of the casual poor, the subject on which he was the acknowledged expert. Continuing to live in Oxford, he was to be an honoured guest at events in the college until his death in 1936. His successor, William David Ross, held office until 1947 and was to see Oriel through the Great Depression and the Second World War. A Scot, he continued Oriel's penchant for choosing one known to it. Born in Thurso in 1877, his early education was at the Royal High School in Edinburgh and Edinburgh University, where he took a first in classics in 1895. Academic success followed him at Balliol with firsts in mods and Greats. His first academic appointment, in 1900, was as a lecturer at Oriel. Almost immediately he was elected to a fellowship by examination at Merton, which he held until 1902, when he was elected fellow and tutor in philosophy

---

[62] OR (June 1926), 328–30; Taylor, *Personal History*, 101–4.
[63] OR (June 1926), 366–7.

at Oriel. Unlike his predecessor, Ross was a distinguished academic figure, both as a philosopher and Aristotelian scholar. He was the leading authority on Aristotle of his generation, editing a major series of translations, to which he contributed the *Metaphysics* (1908) and the *Nicomachean Ethics* (1925). He edited six of the works for the series of Oxford Classical Texts, five with revised texts, introductions, and commentary, the last appearing in 1961. Generations of classicists, philosophers, and historians ancient and modern became acquainted with Aristotle through Ross. As a former lecturer in philosophy at Oriel in the 1970s remarked, 'Aristotle in Oxford *was* Ross'.[64] His war service was also highly esteemed, working from 1915 in a variety of administrative positions, in the north-east, Woolwich, and ultimately Whitehall, concerned with the supply of munitions, leaving with the rank of major and an OBE. His academic career burgeoned after the war. From 1923 to 1928 he acted as deputy White's Professor of Moral Philosophy, meanwhile preparing his philosophical work *The Right and the Good* (1930). He continued to serve on public and charitable bodies, including one of the Textile Trades Boards, which arbitrated wages and conditions of work, and for which he was knighted in 1938. Ross brought more than intellectual leadership to the college: for the first time since 1874, a family lived in the lodgings.[65]

Another important change in the leadership of the college had come in 1925 with the appointment of William Charles Wand as dean, fellow, and tutor, in succession to Eric Graham who was moving to be principal of Cuddesdon Theological College. In 1945, 'Jimmy' Wand would be selected by Churchill to be bishop of London, charged with the recovery and revitalization of the largest diocese in the country. 'Wand of London' had served from 1919 as vicar of St Mark's, Salisbury; alongside his duties as parish priest he conducted lectures at the local theological college, whetting his appetite for further scholarly activity. But he also brought to Oriel the experience of his war service, as chaplain from 1915 to 1918 in Gallipoli and on the Western Front. Like many of his generation, his experience ministering to the spiritual needs of inter-war Oxford was founded on front-line service of an altogether more challenging kind. As chaplain on a hospital ship ferrying the wounded between Gallipoli and Egypt, he conducted funerals at sea, attended the dying, and visited the wards daily, prompting in him the suggestion that the Church of England needed a more 'efficient' service for the dying, casting envious eyes at the last rites of the Roman Catholic chaplains. In France, he was 'priest-in-charge' of the military church of St George at the Rouen Base Camp, a wooden structure in which he organized a highly successful library and lecture room as a rival to the bars and bordellos

---

[64] ODNB s.n.; personal communication from Professor Howard Robinson.
[65] OR (1948), 5–6.

ILLUSTRATION 21.5
J. W. C. Wand (1885–1977), fellow 1925–34, as archbishop of Brisbane, 1934
Oriel College

all around.[66] Undoubtedly recommended to Oriel by Graham, Wand's biographer believed that a major motive in his moving to Oriel was to advance his own studies and to write. But in coming to Oriel he was, as a devotee of Keble and the Oxford Movement, very conscious of its place in recent church history, as well as of its strong academic reputation. Moreover a college which had supplied no less than thirty-nine chaplains to the forces and in 1930 counted seven bishops amongst its alumni, rising later to ten, had by no means relinquished its place as a major force in the Church of England. Ironically, whatever his own Anglo-Catholic leanings, by the time of Ross's arrival he had become part of a remarkably ecumenical troika at the head of the college, for Ross was a Presbyterian and the senior tutor, Marcus Tod, was described as a 'warm-hearted Methodist'. 'There go the Right and the Good', opined a college wit, when he saw the three of them strolling in the quad, echoing the provost's venture into moral philosophy and the firm

[66] J. S. Peart-Binns, *Wand of London* (Oxford, 1987), 29–33.

principles of the college officers. Within the college, Wand did nothing ostentatious in his chapel services to disturb what has been described as the 'middle-of-the-road Anglicanism' that prevailed under his immediate predecessors. Services were described as 'quietly dignified without any catholic embellishments'.[67] He worked hard both inside and outside the college. Although living with his family at Bartlemas, an undergraduate living opposite to him on his staircase in college became accustomed to hearing his bathwater flushing away at two or three o'clock in the morning. He had been writing. Four books were written during his years at Oriel, including a textbook for students, *A History of the Modern Church* (1930), and commentaries on Peter and Jude. He contributed an essay to a collection edited in 1934 by the New College tutor and later cabinet minister R. H. S. Crossman, commenting on Moral Rearmament, a movement currently active and controversial in Oxford. Wand's influence in the college was probably greatest through his tutorials in theology and his work as college chaplain. While he failed to persuade Alan Taylor to discuss his religious 'doubts' with him when he refused to attend chapel on the grounds of having no religious beliefs, it was clear that to others he was a formative influence; Richard Wimbush, later bishop of Argyll, wrote: 'I have very much to thank Jimmy Wand for, as he moulded my later course of life by tutoring me into a First Class degree in Theology—something neither I nor anyone else ever dreamt of! He was an all-rounder—a scholar and a parish priest, and a devoted servant of the Church.'[68]

Wand, of course, had a prominent place in college life because he combined the offices of chaplain, tutor, and dean, responsible for discipline. Moreover, the office of the dean still carried the position of vice-provost or more precisely vice-gerent, though when Wand left Oriel to become bishop of Brisbane, the older term was abandoned and the post of vice-provost formally created. Canon Adam remembered that being dean sometimes obscured Wand's impact as chaplain: 'This muscular, kindly priest was somewhat shy and reserved with undergraduates and not so well known as he deserved. Here was an instance where one half of a dual responsibility (Dean) militated against the other half (Chaplain). It was the Dean . . . whom most of the undergraduates knew, and not so many saw in him the Chaplain who had a real pastoral concern for them.' Reggie Burton remembered Wand as 'outgoing, humane and extremely kind, with a merry sense of humour'. His account of Wand's exercise of the office of dean conjured up the relatively easygoing atmosphere towards college discipline in the run-up to the Second World War:

---

[67] Peart-Binns, *Wand of London*, 45–8, 51.
[68] Peart-Binns, *Wand of London*, 47–51; Taylor, *Personal History*, 85–6.

As Dean, he was responsible for the discipline of undergraduates, a duty he undertook with skill and understanding. I well remember that he used on occasions to wait under one of the college walls, where there was a well known way for climbing in after midnight, and catch the young men almost literally in his arms as they jumped down, with some jocular remark such as 'One up to me this time'. Both Dean and undergraduates would regard this as a good sporting game, and there was never any ill feeling on either side.[69]

Under Provost Ross the 1930s could be seen as halcyon days for the college. In spite of the worldwide recession and, later in the decade, growing international tension, there was much to celebrate. An innovation in the *Record* was the presentation of an educational report which revealed that in 1930 the college had achieved the second highest number of firsts in its history, nine, beaten only by the number in 1924–5.[70] It was recognition that academic attainment remained important to the college. Phelps had encouraged hard work, and when one father of an undergraduate told Dean Wand that his son had enjoyed life at Oriel very much but found that he had to work pretty hard, 'Yes', said Wand, 'work is the only fly in the ointment up here.'[71] Oriel was noted for not taking people for pass degrees simply to make up the numbers. The devotion of resources and benefactions to scholarships and new fellowships was clearly bearing fruit. Nor could the college be said to be inward-looking; in the summer term of 1931 G. M. Wilson became president of the Union and in the General Election in the autumn no less than six former members were elected MPs.[72] What lived most in the memory of those who were present was Oriel's almost unprecedented success on the river, beginning in 1933 when for the first time in decades, Oriel became Head of the River, celebrated with a tumultuous bump supper to which the defeated crews and former Oriel oarsmen were invited. A huge bonfire was again lit in the front quad, but this time to the accompaniment of chamber pots full of lighted methylated spirits hoisted onto the roofs of the front quad. This success was the result of something of a collective effort, not just by the oarsmen, but also with the fellows. Dean Wand took a keen interest in all the sporting activity of the college, coached some of the oarsmen, and suggested innovations to the equipment of the racing eights. A degree of hitherto unheard of professionalism was undoubtedly creeping into Oriel rowing when for its final week of training it 'borrowed' as a coach the well-known playwright R. C. Sherriff, then occupying a special scholarship at New College.[73] This was the hey-day of Oriel rowing before the Second

---

[69] Peart-Binns, *Wand of London*, 46–7.
[70] OR (January 1931), 122–3.
[71] Peart-Binns, *Wand of London*, 46.
[72] OR (June 1931), 146; OR (January 1932), 172.
[73] OR (June 1933), 295–8; Peart-Binns, *Wand of London*, 48.

World War with the headship of the river retained in successive years. More tumultuous celebrations in 1934 were the subject of press reports, forcing the *Record* into a disclaimer: 'The Press, which never showed us much favour, excelled itself in its lurid descriptions of the Bump supper. Not content with detailing a series of outrages which never occurred, it drew upon its equally mythical account of last year's events to lend some purple patches to an already colourful story.'[74] But it was not at the expense of academic prowess. Indeed, quite the opposite, when five of the eight that went Head of the River in 1935 took firsts. The following year saw twelve firsts out of the fifty-seven taking finals and the college still Head of the River. The year 1936 was hailed as an *annus mirabilis*. Oriel's dominance on the river was retained for the fourth year in succession while the college hit a new academic record of thirteen firsts, only exceeded in number by Queen's and Balliol. Athletic prowess was not confined to the river, with two cricket blues and a rugby blue, and victory in the University Lawn Tennis Cup. Meanwhile the provost was busier than ever, chairing three Trade Boards, arbitrating a trade dispute in the Yorkshire woollen industry, and achieving the distinction of President of the British Academy, of which he had been a fellow since 1927.[75]

The academic successes of the college under both Phelps and Ross may also have reflected the way in which the nature of the fellowship and teaching arrangements were changing in the inter-war years. They witnessed the rise of the tutorial fellow, who was expected to carry out significant teaching duties as a matter of course. Oriel had inherited from the previous century a structure of about four tutors appointed by the provost from amongst the fellows. This system was still the case in 1919, though then there were only three, including Ross himself. But the college was beginning to appoint fellow-lecturers in a wider range of subjects, including George Clark in modern history, Stanley Cohn in medieval history, Eric Graham in theology, Percy Simpson in English, Eric Hargreaves in economics, and Kenneth Franklin in physiology. Most of them were eventually appointed tutors, forming a senior group of fellow-lecturers, effectively senior subject tutors. Lecturers who were not fellows of Oriel, though they were often fellows of other colleges, worked in harness with them. As a result tutorial teaching in the college came to be closely defined in terms of particular subjects, in response to developments in the university syllabus, among them the new school of philosophy, politics, and economics in 1920. But as late as 1939 there was no fellow tutor in law, and Percy Simpson had no successor as a fellow tutor in English, leaving the teaching in these mainstream subjects to lecturers. A fellowship in two tiers was the consequence, which inevitably

---

[74] OR (June 1934), 363.   [75] OR (January 1937), 158–9.

produced a degree of resentment. College tradition records a compact to induce the college to abolish the distinction, made about 1938 by three younger fellows, Reggie Burton, Billy Pantin, and Arthur Crow, known from its venue as the Treaty of Ross-on-Wye. If that tradition is accurate, however, they did not succeed; the tutorship was not conferred on all teaching fellows until 1952. But the increasing specialization of fellows within the various schools led to more professional teaching and enhanced its intellectual quality. Ross, Wand, and Tod were all distinguished scholars and recruited younger colleagues of similar calibre, whose tutorials brought undergraduates into contact with current scholarly issues and new ideas. Alan Taylor recorded his tutorials in the mid-1920s with the formidable Clark and Cohn, and further essays which he read to Ross as his moral tutor. The presence in the common room of the Regius Professor of Modern History and the Oriel Professor of the Interpretation of Holy Scripture added intellectual weight, enhanced by the occasional visits of G. M. Trevelyan and Sir Henry Tizard as honorary fellows. After the resignation of Phelps in 1929 the atmosphere was perhaps rather solemn and (as Maurice Bowra recalled) somewhat puritan, evoking undergraduate wit at the expense of the Methodist Marcus Tod:

> On weekdays in Oriel Quad
> You may hear Mr Marcus N. Tod
> Discourse upon Greece
> And the Peloponnese,
> And on Sundays in Walton Street, God.

In 1932 there was a highly significant development: the formation of a society of old members. Initially, it was to involve an annual meeting at the end of summer term for a cricket match in return for a modest life subscription of one guinea. By 1933 the Oriel Society had seventy members who met for a cricket match and weekend in the college at the end of Trinity Term. A dinner at the Holborn Restaurant in London was organized in January 1933, attended by seventy-four people; this set the pattern for Oriel Society events, comprising a dinner in London and a meeting in college at the end of Trinity Term for another dinner and a cricket match. The aims of the Society were expressed in a quotation from Dr Johnson, 'friendship should be kept in repair'. The importance of bringing old members together provoked the *Record* into a peroration:

Do we realise how much of the world 'from China to Peru' comes under the influence of our College? Oriel men govern the Sudan, they administer Nigeria, they are missionaries and colonists in Central Africa, they practice law and teach at the Cape, they are Professors in Canada and the United States, Bishops and Civil Servants

ILLUSTRATION 21.6 The college servants, 1939, *OCA*

in India... Go where you will, wherever the English language is spoken the word 'Oriel' is a passport.[76]

Royal events provided an opportunity for the college to celebrate its corporate identity, since the monarch was its Visitor. In 1935 George V's Jubilee was celebrated in Oriel, not without some embarrassment at the lack of an appropriate flag: 'The only flags that could be discovered in College, a Tricolor and the flag of the Mercantile Marine were deemed unsuitable for the occasion...' An expert in heraldry, the Revd Mr E. E. Dorling, was consulted, who designed a college flag following the description of the arms of Oriel, effectively those of Edward II, in the University Calendar. The new flag with its royal lions, eleven feet in height and nine feet six inches in width like a medieval banner, 'by general consent the most handsome flag in Oxford', was first flown on the tower over the gateway on 6 May 1935. The king's health was duly toasted in college.[77] Two years later, the High Street frontage of the college was illuminated and the hall and library floodlit for the coronation of George VI. The king's message was broadcast in hall

---

[76] OR, (January 1932), 183–4; OR (January 1933), 248–50; OR (June 1933), 281.
[77] OR (June 1935), 8.

ILLUSTRATION 21.7 The fellows, 1941, *OCA*

	K. J. Franklin	Percy Simpson	Chasser Moir	W. G. Maclagan	
W. A. Pantin	H. M. Margoliouth	L. W. Grensted	R. W. B. Burton	J. W. Gough	E. Hargreaves
F. M. Powicke	M. N. Tod	Sir David Ross, *Provost*	D. L. I. Hammick	L. Collins	

after dinner, and the following day the provost and fellows were at home to the resident MAs and their wives.[78]

The college which entered the Second World War was still in most respects recognizable as the Oriel which had endured its predecessor. It was larger both in terms of undergraduate numbers and fellows, but not so much larger as to have lost its sense of identity. In 1939, 192 undergraduates were in residence, 30 more than the record number of 1919, which had been thought impossible to exceed. Triumphs on the river and continuing academic prowess gave the college a strong sense of its own distinction and

[78] OR (June 1937), 210.

identity. The development of the *Oriel Record* and the founding of the Oriel Society gave a greater formal cohesion to old members of the college than they had ever had before. This was all the more important as increasing numbers, greater pressure of business, and changing habits made the vast web of correspondence maintained by Phelps and his like unsustainable. The undergraduate body continued to be dominated, as the lists of freshmen attest, by candidates from the public schools. This was still true of the university as a whole, where 62 per cent of male non-graduate entrants in 1938–9 came from independent schools, 13 per cent from direct-grant grammar schools, 19 per cent from maintained schools, and 5 per cent from other schools in the United Kingdom.[79] But entry was being widened and reflected in a wider range of schools sending undergraduates to Oxford and to Oriel than had been the case before 1914. This was partly the result of broad social and educational changes, dramatically increasing the number of secondary school leavers of whom there were more than five times as many in 1937 as there had been in 1895, and of extended financial assistance to candidates. From 1902 local education authorities offered grants to the most able students and by 1937 over a thousand Oxford men and women, approximately a quarter of those in residence, held such awards. The Board of Education also awarded over two hundred state scholarships from assisted schools, mainly at Oxford and Cambridge. College scholarships and exhibitions, of the kind which Oriel had been able to increase substantially after 1918, were also a significant source of financial assistance to those wishing to study at Oxford. Between a quarter and a third of male matriculands held such awards between 1900 and 1939, and by 1939 over half of all Oxford undergraduates were in receipt of some form of assistance.[80] This undoubtedly eased the way into Oriel for more grammar school entrants, who took nine of the fourteen scholarships in the list of freshmen in 1939. The list contained a wider range of schools than it had at the turn of the century.[81] But within a closely knit nexus of schools and university, many schools built up traditional connections with favoured colleges; alumni who became schoolmasters recommended pupils to their old college; and Oriel had a particularly strong cohort of the sons of former members of the college. There would have been at least eleven, a fifth of the total, entering the college in 1940 if military service had not intervened.[82]

With still only seventeen fellows in 1939, and only fourteen in the early 1930s, the senior common room remained a closely knit community. When Phelps spoke at a dinner in hall on his eightieth birthday, he conjured up a world in process of being lost as numbers of undergraduates and senior

---

[79] Harrison, 'College Life, 1918–1939', HUO viii. 94.
[80] D. I. Greenstein, 'The Junior Members, 1900–1990: A Profile', HUO viii. 46–7.
[81] OR (January 1940), 63–4.   [82] OR (January 1940), 55.

members increased. He referred to common room life as 'The family' for, he averred, 'it was a family which gathered round the fire of a winter evening, large enough and varied enough for conversation, free from "shop" or gossip and all vulgar topics.' He remembered too the days when the college had still had its estates and the half-yearly meetings when 'the Bursar gave an account of rents, the outgoings and the surplus was divided up among the fellows; the undergraduates were never mentioned'. 'All this', he concluded, 'in its varied simplicity made life most enjoyable, and he was heartily glad to have shared in it.' It would be easy to see such comments as somewhat romanticized, but the former provost was reflecting widespread and increasing anxieties about the changes which were beginning to affect the hitherto relatively sequestered life of both junior and senior members. By the time he was speaking, it was impossible to ignore the traffic which thundered past the Rhodes Building and congested Carfax, the new 'super cinema' built at Gloucester Green, or the Woolworths and Marks and Spencers chain stores which were changing the look of Oxford's main streets. Phelps's appraisal in 1935 was remarkably prescient: writing in the *Oxford Magazine*, he recognized that increasing numbers, partly due to 'bursarial pressure' during the depression, and the strain placed upon accommodation, threatened the cohesion of college life. He believed that contemporary undergraduates 'are better behaved, they work harder, and are more economical', but worried that the system of the 'moral tutor' was becoming a thing of the past, reading parties rarer, and corporate spirit weaker. Among senior members too, offices which had once been taken by fellows, such as those of the bursar or chaplain, were increasingly being filled by professionals. Of the traffic, he could only despair: 'it would be idle to try to revive a past, when the High Street, paved with cobbles, was a cricket-ground for boys in the Long Vacation.'[83]

If little could be done to recapture the High Street for cricket, the strong community spirit in Oriel bred a sense of fun, epitomized by the treasured college mascot, the tortoise. Allegedly introduced in 1896 by the dean, Francis Hall, it succeeded a bulldog known as 'Oriel Bill'. Readers of *The Times* on 31 May 1938 might have been intrigued to find the following in the birth notices:

On May 28 1938 at Oriel College Oxford, to Georgina, wife of O. C. Testudo—a son (Whalley George).
Georgius exultat, nato testudine, Whalley.
Est bene, si possis credere Temporibus.[84]

Was this a Virgin Birth? The question was long debated before and after the war. Apart from this putative miracle, the months leading up to the war were reassuringly normal. As the war clouds gathered over Europe, and as the

[83] *Oxford Magazine*, 9 May 1935, 568.   [84] OR (June 1938), 316–17.

first air raid precautions literature and the initial steps taken to introduce conscription were being digested by the college authorities, the Arnold Society in Trinity Term debated a motion in favour of 'moral disarmament', proposed by the dean, with other senior members present. It was reported: 'At the meeting... the most unsuspected facts about don and undergraduate life were revealed, and it was decided after a heated discussion that the Oxford of the past was to be preferred to the Oxford of today.' On the eve of war Arnold organized a joint debate with St Hilda's, and the Newlands Society was resurrected for dramatic productions.[85] In the summer of 1939 another part of the college community was recognized with the publication in the *Record* of a photograph of the thirty male servants then employed. The words of the accompanying article were prescient in view of what was to come: 'There are several meanings attributable to the expression "the College". It may mean the buildings, the Governing Body, or those technically on the Books. But no idea of membership can have any reality or sense which does not include those essential collaborators who, through the agency of the photographer, greet the readers of this issue.'[86]

The impact of war was soon to make itself felt in every aspect of college life. In the last class list before the war, seven out of the fifty-seven Oriel finalists took firsts; the largest schools were modern history, with twelve, followed by law with eight, PPE and classics with six each, and six in the various sciences.[87] Of the 193 in residence in 1939, 115 offered themselves for military service, with another 52 prevented by their nationality or by reading subjects classified as reserved, including chemistry, engineering, and theology. In Hilary Term 1940 numbers were reduced to 132.[88] More serious still, the college had been forewarned that its buildings would be requisitioned in the event of war as the government moved administrative services out of London in anticipation of bombing. As a result large parts of the college were left vacant for whatever might be required; only twenty-two were living in college, forty-three were housed in Hertford, while the rest were in lodgings. Nonetheless, the *Record* for 1940 carried reports of a lively range of sporting and other activities. A notable additional activity was table tennis, encouraged by the gift of a ping-pong table to the junior members by the provost and fellows and marked with a match between the senior and junior common rooms.[89] Unlike the previous war, Oxford and Oriel's undergraduate population kept up well, partly because conscription permitted government to regulate the flow of manpower into the armed forces; for those who still had examinations to take, the call-up date was postponed almost to 21. The university agreed to host special courses for probationers in the Royal Signals and for army and air-force cadets, 3,000 of whom had

[85] OR (January 1939), 47. [86] OR (June 1939), 20. [87] OR (January 1940), 61–2.
[88] OR (January 1940), 55. [89] OR (January 1940), 82–91.

matriculated by 1942. In spite of these mitigating factors, the college anticipated its undergraduate numbers settling down at eighty to ninety, in fact dipping as low as seventy-eight in Michaelmas Term 1942, only a small proportion of whom, about twenty, could live in college. This was at least higher than the low point of seven undergraduates during the previous war. Of the eighty-four in residence in Trinity Term 1943, forty-five were in their first year and liable to call-up. Provost Ross anticipated that for the immediate future, at least half of those on the college books would be probationers who came up for their six-month courses before being drafted into the fighting forces.[90] Few, however, could not be conscious of the larger college community contained in the War Register of those serving in the armed forces, totalling 318 former undergraduates and 14 college servants. In addition, most of the dons were called up for war service of one kind or another. The provost was called on for even more duties, serving as vice-chancellor from 1941 to 1944, chairing the National Arbitration Tribunal from 1941, and the Civil Service Arbitration Tribunal from 1942.[91]

It was more difficult for the college to maintain much corporate spirit with most of its premises occupied by various government departments, and the majority of undergraduates only on the books for a short period and mainly living out of college. Wartime routines gave some cohesion to the hybrid community which now inhabited the three quadrangles, cooperating on fire-watching and fire-fighting. The *Record* put a brave face on it: 'We all rub along very well together, but some of our temporary guests are not as averse to litter as others!'[92] The ARP precautions organized by Kenneth Franklin and Billy Pantin proved their efficacy in discovering a small fire in the library, caused by a defective flue, late on the night of 31 January 1943, before serious damage was done.[93] Increasingly, the college took on a unique wartime appearance. The newly laid out lawns in the first quadrangle were converted to tomato-growing, while the St Mary quadrangle was devoted to cabbages and other vegetables.[94] Arriving in 1941, Peter Anstey still found Oxford 'an oasis where the opportunities for self-fulfilment seemed largely undisturbed', though as dons and lecturers became thinner on the ground he found himself 'farmed out to retired or semi-retired giants from the past'. He reflected on the ambivalence of 'Oxford on rations': 'Peace-time delights, such as tea with cakes and crumpets in college rooms were still a part of undergraduate life, provided that one was prepared to queue outside the North Oxford cake factory at 8 a.m. and provided too that a miniscule 2oz. Butter ration delivered promptly each Monday by the staircase scout had been kept intact...' The war was never far away: 'All of us, however, knew

---

[90] OR (January 1944), 239. [91] OR (January 1943), 173.
[92] OR (June 1941), 133. [93] OR (June 1941), 133–4; OR (January 1944), 239.
[94] OR (November 1940), 98.

well that we had but a part-way course to run—Honour Mods in my case in four terms instead of five and little or no prospect of Greats to follow. Then the war would claim our undivided attention for the foreseeable future.' Indeed the war bore in even as he enjoyed his undergraduate courses, called on to help build a dummy airfield north of Witney, taken off in the summer term of 1941 for a crash course in tractor driving and maintenance, otherwise taking weekly bayonet practice in Christ Church Meadow and carrying out fire-watching duties. Called up in early 1942, he was only to return to Oriel in October 1945 after an interval of three years and seven months: 'One day I was a junior administrative officer at a naval air station in southern Ceylon. Barely 72 hours later, having unbelievably been accorded the privilege of an air passage home, I was once more an undergraduate, dining in Hall on the first day of term.'[95]

The War Memorial placed in the gateway leading onto the High Street bore testimony to those who would not return. Once again, the cost in lives had been high, seventy-two in all. This was fewer both as a total figure and as a percentage of those who had served in the armed forces than in the First World War. Approximately one in ten of those engaged had died in a war which had had a longer duration. While it was impossible to minimize the individual impact of losses, it was also the case that there was less of a sense of a 'lost generation' than had been the case in the previous conflict. Casualties had been spread more widely amongst both civilians, the merchant marine, and the different armed forces, reducing the focus upon the recruits from the two 'old' universities and the public schools. Both widely anticipated and with the appalling experience of the Great War as a backdrop, the second world war in forty years had also taken a lesser toll of college lives. These were severe enough but once again Oriel had a distinguished war record in terms of decorations. The college's most highly decorated soldier summed up both the sacrifice and the heroism involved. Michael Allmand VC lost his life leading a company of the Gurkha Rifles in Burma in June 1944. He had matriculated in 1941 from Ampleforth and spent a year at Oriel reading modern history before he was called up. His obituary said of him: 'He was a very friendly and likeable young man with great charm of manner, enthusiasm, and an obvious enjoyment of life... His temperament and tastes meant that soldiering did not at all come naturally or easily to him; he was not, so to speak, a prefabricated hero.'[96]

In many respects the Second World War was felt most keenly almost as much in terms of its disruption to college life as it was in the personal tragedy reflected in the correspondence of Provost Phelps a generation earlier. From the outset the college had effectively been left to maintain such educational activities as it could, fitting them around whatever occupants the government

[95] OR (1993), 39–41.   [96] OR (April 1946), 33–6, 41–3.

ILLUSTRATION 21.8 Sir George Clark (1890–1979), fellow 1919–31, provost 1947–57
Oriel College

ILLUSTRATION 21.9 The library fire, 7 March 1949: the aftermath, *OCA*

deemed fit to give it. Although the college had been able to maintain more academic activity than in the Great War, it had been at the price in its latter years of an almost total suspension of an independent communal life of the kind which had been maintained through the centuries. It was then with evident relief that the provost in spring 1946 could report the departure of the college's 'welcome guests' which had occupied the larger part of the premises up to the beginning of Michaelmas Term 1945. That term saw an intake of 115, rising to 142 in Hilary Term 1946. Soon, however, the college was dealing with a flood of undergraduates as ex-servicemen took advantage of the government's Further Education and Training Scheme grants which were dispersed to 83,000 people between 1945 and 1950, more than half of them taken up at universities. More than half of Oxford's immediate post-war entry was made up of ex-servicemen. More relaxed admissions requirements and shortened honours examinations helped to swell the number of the post-war college entrants.[97] By Trinity Term 1948 Oriel was fuller than ever, with 253 on the college books and more applicants than places.[98] The fellowship had grown too, to twenty-one, now swollen by another of Provost Ross's many activities which was to provide refuge for foreign scholars seeking escape from persecution. As a result the college had extended its fellowship and membership of common room to distinguished refugees, such as the medieval scholars Lorenzo Minio-Paluello and Raymond Klibansky, the orientalist Richard Walzer, and the art historian Otto Pächt. In 1947, at a significant juncture in the life of the college as it recovered from the effects of the war and faced up to the new challenges of the post-war world, Ross retired as provost, having reached his seventieth birthday. Oriel's encomium was simple and heartfelt: 'No one ever presided over the College in more difficult times, nor left it in a more flourishing state.'[99]

It was a fitting celebration of Oriel's survival of two world wars and a depression that in May 1948 it entertained a distinguished royal visitor when Princess Elizabeth visited the college. The photograph which commemorated the occasion was an amusingly inclusive testimony to the most eminent and the most lowly of the college community. The photograph of the future queen and Visitor being guided through the first quad by the provost was notable for including the approach of the college's oldest inhabitant, the college tortoise. For a day at least it was the most widely known mascot in the kingdom. Perhaps those old Orielenses no longer present and commemorated on the college's two war memorials might have been spared leave to chuckle.

---

[97] Greenstein, 'The Junior Members 1900–1990', HUO viii. 48–9.
[98] OR (1948), 8–9.   [99] OR (1948), 5.

22

The College Community, 1950–1990

John Stevenson

When Provost Ross retired in 1947, Oriel was still freeing itself from the repercussions of the Second World War which continued to affect almost every aspect of college life. There was no sudden lifting of wartime restrictions as had happened in 1918; the country remained gripped by austerity, shortages, and rationing well into the late 1940s: bread rationing was introduced for the first time and particularly harsh conditions affected the country in fuel supplies. As after the Great War, however, the first intakes of undergraduates were a mixture of returning ex-servicemen, some of whom were taking up studies interrupted by military service, others taking advantage of government grants for ex-servicemen, and fresh school leavers, younger in some cases by several years than those who were returning to complete their studies. Peter Anstey, returning to Oriel in October 1945 after an absence of three and a half years in the armed forces, recorded his experience:

> Academically speaking, the colleges gave one the impression of emerging from a long period of hibernation—the return to the fold of dons and undergraduates alike had only just begun. But the atmosphere for those of us arriving back as the war finally ended held an indescribable intensity and promise. We had a brave new socialist world to look forward to, we had all that Oxford traditionally offered to build with, and, most of all, we were adults tested by experience. Returning servicemen, I remember, for the first four weeks preferred uniform to gowns in Hall, as if to emphasise the difference.[1]

As both a distinguished scholar and public servant, Ross had a reputation for being, on the surface, rather taciturn and forbidding. Reggie Burton, speaking at his memorial service in 1971, recognized his enormous capacity for hard work: going to see him in his study at seven in the evening, after Ross

[1] OR (1993), 39–41.

had spent a long day in London serving on a government commission, to find him working on his commentary on Aristotle's *Analytics*. But he reminded his hearers of Ross's enjoyment of tennis, and his innate kindliness. Many attested to the latter quality, seen in particular in his efforts on behalf of refugee foreign scholars and support for them and their families.[2] Moreover, what could seem a somewhat unyielding temperament was certainly capable of bending when circumstances required it, no doubt a quality which his many years of work on arbitration tribunals had taught him. Zelman Cowen encountered both aspects when he arrived as a Rhodes scholar from Australia in 1945 to read for the degree of bachelor of civil law, already possessing a master's degree from Melbourne. As the college was short of tutors, he was soon given some tutorial teaching: he was appointed to a lectureship at Oriel the following year, which carried with it dining rights at high table. He was somewhat concerned and not a little embarrassed about the ticklish problem of what gown to wear in hall; in Oxford terms he was a mere undergraduate, entitled only to the skimpy commoner's gown, and looking, he felt, somewhat out of place. He sought an interview with Ross to resolve the dilemma, not without a little trepidation. 'He was not ... a laughing or even a smiling man, so that encounters with him were usually serious.' At the meeting 'I outlined the problem to him, pointing out that, although I was only a commoner of Oxford, I was a Master of Laws at Melbourne. He came straight to the point, my Melbourne status was irrelevant, my Oxford standing was decisive. So for some time, I joined the High Table procession wearing my commoner's gown.' But as Cowen recalled, following a dinner attended by the chancellor at which full academic dress was worn, doctors in scarlet and masters of arts with their hoods at the end of the line, stood 'this sans-culotte, me'. The next day he received a summons from the provost: 'I came and he said, "Perhaps, Cowen, when you are dining, it would be better if, until you take your degree in this university, you wore no gown at all." There was a temptation to say something, but all that came was: "Yes, Provost".' Nor was Ross unversed in that vital feature of his college, the life and times of the college mascot. In his after-dinner speech on his retirement, he recalled numerous college stories, in case they had been forgotten in the 'exigencies of war': 'He assured us that in 1938, the tortoise had actually laid an egg—in Eights week. As he put it, on the first night of Eights week, the College Boat made a Bump, and the college tortoise laid an egg, and on the second night of Eights week, the College boat made a further bump, and the College tortoise laid two eggs. But on the subsequent night of Eights week, the college boat made no further bumps, nor did the tortoise lay any further eggs.' He added in his dry voice: 'so it was impossible to determine

[2] OR (1971), 23.

whether the series which the tortoise had begun, would have continued in arithmetical or geometric progression.' Further: 'he then went on to remind us that only the Provost's wife or daughter could properly give birth within the college precincts—and continued to say that some time after the appearance of the Oriel College Testudo notice in *The Times*, he had a letter from an academic colleague (I forget from where) in which the colleague mentioned that he had not known that Ross's daughter had married an Italian!'[3]

Ross's successor was Sir George Clark, a distinguished historian with Oriel connections going as far back as 1919, when he had been elected a fellow. A Yorkshireman, born into a business family from Halifax, and educated at Bootham's School, York, and Manchester Grammar School, he was elected to a scholarship at Balliol in 1908. A first in literae humaniores in 1911 and another in modern history in 1912 were followed by a prize fellowship at All Souls. A former member of the Officers' Training Corps, he was commissioned when war broke out in the First Battalion of the Post Office Rifles. Wounded twice and taken prisoner in May 1916 at Vimy Ridge, he put his time in captivity to good use improving the languages he had begun to study before the war, with a period on parole in neutral Holland where he had family connections. Appointed a fellow of Oriel on his return from captivity, he took on the prestigious editorship of the *English Historical Review*, and completed his major study *The Later Stuarts, 1660–1714* in 1934. With a rising reputation as an historian, he was elected in 1931 to the newly established Chichele chair of economic history at All Souls, which he occupied until just before the outbreak of the war when he joined Chatham House. There he put his specialized knowledge of the Low Countries at the service of the government. He returned to full-time academic life in 1943 when he became Regius Professor of Modern History at Cambridge.[4] Once again, Oriel had chosen one of its own: a distinguished scholar, who had been awarded many honorary degrees, including a D.Litt. at Oxford in the year of his election as provost, and subsequently another at Cambridge. Clark presided over the transition of the college from the exceptional conditions of post-war austerity to the resumption of something like normality in terms of intake and teaching arrangements.

Of the eighty-one undergraduates admitted in 1951, the majority were still representatives of the major public schools, but now, continuing the pre-war trend, joined by a substantial body of state school pupils who had been assisted by the introduction of mandatory grants for university study. The fellowship stood at twenty, three more than in 1939; it was still in many ways the relatively close-knit family which Phelps had memorably evoked in the

---

[3] Z. Cowen, *A Public Life: The Memoirs of Zelman Cowen* (Carlton, 2006), 133–4; OR (1993), 38.
[4] ODNB s.n.

1930s. It was now supplemented by eight lecturers. One, Zelman Cowen, later remembered the magical allure of high table to someone encountering it for the first time; in particular, guest nights with the progress from high table in hall to the senior common room for dessert and then on to the small common room for coffee and drinks:

> All this was done at a comfortable pace... There were those who were regulars and those who came in less frequently. For me, quite new to it, it was a recurring source of delight. First of all, there was the visual pleasure of the High Table in the College Hall and of the table in the elegant, late eighteenth-century common room, both handsomely bedecked with college silver... To me, deeply in love with it all, these occasions were primarily memorable for the table talk, The Provost and his colleagues, fellows of the college and others, were, as it seemed to me as a young don, learned, cultured and skilled in the art. If the conversation happened to be, as one night it was, about birds, it had a scholarly depth and richness: there were birds behind birds behind birds.[5]

It was still a largely though not exclusively male world. Ross and his wife and daughters had resided in college, as had the treasurer and his wife, and Cowen recorded his own (not quite accurate) impressions, as a young lecturer, of the place of women in the senior common room:

> The High Table was predominantly male, and the rules for inviting women varied between the colleges. It seemed that, in general, the only unacceptable guest was one's wife, although Oriel was more liberal. Here, the imbalance was recognised by the institution of a ladies' night, a night on which fellows brought their wives to a special dinner. Despite this appeasement, my wife felt that Oxford was a celibate society without the courage of its convictions.[6]

Nonetheless, Oriel's more liberal policy of holding a dinner for fellows' wives was only a recognition that even in the post-war decade, Oxford as a whole was loosening some of the conventions that governed relations between men and women, in ways which would have shocked earlier generations by their boldness, and later eras by their timidity. In March 1946 the governing body had followed a general declaration by heads of houses, determining that after 7.30 p.m. 'women should not be present in College' and banning them from undergraduate rooms after 7.00 p.m. But only two years later, women visitors were allowed in college until fifteen minutes before the closing of the college gate at 9.00 p.m., and a ladies' lavatory was commissioned.[7]

Visible change was most evident outside the college walls, as the growth of Cowley and the increase in traffic added immensely to the bustle of the High Street and threatened, as Phelps had feared, to end any sense of the colleges as

---

[5] Cowen, *Public Life*, 132.   [6] Cowen, *Public Life*, 133.
[7] OCA Governing Body Minute Book, 1941–57, 9 March 1946, 84–5; 12 June 1948, 190.

tranquil havens of scholarship and civilized life. Within the walls, much remained as it had been. A pre-war undergraduate entering Oriel in the 1950s would have found it physically little changed from a generation earlier. Before the great cleaning of the 1960s its visual impact was what it had been for decades, if not for centuries. Blackened stonework, distant bathrooms, and rooms innocent of central heating framed the life of undergraduates. Their day still revolved around hall, chapel, junior common room, and library, though the construction of the beer cellar under the hall provided a new and lively venue for thirsty college men. The river and Bartlemas remained twin poles for sportsmen; undergraduates who had gone to war in 1939 would have found all the sports clubs thriving in the 1950s. So too were its other societies, the Arnold, the Newlands, the dramatic, and the music societies. If the physical and social circumstances of the college were in many ways remarkably similar, numbers had crept up. The 192 undergraduates of 1939 had grown to over 260 by 1949.[8] But academic routines, lectures, tutorials, and work in library or laboratory remained as they had been since before the Great War, conducted largely by dons who had been in fellowship since the 1930s. The younger group of tutors recruited before the war were now the college's senior establishment, among them Reggie Burton, Jack Gough, Eric Hargreaves, Billy Pantin, and Arthur Crow. Honorary fellows such as G. M. Trevelyan, Sir Henry Tizard, and Sir Maurice Powicke, distinguished men in arts and science, not only provided links with the past but also added scholarly lustre to the senior common room. There was one significant loss. In 1949 the tortoise was found fatally wounded about the head in the wine cellar, the victim, it was believed, of rats. As the *Record* dolefully recorded: 'this lamentable event has been commented upon by almost every newspaper except *The Times*, which alone announced the arrival of Whalley George Testudo. *The Times* notice of his birth, and his far more famous appearance before Princess Elizabeth, made him the most widely-known tortoise in the world, a position which he filled with great dignity.' Further, the *Record* noted that the 'writer of the standard account' of the college mascot tells us that 'The family history of the Testudos is not free from tragedy, and the succession has been maintained by adoption rather than the more usual oviparous practice.' Precedent, the *Record* was able to confirm, 'has again been followed and the College has accepted the gift of another tortoise from G. C. Fisk who represented us this year in the Boat Race'.[9]

But there were happier occasions to celebrate. After the college had marked the death of George VI in 1952 with a formal message of condolence, it celebrated the coronation of Queen Elizabeth II, its new Visitor, in June

[8] OR (1949), 6.   [9] OR (1949), 7.

1953. Her Majesty's coronation broadcast was transmitted by loudspeakers installed in the hall and her new reign toasted appropriately. During the coronation period the hall and its entrance were floodlit, as were the library and the High Street frontage of the Rhodes Building.[10] The provost was knighted for his many and continuing public duties.[11] The following year the Jubilee of the Rhodes scholarships and the centenary of Rhodes's birth were celebrated in similar style: the Rhodes Building was again floodlit, particularly the statue of Rhodes; three marquees were erected to welcome the guests, including former Rhodes scholars and their wives, numbering some seven hundred in all; and plans for the construction of the Rhodes Building exhibited. Rhodes's last resting place was not neglected: an occasion was found in August 1953 to place a wreath on his grave in the Matoppo Hills.[12] Both the coronation and the celebrations of Rhodes's life and bequest to Oriel were reminders of the still powerful influence of empire and Commonwealth on the Oxford of the 1950s. The new queen would make the Commonwealth a principal theme of her reign, and appropriately her college remained deeply involved in it, not only through the Rhodes scholarships but through the continuing involvement of Oriel men in colonial service. In the 1950s Commonwealth studies flourished at Oxford, as subjects deemed appropriate for colonial development were incorporated into the university curriculum for graduate students and others. Nearly half of the degrees of Doctor of Philosophy were awarded to overseas students, among whom Rhodes scholars, many of them at Oriel, made up a third. Phelps had taught the probationers' course for entrants to the Indian Civil Service; Oriel men continued in his wake to find employment in the Commonwealth up to and even beyond Rhodes's centenary.[13]

Sir George Clark retired in 1957. His decade as head of the college had not been easy; returning it to normal academic routines after the upheavals of war and its difficult aftermath was a considerable achievement. The financial situation was much less secure that it had been before the war, and shortages of materials in the austerity that followed made repairing the wear and tear of college buildings a formidable task. The college had had to meet the unforeseen need to repair the library after the fire of 1949. Requests from the government to take in the post-war 'bulge' of ex-servicemen had put enormous pressure on accommodation and teaching resources, and even when that was relaxed, financial circumstances dictated that the college keep up its numbers. As the *Record* candidly admitted in 1950, the 'strain' showed no sign of lessening as 'like other Oxford Colleges, we find that in the interests of our finances we have to keep [numbers] above the old level'.[14] One result was that under Clark the college undertook the rearrangement of the

---

[10] OR (1953), 5.   [11] OR (1953), 7.   [12] OR (1954), 5–6.
[13] HUO viii. 616–18; OR (1996), 31.   [14] OR (1950), 8.

buildings on the western side of Oriel Street, the Island Site, 'to give more undergraduates rooms, better lecture rooms, and more revenue...'. It was typical of the frustrations with which he had to deal in the highly regulated environment of the post-war era that though it had been hoped to announce the completed refurbishment in the *Record* for 1950 'the officials in the various ministries have got to work and seen to it that nothing much can happen before this time next year'.[15] There were other improvements to the college fabric, catching up on what had not been possible since 1939. The chapel was redecorated, the porter's lodge remodelled, and 'various reforms' made to the college's increasingly antiquated bathrooms and heating. With the new beer cellar made and the library fully restored, it was a considerable achievement.

Much more remained to be done, both to refurbish the premises and to expand the teaching strength of the college. The only way forward lay in strengthening the college's financial resources, and in 1955 an appeal was launched, remarkably the first since the War Memorial appeal of 1919. Writing in the *Record* the provost explained candidly why it was needed:

Since then [1919] our expenses have risen, but the gifts and legacies which we have from time to time gratefully received have not increased our endowments in anything like the same proportion. We have made economies, and we have, I believe, husbanded our resources well; but like all Oxford colleges, we have found it increasingly difficult to maintain the fundamental condition on which the College system depends, that the Colleges should make a contribution of their own to Oxford education equal in quality to that of the university, though different in kind.[16]

For Clark, as for other heads of houses, it was essential that colleges should be able to command sufficient resources of their own to ensure their survival as effective teaching institutions within the framework of an increasingly state-funded university, as well as providing for the upkeep of their fabric and facilities. As a member of the University Grants Committee from 1951 to 1958, Clark was at the heart of these issues, well aware of the growing government role in university finance and the implicit challenge it posed to the vitality of colleges as self-governing institutions. Government funding for Oxford between 1938–9 and 1951–2 had grown sixfold, allowing an expansion of university facilities, the augmentation of academic salaries, and the funding of university-wide teaching. Colleges were ineligible for state aid, and while for the richest this could be compensated for by their endowments, many were in the position which Clark had indicated, and which the Franks Report was later to describe with equal bluntness as being 'insufficiently endowed to achieve the level of financial security necessary to the unfettered...performance of their academic tasks'.[17] Faced, as many

[15] OR (1950), 8–9   [16] OR (1955), 9–10.   [17] HUO viii. 652.

colleges found themselves, with the maintenance of historic buildings often in dire need of expensive repairs, and with an equal imperative to improve academic and domestic facilities, fund-raising was to become a major concern for Oriel. Jointly funded posts, or posts funded primarily by the university, would be one way forward. In addition, Oriel, along with other colleges, benefited from the Historic Buildings Fund, which would pay for the refacing and repair of its crumbling stonework. But, as Clark recognized, any effective claim to continued independence by the majority of Oxford colleges, not just the wealthiest, required that they raise money on their own account for their core activities. The first fruit of the appeal fell into that category, with the appointment in 1956 of a fellow in physics, J. H. Sanders, bolstering the college's teaching in science.[18] Naturally, the appeal owed most to college members. The Oriel Society had revived after the Second World War, holding its first Annual General Meeting and dinner since the war in December 1949, which eighty alumni attended.[19] By the time of the appeal, the Oriel Society boasted 1,300 members. Partly through its efforts, the Oriel Endowment fund raised £40,000 in its first two years, on very modest outgoings of £200.[20]

On his retirement as provost, Clark took the opportunity to reflect on the changes in the position of heads of houses. They had once been appointed for life or until they chose to retire, and one consequence, he pointed out, was that when he became provost there were only two ex-heads of Oxford colleges alive. When he retired there were seventeen, and their length of service was diminishing: only three heads in place when he was appointed were still in office in 1956. These changes led him to reflect that being provost was no longer a job for the elderly. Citing Phelps's remark that people ought to retire at the height of their powers, he went on:

...when I was elected to a Fellowship my senior colleague was a lively old gentleman who had been elected in 1846. To be a link with the past is not, however, necessarily a good qualification for acting as a link with the future. The leadership of a small College in revolutionary times is an exacting office, and when the retiring age for Professors was recently raised from 65 to 67, I wondered whether my own retiring age ought not to be changed from 70 to the same or even lower figure.[21]

In accord with these sentiments, the new provost, Kenneth Turpin, was at 42 relatively young; he had been an Oriel undergraduate and was currently a fellow. Born in Ludlow, the son of a civil servant, he was educated at

---

[18] OR (1956), 6.   [19] OR (1949), 14.
[20] OR (1955), 15; OR (1956), 10–11. Clark must have been referring to his election to All Souls in 1912, and to Dr Francis Compton who was elected fellow there in 1846.
[21] OR (1956), 9.

ILLUSTRATION 22.1 W. A. Pantin in his study, c.1966, OCA

Manchester Grammar School. Starting his Oxford career late as a result of illness, he took a first in history in 1939, followed a year later by a B.Litt., for which he wrote a dissertation on early eighteenth-century politics. Judged unfit for military service, he entered the Treasury as a temporary civil servant. After 1943 he was close to the heart of the wartime coalition as assistant private secretary to Clement Attlee, the Deputy Prime Minister. From national affairs he moved in 1945 to administering the University of Oxford, as an assistant registrar. In 1947, he took over as secretary of faculties, described somewhat ambiguously in the *History of the University* as 'an unobtrusive official of mounting importance'; the door between his and the registrar's office was described by one official as the most important in the Clarendon Building. One aspect of his duties was the increasingly complex relationship between university administration and the still largely independent colleges.[22] The post carried with it a fellowship at Oriel, and with his insider's view of university government his appointment was welcomed by the provost along with that of the new Regius Professor of Modern History, Vivian Galbraith, formerly the director of the Institute of Historical

[22] HUO viii. 692.

ILLUSTRATION 22.2 Kenneth Turpin (1915–2005), fellow 1947, provost 1957–80
Oriel College: David Poole, 1970

Research at the University of London, as useful helpmates in Oriel's struggle in the more complex and regulated world in which it had to operate:

> In College meetings we shall now profit from the advice of both these high authorities on University administration, and this is no small advantage in these days, when we have to pick our way through the maze of regulations made by Government departments, and by many other bureaucratic authorities, in matters concerning military service, educational grants, quotas of students for particular studies, building licences, rationing, ecclesiastical benefices, and almost everything else we have to do.[23]

Turpin combined his onerous university post with the activities of a resident fellow, taking on the duties of domestic bursar in difficult circumstances. Acknowledged equally for his administrative efficiency and his 'genial and accessible' character, he later continued the academic interests of his predecessors with work on the history of the university in the nineteenth century.[24]

The college of which he was now head was enjoying in the 1950s a relatively balmy period of stability, in which Oxford and Cambridge remained substantially unchallenged at the apex of the British educational

[23] OR (1948), 7–8. [24] OR (2006), 68–9.

ILLUSTRATION 22.3 Sir Michael Swann, Lord Swann (1920–90), provost 1980–1, OCA

system. Although not without critics, they were still the most favoured destination for the brightest pupils from the public and grammar schools; only a few local authorities had at this point experimented with the new comprehensive schools. The first new universities created under the recommendations of the Robbins Committee set up in 1960 would challenge many of the traditions which Oriel and other colleges had painstakingly recreated after the war, but that lay in the future.[25] College life remained much as it had been, with subtle changes that took a shrewd and experienced eye to discern. The editor of the *Record* noted in the early 1950s the changes he had perceived from pre-war. Undergraduates were generally a little older, some of them coming to university after national service or a third year in the sixth form, but they were 'not noticeably harder working' or 'noticeably more impecunious'. The most marked change in recreational activities compared

---

[25] For Robbins see V. H. H. Green, *The Universities* (Harmondsworth, 1969), 135–6, and for a contemporary assessment of the new universities, M. Beloff, *The Plateglass Universities* (London, 1968), reviewed in the *Oxford Magazine*, 30 January 1970, 130.

ILLUSTRATION 22.4 Sir Zelman Cowen (1919–2011), fellow 1947–50, provost 1982–90

Oriel College: Jeff Stultiens, 1988

to pre-war was 'the proliferation of College plays' with productions by the Oriel Dramatic Society and the Newlands Society. Some old rules and formalities had fallen into disuse, the gates not shutting until 10.30 and undergraduates no longer obliged to attend college chapel. Scholars and commoners were no longer strictly segregated in hall. There was, he thought, 'perhaps more social mixing between senior and junior members of the College than before the war'; a dinner given by the junior common room to the dons had 'apparently become an annual event', usually followed by a table tennis tournament. Since 1939, guest nights had been instituted for undergraduates on Thursdays and Sundays, with a separate guest table where wine could be ordered, though beer remained 'the favourite drink'. The new beer cellar, he noted, was patronized by senior as well as junior members.[26] The Educational Report, re-established in the *Record* in 1952, revealed other changes. Out of seventy finalists, twelve were scientists, and the largest school was now modern history with fifteen, followed by classics

[26] OR (1952), 12.

with ten and modern languages with nine. New final honours schools introduced since the war were represented in agriculture, forestry, music, and the joint school of psychology, philosophy, and physiology. A further change for incoming undergraduates had been the abolition of universal pass moderations and the substitution of 'prelims' in most arts subjects.[27]

While some like Clark and his successor could perceive that the ground was shifting under the feet of the colleges, that greater state intervention through the University Grants Committee was being felt in Oxford, not just in the 'redbrick' universities, and that the university, its faculties, and departments were playing an increasingly vital part in what colleges did, much of college life continued in time-honoured routines, refreshed by each new generation. The nightmare of the Bursars' Committee in 1920, that state support for Oxford would mean the colleges becoming little more than halls of residence, was no nearer reality in the 1950s and 1960s than it had been between the wars. Colleges retained their distinctive character, grand, sporty, political, or intellectual, small and intimate, or large and amorphous. The rule that candidates still applied to individual colleges, and the convention of tutors' responsibility for admissions in their subjects, preserved the crucial attachment of individuals to the society they had chosen, and meant that college loyalties remained generally strong. Intercollegiate sport flourished, and new developments, like the rise of college drama societies, sharpened undergraduates' identification with their college and even promoted artistic rivalry, eventually leading to intercollegiate drama competitions. Academic competition too was lively, the Franks Report commenting that there was much public discussion about the number of firsts and seconds long before the publication of the first Norrington Table in 1964; at Oriel, the pre-war Educational Report in the *Record* was revived.[28] It was recognized, however, that college loyalty was diluted as a more diverse range of subjects was taught, some of them entirely out of college; some undergraduates spent the majority of their working time in laboratories and departments. Graduate students with supervisors out of college identified even less with their colleges. Fewer fellows lived in; by 1964 only one in five Oxford dons was resident.[29] But Oriel retained much of the intimacy missing in larger and more dispersed colleges. In spite of a larger undergraduate population, the gradual colonization of Oriel Street and the subdivision of sets allowed most undergraduates to live in for two years. The majority continued to study mainstream subjects taught by fellows in college, a core of whom continued to live in, maintaining the personal relationships upon which collegiate life depended.

[27] OR (1952), 14–15.   [28] HUO viii. 196.   [29] HUO viii. 197.

Life for undergraduates at Oriel in the decades after the war remained varied and individual. The flamboyance of the pre-war aesthetes had been moderated, as had the excesses of the hearties. Both models survived, without the sharp divisions noted in pre-war memoirs. The spread of dramatic societies to almost all colleges, including Oriel, and the growth of music and drama in university and city through well-patronized subscription concerts and through the Playhouse, brought more undergraduates into contact with cultural life and mitigated the philistine tone prevalent before the war. University sport, the Oxford Union (where an Oriel man, Ian Lyon, was president in 1960), and university-wide clubs also offered ample diversions which took undergraduates outside their college, but there was no evidence that they had seriously undermined Oriel's own sporting activities, its societies, and a flourishing junior common room. Critically, the tutorial system, with its weekly essays demanded of most undergraduates, maintained their bond with Oriel. Tutorials were increasing in frequency and becoming more serious; many tutors issued typed reading lists, scornfully rejected as spoon-feeding by older dons.[30] By the 1960s a typical course might require two pieces of written work a week for prelims and three or even four essays a fortnight for finals. Although most courses involved lectures and tutorials outside college, their foundation was generally tutorial teaching with the college's own tutors in the subject. The appointment of fellows in new subjects such as physics ensured that undergraduates reading them did not become completely detached from college teaching. Not unnaturally, many chose courses taught by tutors they knew. Their progress through an increasingly complex syllabus involved intricate arrangements for teaching outside college, which had to be made by their tutors through a blizzard of handwritten notes. Oriel tutors such as Reggie Burton and Peter Brunt in the classics, Jack Gough and Billy Pantin in modern history, Arthur Crow in modern languages, and Ben Brown and John Sanders in the natural sciences were well used to the routine administration of undergraduate courses.

College tutors were generally the first call for references or advice about careers, in which long-established relationships in the City, the professions, and academic life played an essential part. Occasionally, undergraduate studies proved directly relevant to later careers. Ewen Fergusson, British ambassador in Paris in the 1980s, recalls reading modern history on an open scholarship in the early 1950s:

'Prelims', encountered in the first two terms, to a newly-arrived undergraduate, intoxicated by the discovery of all that Oxford had to offer, it was a matter of scraping through with the minimum of effort but one wanted to get through so that one's first summer term could be enjoyed to the full, without any but the most distant thought

[30] HUO viii. 196.

of the exams that would impend at the end of three years... I cannot say that I worked very hard at Oriel. There were many distractions, notably sporting. Only one of my tutors used his acerbic tongue, clarity of thought, and penetrating knowledge of his subject to goad me into serious study; the second, delightful and learned, was over tolerant: 'I see Fergusson, that your contribution is not to be an academic one'... Nevertheless, I came down from Oxford, having passed into the Foreign Service, with my passion for history enhanced and with permanent gratitude for the base which the historical syllabus, unevenly as I pursued it, gave me for the thirty-six years of my career in diplomacy, and my private enjoyment to this day.[31]

Oriel continued to maintain its distinctive traditions, among them mascots of the family *testudinidae*. John Albert recalled an attempt to make an exotic addition to the long-established variety:

I was in the second quad some sunny day in 1957 (I think it was), and a large wooden packing case was opened to reveal a giant Galapagos tortoise. This was a gift from an Orieliensis travelling there. A gathering of dons and undergraduates, together with the Provost watched in wonderment as this giant creature stepped out blinking. It just stood there looking at us all and at its new surrounding... We gradually moved away. A signwriter/painter was sent for to paint the College arms on the creature's shell, as was always the tradition with Oriel tortoises. Some two or three days later the tortoise recovered from its jet-lag, and during the night it must have felt very hungry. During the night it ate every single plant growing in the second quad. It was a total demolition job, leaving only the stumps of the plants about three inches above the ground. The Provost was very upset, and sent for Mr Phillips, the Steward, to retrieve the packing case and repack the tortoise. I understand that it was sent straight back to the Galapagos. Whether or not the college arms had been painted in its shell I know not.

This was not, however, to be the end of attempts to flesh out the college stock of *testudinadae*. Unabashed by the failure to populate the college from the far Pacific, a group of undergraduates had recourse to a source more convenient than the Galapagos Islands, namely Oxford Market. John Albert records:

Enthused with the tortoise theme, a group of undergraduates went to the covered market, and we bought about a dozen small tortoises, carefully chosen for their likenesses to various dons. We then painted the backs of them all with the names of the chosen dons, and let them loose on the College.

It was rumoured that 'a competition then took place amongst the dons to find their named tortoise and to discover the accuracy of the likeness'.[32]

In 1960 as in 1950 the fellowship stood at twenty, with ten lecturers, two more than a decade earlier. Almost all fellows, apart from holders of chairs

---

[31] *The Oxford Historian*, 2 (2004), 13.
[32] Private communication to the author from John Albert, 3 June 2008.

such as Hugh Trevor-Roper, the Regius Professor of Modern History, or college officers like the treasurer, Brigadier Ralph Bagnall-Wild, were now tutors in college and lecturers in their faculty or department. Combined tenure proved a relatively durable compromise between university and college into the next century, though Oriel, like other colleges, employed lecturers in addition to enhance teaching in particular areas. Normally academic appointments at Oriel attracted little attention outside Oxford. Trevor-Roper's appointment to the regius chair was an exception. In 1957 Oriel found itself under scrutiny in the national press, in a public controversy involving the Prime Minister, in whose hands the appointment lay after consultation on the part of his patronage secretary with the university authorities, the modern history faculty, and the college. Soundings had been conducted discreetly in the past almost without comment or discussion outside academic circles. Previous incumbents, such as Firth or Galbraith, while distinguished scholars in their own right, had not been public figures, but in 1957, the two most eligible candidates were well known and controversial. Hugh Trevor-Roper, a student of Christ Church, was a distinguished scholar of seventeenth-century England. But in addition to his principal scholarly interest, he had established an international reputation for his definitive study of the fate of Adolf Hitler, *The Last Days of Hitler*, published in 1947, and was widely known for his essays and reviews in national periodicals. Alan Taylor, himself an Oriel man and now a fellow of Magdalen, was even more widely recognized. His hugely successful early morning lectures at Oxford were distilled in numerous popular books on modern European history, and he was even better known as one of the first television dons. Puckish, opinionated, and usually controversial, his live, unscripted lectures direct to camera on historical themes reached an audience of millions. In his newspaper columns, first in the *Daily Herald* and later in the *Sunday Express*, Taylor made no secret of his anti-establishment views. At 50, and at the height of his powers, he was the favourite and most obvious choice, and thought to be preferred by Provost Clark, his former tutor. The press saw the election as a gladiatorial battle between Taylor and Trevor-Roper, *The Observer* and the *Oxford Mail* citing undergraduate opinions on them.[33] Whatever the outcome, Oriel would be acquiring a controversial figure. In the event Taylor was eliminated, in part because of his involvement in popular journalism and his irreverent political stance. Taylor would later claim that he would have turned down the post if he had been offered it.[34] The less well-known but much respected historian Lucy Sutherland, the principal of Lady Margaret Hall, was also excluded when it became clear that she would only take the chair if she could combine it with her position at her

---

[33] Adam Sisman, *Hugh Trevor-Roper: The Biography* (London, 2010), 278–9, 282.
[34] Sisman, *Trevor-Roper*, 286; Taylor, *A Personal History*, 275–9.

college. This being unstatutory, the chair was offered to Trevor-Roper. Although he had certainly, if discreetly, campaigned to obtain it, he frankly recognized his rival's claim, writing to Sir Lewis Namier:

> I must admit, I felt a bit of a fraud. I remain stubborn in my belief that Alan Taylor ought to have had the Chair, and that politics ought not to have excluded him; but I suppose he was *vix papabilis*, so I must try to wear with dignity the mantle which has been stolen from him.[35]

Trevor-Roper made little secret of his displeasure at having to exchange the grandeur of Christ Church for the more modest circumstances of Oriel. He continued to live in a Christ Church house on St Aldate's. Writing to Berenson, he described his new society as 'the dingiest, dullest college in Oxford'.[36] Trevor-Roper was even more scathing in the late 1960s, reviewing his first decade as a fellow of Oriel. He claimed:

> The intellectual level was low, very low; whatever method of calculation was used, Oriel always came out at the bottom of the list of colleges, measured by results in Schools. The teaching was ineffective; all mental stimulus had long been extinct; the college societies had all died through lack of it; and the Senior Common Room was characterized by a tepid cosiness...[37]

This was exaggerated and in part demonstrably untrue; Trevor-Roper gradually warmed to his new college, and played a prominent part in supporting it in the student unrest which was developing as he wrote these words. Undoubtedly, its traditions and routines were easy to caricature as 'cosy'. The *Record* commented in Trollopean mode on its sixteen livings, 'If the College can on such occasions present an Oriel man who is suitable and willing to undertake the charge it always prefers to do so.'[38] Four bishops attended the Gaudy in 1960, to which matriculands between 1897 and 1923 were invited.[39] Ancient traditions died hard: in 1959 the centenary of college accounts rendered in English was celebrated in the treasurer's office. It was recalled on that occasion that Arabic numerals had only been employed in them in 1628.[40] Long-standing college servants such as Mr Bond, who had worked for the college since 1913, and Mr Hedges who had retired after fifty years' service, were remembered with gratitude.[41] But the college had at the same time been intimately involved in contemporary affairs, as the death of the great scientist Sir Henry Tizard in 1959 reminded its members. He had gone on from his fellowship to become a key scientific adviser to government, with a critical role in the development of radar before the Second

---

[35] Sisman, *Trevor-Roper*, 282.
[36] Hugh Trevor-Roper, *Letters from Oxford*, ed. Richard Davenport-Hines (London, 2006), 234 (10 July 1957); Sisman, *Trevor-Roper*, 299.
[37] Sisman, *Trevor-Roper*, 299–300.   [38] OR (1958), 8.   [39] OR (1960), 6.
[40] OR (1959), 10–11.   [41] OR (1960), 6.

World War, and had conducted a wartime mission to the United States to further Anglo-American scientific cooperation. After a period as president of Magdalen, he had chaired vital committees for the Attlee government advising the armed services and the Ministry of Defence on the implications of new scientific developments. He retired from Whitehall, loaded with honours and with honorary fellowships in both his colleges, in 1952. By his request his ashes were buried in the floor of the Oriel ante-chapel.[42]

But some of Trevor-Roper's disparaging remarks as an 'outsider' from a larger, richer and much grander college than Oriel found echoes within the college itself. Provosts Clark and Turpin, both well versed in developments in the wider world of higher education, were all too familiar with the challenges faced by Oxford, and especially by relatively small colleges without great endowments. Both, as products of northern grammar schools, were well aware of the demands for a demonstrably meritocratic system of recruitment to the older universities. In 1969 V. H. H. Green, the chaplain of Lincoln, reflected: '... there was no doubt that Oxford and Cambridge retained their pre-eminence among the British universities, even if the complacency of earlier years had given way by 1960 to a good deal of self-criticism and even a hint of introspective anxiety.'[43] That anxiety rested upon charges of social exclusiveness, the failure of the older universities and their colleges to provide what the country required for its future prosperity, and increasing competition from the wave of new universities set up in the wake of the Robbins Report, with a radical increase, by 60,000, in the number of university places during the 1960s.[44] In 1965 Oxford had joined the central clearing house for university admissions, the Universities' Central Council on Admissions set up in 1961. Provost Turpin was instrumental in reorganizing Oxford admissions by dividing the colleges into three groups, to one of which prospective undergraduates made their application, while expressing a college preference. By 1965, undergraduates from maintained schools had doubled in number since 1939, and it was clear that the ability to attract the best candidates from every type of school improved colleges' results in finals.[45] Oriel had sustained a high academic reputation between the wars, though it did not consistently score the best results; it was one of only five colleges not to take passmen. Between 1940 and 1960, however, its performance had fallen steeply, from an average of sixteenth place to twenty-fifth; by comparison, Christ Church had fallen to twenty-sixth place. In the 1960s the Education Report in the *Oriel Record* told an even gloomier story: a summary at the end of the decade revealed that between a fifth and a third

---

[42] ODNB s.n., and see S. Phelps, *The Tizard Mission: The Top-Secret Operation that Changed the Course of World War II* (Yardley, Pa., 2010).
[43] Green, *Universities*, 129.   [44] Green, *Universities*, 139.
[45] OR (1965), 9; HUO viii. 213.

of undergraduates were taking third class degrees or below, reaching nearly two-fifths in 1968.[46] Although Oriel was not, as alleged, bottom of the lists, it was nonetheless a worrying trend and one for which remedies were not easily available. Some colleges had a well-established intellectual cachet, notably Balliol, while others such as Queen's and Wadham had made deliberate attempts to cultivate the brightest candidates from maintained schools.[47] Richer colleges tended to offer more scholarships and exhibitions, attracting the best from other colleges' lists. The *Oriel Record* was candid about the need to improve academic performance, noting the need to cater for a larger number of candidates in science subjects, and hoping to attract 'good undergraduates' to Oriel.[48]

If Trevor-Roper's assessment was unduly bleak, therefore, it addressed an objective problem. The undergraduates of the 1930s had achieved, on the whole, comparatively good results. This was no longer the case in the 1950s, although there was no obvious decline in the quality of the candidates admitted, as the distinguished subsequent careers of a good many of them testified. The vigorous body of young tutorial fellows of the 1930s, Eric Hargreaves, Reggie Burton, Jack Gough, Billy Pantin, and Arthur Crow, were still tutors into the 1960s and beyond. It was inevitable, however, that a tutorial body the core of which had remained in place for so long would lose some of its energy, and would dilute the constructive intolerance necessary in the forging of first class degrees. As scholars, they were productive: Burton's edition of Pindar, Gough's books on political thought, and Pantin's pioneering work on medieval vernacular architecture were considerable contributions to their subjects. But their pupils did not achieve, after 1950, grades in the final honour schools to match their predecessors' before the war. There was one striking exception. Peter Brunt, himself an Oriel classicist of the 1930s and ancient history tutor from 1951 to 1967, had been recruited by Provost Clark as (it was said) 'a good knockabout tutor'. He turned out to be much more, as a highly original Roman social historian and authority on the demography of the ancient world, and eventually succeeded to the Camden chair of ancient history.[49] Vigorous both as scholar and tutor, he was probably the most dynamic of the tutorial corps of the 1950s.[50] In any case, as the older generation retired, it was replaced by a more competitive body of tutorial fellows who were determined to improve the college's educational record. Some of them moved on after only two or three years, but others,

---

[46] HUO viii. 105–6; Education Report, OR (1970), 26.
[47] HUO viii. 213–14. Queen's College took only 25 per cent of its undergraduates from independent schools in 1965.
[48] OR (1960), 5–6.
[49] See P. A. Brunt, *Italian Manpower, 225 B.C.–A.D.14* (Oxford, 1971).
[50] See ODNB s.n.; M. H. Crawford, 'Brunt, Peter Astbury', *Proceedings of the British Academy*, 161 (2009), 63–83.

notably Bill Parry, elected in 1961 to a new fellowship in theoretical physics, had a long tenure, and in the 1970s and especially the 1980s results in finals were gradually bettered.

The 1960s offered many forms of renewal, the outward and visible signs of which were the cleaning and refacing of the quadrangles, and a new pavilion and squash court at Bartlemas. Five new fellowships were established, in law, in theoretical physics, in engineering, in inorganic chemistry, and in mathematics. Twenty more graduate students were recruited, in response to university policy and with the deliberate aim of rebalancing the college community.[51] The junior common room was first represented on television in University Challenge (which it won) in 1966.[52] In the same year the first eight, coached by the bishop of Buckingham, was Head of the River. College customs were modified: after 1966 junior members could be guests on high table; women guests had been permitted since 1964.[53] In 1967 the more conservative junior common room instituted a women's guest night on Fridays only.[54] In 1968 Queen Elizabeth dined on high table before visiting the Oxford Union, her first visit for twenty years and the first of a reigning sovereign.[55] In the same decade three of the college's longest serving dons retired. Hargreaves, who retired in 1963, had been elected in 1925, the first tutor in economics in the newly established school of philosophy, politics, and economics. He had served in the Ministry of Supply and Reconstruction during the war, the official history of which he wrote, with Margaret Gowing.[56] Gough, who had been a fellow since 1932, retired in 1967, and Pantin, elected in 1933, in 1969. When Pantin joined the college, the *Record* remarked: 'he has won a place as one of the ablest and most learned of the younger medievalists in this country and will be a great accession to the teaching strength of the College.'[57] In addition to his contribution to medieval ecclesiastical history, he developed a unique knowledge of the medieval domestic architecture of Oxford, including the earliest buildings in the college, his contribution to the understanding of which is acknowledged elsewhere in this volume. Like Phelps he was eccentric in the ancient Oxford mode, but where Phelps had been renowned for his mannerisms of speech, Pantin's rooms were in a notorious state of chronic and acute disarray, with every available flat surface covered in books and papers, the telephone unanswered because it could not be found under heaps of scholarly debris. Undergraduates relate having to read out their essays standing up, a discomfort relieved when he was ill and they could sit on the end of his bed to read.[58]

---

[51] OR (1967), 9; OR (1968), 7–8.   [52] OR (1966), 36–7.
[53] OR (1964), 7; OR 1966, 9.   [54] OR (1967), 8.   [55] OR (1968), 5, 15–16.
[56] OR (1941), 135. E. L. Hargreaves and M. M. Gowing, *Civil Industry and Trade*, History of the Second World War, Civil Series (London, 1952).
[57] OR (1933), 280.
[58] OR (1966), 33; private communication to the author from John Albert, 3 June 2008.

Together with Reggie Burton he was a leading light in the common room and contributed greatly to its convivial atmosphere.

Pantin besides his college roles was university archivist, in which office he annually addressed the delegates on a topic of current concern in its historical context. In 1968, as riots spread across the world's universities, his subject was student disturbances, on which he was able to evoke the long perspective: the ancient battles of northern and southern students, and town and gown conflicts, notably on St Scholastica's day, 1355.[59] The High Street had remained a scene of occasional battles between town and gown well into the twentieth century, one historian going so far as to claim that there are historic battlefields on which less blood has been spilt.[60] Town-and-gown brawls continued into the post-war period, with Guy Fawkes night being the most frequent occasion for violence. Into the late 1960s, the proctors urged undergraduates to remain in college on the evening of 5 November, and the police maintained a prominent presence on the High Street. The tradition of bonfire night rowdyism appears to have been broken in that decade.[61] By then undergraduate hostility was directed not against the town but against university and college authorities. Student protest in the 1960s was a universal phenomenon, in which Oxford played a relatively minor part compared with Paris, Berlin, and some American universities, and in England some of the new universities and the London School of Economics. Although rooted in broad ideological movements and sharpened by international conflicts, the causes of student unrest were often more mundane, as current youth culture was putting strain upon traditional notions of college discipline and acceptable behaviour. As Pantin put it: 'These modern [disturbances] seem to stem either from students chafing against university discipline, or from strong political feelings, or from a lack of contact between seniors and juniors and a sense of unfair treatment by the former.'[62] Women's guest nights, gate hours, or the provision of keys to undergraduates, greater representation for junior members in college decisions, and increases in charges were common issues, underlying which was the reasonable demand that undergraduate voices should be heard more directly in college affairs. The minutes of college meetings at Oriel show that most of these questions were raised in 1968. In January a joint committee of the junior and middle common rooms with the governing body was set up.[63] Joint committees, however, did not necessarily bring consensus. In March the governing body rejected an undergraduate request that college keys be issued to them, and in December 'noted', though

---

[59] W. A. Pantin, *Oxford Life in Oxford Archives* (Oxford, 1972), 68–9, 72–3.
[60] Cited in Pantin, *Oxford Life*, 68; J. Prest (ed.), *The Illustrated History of Oxford University* (Oxford, 1993), 4–5 cites Hastings Rashdall (1858–1924), the historian of European universities.
[61] Prest, *Illustrated History*, 37.
[62] Pantin, *Oxford Life*, 75.
[63] OCA, Governing Body Minute Book 1964–70, 28 January 1968 and 13 March 1968, 106, 106a.

clearly did not accept, a motion passed by the junior common room in favour of the admission of women.[64] The temperature of these discussions rose during 1968, the 'year of revolutions'. Student demands at their most radical sought to remove traditional features of college life, high table, the separation of common rooms, and challenged the college authorities' right to act independently of undergraduate opinion.[65]

In the absence of the provost, who had unexpectedly been called to the office of vice-chancellor for most of the academic years 1966–8, the fellows' reaction was uncertain. A series of concessions on college discipline was sharply checked in Trinity Term 1968, when the acting provost (the vice-provost and politics tutor, Christopher Seton-Watson) proposed a compromise with student leaders which was rejected by the fellows.[66] Provost Turpin's return in October saw the more militant demands stalled, and the undergraduate role in the governance of the college set within limits. On 12 November 1969 the governing body discussed a resolution from the junior common room that college rules should apply equally to senior and junior members, a principle it did not accept.[67] By that time the fellows were beginning to take a more determined line in resistance to radical demands, following the lead of the dean, Ben Brown, and the recommendations of Hugh Trevor-Roper. The latter had experienced radical student action in December 1968, when he had faced down protesters during his lecture at the London School of Economics, and as a result argued that the college was being deluded into concessions which played into the hands of the militants. Paternal and well-meaning fellows were being manoeuvred into surrendering their ultimate authority over the college.[68] A small number of them may have been sympathetic towards the more radical demands; the majority were prepared to meet reasonable grievances, but resisted the militants with increasing firmness. But a fresh ingredient to unrest was added by a dispute over an increase in college charges, which provoked an incident at a college meeting on 21 January 1970. The junior common room's petition against the increases was presented by the president, Guy Mansfield, while a crowd of undergraduates assembled outside to await the response. They were informed that the petition could not be accepted, and in the terse words of the college minutes, 'almost immediately afterwards several members of the J.C.R. interrupted the meeting of the governing body by entering the S.C.R. uninvited. The Provost therefore adjourned the meeting.'[69] At the

---

[64] OCA, Governing Body Minute Book 1964–70, 4 December 1968, 127.
[65] See HUO viii. 703–5.
[66] OCA, Governing Body Minute Book 1964–70, 24 May 1969, 147.
[67] OCA, Governing Body Minute Book 1964–70, 12 November 1969, 163.
[68] Christ Church Archives, Dacre Papers, 11/8, memorandum on the Oriel 'revolution'. See Sisman, *Trevor-Roper*, 400–4.
[69] OCA, Governing Body Minute Book 1964–70, 21 January 1970, 176.

adjourned meeting held the following day, the fellows received the dean's report and resolved 'to circulate to all junior members of the College a communication from the Governing Body setting out the course of events on the previous day, and stating that the Governing Body would rusticate or send down any member of the College engaged in any kind of disruptive action affecting the College, and that in the case of collective action it reserved the right to adjust the penalties to what in its view was the degree of culpability of the various persons concerned.'[70] The imperative to restore college discipline was balanced by the resolve to address all the aspects of relations with junior members, and at a meeting the following month it was agreed to consider how to put them on a more satisfactory footing.[71] It was decided eventually to dissolve the existing joint committee with junior members and replace it with a new body of which any special meeting could only be called at the discretion of the provost.[72] At the same time it was decided to give newcomers a friendlier introduction to the college, the old arrangements being deemed rather cold.[73]

Kenneth Turpin knew more than most about the challenges posed to the university and the colleges by the new wave of undergraduate unrest. In 1968, as vice-chancellor, he had instituted the Hart Committee on relations with the junior members following the first signs of unrest in Oxford. It reported in 1969 and, after much debate, the report formed the basis for a system of greater representation for junior members in university governance, enacted in 1971, and for a new statute on discipline. The provost had acted as principal spokesman for the university council when these moderate recommendations were proposed in congregation; they took the edge off student militancy in Oxford, at a time when direct action in universities was declining generally.[74] When further action took place in Oxford in 1973 and 1974, it was dealt with firmly by the university authorities, who suspended some of the militants. Much of the decline in Oxford's revolutionary fervour was due to the 'close relations between young and old, characteristic of a collegiate university and of the tutorial system'.[75] Oriel, in the wake of the militancy of January 1970, was no exception. Although differences continued to exist between some junior members and the college authorities on a range of issues, they did not again reach the same level of acrimony. Subsequently the provost was praised for the way he had dealt with the unrest in college: 'his response was firm, calm and conciliatory, with the result that the

---

[70] OCA, Governing Body Minute Book 1964–70, 22 January 1970, 177.
[71] OCA, Governing Body Minute Book 1964–70, 11 February 1970, 181.
[72] OCA, Governing Body Minute Book 1970–7, 10 March 1971, 22.
[73] OR (1971), 7.
[74] A. H. Halsey, 'The Franks Commission', HUO viii. 703–6; Michael Brock, 'The University since 1970', HUO viii. 744–5.
[75] Brock, 'The University since 1970', HUO viii. 745–6.

ILLUSTRATION 22.5 The dons' eight, June 1975, *OCA*

(*left to right*) Simon French, S. R. Critchley, C. K. Badenoch, Derek Morris, Graham Vincent-Smith, Bill Parry, Jonathan Barnes, B. K. Flynn, Michael Bryan

College's relations with its junior members were soon warm and co-operative.[76] Writing in the *Record* after his term of office as vice-chancellor, the provost argued that undergraduate participation in college policy was a necessary development. 'Oxford undergraduates', he wrote, 'today echo pretty closely the general aspirations of their generation, and ask for them to be listened to and satisfied in ways appropriate to Oxford.' He noted that although there were more people prepared to challenge the established order, only a small minority wished to overturn it altogether. The new generation insisted on being treated as adults, with more personal freedom, and greater participation in college and university affairs. He was optimistic that Oriel could rise to the challenge: '... if there is a gap between the generations, then let us try to bridge it. If an Oxford College, with all its advantages, cannot do it, then it is unlikely to be done anywhere else.'[77] These sentiments were not misplaced. While the alarums of student protest attracted attention in the press, the normal routines of tutorials and examinations continued as before. College societies and sports flourished, indifferent to student militancy. Only two months after the

---

[76] Obituary of Kenneth Turpin, OR (2006), 69.   [77] OR (1969), 9–14.

confrontation of January 1970, the fellows gave permission to the Dramatic Society to produce the old-fashioned Oxford farce *Charley's Aunt*.[78]

In the event the 1970s proved to be a period of generally harmonious relations between fellows and junior members, though the question of the latter's representation on the governing body continued to be raised from time to time. The provost's hope in 1971 that relations between junior and senior members could be improved was, in general, amply fulfilled.[79] In large part this was due to unpredictable changes in the fellowship: by 1970 more than a quarter of it was under 40, several of whom for at least part of the decade lived in college. They were reinforced by the new phenomenon of full-time college lecturers, who tended to be in their twenties and who were for the most part accommodated in college. This younger element was generally more competitive and more intolerant of poor results in finals, and the college's position in the ranking of colleges gradually, and within limits, improved. At the same time they participated in undergraduate activities much more regularly than their predecessors. Some of them formed a 'dons' eight' on the river which performed creditably in the lower divisions of the spring and summer races; Bill Parry and the new fellow in economics, Derek Morris, later the provost, were among them. Green-garbed fellows and lecturers, including the present author, played a chorus of 'academical frogs' in the college's version of *The Frogs* of Aristophanes. The provost played his part, giving keen support to the Boat Club and attending tumultuous bump suppers after the first eight became, and remained, Head of the River, which were celebrated traditionally with the burning of a boat in the first quadrangle, undergraduates leaping though the flames.

The younger element in the fellowship which emerged in the 1970s began to restore the college's academic standing to the place it had occupied during Ross's provostship. The size of the fellowship had increased, from about seventeen to twenty between 1946 and 1964, and then to twenty-seven by 1982. Bill Parry as librarian made great efforts to bring the collections up to date, helped by the accession of Pantin's and other private libraries and by the funds made available from the Pantin Trust. New stacks were constructed between the senior and junior libraries, which allowed more space for study, a development which palpably improved the college's results in the final honour schools. Jonathan Barnes (fellow 1968–78), Robert Parker (fellow 1976–96), and Simon Hornblower (fellow 1978–97), all of whom went on to distinguished careers elsewhere, brought the reputation of classics at Oriel back to its pre-war level, amply justifying the college's decision to continue literae humaniores at its full strength.[80] David Brown, chaplain and tutor in

---

[78] OCA, Governing Body Minute Book 1964–70, 11 March 1970, 183.   [79] OCR (1971), 7.
[80] Jonathan Barnes, Professor of Ancient Philosophy, University of Geneva, 1994–2002, University of Paris, 2002–6; Robert Parker, Wykeham Professor of Ancient History, 1996; Simon Hornblower, Grote Professor of Ancient History, University of London, 2006–10.

theology (1976–90), created a very successful new school of philosophy and theology before going on to chairs at Durham and St Andrews.[81] College investment in new posts in English literature, modern languages, geography, mathematics, and the sciences were equally fruitful. By 1980 much of the ground lost in the mid-century had been regained.

Apparently radical changes, therefore, turned out to have altered the college less than expected, much as the equivalent changes of a century before, at the end of Edward Hawkins's provostship, had not been as far-reaching as his contemporaries had hoped, or feared. The academic composition of the undergraduate body was changing: almost a third of finalists took science degrees in 1969, compared to a fifth or lower even ten years earlier. Reggie Burton reflected from his long experience in 1973 that a fellowship with only two scientists in the 1930s now had nine. While much of the fabric of communal life remained, in his personal view of Oriel since the 1930s, he could specify numerous changes. Most obvious was the decline in the personal services of a scout, bringing hot water and coal, lighting fires, and providing undergraduates and fellows alike with 'commons' of bread, butter, and cheese in their rooms: 'Now an anachronism...but in those of us who knew it as it was before the war the thought of it awakens nostalgic memories of a vanished world.' More subtle was the effect of grassing the front quad before the Second World War: 'the aesthetic gain was enormous, and there was a decrease in noise, especially at night, whether from the beat of running or staggering feet or from the sound of outdoor singing and annoyingly nocturnal games.' In his view the decline in noise was part of a change in behaviour amongst undergraduates over the long term, with fewer 'high spirits' and feats of individual self-assertion which produced baths on the library roof and bicycles hanging from the tower. Undergraduates were now more likely to engage in collective demonstrations than individually outrageous acts. On the other hand, he saw more visible concern for the underprivileged, something of which he believed the seeds had been sown in the depression years of the 1930s, but which had developed apace in the post-war period in the era of Oxfam and the proliferation of societies and voluntary associations of many kinds. As a classicist he was inevitably aware of the relative decline of his own subject, making space for new and especially scientific disciplines; but the most notable change in academic studies was the great increase in graduate studies. Prospective undergraduates were now less well drilled in their particular subject, but had gained from wider reading.[82] Neither the size nor the composition of the fellowship or the undergraduate community, however, made any fundamental alteration in the life of the college. The traditions of the past were, as always, carried on

---

[81] David Brown, Van Mildert Professor of Divinity, University of Durham, 1990–2007; Wardlaw Professor of Theology, University of St Andrews, 2007.

[82] OR (1973), 15–19.

by the college servants, some of whom had outlasted even the longest-serving fellows. In 1970 the college unwillingly parted with Mr F. H. Hicks, who retired after fifty years of service: he had been appointed in April 1919. Six years later the common room butler, Mr Fred Long, followed him; he had served since 1955. But he continued to work in the college bar, and by particular request to look after the chancellor of the university, Harold Macmillan, on his occasional visits.[83] Mr Bertram Franklin, an ex-naval man who had been a porter and then head porter since shortly before the war, retired in 1974. It was a reminder that long service to a single college had not died out completely in the very different employment conditions of the post-war years.

If relations within the college seemed to be taking a more 'warm and cooperative' turn, there remained other difficulties which the provost had to address, above all the financial position of the college, and the looming expense of restoring its fabric, especially the decaying houses in Oriel Street—the Island Site—was causing concern. The support of old members was necessary, and it was decided in 1971 to set up a Development Trust.[84] Two years later a development plan to cover the next fifteen years was drawn up. A further three tutorial fellowships would be funded, two junior research fellowships established, and considerable renovation undertaken of the college buildings, at a cost of over a million pounds, of which Oriel would find approximately a fifth from its own resources. The remodelling of the Island Site was an integral part of the plan; its accommodation was essential to allow undergraduates at least two years in college as alternative living space in the town declined.[85] The plan however coincided with the global oil crisis of 1973–4, which with the declining value of investments precipitated an acute financial problem. It was fortunate for Oriel that in 1974 it recruited a new treasurer, Eric Vallis, who gradually and systematically, with a clear understanding of the limits of manoeuvre of an Oxford college, proceeded in concert with the Development Trust to restore the college's revenues. As a result in the second half of the 1970s it was possible to see, if not yet to bring to fruition, a way of making the college site fit for the demands which would be made on it in the competitive world of higher education. After the difficult year of 1973–4 the future seemed a little brighter. Success on the river in 1972, when the Boat Club secured the headship in Torpids which it held until 1990, and then in Eights (1976 and 1978–84), improved undergraduate morale. The six hundred and fiftieth anniversary of the foundation was celebrated in 1976. In June the provost and fellows were hosts to 400 Orielenses, and shortly afterwards received the queen and the duke of

---

[83] OR (1970), 11; OR (1990), 79.
[84] OCA Governing Body Minute Book, 1970–7, 10 March 1971, 35.
[85] OR (1973), 5, 8–9. The redevelopment of the Island Site is discussed elsewhere in this volume.

ILLUSTRATION 22.6 The Regius Professors of Modern History in 1998, *OCA*

Robert Evans (1997–2011), Michael Howard (1980–9), Hugh Trevor-Roper (1957–80), John Elliott (1990–7)

Edinburgh, who met members of the college in the senior library.[86] In this atmosphere issues of policy seemed less fraught. Financial considerations were foremost in the decision to increase the number of undergraduates: in the year of the anniversary Oriel was still admitting annually seventy to seventy-five undergraduates to read for first degrees, the figure established twenty years earlier as the norm.[87] In 1977 it was decided to increase the number to eighty-five and in the following year to pursue a more active policy of recruitment.[88] The other important question was the admission of women members of the college. The question had been raised in most of the men's colleges at the beginning of the decade, but the decision of Congregation in 1972 that no colleges beyond the initial five should become co-residential for five years placed it outside active consideration until 1977. Then it was raised again, with a clear simple majority of the fellows (though not the provost) in favour; the necessary two-thirds majority required to change the statutes was not attained.[89] One implication of co-residence was to make improvement of college accommodation even more imperative, a matter which needed funding not yet available.

[86] OR (1976), 34–5.
[87] OCA Governing Body Minute Book 1970–7, 21 February 1973, 100–1.
[88] OCA Governing Body Minute Book 1970–7, 5 October 1977, 3; 18 January 1978, 18.
[89] OCA, Governing Body Minute Book 1977–85, 8 March 1978, 22.

As Provost Turpin neared retirement, then, there was still unfinished business; but in 1980 when he left office he had the satisfaction of having seen the college through an unprecedented period of student unrest and an acute financial crisis. Oriel had expanded on every front since his election in 1957, in the size of the fellowship, in the number of undergraduates, and in the emergence of a considerable body of graduate students. His concern for an improvement in the quality of finals results, frequently referred to in the *Record*, was also in part vindicated to some degree: there were signs of progress up the Norrington Table. In 1972 he had welcomed eight firsts in Schools but looked forward to reaching double figures; in 1979, the year before his retirement, the finalists achieved fifteen.[90] Several alumni of these years achieved notable success, including (to take a few examples at random) David Manning (1968), later ambassador in Washington, John Varley (1974), chief executive officer of Barclays, Jim Mellon (1975), a future benefactor, and John Vickers (1976), who would be director of the Office of Fair Trading and warden of All Souls. Turpin's support for the Boat Club was also rewarded when the first eight was Head of the River for three consecutive years before his retirement. In his final bump supper the departing provost was presented with an oar.[91] In his valedictory reflection in the *Record*, which he had edited since 1971, he returned to what he saw as the proper priorities for Oriel: 'Of course in the life of the college one does not want too much excitement except such as is generated by successes in Schools, on the river and in various sports and other activities…'[92] His college obituary in 2006 gave testimony to his role in facing up to and seeking a resolution to undergraduate protest, his support for their other activities, notably the Boat Club, and the way in which he had earned the affection of undergraduates. More generally, he was credited with having laid the foundations for the future well-being of the college in adverse financial circumstances and the establishment of good management of its resources.[93]

It was not easy to find a successor who would be supported by all the strands of college opinion, and the election was delayed for a year. Eventually the fellows' choice settled on a public figure who, uniquely in its history, had no previous connection with Oriel. On 18 June 1980 they formally elected Sir Michael Swann. Born in 1920, a Wykehamist and graduate of Caius College, Cambridge, he had been professor of natural history at Edinburgh University and subsequently its principal and vice-chancellor. Knighted in 1972, he was next year appointed chairman of the Governors of the BBC, a post which he filled with considerable distinction. His period as provost, however, was to be brief. In July 1981 he resigned his position, citing, in a press statement, the pressure of outside commitments which were preventing

---

[90] OR (1972), 5; OR (1979), 6.　　[91] OR (1980), 6.
[92] OR (1980), 9.　　[93] OR (2006), 68–9.

him devoting the amount of time required to be the 'excellent Provost he would wish to be' and that he 'has been asked to do far more in the outside world than he had ever expected', particularly since his elevation to a life peerage earlier in the year.[94] These sentiments were reiterated in his private correspondence with senior members of the college.[95] A subsequent judgement was that 'he found it difficult to cope with the minutiae of college life after facing the demands of public life for so long, and the college itself was unprepared for the amount of time that his outside activities were to take up'.[96] Certainly, he had arrived when numerous weighty issues were in flux: co-residence was once again under active discussion, as was the possibility of a formal link with a women's college as an alternative; the development of the Island Site was also now in consideration, and various necessary financial expedients being considered, including the sale of the Bartlemas sports ground.[97] In addition, the college was about to overhaul its admissions policy, aiming to attract more candidates from schools with little tradition of sending applicants to Oxford.[98]

With so many important issues in play, it was hardly surprising that the college was, in the words of its subsequent provost, 'severely discomfited' by the circumstances of Lord Swann's resignation.[99] Occurring near the beginning of the long vacation, it was impossible to gather the fellows and organize an election within the ninety days allowed in case of a vacancy by the statutes. The incoming vice-provost, Bill Parry, who stepped into the breach as acting provost for the following year, found it necessary to inform the Visitor, represented by the Lord Chancellor, Lord Hailsham, of the situation; the right of appointment in these circumstances devolved upon the Visitor. The Lord Chancellor graciously permitted the college to go through the form of election on the understanding that the Visitor would appoint the chosen candidate. With this assurance it was possible to proceed towards an election. As it happened, the college was able to find a candidate who was not only a former fellow, but had the skills and contacts required to bring to fruition its plans for the future: Zelman Cowen. Following his resignation as a fellow in 1950, he had returned to Australia to a distinguished career as scholar, constitutional lawyer, and public servant. He was professor and dean of Melbourne University by the age of 31. Credited with having revolutionized legal education in Australia, he had become one of the country's best-known public intellectuals, addressing such issues as an Australian republic and capital punishment. Serving as vice-chancellor of Queensland

---

[94] OCA Governing Body Minute Book 1977–85, 27 July 1981, 133.
[95] Private communication to the author from Ernest Nicolson.
[96] ODNB s.n.
[97] OCA Governing Body Minute Book 1977–85, 20 May 1981, 125–6.
[98] OR (1981), 7.
[99] Zelman Cowen, *Public Life*, 328.

University during the 1970s, he too had experienced turbulent student dissent, and left academic life on appointment as Governor-General of Australia in 1977. In 1981 his term of office was coming to an end. His interest in returning to his former college was communicated to the fellows, who, as he could not be invited to Oriel as candidates normally would be, sent a delegation of four to Canberra to see him. In November 1981 Sir Zelman Cowen was elected provost, on the understanding that he would take up office the following September; in the interim the acting provost would preside. It was necessary that the fellows kept the election secret until the government of Australia had been informed and was ready to announce a successor, a period as it turned out of about three months; surprisingly perhaps, in an Oxford alert for gossip, the secret was kept. His arrival was preceded by the departure of one of the few who had served in college during his fellowship: Mr Phillips, the steward, retired in December 1980, after working in Oriel since 1937.[100]

As the new provost wrote in his memoirs, he returned to Oxford 'expecting to devote myself to the affairs of the college', though with the fellows' concurrence he was to chair the British Press Council for five years. Moving with his wife into the lodgings in which as a young lecturer he had waited upon Provost Ross to discuss gowns, he noted the changes which had occurred in Oxford in the thirty years since his fellowship: 'there were great expansions in numbers, a great increase in graduate studies; there were many more female students and academics; and there was a broader range of opportunities for entry into the university.'[101] The Oxford he had left in 1951 was 'still very much an undergraduate society', the coming of graduates in substantial numbers had made colleges 'triple-tiered' with senior, middle, and junior common rooms. The other obvious difference he had observed, that women were much more in evidence in 1982 now that all the former men's colleges were mixed, as were some of the former women's colleges, led to the first significant alteration to the Oriel over which the new provost presided. He recorded that he had proceeded cautiously on what was clearly a contentious matter; as he wrote later: 'Oriel had been deadlocked over the issue for years. Some wished to preserve the traditional college. Others felt that society had changed and that our anomalous situation discouraged applications from good students. When I was quizzed by the delegation of Oriel fellows who came to see me in Canberra, I was asked my view of the desirability of opening the last male preserve to women. I replied that the question should wait until I got to Oxford, rather than divide the college further by making a statement before hearing the views of its members.' Having settled in, it was not long before the issue was raised again, and a

[100] Cowen, *Public Life*, 328–9; OR (1981), 9. [101] Cowen, *Public Life*, 336–7.

motion to admit women brought before the college. As the provost recorded: 'I strongly believed the college should admit women, and I decided it was time to act. I consulted among the fellows, among the students and among our alumni...There was searching debate and calm discussion. Whatever had divided the college in earlier times, the decision to admit women was taken quickly, decisively and with no lasting division; as one fellow later wrote, within a year we had forgotten what all the fuss was about.'[102] The decision to admit women taken in May 1984 was implemented gradually, with women graduates admitted in 1984 and the first cohort of twenty-one undergraduates in October 1985. As elsewhere in Oxford, the admission of women proved remarkably uneventful, with little effect on examination results. Fears that women might receive a hostile reception in the last all-male bastion were certainly misplaced. One of the first intake of women, Susanna Phillippo, wrote subsequently that being a small minority initially helped to get people 'on their side' and 'We had on our side, too, the fun and adventure of paving the way, of notching up our own "firsts"...Did we change things? Probably not much. Our business, had we thought about it in those terms, was rather to make a place for women at Oriel, gain acceptance, prove that women with a whole range of personalities could survive there quite happily.'[103] Acceptance was not slow in coming: in 1989 the junior common room elected its first female president, Laura Hawksworth, who also took a first in classics. Fears that the admission of women would undermine the college's success on the river and its sporting activities were also somewhat misplaced. Women adopted college sport with a vengeance. Eighteen of the first intake took to the river, and provided two eights in short order.[104] They were equally enthused by the rites associated with success on the river. An unfortunate accident to one of them, jumping over the burning boat after a bump supper, finally brought that ceremony to an end: the college, painfully aware of the danger of incinerating undergraduates as well as old boats, and mindful of the requirements of modern Health and Safety, was compelled to prohibit the practice, and to place the burning of boats on probation.[105] Some older members who regretted the end of decades-long tradition could remember the first quadrangle before it was paved and grassed in the 1930s; the modern ritual of boat burning was a mere Lilliputian reflection of earlier times, when the 'pyre rising nearly thirty feet' had been lit by the provost, carried shoulder-high out of the hall, to mark the college being head of the river for the first time in ninety years.[106]

If the admission of women had been carried through with little upheaval to college life, the 'central issue on the college agenda' which faced the new

---

[102] Cowen, *Public Life*, 337.   [103] OR (1996), 36–9.   [104] OR (1996), 36.
[105] OCA Governing Body Minute Book 1985–93, 30 April 1986, 46; 29 April 1987, 109.
[106] Reggie Burton's reflections, OR (1973), 15.

provost was providing both sexes with enough rooms of a reasonable standard to enable them to live in for the duration of their studies. All colleges were under pressure to expand their accommodation; as Zelman Cowen put it, 'central to the notion of the Oxford collegiate university is residence, and an undergraduate who does not live in college could be disadvantaged'. Only a few of the richest societies had been able to offer three years of living in college; two years had been the norm; but as the feasibility of living out of college diminished, most of them were developing their central sites, or building annexes.[107] Colleges with limited facilities were disadvantaged in attracting applicants. As Oriel had not shared in the wave of rebuilding which had created new quadrangles and buildings in many colleges from the 1960s, there was a real sense of urgency about the task. On the other hand, there was the advantage of an underexploited site next to the college. The Island Site was therefore critical, and the challenge of funding its redevelopment urgent. As the provost wrote with feeling, 'If Queen Mary Tudor had "Calais" engraved on her heart, it is likely that, if there is space enough, the words "Island Site" will be found engraved on mine; its development was a concern from my beginning to my finishing day.'[108] Equally colourful was his description of how the site appeared by the time he assumed office: 'the site was a collection of houses, properties and structures of varying levels of antiquity and repair, all of which belonged to the college... part of the site, already much degenerated, was used for the accommodation of students. In some places, one might have thought that a borstal provided better for less.' Lady Cowen, no less forthrightly, feared her husband had crossed the oceans to become a slum landlord.[109] Outline plans to remake the whole site in stages were already in existence; what was needed was an unprecedented fund-raising effort for the estimated cost of £5 million. The burden fell upon the provost and his fund-raising team. Orielenses gave generously, but the Development Trust, led from 1988 by Sir Bryan Nicholson, was tasked with searching for potential donors outside their ranks. Several companies contributed substantially because of their association with the provost, or with Cecil Rhodes, notably De Beers, Consolidated Gold, Rothmans, and Tube Investments. Sir Philip Harris, later Lord Harris of Peckham, pledged £1.25 million for the conversion of the old real tennis court into a complex for student accommodation and teaching rooms in memory of his father, together with a mathematics fellowship.[110] As the provost approached retirement, the success of the appeal was clearly assured. In 1989–90, his final year, the fellows and Development Trustees fully acknowledged his unprecedented success in raising funds, which had allowed

---

[107] OCA Governing Body Minute Book 1985–93, 2 November 1988, 189.
[108] Cowen, *Public Life*, 340–1.   [109] Cowen, *Public Life*, 341.
[110] Cowen, *Public Life*, 344–5.

The Fellows, 9 October 1991   *Gillman and Soame photograph*

ILLUSTRATION 22.7 The fellows, 1991, *OCA*

		David Charles	Simon Hornblower			
	Michael Stephens	David Maskell	Eric Vallis	Jeremy Catto	Eric Barratt	
Robert Parker	Mark Philp					
	Gordon Macpherson	Richard Swinburne	Bill Parry	Richard Tur	David Barlow	John Heath
	Alan Segar	Glenn Black	Michael Williams	John Sanders	Ben Brown	Keith Prout
Derek Morris	Denis Mustafa	Sarah Coakley	Ernest Nicholson *Provost*	John Barton	Andrew Boothroyd	Graham Vincent-Smith

the massive redevelopment of the Island Site and the funding of four fellowships, with a fifth in prospect. He had also supervised the integration of women students into college life; and he had proved a keen supporter of the Boat Club, which had enjoyed a decade of 'unparalleled success on the river'. Oriel's results in finals were improving, with a much greater number of first class degrees.[111]

His successor as provost, Ernest Nicholson, already knew the college well. A graduate of Trinity College, Dublin, and Glasgow University and a former

[111] OR (1990), 18–24.

ILLUSTRATION 22.8 Oriel women with Bill Parry at the Women's Tenth Anniversary Dinner, 1995, *OCA*

fellow of Pembroke College, Cambridge, he had been Oriel Professor of the Interpretation of Holy Scripture since 1979, and was already active in college business. He had been involved in the development plans, and would bring them to completion. At his installation he was able to report on the final stage, a significant moment in the evolution of the college. Though Oriel had grown considerably in numbers in the forty-five years since the Second World War, and in addition was part of a much larger and more diverse university, the vast majority of undergraduates and graduates could now live in; the college buildings had never been in such intensive use. Thirty years earlier almost all college administration outside the bursary was conducted by Eleanor Mary Harris, the college secretary. Her role was now filled by tutorial, admissions, and development offices, a more than eightfold increase of staff which was accompanied by a similar increase in the bursary. The returning serviceman of 1945, transported to 1990, would have found the physical conditions of life much easier in terms of personal comfort and facilities. The 'chilblained American' undergraduate in 1953 for whom central heating was 'a distant dream' and who found only one telephone available to undergraduates in the whole college, would doubtless have appreciated the redeveloped Oriel. He would have been surrounded by almost pristine stonework, in stark contrast to the ivy-clad and smoke-blackened walls of the past. But there was much that was familiar. The first and second quadrangles were almost unchanged since 1820, the St Mary quadrangle since 1911. Internally however, some staircases had been ingeniously remodelled; en-suite facilities were installed for a large proportion of junior members. If he penetrated the new tunnel under Oriel Street, he would have found an apparently new though hidden part of the college, where old houses stood in a new perspective. College societies and sport flourished, and bumps were still chalked up around staircase doorways. The Library had been vastly expanded. Eminent academic figures such as Sir David Ross had been worthily succeeded by a plethora of younger scholars in the tutorial body. Zelman Cowen himself had been a fellow in 1947, when Ross had been provost. There were several notable anniversaries in 1991: seventy years since Richard Robinson, philosophy tutor from 1946 to 1969, had matriculated at Oriel; sixty years since Reggie Burton had been in fellowship; while Arthur Crow, in the same year, celebrated his eightieth birthday. At the same time George Moody, who had matriculated in 1932, and who had endowed a fellowship in biochemistry, was elected an honorary fellow.[112] Spanning the decades, the *Oriel Record* continued to be printed. F. H. Hall, its first editor, who had been a fellow since the time of Edward Hawkins, might have been surprised by its vigour, but hardly by its contents. He would not have been disconcerted that *The Times* had been induced to record the Oriel tortoise's egg in its notices of birth, nor surprised that half a century after, Orielenses were quite unrepentant at having, some years later, populated the quadrangles with more baby tortoises, honouring in this slow but strong-willed species the traditional emblem of Oriel.[113]

---

[112] OR (1991), 9.
[113] Michael de L. Wilson, 'Testudo and *The Times*: A Letter', OR (1984), 25; OR (1992), 27.

23

Epilogue

Oriel 1990–2013

Jeremy Catto

Though no tortoise wandered about the Oriel quadrangles in 1990, the college proceeded in the direction set by Sir Zelman Cowen with the deliberation of its proprietary creature. In the previous year, in anticipation of Sir Zelman's retirement, Ernest Nicholson had been elected provost; a distinguished biblical scholar and as Oriel Professor of the Interpretation of Scripture already a fellow, he had participated in the college's upward trajectory in the previous decade and would maintain its momentum, completing the internal changes made by his predecessor and setting out an active programme of fund-raising. In accord with the new confident spirit in the college, he was installed in the chapel on 19 October 1990 by the Visitor herself, in recognition of his being the fiftieth provost. Less than a week later, President Francesco Cossiga, the President of the Italian Republic and a Newman scholar who had been elected to an honorary fellowship some years earlier, visited the college in the course of his state visit to the United Kingdom. This unaccustomed prominence was the direct result of the higher profile the college had assumed in the Cowen era; it in no way implied that the recasting of the college as a mixed-gender society in a renewed and reconfigured physical setting had been completed. The first task of the new provost was to oversee the last and most complex stage of the rebuilding of the Island Site, the refashioning of the old and dilapidated tennis court which filled the centre of the site, to accommodate more undergraduate and graduate students and to provide a new seminar room and lecture theatre.[1] The substantial problems of construction and environmental planning were in the capable hands of the new bursar, Brigadier Mike Stephens, another military engineer, who had succeeded Hugh Browne at the beginning of the year; it

---

[1] On this and subsequent building projects see the fuller account in Chapter 17.

would take four years to complete the building and even longer to effect all the detailing and consequent work on adjacent structures. But it was in accord with the college's new visibility that it attracted large benefactions, and that its first stage was inaugurated by the Prime Minister, John Major, on 10 August 1993. The Harris Building was dedicated to Captain Charles William Harris, whose son Sir Philip Harris was the principal benefactor. From October of that year it was possible to accommodate nearly the entire college for the three years of the undergraduate course. Even on the completion of this project, however, accommodation was not quite sufficient when the opportunity of lodging outside the college walls was rapidly diminishing. The new estates bursar, James Offen, was active in the search for properties not too distant from Oriel, and managed to acquire Nazareth House in 1995; the site, however, required rebuilding, of which the first and most radical phase was completed in 2000. By then the whole undergraduate population could live in college or in the new annexe throughout their course, and graduates for two years. The problem which had become acute in the later years of Turpin's provostship, and which had caused Cowen such anxiety on assuming office, was now, for the foreseeable future, solved.

The second concern of the closing years of the century was the quality of collegiate life and study within the new, more spacious premises. Results in the final honour schools, treated comparatively in the Norrington Table, fluctuated between eleventh and twenty-third place; judged more objectively by the number of first class degrees, they showed a fairly continuous improvement. The college at least kept up with its competitors, with a few individuals achieving a spectacular success. Progress towards a balanced mixed-sex undergraduate body continued: 36 per cent of candidates admitted in 1990 were women, 43 per cent in 2003. The much slower process of electing women fellows began in 1991 with the election of Sarah Coakley as theology fellow; though she was in fellowship for only two years, others followed and by 2003 there were five women fellows. Greater available space for residential accommodation changed the balance of the collegiate body in another way: though the number of undergraduates admitted was subject to university rules and was stable at about eighty-nine, the number admitted to read for higher degrees changed dramatically, from nine in 1990 to fifty-one in 2003. A modest increase in the number of junior research fellows and senior scholars, and in the 'welfare team' of chaplain, dean, junior dean, and adviser to women students, swelled the number of residents younger than the fellowship but older than most undergraduates. A new initiative, the election of visiting fellows, began with the appointment in 1992 of the musician Barry Douglas, and in 1993 the authority on business organization Charles Handy (Oriel 1953). These developments brought a larger fluctuating population into the college community, furthering the process of engagement with the larger life of the university and above all with the world beyond. More immediately, junior research fellows, college lecturers, and the arrangements for discipline and welfare which placed much greater responsibility on younger members of the community, bonded the undergraduate members more closely with the burgeoning body of graduates and with members of the senior common room. By the end of the century a sense of belonging and of mutual responsibility among junior members was beginning to distinguish Oriel from other colleges. The achievement of the Boat Club in retaining the headship of the river in nearly all years from 1990 to 2002 certainly helped to maintain college pride; the pleasure taken by a large proportion of undergraduates and graduates in maintaining the full traditions of dining in hall, customs deliberately fostered by college policy, was a mark of Oriel's sociability, especially when a contrary trend to curtail college dining was gaining strength elsewhere in Oxford. As James Methven, dean from 1997 to 2008, would remark on demitting office,

> ... Orielenses showed their character. In my experience, they surpassed the maturity of members of any other College by readily acknowledging their excesses and participating in the consequences. This is a huge achievement of theirs which will make its mark throughout the world for some time to come. (Other Deans at those termly meetings [of deans] always looked surprised when I declared that students in Oriel, on the whole, owned up when asked to, and usually very promptly—the record being under twenty minutes.)[2]

To keep a course against the prevailing winds, when other craft are drifting effortlessly by in the opposite direction, is strenuous, and demands continual tacking. It would not have been possible without the keen involvement and support of the body of Orielenses, in the Oriel Society and the Development Trust, and through their connections in the City and in industry. These bodies had been galvanized by Zelman Cowen's fund-raising campaign, and with Jeffrey Bonas (Oriel 1963) chairman of the Trust and Peter Collett (Oriel 1952) its secretary, and with the support of Helen Kingsley, were now extremely active. The provost embarked on numerous journeys to the United States, to South-East Asia, and elsewhere; at home, an unprecedented number of visitors was entertained, not least undergraduates at Sunday lunch. The response, both among Orielenses and in the wider group of friends of the college, was magnificent. One of the first great benefactors had already made a generous gift: Sir Philip Harris, later Lord Harris of Peckham, had funded the complex development of the old tennis court on the Island Site, and would do more in 1993. Michael Garston, through the Muller Foundation, William Turpin, Barbara de Brye, the Clothier family, and others funded the development of other parts of the Island Site, while George Moody (Oriel 1932) and Ron and Marina Hobson would support

---

[2] James Methven, 'On Deaning Considered as One of the Fine Arts', OR (2008), 58.

new work on the main site. The chapel and its new Newman oratory were endowed by Norma Dalrymple-Champneys, Valerie Eliot, and Vivien Greene. The Singaporean businessman Lee Seng Tee, with a magnificent gift, made it possible to refit the library and common rooms. Sir Ewen Fergusson (Oriel 1951) and Hugh Norwood Collins (Oriel 1954) were equally generous in other ways. Numerous benefactors would fund teaching fellowships and junior research posts: Sir Kirby and Lady Laing, Lord Iliffe, David Arculus (Oriel 1965), Colin Prestige (Oriel 1948), Strone MacPherson (Oriel 1967), Robin Stainer (Oriel 1967), and an impressive number of Orielenses. David Paterson (Oriel 1963) funded Chinese scholars at Oriel, and provided a new building, Paterson House, in the new development at Nazareth House. Major-General Sir Henry Lascelles (Oriel 1930) was the benefactor of its squash court. The new annexe was rebuilt thanks to the exceptionally generous support of James Mellon (Oriel 1975), after whom it is named. They, and an unusually large number, for Oxford, of alumni contributing what they could, made possible a renewal of Oriel life, both in its physical environment and in its commitment to learning and ideas. Their work coincided with the progressive withdrawal of government funds from colleges, as forecast in the Dearing Report in 1998; as a result, by 2003 the college was more financially independent than it had been at any time since the 1920s. This position was enhanced by an active development of Oriel's endowments. Jeffrey Bonas, the chairman of the Development Trust who acted as estates bursar after the retirement of James Offen, together with Graham Vincent-Smith as acting treasurer and then treasurer, took advantage of the current market to acquire a number of business premises, culminating in the purchase of the Cheltenham Business Park in 2003. Oriel's endowments now edged into the upper half of the table of wealth of Oxford colleges.

On the provost's retirement in 2003 the fellows elected Sir Derek Morris, a distinguished economist who had been a fellow and tutor since 1970, and who had resigned his fellowship in 1998 on his appointment to the chairmanship of the Competition Commission. Like his predecessor, on election he was already a familiar figure in the college, and his experience of government and clear notion of Oriel's prospects in the light of university and public policy gave him a strong base from which he could lead the college over new, unstable ground. One feature of the emerging landscape was the award of public funds to colleges according to their research profiles in addition to their educational activities; it was therefore necessary to strengthen the fellowship in response. Like the number of undergraduates, which was more or less stable, the fellowship had only increased from twenty-nine in 1990 (not including two professorial vacancies) to thirty in 2003; but in the next decade it was enlarged by more than half again, reaching forty-seven in 2011. In addition, its balance was altered: whereas in 2003 twenty-three tutors were afforded by two officers and five professors and research fellows, in 2011, twenty-nine fellows were tutors, two were college officers, one a university officer, and fifteen were professors or research fellows. An association with the Said Business School had brought three of its staff into the fellowship. The expansion of the fellowship was concentrated round specific themes: environmental science, neuroscience, the nexus of law, economics, and finance, and the common ground of classics, philosophy, and theology. The enhanced number of established fellows more or less kept up with the growing body of junior research fellows, college lecturers, and deans, to which the new category of graduate teaching assistants was added in 2005. Graduate students were about half as numerous again as in 2003, and only undergraduate numbers remained about the same. While the new shape of Oriel may have alarmed the more traditional fellows and alumni, it allowed the college to take advantage of the changing pattern of university funding.

These further additions to the college community demanded yet more accommodation, though not on the scale of the previous twenty years' expansion. The most substantial project was the extension of Larmenier House, part of the James Mellon Hall complex, in 2007–9, which replaced some small houses in Rectory Road and provided thirty-eight new rooms and a flat for the junior dean. Under the direction of Wilf Stephenson, treasurer since 2005, and the Master of Works, Gerald Inns, this intricate project was a model of what could be done on a constricted site with limited funds and to a tight timetable.[3] Within the college bounds, it was possible to find more rooms on the King Edward Street side of the Island Site. Plans were drawn up to add a new floor to the Rhodes Building, which could be done without violence to Sir Basil Champneys's conception, to extend the library into the old junior common room, and to 'improve the public facilities around the Hall—the College Bar and JCR facilities—and the kitchen and servery...[which] will add to the capacity of Hall, provide additional flexible public space and provide a long term replacement for the JCR'.[4] Conceived in the conservationist spirit of the Island Site renewal of the 1980s, these projects were a logical sequel of the small-scale practical improvements which had been made in every generation since 1329.

Within the continually adjusted, apparently formless but in fact highly organized premises of the college, the student body's strong corporate sense and generally high morale was maintained, given focus by the Boat Club's struggle to regain the headship of the river which it had dominated since the 1970s, but lost in 2003; after seven strenuous years, this was achieved in 2011. If college sport was still the most powerful unifying force among Oriel undergraduates, it was not the only form of sociability. James Methven, the

---

[3] Wilf Stephenson, 'Treasurer's Notes', OR (2010), 73–4.
[4] Wilf Stephenson, 'Treasurer's Notes', OR (2011), 66–7.

dean until 2008, had a unique rapport with junior members which allowed him to direct their revels into harmless if frequently eccentric patterns, and as senior member of the Dramatic Society occasionally to endow them with significant form, such as in the series of plays conceived and performed at twenty-four hours' notice in 2005–10. The inauguration of a Music Room on staircase XV, together with the grand piano installed in the senior library, made possible an enhanced number of performances; the Music Society, divided into an undergraduate and an alumnus branch, sponsored lunchtime concerts in St Mary's, while the champagne concerts in the senior library regularly brought alumni back to Oriel.[5] Like rowing, music came to be a focus of unity in the Oriel community: an annual distinguished visiting musician, a chapel choir of the highest standard, and a student orchestra all contributed to its growing place in college life. The fellowship continued to encourage junior members' formal dining in hall, which remained popular, in contradistinction to other colleges' experience, and instituted a college St George's Day dinner in addition. The performance of undergraduates in the schools was less satisfactory, in terms of the conventional measurement of the Norrington Table (effectively a measure of first class degrees alone), which placed Oriel in the lowest third consistently from 2002 to 2007; thereafter there was a significant if patchy revival. This statistic was not the whole story, as the record of university prizes and awards showed; the measure of firsts plus upper seconds, arguably a more balanced criterion for an education never intended to be purely academic, ranked the college on average eleventh out of thirty. In 2008, a year of much better attainment of first class degrees, they clustered in particular subjects, showing the role of emulation and morale among peers in their year group. But beside the undergraduate body flowed another stream of graduate students, continually growing in volume. The work of graduates proceeded outside the college tutorial structure, in faculties and departments, but as many more of them lived in college for two years they played a growing role in its life, from their newly refurbished base in the middle common room. In 2009 they organized an Oriel Interdisciplinary Student Conference, addressed by two distinguished alumni, the economist Sir John Vickers, warden of All Souls, and Colin Mayer, the director of the Said Business School, and by its own members on subjects as diverse as American literature and quantum computing.[6] This brave reassertion of the unity of knowledge fell squarely within the most ancient intellectual tradition of Oxford. The college as a body was now more sharply aware of its own traditions, which had been celebrated in *son-et-lumière* in the front quadrangle in 2003, and which were explored in

---

[5] David Maw, 'Music', OR (2009), 116–17.
[6] Jennifer Hauschild, 'The Middle Common Room', OR (2009), 51, and see Lise Arena and Ed Tarleton, 'Why do IT Projects Fail in Organisations?', OR (2009), 52–4.

addresses to the Harriot Society, the Newman Society, and in the annual Lee Seng Tee lectures on topics of college history. Few members were insensible to the beatification of John Henry Newman on 19 September 2010 by Pope Benedict XVI, a ceremony to which a delegation of Orielenses was invited; Newman, an unlikely focus of college unity during his fellowship, had become its *genius loci*.[7]

The expansion of the college in the first decade of the twenty-first century rested on the stronger endowment secured and active fund-raising established in the previous twenty years. College finance was complicated by the changing nature of government funding for universities. Oriel emerged from the complex fee settlement of 2004–6 without significant disadvantage, but it was becoming clear, as the provost wrote in 2008, that 'apart from putting all our buildings in good order, we need to have an unencumbered endowment in the £70–80m range if we are to meet all our academic and eleemosynary objectives'.[8] The total endowment in that year stood at about £45m. The shortfall was made up from funds raised by the Development Trust which averaged about £2m p.a. Fund-raising remained, therefore, an essential part of the college's continuing operation. A new Development Director, Mark Curtis, was appointed in 2005 and elected to a fellowship; it was to be a permanent office, to which Sean Power succeeded in 2011, although the legally separate Development Trust was merged with the college in the same year. The director could depend on two great assets: the external friends and benefactors of the college who had been assembled by Zelman Cowen and Ernest Nicholson, and who had been afforced by a large new group of donors since 2004; and the immense good will of Orielenses whom the development trustees represented, which showed no sign of diminishing among the new generations matriculated after 1970—many of whom now occupied positions of power in investment banking, the legal profession, and the political world. A large proportion of the funds raised took the form of legacies, pledged according to a very successful scheme organized by Robin Harland (Oriel 1951). Benefactors who had pledged legacies were members of the Adam de Brome Society; other major benefactors, whose gifts took another form, of the Raleigh Society. A longer-term programme to increase the endowment to around £80m, the 2026 fund, was set up in 2004, with the aim of making Oriel wholly self-sufficient by the septencentenary year. It was a mark of the general enthusiasm for fund-raising that a great deal of money was raised by teams of undergraduates telephoning alumni and soliciting donations. Among the largest gifts and legacies were those of Colin Prestige (Oriel 1948) and Kevin Sharer, an American benefactor who provided an endowment for biochemistry. The stream of benefactions from within and outside the

---

[7] William Wood, 'Oriel at Cardinal Newman's Beatification Mass', OR (2010), 65–6.
[8] 'Provost's Notes', OR (2008), 15.

body of alumni assumed increasing importance as the decade advanced, bringing effectively to an end the period of dependence on government funding which had been in operation since the early 1920s. With its restored and expanded physical assets, the college was able to generate funds itself from conferences and summer schools, to which it let space in a progressively more professional fashion; over £1m was raised from this source in 2010–11.

It was a further consequence of the expansion of the fellowship that it could no longer be governed directly by meetings of fellows which might number nearly fifty persons. The governance of the college now had to conform to criteria laid down for charities, and in this respect it was bound to answer to the Charities Commission. Arrangements had to be 'rigorous and effective, fit for the purpose of running a substantial institution, compliant with new charities legislation', and the college must 'operate with proper accountability, whilst retaining the strongly consultative and participative ethos which colleges have historically exhibited and which their trustee status requires'.[9] The need for accountability was met by new investment, audit, and remuneration committees, largely recruited from among alumni; the efficient flow of business was enhanced by a general purposes committee, which would review and prepare the questions which only the governing body, according to its statutory responsibilities, could determine. Representatives of the graduate and undergraduate bodies would participate in college business within the limits permitted by the statutes. The provost and fellows, as trustees now regulated by the Charities Commission, therefore remained fully and uniquely responsible, in accordance with the principle of independent government laid down in 1326, retained in subsequent revisions of the statutes, and confirmed by successive acts of parliament. They had of course been reliant from the foundation on benefactions for their livelihood, soliciting support as early as the fifteenth century from former fellows in public office, and orchestrating fund-raising campaigns in the 1630s and 1780s. If the current and prospective alumni of the college now in their turn had implicit responsibility for its welfare, it underlined the primacy of their support in maintaining its educative function.

It is not possible for any writer at the present time to see the events of the last twenty years in accurate perspective. The size and shape of the college community had changed; but so far as can be seen, its nature and spirit were the same. All that can be said with reasonable certainty is that an ancient institution had been able to develop itself to meet new circumstances with energy and intelligence, and that its responsible members can still 'shine their light like stars in their courses, and educate their people equally by learning and example', within the University of Oxford, 'the mother and nourisher of lettered persons'.[10] Perhaps it is enough.

---

[9] 'Provost's Notes', OR (2008), 15–16.
[10] Foundation charter of Oriel, 21 January 1326, OCR 3.

Appendix: College Officers

(A) PROVOSTS

The office of provost was established in the statutes of 21 January 1326 (OCR 6).

1326–32	Adam de Brome
1332–48	William de Leverton
1348–9	William de Hawkesworth
1349–73	William Daventry
1373–85	John Colyntre
1385–94	John Middelton (*in dispute 1385–7*)
1394–1402	John Maldon
1402–14	John Possell (*in dispute 1402*)
1414–15	John Rote (*in dispute 1414–15*)
1415–17	William Corfe
1417–21	Thomas Leintwardine (*in dispute 1417–19*)
1421–22	Henry Kayll
1422–4	*vacant*
1424–7	Nicholas Herry (*in dispute 1424–26*)
1427–35	John Carpenter
1435–46	Walter Lyhert
1446–9	John Hals
1449–75	Henry Sampson
1475–8	Thomas Hawkins
1478–92	John Taylor
1493–1507	Thomas Cornysh
1507–16	Edmund Wilsford
1516–30	James More
1530–8	Thomas Ware
1538–40	Henry Myn
1540–50	William Haynes
1550–65	John Smyth
1565–66	Roger Marbeck
1566–74	John Belley
1574–1618	Anthony Blencowe
1618–21	William Lewis
1621–44	John Tolson

(*continued*)

Continued

1644–53	John Saunders
1653–91	Robert Say
1691–1708	George Royse
1708–27	George Carter
1727–57	Walter Hodges
1757–68	Chardin Musgrave
1768–81	John Clark
1781–1814	John Eveleigh
1814–28	Edward Copleston
1828–82	Edward Hawkins
1882–1905	David Binning Monro
1905–14	Charles Lancelot Shadwell
1914–29	Lancelot Ridley Phelps
1929–47	Sir David Ross
1947–57	Sir George Clark
1957–80	Kenneth Turpin
1980–1	Sir Michael Swann, Lord Swann
1981–2	W. E. Parry (*acting provost*)
1982–90	Sir Zelman Cowen
1990–2003	Ernest Nicholson
2003–13	Sir Derek Morris
2013	Moira Wallace

(B) VICE-PROVOSTS

The office of vice-provost was instituted for David Binning Monro in 1874, when he undertook the duties of the provostship in the last years of Edward Hawkins. It ceased in 1882 when Monro became provost. It was revived in 1934.

Date	Vice-provost
1874–82	David Binning Monro
1934–45	Marcus Tod
1945–8	Dalziel Llewellyn Hammick
1948–50	L. W. Grensted
1950–3	R. W. B. Burton
1953–6	J. W. Gough
1956–9	W. A. Pantin
1959–62	Arthur Crow
1962–5	John Chassar Moir
1965–9	Christopher Seton-Watson
1969–72	Graham Weddell

1972–5	H. F. D. Sparks
1975–8	Ben Brown
1978–81	John Sanders
1981–3	W. E. Parry
1983–86	Keith Prout
1986–9	Robert Beddard
1989–92	Graham Vincent-Smith
1992–95	Jeremy Catto
1995–98	Alan Segar
1998–2001	Gordon McPherson
2001–2	Michael Williams
2002–5	Glenn Black
2005–8	David Charles
2008–11	Mark Philp
2011	Andrew Boothroyd

(C) DEANS

The office of dean was established in the January 1326 statutes (OCR 6–7) and confirmed in the May 1326 statutes (Statutes 1853, i. Oriel, 6–7). Provision was made for subdeans to be elected from time to time (OCR 7; Statutes 7). They became regular from 1826 to 1903, and subdeans were appointed from 1915 to 1919 and from 1975 to 1986. After 1988 the title of dean was changed to senior dean, and that of subdean to dean.

Date	Dean	Subdean or deputy
1326–32	*implicitly* John de Laghton	
1332	*implicitly* William de Leverton	
1332–1409	*unknown*	
1409–13	John Rote	
1413–14	*unknown*	
1414–15	Henry Kayll	
1415–17	*unknown*	
1417–18	Henry Kayll	
1418–50	*unknown*	
1450–1	John Weston	
1451–3	Andrew Mankswell	
1453–4	Thomas Wyche	
1454–5	Richard Wiltshire	
1455–7	Thomas Wyche	

(continued)

Continued

Date	Dean		Subdean or deputy
1457–9	Henry Popy		
1459–60	Thomas Wyche		
1460–1	Henry Popy		
1461–2	Thomas Parys		
1462–3	William Fewers		
1463–4	Henry Popy		
1464–5	Robert Grafton		
1465–6	Robert Karver		
1466–8	Thomas Sadler		
1468–9	Robert Karver		
1469–71	Thomas Sadler		
1471–2	Robert Karver		
1472–8	John Taylor		
1478–81	John Perot		
1481–4	*unknown*		
1484–5	Thomas Wormeswell		
1485–97	*unknown*		
1497–8	Edmund Wilsford		
1498–9	Edmund Alyard		
1499–1500	*unknown*		
1500–1	Edward Powell		
1501–2	John Taylor		
1502–3	John Baker		
1503–4	*unknown*		
1504–5	James More		
1505–7	John Goodrich		
1507–10	Edward Trowbridge		
1510–11	*unknown*		
1511–12	Edward Trowbridge		
1512	Thomas Richards		
1512–13	William Broke	1513	Thomas Richards
1513–16	*unknown*		
1516–17	Thomas Stock	1517	Thomas Ware
1517–18	Thomas Ware		
1518–21	William Canynges		
1521–2	Thomas Ware		
1522–3	Thomas Schoppe		
1523–4	Walter Mey		
1524–5	Thomas Ware		
1525–7	Richard Crispin		
1527–31	Richard Lorgan		
1531–5	John Ryxman		

1535–7	Alexander Ryshton		
1537–41	John Griffith		
1541–3	William Pye		
1543–5	John Durston		
1545–50	John Smyth		
1550–2	William Collinge		
1552–3	*unknown*		
1553–6	William Norfolk		
1556–64	John Rawe		
1564–5	Francis Webber		
1565–6	William Jones		
1566–7	John Hurlock		
1567–9	Richard Pigot		
1569–70	Thomas Cogan		
1570–1	John Jackman		
1571–2	Anthony Blencowe		
1572–3	John Jackman		
1573–5	Thomas Philipson		
1575–9	John Jackman		
1579–80	*unknown*		
1580–1	Thomas Cooke		
1581–2	John Jackman		
1582–3	Anthony Tye		
1583–4	William Bond		
1584–5	Henry Ashworth	1585	Richard Pigot
1585–7	Richard Wharton	1587	Richard Pigot
1587–8	George Dale		
1588–9	Richard Wharton		
1589–90	Henry Scott	1589	Richard Wharton
		1590	Richard Pigot
1590–1	Thomas Hill		
1591–2	Richard Pigot		
1592–3	Thomas Dent		
1593–4	Cadwallader Owen		
1594–5	David Griffith		
1595–6	Cadwallader Owen		
1596–7	Abel Gower		
1597–8	William Wilmott		
1598–9	Cadwallader Owen		
1599–1600	Richard Harris		
1600–1	John Day		
1601–2	John Charlett		
1602–3	Abel Gower	1603	Richard Wharton
1603–4	Richard Wharton		
1604–5	William Wilmott		

(continued)

Continued

Date	Dean		Subdean or deputy
1605–6	Abel Gower		
1606–7	John Tolson		
1607–8	William Whetcombe		
1608–9	Abel Gower	1609	William Wilmott
1609–10	Thomas Wyatt		
1610–11	Ralph Fawconer		
1611–12	John Day		
1612–13	John Tolson		
1613–14	Richard Cluett		
1614–15	John Saunders		
1615–16	John Day		
1616–17	John Rouse		
1617–18	James Battye		
1618	William Lewis	1618	Barton Daniell
1618–19	Barton Daniell		
1619–20	Giles Widdowes		
1620–1	John Taylor		
1621–2	Nicholas Brookes		
1622–3	Robert Forward		
1623–4	Nicholas Brookes		
1624–5	John Cowling		
1625–6	Hugh Yale	1626	John Rouse
1626–7	Robert Forward	1627	John Rouse
1627–8	John Potticary	1628	Robert Forward
1628–9	John Horne		
1629–30	Maurice Williams	1629	John Rouse
		1629–30	Robert Forward
1630–1	Nicholas Brookes	1631	John Rouse
1631–2	Robert Forward	1632	Nicholas Brookes
1632–3	Richard Fowler	1633	Nicholas Brookes
1633–4	Edward Witherstone		
1634–5	Daniel Lawford	1634–5	John Rouse
1635–6	Richard Owen		
1636–7	John Gandy	1637	John Rouse
1637–8	John Duncombe		
1638–9	Henry Eccleston	1639	John Rouse
1639–40	Humphrey Lloyd		
1640–1	Nicholas Brookes		
1641–2	William Wyatt		
1642–3	John Duncombe		
1643–4	James Farren		
1644–5	Richard Saunders		

APPENDIX: COLLEGE OFFICERS

1645–7	William Washbourne		
1647–8	Robert Say		
1648–9	*unknown*		
1649–50	James Farren		
1650–1	Arthur Acland		
1651–2	Thomas Sheppard		
1652–3	Sharington Sheldon		
1653–4	Arthur Acland		
1654–5	William Bragge	1655	Sharington Sheldon
1655–6	Thomas Ofield		
1656–7	Thomas Sheppard		
1657–8	Henry Hawley		
1658–9	Charles Perrott		
1659–60	George Davenant		
1660–1	John Washbourne		
1661–2	Francis Barry		
1662–3	George Moore		
1663–4	John Washbourne		
1664–5	John Broderwick		
1665–6	John Whitehall		
1666–7	Edmund Thorne		
1667–8	Sharington Sheldon		
1668–9	Robert Swinglehurst		
1669–70	Edmund Thorne		
1670–1	James Davenant		
1671–2	Robert Kellway		
1672–3	John Wilcocks		
1673–4	Robert Kinsey		
1674–5	John Stonehouse		
1675–6	William Harvey		
1676–7	John Haslewood		
1677–8	George Barbour		
1678–9	Joseph Woodward		
1679–80	Henry Gandy		
1680–1	Joseph Crowther		
1681–2	Philip Foster		
1682–3	Richard Dyer		
1683–4	James Davenant		
1684–5	Robert Kinsey		
1685–6	William Harvey		
1686–7	Henry Gandy		
1687–8	John Haslewood		
1688–9	Henry Gandy		
1689–90	John Stonehouse		
1690–1	William Walker		

(continued)

Continued

Date	Dean	Subdean or deputy	
1691–2	Gerard Thurston	1692	James Davenant
1692–3	Peter Randal		
1693–4	Thomas Eyre		
1694–5	Richard West		
1695–6	Richard Dyer		
1696–7	Peter Randal		
1697–8	Richard West		
1698–9	Bradley Whalley		
1699–1700	Peter Randal		
1700–1	Edmund Brickenden		
1701–2	George Carter		
1702–3	Richard Dyer		
1703–4	Richard West		
1704–5	George Carter		
1705–6	Thomas Whalley		
1706–7	Richard Ibbetson		
1707–8	Nicholas Rogers		
1708–9	Edward Beckham		
1709–10	Thomas Ward		
1710–11	Richard Ibbetson		
1711–12	Nicholas Rogers		
1712–13	Edward Beckham		
1713–14	Thomas Ward		
1714–15	William Dering		
1715–16	Thomas Weeksey		
1716–17	Nicholas Rogers		
1717–18	Edward Beckham		
1718–19	Thomas Ward		
1719–20	Thomas Weeksey		
1720–2	Nicholas Rogers		
1722–3	Walter Hodges		
1723–4	Thomas Weeksey		
1724–5	Samuel Catherall		
1725–6	Thomas Weeksey		
1726–7	Samuel Catherall		
1727–8	Robert Fysher		
1728–9	John Woollin		
1729–30	Henry Edmunds		
1730–1	Philip Pipon		
1731–2	Robert Fysher		
1732–3	Henry Edmunds		
1733–4	Christopher Robinson		

APPENDIX: COLLEGE OFFICERS

1734–5	Robert Fysher		
1735–6	Edward Rayner		
1736–7	Thomas Myddelton		
1737–9	Edward Bentham		
1739–40	Humphrey Perrott		
1740–1	Edward Bentham		
1741–2	Charles Whiting		
1742–3	Humphrey Perrott		
1743–4	Edward Bentham		
1744–6	John Frewen		
1746–9	Edward Bentham		
1749–50	John Frewen		
1750–1	Chardin Musgrave		
1751–2	Edward Bentham		
1752–3	Gilbert White		
1753–4	Charles Whiting		
1754–5	Thomas Maunder		
1755–6	Edward Blake		
1756–7	James Beaver		
1757–8	John Frewen		
1758–60	Thomas Nowell		
1760–1	John Clark		
1761–2	John Dodson		
1762–8	John Clark		
1768–72	James Morgan		
1772–3	John Fleming		
1773–4	Robert Penny		
1774–5	Edward Marshall		
1775–81	John Eveleigh		
1781–7	Henry Beeke		
1787–97	Daniel Veysie		
1797–9	George Cooke		
1799–1800	James Landon		
1800–10	John Woolcombe		
1810–14	Edward Copleston		
1815–17	John Davison		
1817–19	William Bishop		
1819–20	Richard Whately		
1820–6	James Endell Tyler	1825–6	Edward Hawkins (*subdean*)
1826–8	Edward Hawkins	1827–8	Joseph Dornford
1828–32	Joseph Dornford	1828–31	Robert Wilberforce
		1831–5	George Denison
1832–3	William Copleston		
1833–5	John Henry Newman		

(*continued*)

Continued

Date	Dean	Subdean or deputy	
1835–8	William Copleston	1835–8	Clement Greswell
1838–42	Charles Page Eden	1838–41	Charles Daman
		1841–4	Charles Marriott
1842–3	Henry Shepheard		
1843–4	Edward Litton		
1844–50	Charles Marriott	1844–7	James Fraser
		1847–8	Arthur Hugh Clough
		1848–50	Charles Chretien
1850–9	Charles Chretien	1850–2	George Buckle
		1852–9	John William Burgon
		1859–62	Henry Earle Tweed
1859–67	Francis Harrison	1862–74	David Binning Monro
1867–74	William Collett		
1874	David Binning Monro	1874–5	William Collett
1874–81	Arthur Butler	1875–91	John Cook Wilson
1881–1915	Francis Henry Hall	1891–1903	F. C. Montague
1915–19	Charles Firth	1915–19	Frank Barry
1919–25	Eric Graham		
1925–34	John C. Wand		
1934–6	John Frank Russell		
1937	R. W. B. Burton		
1937	Arthur Crow		
1938–48	John Collins		
1948–61	Christopher Seton-Watson		
1961–4	Peter Brunt		
1964–72	Ben Brown		
1972–5	Derek Morris		
1975–86	Jeremy Catto	1976–86	David Brown
1986–8	Glenn Black		
1988–90	Glenn Black (*senior dean*)	1988–91	David Myers (*dean*)
1990–2	Simon Hornblower	1991–3	R. B. Moore
1992–4	Glenn Black	1993	David Myers
1994–5	Jeremy Catto (*acting senior dean*)	1994–7	James Burns
1995–2006	Jeremy Catto	1997–2008	James Methven
2006–10	Theresa Morgan	2008–9	Kathryn Bevis
		2009–12	Elizabeth Russell
2010	Juliane Kerkhecker	2012	Alexander Blake Ewing

(D) TREASURERS

The office of treasurer, to be occupied by an unspecified number of fellows at any one time, was set up under the Statutes of 26 May 1326 (Statutes, 1853, i. Oriel, 11–12) and specified as two in the amendment of 8 December 1329 (Statutes, 1853, i. Oriel, 15–16). After 1889 a single treasurer served, until 1918 formally holding both offices. From 1975 to 2005 a bursar or acting bursar was appointed in addition.

Date	Senior treasurer	Junior treasurer
1326–1409	*unknown*	*unknown*
1409–10	John Rote	Richard Garsdale
1410–11	John Rote	Richard Garsdale
1411–12	John Rote	Richard Garsdale
1412–50	*unknown*	*unknown*
1450–1	Roger Stephens	Henry Francys
1451–2	Richard Wiltshire	Thomas Hawkins
1452–3	Thomas Hawkins	John Brews
1453–4	Roger Stephens	Henry Popy
1454–5	William Edwards	Henry Popy
1455–6	Andrew Mankswell	John Brews
1456–7	Thomas Parys	Robert Grafton
1457–8	Thomas Parys	Robert Grafton
1458–9	Thomas Wyche	David Fairwater
1459–60	Thomas Parys	Roger Stephens
1460–1	Thomas Parys	Robert Grafton
1461–2	William Fewers	Robert Karver
1462–3	Thomas Parys	John Springbet
1463–4	Robert Grafton	John Springbet
1464–5	Robert Karver	Thomas Sadler
1465–6	Thomas Parys	Thomas Sadler
1466–7	Robert Karver	Edmund Alyard
1467–8	Robert Sheffield	Edmund Alyard
1468–9	Robert Sheffield	John Hyll
1469–70	Edmund Alyard	John Taylor
1470–1	Robert Sheffield	John Taylor
1471–2	Robert Sheffield	Thomas Sadler
1472–3	Robert Sheffield	John Perot
1473–4	Robert Karver	John Perot
1474–5	Robert Holcot	John Perot
1475–6	Robert Holcot	James Laws
1476–7	Edmund Alyard	James Laws
1477–8	John Perot	John Drake
1478–9	John Drake	Thomas Cornysh
1479–80	Robert Holcot	William Lynch

(continued)

Continued

Date	Senior treasurer	Junior treasurer
1480–1	Thomas Cornysh	William Lynch
1481–2	John Perot	Thomas Wormeswell
1482–3	John Perot	Thomas Wormeswell
1483–4	Edmund Alyard	William Wright
1484–5	Nicholas Flint	Richard Martyn
1485–6	William Wright	Roger Sutton
1486–7	Thomas Wormeswell	Richard Martyn
1487–8	Edmund Alyard	Richard Martyn
1488–9	Thomas Wormyswell	Edmund Wilsford
1489–90	William Wryght	Walter Goodyer
1490–1	Richard Gardener	Walter Goodyer
1491–2	Richard Gardener	John Taylor
1492–3	John Taylor	Rowland Phillips
1493–4	Edmund Alyard	Rowland Phillips
1494–5	Richard Gardener	James More
1495–6	James More	William Wodehoke
1496–7	Richard Gardener	William Wodehoke
1497–8	Richard Gardener	John Taylor
1498–9	John Taylor	Robert Norreys
1499–1500	John Taylor	Edward Powell
1500–1	John Taylor	John Baker
1501–2	John Baker	Richard Vaughan
1502–3	Richard Dudley	John Goodrich
1503–4	John Baker	Edward Trowbridge
1504–5	John Goodrich	Edward Trowbridge
1505–6	Edward Trowbridge	Henry Myn
1506–7	Henry Mynne	Thomas Richards
1507–8	John Goodrich	Edward Trowbridge
1508–9	Thomas Richards	William Broke
1509–10	Thomas Richards	William Broke
1510–11	William Broke	Matthew Smyth
1511–12	William Broke	Thomas Stock
1512–13 1513	John Morys (to June) Thomas Stock (13 June)	John Stephens
1513–14	Thomas Ware	John Stephens
1514–15	Thomas Ware	William Canynges
1515–16	Thomas Ware	John Stephens
1516–17	John Stephns	William Canynges

APPENDIX: COLLEGE OFFICERS 805

1517–18	William Canynges	William Rose
1518–19	John Stephens	William Rose
1519–20	Walter May	Thomas Mawnfyld
1520–1	Walter May	Richard Crispin
1521–2	Thomas Mawnfyld	Richard Crispin
1522–3	Richard Crispin	William Upton
1523–4	Richard Crispin	William Upton
1524–5	William Upton	Richard Lorgan
1525–6	William Upton	Richard Lorgan
1526–7	*unknown*	*unknown*
1527–8	Robert Charde	John Ryxman
1528–9	John Ryxman	*unknown*
1529–30	John Ryxman	*unknown*
1530–1	*unknown*	*unknown*
1531–2	Alexander Ryshton	John Griffith
1532–5	*unknown*	*unknown*
1535–6	William Pye	*unknown*
1536–41	*unknown*	*unknown*
1541–2	William Cocks	John Durston
1542–3	*unknown*	*unknown*
1543–4	William Cocks	William Collinge
1544–5	William Collinge	John Smyth junior
1545–8	*unknown*	*unknown*
1548–9	John Smyth junior	*unknown*
1549–82	*unknown*	*unknown*
1582–3	William Nelson	George Dale
1583–4	Richard Wharton	George Dale
1584–5	Richard Wharton	George Dale
1585–6	Simon Lee	Robert Heighley
1586–7	Thomas Dent	Henry Scott
1587–8	Robert Cockram	David Griffith
1588–9	Robert Cockram	David Griffith
1589–90	Cadwallader Owen	Abel Gower
1590–1	Thomas Dent	William Wilmott
1591–2	Cadwallader Owen	Abel Gower
1592–3	William Wilmott	John Charlett
1593–4	John Day	Richard Harris
1594–5	Thomas Hill	Richard Parkinson
1595–6	Richard Harris	Matthew Lister
1596–7	Richard Wharton	Richard Butler
1597–8	Richard Wharton	John Charlett
1598–9	Richard Parkinson	Matthew Lister
1599–1600	William Whetcombe	John Tolson
1600–1	Abel Gower	William Wilmott
1601–2	Richard Wharton	John Day

(*continued*)

Continued

Date	Senior treasurer	Junior treasurer
1602–3	Ralph Fawconer	Thomas Johnson
1603–4	John Tolson	Thomas Wyatt
1604–5	John Day	John Rouse
1605–6	Ralph Fawconer	Thomas Johnson
1606–7	David Lloyd	John Saunders
1607–8	Thomas Wyatt	Richard Cluett
1608–9	John Rouse	John Lloyd
1609–10	John Day	Ralph Fawconer
1610–11	John Tolson	Walter Pargeter
1611–12	John Saunders	Richard Cluett
1612–13	Robert Cockram	John Lloyd
1613–14	George Cockram	William Lewis
1614–15	John Tolson	John Lloyd
1615–16	James Battye	Barton Daniell
1616–17	Giles Widdowes	Joshua Eliot
1617–18	Barton Daniell	Nicholas Brookes
1618–19	John Rouse	Robert Forward
1619–20	John Rouse	Nicholas Brookes
1620–1	Edmund Brockhurst	John Cowling
1621–2	John Taylor	Hugh Yale
1622–3	Francis Duncombe	Robert Tooker
1623–4	John Horne	Robert Tooker
1624–5	John Potticary	Maurice Williams
1625–6	Robert Forward	Richard Fowler
1626–7	John Cowling	Thomas Cole
1627–8	Nicholas Brookes	Hugh Yale
1628–9	John Potticary	Edward Witherstone
1629–30	John Rouse	Daniel Lawford
1630–1	Robert Forward	Pauncefoot Wall
1631–2	Hugh Yale	John Gandy
1632–3	Thomas Cole	Richard Owen
1633–4	Richard Fowler	John Duncombe
1634–5	Edward Witherstone	Henry Eccleston
1635–6	Nicholas Brookes	John Warren
1636–7	Daniel Lawford	Humphrey Lloyd
1637–8	Richard Owen	Richard Winch
1638–9	John Duncombe	William Wyatt
1639–40	Henry Eccleston	Edward Smallbone
1640–1	Humphrey Lloyd	James Farren
1641–2	Nicholas Brookes	Robert Say
1642–3	William Wyatt	Richard Saunders
1643–4	John Duncombe	William Washbourne

1644–5	James Farren	Thomas Sheppard
1645–6	Richard Saunders	Henry Chamberlaine
1646–7	William Washbourne	Sharington Sheldon
1647–8	Thomas Sheppard	Arthur Acland *deputed to* William Washbourne
1648–9	William Bragge	Henry Lomax
1649–50	Robert Say	William Bragge
1650–1	William Washbourne	John Eston
1651–2	Arthur Acland	Henry Long
1652–3	Thomas Sheppard	Thomas Ofield
1653–4	Sharington Sheldon	Samuel Dyx
1654–5	Arthur Acland	Thomas Gybons
1655–6	William Bragge	Henry Hawley
1656–7	Thomas Ofield	George Davenant *deputed to* Henry Hawley
1657–8	Thomas Sheppard	Charles Perrott
1658–9	Henry Hawley	John Washbourne
1659–60	Charles Perrott	Francis Barry
1660–1	George Davenant	George Moore
1661–2	John Washbourne	Richard Garland
1662–3	Francis Barry	John Broderwick
1663–4	George Moore	Robert Swinglehurst
1664–5	John Washbourne	John Whitehall
1665–6	Sharington Sheldon	Edmund Thorne
1666–7	John Whitehall	James Davenant
1667–8	Edmund Thorne	Robert Kellway
1668–9	Sharington Sheldon	John Wilcocks
1669–70	Robert Swinglehurst	Robert Kinsey
1670–1	Edmund Thorne	Henry Clayton
1671–2	James Davenant	George Cowslade
1672–3	Robert Kellway	William Harvey
1673–4	Charles Perrott	John Stonehouse
1674–5	Robert Kinsey	John Haslewood
1675–6	John Stonehouse	George Barbour
1676–7	William Harvey	Joseph Woodward
1677–8	John Haslewood	Henry Gandy
1678–9	George Barbour	Joseph Crowther
1679–80	Joseph Woodward	Philip Foster
1680–1	Henry Gandy	Richard Dyer
1681–2	Joseph Crowther	George Royse
1682–3	Philip Foster	Samuel Desmaistres

(continued)

Continued

Date	Senior treasurer	Junior treasurer
1683–4	Richard Dyer	William Walker
1684–5	James Davenant	William Harvey
1685–6	John Stonehouse	Joseph Woodward
1686–7	William Harvey	Richard Dyer
1687–8	Henry Gandy	George Royse
1688–9	John Haslewood	William Walker
1689–90	Robert Kinsey	Gerard Thurston
1690–1	John Stonehouse	Peter Randal
1691–2	William Walker	Thomas Eyre
1692–3	Gerard Thurston	Richard West
1693–4	John Stonehouse	William Walker
1694–5	Thomas Eyre	Bradley Whalley
1695–6	Richard West	Edmund Brickenden
1696–7	Richard Dyer	Nicholas Tripe
1697–8	Peter Randal	Andrew Crispe
1698–9	Richard West	George Carter
1699–1700	Bradley Whalley	George Rye
1700–1	Peter Randal	Thomas Whalley
1701–2	Peter Randal	Alexander Ashe
1702–3	George Carter	Richard Ibbetson
1703–4	Andrew Crispe	Nicholas Rogers
1704–5	Richard West	William Hawkins
1705–6	George Carter	Edward Beckham
1706–7	Thomas Whalley	Thomas Ward
1707–8	Richard Ibbetson	William Dering
1708–9	Nicholas Rogers	George Rye
1709–10	Edward Beckham	John Salmon
1710–11	George Rye	George Parry
1711–12	Richard Ibbetson	Thomas Weeksey
1712–13	Nicholas Rogers	William Cary
1713–14	Edward Beckham	Charles Cotes
1714–15	Thomas Ward	Edward Talbot
1715–16	William Dering	Nicholas Rogers
1716–17	Thomas Weeksey	Edward Beckham
1717–18	Nicholas Rogers	Thomas Ward
1718–19	Edward Beckham	Thomas Weeksey
1719–20	Thomas Ward	Samuel Catherall
1720–1	Thomas Weeksey	Walter Hodges
1721–2	Walter Hodges	John Evans
1722–3	John Evans	Joseph Bowles
1723–4	Walter Hodges	Henry Brooke
1724–5	Thomas Weeksey	Alexander Rayner

APPENDIX: COLLEGE OFFICERS

1725–6	Henry Brooke	Alexander Rayner
1726–7	Henry Brooke	Alexander Rayner
1727–8	Philip Pipon	John Woollin
1728–9	Robert Fysher	Henry Edmunds
1729–30	Robert Fysher	Philip Pipon
1730–1	Henry Edmunds	Christopher Robinson
1731–2	Christopher Robinson	Edward Rayner
1732–3	Edward Rayner	James Hawley
1733–4	James Hawley	William Seaman
1734–5	Edward Bentham	Thomas Myddelton
1735–6	Thomas Myddelton	Edward Bentham
1736–7	Robert Fysher	Christopher Robinson
1737–8	Thomas Myddelton	Humphrey Perrott
1738–9	Humphrey Perrott	William Carter
1739–40	William Carter	Thomas Myddelton
1740–1	Thomas Myddelton	Robert Fysher
1741–2	Humphrey Perrott	John Frewen
1742–3	John Frewen	Charles Whiting
1743–4	Charles Whiting	Robert Fysher
1744–5	Robert Fysher	Humphrey Perrott
1745–6	Humphrey Perrott	Charles Whiting
1746–7	Charles Whiting	John Frewen
1747–8	John Frewen	Chardin Musgrave
1748–9	John Frewen	Chardin Musgrave
1749–50	Chardin Musgrave	Henry Davies
1750–1	Henry Davies	John Bosworth
1751–2	John Bosworth	Thomas Maunder
1752–3	John Frewen	Thomas Maunder
1753–4	Thomas Maunder	James Beaver
1754–5	James Beaver	John Frewen
1755–6	James Beaver	Thomas Nowell
1756–7	John Frewen	Thomas Nowell
1757–8	Thomas Nowell	John Dodson
1758–9	John Dodson	John Clark
1759–60	John Clark	William Thomas
1760–1	William Thomas	John Frewen
1761–2	John Frewen	Thomas Nowell
1762–3	Thomas Nowell	William Thomas
1763–4	William Thomas	John Frewen
1764–5	John Frewen	John Dodson
1765–6	John Dodson	James Morgan
1766–7	James Morgan	Richard Head
1767–8	Richard Head	Stephen Pemberton

(continued)

Continued

Date	Senior treasurer	Junior treasurer
1768–9	Stephen Pemberton	Edward Marshall
1769–70	Edward Carne	William Walker
1770–1	William Walker	Edward Norwood
1771–2	Stephen Pemberton	John Fleming
1772–3	Stephen Pemberton	John Eveleigh
1773–4	John Eveleigh	John Fleming
1774–5	John Fleming	Robert Wood
1775–6	John Fleming	John Pitman
1776–7	John Fleming	Bartholomew Sclater
1777–8	John Fleming	Henry Beeke
1778–9	Henry Beeke	Daniel Veysie
1779–80	Henry Beeke	James Rogers
1780–1	Henry Beeke	Richard Twopeny
1781–2	Richard Twopeny	Thomas Shore
1782–3	Richard Twopeny	Thomas Shore
1783–4	Richard Twopeny	John Williams
1784–5	Daniel Veysie	James Pitt
1785–6	James Pitt	James Rogers
1786–7	James Rogers	Jeremiah Curteis
1787–8	Jeremiah Curteis	George Cooke
1788–9	George Cooke	John Elmsly
1789–90	George Cooke	James Landon
1790–1	James Landon	George Cooke
1791–2	George Cooke	James Landon
1792–3	James Landon	George Richards
1793–4	George Richards	George Cooke
1794–5	George Cooke	Richard Walwayn
1795–6	George Cooke	Joseph Pickford
1796–7	George Cooke	John Woolcombe
1797–8	John Woolcombe	Edward Copleston
1798–9	Edward Copleston	James Bordman
1799–1800	Edward Copleston	Edward Bullock
1800–1	Edward Copleston	Edward Holwell
1801–2	Richard Mant	Edward Holwell
1802–3	William Bishop	Edward Berens
1803–4	William Bishop	Edward Copleston
1804–5	Edward Copleston	William Bishop
1805–6	Edward Copleston	Thomas Scott Smyth
1806–7	Edward Copleston	Thomas Scott Smyth
1807–8	Edward Copleston	William Bishop

1808–9	Edward Copleston	William Bishop
1809–10	Edward Copleston	William Bishop
1810–11	John Davison	William Bishop
1811–12	John Davison	William Bishop
1812–13	John Davison	Edward Marsh
1813–14	William James	John Keble
1814–15	William James	James Endell Tyler
1815–16	William James	James Endell Tyler
1816–17	William James	Edward Hawkins
1817–18	William James	Edward Hawkins
1818–19	James Endell Tyler	Thomas Arnold
1819–20	James Endell Tyler	John Keble
1820–1	John Keble	Henry Jenkyns
1821–2	John Keble	Joseph Dornford
1822–3	Edward Hawkins	William Brudenell Barter
1823–4	Edward Hawkins	Joseph Dornford
1824–5	Edward Hawkins	John Henry Newman
1825–6	Joseph Dornford	William Churton
1826–7	Joseph Dornford	John Henry Newman
1827–8	Joseph Dornford	John Henry Newman
1828–9	Joseph Dornford	John Henry Newman
1829–30	John Henry Newman	Richard Hurrell Froude
1830–1	John Henry Newman	Richard Hurrell Froude
1831–2	Henry Jenkyns	Richard Hurrell Froude
1832–3	Henry Jenkyns	John Frederic Christie
1833–4	William Copleston	John Frederic Christie
1834–5	William Copleston	John Frederic Christie
1835–6	George Antony Denison	Thomas Mozley
1836–7	George Antony Denison	Charles Page Eden
1837–8	George Antony Denison	Charles Page Eden
1838–9	Frederic Rogers	John Henry Newman
1839–40	Frederic Rogers	Richard William Church

(continued)

Continued

Date	Senior treasurer	Junior treasurer	
1840–1	Frederic Rogers	James Prichard	
1841–2	Richard William Church	Thomas Cornish	
1842–3	Richard William Church	Albany Christie	
1843–4	Richard William Church	Albany Christie	
1844–5	Richard William Church	Drummond Percy Chase	
1845–6	Charles Neate	Drummond Percy Chase	
1846–7	Charles Neate	Drummond Percy Chase	
1847–8	Charles Neate	Drummond Percy Chase	
1848–9	Charles Neate	Drummond Percy Chase	
1849–53	Drummond Percy Chase	John Earle	
1853–9	Drummond Percy Chase	John William Burgon	
1859–60	Charles Chretien	John William Burgon	
1860–1	Charles Chretien	Drummond Percy Chase	*with* Henry Earle Tweed
1860–2	Drummond Percy Chase	Henry Earle Tweed	
1862–6	Drummond Percy Chase	David Binning Monro	
1866–73	Drummond Percy Chase	Charles Lancelot Shadwell	
1873–4	Drummond Percy Chase	Charles Lancelot Shadwell	
1874–6	Charles Lancelot Shadwell	Charles Lancelot Shadwell	
1876–9	Charles Lancelot Shadwell	Francis Hall	
1879–83	Charles Lancelot Shadwell	Lancelot Ridley Phelps	
1883–7	Charles Lancelot Shadwell	Charles Lancelot Shadwell	
1887–8	Charles Lancelot Shadwell	John Cook Wilson	
1888–9	Langford Lovell Price	John Cook Wilson	
1889–1918	Langford Lovell Price	Langford Lovell Price	
1918–28	Percy Lyon (*sole treasurer*)		

1928–46	Cecil S. Emden		
1946–51	J. W. Gough		
1951–5	Hugh Lambrick		
1955–6	Ian Ramsey (*acting treasurer*)		Kenneth Turpin (*acting bursar*)
1956–69	Ralph Bagnall-Wild		
1970–3	Derek Shorthouse		
1973–4	H. F. D. Sparks (*acting treasurer*)		Ben Brown (*bursar*)
1974–86	Eric Vallis	1975–8	John Baker (*bursar*)
		1978–9	Jonathan Barnes (*acting bursar*)
		1979	Alan Segar (*acting bursar*)
		1979–90	Hugh Browne (*bursar*)
1986–2000	Eric Barratt	1986–93	Eric Vallis (*estates bursar*)
		1990–9	Michael Stephens (*bursar*)
		1993–2000	James Offen (*estates bursar*)
		1999–2004	Alexander Hardie (*bursar*)
2001–3	Graham Vincent-Smith (*acting treasurer*)		
2003–5	Graham Vincent-Smith	2004–5	Michael Stephens (*acting bursar*)
2005	Wilf Stephenson		

Index

Abbot, George, archbishop of
    Canterbury 102, 115, 143
Aberford, Yorkshire, Oriel living 16, 17, 19,
    21, 22, 25, 40, 91n, 144, 200, 204, 208,
    210, 477, 485, 487, 488, 489, 497,
    498–500, 512, 533
Abraham, Sir Edward Penley 670
Acland, Arthur 103, 132, 799, 807
Acland, Sir Henry 272, 415n, 661, 662
Adam de Brome Society 791
Adam, John Marshall William 734
Adams, Richard 230
Addison, Joseph 257
Adelaide, queen of Great Britain 601
Aeschylus 101
Aesop 102
Agricola, Georgius 650–1
Aikin, John 653
Albert, John 763
Alberwyk, William de 21
Alfonso X, king of Leon and Castile 25
Alfred Street, Oxford, Oriel property
    in 539, 585
Alfred, king of England 2
Alington, Robert 46
All Souls College 49, 65n, 69, 130, 164, 166,
    170, 177–8, 193, 220, 239, 491, 494n,
    496, 509, 514, 526, 570, 598, 602
Allen, Mr, barber 239
Allen, Thomas 109, 147–8, 648
Allen, William Cardinal 82, 86, 87–8, 90, 136,
    139, 147, 159, Ill. 3.5
Allmand, Michael, VC 746
Althorp, John Charles, Lord Althorp, third
    Earl Spencer 381
Alyard, Edmund 54, 56, 67, 93, 796, 803, 804
Ambrose, bishop of Milan 55, 350
Amhurst, Nicholas 170, 171n, 216
Ammonius 101
Anderson, Hector James 454, 455
Andreas, Antonius OFM 73
Andrewes, Lancelot, bishop of Winchester 158n
Andrews, Len 635
Anne of Denmark, queen of Great
    Britain 650
Anne, queen of Great Britain 168, 171,
    198n, 241
Annetts, Arthur 712n
Anstey, Peter 745–6, 749
Antonio, Prior of Crato, claimant king of
    Portugal 451
Anyan, Thomas 118
Apperley, Thomas 183, 226
Appleyard, Sir Matthew 129
Aquinas, Thomas OP 54n, 55, 62, 85, 101, 102
Arabic, study of 120
Arc, Joan of 51–2
Archer, Andrew 230
Archer, Simon 230
Archery 601
Arculus, David 788
Aristotle 12, 28, 30, 32, 40, 57, 60, 72, 76, 85,
    101, 102, 260, 270, 312, 331, 368n, 412,
    414, 475, 645, 733, 750
Armstrong, C. G. (Sir Godfrey) 462
Arnold, Matthew 260n, 330, 354, 365, 423–4,
    Plate 5
Arnold, Thomas 280, 283, 284, 296, 297, 300n,
    302, 305, 333, 335–6, 338n, 339, 340,
    341–2, 343, 354, 365, 369, 370, 375, 382,
    387, 404, 409, 412, 603, 610, 643, 707,
    811, Plate 3
Arnold Society 717, 727, 744, 753
Arundel, Richard Fitzalan earl of Arundel
    (d.1376) 34, 551
Arundel, Thomas, archbishop of
    Canterbury 30, 34, 37, 38–9, 40, 42, 43,
    45, 47, 58, 443, 551, Ill. 2.3
Ashdown, John 586
Ashe, Alexander 808
Ashe, John 161n, 245n
Ashe, Joseph 245n
Ashenden, John 47
Ashworth, Henry 105, 125, 797
Asquith Commission 524, 527–8, 679, 685–8,
    689, 694, 705
Asquith, Herbert Henry, earl of Oxford and
    Asquith 685
Aston, Elizabeth 511
Aston, John 19, 26, 27

Aston, Sir Richard 194–8, 495, 510–11
Aston, Sir Thomas 197n
Aston, Sir Willoughby (m.1730) 195, 245n, 485, 487, 498n, 506n, 511
Aswardby, John 45
Athanasius, bishop of Alexandria 142
Athletics 615, 631
Atwater, William, bishop of Lincoln 70, 78
Aubrey, John 148
Aubrey, John, of Boarstall 485
Auden, Wystan Hugh 731
Augustine, bishop of Hippo 61, 62, 379
Aungevyn, Ralf 553
Aungevyn's tenement 553
Austen (Godwin-), Robert 657
Austin, Sir Robert 245n
Averroes 55
Avicenna 55
Awdry, Sir John 281, 427–8
Aylesbury, Oriel property at 534, 542
Aylmer, John, bishop of London 137

Backhouse, Maxwell Vaughan 467
Bacon, Sir Francis, earl of Verulam 102, 114, 115, 116, 117, 118, 145, 146
Badcocke, Katherine 110
Badlesmere, Henry Lord 24
Badminton 615, 631, 633
Badnoll, Henry 490
Badnoll, Thomas 483, 490
Bagnall-Wild, Ralph E. 536, 537, 538, 548, 585, 764, 813
Bagot, Sir Walter 191
Baker, John (fellow 1493–1509) 65, 66, 72, 74, 796, 804
Baker, John (fellow 1975–8) 813
Baldock, W. S. 459–60, 466
Balfour of Burleigh, Alexander Lord 622
Balliol College 10, 111n, 131, 193, 224, 241, 247, 371, 407, 414, 416, 446, 452n, 467, 483, 488, 493n, 496, 505, 512, 527, 544, 566n, 616, 636, 645, 663, 733, 738, 767
Balliol, John earl of Galloway 14
Bampton Lectures 249, 250, 256, 259, 260, 263, 266n, 275, 280, 284, 293, 297, 301, 305, 306, 340–1, 343, 346, 409
Bampton, John 249n
Banbury School 63
Bancroft, John, bishop of Oxford 152
Bancroft, Richard, archbishop of Canterbury 143

Bandinel, James 249
Baner Hall 25, 27
Bankes, John, junior 133
Bankes, Sir John 129
Barbour, George 167, 799, 807
Barclay, John 126
Barclays Bank 529
Bardelby, Robert de 16, 17, 33
Barge, Oriel College 634–5, 718
Baring, Alexander, first Lord Ashburton 382
Baring, William Bingham, second Lord Ashburton 387
Barker, Henry 125
Barker, Sir John 486
Barker, Sir John Fitch 486
Barker, Scorey 161n, 245n
Barlow, David 672
Barlow, Robert 146
Barlow, Thomas 161
Barlow, William, bishop of Lincoln 103, 106, 110
Barnes, Jonathan 643, 773, 813
Barratt, Eric 540, 543, 813
Barret, Richard 84, 88, 136
Barrington, Daines 653
Barrington, Robert 642n
Barry, Francis 799, 807
Barry, Frank Russell 714, 802
Barter, William Brudenell 273n, 811
Bartlemas 22, 25, 133, 144, 476–7, 480, 485 488, 489, 492, 493n, 495, 528, 530, 533, 535, 541, 542, 544, 554, 616, 626–7, 643, 713, 717–18, 727, 753, 768, 778
Basel, university of 106
Basil, bishop of Caesarea 107
Baskerville, Hannibal 126
Basketball 631
Bastwick, John 151
Bath, Robert 156n
Bathwick 16
Battye, James 154n, 798, 806
Baxter, Richard 156
Bayly, Richard 155
Baynes, Arthur Hamilton, bishop of Natal 456, 465
Beak, David 637
Beam Hall 67, 76
Beard, Geoffrey 564
Beattie, Ian 674
Beattie, James 261–3
Beauchamp heraldic shield 551

Beauchamp, Philip 34, 40
Beaufort exhibitioners 163, 188, 228, 229
Beaufort, Charles Somerset fourth duke of 188, 190, 238, 246, Ill. 6.2
Beaufort, Henry Somerset third duke of 188, 228
Beaufort, Henry Somerset, fifth duke of 190, 191, 203, 220, 226, 233, 238, 242n, 246, 252–3
Beaver, James 190, 801, 809
Beckham, Edward 173, 199, 205n, 800, 808
Beddard, Robert 586, 795
Bede 55
Bedel Hall 32, 37, 39, 53, 54, 57, 67, 77, 477n, 479, 569
Bedmystre, Thomas 41, 42
Beeke, Henry 5, 11, 255, 256n, 266n, 271, 381, 566, 652, 653, 801, 810
Belfield, Alan 228n
Belfield, Finney (m.1720) 228n
Belfield, Finney (m.1775) 228n
Belfield, John (m.1688) 228n, 245n
Belfield, John (m.1720) 228n
Belfield, Samuel 228n
Bell, Harold Idris 435
Bellarmine, Robert cardinal 126, 142–3
Belley, George 91
Belley, John, provost 87, 89, 91, 485, 793
Bellingham, Lady Katherine 195
Belson, Thomas 136n
Bence-Pembroke, Reginald Arthur 469
Benedict XVI, pope 791
Bennett, James 71
Bent, George 229n
Bent, William, junior 229n
Bent, William, senior 229n
Bentham, Edward 3, 6, 188, 190, 208, 216, 218, 232, 241, 801, 809
Bentham, Jeremy 226
Bentham, Thomas 208n
Benwell, Thomas, tailor 235
Berens, Edward 810
Berenson, Bernard 765
Bergueny, William de 553
Berkeley, Charles Berkeley, earl of 211
Berkeley, George Berkeley earl of 169
Berkeley, George, bishop of Cloyne 261
Berkenhead, John 130, 155, 161
Berkshire, Henry Bowes Howard earl of 226
Bernard of Clairvaux 55
Bernard, Robert 173, 177n, 178n, 180

Berry, John 155–6
Best, John 124
Best, Richard 124
Bethersden, Kent property 545
Beveridge, Sir William, Lord Beveridge 406n, 685, 710
Bevis, Kathryn 802
Beza, Theodore 143
Bilham Farm, Kent, Oriel property 480, 522
Bill the bulldog 631
Bingham, Isaac Moody 224n
Birch, John 42, 43, 45
Bird in Hand Inn 584
Bishop, Henry 390
Bishop, Mr, of Dean 498
Bishop, William 273n, 390, 801, 810, 811
Bismarck, Otto von, Prince Bismarck 473
Black, Glenn 795, 802
Blackstone, Sir William 190, 202
Blackwell, A. F. 729
Blake, Edward 801
Blake, Mr, of Swainswick 495
Blakeway, Cyril Tennant 455
Bland, Sir Thomas 489, 495, 498
Blandford, Walter 161
Blencowe, Anthony, provost 9, 73, 84, 89, 91, 92, 99, 103–4, 105, 106, 107, 108–10, 111, 113–14, 115, 117, 120, 123, 136, 145, 147–9, 159, 555–6, 793, 797, Ill. 4.1
Blencowe, George 109, 112
Blencowe, John 245n
Blenkinsop, R., barber 235
Bliss, Nathaniel 656
Bliss, Robert, bookseller 235
Blois, Peter of 55
Blomfield, Charles James, bishop of London 293n
Blund, Andrew 25
Boardman, Elizabeth 8
Boarstall 478
Boat Race, Oxford and Cambridge 608, 612, 616, 630, 633, 637–8
Boathouse of Oriel 635
Bodin, Jean 101
Bodley, George Frederick 561, 572
Bodley, Sir Thomas 103, 107, 120, 124, 139, 148, 159
Bohun heraldic shield 551
Bonas, (Bonus), Arthur Rivers (Balliol) 459
Bonas, Jeffrey 540, 633, 787, 788
Bonaventure 143

Bond, Mr, college servant 765
Bond, Nicholas 107
Bond, William 797
Boniface IX, pope 42
Bookbinder, Adam the 553
Bookbinder's tenement 553
Booth, Charles 403
Booth, Sir George 134
Boothroyd, Andrew 675, 795
Bordman, James 810
Borlase, Sir John 161n
Bosanquet, Bernard James Tindal 617, 618, 624
Bosanquet, Helen 405
Bosanquet, Oswald 460
Bosanquet, Samuel 396, 397, 398, 399, 401
Boswell, Martin, of Oxford 487
Bosworth Lectures 298
Bosworth, John 188, 206, 809
Boteler, Charles 224n
Bourchier, Charles 485
Bourke, Sir Richard 387
Bourne, George Drinkwater 613
Bourne, Sturges 401
Bournemouth, Oriel property in 533, 534, 542
Bowden, Edward 69
Bowden, Elizabeth 355
Bowerman, John 65n, 75
Bowles, Joseph 171, 173, 174, 177, 178, 180n, 181, 187, 224, 808
Bowls 601–2
Bowra, Sir Maurice 739
Bowring, Sir John 380
Box, Graham 632–3
Box, Henry 128
Box, Mary 128
Boxing 604, 615, 632, 633
Boyce, Sir John 485
Boycott, Arthur Edwin 665
Boyle, Robert 262
Braddell, Maurice Lee 626
Braddyll, Ralph 100, 104, 106, 122
Bradley, James 656
Bradwardine, Thomas, archbishop of Canterbury 28
Bradwell Hall 477n
Bragge, William 133, 807
Brasenose College 63, 84, 122, 129n, 133, 135, 138, 163, 479, 494n, 496, 505, 509, 514, 528, 538, 547, 554, 566n, 580, 603n, 607, 644, 671, 682

Brasenose Hall 63
Brathwaite, Richard 126, 127–8
Bray, Sir Reginald 63n
Braziers (108 High Street) 582
Brearley, Mike 632n
Brechin, Alexander 90
Bredin, George Richard Frederick 468–9, 44
Bredon, Simon 645–6
Brenton, Charles Lancelot Lee 294n
Brewer, Anthony 483
Brews, John 803
Brickenden, Edmund 171n, 199, 203n, 800, 808
Bride Hall (14–15 Oriel Street) 584
Bridford, Devon 16
Bridge 632
Bridge, Peter 638–9
Bridgeman, George 121
Bridgeman, Henry, bishop of Sodor and Man 146, 161
Bridgeman, John, bishop of Chester 121
Bridgeman, Orlando 229n, 245n
Bridgeman, Sir John 229n
Bridges, John Henry 620n
Bridges, John, bishop of Oxford 109, 148
Bright, John 422
Brigit of Sweden, St 73
Brindle, C. 527
Britton, Richard Berry 632
Brockhurst, Edmund 806
Brockis, Edward, innkeeper 235–6
Broderwick, John 160, 799, 807
Broke, William 65, 66, 69, 78, 796, 804
Brome, Adam de 10, 14, 15–27, 29, 30, 33, 34, 77, 115, 181, 356, 433, 476, 477, 550, 553, 582, 587, 793, Ill. 1.3, 1.4
Brome, Sir Christopher 147
Brome, Mrs 147
Bromley, William 171, 187, 245n
Brooke, Henry 173, 177n, 180, 184, 186, 205n, 245n, 808, 809
Brooke, Rupert 690
Brookes, Nicholas 122, 798, 806
Brown, Ben 540, 667, 673, 762, 770, 795, 802, 813
Brown, David 773, 802
Brown, Ron, property agent 543
Browne, Hugh 543, 585, 586, 785, 813
Browne, James 157
Brudenell, Robert 229n, 245n
Brummell, George (Beau Brummell) 284
Brummell, William 284

Brunt, Peter 762, 767, 802
Bryce, James, Lord Bryce 426–8, 429, 431, 437, 446, 448–51, 455, Plate 9
Bucketrowte, William 91n
Buckingham heraldic shield 551
Buckingham, George Villiers duke of 118
Buckingham, Katharine Villiers duchess of 129n
Buckingham, Richard Earl Temple, duke of 284, 288, Ill. 9.3
Buckingham, Thomas 28
Buckland, Robert 41, 43
Buckland, William 288, 415n, 657, 658
Buckle, George 802
Buckle, William 613
Buckler, Edward 156, 159
Buckler, John Chessell 584
Buckley Hall 587–9
Bucktrout, Thomas 489
Budd, Mr, of Boarstall 494
Buffon, Georges Louis de Clerc, comte de 258, 262
Bulkeley, James 226n, 245n
Bulkeley, Richard 587
Bulkeley, Richard, fourth Lord Bulkeley 226n
Bull, C., common room steward 230, 235, 237
Bull, E., college servant 235
Bull, George 241n
Buller, William, bishop of Exeter 245
Bullingdon Club 605
Bullock, Edward 810
Bulteel, Henry Bellenden 294–5, 299, 307
Buncombe, William 602n
Bunsen, Christian Charles Josias, Baron 373
Burdon, Richard *see* Sanderson (formerly Burdon) 273n, 292n, 408n
Burgess, Nicholas 637
Burghersh, Henry, bishop of Lincoln 3, 23–5, 26, 30, 77
Burghersh, Matilda 23
Burghersh, Robert, magister 23
Burghersh, Sir Robert 23
Burgon, John William 264, 353n, 358, 362, 364, 429, 430, 432n, 802, 812, Ill. 13.2
Burke, Edmund 246, 248–9, 261
Burnet, Gilbert, bishop of Salisbury 200
Burnham, Thomas 600n
Burns, James 802
Burton, Henry 151
Burton, Mr, of Swainswick 487, 508
Burton, R. W. B. 730–1, 736, 739, 749–50, 753, 762, 767, 769, 774, 784, 794, 802

Burton, Thomas 69
Bury, Richard de, bishop of Durham 26, 28, 29
Butler, Arthur Gray 430, 433n, 434, 438–9, 802
Butler, Joseph, bishop of Durham 216, 231, 245, 259, 260, 262, 263, 283n, 300n, 305, 313, 331, 375n, 414, 424, 443, Ill. 7.2
Butler, Lilly, prebendary of Canterbury 212
Butler, Richard 103, 805
Button, Francis 240n

Cadogan, William 7, 654
Cairns, Hugh McCalmont, Earl Cairns 430–1
Cairns, Sir Hugh 672
Calcott, Thomas 494, 497
Calley, William 232, 236, 243
Calvin, John 140, 143
Cambridge, university of 35, 53n, 414, 416, 527, 608, 612, 613, 615, 616n, 625, 627, 630, 633, 644, 665, 670, 673, 686, 700
Camden, Sir William 148
Cameron, Catherine Lady Fairfax of 223
Campbell, Ewen 469
Campbell, William Grahame 632
Campione, picture framer 235
Canning, George 278, 391
Canonicus, John 72
Canterbury College 69, 70
Canynges, William 66, 67–8, 74, 80, 82, 93, 796, 804, 805
Capel, Arthur Lord 129
Cardigan, George Brudenell fourth earl of 226n
Cardigan, James Brudenell fifth earl of 226n, 245n
Cardus, Neville 620
Cardwell, Edward, principal of St Alban Hall 416
Carey, Henry, Lord Falkland 134
Carlyle, Thomas 403
Carmarthen, Edward de, OP, bishop of Ardfert 26
Carne, Edward 810
Caroline, Princess of Wales 256
Carow, Robert 549, 588
Carpenter exhibitioners 228
Carpenter fellowship 61, 70, 99, 162, 173–4
Carpenter, John, common clerk of London 49
Carpenter, John, provost, bishop of Worcester 39, 43, 48–9, 50, 51–2, 54, 57, 58, 59, 62, 67, 77, 80, 173, 478, 479, 569, 793
Carter Building 233, 275–7, 556, 563–4, 570, Ill. 17.7

Carter, George, provost 8, 10, 171–84, 185–7, 202, 204, 205n, 208, 211, 212, 213n, 216, 223, 224, 230, 232, 480, 563, 651, 794, 800, 808
Carter, Samuel 160
Carter, William 654, 809
Carteret, John Carteret Lord 179
Cartwright, Edward 633
Cary, William 167n, 808
Case, John 101
Castle Combe, Wiltshire, Oriel property at 480, 483, 492
Catcher, Edward 136n
Catherall, Samuel 167n, 177n, 179n, 184, 215–16, 800, 808
Catto, Jeremy 586, 795, 802
Caulfeild, James William, Viscount Caulfeild 403
Cave, Richard 97
Cave, Sir Thomas, Bart 97, 121
Cave, Sir Thomas, of Stanford 97
Cavendish, Thomas 648
Cavill, William Victor 627
Cecil, Sir William, Lord Burghley 89
Chadwick, Edwin 383
Chafin, George 245n
Chain, Sir Ernest 670
Chalford manor 478–9, 481, 483, 492, 497, 505n, 508, 512, 522, Map 4
Chalmers, Robert, Lord Chalmers 454
Chalmers, Thomas 379, 399
Chamberlain, Joseph 450, 465n
Chamberlaine, Henry 158, 160, 807
Champernowne, Charles 91–2
Champneys, Sir Basil, architect 440–1, 442–3, 549, 572–81, 708–9, 789
Chapman, Henry 137
Chapman, William, ironmonger 117, 137–8
Charde, Robert 80, 805
Charles I, king of Great Britain 94, 99n, 105, 118, 124, 126, 127, 129, 130, 141, 153, 168, 170, 239, 558, 592, 600
Charles II, king of Great Britain 133, 160, 162n, 164–6, 505
Charles, David 795
Charlett, Arthur 172
Charlett, John 138, 143, 797, 805
Charlton-on-Otmoor farm, Oxfordshire 480
Charterhouse School 228, 456–7, 615, 620, 709
Chase, Drummond Percy 412n, 427, 428n, 429, 432–3, 452n, 516, 568, 582–3, 594, 812
Chase, Philander, bishop of Ohio 291
Chater, Leslie 540
Chaucer, Geoffrey 126
Chaundler, Thomas 35, 56, 61
Chess 598, 621n
Chester, St John 180
Chester, Thomas 245n
Chichele, Henry, archbishop of Canterbury 43, 48
Child, Charles 117
Child, Thomas 492
Cholderton, Wiltshire, Oriel living 200, 204, 205n, 208–9, 394
Cholwell, Sir Thomas 204
Chretien, Charles 802, 812
Christ Church 83, 85, 89, 93, 108, 122, 129, 193, 204, 336, 246, 251, 434, 494n, 496, 498n, 505, 526, 538, 547, 548, 554, 566, 584, 585, 600, 603, 608, 633, 635, 652, 663, 666, 671, 679, 682, 765, 766
Christian Malford, Wiltshire 480, 495
Christie, Albany 345, 350–1, 355, 357, 812
Christie, John Frederic 321, 332, 336n, 348, 349–50, 355, 356, 292, 811
Church, Richard William 266, 331, 344, 348, 349–50, 353, 354, 355, 358, 359, 360n, 368–9, 370, 393, 410, 420n, 515, 811, 812, Ill. 11.7
Churchill, Sir Winston 734
Churton, William 811
Cicero 101, 102, 107
Clare, Bogo de 25
Clarendon, Henry Hyde earl of 162n
Clark, Andrew 4
Clark, John, provost 10, 183, 191–2, 194n, 203, 205–8, 212–13, 232, 234, 236, 250, 794, 801, 809
Clark, Sir George, provost 7, 526, 527, 635, 682, 694, 696, 738, 739, 751, 754–5, 756, 761, 764, 766, 794. Ill. 21.8
Clarke, George 507
Clarke, Nathaniel 493
Clarke, William 214, 229
Clavell, William 106–7, 128
Clayton, Henry 807
Clerke, George 153n
Cleveland Commission 435, 481n, 482, 517–18, 520
Cleveland, Lord Harry Vane, fourth duke of 284, Ill. 13.6
Clif, Henry de 16, 17
Clifton, Robert 656

Close-Brooks, Jonathan 635
Clothier family 787
Clough, Arthur Hugh 331, 353–4, 359–60, 369, 412, 423–4, 426, 802, Ill. 13.3
Cluett, Richard 107, 143, 144, 145–6, 152, 154n, 798, 806
Coakley, Sarah 786
Cobb, Thomas 180
Cobbett, William 378, 403
Cobbledik, John 30, 31
Cobham, Jonathan Blenman 452
Cobham, Thomas, bishop of Worcester 17, 21, 24, 29, 30, 33, 34, 43
Cockman, Thomas 186n
Cockram, George 806
Cockram, Robert 805, 806
Cocks, William 805
Coconut Cup 80n
Codd, Frederick, architect 583–4
Cogan, Thomas 9, 77, 89, 91, 107, 125, 599, 643, 650, 797
Cohn, Stanley 729, 738, 739
Coke, Sir Edward 213
Cole, Thomas 122, 806
Coleby, Lincolnshire, Oriel living 15, 19, 25, 113n, 137, 144, 204, 477, 480, 483, 485, 487, 488, 493, 495, 500, 512, 513, 518
Coleridge, Hartley 281
Coleridge, Henry James 352, 356, 357–8
Coleridge, Samuel Taylor 281
Coleridge, Sir John Taylor 328n, 351–2, 358
Colet, John 35, 61, 71, 74
Collet, Elizabeth, laundress 235
Collett, Peter 787
Collett, William 802
Collinge, William 85, 86, 493, 797, 805
Collins, Hugh Norwood 788
Collins, John 802
Colne, scholar 41
Colquhoun, John Campbell 292, 295n
Colyer-Fergusson, T. R., VC 722
Colyngtre, John, provost 33, 34, 35, 553, 554, 793
Combe, James 494
Combe, William 108
Comper, Sir Ninian 561
Comport, Christopher 486
Compton, Francis 756n
Conington, Nicholas 637
Conquest, Richard 129
Constable, John 76

Constance, council of 45, 48
Conyers, Lord Conyers Osborne 247
Cook, James 258
Cooke, George 253, 801, 810
Cooke, Thomas 797
Cooke, William 98
Cooper, James 229n
Cope, John 245n
Cope, Mr, prospective undergraduate 222, 231, 233
Cope, Sir Anthony 134
Copleston, Edward, provost, bishop of Llandaff 5, 11, 247–8, 250, 255n, 264–78, 282, 283, 284, 287, 288–90, 291, 295, 297, 298, 299, 300, 301–2, 316, 318, 319, 320, 324, 333, 337, 340, 343, 351, 353, 355, 359, 366, 368, 369, 372, 375, 376, 380, 381–2, 383, 385, 387, 388–9, 391, 398, 401, 408, 409, 413, 415, 418, 435, 512, 602, 660, 794, 801, 810, 811, Plate 1
Copleston, William James 5, 333, 340, 350, 359, 412, 801, 802, 811
Coppen, John 178
Corbett, Bertie Oswald 620n
Corbett, Clement 109n
Corfe, John 48
Corfe, William, provost 43, 44, 45, 48, 793
Cornbury, Henry Hyde Lord 197n
Cornish, Thomas 812
Cornysh, Thomas, provost, episcopus tinensis 62, 64–6, 68, 793, 803, 804
Corpus Christi College 61, 74, 93, 111n, 118, 123, 193, 219, 220, 340, 491, 494n, 496, 538, 547, 598, 616, 722
Coryngham, Roger 43
Cosier, Benjamin, saddler 235
Cossiga, Francesco 785
Cotes, Charles 167n, 174–5, 213–14, 808
Cotes, John 175
Cotta, John, physician 105
Cottington, Francis 129
Cottle, Joseph 514
Cotton, Richard Lynch 420n
Cotton, Sir Robert 148
Couldrey, Oxford supplier 235
Courtenay, Kelland 245n
Courtenay, Richard, bishop of Norwich 43
Courtenay, William, archbishop of Canterbury 45
Coventry, Henry 214
Coward, Noel 626n

Cowen, Anna, Lady Cowen 781
Cowen, Sir Zelman, provost 540, 586, 643, 750, 752, 778–82, 783, 785, 787, 791, 794, Ill. 22.4
Cowling, John 798, 806
Cowling, Thomas 498
Cowslade, George 214, 807
Cowton, Robert OFM 41
Cox, George Valentine 607
Cox, Lynne 676
Cox, Richard 82
Coxed, John 203
Craigie, William Alexander 524, 527, 528
Cranmer, Thomas, archbishop of Canterbury 82, 87, 281
Craster, William 180, 184, 185
Craven, William, Lord Craven 251
Crawley, John 632n
Crawley, Mark 632
Creighton, Mandell, bishop of London 434
Crellius, Johannes 339
Cricket 601, 604, 605 608, 612, 616–20, 624, 627, 632, 633
Crispe, Andrew 808
Crispin, Edmund 85
Crispin, Richard 78, 80, 82, 85, 796, 805
Croft, Francis 153n
Croft, George (fellow 1513–21) 82
Croft, George, Bampton lecturer 249
Crofts, Mr 183
Cromer, Evelyn Baring Lord 465
Cromhall, Gloucestershire, Oriel living 204–5, 208, 209, 229
Cromwell, Oliver, lord protector 122, 133, 154, 156, 158
Cromwell, Thomas, earl of Essex 83
Crossman, R. H. S. 736
Crow, Arthur 739, 753, 762, 767, 784, 794, 802
Crowther, Joseph 807
Crucknell, Henry 429
Crutch, Thomas 230
Curson, Sir John 485
Curteis, Jeremiah 810
Curten, Sir William 483, 22
Curtis, Mark 791

d'Alembert, Jean-Baptiste de Rond 262
Dackam, John 113n, 483, 485
Dagenham manors (East Hall and Valence) 479
Dalby, John 69
Dale, Christopher 122

Dale, George 104, 125n, 805
Dallas, Linwood Forbes 455
Dallaway, James 566–7
Dalrymple-Champneys, Norma Lady 559, 787
Dalrymple-Champneys, Sir Weldon, Bart 539, 564
Daman, Charles 802
Danby, Henry Danvers earl of Danby 557
Dandridge, Mr, college servant 230
Daniell, Barton 97, 798, 806
Darts 632
Darwin, Charles 281, 426, 661
Dash, Walter 45
Daubeny, Charles 415n, 661, 662
Dauncey, Philip 229n
Davenant, George 132, 160, 799, 807
Davenant, James 2, 164, 169, 202, 214, 799, 800, 807, 808
Davenport, Dr 222, 231
Davenport, Mr 222
Daventry, William, provost 29, 33–4, 582, 590, 793
Davie, Joseph 487
Davies, Henry 809
Davies, Thomas 273n
Davison, John 255n, 273n, 274, 278, 280, 283, 295, 300, 302, 304, 316, 343, 375, 381, 388, 390, 391, 801, 811
Davyes, Rebecca 137n
Davyes, Richard 137, 144n
Day, John 99, 101, 103, 106, 107, 115, 119, 124, 138, 139–41, 143, 159, 797, 798, 805, 806
Day, Lionel 99
Daye, Mr, tailor 242
De Beers Company 440
de Brye, Barbara 787
de Gaulle, Charles 693
de Witt, Cornelius 240n
de Witt, Jan 240n
Dean, manor of 53, 64, 77, 90, 197, 478, 483, 485, 487, 489, 492, 493, 495, 497, 498, 505n, 507–8, 516 n, 517, 522, 524n, Plate 11, Map 4
Dearing Report 788
Delane, John Thadeus 393
Demosthenes 101
Deneke, R. H. 466
Denison, Edward, bishop of Salisbury 657
Denison, George Anthony 296, 362, 412, 801, 811, Ill. 13.1

Denison, William 182n, 184, 185, 186n, 188
Dent, Thomas 797, 805
Denton, William 105
Dering, Sir Cholmley 175
Dering, Sir Edward 175, 242, 243, 245n
Dering, William 167, 174–6, 178n, 187, 239–40, 800, 808
Dervorguilla, countess of Galloway 14
Descartes, René 261
Desmaistres, Samuel 204, 218, 807
Despenser, Hugh, the younger 21, 24, 25
Development Trust 775, 781, 787, 791
Devereux, Robert, earl of Essex 123
Deverose, John 57
Dewe, John 178
d'Eyncourt, Oliver 15
Dibdin, T. F. 607n
Dickens, Charles 402, 403
Dickinson, Charles 342
Diderot, Denis 262
Dilke, Fisher Wentworth 221n
Dilke, Thomas 221, 231
Dillon, Terry 638
Dimroth, Otto 666–7
Dioscorides 651
Disraeli, Benjamin, earl of Beaconsfield 403
Dix, Samuel 155
Dobson, Kenneth 466
Dochen, Lady, of Shenington 487, 490
Dod, John 141
Dodd, John 245n
Doddington, Sir William 126
Dodoens, Rembert 651
Dodson, John 232, 801, 809
Dodwell, Henry 170
Dolben, Sir William 191
Doll, Robert 65–7, 72n
Domus Zacharie 550
Dorking, Oriel property at 534
Dorling, E. E. 740
Dormer, Sir Michael 120n, 147
Dornford, Joseph 281, 303n, 362, 412, 801, 811
Douai, Catholic college at 136n
Douglas, Barry 786
Doull, Alexander John, bishop of Kootenay 465
Dover, Robert 126
Dowle Street farm, Ashford 544
Downing, Carybute 153
Drake, John 803
Drake, Sir Francis 451
Drake, William 245n

Dramatic Society 753, 760, 772, 790
Du Bois, Charles 24n
Ducie, Matthew Ducie Moreton Lord 204
Dudley exhibitioners 3, 67, 76, 80, 83, 90, 98, 102, 103, 108, 122, 137, 163, 228, 480
Dudley, Edmund 71, 80
Dudley, George 80n, Ill. 3.4
Dudley, John Ward, first Lord 226n
Dudley, John Ward, second Lord 220, 226n, 239n, 253
Dudley, John William Ward, first earl of 296n, 380
Dudley, Richard (fellow 1495–1506) 67, 71, 74, 77, 80, 82, 83, 87, 103, 204, 480, 804
Dudley, Richard, of Yanwith 83–4
Dudley, William Ward, third Lord 226n
Duncannon, John William Ponsonby, Lord Duncannon, fourth earl of Bessborough 385
Duncombe, Francis 806
Duncombe, John 160, 798, 806
Duns Scotus OFM 12, 36, 55, 73
Dunster, Thomas 170
Dunwich Hospital 16
Durram, Nicholas 490
Durston, John 797, 805
Dyer, Richard (fellow 1674–1728) 10, 166, 173, 174, 175, 176, 177, 178, 179, 180, 181, 202, 205, 214, 215, 229n, 237n, 651–2, 800, 807, 808, Ill. 19.2
Dyer, Richard, gentleman 229n
Dyer, William 229n
Dykes, Robert 41, 42, 45
Dyson, Peter 668

Earl, Goody, scout 230
Earle, J., of Swainswick 487
Earle, John 412, 812
Eccleston, Henry 131, 798, 806
Eckington 16
Eden, Charles Page 6, 321, 347, 350, 353, 356, 363, 802, 811
Eden, Thomas 109n
Edge, Edward, builder 566
Edgeworth, Francis 405–6
Edgeworth, Roger 64, 71, 72n, 74–5, 82, 87, 93
Edinburgh, Philip duke of 775
Edmonds, James, bedel 590
Edmund earl of Cornwall 15
Edmunds, Henry 173–4, 176, 181, 187, 213, 214, 800, 809

Edmunds, John 493
Edward I, king of England 14, 15, 16, 201
Edward II, king of England 3, 13, 15, 17, 19, 22, 23, 24, 77, 111, 181, 476, 551, 558, 595, 740
Edward III, king of England 22, 25, 26, 29
Edward IV, king of England 54, 58, 478, 479
Edward VI, king of England 82, 86, 257
Edward VII, king of Great Britain 592, 601
Edward, Mr, of Magdalen Hall 180
Edwardes, John 86, 87, 493
Edwards, John 131n
Edwards, William 803
Edwards, William Gerald 466, 467
Eedes, Richard 108–9, 148
Egerton, John, bishop of Durham 220, 245
Eglesfield, Robert de 14
Eldon, John Scott earl of 274
Eleanor of Castile, queen of England 25, 26n, 550
Eliot, George (Mary Ann Evans) 403, 423
Eliot, Joshua 117, 806
Eliot, Valerie 788
Elizabeth I, queen of England 90, 111, 147, 257, 333, 525, 649
Elizabeth II, queen of Great Britain 595, 748, 753–4, 768, 775, 785
Elliot, Robert 675
Ellis, Clough Williams, architect 624n
Ellis, James 244
Elmsly, John 810
Eltham, Kent, living of 145, 480, 483, 485–6, 487
Emden, Alfred Brotherston 6
Emden, Cecil Stuart 6–7, 532, 534, 536, 813
Emmanuel College, Cambridge 94, 491, 496
Erasmus, Desiderius 51, 74, 75, 93, 119n, 249n, 257
Eston, John 155, 807
Estwick, Sampson 173n
Etherington-Smith, Thomas 621n
Eton College 52, 60, 63, 83, 467, 607–8, 609n, 615, 641–2
Euclid 47, 647, 660
Eusebius, bishop of Caesarea 54, 111
Evans, Alfred Henry 617
Evans, Alfred John 619–20, 624
Evans, John 180, 808
Evans, Thomas 485
Evans, William Henry Brereton 459, 462, 467, 469, 471

Eve, Henry 241
Eveleigh, John, provost 5, 10–11, 200–1, 217, 232, 236, 238, 247–54, 256–64, 266–9, 272–4, 278, 284, 371–2, 375, 378, 409, 412n, 565–6, 568, 596, 615, 664, 794, 801, 810, frontispiece
Eveleigh, John, senior, rector of Winkleigh 250
Eveleigh, Martha 250
Evelyn, John 158
Everdon, John de 17
Ewing, Alexander Blake 802
Exeter College 13, 14, 21, 163, 182, 193, 355n, 360, 496, 538, 547, 555, 645, 663
Exton, Sir Thomas 161n
Eyre, Thomas 800, 808

Facer, Albert William 469–71
Fairbairn, Steve 630
Fairfax, Henry Culpeper (m.1714) 226n, 240
Fairfax, Sir Thomas Fairfax, third Lord 131
Fairfax, Thomas Fairfax, fifth Lord 223, 226n, 242–3
Fairfax, Thomas Fairfax, sixth Lord 226n, 240n
Fairwater, David 803
Falconer, Thomas 271
Faraday, Michael 415
Farnell, Vera 725
Farren, James 132n, 156, 798, 799, 806, 807
Faussett, Godfrey 275
Fawconer, Ralph 106, 145, 798, 806
Felkirk, John 31, 32, 40
Fell, John, bishop of Oxford 164–6, 215, 652
Fellowes, Edmund Horace 622, 624, 629–30
Fencing 598, 601, 615
Fergusson, Sir Ewen 632, 762–3, 788
Feribrigge, Richard 32
Ferrars heraldic shield 551
Feteplace, Adam 25
Fewers, William 796, 803
Field and Castle, land agents (Francis Field) 441, 582–3
Fillary, Edward William Joseph 632
Finch, William 263n
Firth, Sir Charles 714, 764, 802
Fisher and Hobdell, builders 583–4
Fisher, Herbert Albert Laurens 685–6
Fisk, Graham 633, 753
Fitch, Alice 486
Fitch, Sir Comport 486
Fitch, Sir Thomas 486
Fitzalan heraldic shield 551

Fitzjames, Richard, bishop of London 55
Fitzralph, Richard, archbishop of Armagh 28, 29
Flacius, Matthias 143
Flag of Oriel 740
Flaxney, Thomas 109
Fleetwood, John 245n
Fleming, John 801, 810
Fleming, M. H. V. 464
Fletcher & Parsons' Bank 494
Flint, Nicholas 804
Florey, Howard, Lord Florey 670
Floyd, John, shoemaker 235
Foley, Thomas, second Lord Foley 191
Fonseca, Pedro de 101
Football 615, 620–1, 624, 626, 627–8, 632, 732
Forbes, V. N. 454
Forster, Arnold 456, 469
Forsthulle, Nicholas de 554
Forsthulle, Thomas de 554
Forward, Mr, of Shenington 493
Forward, Robert 98n, 116, 145, 146, 798, 806
Forward, Thomas 146n
Foster, Philip 213, 807
Founder's Cup 63, 277
Fowler, Gerald 617
Fowler, John 568
Fowler, Richard 798, 806
Fowler, William Warde 434
Fownes, Richard 161n
Fox, Richard, bishop of Winchester 61, 74
Foxe, John 138
France and England heraldic shield 551
Francys, Henry 803
Frank fellowships 10, 61, 67, 70, 99, 162, 250, 263, 265, 278n
Frank, John 52, 478
Franklin, Bertram, head porter 775
Franklin, Kenneth James 668–9, 672, 693, 738, 745, Ill. 19.5
Franklin, Mr, college servant 230
Franklin, Willingham 273n
Franks Commission and Report 537, 538, 698–9, 755, 761
Fraser, James, bishop of Manchester 354, 356–7, 363–4, 412, 603, 802, Ill. 11.9
Frederick the Great, king of Prussia 473
Freeman, John 498
Freeman, Richard 153n
Freeman, Thomas 75

Freeman, William 485, 493
Freke, William 102
Frewen, John 183, 190, 202, 209, 801, 809
Frewin, Richard 202n
Frith Farm, Ashford 544
Froude, Catherine 360n, 368n
Froude, James Anthony 360–1, 366, 369, 370, 424–6, 445, 446, 447–8, 450, 451, Ill.11.8
Froude, Richard Hurrell 6, 265, 280, 290, 296n, 308, 309, 310, 313–16, 317–20, 322, 324–5, 328–9, 335n, 339, 344, 360, 365–6, 369, 370, 376, 377, 391, 392, 410, 412, 424, 811, Ill. 11.3
Froude, William 360, 658
Fry, Roger 160, 230
Fuller, William, bishop of Lincoln 164–6, 210
Fuller-Maitland, Guy Alexander 454
Fysher, Robert 173, 176, 181, 214, 800, 801, 809

Gaines estate, Worcestershire 533, 535
Galbraith, V. H. 757–8, 764
Galen 75, 599, 650
Galilei, Galileo 649
Gandy, Henry 168, 170, 799, 807, 808
Gandy, John 154n, 158n, 168n, 798, 806
Gardener, Richard 804
Gardiner, Bernard 170, 171n
Gardiner, Lady 129
Gardiner, Robert 129n
Garland, Richard 807
Garlick, George 454
Garner, Thomas 561, 572
Garsdale, Richard 40, 42, 44, 46, 49, 803
Garston, Michael 787
Garvey, Robert 89
Gascoigne, Sir Edward 485, 497, 498
Gascoigne, Sir Thomas 499
Gascoigne, Thomas (died 1458) 9, 37, 41, 48, 49–51, 58, 551, 552
Gastrell, Francis, bishop of Chester 180
Gatehouse 39, 558
George I, king of Great Britain 168, 171, 172, 177, 239
George III, king of Great Britain 190, 261
George IV, king of Great Britain 246, 274, 570
George V, king of Great Britain 438, 733, 750
George VI, king of Great Britain 750–1, 753
Ghent, Henry of 55
Ghose, Khetrapal Das 463
Gibbon, Edward 248–9, 257, 258–9, 262, 267n
Gibbs, William 498

Gibson, Edmund, bishop of Lincoln 171, 173–6, 183, 212
Gilbert, A. T. 352n
Gillett, M. J., head cook 713
Gillmor, Eric Robert Wilfred 467
Gilpin, Bernard 83
Gilpin, James, recorder of Oxford 190, 202–3
Gish, Peter 638
Gladstone, William Ewart 353, 380, 418–19, 420n, 421–2, 450, 715
Gloucester Hall 135, 147, 648
Glower, John 69
Goderich, Frederick John Robinson Lord, earl of Ripon 289
Godley, A. D. 526
Godstow Abbey 584
Godwin, William 263, 267
Goldie, Edward, architect 594
Goldsmith, Laura 642
Goldwell, Thomas, bishop of St Asaph 82n
Golf 615, 624
Golightly, Charles Portales 346–7, 349, 355, 368
Gooch, Barnaby 109n
Goodrich, John 64–7, 70, 71, 72, 74, 75–6, 82, 83, 796, 804
Goodyer, Walter 804
Googlies (or Bosies) 618–9
Gore, John 483
Goschen, George, Viscount Goschen 413–14, 428, 431–2, Ill. 13.9
Gott, John Bury 467
Gough, J. W. 534, 536, 753, 762, 767, 768, 794, 813
Gough, Robert 485
Gough, Sir Henry 220, 245n
Gower, Abel 104, 106, 106n, 110, 112, 797, 798, 805
Gower, Henry de, bishop of St David's 21
Gower, John Leveson-Gower Earl 188
Gowing, Margaret 768
Grace, W. G. 620n
Grafton, Robert 54, 55, 796, 803
Graham, Eric 734, 735, 738, 802
Graham, Henry, principal secretary, lord chancellor's office 430–1
Grant, Alexander 410, 412
Grant, Anthony 335
Grant, Elizabeth 291n
Graunt, Thomas 48, 49n, 51
Gray, John 102

Greek, study of 35, 61, 75, 76, 93, 101, 102, 648
Green T. H. 263n
Green, John 486
Green, John, junior 486n
Green, Lady Ann 486n
Green, V. H. H. 766
Greene, Vivien 788
Greenley, Thomas 42
Gregory I, pope 55
Grensted, L. W. 794
Grenville, George 384
Grenville, Sir Richard 445, 649
Grenville, William Wyndham, Lord Grenville 262, 381
Gresham's School, Holt 667
Gresley, William 396
Greswell, Clement 412, 802
Greville, Robert, Lord Brooke 141
Grey, Charles, second Earl Grey 386
Grey, Sir Charles (m.1802) 273n
Grey, Sir Edward, Lord Grey of Fallodon 448
Grey, Sir George 287, 332, 380, 413, Ill. 9.4
Grieve, Angus McLeod 467
Griffin, Ann, coal merchant 235
Griffith, David 99, 805
Griffith, Evan 229
Griffith, James 291n
Griffith, John 83, 485, 797, 805
Griffith, Richard 797
Griffith, Thomas 87
Griffith, William 71, 72n, 73, 76
Grimes, Daniel 495
Grimes, John 490, 495
Grimes, Richard 490
Grocyn, William 61, 62
Grossesteste, Robert, bishop of Lincoln 55
Grosvenor, Richard Grosvenor Earl 220, 245n, 253
Grosvenor, Sir Thomas 245n
Guildford, Henry 14
Gunn, James Andrew 669
Gunning, John 495
Gunning, Peter 487, 505, 508
Gwinear, Cornwall 21
Gwyn, Francis 245n
Gybons, Thomas 807
Gye, Denison Allen 459, 463–4

Hadley, Henry 239n
Haggar, Henry 157

INDEX 827

Haig, Lady Vivienne 559
Hailsham, Quintin Hogg, Lord Hailsham 778
Hakewill, Henry, architect 276–8, 564
Hakluyt, Richard 648
Hale, William 287–8, 293
Hales, Thomas 240n, 245n
Haley, Francis 229–30
Hall, A. W., Oxford brewer 406
Hall, Francis Henry 5, 428, 434, 577, 616, 620, 621, 622–3, 624, 626–7, 631, 634, 643, 644, 710–11, 714, 720, 743, 784, 802, 812, Ill. 18.3
Hall, Mr, of Chalford 512–13
Hals, John, provost, bishop of Coventry and Lichfield 2, 48, 51, 53–4, 58, 59, 62, 478, 793
Halse, James, upholsterer 234n, 235
Halse, Nicholas, saddler 235
Hamersley, Hugh Montolieu 614
Hamilton, Douglas 586, 676
Hamilton, Sir David 241n
Hamilton, Sir William (1731–1803), diplomat 258, 262
Hamilton, Sir William (1788–1856), ideologue 417–18, 419–20, 658–9
Hamilton, Thomas 240n, 241
Hamilton, William 245n, 246
Hammick, Dalziel Llewellyn 533, 666–8, 672–3, 794, Ill. 19.4
Hammond, Henry 156
Hampden, Henrietta 368
Hampden, John 127–8, 141
Hampden, Renn Dickson, bishop of Hereford 11, 259, 260, 280, 281, 290, 295, 298, 299, 305–6, 312, 320, 333, 334–5, 336–7, 338n, 339–44, 346, 347, 352, 360, 362–3, 368, 370, 375, 376, 377, 382–3, 412, 416, 418, 572, Ill. 11.4
Hampson, Dennis 243
Hampton School 641–2
Handball 598
Handsworth 16
Handy, Charles 786
Hanmer, John, bishop of St Asaph 146
Hansard, Richard Massey 467
Hardaway, Thomas, corn dealer 600
Hardie, Alexander 813
Hardway, John 236
Hardwicke, Philip Yorke Lord 244
Hardy, Gathorne, first earl of Cranbrook 413, Ill. 13.8

Hardy, Thomas 41
Hare, Julius 373
Hare, Robert 234
Hargreaves, Eric 738, 753, 767, 768
Harkes, Garbrand, bookseller 588, 590
Harkes, Tobias 588n
Harland, Robin 791
Harle, Mr, of Oriel 240n
Harley, Edward (Ned) 153
Harley, Robert (died 1774) 188
Harley, Sir Robert 7, 97, 120–1, 129 136n, 141, 153, 154, 159, Ill. 5.1
Harper, Julian Francis Howard 465, 467
Harrington, Mr, candidate for fellowship 183
Harriot Lectures 647n
Harriot Society 791
Harriot, Thomas 92, 148, 445, 596, 647–50
Harris Building 593, 601, Ill. 17.13
Harris, Eleanor Mary, college secretary 783
Harris, Group Captain Charles William 593, 786
Harris, Richard 797, 805
Harris, Sir Philip, Lord Harris of Peckham 593, 781, 786, 787
Harrison, Francis 428n, 429, 663–4, 665, 666, 802, Ill. 19.3
Harrow School 608, 609n, 615
Hart Committee and Report 771
Hart Hall 224, 240
Hart, John 142
Hart, Thomas 170
Harvard University 616
Harvey, Sir William 668
Harvey, William 799, 807, 808
Haslewood, John 162, 799, 807, 808
Hastings, Lady Betty 210
Hastings, Theophilus, earl of Huntingdon 161n
Hawkesworth, William 27, 32–3, 793
Hawkins, Edward, provost 3, 4, 5, 9, 247n, 265, 273n, 279, 280, 283, 290, 292, 293, 294, 295, 296, 297, 299, 303n, 304–5, 306, 307, 316–17, 319–20, 322, 329, 333, 337, 340, 341, 343, 344, 346–54, 355, 356, 357, 358, 359, 363, 367–9, 375, 376, 377, 408–14, 418–19, 421–30, 431, 433, 437–8, 515, 516, 715, 774, 784, 794, 801, 811, Plate 4
Hawkins, Edward, senior 408
Hawkins, Henry Caesar 438
Hawkins, Margaret 408
Hawkins, Mary Ann 410, 433

Hawkins, Thomas, provost 35, 57–8, 62, 793, 803
Hawkins, William 213, 808
Hawksworth, Laura 642n, 780
Hawley, Henry 799, 807
Hawley, James 809
Hawten, John 495
Hayles, Thomas 117
Haynes, Stephen, glovemaker 235
Haynes, William, provost 83, 85, 86, 793
Hayward, Thomas 224n
Head, Edmund 600
Head, Philip 637
Head, Richard 214, 809
Heaney, Leonard Martin 458, 466
Hearne, Thomas 2, 5, 8, 166–7, 168–75, 177–85, 187, 200, 202, 210, 213, 214–15, 217–18, 219, 220, 224, 230, 237n, 239, 241, 246, 562–3, 652
Heath, James 161
Heath, John 676
Hebbes, John 639
Hebrew, study of 101, 126
Hedges, Mr, college servant 765
Hegel, Georg Wilhelm Friedrich 260n, 263
Heidelberg, university of 106, 120
Heighley, Robert 805
Hemming, John 87, 88
Hendley, Walter 486n
Henley Races 608, 613, 621, 623, 628, 630, 635, 644
Henley, Edward Francis 621n, 634
Henley, Sir Robert 204
Henrietta Maria, queen of Great Britain 148
Henry Box School, Witney 128
Henry IV, king of France 106
Henry of London, archbishop of Dublin 25
Henry V, king of England 58
Henry VI, king of England 51, 54, 201
Henry VII, king of England 71, 80, 588
Henry VIII, king of England 71, 81, 82, 198, 257, 485
Henry, prince of Wales 139
Herbert, Richard 129
Hereford, Nicholas 45
Heritage, Thomas 65, 66, 67, 72, 552
Herleston, William de 17, 19
Herniman, John 84, 87, 88, 90
Herodotus 102
Herring, Herbert Ralph 466
Herry, Nicholas, provost 40, 42, 44, 48, 793

Hertford College 224, 538, 544, 547, 672, 692, 744
Hertford, William Seymour marquess of 160
Hewens, Mr, of Shenington 486
Heywood, James 418, 422
Hickes, George 169, 239, 245n
Hickey, William 607
Hicks, F. H. 774
Higden, Ranulf (Radulphus Cestriensis) 201
Hill, Edward 229n
Hill, John 294, 331
Hill, Joseph, receiver 254, 255
Hill, Robert 136
Hill, Thomas 797, 805
Hill, Vernon Tickell 617
Hill, Sir William 485
Hinds, Samuel, bishop of Norwich 281–2, 283, 296, 300, 305, 338n, 359, 375, 386–8
Hinshelwood, Sir Cyril 670
Hinxey Hall 594
Hitler, Adolf 473, 764
Hoadly, Benjamin, bishop of Winchester 170
Hoare's Bank 494, 529
Hobart, John Henry, bishop of New York 291n
Hobbes, Thomas 475
Hobbs, Charles 206–7
Hobson, Marina 787–8
Hobson, Ron 787–8
Hockey 615, 624, 631, 642n, 644
Hodges, Walter, provost 177n, 179, 183–90, 200, 202, 203, 205–8, 213, 216, 223, 229, 653, 794, 800, 808
Hodges, William 203
Hodgkin, Dorothy 660
Hodgson, Arthur Brian 630
Hodson, Dudley 204
Hogben, Sidney John 460–1, 467
Hogg, Douglas, stained glass artist 559
Holbrooke, John 163
Holcot, Robert (fellow c.1463–79) 803
Holcot, Robert, OP 28
Holland, Henry Edward Fox, third Lord Holland 383
Holland, Henry Richard Fox, second Lord Holland 298n, 383
Holland, Nicholas 637
Holland, Robert Erskine 454
Holland, Thomas 137, 143, 159n
Holt, Sir John 7, 161
Holte, William 88, 136

Holt's Bank 540, 541
Holwell, Edward 273n, 810
Homer 101
Hoods crew 640
Hooker, Richard 140, 143, 158n, 257, 300n
Hooper, James 429
Hooper, Mr, of Swainswick 507
Hopgood and Sons, builders 595
Hopkins, William 505
Hopton, John 32
Hopton, Richard 52
Hopton, Robert 69
Hore's tenement 553
Horn, C. F. 527
Hornblower, Simon 773
Horncastle, Alan de 17, 27
Horne, John 144, 153n, 154, 798, 806
Horne, Robert, bishop of Winchester 136
Horne, Thomas 153n
Hornie, Mr, of Stowford 493
Hornsby, Thomas 656
Hose, Sir John 458, 459
Hotham, Thomas 18, 21
Howdill, Ian 586
Howell, Miles 625, 626, 627
Howick, Henry Grey Lord Howick, third Earl Grey 390
Howley, William, archbishop of Canterbury 340
Howson, John, bishop of Durham 152
Huber, John 676
Huber, Samuel 143
Hudson, John 169n
Hues, Robert 648–9
Hughes, Edward 487
Hughes, George 603, 612–13, 614, 644
Hughes, John Osborne 467
Hughes, Robert 87
Hughes, Thomas 364, 366–7, 428, 603, 609–10, 612–14, 621, 643, Ill. 18.2
Huish Barton Farm, Barnstaple 534
Hull, Richard 638
Hume, David 248, 257, 258, 260–3, 267n, 301
Hunt, Brigadier-General E. 720
Hunt, Henry (Orator) 378
Hunter, David 633
Hunter, John, surgeon 654–5
Hunter, William 654
Hunting 602–3
Huntman, John (Johannes Venator) 30, 32, 45, 46

Hurlock, John 89, 90, 91, 136, 137, 797
Huse, George 630
Hutchinson, John 216
Hutt, Sir William 387
Hutton, Sir Richard 128
Huxley, Thomas Henry 423, 426
Hyll, John 803

Iarpomuylle, Henry 553
Ibbetson, Richard 167, 170, 171, 184n, 216, 800, 808
Ice hockey 615
Iffley, Oriel property at 541, 542, 544
Iliffe, Robert Peter Richard, third Lord Iliffe 788
Imam, Syed Mehdi 463
Ingham, Robert 281
Inglett, John 245n
Ingolmeles, John 26
Ingram, Charles 226n, 240
Ingram, George see Irvine, George Ingram
Innes, Graham 637
Inns, Gerald 789
Ireland, John 227–8, 409
Irenaeus 142
Irvine, Arthur Ingram, sixth Lord 226n, 245n, 498
Irvine, Charles Ingram, ninth Lord 499
Irvine, George Ingram, eighth Lord 167, 173, 199, 226n, 240, 499
Irvine, Henry Ingram, seventh Lord 226n, 245n, 498–9
Irvine, Rich Ingram, fifth Lord 226n
Isabella, queen of England 21, 23, 24
Island Site, Oriel property in Oxford 526, 541, 542, 544, 548, 549, 581–7, 593–4, 754–5, 775, 778, 780–1, 782, 785–6, 787, 789
Ives, William, apothecary 591

Jackman, John 9, 73, 89, 91, 98, 105, 107, 125, 136, 650–1, 797
Jackson, Henry 140, 143
Jackson, Sir Thomas Graham, architect 559, 572, 580, 634
James I, king of Great Britain 105, 111, 112, 135, 139, 145, 194, 510, 558, 650
James II, king of Great Britain 167, 168, 182
James Mellon Hall 549, 594–5, 788, 789
James, Godfrey Warden 471–2, 534
James, John, junior 232n

James, John, senior 232
James, Robert 485
James, Thomas 2
James, William (fellow 1809–37) 273n, 274, 307, 811
James, William Owen 670
James, William, fellow of Merton 46
Jardine, Douglas 620
Jelf, William Richard 281, 348–9, 364, Ill. 10.4
Jenkinson, Charles, earl of Liverpool 191
Jenkyns, Henry 281, 319n, 811
Jennings, Philip 245n, 246
Jerome, St 50, 51
Jesus College 94, 120, 191, 193, 496, 512, 554, 601n, 608, 663, 671
Jewel, John 143
Johnson, Mr, of Christ Church 167
Johnson, Robert 102
Johnson, Samuel 7, 183, 226, 246, 257, 261, 654, 739
Johnson, Thomas 143, 806
Jokys, Thomas 65
Jones, William 797
Joseph, Robert, OSB 76
Josephus 55
Jowett, Benjamin 260n, 263, 419, 426, 432, 455
Justin Martyr 101
Justinian I, emperor 101
Juvenal 119n

Kames, Henry Home Kames Lord 258, 262
Kant, Immanuel 260n, 263
Karver, Robert 77, 83, 796, 803
Kayll, Henry, provost 41, 43, 44, 47, 48, 647, 793, 795
Keane, John 245n
Keble College 368, 370, 471, 632n, 633, 635, 663, 666
Keble, John 5, 263, 265, 273n, 279, 280, 281, 290, 300n, 309, 310–14, 315, 316–17, 322, 326–7, 328–9, 331, 336n, 343, 344, 345, 348, 359, 365–6, 368n, 369, 382, 391–2, 396, 409, 410, 411, 412n, 422, 516, 735, 811, Ill. 10.1
Kellway, Robert 164, 799, 807
Kempe, Charles Eamer 561
Kemys, Arthur 99
Ken, Thomas, bishop of Bath and Wells 168
Kennicott, Benjamin 257n

Kennion, George Wyndham, bishop of Bath and Wells 465
Kent, John 43
Kent, Thomas Holland earl of, heraldic shield 551
Kerkhecker, Juliane 802
Kettel Hall 476
Kettlewell, William Wildman 435
Kevelyngworth, Ralph de 19, 26n
Key, Kingsmill James 617
Keynes, John Maynard, Lord Keynes 545
Kight, Arthur 230
Kilby, Richard 115
Kilvington, Richard 26, 27, 28–9, 30–1, 32, 34, 48, 49, 645
King Edward Street, Oxford 516, 530, 539, 540, 545, 581, 582–4
King, A., grocer 235
King, Edward, bishop of Lincoln 11, 414, 608, Ill. 13.4
King, Edward, cook 230
King, Godfrey James 455
King, James 258
King, John Richard 429, 431, 434, 577
King, John, bishop of London 115, 145, 146, 152
King, Peter, Lord King 184, 186–8
King, Walker, the younger 608
King, William 174, 232, 569
King's College, Cambridge 524, 545
King's Hall, Cambridge 18
Kingerlee, T. H., Oxford builder 406
Kingsley, Charles 609
Kingsley, Helen 787
Kingston, Robert Pierrepont earl of 97, 124–5, Ill. 4.4
Kington, Thomas 487, 514
Kinsey, Robert 799, 807, 808
Kipling, Rudyard 448–9, 458, 536
Kirby, Richard 137
Kirkham, William de 19, 26
Kitchen 530
Kitchener, Horatio Herbert, Earl Kitchener 438, 681
Kleinwort Benson 539
Klibansky, Raymond 748
Knapp, Sir Arthur 46
Knight, Richard Payne 270n
Knight, Robert 197n
Knightley, John 141
Knightley, Richard, (1593–1639) 141

Knightley, Sir Richard 141
Knightley, Sir Valentine 112, 193–4, 510
Knolles, Thomas 83
Korfball 632, 633
Kylyngworth, Peter de 590
Kylyngworth's (11–12 Oriel Street) 582, 590–2
Kynaston, Edward (1583) 100, 126
Kynaston, Edward (1631) 100
Kynaston, Francis (1601) 99, 126–7
Kynaston, Francis (1655) 100

Lacrosse 615, 631
Lady Margaret Boat Club 607n
Lady Margaret lecturer 63, 71, 86
Lagden, Ronald Owen 464, 624, 625
Laghton, John de 18, 26, 27, 795
Laing, Isobel Lady 788
Laing, Sir Kirby 788
Lamb, Charles 256
Lambrick, Hugh 474–5, 536, 813
Lamplugh, Thomas 161
Lancaster heraldic shield 551
Landon, James 253n, 801, 810
Lane, John, SJ 88, 451
Lane, Mr, of Merton 178
Lang, William 137
Langbaine, Gerard 2, 122
Lardner, Dionysius 424
Lascelles, Sir Henry 788
Latimer, Hugh, bishop of Worcester 74, 82, 87
Latter, Edward 228n
Laud, William, archbishop of Canterbury 9, 100n, 118, 125, 129, 130, 135, 149, 151, 153, 159, 322, 558–9
Lawford, Daniel 798, 806
Laws, James 803
Lawson, Sir Wilfred 197n
Lee, George 197n
Lee, Lady, of Dean 487
Lee Seng Tee 788
Lee, Simon 109, 808
Leeds, Oriel property at 533
Legh, Thomas de 553
Legh, Thomas de, junior 553
Legh's chantry 553, 554
Leicester, Robert Dudley earl of 90, 148, 483, 485
Leigh Library 250–6, 276, 549, 564–8, 581
Leigh, Charles Leigh Lord 254

Leigh, Edward Leigh Lord 9, 203, 220, 226, 250–1, 254n, 564, 655–6
Leigh, James Henry, of Adlestrop 254
Leigh, Mary 251, 254
Leintwardine, Thomas, provost 2, 40, 41, 43, 44, 47–8, 793
Lenton, Mary 642n
Leverton, William de, provost 19, 26, 27, 29, 32, 77, 793, 795
Lewis, Francis Frederic Compson 455
Lewis, John 65, 66, 70, 71–2, 73, 75
Lewis, John, of Iffley 107
Lewis, William James 438n, 443n, 664–5, 729
Lewis, William, provost 99, 103, 109, 114–19, 129, 146, 152, 154n, 159, 556, 793, 798, 806, Ill. 4.6
Leyborn, Dr, of Dean 507
Leyland, Norman 540
Lhuyd, Edward 652
Lichfield, George Henry Lee earl of 191
Liddon, Henry Parry 309, 368n
Lidgould, John 166, 171n
Linacre, Thomas 61
Lincoln College 163, 193, 222, 247n, 434, 479, 494n, 496, 509, 514
Lion Hall 585–6
Lister, Joseph Storr 455
Lister, Sir Matthew 103, 105, 106, 125, 650, 805, Ill. 4.3
Literary Society 717, 727
Littlemore, Oriel property at 75, 199, 347, 352, 356, 476, 485, 538, 541, 542, 547, 582, 584, 635
Littleton, Edward Lord 129n
Littleworth, manor of 54, 58, 62, 120, 478, 481, 483, 485, 490, 495, 497, 507, 514, 516n, 517, 522, 523, 524, Map 3
Litton, Edward Arthur 295n, 354, 362, 364, 802
Liverpool, Robert Jenkinson, second earl of 288, 381
Llewellin, Martin 122
Lloyd, Charles, bishop of Oxford 288, 315
Lloyd, David (fellow 1602–9) 806
Lloyd, David (m. 1653) 160
Lloyd, Hugh, bishop of Llandaff 146
Lloyd, Humphrey, bishop of Bangor 103, 106, 146, 159n, 161, 798, 806
Lloyd, John 806
Locke, John 261
Loder brothers 229n

Lodge, Thomas 229
Lomax, Henry 133, 807
Lombard, Peter 12, 28, 60
Londonderry, Ridgeway Weston, earl of 219n
Long, Christopher 637
Long, Fred 775
Long, Henry 155, 807
Long, Sir James 245n, 246
Longland, John, bishop.of Lincoln 76, 78, 84, 85
Lorgan, Richard 78, 80, 82, 83, 86, 796, 805
Lorimer, Emily Overend 725
Lovel, John Lord 41
Lovel, Ralph 41
Lovell, Alan 601n
Lovell, John, junior 234, 238, 243
Lovell, John, senior 233n, 235, 236
Lovell, Peter Harvey 233–4, 236–8, 243
Lowe, Rob 641
Lower, Richard 668
Lowth, Robert 257n
Loyd, William 161
Lucian 248n
Ludwell exhibitioners 163, 228
Ludwell, Elizabeth 228, 480
Ludwell, Joanna 77
Lugard, Frederick, Lord Lugard 461
Lupset, Thomas 75
Luther, Martin 71, 74, 75
Lutterell, John 15
Lyhert, Walter, provost, bishop of Norwich 48, 49, 51, 52, 53, 54, 56, 58, 59, 77, 93, 793
Lynch, William 582, 588, 803, 804
Lynch's (105 High Street) 582
Lyne, Mr, treasurers' servant 494
Lyon, Ian 762
Lyon, Percy Comyn 454, 523, 527, 528–9, 530–1, 532, 534, 812
Lyons, Dan 638
Lyre, Nicholas of OFM 55
Lyttelton, William Henry, fifth Lord Lyttelton 380

Mackrell, John Edward Colborne 461–2, 468–9
Macmillan, Harold, earl of Stockton 681, 775
MacPherson, George Philip Stewart 535, 539, 627, 632
MacPherson, Gordon 542–3, 675, 795
MacPherson, Strone 788

Magdalen College 35, 61, 63, 93, 135, 163, 179, 182, 193, 219, 224, 226, 246, 295, 467, 483, 491, 496, 521, 538, 547, 548, 566n, 624, 626, 629, 663, 666, 671
Magdalen College School 60
Magdalen Hall 153
Magna Scola 553
Magpie Lane, Oriel property in 585–6
Mahoney, Christopher 637
Maiden Hall 477n
Maidstone, Richard OC 45n
Mainwaring, Roger, bishop of St David's 146
Major, Sir John 593, 786
Makepeace, William 173, 177n, 178n, 180n, 184, 187, 211, 214
Maldon, John, provost 44, 48, 793
Malebranche, Nicolas 261
Malins, William 230
Mallward, L. W. 455
Malmesbury, James Howard Harris Lord Fitzharris, third earl of 284–6, 320, 413, Ill. 9.6
Malthus, Thomas 377–9, 383, 388
Maltravers heraldic shield 551
Malvern College 620
Manasseh, Maurice 632
Manchester Grammar School 89, 173, 632, 650
Mander, John 485, 506–7
Mankswell, Andrew 803
Manning, Henry, cardinal archbishop of Westminster 281
Manning, Sir David 777
Mansbridge, Albert 686
Mansel, Henry 263
Mansell, Sir Robert 128
Mansfield College 572
Mansfield, Guy 770
Mant, Richard 269, 810, Ill. 9.1
Marbeck, Edward 90, 483
Marbeck, Roger, provost 89–90, 91, 483, 793
Marcus Aurelius 216
Mareschal, Roger le 587
Margaret of Anjou, queen of England 52, 53
Margaret Street, London, Oriel property in 533
Markes, John 105
Markham, William, bishop of Chester 261n
Marlborough College 615, 622
Marlborough, John Churchill, first duke of 169
Marlborough, John Spencer-Churchill, seventh duke of 413, Ill. 13.7

Marre's tenement 585
Marriott, Charles 6, 321, 332, 344, 346, 347, 348, 353, 354, 355, 356–7, 358, 392, 414, 420n, 802, Ill. 11.5
Marsh, Edward Garrard 247n, 811
Marshall, Edward 801, 810
Marshall, Howard Percival 627
Martill, John 41, 43, 46, 49
Martin Hall 32, 37, 39, 68, 72, 74, 77, 80, 477n, 550, 552–3
Martin, Samuel 176n, 181
Martyn, Bartholomew 203n
Martyn, Henry 213
Martyn, John 203n
Martyn, Richard 63, 77, 83, 804
Martyr, Peter 85
Mary I, queen of England 82, 86, 87, 138, 257, 588, 781
Mary II, queen of Great Britain 168
Mary Queen of Scots 147
Mason, Francis 138
Master, Thomas 245–6
Matthew, Richard 129n
Matthew, Tobias, archbishop of York 108
Maude, J. P., of Swainswick 487
Maunder, Thomas 801, 809
Mawdesley, Robert, junior 229n
Mawdesley, Robert, senior 229n
Mawdesley, Thomas 229n
Mawnfyld, Thomas 805
Mawnsell, John 52
May, Alston James, bishop of Northern Rhodesia 465–6
Mayer, Colin 790
Mayerne, Theodore de 650
Mayers, Walter 306
Mayhew, Henry 403
Mayo, John 256, 266n, 273n
Mayo, Thomas 408n
McCall, Robert Forster 457
McCarthy, W. F., architect 584
McGregor, Alexander John 455
McKerron, Robert Gordon 455
McLachlan, Andre Kenneth Wearing 455
McNeile, Robert Fergus (Balliol) 465
Meake, Martin 490
Mehta, Alex 633
Melanchthon, Philip 102
Melbourne, William Lamb, second Lord 340, 373, 383, 384
Mellon, James 594–5, 777, 788

Menzies, Fletcher 612–3
Merewether, Wyndham Arthur Scinde 620n
Merivale, Charles 608–9
Merivale, Herman 397, 608–9
Merton College 13, 14, 26, 30, 32, 46, 55, 62, 73, 108, 123, 129n, 138, 163, 167, 170, 173, 179, 193, 414, 434, 496, 566n, 572–3, 645–6, 647, 695
Merton, Walter de, bishop of Rochester 14
Methven, James 787, 789–90, 802
Mews, Peter 164
Mey (Maye), Walter 74, 78, 527, 796, 805
Meyronnes, François de, OFM 55
Michaelopoulos, Andreas Constantine 454
Middelton, John, provost 43, 44, 47, 554, 793
Midland Bank, Oxford Street, London, Oriel property 533
Miles, Philip John 514
Mill, James 384
Milton, John 124, 410
Milverley, William 46
Milward, Henry, haberdasher 592
Minio-Paluello, Lorenzo 748
Mirandola, Pico della 102
Misterton, Nicholas 27
Mitchell, Henry 87
Moberly, George 352n
Moir, John Chassar 672, 794
Monk, John 245n
Monro, David Binning, provost 5, 370, 408, 413, 429, 430–1, 433, 434, 435, 437, 439, 443, 574–6, 593–4, 715, 716, 794, 802, 812, Plate 6
Montague, Francis Charles 5, 802
Montaigne, George 115
Montaigne, Michel de 102, 257
Moody, George 540, 639, 784, 787
Moody, Henry Riddell 288
Moore, E. A. L., bishop of Travancore and Cochin 473
Moore, George 160, 162, 799, 807
Moore, R. B. 802
Mordaunt, Colonel 197n
More, Cresacre 69–70
More, George 160, 162
More, James, provost 70, 74, 76, 78, 79–80, 485, 793, 796, 804
More, John, stationer 55
More, Sir Thomas 35, 61, 69–70, 75, 76, 485, Ill. 3.2
Morebreade, Anthony 110

Moreton Pinkney, Northamptonshire, Oriel living 144, 204, 208, 210, 229, 480, 481, 483, 487, 494–5, 509
Moreton-in-the-Marsh, Oriel property at 544
Morgan brothers (m. 1757) 229n
Morgan, Henry 83
Morgan, James 209, 487, 801, 809
Morgan, Theresa 802
Morison, Robert 651
Morley, David, architect 595
Morris, John 72n
Morris, Sir Derek, provost 773, 788, 794, 802
Morrison, John Knerston King 469
Morse, Mark 230
Morshead, John 245n, 246
Morshead, Leonard Frederick 458
Mortimer heraldic shield 551
Morton, John, cardinal archbishop of Canterbury 69
Morton, Robert 42, 44
Morys, John 804
Moyses Hall 25, 27
Mozley, Anne 344
Mozley, Henry 401
Mozley, James 344, 345, 347, 361, 393–4
Mozley, Thomas 3, 5, 266, 278, 280, 294, 296, 298, 303n, 313, 320, 321, 332–3, 334–5, 343n, 344, 353, 354–5, 360, 371, 372, 393, 394, 395, 396, 398, 400, 401, 402, 403, 412n, 657–8, 659–60, 811, Ills. 11.3, 12.2
Muckleston, Richard 90
Muller, Karl Alexander von 712
Muller, Leopold 592
Mulso, John 188–90, 193, 203, 204, 208–9, 218, 222n
Murray, Sir Charles Augustus 320, 600–1, 602
Musgrave, Chardin, provost 190, 191, 201, 203, 212, 222, 233, 653, 794, 801, 809
Musgrave, Christopher (m.1731) 229n
Musgrave, George 229n, 245n, 246
Musgrave, Hans 229n
Musgrave, John Chardin 229n
Musgrave, Joseph 229n
Musgrave, Sir Christopher 229n
Musgrave, Sir Philip 190, 229n, 245n
Musgrave, Thomas, archbishop of York 373
Music Society 753, 790
Myddelton, Thomas 801, 809
Myers, David 802
Myn, Henry, provost 65, 66, 72, 83, 793, 804

Nairne, Edward, instrument maker 655
Namier, Sir Lewis 765
Nanney, Henry 434
Nanney, Hugh John Ellis 434
Napier, H. 720
Napier, Sir Nathaniel 161n, 559
Napoleon Bonaparte, emperor of the French 247n, 248, 409
Nares, Edward 257n, 262n, 263, 267n
Nassau, Robert 486
Nazareth House, Rectory Road 545, 548
Nazianzus, Gregory of, archbishop of Constantinople 102
Neale, Edward Vansittart 428, 435
Neate, Charles 263n, 420n, 428, 429, 515, 517, 812, Ill. 11.10
Neile, Richard, archbishop of York 149
Nelson, William 805
Nernst, Walter 666, 681
Nerses II, Armenian patriarch of Constantinople 449
Netball 631
Neve, Frederick 357
New College 10, 61, 35, 49, 54, 138, 193, 219, 223–4, 239, 241, 246, 467, 491, 494n, 496, 505n, 509, 514, 522, 559, 566n, 567, 572, 598, 607, 665, 666, 671, 682
Newbold, Douglas 469
Newbold, Philip 467
Newdigate, Sir Roger 188
Newlands Society 744, 753, 760
Newman, Charles 307
Newman, Christian 230
Newman, Harriett 332, 394
Newman, John Henry 3, 6, 5, 11, 265, 272, 277, 278n, 279, 280, 283n, 290, 291n, 292, 293, 294n, 300n, 302n, 306–11, 313, 314–16, 317–27, 328–42, 343, 344, 345, 346–57, 358, 359, 361, 362, 367–70, 372, 376–7, 382, 391, 392, 394–6, 397, 398–9, 400, 401, 409, 410, 411, 412, 443, 516, 559, 596, 658, 660, 707, 791, 801, 811, Ills. 11.1, 11.2, 11.3
Newman, Thomas 160
Newman Society (Oriel) 791
Newry, Francis Jack, Viscount, earl of Kilmorey 607
Newton, Richard 224
Newton, Sir Isaac 262
Niblett, Stephen 203, 205

Nicholas IV, pope 201
Nichols, Thomas 224n
Nicholson, Ernest, provost 586, 782–3, 785, 791, 794
Nicholson, Sir Bryan 781
Niebuhr, Barthold Georg 368n
Norfolk, William 85n, 86, 797
Norreys, Robert 78, 804
Norris, Henry Handley 306, 324
Norris, Sir John 451
North Wraxall, Wiltshire, Oriel living 480–1
North, Frederick North Lord, earl of Guilford 261n, 284
Northampton, Henry Howard earl of 112, 510
Northumberland, Henry Percy, ninth earl of 647, 649
Northumberland, John Dudley duke of 87
Norwood, Edward 810
Nowell, Elizabeth 205
Nowell, John 183
Nowell, Thomas 191, 570, 801, 809
Nowell, William 205–8
Nuffield College 698
Nuffield, William Morris, Viscount 694

O'Brien, Edgar 541, 542, 592
Ockham, William of OFM 12
Offen, James 545, 594, 786, 788, 813
Offinton, John de 25
Offinton, Robert de 25
Ofield, Thomas 133, 799, 807
Old Mortality Club 3
Opizzoni, Giovanni Baptista 650
Oriel College
  astrolabe 645–6, Ill. 19.1
  barge 634–5, 718, Ill. 18.8
  benefactors 52–3, 58, 63–4, 80, 188, 251–4, 437–40, 476–80, 521, 556–7, 562–3, 564–5, 572, 593–5, 781–2, 786, 787–8, 791–2, Ill. 8.1
  boathouse 635
  Carter Building 233, 275–7, 556, 563–4, 570, Ill. 17.7
  catholic sympathies 81–3, 87–8, 135–6
  caution money 100
  chapel, 14th-century building 38–9, 551
    15th-century building 39, 551
    17th-century building 559
    attendance at 77, 291, 364–5, 712, 731
  chaplain 21, 39, 40, 55, 199–200, 734–6
  common rooms 234–5, 251–2, 254, 264, 283, 296, 310, 328, 334, 347, 391, 568, 694, 752, 753, 762, 765, 769, 770–1, 780
  cricket pavilion 616, 626–7
  customs 4, 72, 77–8
  ecclesiastical livings 137, 144–5, 198–9, 204–10, 477, 480
  endowments and estates 18, 24, 25–6, 52–3, 58, 63–4, 80, 193–8, 476–525, 527–8, 532–3, 534–5, 542–8, Map 1, Map 2
  exhibitions
    Beaufort 163, 188, 228, 229
    Dudley 3, 67, 76, 80, 83, 90, 98, 102, 103, 108, 122, 137, 163, 228, 480
    Ludwell 163, 228
    Robinson 228
    St Antony 3, 54, 69n, 77, 80, 83, 88, 98, 110, 122, 123, 137, 146, 228, 479
  fellows
    accommodation 18–19, 25–6, 233, 561
    age 41, 767, 773
    books 49, 54–6, 101–2, 107–8, 118–19, 124, 216–18
    careers 28–9, 47–52, 74–6, 125, 194, 214–16, 380–88, 392–4, 402–5
    diet 77
    dress 78
    election 10–11, 45–6, 64–7, 78, 163–7, 173–82, 187, 264–7, 278–81, 325–6, 332–3, 344–5, 355, 414, 427–8, 429
    emoluments 18, 76–7, 193–4, 198–203, 496–7, 509, 512
    financial inexperience 445, 526
    governance 173–83, 426, 769–72, 792
    literary interests 75–6, 118, 215–18, 255–8, 270–1
    misconduct 41–5, 71–2, 78–9, 85, 167
    number 14, 18, 41, 434, 526, 691, 696, 709, 777, 788–9
    regional origin 10, 27–8, 42, 44–5, 52, 64–7, 78, 99, 264–5
    studies 28–9, 30–2, 46–52, 54–6, 74–6, 89, 101–18, 309–10, 325–6, 345–6, 645–7, 650–6, 659–61, 663–5, 666–9, 672, 673–6, 715, 751, 767, 768, 773–4
    teaching 31–2, 39–40, 56–7, 72–4, 80, 84, 87, 96–7, 100, 138–9, 231–2, 268–9, 278–9, 287, 294, 301, 310–13, 314, 317–21, 337–9, 350, 362, 410, 412–3, 430, 434–5, 663–4, 666–70, 672–6, 715, 734, 738–9, 753, 762–3, 767–8, 773–4

Oriel College (cont.)
  flag 740
  foundation 18–26, Ill. 1.1, Plan 1
  garden 37–9, 554, Plan 2
  gatehouse 39, 558
  graduate students 539, 754, 761, 768, 774, 777, 779, 787, 789, 790
  hall, first (old hall) 39, 552
  hall, second 80–1, 552
  hall, third 559–61
  Harris Building 593, 601, Ill. 17.13
  incorporation 110–1
  island site 526, 541, 542, 544, 548, 549, 581–7, 593–4, 754–5, 775, 778, 780–1, 782, 785–6, 787, 789, Plan 7
  James Mellon Hall 549, 594–5, 788, 789, Ill. 17.14
  kitchen 530, 532, 548, 552, 558
  La Oriole 17, 25–6, 33, 550, 551
  library 30–1, 39, 50–1, 54–5, 73, 107–8, 124, 142–3, 152, 250–6, 276, 549, 551, 561, 564–8, 569, 581, 773, 784, Ill. 17.8, 21.9
  parliamentary visitors 131–3
  provost
    election, disputed 43–5, 115–16, 183–7
    emoluments 63, 91, 211–14, 479, 497, 529–30
    laicisation 430–2
    lodgings 113, 275–8, 553, 554, 561, Ill. 17.11
  Rhodes Building 439–41, 521, 540, 542, 549, 569, 572–81, 595, 679, 707–9, 712, 753, 754, 789, Ill. 21.1, Plan 8
  Robinson Building 233, 275, 562–4, Ill. 17.6
  scientific instruments 645–6, 655–6
  seal Ill. 1.2
  servants 43, 56n, 117, 230–1, 277, 529, 530, 713, 718, 733, 744, 745, 765, 774–5, Ill. 21.6
  silver
    Founder's Cup 63, 277, Ill. 2.3
    Coconut Cup 80n, Ill. 3.3
  societies
    Adam de Brome Society 791
    Arnold Society 717, 727, 744, 753
    Book Club 288
    Dramatic Society 753, 760, 772, 790
    Harriot Society 647n
    Music Society 753, 790
    Newlands Society 744, 753, 760
    Newman Society 791
    Oriel Society 739–40, 756, 787
    Plantagenet Society 727
    Raleigh Society 791
    Whately Society 733
  sojourners 17, 33–4, 41, 47, 50, 68, 71, 76, 80, 83
  Tackley's Inn 18, 22, 25, 476, 550, 587–90, 595, Ill. 17.12, Plan 10
  tennis court 582, 592–4, 600–1
  tortoise 631, 743, 748, 750–1, 753, 763, 784
  treasury, old 551–2
  tutorship 312, 314, 317–22, 337–9, 350, 362, 412–13, 430, 434–5, 738–9
  undergraduates
    accommodation 113, 222–4, 703–4
    admission 99–100, 700–1, 742
    age 226
    books 101, 102, 287–8
    expenses 102–3, 232–4, 236–8, 731
    careers 124–8, 241–6, 284–7, 386–8, 413–4, 435, 451–75, 777
    commensales 97–8, 226–7, 284–6, 435
    commoners 97–8, 228
    general strike and 689–90, 731, 733
    family background 98–9, 228–30, 709–10, 742, 751–2
    misconduct 239–41
    number 61, 97, 284, 679, 682, 689, 691, 692, 699, 704, 709, 753, 776, 789
    protest 769–72
    recreation 234–6, 288, 597–644, 731–2, 762
    regional origin 98–9, 230
    servitors 97–8, 227–8
  visiting fellows 786
  war conditions
    1914–18 678–85, 716–24
    1939–45 691–4, 741–8
  War Memorials 569, 581, 693, 696, 704, 772–4, 746
  women at 129, 642–3, 701–4, 769, 776, 779–81, 786
Oriel Lake, Waterperry 477
Oriel Record 711–12, 720–1, 742, 744, 784
Oriel Society 739–40, 756, 787
Oriel Square 585, Plan 9
Oriel Wood, Boarstall 477, 481, 485, 487, 491–2, 494, 495
Origen 142, 298
Ormonde, James Butler first duke of 162n, 165
Oswestry School 126
Overton, Richard de 17, 25, 27, 553

Owen, Cadwallader 99, 107, 121, 138, 141, 143, 154, 797, 805
Owen, Edward 229–30
Owen, John 245n
Owen, Richard 98n, 99, 121, 145n, 154, 158, 159, 798, 806
Owen, Sir Robert 161n, 245n
Oxford Blues, film 641
Oxford, Robert Harley earl of 180

Pächt, Otto 748
Padua, university of 36, 97, 106
Page, J. H. 629, 630, 635
Pagès, Pierre Marie François de 257
Paget, Francis Edward 396, 401–2
Paget, Richard 224n
Paine, Thomas 259, 263, 267, 378
Palairet, Lionel Charles Hamilton 617–18, 623
Palairet, Richard Cameron North 617–18, 620, 624
Paley, William 283n, 424
Palladio, Andrea 564
Palmer, William, provost's butler and secretary 277, 490, 494, Ill. 9.7
Palmer, William, fellow of Worcester 328
Palmer, William, of Shenington 494
Pantin, William Abel 7, 533, 585, 693, 739, 745, 753, 762, 767, 768–9, 773, 794, Ill. 22.1
Panting, Samuel 229n
Pargeter, Walter 806
Paris, university of 36, 41, 71, 74
Parker, Henry 429
Parker, James 176n, 181
Parker, John 64–6
Parker, John Oxley 721
Parker, Robert 773
Parker, W. L. O. 721
Parkhurst, John 76
Parkinson, Richard 805
Parry, Edward Archibald, archbishop of the West Indies 465
Parry, George 200, 210
Parry, W. E. 586, 643, 674, 675, 768, 773, 778–9, 794, 795, Ill. 22.8
Parsons, Bartholomew 125–6, 159
Parsons, John, hatter 235
Parsons, Robert, SJ 451
Parsons, Sir Mark 220
Parys, Thomas 57, 796, 803
Pasor, Matthias 120

Paston, John I 53n, 56
Paston, Margaret 56
Paston, Walter 53n, 56, 67, 93
Pater, Walter 3
Paterson, David 594–5, 788
Pattison, Mark 5, 247, 260n, 263, 265, 266, 283, 284, 288, 330n, 331, 344n, 345, 360, 364, 366, 372, 412, 419, 603, 607
Paule, tutor of St Mary Hall 102
Paxton, John 44
Payne, Peter 46
Peake, Edward 616n, 622
Peake, Henry 720
Peake, Kenneth 720
Pearce, Thomas 229n
Pearson, N. J. 527
Peckitt, William 559
Pecock, Reginald, bishop of Chichester 11, 48, 49–50, 52, 59, 596
Peel, Sir Robert 282, 284n, 288, 321–2, 323, 324, 380, 381–2, 388, 391, 515
Pegge, Sir Christopher 256, 652–3
Pemberton, Stephen 809, 810
Pembroke College 193, 211n, 496, 538, 546, 547, 624
Pembroke, Philip Herbert earl of 123
Pembroke, William Herbert earl of 115
Penbegyll, William 41, 46
Peniston, Thomas 483
Penney, José Campbell 464, 469
Penny, Robert 203, 210, 238
Penrose, Emily 686, 724–6
Pepys, George Christopher Cutts, bishop of Buckingham 630, 635, 768
Pereira, Benito 101
Perilous Hall 18, 22, 476
Perkins, Edward 153
Perot, John 796, 803, 804
Perrott, Charles 133n, 162, 214, 218, 807
Perrott, Humphrey 801, 809
Perrott, Thomas 799
Persius 119n
Peterson, John Magnus 627, 632
Petre, Robert 8
Petty, Edmund 125, 159
Phelps, Lancelot Ridley, provost 9, 403–6, 429, 434, 437, 455–74, 523, 524, 527, 533, 623, 624, 643, 665, 695, 705, 714–16, 717, 719–21, 724, 725–6, 729–30, 732, 733, 737, 739, 742–3, 746, 751–2, 754, 756, 768, 794, 812, Plate 10

Philip, scholar of Knutsford 69
Philippa of Hainault, queen of England 34
Philipson, Thomas 89, 91, 122, 797
Phillippo, Susanna 780
Phillips, Cyril, steward 763, 779
Phillips, Morgan 83, 85, 86, 87–8
Phillips, Rowland 71, 74, 82, 804
Philp, Mark 795
Philpot, Joseph Charles 294
Philpotts, Henry, bishop of Exeter 358
Picard's tenement 553, 554
Pickford, Joseph 810
Pickwick, Eleazor 514
Pigot, Richard 73, 91, 92, 106, 108, 122, 137, 143, 493, 647, 649, 797
Pipon, Philip 176n, 179, 181, 800, 809
Pirie-Gordon, Patrick 540–1, 544
Pitman, John 810
Pitt, Clifford George 467
Pitt, James 810
Pitt, William, the younger 246, 255, 378, 381, 512
Plantagenet Society 727
Plato 61, 107, 263n, 372, 47
Playfair, John 270n
Plumb, John 494
Plumer, Walter 197n
Plumer, William 384
Plummer, John 40
Plumpton, Adam de 553
Plumptre, Frederick Charles 366
Plutarch 102, 143
Plymtree, Devon, Oriel living 205
Pole, Reginald, cardinal archbishop of Canterbury 82n
Pole, Willam de la, duke of Suffolk 49, 52
Pollen, John 197n
Ponteland, Northumberland 13, 21
Pool 632
Popham, Dorothy 203n
Popham, Edward 203n
Popham, Francis 203n
Popy, Henry 54, 57, 796, 803
Porter, Thomas 157
Possell, John, provost 41, 43, 48, 793
Poste, Edward 428, 429
Postlethwaite, Ian 675
Potter, John, archbishop of Canterbury 511
Potticary, John 798, 806
Powell, Baden 272, 281, 283, 288, 295, 300n, 306, 336–7, 341, 342, 346, 362–3, 364, 375, 415, 659–61, Ill. 9.2

Powell, Edward 11, 71, 74, 82, 87, 93, 796, 804
Powell, Thomas 101
Power, Sean 791
Powicke, Sir Maurice 753
Praepositinus 55
Praty, Richard, bishop of Chichester 48, 51, 52, 59
Prestige, Colin 788, 791
Preston, John 141
Prevost, Sir George 321
Price, Langford Lovell 439, 440n, 482, 516, 519–20, 521, 523, 527, 534, 572, 812
Prichard, James 812
Prideaux, Edmund 245n
Prideaux, John, bishop of Worcester 122
Prince, Daniel, bookseller 235
Pringle-Pattison, Andrew Seth 423
Prout, Keith 674, 795
Provost's Lodgings 113, 275–8, 553, 554, 561
Prudentius 55, 62
Pryce, Phillip, architect 595
Prynne, Marie (mother of William) 137n
Prynne, Mary 99n
Prynne, Thomas 99
Prynne, Thomas junior 99
Prynne, William 11, 99, 103, 118, 124, 129, 131, 135, 137n, 148–52, 159, 161, 214, 229, Ill. 5.2
Pullan, C. E. A. 720n
Purefoy, George 490
Purefoy, Sir Henry (m.1671) 195, 229, 485
Purefoy, Henry (m.1719) 195, 233
Purefoy, Knightley 195
Purleigh, Essex, Oriel living 205, 212, 213, 529, 534
Purnell, William 229n, 244–5
Pusey, Edward Bouverie 280, 300n, 309–10, 315n, 331, 337, 339–40, 345, 347–8, 352–3, 355, 367–8, 392, 396, 399, 422, 426, Ill. 10.5
Pusey, Philip 396
Putt, Sir Thomas 161n, 245n
Pye, Charles 485, 511
Pye, William 79, 82, 83, 86, 87, 797, 805
Pym, John 130

Quatermain, John 492
Queen Elizabeth's Grammar School, Blackburn 632

Queen's College 15, 32, 121, 123n, 163, 196, 210n, 239, 496, 535, 551n, 598, 635, 645, 738, 767
Queens' College, Cambridge 491n
Quiney, Richard 103

Rabelais, François 257
Radcliffe, Roger 41
Radley School 621
Radnor, Jacob Pleydell-Bouverie, third earl of 383
Raikes, Thomas Digby 621–2
Rainolds, John 101, 123, 142, 159n
Raisman, Geoffrey 675
Raleigh Society 791
Raleigh, Sir Walter 7, 11, 89–90, 97, 102, 444–5, 446, 451, 647–9, Ill. 3.6
Ramsey, Ian, bishop of Durham 536, 813
Randal, Peter 171, 173, 202, 217–18, 800, 808
Rannie, David Watson 4–6, 11
Rao, Srinivasa Raghunatha 462–3
Ratcliffe, John 205–6
Rauton, William 77
Ravis, Thomas, bishop of London 137
Rawe, John 144n, 797
Rawlinson, Richard 239–40
Rayner, Alexander 173, 177n, 179n, 808, 809
Rayner, Edward 203, 801, 809
Reid, Frank 455, 472
Reid, Norman 455
Reid, Thomas 258, 261
Repingdon, Philip, bishop of Lincoln 40, 45, 49n
Repton School 620, 621n
Rewley Abbey 16
Reynham, John 29
Reynolds, Gerald Nairne 459
Reynolds, Mr, of Faringdon 507
Reynolds, Richard, bishop of Lincoln 136, 176–81, 184–6
Reynolds, Sir Joshua 261n
Rheims, Catholic college at 136
Rhodes, Cecil 437–9, 440, 443, 444, 445–6, 452, 468, 472, 520n, 521, 526, 545, 572, 580, 581, 704, 707, 754, 781, Plate 7
Rhodes Building 439–41, 521, 540, 542, 549, 569, 572–81, 595, 679, 707–9, 712, 753, 754, 789, Plan 8
Rhodes Scholars 443, 452, 455, 472, 709–10, 728, 750, 754
Rhodes Trust 456, 521n, 540, 702

Ribbentrop, Joachim von 690
Ricardo, David 372, 380, 383
Richard III, king of England 62
Richards, George 253n, 256, 266n, 810
Richards, George Chatterton 6, 434, 443n, 577–81
Richards, Thomas 65, 796, 804
Richardson, John Noel 468
Rickards, Samuel 281, 307–8, 318–19
Rigaud, Stephen Peter 656
Ritchie, William 455
Robbins Committee and Report 759, 766
Roberts, Thomas 76, 93
Robertson, Daniel, architect 570
Robertson, William 257, 262
Robinson Building 233, 275, 562–4, Ill. 17.6
Robinson exhibitioners 228
Robinson, Christopher 199, 800, 809
Robinson, John Martin 565
Robinson, John, bishop of London 5, 13, 162, 171, 176, 198, 211, 212, 214, 228, 452, 562–3, Ill. 7.1
Robinson, Richard 784
Robinson, Sir Robert 670, 673
Rochester Cathedral, provost's prebend at 171, 211–12, 250, 289, 408, 430–2, 518n
Rogers, Frederic, Lord Blachford 320n, 321, 325–6, 332, 335n, 347, 348, 353, 354, 355–6, 358, 359, 392, 811, 812, Ill. 11.6
Rogers, James 810
Rogers, Nicholas 170, 174n, 199, 205n, 800, 808
Rogers, Thorold 405
Roper, Anthony 485–6
Roper, John, attorney general 485
Roper, John, vicar of St Mary's 71
Roper, scholar 68
Roper, William 485–6
Ros, William Fitzgerald de, Lord de Ros 608
Rose, Hugh James 319n
Rose, William 75–6, 93, 493, 650, 804
Ross, John 228
Ross, Sir David, provost 434, 527, 672–3, 694, 714–15, 733–4, 735, 737, 738, 739, 745, 748, 749–51, 752, 773, 779, 784, 794, Plate 12
Rote, John, provost 40, 42, 43, 44, 48, 793, 795, 803
Rothbury, Gilbert de 14
Rotherham, Thomas, bishop of Lincoln 57n

Roundell, Charles 432–3
Rouse, John 103, 106, 116, 124, 127, 132, 148, 159, 798, 806, Ill. 4.5
Rousseau, Jean-Jacques 257, 475
Routh, Martin 256, 257, 272, 295, 366, 511–2
Row, C. A. 418n
Rowing 604, 605–9, 610–15, 616, 621–4, 626, 628–31, 633–42, 644, 737–8, 773, 775, 777, 780, 787, 789
Rowntree, Seebohm 403
Rowsam, Stephen 136
Royse, George, provost 168–71, 211, 217, 794, 807, 808
Royse, William 168n
Rudd, Edward 273n
Ruel, Jean 651
Rugby football 624, 627, 631, 632, 642
Rugby School 280, 297, 342, 359, 365, 603, 610, 612, 615, 709
Rupert of the Rhine, Prince 130, 592, 600
Rusbridge, Edward 487
Ruskin, John 403
Russell, Elizabeth 802
Russell, James, tennis court keeper 601
Russell, John Frank 802
Russell, Lord John, Earl Russell 383, 384, 387, 401, 418, 419
Rutter, Ferriman 126
Rye, George 170, 171, 199, 808
Ryles farm, Wiltshire 480, 495
Ryshton, Alexander 82, 552, 797, 805
Ryves, Bruno 130, 131n, 155
Ryves, Thomas 131n
Ryxman, John 82, 87, 796, 805

Sabin, William, tennis court keeper 601
Sadeel, Anthony 140
Sadler, Thomas 803
St Alban Hall 300n, 308, 324
St Antony exhibitioners 3, 54, 69n, 77, 80, 83, 88, 98, 110, 122, 123, 137, 146, 228, 479
St Antony's College 633n, 698
St Antony's Hospital 51, 52, 53, 479
St Aubyn, Sir John 245n
St Creed, Cornwall 16
St Edmund Hall 46, 98, 168, 191, 294, 295, 633, 635, 674–5, 697,
St Edward Hall 477n, 585
St Frideswide's Priory 24, 550
St Frideswide's tenement, Magpie Lane 553, 554

St Germans, Richard of 25
St Hilda's College 744
St John, Paulett 245n
St John's College 107n, 193, 494n, 496, 529, 538, 547, 558, 559, 570, 603n, 671, 697
St John's College Cambridge 608
St Lawrence Hall 67
St Mary Hall 19, 32, 37, 39, 52, 56–7, 59, 63, 67, 69, 72, 80, 84, 85, 86, 87, 89, 90, 91, 93, 100, 102, 106, 122–3, 131, 136n, 137, 148, 174, 191, 217, 232, 241, 341, 416, 429, 433–4, 477n, 549, 550, 553, 554, 568–72, 587, 595, 598, 611n, 647, 648, 650, 679–80, 683, 692–3, 704, Plan 4, Plan 5, Plan 6
St Mary the Virgin, Oxford, church of 12, 13, 16, 25, 29, 33, 41, 42, 45, 71, 85, 120, 122, 139–40, 144, 153, 168, 170, 171, 199, 200n, 204, 250, 273, 291n, 293, 294–5, 300n, 303, 307, 327, 330–1, 331, 350, 352, 355, 356, 393, 410, 476, 487, 490–1, 549, 553, 559, 568, 718
St Peter's College 526
St Thomas Hall (109–10 High Street) 477n, 582
St Thomas's chantry 592
St Valery, Bernard of 25
Salisbury, Fulk 71
Salisbury, Robert Cecil, first earl of 113n, 485
Salisbury, Robert Arthur Talbot Cecil, third marquess of 431
Salmon, John 170, 199–200, 217, 808
Salter, Herbert Edward 6, 8
Saltfleetby St Peter, Lincolnshire, Oriel living 204
Salutati, Coluccio 34
Salusbury, Sir William 129, 152
Sampson, Henry, provost 48, 53, 54, 57, 74, 77, 808
Sancroft, William, archbishop of Canterbury 169
Sancta Fide, Gilbert de 15
Sanders, John 671, 673–4, 675, 712, 762, 795
Sanderson, Anthony 224n
Sanderson (formerly Burdon), Richard Burdon 273n, 292n, 408n
Sandford, Francis 103n
Sandford, Martin 102–3, 129
Sandford, Thomas Frederick 454, 464, 466, 471, 472
Sandwich, Edward Montagu earl of 162

Sandys, George 203n
Sandys, Samuel 205
Sanford, Dorothy 250
Sanford, William 250, 485
Sankey, Peter 98–9
Sankey, Richard 98–9
Sankey, Samuel 98–9
Sarasin and Partners 543
Saumur, Protestant seminary at 106
Saunders, Humphrey 156n
Saunders, John, provost 100, 103, 105, 122, 131–2, 569n, 794, 806
Saunders, Richard 132, 195, 798, 806, 807
Sawy son of Langrif 25
Sawyer, George 239n, 243
Saxon, Eric 457
Say, Robert, provost 103, 132, 133, 155, 158, 160–1, 165–6, 168, 169, 794, 799, 806, 807, Ill. 6.1
Say, William 161
Saye and Sele, William Fiennes Lord 141
Sayer (Sawyer), Henry 243, 246
Scanlen, Sir Thomas 452
Scawen, Robert 232n
Scawen, Alderman Sir Thomas 232
Schoppe, Thomas 796
Schrider, Christopher, organ builder 559
Schwartze, Helmuth Eric 464–5, 46
Sclater, Bartholomew 810
Scott, Christopher Fairfax 467
Scott, George Gilbert, junior, architect 572
Scott, Henry 797, 805
Scott, Thomas, of Aston Sandford 306
Scroggs, Sir William 161
Scrope, Richard 224n
Scrope, Thomas, of Coleby 485, 500
Scrope, William (d. 1463) 41
Scudamore, John 68
Scudamore, Richard 68
Scudamore, William 68, 69n
Seabrook, Peter 601n
Seaman, William 224, 809
Secker, Thomas, archbishop of Canterbury 216
Seeley, Sir John 446, 451
Segar, Alan 674, 795, 813
Selborne Commission 431, 432, 433, 665
Selden, John 148
Seldon, Arthur Arnold 467
Sellar, Walter Carruthers 728
Selwyn, William 245n
Sen, Dhirendra Kumar 463

Senior, Jane 390
Senior, Nassau 279, 338n, 342n, 375, 383–5, 386, 389–90, 391, 400
Seth-Smith, Donald Farquharson 454, 467
Seton-Karr, Heywood Walter 620n
Seton-Watson, Christopher 770, 794, 802
Sevington, Wiltshire, Oriel property at 480, 483
Sewall, Richard 87
Shacksnovis, Arthur 455
Shadwell, Charles Lancelot, provost 3, 5, 6, 7, 8, 429, 430, 434, 439, 440, 442, 459, 516, 528, 576, 581, 624, 644, 680, 705, 707, 709, 711, 713, 714, 717, 727, 794, 812, Plate 8
Shakerley, George 183, 199
Shakespeare, William 103, 124
Sharer, Kevin 791
Sharpe, Thomas 695
Shaw, Edward Domett, bishop of Buckingham 465, 644
Sheffield, Nicholas 90
Sheffield, Robert 54, 55, 803
Sheldon, Edward 120n, 147
Sheldon, Gilbert, archbishop of Canterbury 154–5, 161n, 164
Sheldon, Ralph 90, 99, 132n, 147–8, 483
Sheldon, Sharington 132n, 799, 807
Shellord, Stafford, of Shenington 497
Shenington, Oxfordshire, manor of 63, 77, 479–80, 481, 482, 486–7, 489, 490, 493, 494, 495, 498, 505, 506, 512, 516n, 517, 522, 524, Map 5
Shepheard, Henry 350, 802
Sheppard, Elizabeth 211n, 213, 238
Sheppard, Thomas 98, 132n, 160, 163, 799, 807
Sherriff, R. C. 737
Sherrington, Charles 670
Sherwood, W. E. 606, 608, 611
Shippen, Robert 184, 187, 213
Shippen, William 197n
Shore, Thomas 810
Shorthouse, Derek 539, 540, 813
Shrewsbury School 620
Shrewsbury, Charles Talbot duke of 239
Shrewsbury, Gilbert Talbot earl of 124
Shrewsbury, Oriel property at 534, 542
Shrewsbury, Ralph de, bishop of Bath and Wells 21, 26
Sidney Sussex College, Cambridge 94

Simpson, George William, builder 573
Simpson, Percy 738
Sinclair, John Stewart 620n
Sinclair, Sir John 268
Skelton, John, underbutler 56n
Skinner, Robert, bishop of Oxford, translated to Worcester 114–15, 158
Slack, Samuel 514
Slack, William 514
Slade, Thomas 78
Slough, Oriel property at 534, 542
Smail, William Mitchell 455
Smallbone, Edward 806
Smedley, Edward 325
Smiles, Samuel 401
Smith, Adam 373, 380
Smith, Assheton 402
Smith, Clement 57
Smith, Eleanor Elizabeth 429n
Smith, Goldwin 445–6, 449–50, 451
Smith, Griffith 102
Smith, John, gentleman commoner 242
Smith, Joseph 602n
Smith, Michael 239
Smith, Richard 229n
Smith, Robert 224n
Smith, Rupert Barkeley 454
Smith, Sidney, college butler 721
Smith, Sydney 270n, 383
Smith, Thomas 169
Smith, William 129, 130–1
Smyth, John, junior 805
Smyth, John, provost 85–6, 89, 107, 552, 793, 797
Smyth, Matthew 63, 64, 804
Smyth, Thomas Scott 810
Smyth, William, bishop of Lincoln 63, 77, 479
Snetisham, Richard 41, 43
Socinus (Fausto Paolo Sozzini) 339
Soddy, Frederick 670
Somaster, Joseph 224
Somerset, Edward Seymour first duke of 86
Somerset, Edward Seymour thirteenth duke of 219–20, 226, 242n
Somerset, Lord Noel 197n
Somerville College 573, 683, 703, 717, 724–6
Sophocles 101
South London, Oriel estate in 543, 545, 546
Southby, John 484, 490
Southey, Robert 607n
Southwood, Dick, property entrepreneur 543

Spain, James of 17–18, 25–6, 37, 476, 550
Spalding's tenement 553
Sparks, H. E. D. 540, 795, 813
Spence, Thomas 378
Spencer, George John, second Earl Spencer 381
Spender, Sir Stephen 731
Spenser, John 140
Spivey, Michael 676
Springbet, John 803
Springer, Ferdinand 709
Spring-Rice, Sir Cecil 446n
Spry, John Hume 298n, 324
Squash 627n, 631
Stadhampton farm, Oxfordshire 480, 495, 509
Stafford, Mr, of Oriel 241
Stainer, Robin 788
Staines, Oriel property at 534, 542
Stallworthy, Sir John 672
Stallybrass, William 671
Standish, Richard 229
Stanford, Ralph 136
Stanhope Smith, Samuel 258, 262
Stanley, Arthur Penrhyn 342, 369, 419
Stanway House 558
Stapeldon, Walter de, bishop of Exeter 14, 25
Stephens, John 72n, 804, 805
Stephens, M. J. F. 586, 785–6, 813
Stephens, Roger 803
Stephenson, E. W. 789, 813
Sterling, John 373
Stevenes, Roger 54, 55
Steward, Charles (1656) 133
Steward, Charles (1847) 613
Steward, Richard 129
Stewart, Dugald 258, 262n, 383
Stewart, Duncan 460
Stillingfleet, Edward, bishop of Worcester 182
Stock, Thomas 64–7, 72n, 76, 78, 796, 804
Stockdell, William 110
Stockford, Samuel 230
Stodle, John de 553
Stodle's tenement 553
Stokes, Hopetoun Gabriel 454
Stone Farm, Longcot (Faringdon) 534
Stone, Charles 224n
Stone, John 242
Stone, Nicholas 557
Stonehouse, John 799, 807, 808
Stow, archdeaconry 16

Stowford farm 477, 485, 487, 489, 491, 492, 493
Stowlangtoft, living of 308
Strabo 270, 271
Strafford, Thomas Wentworth earl of 125, 145
Strange, William 235
Stratford, William 172, 179, 180, 182
Strauss, David Friedrich 423
Strauss, Richard 680
Strickland, Hugh Edwin 657
Strong, Thomas Banks 681
Strong, Timothy 549, 557–8
Strutt, John James, Lord Rayleigh 288
Stubbs, William, bishop of Oxford 429
Sturdy, Mr, of Dean 498
Stylyngton, John de 553
Stylyngton's tenement 553
Sumner, John Bird, archbishop of Canterbury 379
Sunderland, Charles Spencer earl of 212
Sutherland, Dame Lucy 764–5
Sutton, Roger 63, 804
Sutton, Surrey property 533, 542
Swainswick, Somerset, manor of 80, 83–4, 91, 99, 137, 144, 204, 209, 210, 214, 229, 480, 481, 484, 485, 487, 489, 490, 492, 495, 505, 506, 507, 508, 512, 513, 514, 521, 524, 689, Map 6
Swan on the Hoop Inn 582, 584
Swann, Sir Michael, Lord Swann, provost 777–8, 794, Ill. 22.3
Sweit, Giles 125
Swift, Jonathan 257
Swimming 602, 615, 631
Swinglehurst, Robert 799, 807
Sword and buckler play 598–9
Sydenham, William 156
Sylvester, Thomas 495
Symond, William 41, 42
Symons, Benjamin 352
Szurko, Marjory 9

Table tennis 631, 642, 744
Tackley's Inn 18, 22, 25, 476, 550, 582, 587–90, 595
Talbot, Charles Talbot Lord 170, 238, 239, 244, 245
Talbot, Edward 210, 216, 238, 245, 808
Talbot, William, bishop of Durham 239, 245
Tanner, Benjamin 144n
Tasker, F. W., architect 594

Tatham, Edward 271–2
Taylor, A. J. P. 11, 628–9, 678, 690, 729, 730–3, 736, 739, 764, Ill. 21.4
Taylor, George 390
Taylor, John (fellow 1489–1502) 796, 804
Taylor, John (fellow 1611–27) 98n, 116, 144, 798, 806
Taylor, John, provost 54, 55, 58, 61–2, 74, 78, 92, 793, 796, 803
Taylor, John, the Water Poet 606–7
Tennis 598, 599–601, 615, 624, 626, 631
Tennis Court, 104 High Street 582, 592–4, 600–1
Tenterden, Oriel property at 544
Tertullian 107
Theodosius of Tripoli 47, 647
Thirlwall, Connop, bishop of St David's 373
Thomas, Vaughan 340
Thomas, William 201, 809
Thompson, S. 730
Thomson, Henry Arthur 455
Thorne, Edmund 167, 799, 807
Thorne, Mr, college servant 230
Throckmorton, John 78
Throgmorton, Sir Robert 507
Throwley farm, Kent 480
Thurston, Gerard 800, 808
Thynne, Lord Edward 602
Thynne, Thomas 165–6
Tighe, Bert 586
Tillotson, John, archbishop of Canterbury 168, 211
Tinney, William 273n, 274
Tizard, Sir Henry 522–5, 527, 666, 681, 682, 684, 694, 739, 753, 765–6, Ill. 21.3
Tod, Marcus Niebuhr 434, 534, 683, 726, 735–6, 739, 794
Todd, Alexander, Lord Todd 673
Toledo, Francisco de 101
Tolson, John, provost 99, 103, 105, 110, 114, 115, 116, 119–22, 123, 129, 131, 144, 148, 152, 159, 556, 793, 798, 805, 806, Ill. 4.7
Tooker, Charles 125, 155
Tooker, John 149, 155
Tooker, Robert 806
Topolski, Daniel 633–4, 637, 638
Torpids 611, 622, 636–7, 641n, 642
Tortoise Club 631, 641
Tortoise, college 631, 743, 748, 750–1, 753, 763, 784

Tortworth, Gloucestershire, Oriel
    living 204–5, 208
Tostado, Alfonso, bishop of Avila 118
Towne, Robert 156–7, 159
Townesend, William, architect 549,
    562–3, 564
Townsend, John 487
Townsend, Lady Elizabeth 487
Townshend, Charles Townshend Lord 182
Townshend, Thomas 197n
Tracy, Robert (m. 1672) 226n, 244
Tracy, Robert, Lord Tracy of
    Rathcoole 226n
Trampolining 632
Treasury, old Oriel 551–2
Trelawney, Sir Jonathan, bishop of
    Exeter 182
Trench, Francis 600, 602
Trenchard, William 160n, 245n
Trevelyan, George Macaulay 739, 753
Trevor-Roper, Hugh, Lord Dacre 568,
    764–6, 770
Trinity College 193, 222, 226, 291n, 370,
    427, 476n, 496, 505, 538, 547, 613,
    648, 653, 663
Trinity College, Cambridge 609n
Tripe, Nicholas 808
Trollope, Mr, of Dean 497
Trott, Edmund 229
Trott, John 229
Trowbridge, Edward 65, 66, 67, 796, 804
Tuckwell, William 5, 296n, 302n, 372, 375,
    411–12
Tudway, Clement 245n
Turberville, James, bishop of Exeter 82
Turnbull, Alexander 542–3, 672
Turner, Gilbert 86
Turner, William 651
Turpin, Kenneth, provost 536, 643, 701,
    756–7, 766, 770–3, 777, 786, 794, 813,
    Ill. 22.2
Turpin, Nancy Bisell 592
Turpin, William 787
Turpin, William Nelson 592
Tweed, Henry Earle 802, 812
Twerton, Somerset, Oriel living 480, 481
Twitty, Thomas 164–6
Tye, Antony 98, 101, 797
Tyler, James Endell 273n, 274, 318, 335, 359,
    368, 801, 811, Ill. 10.2
Tyrconnel, John Brownlow Lord 197n

Ufton Nervet, Berkshire 204–5, 209
University College 2, 13, 111n, 138, 159, 163,
    179–80, 188, 193, 226, 291n, 437, 445,
    449, 493, 496, 585, 624, 645
Unton family 485
Unton, Alexander 68n, 194, 476
Unton, Edward 91–2, 451
Unton, Francis 91
Unton, Sir Henry 91–2, 97, 106, 451, Ill. 4.2
Unton, Thomas 68
Unton, Thomas, junior 68n
Upton, William 80, 805
Ussher, James, archbishop of Armagh 51

Vale, W. S., of Swainswick 487
Vallis, Eric 540–1, 542, 543, 545, 586, 594,
    775, 813
Van Mildert, William, bishop of Durham 293
Vanbrugh, Sir John 564
Vansittart, Nicholas 255, 381
Vansittart, Robert 261n
Varley, Frederic John (m.1891) 7, 729
Varley, John (m.1974) 777
Vaughan, Henry Halford 345, 354, 419
Vaughan, Richard 69, 804
Vaughan, Robert 126
Ventris, Edward 224n
Ventris, Francis 224n
Vesalius, Andreas 650
Veysie, Daniel 11, 229n, 253, 264, 266n, 801, 810
Vickers, Sir John 777, 790
Victoria, queen of Great Britain 570
Vidal, Montague Richard Reynolds 467
Vincent Smith, Graham 539–40, 586, 675, 788,
    795, 813
Vitelli, Cornelio 61
Volney, Constantin de Chasseboeuf, comte de 258
Voltaire, Francois-Marie 249n, 257
Von Polier, Ferdinand Rudolph Helmuth 466
Voyle, William 141

Wadham College 94, 163, 167, 170, 171, 193,
    295, 491, 494n, 496, 509, 514, 538, 547,
    554–5, 557, 558, 561, 570, 623, 697, 767
Wadham, Dorothy 554–5
Wadham, Nicholas 554–5
Wadley, Oxfordshire, manor of 8, 52, 54, 58,
    62, 68, 78, 111, 194–5, 229, 476, 478,
    484, 485, 487, 489–90, 494, 498n, 506,
    507, 509–11, 514, 516, 517, 518n, 522,
    523, 524, 532–3, Map 3

INDEX

Wagner, Abram Isaac 455
Wake, William, archbishop of Canterbury 172, 212, 232
Wakefield, Edward Gibbon 386
Walford, Arthur 464–5
Walker, Elizabeth, of Dean 498, 507
Walker, J. W. and Sons, organ builders 559
Walker, Robert 656, 661
Walker, Thomas 160n
Walker, William (fellow 1680–1700) 799, 808
Walker, William (fellow 1767–74) 810
Walker, William (m. 1722) 224n
Wall, Pauncefoot 125n, 806
Wallace, Moira, provost 794
Waller, Robert 245n
Walpole, Horace, fourth earl of Orford 565
Walpole, Sir Robert, first earl of Orford 179n, 188, 197n, 511
Walsall, John 167, 173
Walsh, Donald 674–5
Walsh, Walter, hair dresser 235
Walsingham, Sir Francis 123
Walter, Hubert, archbishop of Canterbury 25
Walter, John, the third, proprietor of *The Times* 394, 401
Walter, William 117
Waltham, Roger of 49n
Walton, Brian 119, 128n
Walwayn, Richard 810
Walzer, Richard 748
Wand, John William Charles, bishop of London 690, 734–7, 739, 802, Ill. 21.5
Wandesford, Walter de 31, 32, 553, 554
War Memorials 569, 581, 693, 696, 704, 722–4, 746
Ward, John (1805–90) 382, 387–8
Ward, Richard 549, 586
Ward, Thomas 174, 218, 226, 230, 800, 808
Ward, Tony 638
Ward, William George 353
Ward-Clarke, Harry Martin 627
Ware, Thomas, provost 70, 72n, 73n, 74, 80–3, 552, 793, 796, 804
Warenne heraldic shield 551
Warner, Hugh Compton 458
Warner, Mrs Winifred 458
Warner, Sir Pelham 616n, 617, 619–20, 621, Ill. 18.6
Warre, Sir Francis 161n, 245n
Warren, John 256, 266n, 806
Warton, Joseph 7, 245, Ill. 8.2

Warton, Thomas 257
Washbourne, John 799, 807
Washbourne, William 798, 806, 807
Water polo 615, 631
Waterhouse, Alfred, architect 584
Waterperry, Oriel property at 477, 485
Watson, Hugh 187
Waugh, Evelyn 581, 708, 729
Way, Benjamin 155
Webb, Allan 452
Webb, Beatrice 406, 716
Webb, Francis 229n
Webb, John 229n
Webb, Nicholas 229n
Webb, Sidney, Lord Passfield 406
Webb, Thomas, butler 230
Webber, Francis 88, 89, 90, 797
Weddell, Graham 672, 675, 794
Weeksey, Richard 203
Weeksey, Thomas 167n, 179n, 180, 183–7, 200–1, 203, 213n, 242, 800, 808
Wellington, Arthur Wellesley first duke of 352n, 416
Wells Cathedral School 60
Wells Street, London, Oriel property in 533
Wells, Alice 181
Wells, H. G. 464n
Wenman, Philip Wenman, seventh Lord 220, 226n, 238, 245n
Wenman, Philip Wenman, sixth Lord 226
Wenman, Richard (m.1744) 226n
Wenman, Richard Wenman, fourth Lord 226n
Wenman, Sir Richard 161n
West, Richard 800, 808
Westbury on Trim College 53
Westerman, William 111
Western Farm, Oakford, Devon 534, 535
Westmacott, Richard, the first 254, 568
Westminster School 607–8
Weston, John 795
Weston, Thomas 133
Whalley, Arthur George Cuthbert 630
Whalley, Bradley 203n, 800, 808
Whalley, Thomas 175, 202, 204, 800, 808
Wharton, Richard 106, 108, 122n, 138, 797, 805
Whately Society 733
Whately, Elizabeth 368
Whately, Richard, archbishop of Dublin 5, 255n, 260, 264, 265, 266, 269, 273n, 278–9, 281, 282, 283, 284, 290, 295, 296, 297, 299, 300–5, 306, 307–10, 311n, 314,

Whately, Richard, archbishop of Dublin (*cont.*) 322, 324, 331, 333–4, 336, 338n, 340, 342, 343, 355, 357, 359, 360, 362–3, 365, 368, 369, 375, 376–7, 378, 380, 382, 383, 384–91, 396, 398, 401, 405, 409, 412, 801, Plate 2
Whately, Thomas, rector of Cookham 389, 401
Whately, Thomas, secretary to the Treasury 384, 386
Wheathamstead, John, abbot of St Albans 47
Whetcombe, William 110, 798, 805
Whitaker, William 143
White, Alderman, of Oxford 245n
White, Gilbert, bishop of Willochra 465
White, Gilbert, of Selborne 7, 10, 189, 190, 193, 202–3, 204, 208–9, 218, 222n, 232, 233, 234, 237, 597, 653, 695, 801, Ill. 7.3
White, John Meadows 390
White, Joseph 249, 256, 257n
White, Joseph Blanco 282, 283, 296, 298–9, 300n, 308, 316, 322, 341, 356, 375, 376, 377, 383, 386, 390, Ill. 10.3
White, Mrs Jenny 245n
White, Peter 87, 88
Whitehall, John 799, 807
Whitelocke, Bulstrode 123
Whitgift, John, archbishop of Canterbury 109, 148
Whiting, Charles 189, 199, 200, 210, 216, 217, 801, 809
Whittington College, London 52
Wickensham manor, Berkshire 111, 514, 516n
Wickes, Thomas 208
Widdowes, Giles 103, 130, 148–52, 159, 798, 806
Wight, Robert 229n
Wightwick, Walter 229
Wigmore, Michael 117, 144, 145
Wilberforce, Henry 247n, 281, 308, 320, 334, 338, 339, 355, 392–3, 395, 400, 657–8
Wilberforce, Robert 247n, 280–1, 310, 314, 315, 317, 320, 359, 392–3, 412, 657–8, 660, 801
Wilberforce, Samuel, bishop of Oxford, bishop of Winchester 247n, 295, 296n, 301n, 331–2, 355, 372, 426, 657–8. Ill. 13.5
Wilberforce, William 247, 280, 295, 392–3
Wilberforce, William, junior 247n
Wilberforce, William, the younger (m.1840) 613
Wilcocks, John 799, 807
Wilcottes, Thomas 53n
Wilcox, Joseph, bishop of Bristol 178n
Wild, George 155
Wilfrid, bishop of York 354n
Wilkins, H. R., of Swainswick 487
Wilkinson, Francis 461
Wilkinson, William, architect 584n
Willement, Thomas, stained glass artist 570
Willes, Edward, bishop of Bath and Wells 245
William II, emperor of Germany 681
William III, king of Great Britain 168, 169
Williams Ellis, Clough, architect 624n
Williams Wynn, Sir Watkin 190n, 220, 243, 245n, 253
Williams, Anne 90
Williams, Isaac 291n, 310–11, 313–4, 316, 325, 329–30, 352, 358
Williams, John (fellow 1780–6) 810
Williams, John Milton 468, 469
Williams, John, bishop of Lincoln 144, 149n, 153
Williams, Michael 586, 795
Williams, Mr, cook 230
Williams, Owen 614
Williams, Sir Maurice 123, 129, 145, 798, 805
Williams, William 278n
Williamson, Joseph 162, 214
Willoughby de Broke, Henry Verney Lord 284
Wilmot, John, of Shenington (1585) 490
Wilmot, John, of Shenington (1635) 493
Wilmot, Sir Robert 222
Wilmott, William 104, 106, 110, 797, 798, 805
Wilsford, Edmund, provost 63, 66, 71–2, 74, 75, 76, 79, 80, 82, 84, 86, 89, 93, 793, 796, 804
Wilson, John Cook 4, 429, 434, 802, 812
Wilson, Robert Francis 321, 336n
Wilson, Sir Geoffrey 737
Wilson, William 126
Wilton, Thomas 41, 43, 44, 45
Wiltshire, Richard 57, 795, 803
Wimbush, Anthony 454
Wimbush, Richard, bishop of Argyll 736
Winch, Richard 131, 133n, 806
Winchester College 10, 60, 223, 245, 467, 601n, 609n, 620, 667, 709
Windsor, Andrew Lord 68
Windsor, Anthony 68
Windsor, dean and chapter of 110, 113
Windsor, Miles 68, 69–70
Winstanley, Elizabeth 675

Wint, Guy 473
Winter, Reginald Keble 454, 464, 468, 469
Wise, Alfred Roy 457, 460, 471
Witherstone, Edward 798, 806
Wodehoke, William 804
Wolcombe, Robert 133n
Wollstonecraft, Mary 263, 267n
Wolsey, Thomas, cardinal archbishop of York 71, 74, 78, 493n
Women, admission of 769–70, 776, 778, 779–80
Women's sport 642–3
Wood, Anthony 2, 95, 99, 116, 139, 145, 149n, 150, 167, 195, 218, 229, 230, 239, 242, 550–1, 569, 600
Wood, Charles, first Viscount Halifax 286–7, 332, 380, Ill. 9.1
Wood, George 416
Wood, Mr, surgeon 183
Wood, Robert 214, 810
Wood, Samuel Francis 321, 331, 344, 392
Wood, William 86
Woodforde, James 223
Woodgate, 'Guts' 620n
Woodgate, Henry 310
Woodridge & Simpson, builders 441
Woodridge, John, builder 573
Woods, Thomas, tennis court lessee 600
Woodward, Joseph 176n, 177, 178, 179n, 202, 214, 799, 807, 808
Woolcombe, Edward Cooper 331
Woolcombe, John 253, 269, 801, 810
Woollin, John 173, 177n, 179n, 800, 809
Woolton, Frederick Marquis, Lord Woolton 710
Worcester College 526, 566n
Wordsworth, Charles, of Christ Church 600–1, 608–9
Wordsworth, Matthew Charles 469
Wormeswell, Thomas 62, 796, 804

Wreford-Brown, Charles 620–1
Wren, Sir Christopher 559
Wright, Paul 637, 641–2
Wright, William (fellow c.1479–92) 62, 804
Wright, William, recorder of Oxford 182, 213
Wyatt Building see Leigh Library
Wyatt, James, architect 251, 254, 549, 564–7, 596
Wyatt, Thomas 105, 106, 130, 143, 145, 152–3, 154n, 798, 806
Wyatt, William 131, 798, 806
Wyche, Thomas 49n, 51, 54, 55, 795, 796, 803
Wyck Rissington, Gloucestershire 16
Wyclif, John 32, 35, 45, 46, 49, 54
Wyght, Joan 553
Wyght, Simon 553
Wyght's tenement (Adam Faber's) 553, 554
Wylyot, John 33
Wyndham, John Eveleigh 615
Wyndham, Sir William 197n
Wyndham, Thomas Heathcote Gerald 664
Wyndham's race 615, 622, 639, 642

Yale, Hugh 117, 798, 806
Yate, James 167n
Yates, Theodore 732
Yates, Thomas 164
Yeamans, John 239n
Yeatman, Robert Julian 728
Yerworth, Samuel 126
Yonge, Francis 124n
Yonge, Sir William 197n
Yorke, Charles 208
Young, Francis, of Wadley 490
Young, Maria, fruiterer 235

Zanchius, Hieronymus 143
Zuloaga, Ignacio 428n